A CRITICAL DICTIONARY
OF THE FRENCH REVOLUTION

A CRITICAL DICTIONARY
OF THE
French Revolution

EDITED BY

FRANÇOIS FURET AND MONA OZOUF

Translated by Arthur Goldhammer

THE BELKNAP PRESS OF

HARVARD UNIVERSITY PRESS

Cambridge, Massachusetts

London, England

1989

First published as *Dictionnaire critique de la révolution française,* © Flammarion, 1988.

The preparation of this volume was assisted by a grant
from the French Ministry of Culture and Communication.

This book is printed on acid-free paper, and its binding
materials have been chosen for strength and durability.

Library of Congress Cataloging-in-Publication Data

Dictionnaire critique de la révolution française. English.
   A critical dictionary of the French Revolution / edited
by François Furet and Mona Ozouf ; translated by Ar-
thur Goldhammer.
      p. cm.
   Translation of: Dictionnaire critique de la révolution
française.
   Includes index.
   ISBN 0-674-17728-2 (alk. paper)
   1. France—History—Revolution, 1789–1799. 2.
France—History—Revolution, 1789–1799—Historiog-
raphy. I. Furet, François, 1927– . II. Ozouf,
Mona. III. Title.
DC148.D5313 1989   89-30656
944.04—dc19   CIP

CONTENTS

CONTENTS

3   INSTITUTIONS AND CREATIONS

CONTENTS

CONTENTS

5 HISTORIANS AND COMMENTATORS

ILLUSTRATIONS

EVENTS
(following page 106)

Cholat, *The Taking of the Bastille.* Musée Carnavalet, Paris. Photograph: Dagli Orti.

Houel, *A Cell in the Bastille.* Musée Carnavalet, Paris. Photograph: Giraudon.

Oath of the King, Queen, and Nation at the Festival of the Federation. Musée Carnavalet, Paris. Photograph: Giraudon.

Lafayette's Oath at the Festival of the Federation (detail). Musée Carnavalet, Paris. Photograph: Dagli Orti.

Cornu, *Festival of the Federation.* Musée des Beaux-Arts, Besançon. Photograph: Giraudon.

Arrest of the King and His Family at Varennes. Musée Carnavalet, Paris. Photograph: Dagli Orti.

Taking of the Tuileries, or, Foundation of the Republic. Musée Carnavalet, Paris. Photograph: Dagli Orti.

Painful Leavetaking of Louis XVI from the Queen and His Family. Musée Carnavalet, Paris. Photograph: Artephot/Nimatallah.

Execution of King Louis XVI. Musée Carnavalet, Paris. Photograph: Giraudon.

Tassaert, *Hérault de Séchelles Harangues the Crowd.* Musée Carnavalet, Paris. Photograph: Bulloz.

Deray, *Execution of the Demoiselles de la Métaierie (Charette's Cousins) at Nantes.* Musée des Beaux-Arts, Nantes. Photograph: Giraudon.

After the capture of Chemillé, d'Elbée saves the Blues from massacre. (*The Pater d'Elbée.*) Musée de Cholet. Photograph: Golder.

Vendean Insignia. Musée Dabrée, Nantes. Photograph: Hemon.

Béricourt, *Unloading Victims after a Revolutionary Journée.* Musée Carnavalet, Paris. Photograph: Edimedia.

Tellier, *Boissy d'Anglas Saluting the Head of Féraud.* Château de Versailles. Photograph: Lauros-Giraudon.

The Rapes of the Constitution. Musée Carnavalet, Paris. Photograph: Edimedia.

Entry of the French Army into Rome. Château de Versailles. Photograph: Dagli Orti.

General Bonaparte's Generosity during the Campaign in Italy. Musée Carnavalet, Paris. Photograph: Dagli Orti.

ILLUSTRATIONS

ACTORS
(following page 362)

Ducreux, *Last Portrait of Louis XVI*. Musée Carnavalet, Paris. Photograph: Edimedia.

Montigny, Bust of Mirabeau. Musée Arbaud, Aix-en-Provence. Photograph: Jean Bernard.

Kucharsky, *Marie Antoinette*. Château de Versailles. Photograph: Bulloz.

David, *Marie Antoinette on the Tumbril*. Musée Carnavalet, Paris. Photograph: Bulloz.

Wille, *Portrait of Danton on His Way to Execution*. Musée Carnavalet, Paris. Photograph: Edimedia.

Danton (Alexandre Koubitzky) in Abel Gance's *Napoleon*. Photograph: Christophe.

Bust of Marat. Musée Carnavalet, Paris. Photograph: Edimedia.

Marat (Antonin Artaud) in his bathtub in Abel Gance's *Napoleon*. Photograph: *Cahiers du cinéma*.

Delaroche, *The Girondins on Their Way to Execution*. Musée Carnavalet, Paris. Photograph: Bulloz.

Boilly, *Maximilien de Robespierre*. Musée des Beaux-Arts, Lille. Photograph: Giraudon.

Emigration: Four Caricatures.
  The Prince of Condé. Musée Carnavalet, Paris. Photograph: Edimedia.
  The Return of an Emigré. Musée Carnavalet, Paris. Photograph: Edimedia.
  Parisian Sans-culotte. Musée Carnavalet, Paris. Photograph: Dagli Orti.
  October 16, 1793. Musée Carnavalet, Paris. Photograph: Edimedia.
Revolutionary Patrol. Musée Carnavalet, Paris. Photograph: Edimedia.

Ronot, *The Last Montagnards*. Musée de la Révolution Française, Vizille. Photograph: Dagli Orti.

Bacler d'Albe, *General Bonaparte in Milan in Year V*. Château de Malmaison. Photograph: Dagli Orti.

INSTITUTIONS AND CREATIONS
(following page 522)

Brenet, *Louis XVI Swears Allegiance to the Constitution on the Altar of the Fatherland*. Musée des Beaux-Arts, Quimper. Photograph: Giraudon.

Monsiau, *The Abolition of Slavery Proclaimed to the Convention on 16 Pluviôse, Year II*. Musée Carnavalet, Paris. Photograph: Dagli Orti.

National Assembly, Session of September 14, 1791. Bibliothèque Nationale, Paris. Photograph: Bibliothèque Nationale.

Patriotic Priest Taking the Civic Oath in Good Faith. Musée de l'Arsenal, Paris. Photograph: Hubert Josse.

Aristocratic Priest Fleeing the Civic Oath. Musée de l'Arsenal, Paris. Photograph: Hubert Josse.

ILLUSTRATIONS

ILLUSTRATIONS

Fraternal Meal. Watercolor. Bibliothèque Nationale, Paris. Photograph: Bibliothèque Nationale.

Freedom of the Press. Private collection. Photograph: Explorer Archives.

Lesueur, *Vandalist, Destroyer of the Productions of the Arts.* Musée Carnavalet, Paris. Photograph: Lauros-Giraudon.

Pillage of the St. Lazare House. Photograph: Hubert Josse.

PREFACE

The birth of democracy: this definition of the French Revolution carries such intellectual weight that no one can dismiss it, for here the partisan finds his vindication and the adversary, grounds for his opposition. But early on, both sides recognized in the Revolution a temporal dividing line which separated them. While the Ancien Régime meant inequality and absolute monarchy, under the banner of 1789 appeared the rights of man and the sovereignty of the people: this sharp divergence is the most profound expression of the nature of the French Revolution, at once philosophical and political. It is this that gives the Revolution the dignity of an idea and the character of a commencement. In order to understand the event, we must begin with this rupture, which remains an enigma despite two hundred years of scholarship and controversy.

In the vast tradition of commentaries on the Revolution, which have become inseparable from their subject, one body of ideas has dominated twentieth-century interpretations: the majority of contemporary historians have attempted to minimize the Revolutionary rupture by emphasizing the emergence of the bourgeoisie into the national political arena. The Revolution is said to have marked the political culmination of the long social development of the middle class—what was called in the nineteenth century the "declaration of its preponderance." This view has not been without pertinence or fruitfulness. Elaborated by liberal thinkers and reworked by Marx, the idea of the class struggle does have a legitimate place in a history of the French Revolution. One whole aspect of the Revolution involves the interplay of the social classes, their changing relations in the eighteenth century, and the extraordinary new arena for class alliances and conflicts made available by the advent of the ideas of liberty and equality. The history of the peasantry, addressed only in the twentieth century, is in this respect a good example. It enables us to understand why rural society welcomed the antiseigneurial principles of 1789 and the sale of Church property; but it should also make it possible to recognize a subsequent turn against the Revolution by peasants, as would occur in western France, for if class interests are taken as the only factor guiding events, the result is a logical impasse. Or consider an example drawn from urban class analysis. The destruction of the old society, largely accomplished by the Ancien Régime and consecrated by the events of 1789, revealed social divisions with a clarity typical of modern, individualistic societies. The Revolution, while assuming that its role was limited to eliminating aristocracy, actually inaugurated a powerful tension between rich and poor, *bourgeoisie* and *peuple, muscadins* and *sans-culottes:* the very uncertainty of the period's nomenclature reflects the degree to which social realities were overinvested with political ideas and passions.

PREFACE

What was overturned between 1787 and 1800 was not the substance of society but its principles and government. Absolute, divine-right monarchy gave way to the rights of man. Louis XVI's successors were Robespierre, the Thermidorians, and Bonaparte. The purpose of this book is to restore to this upheaval in French history its cultural and political character, which is also the basis of its strangeness. True, Enlightenment philosophy had set the stage. But how? And how was the transition made from the world of philosophy to that of the French Revolution? These are old questions, and enormous ones, which the social interpretation of the Revolution believed it could sidestep but which must inevitably be confronted.

It was the proposal to reconsider this issue that brought together the authors of the *Critical Dictionary*. Credit for the conception of the enterprise belongs to Louis Audibert, who is social sciences editor at Flammarion. This book was his idea originally, and he has followed it all the way through to completion. As for our coauthors, the core group consists of historians and philosophers who work on subjects of common concern and interest at the Institut Raymond-Aron (Ecole des Hautes Etudes en Sciences Sociales). A number of historians from other countries, chosen for their scholarship, joined with us in discussions held at a series of international colloquiums to explore a common set of issues and have also consented to contribute pieces to this book. To all, and especially to the English-speaking historians whose contribution to the history of the French Revolution has been so crucial since World War II, we wish to express our debt and our gratitude.

This book is not an encyclopedia or even a dictionary in the ordinary sense of the word. The revolutionary text is vast, and we do not pretend to have spelled out its full alphabet. How could anyone even think of compressing an event as complex as the French Revolution, as extravagant, as often retold and as overburdened with interpretations and commentaries, into the 1200-odd pages of a dictionary? We have produced a "dictionary," rather, in the sense made familiar by the Enlightenment. Its principle: a set of key words, which suggest not only the state of current scholarship but even more a shift in the nature of the questions posed. Its objective: to recover both the strangeness and the disruptive force of the founding event of modern French history. Its unity: the stress placed on the political event and its creative capacity.

Unlike an ordinary dictionary, our work is also distinguished by the grouping of its articles—or brief essays—into five major sections organized around convenient themes: events, actors, institutions and creations, ideas, historians and commentators.

Events. Is it not the essence of the Revolution to have given the word "event" its modern meaning, to have been prodigious to the point of excess in creating events, and to have profoundly altered the way in which they were perceived and interpreted? Some were events in the purest sense of the word, recognized as they happened for their disruptive power: the Great Fear, the Night of August 4, Varennes. Others were repetitious, almost rituals: Coups d'Etat, Revolutionary *Journées*. Still others were crucial constellations of events, whose many facets historians have yet to explore fully: The King's Trial, the Terror, the Vendée.

PREFACE

Actors. There were collective actors, which the Revolution engendered and devoured, from the Enragés to the Sans-culottes, from the Monarchiens to the Thermidorians. And there were individual actors, from Louis XVI to Napoleon Bonaparte. Their small number may come as a surprise, given that the French Revolution offered brilliant roles to so many talents that would have gone unemployed without it. It was our view, however, that beyond the first circle of renown, where the selections were beyond dispute, the inclusion or exclusion of figures of the second rank could have been debated forever and furthermore that on this vast stage the libretto mattered more than the cast: the grandeur of the revolutionary drama dwarfed its interpreters.

Institutions and creations. Some were chosen because they developed into institutions that still form the basis of civic life in France, such as Suffrage, Département, and Civil Code. Others were included because they exemplified the spirit of the Revolution, such as the Paris Commune, the Clubs and Popular Societies, and Revolutionary Religion.

Ideas. Some enabled the Revolution to name itself and identify the enemy (Revolution, Ancien Régime, Feudal System, Aristocracy). Others enabled it to define its goals and principles (Sovereignty, Rights of Man, Nation). Still others allowed us to acknowledge the Revolution's debts (Enlightenment) and hail its innovations (Regeneration, Republic). To give these "ideas" their due, one must first deal with the disparity between inaccessible, little-read works and revolutionary practice. The distance between the *Social Contract* and an obscure speech by a Jacobin militant is so readily apparent that it is tempting to conclude that one is dealing with two sets of fundamentally independent phenomena. One then has on one side the philosophers of the Enlightenment, unprogrammatic and bearing no responsibility, and on the other a Revolution without precursors, in which what was played out had no intellectual content whatsoever.

All the essays here reject this judgment in both its parts. The ideas at issue here did not arise out of purely theoretical debate. They were put into practice and embodied in institutions. They were disseminated through a pedagogy. They were modified by events (see Sovereignty, Fraternity, Revolution). They became issues in political combat. If the men of 1789 took their ideas from the great minds of the century, whom they themselves identified as the sources of their inspiration, and if, moreover, they were convinced that the Enlightenment, which began the Revolution, also ought to end it, then the task they confronted was infinitely more complex than that of writing. Thus nothing could be more unjust than to look only at the bookish, philosophical, abstract aspect of their work. They continually reflected on the almost insurmountable difficulties of applying the new principles to the old French monarchy and constantly said so, much more aware of their digressions, much more conscious of their failures to live up to their principles, than suspicious historians—for whom the actor is always blind and the interpreter always lucid—have led us to believe.

Historians and commentators. We find, of course, not only those who attempted to restore wholeness to the phenomenon (Michelet, Jaurès, Buchez, Blanc) and those who so quickly set the terms of interpretation (Constant, Burke, Michelet) but also those who never ceased to ponder one or another of the problems that the Revolution raised for the modern world: Kant and regicide, Hegel and the Terror, Quinet and religion. Historiography occupies a fundamental place in this book—it can be found in nearly all the articles— because of one idea: that there is in historical knowledge both a cumulative aspect and a noncumulative aspect. Cumulative, because no one can write about the Revolution today without taking account of the knowledge that has been built up over the past two centuries, especially during those two nine-teenth-century high points of scholarship, the Michelet period and the Aulard-Jaurès period. Concerning popular movements, both rural and ur-ban, the Vendée, and the nobility, our knowledge today is more reliable and more extensive than in the past, as a number of articles make clear: consider, for example, Taxes, Aristocracy, and Suffrage. But historical knowledge is also noncumulative, for progress does not cover its tracks. To neglect the his-tory of this history would be to blot out the intellectual landscapes that have been traversed and to ignore the way in which problems have been laid down layer upon layer: the great interpreters of the French Revolution approached the event through books—Marx through Hegel, Taine through Burke and Tocqueville—so that the historiography of the Revolution invariably com-bines a variety of eras, questions, and issues. Furthermore, ignoring the evo-lution of historiography means overlooking an important aspect of the event itself: the freshness and force with which certain questions were immediately posed. No one has understood better than Benjamin Constant the danger to political liberties represented by the assertion of absolute sovereignty. No one has portrayed more profoundly than Burke, a half century before Marx, the philosophical coup de grace that swept away the diversity of conditions and erected in its place the abstract universality of democracy. The development of revolutionary historiography contradicts the conventional wisdom that the longer ago an event took place, the "truer" our knowledge of it is. The most profound questions about the Revolution were posed very early. Our purpose here is therefore to help the reader rediscover this forgotten history, to incor-porate not only the variety of different schools but also the complexity of the issues, in short to point up all the richness of the intellectual space that stands between us and the Revolution.

Events, actors, institutions and creations, ideas, historians and commen-tators. The assignment of articles to these five thematic groups is open to debate, for they naturally overlap. Echoes reverberate from one to another, information flows back and forth, and readers will not necessarily find what they are looking for where they expect it. The question of revolutionary pedagogy is taken up in the article Regeneration; that of the press in Public Spirit; while the religious essence of the Revolution is considered by way of Michelet, Tocqueville, and Quinet. A subject such as representation may not be treated in any specific article but may be approached through a host of entries (Suffrage, Elections, Rousseau, Sieyès, Democracy). An actor whom we did not consider worthy of a full portrait may appear in another context (Brissot in Girondins, Saint-Just in Revolutionary Government). The index, thanks to the scrupulous vigilance of Jonathan Mandelbaum, and the list of related topics that accompanies each article should make it possible for readers to find their way through the book and proceed from article to article. These tools invite the reader to fill in the lacunae in our work, and the suggestions for further reading should help not just in learning the standard answers but in discovering the important questions and thus extending a work that is obviously incomplete.

This incompleteness is an essential component of a project deliberately intended to be "critical." The adjective is incompatible with the dogmatism of a closed system, acknowledges that research is open-ended, and suggests that our aim was not to give an exhaustive inventory of the facts but to measure their uncertainties and gaps. The critical work does not immediately adopt the standpoint of totality. The systematization of the revolutionary phenomenon—the Revolution as a "bloc"—is implicit in the way in which the men of 1789 conceived of it as the advent of reason and liberty. As early as 1790 Burke had turned the idea against them: with him began a counterrevolutionary philosophy that gave a radically negative sense to the whole phenomenon and enabled him to condemn the terrorist deviation before it occurred. For the Revolution's actors it was a thornier affair, because they had to live through all its stages. The Convention set the dawn of Year I on the date of its first meeting, the date of the abolition of monarchy. By relegating 1789 and the Constitution of 1791 to the dark age of the old calendar, it defined a new revolution, the successor to an abortive one. Less than two years later, the Thermidorians, after overthrowing Robespierre, continually asked how they might piece together the various bits of their past to make one whole from many parts.

The question runs through the whole nineteenth century and has given rise to diverse, often contradictory answers in the fragmented camp of the Revolution's heirs. It took the left a long time to take over for its own ends, and in the process invert the meaning of, the imperious explanatory model of the bloc; the path was blazed by Michelet, not just against liberals such as Mme. de Staël and socialists such as Louis Blanc but against his own closest ally, Quinet. As this model became widely accepted, it led to the historical-political synthesis of the Third Republic from Aulard to Clemenceau. Subsequently threatened by the occurrence of the Soviet revolution and the concomitant shift of interest from 1789 to 1793, the bloc model has been refurbished in the latter half of the twentieth century, but more as the last resort of a Jacobin historiography on the defensive than as a research hypothesis.

This is a truly controversial model, since it is shared by both counterrevolutionary historiography and left-wing ecumenicism, and the *Critical Dictionary* seeks to examine it for what it contains by way of both intellectual commonplace and political ambiguity. Whatever historians may say, they have been paralyzed by the all-encompassing and massive certainty of the bloc model, which has hidden the ambivalent stakes and incredible complexity of circumstances and events. It is not really defensible except at a very high level of abstraction, which dispenses with the ebb and flow of events. Even in its classical sense, the French Revolution exhibits no unity as regards its heroes or leaders, its actors' justifications, or its political forms. This is a book of history, and the reader will learn how much the diversity of the event exceeds the unity of the concept. Before conceptualizing the Revolution as a unified whole, we must measure its disparities, discordances, and even contradictions, and we must not dismiss what was random in it: these are the exigencies to which a critical inventory must respond.

But here something more needs to be said. To refuse to adopt the point of view of finished science—to draw the conclusion, for example, that the events of 1789 and 1793 were radically heterogeneous—is by no means to refrain from linking the episodes of the Revolution to one another. The entire *Critical Dictionary* is a protest against this surgical distinction. One of its contributions, perhaps, is to have restored the year 1789 to a central position and to have seen the weeks between the elections to the Estates General and the October Days of 1789 as not only the overture to the Revolution but also its laboratory: a very brief expanse of time and yet the most important in French history, during which everything there was to say about the new principles was said. Turn, for example, to the article on the Declaration of the Rights of Man, and you will discover that it is hindsight that has dramatized the differences between the words and deeds of the actors of 1789, 1793, and 1795. You will find that the intellectual space within which future debates would take place had already been carved out in the summer of 1789 and that the whole range of arguments was already in place, anticipating all that was to come from the radical escalation of the Jacobin period to the sober retreat of the Thermidorian era. Thus, to describe these arguments in their disparity should not stand in the way of rethinking the intellectual unity of a Revolution founded on the rights of man. But that unity remained a normative requirement, a philosophical horizon, not a moral and affective datum whose consequences merely had to be unfolded.

Finally, the adjective "critical" is also to be applied by the authors to themselves. To sift through the composite episodes and controversial issues of the French Revolution, to revisit the various accounts of the historians, does not imply that we are adopting a position of neutrality. No narration is neutral, no research is free of cultural baggage, and both are imbued with current concerns and values. As a critical work, this *Dictionary* is therefore obligated to include a reflection on the background and roots of its own questions: to do this we must reflect on the relation of the present to the past, which is what gives all history its depth.

The simplest way to illustrate that relation is to note the *Critical Dictionary*'s date of publication. It comes at a time of celebration. It is therefore commemorative, while at the same time it is intended to be critical of the commemoration as a phenomenon. To call oneself a "child of the Revolution" has often implied a total acceptance, which precluded any distance and made it necessary to share and even to relive the emotions and convictions of the actors. It is often said that the Revolution is our "mother," but Quinet long ago denounced the implicit blackmail in that idea, the insistence on unconditional piety and compulsory devotion. The argument has outlived him: the theme of the Revolution's centennial and sesquicentennial was that of a legacy not only to be honored but also to be relived in order to carry it on. In the tension between the abstract rights of man and their realization there is a legacy of infinite elasticity, present since 1789 and certain to live on. Here the commemorative passion seeks to gather the children of the Revolution around their ancestors and in the name of their offspring: a dizzying continuity that serves as, and supplants, justification of the desire to appropriate the Revolution as one's own possession.

This emotional bond, presented in an intellectual guise, is what a critical work must reject. The French Revolution belongs to all citizens. Even those who do not like it are its children, for they have no other choice. This book seeks to establish the presence of the past in us by showing how for two hundred years the idea of the universality of mankind has been at work. What is astonishing is not only that some people still detest the French Revolution but that those who profess to love it ignore its force and effects.

The French Revolution is by now remote, yet we live more than ever in the world that it created. A new kind of proximity is born of distance. The two hundred years that stand between us and 1789 have included events that we must recross in order to approach and understand it—events that have made certain of our questions about the French Revolution more urgent than ever. It is because our view of the Revolution has been weighed down by the perplexities and anxieties of the intervening years that today we have new questions about the democratic experience it inaugurated. The discovery in the twentieth century of an unprecedented form of despotism in no way implies that the Enlightenment was the cause of the gulag or even that democracy must necessarily veer toward totalitarianism. But it does make us more aware of the possibilities of a dissolution of democratic politics and more aware of its despotic potential.

How could we feel any other way about the French Revolution? Lenin and Trotsky were obsessed with the example of the Jacobins. And in return, Albert Mathiez and his successors were obsessed with the Russian Revolution. Today, this oversimplified yet greatly influential analogy has come back like a boomerang to strike those who imprudently wielded it as though it were holy writ. Historians have been relieved of an anachronism, not so much by the fruits of their research as by the course of events. But their subject has been enriched by the addition of yet another layer of history, whose meaning must be established. Accordingly, the late twentieth century has rediscovered, by force of circumstance, certain old questions, to which we have accorded due place in the *Critical Dictionary*. That is the reason for the large number of articles that insist on the tension in revolutionary politics between the will of the majority and the general will; on the anonymity of the sovereign power, all the more constraining for being more neutral; on the permanent possibility that sovereignty will be usurped by a faction; and on the lack of any recourse for the opposition in a system in which the representation of the sovereign people is conceived as being indivisible and omnipotent.

Nevertheless, the proximity and even urgency of these questions must be set against a growing estrangement. To put it in the most banal terms, a great deal of time has passed since 1789, and with it memories of the events of the Revolution—still remarkably fresh in the first nineteenth-century historians—have dimmed, and people's sense of familiarity and solidarity with the actors has diminished. Nothing seems more dated today than those histories that revolve around a choice of hero, whether Robespierre or Danton, and it is hard for us to understand how so many things—careers, works, friendships—could have been dramatically determined by such preferences. More pointedly, when the centennial of the Revolution was celebrated, the political issues it raised were still alive. At that time one France was celebrating its birth in defiance of another France, a situation that inevitably encouraged people to feel that they were reliving the events of the past and opposing the enemies of the past. At the time of the sesquicentennial celebration this spirited solidarity remained intact: the Vichy regime cannot be understood without taking its counterrevolutionary inspiration into account. By the same token, the communist hold on the left-wing electorate in France over the half century from the Popular Front to the election of François Mitterrand is inseparable from the Jacobin heritage. In both cases, moreover, this ancestry was explicitly acknowledged and proclaimed.

Since the war, however, this beacon has vanished from the national horizon. The postwar period was a time of upheaval in the economy, growth in the national product unprecedented in the history of France, inclusion in the international economy, and influx of foreign goods and ideas. Today's France bears little resemblance to the France of our childhoods, which until 1950 remained the France of the nineteenth century. There are no longer many peasants, and the middle class is much larger than it was. The exile of the working class, to which the communist party lent dignity, is ending before our eyes. The society is more modern, and the French people are much more similar to one another than they were a century ago. As a result, however, they have less need of the unity that teachers once tried to foster by keeping memories of the Revolution alive. Absorbed into a common culture, less dependent than in the past on outspoken and militant loyalties, the republican memory is fading as a consequence of its own success.

Not that French democracy is today without enemies capable of being roused to action. From yesterday's battles old antagonists remain. But they can do battle now only under colors borrowed from the new age. Since the philosophy of the universal rights of man has no more open adversaries, the unanimity of approval has tended to obscure the difficulties inextricably associated with this subjective foundation of the social realm. Hence modern society exhibits as never before the gap between its principles and their application. This gives rise to new civil tensions, superimposed on the old ones, yet without precedent.

Another element of the revolutionary culture firmly fixed in thought and custom is also beginning to change, and it is of no small importance: the idea of the nation. Our generation has witnessed the death of the soldiers of Verdun and the aging of the men of the Resistance. For all the differences between the two episodes, both nevertheless attest to a similar collective passion: the habit, born in the Revolution, of investing the nation with a universal significance. But World War II has dramatically reduced the role of old European nations such as France in world history. Prosperity and evolving customs have also altered the sense of membership in a community. It is difficult for a young French person today to imagine the war of 1914, much less the Napoleonic campaigns. For such a person the issue of the day is the problematic one of European unity, since it is easier to unify economies than to unify histories. What capacity to forget, or what power to synthesize, will be needed by the citizens of the oldest nation-states in the world, who struggled so long to create their unified polities? In tackling this question France need not forget any of its past, least of all the Revolution, for that unique epic was intended to herald the collective emancipation of humanity. But the country is less and less able to think of that past as a model without parallel.

Finally, if habits have changed, so have laws and institutions. The end of the nineteenth century saw the establishment of a durable republic. The end of the twentieth century is witnessing the creation of a consensus around a new constitution at first disavowed by the republican tradition stemming from the legacy of the Revolution and the nineteenth century. Not only was the Fifth Republic born in 1958 in a kind of coup d'état; it also instituted, in 1962, the election of a president by universal suffrage. Both circumstances were reasons for its rejection by the heirs of the Revolution, from the radicals to the communists, followers of 1789 and 1793 alike. But public opinion took a different view: the 1962 provision for presidential elections completely erased the regime's dubious origins. The right of the people to choose the chief executive by direct election came to be seen as a right neglected for far too long, and de Gaulle apparently hit on the key to creating a monarchical republic that after two hundred years has reconciled Ancien Régime and Revolution.

At the same time a body of magistrates was created to oversee the constitutionality of the laws, and it has rapidly taken root. This court, whose members are appointed by the leaders of the Republic, therefore derives its authority, just as the president does, from the suffrage of the people, but indirectly. The aim was to divide the power of the sovereign people in the manner of the U.S. Constitution so as not to pose a threat to the liberty of citizens. Over the years the jurisdiction of the Constitutional Council has been broadened, making it into one of the fundamental institutions of the Fifth Republic. This evolution, so gradual that it seemed almost natural, marked yet another break with the republican spirit as it had formed in the years after 1789. The idea of a power superior to the National Assembly in constitutional matters is related to a logic of "checks and balances," a notion with a respectable pedigree in France since Montesquieu but foreign to the rationalism of the revolutionaries and their heirs. To the extent that the Constitutional Council is not merely a check on the legislature but also a dissuasive force, its spirit is at odds with the notorious legicentrism of both the Revolution and the Republic, which was so ably analyzed by Carré de Malberg between the first and second world wars.

Weakening of the legislature, election of the executive by universal suffrage, constitutional checks and balances: in all three ways the last thirty years of French history have marked a break with republican orthodoxy. But that break has also been the occasion of the rediscovery of aspects of the French Revolution that did not give rise to any tradition and were therefore somewhat neglected. We have rediscovered the paradox of a Declaration of Rights that surely excluded the idea of a fundamental law above the will of the legislature but that nevertheless recognized the absolute and inalienable character of the rights of man, superior to the constitutional order. We are reminded that while the revolutionary enterprise may be interpreted as an attempt to eliminate or reduce the uncertainties of the future, there were some revolutionaries, such as Condorcet, who refused to restrict even the Declaration of Rights to a definitive formulation and who insisted on the right of future generations to interpret the Constitution for themselves. Our attention has been drawn once again to such powerful and original voices as Sieyès, who in distinguishing between the "constituent power" and the "legislative power" proposed creating a special court responsible for monitoring the constitutionality of laws. Thus it is as though by following the path of the nineteenth century back to its source, France has once again rediscovered the great event in its history, with all its extraordinary wealth of ideas and possibilities. Would that this critical inventory may help give some sense of that event. That, in any case, is its ambition.

François Furet
Mona Ozouf

EVENTS

1

CHOUANNERIE

The term *chouannerie*—from *Chouan,* a word drawn from a nickname given to one of the rebels—refers to a peasant resistance movement opposed to the French Revolution, which spread gradually over much of western France in 1791, after priests had been required to take an oath to support the Civil Constitution of the Clergy. (The term *chouannerie* was not used in official documents, however, until 1794.) Although the rebel Vendeans of 1793 were also "Chouans," the definition of chouannerie does not include the Vendée insurrection as such. Indeed, one way to pinpoint the precise meaning of the word is to examine the way in which chouannerie differed from the Vendée uprising.

South of the Loire, in a military zone of roughly rectangular shape comprising the Mauges, the *bocage* (or area of hedged-field agriculture), and the marshes of the Vendée, the insurrection had the character of a genuine war with armies and pitched battles, a war ended late in 1793 by the rout of Savenay; the last pockets of resistance were wiped out with the capture and execution of Stofflet and Charrette in February and March 1796. By contrast, chouannerie never involved armies or even remnants of armies. It was never more than a series of sporadic, isolated guerrilla actions, which often degenerated into pillage. It covered a vast territory, however, compared with the relatively limited rectangle of rebellion south of the Loire. It included all of western France north of the river from the Perche to lower Brittany, that vast region of *bocage* so distinct from the open fields around Paris that Vidal de la Blache was moved to write that "the inhabitant of the plains of the Paris Basin is a villager; the inhabitant of the west is a peasant." Chouannerie continued throughout the Directory, ending only with the Consulate.

Yet this distinction is as misleading as it is clear. Simply because the war in the Vendée and the guerrilla warfare waged by the Chouans differed in scope, intensity, and duration, it does not follow that the two movements, the two episodes of resistance, were also different in nature. After all, the war in the Vendée in its final phase was nothing but chouannerie, and its early liquidation, in 1796, was simply the result of the fear that memories of the great "royal and Catholic army" caused to weigh upon the Republic. Both north and south of the Loire, moreover, the typical insurgent was the same: the peasant of western France, who left his isolated farm and hedgerows to do battle against the Republic, while the cities and the towns remained in republican hands. Hence the Vendée and chouannerie are perhaps best thought of as two aspects of a single historical phenomenon, each of which sheds light on the other.

EVENTS

By its very nature the story of chouannerie is not easy to relate, for it was a vast movement of rural resistance, a silent, massive repudiation of the Revolution punctuated by sporadic attacks and outbreaks of violence and contemporaneous with innumerable restorationist conspiracies. There is no comprehensive work treating all aspects of this latter-day Jacquerie, which so delighted the castle-dwelling class that it gave rise in the nineteenth century to a vast reactionary literature. Owing to the sheer number of incidents and sources, our picture of the phenomenon is at best fragmentary.

As early as 1790 there is evidence of rural discontent with the Revolution not only in the Vendée, not only in the west, but in other regions of France as well, such as the area near the border between Rouergue and Lozère. Many factors entered into this latent hostility; some reawakened old sentiments, such as rural distrust of the city and resistance to the government and its taxes; others stemmed from disillusionment with the Revolution. Greeted everywhere with hope in 1789, the Revolution had not abolished seigneurial rights but had sold them off. In the cities and towns it had established bourgeois administrations eager to dominate the surrounding countryside and without much sensitivity to rural traditions. Worst of all, it had undertaken to force the Church to accept administrative rationalization of the old kingdom and priests to swear an oath of loyalty. By the second half of 1790 it was the loyalty oath that was causing the greatest trouble; what is more, it provided the resistance with ready-made spokesmen in the person of refractory priests.

Despite what is said in most nineteenth-century republican histories (such as that of Chassin), the nobility played no part in stirring up this peasant frustration. Not that aristocrats here and there failed to act on their counter-revolutionary hopes; but they never even sought, much less gained, the support of the rural masses. In the west, a conspiracy hatched in the château of the baron de la Lézardière near Saint-Martin-sous-Mouzeuil in the Vendée was put down without difficulty. In the spring of 1792 the marquis de La Rouërie in upper Brittany led a network of committees of noblemen organized as military units, but these took no part in the armed actions of the peasantry.

Attacks by armed peasants also began in 1792, the main grievance being the religious question as well as the ever-unpopular conscription of soldiers by lot. Mayenne rose in rebellion in August 1792. But, as in the Vendée, the fatal date was March 1793: between the tenth and thirteenth there were armed uprisings throughout the west, from the Sarthe to the ocean. Bands of peasants sprang from the hedgerows and challenged the republican authorities more or less everywhere, but in sporadic fashion; there were clashes in Perche, Mayenne, Maine, and Brittany. In most places quick action by government troops reestablished order, that is, saved the towns from occupation by insurgent peasants. This was the great—the huge—difference between what happened in these places and what happened in the Mauges and the *bocage* of Vendée, where things began in much the same way but took a very different turn: on March 19 a republican army of 3,000 men was routed by a ragtag troop of peasants. The spread of the insurrection to a vast territory controlled by veritable rebel armies was made possible in large part by this initial success. By contrast, the uprisings north of the Loire were put down and the revolutionary authorities continued to control the cities and towns. Thereafter peasant anger was funneled into sporadic actions by scattered guerrilla bands, which posed less of a threat to the Revolution but were also less vulnerable to decisive repression.

In Brittany agitation over the religious question and, later, over conscription by lot affected mainly the so-called *pays gallo* east of the famous linguistic boundary, and the troubles of March 1793 reignited a flammable situation. In Breton-speaking territory in the center and west of the peninsula, only Léon and the area around Vannes took arms against the Republic. Saint Pol de Léon to the north and Pontivy and Vannes to the south were threatened by numerous bands; but without military experience or leaders (except for Cadoudal, who began his career as a counterrevolutionary soldier in Morbihan), these were quickly and decisively defeated. The prison sentences and fines imposed on the insurgent communes proved sufficiently dissuasive to keep Léon quiet for the rest of the Revolution and Empire. Of all the Breton-speaking areas of Brittany only the eastern Vannetais resumed its attacks on the Revolution (but more than a year later, in the summer of 1794), a lower-Breton chouannerie that was part of a wider action, centered mainly in upper Brittany.

In fact the epicenter of Breton chouannerie was located in a triangle formed by Rennes, Fougères, and Nantes. The peasant agitation also extended further west, into Maine and Mayenne, where it had been smoldering since 1791. It reached a peak in 1794 after the defeat of the more organized rebellion in the Vendée without ever having developed into a major insurrection or having gained permanent control of any territory. Three or four substantial groups did manage to operate in the forests of Paimpont, Liffré, Champaufour, and Pertre between Laval and Rennes; these comprised several thousand men, many of whom had refused conscription. Arrayed around these potential counterrevolutionary vanguards and their local leaders were networks of intrigue that reached as far as the comte d'Artois and the English government.

In this respect the history of chouannerie coincides with that of the final phases of the war in the Vendée, for the hopes of the émigrés were vested in these relatively large and readily mobilized guerrilla bands as well as in the two small Vendean armies that had resumed combat, one led by Stofflet, the other by Charrette. But the disaster that followed the émigrés' landing at Quiberon (July 1795), the capture and execution of the last two Vendean leaders early in 1796, and the success of Hoche's policy of pacification deprived the chouannerie not only of its hopes for a quick restoration but also of a portion of its rural base. At this point began what Dubreuil has called the "second chouannerie," more than ever an affair of sporadic, scattered guerrilla action and divided leadership. Such resistance was relatively easy to contain but by its very nature almost impossible to root out entirely. The pacification of 1796 reestablished the authority of the Republic but could not guarantee the security of all persons and property.

Prior to the coup d'état of 18 Fructidor 1797, which was directed against the royalists, the bands of Chouans still enjoyed support from certain local government quarters. Cadoudal in Morbihan, Frotté in the Avranches-Alençon area, and Scépeaux in Mayenne and Maine could still share with their troops of young draft evaders the hope of a quasilegal return of the monarchy. But the eighteenth of Fructidor reinstated the policies of "public safety" and the republican Terror, most notably against the refractory priests, the preachers of chouannerie. The episode marked a stiffening of local resistance, now less likely than ever to succeed and ready to resort to every form of guerrilla warfare from ambush to surprise attack, not to mention outright robbery. The final resurgence of rebellion came in the middle of 1799, when the Directory's difficulties at home and abroad lent credence to the old rumor of an English landing and a return of the princes. From Brittany to the Perche sixty miles from Paris, the Chouans dreamed of a unified offensive against the cities and the Republic.

That autumn the coup d'état of 18 Brumaire revealed that the movement's principal strength had been the Republic's weakness. Bonaparte was able to avail himself of the ambiguity of the situation and of a vain hope cherished by royalist activists (with the exception of intransigents such as Cadoudal and Frotté), namely, that the new ruler would restore the monarchy. The people, however, expected him to restore domestic peace, to calm the political and religious situation. He not only fulfilled that wish but followed up by concluding an agreement with the Church, the Concordat of July 1801, thus winning the Consulate the support of the rural west and leaving the Chouan leaders with no option but assassination. The chouannerie ended in conspiracy. Its most emblematic leader, Georges Cadoudal, would mount the scaffold in 1804, convicted of plotting to restore the monarchy by murdering the usurper.

The Chouans are the great heroes of the royalist tradition. Brittany and the Vendée would rise again in 1815, during the Hundred Days, to restore Louis XVIII to the throne. Defeated on the field of battle in June, the rebels were avenged at Waterloo. In 1832 the same scenario was played out one more time—this time as parody by the duchesse de Berry, mother of the legitimate heir to the throne usurped by Louis Philippe.

Like the Vendean war, chouannerie has been the subject of many books over the past two centuries. Many works treat both insurrections together, for to some extent the chouannerie was an abortive Vendée and the Vendée a triumphant chouannerie. The literature on both subjects exhibits the same political passions and the same types of analysis.

Some authors hold that both chouannerie and the insurrection in the Vendée were the result of an aristocratic plot, a common theme in nineteenth-century republican historiography. The assumption is that the population of western France was particularly malleable owing to the prevalence there of a form of "obscurantism" peculiar to the vast *bocage*, with its scattered homes in which peasants lived in isolation. Living nearby in châteaux and presbyteries were men ready to manipulate them: the noble unwilling to relinquish his privileges and the refractory priest, whom the west produced in great numbers. Most typical of this line of argument is the monumental work of Charles-Louis Chassin, which even today remains a treasure trove of sources and documents. But the argument of these *Etudes documentaires sur la Vendée et la chouannerie* (1892–1900), the aspect of the book that most endeared it to republican militants, has not aged well.

Elsewhere the republican interpretation is divorced from the idea of a conspiracy and rests simply on the proposition that the peasants of western France were docilely obedient to the "natural" authorities: the lord and the curé—openly so in periods of calm and secretly in the maelstrom of the Revolution. Such obedience can be seen, it is argued, in nineteenth-century voting patterns as well as in the civil wars of the eighteenth century. The problem, then, is to explain the existence of these persistent patterns, which André Siegfried made one of the cornerstones of his *Tableau politique de la France de l'ouest* (1913). Siegfried adduces geographical and even geological factors and in the final analysis argues that the observable patterns grew out of the very nature of the western countryside: the granite-based *bocage* was Chouan country, the limestone-based open-field regions were republican.

Interpretations of this type deprive the rebellious peasant of the freedom and nobility of his choice, and royalist historians have long responded by arguing that the peasants of the west heroically defended patriarchal society because it had been good to them and they mourned its passing. The marquise de La Rochejaquelein set the tone in her *Memoirs,* written during the Empire: "This war was not, as some say, fomented by nobles and priests. . . . There was no plan, no conspiracy, no secret compact. The entire populace rose at once."

The strength of this argument, even today, is that it accounts for the spontaneity of the peasant uprising. The fact that chouannerie was a people's movement, so embarrassing to republicans, proves to royalists that there was a natural alliance between lord and peasant, those two sons of the earth and of tradition. The problem is that the same peasant who rebelled in 1793 had enthusiastically hailed the abolition of feudal rights in 1789. How can he be made over into a votary of the Ancien Régime? Thus, republican prejudice is contradicted by 1793, royalist conviction by 1789, whereas we are trying to explain both periods in the history of the west.

Recent historiography, less impassioned than that of earlier times, has attempted to reconcile the two extremes by providing a socioeconomic interpretation of rural behavior. The new approach involves borrowing Siegfried's deterministic assumptions and methods, but in place of his geological and sociopolitical arguments (granite and domination by large landowners) substituting concepts based on a Marxist analysis updated by an infusion of social scientific methods (class relations and peasant consciousness). The most important work to come from this approach is Paul Bois's *Paysans de l'ouest,* published in 1960.

Despite the broad title, the book is a detailed, retrospective monograph that examines the département of the Sarthe as a paradigm: an intelligent choice, because the département is divided in two by a north-south line separating the conservative right and the republican left, a dichotomy that is observable in voting patterns from 1848 to the present. Bois, in attempting to trace the origins of this geopolitical division in the Sarthe back to the time of the Revolution, found that in the late eighteenth century two very different sorts of peasantry lived on either side of the line. To the east the peasants were poor, the land they worked was infertile, and they were often obliged to take in weaving in order to make ends meet. Hence they were dependent on urban merchants. To the west the peasants were more prosperous and productive and formed a relatively homogeneous group that aspired to ownership of the land. Noble lords lived far away and were treated with respect, and in their absence the chief obstacle to peasant advancement lay in competition with the bourgeoisie for ownership of the land. When the Revolution came, it crystallized two different political ideologies in these two rural societies. The poorer peasants joined forces with the republican towns, with the peasant weavers offering the most fervent support. The more prosperous peasants in the west, however, became Chouans, rebelling against the revolutionary bourgeoisie with all the more vehemence because 1789 to them meant principally new taxes, acquisition of "national properties" by the townsfolk, and conscription.

In other words, chouannerie is explained as the product of a class consciousness peculiar to a segment of the *bocage* peasantry, which felt no hatred for an absent nobility (the burden of feudal dues having been considerably alleviated by the end of the Ancien Régime) and which was ambitious enough to mount an opposition to the bourgeoisie. Bois's book was thus part of a broad current of twentieth-century works in social science, which rediscovered the political autonomy of the peasantry, in contrast to nineteenth-century writers who by and large had seen the French peasant as a dependent, a plaything of the other classes of society. Unlike Michelet, Tocqueville, and Marx, Bois asked not who kept the peasant in a state of dependency but what made him form a particular type of society. What made the peasants of the Sarthe so bold that they were ready to launch a civil war? No longer was chouannerie seen as the product of a conspiracy manipulated by the few, working behind the scenes to stir up the uneducated masses. For Bois it stemmed, rather, from the crystallization of the collective consciousness of the peasantry, which, depending on the situation and the circumstances, could be directed against either the bourgeoisie or the nobility.

The advantage of rehabilitating the peasant in this way is that it enables us to understand something that could not be explained by those who sought to exalt the heroism of the Vendée rebels in their zeal to defend the Ancien Régime: namely, the fact that the peasants of western France were as favorably disposed toward the Revolution of 1789 as peasants elsewhere in France until the time when they rose in rebellion against the revolutionary dictatorship of 1793. Bois even goes so far as to suggest that the *cahiers* of the future Chouans on the eve of the Revolution reveal a greater hostility to the nobility than do *cahiers* from the section of the département that would remain republican in 1793. At first peasant suspicions were directed against the nobility, but later they gave rise to rebellion against the bourgeoisie, which had become the sole enemy.

The problem with such an interpretation, however, is that it assumes a strict determination of the political by the social. Not only is this not obvious on its face, but by emphasizing a single causal chain it can yield contradictory results. In Bois's work it is the relatively prosperous peasants who rebel; but in the work of Faucheux or Sutherland it is the poor peasants. For Bois the weavers play a key role in conveying republican ideas from town to country-side, while Claude Petitfrère shows that most of them joined the "royal and Catholic army." To be sure these works focus on different regions of western France. But since they all rely on the struggle between town and countryside as the sole explanatory factor, they adduce such a variety of mutually incompatible causes for that struggle that in the end they undermine the idea that the west rebelled as a peasant society defending its own interests against its new rulers.

Like the Vendean insurrection and the rural rebellion in Lozère, the chouannerie cannot be understood without reference to the unifying role of religion. The peasants of the west were surely appalled by the new taxes voted by the Constituent Assembly and by the new division of France into administrative départements. But it was the Civil Constitution of the Clergy and the affair of the priests' oath that consummated the sense of a definitive break in all the regions where rebellions broke out in 1793. This powerful rural attachment to traditional religion and the Church, evident as early as 1791 in the *bocage* of western France and the southeastern Massif Central, itself raises questions that have yet to be explored, such as the inroads made by the Counter Reformation and religious practices in Ancien Régime France.

What can be said with assurance is that the Revolution's reformist activism in religious matters drove the rural west into overt hostility, as can be seen from a glance at the map of disturbances relating to the priests' oath. The area was already a minefield, and the conscription of March 1793 acted as a detonator. The explosion of discontent took two forms, depending on the nature of the resistance encountered. The insurrection in the Vendée was destined to grow, because it met with immediate victory. Elsewhere the National Guard held its own against the peasant bands, and the rural wrath thus contained gave rise not to war but to chouannerie.

Thus chouannerie had many causes, many of them shared with the war in the Vendée. But in the Vendée the peasants were initially victorious, whereas elsewhere guerrilla bands borrowed the more traditional forms of the Jacquerie. What distinguished the west from other regions in more or less open rebellion against Jacobin Paris is a question that has yet received little study, for until recently it has been overshadowed by the vehemence of the insurrection in the west and the idea that there was something unique about the *bocage*. It is not at all certain, however, that there was any fundamental difference between what happened in the Vendée, Brittany, or Maine and rural resistance to the Revolution that erupted in 1793 in such other places as Flanders, Puy de Dôme, Lozère, the Cévennes, and the Rhône valley. In this widespread rural discontent with the escalating tendency of the Revolution the religious question was surely the key factor, and the particularly violent character of the rebellion in the west may have been due to the relatively low level of urbanization there, which deprived the republican forces of bases from which to operate.

François Furet

FURTHER READING

Bois, Paul. *Paysans de l'ouest: Des structures économiques et sociales aux options politiques depuis l'époque révolutionnaire dans la Sarthe.* Le Mans, Paris, and The Hague, 1960; abridged edition, Paris, 1971.

Chassin, Charles-Louis. *Etudes documentaires sur la Révolution française: Les pacifications de l'ouest, 1794–1801 [–1815],* 3 vols. Paris, 1896–1899.

Dubreuil, Léon. *Histoire des insurrections de l'ouest,* 2 vols. Paris, 1929–1930.

Dupuy, Roger. *Aux origines de la chouannerie en Bretagne, 1788–1794,* 3 vols. Unpublished thesis, University of Rennes, 1986.

Lewis, Gwynne. *The Second Vendée: The Continuity of Counter-Revolution in the Departement of the Gard, 1789–1815.* Oxford, 1978.

Petitfrère, Claude. *Blancs et Bleus d'Anjou, 1789–1793,* 2 vols. Lille (University of Lille III, Thesis Reproduction Center); distribution: Paris, 1979.

Sutherland, Donald M. G. *The Chouans: The Social Origins of Popular Counter-Revolution in Upper Brittany, 1770–1796.* Oxford, 1982.

RELATED TOPICS

Civil Constitution of the Clergy   Counterrevolution   Emigrés   Vendée

COUPS D'ÉTAT

I n its original meaning the concept of *coup d'état* had nothing to do with what occurred in France between 9 Thermidor and 18 Brumaire. The term *coup d'état* had been in use since the early seventeenth century, but paradoxically it was not until the nineteenth century—especially after December 2, 1852—that it entered the political vocabulary with a meaning derived from the experience of the Revolution.

The term first gained currency in the 1630s among *libertins* influenced by Italian Quattrocento literature. Guez de Balzac's *Le prince* and especially Gabriel Naudé's *Considérations sur les coups d'état* (1632) used it to refer to an "extraordinary" measure taken by the sovereign out of concern for the public good. The coup d'état was thus a concrete application of *raison d'état:* a blow that had to be struck for "reasons of state." In this way Naudé was able to justify the Saint Bartholomew massacres and the murders of the Guise at Blois in 1588 on orders of Henri III. Seventeenth- and eighteenth-century dictionaries give only this meaning, referring exclusively to something done for the public good or for reasons of public utility. Consider, for example, Furetière's dictionary (1684): "The seizure of La Rochelle was a *coup d'Estat*." Or the first edition of the *Dictionnaire de l'Académie Française* (1694): "*Coup d'Estat*, that is, what is useful to the good of the State." The 1771 edition of the *Dictionnaire de Trévoux* merely copied its predecessors: "A *coup d'Estat* is a coup useful to the public good. The seizure of La Rochelle was a *coup d'Estat*." Not until the sixth edition of the Academy's dictionary (1823) do we find an emphasis on the extraordinary and violent character of the action, but still subsidiary to the notion of the public good: "An extraordinary and always violent measure to which a government resorts when it deems the security of the State to be in jeopardy." And this is twenty years after 18 Brumaire! In other words, unlike so many words or expressions coined before the things to which they referred became realities, the modern coup d'état, as it developed in the nineteenth and twentieth centuries, was a reality before it was baptized with a name. When Chancellor Maupeou abolished the parlements, people spoke of "Maupeou's revolution," not of "Maupeou's coup d'état." When Louis XVI dismissed Necker shortly before July 14, 1789, people referred to an "aristocratic plot," as they did again in October, despite the use of troops. Hence we are obliged to study the revolutionary coups d'état without benefit of dictionaries. As a preliminary hypothesis, I want to distinguish three types of coup d'état. Then as now, a coup d'état was a sudden overthrow of the government by means of military force. But such a blow could be struck first of all by a legislature against a government of which it had tired (9 Ther-

11

midor). Or it could be struck by the legislature against the executive (as in Floréal and Prairial). Or it could be struck by one agency of the executive against another (as on 18 Fructidor and 18 Brumaire). In all three cases preparations had to be made more or less secretly, a premeditated political plan was required, and support had to be sought outside official institutions.

**

Was 9 Thermidor, Year II (July 27, 1794) a coup d'état? Not in appearance, because the Convention chose either to exclude or confirm the members of the Committee of Public Safety, which was then acting as the executive branch. In reality, however, it was a coup d'état, because the carefully prepared charges leveled against Robespierre, Couthon, and Saint-Just brought down the "revolutionary government" and installed a new regime. A great deal is known about the preparations for what can rightly be called a plot. Four groups of politicians took part. There were the former *représentants en mission*, representatives sent by the government to the provinces, who according to Robespierre had "abused the principles of the Revolution" and were recalled by the Convention for terrorist excesses and exactions on local populations. This group included Tallien (whose mistress, the beautiful Theresa Cabarrus, had been in prison since Prairial and was awaiting judgment), Barras, Fréron, and, most important of all, Fouché, whose mission to Nièvre and Lyons had left a bloody trail in its wake. Fouché was openly attacked by Robespierre on 23 Prairial (June 11) and again on 23 and 24 Messidor (July 11 and 12) at the Jacobin Club, since Robespierre no longer spoke before the Convention. He accused the former proconsul of Nièvre of having pursued a policy of materialism and atheism. Feeling threatened, Fouché quit the Jacobins but passed the word to the Convention—the "rogues," as Robespierre would call them—that they were all in jeopardy and must seize the opportunity to act.

The Committee of Public Safety was divided. Feeling isolated and weak, Robespierre ceased to take part in its labors as of early Messidor, forty days before his fall. In his absence who was the leader of the opposition? Carnot, as Georges Lefebvre believed? To be sure, there had been violent disputes between Carnot and Robespierre (on the subject of Bonaparte) and especially between Carnot and Saint-Just (on the subject of General Jourdan's appointment). But it is difficult to believe that this hardworking captain of engineers, whose mediocrity was demonstrated by his subsequent career, was tough enough to bring down the Incorruptible. The Committee's technicians—Prieur of the Côte d'Or and Lindet, for example—confined themselves to their specialties, whether military or economic, and in any case were frequently absent. That leaves two men whom the Committee had been forced to accept by the Club des Cordeliers after the events of September 4 and 5, 1793: Collot d'Herbois and Billaud-Varenne. Believing themselves to be in jeopardy, they made the decisive contacts with others.

What others? The Committee of General Security, led by Vadier and Amar, had never accepted being relegated by the Terrorist Law of Prairial to a subsidiary role relative to that of the Committee of Public Safety. Its atheist leaders laughed at Robespierre's cult of the Supreme Being, whose great festival, staged by the painter David on 20 Prairial (June 8), seemed to cast the former Arras lawyer in the role of the Messiah. Then there was the obscure affair involving Cathérine Théot, a religious crank who was rumored to have prophesied the coming of a new era in which Robespierre would be called upon to save mankind. Everything about the rumors was suspect, as Albert Mathiez has shown. But the Committee of General Security seized on them, amplified them, and used them as a weapon against a man whose deism—and power—they detested.

Robespierre had felt isolated for more than a month. The law of Prairial had heightened the Terror without giving him a free hand in the choice of the accused. Between June 10 and July 27, 1,285 people were condemned to death, including André Chénier. Robespierre sensed people's revulsion at this turn of events. The cult of the Supreme Being, which though despised by the de-Christianizers did nothing to reassure the Catholic faithful, accentuated his isolation. Most important of all, there had been a dramatic reversal in the military situation: on 7 Messidor the army of Sambre and Meuse took Charleroi, on the eighth it took Fleurus, and on the twenty-second it entered Brussels. As Barère would put it later, "victories descended on Robespierre like furies."

Barère represented the Plain, which had supported the revolutionary government as long as it seemed indispensable to save the Revolution, but which was eager to end the Terror and the dictatorship once it seemed secure. He was the intellectual leader of the Thermidorian reaction. Danton's gamble—to back liberty and peace without certainty of victory—had failed. But now that victory was at hand, was that not grounds for reinstating liberty? Everyone hoped so, and Robespierre, who clung to the contradictory formula of terror plus victory, would pay with his life for his stubborn refusal to accept reality.

Robespierre brought matters to a head. On 8 Thermidor (July 26) he mounted the podium of the Convention, confident of the persuasive powers of a voice that had so often served him well. He defended the Committee—and himself—against the charge of dictatorship. He denounced a handful of scoundrels. Unwilling—or unable—to name them, he placed himself in a hopeless position. Charlier took it upon himself to respond: "When one boasts of having the courage of virtue, one must have the courage of truth. Name those whom you accuse."

That same night the coup was meticulously prepared. Recalled from the army, Saint-Just was approached by Billaud-Varenne and asked to take part. Despite his disagreements with Robespierre, he refused to abandon him. Collot d'Herbois, who was to chair the meeting of the Convention on the ninth, was ordered to prevent Robespierre and Saint-Just from speaking. Contacts were made with the Plain, which agreed to abandon Robespierre in exchange for an end to the Terror. At around noon on the ninth Saint-Just took the floor but was able to utter only a few sentences. Tallien interrupted him and Billaud-Varenne attacked Robespierre: "An abyss has opened up beneath our feet. We must not hesitate either to fill it with our corpses or vanquish the traitors."

Robespierre attempted to mount the podium, but the chairman, Collot d'Herbois, rang his bell to drown him out while the floor resounded with shouts of "Down with the tyrant!" At Tallien's behest the assembly voted to arrest Hanriot, commander-in-chief of the National Guard. Louchet called for warrants to be issued for the arrest of Robespierre, Saint-Just, and Couthon. Augustin Robespierre and Le Bas insisted upon the honor of having their names included in the warrant: "The Republic is lost, the brigands have triumphed."

Sent to various prisons around the capital, the five were soon freed. The Commune and Hanriot sounded the alarm and called for a demonstration by the sections late that afternoon, while Barras and Bourdon rallied sections loyal to the Convention, which invaded the Hôtel-de-Ville. Robespierre and his friends did not believe in a genuine insurrection. Their enemies were parliamentarians, not rioters. Robespierre was found with a broken jaw. A legend to the contrary notwithstanding, he had injured himself. Le Bas killed himself with a pistol shot, and Augustin Robespierre leapt from a window. On the night of the tenth, the triumvirs and nineteen of their supporters were guillotined on the Place de la Révolution. Seventy-one others were put to death on the eleventh—the heaviest single day's tribute to the guillotine in all the Terror. Twelve more died on the twelfth. The Terror could not be ended without more terror.

The Thermidorian Convention did not have to contend with any coups d'état. It managed to ward off pressures from the street (including neo-Terrorist demonstrations in Germinal and Prairial, Year III, and royalist disturbances on 13 Vendémiaire, Year IV) while keeping its power intact. On one point, however, it bowed to necessity, relying on the army to crush its enemies. Its indispensable agents were General Menou in Prairial and Generals Brune and Bonaparte in Vendémiaire. The danger, of course, was that these agents would become arbiters of the government's fate. The new constitution was approved by the Convention on 5 Fructidor, Year III (August 22, 1795), shortly before it disbanded. The Constitution was inspired by the principles of 1789 but revised and corrected in light of the experience of 1793 and 1794. It was intended to be liberal and to embody the principle of separation of powers. In fact, however, it institutionalized the practice of resorting to extraordinary procedures, a sort of permanent small-scale coup d'état in anticipation of what was to come in Fructidor and Brumaire. The legislature consisted of two houses, a Council of Five Hundred, which proposed new legislation, and a Council of Anciens, which transformed bills into law. Executive authority was vested in a Directory of five members chosen by the Anciens from a list of fifty proposed by the Five Hundred. Each year one of the five directors and one of every three representatives were required to stand for reelection. The resulting instability imposed a heavy burden on a country at war both at home and abroad, and every year the founders of the Republic were forced to circumvent their own Constitution. The circumvention began even before the Constitution took effect, when the Convention passed the "two-thirds law" of August 22, requiring that two-thirds of the representatives to the new councils be chosen from among present members of the Convention. The events of 13 Vendémiaire grew out of this Hobson's choice. *Les perpétuels,* as their enemies called them, sought to protect what the Revolution had wrought over and against any constitution. In the first elections, held in Brumaire, Year IV (October 1795), the republicans won a majority of the seats, although it is futile to count deputies, since the labels they wore did not always reflect their true positions. The by-elections of Prairial, Year V (October 1796) revealed a marked shift to the right, however. Nearly 170 avowed or covert royalists were elected to the two councils. What is more, the previous councils' incumbents ceased to be *perpétuels:* only 11 of 216 were reelected.

For the Directory the only way out of the impasse was a coup d'état. As chairman the Council of Five Hundred chose General Pichegru, a convinced royalist and member of the Council of Clichy, a society of prominent royalist moderates. The Anciens chose Barbé-Marbois as their chairman and selected Barthélemy to replace Letourneur as director. The events of the spring of 1797 forced both camps to clarify their positions and organize. The royalists and moderates in the two councils were divided and indecisive: some were constitutional monarchists, heirs of the monarchiens and Feuillants, while others supported the rebellious Chouans and Vendeans. They could not agree about the wisdom of seizing power by force. In the spring of 1797 two of the five directors, Reubell and La Révellière, decided to take decisive action against the reactionaries. Barras sat on the fence for quite some time, playing a double game as was his wont. He made contacts with the Agence Royaliste in Paris, but at the same time he sent a trusted friend, Fabre de l'Aude, to Milan to see General Bonaparte and secure the support of his army for use against the majority in the councils. When Bonaparte sent proof of Pichegru's treason, Barras made up his mind to act: his career was at stake, perhaps even his life.

The only option was to call on the army, since calling on the people was out of the question. And the army came down to three men: Moreau (commander of the army of the Rhine), Hoche (commander of the army of Sambre and Meuse), and Bonaparte (victorious in Italy). Moreau vacillated throughout the summer, not because he had been won over by the royalists but because he was reluctant to denounce Pichegru. Like all the republican armies, Moreau's staunchly supported the Republic. Bonaparte acted as he had done before, on 13 Vendémiaire, and as Barras was already doing: he made contacts with both sides and steered a careful course between them. To Carnot he sent his aide-de-camp, Lavalette, who had ties to the moderates. But he feared that credit for the treaty with the Austrians would be stolen from him, and criticism from right-wing deputies and journalists in Paris convinced him to support Barras, Reubell, and La Révellière. He therefore sent Augereau to back the Directory. The army of Sambre and Meuse was closer to home, and no one suspected Hoche, its commander, of counterrevolutionary sympathies. On the pretext of shifting a portion of his army to Brest for a foray into Ireland, he sent 9,000 men marching toward Paris on July 1. On

July 15 his cavalry reached La Ferté-Alais, within the "constitutional radius" from which the army was excluded under the Constitution of Year III. This triggered sharp debate in the councils and the Directory. On 14 Thermidor the triumvirs responded to Carnot, who had been calling for a shake-up in the ministries in favor of the moderates, by dismissing his supporters and appointing Hoche minister of war, François de Neufchâteau minister of the interior, and Talleyrand minister of foreign affairs. By 17 Fructidor (September 4), when the councils brought charges against the triumvirs, it was too late. That night Hoche's soldiers infiltrated the capital, and Augereau took command of the Paris division. Pichegru and Barthélemy were arrested. Only Carnot escaped. On the nineteenth the councils were forced by the victors to approve two emergency measures. Elections in forty-nine départements were nullified; fifty-three deputies and two directors, Barthélemy and Carnot, were sentenced to imprisonment in Guiana. Also approved were harsh new laws applying to émigrés and refractory priests.

Meticulously planned and carried out, the coup d'état of 18 Fructidor at first seemed to mark the beginning of a new Terror, but it proved to be nothing of the kind. It was a Terror without a scaffold. But it did mark the end of a regime: the Directory established by the Constitution of Year III. Some historians refer to a "second Directory": although on the surface it might have seemed that nothing had changed, in reality the house had been abandoned and was available to anyone who wished to occupy it.

After Fructidor this second Directory lived only in anticipation of the annual elections to be held in May 1798. The expulsions in the wake of the coup and the requirement that half of the *perpétuels* left over from the Convention be replaced were hard for the Directory to swallow. Barras waged war on two fronts: against "royalists with red caps" (that is, those who pretended to support the Revolution) and against anarchist levelers. The elections, which went well for functionaries and neo-Jacobins, were hardly of a sort to satisfy the directors, who chose to strike the first blow themselves. With the Law of 22 Floréal, Year VI (May 11, 1798), they "florealized"—disqualified— 106 deputies and dismissed some 200 functionaries and administrators. For the first time the term *coup d'état* was used. Jourdan summed up the situation: "From now on deputies are to be appointed by the executive. The Republic is finished. It is obvious that a regime that systematically nullifies elections in order to create an assembly that pleases the government is no longer a republic; it is a dictatorship." Meager though the fruits of 22 Floréal may have been, it was on that day, and not 18 Brumaire, that the coup d'état was born. The elections of Year VII (March 1799), feebly managed by the Directory, left the country divided between those who wished to maintain what the Revolution had wrought and others, more moderate, who were willing to accept something in the nature of a limited monarchy. The choice fell to the army. The Directory had lost the elections: of 79 incumbent deputies—more or less official candidates—43 were rejected by the voters. Of 64 new candidates proposed by the government, 39 were defeated. Sieyès, whom Robespierre called "the mole of the Revolution," was elected director on May 16 and decided to precipitate yet another crisis. On 30 Prairial, Year VII (June 18, 1799), he persuaded the councils to dismiss those of his colleagues who displeased him and to elect three minor figures of the revolutionary period: Roger Ducos, Gohier, and Moulin. In appearance, 30 Prairial was revenge for 22 Floréal, since it was a reassertion by the councils of a power that had been taken away from them, a pallid reprise of 9 Thermidor. In reality, however, it was a victory for the generals and the army. The first tentative steps toward civil government were overshadowed by a deep-seated movement toward "revisionism."

The roots of the revisionist movement can be traced back to the beginning of the Directory. Nobody—and certainly not Sieyès, embittered by the Convention's rejection of his proposed constitution—believed that a regime designed for stability could survive for long in a time of constant flux. The issue was raised for the first time in a speech to the Five Hundred by the deputy Rouault: the Constitution, he said, contained the "seeds of death." Even some of the men who had drafted the Constitution of Year III, such as Daunou, were convinced of the need for revision. Many who contributed to the strength of the movement later became its victims. Mme. de Staël and the young Benjamin Constant advocated the kind of constitution that would have suited them: liberal and elitist. Much of the right wing, apart from the Chouans and Vendeans, favored revision. Old revolutionaries, depressed and depleted after innumerable failures, no longer had faith in the *perpétuels* and their unpredictable reversals. Since the Commune had been liquidated and the faubourgs crushed, only the republican armies represented their wishes. The "political class" was worn out. After repeated purges, it survived only as a tradition and a myth. The tradition: that of 1789, of 1793. The myth: that a group of men stood for and embodied the Revolution as such—an honorable group for the most part, but not the Revolution.

In contrast to 18 Fructidor, 18 Brumaire was the occasion of a coup d'état that was well planned but badly executed. It all began with a man—and certain forces. The man was Sieyès. The Oratorian regicide who had failed in every attempt to gain power passed for a misunderstood theoretician: "Enigmatic and deliberately unintelligible, he seemed to carry within him a great mystery of public salvation" (Vandal). In the summer of 1799 he became the rallying point for all the Revolution's malcontents: for Jacobins tired of repeated coups, moderates like Daunou, Benjamin Constant, Roederer, Talleyrand, protégés such as Ducos, Cambacérès, Fouché, and Lefebvre—and then Barras, who was both an insider and an outsider. Sieyès' long-term goal was a restoration of the monarchy under the Orléanist dynasty. For the short term he envisioned a coup d'état backed by the Council of Anciens, the purpose of which would be to entrust power to three consuls. But nothing could be done without the army and its generals. Sieyès thought of Moreau, but he was suspected of royalism; of Joubert, but he died at Novi; and then of Brune and Masséna, but they were busy racking up victories.

Then, on October 9, 1799, Napoleon Bonaparte landed at Fréjus. It scarcely mattered that he had left a defeated army bogged down in the sands of Egypt to the hapless Kléber; his legend was born. A contemporary report noted: "Bonaparte's return is regarded as a good augur for our armies, as a guarantee of victories as quick as they are brilliant." The public enthusiasm spread to the Five Hundred and even the Jacobins. The Directory was anything but pleased, but it was not powerful enough to stand in the way. Bonaparte made some modest statements and did not disdain to receive such "Jacobins" as Moulin and Gohier. According to his brother Lucien, then chairman of the Five Hundred, "the unanimous welcome that he received seemed to him to require initially that he turn no one away." In serious matters, however, Lucien acted as intermediary between Napoleon and Sieyès.

Most serious of all the business transacted was the formation of the group that came to be known as Brumairiens, consisting of moderate politicians and intellectuals from the Institute, courted by Bonaparte, who replaced Carnot as a member after Fructidor and who also courted the generals whose support he would need. On 10 Brumaire Bonaparte finally met with Sieyès at Lucien's home. He approved the idea of moving the two councils to Saint-Cloud but rejected Sieyès' initial plan. Napoleon's counterproposal was this: a provisional government of three consuls, with Napoleon as first consul, was to be entrusted with the task of drafting a new constitution. Otherwise "you must count on me no longer." Sieyès gave in: "One is always obliged to trust some things to chance." But in this case chance was named Napoleon Bonaparte.

On 18 Brumaire the coup went off as planned. While Bonaparte met with the generals of all the armies on the rue de la Victoire, a decree was issued transferring the Five Hundred and the Anciens to Saint-Cloud and entrusting Bonaparte with the task of "saving the Republic." At the Tuileries the new consul spoke: "In what state was France when I left it, and in what state did I find it on my return. I left you in peace, and I return in war. I left you conquests, and now the enemy is crossing our borders." Rarely have such dishonest words proved so effective. On the nineteenth everything hung in the balance at the Château de Saint-Cloud. The deputies of the Five Hundred were asking themselves, Why this transfer, why this mobilization of troops? The Anciens sent the Directory a message demanding an explanation, which persuaded Bonaparte of the need to make a personal appearance. His speech to the assemblies was inept and provocative. Jostled, slapped about, and forcibly detained by soldiers under Murat and Lefebvre, he was saved by his brother Lucien and his generals.

*
**

To contemporaries 18 Brumaire was an unexceptional episode, less important than 18 Fructidor or 22 Floréal—merely another change of course in the Revolution's erratic trajectory after 9 Thermidor. The Brumairiens were a disparate coalition. Moderates such as Daunou and Roederer were hoping for stability and peace: they had mistaken Napoleon for Louis Philippe. Yet the coup brought to power a government from which France, to say nothing of Europe, would not recover until after 1815. It was the birth of modern Europe—and a most difficult and painful birth it was.

Although contemporaries may not have seen anything remarkable in the events of 18 Brumaire, the episode has come to be regarded as the very model of the *coup d'état*. When the Eagle's nephew seized power from the Second Republic on December 2, 1852, Marx had every reason to entitle his account of the events *The Eighteenth Brumaire of Louis Bonaparte*.

Denis Richet

FURTHER READING

Bainville, Jacques. *Le dix-huit brumaire*. Paris, 1925.
Lefebvre, Georges. *La France sous le Directoire, 1795–1799*. Paris, 1977.
Ollivier, Albert. *Le dix-huit brumaire, 9 November 1799*. Paris, 1959.

RELATED TOPICS

Carnot
Committee of Public Safety
Constant
Constitution
Danton

Napoleon Bonaparte
Paris Commune
Revolutionary Government
Robespierre

Sieyès
Staël
Terror
Thermidorians

DE-CHRISTIANIZATION

Applied to the French Revolution, the word "de-Christianization" is full of ambiguities. In the first place there is a question whether it can or cannot be used to characterize the Revolution as a whole. Some interpreters, such as Maistre and Bonald, have viewed the whole Revolution as having been entirely anti-Christian in inspiration. But others insist that de-Christianization was by no means the Revolution's dearest project. At the outset there was nothing to suggest that a series of unrelated decisions would inexorably lead to a conflict between the Revolution and the Church that the leaders of the Revolution did not want. Proponents of the first interpretation see the desire to de-Christianize everywhere: in the early days of the Constituent Assembly, in the elimination of the tithe, and in the confiscation of Church property in the name of the nation. But those who take the second view see de-Christianization as having been confined to the years 1793 and 1794 and as incompatible with what went before and what came after. Quickly launched and just as quickly forgotten, the whole episode was a sideshow without great significance: such is the view of Richard Cobb.

Yet both groups of interpreters, however broadly or narrowly they construe the extent of revolutionary de-Christianization, agree that its aim was to rid France of the influence of the Catholic Church. It is assumed that this was a goal consciously held by the leaders of an organized movement, and the only question is whether they succeeded or failed. Yet the very notion of de-Christianization suggests a quite different view. Antireligious sentiment was something that developed gradually over centuries, that was experienced rather than philosophized; it was spontaneous rather than coerced, arising out of the depths of society rather than being imposed by the political authorities. The issue of de-Christianization in the Revolution therefore raises complex questions about the relation between specific events and long-term historical trends. Was this episode conditioned by a much earlier history? Was de-Christianization a cause—an aggressive and voluntary movement—or a much less self-conscious effect? In order to speak of revolutionary de-Christianization we must therefore either give up the hypothesis that it was the work of men of ill will or else spread the blame so that it is shared in part by the spirit of the times.

In choosing to view de-Christianization as a long-term phenomenon brutally revealed by the revolutionary convulsion, we do not ignore willful de-Christianization by the men of the Revolution but rather elect to view it in its proper perspective. Their initiatives were preceded by a long and silent process, but they hastened and intensified that process and simultaneously helped to create an entirely new situation. When it came to de-Christianization, the Revolution was less inventive than it has been accused of being. Nevertheless, the Revolution did mark the end of a world in which obedience to religion went unquestioned and the advent of a world in which ever broader segments of the population drifted into religious indifference. Seen in this way this violent and incongruous episode was far more than a sideshow.

The problem is further complicated, moreover, by the various meanings that can be attached to the word "de-Christianization": secularization, elimination of the role of priests, and changes in religious practice can be quantitatively measured, but the weakening of religious feeling is an intangible. Because this reality is so hard to get at, it has encouraged polemic. Historians such as Jean Delumeau, unwilling to judge the degree of religious fervor by such measures as the density of priests or the regularity of church attendance, speculate that the Revolution produced effects of two kinds: de-Christianization of the majority (in the sense of a curtailment of religious practice) coupled with re-Christianization of a minority (in the sense of a heightening of religious fervor). This is not the place to enter into a discussion of Delumeau's hypothesis, whose validity is very difficult to judge. Note, however, that it contrasts two different definitions of Christianity: one internal and incommunicable, the other communal and observable. Obviously the historian who is resigned to judge inner emotions only indirectly is obliged to focus attention on the latter aspects of religious behavior. And it was precisely those aspects on which the men of the Revolution set their sights, their aim being to destroy not religion as such but what they called "its outward signs."

It is a commonplace to think of France as a uniformly and tranquilly Christian nation on the eve of 1789, disrupted from top to bottom by the aggressive de-Christianization of the Revolution. Before the Revolution nearly all of France's peasant population attended Easter mass. Receiving the sacraments was all the more difficult to avoid because the priest controlled the parish register and thus the civil status of every person in the parish. To be born and to die, therefore, meant to be born and to die in the Catholic faith. Although Protestants were granted civil status, France remained so Catholic a country that Protestants were denied positions in the courts, police, and schools. Even those who would become the most zealous of patriots, such as Fauchet, argued that Catholicism was the most natural religion for a monarchy because it refused to subject religious worship to the anarchy of private opinion. But the actual religious history of Ancien Régime France does not exactly confirm the notion that before the Revolution the country was united by a uniform, ancient, and unshakable Catholic faith.

Let us first examine the question of uniformity. As soon as one begins to look at French Catholicism in detail, its uniformity becomes questionable. Even before the Revolution there were social differences in religious practice, which pointed to nonconformist behavior in mobile or poorly controlled groups: hawkers, weavers, soldiers, and tavernkeepers, to name a few. There are also early signs of a sexual dimorphism in religious practice: a disparity between male and female observance (invariably an indication of declining practice overall) had begun in rural central France. Necker had already noticed that men were likely to leave church before the sermon and return just in time for the consecration, a practice that would become common in the nineteenth century. Finally, there was a geographical differentiation of religious practice well before the Revolution, which solidified those boundaries. Montfortian missionaries to western France were not mistaken about the degree of religious fervor they encountered there or about the mixed reception that awaited them. They took note of the *pays durs,* those regions of open countryside, close to urban influences, and maritime regions where constant traffic and sea trade were already creating "a republican people." Elsewhere, in Provence for example, the boundaries were different: the seacoast was more devout than the inland areas. But the important point to make about these early regional differences is that they challenge the notion of religious uniformity. If, moreover, the study of regional differences were to show that the places and milieus in which religious fervor was already on the wane were those most affected by revolutionary de-Christianization, then we would have to revise our notions about the violence of this phenomenon.

Let us now turn to the question of the ancientness of French Catholicism. Recent historiography has also cast doubt on another cliché: the idea of an immemorially Christian France. It has been shown that medieval society was not as thoroughly Christianized as was once thought, and that the real Christianization of France did not begin until the sixteenth century, when post-Tridentine Catholicism attempted to reassert its dominion. The Church then sought to improve its priests intellectually and morally by building seminaries throughout the country and establishing a regular schedule of pastoral visits. Missionary teachers were dispatched to instruct the faithful: Montfortians, Lazarists, and Eudists took to the highways carrying icons and pamphlets; they taught canticles, established missions, and perfected the preacher's art to the point where the abbé Pluche could say that "in the Catholic Church preaching is everything." (Catholic preaching impressed revolutionary anticlericals so much that they sought to copy its methods.) Last but not least, the Church stepped up its efforts to rechannel energies wasted in suspect pre-Christian rituals and superstitions. This took time. Contrary to conventional wisdom, the eighteenth century can therefore be seen as *the* truly Christian century. By that time the faithful could call upon the services of an excellent parish clergy. (Never was there a more remarkable clergy, said Tocqueville, than that of France when the Revolution took it by surprise.) Priests read more, abstained from dance and drink, and wore the cassock, a recent innovation that distinguished them from their parishioners and gave them newfound dignity. A new generation of bishops made up its mind to reside in its dioceses and devote its attention to ecclesiastical administration. And finally, the faithful themselves, thanks to the catechism and lessons they received, knew what the Church required of the Christian and did what they were supposed to do, taking part in morning and evening prayer, Easter communion, and Sunday mass. To those who remembered the complaints of seventeenth-century bishops about the ignorance of their flocks, it was clear that considerable gains had been made.

Consider, finally, the question of the Church's strength. In this solid edifice, controlled more tightly than ever by a hierarchy whose prescriptions were more widely observed than ever before, cracks were already visible, premonitory signs of the de-Christianization to come. Within the Church itself, monastic vocations had declined sharply, for this was an era that wasted no tenderness on vain and useless monastic life. Ordinations of priests also dropped. What is more, extreme disparities of income created tensions within the clergy and fostered unrest within a small avant-garde led by Richer. By the end of the century the Jansenist controversy had abandoned the realm of theology for that of politics, thereby gaining in vehemence what it had lost in loftiness. We have probably underestimated the extent to which the whole interminable affair shook the faith of many. Hume, who observed the controversy with astonishment, noted that it made religion appear to be the opposite of what it should be, an explosive rather than a unifying factor in the community. Although it is not easy to say how much Jansenism contributed to the weakening of religious fervor, it is certain that it fostered the habit of protesting both papal despotism and royal authority, and that by favoring infrequent communion as a way of enforcing respect and awe for the sacraments it hastened the decline of devotion. Of course there was Jansenism and there was Jansenism: as Pierre Chaunu has shown in the case of Lorraine, Jansenism did not necessarily encourage de-Christianization in areas bordering on Protestant countries. It did, however, encourage the faithful to enter into personal relations with God and thus promoted emancipation from the ecclesiastical authorities and autonomy of the individual conscience. Hence, despite all that was archaic in its vision of the world as evil, it helped blaze a trail toward modernity.

Among the Catholic faithful too we find signs of growing individualism. Michel Vovelle has shown how in one century wills became secularized: introductory passages commending the soul of the deceased to God grew shorter, ostentatious funerals ceased to be fashionable, and testators indicated less concern about their place of burial. Burial in outdoor graves in enclosed cemeteries rather than in the dark haven of the church, a change recommended in any case by contemporary hygienists, became the rule and the symbol of a growing separation between religion—the Christian life—and life in the broader sense. The decline in the importance of confraternities and the secularization of their activities also points to this growing rift. Less direct but no less eloquent symptoms of change include the rise of illegitimate births and increased recourse to contraceptive practices.

Finally, mention should be made of the success and popularization of Enlightenment philosophy. At bottom the men of the Enlightenment were not antireligious, for they were animated by the creative energy of a new faith. Nor were they necessarily anti-Christian. Some believed in the spirit of early Christianity, which they claimed had been betrayed by the Roman Catholic Church. Above all, they said that Christianity should be pursued as a political force, not as a belief. Still, it was often difficult to distinguish between power and belief. Anticlericalism quickly shaded into anti-Christianity, and the Enlightenment was decidedly anticlerical. The Catholic Church, having sealed its alliance with the monarchy through the revocation of the Edict of Nantes, became the philosophes' favorite target. The great works of Pierre Bayle (1647–1706) date from a period when Protestants were faced with the choice so contrary to the national interest of accepting either exile or conversion. From Bayle's writings the philosophes drew some of their most powerful ideas (all the more readily in that Bayle, though a Protestant, never spoke in the name of the defeated sect and detested Calvinist intolerance as much as its Catholic counterpart): namely, that no religion can claim decisive proof of its truth, and that therefore the state should not intervene in matters of faith; that no religion is a guarantee of morality; and above all that any form of coercion in religious matters is absurd. By the time of the Revolution these articles of the new faith had already won over an enlightened elite that was ready to make trouble if the opportunity arose. This readiness became apparent in 1790 when conflict broke out between anti-Catholic local authorities and a Christian peasantry. The Enlightenment spirit also affected pastors themselves: in their sermons the image of a cruel God and eternal torture was toned down and the obsessive presence of sin faded. One went so far as to publish an "Easy Method for Being Happy in This Life While Insuring Eternal Bliss," a title that must have caused more than one Jansenist to turn in his grave and which confirms the view of a contemporary that religion had turned "soft and soothing." Boisgelin, the archbishop of Aix, admitted that "the color of the eighteenth century cannot be that of primitive times." Surely the most striking symptom of growing unbelief was that religion seemed bent on shedding its pomp and identifying itself with morality. In *Questions sur l'incrédulité* Le Franc de Pompignan remarked that whereas the category of unbelievers had once been quite simple, it now took a very sophisticated system of classification to capture all the varieties of incredulity.

Exaggeration is to be avoided, however. Though less uniform, ancient, and stable than it appeared, Christianity structured the world in a way that nearly everyone accepted. Voltaire's influence might have won over the elite, but the masses continued to live the religious life. The relation of priests to society had evolved in two ways: integration and separation. On the eve of the Revolution the clergy was more separate from the rest of society than it had been two centuries earlier: distinguished by its clothing, its code of conduct, and its enlightened attitudes. The man with knowledge, living among those without it, may have scorned popular traditions and thus encouraged religious indifference and, by attempting to enforce a higher standard, may have driven a moral wedge between the Church and its flock. At the same time, however, eighteenth-century priests were wholehearted supporters of the ideal of social utility. The priest's new duties of charity, assistance, and education linked him to his parish more closely than in the past. Both a stranger in the lay community and a part of it, exigent when it came to religious practice but indulgent in regard to the quest for worldly happiness, he was able to achieve a certain equilibrium in this paradoxical situation. But the

Revolution upset this equilibrium: by attempting to force the clergy toward integration, it only condemned them to separation.

The process of de-Christianization had been under way for centuries, and at first the Revolution simply marked an acceleration of its pace. From the Constituent Assembly's first actions to the completion of the Civil Constitution of the Clergy, a series of legislative measures gave rise to suspicions that the Assembly was hostile to the Catholic religion. After August 4 the tithe was eliminated—and without indemnities, in contrast to other feudal dues. On November 2 the Assembly confiscated ecclesiastical property to reduce the deficit. In both cases it justified the dispossession of the Church on the grounds that the Church did not own its properties but simply enjoyed their usufruct for the traditional purposes of education and charitable relief. In February a law was passed concerning monastic vows. Yet none of these new laws led to open conflict; the Church, it is true, was used to submitting to the law of political power. It was no longer constrained by the crown but in the name of the sovereign people.

Trouble first began brewing in parts of France where there was a strong dissident minority, where a wealthy Protestant bourgeoisie lived in proximity to a Catholic proletariat agitated by the counterrevolution. The ire of Catholics was aroused by the Assembly's dismissal of Dom Gerle's motion that Catholicism be declared the official state religion (April 1790). Immediately supported by the high clergy, the motion was denounced by certain Jansenists in the Assembly as a trap. And the trap was indeed sprung in Languedoc, Poitou, and above all in the cities of Montauban (May) and Nîmes (June), where bloody clashes made it seem that civil war had come.

Conflict merely smoldered, however, until the difficult process of ratifying the Civil Constitution of the Clergy was complete. The Pope took eight months before issuing his negative opinion of the decision, thus creating a void, for the bishops had let it be known that they would await the views of the supreme spiritual authority before coming to a judgment of their own. In the meantime, on November 26, 1790, the Assembly decided to insist that all priests swear an oath of allegiance to the Constitution, which would imply allegiance to the Civil Constitution of the Clergy as well, and which would have to be made publicly, after mass, to an assembly of the faithful. Municipalities made preparations for these ceremonies and agreed to certify the oaths. The validity of these proceedings was frequently challenged, for the oaths often contained appended commentaries that altered their meaning. At the conclusion of this process, whereby the lay community arrogated to itself the right to judge the validity of the clergy's oaths, France had two clergies, one consisting of priests who had taken the oath, the other of so-called refractories (estimated to have numbered around forty-five percent of the total). In fact there was also a third group, consisting of priests who had taken the oath but who refused all contact with priests chosen to replace the "refractories," who were stigmatized as "intruders."

Timothy Tackett has recently examined the question of what motives priests might have had for taking or not taking the oath. Which priests went along, and which refused? And in what regions were priests most likely to cooperate? Economic motives played a part: in the west, where the clergy was relatively prosperous, large numbers of priests refused to take the oath. By contrast, in the Paris basin, Champagne, and central France, it was the poor priests who submitted. The geographical distribution of a disciplined, organized clergy also played a large role. Where priests felt that they were supported by a concentrated, cohesive group, and where they felt least personally exposed to criticism (as in the cities), they refused to go along. The most important factor was the nature of the religious environment: wherever there was a strong Protestant community, priests were reluctant to be seen taking the oath in the face of the enemy. Last but not least was the attitude of the populace. Although it would be wrong to suggest that the priest's choice merely reflected the sentiments of the community, it is remarkable that the geographical distribution of oaths largely anticipates the map of religious practice as recently as the 1960s: the oath was widely refused in those areas where religious practice has remained strong, namely, western, northern, and northeastern France and the southeastern portion of the Massif Central. By contrast, the oath was successful in the Paris basin and in central France and the northern Massif Central, where the degree of religious observance in the twentieth century has been low. Although local situations were extremely diverse and the event was unique in French history, it nevertheless established a durable division between a clerical France and an anticlerical France; this mitigates the importance of the priest's personal choice and highlights the role of the attitude held by the religious communities.

In any case, the cost of this first revolutionary shock was high. While it was relatively easy to replace the eighty bishops who refused to sign, it was far less easy to find new parish priests. Some of the priests chosen refused to accept their posts, while others were boycotted by their parishioners, and the Constituent Assembly was obliged to leave in place some refractories for whom no replacement could be found. Did this stalemate contribute to the coming de-Christianization? It could be argued that the crisis affected only the clergy, the spiritual supervision of the flock and not its Christian sentiments. But aside from the disarray engendered by the existence of rival clergies, would not the practice of electing curés and bishops have shaken the traditional sense of dependence on and deference toward the priest? A priest who was also a government official was no longer shielded from the fray.

Nevertheless, the muddle created by the intransigence of both the Pope and the Assembly can be seen as the result of ineptness rather than of a deliberate policy of de-Christianization. Within a year, however, the government had clearly moved toward a policy of deliberate hostility toward the Church. After August 10 it decided to deport refractory priests in order to prevent them from influencing the elections. Even more important was the decision to establish a secular department for recording vital statistics, traditionally a responsibility of the parish priest. This measure struck directly at the constitutional clergy, which, in addition to administering the sacraments, kept the parish registers. The parish priest lost one of his primary functions and thus a new blow was struck at the heart of this loyal clergy. Henceforth the only legitimate certificate of marriage was to be the civil marriage contract; hence the state alone would have the exclusive right to determine what constituted impediments to marriage. Divorce and remarriage would therefore become permissible. Even monks and priests could legally marry. The new law made a mockery of ecclesiastical law. And once again, on this extraordinarily important issue the constitutional bishops were divided: Lindet, bishop of Eure, took a wife just one month after the decree (November 24, 1792). Others, such as Grégoire and Fauchet, moved even more quickly to forestall such action, declaring that the Church had a sacred interest in the rule that ordination was an impediment to marriage and grounds for nullification. All viewed secularization as a portent of the violent de-Christianization to come.

The first violence came in early autumn of Year II, and despite Robespierre's quick action in Frimaire to nip the movement in the bud, sporadic episodes continued until spring in outlying areas. The nature of the violence varied widely depending on the place and the individuals involved. In some cases priests were forced to abdicate and soon thereafter to marry. In others churches were closed and services prohibited. In still others church silver and bells were confiscated for the "national melting pot" as contributions to the war effort. Elsewhere there were incidents of icon smashing, pillaging of precious objects, and destruction of paintings and statues (Michelet would later speak of a "Saints' second of September"). There were also anticlerical masquerades, and virtually everywhere there were attempts to substitute revolutionary rituals for Christian ceremonies. Of course there were many degrees of violence. The scenes that bulk largest in collective memory are those of transgression (which revived images of the wars of religion): saints demolished by hammer blows, cassocks burned in bonfires, and priests, after committing their letters of ordination to the flames, forced to ride backwards on asses. Elsewhere, however, there were peaceful scenes in which sacred objects were turned over to the authorities.

Who initiated these episodes, and who participated in them? With the exception of Michelet and Quinet, who both looked favorably on the de-Christianization movement (although the former felt that it came somewhat too late and the latter that it did not go far enough), most historians have been rather harsh about the whole business, in which they detect the machinations of a political faction. Albert Mathiez and Daniel Guérin, following a view shared by many others, including Robespierre himself, have named the guilty parties—adventurers and unscrupulous foreigners who gravitated around Hébert—and identified their motives, the very same motives attacked by Robespierre: by rousing the populace to a militant campaign of de-Christianization these dubious characters hoped to divert attention from their own dishonest activities. In favor of this argument is obviously the brevity of the episode, as well as the role played by government liaison officials, who were everywhere among the instigators. Dumont in the Somme and Fouché in Nevers staged pagan ceremonies and smashed icons well before the incident usually taken to have initiated the de-Christianization movement: the solemn abjuration of the bishop of Paris at the famous session of the Convention on 17 Brumaire, Year II. Sent to the provinces to combat federalism, these men made de-Christianization into a "campaign," whose progress faithfully followed their itinerary and whose violence and systematic character were products of their personal zeal. The role of outside agitators suggests that de-Christianization was foisted upon a population that had no choice in the matter. Indeed, detachments of the Revolutionary Army were sent ostensibly to maintain communications and protect the flow of food, and even if they did not instigate the movement, they did offer energetic assistance. This explains how the wave of de-Christianization followed the routes taken by these political soldiers, proceeding from town to countryside and avoiding the harder-to-reach mountainous areas. Thus, the movement came from outside; it was foreign to the regions involved and artificial, coercive. Inaugurated by a political initiative, it ended in the same way, with the intervention on 1 Frimaire of Robespierre, who quickly obtained the support of Danton, effecting a first halt that would thwart the sans-culottes. The report of 18 Floréal defining "the relationship between religious ideas and republican principles" heralded the Supreme Being and definitively ended the episode.

But this political interpretation, which deprives the popular movement of any autonomous role in de-Christianization, is today viewed with widespread skepticism by historians concerned with reconstructing the role of actors at the grass roots. This skepticism has produced, among other things, an interpretation of the movement as a spontaneous uprising. Seeking to deprive Robespierre of credit for halting the de-Christianization process, some historians have preferred to paint him as an inspired interpreter, the decipherer of popular sentiments, which, we are told, had "since Germinal" mandated an end to the disrespect being shown sacred things. The merit of this view is that it casts the Floréal report as the expression of a deep-seated popular need. Unfortunately, it cannot stand up to serious scrutiny. What kind of religious sentiment waxes and wanes over the course of a few months?

There are at least two ways of arguing more reasonably for an active role of the populace in the movement. First, we might identify, in addition to government liaison officers and soldiers of the Revolutionary Army, participants less external to the regions concerned, activists in popular societies and local militants. Their active participation and even their sometimes excessive enthusiasm (for they occasionally went beyond the orders of the liaison officers) explains why even some out-of-the-way villages experienced violent outbursts. It seems quite reasonable to conclude, therefore, that de-Christianization was particularly intense where initiatives emanating from the central authorities met with popular assent. We must be clear about the meaning of "popular": local participation was the work of the militant members of popular societies. Scarcely "men of the people," many were activists skilled in public speaking and in leading and convincing others.

DE-CHRISTIANIZATION

There is a second way to give the people back their role: to show that the geographical pattern of events, like the pattern of priestly opposition to the oath, was less arbitrary than one would expect if all the trouble had been fomented by revolutionary officials and soldiers. Michel Vovelle has studied abdications by priests in the southeastern quarter of France and identified three distinct zones. In central France, where great numbers of priests took the constitutional oath, that foremost sign of lukewarm religious sentiment, there were also numerous incidents of de-Christianization, and in the nineteenth and twentieth centuries this area has been one in which the level of religious practice has been low. The second region—the mountainous areas in the Alps and along the fringes of the Massif Central—was a rebellious one, where the oath was accepted in some places, rejected in others. Here, occasional violent incidents of de-Christianization were the work of small groups of activists without popular support. Where the oath was resisted, religious fervor remained strong in the nineteenth century. The third and last zone, consisting of the Rhône valley, Hérault, and Gard, was one of mixed attitudes. Some priests took the oath, others refused; the pressure to de-Christianize was itself very uneven, and religious behavior in the nineteenth and twentieth centuries continued to be diverse. The consistency of these maps over time suggests that a variety of factors was at work in de-Christianization. Vovelle's hypothesis is that the whole episode was less traumatic than is usually assumed because it was part of a long-term de-Christianization. Nevertheless, while this evidence helps us to restore the shading of the portrait, it cannot refute the view that the movement was generally aggressive and instigated by outsiders.

To say that a movement was instigated from outside is not to say that it had no consequences, nor is it to say that it did not take longer to forget than it took to launch. These few months or even weeks of coercive de-Christianization left profound traces. Among the "outward signs" of religion targeted by revolutionary troops, how many steeples, crosses, church porches, and statues disappeared forever? How many parishes were left without a priest? In addition to those priests who refused to take the oath, 20,000 others abdicated their posts, and despite later efforts by the hierarchy to bring them back, the damage was never completely undone. In the absence of a clergy, it is not inconsequential that many people began to hold services at home, accentuating independence from the Church hierarchy. Even more important, popular protests against the de-Christianization campaign were inspired and led by women. Women were the first to boycott priests who had taken the oath: Grégoire complained that his constitutional church was "strangled by dissolute and seditious women." It was women who camped on the doorsteps of sacristies, defended their ciboriums, reclaimed their bells, and molested administrators. Women also refused to accept the republican calendar and the substitution of revolutionary for Christian ceremonies. It was their resistance that gave a feminine visage to the French Catholic Church in the nineteenth century.

After the brief period of violence came a time of confusion. Robespierre, who had done all he could to put an end to a de-Christianization whose political stupidity worried him and whose ostentatious character repelled him, was deposed on 9 Thermidor; his successors were committed anticlericals who had had a hand in the de-Christianization movement. Though they were influenced by Voltaire, their accession to power did not mark the triumph of Voltaire over Rousseau, for not only the logic of their policies but also public opinion demanded a restoration of religious freedom; besides, pacification seemed impossible without it. The Thermidorian Convention therefore reluctantly accepted freedom of worship and agreed to a trial separation of church and state: the government would no longer pay clerical salaries and would end its attacks on churches and on religion's "outward signs." At long last the Catholic religion could emerge from its subterranean existence. Despite the leadership's firm intention to confine religion to private oratories, churches began to reopen. Under the Directory the legislature's religious policy was inconsistent. Sometimes it simply shut its eyes and allowed the Church to reestablish itself in many parishes. Services were held and bells were rung. Concessions were made to "peaceful priests." Yet on occasion, most notably after Fructidor, Year V, persecution was reinstituted. Priests were again required to take oaths: one, which contained a promise to "hate royalty and anarchy," earned priests who took it the sobriquet "hatefuls." The government granted itself the right to deport anyone who disturbed the peace, reviving memories not so much of the Terror (for the laws were ignored and executions were rare) as of arbitrary rule. In this combative atmosphere no particular benevolence was shown toward the Gallican Church, which had to fight a war on two fronts: against the competition of the "Romans" on one side and against the substitute religions dreamed up by the Revolution on the other. But the latter never took hold (the Revolution, Michelet remarked sadly, had been able to close the churches but not to open the temple) and peasant resistance to "republican institutions" did not diminish. In Messidor, Year VII, Boulay de la Meurthe gave voice to a widespread sentiment when he observed that "the people are more attached to independence of religious opinion than to any notion of liberty," which led him to prophesy that "a skillful usurper, even one with relatively limited forces, could win himself support by guaranteeing that liberty." And Bonaparte would do just that from the very beginning of the Consulate, even before any steps were taken to resolve the religious problem as a whole, by showing through conciliatory gestures that the government had given up any thought of imposing de-Christianization.

This inglorious end to a revolutionary experiment might suggest that nothing remained of the Revolution's religious policies and that "revolutionary de-Christianization" became a meaningless phrase. But if de-Christianization is reinterpreted as declericalization, it retains its meaning. Thousands upon thousands of priests emigrated; others abdicated, many of them never to return, leaving a shambles behind: pastorless parishes, abandoned presbyteries, the faithful in need of sacraments. And if by de-Christianization one means secularization, the term still makes sense. The Church, which had ceased to preside over social activities, would never regain its control over individual lives, nor would it ever repair its most significant loss: clerical control over public records and vital statistics. If de-Christianization means a decline of religious practice, again the results were dramatic. The Revolution aggravated existing differences in religious observance by men and women, hastened male abstinence from Easter communion, and inaugurated the two antagonistic centers of village social life of the nineteenth century, the church for women and the tavern for men. Geographical differences appeared for the first time. The response to religious persecution strengthened or, as in the Vendée, created feelings of regional identity. In areas where no one minded the absence of the priest or the interruption of services, religious observance quietly declined. The constitutional priest who took over the diocese of Limoges after its bishop emigrated painted this sad portrait of his flock under the Directory: "When they were exhorted to show that they were Christians and Catholics, they pleaded that they were awaiting the return of their legitimate priests to confess and take communion, even at Easter. But in truth this was only an excuse. When they begged their priests to return to their churches in 1795, they came apparently full of zeal, but when the reaction set in, they ceased to attend. Most awaited death before taking a step toward the sacraments, and God knows how they received them." And a Burgundian mayor observed: "A good third of the inhabitants no longer wished to observe the sabbath. They went to the tavern and played cards during mass and vespers." In many regions of France the Revolution was an open-ended episode, and it marked the beginning of indifferent and intermittent religious practice, further attested to by children without religious instruction and increasingly late baptisms.

If by de-Christianization one means loss of religious feeling, however, the question is far more difficult if not impossible to settle. Some have even argued that religious feelings were rekindled by the Revolution. Canon Duchastanier wrote: "Never were more good masses celebrated than under the Terror. . . . Robespierre filled heaven and purified and saved religion in France, yet the ignorant maintain and believe that he destroyed it." Such a judgment takes away with one hand what it grants with the other, however, for it assumes that this miraculous renaissance came about because the Christian community rid itself of the only mildly religious and purged itself of mere conformists, thus effecting a divorce from a society that had ceased to be religious and claimed to stand on its own. In other words, the price of this renaissance was that religious commitment increasingly became a matter of individual choice. A further cost was a widespread belief that would continue to be influential in French politics for a long time to come, in the words of Mme. de Staël, that "the friends of liberty appear to be the enemies of religion." The course of the Revolution lent substance to an idea that was difficult to accept for those who held that liberty and equality were values derived from the gospel and applied to civic life, an idea that would have seemed ridiculous to most of those who participated in the Revolution at the outset, namely, that the new principles of political life were incompatible with the old religion.

Mona Ozouf

FURTHER READING

Annales historiques de la Révolution française, no. 233, July–September 1978. Special issue, "De-Christianization in the Year II."

Cobb, Richard. *Les armées révolutionnaires, instrument de la Terreur dans les départements, April 1793–Floréal An II*, 2 vols. Paris and The Hague, 1961–1963.

Delumeau, Jean. *Le Catholicisme entre Luther et Voltaire*. Paris, 1971.

Dupront, Alphonse. "Vie et création religieuse dans la France moderne (XVIe–XVIIIe siècle)," in Michel François, ed., *La France et les Français*. Paris, 1972.

Groethuysen, Bernard. *Origines de l'esprit bourgeois en France*, vol. 1, *L'Eglise et la bourgeoisie*. Paris, 1927.

Hufton, Olwen. "The Reconstruction of the Church," in Gwynne Lewis and Colin Lucas, eds., *Beyond the Terror: Essays in French Regional and Social History, 1794–1815; Essays for Richard Cobb*. Cambridge, 1983.

Leflon, Canon Jean. *La crise révolutionnaire, 1789–1846*, vol. 20 of *L'histoire de l'Eglise depuis les origines à nos jours*, Augustin Fliche and Victor Martin, eds. Paris, 1951.

Pérouas, Father Louis. "Sur la déchristianisation: Une approche de la pratique pascale sous le Directoire, Le cas de la Creuse," *Revue d'histoire de l'Eglise de France*, no. 189, July–December 1986.

Tackett, Timothy. *Religion, Revolution and Regional Culture in Eighteenth-Century France: The Ecclesiastical Oath of 1791*. Princeton, 1985.

Vovelle, Michel. *Religion et révolution: La déchristianisation de l'an II*. Paris, 1976.

RELATED TOPICS

Civil Constitution of the Clergy
Clubs and Popular Societies
Enlightenment
Hébertists

Michelet
Necker
Revolutionary Religion

Robespierre
Staël
Tocqueville

ELECTIONS

E lections constitute an important yet neglected chapter of the French Revolution. They were important, first, because various revolutionary assemblies, by carefully elaborating electoral legislation, attested to the privileged position reserved for suffrage in the new political order. They were also important because of their number and frequency: some twenty elections (both first- and second-stage) were held during the revolutionary decade.

Despite the frequency of elections and the scope of the debates to which they gave rise, one cannot help being struck by historians' general indifference to them. This indifference is more noticeable for the elections of the period 1789–1792 than for those of the directorial period, which have been the subject of systematic study by J.-R. Suratteau and others.

Of the elections held in the early years of the Revolution, the only one that has received extensive scrutiny is the spring 1789 election of the Estates General. The unusual interest in this particular election is due primarily to its unique location in the chronology of the Revolution, at the dividing line between two eras. The election of 1789 could be seen as either the final political act of the Ancien Régime or the inaugural act of the Revolution. Prior to the innovative work of Auguste Cochin, however, historians were primarily interested in the *cahiers de doléances,* that is, in the most old-fashioned aspect of this consultation with the electorate rather than in the election of deputies per se. If the *cahiers* offer a summary of Ancien Régime society, the nomination of deputies empowered to transmit them to Versailles was the prelude to the birth of the first French representative assembly on June 17, 1789.

Michelet, the exception to the rule, reveals the reason for the nineteenth century's widespread lack of interest. The only historian of the period to offer penetrating analyses of the elections, especially those of 1792, he was also the only one to delve into the treasure stored in the archives. It was not until the centenary of the Revolution, at a time of transition from "philosophical" to scholarly and soon academic history, whose mission was to chronicle the "Great Revolution" cherished by the nascent Third Republic, that it became possible to exhume revolutionary electoral events. Not only the many studies of "the public spirit" but also more illustrious works, such as that of Aulard, contributed to the task. Yet the context in which these undertakings were framed—namely, to uncover the roots of a republican consensus—dictated that elections would occupy a marginal position: they were used solely as a way of establishing an implausible and not very pertinent X-ray of public opinion.

That this enterprise was abandoned is unfortunate, in spite of its weaknesses. Twentieth-century historiography, interested primarily in social history and extralegal modes of political action, has for the most part ignored the electoral question.

*\
* *

In the history of elections the Constitution of Year III marks an important dividing line. Subsequent elections became a major factor in political life. Earlier, their character was ambiguous, defined on the one hand by their inability to fulfill the role assigned to them and on the other hand by the progressive confiscation or diversion of an essential institution by groups engaged in a struggle for power. The fact that it is hard to get a handle on the elections held between 1790 and 1793 partly explains why historians generally have been indifferent to them or have treated them in a marginal and anecdotal way.

Traditionally divided into chronological sequences—constitutional monarchy, Republic and Terror, Directory, Consulate—the Revolution was in fact punctuated by a series of major crises, insurrections, and coups d'état: Varennes, August 10, May 31, 9 Thermidor, and finally 18 Brumaire. These upheavals marked transitions between principal periods of the Revolution and defined their meaning. In the genesis of political upheaval and change, elections were always subsidiary episodes, at least until the Directory. At most they confirmed, by changing the groups in power, changes and purges that had *already* taken place.

Thus, two parallel histories of the Revolution are possible: one a history of upheavals, whose spiraling course would define the central thread of history, the other that of fragmentary institutions, of continuity barely formed yet already compromised. Until Year III, the essential factor in political life was the constant melding of legitimacy conferred by suffrage with de facto legitimacy, granted and withdrawn by "opinion." The former bestowed power, at least nominally, but one could not remain in power without the latter. The electorate designated, but the "people" remained vigilant; at each election the Jacobins of course sought to elect as many of their supporters as possible, but they placed even greater emphasis on the need to monitor those elected in the name of the "popular will," which the electors might have betrayed.

This situation is explained in part by a long popular tradition of hostility to government, a sentiment that the *régime censitaire* (1789–1792) may have encouraged by limiting the suffrage to so-called active citizens. This explanation is insufficient, however, since doubts about the capacity of suffrage to express the true wishes of the citizenry persisted as vigorously as ever after the establishment of universal suffrage in August 1792.

More decisive, apparently, was the Revolution's inability to provide the new institutions with durable roots. Under the representative system elaborated by the Constituent Assembly, the purpose of elections was not to inventory the voters' wishes nor even (through synthesis) to ascertain the general will, but only to select the deputies who would exercise sovereignty, free of any checks or balances, in the name of the indivisible nation. Election was merely a function entrusted by the nation to certain citizens recognized as able to perform it, an instrumental mediation intended to constitute and legitimize the assembly of representatives.

The law was precise: electors were to gather upon convocation, verify the credentials of the citizens present, elect a *bureau,* and proceed to nominations. These assemblies were forbidden to deliberate, issue orders, draft instructions or strict mandates, or correspond with one another, and they were required to disband as soon as the purpose of their meeting was complete. From the moment the results were announced, the elected ceased to be subject to the control of their electors: though chosen by electors of a particular circumscription, their authority stemmed from the nation as a whole.

According to this doctrine, whose impracticality was soon demonstrated, elections were supposed to take place in a total political vacuum and, more specifically, without public competition between rival candidates and programs. To be sure, frequent replacement of the assemblies offered the electorate a kind of veto power over those whom the assemblies had elected, whose mandate could be either renewed or terminated. Nevertheless, the character of elections differed profoundly from what it had been as late as 1789, when corps and communities had expressed their grievances and chosen proxies to represent them in strict accordance with their wishes. The decrees of December 1789, which liberated deputies from strict control by their constituents and thus caused a profound change in the nature of the political bond, gave rise to vigorous and prolonged resistance, especially in Paris districts.

Because it became the rule for the electoral process to unfold in a political vacuum, debate over political issues was relegated to the margins, outside any legally sanctioned arena, in organizations that dispensed a "popular" form of legitimacy distinct from the suffrage. At the same time, the consequences of this political vacuum—the absence not only of issues but also of declared candidacies, the law recognizing no intermediate entity between the state and its individual citizens—encouraged seizure or confiscation of the electoral machinery by those best equipped to select candidates and establish implicit agendas.

*
**

Whether suffrage was *censitaire* or universal, voting was an affair of minorities, for whose votes "candidates" competed. The overall evolution of electoral participation can be sketched despite gaps in data, dispersal of documentation, and uncertain reliability of sources.

In the initial phase, participation—independent of the transition from a community-based vote (in 1789) that favored traditional solidarities to an individualized vote (in 1790) that appealed to the civic consciousness of the citizenry—was high, perhaps because the reforms had gained widespread support, or perhaps because the new and poorly understood electoral laws had not yet altered the situation created by the mobilization of 1789. Generally speaking, participation in the elections of 1790 exceeded fifty percent and sometimes reached eighty or ninety percent, particularly in rural cantons. Parisians were considerably less ardent, since only a quarter of the active citizens attended the assemblies.

The year of the great reforms was also a veritable "golden age" of electoral history. Michelet observed that 1793 was not at all the year in which popular enthusiasm for the Revolution reached a climax but in fact the year in which the people "returned to their homes," as they had begun to do by the end of 1792. Indeed, from our point of view citizens began to turn away from public affairs as early as the spring of 1791; the primary assemblies of June failed to attract even half as many voters as those of 1790. By August 1792 the collapse was confirmed, despite the fact that universal suffrage was now in force for the first time. In many cases, as in Paris where less than ten percent of the eligible voters went to the polls, the rate of participation was inversely proportional to the size of the electorate.

Intermediate elections, which chose second-stage electors, were not the only ones affected by a high rate of abstention. An attenuated version of the same phenomenon is evident in municipal elections. Electoral participation did not increase significantly in subsequent years, except in the carefully controlled referendum of July 1793, whose purpose was to obtain formal approval of the new Constitution. The end of the Terror and the return of institutions to normal operation did not reverse the trend: from 1795 to 1799, electoral participation was generally below twenty percent.

What were the reasons for the high rate of abstention? The irreversible collapse after the initial successes of 1790 undercuts sociological explanations, such as the argument that the urban vote was more individualized than the rural vote, hence likely to favor a high rate of abstention. The type of analysis that attempts to establish hierarchies of interest between local and national elections also fails for the same reason. To be sure, the features of particular elections can be explained in such terms, as can regional differences, but not an overall evolution characterized by early and massive disaffection.

Factors affecting major segments of the electorate—the weather, the agricultural calendar, the costs of travel and lodging, the location of elections in cantonal capitals, the fatigue induced by interminable meetings, or problems stemming from linguistic differences—also fail to provide an explanation of the larger trend.

What remains is indifference toward public affairs, what Michelet characterized as a *marais,* or swamp. Was this indifference the result of inadequate political education and inability to understand the scope and mechanics of the new institutions, as Jaurès and Aulard believed? The Constituent Assembly itself had already advanced similar arguments to justify the *cens,* or property qualifications for electors, yet those arguments cannot account for disaffection among active citizens, who allegedly possessed the intellectual equipment and material resources necessary for participation in political life. Was not the indifference rather the manifestation of a refusal, an opposition perhaps associated with the intensification of political conflict? The assemblies of August 1792 and Fructidor, Year III, were in fact affected by measures of proscription aimed in the one case at moderates and royalists and in the other at the Terrorists of Year II. More generally, a search for unanimity seems to have been the rule from as early as 1790. There was no room for minority opinions; majorities in most assemblies were overwhelming. Those whose "candidate" appeared not to be in a position to win often preferred to withdraw, possibly to form a parallel assembly that met alongside the regular one, rather than suffer defeat. This practice became quite common under the Directory. To be sure, withdrawal was not always voluntary, but the use of coercion only accelerated a tendency to shun regulated competition and pluralism of opinion, the indispensable prerequisites of democratic elections.

Indifference in the narrow sense should not be neglected. It should probably be viewed as a consequence of lack of interest in a formal exercise whose purpose was to select the "representative elite," as Sieyès put it in 1799, rather than to offer a verdict on a political program or direction. To grasp the stakes implicit in an election one had to make an effort, and it was unlikely that such an effort would be made by anyone who was not already interested in the electoral competition. The immobile majority of France, which the Revolution did not shake until the next century, remained outside a political arena monopolized by minorities. Contemporaries were already remarking on the astonishing contrast between the low level of electoral participation and the size of the crowds involved in uprisings, riots, and pillage. Enlightened opinion worried about the disdain of the French for the lawful political practices stemming from the Revolution of 1789 and their preference for violent forms of activity typical of the previous centuries of "despotism."

The suffrage was co-opted by the contending political forces through manipulation of defects and flaws in the electoral system. The absence of public debate, while it did not prevent topical issues from influencing elections, did mean that the results depended strongly on local and individual factors: in a sense men counted more than ideas. Of course the electorate was not blind, and its decisions, especially after 1792, were determined by national events. In the absence of party affiliations, electors voted primarily for individuals, and ideas and options were taken into account only to the extent that "unofficial" candidates were obliged to accommodate themselves ideologically to successive sets of dominant revolutionary "values": the Constitution in 1790–1791, equality in 1792, Thermidor in 1795. The composition of the electoral assemblies, whether administrative or parliamentary, clearly demonstrates the overrepresentation of notables in the broad sense of the word, relative to shifting and secondary political cleavages. In many places, the integration of new representative institutions and new political discourses into old divisions and cleavages in local society reinforced the influence of kinship and clientage networks and merely papered over ancient arrangements with an appearance of modernity.

The most striking feature was not the domination of political life by notables—who alone possessed the taste, time, and resources required for participation in public affairs—but the rapid formation of a homogeneous political class. Indirect elections—the "two-stage system"—contributed to this outcome by turning the second-stage assemblies into the breeding ground from which nearly all deputies and public functionaries were chosen, even though the law required nothing of the kind. As early as 1791, we find that local officials elected the previous year frequently occupied more than half the seats in the electoral assemblies: a veritable system of co-optation was thus functioning, carrying some men from relatively low-level positions to more important offices while others, such as former members of the Constituent Assembly, rejoined local administrations. In September 1792, numerous deputies of the Legislative Assembly who were too moderate to be reelected to the Convention were nevertheless chosen by the same electors for less risky offices. Conversely, more than eighty-five percent of the Convention's deputies had previously served as public officials, and almost all who were elected for the first time had been second-stage electors. This unfortunately little-noticed characteristic of revolutionary elections contributed to the formation of a tested and competent political class that steadily gained experience of public affairs via a kind of *cursus honorum;* in a negative sense, however, it also reflected a very real tendency toward oligarchy often denounced by contemporaries, although the use of this rather pejorative term is perhaps mitigated by the observation that there were nearly a million elective public offices in 1790. Despite a variety of purges and proscriptions, this political class survived difficult years without serious damage and ultimately—speaking very broadly, of course—monopolized official posts under the Directory and the Consulate.

The elections of the revolutionary decade do not fit the pattern of the strictest *censitaire* regimes, however, in which one of the most prominent characteristics is the power of notables. For one thing, the *censitaire* regime, under which access to voting was subject to modest fiscal requirements, alternated with periods of universal suffrage. For another, the same groups tended to remain in power owing to the political vacuum that existed in the legal sphere, and this permanent presence coexisted with a burgeoning political debate on the margins.

Indeed, although there was no legal way to declare one's candidacy, declarations were nonetheless made. Elected officials generally enjoyed the support of more or less formally organized groups. Elective assemblies were invariably pitiless in their vigilance against "intrigues," "cabals," and "conspiracies" organized by those who, lacking needed support and unable to rely solely on their own strength, were inevitably compelled to resort to crude methods such as intimidation, violence, fraud, or vote-buying.

Although an appearance before the assembly of voters was the final stage in any election, the decisive test took place earlier, outside the electoral mechanism and particularly in the network of Jacobin clubs. Electoral competition was in the first place a competition for an endorsement, to obtain political accreditation in the form of a label of "civism" along with the practical means necessary for victory. One sees this clearly in the preparatory work of the clubs, which generally held special meetings devoted to elections in which candidacies were discussed and endorsements granted or on occasion refused or withdrawn. What was given could also be taken away, as when the club of Bagnères-de-Bigorre in August 1792 opposed the reelection of a deputy it had helped to nominate the year before and denounced "the soul no less wicked than the conduct of the man Loustalot, which . . . justifies what opinion had always thought of him, and must disappoint those who conspire in the cabal of his deputation; contempt and total exclusion from the French family are the only sentiments this man deserves, and these are what he gets from society." As this example shows, the plasticity of the language and the accusations made it possible to withdraw confidence without going into detail about the reasons, while implying a guilt so obvious and beyond challenge as to convince the undecided.

If isolated candidacies almost always failed, with the exception of local luminaries enjoying unchallenged prestige, candidates backed by organized and "legitimate" support groups were able to impose themselves upon divided and directionless assemblies. The choices made by the second-stage assemblies reflected not so much "the public spirit" or majority opinion as the efficacy of pressure groups: this was manifestly the case in the Vendée and Brittany, where the massive mobilization in favor of the refractory clergy did not prevent the election of "patriotic" deputies, defenders of state interests against local passions.

The technical modalities of election lent themselves particularly well to manipulation. Assembly votes were by roll call. The first consequence of this system was that voting took an extremely long time, since all registered voters, whether present or absent, were called to fill out ballots and take the oath. The roll call was repeated with each round of balloting, and it is not hard to imagine how voters might have been subjected to suggestions and pressures or how, in a disorganized, chaotic situation, secret caucuses might have exerted influence on undecided electors.

Although the law required voting by ballot, could there really be a secret ballot and free choice without voting booths? In 1792 nearly half the deputies elected by "secret" ballot were elected on the first round, and a quarter of them received more than ninety percent of the votes cast. During the same election, continuation of the voice vote in certain assemblies further reduced a precarious margin of liberty while undoubtedly speeding up the proceedings; more than sixty percent of the deputies in these assemblies were elected on the first round, half of them by nearly unanimous votes. Where the outcome was not determined in advance, the totally open range of choices resulted in anomalies favorable to minorities: the voting on the first round might be so fragmented, for example, that even though the leader had only a small number of votes, he was nevertheless in a favorable position for subsequent balloting.

The inadequacies and untenable assumptions in the electoral system opened the way to manipulations and minority strategies. Examples exist from two very different periods of the Revolution: the dawn of the Jacobin phase, when elections were used gradually to destabilize institutions, and the Directory, when election results were ignored so that the victors of Thermidor could hold on to a power that was soon discredited. In both cases the electoral process was diverted from its legal ends for political purposes. This politicization was not a sign of normalization or pacification of political conflict but proof of the Revolution's inability to implant the new institutions.

At the beginning of 1790, in application of recent laws on administrative reorganization, elections brought large numbers of notables into municipal and administrative posts at all levels. The network of Jacobin societies, then still in the process of formation, was able to exert its influence only locally and in support of certain individuals. In Paris, at the behest of Brissot, a minority of electors formed a "Society of Patriotic Electors," which had no significant influence on the results.

A year later, the Jacobin movement had considerably more weight, especially in the cities, and the assemblies that convened on June 16, 1791, to name second-stage electors demonstrated the Jacobins' ability to control the electoral machinery. Their initial success did not carry over, however, to the second-stage elections, which chose deputies to the Legislative Assembly. Two explanations may be proposed: the flight of Louis XVI on June 21 and the rift in the Jacobin Club on July 16, 1791. After Varennes the meeting of the intermediary assemblies was postponed. But the primary assemblies, on June 16, were usually content to reelect the electors chosen the previous year. As a consequence of Varennes, the Jacobin Club split on July 16 into a radical minority and a Feuillant majority. The minority, led by Robespierre and Brissot, quickly secured the allegiance of most of the affiliate societies. Electorally speaking, however, the damage was done: the results of the June primary elections fairly accurately reflected the state of affairs prior to June 21: a moderate, constitutional majority. For the minority, the second-stage elections, which began at the end of August, were a delicate affair. In Paris, two societies of electors, the Society of the Evêché and the Society of the Sainte-Chapelle, which reproduced in the electoral assembly the split between Jacobins and Feuillants, battled fiercely on behalf of their respective candidates. The *chapelains* won handily, while the Society of the Evêché for all its dogged efforts managed only to elect Brissot and Condorcet. In the provinces things went a little better for the Jacobins, with urban electors generally managing to impose their candidates on a majority of isolated and divided rural electors: 136 of the 745 deputies of the Legislative Assembly joined the Jacobins, 260 the Feuillants.

The municipal elections of late 1791 showed that the relative lack of success in September had been due to both the July split and the indirect method of election. Since municipal elections were by direct ballot, the Jacobins exacted a stunning revenge, which contributed greatly to the subsequent aggravation of the crisis of the regime in June and July 1792, at which time the municipalities served as bastions for an all-out offensive against the Constitution and the king. That vote proved a harbinger of the very special elections of August–September 1792, in which the Jacobin machine effectively seized control of the electoral system.

With the suspension of the king and the convocation of a National Convention on August 10, 1792, preparations for the elections began. In Paris, under the discipline of the Jacobins, the Cordeliers, the Commune, and some sections, Feuillants and moderates were purged from electoral assemblies or declared ineligible in order to prevent a repetition of the previous year's delicate situation. This weeding-out was essentially complete before August 26, when the primary assemblies met. The Jacobins eliminated all danger by exercising tight control over the assemblies' operations: they were obliged to use voice votes, and the second-stage assemblies reserved the right to "revise" the choices of the primary assemblies by verifying the credentials of their members. Some electors were excluded in this way. At the second stage, balloting was again by voice vote, and to make things more efficient the electors abandoned the hall in the Evêché for that of the Jacobins, where sessions were open to the public.

Almost a caricature, the Paris session offered no surprises. The principal leaders of the Jacobins, the Commune, and the Cordeliers were elected to the Convention. The Jacobins had eliminated not only the Feuillant deputation, which had been defeated politically since August 10, but also Pétion, Brissot, and the major Girondin leaders.

In the provinces, however, most of the prominent Girondins were reelected. Purgative and disciplinary measures adopted in numerous assemblies in line with the Paris model did not prevent the election of resolute adversaries of the new masters of the capital. What accounts for this contrast between Paris and the départements? Paris was then in an unusual situation, in which the opposition was not able to declare itself. But the most important factor was the Jacobins' two-tier strategy. In the capital they controlled the elections in order to eliminate the "Brissotins," who had been saved from disaster by the insurrection of August 10, which had forged the myth of a "sacred union" against treason and a domestic plot. At the same time, the Jacobins were able to put together a Parisian deputation that would be an extension of the club within the Convention. In the provinces, less certain of the affiliated societies whose convictions were in some cases too moderate and often behind the times with respect to Parisian cleavages, the club preferred to adopt a minimalist strategy, which would eliminate the Feuillants from the Convention and offer the electors not the alternative of Jacobins and Commune versus Girondins and legal power, but rather a choice between those who had lost on August 10 and the whole range of those who had gained. This was the meaning of the well-known *Tableau comparatif* circulated by the club and the Legislative Assembly, which treated all "patriotic" deputies—those who had voted on August 8 against Lafayette, Jacobins and Girondins alike—as a bloc. The success of this strategy was undeniable, since of the 406 deputies who had voted in favor of the general, only five were reelected, compared with 167 of the 235 who had voted against him.

The elections for the Convention were truly Jacobin elections: through the Parisian deputies and their allies, the club was able to rule the Convention and, once the king had been executed, to begin the process of liquidating the Girondins. The different treatment of Paris and the provinces illustrates a fundamental feature of the revolutionary elections: while choices were made *prior* to the electoral operations as such, the decisive struggles for legitimacy did not begin until *afterward*.

*
* *

My second example is the Directory period, during which elections constituted a major part of political life. J.-R. Suratteau has studied the issues of the day, categorized the various deputies, and defined "parties" essentially by their relation to the legacy of the preceding years. At first sight nothing in the Constitution of 1795 would seem to have dramatically altered the nature of elections. It was rather the conditions created by 9 Thermidor, by the dismantling of the clubs and other groups that for six years had arisen in opposition to the legal government, that turned the elections into a key to understanding the directorial period. In the hands of a government anxious to perpetuate itself but whose credibility had been impaired by its involvement in regicide and the Terror, elections, which hitherto had embodied a fragile legality, became either the instrument or the prize in repeated coups d'état. Under a Constitution that finally permitted a lawful democratic life, the electoral farce revealed the rottenness of the civilian government and thus paved the way for the generals.

With the decrees of 5 and 13 Fructidor, Year III, which required electors to choose two-thirds of the new legislative body from among the outgoing members of the Convention, the Thermidorians intended to hold on to the fruits of their victory of the summer of 1794. They also hoped to avoid a repetition of the disastrous experience of 1791, when the Constituent Assembly had yielded to an assembly composed entirely of new men without experience at the national level. After the end of the Terror, these decrees were justified on grounds of "public safety," according to whose logic the Revolution had to be defended even at the cost of violating its own principles.

Nevertheless, by enabling the Convention to succeed itself, the two-thirds decree primarily aided the more moderate members, as is shown by the crushing defeat of those who had participated in 9 Thermidor, for the most part former "ultras" of terrorism in search of a new virginity. The electorate confirmed these initial moderate results, for fully half the deputies in the newly elected third of the Assembly were out-and-out monarchists.

One-third of both houses of the legislative body was supposed to be reelected each year, so new elections were held in Germinal, Year V (April 1797). They confirmed the moderate trend already evident in the autumn of 1795. The Directory intervened, however, to ensure that the results would be consistent with both political stability and its own interests; the number of outgoing deputies was reduced as much as possible by counting those who had died since 1795, so that even an unfavorable outcome would not upset the balance of power in the legislature. Repressive measures in the wake of the abortive Babouvist plot made it possible to get rid of those still nostalgic for Jacobinism, while, at the other extreme, émigrés who had returned to France were prevented from voting. These measures proved futile: 170 of the 248 seats to be filled were captured by monarchists, who now controlled 330 of the 730 seats in the two houses.

The stabilization in the center that elections had been unable to secure was obtained by force. After six months' guerrilla warfare between councils and the Directory, the latter decided to take action. On 18 Fructidor (September 4, 1794), with the support of the army, it nullified elections in 49 départements and deported or proscribed 53 deputies. Nearly a third of the legislature was purged, some 200 moderate and monarchist deputies paying the price.

Intended to head off a new political adventure and born of a desperate determination to reconcile French society to the legacy of the Revolution, the anti-electoral coup d'état of 18 Fructidor actually disrupted the nation's institutions one more time, as a government sought to obtain at any price the approval of an electorate that obstinately refused to give it. Barras was the orchestrator of the initial coup, and the following year, Merlin de Douai, faced with a similar problem of political survival, was the organizer of a second anti-electoral coup on 22 Floréal, Year VI (May 11, 1798), this time directed against the neo-Jacobins whom the coup of 18 Fructidor had enabled to make a spectacular political comeback.

In the elections of 1798 the second and third "thirds" of the conventionnels reelected in 1795 were to be replaced. With this change in mind, the Directory took charge: local officials and commissaires of the central government were sacked and replaced, and circulars expressing the wishes of the executive were sent out. Above all, in order to avoid a new post-electoral coup like that of 18 Fructidor, the Directory chose to manipulate the outcome in advance: Merlin de Douai and Letourneux, the minister of the interior, sent agents to the départements for the official purpose of preparing a report on the state of the highways and the unofficial purpose of sowing dissension in the assemblies between supporters of the Directory and their Jacobin and royalist opponents, among whom the government could pick and choose to serve its own interests. The operation was effective, but not sufficiently so: while 370 of the 510 newly elected deputies had the approval of the Directory, the latter could count on only 467 of the 807 deputies in the legislature as a whole. Furthermore, the widespread reliance on factional dissension had increased the number of deputies elected: in most départements there were more deputies than there were seats to be filled as a result of two or even three simultaneous assemblies. It was up to the legislature to determine which deputies to seat. In order to make sure that its stratagem could not be used against it, the Directory, in preparing for the elections of Germinal, had seen to it that the incumbent legislators (purged of their "Fructidorized" opposition) were granted the power to validate the credentials of their successors. The legislature docilely acceded to this new affront and on 22 Floréal invalidated the election of 106 deputies, nearly all neo-Jacobins.

The mechanism of purges had run out of steam. The elections of Germinal, Year VII (April 1799), resulted in a crushing defeat for the candidates officially supported by the Directory. The latter then attempted a repeat of the operation of May 1798, but the councils, strengthened by the government's failure, refused to go along. In June 1799, divided, discredited, sapped from within, the Directory fell apart; the men of 1798, Merlin de Douai and La Révellière-Lépeaux, were eliminated. The new prominence of Barras, the last survivor of a foundering regime, and the return to public life of Sieyès, heralded the coming 18 Brumaire, the end of a period of drift, and, on the ruins of legality, the birth of modern institutions.

Patrice Gueniffey

FURTHER READING

Baticle, René. "Le plébiscite sur la Constitution de 1793," *La Révolution française,* vol. 57, 1909, 496–524; vol. 58, 1910, 5–30, 117–155, 193–237, 327–341, 385–410.

Cochin, Augustin. *L'esprit du jacobinisme* (reprint of *Les sociétés de pensée et la démocratie: Etudes d'histoire révolutionnaire,* Paris, 1921). With an introduction by Jean Baechler. Paris, 1979. See esp. pp. 49–93.

Marx, Roland. *Recherches sur la vie politique de l'Alsace prérévolutionnaire et révolutionnaire.* Strasbourg, 1966.

Rémond, René. "L'apport des historiens aux études électorales," in Daniel Gaxie, ed., *Explication du vote: Un bilan des études électorales en France.* Paris, 1985, pp. 35–48.

Suratteau, Jean-René. "Les elections de l'an IV," *Annales historiques de la Révolution française,* 1951, 374–393; 1952, 32–63.

——"Les opérations de l'Assemblée Electorale de France," *Annales historiques de la Révolution française,* 1955, 228–250.

——"Les elections de l'an V aux Conseils du Directoire," *Annales historiques de la Révolution française,* 1958, 21–63.

——*Les elections de l'an VI et le "Coup d'Etat du 22 floréal" (11 mai 1798).* Paris, 1971.

RELATED TOPICS

Academic History of the Revolution
Clubs and Popular Societies
Condorcet
Coups d'Etat
Estates General
Feuillants
Girondins
Jacobinism
Michelet
Revolutionary Assemblies
Sieyès
Sovereignty
Suffrage
Thermidorians

ESTATES GENERAL

U nder the Ancien Régime, the Estates General were an expedient for use in exceptional circumstances. Possessing no autonomy and no permanence, they left no trace of their activities. They owed their existence to an initiative of the government, which convoked and dismissed them at will. They lacked all authority in matters of government and even legislation. Although they sometimes took part in the drafting of certain ordinances, the king remained the only legally authorized legislator in the realm, both as author of the laws and as dispenser and guarantor of privileges. Until 1789 this essential attribute would remain an intangible principle of monarchical authority: faced with an exceptional situation, the monarch called upon the kingdom's "representation" in order to build a consensus around his policy or, more simply, to raise emergency revenues. Upon the death of Louis XI in 1483, the Estates General were invited to give their opinion concerning the organization of the regency. After a long interval François II convoked them in 1560 to resolve a financial crisis and to calm tempers in the wake of disturbances provoked by religious innovations. Estates General were also held in Blois: in 1576–1577 to deal with the religious situation after the formation of the League; in 1588–1589 for the same reasons, complicated by the dynastic question raised by the existence of a Protestant heir. After the assassination of Henri IV, the regent Marie de Médicis, at grips with the Condean rebellion, was forced to convoke the Estates in 1614. They would not be convoked again for a century and a half.

From the end of the Middle Ages to the Revolution, the act of *representing* retained the very narrow sense ascribed to it by both governors and governed: the people, by delegation but without intermediaries, held out to the monarch a mirror of his realm; they did so by making known their wishes, complaints, and remonstrances. This act revealed the very nature of Ancien Régime society, in which the individual had no political existence except through his organic affiliations: orders, corps, communities, privileges. Before 1789, therefore, "to represent" did not necessarily imply representativity or even election. It meant first of all to communicate or transmit, an operation to which the designation of deputies remained clearly subordinate, such designation being merely *recognition* of the attributes that qualified a particular individual to convey his community's grievances to the Estates. In fact, the old form of the strict mandate (*mandat impératif*) made the person with the mandate not the author of a political will but a mere messenger, who scrupulously reported the precise contents of a *cahier* that precluded all personal initiative and autonomy. Hence before 1789 the election of deputies to the Estates was a strictly secondary affair, just as recourse to suffrage was a form of procedure devoid of the political significance that it would take on much later under modern democracy.

*
**

In 1788 as in the past, it was a political crisis that caused Louis XVI to consult his "Estates." He was obliged to do so by the combined effects of temporary circumstances, the crisis of absolutism, and the pedagogy of the age: food shortages, popular uprisings, a deficit that could no longer be dealt with by a state that had run out of fiscal resources and expedients, the imperious pressure of public opinion, and above all resistance from notables and parlements opposed to any reform in the royal finances not sanctioned by the Estates General. No sooner did the government consent to call the Estates, however, than other issues arose, and a new actor appeared on the scene: the Third Estate. Momentarily united by popular wrath, the appeal to natural rights, and egalitarian demands, the Third Estate joined in denunciation of nobles, privileges, and despotism; the Third aspired to obtain representation equal to that of the first two orders combined and, by demanding voting by head rather than by orders, sought to achieve power commensurate with its numerical preponderance. In late winter 1789, after a turbulent election campaign, France set about drafting its remonstrances and designating its representatives—the very same representatives who, a few months later, would take possession of the national sovereignty.

Yet elections to the Estates General, like other revolutionary elections, are all but ignored by the revolutionary historiography of both left and right in the nineteenth and twentieth centuries. The episode, often summed up in a few dull lines, is reduced to a sort of mechanical link between the demands of the patriots—especially deliberation in common and voting by head—and the collapse of the Ancien Régime, as if it had no meaning or interest except for its remote consequences. This assumption is shared all the more widely because it can be adapted to fit the most incompatible interpretations of the coming of the Revolution. Whether celebrated or reviled, the victories of the Third Estate (National Assembly, night of August 4, Declaration of Rights) are presumed to resolve any question that might be asked about these elections. They fully reveal the meaning of the event, explain its outcome, and therefore make it unnecessary to dwell on its details, or so we are told.

This unanimity of silence and indifference obscures more profound causes, however. It reflects the difficulty of taking account of both suffrages and grievances, electoral issues and political issues. But the major difficulty is that of reconciling the fundamental rupture of 1789 with an episode that inevitably raises questions about the significance of that moment.

In fact, the elections of 1789 mark an end as well as a beginning. They were the last elections of the Ancien Régime and the first of the Revolution. They sufficiently resemble both that they remain unclassifiable: a traditional procedure of the monarchical institutions was also a prize in a contest for power. Although the *cahiers* called for reform of the regime, they paved the way for its dissolution by sending to Versailles delegates who would become the authors of a new political legitimacy, instituted by national sovereignty and the rights of man.

The old monarchy played an unwitting yet undeniable part in this transition. When it resurrected an abandoned tradition after a century and a half of disuse, it established the legal and political machinery that would make possible the triumph of the Third Estate. It set the terms, so to speak, and prescribed the modalities of change before offering the first victim. In other words, the Revolution owed as much to the electoral regulations of January 24 as to its authors.

The extreme novelty of this document stems first of all from its very existence. In 1789, for the first time, the letters of convocation, which in the past had been merely a formal declaration of the Estates' meeting date, included a veritable electoral code, whose detail, complexity, and unprecedented concern with unity and equity imply an obvious change in public law.

Yet the letters are an ambiguous, contradictory text, caught between tradition and innovation, experimentally juxtaposing ancient customs with a new spirit. On the one hand they borrow the context and form of earlier convocations, stipulating that the inhabitants of large cities should assemble by occupational corps and companies, and they preserve the old form of representation by strict mandate and the traditional procedure of drafting grievances. They mention numerous exceptions and derogations in deference to established privileges. Most important of all, they preserve the separation of orders and remain silent about the principal demand of the Third Estate: deliberation and voting in common.

On the other hand, they grant the Third Estate at least double representation and honor the principles that form the basis of modern political representation. The phrases with which the January 24 regulation begins are eloquent in this regard: "The king, in addressing to the various provinces subject to his obedience letters of convocation for the Estates General, has wished that all his subjects be called to participate in the elections of the deputies who are to form this great and solemn assembly. His Majesty has desired that from the extremities of his kingdom and most remote locales every person be assured that his wishes and requests will reach his presence." The grievance structure was thus maintained: the king consulted the nation through the petitions of the corps. Yet every member of the third order above the age of twenty-five who was inscribed on the tax rolls was recognized as possessing a right of suffrage. No distinction was established between the right to vote and the right to stand for office: any individual admitted to the electoral assemblies automatically acquired the capacity to submit to the suffrage of his fellow citizens. Political equality, formerly contingent and subject to the will of individuals, pressure groups, and royal arbitration, here found juridical sanction: for the first time the people *by law* gained access to public life on a broad scale.

Inseparable from political equality was citizenship, which, in the name of progress, transformed the subjects of the realm into members of the body politic. It is impossible, Necker told the notables, to exclude from public life

47

a whole class of men so intimately involved in the prosperity of the state through commerce, industry, science, and the arts: "We are surrounded by precious citizens, whose works enrich the state and to whom the state, in just recompense, owes esteem and confidence" (November 6, 1788). The development of the economy, the spread of Enlightenment, and the generalization of citizenship all contributed to undermining the permanence of past customs and weakening the association with previous convocations. For the government to acknowledge this before the notables was to yield to the verdict of historical reason, now embodied not in the monarchy but in a new figure, sovereign and ungovernable: public opinion.

The idea of a just proportionality between the size of representation and the size of the district represented was also a product of the times. Equality of rights in effect prescribed a modern type of representation, which established a stable relation between representatives and represented in the formation of political power. Thus, in order to forestall declarations claiming—with good reason—to be founded on "ancient usages," it was also decided to increase considerably the number of deputies to the Estates: the text specified a thousand, nearly double the number of seats allotted in 1614. Still, the principle of proportionality was incompatible with the idea of the strict mandate, according to which the wishes of the mandaters were infinitely more important than the number of mandatees. That so many contemporaries, beginning with the least accommodating of aristocrats, were equally vigorous in support of *both* the strict mandate *and* proportional representation is not the least of paradoxes.

As had been the case a century and a half earlier, it was the *bailliage* (or, in some areas, the *sénéchaussée*), an ancient judicial district that had fallen into total disuse by the end of the Ancien Régime, that was chosen as the basic electoral district. The nobility directly designated its delegates to meet in plenary session in the district's main town. The right to elect and be elected devolved upon all members of the second order, regardless of whether or not they owned land. Those who did own land were convoked individually and could vote wherever they possessed fiefs, whether directly or by proxy (as was the case with women and minors). Those who did not own land were convoked by posted bills and participated in assemblies only in the places where they resided.

For the clergy, two distinct registers coexisted. Cardinals, archbishops, bishops, and all holders of benefices or parish offices held direct elections. Canons and religious held two-stage elections. Each community generally designated a representative to go to the *bailliage*, which assured the lower-level clergy of a marked preponderance in the electoral assemblies and later in the Estates General (at least 204 curés compared with some 50 bishops and coadjutors and 18 vicars-general).

Election of deputies to the Third Estate was also in several stages—at least two, often three, occasionally four. In the countryside the primary assemblies, held in each parish, chose two deputies in parishes of up to 200 households, three in parishes of up to 300 households, four in parishes of up to 400 households, and so on. Towns and small cities invariably chose four delegates. Larger cities used a two-step procedure: each occupational corporation chose one deputy per 100 members; corporations of the liberal arts and residents who were free or not included in any corporation were allowed two representatives per 100. All these representatives constituted the Assembly of the Third Estate of the city, which then selected deputies to attend the *bailliage* assembly.

There the procedure was complicated by the distinction between two types of jurisdictions. So-called principal *bailliages* sent delegates directly to the Estates General—that is, deputies elected by the various localities of the district met in the chief town, drafted the *cahier* of the Third Estate, and elected deputies. Other circumscriptions comprised several *bailliages*, however, including one principal *bailliage* and several secondary ones. In that case each *bailliage* assembly initially proceeded independently. After grievances were combined into a single *cahier*, each assembly would choose a quarter of its members to go to the chief town of the principal *bailliage* for the final stage of the process, choosing deputies to the Estates General. The quartering (or supplementary stage of election) was intended not only to "prevent overly large assemblies" and to "diminish the pain and costs of travel" (article 34) but also to keep illiterates who survived the primary assemblies from being chosen as deputies.

Paris, which did not vote until the end of April, did so under a special regime: sixty arrondissements, meaning sixty primary assemblies in the *quartiers*, chose delegates to attend a citywide meeting, which made the final selection of twenty deputies to the Estates General. Here the financial and status qualifications for voting were considerably more stringent than in the provinces. A minimum of 6 livres in *capitation* was required of all who were not convoked *ex officio*, including graduates of the faculties, holders of offices and commissions, and those in possession of *lettres de maîtrise*.

Finally, the mode of election adopted by the government involved a list of candidates who were required to receive an absolute majority in several rounds of voting: electors voted for a man, not a list. Hence representatives had to be chosen one by one, and each successful candidate had to receive an absolute majority. At the lower levels of the electoral hierarchy, the vote was public; at the final stage, however, it was secret.

Ex officio access to the electoral assembly for the privileged, quasi-universal suffrage for the Third Estate—these two traits sum up the contradictions in a procedure that mixed the "organic" with the "democratic" to the point of paradox. Nevertheless, the process exhibits a profound overall unity not unlike the modern system of voting by arrondissement.

Genuine efforts were made to arrive quickly at a just distribution of electoral districts. Officials were nevertheless unable to dispel uncertainties that remained from hasty investigations into earlier convocations—uncertainties as to the number, population, tax contributions, and above all boundaries of each district. Bailiffs and other local officials asked to indicate the exact contours of their district often admitted their ignorance. At the time there existed a multitude of jurisdictions whose limits did not necessarily coincide with the supposed boundaries of the *bailliages*. Of the more than 400 *bailliages* few were without parishes either shared or disputed with another *bailliage*, and representatives of these were required to appear, often on the same day, at two or more assemblies. And there were some parishes that, "in order to preserve influence," did not hesitate to send delegates to more than one assembly. One community in the Loudunais went so far as to send delegates simultaneously to Chinon, Saumur, and of course Loudun, even though the jurisdiction of the last extended to only one of its households.

These confusions and uncertainties show how incapable the government was of adapting its old circumscriptions to the new election rules. It was therefore forced to revise those rules constantly as protests streamed in from all quarters. In this respect, at least, the existence of regulations changed little in the old practices of bargaining and compromise characteristic of previous convocations.

What made this confusion even more apparent was the fact that many privilege-holders—cities, groups, individuals—treated the modalities of consultation as mere guidelines rather than hard-and-fast rules. This attitude prevailed at all levels of society, from the duc d'Orléans with his celebrated *Instructions* on down to certain ministers anxious to indulge the nobility and especially the high-ranking clergy, which privately feared the preponderance of curés in the electoral assembly.

Elsewhere, defects in electoral districting made Necker's regulations pointless, absurd, and worst of all inequitable. Since each separate roll was entitled to two representatives, it sometimes happened that two or three isolated hamlets had as many representatives as the principal town of a *bailliage*, if not more. Sometimes, too, a parish, uninhabited estate, or community consisting of a single hearth was declared extinct, for otherwise its sole elector would have been required to deliberate (if it makes sense to speak of deliberation in such a case), record his grievances—and elect *two* deputies.

Overrepresentation on the one hand, "chimerical" communities on the other: the imbalance seems all the more paradoxical in that it was both consistent with the regulations and incompatible with one of their fundamental elements, the principle of proportionality.

In rural France meetings of electors were quite similar from parish to parish. If the scene was always filled with peasants, it was orchestrated by the assembly presidents, who transformed an official post into an instrument of political ambition. The procedural control exercised primarily by members of the *noblesse de robe* and duplicated at each level of the hierarchy was at once legal and unanticipated. In requiring that every primary assembly be presided over by the judge of the district or, in his absence, by another public official, the regulations authorized a frenetic contest to accumulate presidencies. By doing so, a local judge could increase his influence not only over assembly deliberations and the drafting of grievances but also over the elections themselves. There were limits to this influence, however. While *cahiers de doléances* often drew their inspiration from existing models, they never reproduced those models verbatim. Behind the legal and notarial prose there invariably lay a wealth of demands whose tenor and spirit were unmistakable. Humble country folk paid only intermittent attention to public affairs and confined their boldest demands to social and administrative matters. They were less "revolutionary" than Tocqueville imagined but much less timorous than Taine believed or than might be thought from their eclipse in the actual voting despite an overwhelming numerical majority.

In effect, those who went to the *bailliage* were primarily the more prosperous and better educated: the independent yeomen who constituted the "political" stratum of rural society and the lawyers and administrators who served as its spokesmen. Hired hands, vine growers, and day laborers all but vanished—an outcome that might have seemed predictable to anyone who understood how rural notables controlled the proceedings. Yet this prosaic fact does not tell the whole story, for at this grass-roots level of consultation selection probably had more to do with an accepted compromise than with an unforeseeable competition; it was less a matter of "manipulation" from above than of consent emanating from below. A peaceful division of labor was thus established between representatives and represented: the latter enjoyed the prerogatives of remonstrance while the former received the honors of the mandate. On the one hand the voice of the community, on the other the ambition of an individual: two logics of representation indiscriminately amalgamated in obedience to the royal letters.

Lists of electors in the principal and secondary *bailliage* assemblies are now available, albeit in rudimentary form. Direct electors to the Estates General (all orders combined) numbered between 105,000 and 110,000. Of this total the Third Estate alone accounted for some forty percent, the clergy for about a third, and the nobility for approximately a quarter. In terms of sheer numbers, the privileged orders accounted for roughly sixty percent of the "electoral mass," owing mainly to the "quartering" of the representation of the Third Estate from combined primary and secondary *bailliages*. By contrast, in principal districts without secondaries, the Third Estate maintained a fairly substantial numerical superiority. Obviously the overall majority of the privileged orders could have no effect on electoral operations as such, since in principle the orders deliberated and voted separately. Nevertheless, this advantage gives a particular resonance to the demand to vote and elect in common. If this demand had been met, and assuming that the government had continued to insist on multistage elections to the Third Estate, the Third might have found itself in the minority in a large number of assemblies.

It was at the *bailliage* level that the election of 1789 differed markedly from past convocations. No elections at this level were decided in advance, and no votes were taken without debate, conflict, and surprise. Pamphlets, slogans, discreet machinations, novel coalitions, "invisible" candidates, unforeseen results: the final stage of the electoral mobilization offers a thousand examples to illustrate Augustin Cochin's analysis. What Cochin demonstrated was the fundamental paradox of a procedure that juxtaposed a "democratic" vote with a "traditional" consultation, the division of votes with the unanimity of voices. This confusion of principles had inevitable consequences: separate voting of the three orders, which cut the nobility off from its natural sphere of influence, and the imposition on the Third Estate of a series of preliminary elections. These actions neutralized the influence of the traditional notables, and left the field open to a new personnel of specialists, anonymous and powerful. Experienced in the methods of purge and exclusion, these men found their task made easier by the fact that the elections were held, as was customary, without candidates or platforms and without the necessary confrontation of ideas and programs. The vacuum was filled by the new networks of power, promoters of "democratic sociability" formed in "societies of thought" on the fringes of organic society: circles, clubs, museums, patriotic societies, reading rooms, and Masonic lodges. In the theater of confrontation inaugurated by the convocation, only these groups were able to offer "ready-made structures, phrases, and men." Only these practitioners of "direct democracy" knew how to mobilize votes, "neutralize" troublesome adversaries, and "filter" a horde of unorganized voters.

This analysis reveals the fluid, uncertain, ambiguous nature of the relations between electoral mobilization and the campaign of opinion, between the weight of the written word and that of organization. The vast literature of *Observations, Instructions, Memoirs,* and brochures (about whose reception by the public we know very little, incidentally) does not yield the key to the election. On the contrary, it often masks the real issues, which were far more prosaic but less easily identifiable.

In short, for all the egalitarian rhetoric, access to the deputation was a long way from being equal at all times and in all places. How many noisy opponents of absolutism, promoters of reforms and political protest, were turned aside in favor of unknown and sometimes absent candidates in the fatal moment of voting? How many obscure deputies (including some seventy percent of the deputies of the Third Estate), who would play no active role in the work of the Constituent Assembly, owed their election to solidarities forged long before 1789 and outside the arena of political debate? If Cochin's thesis were to prove correct, one could argue that the Ancien Régime, prior to its demise, organized the first purge of the French Revolution.

Ran Halévi

Estates general

Further reading

Brette, Armand. *Recueil des documents relatifs à la convocation des Etats Généraux de 1789*, 4 vols. Paris, 1895–1915.

Cadart, Jacques. *Le régime électoral des Etats Généraux de 1789 et ses origines (1320–1614)*. Paris, 1952.

Chartier, Roger, and Denis Richet, eds. *Représentation et vouloir politique: Autour des Etats Généraux de 1614*. Paris, 1982.

Cochin, Augustin. "La campagne électorale de 1789 en Bourgogne" and "Comment furent élus les députés aux Etats Généraux," in *L'esprit du jacobinisme* (reprint of *Les sociétés de pensée et la démocratie: Etudes d'histoire révolutionnaire*, Paris, 1921). With an introduction by Jean Baechler. Paris, 1979, pp. 49–93.

Furet, François. "Les élections de 1789 à Paris, le Tiers Etat et la naissance d'une classe dirigeante," in Albert Cremer, ed., *De l'Ancien Régime à la Révolution française*. Göttingen, 1978, pp. 188–206.

Halévi, Ran. "Modalités, participation et luttes électorales en France sous l'Ancien Régime," in Daniel Gaxie, ed., *Explication du vote: Un bilan des études électorales en France*. Paris, 1985, pp. 85–105.

Related topics

Ancien Régime	Equality	Suffrage
Clubs and Popular Societies	Louis XVI	Taine
Elections	Necker	Tocqueville

FEDERALISM

B rissot, questioned during his October 1793 trial about Condorcet's "feuillantine" constitution, protested: no more democratic constitution had ever existed, he said, adding that "I might mention that of the United States, which is far less so." The presiding judge of the Tribunal seized upon these unfortunate words as though they constituted a confession: "No more convincing proof can be given of the accused's intention to federalize the Republic than Brissot's reference to the Constitution of the United States, which all the accused used to invoke continually."

Were there really men among the revolutionaries with whom federalism had attained some credit? The terms "federative republic" and "federative constitution" were not unfamiliar to readers of Locke, Mably, Montesquieu, and Rousseau. They were used primarily to refer to either diplomatic alliances or federations of states, "societies of societies" as Montesquieu put it. These writers were indeed sympathetic to this "very new subject," the principles of which as Rousseau noted had yet to be established. Furthermore, the members of the Constituent Assembly were thoroughly familiar with and often cited the propaganda of the "Federalist." Two new editions were published in 1792, and on August 26 of that year the Legislative Assembly included Hamilton and Madison on the list of celebrated servants of humanity.

It is doubtful, however, that the men of the Revolution, with a few exceptions such as Buzot, were able to appreciate the subtle distinctions that the American authors established between "confederation," a system in which a decision could be blocked by the vote of a single state, and "federation," based on a division of powers between the several states and the federal government. So much is clear from their indiscriminate use of the words "federation" and "confederation." Their sympathy for the American model quickly succumbed, moreover, to bedazzlement by the French: what was the significance of compromise compared with the inception of a new political and social system? It is striking that suspicion toward any kind of federal system arose quite early, in discussions of the division of France into départements, and almost immediately cast discredit on provincial and local aspirations. The enthusiasm aroused by Sieyès' plan stemmed, according to Rabaut Saint-Etienne, from the fact that it guaranteed unity and dispelled the specter of "federative republics." On September 7, Virieu described the misfortunes that such republics inevitably would bring: "Certain provinces would be oppressed by neighboring powers, others by the border provinces." For Virieu, secession of provinces and federalism were clearly one and the same. Even the autonomous movement of the federations, though deprived at its inception of an official program and arising out of the depths of France (Proudhon saw it as a "resurgence of the federative idea, indigenous to old Gaul"), exhibited centripetal tendencies far more convincing than its centrifugal ones. Michelet no doubt exaggerated the former out of fervor for "our beautiful centralization." He was nevertheless correct in saying that the federations helped to place the various parts of French territory on an equal footing. The federations were fated, he said, to cancel one another out: "No more federations; they are useless. Only one is necessary: France."

Montagnard accusations notwithstanding, what needs to be explained is therefore not the lure of federalism but rather the intellectual obstacles that prevented acceptance of a model at first sight so attractive and supported by such authorities. What compromised the federative system in the eyes of the revolutionaries was its tenacious association with two apparently contradictory principles: democracy on the one hand and aristocracy on the other. Democracy, because to the classic question of whether a democratic regime was viable the eighteenth century provided a classic answer: democracy, which is defined by direct participation of all citizens in the formation of the law, was suited only to states of relatively small size. Inextricably associated with the republics of antiquity, democracy's time was past. What is more, it almost inevitably gave rise to factions. If, as Sieyès argued in the debate of September 1789, *bailliages* and *sénéchaussées* had the capacity to participate directly in the formulation of law, "to express their separate wishes," then soon "there would be as many states as *bailliages*," and France would succumb to "chaos and anarchy." Distrust of pure democracy, distrust of local and special interests (wherein lay incomprehension of the American system, which in fact consisted in entrusting such interests to local legislatures), and distrust of federalism were all of a piece for Sieyès. After pointing out that France "is not and cannot be a democracy," he immediately added that "it should not be a federal state, composed of a multitude of republics united by some kind of political bond." An extensive, civilized, commercial nation, France required a monarchical form (of this no one in September 1789 harbored the slightest doubt). Sieyès, in the name of indivisible sovereignty, therefore argued that the French monarchy was incompatible with federalism. This incompatibility was so vehemently felt that it still roused Buzot to indignation in his *Memoirs*. What aberration, he asked, had made it possible to accuse the Girondins of both royalism *and* federalism? "Surely these two words are quite astonished to find themselves together." The Jacobins had created a monster for polemical purposes.

Another spontaneous association linked federalism with aristocracy or even feudalism, the latter two words having become almost synonymous. Barante recounted Royer-Collard's jest that "if the feudal government had had philosophes, they would have said that it bore the Constitution of the United States in its belly." The idea of the feudal order as an unconscious blueprint for the federative order had already been suggested to Barnave by his distrust of both systems: "Federation is republican feudalism; feudalism is monarchic federation." For Barnave a conservative and territorial spirit marked the federative system; it ensnared the individual in local dependencies and subjected him to the influence of great families, which styled themselves guardians and guarantors of diversity. He therefore expressed a decided hostility to what he called "division into cantons" and doubted, moreover, that France felt a sufficiently powerful or conscious need for unity to prevent "the South and the North from forming two nations." Only "the immense energy of the monarchy" seemed to him capable of guaranteeing a unity that a Congress would be powerless to secure and of maintaining the power of the whole over the parts.

Whether factions of democratic society or fractions of aristocratic society, federalism always seemed to bear within itself seeds of dissolution and inequality. By contrast, the monarchy—to which the Revolution, as Mirabeau pointed out to Louis XVI, had just presented the priceless gift of a future "without parlements, without *pays d'états*, without privileged corps, without clergy, without nobility"—was working toward unification of the territory, equality of the citizenry, and rationality. And the Revolution, which had kept the monarchy but broken with aristocratic anarchy and which remained fearful of democratic anarchy, was doubly impervious to the allure of the federative idea.

Accordingly, the French Revolution knew only a brief "federalist" moment, which was neither the time of the federations nor that of the Girondin struggle against Paris. Federalism's moment came after Varennes, when one of the intellectual obstacles to acceptance of the federative idea was removed. Once monarchy was condemned, in people's minds at any rate, the idea of federalism, as well as the word itself, was free to surface at the *Cercle Social*, admittedly still in the form of a federation of nations. For federalism to appear in the form of an intermediary power between the central government and individuals we must await the end of 1791 and the drafting of a surprising text by Billaud-Varenne. Billaud—as the Girondins accused of federalism were quick to remind him later—granted to the eighty-three départemental administrations a "power of sanction" such that no decree would have force of law unless approved by three-quarters of them, a system which he presented as the solution to the problem of the viability of a republican government in a large state. This view was precisely that of Buzot, who presented it as a strictly personal opinion and not at all as a Girondin commonplace; well suited to large territories, federalism combined "the advantages of a well ordered liberty internally with those of a powerful union of all the forces of the state externally."

Probably because the war revived the threat and fear of fragmentation, however, interest in the federalist solution was shortlived. In September 1792, on the eve of the proclamation of the Republic, the Jacobin Club placed the federative question on the agenda, and Chabot was already characterizing it as a "Brissotin plan" to reestablish the monarchy. The true meaning of the plan would be revealed by Brissot two months later. His system, he said, was this: "Unity of the départements of France, extension to the boundaries prescribed for it by nature, and beyond, a belt of federative republics." A unified France, in other words, extending to its natural borders and protected by a buffer of allied republics: such were the limits of Brissot's federalism, without a trace of monarchy or of a federal state. The misunderstanding was thus total, and the whole history of the Revolution would only deepen it.

*
**

The Girondins, it is true, took it upon themselves to aggravate the situation and fan the suspicions of Chabot. On September 23, 1792, all the more shaken by the September massacres because they had had to absorb the shock, the Girondins in the person of Roland issued an appeal that the Assembly be defended against the possibility of similar events in the future. By what? By the départements themselves, which would recruit a public force, answered Vergniaud, Lanjuinais, and Buzot, all three speaking with one voice. Immediately thereafter came the conflict between Lasource and Danton. The former claimed to fear the despotism and "intrigue" of Paris. Danton, as usual, responded with extreme words—calling for the death penalty for those who wished to carve up France—and moderate thoughts: the threat of death ought to be enough to "drive out absurd ideas." For Danton, federalism was obviously a phantom. Buzot, who intervened at this point, made a purely defensive argument: the only purpose of calling upon the départemental army was to quell "federative divisions." Robespierre was thus left in the advantageous position of concluding the debate. In a single condemnation he lumped together—in an amalgam that would prove quite durable— those who attacked the Commune, those who waved the red flag of the agrarian law as though it had already been passed, and those who harbored the "finished plan of creating a federative republic." He scored a decisive point by playing on the passion for unanimity that existed in the Convention and rallying it around the vote for unity and indivisibility of the Republic. This unity was indeed everyone's wish, but now the call for a départemental army was definitively branded with the mark of infamy, for it was against this proposal that the vote was obtained.

By September 1792 everything was therefore in place: suspicion of the word "federalism," which was shared by the Gironde itself and was powerful enough to make even the glorious word "federation" inopportune, the only ones still to use it with any enthusiasm being those *fédérés* who arrived in Paris during the summer; trading of charges of federalism between the two camps; the use by both sides of historical allusions, the Girondins comparing Paris to the Rome of the Empire, the Montagnards harking back to Cromwell ("It has been proposed that you place yourselves on a par with tyrants by surrounding yourselves with a guard"); the idea, which arose quite early on the Girondin side, of finding another city to take the place of Paris and become a capital of *the* peaceful Revolution to oppose to a capital of anarchic revolutions (an idea, incidentally, that points up a centralism that was as vigorous on the Girondin side as on the Montagnard); and finally, a panicky fear, which grew throughout the year, of borders left undefended as départemental volunteers marched on Paris. This argument, which the Mountain exploited to the full, became irresistible when the difficulty of recruiting 300,000 men became apparent; but even before that it was powerful enough for Boyer-Fonfrède himself to ask the volunteers who had already answered the call to head back to their départements.

Nothing was more striking throughout that year than the contrast between the menacing flood of provincial petitions that converged on Paris, announcing the recruitment and departure of armed units, and the meagerness of the results. The *conseils généraux* of the départements nevertheless began recruiting troops here and there, issuing marching orders, and setting soldiers' wages, and in fact some small detachments reached Paris at the beginning of winter. But by January the Montagnards won postponement of the debate that would have authorized the départemental administrations to vote on public expenditures. In February Cambon asked that the battalions recruited by the départements be placed at the disposal of the Executive Council, and his request was granted. In March, in the climate of panic created by military defeats and the Vendean uprising, the Girondins retreated. The départemental force remained at the heart of the political problem until May 31, however, and already, well before the revelations of the federalist insurrection, demonstrated the paralysis of the départemental administrations. The latter were able to stir up a little agitation in clubs that had broken with the mother society, to arouse the national guard, and, thanks to the power of hierarchy, to obtain the support of subordinate administrations. But their meager success in raising troops was a harbinger of other difficulties to come.

In the area where they were most successful—mobilizing moderates and inspiring them to make threatening declarations—can we find traces of the localist aspirations for which they were so severely criticized? The texts inspired by this agitation actually contain few traces of regional sentiment. It might be objected that this was a strategy on the part of men who sensed that the accusation of federalism would prove fatal and who were obliged to advance under cover. Yet these precautions would not have sufficed if a strong sense of provincial identity had existed. In fact, apart from standard references to shared soil and climate (mountain and plain, North and South), the only allusions to regional identity touched on the recent past of the Revolution itself (the republican vocation of the Marseillais, the anti-despotic enthusiasm of the Bretons), as if local pride had been reduced to having shared in the national sentiment. The administrators of the Finistère even went so far as to hold up as an example to Parisians forgetful of their qualities as Frenchmen the national consciousness of those who, though Breton by origin, were true French patriots. Thus, it was the Montagnard adversary alone that detected signs of secessionist sentiment in the behavior of the moderate administrations. Dubois-Crancé, dispatched on a mission to Isère, reported that he had seen départemental administrators bold enough "to lay a map of France on the table and prove by geography that the South could get along without the North." Of a piece with this partisan observation is a confidence that Mme. Roland let slip in her *Memoirs:* "In thinking about the bad situation and the fear of despotism in the North, we conceived a tentative plan for a Republic in the South. Servan studied the military posts. We traced on the map lines of demarcation determined by rivers, mountains, and cities. We discussed territorial production and resources." What is evident here, however, is in no sense a regional, much less a separatist, sentiment but a childish excitement at recreating politics with a clean slate.

What is even more evident is hatred of Paris. In various départemental petitions Paris was sometimes the dominating, arrogant, rebellious city of the Commune, sometimes the humiliated and abject city of the Convention, but always the city that stood apart, the true federalist city. Roger Dupuy, who has examined all the texts pertaining to Paris in the correspondence of the Ille-et-Vilaine deputation, points out that the deputies' hostility was directed less toward the Mountain than toward the Commune, less toward Robespierre than toward Marat, less toward the manipulated but not inherently evil Parisian masses than toward a handful of ambitious or fanatical men. Still, the existence of this enormous armed mass was interpreted by the magistrates of Rennes in terms of their own cultural categories: Paris, for them, was the Rome of the late Republic, beset by plebeian demands and egalitarian pressures. They saw the provincial representatives of the central government as agents sent to govern the départements like Roman provinces. The theme they harped on was not so much one of alleged Parisian contempt for the provinces as one of protest against Jacobin centralization.

This same protest inspired a moderate sectional movement in the spring of 1793. After Parisian sections began in April to press for the purge of Girondin deputies, the provinces responded with a move to maintain the moderate sections—agitation intended as a response to interference in local affairs by representatives of the central government, whose arrival that spring to oversee troop recruitment activities was taken as a challenge. These representatives became the focus of provincial hatred. In some cities the moderate sections were content to issue Platonic petitions. But in others, such as Marseilles and Lyons, they took charge of municipal affairs; arresting Jacobins and ransacking their clubs, they were already resorting to illegal methods. Even in Paris, "the springtime of moderatism" permitted some sections to throw off Montagnard hegemony. From the existence of this movement one can infer that the federalist revolt was far from a simple reply to the coup d'état of June 2, 1793. On May 23 the citizens of Dijon told the Convention that if it continued to warn against the federalist wolf, it would ultimately cause such a beast to appear; the idea of the départements banding together in response to an eventual coup by the Commune was described a thousand times before it actually occurred.

When news of the coup of June 2, 1793, reached the provinces, it seemed at first to fulfill the prediction made by the citizens of Dijon, for it provided all the fragmentary protests with a pretext, hastened their development, and gave them substance. The first thing to be fixed was the geography of revolt. Départements forming a circle around Paris remained calm. In addition to these areas under Parisian influence, the border départements of the Nord and Pas-de-Calais, as well as the départements of Lorraine and Alsace, which were somewhat more hesitant but where protest was stifled by internal dissension, constituted a northeastern corner of France that remained loyal to the Convention. Central France also remained quiet, though Bourges would ultimately become the capital of a new Convention. The traditional historiography of the federalist movement therefore counted some thirty loyal départements and described two-thirds of the départements as being in a state of rebellion against the mutilation of the Convention. What Jaurès called the "federalism of despair" was almost a reality.

But the magnitude of the phenomenon was exaggerated by both the Gironde, which hoped to envelop the movement in rumors of success, and the Mountain, which needed to justify repressive measures. The insurrection, like the agitation of the preceding months, was centered in the départemental administrations, controlled now as in the past by a very moderate segment of the bourgeoisie—the electors of 1792, despite the advent of universal suffrage, generally chose the same men as their predecessors—that hoped for peace and financial security. Upon receiving news of the coup, these départemental administrations convoked an extraordinary assembly of all or some of the constituted corps. Several outcomes were possible. In some places the insurrection failed owing to dissension within the assembly; in the Orne, for example, the départmental administration, dominated by Valazé and associated with the Girondins of Caen, found itself at loggerheads with a municipality loyal to the Convention and led by Argentan, who proposed a wait-and-see attitude in response to bellicose resolutions and ultimately succeeded in paralyzing the entire assembly. In other places the resistance went further: the assembly established a committee or commission of public safety, arrested the Convention's representatives, and attempted to recruit troops, yet retained sufficient respect for legal procedure to notify the Convention of the steps taken. Initially this was what took place in Caen. In still other places, the assembly broke with the Convention and sent liaison officers to neighboring départements to arrange for common action; such concertation gave federalism what substance it had.

Of the five centers of declared insurrection—Caen, Bordeaux, Marseilles, Lyons, Toulon—two were dealt with fairly easily. The Assembly of Calvados, meeting in Caen, which had become the refuge for fugitive Girondin leaders after June 2, decided a week later not to lay down its arms until the liberty of the Convention had been restored. Its first acts were to arrest Romme and Prieur of the Marne, the representatives of the Convention, and to place an embargo on food shipments to Paris. Then it formed an Insurrectional Committee of the départements of the Northwest. It had a much harder time enlisting volunteers. After drawn-out preparations, a battalion left Evreux on July 12 without waiting for another battalion to arrive from the Finistère. Begun without enthusiasm, the expedition was surprised by Republican troops and ingloriously routed at Brécourt on July 13, 1793. There the march on Paris came to an end. When Jullien, in a "Report on the Rebellious Administrations" that became the bible of the Montagnard prosecution, said that the purpose of the Caen operation was to establish a system of federal republics modeled on the Swiss, the accused had no difficulty defending themselves. They had a harder time absolving their leaders of the charge of royalism: Wimpfen had been only an ephemeral Jacobin and Puisaye would eventually go over to the Vendée.

The scenario was not very different in Bordeaux, where out of the Extraordinary Assembly of June 7 came a popular commission that began by abolishing the *maximum* and sending agents to spread propaganda in neighboring départements. As in Caen, the great failure was in recruiting troops; it was hard to find volunteers or to stem a high rate of desertion. Despite the formation of a military committee, Bordeaux was unable to field the prescribed 1,200 men; it was a meager army of 400 that, after a thirty-mile march, was scattered in the vineyards on July 31—an end comparable to that of the movement in Caen. Although royalism had made few inroads in Bordeaux, the two examples have much in common. Both were replies to the coup d'état. Both were connected with the expulsion of the Girondins (Bordeaux was their native city, Caen their refuge). Both erupted in cities where the sectional movement of that spring had been lacking in vigor, and where Jacobin activism, even among the poor classes, remained measured. Finally, federalism in both places lacked popular support.

Things went quite differently in the three other centers of revolt, where it took much longer and proved much more difficult to put down the rebellion. In Marseilles, Lyons, and Toulon the insurrectional movement was not a response to the expulsion of the Girondins. In those cities the conflict was long-standing. Even before September 1792 Marseilles had been the scene of a massacre of merchants and priests, hanged by the Jacobins. The Jacobin sections had taken the initiative in setting up a popular tribunal that administered a justice of its own. The arrival of agents of the central government in the spring of 1793 led to a renewal of tax assessments on the rich and removal of administrators. The moderate sections responded by driving out the agents and declaring themselves to be in a state of insurrection. In Lyons after the elections of November 1792 there was dissension between the départemental authorities, which feared the revolutionary measures, and the very advanced communal council. Conflict raged throughout the winter in a series of ambiguous episodes, with the Jacobins victorious in some, the moderates in others. All this turmoil exploded in the insurrection of May 29, which erupted *before* the events in Paris and which led to elimination of the Jacobin municipal council and the downfall of Chalier's dictatorship. It was a bloody insurrection made unpardonable by the execution of Chalier. Finally, Toulon had long been a center of serious disturbances, purges, arrests, and exactions; as early as July 1792 a Jacobin municipal council had taken part in the massacre of départemental administrators.

Thus we have three cities in which political conflict was long and bitter. Three cities in which the Jacobins had been in control for long periods and had stirred opposition even in popular quarters. Three cities in which armed resistance met with remarkable success. What distinguished Marseilles was the département's ability to mobilize an army of 3,500 men, which made several victorious sallies aimed at establishing a link to the forces of Lyons. On their way to Paris the Marseillais occupied Avignon on July 7, but the city was recaptured by General Carteaux ten days later. Still, it took two more battles to put down the Marseilles rebellion. And bitter and bloody sieges were needed before Lyons and Toulon would yield.

Furthermore, these were three cities in which, in contrast to the first two examples, royalism clearly had a hand in the insurrectional movements, though probably not at the very beginning. According to Joseph de Maistre, "royalism played no part in the Lyons affair; it was one republican faction striking at another." But the geographical situation of Lyons as a crossroads city situated close to a Switzerland filled with émigrés made it easy for royalists to infiltrate the rebellion. The siege forced the city to find an army to defend it, moreover, and at the head of that army it placed a royalist general. The increase in royalist influence during those terrible weeks explains why, in contrast to what happened in Bordeaux, the Lyons sections opposed supplying materiel to the army of the Alps, because Lyons openly counted on a Piedmontese offensive. Toulon, for its part, set an example of treason, since the General Committee of the Sections, after a period of relative independence, finally surrendered in August to the English, after which it did nothing all autumn but carry out English orders until the city fell on December 18.

From study of these three cities, finally, one can conclude that what sustained the rebellion was not so much the insult to the representatives of the nation as the fear of another revolution, sparked by rumors of an agrarian law and taxation of the rich. If royalists infiltrated the rebellion, moreover, they did not plot to bring it about: the anti-Jacobin movement was born in the assemblies of the republican sections and in patriotic circles, as is shown by the example of Marseilles, where the "federalists" were former Jacobins. If the urban elite of major merchants and rentiers played an important role in the revolt of these commercial and industrial cities, shopkeepers and artisans—the very same individuals who would have been sans-culottes in Paris— also took part, along with (in Marseilles at least) even more popular elements. In short, the federalist revolt was a little less bourgeois than it has been accused of being, much less royalist, and infinitely less "Girondin." It was most firmly rooted where conflict was long-standing, where anti-Jacobinism was fostered by the exactions of the clubs, and where local notables had been unable to assume firm direction of their cities. The violence of local politics accounts for the success of the federalist revolt.

It was all over by the end of 1793, with the surrender of Toulon. Now came the merciless repression, executions of insurgents by firing squad, demolition of houses, renaming of the guilty cities. One reason for the failure of the movement was the rapid approval of the Constitution by the Montagnard Convention, which definitively won over hesitant administrations. Even in the regions most clearly in the anti-Jacobin camp, there were some cantons, districts, and municipalities ready to send petitions of support to the Convention, and even certain federalist départements (such as the Gironde) agreed to organize the referendum on the Constitution. The slowness of communications made it possible for the Convention to exploit provincial procrastination by sending representatives sufficiently energetic to ward off a break. The food crisis also played a restraining role at a time of year marked by anxiety over whether supplies would hold out through the winter. Furthermore, in many départements worries about the threat of foreign invasion and about the Vendée uprising encouraged doubts as to the wisdom of breaking with the Mountain. Finally, the rural masses everywhere remained indifferent to the movement in the cities. This was true to such an extent that one might interpret the "federalist" reverses as a definitive failure for the maritime, commercial, liberal France of the ports as opposed to what E. Fox in a brilliant book characterized as agricultural, peasant, authoritarian, centralizing France.

*
**

Baudot wrote in his *Memoirs:* "I know that on several occasions the Committee of Public Safety discussed drafting a report on federalism, and that this report was always postponed for lack of proof. Yet this was a time when no one was very demanding when it came to evidence." We agree with Baudot and disagree with Albert Soboul when he says that "the persistent reality of provincial and regional differences caused the federalist crisis in 1793." Nowhere do such "differences" figure in the origin of the crisis, which everywhere involved rejection of Jacobin measures and of the *représentants en mission* who embodied those measures.

This error has proved persistent, however. Regionalist movements in France were permanently marked by the memory of the insurgent regions, which in a time of national danger dared to attack on a second front and at times did not disdain foreign help. The revolt of the cities against Jacobin policy became synonymous with threats to national unity. The memory of federalism has always been used to frustrate even the most modest regional aspirations. If the Jacobin spirit or Jacobin activism still enjoys the reputation of having saved the country, regional claims are suspected of posing a covert challenge to its unity and indivisibility. That is why such claims have been urged so timidly over the two centuries since the Revolution. La Révellière-Lépeaux tells us that under the Directory men of both the left and the right were in tacit agreement when it came to "heaping abuse on the federative system." Out of this common rejection there even arose a "right-wing Jacobinism," a political orientation that would have been totally out of place during the Revolution itself. Even those parties that might have had some sympathy for the regional cause owing either to their regional roots (the Radical party) or their principles (Christian Democracy) were never able to express that sympathy in the face of their leaders' Jacobinism and nationalist reflexes revitalized by war. And the Jacobins also won a victory of another order: after them the French went right on—until very recently, in fact—inventing "federalist" enemies.

Mona Ozouf

FURTHER READING

Baudot, Marc-Antoine. *Notes historiques sur la Convention Nationale, le Directoire, l'Empire et l'exil des votants.* Paris, 1893.

Buzot, François-Nicolas-Louis. *Mémoires sur la Révolution française.* Paris, 1823.

Dupuy, Roger. "Aux origines du fédéralisme breton: Le cas de Rennes, 1789–mai 1793," *Annales de Bretagne et des pays de l'Ouest,* no. 3, 1975.

Edmonds, Bill. "Federalism and Urban Revolt in France in 1793," *Journal of Modern History,* 55, March 1983.

Forrest, Alan. *Society and Politics in Revolutionary Bordeaux.* Oxford, 1975.

Fox, Edward Whiting. *History in Geographic Perspective: The Other France.* New York, 1971.

Goodwin, Albert. "The Federalist Movement in Caen in the Summer of 1793," *Bulletin of the John Rylands Library* (Manchester), 42, March 1960.

Herriot, Edouard. *Lyon n'est plus,* 4 vols. Paris, 1937–1940.

La Révellière-Lépeaux, Louis-Marie de. *Mémoires,* 3 vols. Paris, 1873.

Nicolle, Paul. "Le mouvement fédéraliste dans l'Orne en 1793," *Annales historiques de la Révolution française,* 1936.

Voyenne, Bernard. *Histoire de l'idée fédéraliste,* 3 vols. Paris and Nice, 1973–1981.

Wallon, Henri-Alexandre. *La révolution du 31 mai et le fédéralisme en 1793 ou la France vaincue par la Commune de Paris,* 2 vols. Paris, 1886.

RELATED TOPICS

Aristocracy
Barnave
Centralization
Condorcet
Constitution

Democracy
Département
Federation
Feudal System
Girondins

Jaurès
Maistre
Michelet
Montesquieu
Paris Commune

Robespierre
Rousseau
Sieyès

FEDERATION

The prestige of the Federation, and of all that the word implies (for it was also used, often somewhat negligently, to denote efforts to unify the National Guards in the summer and autumn of 1789, as well as the federative movements of the spring of 1790 and the National Federation of July 1790), comes from its having been the least contested episode of the French Revolution. This distinction it owed to several merits. It extended, first of all, over the whole country, the sign of a spontaneous, simultaneous, and unanimous will; "One instinct," Jaurès wrote, "warned all citizen groups and all cities at the same moment that liberty would be precarious and feeble so long as it rested solely in the National Assembly, and that it needed to be provided with as many centers as there were communes." Second, the Federation was a demonstration of fraternity—a return, in Michelet's words, to "that cornerstone of human nature," sociability, and thus a true invention of that "universal Church that knows no temple other than the vault of heaven, from the Vosges to the Cévennes and from the Pyrenees to the Alps." Last but not least, the inception of the federations was seen as the birth of French patriotism, as a product, according to Michelet, of France's wedding with itself, which seemed to have abolished local and regional differences; the federations, Michelet said, were "the death of geography." For the first time in history they gave men the strength to escape the confines of the village and its parochial spirit. People abandoned, in the words of Louis Blanc, "the bell that sounded at the birth of their children and the wooden cross that protected the ashes of their forebears." The federations also established the prestige of Paris as center. The federative movement embodied in images both the French passion for unity and the sense of a convergence toward the center, for it explicitly renounced particularisms and concretely illustrated the march of the provinces toward Paris. Even Taine, the author of the most tepid account of the Federation, conceded that those who participated in the events of July 14, 1790, were "transported, raised above themselves."

Of course he added that it lasted only one morning, just long enough for an embrace and an oath. The next day the participants "again became what they always were." Since Taine, critical reexamination of the Federation has generally cast doubt on historians' euphoric accounts. Its unanimity has been challenged by pointing out that its principal actor, the National Guard, was scarcely representative of the nation. Its spontaneity and enthusiasm have been questioned by showing that laborious preparations preceded the event and by stressing its association with the restoration of order after the riot and the Great Fear. Its ceremonial arrangements have been ridiculed by showing that they were the result of a hard-won compromise rather than a true dramatization of unity. And its usefulness has been questioned by enumerating the many ways in which it bore the seeds of future conflict. The debate over dissension within the Federation has added to our knowledge of the National Guard and the federative movements, though gaps still remain. But it has not resolved the major question raised by the Federation, which is that of the power of the symbol and the truth of the legend.

The central actor in the federations was the National Guard, baptized on July 16, 1789, by Lafayette. The date on the baptismal certificate says all that needs to be said about the connection with the riot and the need to control it. A deputation from the National Assembly—eighty-eight men including Lafayette and Bailly—arrived in Paris on Wednesday, July 15, to find a permanent committee, an organized bourgeois militia, and a city filled with men in arms. After Lafayette was named colonel-general of the bourgeois militia, his goal was to disarm those who posed a threat to the social order but to maintain a citizens' army to counter the threat from royal troops. With the aid of a military committee this plan was promptly carried out, for by July 31 the guard was organized (400 men in each of the sixty districts) under the orders of an elected commanding general, with membership restricted de facto to prosperous citizens by way of a regulation requiring each soldier to pay for his own arms and handsome tricolor uniform. The purpose of this Paris creation was therefore unambiguous: it was to normalize an insurrectional situation.

In the provinces things were more complex. There had been turmoil well before July 14, 1789, and here and there improvised bourgeois militias had been set up under a variety of names including "civic guards" and "volunteers of the Third Estate." On this well-prepared terrain news of the Bastille's fall caused people to arm themselves, but in a variety of ways: at times in opposition to, at other times in alliance with, the municipal councils (old councils having been abolished in some cases but preserved in others, while in some places two rival councils coexisted with difficulty); at times in opposition to the military authorities but more often with their consent and complicity in supplying arms and surrendering citadels and fortresses. Yet this extreme diversity cannot conceal the essential fact, which is that militias simultaneously sprang up all over France. Thus, the movement did not originate with the Great Fear, but the Fear did reinvigorate it, leading to hasty conscription in cities and towns in the last week of July and the first few days of August. Everywhere men took arms, organized to sound the alarm, and established regular patrols and watches. When professional soldiers described these improvised troops, they stressed their irregular nature: "This type of troop is absolutely without discipline, without obedience, and without instruction of any kind," said a colonel from Epernay, speaking of his city's militia.

This anarchy of the bourgeois militias, as well as their propensity to stray beyond strictly municipal limits, accounts for the fact that as early as August 10, 1789, the deputies submitted for royal approval a decree granting official status to the National Militias and assigning to the municipal councils the tasks of calling the militias up when needed to keep the peace and of enlisting the aid of royal troops to disperse seditious assemblies. The decree did little to settle conflicts over authority between the municipal councils and the militias, however, since militia members took an oath (which Barnave deemed indispensable at a time when "the bonds of subordination appear to be broken") to their commander but not to the municipal council. Nevertheless, it clearly delineated the militia's police functions and in particular assigned it the mission of monitoring the conduct of "men without visible means of support, trade, or profession."

The contagious nature of this nationwide call to arms raises numerous problems, not all of which have been equally well resolved. Was it as novel as revolutionary historiography has maintained? Was it urban or rural? How were militiamen recruited? What links were there between the militias and the municipal councils?

Bourgeois militias, watches, and regiments were not an invention of the Revolution. Under the Ancien Régime the militias were still an organized force, sometimes limited to ceremonial duties—in processions and fireworks displays—sometimes assigned to police functions. But the revolutionary shock did not merely reactivate these militias; it transformed them profoundly. Studying the case of Rennes, Roger Dupuy has shown the novelty of the new National Guard compared with the old bourgeois militias. The National Guard of Rennes was born well before July 14, 1789, a result of the activism of the town's youth, which was responsible for the riotous days of January 26 and 27, 1789. The declarations made by these young men are astonishing documents, which already contain not only the word and idea of confederation but also the motto and emblems of the future National Guard. When these restless youths again entered the scene after July 14, 1789, it was to proceed with the organization of a short-lived "National Army," which was quickly taken in hand by the municipal council (whose reply to this creation was the National Guard Regulation) but whose name was in itself a protest against the memories associated with the word "militia." The point the young men wished to make was that the Third Estate had taken possession of the army.

The simultaneity of the movement points to the concerted underground influence of the deputies of the Third Estate. But the debates that began in the Assembly on July 18, 1789, in which the monarchists not surprisingly displayed their opposition to a France covered with revolutionary militias liberated from royal authority, do not reveal a very united front among the deputies of the Third Estate. Owing to this lack of unity, the debate very quickly bogged down. Mirabeau, for example, would have liked first to organize the municipal councils, in order to make sure that the militias would remain independent of the old oligarchies. Barnave, though not very explicit in the Assembly, wrote to correspondents in Grenoble that he wanted "militias ready to march." These doubts show that, while the Third Estate did wish to control a movement that threatened to overwhelm it, it had no clear doctrine on the subject.

Was the movement essentially urban, as nearly all historians of the Revolution have agreed? Paul Bois saw this urban character as one of the sources of peasant opposition to the Revolution. Since petty bourgeois and artisans were the mainstay of the National Guard's battalions in the countryside, while peasants were prevented by farm chores from taking part, rural opinion for a long time identified the Blues with the bourgeoisie. Though statistically correct, this assertion as it stands is too simple, for there were rural cantons that joined in events in nearby capitals, and there were rural National Guards with peasant captains. Nor is it true that the militia everywhere participated in and was therefore identified with repressive actions undertaken in the countryside for the protection of landlords; there are many instances in which national militiamen took part in attacks on châteaux or spontaneously went over to the side of the "mob." This very diversity shows clearly enough that the militias were unreliable and their functions ambiguous. They were also internally divided: a single city might have both patriotic companies and aristocratic companies, which explains how the National Guard in some places could have been lured to the camp of counterrevolution.

That division explains why the National Assembly soon sought to regularize the National Guard. It initially attempted to control recruitment. The social composition of the militias recruited before the Great Fear was rather limited, but danger in some cases caused the doors to be opened wide enough to admit, as in Toulouse, "everybody, without distinction, from the premier président down to the last artisan." Once the alert was over, attempts were again made to limit access through various property qualifications that in many cases anticipated the distinction between active and passive citizens. In some places only landowners were admitted, in others payment of a certain amount of tax was required, in still others it was enough to be inscribed on the roll of taxpayers. Domestics were of course excluded, sometimes along with "citizens needing to work every day for their subsistence." This diversity in recruitment was ended by the decree of June 12, 1790, limiting access to the National Guard to active citizens and their sons, who were obliged to enlist. Even if the Constituent Assembly did not dare disarm the "passive citizens" who had enlisted in the hour of danger, this restriction spelled the end of the volunteer militia and marked the closing of the doors to less prosperous citizens. Command of the militias continued to be exercised either by nobles (often chosen for their military experience) or by the *haute bourgeoisie* of professionals, administrators, and financiers.

Furthermore, the Assembly through a series of decrees concerned itself with limiting the autonomy of the militias and ensuring their subordination to the municipal councils; as of February 2, 1790, the latter were granted authority over "citizens organized in armed companies." In a sense the federative movement was a response to this loss of authority in the municipal arena. Through the movement the National Guard was able to claim a regional and later even a national role.

Where did the idea of the Federation—in the view of Michelet and

Jaurès a spontaneous creation—come from? With this question we come to a much debated problem of attribution. Some say that it originated with a pact concluded on November 2, 1789, among the fourteen cities with *bailliages* in the province of Franche-Comté. Others mention the federative oath of the national guards of Dauphiné and the Vivarais on November 19, 1789. Still others cite a meeting of sixty-nine town and city militias from Brittany in an assembly held at Pontivy on January 15, 1790. But the answer depends on whether one is interested in the idea of a national federation (in which case it would appear to have been coined in Pontivy: "Does not the new order of things require that you extend your pact of Union and make it common at the capital?") or simply in that of federation. The latter appeared quite early: on August 8, 1789, the municipal council of Millau, where Bonald was mayor, in concert with all inhabitants of the town founded a "Confederation with the cities of Rodez and Villefranche and any other city that might wish to join." On August 9 a small commune in Ariège proposed to its municipal council a "federative pact" with neighboring cities and villages. It was thus a question of innumerable local initiatives born of the Great Fear. Very likely, too, the need for federation, and even the word itself, arose out of more localized fears as early as the winter of 1789; young citizens of the Third Estate of Rennes used it in February 1789 in signing a pact of union with other young men who had come to the city from Brest and Anjou.

Through these various movements, all bound together by anxiety, the word "federation" gradually took hold. For a long time the terminology used to designate pacts between cities remained fluid: among the words and phrases used were "union," "reconciliation," "coalition of cities," ceremonies of "fraternity" and "patriotism," and "federation." The last, long fallen into disuse and overlooked by eighteenth-century dictionaries, came back into fashion in the language of politics (where it was used by Montesquieu, Mably, Rousseau, and Dupont de Nemours) and took on new luster from the example of America, which played a large part in popularizing the nouns "federation" and "confederation" and in fostering admiration for nations that "confederated." Still, these new terms did not take root without difficulties. For one thing, they sometimes had pejorative connotations, since thieves, too, joined in "infernal confederations" (so that militias thought it wise to refer to themselves as "holy confederations," "federations of fraternity, honor, union, and aid"). For another, the word "federation" sometimes put people off: when members of a special deputation from Brittany and Anjou reached the National Assembly on March 20, 1790, some deputies tried to prevent them from reading their declaration, on the grounds—or pretext—that it referred to a "federative pact," in which these deputies thought they saw the menace of federalism. Ultimately, however, they accepted the argument of the president of the Assembly: the declaration, which contained a formal renunciation of the title Bretons and Angevins, actually seemed to "demolish the federative system forever." Here we see a sign of the ambiguity of the word "federation" and a glimpse of its complex future relations with the word "federalism."

In the end, however, "federation" did take hold (triumphing over "confederation" by virtue of simplicity). From now on there were regional federations and *fédérés,* whose numbers grew during the spring of 1790 and which enjoyed the support of the patriotic party in the Assembly. The federations, apparently amenable to the dictates of the clubs, were also a way for the militias to escape from the control of aristocratic municipal councils: they were both objects of control and instruments of control. This duality is also apparent in the twin aims of the federations, which opposed both popular violence and the aristocratic threat. Certain federations preferred to emphasize one or the other of these objectives: that of Pontivy, for example, opposed only "enemies of the present regeneration" and breathed not a word about repression of the peasant movement. But most avowed both purposes in a cautious alternation between "brigands" on the one hand and "those who distinguish between the title of citizen and that of noble" on the other.

All these ambiguities—of vocabulary and purpose—as well as the very real conflicts between municipal council and National Guard (or between two rival National Guards) in places such as Montauban and Nîmes gave rise to the idea that the National Guard was not always a promoter of unity. Such suspicions were supposed to be erased by ceremonies organized to celebrate the signing of pacts of federation. Not that anything very new was proposed; these were military celebrations in which officers of the regular army and officers of the National Guards marched together, swore an oath with sword in hand, listened to an outdoor mass, and accepted the blessing of the flag— masculine affairs, celebrations of notables, between the altar of the fatherland and the town hall in which the pact of federation was drafted and signed. Embroidered upon these rather stiff ceremonies, however, were speeches that enthusiastically expressed the wish and desire for identity. A glance at these texts reveals that the interpretation of the movement as "provincialist" (which tempted the Assembly, as we saw earlier, and later Mirabeau, who portrayed Lafayette, the central figure of the Federation, as the "man of the provinces") is untenable. When the militiamen of Bourg l'Etoile declared "we are no longer Dauphinois, you are no longer Languedociens, we are all Frenchmen," the Bretons and Angevins responded by abjuring their "particular privileges." Participants in the federations, or at any rate their orators and petition writers, imagined an association of individuals identical in every respect— interchangeable links in an indestructible chain, to use a metaphor that recurs constantly in these texts. The federations, as La Tour du Pin put it quite clearly on January 4, 1790, were not "a system of local associations." It was not to muzzle "provincialism" that Paris sought to take control of them.

The idea of taking control arose instead out of the fear inspired by the contagious effect of the National Guards on the regular troops. It was this "Federation of line troops and National Guards," designed to control the latter, that Bailly stressed when he suggested, in the name of the Paris Commune, a "Great Federation," for which he proposed the date July 14. The proposal also served the purposes of Lafayette, who was increasingly estranged from the patriotic party and not displeased at the prospect of an opportunity to shore up his declining popularity. The participation of civilians in this anniversary celebration was briefly considered by the Commune but in the end rejected: according to Talleyrand's report, it was "armed France that will assemble, not deliberating France." Thus no one could participate in the ceremony except as a soldier. These exclusionary measures were further tightened in the course of the preparations: national guardsmen were to be named in a two-stage election, while only the most senior line troops were to be selected. An official oath was to be drawn up. And on the recommendation of Le Chapelier, efforts were to be made to economize; we are a long way from the youthful and tumultuous dawn of the first pacts between militias.

The festival itself did not exactly belie these fearful, conservative provisions. On July 14, 1790, 50,000 armed men marched before a crowd of 300,000 on a rain-drenched Champ de Mars. The celebration, whose only innovation was the inclusion of a battalion of children and a battalion of old men, showed signs of having been put together hastily: an interminable military parade, a mass on the altar of the fatherland, which, though celebrated by three hundred priests who assisted Talleyrand, was lost in the immense, theatrical setting of the Champ de Mars, and a very casual oath by the king (no one, not even Mirabeau, had been able to convince Louis XVI to take the oath at the altar). Enthusiasm was evident only in the rounds of *fédérés* who ignored the ceremonial script and braved the wind, and the triumph seemed to be Lafayette's and Lafayette's alone.

How, in spite of all this actual gloominess, did the Festival of the Federation acquire its extraordinary symbolic significance? Note first of all that the historians who, like Michelet, gave an effusive account of it placed the accent on the July 14 federative festivals *in the provinces*. These were able to proceed uncoerced, since Paris had neglected to dispatch instructions. While all the provincial occasions included, like the one in Paris, a military parade, "celebration of the holy mysteries," and an oath, the organizers were able to embroider on this canvas. Some added unexpected new participants, including women and girls. Others drew on the old corporative order, as in Strasbourg, where gardeners, fishermen, and farmers marched in the parade. Some celebrated first baptisms and civil marriages on the altar of the fatherland. Others invented backdrops that borrowed indiscriminately from ancient forms and exotic and allegorical motifs. There were fireworks and balloons—not a novel kind of ceremony, in short, so much as a joyous mingling of disparate elements, whose verbal and visual syncretism has delighted historians.

The simultaneity of all these celebrations is another fact that historians like to point out. The only requirement to be observed in the provinces was that the federative oath be sworn "at the hour of noon, in concert and at the same moment in all parts of the Empire." People were extraordinarily struck by this simultaneity. Another point that has caught the attention of historians is the dynamic nature of the event, exemplified by the *fédérés'* march to Paris. Both those who made the trip—for some the first journey of their lives—and those who watched them march past on roads suddenly filled with people, where according to a thousand witnesses speech itself was in motion, saw the image of a vital and busy nation on the move. Actors and spectators alike learned a lesson about the homogeneity of French territory as they actively experienced the crossing of ancient boundaries. Louis Blanc saw this quite clearly: "1,200 internal barriers disappeared; mountains seemed to lower their peaks, and rivers ceased to be anything more than moving belts linking populations separated for far too long." This experience of homogeneity was not even contradicted by the sacred position of the terminus and focus of all the journeys, Paris. For if the *fédérés* entered Paris, in Quinet's words, as "a holy city," it should be remembered that the king was in Paris and that many travelers spoke of the religious emotion with which they came to "contemplate" him, evidence of the popularity that the monarch still possessed but of which, to Mirabeau's dismay, he had no idea how to take advantage. Furthermore, the travelers were all mindful of the other end of the road, the city to which they would return laden with relics, insignia, and banners at the end of a second journey no less important than the first. In this respect, the Federation illustrated, by way of this round-trip pilgrimage, the fact that every point on French soil was of equal dignity.

Simultaneity, topographical equality, dynamic image of unity, and also perhaps, as Jaurès suggested, a revolutionary ferment injected into the ranks of a regular army not particularly favorable to the Revolution: it was in these ways that the Federation left a durable imprint on the national imagination. Can unanimity be added to the list? Obviously there was a unanimity of patriots, which left out the aristocrat in opposition to whom the patriot defined himself. It was also a bourgeois unanimity, which excluded the "passive citizens." Yet this double exclusion cannot be said to have been a deliberate fraud: the first was functional, and without it the festival would not have existed; the second seems shocking to us only by dint of an anachronism and could hardly have been experienced as such in 1790. The participants in the celebration were chosen that year in a cascade of elections. It was the active nation, the duly authorized revolutionaries who gathered on the Champ de Mars. Jaurès wrote: "When the Constituent Assembly called four million men to the polls, it could imagine that it had called the entire nation." The same could be said of the Federation.

Unanimity was therefore not a deliberate lie but a widely shared illusion, or even better, a promise: the fact that common people in the towns and villages demanded, and by breaking down the barriers that excluded them from "notability" sometimes obtained, the right to "federate" themselves, shows that it was indeed interpreted in this way. Thus the Federation could be disappointing as a unity rally yet embody a unifying dynamic; it could be an imperfect illustration of the social bond but also be "the highest vision of the future that any nation has ever had." Therein lies the truth of its legend.

This symbolic charge also meant that the Federation could not be contained entirely in the brief pause it marked in the history of the Revolution. Though the event itself may have been marred by cautious preparations, its future was filled with conflict. The *fédérés,* who in 1790 displayed both devotion to the king and revolutionary fervor, would soon express the Revolution's radicalization. On April 18, 1791, it was the National Guard that, in spite of Lafayette's objections, opposed the king's departure for Saint-Cloud. It was the arrival of the *fédérés* in Paris after July 8, 1792, that set the stage for the Tenth of August. It was they who called for the suspension of the king and the election of a National Convention. While the significance of the Federation is not exhausted by the federative episode, the former should not be allowed to hide the precariousness of the latter. "It is good," Jaurès writes, "that penetrating and keen minds look beyond the prestige of the festivals and the bedazzlement of universal joy to identify the persistent causes of disorder, distrust, and violence, which would soon produce further effects."

Mona Ozouf

FURTHER READING

Arches, Pierre. "Aspects sociaux de quelques gardes nationales au début de la Révolution, 1789–1790," *Actes du 81e congrès national des sociétés savantes, Rouen-Caen, 1956*. Paris, 1957–1960.

Carrot, Gérard. "Une institution de la nation: La Garde Nationale 1789–1871." Doctoral dissertation, Faculté de Droit et de Sciences Economiques, Université de Nice, 1979.

Dupuy, Roger. *La Garde Nationale et les débuts de la Révolution en Ille-et-Vilaine*. Paris, 1972.

Lambert, Maurice. *Les fédérations en Franche-Comté et la fête de la Fédération du 14 juillet 1790*. Paris, 1890.

Leclercq, Dom Henri. *La Fédération (janvier–juillet 1790)*. Paris, 1929.

Thoré, P.-H. "Fédérations et projets de fédérations dans la région toulousaine," *Annales historiques de la Révolution française*, October–December 1949.

RELATED TOPICS

Barnave	Jaurès	Michelet	Quinet
Blanc	Lafayette	Mirabeau	Rousseau
Federalism	Louis XVI	Montesquieu	Taine
Great Fear			

GREAT FEAR

Among events of the first months of the Revolution the Great Fear stands out as a distinct episode that in some ways has never ceased to be an embarrassment to historians. It is one of the unexpected incidents of 1789, which surprised contemporaries before it baffled specialists. It is hard to integrate into any account of the origins of the Revolution because it often looks like an archaic throwback and seems to contrast with the awakening of national political consciousness. Doubtless that classification is why it was all but left out of the major nineteenth-century histories of the Revolution and for a long time interested only local scholars, who approached its study in a narrowly regional framework. The Great Fear did not find its historian—and at the same time its place and its interpretation—until the publication of Georges Lefebvre's magisterial synthesis in 1932. After more than half a century his book still has not been replaced, nor have its results been subjected to major revision. Hence it is appropriate that we begin with this classic analysis.

Lefebvre's primary concern was to distinguish carefully among the various aspects of the peasant movement of the spring and early summer of 1789. Strictly speaking, the Great Fear was the final stage of that movement, and its distinguishing characteristics need to be identified. But it cannot be understood in isolation from a broader context that has to be reconstituted first.

We begin, therefore, with the situation in the countryside, the seriousness of which does not seem to have been properly appreciated by any of the major political actors in Versailles, Paris, or the provincial capitals. Things came to a head in the final year of the Ancien Régime as proximate and remote factors converged and their effects reinforced one another. Among the more immediate factors was the disastrous harvest of 1788, which once again raised the specter of high prices and even shortages in most provinces. Add to this situation the unfortunate effects of a hesitant and contradictory grain trade policy, which inevitably encouraged speculation. Taking a somewhat longer view, a recession in the early 1770s interrupted a long-term growth trend spanning much of the eighteenth century. The effects of the recession were particularly severe in certain sectors of agriculture (such as grape production) and among certain independent farmers and wage earners, who suffered more than a simple reduction in consumption. Finally, looking at the century as a whole, some of the effects of growth had proved perverse, particularly the nearly insupportable weight of a rapidly increasing population. In short, what we see is, in the words of Denis and Pierre Goubert, "the conjunction of the day before yesterday's prosperity with yesterday's stagnation and today's crisis." The resulting tension reached a peak on the eve of the next harvest, in July 1789. It was accompanied, as usual, by skyrocketing food prices, particularly cruel because they came at a low point in the income cycle, and by rising anxiety and suspicion of hoarders who battened on the people's misery. Increasing numbers of vagabonds wandering the roads in search of scarce supplies—defenseless sometime mendicants mingled with those who made a profession of surviving on the fringes of society—further compounded the worries of those who stayed at home. Their fears probably heightened the drama of an already difficult situation. The result was the first series of food riots, traditional in form and, what is more, not exclusively rural.

These tensions were contemporaneous with the lengthy process of political consultation that preceded the meeting of the Estates General. To be sure, most peasants were only remotely associated with the drafting of *cahiers de doléances* and the electoral procedure per se. And contemporaries doubtless paid little attention at the time to the distress of the countryside, much less to the possible political consequences of that distress. Nevertheless, preparations for the elections during the winter of 1788–89 seem to have aroused great hopes. People began to expect that the sovereign, finally forced to look into the woes of his subjects, would be moved not only to provide compassionate aid and to restore order in the realm but also to right past wrongs. Peasants contrasted the good and charitable king with all whose domination and predation they were obliged to endure, above all the lords "ever busy sucking their blood." Though expressed with unprecedented vigor, the protest itself was not new. It followed on the heels of a half-century of rebellions that grew steadily more bitter in the final years of the Ancien Régime, as Emmanuel Le Roy Ladurie, following Saint-Jacob and others, has shown.

Once again, the short-term situation must be viewed in relation to a longer-term evolution. By doing so we see more clearly why the political opportunity of 1789, though only dimly comprehended, immediately gave rise to hopes and demands. And also to acts: well before August 4 some were convinced that it had been easier to abolish unjust dues and rents because a struggle had already been waged against them in the form of overt violence and strikes. The electoral assemblies no doubt contributed to the spread of such actions and to the organization of resistance. The privileged (as well as royal tax collectors) became targets of peasant agitation. Between March and May, Provence, Dauphiné, Hainault, Cambrésis, Picardy, and the Paris region became theaters of violent actions against the seigneurial order, and there were also more sporadic outbreaks of violence in Franche-Comté, the Lyonnais, Champagne, and Languedoc. Often these actions were superimposed on hunger riots.

Early that summer the movement took a tougher stand, and protests over dues to landlords took a more radical turn. In the second half of July veritable revolts almost simultaneously shook the Norman bocage, Franche-Comté, Alsace, Hainault, and the Mâconnais. The violence was uneven (as was the repression that followed). All the riots appear to have involved people of rather different backgrounds, however, from wage earners to independent farmers, artisans, and even minor rural notables. The authorities chose to view the incidents as the work of looters out to enrich themselves. Yet the insurgents usually struck at the proofs and symbols of oppression. They burned land registers and seigneurial court records and attacked royal tax offices. Sometimes they attacked a château or abbey and insisted that the master renounce his dues. Weathervanes and dovecotes were knocked down. The violence, though determined and impressive, was not very bloody, despite Taine's claims to the contrary, and often it took very little to transform it into celebration.

Fear was the third aspect of the emotion that gripped the French countryside. It, too, was born of the conjunction of several motifs. Fear of famine had heightened tempers. The growing numbers of vagabonds, who revived images of famous brigands as well as distant memories of invasion, posed an intolerable threat; "We cannot lie down without fear; the nighttime paupers have tormented us greatly, to say nothing of the daytime ones, whose numbers are considerable," wrote a man who owned land on the outskirts of Aumale. As the harvest season drew near, fears grew that these beggars would seize the long-awaited harvest. The spring riots only reinforced this general feeling of insecurity. In a sense the movement sustained itself. It also had repercussions in the cities, which soon began to arm themselves against the "fourth estate." The alarm spread, amplified, from city to city, that the kingdom was rife with thieves. Finally, worries of a more political order emanated from Versailles and Paris. The crisis that began on June 23 in the Assembly led people to anticipate a firm reaction by the privileged, the form of which they could already imagine. After the *journée* of July 14 and the spectacular début of emigration, people were even more prepared to believe in such a reaction. From the political center rumors spread of an aristocratic plot against the Third Estate, rumors that seemed fully justified by events. Spread in the provinces by the municipal councils of cities and towns, when these rumors reached the countryside, they were transformed on contact with the anti-seigneurial movement. The aristocrats who wished to halt recent progress and disobey the will of a king now reconciled with his people were alleged to be the very same nobles against whom the countryside had risen in rebellion over the past three months. Hence the rebellion was legitimate. But the threat was still more plausible.

This is where the Great Fear per se comes into the picture. It cannot be understood in isolation from the several movements just discussed, from which it borrowed themes, episodes, and a sensibility. But neither can it be identified with those movements; it formed an autonomous sequence of events. Starting on July 20, 1789, panic spread from a series of independent epicenters: from Franche-Comté to the northeast and simultaneously to the southeast as far as the Mediterranean; from the Mauges and Poitou; from Maine; from the Clermontois and Soissonnais northward to Paris; and finally from southern Poitou into Aquitaine and as far as the Pyrenees, which felt the effects in the first few days of August. The situation differed in each region. In the northeast the fear was associated in various ways with the rural revolt. In the west, famine and political anxiety seem to have played a more decisive role. Whatever the circumstances of these "original panics," however, they soon began to obey a law of their own. Like an epidemiologist, Lefebvre traced the circulation of the "monstrous false news" throughout the kingdom (large areas of which were spared, including most of the regions where the anti-seigneurial rebellion was most overt). His conclusion is clear: although the fear initially may have reflected the real situation, it soon developed an autonomous interpretation, which became for those affected by it a way of perceiving reality. In the days following the fall of the Bastille, reports of the vengeance of the privileged circulated throughout France. People thought they had seen—and soon were certain that they had seen—English, Piedmontese, and German mercenaries to whom these traitors had surrendered the country. Armies of brigands had been caught making ready to cut down wheat still in the field and to hold for ransom or even to massacre whole communities. As the rumors made their way from place to place, they swelled with new details that made them more credible. Suddenly every sign was spontaneously interpreted so as to fit the myth racing through the countryside.

In many cases people did more than merely repeat rumors. Communities reacted to the threat. They organized to confront, with whatever means were at hand, the imaginary enemy (a reaction that sometimes added to the confusion). With the moment of truth believed to be at hand, the sentiment of solidarity forged in the struggles and hopes of the previous months was reinforced. It pointed to one adversary: the lord, responsible for these ills as well as all the others. The fear completed the task of forging an anti-seigneurial coalition, and as rural people invented ways of responding to the danger the effects of the agrarian revolt spread to regions hitherto unscathed.

Such was the way in which the peasants joined the Revolution. They did so on a vast scale. Their participation was also unexpected. It worried the provincial bourgeoisie, which liked order and which also was often involved in seigneurial exploitation, speculation in grains, and the fiscal apparatus. Nor was the problem less urgent in Paris or in the Assembly. Could the rural insurrection be allowed to spread little by little? Should the government respond with the usual repression, which would restore the initiative to the king, or should the Assembly attempt to retain the initiative with support from the movement? The night of August 4 was among other things a response, at once shrewd and ambiguous, to this dilemma.

For a long time the Great Fear evidently embarrassed historians of the Revolution. Soon after the publication of Lefebvre's study Marc Bloch asked whether "this was because of [its] almost anodyne character or because it was agreed that the decisive events of the Revolution had for their theater the streets of the great cities?" Compared with France's majestic entry into politics, the episode seemed to partake more of an ageless past than of the new age of reason. Did not Denis Richet insist as late as 1964 on the inertia of a

"France in which popular mentalities were still rooted in the irrational?" The interpretation was not new. Nineteenth-century historians were also at a loss when it came to interpreting the rural drama of the summer of 1789. Neither Michelet, for all his sensitivity to the emotions of the crowd, nor Louis Blanc paid much attention to it. Less lyrical, more skeptical, Thiers was more inclined to accept the idea of a plot, which some contemporaries had already proposed as the key to the enigmatic event: "This stratagem, which made the Revolution of July 14 universal by provoking the nation to take arms, was attributed at the time to all the parties, and since then it has been blamed chiefly on the popular party that reaped the benefits. . . . It is curious that one should thus have shunned responsibility for a stratagem more ingenious than criminal." Jaurès, in his *Histoire socialiste,* does not question the spontaneity of the movement and stresses its importance. But he strives to reconcile its contradictory aspects and quite frankly succeeds only by prophesying the advent of a still nonexistent class consciousness. Among the leading academic historians, neither Aulard nor Mathiez dwelt on the rural revolt. Before Lefebvre only Taine paid any attention to it, in long, lyrical pages of his *Origines de la France contemporaine* (1878). But that was because he saw it as a detestable illustration of the "spontaneous anarchy" that he claimed had established itself on the ruins of the monarchical order in the early days of the Revolution. In powerful, obsessional passages he uses the episode to denounce the dissolution of the social bond, the resurgence of animal instincts, and the abdication of conscience in communities that came together and dissolved at the whim of events. In this very special sense Taine was the first historian to take the Great Fear seriously and not to see the rural tumult as a mere prelude to the great settlement of August 4. It was Taine, moreover, to whom Lefebvre was explicitly responding when he wrote his book a half century later, as well as in his pioneering 1934 essay on "revolutionary crowds." The episode was finally treated in its own right, in a way that modified to a not insignificant degree what we know about the origins and beginnings of the Revolution.

Lefebvre suggests, first of all, reevaluating the role of the peasantry, which contemporaries and historians after them often viewed as a passive mass. To reduce the fear to a panic phenomenon, probably manipulated from outside, was simply to confirm that view. Because rural residents did not take part in the preparations for the Estates General (were not the *cahiers* most hostile to feudal and seigneurial dues often of urban origin?), and because their grievances were frequently transmitted via local notables, it was long held that peasants suffered from a kind of collective inertia. The very complex and even contradictory nature of the movement of the spring and summer of 1789 corrected that view. In particular, it pointed up a need to look for the beginnings of anti-seigneurial resistance earlier in the eighteenth century, particularly in the northeastern quarter of the kingdom. Common objectives were gradually defined, and forms of struggle were worked out in common, along with ways of organizing to present demands. To be sure, the tendency was not to be found everywhere. And surely the notion of a "seigneurial reaction" has been seriously undermined in recent years. Nevertheless, in whole regions such as Burgundy, an awareness of shared interests brought together in a common front not only the poorest peasants but also the rural elites, who were ultimately forced to bear the brunt of taxation as a result of the impoverishment of the countryside. Following Saint-Jacob, Root has shown that violence and strikes were not the only means employed by a protest movement that precociously adopted the law as its battleground. Of course the burden of ancient oppression varied widely from region to region, and rural uprisings (to the extent that we know about them, for the map has yet to be completed) were not uniformly distributed in the eighteenth century. The awakening of 1789, the circulation of model grievances, the news of peasant revolts, and finally the almost epidemic spread of fear further contributed to unifying expectations and actions throughout the kingdom. In this respect it scarcely matters that this unification was the result of false rumors. Those rumors were believed only because they were plausible—that is, because they provided similar terms in which people could make sense of a common situation of which they had not always previously been aware. At the same time, they rallied, for a time at least, a very diverse rural world around the banner of the Third Estate.

The modalities of the revolt and the fear raise a second series of problems. Nothing is more difficult to understand or conceptualize than large-scale collective action in an immense country where news, which already traveled slowly, was further slowed by the day's disorder. An explanation that occurred to many people almost spontaneously was that there must be some kind of plot: an aristocratic plot hatched to bathe the nation in blood as punishment for its uprising; a plot by the Assembly to rally people in outlying areas behind a cause whose victory was not yet assured, behind which people imagined intrigues by such important personages as the duc d'Orléans, Sieyès, and Mirabeau; a plot by stockjobbers and hoarders who starved the people for their own profit; a plot by the cities against the countryside; a plot by brigands and mercenaries. It was perhaps Georges Lefebvre's primary merit to have done justice to such contemporary accusations, which historians have all too often accepted at face value. By following the progress of the fear he was able to reconstruct its substance in minute detail, allowing us to understand how and above all why information circulated, how it was appropriated by those who received it, and how it affected the areas in which it was received. Few events of the Revolution have been subjected to such scrutiny. Yet even though the idea of a plot is a red herring, the theme is worthy of attention; straddling the imaginations of both the old order and the newly emergent democratic society, it shows, as Marcel Gauchet has suggested, how difficult it was for a collectivity that aspired to assume control over its own workings to produce an intelligible interpretation of events.

The vocabulary of the episode—its gestures and cries—was long thought to link it to traditional forms of peasant protest, characterized by irrational panic, obsession with hunger, and a folklore of pillage. If that association were true, the Great Fear would belong to the prepolitical age. Today, however, this somewhat hasty conclusion is subject to revision. For one thing, Lefebvre's study clearly points up the constancy of objectives and stakes. The peasants of the summer of 1789 knew against whom they were defending themselves and against whom they were ready if necessary to fight, even if they draped their adversaries in tawdry finery and furnished them with imaginary allies. Furthermore, although the Great Fear was to a large extent part of a long tradition of peasant revolts, it was accompanied by forms and symbols whose political dimension cannot be denied simply because it was expressed in nonpolitical terms. The work of Bercé shows that this finding holds true of earlier revolts as well. It is also true of later ones, as is shown by the revolts that took place in the winter of 1789–90 in Aquitaine and that have recently been studied by Boutier; or, again, by recurrences of the fear already noted by Lefebvre himself and still later instances of peasant violence in the early nineteenth century. Accordingly, the question of tradition versus modernity seems poorly framed. From the persistence of symbolism one cannot deduce that behavior too was unchanged, much less the situation. In the summer of 1789 communities were often still unanimously opposed to the lord, as they had been so frequently in the past; this was the predominant fact. Already, however, new solidarities were here and there taking shape against new enemies: bourgeois rentiers, grain merchants, urban communities. Taine saw only the erratic character of collective violence. Today the tendency is the opposite: to insist on what was repetitious in highly ritualized types of behavior. But that behavior was not inert. It shaped common action, furnished it with occasions and immediately intelligible goals, and made it possible to represent new phenomena in comprehensible language. Nor was such experience peculiar to the peasantry; think of all that the sans-culottes borrowed from the old corporative idiom. What is interesting about the Great Fear (here using the term in the broad sense) is that it teaches us how diverse, complex, and contradictory was the political apprenticeship of the Revolution's early stages.

Jacques Revel

FURTHER READING

Conrad, Pierre. *La peur en Dauphiné (juillet–août 1789)*. Bibliothèque de l'Histoire Moderne, vol. 1, series 1, Paris, 1904.

Lefebvre, Georges. *La Grande Peur*. Paris, 1932.

——— "Foules révolutionnaires," in Centre International de Synthèse, *La foule* (Fourth International Synthesis Week). Paris, 1934. Reprinted in Lefebvre, *Etudes sur la Révolution française*. Paris, 1954; reprinted 1963.

RELATED TOPICS

Feudal System Jaurès Night of August 4 Taine

Italian Campaign

The Italian campaign, the springboard from which Bonaparte launched his career, began in April 1796 and ended in April 1797 with the signing of a preliminary peace accord by Austrian representatives at Leoben. Ever since it has been a matter of controversy among opposing schools of French and Italian historians. At issue in these controversies are four major questions: Why Italy? Why Bonaparte? What was the nature of the Italian reaction to the French Revolution in 1796? And was Bonaparte merely the executor of a policy and strategy ordered by the Directory, or was he a military genius who developed during the Italian campaign into an independent statesman?

Made necessary by the failure of negotiations with the states of the coalition (Austria, Russia, and England), the military campaigns of the spring of 1796 were planned under Carnot's guidance by the "historical and topographical unit" commanded by Clarke and Dupont. After consulting with his generals, Carnot had these plans approved by the Directory. As Carnot saw it, the main thrusts against Austria should proceed through Germany, using the army of the Sambre and Meuse (commanded by Jourdan) and that of the Rhine and Moselle (commanded by Moreau). Their mission was to cross the Rhine and head for the Danube. The so-called army of Italy, under the command of Scherer, occupied little more than Liguria. Carnot drew on proposals made over the past two years by the general of the interior, Bonaparte, and summarized by him in a note dated 29 Nivôse, Year IV (January 19, 1796): in order to eliminate the Piedmont from the coalition, the army should invade Piedmontese territory and continue into Austrian Lombardy. Unhappy with this plan, Scherer resigned. He was replaced on March 2 by Bonaparte. If Barras' memoirs can be believed, it was he who was responsible for this choice. According to La Révellière, however, Bonaparte was the unanimous choice of the Directory. It seems clear that Carnot played the key role. He had read all the plans for a northern Italian campaign submitted by Bonaparte between 1794 and 1796 and knew that this artillery officer had the training and experience necessary to make a good commander.

Nevertheless, the nomination of Bonaparte caught many by surprise. An army commander was supposed to be an old campaigner risen through the ranks or a young hero of the battles of Year II. Astonishment was often tinged with contempt. Most people had little conception of the importance of the *armes savantes,* the artillery and engineers, in modern warfare—a limitation that Carnot did not share. Others were contemptuous of soldiers who became involved in police operations, and for many of these Bonaparte was still "General Vendémiaire." And some, it must be said, were dubious of the loyalties of Corsicans. Dupont de Nemours wrote to Reubell: "Do you not know what Corsicans are? . . . For two thousand years no one has been able to rely on them. They are fickle by nature and obliged to make their fortune." This latent chauvinism, which produced still stronger prejudices against Italians (even those who had joined the Revolution), was strengthened by the recent nomination of Saliceti to the post of *commissaire* of the army of Italy. The anti-Napoleonic legend was born before the Napoleonic one. For royalists and moderates there was no problem: the "Jacobin of Vendémiaire" who presided over ceremonies marking the anniversary of the execution of Louis XVI on January 21, 1795, was not a serious adversary. Mallet du Pan was singularly unperceptive when he spoke of "this Corsican terrorist named Bonaparte, Barras' right-hand man," a general "who is not thirty years old and has no experience of war," a "tiny freak with thinning hair, the bastard son of Mandrin [a notorious thief]." The Austrian generals would pay dearly for their illusions about the *giovinastro* (adolescent) whom the Directory had sent into battle against them. For the Directory, the choice of Bonaparte was a reasonable gamble. On March 12 the young general set out for Italy.

But which Italy? The map reveals two prominent features: the country's long-standing internal divisions and the influence, direct as well as indirect, of the Hapsburgs. In the north, that is, the foothills of the Alps, the Piedmont, and the plains, there were seven "sovereign" states, two of them oligarchic republics: Genoa, which controlled a much-reduced inland territory, and the Serene Republic—Venice—which stretched from Venezia to the Ionian Islands. Emilia was divided among Parma (ruled by a Bourbon), Modena (whose duke had married his only daughter to a Hapsburg), and the northern appendage of the Papal States (known as the "Legations"). For the French Republic, however, only two states mattered: Lombardy, which had been Austrian since 1713, and Piedmont, base of the House of Savoy or "Kingdom of Sardinia," whose only capital was Turin. The Directory's "instructions to the commanding general of the army of Italy" concentrated on these two states. A wedge was to be driven between their armies by a rapid offensive. Turin was to be compelled to sign a peace treaty, and the Austrians were to be driven from Milan: "Details of execution will be left to the commanding general." Nothing was said about central Italy, where the two most important powers were Ferdinand of Hapsburg's Grand Duchy of Tuscany (the first state to withdraw from the coalition in 1795) and the Papal States. Of even less concern were Naples and Sicily, whose queen, Marie-Caroline, was also a Hapsburg. Not only was Italian territory divided into innumerable small states; its economic and social development had for centuries been remarkably uneven. The most advanced regions were northern Italy and Tuscany, whose cities and countryside had been transformed in the eighteenth century. An "enlightened despotism" had developed in these areas, and after 1789 (or 1791) a Jacobin democratic movement that supported the French Revolution. Italian historians have recently argued that this movement was less isolated than had been thought. Prior to the campaign of 1796 the mass of the population had shown no hostility to the Revolution. Nevertheless, most French observers with first-hand knowledge of Italy in this period were either contemptuous or skeptical of Italian Jacobinism. When the minister Delacroix consulted French diplomatic representatives in Italy in July of 1796, one consul, Fourcade, replied: "Italians in general value the human race only through the forms that distinguish it and the vices that dishonor it." Others more subtly held that the Italians were not ripe for freedom and that the Italian Jacobins who had been exiled to France and who returned with Bonaparte's army were mere dreamers without popular roots. For Carnot, moreover, Italy was simply a lemon to be squeezed, a minor prize in the great battle with Austria, which would be decided between the Rhine and the Danube. He failed to reckon with Bonaparte.

Before turning to the campaign proper, I want to consider briefly a controversy inaugurated in 1936 by the Italian historian Guglielmo Ferrero. In his view, Bonaparte in Italy was merely carrying out orders, acting as the disciple of his one true master. A mediocre strategist, he did nothing, Ferrero argued, but enact the ideas of Guibert, whose works overthrew the accepted military doctrine of the eighteenth century, based on limited war, and heralded the kind of total war made possible by the Revolution. Bonaparte merely expounded a plan elaborated by others (a patently false assertion), and he was able to do this only by violating the neutrality of the Italian states and taking advantage of concessions made by his adversaries. Critics have pointed up many weaknesses in this theory. To be sure, Bonaparte had read Guibert, whose *Essai de tactique général* advocated mass action and rapid movement. But he had also studied the campaigns of Frederick II and pondered the works of the English writer Lloyd, Chevalier Du Teil, and Bourcet. He was not the student of a single master. Throughout the campaign he displayed remarkable adaptability and extreme prudence. No one today doubts Bonaparte's military genius. His political independence with regard to the Directory would increase with each new victory.

The campaign was rather like a movie with a scenario composed of "sequences." The first was the introduction of the commanding general to his troops at Nice on March 29. The army of Italy consisted of some 45,000 men, most recruited in the major *levées,* or troop levies, of 1792 and 1793 in the Alps, Provence, and the Cévennes. After the Treaty of Basel these were reinforced by contingents from the Pyrenees led by Augereau. There were few cavalrymen, and the lack of heavy cavalry would prove damaging in the Po Valley. There was adequate artillery but an almost total lack of horses and wagons to transport it. Everything depended on the infantry. Ill-fed, ill-clad, and ill-shod, the troops resorted to pillage. They sowed terror wherever they went. Alfieri speaks of "all the lepers of Provence and Languedoc" descending upon his country. Apart from Sérurier, an officer brought up on the strict habits of the old army, and the German Stengel, in command of the cavalry, the generals mirrored their troops. Two were beloved by the men who served under them: Masséna, more of a brigand than his men, and Augereau, legendary for his courage and notorious for his vain braggadocio. There was no real chief-of-staff. Bonaparte brought with him from the army of the Alps an officer who in subsequent campaigns proved to be the wisest and best of aides: Berthier.

From the moment he arrived the new commander showed his subordinates who was in charge. Two days later he addressed his troops, and from words spoken that day he later composed a stirring declamation: "Soldiers, you are naked. I am about to lead you into the world's most fertile plains. Rich provinces and great cities will be in your power, and in them you will find honor, glory, and riches. Soldiers of Italy, why should you want for courage and steadfastness?" This was the beginning of a publicity campaign that Bonaparte himself composed out of speeches and letters, with considerable success.

The second sequence in our film is the Piedmont campaign. The French forces faced two enemy armies: 15,000 Piedmontese under the command of Colli, whose camp was at Ceva in the Tanaro Valley, and 25,000 Austrians under the command of Beaulieu, who had withdrawn to the north. Bonaparte decided to attack Ceva from two directions in order to crush Colli's army before Beaulieu's could come to its aid. A surprise attack by the Austrians at Voltri (in Genoan territory) forced him to modify his plans. Within two weeks his army managed to drive a wedge between the Austrians and the Piedmontese, and on April 23 Colli asked for an armistice. On April 28 the Piedmontese government, harassed by revolutionary movements stirred up by Augereau, added its signature to the Cherasco armistice, which gave Bonaparte possession of Coni, Tortore, and Alexandria. The general knew how to exploit his victories. He wrote to Barras—who he knew would make sure the news got out—that in ten days he had taken 12,000 prisoners. He personally wrote a statement to his soldiers that soon found its way into Paris newspapers: "Soldiers, in two weeks you have won six victories. . . . But soldiers, you have done nothing, because there is still work to do. . . . Everyone wants to be able to return to his village and say, 'I was in the conquering army of Italy.'" With the Piedmont neutralized and forced to pay heavy reparations (5 million livres taken out of the area surrendered to France under the treaty of Cherasco), the big prize and principal adversary still lay ahead: Austrian Lombardy.

The third sequence in the film includes the rapid drive to Milan and the first signs of discord between the commanding general and the authorities in Paris. French progress was rapid because Beaulieu avoided combat. The battle of Lodi Bridge, glorified by a famous engraving—a pure propaganda instrument, engraved at Genoa on Faipoult's orders for distribution in France—and transformed into a great victory by bulletins sent to Paris by Bonaparte and Saliceti, was nothing more than a skirmish with a rear guard left at Lodi by Beaulieu. Far from being destroyed, the Austrian army executed an orderly withdrawal. But the French were able to occupy Milan by May 14, and Bonaparte made a triumphant entry into the city. He promised liberty to the Milanese: "You will be free, and more certain of being free than the French. If Austria counterattacks, I will never abandon you." This was the first overt sign of a personal policy, which, Ferrero's opinions to the contrary notwithstanding, would eventually lead to friction between the general and the Directory. On the eve of his entry into Milan Bonaparte had received a missive from Carnot containing new directives from the government. The Austrians were not to be pursued into the Tyrol; French troops were to march toward central Italy; command of the troops remaining in Lombardy was to be turned over to Kellermann; and revolutionary action in Italy was to be avoided. Bonaparte was not troubled by the first two instructions from Paris, for an attack on Tyrol would be risky as long as the armies of Morea and Jourdan remained bogged down. As for the final instruction, concerning the attitude toward Italian revolutionaries, Bonaparte judged each situation individually. In Cherasco he had sacrificed the Piedmontese republicans to the king of Sardinia. But in Milan he was obliged for the time being to rely on the only political element favorable to the French occupation: the Jacobins. The Milanese liberals, who had inherited the mantle of enlightened despotism, chose to wait and see how things turned out before compromising themselves through affiliation with revolutionary France. Hence for several months Jacobin propaganda went unchallenged in the Lombard press. As for the third instruction, however, Bonaparte haughtily rejected Carnot's directive: "If you destroy the unity of military thinking in Italy, then I am distressed to say that you will have lost a wonderful opportunity for establishing laws" in the country. "To assign both Kellermann and myself to Italy is tantamount to losing the war on purpose." Bonaparte was not ready to give up his army. The Directory understood this and, like it or not, confirmed Bonaparte as sole commander.

The fourth sequence in our movie is the raid into Emilia and Tuscany. Repeated missives persuaded Bonaparte in June to launch the attack on central Italy that Paris desired. There were three objectives: to extract ransom from prosperous, wealthy cities; to drive English ships away from the Italian coast; and to compel local sovereigns to compromise. Before starting out Bonaparte extracted from the king of Naples' envoy an agreement of neutrality (June 6). The Neapolitan contingent withdrew from the coalition. Then Bonaparte headed south. The Papal Legations were occupied between June 18 and June 23. In Bologna the envoys of Pope Pius VI were forced to sign an armistice, which enabled Bonaparte to dispense with a Roman expedition. The Pope was given Ravenna but surrendered Bologna and Ferrara in anticipation of a French occupation of Ancona. He further pledged to pay 21 million livres and to surrender 100 works of art and 500 manuscripts. After the Pope came the grand duke of Tuscany, even though he had been the first to choose neutrality in February 1795. Along the way Bonaparte occupied Pistoia (June 26) and forced the republic of Lucca (which had never joined the coalition) to pay a ransom in cash and arms in exchange for an agreement to keep French troops out of the city. General Vaubois's division then occupied Livorno (Leghorn). That great Tuscan port, which the grand duke had opened to free trade with foreign countries, was a crucial objective in the war against England. The English, however, had time to reembark most of their merchandise, and this loss exasperated Bonaparte, who had counted on a profit of 10 million livres and had to settle for a third that amount. Received in Florence by the emperor's brother, Grand Duke Ferdinand, Bonaparte left quickly for Milan, where he arrived on July 13.

The central Italian expedition was important for three reasons. First, it was a profitable venture: the pillage of Italian money and art works had already begun in Piedmont and Lombardy, but Emilia and Tuscany considerably expanded the scope of the affair in accordance with the avowed intentions of the Directory. Its wishes were conveyed in a directive to the commanding general dated May 7: "The executive Directory is certain, Citizen General, that you look upon the fine arts as adding to the glory of the army under your command. To the arts Italy owes much of its wealth and renown, but the time has come when supremacy in art must pass to France to strengthen and embellish the reign of liberty. The National Museum must embrace celebrated developments in all the arts, and you will not neglect to enrich its holdings with the treasures it expects from the army of Italy's present conquests as well as those yet to come. This glorious campaign, which will allow the Republic to make peace with its enemies, must also repair the ravages of vandalism and join to the luster of military trophies the charm of beneficial and consoling arts. The executive Directory therefore urges you to seek out, collect, and transport to Paris objects of this type."

Bonaparte fully agreed with Carnot as to the wisdom of "squeezing the lemon." After extracting 5 million livres from the sections of the Piedmont surrendered to him at Cherasco, he wrote the Directory on April 28: "In passing I intend to ransom the duke of Parma." In Lombardy: "We shall extract 20 million from this country" (May 17). The duke of Modena was compelled to pay a ransom of 10 million livres and to surrender some twenty paintings, including Correggio's *Saint Jerome*. Profits rose sharply in the wake of the central Italian expedition. According to an estimate made in December 1796 the pillage had already yielded 46 million francs in cash and 12 million in kind. To this "legal" booty one must add the private benefits reaped by soldiers and generals, particularly Masséna, Berthier, and Bonaparte himself, who took nearly 3 million francs out of Italy, not counting the gifts he sent to his family, which had been on the verge of starvation only a short while before. Yet he was determined to control the looting and keep the booty out of the greedy hands of suppliers, speculators, and parasites of every sort who had attached themselves to the army, which it was Bonaparte's chief aim to satisfy. The key decision was taken on May 20: his soldiers' wages would be paid in hard cash, even though the soldiers of the army of the Rhine were paid only in assignats. It is not hard to understand why the commanding general of the army of Italy became popular among soldiers of all the Republic's armies. For him the pillage was a grand investment opportunity.

The drive into central Italy marked an important turn in Bonaparte's career. Yesterday an unknown, the young general who had made a pope tremble and been invited to dinner by a Hapsburg was now transformed into a politician eager to secure his independence. He was no longer disposed to remain docile and allow a government of lawyers to clip his wings. He openly complained about the civilian *commissaires* attached to his command: "They have nothing to do with my policy." In Emilia that policy at last became clear.

There he found a situation very different from the one in Milan, where he had been obliged to allow the Jacobin "patriots" a free hand. In Ferrara with its council of centurions and Bologna with its Senate, he met liberal aristocrats and enlightened bourgeois whose devotion to their municipal liberties in no way impeded their acceptance of the French presence. Bonaparte saw the possibility of a third way between Italian Jacobinism, which he already found oppressive, and the brutal policies dictated by Paris. Here was the embryo of an "aristo-democratic republic," as he wrote to Carnot on July 2. As Albert Sorel has remarked, these Italian patricians had affinities with both the Feuillants of 1789 and those who would later become the post-Brumaire republicans. In the short term Bonaparte's experience in Emilia determined his policy for the reorganization of Italy. In the long term it prefigured France under the Consulate—from one enlightened despotism to another.

The fifth sequence started badly. Battle raged around Mantua, where Beaulieu had left an army of 13,000 men. Hemmed in on two sides by marshes traversed by four roads, and with approach from the north and west cut off by the broad arms of the Mincio, the city seemed to have been granted nature's protection. Some historians have wondered why Bonaparte, rather than pursue Beaulieu into the Tyrol, stubbornly insisted on taking Mantua. In fact he had no choice, for had he proceeded northward he would have risked attack from the rear by the city's Austrian garrison. Stendhal saw the situation quite clearly: "As long as Mantua was not taken, the French could be said to have passed through Italy but not to have conquered it." Wurmser, who replaced Beaulieu in the Tyrol, commanded an army of 50,000 men, against which Bonaparte could muster no more than 39,000. At the end of July the Austrians launched a three-pronged offensive. On July 29 Bonaparte was forced to evacuate Adige. The western flank of his army, commanded by Sauret, was overwhelmed by Quasdanovich's troops. On July 31 Bonaparte wrote to Augereau: "The enemy has broken through our lines at three points. They control Corona and Rivoli. . . . Masséna and Joubert have been pushed back. Sauret has abandoned Salo. The enemy has taken Brescia." He said nothing about his own responsibility, however. For three days he had left his division commanders to their own devices while he went off to Brescia for an encounter with his ever unfaithful Josephine. In early August he decided to lift the siege of Mantua temporarily and attack the divided Austrians, massing his troops to strike separately at each of the two Austrian corps. He was gambling on speed, mobility, and concentration of his forces to overcome the enemy's superior numbers. The battles around Castiglione finally forced the Austrians to retreat into the Tyrol (August 6). Castiglione was not a great victory, but it inaugurated what would become the Napoleonic strategy. The victory bulletins and letters sent to the Directory concealed the true situation: "The Austrian army has vanished like a dream," wrote Bonaparte. Berthier added: "Italy is surely ours." In reality, Wurmser had lost hardly any men and soon obtained reinforcements, and it was no longer possible to mount a siege of

Mantua owing to a shortage of supplies. A blockade was the best the French could manage. The army of Italy was exhausted when Carnot ordered it to coordinate its efforts with those of the armies of Germany, now entering Bavaria, and to "carry the conquests of the Republic on to Innsbruck." Throughout August the army remained dormant, unable to move. Reinforcements from France enabled Bonaparte to resume the offensive on September 1. Wurmser took refuge in Mantua. When he attempted to break out, the French attacked, and the upshot of the battle of San Giorgio (September 15) was that Wurmser was driven back into Mantua. But the outcome was still in doubt. It took more than a month (from September 15 to the end of October) for Bonaparte to reorganize his army, stanch the flow of deserters, halt the looting, and reestablish discipline. During that month he also established his policy and confirmed his independence. The citizens of Reggio rebelled against the duke of Modena on August 26 and set up a provisional government that sought French protection. Bonaparte gave his support to the revolutionaries, unilaterally broke the truce signed by the duke of Modena (October 4), and authorized the meeting of a congress in Modena including delegates from Ferrara and Bologna (October 16). Thus was born the Cispadane Confederation with an Italian legion and tricolor cockade (red, white, and green, which would remain the colors of the Italian flag). Militarily, Austria took the initiative. Under the command of the Hungarian Alvinczy, an army of 50,000 men prepared to end the blockade of Mantua. For the first time in the Italian campaign the French forces were numerically inferior, and its leaders were demoralized. "The troops fight nonchalantly and almost with repugnance; even the leaders are disgusted," Garrau wrote on November 13. But neither Bonaparte nor Berthier was prevented from sending victory bulletins to Paris. On November 15 they decided to respond by attacking Alvinczy's rear through swamps flanking a small tributary of the Adige, the Alpone. The Arcole bridge was attacked, but the troops, according to the testimony of an aide-de-camp, Sulkowsky, displayed "unprecedented cowardice." To stem the panic Bonaparte was forced to dash onto the bridge with a flag. Although he took Arcole the next day, this hardwon victory changed nothing fundamental in the situation.

The next few weeks were probably the most difficult of his entire career. At stake were both Italy and his own future. He had lost 7,000 men (of whom he acknowledged only 1,000), and at Arcole the troops had shown obvious signs of fatigue and flagging will. In Paris, Carnot, in search of a way to end the fighting, decided to send General Clarke to Italy on a twofold mission: to investigate Bonaparte's army and to negotiate with Austria a treaty that would have sacrificed both Lombardy and the Cispadane Confederation. To danger and weakness Bonaparte responded on all fronts. He took the army in hand, broke all mutinies, increased rewards and promotions, and named new division commanders, most notably Joubert. Politically he continued to make his views known. The second Cispadane Congress, which met in Reggio from December 27, 1796, to January 9, 1797, transformed the Confederation into the Cispadane Republic, while in Milan people were all but openly talking about a "Transpadane Republic." Clarke, initially contemptuous of his "young comrade," was soon won over. Military operations resumed in January 1797. When Alvinczy launched an offensive, the die was cast. On February 2 Wurmser surrendered Mantua to the French. The door to Italy was open. After Rivoli (January 14), the capitulation of Mantua opened a multitude of possibilities to the victor: Bonaparte could compel Austria to sign a treaty, pursue his Italian policy, or force himself—with the help of a shrewd publicity campaign—upon a government in Paris riven by internal contradictions and fatally weakened by the impossibility of making peace without undermining its revolutionary power base. Bonaparte now emerged at the crucial moment as an almost magical medicine when no other remedy seemed available.

Good times were at hand. The capture of Mantua, news of which was magnified by publicity, created a heady atmosphere in Paris. "Bonaparte . . . knows everything," Brune wrote to Barras. Countless copies were made of Horace Vernet's painting glorifying the battle of Arcole bridge. Did the directors succumb to the enthusiasm? They were preoccupied with domestic problems. The royalist menace had once again reared its head. To oppose Carnot and Letourneur, Barras and Reubell needed a fifth man: La Révellière, inheritor of Girondin passions, enemy of Catholicism, spokesman for the "sister republics." This triumvirate of the moment—a cartel of consent—issued Clarke new orders: Do not sacrifice Lombardy or the Cispadane Confederation and attempt no negotiation without Bonaparte's consent. This was merely a recognition of the facts: nothing could be done without the support of the army of Italy's commander, the Revolution's prodigal son. But Bonaparte was little troubled by the directors' calculations and took orders from the Directory only to the extent that they coincided with his own views. This was clear in his behavior toward the Pope in February. Irritated by pro-Austrian sentiment in the papal entourage on the eve of Rivoli, the triumvirate advised Bonaparte (February 3) "to snuff out the flame of fanaticism" and "destroy the center of Roman unity." Bonaparte shared the republicans' contempt for the "priestly rabble," the "old machine," and the "imbecile doddering of aging cardinals." But he was a politician, a soldier, a diplomat, and a cynical realist. In a hurry to wear down Austrian resistance, he wanted nothing to do with a Roman expedition. After entering Ancona on February 5, he forced the papal envoys to sign the treaty of Tolentino on the nineteenth. Unconcerned by spiritual matters, he obtained Romagna and 15 million francs from Pius VI: a supplement to the bill presented at the time of the Bologna armistice. This policy was summed up in a short sentence: "For us 30 million francs are ten times more precious than Rome."

But the Austrians still had to be convinced to lay down their arms, and this took until March. Archduke Charles was short of men. Later, Bonaparte—now Napoleon—conceded his adversary's desperate situation: "Austria, after sending into battle armies without a general, in the end sent a general without armies." The battle, in northeastern Italy and the Tyrol, was brief. On March 31 the Austrians asked for an armistice. Negotiations in Leoben led to a preliminary peace accord (April 18, 1797). This agreement contained both public articles and secret ones. Publicly Austria surrendered Belgium and Milan. The secret articles specified a redrawing of the map of Italy. Milan and the duchy of Modena were to be fused into an independent republic, to which Venice would surrender Bergamo and Cremona. In exchange the republic would be obliged to give Istria, Dalmatia, and the terra firma as far as Oglio to Austria and the Ionian Islands to France. Venice was theoretically supposed to be "compensated" with the old Papal Legations. As for the left bank of the Rhine, Austria stipulated that any decision would have to be made later by the Imperial Diet, which would convene at Rastatt for discussions with the French envoys.

Ever since, Leoben has been the object of historiographical polemics and debates. Ferrero's judgment was that "Bonaparte retreated on all fronts in exchange for a colossal deception in which the court of Vienna agreed to participate." Others say that the treaty was a "miracle" for Austria, which obtained a piece of Venice's territory without giving up the Rhineland. Bear in mind, however, that Vienna was in a panic over the threat of a French invasion and that Bonaparte's ultimatum was unambiguous: either surrender the left bank of the Rhine and give up all of Italy, or keep the Rhineland and trade Lombardy for Venice. Austria chose to minimize the damage. Is Raymond Guyot correct that for France the treaty marked "the definitive abandonment of the policy of public safety for the sake of Bonaparte's ambitions"? Although the Directory declared that its primary objective was the left bank of the Rhine, it was attracted by the idea of annexing Lombardy. And Bonaparte held out the prospect of an "improvement" in the terms of the Leoben accord, possibly including an adjustment of the Rhine boundaries. In the short run, in fact, there was only one loser: the Venetian Republic. Just as France had hypocritically agreed in Basel in 1795 to allow Prussia a free hand in Poland, so now it sacrificed Venice on the altar of peace. Bonaparte himself justified the dismemberment of the Serene Republic on April 19: "The government of Venice is the most absurd and tyrannical of governments. There is no question that it was waiting until we had entered the German heartland to do us in. Our Republic has no more determined enemy." Thus the Venetian Republic was stricken from the map. Taking advantage of pseudo-revolutions that had broken out in the neighborhood of Verona, Bonaparte unilaterally declared on May 2 that a state of war existed between Venice and the French army. France's price was 3 million francs, 5 ships, 20 paintings, and 500 manuscripts. And Venice became Austrian.

In Mombello Castle near Milan Bonaparte held court, receiving admirers from Paris and envoys from the Italian cities. At this court, out-and-out parasites—the general's own family foremost among them—jostled with the most distinguished representatives of the sciences and the arts, such as Monge and Berthollet. The general himself was preoccupied chiefly with the reorganization of Italy. In a letter to the Directory dated May 19 he laid out his

plan: to sow dissension in the Cispadane Republic, split off the Papal Legations and Romagna (in order to make good on the secret articles of the Leoben accord), and join the rest (the old duchy of Modena, Massa, and Carrara)
to Lombardy, thereby creating a Cisalpine Republic. Bonaparte would have
liked to extend that republic as far as Genoa, but agents of the Directory beat
him to the punch and fomented a revolution in Genoa on May 22, which
resulted in the formation of a new "sister republic": the Ligurian Republic—
to remain separate from the Cisalpine—was proclaimed on June 29. Internal
political considerations played a part in this carving up of Italy. Democrats
were more numerous and more active in Milan than in central Italy. To swallow them up in a vast "republic," which the Papal Legations and Romagna
joined on July 27 in spite of the Leoben accord, would have strengthened
support for Bonaparte's plan by shifting the balance of power toward a semi-
aristocratic, semibourgeois stratum and away from the "priestly rabble" and
the "anarchists." Earlier, in October 1796, the general had written to the Cis-
padanes: "You are more fortunate than the French. You can achieve liberty
without revolutions or crimes." This objective, born of Bonaparte's experience
in central Italy, was made concrete by the new constitution that he forced on
the Cisalpine Republic on July 8, 1797. It was inspired by the Constitution of
Year III, but with one major difference that presaged the coup d'état of 18
Brumaire: the general himself was given the power to appoint the members
of the Directory and Legislative Council. In other words, this would be a
government of prominent citizens presided over by a sovereign commander-
in-chief. If at the same time Bonaparte permitted disturbances led by democrats in Venice, Padua, and Verona, it was only to hasten the fall of the Serene
Republic.

In order to conclude a peace treaty with Austria, Bonaparte had to
loosen the brake that was being applied in Paris. These were turbulent times
at home, and the general made contact with all parties (as he had done on
the eve of 13 Vendémiaire). For him, however, the principal threat came from
Carnot and Barthélemy, who were committed to a compromise peace settlement rather than an unconditional surrender. He therefore sent Augereau
to help the triumvirs "Fructidorize" their adversaries. After 18 Fructidor
(September 4, 1797) his hands were free. The new Directory was in his debt,
and he collected by dictating his terms for peace. The treaty was signed at
Campo-Formio on October 18. He hurried the negotiations for fear that a
new campaign in Germany might diminish the luster of his Italian victories.
In addition to Istria and Dalmatia, already acquired at Leoben, Austria received Venice and the terra firma as far as Adige. To the Cisalpine Republic
it surrendered Bergamo, Brescia, and Cremona, as well as the Papal Legations. From the spoils of Venice France took the Ionian Islands and territories
in Albania. In Germany, however, the Austrian "sacrifices" were illusory. The
surrender of the left bank of the Rhine still depended on ratification by the
Imperial Diet. Sadly the directors ratified this treaty. Did they have any other
choice? Italian patriots resented it bitterly. Foscolo, who had praised Bonaparte to the skies only a few weeks earlier, expressed his indignation over

Venice in some of his last letters to Jacopo Ortis. But the Italian patriots had little choice, either: they could vest their hopes in the Cisalpine Republic, as the majority chose to do, or suffer again under Austrian rule.

✳︎✳︎

In assessing the results of the Italian campaign, let me consider three separate subjects: Italy, French policy, and Bonaparte. For the Italians, the campaign raised great hopes but only to prepare the way for an even greater disillusionment. Paris was full of Italian émigrés, inevitably drawn to Jacobinism, the most notable of the group being Buonarroti. In perceptive notes sent to Bonaparte through the minister Delacroix, Buonarroti divined the contradictions that were already emerging: "You French must not forget that Italy was your downfall in the past and could become so again if you do not go as friends of peoples of whom you ought to be the liberators. . . . Do not allow the indiscipline of the army and above all the barbarous greed of the military governors, which is devastating the conquered territories in Italy, to turn the people's love into hatred and tighten the chains we should be trying to break." For this hatred there were obvious reasons. An excellent observer, Stendhal, wrote: "The good people of Milan did not know that the presence of an army, even a liberating one, is always a calamity." Anti-French uprisings began immediately after the capture of Milan. Disturbances broke out in Milan itself on May 21, 1796, and more serious ones occurred in the vicinity of Pavia between the twenty-third and the twenty-sixth. In Binasco and Arquata-Scrivia soldiers were killed. Bonaparte had ordered Binasco burned by Lannes's troopers and permitted his soldiers to run wild in Pavia for twenty-four hours. "I have no doubt," he wrote the Directory, "that this lesson will prove instructive to the peoples of Italy." In central Italy, in Ferrara and Bologna, there were demonstrations against the French. The city of Logo rose in rebellion, and it took a full-scale assault to put down the insurrection. In April 1797 the region around Verona rebelled, and this "Veronese Easter" served Bonaparte as a pretext for destroying the Venetian Republic: "You and your Senate are disgusting, drenched with French blood," he told the envoys of the Serene Republic. French historians, not always exempt from chauvinism, have often interpreted these uprisings as counterrevolutionary rebellions on the model of the Vendée, fomented by the "priestly rabble" and proponents of a return to the old system. Nothing could be farther from the truth. Discussing Bologna in one of his letters, Captain Sulkowsky described the anti-French elements as extremist republicans: "A large and widely spread (but fortunately unarmed) faction hopes to create disorder. They characterize themselves as revolutionaries, but their intentions are to massacre any Frenchmen who fall into their hands, refuse to pay taxes, ransom priests, and pillage nobles. Such is what they nowadays call the republican party in Romagna." After Campo-Formio and the demise of Venice, anti-French sentiments increased among patriots. In 1798 the Black League was formed in Italy, which the physician Dotta described thus: "The adepts of this sect detested the French as much as the Germans. . . . They wanted to use the former to drive out the latter, then draw upon the forces of a unified Italy to drive out the former." Uprisings at Montferrat and in the Asti region in 1799 attest to the persistence of this movement: it was possible to love the Revolution without loving France. Events in Spain in 1808 and Germany in 1811 were prefigured by these rebellions. The campaign of 1796–1797 left Italy only two blessings: the Cisalpine Republic, out of which grew an enlightened reform movement, and the red, white, and green colors first flown by the Cispadane Confederation.

What did the transalpine expedition of 1796 mean to revolutionary France and the Republic? Leave aside the immediate gains: of the 46 million francs extorted from the conquered territories, the Directory received only 10 million, which were turned over at once to the armies in Germany. The political situation changed in two respects. From the first, France's post-Thermidorian foreign policy had been erratic, owing in part to the changing military situation, and in part to a major contradiction in the nation's outlook: although everyone knew that a durable peace was necessary and could be obtained only by making concessions, a significant segment of public opinion viewed the Revolution as a crusade on behalf of liberty and clamored loudly in favor of expansionism. Pushing the borders of France back to the Rhine remained an all but untouchable dogma, even though none of the leaders except Reubell really believed that it was possible. With the treaties of Leoben and Campo-Formio Bonaparte led France in two new directions at once. The Rhine frontier, despite the promises and hopes, was in fact sacrificed in return for the Italian protectorates. And that sacrifice led to another—of Venice, a neutral state. This required quite a twisting of the ideology expressed in 1792 and 1794, which affirmed the right of all nations to self-determination. The Fructidorians were aware of this, but they averted their eyes. After all, France now "had" Italy, or at any rate its wealthiest, most prosperous parts, and the mirage of the Rhine persisted still. But France's internal politics had been permanently altered. Now the army's heavy hand was felt on the tiller at each new change in direction, from Prairial to Fructidor. From here on out, Bonaparte was a force to be reckoned with.

For him Italy provided a tremendous opportunity. The night after the battle of Lodi the fledgling eagle spread his wings: "That night I saw myself for the first time not as a mere general but as a man called upon to influence the fate of a nation. I saw myself in History." Shortly thereafter he confided to Marmont: "My Dear, they have seen nothing yet. . . . No one in our time has conceived anything great. It is up to me to set an example." In central Italy he found the key to his political future: an alliance with prominent citizens who accepted the authority of a military government camouflaged as a civilian one and wreathed in the prestige of intellectual brilliance—a Revolution without a Terror. When, on December 28, 1797, he replaced the unfortunate Carnot, forced into exile by the triumvirs of Fructidor, as a member of the Institute, Bonaparte reaped the benefits of an Italian campaign that for him at least had been most fruitful.

Denis Richet

Further reading

Candeloro, Giorgio. *Storia dell'Italia moderna*, vol. 1. Milan, 1956.

Ferrero, Guglielmo. *Aventure, Bonaparte en Italie (1795–1797)*. Paris, 1936.

Godechot, Jacques. *Les commissaires aux armées sous le Directoire: Contribution à l'étude des rapports entre les pouvoirs civils et militaires*. Paris, 1937.

——— *La grande nation: L'expansion révolutionnaire de la France dans le monde de 1789 à 1799*. Paris, 1956.

Guyot, Raymond. *Le Directoire et la paix de l'Europe, des traités de Bâle à la deuxième coalition (1795–1799)*. Paris, 1911.

Procacci, Giuliano. *Storia degli italiani*, 2 vols. Bari, 1968.

Reinhard, Marcel. *Avec Bonaparte en Italie, d'après les lettres inédites de son aide de camp, Joseph Sulkowski*. Paris, 1946.

Sorel, Albert. *L'Europe et la Révolution française*, 8 vols. Paris, 1885–1904.

Related topics

Army
Carnot
Napoleon Bonaparte

Natural Borders
Treaties of Basel and The Hague

KING'S TRIAL

D uring the riotous night of August 9–10, Louis XVI sought refuge along
with his family in the Manège, where the Assembly was meeting. The
Commune assumed responsibility for guarding the royal prisoners and had
them interned at the Temple. The Assembly was content to suspend the executive power and leave the king's fate to a Convention elected by universal
suffrage. In so doing it bequeathed a host of difficulties to the new Assembly.

The guilt of Louis XVI was not in doubt for the August 10 insurgents,
convinced that the *fédérés* had been allowed to mount the great staircase of
the Tuileries only to facilitate their slaughter by the Swiss Guards, thus deliberately transforming a scene of fraternization into one of carnage. When the
insurgents demanded vengeance for their dead and were granted, on August
17, a "Tribunal of August 10" to judge crimes committed that day, how could
anyone believe that the man who seemed most responsible for what had happened would be left unjudged and unpunished? Nevertheless, throughout
August and September, the Paris sections that applauded the suspension of
the king and later the decree abolishing royalty showed no hostility toward or
even interest in the person of Louis XVI. It was not until the end of September that the fate of the king was discussed in the Paris sections and the Jacobin
Club. Clubs and sections, preceding the Assembly, issued vigorous calls for
punishment but not for quick trial or denial of due process. In the Convention the issue of the king's trial came up in somewhat oblique fashion on
October 1: in order to obtain from the Commune's Committee on Surveillance the papers seized at the Tuileries, documents that would be needed in
any trial, the Convention promised to turn them over to a parliamentary commission of twenty-four deputies, all Girondins, who would then report on the
charges pending against the prisoner held in the Temple. Thus began an
inexorable process, which led ultimately to the trial of the king.

Though the trial was a primal and central scene of the Revolution, it
has received little attention from historians, in part because they view it as
implicit in earlier episodes: the king's suspension and internment, the election
of the Convention, the proclamation of the Republic. Deciding the king's fate
seemed a mere formality. Even counterrevolutionary historians have come to
the same conclusion: neither Maistre nor Bonald pays much attention to the
royal person. In part, too, historians have seen the trial as a strategic focus in
party conflict; Aulard treats it simply as one of many episodes in the battle
between the Girondins and the Montagnards. Either way, scholars have remained indifferent to the high symbolic stakes of the face-to-face confrontation between the king and the Revolution. Only Michelet illuminates the

scene, upon which he casts a violent light, devoting to it no fewer than a hundred pages of his history. He did so because for him the power of the monarchy was a power of incarnation, and the Revolution was the advent of royalty's antithesis, Law: "The French Revolution is the judgment of kings." Whoever adopts such a definition obviously charges the episode of the trial with its maximal significance.

"A king killed," Michelet writes, "was nothing new. Charles I had perished without shaking the religion of monarchy. Louis XVI in perishing restored strength to that religion." In three sentences Michelet goes straight to the heart of the matter. Did not killing the king risk reviving a nearly exhausted blood line and resurrecting royalty? Michelet's fear underlies his hostility to the execution. Would it not have been better to spare the king's life while bringing out the inanity of royal power in the trial? By so doing one would have separated kingship from the king and transferred it to the people, and one would have put an end to the mystery of royal incarnation. Michelet's fondness for this solution stems from the fact that it reverses the old politics of killing kings while sparing the royal institution; here was a chance to kill the monarchy while sparing the king. For Michelet, moreover, the only king worth judging was not the insipid functional king of the 1791 Constitution but the "handsome golden head" of the absolute monarch. Clearly, his account touches on all the issues not only raised by but also dealt with in the course of the king's trial, in which political stakes were never distinct from symbolic and legal ones.

The image of a king put to death and thereby giving new life to royalty was not absent from the debates of autumn 1792. Brissot's words had caused a shudder to pass through the Assembly: "The blood of Charles I gave new life to royalty." Indeed, the English precedent, so vital in the mind of Michelet, was just as vital in the minds of the actors. As dauphin, Louis XVI had spent a great deal of time with the work of Hume. The story of Charles I, as we know from Bertrand de Moleville and Mme. Campan, was for him a negative model; the English monarch had committed the high crime of making war on his own people. Throughout the debates the conventionnels made the same comparison. Some did so in order to call attention to a certain similarity, to raise fears, almost to point to another Cromwell "behind the arras": the theme was touched on by Buzot, Louvet, Rabaut, Bancal, Vergniaud, and all the Girondins. Others pointed out the differences, contrasting the English High Court, which did not represent the nation, with a fully legitimate Convention. A majority of the deputies wished to hold up, in opposition to the irregularity of the English case, the edifying spectacle of the Convention's "tranquil debates," of a "philosophical conference on what kings are or ought to be" (Léonard Bourdon).

If the aim was to engage in disinterested, elevated speculation, would it not have been better, as Michelet suggested, to have abstained from punishment? Michael Walzer, comparing the English trial to the French, pointed out that history has known many regicides, but that the murderers of kings, far from murdering mythic royalty, actually strengthened it; subjecting a king to public trial, on the other hand, disposes of the myth of royalty as well as the king. When kings cease to be simply killed and are instead publicly judged, monarchy is done for. Even when it lingers on, as in the English case, kings never again claim to embody the monarchy. Thus, one can accentuate the analogy between the two histories by invoking a distinction between the murder of kings, which leaves royalty intact, and the trial of kings, which uncrowns them. Kant said much the same thing in his own way: the murder of kings is an abomination, but it is an exception that confirms the rule. A judicial process is a worse abomination, for it involves a complete reversal of the principles that govern the relations between kings and peoples.

Who exactly was to be tried? The monarchy as a whole, including past and future kings, as Michelet would have liked? Or this particular king? And in this king, what monarch? The absolute monarch that Louis XVI remained in his own mind? Or the monarch defined by the Constitution of 1791? The divinely anointed king or the king of the French? The issue did not really come up in the trial of Charles I. For one thing, the indictment of Charles was a very sober document, focusing on the charge of civil war. For another, he had answered his accusers in full awareness of what sort of king he was. He repeatedly asked to be told what legal authority justified his being held, and he denied his judges' right to judge him, stubbornly clinging to the idea that England, far from being an elective monarchy, had for more than a thousand years been a hereditary one. He was, as Napoleon noted in his Saint Helena *Memorial,* "intimately convinced of the rights of his prerogative." By contrast, Louis XVI did not seem fully convinced. And the conventionnels were in so little agreement as to which king they were about to judge that they devoted the first phase of the trial to an interminable verification of identity.

On November 6 the Assembly heard Valazé, speaking for the Girondin Commission of Twenty-Four, set forth the charges against Louis XVI. The commission's report was so mediocre, however, that the Girondin Barbaroux himself called for a supplementary indictment. The next day it was the turn of the Convention's Committee on Legislation to submit its report and deal with the juridical aspect of the question. Speaking through its secretary, Mailhe, the Committee concluded that Louis was subject to judgment and that he could be judged by the Convention. Mailhe's aim was to establish first that the king being judged was indeed the constitutional king of 1791 and second, that the Constitution, which had made his person inviolable, nevertheless permitted him to be tried. The essence of the argument was to show that the Constitution of 1791 had established two limits to the king's inviolability. First, inviolability did not apply to acts committed outside the king's legal functions, beyond which boundary the king became a citizen subject to indictment as an individual (and Mailhe in fact argued that Louis XVI was no longer a king: "He has resumed his original title; he is a man"). Second, although Louis XVI had not committed any of the three types of acts that would have jeopardized his immunity (abandoning the kingdom, assuming command of a foreign army, refusing to take the constitutional oath), he had nevertheless broken the law from the outset, for he had never accepted the contract that made him a constitutional king. Hence as a public functionary he was guilty of perjury, well before committing the specific infractions noted in the Constitution. This argument was a device for overcoming the objection of ex post facto prosecution, which the Committee rightly expected would be raised. Mailhe subtly but not without difficulty steered a course between the desire to judge the king according to the terms of the Constitution and the need, in order to judge him, to suspend the immunity promised by the Constitution. This embarrassment, felt on both sides in the Assembly, would be exploited in two ways: by the right, which attempted to show that the letter of the Constitution absolutely prohibited dressing the trial up in legal costume; and by the left, which refused to allow itself to be confined by the constitutional text.

When debate resumed in the Convention on November 13, it was the voice of the right that was heard first, speaking through Morisson, deputy for the Vendée. He argued that the text of 1791 had erected an impregnable fortress around the king. It had done this by granting him the extraordinary favor of declaring his person inviolable, and by specifying three and only three cases in which he might be considered to have abdicated. To be sure, it was not stated that it was impossible for the nation to alter these provisions, but no law substituted for that of the Constitution could have retroactive effect. Hence Louis might well be guilty—no one in the Convention dared to argue his innocence—but he was not subject to a law that said nothing about his case. Let it not be said, moreover, that no one has the right to invoke in his own defense a law that he has violated. Not only would such an assertion spell the end of all law, but more than that, it was the general will that gave the Constitution its validity, not the individual consent of the king. Louis was therefore untouchable.

Mailhe and Morisson, despite their opposite conclusions, shared the same legalistic philosophy. That same November 13 it was left to a twenty-five year old deputy, appearing on the podium for the first time, to establish a limit beyond which the debate would not go. Thunderstruck, the Assembly listened to Saint-Just assert that Louis XVI was not a traitor and that it was a case not of judging but of punishing him. Saint-Just shifted the grounds of the debate from the immediate question of the king's guilt to the global conception of the social pact. Within that pact, bound by relations of justice, equal individuals might fail to meet their commitments and therefore be judged. But a king had never been a member of the community of citizens, hence he could not violate commitments he had never made. Consequently, he could be tried in a civil trial and must be treated for what he was, for what any king would be, regardless of his merits or actions, namely, a stranger to the social contract: as an enemy and rebel, and outside the ordinary procedure.

A pistol shot in an Assembly by this time inured to the drone of legal argumentation, Saint-Just's speech lacked the logical brilliance with which it was later credited (especially in light of the ambiguity it encouraged with respect to "judgment" versus "punishment"). But the clubs and sections were alert to the essence of the case (to the argument that the contract of 1791 was null and void and to the note of danger to the fatherland) and were inclined to repeat after Saint-Just that it was political blasphemy to question whether the king would be judged. The discovery on November 20 of documents in an iron chest that Louis XVI had had installed at the Tuileries added new charges to the indictment drawn up by the Commission of Twenty-Four and further heightened the atmosphere of drama. Robespierre, after a long silence, grasped the need to use Saint-Just's fundamentalist axiom as a basis for a more sober and political argument. (On December 3 he said that to begin the trial of the king would be to entertain the possibility of his innocence, hence tantamount to putting the insurgents of August 10 and the Convention itself on trial.) Robespierre's conclusion was the same as Saint-Just's, however: that in this case respect for judicial forms would amount to disrespect for principles, and that one cannot try an individual who, being inextricably both monarch and monarchy, was a monstrous exception to natural law.

Saint-Just and Robespierre in effect addressed not "the man Capet" (that is, the individual shorn of his royalty) but rather the extravagant status of the monarch. They alone took seriously the Ancien Régime notion of monarchy as undivided sovereignty, which necessarily occupies all public space. Hence the Revolution, being the sovereignty of the people, could not compromise with it. They alone asserted that it was incompatible to be both king and citizen. They alone understood that, in order to make the Revolution sacred, it was necessary to contrast it with the sacred character of monarchy— the better to deny monarchy such sacredness. Therein lies the meaning of the celebrated maxim: "Louis must die in order that the fatherland may live."

Between Morisson and Saint-Just the moderate majority of the Assembly was caught in an uncomfortable situation. It could not accept the radical argument of Robespierre and Saint-Just, much too strong, as Jaurès noted, to make headway "in a hesitant and confused Convention." Yet it shared their intuition of the danger that Louis represented as long as he lived, and it paid no heed to the few voices that called for sparing Louis and condemning the institution of monarchy (the very solution of which Michelet was so fond). It did not listen to Grégoire, nor did it pay attention to Paine, though he composed an edifying didactic novel in which Louis, rehabilitated and enjoying a virtuous old age in Philadelphia, in turn rehabilitated his fellow citizens. It clung instead to Mailhe's arguments and occasionally attempted to refine them, as when Condorcet, in a gesture rare in the Assembly, replied to Saint-Just. There was, he conceded, no contract between king and people. Nevertheless, every citizen who accepts public office and thereby asks for public confidence enters into a contract with the nation as a whole.

Condorcet's scrupulous and rather desperate effort to judge the case in constitutional terms while attempting to indicate where Louis XVI's constitutional protection ended is a useful stopping place, in part because this was in fact the solution chosen by the Convention on December 3: Louis, despite his inviolability, was declared subject to judgment and was therefore judged. In addition, Condorcet's argument illustrates both the egalitarianism and the formalism of the Convention's majority. Formalism, because the Convention tried, against all probability, to make the king's trial resemble an ordinary trial. Egalitarianism, because it was not at all reluctant to sever the connection between monarch and monarchy, to treat Louis as an ordinary citizen, thereby signifying that, far more than the Jacobin extremists, the Convention majority had abandoned the image of the Ancien Régime monarchy.

In so doing, the Convention also ratified Mailhe's second argument. By whom should Louis be judged? Among the various possibilities—ordinary tribunals, high court, primary assemblies, the Convention itself—opinions at first seemed divided. Would not entrusting the king's fate to the ordinary courts run the risk of encountering judges favorable to the Ancien Régime? But setting up a special court might produce a tribunal less representative of the nation than was the Convention (the memory of the English trial was significant in this respect). To submit the judgment to primary assemblies would be to pretend that the people were less interested in the outcome of the debate, less judge and party in the case, than the conventionnels themselves. Who, in any event, could claim to be disinterested in the outcome of this case? The planets perhaps, Amar sarcastically observed. Hence the Convention would sit in judgment.

Was this lengthy first act a mere formality? Hardly. For one thing, the Convention was wholeheartedly involved: hundreds of speeches were printed, and countless obscure deputies who would never be heard from again took part in the debate. Furthermore, the question was one of fundamental importance: the representation of power. Last but not least, the fate of the king was really decided here: the legal discussion of inviolability was, in the words of Joseph de Maistre, the "staircase to the scaffold."

Let us borrow from Michelet the portrait of the man who, on December 11, finally appeared at the bar of the Convention: "A man like so many others, who looked like a bourgeois, a rentier, a father, of simple appearance, somewhat nearsighted, with a complexion already pale from prison and tinged with the color of death." Many deputies, just arrived from their provinces and never having seen the king before, were apt to be touched by Louis XVI's great simplicity and calm. The king, moreover, said that he was prepared to behave "better" than Charles I. But with the first questions of the interrogation, for which Lindet's "enumeration of the crimes of Capet" had set the stage, he revealed the rather narrow defensive strategy he had chosen: for crimes prior to the Constitution of 1791, to plead that the Constitution was supposed to have effaced the past in its entirety; for the period after September 1791, to take refuge behind the responsibility of his ministers; and finally, in a move that the deputies found aggravating, to recognize none of the evidence presented—neither the documents themselves, nor the seals, nor the writing, nor his own signature.

This strategy was also adopted by the lawyers whom the Convention had assigned to represent the king. They had been allowed such a brief time to prepare the defense that Tronchet, whom the king had chosen, and Malesherbes, who had courageously offered his services, asked the Assembly to grant them the aid of a third, more experienced and younger man, De Sèze.

100

On December 26, the date of the king's second appearance, it fell to De Sèze to read the opening statement, based entirely on Morisson's argument: "Where there is no law that can be applied, there can be no judgment."

The most striking thing about this text is the degree to which the king's defenders chose to avoid mention of the sacred monarchy. "Louis," they assured the Convention, "has no more prestige." Their argument was cast in the contractual terms most likely to appeal to the majority of deputies. The constitutional pact had erased all prior crimes; as for crimes subsequent to the Constitution, those covered by ministerial responsibility had to be eliminated from the indictment. This left only a handful of personal acts, quite minor despite the discoveries made in the iron chest and not proven beyond reasonable doubt: among these was the king's payment of the Koblenz bodyguards, which De Sèze refuted only to be obliged a few days later to recognize the validity of the accusation.

Historians have taken a dim view of this line of defense. According to Rehberg, it was what killed the king. Jaurès found it "so weak, so sedative," that he provided his own, more flamboyant defense: a Louis XVI somehow miraculously rendered intelligent and firm could and should have made the deputies realize that his death, by dividing the revolutionary camp, would presage the death of the Revolution. Yet the only weakness of the defense as it stood was that it shared the intellectual assumptions of the deputies. As a result, De Sèze in effect ruled out a political defense. Yet he might have hoped to place the Convention's moderate majority, so concerned about the decency of the process, in an embarrassing situation by showing that the king had not enjoyed the same guarantees as the ordinary citizen (to hear witnesses and call handwriting experts) and by portraying the conventionnels as accusers in the guise of judges, who had already decided the fate of the man whom they pretended to be trying.

To this legalistic defense Louis wished to add only one thing: his indignation at the accusation of having deliberately spilled blood on August 10. He then reverted to his "stonewall" defense, pretending not to recognize any of his own notes. Because the Convention and the king failed to engage, this second act lacked grandeur.

The third act proved more political. Throughout the trial the Gironde had resorted to delaying tactics. At the end of December these culminated in a final attempt to have the verdict ratified by the people in primary assemblies as a way of both relieving the Convention of the burden of the trial and obtaining clemency.

The idea of an appeal to the people had arisen previously in the debate and was not strictly speaking a Girondin idea. But all the Girondin leaders defended what appeared to be a brilliant maneuver because it seemed difficult to combat in the name of "principles." The appeal to the people made ratification of the verdict as important a matter as ratification of the Constitution, removed the verdict from the influence of the Paris sections and restored it to the nation as a whole, and seemed to be a posthumous homage to Rousseau. And it was indeed over the issue of direct democracy that the two great orators in this new debate clashed. Against Barère, who defended the representative and parliamentary system, Vergniaud based the appeal to the people on a critique of representation.

On both sides the danger to the fatherland introduced a note of tragic urgency: the Girondins argued that the death of Louis XVI would lead to a break with England and Spain; the Montagnards maintained that to refer the verdict to the primary assemblies just as spring brought renewed warfare would be to furnish royalist propaganda with an unhoped-for platform. Although Barère appeared to be even-handed in his treatment, he in fact persuaded the Assembly to accept the Montagnard case by raising the decisive issue of the Convention's responsibility. Legislators, the Girondins argued, could not be judges of offenses against them. Did the people then have the right to be both judge and party? You must not, Barère concluded, "shift to the sovereign the burden that the sovereign asked you to bear." This appeal to courage was heeded.

The great weakness of the Girondin case was to envisage the appeal, theoretically open to a free decision of the people, as implying a certainty of clemency. The party of *appelants* thus became (with the help of opportune revelations concerning Girondin transactions with the king in July and August) the party of the king—a wholly unjust accusation. The Girondins were in no sense royalists. Their evolution toward clemency had to do chiefly with the terror inspired in them by the Paris sections with their crude attacks on the authors of the September massacres and their pressure on the Assembly. Vergniaud's great speech thus entertained the hope that the départements would not have to contend with this horde of agitators "that a shameful weakness has allowed to usurp power in Paris." The obsession with Paris is also evident in the many petitions submitted by the départemental administrations. That obsession was revived once more by a new rumor of prison massacres that raced through Paris in January. The tragedy of the Girondins was that this fear could henceforth be baptized "royalism" by Paris clubs and sections unremitting in their harassment of the *appelants,* who would survive only six months after this venomous charge was raised.

For these men living on borrowed time, the adoption of the roll-call vote was yet another defeat. Obtaining the roll-call was a point for the party of death. The order in which questions were to be voted on was another point. Appeal to the people, guilt, sentence was the order desired by the Girondins; guilt, sentence, appeal to the people the wish of the Montagnards. The Plain appeared to reject both sides by favoring guilt, appeal, sentence. In reality, however, the Plain's position gave a decisive advantage to the Mountain; to vote in favor of guilt—and it was clear that the Convention would vote overwhelmingly for conviction—was already to exercise sovereign judgment, and it would be contradictory afterward to subject that sovereignty to another sovereignty. Some Girondins agreed with this logic, moreover; not all the Girondin départements voted the same way, and forty-one Girondin deputies refused to vote for an appeal to the people.

In the end the Assembly rejected the appeal to the people by a vote of 424 to 287. Contrary to all expectation—for even the royalists remained confident—it then voted in favor of death by a one-vote majority. Yet some forty-six deputies combined their harsh verdict with a call for some kind of stay of execution. The most ambiguous case was that of Mailhe, who had voted both for the death penalty and for consideration of a stay while refusing to say whether the latter was a condition of the former. Hence a fourth roll-call vote was needed on the question of a reprieve. Deemed a final delaying tactic, it produced an even more comfortable majority for the Mountain: the Assembly rejected a stay of execution by 380 to 310.

This dramatic and confused debate, not without examples of individual inconsistency (one deputy in five contradicted his own judgment along the way, voting now for clemency, now for severity), weighed heavily on the Convention and the entire Revolution. It traced with inescapable clarity frontiers that had previously been nebulous. The first roll-call vote isolated a tiny group of deputies in the Convention who did not even wish the question of the king's guilt to be raised. The second was a test of shrinking Girondin influence. The third and fourth, concerning the sentence and stay, showed the extent to which the influence of the Mountain had already extended into the Plain.

The Gironde owed its defeat to its political inconsistency: while all ears still rang with the inflammatory speeches of its orators calling for war ("We will not be tranquil until all Europe is in flames"), the Gironde raised the dangers of extending the conflict; it argued at once for the principle of popular sovereignty and against the principle of revolutionary justice equal for all. It was by turns realistic and lucid about the external threat and unrealistic and blind to the danger of civil war. Moral inconsistency also played a part: the Gironde constantly complained of unacceptable pressure from the galleries yet surrendered sufficiently to cause internal dissension while provoking the galleries through ill-advised diversionary tactics. It was confronted by a Mountain that was far more consistent in its choices and votes and no doubt was already far less of a minority in the Assembly than was believed, and which was able to persuade the Plain of its duty not to shirk the responsibility incumbent on the people's representatives. Through the voice of Robespierre the Mountain was able to boast of having given a "great character to the National Convention."

The verdict, finally, was pregnant with all the Revolution's future conflicts. Not only did a European war ensue as the Girondins, perhaps as a pretext, perhaps out of genuine conviction, had predicted. (England declared war just eight days after the execution.) Not only were the themes of the conflict between Gironde and Mountain enumerated, tested, and sharpened for battle. But above all it was proven once again that anyone who attempted to put an end to the Revolution signed his own death warrant. The Gironde, Jaurès tells us, had noted a similarity between the king's fate and its own.

As dauphin, Louis XVI had been an assiduous reader of *Telemachus* and had himself printed its maxims. He knew by heart the scene in which a Cypriot soldier holds by the hair and exhibits to the victorious army the bloody head of the king. His exemplary death after a pitiful defense at his trial therefore does not need to be explained as the result of a "purification" of his personality by a miserable ordeal. More simply, his royal and Christian education, which had taught him nothing about courtroom procedure, had taught him how to die—which he did as Most Christian King, thereby transforming, as Ballanche so perspicaciously observed, regicide into deicide.

After his flat denials during the trial, Louis XVI's testament is striking for its tone of truly royal dignity. There was "more church than monarchy" in him, according to Jaurès, and in fact the only true remorse that the king expressed was to have given his consent to the Civil Constitution of the Clergy. Nevertheless, one can read the document as containing, still intact, the traditional theory of monarchy. "To reign in accordance with the laws" but to be bound by the laws "only in its operations" is indeed the theory of royalty according to Telemachus, who has "all power over peoples" but over whom "the laws have all power." In expressing the hope that his son, should he have "the misfortune to reign," will have the "authority necessary" to the sovereign, Louis XVI showed that, in contrast to the strategy that he had adopted in his trial, he had never recognized the law of the Revolution.

Was this ancient royalty regenerated by the blood spilt on the Place de la Révolution? Michelet suggested as much. Quinet feared it: "Louis XVI wandering the world would have been a hundred times less fearsome than Louis XVI tortured in the Temple through his wife and children, his hands tied behind his back, guillotined opposite his palace." Louis Blanc affirmed it: "All royalism flourished on that cadaver, like mistletoe on a dead tree."

Yet the death of the king did not give rise to the miracles, convulsions, and prodigies that had marked the days following the execution of Charles I. Sébastien Mercier reports that after Louis's head had fallen he saw people walking about and "talking familiarly as if returning from a celebration." When the news reached Grenoble, the young Stendhal was "gripped by one of the joyful emotions of my life." Occasionally a text, especially from the provinces, mentions a feeling of horror, or again, an obscure sense of relief that the regicide did not, as an indication of sin, lead to any cataclysmic upheaval. But all of this reaction was fleeting. What is more, the revolutionaries even thought of celebrating the king's death and from 2 Pluviôse, Year II, until Brumaire they clung to the idea of a regular commemoration. Even if the occasion reveals signs of resistance to celebration (there being few effigies of Louis XVI in the procession, his death was barely represented, and the evocation of the guillotine—"the sword of the nation"—was left to a metaphorical speech), an oath of hatred to kings was publicly sworn every year by government officials. The revolutionaries stood firm on this holiday despite the adversities of the season and swore that it would be "eternal, like the Republic." Membership in the syndicate of regicides was explicitly claimed and celebrated, even more than the tacit rule of political designations under the Directory. It remained (think of the exiles of the Restoration, for example) a matter of somber pride, which Hugo captured by depicting Monseigneur Myriel on his knees before the dying regicide.

After the Restoration, a royalist cult seemed to flourish around images of the king on the scaffold as the "divine representative of human nature with a crown of thorns and a scepter of reed." But royalist tradition offered little sustenance to this new cult. Ballanche, who described the scaffold as a cross and Louis XVI as a Christ, was unable to see the official ceremonies of expiation (tirelessly and didactically staged to make the people feel the miracle of the Bourbons' return) as an authentic cult. It was imposed from above, aroused no sympathy, and was limited to a few places (the Vendée) and milieus. It also lasted for a very short time: the flourishing of monarchic idolatry, the religion of souvenirs, the devotion to the "child of the miracle," and the sentiment of pity that encouraged the growth of what Michelet called the "tearful party" did not outlive the Restoration.

The royal cult had no sacred significance—no one still saw the king as the captain of God, for whom the Angels did battle—and was without popular support. Cournot reports in his memoirs that by 1814 no one knew what had become of Louis XVI's brothers and nephews, nor had anyone at the trial called for their death or for the death of the dauphin, for these potential kings were not seen as posing a great threat. "The destinies of the old monarchy were foreclosed," and even after the monarchy had been restored it continued to think of itself in light of the scaffold. Jaurès captured the new reality when he wrote that "the people acquired terrible habits of familiarity with the monarchy, which nothing could efface." The death of the king therefore signified the death of a system of representation of power.

In other words, the apparent suddenness of the end of the monarchy is misleading; sacred royalty was dead in France long before the king's trial. When exactly did the disenchantment of the realm begin? This is an embarrassing question for a historian, although the reign of Louis XIV does suggest certain hypotheses. By accentuating the ideology of transmission by blood to the detriment of the public law of monarchy and by linking divine right not so much to a principle as to a concrete person, Louis XIV and Bossuet weakened the king in ways concealed by the dazzle of the Sun King. By pursuing a policy of emancipation with respect to the priesthood, royalty, in Quinet's well-turned phrase, "spent its genius in separating itself from the sanctuary" and thus exposed "its isolation and nudity." By throwing off all legal and religious bonds, the king became lawless and faithless. Add to these weaknesses the ferocious leveling accomplished by Jansenism, which showed that all creatures were equal in abjection and in the face of a death equally merited by all, resulting in what Louis Blanc called "the prodigious abasement of majesties of convention," and it becomes clear why pathos deserted the scene of the king's trial and death.

Mona Ozouf

FURTHER READING

Bongie, Laurence L. *David Hume, Prophet of the Counter-Revolution.* Oxford, 1965.

Jaurès, Jean. *Histoire socialiste de la Révolution française,* vol. 4, *La Convention.* Paris, 1969.

Kant, Emmanuel. *Elements métaphysiques de la doctrine du Droit.* Paris, 1853.

Michelet, Jules. *Histoire de la Révolution française,* vol. 2, book 9. Paris, 1952.

Patrick, Allison. *The Men of the First French Republic: Political Alignments in the National Convention of 1792.* Baltimore, 1972.

Seligman, Edmond. *La justice en France pendant la Révolution, 1791–1793,* vol. 2. Paris, 1913.

Walzer, Michael. *Regicide and Revolution.* Cambridge, 1974.

RELATED TOPICS

Blanc
Clubs and Popular Societies
Condorcet
Constitution
Girondins

Jaurès
Kant
Louis XVI
Maistre
Michelet

Montagnards
Napoleon Bonaparte
Paris Commune
Quinet
Robespierre

Cholat, *The Taking of the Bastille, July 14, 1789.* Eighteenth century. Musée Carnavalet, Paris.

Houel,
*A Cell in the
Bastille,
July 14, 1789.*
Musée Carnavalet, Paris.

Oath of the King, Queen, and Nation at the Festival of the Federation, July 14, 1790.
Anonymous, eighteenth century.
Musée Carnavalet, Paris.

Cornu, *Festival of the Federation.* 1790. Musée des Beaux-Arts, Besançon.

Arrest of the King and His Family at Varennes, June 21–22, 1791. Musée Carnavalet, Paris.

Taking of the Tuileries, or, Foundation of the Republic, August 10, 1792. Musée Carnavalet, Paris.

Painful Leavetaking of Louis XVI from the Queen and His Family. Musée Carnavalet, Paris.

Execution of King Louis XVI, January 21, 1793. Denmark, late eighteenth century. Musée Carnavalet, Paris.

Deray,
Execution of the Demoiselles de la Métaierie
(Charette's Cousins) at Nantes. 1793.
Musée des Beaux-Arts, Nantes.

Vendean insignia.
Musée Dabrée, Nantes.

After the capture of Chemill
d'Elbée saves the Blues from massacr
(The *Pater d'Elbé*
Musée de Chol

Béricourt,
*Unloading Victims after
a Revolutionary
Journée.*
Musée Carnavalet, Paris.

Tellier,
*Boissy d'Anglas
Saluting the Head
of Féraud,
May 20, 1795.*
Château de Versailles.

En mo violant trois fois ils m'ont causé la mort !!!

*The Rapes of the
Constitution:
Fructidor, Floréal,
and Prairial.*
Etching.
sée Carnavalet, Paris.

Entry of the French Army into Rome, February 15, 1798. Château de Versailles.

General Bonaparte's Generosity during the Campaign in Italy: Honor to Defeated Courage.
Musée Carnavalet, Paris.

NIGHT OF AUGUST 4

The night of Tuesday, August 4, 1789, is the most famous date in French parliamentary history: it marks the moment when a juridical and social order, forged over centuries, composed of a hierarchy of separate orders, corps, and communities, and defined by privileges, somehow *evaporated*, leaving in its place a social world conceived in a new way as a collection of free and equal individuals subject to the universal authority of the law. The debate of August 4, 1789, held at night, was in fact associated with a very powerful feeling in all the deputies that they were witnessing a twilight and a dawn. But even this classical simile cannot do full justice to the emotions of the participants in this celebrated session, who for a few hours felt as though they were virtually divine mechanics helping to bring about this incredible spectacle. This twilight and this dawn were their work.

As for the collective enthusiasm invested in the destruction of the "feudal regime," the usual twentieth-century interpretation emphasizes its rather forced character: the session of August 4 was in fact an improvised parliamentary response to an emergency situation, made possible by a change in the agenda.

In the latter half of July, rural discontent, latent since springtime, began to take on the aspect of an uprising. In a kingdom where insurrection traveled slowly and badly, news of the fall of the Bastille nearly everywhere triggered what historians have called the "Great Fear," a huge flare-up of false rumors generally involving a reported conspiracy among enemies of the new age inaugurated by elections to the Estates General and National Assembly. Peasants banded together and armed themselves as best they could. In some parts of the territory—the Norman *bocage*, Hainault, Alsace, Burgundy, Franche-Comté—they hastened to the nearest château to burn records of their servitude: namely, the land registers in which the lords recorded their various "dues"—*droits, cens, champart, lods et ventes*, and so on, all duly certified by specialists in feudal law.

The insurrection was limited to seigneurial property, the châteaux being the Bastilles of feudalism, but at the same time it posed a threat to property in general, not only because many commoners in late eighteenth-century France owned seigneurial estates and properties, but also because "feudal" dues constituted a particular type of property, rooted in a very ancient past but still incontestably property. Criticism of the "gothic" irrationality of such feudal dues was a theme common to Enlightenment philosophy and statecraft, but the only solution was to substitute for these archaic obligations the universality of free contract between individuals. By burning the land registers the peasants purely and simply liquidated feudal dues by violence.

Whence the embarrassment of the Assembly, which in the latter half of July received alarming news of disturbances that had erupted throughout the country despite the efforts of the recently organized bourgeois militias. The deputies were then debating the Rights of Man and its relation to the future Constitution when news of the growing disorder forced it to alter its calendar. On the night of August 3 the spokesman for the *comité des rapports* made no attempt to embellish the situation: "Letters from all provinces make it appear that properties of all kinds have fallen prey to the most criminal looting. Everywhere châteaux are burned, convents destroyed, farms abandoned to pillage." The committee drafted a bill reaffirming the value of all forms of property and dues. A little later that evening, Malouet, one of the monarchien deputies, expounded a vast program of poor relief through aid offices (*bureaux de secours*). But in the eyes of "patriotic" deputies the first proposal had the disadvantage of committing the Assembly to a course of repression and thus restoring force to what remained royal troops while at the same time putting the king in the position of arbiter. The second proposal was a long-term project unlikely to have any effect on a situation that called for an urgent political response.

The idea of August 4—to distinguish between feudal property and property as such and to convert whatever was legitimate in the former into good bourgeois currency—was born as a solution to this impasse. It probably originated at a meeting of the Breton Club on the night of August 3–4, the club being a small group of deputies of the Third Estate who since May had formed the habit of meeting with the Breton delegation before Assembly debates to work out a concerted strategy. The key testimony here is that of Parisot, a deputy for Bar-sur-Aube, who in a letter written on the fifth recounted what had happened on the night of the third: "We, that is to say, about a hundred of us, met in private committee for practically the entire night. There it was resolved to use a kind of magic, a temporary suspension of the Constitution, in order to destroy all privileges of classes, provinces, cities, and corporations. It was with this intention that we entered the hall yesterday at five o'clock. Our committee alone was in on the secret."

As so often happens in the parliamentary history of the Revolution, we know little else about the discussions that preceded the session of August 4. Nor do we possess verbatim or incontestable minutes of that session: the report of the meeting, drafted by one of the Assembly's secretaries, was drawn up and submitted the following day and debated until the twelfth, as the situation evolved. Yet it remains, along with newspapers of the day, our primary source concerning the event. The session began at eight in the evening with a discussion of the bill, drafted the night before, on the need to respect property and persons. But two unexpected interventions immediately transformed the debate, one by the vicomte de Noailles, the other by the duc d'Aiguillon, both members of the liberal nobility: a younger son with no fortune and a very wealthy landowner. The rebellious peasants were criminals, they argued, but criminals whose crimes were excused by the oppression they had endured from lords and their stewards. In opening the debate, Noailles shifted the focus from the security of property and persons to the wrath of the peasantry and indicated a possible way out of the dilemma confronting the Assembly: redemption of feudal dues and abolition without indemnity of seigneurial corvées and what remained of personal servitude. The duc d'Aiguillon, who also denounced the "vexations" to which peasants had been subjected "for so many centuries," was nevertheless careful to submit an elaborate motion proposing redemption *"au denier trente"* (meaning that feudal dues would be redeemed for a sum equivalent to thirty times their annual yield, thus establishing a ratio of income to capital of 3.33 percent).

These two speeches indicated the political solution to the crisis. They also set the tone of the debate: a general denunciation of "feudalism" as the greatest curse in the national past, a source of dissension in the nation rather than unity. But this collective exaltation of the new nation against the "gothic" edifice of particular privileges was accompanied by a constant concern to translate the abolished "dues" (or at least most of them) into good bourgeois currency. Historians, particularly twentieth-century historians, are sometimes astonished by the coexistence of these two themes; obsessed by the socialist idea, they see nothing in August 4 but bourgeois inequality supplanting aristocratic inequality. In reality, money was in this period the great equalizer of conditions, the instrument for the destruction of privileges and of the old society of orders. It was the universal character of the new property, henceforth open to all, that excited people; this was the world that the enthusiasm of the deputies celebrated on the night of August 4.

In order to understand the "patriotic" emotion that constantly enveloped the debate, we have only to imagine how the actors saw themselves. A vast literature, at once philosophical and juridical, had long since instructed them in the misdeeds of *la féodalité*, the feudal system, by which they meant not only what remained of the rights of fiefs but the whole corporate structure of society as reshaped by the monarchy. The idea of unifying property and making it the rational basis of the state had been the cornerstone of physiocratic thought; ultimately it suggested how absolutism might be reformed. The last person to develop systematically this whole body of ideas, and to accommodate them to the circumstances of 1789, was Sieyès, in his *Essai sur les privilèges* and *Qu'est-ce que le Tiers-Etat?* "We must go back to principles," he had proclaimed in the second of these brochures, in which he also argued the need to oppose the pseudo-authority of centuries with the rights of reason.

The night of August 4 celebrates the advent of reason in the exaltation of hearts: an extraordinarily modern event in that it revealed a deep emotional investment in the belief that an Assembly could, through its political will, change the course of the nation's history. The unfolding of the session from eight in the evening until two in the morning dramatized the culture of the century; the deputies—clergy, nobility, and Third Estate meeting together—moved from feudal dues to the privileges of corps, cities, and provinces, from the land to society, and from the social to the national. One after another they mounted the podium to sacrifice to the "nation" the special rights of the communities and corps that had elected them. What is more, their procession, as many of them noted with a twinge of anxiety, marked the end of the old idea that deputies are bound to their electors by a strict mandate. When, at two in the morning, Lally-Tollendal managed to associate the name of Louis XVI with the spirit of the session, the whole structure of the old society came tumbling down: not only feudal dues but the whole social order defined in terms of collectivities granted certain privileges by the king—cities as well as provinces, ecclesiastical benefices as well as exclusive hunting rights, tithes, and the sale of offices. The admission of everyone to all employments consecrated the equality of individuals before the law, a condition of their union with the nation. All these historic decisions were taken on the night of August 4 before the deputies finally went to bed. Some made their approval contingent on the consent of their constituents, which they confidently anticipated receiving. The more difficult problem was the one that arose the next day, August 5: how to cast the decrees in proper legal form.

The ensuing debate, held between August 5 and August 11, was largely faithful to the spirit of August 4. Two points should be noted in particular. The first concerns trade guilds; the text approved on August 4 provided only for a "reform of the *jurandes*." The traditional organization of labor would remain untouched by the legislation of these few days; the guilds were not abolished until 1791. The second point has to do with the tithe, which under the Ancien Régime was the clergy's fundamental resource, based on a payment in kind of a fraction of the harvest (ranging from 1/15 to 1/20). Declared vulnerable to confiscation in return for compensation on the night of August 4, the tithe was ultimately abolished without indemnity. The question became the focus of a major debate, participants in which included Mirabeau and Sieyès, the two most important figures not present during the session of August 4. The argument of the deputies hostile to the indemnity was put forward as early as August 6; the central idea was that ecclesiastical property belonged to the nation. Mirabeau made himself champion of this view on August 10. The tithe, he argued, was not property but only a contribution to the Church in exchange for its assumption of part of the burden of public service; but this contribution had proved too costly, and Mirabeau proposed something less onerous, though he offered no further details. In opposition, Sieyès on the same day delivered a great speech, less as a defender of the clergy, as some historians still argue, than as a theorist of the equality of individuals before the law. The origin of the tithe, he argued sagely, was neither more nor less obscure than that of many other forms of property. Its abolition was tantamount to an arbitrary gift to landowners, since this sum was traditionally subtracted from the price they paid for their land.

The final text, of which the principal author was Duport, was passed during the session of Tuesday, August 11, in the evening. The first sentence crashes down like a falling curtain: "The National Assembly entirely destroys the feudal regime." It is followed by other provisions already approved on the fourth: abolition without indemnity of dues involving personal servitude, all other dues being redeemable against compensation. But in the articles that followed (nineteen in all), what was abolished was not always associated with *féodalité* in the strict sense of the word. The right to keep a dovecote, hunting rights, seigneurial courts, *cens* and *champarts* were indeed feudal rights (articles 2, 3, 4, and 6). But article 6 abolished without indemnity tithes of all kinds, with application of the provision "pending notice of other means of subsidizing the expenses of divine worship," meaning, in other words, that the tithe would continue to be collected until the Assembly had decided on some other means of supporting the Church. So the first part of the provision was unrealistic, and the second would involve the deputies, from the fall of 1789 until July 1790, in the spoliation and complete reorganization of the former first order of the realm; the "placing at the disposal of the nation" of the property of the clergy was already legible between the lines of the simple abolition of the tithe.

The sale of offices was no more part of the "feudal" regime than the tithe. It was a later institution, not definitively established until the beginning of the seventeenth century, which the monarchy used to fill its coffers by selling hereditary offices in its judicial, financial, and municipal administrations. Article 7 of the decree of August 11 abolished the sale of offices and at the same time affirmed the principle of a feeless administration of justice. The Revolution thus resolved in the name of new principles a problem before which the monarchy had recoiled—in the final years of the reign of Louis XV, in 1771, Chancellor Maupeou had attempted to break opposition in the parlements by abolishing the sale of judicial offices as well as fees (known as *épices*) paid to judges for hearing cases, but when Louis XVI acceded to the throne in 1774, he capitulated to the protests of the corps. The deputies of 1789 portrayed the end of the parlements as a consequence of the new principles, which did away with the entire corporate structure of the kingdom, thereby cutting the Gordian knot of the Ancien Régime, which both dispensed privileges and found itself threatened by them. But here, too, the Revolution kept faith with the idea of property. By declaring all offices redeemable, the Assembly opened the door to a long controversy over evaluation and reimbursement.

Along with the corps, all private rights attached to them were also abolished. The liberties of the king's subjects were replaced by the liberty of each citizen, a liberty which was therefore intimately associated with equality. Article 9 prohibited "forever" all "pecuniary privileges," personal or real, "in the matter of allowances," in favor of a uniform assessment of taxes. The next article abolished any type of exemption or privilege granted to any territorial entity: province, region, city, or community. Henceforth one common law would apply universally to all French citizens, and there would no longer be any intermediary structures or corps to serve as screens between the individual and the public sphere of the law. Accordingly, article 11 provided that "all citizens, without distinction as to birth, may be admitted to all ecclesiastical, civilian, and military employments and dignities, and no useful profession shall constitute derogation."

This general liquidation, which established a new social contract, even included a promise, in article 15, to keep an eye on the activities of the king: the Assembly would insist on an accounting of "pensions, favors, and bonuses" awarded by Louis XVI in order to do away with arbitrary favors granted under the Ancien Régime. When the list of those favors was published the following year, it revived the detested ghost of the Court. In return, Louis XVI was in the end proclaimed, as Lally-Tollendal had urgently demanded, "Restorer of French liberty." It is not clear that this "monarchien" formula, at odds with the rationalist spirit of the *tabula rasa,* accurately reflected the sentiment of the Assembly. The near future would tell the tale. Yet the proposal did indicate a temporarily successful attempt to separate the royal person and institution from the end of the "feudal regime."

In fact, neither Louis XVI nor his entourage approved of the decisions taken by the Assembly between August 4 and August 11. Officially granted, as of September, a suspensive veto over laws of the Assembly, the king for many long weeks refused to give his sanction to the destruction of the old society. On September 18, just after receiving the suspensive veto under the terms of the draft Constitution, the king transmitted to the Assembly a lengthy series of remarks prepared by Necker. He gave his accord to the principle of redeeming seigneurial rights but disputed the list of rights declared to be abolished without indemnity. He objected to the special treatment of the tithe and favored preserving the *cens* and the *lods et ventes,* which he deemed useful for maintaining small holdings. In effect, these rights dissuaded wealthy landowners from extending their holdings indefinitely by allowing them to retain certain honorific prerogatives—an interesting argument, entirely in keeping with Necker's social concerns, but utterly alien to the spirit of the times, which favored a clean slate and rational reconstruction. The king gave in only when forced to do so in October, when he was led back to Paris from Versailles by an insurgent crowd. During August and September the question of the king's approval of August 4 was one of the major themes of agitation in Paris and throughout the country.

The most important thing about the decisions taken in this fateful week of August 1789 was that they survived. The French Revolution created many temporary institutions and often legislated for the short term. But the decrees of August 4 to August 11 number among the founding texts of modern France. They destroyed aristocratic society from top to bottom, along with its structure of dependencies and privileges. For this structure they substituted the modern, autonomous individual, free to do whatever was not prohibited by law. August 4 wiped the slate clean by eliminating whatever remained of intrasocial powers between the individual and the social body as a whole. The program was completed in 1791 with passage of the Le Chapelier Law prohibiting associations. The Revolution thus distinguished itself quite early by its radical individualism.

It was also a proprietary individualism. The juridical revolution accomplished by the August decrees was not a spoliation except as regards the Church. Compensation was offered for most abolished seigneurial rights and dues, and offices were to be redeemed at market value. Socialist historiography has tended to underestimate the importance of August 4 on the grounds that it simply converted an older form of property into contractual bourgeois property. Yet while offices were indeed reimbursed after protracted proceedings, seigneurial dues declared redeemable were never actually redeemed, owing to the passive or violent resistance of the peasantry; they were abolished without indemnity in August 1792 and July 1793. And abolition of the tithe was the prelude to confiscation of Church properties. The texts of August 4–11 were of immense significance, moreover, because they struck down the whole legal and administrative structure of society, leaving only free and equal individuals with whom it then became necessary to reconstruct a new body politic. The difficulties that the Revolution encountered in equipping the old kingdom with a new Constitution were not unrelated to this creation, without concessions and in the space of a few days, of a wholly modern, individualistic society. What had to be worked out now, for this society of free and equal individuals, was not only the meaning of liberty but also the sense in which those individuals were unified in the new nation.

The night of August 4, prelude to the great decree of August 11, was thus one of the key dates of 1789. Of the general spirit of that famous year, or rather of those famous few months between May and October during which the history of France changed course, the event shared and exhibited characteristic traits: repudiation of the past, the ambition to reconstruct society on rational principles, philosophical radicalism combined with political management of revolutionary circumstances. What was durable and even irreversible about August 4 was that by inaugurating the *civil* legislation of the Revolution, it established the universality of law in the sphere of society. Quinet strongly emphasized this legislation when he contrasted the solidity of this act of foundation with the fragility of the political Constitutions (*La Révolution*, IV, p. 6). For him, the laws so solemnly passed between August 4 and August 11 were so much a part of the Age of Enlightenment that they were almost a natural culmination. Enjoying a profound and well-prepared consensus around liberty, equality before the law, and property, subsequent civil legislation of the revolutionary assemblies and the Consulate would remain within the legal framework defined during these "historic" days; the abolition of nobility, equality in inheritance, and limitations on the right to make a will were logical consequences of the spirit of August 4. The differences between the Convention's debates and those of the Consulate concerning the future Civil Code, finally completed in 1804, were more than minor, but the principles common to both periods were established in August 1789. On that date, in a sense, the Revolution was complete. But it had yet to be inscribed in the sovereignty of the people; in that sense it had only just begun.

François Furet

EVENTS

FURTHER READING

Aulard, Alphonse. "La nuit du 4 août," *La Révolution française,* 1913.

Hirsch, Jean-Pierre. *La nuit du 4 août.* Paris, 1978.

Jaurès, Jean. *Histoire socialiste de la Révolution française,* vol. 1. Revised and annotated by Albert Soboul, preface by Ernest Labrousse, foreword by Madeleine Rebérioux. Paris, 1969.

Sieyès, Emmanuel. *Essai sur les privilèges* (1788) and *Qu'est-ce que le Tiers Etat?* (1789), reprinted Paris, 1982.

——— *Vues sur les moyens d'exécution dont les représentants de la France pourront disposer en 1789* [1788?].

Tocqueville, Alexis de. *L'Ancien Régime et la Révolution,* 2 vols. (Paris, 1856). Reprinted as vol. 2 of *Oeuvres complètes.* Paris, 1952.

RELATED TOPICS

Aristocracy	Equality	Louis XVI	Physiocrats
Civil Code	Feudal System	Mirabeau	Quinet
Civil Constitution of the Clergy	Great Fear	Necker	Sieyès

THE REVOLUTION
AND EUROPE

The French Revolution was far from being the only challenge to the political order of Ancien Régime Europe. Before 1789, there had been revolutions in Switzerland, Holland, and Ireland—to say nothing of the American War of Independence against the British monarchy. In the 1790s there would be further outbreaks of revolution in a whole cluster of European countries—in Holland and the Rhineland and in Italy and Switzerland, as well as in Malta and along the eastern Mediterranean. These cannot be dismissed as wholly isolated phenomena, uninfluenced by what was happening elsewhere. The French Revolution, in particular, inspired deep loyalties and excited emulation. But we must beware of the simplistic attractions of any catch-all explanation such as the idea of a single, democratic, Atlantic Revolution, which enjoyed an extraordinary vogue during the 1950s and 1960s. For in reality there was no single ideology, and many of the resolutions adopted by the Atlanticists had very little to do with democracy. T. C. W. Blanning, discussing the effects of the French Revolution in Germany, rightly warns against any all-embracing ideological interpretation of events in these years. "What is portrayed by the Atlantic school as a great democratic revolution," he argues, "was in reality nothing more than the military expansion of the French Republic." And he dismisses any notion of a Europe-wide revolutionary movement in the 1790s. "Against the scale, duration, intensity, and above all success of the French Revolution, the disturbances elsewhere in Europe shrivel into insignificance."

If European liberal opinion was excited by the ideals of the French Revolution, the revolutionaries themselves did much to arouse and sustain that excitement. They claimed, quite explicitly, to be following in the philosophical traditions of the Enlightenment. They spoke a language that in many respects was the shared language of secular and progressive thinkers everywhere. Coming so soon after the American colonists had thrown off the yoke of British domination, moreover, 1789 seemed to offer hope for the oppressed of the old continent, too. Constitutionalist notions of a kind that had exercised the people of Geneva in 1768 and the leaders of the new United States were being discussed in one of the most powerful monarchies in Europe. The Declaration of the Rights of Man was a clarion call of enlightened thinking. And the French went far beyond the relatively cautious claims of the Americans to advocate ideas of democracy and popular sovereignty and to urge revolutionary changes in society as well as in politics. At one moment or another they denounced the iniquity of feudalism and the tyranny of kings; offered help to others who might wish to achieve their own liberation; and publicly embraced the principle of national self-determination. "The National Convention," in the words of La Révellière-Lépeaux's decree of November 19, 1792, "declares in the name of the French nation that it will grant fraternity and aid to any people that may wish to recover its liberty." Those living under benighted or oppressive regimes were invited to take the law into their own hands: insurrection was no longer a crime, but a right to be exercised by the peoples of the world. They were, in the Convention's words, to "free themselves . . . to give themselves as legitimate sovereigns a free government . . . to regenerate themselves through a universal change in accordance with the principles of liberty and equality." It was a heady doctrine, which the Revolutionary leaders rightly saw would give them a tremendous propaganda advantage among the subjects of kings and emperors. To a Europe still accustomed to autocratic kingship and clerical authority, such ideas could easily be seen as offering a panacea for a multiplicity of political ills.

But who exactly read the speeches of the Revolutionaries or responded to the ideals that they preached? Who, indeed, would be in a position to read them or be influenced by them? European society was predominantly a society of peasants in which literacy levels were miserably low; in much of central and eastern Europe there were few cities of any size, trade was slow to develop, and the emergence of an educated middle class was necessarily retarded. Reading circles and *salles de lecture* had no chance to establish themselves in the way they had in France or Belgium or Holland. Besides, in the majority of European states rulers had no interest in allowing their people to be subverted by news from elsewhere. Political information was severely censored. Even the most liberal among them, the so-called "enlightened despots," did not take Enlightenment so far as to pose a challenge to their own security, while the outbreak of revolution in France quickly revealed Catherine the Great of Russia for the arch-reactionary she was. It was, quite predictably, in western Europe that the ideals of the Revolution achieved their widest audience and evoked the most significant intellectual response—in England, where intellectual opinion flattered itself with the thought that the French were following their own example of the Glorious Revolution of 1688; in Switzerland, where republican government had already been achieved and where the idea of revolution was hardly novel; and in the commercial cities of Belgium and Holland, where economic prosperity and freethinking were well-established and where interest in French politics had been fostered by a vigorous political press, by papers like the *Gazette de Leyde*, during the last years of the Ancien Régime.

The most immediate response to the ideas of the Revolution came from writers and intellectuals who saw the events of 1789 as a milestone in the history of mankind, as the natural consummation of the intellectual ferment of the eighteenth century. It was an obvious conclusion to draw at a time when the National Assembly was liberating the people from age-old abuses and when the spirit of the Revolution seemed to be encapsulated in the Declaration of the Rights of Man. In this early period, before its image became soiled by the bloodletting of the Terror or by the intolerance of de-Christianization, France seemed to offer hope to all enlightened humanity. It was still easy to portray the Revolution as a guarantor of individual rights and freedoms, and William Wordsworth was not alone in his belief that "Bliss was it in that morn to be alive, and to be young were very heaven." In England admiration for the events of 1789 extended to scientists like Joseph Priestley and political leaders like Charles James Fox; Tom Paine was not only inspired to write his Rights of Man, but came to France as an honorary French citizen and took his seat in the Assembly. The same intellectual enthusiasm was evident in many of France's continental neighbors. In Holland Patriots like Valckenaer were thrilled by the liberationist language of the National Assembly and read into its declarations of fraternity a universal promise that would bring freedom for the Dutch as well. Similarly in Italy, where eighteenth-century physiocracy had become closely tied to nationalist hopes and aspirations, intellectuals turned avidly to the message emanating from Paris. And in Germany, especially in the south German states, the Revolution met with an enthusiastic response from writers, journalists, and members of masonic lodges.

Yet the historian must view such expressions of solidarity and hope with a certain caution. The writings of a few radical or liberal thinkers are a poor guide to popular feelings and reactions. The Patriots in Holland were little more than a tiny and privileged elite, tightly centered on Amsterdam, whose houses had been angrily sacked by a mob in 1787. In England, too, popular opinion failed to rally in force to the ideas of the National Assembly; popular patriotism was always a potent force and anti-French feelings could be rapidly aroused in defense of the existing order. Priestley, for instance, suffered the humiliation of being stoned and abused by a monarchist crowd in Birmingham in 1791; while, for all his passion for popular causes, Paine never enjoyed more than a fraction of the popularity of his conservative rival, Edmund Burke. In assessing the impact of radical writing and intellectual support for the Revolution, indeed, it must not be forgotten that the 1790s also produced philosophical works that were utterly hostile to the premises on which the Revolution was based, arguing the case for absolute monarchy and for the natural division of society into estates and orders. Such works were often highly influential, and not just among the political establishment. Besides, much of the opposing radical opinion was expressed in such abstract language and on such an ethereal plane that it could aspire to little genuine influence over the population at large. Nowhere was this more true, as Jacques Droz has pointed out, than in Germany, where radicalism was expressed in terms of cosmopolitan humanism, which related only very indirectly to political debate or national institutions. In Germany, according to Droz, the divorce between the intellectual and the political was virtually total. In consequence, philosophers like Immanuel Kant judged the Revolution by its moral effect on the human soul; and German intellectuals concluded that in a humanist culture like their own the errors that the French had made could have been more easily avoided. "Drained of its historical substance, the

Revolution was seen by the German intelligentsia as a metaphysical fact, of which they calculated the ethical value."

The part played by political philosophers in preaching the ideals of the Revolution would not become fully apparent until well into the following century, when Fichte and Herder helped link the Revolutionary tradition to a new and highly romantic German nationalism and Buonarroti preached the value of spontaneous revolution to a new generation of Italian radicals. Their role would be crucial in creating a revolutionary myth that continued to inspire loyalties in the Europe of 1830, 1848, and beyond, by giving some substance to the idea of "la grande Nation" to which the revolutionaries themselves were so attached. But in the context of the 1790s their contribution remained limited. The same is largely true of the small groups of political radicals, generally calling themselves "patriots" in the early stages and "Jacobins" after 1793 and 1794, who founded clubs and popular societies in the larger towns in imitation of the revolutionaries in France. Like the political philosophers whom they read and admired, such men were drawn largely from among the liberal professions of urban Europe. Although they have been accorded considerable prominence in their respective national historiographies, often for launching or fostering infant nationalist movements, they were few in number and often uncertain in their aims. As for the societies over which they presided, they generally emerged from existing reading circles or masonic lodges, renamed to conform to the mores of the times. Despite their own enthusiasm for the French revolutionary cause, their influence over their fellow citizens remained consistently small. In none of the Italian states did they establish a large or lasting support. In the Swiss Confederation their bridgehead was largely restricted to the Pays de Vaud, where French influence had always been strong. And despite the high reputation that the so-called German Jacobins still enjoy, the number who were prepared to welcome the French as liberators in 1792 was very small indeed. Those who were, like Georg Forster, were left terribly isolated.

At a popular level, too, the French Revolution could command a limited but fervent support. In England, for example, popular radical politics was given a new lease on life by events in France, as the movement for parliamentary reform assumed a new and more egalitarian character. From being a movement of country freeholders in the 1780s, the reform movement became the domain of urban radicals, men who took from the French Revolution its concern for natural rights and turned their venom on surviving feudal privileges in their own society. Groups like the London Corresponding Society ensured that the latest news from Paris reached a wide audience throughout England, and in major industrial cities like Manchester and Sheffield artisans and workers campaigned actively against the oppressive stance of Pitt's government. Given that from 1793 Britain and France were at war, it was difficult to cite the French example without incurring charges of sedition, and English radicals of the period often defended parliamentary reform by reference to Anglo-Saxon liberties rather than to the achievement of the Convention. But the influence of the Revolution was not in doubt. English, Scottish, and Irish radicals used the same revolutionary language and borrowed the same sans-culotte symbolism. Trees of liberty were planted in the unfamiliar soil of British cities, and strikes were called in support of the French; in 1797 even the sailors of the Royal Navy at Spithead mutinied in a rare display of solidarity. Perhaps the most frightening development from the point of view of the British government was the summoning of a British Convention, a gathering of radical spokesmen from England and Scotland, to meet in Edinburgh in November 1793. It was a gesture of defiance to Pitt's government, which used spies and secret agents to report on the activities of the radicals and, through the agency of Lord Braxfield and the Scottish courts, imposed draconian sentences on their leaders. In the short term Pitt emerged the winner. The radicals were broken as a political force, the London Corresponding Society effectively gagged, its links with the northern and midland cities destroyed. But the legacy of the radicals to the nineteenth century would be powerful and emotive.

Britain provides a good instance of popular enthusiasm for the ideas of the Revolution—and especially for the Paris popular movement—precisely because that response was genuinely spontaneous. Unlike most of France's continental neighbors, Britain was not invaded by the revolutionary armies and was not subject to the sorts of pressures that military defeat and occupation implied. Elsewhere in Europe, it was always more likely that the effects of the Revolution would be imposed by force than that they would be sought by the free choice and expression of the people. However sincerely the French government might have committed itself to the principle of national self-determination in 1792, there could be little doubting the real impact of invasion by the revolutionary armies. Lofty ideals were soon superseded by practical necessity, the universalism of the Revolution by the everyday needs of war. In 1790 the National Assembly had received a colorful international deputation, led by Anarcharsis Cloots, asking France to bring freedom to the peoples of Europe. Yet the first annexations, of Avignon and the Comtat, were halting, rather timid ventures in which French interests were carefully weighed and assessed. And by 1793, when the French found themselves at war with most of monarchical Europe, it was the interest of France and of the French military machine that was paramount. Already, generals like Custine and Jacobin politicians like Danton were expressing the view that national interest required strong, natural frontiers and buffers against France's counterrevolutionary neighbors.

Pays ennemis and *pays conquis* could not expect to receive unrealistically generous terms, and if the method of their attachment to the French Republic might vary widely, French control was always assured. Thus Belgium in 1795 and Piedmont in 1802 were simply annexed and divided into French-style départements, arbitrarily and without consultation, whereas the Rhineland was added only after the solemn protocol of a treaty had been entered into by both sides. Similarly, if the Batavian Republic could be presented as the initiative of Dutch patriots when the French crossed the frontier into their country, the Cisalpine Republic was the arbitrary creation of Bonaparte. In some cases the birth of a sister republic could be presented as the stated wish of the most advanced patriots in the territory concerned: the Helvetic Republic, for example, could plausibly be presented as a Swiss objective, espoused by Frédéric-César de la Harpe and Pierre Ochs. But such arguments were always rather specious. Seldom did the policy conflict with immediate French military strategy, and often it was undertaken solely for short-term strategic ends. In Italy it was in the French interest that the individual republics were kept weak so that they could be efficiently exploited. In Switzerland, despite repeated declarations of friendship by Paris, the Confederation was invaded and annexed when military priorities made such action necessary. Indeed, in virtually every case the political solution that was reached was a solution imposed by Paris; the right of self-determination had very quickly given way to the needs of national security, and after Thermidor France was once again committed to her age-old ambition for natural frontiers. Hence those countries that were overrun were not given any choice about the form of government they should have. Liberty was not negotiable.

French intervention extended far beyond the simple act of drawing new political boundaries. Political institutions and ideological priorities, often carbon copies of those pertaining in France itself, were established in each of the sister republics, and these priorities were eagerly espoused by local patriots. Thus French administration and French justice were implanted in many parts of western Europe, with departments and districts, cantons and communes; while attempts to influence the local fiscal system were more sporadic and far less successful. A political press was nurtured to reflect the prevailing orthodoxies in Paris. And in many parts of occupied Europe, clubs and popular societies were encouraged to spread revolutionary ideas amongst the native population—though, as Jacques Godechot has remarked, they often took on the configuration of their local community, or else became outposts of neo-Jacobinism through their large and highly politicized membership of French army officers. As in France, too, reforms were passed that attacked the bases of seigneurialism and tried to undermine the spiritual hold of the Catholic Church. In these respects the revolutionaries did believe that they were working for the betterment of the peoples over whom they held sway, and in many of the sister republics their principal political goal was to draw up a constitution that would guarantee stability and certain basic freedoms. In the majority of cases the outcome was a republican constitution, based on a limited property franchise and guaranteeing strong executive authority—a constitution, that is to say, that bore more than a little resemblance to the French Constitution of Year III.

Although such reforms might seem to show that the French were bringing to the peoples they conquered some of the benefits of their own Revolution, few Belgians or Italians would have seen it that way. All these reforms, however worthy they might be in principle, risked being damned in local eyes, since they had been imposed by conquest, not by consent. Besides, such political and social benefits paled into insignificance when compared to the economic cost of the French presence. The extension of the war in 1793 made it unavoidable that the French armies would seek to live off the land, and the Committee of Public Safety soon made it plain that the main purpose of annexation was not the liberation of peoples suffering under tyranny but the acquisition of food and supplies for the military. The invasion of northern Italy, for example, was undertaken to provide a new granary for the French armies and new funding to help pay for the costs of war. The interests of the Italians were never more than secondary. If seigneurial and clerical lands were converted into national properties on the French model, it was for the French treasury, not for the benefit of the Italian population, that they were seized. The famous revolutionary slogan, *"Guerre aux châteaux, paix aux chaumières"* ("War on castles, peace to cottages"), was largely forgotten as all sections of the population were made to play their part in the French military effort. On September 18, 1793, the Committee ordered that the commanders of French armies in occupied territory "procure, as far as possible from enemy territory, the supplies necessary to provision the army, as well as arms, clothing, equipment, and transport." In May of the following year four *agences de commerce* were established to organize the evacuation of essential materials; they were to be stationed in Spain and in the Alps, in Belgium and on the Rhine. Their role was crisply defined—to take everything out of the locality that had a strategic importance, to "transport to France such supplies, commercial items, and artistic and scientific objects as may be of use to the Republic." It was a wide-ranging brief. In addition, *commissaires militaires* were instructed to tax and requisition on the spot, and to reserve exemplary punishment for those who resisted. The fact that they paid for all requisitions in devalued assignats did little to increase their popularity.

The economic cost to France's neighbors of invasion and conquest was often cripplingly high. There was little consideration for the feelings of the local people, or for the practical limits to what they could afford. Thus in Belgium the *commissaire-ordonnateur,* Sabin Bourcier, would demand in Year III that "half the supplies of grains, wheat, rye, oats, hay, and straw in Belgium and the conquered territories" be seized for the use of the French troops. And Hoche, on the Moselle, told his divisional commanders that there was only one thing that he expected them to bear in mind—the fact that they were in a rich country, a country that could afford to pay its share of the French military bill. They should therefore have no qualms about the policy they were executing, especially since they must know that if the French were to suffer a reverse, local people would rush to take up arms against them. The conquered territories were deemed to owe it to France to participate fully in the costs and obligations of the war. They were to provide their share of troops for the French levies; to provide carts, horses, and oxen for the task of supplying the armies on their soil; and to pay huge sums in *contributions de guerre,* additional taxes arbitrarily imposed to purchase military supplies. In the Helvetic Republic, the cantons of Berne, Zurich, Soleure, and Fribourg were collectively assessed in 1798 to pay a sum of sixteen million livres, with the express order that the first fifth must be handed over within a period of five days. If these obligations were not met, the French would resort to the armory of punitive measures at their disposal—among them the taking of hostages and the billeting of soldiers.

Requisitions and contributions represented the semilegal face of the military occupation. But the presence of the French armies left other scars, too, which helped to confirm the reactions of those they conquered to the Revolution in whose name they served. Like all armies of the period, the French could be brutal and callous in their treatment of the local people through whose towns and villages they passed. Booty was a traditional and much prized privilege of the victor, and in the conquered territories civilians often seemed to present fair and highly attractive targets. But if that assumption was true of all eighteenth-century armies, the sheer size of the French forces, combined with their greater youth and inexperience, made them especially feared among the civilian communities through which they passed. Even their generals, though conscious of the grave threat that looting posed to military discipline, recognized that there were occasions when they had no choice but to turn a blind eye. For given the unreliability of food convoys, the soldiers often had little choice but to steal and pillage if they were to survive. Pillage blended unhappily into unofficial requisitioning, with the troops helping themselves to horses and cattle, money, bedding, articles of clothing, and kitchen utensils. Fields were regularly stripped of their crops, and livestock rounded up to feed starving battalions. Looting of this kind was generally accompanied by violence and drunkenness, as the troops, momentarily freed from the discipline of the barracks, found themselves unleashed on the civilian population; there were constant complaints in occupied territories of debauched and undisciplined soldiers streaming into private houses, stealing what caught their fancy, indulging in acts of wanton vandalism, and beating or raping all who stood in their path. Few were ever brought to justice, despite occasional bursts of repression by either deputies on mission—like Saint-Just with the armies in the East and the North—or generals intent on reimposing a minimal level of discipline in the ranks. The problem was never properly resolved, and booty continued to be taken by the French armies throughout the decade, to the hurt and anger of countless Belgians, Italians, and Rhinelanders. As Blanning rather poignantly notes, in the context of the Rhineland, "To cap it all, the various booty was to be removed to French depots in requisitioned carts pulled by requisitioned horses steered by requisitioned carters."

It is, of course, tempting to adopt the missionary language of the revolutionaries themselves and to see the French Revolution in ideological terms, bringing liberty, equality, and fraternity to the European continent. Perhaps in the long term there may be some truth in that view. At the time, however, many Europeans, the peasants in their cottages as well as the nobles in their châteaux, saw the Revolution through the actions of the politicians, administrators, and soldiers whom it sent among them. They awaited with trepidation the arrival of the next demand for requisitions, the next order billeting yet more hungry and undisciplined troops within their communities. They believed the worst of the rumors that presaged the arrival of the French, the image of the revolutionaries as bandits and atheists, defiling churches and profaning shrines. They viewed the Revolution not with gratitude, but as a conquered people views its conquerors; and in the manner of that conquest they saw little evidence of liberty and none of fraternity. Indeed, the most lasting memory of these years for many of the people of Europe was one of fear and insecurity, an indelible image of military occupation and grinding poverty. In these circumstances it is hardly surprising that they should have resisted their conquerors, or that a nationalist spirit should have been founded upon a mood of reaction against the French. Nor is it surprising that, when the opportunity presented itself, so many of them responded by rejecting the unrepresentative Patriot cliques whom the Revolution had forced upon them.

Alan Forrest

FURTHER READING

Blanning, T. C. W. *The French Revolution in Germany: Occupation and Resistance in the Rhineland, 1792–1802.* Oxford, 1983.

Devleeshouwer, Robert. *L'arrondissement du Brabant sous l'occupation française, 1794–1795, aspects administratifs et économiques.* Brussels, 1964.

Droz, Jacques. *L'Allemagne et la Révolution française.* Paris, 1949.

Elliott, Marianne. *Partners in Revolution: United Irishmen and France.* New Haven, 1982.

Godechot, Jacques. *La grande nation: L'expansion révolutionnaire de la France dans le monde de 1789 à 1799.* Paris, 1956.

Goodwin, Albert. *The Friends of Liberty: The English Democratic Movement in the Age of the French Revolution.* Cambridge, Mass., 1979.

Occupants-occupés, 1792–1815: Colloque de Bruxelles, 29 et 30 Janvier 1968. Brussels, 1969.

Rufer, Alfred. *La Suisse et la Révolution française,* ed. Jean-René Suratteau. Paris, 1974.

Schama, Simon. *Patriots and Liberators: Revolution in the Netherlands, 1780–1813.* New York, 1977.

Tassier, Suzanne. *Histoire de la Belgique sous l'occupation française en 1792 et 1793.* Brussels, 1934.

Woolf, Stuart. *A History of Italy, 1700–1860: The Social Constraints of Political Change.* London, 1979.

RELATED TOPICS

American Revolution   Burke   Italian Campaign   Natural Borders
Army   Fichte   Kant

REVOLUTIONARY
JOURNÉES

The old France had known *journées* (in the sense of historically momentous days) of its own, especially days of barricades. On May 12, 1588, such days were an innovation; August 26–28, 1648, repeated the experiment; and by the eighteenth century a vigorous tradition had been established. In 1731 the marquis d'Argenson wrote: "The king does not think enough about the security of Paris, which is often of great consequence for his authority. Barricades have been seen, an invention that became popular in the time of the duc de Guise, that has seen use since, and that Parisians have not forgotten. They will use it at the first opportunity. . . . Anything can cause sedition among cityfolk: a slightly high price for food, a fiscal edict, a favorite of the people mistreated." It was *night,* however—the time between vespers and matins—that was most propitious for all kinds of collective disturbances: think of Saint Bartholomew's Day. Racine's tragedies with their bloody, torchlit nocturnal scenes reflect this fascination with the night, which obsessed generation after generation.

The Revolution innovated in two ways. It mobilized the masses, which were formed into columns. And it shunned barricades, except for a brief moment on July 13, 1789, and again in Germinal, Year III, in the faubourg Saint-Antoine. Was there anything surprising in this tactic? The people were in control of the streets, and their capture of the streets was the sign of their capture of sovereignty. What good were barricades (a defensive strategy), when the initiative and the offensive thrust came from below? For four years Paris was an open city. The word *journée* did not appear in Richelet, Furetière, or in the first five editions of the *Dictionnaire de l'Académie Française.* More precisely, it did appear, but only as a synonym for battle, as in *la journée de Rocroi*—but not the *journées* of May 1588 or August 1648. One may ask whether the revolutionary *journées* were not also the occasion of a certain theatricalization of political life, of a transition from the stage to the public arena. To associate *Père Duchesne* with the Revolution was one thing, but to bring the masses into the streets as actors was to expand the theater of the boulevards to a larger stage, the capital as a whole.

If we are to follow the succession of great *journées* from 1789 to 1793, a three-stage typology suggests itself. From July 14, 1789 to August 10, 1792, mobilization was directed against the king. On May 31 and June 2 and during the "September days" of 1793 the targets were the representatives of the nation, a momentous change in light of the objectives of the Constituent Assembly of 1789. Then came a period of ebb, noticeable after 9 Thermidor, Year II, unmistakable after the days of Germinal and Prairial in Year III. Power was no longer in the streets, and Pretorian guards supplanted the sections.

*
**

In the overheated atmosphere of Paris in July 1789, the idea of an "aristocratic plot" menacing the Revolution's first steps existed in a latent state. Not that Parisians were ready to rush to the aid of the National Assembly. It was themselves they were thinking of, themselves and the danger to the capital posed by royal troops. On Sunday, July 12, around noon, Paris learned that the previous night the king had dismissed and banished from France the minister Necker, whose popularity—to some extent usurped—was associated with that of the duc d'Orléans. The latter had opened to the public his gardens at the Palais Royal. The weather that Sunday was fair, and the crowds in the Palais Royal gathered around orators who, only the day before, were still unknown, men such as Camille Desmoulins. Later they formed processions and carried busts of Necker and the duke in triumph. On the Place Louis XV they were met by cavalry of the Royal German regiment, which brought the French guards out of their barracks to join the demonstrators. That night, the baron de Besenval, who commanded the royal troops in Paris, ordered his soldiers to fall back on the Champ de Mars. But the Parisians, in the grip of panic (owing to rumors that the city would be bombarded and then pillaged), did not back down. After smashing customs offices (*octrois*) and giving chase to employees of the Ferme Générale, they began searching for weapons. Throughout the day of the thirteenth they massed around the Hôtel-de-Ville to demand arms. Meanwhile there was a spontaneous municipal revolution; electors from the Paris districts—chosen to prepare for the meeting of the Estates General—appointed a permanent committee and organized a bourgeois militia to protect the security of the public. The situation was akin to that of the Day of Barricades two centuries earlier: Paris wished to protect itself against the royal troops and at the same time to prevent the dubious population of the sewers from rising up to threaten the landlords' order. This event was a revolution, the birth of the National Guard. On the morning of the fourteenth, rifles were seized at the Invalides. The crowd then marched on the Bastille, no doubt in search of more arms. And no doubt there was also a more profound reason for the choice, since the depressing fortress that dominated the entrance to the faubourg Saint-Antoine was the symbol of a regime they no longer wanted. The governor, Launay, had only a skeletal garrison at his disposal: twenty-four disabled veterans and thirty Swiss. Attempting to negotiate, he pledged not to open fire if the crowd did not attack. At about one o'clock, however, the crowd having entered the courtyard of the fortress, he panicked and gave the order to fire. A hundred or so casualties were left on the field of battle. At around five o'clock, a huge crowd returned with four cannon seized at the Invalides and accompanied by French Guards.

Launay tried to surrender, but the crowd rejected his offer and invaded the prison. Three officers and three soldiers were killed. Launay, taken to the Hôtel-de-Ville, was murdered on the Place de Grève. That same night, Flesselles, the provost of merchants, was also killed. The severed heads of the two men were paraded on pikes to the Palais Royal. Today we know the social composition of the crowd that participated in the attacks. It was a microcosm of Paris society, including masters, journeymen, and merchants, but with a marked preponderance of artisans from the faubourg Saint-Antoine. Besenval withdrew with his troops to Saint-Cloud.

Was Paris a free city? No miracle put an end to the fear, and disturbances continued for more than a week. The intendant of Paris, Bertier de Sauvigny and his father-in-law Foullon de Doué, were seized and hanged. But Louis XVI, despite the reactions of the comte d'Artois and the prince de Condé (who emigrated), had already capitulated. On the fifteenth he had announced the troop recall to the Assembly. On the sixteenth he recalled Necker. On the seventeenth he went to Paris and accepted, at the Hôtel-de-Ville, the blue and red cockade—the colors of the city. With Lafayette named commander of the National Guard and Bailly mayor of Paris, a new group came to power in the capital. The revolution of the lawyers had unwittingly been saved by the taking of the Bastille. But the king and the Assembly remained in Versailles.

The days of October 5 and 6, 1789, put an end to this anachronistic duality. Three factors were responsible. Economic difficulties had been accumulating since July. Although the summer harvest was good, supplies were still not adequate to compensate for the previous year's shortfall, and the price of bread—a scarcity price—was cruelly felt and heightened housewives' discontent. The beginnings of emigration affected the labor market; the market for luxury items on which many Parisian artisans depended was hard hit. But the crucial factor was political. Louis XVI had not approved either the decrees of August 4 or the Declaration of the Rights of Man and of the Citizen. The Assembly had refused to grant the king the absolute veto power that the moderate minority—the monarchiens—wished to give him, but it had granted him a so-called suspensive veto on the understanding that this power would not be used to block the decrees of August 4 or the Declaration. But the king did not give in. The idea of an "aristocratic plot," spread far and wide by the "patriotic" press (Marat had founded the *Ami du peuple* in September), found support in the slightest incident. A march on Versailles had been proposed as early as the end of August by speakers at the Palais Royal. The new order in Paris was fragile, despite Lafayette's determination (and the thirty thousand national guardsmen recruited since July). A rumor was all it took to ignite the powder keg. On October 1, during a dinner that the officers of the king's bodyguard gave at Versailles for those of the regiment of Flanders recently arrived in the city, the tricolor cockade was trampled underfoot and the colors of the queen were hoisted, as the royal family looked on from its loge. The news reached Paris on the third, and the districts called for withdrawal of the Flanders regiment and royal approval of the Assembly's decrees.

We do not know what preparations were made for the insurrection, though surely there were preparations. Women from the faubourg Saint-Antoine and Les Halles formed the first procession to set out for Versailles. In Paris the tocsin was sounded, and Lafayette, who arrived late in the morning, tried in vain to calm national guardsmen eager to follow the women. He was obliged to accede to the wishes of his troops, and at around four o'clock a second procession (of fifteen thousand guardsmen along with bourgeois and artisans) set out for Versailles. Meanwhile, the first group had reached the château (at around four-thirty), and a delegation of women was received by Louis XVI, who had returned hastily from a hunt. He promised them provisions for Paris and sent them away with reassuring words. Some started back to Paris, but most hung about outside the palace. Eleven deputies of the Assembly, led by Mounier, remained inside awaiting the king's approval of the decrees. In order to head off a new crisis Louis XVI finally gave in. But the arrival of the second procession, headed by Lafayette flanked by two *commissaires* designated by the Paris Commune, dramatically altered the situation: the *commissaires* demanded that the royal family return to Paris. Louis XVI postponed his decision until the following day, and all the responsible leaders—Lafayette, Mounier, the king—went to sleep, while the crowd remained awake. At six in the morning it invaded the courtyard of the château. Hastily awakened, Lafayette appeared with the king, the queen, and the little dauphin on the balcony of the marble court. "To Paris, to Paris," shouted the crowd. Louis XVI capitulated: "My friends, I will go to Paris with my wife and children. To the love of my good and loyal subjects I entrust what I hold most precious."

The Assembly decided to follow the king to Paris. At one in the afternoon, a diverse procession of thirty thousand men and women set out for the capital: national guardsmen in the lead, followed by wagonloads of wheat and cannons escorted by women armed with pikes, the carriage of the royal family accompanied by Lafayette, the carriages of the deputies, and finally the crowd itself. "We are bringing back the baker, the baker's wife, and the baker's boy": this cry of the people is etched in the collective memory of France, as if the symbolism of bread summed up the meaning of the October days. But the real significance of those days lay elsewhere: the sun had ceased to set at Versailles in the splendid isolation willed by Louis XIV. The October rain brought the king back to the Tuileries, from which he would emerge only to enter prison and mount the scaffold.

*
**

But he did attempt to escape. As early as April 1791, when he sought, as he did every year, to leave the Tuileries on his way to Saint-Cloud, the crowd obliged him to turn back. The revolutionaries' suspicions, heightened by the emigration of Mesdames, the king's aunts, were stirred up by the popular clubs (the most important of which was the Society of the Rights of Man and of the Citizen, founded at the Convent of the Cordeliers) and the fraternal societies that sprang up nearly everywhere and that formed a federation with a central committee in May 1791. The democratic press, especially Marat's paper, warned constantly of the danger of the king's flight. And we know, of course, that the king did flee to Varennes on June 20. The people reacted angrily, smashing busts of the king and destroying *fleurs de lys*. But they reacted even more with fear: fear of an aristocratic plot led by émigrés and foreign powers, which it was alleged had only been waiting for the signal of Varennes to declare itself openly. When the king returned on June 25, he was met by an immense and silent crowd. Pétion, one of the *commissaires* sent by the Assembly to meet him, described this extraordinary scene: "The participation of the people was immense. It seemed that all Paris and its environs had come together. The roofs of the houses were covered with men, women, and children, the fences bristled with them, the trees were filled. Everyone wore hats, and the most majestic silence reigned." By fleeing, one king had renounced his sovereignty, while another king, the people, grimly looked on.

In the face of the vacuum created by Varennes, the majority of the Assembly and the Paris authorities agreed to accept the fiction that the king had been "abducted." Only a minority opted for either the republic, a regency with the duc d'Orléans as regent, or—Marat's idea—a Roman-style dictatorship. Robespierre wanted to avoid raising the question of the regime. The investigating committee appointed by the Assembly submitted its report on July 15: the king was innocent, and only those who organized and carried out the abduction were guilty. The Cordelier Club and the fraternal societies did not see things that way, however. They demanded a consultation with the people and punishment of Louis XVI, and called for a demonstration on the Champ de Mars on the seventeenth, where a petition was to be placed on the altar of the fatherland. The Jacobins, Robespierre in the lead, refused on grounds of respect for the law to take part in the demonstration, against which Lafayette unleashed the National Guard. This was not a true *journée:* it lacked unanimity. Nor was it a "massacre": fifteen victims fell after a shot was fired, no one knows from where. But for the first time the bourgeois militia had fired on the people. And for the first time the red flag—the flag of martial law—made its entry into History.

Varennes had two contradictory consequences. In the short term it reinforced the moderate and royalist element, and when Louis XVI was reestablished after taking an oath to the Constitution on September 14 and the Legislative Assembly met on October 1, it was possible to believe that the Revolution had been stopped. Nothing could have been farther from the truth. The war and the economic crisis (caused by the assignat and the sharp rise in the cost of food from the colonies) again, in the spring of 1792, mobilized those whom people had begun to call sans-culottes around a set of economic, political, and ideological issues: price controls, anti-hoarding policies, and monitoring of a bourgeois Assembly suspected of connivance with both domestic and foreign enemies. The first defeats, coupled with the king's veto of two decrees (one concerning refractory priests, the other establishing a camp of twenty thousand *fédérés* just outside Paris), led to a resumption of agitation. On May 20 the faubourg Saint-Marceau organized to the sound of "*Ça ira.*" But on June 20 a great *journée* was organized to celebrate the anniversary of the Tennis Court Oath. Neither the Girondins—excluded from the royal government but in favor of a peaceful banquet—nor Robespierre, whose tactic was always to defend the Constitution, were responsible for this movement, which was led by hitherto obscure agitators such as Santerre, a brewer from the faubourg Saint-Antoine. The mayor of Paris, Pétion, was inspired by the precedent of the October days: imitate Lafayette and use the National Guard to channel the energy of the masses in the hope of intimidating the court without really threatening it. This hope was disappointed. June 20 was a failure. Starting from the faubourgs at dawn, the sans-culottes—armed this time—went to the Salle du Manège where the Assembly was in session and forced admission of their delegates, as a host of pikes and red caps milled about in the neighboring streets. Then the crowd broke down a gate that separated the Manège from the garden of the Tuileries, occupied the Place du Carrousel, and entered the château. Cornered for more than two hours in the embrasure of a window, Louis XVI listened unflinchingly as petitioners shouted, "Down with the veto!" He accepted a red cap, raised his glass to the health of the fatherland, but for the first time refused to give in to popular pressure. That evening the Tuileries were evacuated. For another week there were further disturbances in the faubourg Saint-Antoine, but the springs of the insurrection were broken. The halt was temporary, however. The royalists and moderates, Dupont de Nemours and Lafayette, who came to the Assembly to demand the dissolution of the clubs and fraternal societies, thought they would benefit from a certain shift in bourgeois opinion after Louis XVI's firm stand. They were mistaken.

In order to overcome the royal veto, the Paris sections, supported by provincial municipal councils, decided to call the *fédérés*, or provincial militias, to Paris. Their pretext was the celebration of July 14. The Assembly gave legal sanction to this initiative, the impetus for which came from elsewhere, and on July 11 proclaimed the fatherland to be in danger. A civic mobilization, directed as much against the internal enemy as against the Prussian armies, was therefore justified. Starting on July 8 the *fédérés* began to arrive, bringing with them attitudes toward the executive still more radical than any in Paris. Had not the municipal council of Marseilles called on June 27 for the removal of the present executive and the nomination of another by the people? The battalions from Marseilles entered Paris on July 30 singing the words of Rouget de l'Isle. Thus *La Marseillaise* was born owing to an error of attribution. Its birthdate should have been August 10.

The manifesto signed by the Duke of Brunswick, commander-in-chief of the enemy forces, became known in Paris on August 1. Threatening to subject Paris "to military rule and total subversion" if the royal family were insulted in any way, it was received by an already tense capital bolstered by the arrival of the *fédérés*. On July 17 the latter had submitted a petition calling for suspension of the king and election of a national convention by universal suffrage. The Paris sections underwent another revolution; everywhere the passive citizens—excluded from the right of suffrage by the Constitution—

flocked to sectional assemblies and in many cases seized control. At the Hôtel-de-Ville they set up a central bureau and established a liaison with the central committee of the *fédérés*. This was a well-prepared insurrection. How did the patriotic party in the Assembly react? The event brought about the final break between the future Girondins and the future Montagnards. While Brissot's friends, harboring the illusion that their return to power could defuse the bomb, made overtures to the Court, Robespierre changed his tactics. The "defender of the Constitution" saw that the movement was irreversible, the outcome inevitable. In a great speech on July 29 he adopted the slogans of the *fédérés* and the sections: down with the king, election of a national convention by universal suffrage. But neither he nor other leaders of the Jacobin left wing personally participated in the popular *journée*. The dirty work was left to others.

On the night of August 9 and the morning of August 10, while the tocsin sounded, *commissaires* deputed by the sections went one after another to the Hôtel-de-Ville, where at dawn they formed an insurrectional commune and did away with the old municipal council. The commander-in-chief of the National Guard, Mandat, was removed and killed. He was replaced by Santerre. The Tuileries were to be attacked in a pincers' movement by two columns, one from the faubourg Saint-Antoine, the other from the Left Bank, together with contingents from Marseilles and Brest. The Saint-Antoine column arrived first. Roederer, the *procureur général syndic*, loyal to the Girondins, had persuaded Louis XVI to leave the château and take his family to the Manège, where they would be placed under the protection of the Assembly. After his departure, however, the Swiss Guards and nobles who remained in the palace could not prevent the demonstrators from invading it. The demonstrators refused to accept the surrender ordered by the king and massacred more than fifty of the Swiss Guards. Three hundred seventy-six of the attackers were killed or wounded, nearly a quarter of them *fédérés*, all bourgeois from large provincial cities. Paris was represented by small merchants, artisans, and workers, with a marked preponderance of residents of the faubourgs. The Assembly did not protect the king. Under pressure from the people and its pikes, it decided to suspend Louis XVI—whom the new Commune imprisoned at the Temple—and to replace him with a provisional Executive Council, reserving final judgment to a Convention elected by universal suffrage. Legally the king had not been deposed; politically he had been, for good.

But August 10 was also the first attack on representative government. One group of deputies—friends of Barnave and Lafayette—recognized this fact and quit an Assembly that was doomed to vanish. The others—the "democrats"—remained at their posts: they were not yet done watching the sun set.

The Revolution pursued its new course. After the initial phase of the Terror—the massacres of September 1792—there was a brief pause, owing to the calm of the first few months of the Convention and the victories, won by the Republic in the autumn of 1792 and the winter of 1792–93, which may have suggested to the Girondins, like the Feuillants before them, that the worst was over. The spring of 1793 was a tragic time: defeats abroad, the Vendée insurrection at home, and a resumption of popular agitation in Paris, driven by rising prices and inflation. The first terrorist measures approved by the Convention between March 10 and May 20 did not resolve the struggle for power. The Paris sans-culottes wanted to get rid of the Girondins, whose program was tilting more and more openly toward the wishes of the country's moderate and conservative forces. "They are inciting warfare between the haves and have-nots," wrote Pétion in a "Letter to Parisians" published at the end of April. The left wing of the Assembly, the Mountain, while hesitant about the sans-culotte demands, recognized the danger of isolation. In a letter to Barère, Jean Bon Saint-André acknowledged: "It is absolutely imperative to help the poor man live if you want him to help you complete the Revolution." For the sans-culottes there was only one way out: yet another revolutionary *journée*. The Girondin Isnard was oblivious enough to repeat the mistake of the Brunswick manifesto. On May 25 he told a delegation from the Commune: "If ever the Convention were abased, if ever through one of these endless insurrections some harm were to come to the representatives of the nation, then I declare to you in the name of all of France that Paris would be annihilated. Soon they would be searching the banks of the Seine to find out whether Paris had ever existed." One cannot wave a red flag in front of a bull without paying the price.

The initiative for the insurrection of May 31, the work of obscure agitators, came from the Cité section, which on May 28 had invited the other sections to send *commissaires* to the Evêché, where an unofficial electoral committee had been meeting for some weeks. On May 29 *commissaires* from thirty-three of the city's forty-eight sections met with a mysterious Committee of Six, including the engineer Dufourny, which was the true organizer of the *journée*. The Paris and national authorities were kept informed. Danton attempted to defuse the mine. Robespierre declared: "When all the laws are violated, when despotism is at its height, when good faith and decency are trampled underfoot, then must the people rebel. That moment has come." But his conclusion stayed within strictly parliamentary bounds: "I urge all Montagnard deputies to rally and fight aristocracy, and I say that for them there is only one alternative: either resist intrigue with all their might or resign." A "moral" insurrection, then—no armed force. At the Commune, whose mayor, Pache, was suspected of moderatism, and in the département, whose *procureur syndic* Luillier was a friend of Robespierre, efforts were made to halt or at least moderate the movement, but to no avail. The Insurrectional Committee dissolved the Commune on the night of May 30–31 only to reconstitute it immediately: the sovereignty of the revolutionary people had to be affirmed. Hanriot, a customs clerk who commanded the battalion of the "sans-culotte section" (the *quartier* of the Jardin des Plantes), was named head of the National Guard. But unanimity no longer existed. Several sections, such as that of the Marais, condemned the movement. Others were content simply not to take part. Thanks to the efforts of Jacques Roux and Varlet, the insurgents managed to invade the Convention at five that evening and present several petitions calling, first, for the arrests of the twenty deputies who had voted to allow the king to appeal the verdict of his trial to the people, and of the twelve members of the Commission set up by the Girondins; second, for the creation of a sans-culotte army; and third, for a temporary restriction of the right to vote to sans-culottes. The majority was satisfied with voting to abolish the Commission of Twelve. For the insurrection, this meeting was a failure.

It did not lay down its arms. On the night of May 31–June 1, the Insurrectional Committee ordered the arrest of the deputies it had designated. Methodically prepared, June 2 was the most impressive of all the revolutionary *journées*. It was a Sunday, so many employees and artisans were free. A crowd of eighty thousand men, with more than a hundred cannon, encircled the Convention in the early afternoon.

A majority of deputies, led by Barère and Hérault de Séchelles, wanted to play at being Roman senators and go out in procession to meet the rioters. Hanriot, saber in hand, asked Hérault, who was presiding over the Assembly, whether it was prepared to hand over the "guilty" deputies. The deputies were obliged to return to their seats. Levasseur's *Memoirs* describe the atmosphere in the hall: "A sort of stupor reigned in the Assembly. We ourselves, members of the Mountain, could not watch without pain as the popular insurrection attacked the only constituted body capable of saving the country. No one asked to speak; no deliberation was begun." Couthon proposed the arrest of the twenty-nine Girondin deputies and the ministers Clavière and Lebrun. With this amputation the Montagnards paid the price required to hold on to their base of power: the Convention. The Insurrectional Committee was abolished on June 8 and replaced by a départemental Committee of Public Safety.

June 2, 1793, marked an important turning point in the history of the Revolution. Until then the whole bourgeois revolution rested, even in democratic dreams, on the dogma of representative government. This was a late-eighteenth-century innovation. By reawakening the old popular passion for direct power, June 2 dealt a mortal blow to parliamentarism. The Assembly found itself a prisoner, and it mattered little whether it was held today by the sections or tomorrow by the army. As Michelet saw clearly, June 2 presaged "both Fructidor and Brumaire." It was not only the Girondins who were defeated; it was the Revolution. The Thermidorians would always think so; Levasseur wrote, "Yes, the Gironde was republican. . . . Yes, its proscription was a misfortune." And Thibaudeau referred to "the outrage committed on May 31 against the inviolability of [its] representatives." The day it accepted the violation of the representative principle, the parliament renounced its own legitimacy.

**
***

June 2 did not put an end to the agitation of the sans-culottes. Led by what came to be known as "enragés"—Varlet, Jacques Roux—and exasperated by a subsistence crisis due to inflation (the assignat lost seventy percent of its nominal value), that agitation mobilized around several themes: general price controls on food (the *maximum* on grains, passed on May 4, was not actually applied) and the death penalty for stockjobbers and hoarders. In July and August other demands, this time backed by the Cordeliers ("Hébertists"), stemmed from the Republic's defeat in the Vendée and abroad on all fronts: calls for price controls were mingled with terrorist demands, the arrest of suspects, judgment of the guilty, and mass conscription. It was feared that August 10, the festival of the Revolution, might become the pretext for a popular *journée*. The Committee of Public Safety managed to halt the movement by resupplying Paris and having Marat's widow condemn the enragés. By the beginning of September, however, exasperation was at its height. Drought made the food shortage acute. On September 2 the news arrived that Toulon had surrendered to the English. Preparations began for the *journées* of September 4 and 5. The insurrection began on the morning of the fourth. Groups of workers and employees of the Ministry of War (infiltrated by Hébertists) formed on the boulevards and invaded the Place de Grève, shouting, "Bread!" The Montagnard left joined the movement. Chaumette, speaking for the Commune, proclaimed: "It is open warfare of the rich against the poor. They want to crush us. Well, we have to stop them. We must crush them ourselves." And Hébert shouted: "Everyone, tomorrow, to the Convention!" Was another June 2 in the works? On September 5 the armed sections surrounded the Convention, and in their name Pache and Chaumette demanded the creation of a revolutionary army, the arrest of suspects, and the purge of the revolutionary committees. On all these points the Convention gave in and made the Terror "the order of the day." Throughout the month steps were taken, under pressure from the sans-culottes, toward both the Terror and state control of the economy. Politically, the Committee of Public Safety accepted as members Billaud-Varennes and Collot d'Herbois, who had supported the Hébertist movement. In contrast to June 2, however, it held on to power. It had the enragé leaders arrested. It limited sectional assemblies to two days a week. On October 10 it set up a government of exception, which gave it the right to supervise all constituted corps. In this sense the September days were a partial failure for the leaders of the sans-culotte movement. Henceforth the Commune, the sections, the Cordeliers, and the clubs were reduced to a semipowerless state and kept under close surveillance by the Committee and the Convention. In the short term it was the end of pressure from the street. The Cordeliers—among whom Vincent and the members of the war office played an increasingly important role—would attempt to organize yet another *journée* in February and March of 1794, a threat made credible by popular discontent owing to high prices and scarcity of food. On March 4 (14 Ventôse) the Cordeliers veiled the Rights of Man, and Carrier called for a "holy insurrection." Ill prepared and not supported by the sections or by Chaumette and Pache, this was a fiasco. The Cordelier leaders were arrested on the night of 23–24 Ventôse (March 13–14) and tried from 1 to 4 Germinal; Hébert, Vincent, Ronsin, Momoro, and later Chaumette were condemned to death and beheaded. From that date on Paris had no more autonomous institutions, and the new—Robespierrist—Commune merely transmitted orders from above. Michelet perspicaciously commented that "the spirit of Paris vanished with its Commune."

We can see why, on 9 Thermidor, Year II (July 27, 1794), the Commune and Hanriot, despite the sounding of the tocsin and the orders issued to the sections, were unable to mobilize the people to save Robespierre, Couthon, and Saint-Just. Faced with armed troops of which Barras had assumed command with the help of contingents recruited in the western and central sections, the Commune and Hanriot were able to link up with reinforcements from only sixteen of the forty-eight sections. Little by little these contingents were put to rout. It was not the rain, as has too often been written, that reduced the people to inaction on 9 Thermidor. It was, as Saint-Just rightly remarked, that the Revolution had been "chilled."

*
* *

The Thermidorians experienced two more *journées:* 12 Germinal, Year III (April 1, 1795) and 1–5 Prairial (May 20–24)—two convulsions of a single revolt, by this time powerless against an Assembly that had received a costly political education.

The winter and spring of 1795 were atrocious. Paper money collapsed, and those who lived on fixed incomes could no longer make ends meet. The abolition of the *maximum,* though desired by public opinion, led to price hikes and scarcity. After blaming the troubles on coercion, the people began to blame them on liberty. Never were social contrasts more visible. Georges Duval recounted that he was able to purchase brioches daily for 100 francs apiece at a time when three-sou loaves were nowhere to be found: "The balls continued, and so did the famine, so that upon leaving the dance halls between midnight and one in the morning, the first thing one saw was lines already formed at the bakers' doors." Discontent with the Thermidorian Convention, reflected in posters, assemblies, petitions, and brawls, crystallized on 10 Germinal in sectional assemblies, in the faubourgs, and in the historic center of the city (the great crossroads of Paris); the rallying cries were bread, the Constitution of 1793, and the liberation of imprisoned patriots. But Paris was divided, as it had been on 9 Thermidor. Sections in the west and around the Bourse called for punishment of the four "terrorists" (Barère, Collot d'Herbois, Billaud-Varenne, and Vadier) whom the Convention had begun to try in a raucous session. The insurrection of the twelfth began on the Ile de la Cité. That morning, women massed and induced men to gather in front of Notre-Dame. A revolutionary assembly there voted to march on the Convention. Reinforced by malcontents who rushed in from all sides, the crowd broke down the gates of the Tuileries between one and two o'clock. Demonstrators entered the hall where the Assembly was in session and were able to remain for four hours, during which they read petitions and shouted, "Bread! Bread!" In the end they heeded the deputies of the Mountain, who advised them to evacuate the hall. Around the Tuileries an angry crowd continued to gather. At about six o'clock the arrival of battalions from the west caused the crowd to disperse: not a single person was killed. The right wing in the Assembly took advantage of this "victory" to heighten its repression, while sporadic agitation continued.

Rioting resumed in earnest on 1 Prairial (May 20), this time with a program and a slogan. The program: enforcement of the Constitution of 1793, arrest of counterrevolutionaries, new elections. The slogan: "Bread and the Constitution of '93." At the sound of the tocsin the historic faubourgs of the Revolution, Saint-Antoine and Saint-Marceau, began to stir, and the movement gradually spread to the sections of the east and center: Gravilliers, Arsenal, Ancis. Once again it was the women who incited the men. And this time people took the trouble to arm themselves with pikes and cannon. The Convention had already begun its session (at around eleven o'clock), declared "leaders of demonstrations" to be outlaws, and called "all good citizens" to arms. Then the committees issued orders to all line troops around Paris to rendezvous at the Camp des Sablons and mobilized the National Guard. In fact, while the leaders of many of these battalions came to defend the Convention, many guards wore the insignia of the rioters. Between three and seven o'clock the insurgents invaded the hall, and one member of the Convention, Féraud, was killed by a pistol shot. While the demonstrators read petition after petition, the committees assigned Raffet to mobilize the battalions of the west. By eleven-thirty it was all over. Rioters fled through doors and windows. Over the next few days the insurrection petered out, while the committees, determined to put an end once and for all to the "insurrectional machinery," amassed an army of twenty thousand men under General Menou with orders to clean out the faubourg Saint-Antoine. Although barricades went up, the faubourg capitulated on 4 Prairial. The committees of the Convention finished off the repression; purging the Paris sections, they imprisoned some members and stripped others of their rights while reorganizing the National Guard to exclude the poorest citizens. All were obliged to surrender their pikes.

Germinal and Prairial of Year III finished what had begun a year earlier with the execution of the Hébertists. "Class discipline," in the words of Georges Lefebvre, consolidated the unity of the bourgeoisie both temporarily and permanently—permanently vis-à-vis the street, temporarily because the politicians remained divided. Henceforth the army, which the bourgeois had needed to wage the battle of the streets, was able to play the role of arbiter. The revolutionary *journées* were over; the time of the coup d'état had come. On 13 Vendémiaire the royalists attempted to play the game of the "popular" uprising. But as Mme. de Staël predicted: "You are quite new at talking about the sovereignty of the people. You stammer a language that they know better than you, a language they forged for their own use." Much later, of course, there were the "*journées*" of the nineteenth century: July 1830, February and June 1848, May 1871. But those days of barricades, harking back to an ancient past, had nothing in common with the cohorts of men and women who took the Bastille, went to Versailles in search of the king, drove him from the Tuileries, and obliged the Assembly to amputate its own members.

Denis Richet

Events

Further reading

Braesch, Frédéric. *La commune du dix août 1792: Etude sur l'histoire de Paris du 20 juin au 2 décembre 1792.* Paris, 1911.

Lefebvre, Georges. *Quatre-vingt-neuf.* Paris, 1939.

Mathiez, Albert. "Etude critique sur les journées des 5 et 6 octobre," *Revue historique,* 1898.

———— *Le dix août.* Paris, 1931.

Pitra, Louis-Guillaume. *La journée du 14 juillet 1789: Fragment des mémoires inédits de Louis-George Pitra, électeur de Paris en 1789,* with an introduction and notes by Jules Flammermont. Paris, 1892.

Rudé, George. *The Crowd in the French Revolution.* Oxford, 1959.

Soboul, Albert. *Les sans-culottes parisiens en l'an II: Histoire politique et sociale des sections de Paris, 2 juin 1793–9 thermidor an II.* La Roche-sur-Yon, 1958. Reprinted Paris, 1958, and 1962 with the subtitle *Mouvement populaire et gouvernement révolutionnaire.*

Tonneson, Kare D. *La défaite des sans-culottes: Mouvement populaire et réaction bourgeoise en l'an III.* Oslo and Paris, 1959.

Related topics

Barnave
Clubs and Popular Societies
Danton
Enragés
Federation
Girondins
Hébertists
Lafayette
Louis XVI
Marat
Montagnards
Necker
Paris Commune
Robespierre
Sans-culottes
Sovereignty
Staël
Terror
Varennes

TERROR

On September 5, 1793, the Convention made "the Terror" the order of the day. By this action it signaled its intention to organize, systematize, and accelerate repression of the Republic's domestic adversaries and to ensure quick punishment of "all traitors." But this blunt and candid declaration, this inaugural vote of the Terror, came in unusual circumstances. That morning, the sans-culottes had invaded the Assembly demanding both bread and the guillotine—the guillotine in order to have bread. What they wanted, and what they would obtain a few days later, was a "revolutionary army" of the interior, intended to strike terror in the hearts of hoarders and enemies of the Republic with the aid of a terrifying machine that would be part of its standard equipment, "the fatal instrument that with one blow cuts short both conspiracies and the lives of their authors." Shortly thereafter, a delegation of Jacobins offered a version of the same rhetoric less directly concerned with bread: those to be guillotined were "traitors." It was in order to give official satisfaction to the Paris militants that the Committee of Public Safety declared the Terror to be the order of the day.

The circumstances surrounding this celebrated vote indicate that before becoming a set of repressive institutions used by the Republic to liquidate its adversaries and establish its domination on a basis of fear, the Terror was a demand based on political convictions or beliefs, a characteristic feature of the mentality of revolutionary activism.

As such, it predated the dictatorship of Year II, the Republic, and the war with Europe. It had existed since the early summer of 1789, along with the related idea that the Revolution was threatened by an aristocratic plot that only prompt measures could thwart. The popular violence that engulfed Paris on July 14 was an early consequence of the partly economic, partly political logic that characterized the actions of the Paris crowd; the murder of the minister Foullon de Doué on July 22, followed by the murder of his son-in-law Bertier de Sauvigny, the intendant of Paris, was a summary punishment that temporarily quieted the obsession with grain hoarding and the Versailles plot. In September the terrorist idea found in *L'ami du peuple* and its publisher Marat its newspaper and its champion. The man whom the people of Paris led back to their city on October 6 was less a king than a hostage: in the return of "the baker, the baker's wife, and the baker's boy" the people saw a guarantee that Paris would henceforth be supplied with food as well as an assurance that they would at last be able to monitor the king's activities and the maneuvers of the queen and the royal entourage.

This general, systematic suspicion was inextricably associated with a persistent overestimation of the degree to which the enemy's strategy was deliberate and his resources were limitless. The plot drew substance from the idea of the enemy's omnipotence, which only the people could thwart. In its crudest form this image existed among the lower orders of the urban population, but it was also present in the minds of many deputies, since it was rooted in the new political culture: just as the Revolution was the reversal whereby the people reappropriated a power previously alienated to the king and to God, the political universe that it inaugurated was populated solely by wills, so that henceforth nothing remained outside human control. The new realm of power was occupied entirely by the people, which through its actions had reclaimed inalienable rights. Yet the people continued to be menaced by an anti-power, which like the nation was abstract, omnipresent, and all-enveloping, but which was hidden where the nation was public, individual where the nation was universal, and harmful where the nation was good. This anti-power was thus the negative, the inverse, the anti-principle of the nation. Such was the fantastic nature of revolutionary society's discourse on power, and it made the aristocratic plot one of the central figures of the revolutionary mentality. It was almost infinitely malleable, apt at interpreting every circumstance, and sustained most of all by ambiguities in the royal attitude.

Traces of the obsession with a plot can also be found, in less caricatural form than with Marat or the Cordeliers, in the words of deputies of the Constituent Assembly, where even at this early date the Assembly encouraged the notion that in case of public emergency it might be necessary to limit human rights. Consider, for example, the February 1790 debate on the right to emigrate: Mesdames, the aunts of Louis XVI, had been arrested on their way to Rome by local authorities in Burgundy. This led to a debate in the Assembly, ultimately resolved in favor of Mesdames by invoking the rights of man, but tested by a strong contrary case that invoked the national emergency. In the following year, the king's flight to Varennes and return to Paris publicly demonstrated the royal family's true sentiments; this minor plot—ill conceived and ill executed—was construed by revolutionary opinion as proof of the great plot, universal, omnipresent, and omnipotent. The Revolution had really already ceased to have a true constitutional king, despite the temporary fiction of an "abduction." Yet it made of this vanquished, captive, but reinstated monarch a formidable enemy, soon supported by all the kings of Europe.

The war raised both the stakes and the fears. It erased the line between opposition and treason once and for all. It turned nobles and refractory priests into enemies of the fatherland. It quickly dissolved what was left of the royal fiction after the Varennes episode, but not even the fall of the king on August 10 diminished the perceived threat to the Revolution from the conspiracy of external enemies and domestic traitors. On the contrary, the six weeks that separated the fall of the Tuileries from the meeting of the Convention on September 20 marked the entry of the Terror into revolutionary politics.

But the Terror was not yet the policy of the Revolution. For the Legislative Assembly was now only a caretaker regime, and real power had passed to the victors of August 10: the Paris Commune, composed of the former Insurrectional Committee, rounded out through carefully contrived elections to a complement of nearly three hundred members representing the cream of Parisian militancy. Under pressure from the Commune the Legislative Assembly voted on August 17 to establish a special tribunal and declared refractory priests to be criminals. Under the Commune's direct authority the Paris sections organized themselves as surveillance committees, conducting searches and making arrests. The punishment of the "guilty" was the order of the day. By the end of August the bad news from the frontiers heightened the siege mentality and the obsession with punishment, which were responsible for the massacres of prisoners by mobs in Paris between September 2 and September 6.

This baleful episode illustrates the psychological and political mechanism of the Terror. The victims were mostly common law prisoners (nearly three-quarters of the more than a thousand killed), while the murderers were the victors of August 10: shopkeepers, artisans, national guards, *fédérés*, motivated by their obsession with treason. No orders, no identifiable instructions, came from above. The press poured oil on the fire, and the idea of liquidating traitors was of course an old refrain of Marat's, but the crowd needed no visible leader to conduct a slaughter arranged to look like a rough parody of justice. Danton, the minister of justice, did not intervene, and even the Girondin Roland wrote on September 3: "Yesterday was a day over whose events a veil should probably be thrown." A few weeks later, the September massacres would became a theme in the political battle between Girondins and Montagnards. At the time, however, the politicians of the Revolution endured the event as one accepts the inevitable.

In fact, the Terror was gradually established as a repressive system organized from above and institutionalized during the year 1793, as the Montagnards turned to activists in the Paris sections for support in taking control of the Revolution. The question whether the king's trial and execution formed the prelude to or even the first act of the Terror is not easy to answer. One may agree with Kant that the answer should be "yes" if one sees the death of Louis XVI as an illegal violation of the constitutional contract by the Convention. Or one may answer "no," along with Michelet, if one views the trial as the solemn affirmation of the new sovereignty of the people, incompatible with the old sovereignty of the king. The fact remains that the judgment and execution of Louis XVI were extensively and minutely debated and did not entail creation of emergency institutions.

However firm their legal underpinnings, the king's trial and execution did nevertheless signal a key political victory for the Mountain. Since September the Girondins had been banking on relaxation of repressive and coercive measures. The Montagnards relied on their alliance with militants in the sections and on the implementation of a terrorist policy. January 21 was a great symbolic victory for that strategy. In the spring, Dumouriez's military failures (followed by his defection to the enemy), the start of the Vendée war, and economic difficulties in Paris made it possible to move further in the direction of such a policy.

On March 11 the Convention established a Revolutionary Tribunal; on March 21 it set up the Committees of Surveillance, responsible at the local level for keeping an eye on "suspects," a category largely left to the committees' judgment; on March 28 laws against émigrés were codified and strengthened, depriving those who emigrated of their property and providing for the death penalty if they returned to France. The philosophy behind these measures was well summarized by Danton, who had in mind the September massacres: "Let us be terrible in order to dispense the people from being so." The expulsion of the Girondins from the Convention on June 2 hastened the evolution toward terror by offering, in response to sans-culotte demands, an additional—and important—reward. Both domestic and foreign situations at the beginning of the summer justified a dictatorship by the committees and the dispatch of representatives with extraordinary powers to the rebellious provinces and the armies—measures outside common law. But once again it was the invasion of the Assembly by sectional militants on September 5 that placed the Terror on the agenda.

The Terror was from that point on a system of government, or rather, an essential part, the arm, of the revolutionary government. Its administrative structure was simple. At the top were the two committees, especially the Committee of General Security, whose responsibilities included surveillance and police. At the grass roots was a vast network of local revolutionary committees responsible for identifying and arresting "suspects" and issuing certificates of civism. These were complementary tasks, since any grounds for not issuing such a certificate were also grounds for declaring a person "suspect," that is, an enemy of the regime or merely a potential adversary, a fence-sitter. A wave of denunciations took advantage of this incitement by public authority. "Suspects" were judged by special courts; the principal one was the Revolutionary Tribunal in Paris, created in March 1793 and reorganized in September to accelerate its operations. Divided into four sections, two of which functioned simultaneously, it comprised sixteen examining magistrates, a jury of sixty, and a public prosecutor with a staff of assistants, all named by the Convention on nomination by the two committees. The subordination of the court to political power was thus a matter of principle: trial was quick and judges lacked independence; deliberations were hasty and in fact limited to three days by an October decree intended to hamper the defense of the Girondin deputies. The autonomy of the Tribunal consisted in its power to free certain of the accused. Otherwise the stakes were life or death, for it was not long before judgments were reduced to just two: acquittal or execution. Verdicts were rendered by majority vote after secret deliberation, but in the March decree it was stipulated that judges "state their opinions out loud." Michelet and later Louis Blanc commented: "The Terror was in this phrase more than in the whole project."

But the Terror was not contained in any one institution, no matter how symbolic. It was also a ubiquitous means of government, through which the revolutionary dictatorship of Paris would make its iron hand felt everywhere, in the provinces and in the armies. It was exercised by way of "the revolutionary army" created in September, a great reserve of activists under the authority of the sans-culotte Ronsin, a political gendarmerie that, keeping one eye on hoarders and the other on the notorious "suspects," represented the Paris sections in every town and village in the Republic. Its chief operative was the *représentant en mission,* designated by the Convention and the Committee of Public Safety to organize the victory of the Revolution on the frontiers and exterminate the enemies of the Republic in the regions in revolt against or at war with Paris. He had full powers to establish special courts or courts-martial to hasten the work of repression, not to mention the even more expeditious justice meted out in the form of mass executions, as in Lyons and the Vendée. The Terror thus operated through a motley fabric of improvised institutions; special courts modeled after the one in Paris were established in Arras, Cambrai, Brest, Rochefort, and Toulouse in the winter of 1793–94. But most of the organs of repression were "extraordinary commissions," civilian or military, created ad hoc in the civil war zones and rendering judgments from which there was no appeal. It was not until the spring of 1794 that the Revolutionary Tribunal of Paris began asserting its jurisdiction over an increasing number of cases of counterrevolutionary crime. The laws of 27 Germinal (April 16) and 19 Floréal (May 8) capped this development by granting the Paris tribunal exclusive jurisdiction.

This spring of 1794—a year after the creation of the Tribunal—was also the time of the administrative institutionalization of the Terror through the dreadful law of 22 Prairial (June 10), the draft of which is in Couthon's hand. A majority of the personnel serving the Tribunal were replaced, beginning with the public ministry, which had been headed from the beginning by Fouquier-Tinville. The novelty of the law lay in its redefinition of the mission and lethal omnipotence of the redoubtable court. Its fourth article stated that the Tribunal "is instituted to punish the enemies of the people." More political than juridical, this definition prefaced procedures that were more expeditious than judicial. The text eliminated the *instruction,* or preliminary investigation (article 12), and permitted charges to be brought merely on the basis of denunciations (article 9); it deprived the accused of the assistance of an attorney (article 16) and transformed the hearing into a mere formality by eliminating the examination of witnesses. Article 13 stated: "If material evidence exists independent of the testimony of witnesses, the witnesses will not be heard." Robespierre, who presided over the session of 22 Prairial, mounted the Assembly rostrum to defend his loyal Couthon against those few members of the Convention who were frightened by the nature of this revolutionary justice: "We shall brave the perfidious insinuations of excessive severity with which some have sought to attack measures prescribed by the public interest. This severity is redoubtable only to conspirators, only to enemies of liberty."

The law of 22 Prairial was rescinded in the wake of 9 Thermidor. Deprived of its political source of energy and detested by public opinion, the Revolutionary Tribunal ceased its activities. Though later reorganized, it had permanently lost the quasi-legitimacy and frightful utility it had derived for sixteen months from the idea of a government of exception, with terror the order of the day.

From this rise and fall arises a new set of questions, which have less to do with the institutions of revolutionary Terror than with their role and consequences. It is best to begin once again with Paris and with what information we have about the Revolutionary Tribunal. Examination of the monthly summaries of its activities from its inception to the fall of Robespierre reveals that between March and September of 1793 the Tribunal's work was curtailed, though already its verdicts were limited to either death or acquittal: five to fifteen death sentences were handed down each month, compared with a far greater number of acquittals. The number of "cases" rose sharply in October, that is, just after the measures that followed the sans-culotte *journée* of September 5—measures that made Terror the order of the day, established the law of suspects, and reorganized the Tribunal and replaced its personnel. Actually it was in September that the number of judges was raised from five to sixteen and the number of jurors from twelve to sixty. The personnel of the March 10 tribunal had been completely replaced, with hardly anyone left in place other than the public prosecutor Fouquier-Tinville and his two lieutenants. Oversight by the two committees became discretionary. The figures reveal what a spur these changes were to repression: 193 accused went to the guillotine in the final two months of autumn and through early January. Among these "counterrevolutionaries" were not only Marie Antoinette, Mme. Elisabeth, the duc de Biron (who was ex-general of the Armies of the Republic), and the former duc d'Orléans (who in vain had taken up the new name Philippe-Egalité), but also all the Girondins arrested or declared suspect since springtime, with Brissot and Vergniaud leading the way, followed by the remains of what had been the Feuillant group along with Bailly and Barnave. The guillotine exorcised the Revolution's past at the same time as it felled the Ancien Régime.

By autumn the Tribunal was already judging more than a hundred suspects per month but still acquitting more than half of them. Then, in March, as the prisons filled with suspects and the number of accused to be tried continued to increase, the proportion of death penalties rose, and this change was soon followed by a dizzying rise in the actual number of trials. The causes of the two phenomena were different. The first had to do with the sharpening of factional struggle in the first few months of 1794 and the radicalization of conflicts for power, which led in the end to the guillotine first for the Hébertists and later for the Dantonists (late March–early April): death became the universal sanction for political conflict. The second was, in essence at any rate, the result of the previously mentioned decree of 27 Germinal, carried on a motion by Saint-Just, which centralized revolutionary justice in Paris. This evolution culminated in the law of 22 Prairial, which completed the mechanism of the judicial Terror; nearly 700 judgments were handed down in Prairial and nearly 1,000 in Messidor (June 21–July 21), and together these judgments resulted in close to 800 executions. The Paris prisons were overpopulated; they housed over 8,000 "suspects" at the beginning of Thermidor. Only the fall of Robespierre on the ninth (July 27) halted the endless procession of tumbrils that historians have baptized the "Great Terror."

This summary of the results of the Terror in Paris, based on data from the Revolutionary Tribunal, may usefully be compared with a statistical study, published in 1935 by the American historian Donald Greer, of victims of the Terror nationwide. Confirming two earlier works, Greer arrives at a figure of 16,600 victims executed after being sentenced to death by a revolutionary court of justice (including, as we have just seen, 2,625 in Paris). The number of arrests from March 1793 to the end of July 1794 was far higher, probably close to a half-million: this figure gives some idea of the shock caused by a repressive wave of these dimensions. It also indicates that there were not only acquittals but also, occasionally, penalties other than the death sentence, as well as "suspects" who languished in prison until 9 Thermidor without being tried. The Terror's victims came from all levels of society, with each conflict producing its own characteristic shadings: more peasants in the Vendée, more bourgeois in Paris, Lyons, and Nîmes. In proportion to their relatively small numbers, the upper classes and clergy were comparatively hard-hit.

Greer's chronological graph of executions nationwide shows low or very low figures during the spring and summer of 1793, exactly as in Paris. But what followed was different: the number of death sentences peaks sharply in December 1793 and January 1794, with nearly 3,500 executions in each of these two months. The tragic curve drops below 1,000 from February to May and then climbs again in June and July until 9 Thermidor. The difference between these figures and those from the Revolutionary Tribunal in Paris is thus concentrated in the middle of the period, in the months of December and January, when the Terror was at its height in the provinces. This chronology suggests a first comprehensive interpretation.

If we can agree that the Terror began in March 1793 with the creation of the Revolutionary Tribunal and the first measures of public safety, then its least bloody period—indeed not very bloody at all—was the spring and summer of 1793. This was also the Republic's most critical period. The Prussians and Austrians took Condé, Valenciennes, and Mainz in July, and the domestic situation was catastrophic, with the federalist revolt, the victorious Vendean peasants, and the royalist insurgents in control of Lyons, Marseilles, and Toulon, to say nothing of the Paris sections' threats to the Convention. By contrast, when the number of death sentences and executions began to rise sharply in October, the Republic had been saved on the northern frontier by the battles of Hondschoote (September 8) and Wattignies (October 16). Lyons was retaken on October 9, and the Grand Army of the Vendean peasants was defeated at Cholet on October 17. Made the order of the day on September 5, the Terror, when viewed in relation to the war, both foreign and civil, seems to have been a belated response to a situation that had already begun to improve. The diagnosis is still more obvious if we take into consideration the fact that executions reached a peak in December and January and then resumed with even greater ferocity in the spring under Robespierre's personal dictatorship, at a time when the Revolution faced no more threats at home and the armies of the Republic were taking the offensive on the borders; the law of Prairial and the "Great Terror" have lost any semblance of a connection with public safety.

This paradox can be understood with the aid of two examples, which help us to move beyond the abstraction of a chronological curve of executions. The situation under the Terror varied considerably in different localities and regions. In Greer's data, more than half the executions took place in the thirteen départements of western France, and twenty percent in the Rhône valley. Characteristic are the case of Lyons and the repression in the Vendée.

In Lyons class warfare superimposed its effects on the consequences of political struggle. The conflict between the Mountain and the Gironde was embedded in social antagonism between the lower classes and the rich. The crusade of the poor found its Savonarola in the Piedmontese merchant Chalier, who defected to serve the working people in their struggle against the merchant city. The workers lost the mayoralty to a Girondin in November 1792, but the Jacobins held a majority in the Municipal Council and ultimately, in March 1793, obliged the council to approve one of Chalier's men. On May 29 the Girondins (on the eve of their elimination in Paris) took their revenge, thanks to an insurrection triggered by the levying of a special tax. The city quickly passed from the enemies of the Paris dictatorship into the hands of the royalists, who ruled throughout the summer; but it was retaken by troops of the Convention on October 9.

It now became an "Emancipated City," symbolically rescued from its accursed past and destined to endure a partial razing, limited to the "houses of the rich." Couthon, the city's conqueror, carried out a relatively moderate repression in October. But in November he was replaced by Collot d'Herbois and Fouché, who proceeded with numerous hasty trials and summary executions. Leveling of the large residences along the quays of the Saône got under way. Several thousand suspects were guillotined, shot, or cut down en masse by firing squads. The terror lasted until March 1794.

The history of the revolutionary Terror in the Vendée obeyed the same logic and the same chronology. Again it was a case of putting down an insurrection, the most serious that the Revolution had had to confront. And as in Lyons repression not only came after the victory but actually reached a peak several months later. The Vendée rebellion actually began in March 1793, and reports of its victories resounded throughout the spring and early autumn. But it quickly subsided beginning in mid-October, when the peasant army was crushed at Cholet and moved north of the Loire in the hope of joining an English fleet at Granville, until what troops remained were destroyed in December in the battles of Le Mans and Savenay. But the revolutionary Terror—which is to be distinguished from atrocities and massacres committed in the heat of battle—raged from January to March 1794.

For if the war was pitiless on both sides, what began afterward was of a different nature: it was a massive repression organized from above on orders of the Convention with the intention of destroying not only the rebels but the population, farms, crops, villages, and anything else that had served the "brigands" as shelter. For such a task the guillotine was no longer sufficient, and in December Carrier resorted to mass drownings in the Loire. But it was in January that an idea proposed by Barère began to be put into effect: "To destroy the Vendée." The Republican troops divided into several columns, each with its own itinerary, with explicit orders to burn all homes and murder their inhabitants, women and children included. This dreadful operation continued until May, and its sad toll must be added to the strict costs of the war: the territory known as the "military Vendée" (comprising parts of Loire Inférieure, Maine-et-Loire, Vendée, and Deux-Sèvres) lost twenty percent of its housing and a substantial percentage of its population.

Numerical estimates of the loss of human life have remained a subject of polemic. It is impossible to be as precise as one would like for two sets of reasons. In the absence of specific sources, historians must resort to comparisons between prior and subsequent population estimates. The documents, moreover, do not permit a breakdown of the three different types of mortality: persons killed in battle (on both sides), persons killed in terrorist repression (whether condemned by a court or simply massacred), and reduced birth rates and increased death rates in the years following the war. Hence it is impossible to give a precise estimate of the number of victims of the Terror in the Vendée. Nevertheless, taken together, the actions of Carrier in Nantes and of Turreau's infernal columns were responsible for deaths numbering in the tens of thousands. This figure, by far the largest item in the final count of victims of the Terror, is left out of Donald Greer's statistics, based primarily on capital sentences. It must be added in round numbers to the total, which it increases considerably.

The legacy of the Terror poisoned all subsequent revolutionary history and, beyond that, all political life in nineteenth-century France. Throughout the Thermidorian period the Terror lurked about the fringes of the political scene. The royalists used it to forge a weapon of revenge, an instrument for settling local scores in areas where the population leaned toward their camp and Republican troops were thinly scattered, as in the Rhône valley. The republicans would have liked to forget the Terror and root the new institutions of the Year III in the law; Benjamin Constant and Mme. de Staël worked feverishly between 9 Thermidor and 18 Brumaire to exorcise the ghost of the guillotine that haunted the Republic, but to no avail. Thermidor revived the royalist menace and counterrevolutionary violence, and the Directory was unable to accept the election dates legally set by the Constitution. In September 1797 Augereau's army laid siege to Paris at the behest of the director Barras in order to save the Republic from a royalist parliamentary majority. The coup d'état of 18 Fructidor (September 5) was the signal for a new series of "public safety" measures in which deportation to Guiana replaced the scaffold, with refractory priests paying the heavy price. The nation's revolutionary education proceeded on course, and the civil and military putsch of 18–

19 Brumaire 1799 capped it off by establishing a regime "that completed the Terror by replacing permanent revolution with permanent war" (Marx, *The Holy Family*).

In the nineteenth century memories of the Terror imparted a peculiar bitterness to civil struggle, while at the same time adding further passion to the great conflict between Ancien Régime and Revolution. By associating the advent of democracy with a bloody dictatorship, it supplied counterrevolutionaries with arguments and liberals with fears. It embarrassed or divided republicans and isolated socialists. In postrevolutionary France the monarchy was suspect because of the Ancien Régime, but the Republic was unable to cleanse its image of the blood spilled in its name. When it finally triumphed in the 1870s, it was because the republicans had conquered their own demons and presented a pacified version of their great ancestors from which the specter of the guillotine had been exorcised. It was not until the twentieth century, with the injection of bolshevism and the development of a communist extreme left, that a cult of the Terror, associated with that of Robespierre, was established on grounds of revolutionary necessity, where for half a century it flourished in the shadow of the Soviet example.

Thus, there exists a history of the history of the Terror, associated with the vicissitudes of French political history over the past two hundred years. But that history can also be written in a less chronological mode by attempting to reconstitute the various types of interpretation to which the Terror has been subjected.

The most common strategy is to relate the Terror to circumstances external to the Revolution; we are told, then, that the Terror was merely the product of the tragic situation in which the Republic found itself in 1793 and was a terrible yet necessary instrument of public safety. Surrounded by enemies foreign and domestic, the Convention allegedly had no choice but to rely on fear of the guillotine to mobilize men and resources. We find this interpretation being advanced by the Thermidorians in the period immediately following Robespierre's fall, and it was destined to enjoy a brilliant future, for it can also be found in most French public school texts for reasons that are easy to understand: it has the advantage of offering to the ultimately victorious republican tradition a Revolution exonerated of guilt for the terrorist episode, responsibility for which is shifted to its adversaries. That is why this interpretation is favored by many who consider themselves heirs of 1789, for it is a way of escaping the dilemma of contradiction or denial.

The "circumstantial" thesis is often associated with another idea, according to which the Terror coincides with a period during which social strata other than the cultivated bourgeoisie were gaining access to power: specifically, the class of urban artisans and tradesmen from which the sans-culotte activists were recruited and which Mignet, for example, setting the tone for liberal historiography, dubbed the "plebs" or the "multitude" to distinguish them from the bourgeoisie of 1789. Thus circumstances presumably brought to the fore a second revolution, which lacks the historical dignity of the first because it was neither bourgeois nor liberal; its necessity was merely circumstantial, that is, subordinate to the principal course of the event, which continued to be defined by the principles of 1789 and the rise of the bourgeoisie. But the plebeian nature of this episode makes it possible to understand how the Terror was also the product of elementary political reflexes, at once egalitarian and punitive, triggered by military reverses and internal insurrections. The Ancien Régime had not known how to educate its people, and for this it paid a heavy price at the moment of its downfall.

It is not difficult to find elements of historical reality to support interpretations of this type. The Terror did in fact develop in the course of the Revolution at a time of foreign and domestic danger and out of obsession with "aristocratic" treason and an "aristocratic plot." It continually justified itself in these terms as indispensable to the salvation of the fatherland. It was "placed on the order of the day" and exercised in the name of the state and the Republic only under pressure from sans-culotte militants. The Paris prison massacres of September 1792 showed the extremes to which the punitive passions of the people might go. A year later, it was in part to channel those passions that the Convention and the Committees turned the Terror into a banner of government.

Nevertheless, neither the circumstances nor the political attitudes of the *petit peuple* are enough to account for the phenomenon. The "circumstances," too, have a chronology. The risks for the Revolution were greatest at the beginning and in the middle of the summer of 1793, at a time when the activity of the Revolutionary Tribunal was relatively minimal. By contrast, the Terror intensified with the improvement of the situation and the victories, starting in October. It reached a peak during the winter, in a Lyons that had been vanquished for several months and in a defeated Vendée that had to be put to the torch, as well as in countless other places where there were violent clashes as a result of initiatives on the part of local militants or envoys of the Convention. There was indeed a connection between the civil war and the Terror, but it was not that the Terror was an instrument for ending a war; it followed and actually prolonged rather than shortened the war. One cannot credit it with patriotic devotion without falling into inconsistency, because to do so would be to assume—incorrectly, by the way—the existence of a counterrevolutionary France. Nor can one credit it with saving the fatherland or maintaining the Republic, since it came after the victory. "The Great Terror," wrote the republican Quinet as long ago as 1867, "nearly everywhere revealed itself after the victories. Can we maintain that it caused them? Can we argue that, in our systems, effect precedes cause?" (*Critique de la Révolution*).

The explanation involving the role of popular attitudes accounts for only some of the facts. It is indeed true, as we have seen, that the pressure to establish a terrorist dictatorship came chiefly from sans-culotte militants. But it is not a simple matter to establish a dividing line between the "people" and the political elites, between "popular" culture and "high" culture. What about Marat, for example, who may be considered one of the purest ideologues of the Terror? To which group did he belong? This demi-savant, who since 1789 had been denouncing the aristocratic plot and tirelessly calling for scaffolds to be erected, straddled both "cultures." The same can be said of Hébert and the Hébertists, who extended his influence in Paris and played so important a role in the republican repression in Vendée. In fact, in 1793 terrorist discourse was in the mouths of nearly all the leaders of the Revolution, including those who had no special relation to sans-culotte activism, the legists and bourgeois of the committees and the Convention. Barère's demand in the summer of 1793 for the total destruction of the Vendée is enough to make clear the grip of terrorist fanaticism on all the Montagnard deputies.

Of course this call for widespread extermination grew out of the civil war, even if that was not its only cause. But, as Mona Ozouf has demonstrated, from the autumn of 1793 to the spring of 1794 the case for the necessity of the Terror abandoned the circumstantial grounds of the war in favor of a more fundamental justification: nothing less than the Revolution itself. After the end of March and the liquidation of the Hébertists, which put an end to the bloody escalation of what remained of sans-culottism, the Terror, by this point the exclusive instrument of the Robespierrist clan, had ceased to be a matter for learned and sometimes philosophical rationalization. It was less a part of the arsenal of victory than of an ambition for regeneration.

Nor was the climate any longer that of a besieged city, since the frontiers had been liberated and the civil war extinguished. The most obvious use of the guillotine was no longer the extermination of avowed enemies but rather that of "factions": the Hébertists followed by the Dantonists. The Terror raged all the more fiercely because the Robespierrist group had no further support either on its left, among the activists, or on its right, in public opinion; it was a government of fear, which Robespierre portrayed in theory as a government of virtue. Conceived in order to exterminate aristocracy, the Terror ended as a means of subduing wrongdoers and combatting crime. From now on it coincided with and was inseparable from the Revolution, because there was no other way of someday molding a republic of citizens.

Hence the Terror cannot be reduced to circumstances, whether the emergency situation or pressure from the *petit peuple,* surrounding its birth. Not that circumstances played no role; obviously they provided an environment in which ideology developed and allowed terrorist institutions to be gradually put in place. But this ideology, present in the Revolution of 1789, predated the circumstances and enjoyed an independent existence, which was associated with the nature of French revolutionary culture through several sets of ideas.

The first of these ideas was of man's regeneration, in which respect the Revolution was akin to a religious annunciation but in a secularized mode. The actors in the events actually conceived of their own history as an emancipation of man in general. The issue was not to reform French society but to reinstitute the social pact on the basis of man's free will; France represented only the first act of this decisive development. This truly philosophical ambition was unusual, however, in that it was constantly caught up in the test of actual history, as though the truth of a religious promise had been left to empirical verification by the facts. In the gap between facts and promise was born the idea of a regeneration, to reduce the distance between the Revolution and its ambition, which it could not renounce without ceasing to be itself. If the Republic of free citizens was not yet possible, it was because men, perverted by their past history, were wicked; by means of the Terror, the Revolution—a history without precedent, entirely new—would make a new man.

Another idea said roughly the same thing, or arrived at the same result: that politics could do anything. The revolutionary universe was a universe populated by wills, entirely animated by the conflict between good intentions and evil plans; no action was ever uncertain, no power ever innocent. As first Hegel and later Marx recognized, the French Revolution was the theater in which the voluntarism of modern politics revealed itself in all its purity. The event remained ever faithful to its original idea, according to which the social contract could be instituted only by free wills. This attribution of unlimited powers to political action opened a vast field to radicalization of conflicts and to militant fanaticism. Henceforth each individual could arrogate to himself what had once been a divine monopoly, that of creating the human world, with the ambition of recreating it. If he then found obstacles standing in his way, he attributed them to the perversity of adverse wills rather than to the opacity of things: the Terror's sole purpose was to do away with those adversaries.

In the end, the Revolution put the people in the place of the king. In order to restore to the social order the truth and justice ignored by the Ancien Régime, it returned the people to its rightful place, usurped for so long by the king: the place of sovereign. What the Revolution, following Rousseau, called the general will was radically different from monarchical power in the manner of its formation yet identical to it in the extent of its jurisdiction. The absolute sovereignty of the king presaged the sovereignty of democracy. Wholly obsessed with legitimacy, having thrown off divine guidance without establishing reciprocal checks and balances in the American manner, the Revolution was unwilling to set limits to public authority. It had lived since 1789 on the idea of a new absolute—and indivisible—sovereignty, which excluded pluralism of representation because it assumed the unity of the nation. Since that unity did not exist—and Girondin federalism showed that factions continued to plot in the shadows—the function of the Terror, as well as of purging elections, was invariably to establish it. As early as 1795, in the discussion of the Constitution of Year III, Sieyès would blame the Terror on the Revolution's errors regarding the concept of sovereignty (speech of 2 Thermidor); somewhat later this idea was adapted and systematized by Mme. de Staël, Benjamin Constant, and finally Guizot.

This explanation of the Terror is not incompatible with a more sociological type of interpretation, which incidentally can also be found in the work of Constant and Staël. An enthralling chapter of the latter's *Considérations sur la Révolution française* (book 3, chap. 15) in fact suggests that the Ancien Régime bequeathed to posterity not only its conception of sovereignty but also the harshness of its social relations. Aristocratic society, composed of castes created by the monarchy and fiercely jealous of their privileges, left the embers of its violence to the Revolution, which fanned them into conflagration: "Because the various classes of society had almost no relations among themselves in France, their mutual antipathy was stronger . . . In no country were nobles as much strangers to the rest of the nation. When they touched the second class, it was only to give offense. . . . The same scene was repeated from rank to rank; the irritability of a very sensitive nation inclined each person to jealousy toward his neighbor, toward his superior, toward his master; and all individuals not content to dominate humiliated one another." In part, therefore, the "Terror" may have stemmed from an egalitarian fanaticism born of an inegalitarian pathology in the old society. For there is no reason not to think that in the genesis of the bloody dictatorship of Year II, Ancien Régime and Revolution combined their effects.

François Furet

FURTHER READING

Caron, Pierre. *Les massacres de septembre.* Paris, 1935.

Constant, Benjamin. *Des effets de la Terreur.* Paris, 1797. Reprinted in Olivier Pozzo di Borgo, ed., *Constant: Ecrits et discours politiques,* 2 vols. Paris, 1964, vol. 1, pp. 95–112.

Greer, Donald. *The Incidence of the Terror during the French Revolution: A Statistical Interpretation.* Cambridge, Mass., 1935.

Hegel, Georg Friedrich Wilhelm. *The Phenomenology of the Spirit.*

Herriot, Edouard. *Lyon n'est plus,* 4 vols. Paris, 1937–1940, vol. 3.

Lefebvre, Georges. "Foules révolutionnaires," in Centre International de Synthèse, *La foule* (Fourth International Synthesis Week). Paris, 1934. Reprinted in Lefebvre, *Etudes sur la Révolution française.* Paris, 1954; reprinted 1963.

Lucas, Colin. *The Structure of the Terror: The Example of Javogues and the Loire.* Oxford, 1973.

Marx, Karl, and Friedrich Engels. "Critical Battle against the French Revolution," in *The Holy Family.*

Ozouf, Mona. *L'école de la France.* Paris, 1984, pp. 109–127, "Guerre et Terreur dans le discours révolutionnaire."

Quinet, Edgar. *La Révolution.* Paris, 1865, books 16, 17.

RELATED TOPICS

Barnave

Committees of Public Safety

Constant

Counterrevolution

Danton

Girondins

Guizot

Hébertists

Jacobinism

Kant

King's Trial

Louis XVI

Marat

Marie Antoinette

Marx

Michelet

Montagnards

Paris Commune

Quinet

Regeneration

Revolutionary Assemblies

Revolutionary Government

Rights of Man

Robespierre

Sans-culottes

Sieyès

Sovereignty

Staël

Varennes

Vendée

TREATIES OF BASEL AND THE HAGUE

B etween April and July 1795 the French Republic succeeded in removing three powers from the coalition. It was not the first time that such a thing had happened, since the Grand Duke of Tuscany, the Emperor's own brother, had in February signed a treaty guaranteeing him neutrality. But the treaty was a small achievement for revolutionary France; it needed to consolidate its borders, deploy its troops, and establish that a regicide nation could treat with kings. These goals were achieved in three stages, not without difficulties. To follow chronology we would have to begin with the first Treaty of Basel, signed with Prussia on April 5, 1795, then follow the negotiations with Holland that culminated in the "Treaty of The Hague" of May 16, and conclude with the second Treaty of Basel between France and Spain (July 22). But the logic of the Revolution was not determined by calendar dates. Between Holland and Prussia there was a radical difference: on the one hand a *diktat*, a veritable protectorate, on the other an agreement, not without misgivings, between two powers.

The Treaty of The Hague scarcely deserves its name. France dictated its conditions. The once "United Provinces" had been disunited for nearly two centuries, well before July 14, 1789, by the struggle between the stadtholder and liberal bourgeois forces. In 1788 Prussian armies had invaded Holland in support of the stadtholder. In fact, Holland was riven not so much by internal dissension as by its place in the international arena. A key element in English commerce, it covered the French border. The Scheldt was an essential base for Great Britain but a barrier for France. From 1793 to 1795 the Dutch nation had suffered the consequences of the military situation. On February 16, 1795, the Dutch proclaimed the independence of the "Batavian nation" and expressed the wish that they might establish between themselves and France a relation of "sister republics." This was a utopian dream. Sieyès and Reubell were sent to The Hague to remind the Batavians of the conditions of fraternity. With the "treaty" signed on May 16, 1795, France annexed Dutch Flanders (the region of Maestricht and Vanloo) and forced its younger sister to accept occupation by an army of twenty-five thousand men and a tribute of one hundred million florins, to say nothing of the innumerable paintings that found their way to Paris. The two republics were united by a defensive and offensive alliance.

A product of circumstances, the Treaty of The Hague did not count for

151

much in either the history of the Revolution or the history of Holland. It signified a temporary pause in the long struggle between England and France. The idea, cherished by Sieyès, of creating a belt of (junior) sister republics around revolutionary France succumbed to geographical and historical realities. Napoleon made those realities quite clear by establishing a kingdom for his brother, Louis Bonaparte, in Holland.

*
**

With Spain—the Spain of Goya—the dispute was more serious. There were dynastic obligations: Charles IV was a Bourbon and, despite the treaties of Utrecht, he never forgot the bonds of cousinhood that attached him to the House of France. In March 1793 republican France had declared war on Spain, which thus, somewhat against its will, joined the coalition. There had been no territorial dispute between the two countries since Roussillon had been incorporated into France. In September 1794 General Dugommier, who commanded the army of the Eastern Pyrenees, had driven the Spanish from Bellegarde, the last fortress they occupied in France. His troops also entered Catalonia. Godoy, seeking negotiations, sent him a letter and an olive branch. After Dugommier's death, his successor, Pérignon, advanced into Spanish territory, taking Rosas on February 3, 1795. Moncey took Bilbao. Negotiations dragged on owing to the insane hopes of the Spanish Bourbons. Their diplomats in Basel proposed the establishment of a kingdom between France and Spain to be ruled by "Louis XVII" (held prisoner in the Temple). For the Republic the idea of surrendering a kinglet who might one day demand restoration of royal power in France was out of the question. But France wanted peace with Spain, first of all so that it might redeploy the armies that were engaged in the Pyrenees. Then Augereau could use his Basque contingents to reinforce the army of Italy. In addition, France wanted peace because the Spanish colonial empire and the extent of coastline controlled by Madrid in both Europe and America might have served as a major trump card in the conflict with France's principal enemy, England. But for that consideration, France would have had to make sure of Portugal, and Napoleon would have exhausted himself in the effort. Ultimately the treaty was signed in Basel on July 22. Spain ceded half of Santo Domingo to the Republic, and France agreed to evacuate the occupied portions of Catalonia and the Basque regions. The only winner was Godoy, who was made "prince of peace."

Negotiations with Prussia took on tremendous importance for two reasons. In eighteenth-century French foreign policy, Prussia had been a very important prize. The existence of the Prussian state as a counter to the Hapsburg empire, just as important as the belt of northern and eastern states from Denmark and Poland to Ottoman Turkey, had been a consistent focus of French diplomatic interest. The Revolution inherited from the monarchy a dual tradition, momentarily interrupted in 1756 by Louis XV. The shift of alliances, which led to a break with the state of Frederick II and to entente with Maria Theresa's Austria, was interpreted as a mistake by many observers. The two-centuries old rivalry between the Hapsburgs and the Bourbons, the obsession with the empire of Charles V, memories of Pavia and the Treaty of Madrid, and the presence at Versailles of the "Austrian" Marie Antoinette all contributed to France's banking on Prussia. As late as 1797 Reubell wrote: "I detest Austria, and I take the most active interest in the prosperity of Prussia." At the same time, however, the revolutionaries were attached to the security line constituted by northern and eastern Europe, especially Poland. Strategic interests combined with sympathies inherited from the past. When negotiations began with Prussia, Eschassériaux mounted the podium of the Convention on November 9, 1794, to ask: "Are we going to negotiate with Prussia at a time like this in order to give her the means to shift to Poland the troops that she now has on the Rhine?" What is more, Prussian policy was reputed in France to be dishonest and Machiavellian. But if the goal was to isolate Austria, negotiation with Prussia was the only way.

For Prussia there was no escaping the need to withdraw from the coalition. True, King Frederick William was loath to treat with regicides and even less inclined to enter into the alliance sought by the Committee of Public Safety. His cabinet and entourage were divided between hawks and doves. Hardenberg favored a policy of firmness toward France. Haugwitz suggested postponing surrender of the left bank of the Rhine until the general peace treaty and leaving the fate of that area's Prussian possessions, which were territorially of little importance, in suspense. Prince Henry ("Citizen Henry" as Catherine II disdainfully called him) favored an entente with France. The Polish question turned out to be decisive. After the failure of the Prussian armies to take Warsaw, and following the entry into the war of Suvorov's Cossacks, Austria and Russia signed, on January 3, 1795, the Treaty of Saint Petersburg, which erased Poland from the map of Europe. The treaty was kept secret, but the Russian minister Alopeus revealed its main points to the Prussian ministers. Since the French were masters of Holland, the Prussians were threatened with not receiving anything from anyone. They were therefore obliged to acquire German territories through negotiations with France and, using provisions of that treaty, to demand compensations in Poland. Barthélemy, who played the role of a veritable minister of foreign affairs for the Republic, wrote from Basel after his arrival on January 12: "I think that the king of Prussia will make peace. It will be up to us to grant it to him, but let us renounce the idea of making him play a grand role. He will never understand such language. He will easily compensate himself at the expense of Poland and the German princes for what he will lose on the left bank of the Rhine. He will move toward us only when fear of Russian progress forces him to do so" (report of February 1). But Barthélemy was trapped between his own clear vision and the instructions he had received from Paris: settle for the left bank of the Rhine, indemnify the dispossessed princes through division of ecclesiastical territories on the right bank. By this means, "authorized by the Treaty of Westphalia and imperiously prescribed by the enlightenment of the century," the king of Prussia would be able to constitute an alliance in northern Germany that would establish a new equilibrium in the Empire: a seductive allusion to the aims of Frederick II and a prefiguration of what would much later become the policy of Bismarck. Barthélemy was obliged to tell his counterparts that "the Republic regards the Rhine as its natural boundary, which it is determined to maintain." He believed nothing of the kind. To Harnier, a Prussian emissary, he declared in the final days of November 1794 that there were two parties in the Convention: one that wished to "unify" all the territories up to the Rhine, the other, loyal to the Constitution, holding that the Republic ought to renounce all conquest and establish "a beautiful chain of fortresses" along the old boundaries. He added: "I would be of that opinion."

Frederick William's instructions to Count von Goltz, sent to Basel in December 1794, aimed in a different direction: an alliance with France was out of the question, and a definitive treaty would depend on a decision by the Imperial Diet. With Goltz out of the picture, it was Hardenberg who negotiated with Barthélemy at Basel. The treaty was signed on the night of 15–16 Germinal (April 4–5, 1795). For the Republic it was a half-success. Prussia recognized the French occupation of the left bank of the Rhine until a general treaty was signed. But it refused to enter an alliance and obtained neutralization of northern Germany. French opinion was favorable: was this not the first time that a great power had recognized the Republic? But as long as Austria—and behind it the enormous power of Russia—as well as England remained at war, nothing would be settled.

The Directory did not give up the dream of an alliance with Prussia easily. In August 1798 it sent Sieyès on a special mission to Berlin. He was received coolly, and his negotiations ended in failure. Why would the Hohenzollerns trade their freedom of maneuver for an alliance that looked like vassalage?

Denis Richet

FURTHER READING

Fugier, André. *La Révolution française et l'empire napoléonien*, vol. 4, in Pierre Renouvin, ed. *Histoire des relations internationales*. Paris, 1954.

Sorel, Albert. *L'Europe et la Révolution française*, vol. 4. Paris, 1904.

Vivenot, Alfred Ritter von. *Quellen zur Geschichte der deutschen Kaiserpolitik Oesterreichs während der französischen Revolutionskriege, 1791–1801*, vol. 4. N.p., 1890.

RELATED TOPICS

Natural Borders   Sieyès

VARENNES

The flight to Varennes is one of the episodes of the Revolution whose fascination has proved most durable, as evidenced recently by the filmmaker Ettore Scola and the scholar Georges Dumézil, haunted by the image of the "black monk in gray within Varennes" in the prophecy of Nostradamus, supposedly a reference to the fleeing king disguised in the gray livery of a valet. The sources of this fascination are not difficult to understand. Varennes has a marvelous script, complete with emotionally charged situation (the nation holds its breath, waiting for news of whether the king's escape has succeeded or failed), unity of time (five days separate the clandestine departure, nocturnal and joyful, from the public return, by daylight and full of shame), and unity of place (the cramped quarters of the royal berlin, which the returning royal family must share with the enemy). Upon this simple plot a lush variety of episodes have been embroidered, some dramatic, some romantic, others merely prosaic. The result is that Varennes is a story made not for Racine but for Shakespeare, at once tragedy, farce, romance, and enigma.

The drama stems from the magnitude of the stakes: had the escape succeeded, it would have changed not only the fate of those involved (for everyone in the berlin, except the royal children and their governess, would end at the guillotine) but also the phases of the Revolution and the destinies of France. It also stems from the breathtaking alternation of hope and despair (the expedition, which begins well, ends in disaster) and the violent contrasts of the *mise en scène*. One can dream about this runaway king, as gray as the night into which he melted, as undistinguished as the emblematic last name under which he chose to travel: Durand. Or about the prosaic encounter that decided his fate, a meeting with an "obscure postmaster's son, standing idly one night by a village gate" (Lamartine's vivid sketch of Drouet). Or about the respectful violence done to the king by a candle-seller, the *procureur syndic* of Varennes, who refused to release the monarch without express orders from the Assembly. Or about the exhausting return trip, during which Ancien Régime and Revolution sat side by side in the overheated berlin, Barnave squeezed between Louis XVI and Marie Antoinette, while Mme. Royale shifted from Pétion's knees to Mme. Elisabeth's. Or about the waves of people who surrounded the slowing coach, waves swollen by troops described by Pétion as "old men, women, and children, some armed with picks and scythes, others with clubs, sabers, and battered muskets," who "went as to a wedding." Or, finally, about the most impressive of revolutionary processions as it traveled across Paris, packed with silent crowds: this time it was not the remains of a great man being transported to the Pantheon, bound for immortality, but rather a diminished king, already doomed by what Michelet called "the ex-

155

communication of silence," being returned to the Tuileries by a suspicious people.

Nor did this tragic and burlesque tale lack for romantic embellishment. The whole operation originated with the amorous devotion of Fersen. There was also the romance invented, with Don Juanish ingenuity, by the impetuous Pétion, convinced by a glance at Mme. Elisabeth that "if by magic everyone had disappeared, she would have fallen into my arms and abandoned herself to nature's impulse." Finally, there was the understanding supposedly reached by Marie Antoinette and Barnave, a pact sufficiently explained by political calculation but subtly modified by sentiment: esteem on her side ("Barnave is very good") and on his the excitement of success with an unhappy queen.

Finally, Varennes has remained a historical enigma. The fact that the protagonists in this abortive expedition left memoirs intended to justify or absolve them has in no small way helped to obscure what happened. Even today one can still wonder about the nature of the event. Was it a plan hatched over a long time or a last-minute decision? Was it the queen's idea or the king's? Or were there two plans, clumsily merged? The escape plan was old: traces can be found as early as October 1790 in a first-hand account by the marquis de Bouillé, who was charged with making military preparations, and as early as November in the secret correspondence between Marie Antoinette and her brother the emperor. Between that autumn and the following spring there was time enough for the plan to be modified many times as the situation evolved and in light both of the monarchs' distrust of the émigrés and of the hesitation of the king, who at first showed no enthusiasm for the project. That reluctance is grounds for attributing the plan to Marie Antoinette alone, as many historians have done. It is true that her correspondence is the principal source of information concerning the Varennes affair and that there is little testimony coming directly from the king. It is also true that contemporaries themselves speculated about two different policies in the royal couple, as is shown by Bouillé's insistence on having a note in the king's own hand before going ahead with the project. The note leaves no doubt about Louis XVI's participation in the escape, but it also indicates his wish to modify the plan: the king was willing to leave Paris but insisted on remaining in France, and he was sufficiently conscious of public opinion that he rejected the itinerary proposed by Bouillé because it involved passing through a foreign country. Nevertheless, it is impossible to say exactly what part each sovereign played in the preparations. It is probable, in any case, that the crisis of April, when the crowd prevented Louis XVI from leaving the Tuileries for Saint-Cloud, overcame any lingering doubts in the king's mind.

The conditions of the escape also remain mysterious. We do not know exactly what complicity there was inside the Tuileries. Nevertheless, we can identify the reasons for the failure. Contrary to what has often been written, the escape was not that poorly planned; those in the know faithfully kept the secret; the passport was in order; the berlin, far from flaunting the astounding luxury that Sébastien Mercier mocked as "an abbreviated Versailles," was an ordinary carriage; and the only obvious blunder was that the postilions wore the gold-buttoned livery of the prince de Condé.

The schedule, however, was not worked out in sufficiently meticulous detail. First of all, the departure had to be put off until June 20 (the date initially planned was June 19) to allow time to get rid of a chambermaid whom Marie Antoinette judged to be an "enraged democrat." This delay, further aggravated by a departure at two in the morning rather than midnight, was to have serious consequences. The troops assembled by the marquis de Bouillé (chosen for the iron hand he had displayed in putting down the Nancy mutinies), forced to mark time as a result of the delay, soon aroused anxious suspicions along the route. The agitation of people in towns along the way led to the defection of Choiseul, who commanded what was to have been the first support detachment en route. Worried by the lateness of the royal coach, Choiseul made three errors: he dispersed his troops, sent orders to relays down the line to unsaddle their horses, and himself abandoned the most direct route, thereby forgoing whatever chance he had of meeting up with the king. Hence the monarch never saw the detachments that were supposed to be awaiting him at Pont-de-Sommevesle and Sainte-Menehould. At the latter stop, however, he did encounter Drouet, out enjoying the cool air of a June evening, who, suspicions aroused, sought and obtained orders from the municipal council to pursue the berlin.

From that moment on the royal entourage was on the road to disaster. A second hitch came at Clermont-en-Argonne: here the king did indeed meet up with his dragoons, but once again the municipality intervened. Although it allowed the berlin to depart, it forbade the detachment to escort it. Finally the king came to Varennes. Bouillé made the mistake—treasonous, some say—of placing the relay beyond the bridge rather than before it. This gave Drouet time to raise the alarm, bar the bridge, hold the king at the home of the grocer Sauce, and wait for the courier from the National Assembly sent out that morning in pursuit of the royal carriage.

Like so many grains of sand strewn by chance on the road to Varennes, none of these things would have been enough to stop the escape had there not been, surrounding all the soldiers, carriages, and teams of horses, a population alert enough to interpret the movements of the troops (whose lack of aggressiveness was yet another cause contributing to the failure) and to comment on the passage of the carriages. There was no need even to call upon the clubs and popular societies, notoriously absent from the episode. The regular institutions established by the Revolution were enough: first, a small, patriotic municipality made the totally illegal decision to halt a convoy on suspicion that the king might be part of it; and then a *procureur syndic,* one of the most moderate of the lot and quite unwilling to compromise himself, held the king, who by this point had been duly identified. Everywhere along a road to Varennes "haunted," in the words of Louis Blanc, "by the phantom of emigration," we can make out, in the background behind the principal players, the presence of a collective actor, now awake and active: this element, too, accounts for the charge that envelops the event.

The news of the king's departure struck the National Assembly like a thunderbolt. It could not have come at a worse time for the majority, then in the midst of an effort to "establish the Revolution," as Duport had said in May, and revise the Constitution in a moderate direction. The "triumvirs" Barnave, Duport, and Lameth, who had hated Mirabeau, nevertheless inherited his place in the king's councils and adopted his policy. That policy was singularly complicated by the event, since the king's flight, long predicted in radical broadsides, provided the left with the satisfaction of prophecy and the occasion to up the ante.

What Varennes called into question, in effect, was the very heart of the Constitution, the dualist conception of sovereignty. Not that conflicts between the two powers had waited for Varennes to surface. But the Constituent Assembly had deliberately avoided dealing with them. To that end it had conceived the metaphor of a "religious" or "respectful" veil that, it held, ought to be thrown over the respective positions of the two powers. That veil had already snagged on several thorny issues, however. In February and March 1791 the Assembly had even envisaged a possibility suddenly given substance by the king's flight: Should the king be punished if he entered his own kingdom at the head of a foreign army? Lameth had concluded the debate by linking the king's immunity to the performance of his duties, thus pledging the nation's loyalty only to the "king of the Constitution." The decree of March 28, according to which the king could be assumed to have abdicated his throne if he left the kingdom and did not return when summoned by the legislature, confirmed that in the eyes of the Assembly the nation could determine not only the limits of the king's power but its very existence.

The unprecedented situation created by Varennes rent the veil completely. How could the Assembly now avoid considering the very existence of the king's powers? How could it pretend that he was still the king of the Constitution? The deputies' first idea, given their uncertainty about the outcome of the escape attempt and the intentions of monarchical Europe, was to disguise the king's flight as an "attack on his person by the enemies of the public welfare." Born in Lafayette's entourage, first stated by Beauharnais (at that time president of the Assembly), and adopted by Le Chapelier and Lameth, the fiction of the king's abduction—rather soberly set out in the Assembly but much embellished by the time it reached the départements—made it possible to stand firm on the structure of the Constitution. The left had no great difficulty ridiculing this fiction since it was not long before the discovery was made of a manifesto foolishly left behind by the king, a long litany of complaints including an explicit disavowal of the Constitution and a list of the motives for a departure designed to restore his liberty. The address to the French people read by Démeunier in the name of the Assembly therefore had to minimize not only the king's escape but also the import of this document, "wrested prior to the departure from the misguided king."

Thus, the all but untenable thesis of the king's abduction (Robespierre asked "whether nations today are prepared to believe that people abduct kings as they abduct women") was replaced by the notion of a misguided king, a moral kidnapping, an updated version of the hoary myth of a hapless monarch led astray by evil advisers. The official version of the "Committee of Inquiry and Investigation into the Events Surrounding the Escape of the

King and the Royal Family" illogically combined both theses and pointed the finger of blame at the providential scapegoat Bouillé. The gist of the argument was that the king, misled by Bouillé, intended only to leave Paris, not to cross the border—a version of the facts that would have exempted him from the consequences of the March 28 decree. That report might have been the end of the case had it not raised a host of related issues that would force the Constituent Assembly, like it or not, to ponder the nature of constitutional monarchy, the Constitution itself, and even the meaning of the Revolution.

A seemingly minuscule problem led to the debate over the nature of the monarchy, a veritable dress rehearsal for the trial to come. The issue was over who would hear the king's crucial "declarations" concerning the event: the Assembly or a judicial hearing? The left insisted on a formal judicial hearing; the case involved Louis XVI the individual, not the king: "At the time and in the case concerned [the king] was a citizen." (A year later, Robespierre, the author of this definition, would argue instead that the trial of a king is a political, not a judicial, act.) Pétion, going even further, insisted that the king was a "corporeal being" upon whom "one may inflict a punishment." The "inviolability" of this concrete individual was contradicted, moreover, both by the facts (the Assembly was so little persuaded by the king's immunity that it had immediately seized control of executive authority) and by a case based on the royal manifesto: How could a Constitution that the king had violated guarantee his inviolability? The Constitution, said Grégoire, could not be invoked in his favor. It had to be granted that even if the king enjoyed a certain immunity under the law, it was for "acts associated with royalty," a fiction that posed no danger, according to Brissot, since such acts had to be countersigned by ministers; he could not claim any immunity whatsoever for private acts. "Being king," Buzot summed up in a lapidary phrase, "makes one no less a man."

The majority of the Assembly did its best to resist this distinction between the king's two bodies, which left one of them subject to judgment and therefore to eventual punishment. The king was not a citizen but a power unto himself, in whom it was impossible to distinguish between the function and the individual. To be sure, a king found to be demented could be replaced by a regent. In no case, however, could he be heard by judges. Fortified by such arguments, the Assembly therefore decided that it would hear the royal declarations itself.

In the meantime, however, it was also obliged to throw a powerful light on the nature of royal power. "You have placed the king," Duport said, "in a separate class of citizens, in a position in which his individual and political character are united" and, Salle added, "outside the natural state of things." Had it been possible, La Rochefoucauld-Liancourt observed, "they would have made him eternal." The strength of the "constitutionals" in the debate was to show that this extravagant fiction was for the best. From Muguet de Nanthou, secretary of the investigating committee, to Duport and Barnave, a majority attempted to save the work on the Constitution by invoking utility and alluding to the factional dissension that would arise from the slightest attempt to tamper with the king's inviolability: allusion was made to disturbances in England and Russia, and during the minority of Louis XIV in order to justify an unconditional and purely functional definition of inviolability. Such a definition would be workable only if the emotional bonds between nation and king were severed, and this Barnave endeavored to do with great lucidity, for if a king's questionable behavior could shake the faith of citizens to the point where they wished to see him dethroned, laudable behavior might equally well cause them to wish for tyranny. Royalty is therefore justified only by absolute indifference to the personal merits of the king. The flight to Varennes was a godsend, an unhoped-for opportunity to demonstrate that an intellectually and morally bankrupt king was precisely what a constitutional monarchy needed. Legally this argument was impeccable, but politically it was weak: once the king was reduced to such an abject role, how could he stand above other citizens? How could he even continue to be the paternal and beneficent king of 1789 (an image still cherished in the royal manifesto)? What was the point, moreover, of persuading a merely functional king to accept "sincerely" the new Constitution—the now paradoxical wish of the majority? All the themes of the king's trial were here in a nutshell, even if the sides were reversed, for Robespierre in 1792 would speak the same language as Duport in 1791.

Nor could the Assembly further postpone consideration of its own powers and of a legitimacy disputed by both right and left. On one side, in order to save the king, a challenge was raised to the notion that the will of the nation was embodied in the Assembly; it was in the *cahiers*, which obviously did not contain an appropriate strict mandate. On the other side, in order to judge the king, questions were raised as to the Assembly's capacity to sit as judge in its own case, and calls were therefore heard for a Convention. Between these two interpretations, the majority, which would not and could not separate its fate from that of the king, clung to the status quo. It is interesting, however, to see how doubts sown during the debate contributed to the Constituent Assembly's unenthusiastic approval in May of a measure prohibiting incumbents from being reelected to the next Assembly. Varennes made everyone keenly aware of the need for a new deal; by standing aside, in an unprecedented show of humility, in order to make way for a true legislative power, for a constituted rather than constituting authority, the Constituent Assembly presided over the birth of an entirely new legislature. The hope was that this new legislature would coincide with the emergence of a new king, at last convinced that his power would not be disputed. In other words, the hope was for a twofold regeneration capable of erasing the unfortunate event from memory.

Finally, behind the whole debate that grew out of Varennes emerged a new conception of the Revolution itself. Those who had been attempting for months to prove that, in the words of Duport on May 17, "what is called the Revolution is over" now looked, implausibly enough, to the royal escape for an argument in their favor. Before Varennes, the king's position, known according to La Rochefoucauld-Liancourt to "all Europe," was not the position of a constitutional monarch but the consequence of a revolutionary situation. What was missing? "That the king, situated outside Paris, should be able to return to the capital with the complete freedom and dignity of a constitutional king." Varennes was an escape not from Paris but from the revolutionary situation, a clumsy yet effective way of "halting" the Revolution. This was the view of Barnave, the principal voice in this debate. Barnave's case was both general and particular: revolutions can be ended, and this particular revolution had reached its end. This theory was both a matter of fact—everything that was to be destroyed had been destroyed—and of anticipation: if the Revolution were unfortunate enough to take another step "in the line of liberty," royalty would be done for; another step "in the line of equality" and property would be done for, too. The strength of Barnave, who more effectively made the same case that Duport had argued in May, was that he was able to link the fate of property to that of the monarchy and thus make people aware of the link between the republican and the egalitarian dynamic. His policy was to declare that the latter could be halted. His failure was that he did not manage to do so.

On July 15, 1791, however, it was possible to believe that the job had been done. Barnave's eloquence, which had already saved Lafayette on June 23, was decisive in persuading a majority of deputies to accept the report of the Committee, to find only Bouillé and his accomplices guilty of any crime, to exculpate the sovereigns, and to maintain the constitutional monarchy. The Assembly even decided not to circulate an official version of the event in the form of an address to the French nation out of fear "that it would encourage a sentiment of doubt, uncertainty, and controversy." The former left, which had combatted Mirabeau but which now occupied the center of the political arena, seemed to have circumvented the divorce between king and nation.

Obviously this truce was an illusion. At the very moment the Assembly was placing the royal person beyond reach, the Cordeliers began circulating a petition calling for a Republic. The manifesto had been drafted by Robert, who had just reprinted his work on a republicanism tailored to the needs of France with, thanks to Varennes, a new subtitle: "Advantages of the flight of Louis XVI and necessity of a new government." The Republic had in fact been carefully kept out of the Assembly debate by the left itself; from Robespierre to Pétion and Vadier (who hazarded the soon-to-become-popular image of a "crowned brigand" but who nevertheless insisted that he detested the Republic), the Assembly banished all thought of the ancient republics and even recoiled at the word. But the Republic found champions outside the Assembly. Brissot offered lukewarm support in issues of the *Patriote français,* and Condorcet at the *Cercle Social* boldly questioned the utility of the king, the centerpiece of the moderate argument. The progress of reason, Condorcet argued, had discredited the notion of monarchy's usefulness: "We are no longer in the time when one dared count among the means of securing the power of kings that impious superstition that made a man into a kind of divinity." This new political language caught the ear of certain départemental administrations and clubs. In the Jacobin Club, however, it ran up against the subtlety of Robespierre, who was determined not to raise the regime issue. It was among the Cordeliers, who congratulated themselves on "being free and kingless," that the idea of taking a republican petition to the Champ de Mars took shape. The petition of July 16, which became illegal after the Assembly voted to maintain Louis XVI, still bore traces of Orleanism. On July 17 it gave way to a more energetic version, which criticized the deputies for stalling and called for judgment of the king. After incidents in which things got out of hand, the National Guard of Lafayette and Bailly fired on the crowd of unarmed petitioners beneath the red flag of martial law, which became the emblem of the first divorce between the militia of the Revolution and the revolutionary people.

Despite the Assembly's efforts to dress things up, Varennes thus exploded the unity of the Revolution, and the resulting cracks were visible everywhere: in the clubs, the country, and the Assembly itself. In the patriotic societies the aftermath of the Champ de Mars turned things upside down. The Cordeliers were shut down; Danton was forced to flee, Desmoulins to halt publication of his newspaper. The Jacobins, unable either to disavow the Cordeliers or to follow them, split. Slightly over three hundred deputies emigrated to the convent next door, a topographical shift that symbolized a political one. The schism between Jacobins and Feuillants was initially to the advantage of the latter, whose ranks were swelled by the vast majority of constitutional deputies led by the triumvirs and their friends, while at the Jacobin Club a handful of loyal deputies closed ranks around Pétion and Robespierre. The first Feuillant victory lay in preceding the Jacobins in drafting the petition that was supposed to inform the provincial societies of the official version of events. The great majority of the societies were hesitant at first, but seventy-two of them joined the Feuillants in the first two weeks of the schism while only fifteen supported the Jacobins. This triumph was short-lived, however, for by the end of July the return to the mother-society had begun. The Jacobins were acknowledged to have a more efficient network of correspondence, the loyalty of most of the newspapers to which the provincial societies subscribed, and the finesse of Robespierre and Pétion. By the time the Constituent Assembly disbanded, the Jacobin network had been not only patched up but expanded.

The king's flight left visible traces in the political geography, traces that can be evaluated through study of letters of congratulation sent to the valiant municipality of Varennes as well as numbers of volunteers for the National Guard, which had been urged to form battalions to head for the borders. By either measure we find a striking contrast between urban France and rural France (the latter not well informed and in any case viscerally opposed to any kind of militia); and we also find a contrast between central and western France, still faithful to the monarchy, and eastern and southern France, from the Moselle to the Mediterranean, which had consciously turned against it.

In the Assembly, finally, the break between moderates and ultras on both sides was consummated. The right, by refusing to endorse the suspension of an inviolable king, had directly brought about an emigration to abstention. The democrats, despite persecution of their leaders, owing to the shock of Varennes gained the support of a small number of deputies. Hence the majority was left with limited room to maneuver. The reform of the Constitution (accepted by the king on September 15 and coupled with an amnesty that pleased the accused in both the Varennes and the Champ de Mars affairs) lacked the desired scope: the majority, which would have liked to strike the Civil Constitution of the Clergy from the Constitution, a measure that would have made revision possible, was ultimately obliged to put it back in. The revised constitution nevertheless attempted to satisfy that instinctive need for "tranquillity," which Barnave, well before Constant, deemed more imperious than the need for liberty. The *cens* was increased in order to purge the electorate, as Barnave once again explained, of "extreme poverty," which carried with it a risk of corruption, but to make up for this the *marc d'argent* was no longer required for eligibility. Election remained a duty and not a right, however, and was restricted to the "middling class of fortunes," a formula that anticipated the *doctrinaires*. In opposition to the left, which argued that a hereditary king could not *will* for the nation, the Constitution emphasized the king's representative character. Thouret and Barnave sought to prove that even if the king does not "represent" the nation in the strict sense of the word, he "wills" for it in exercising the right of sanction, and as first citizen he represents its "majesty." One has the sense that by reintroducing "grandeur," they were attempting, not without difficulty, to correct the functional argument—which deprived the executive of dignity and moral consistency—even though they had used that argument themselves. Setting up a representative king opposite a representative Assembly seemed to be the only way to keep the two equivalent in status and thus avoid the dreaded issue of the relative power of the two branches. The text, moreover, restored to the king the right to grant pardon, the suspensive veto, and the right to propose laws and granted him the new right to have his proposals defended by ministers in the Assembly. The revision, as Barnave did his utmost to explain to Marie Antoinette, ought to have delighted the king. He could savor the enormous superiority that would accrue to him by virtue of his permanence in office. A legislature lasted no more than two years, so that it "would be enveloped, before, during, and after its formation, by the royal influence."

Barnave's pedagogical zeal reveals both the acuity of his diagnosis and the weakness of his therapy. In order to ensure survival of the alliance between constitutional monarchy and popular sovereignty, just sealed by renewal of the king's oath and hailed by popular ovation, the king would have to accept his role, but in fact he continued to negotiate with the powers. The nation, however, would also have to accept this king, and the fact was that the king who had been brought back from Varennes had nothing in common with the king who had been brought back from Versailles in October 1789, whose mere presence in Paris everyone at the time, including Marat, had hoped would alter the situation. The king of Varennes, as Lamartine wrote, was an "amnestied king," in whom Europe saw only an "escapee from the throne brought back to face punishment, [and] the people only a traitor and the plaything of the Revolution." Varennes illustrates the pathetic effort of the men of the Revolution to soften, efface, and if possible deny the event, yet it also demonstrates the disruptive force of that event, which set the Revolution in motion once again: proof that, contrary to the wishes of Barnave, the "political machine" was not yet in place and that the never-ending task of ending the Revolution continued.

Mona Ozouf

FURTHER READING

Barnave, Antoine-Pierre-Joseph-Marie. *Oeuvres,* 4 vols., published by Alphonse-Marc-Marcellin-Thomas Bérenger de la Drôme. Paris, 1843.

Barnave and Marie-Antoinette. *Marie-Antoinette et Barnave, correspondance secrète (juillet 1791–janvier 1792),* edition compiled by Alma Söderhjelm. Paris, 1934.

Chevallier, Jean-Jacques. *Barnave ou les deux faces de la Révolution, 1761–1793.* Paris, 1936.

Duclos, Pierre. *La notion de constitution dans l'oeuvre de l'Assemblée Constituante de 1789.* Paris, 1932.

Pétion de Villeneuve, Jérôme. *Mémoires inédits.* Paris, 1866.

Reinhard, Marcel. *La fuite du roi.* Paris, 1958.

RELATED TOPICS

Barnave

Blanc

Civil Constitution of the Clergy

Condorcet

Constant

Feuillants

Jacobinism

King's Trial

Lafayette

Louis XVI

Marat

Marie Antoinette

Michelet

Mirabeau

Republic

Revolutionary Assemblies

Robespierre

VENDÉE

The Vendée war (March–December 1793) was the longest and bloodiest of the civil disturbances that characterized the year 1793. It was also the most symbolic conflict, because it pitched Revolution and Ancien Régime against each other in open country. The Civil Constitution of the Clergy had witnessed confrontation between the camp of oath-taking priests and the camp of refractories. The federalist revolt of June–July 1793 aroused the bourgeoisie of the Girondin cities against the dictatorship of Paris. But what began in March of that same year was a war in which armies—one composed of soldiers flying the flag of the Republic, the other composed of the peasant population of Vendée under the banner of God and king—would soon test each other. These antagonistic emblems would survive the fury of combat and fill memoirs after having flown on battlefields; the Ancien Régime had its martyrs, whose testimony the Revolution has continually sought to conjure away.

The revolt began in March as a refusal to submit to conscription. To reinforce the Republic's military manpower, the Convention voted in February to approve a levy of three hundred thousand men, to be chosen by lot among the unmarried men in each commune. The arrival of recruiters, a reminder of the methods of the monarchy, aroused resistance nearly everywhere in the countryside and even the first signs of sedition, quickly put down. But the situation took a particularly serious turn south of the lower Loire in the Mauges and the Vendean *bocage*. In the first days of March, in Cholet, a large textile town located at the boundary between the two regions, youths from the surrounding communes, including both peasants and weavers, invaded the town and killed the commander of the National Guard, a "patriotic" manufacturer. A week later the violence had spread to the western fringe of the *bocage* in the Breton marshes: the small town of Machecoul was overrun by peasants on March 10–11, and several hundred "patriots" were massacred. To the north, near the Loire, a large band of peasants under the leadership of Cathelineau and Stofflet seized Saint-Florent-le-Vieil.

On March 19 a small republican army of three thousand men, on its way from La Rochelle to Nantes, was scattered by the attack of a rural band at Pont-Chassault in Vendée. The revolt had turned into an insurrection. Geographically this conflict was confined to a quadrilateral that is impossible to describe in terms of the usual administrative subdivisions, since it comprised parts of the *généralités* of Poitiers and Tours (to use the nomenclature of the Ancien Régime) or the départements of Maine-et-Loire, Loire Infé-rieure, Vendée, and Deux-Sèvres (to employ the terminology of the redistricting of 1790). The heart of the movement was in the Mauges and the *bocage,* a vast square some sixty miles on each side with Cholet at its center; the immediate periphery of this zone—especially to the west, in the Breton marshes between Montaigu and the sea—never fell completely under the control of the insurgents but passed back and forth from one camp to the other with the fortunes of battle.

The "military Vendée," which slipped completely from the control of Paris for a period of several months, had not been a region morally at odds with the rest of the nation in 1789; at least no trace of moral secession remains in the parishes' *cahiers de doléances,* which were "normally" hostile to seigneurial rights and reasonably reformist with respect to the courts and taxation. Hence it was not the fall of the Ancien Régime that aroused the population of the region against the Revolution but the reconstruction of the new regime: the new map of districts and départements, the administrative dictatorship of towns and cities, and above all the affair of the nonjuring priests, whose refusal to take an oath to the Constitution bestowed the name of God on the clandestine resistance and rewarded it with the active support of the refractory priests. Rebellion had first flared in August 1792 but had quickly been put down. In 1793, however, it was not the January regicide that triggered the insurrection but the return of forced conscription. Here is yet another sign that if the Vendean people inscribed God and king on their flags, they invested those inevitable symbols of their tradition with something other than simple regret for the Ancien Régime, whose death they had witnessed without sorrow.

But the Convention, faced with an insurrection of the people against the Revolution of the people, was unable to see in it anything other than a new indication, the gravest yet, of an "aristocratic plot" to restore the old world on the ruins of the Republic. On March 19 it approved a first decree providing for execution within twenty-four hours of any person caught with weapons in hand or wearing the white cockade. In its own way it also gave the insurrection its banner. Within the first two weeks the die was cast.

The "Whites" were a rather unusual army, a mob of some tens of thousands of peasants, weavers, and minor country notables called together by the village tocsin under the command of the "parish captain" and, once combat had begun, little disposed to venture far from home. The permanent core consisted of perhaps ten thousand men divided among the several Vendean armies, of which they formed the spearhead. Their weaponry was rudimentary, the best of it taken from the enemy. There was little or no cavalry, artillery was rare, and logistical support was nonexistent. Facing small republican units, the Vendean troops owed their summertime successes to their numbers more than to their technique or strategy. The Vendeans chose leaders, or, rather, sought them out, often among nobles who had retired to the region after serving in the king's army: Charette, d'Elbée, La Rochejaquelein, Lescure, Bonchamps. But Cathelineau was a wagoner at Pin-en-Mauges and Stofflet a game warden at Maulévrier. In all cases their authority was as precarious as its origins; with these generals appointed by their troops, command was mingled with persuasion. What is more, there were incessant rivalries among them, and the man elected commanding general (first Cathelineau, then d'Elbée, then La Rochejaquelein) never enjoyed genuine overall command. The "Superior Council" of the Vendée, established in the town of Chatillon-sur-Sèvre in the middle of the *bocage,* was no more successful. The council, in which the principal military leaders joined with a group of priests and royalist notables, functioned more as an ephemeral attempt at civil government, a restoration more symbolic than real of the institutions of old France.

On the ground the bulk of the troops belonged to the great "Catholic and Royal Army." Operating on the border between Poitou and Anjou, in the Mauges, it comprised in the best of times some forty thousand soldiers under the command of the insurrection's principal military leaders. To the south the army of the center, ten thousand strong, dominated the *bocage,* and on the western fringes Charette's bands never left the Breton marsh. By April the Mauges and the *bocage* were in the hands of the insurgents; villages and towns, deprived of regular garrisons of republican troops, fell without resistance. In the west Les Sables d'Olonne resisted, but in the east the cities bordering the insurgent quadrilateral were taken in May: Bessuire, Parthenay, Thouars, and on June 9 Saumur, where a small army of eight to ten thousand republicans was dislodged from its position by the Vendeans with help from counterrevolutionaries in the city. The insurgent leaders then decided to take Nantes, the rich bourgeois metropolis of the west, from which they planned to solicit the assistance of the English and the émigrés. But the city was vigorously defended. Charette's bands attacked prematurely from the south, and two days later, on June 24, Cathelineau's army lost the battle for the streets. Nantes remained in the hands of the Patriots.

During the summer, however, the Vendean armies, on occasion defeating ill-equipped and hastily assembled republican units, remained in control of "their" territory. Meanwhile, in Paris, the failures encouraged the Commune to increase its pressure, forcing the Committee of Public Safety to name as commander of the republican troops an unlikely leader, a sans-culotte activist and journeyman jeweler by the name of Rossignol. On August 1, on a motion by Barère, spokesman for the Mountain and the Committee, the Convention decreed the "destruction" of the Vendée. The order was to evacuate all patriotic civilians, whom the Republic would take it upon itself to feed while the insurgent region was transformed into a desert: burn the forests, raze houses, remove livestock, cut hedgerows—in short, treat the rebellious land as Louis XIV had demonstrated with the Palatinate.

This rhetoric of extermination gave free rein to the soldiers' ferocity and within a few months produced baleful results in the form of deliberate massacres; but it had no immediate effect on the incompetence of the leaders or the divisions within the leadership. In reality, the summer of 1793 saw the confrontation in the Vendée not of two armies but of isolated, disparate units; not of two commands but of carefully watched leaders almost more divided among themselves than united against the enemy; not of two forces but of two weaknesses. The Vendeans failed twice to capture Luçon. Unable to break out of their own backyard, they seemed invulnerable within it.

The situation did not change until September, with the arrival of the "Mayençais," the army that had survived the siege of Mainz and which the Convention now assigned, along with its two generals, Kléber and Marceau, to the Vendée. After a bungled first offensive, the Mayençais recaptured Cholet, at the heart of the insurrection, on October 17 and drove the remains of the Catholic and Royal Army to the north. This was the turning point of the war and the beginning of the end for the insurrection. Deprived of many of their leaders—Cathelineau died at Nantes while Lescure, d'Elbée, and Bonchamps were mortally wounded in the battle of Cholet—and forced to abandon their ephemeral kingdom, the Vendeans crossed the Loire. The idea, perhaps suggested by émigrés, of their new twenty-year-old supreme commander, La Rochejaquelein, was to join up at Granville with the English vessels that patrolled the Breton coast. This order led to an interminable march by a huge horde of Vendeans strung out over several miles and including common folk and people of means, soldiers and families, men, women, and children—some eighty thousand people in all, protected by thirty to forty thousand soldiers, who in passing attacked and looted the poorly defended cities of Le Mans, Laval, and Fougères, only to be thwarted in the end by Granville's high walls. After bloody battles at Pontorson, Antrain, and Dol, the Vendeans began a dramatic retreat, falling back on their home bastion in rain and the first frost of late autumn, and following the same route as on the way out: Fougères, Mayenne, Laval. Pushed back by early December to a position just outside Angers, they set out to the west and were crushed at Le Mans on December 13, one of the most dreadful days in this merciless conflict; the republicans gave no quarter, and the routed Vendean "army" left ten thousand dead on the field of battle. The survivors, hotly pursued by the enemy, were cut to pieces at Savenay just before Christmas. At the other end of the civil war battle zone, Charette was also tracked down in his Breton marsh during the same last two weeks of December, and his base on the island of Noirmoutier was taken on January 3.

The insurrection in the strict sense was over. Not that the fighting had stopped completely, but the surviving leaders, Charette and Stofflet, commanded little more than scattered bands, beating the bush and hard to distinguish from chouannerie in west Normandy and Brittany. It was at this point that General Turreau was sent to Vendée with orders to carry out the terrible decree of August 1 ordering the republican authorities to transform Vendée into a desert.

Even earlier Carrier had set an example in Nantes. Sent there in October, the Convention's representative, a fanatic in keeping with the spirit of the times and supported by the local sans-culottes, ordered numerous arrests, and those detained were joined in overcrowded prisons by captured Vendean soldiers. Carrier soon replaced the comparatively slow guillotine with executions by firing squad (without trial) and mass drownings in the Loire, using large barges that were loaded with suspects and then sunk in the middle of the river. Some ten thousand people were executed, four or five thousand of them by drowning. But Turreau's "infernal columns" were even better at this baleful business. In February 1794 they divided up rebel territory and proceeded to search and destroy. Trees were cut down, villages burned, livestock slaughtered, people murdered indiscriminately. This frenzy of destruction ravaged the area's patrimony of farms and homes and left more than a hundred thousand dead in whatever towns, villages, and hamlets the undisciplined troops happened upon. The dreadful business did not end until May. One consequence was to reignite and spread a residual guerrilla war, whereby the Vendée turned into chouannerie.

Stofflet, a refugee in the forests around Maulévrier, his starting point, and Charette, in his marshy western fief, remained in the field. After 9 Thermidor, the Convention abandoned the policy of repression and made overtures to the two leaders, who signed compromise armistices in February and May of 1795. The Vendée recognized the Republic.

The Republic agreed to accept the refractory priests and not to levy either troops or taxes for a period of ten years. But the two leaders quickly took up arms again when an émigré force attempted a landing at Quiberon in June. Armed by the English, Charette once again sought to incite coastal Vendée to rebel. The peasants were tired, however, and the comte d'Artois, who landed on the isle of Yeu during the summer, refused to commit himself and returned to England. Stofflet remained in the Mauges, supported only by guerrilla bands of mediocre quality. Against them the Revolution finally offered a free hand to an intelligent and moderate general: Hoche. By alternating between tolerance and severity, he sought to keep the population neutral and organized small, mobile units of a few thousand men to pursue the Vendean guerrillas. Stofflet was captured and shot in February 1796, Charette in March.

That was the end of the war, but it did not mark the Vendée's reconciliation with the Republic. Though prostrate, ravaged, and destroyed, the region continued to experience sporadic convulsions up to the time of the Consulate. With the Concordat Bonaparte deprived it of its affiliation with refractory Catholicism, yet he continued to keep an eye on the département, in which he created an imperial bastion at La Roche-sur-Yon. He was right to be wary. Vendée henceforth had an identity that separated it from the nation. It was a region apart, a different people.

The traveler who today visits what was once the military Vendée can see in the place of old churches razed by Turreau's young troopers vast nineteenth-century edifices, mostly graceless and invariably too large for the villages they serve. Rebuilt during the Restoration or the Ordre Moral period, the two high points of triumphant Catholicism, these temples exhibit memories of the insurrection transfigured by the subsequent century. With the return of the kings begins a new history, in which the Vendée stands for the profound essence of western France: sharecroppers, châteaux, and churches in which an interminable counterrevolution, alternately victorious and martyred (more often the latter than the former) yet indestructible, lives on. In part this history is real, because the département and its fringes (southern

Maine-et-Loire and Loire Inférieure, the western part of Deux-Sèvres) did rise up to drive out the Emperor in 1814 and 1815, responded again in 1832 to the duchesse de Berry's call to restore the legitimate king, and later, with the advent of universal suffrage, provided the most traditionalist elements of the right with their most loyal phalanxes of voters. Studies in electoral sociology invariably confirm the existence of a unique conservative tradition in the Vendée, a tradition associated with the formative event and, perhaps for that very reason (and notwithstanding what André Siegfried says in his celebrated *Tableau politique de la France de l'ouest*), more clerical than monarchist per se. In the period between the two world wars, for example, Marc Sangnier's social Catholicism made inroads in the region at the expense of the royalists, and the Action Française never established a foothold even before its condemnation by Rome in 1926.

But this history of Vendée after the Vendée is most of all a matter of the national political imagination, torn between the Ancien Régime and the Revolution. Nineteenth-century Frenchmen and Frenchwomen could not love both parts of their past at the same time: those who loved the Revolution detested the Ancien Régime, and those who longed for the Ancien Régime detested the Revolution. The Vendée was one of the central pieces in this two-dimensional world, which, being one of the world's poles, it helped crucially to structure and perpetuate. As a culture of peasants, priests, and nobles, it was the old society. As an insurrection against the Jacobin dictatorship, it was loyalty to tradition. Finally, through the hatred it aroused, it became the living image of the revolutionary curse. It ennobled the Ancien Régime by adding ingredients of which its inglorious end would otherwise have deprived it: popular fervor and the heroism of resistance.

In order to understand this symbolism, one must read the *Memoirs* of the marquise de La Rochejaquelein, who fought the whole terrible war at the side of her husband Lescure before taking as second husband a brother of the last supreme commander of the Catholic and Royal Army. As far as one can tell from the remembrances of this aristocratic lady, raised at the château of Versailles until October 1789 (when she was seventeen), Vendée was a felicitous Ancien Régime: a society of peasants and lords extraordinarily closely united in respect for the Christian virtues and the Church. When 1789 came, "the inhabitants of the *bocage* looked with fearful and sorrowful eyes on all the changes, which could only disturb their happiness and scarcely add to it. . . . Every day the peasants showed themselves to be more discontent with the new order of things and more loyal than the *gentilshommes*." This long-standing frustration, aggravated by the issue of the priests' oath in 1791 and radicalized after August 10 by the execution of the king and mass conscription, ultimately led to the great insurrection, which the marquise recounts, incidentally, with sensibility and talent. Her book, written during the Empire and published shortly after the legitimate king's return, set the tone for a long line of legitimist and clerical historiography, in which, through a marriage of throne and altar, a heroic tradition is restored to the nineteenth century, along with religious faith and popular approval. Today this historiography no longer touches on issues of national political significance, yet it retains, with the usual poetic charm of a great lost cause, a regional base and audience.

Opposing this history, the party of the Revolution for a long time grav- itated toward a formula used by Barère in speaking to the Convention: "the inexplicable Vendée." This peasant insurrection against a Revolution to emancipate peasants was indeed inexplicable, as was the alliance between the rural populace and their lords and priests against the proclamation of uni- versal equality, this ghost of the Ancien Régime reincarnated in opposition to that which had liberated the French people. Inexplicable, that is, unless one assumed that the people had been deceived and unwittingly manipulated by their enemies: this manipulation was the role of the nobles or the priests or both together. The marquise de La Rochejaquelein depicted the Vendean peasant as the brother of his lord in a feudal idyll to which the benediction of the Church lent an air of eternity. Republican historians also saw the peasant as immersed in the Ancien Régime, but in the sense of being an unconscious object of seigneurial oppression and clerical obscurantism, hemmed in by the narrow horizons of his sharecropper's plot in a region isolated from the rest of the country, a living illustration of the condemned past.

The greatest of all republican historians, Michelet, saw clearly that the revolt was entirely a peasant rebellion; he notes the refusal of conscription, the rural hatred of urban "gentlemen," and the absence of nobles from the March events as the upper classes waited to see what would happen. He has no difficulty refuting the "feudal" version of the insurrection, that of a people risen "under its clan chieftains" (*Histoire de la Révolution française*, book 10, chap. 5). But what he denies the château he gives to the presbytery. Mis- guided western France, trapped by its parochial spirit and divided from the new nation, was the work of priests operating behind the scenes, the product of a spiritual organization of the region by the Montfortian missions. The Vendean peasant was a dependent, half-savage creature, turned fanatic by the Church through the agency of women: "Women and priests: the whole Vendée is there, the whole civil war" (book 8, chap. 2). Between the confes- sional of the refractory priest and the poor sharecropper's marriage bed was hatched the great conspiracy that would send men—and often their wives as well—into the Catholic and Royal Army.

The idea of the political and moral dependency of the Vendean insur- gent vis-à-vis traditional authority was generally extended by republicans to include the power of nobles acting in common with the Church: this associa- tion was the result of an extrapolation into the past of local political conflicts of the nineteenth century, and it gave rise to an image of the Vendée as an inextricably clerical, aristocratic, and monarchist province, an isolated Ancien Régime preserve surviving in the midst of Third Republic France. This por- trait is the background to the great work of Quinet's friend Charles Louis Chassin, whose book, along with that of Célestin Port, an archivist himself and a historian highly skilled in sifting the départemental archives, is the great repository of republican historiography. The most fully developed ver- sion of this thesis may be found in the *Tableau politique de la France de l'ouest*, which appeared just before World War I. Based on electoral data from the cantons, André Siegfried drew a political and moral portrait of the Vendean countryside as a region closed to external influences and dominated by its castellans and curés. The priest remained "as in the past the peasant's true leader," but the nobility was the principal bulwark of the temporal hierarchy; this authority was the crucial difference between "this great region of the Ancien Régime type" (*Tableau politique,* p. 29) and the republican "plain" to the south, the one as different from the other as granite from limestone.

Modern historiography since World War II has retained this deterministic approach to the uniqueness of the Vendée in modern French history but has favored socioeconomic over geographic factors. Most important of all, it has abandoned the idea that the Vendée was nostalgic for the Ancien Régime and dominated by nobles and priests. Instead, it has sought to explain the autonomy of a relatively late popular insurrection against the Revolution. In fact, before becoming an insurgent in 1793, the Vendean peasant was favorable to 1789 and welcomed, along with the rest of the nation, the abolition of feudal dues and the tithe. In March 1793, on the other hand, he knocked at the castle gate to ask for help: not to reestablish the seigneurial regime but in search of military leaders. The new alliance between the peasant and his former lord was sealed more in the war itself than in the Ancien Régime. Hence the question is not why the peasant longed for the old society, that "longing" being a retrospective illusion of the nineteenth century, but why in four short years he became an enemy of the Revolution. The most interesting recent work on the Vendée war arises out of this effort to distinguish between what came before and what came after, between origins and legacy.

Research has focused especially on what might explain the very violent antagonism between the patriotic cities and the insurgent countryside. This antagonism was a common feature of the whole prerevolutionary society, but the war of 1793 revealed its peculiar potency in the rural west and the military Vendée. Following the lead of Paul Bois, who in 1960 published a study of chouannerie in the Sarthe département, scholars have studied such things as the structure of rural communities, peasant production and its relation to the market, the burden of seigneurial charges, and rural poverty, and have compared the results with those of similar studies in regions that remained republican on the periphery of the insurgent areas. Yet none of the attempts to locate the secrets of the insurrection in specific social structures or in the peasant economy is invulnerable to refutation. Instead, what emerges from the history of "Vendean" rural communities is a growing political hostility to upheavals in daily life caused by the Constituent Assembly's reforms: the creation of départements and districts, new taxes, massive purchases of national properties by the inhabitants of cities and towns. In all these changes, equally changed administrations, energized and staffed by bourgeois readers of Voltaire and the *Encyclopedia,* men who acquired a great deal of Church property and affected an air of insuperable superiority in the face of rural backwardness, lent a hand. In many départements in the west, the age-old antagonism between city and country drew unprecedented vigor from conflicts between new interventionist administrations and rural communities jealous of their autonomy and little inclined to innovation.

The great issue, the heart of the conflict from the Civil Constitution on, was the religious question. The insurrection of March 1793 was preceded by a series of local incidents stemming from the compulsory oath and the division of the Church between two warring clergies. All indications are that the principal source of the Vendean revolt was religious and not social or simply political; since the nobles were belated participants, royalism was a secondary factor, a consequence of the appeal to God and to Catholic tradition (January 21 did not rouse the west to revolt). Finally, military heroism in the insurrection—when there was heroism, for the Vendean army was also subject to panics—was inspired by religious fanaticism and the promise of paradise. This communal devotion to the old faith and the old Church, perceived as inseparable and both threatened by the Revolution, transcended the limits of the conflict between town and country. It explains why, as Claude Petitfrère has shown, the Catholic and Royal Army also included many urban artisans, to say nothing of notables, both minor and major.

In order to measure the importance of the religious phenomenon we must abandon the "republican" obsession, inherited from the Enlightenment and much in evidence in Michelet, with manipulation of the half-savage peasant by the refractory priest. We must restore to the Vendean people its traditional faith and its churches, shaped by the past and soon in conflict with a revolutionary reorganization that quickly came to be seen as antireligious. This history is not well known and is still mysterious, and what emerges from the shadows is the most recent phenomenon: namely, that the territory of the future insurrection had been the territory of an eighteenth-century mission by the Montfortians.

The order takes its name from Grignon de Montfort (1673–1715). Following the example of its founder, it revived, at the height of the Enlightenment, the extraordinary intensity of medieval preaching in inculcating the word of the Church in the minds of the illiterate. It systematically covered western France with missions, retreats, and stations of the cross, combining exaltation of poverty and rejection of the world with the modern themes of the Counter Reformation: to root out heresy, extirpate superstition, and organize religion around obligations, rules, and exercises. The center was in Saint-Laurent-sur-Sèvre, a few miles south of Cholet, a small *bocage* town covered with churches and convents, which would also be the heart of the insurrection; from there, following a circular arc, the Mulotins (from Mulot, the name of the order's first director) disseminated with almost military diligence their Marial devotion, Saint-Sulpice's legacy to Grignon de Montfort, which the Mulotins passed on to the insurgents of 1793.

The preaching of the Montfortians extended beyond the limits of what would become the military Vendée, however; it covered a vast territory, from Brittany to Aunis, corresponding to the dioceses of Vannes, Nantes, Angers, Luçon, and La Rochelle. Furthermore, from the accounts left by Father Hacquet, one of the participants, it is clear that the reception of the Mulotins was not uniformly warm. The contrast between plain and *bocage,* which for Sieg-fried distinguished republican territory from royalist territory, already sepa-rated, according to Hacquet, the "hard-hearted" from the "good and docile" people. Hence the peculiar strength of Catholic traditionalism in the Vendée of 1790–1793 cannot be ascribed solely to the Montfortian missions. The mis-sions themselves built on an early base, whose history is unknown and per-haps unknowable. Yet they surely gave the populations of the Mauges and the *bocage,* which honored them, something in the nature of a religious tra-dition, at once popular and clerical, based on frequent and disciplined devo-tions. This tradition was less ancient than revolutionary bourgeois adminis-trators believed, and they were ill prepared to comprehend it; being disciples of the century's other side, the philosophes, they saw in it nothing but super-stition and savagery. The Vendée war was born of the clash between these two mutually opaque worlds, whose features it brought into sharp relief for sub-sequent centuries.

If this relatively brief episode in the history of France has left such significant traces in French politics, it is surely because it immediately became the symbol of the confrontation between revolution and counterrevolution and a source of inexpugnable violence. Violence, first, on the Vendean side, since the rural plebs fighting in the name of God showed no mercy. But above all revolutionary violence, and of all the violence of the Revolution the least excusable on grounds of "public safety," since it was the punitive violence of victors visited upon the Vendée after the Catholic and Royal Army had been wiped out. The slaughter of the Vendeans, along with the destruction of the Vendée, was the greatest collective massacre in the revolutionary Terror, and it cannot be absolved by invoking the notorious excuse of "circumstances."

In fact, it was in the name of salvation of the fatherland that Barère proposed the program of extermination in his speech of August 1. ("Destroy Vendée and Valenciennes will no longer be in the power of the Austrians. Destroy Vendée and the English will no longer occupy Dunkirk." And so on.) But that program was not implemented until January, when the situation was well in hand nearly everywhere, as if Vendée continued to embody, as Barère expressed it on August 1, "the canker eating away at the heart of the Repub-lic"; combat continued as long as the embers of counterrevolution continued to burn, as if in order to be totally victorious the Revolution was obliged to destroy its anti-principle, to erase it from history. The region and its towns were debaptized, the département of Vendée was renamed Vengé; Fontenay-le-Comte was renamed Fontenay-le-Peuple; Noirmoutier, the île de la Mon-tagne. Yet there remained any number of farms and villages where rebellion had reigned and the Ancien Régime still lurked.

Thus, there was no difference in nature between the Terror that mar-tyred the Vendée and the revolutionary Terror in general. The same forces were at work, the forces that underlay the political ideology of the coalition in power, that unstable alliance of the Mountain and the sans-culottes: the identification of the rebellion with conspiracy and treason, repressive passion, faith in the indivisible unity of the Republic, belief that a bloody dictatorship was the indispensable instrument of public regeneration. The Convention and the Committee of Public Safety acted no differently in the Vendée than in Lyons, another hotbed of counterrevolution. To Lyons, too, they sent fanatical representatives who carried out mass executions; in Lyons, too, rebaptized Free City, they began destroying houses. Vendée was surely a vaster, more militarized theater. Yet the Republic's generals until the spring of 1794 carried on there more as representatives of the Terror than as military officers. Indeed, one has to await the end of the Terror to see the Revolution adopt an intelligent strategy—Hoche in 1795—against what was left of the military Vendée.

Nevertheless, the repression that raged in the Vendée at the end of 1793 and during the first few months of 1794 not only revealed massacre and destruction on an unprecedented scale but also a zeal so violent that it has bestowed as its legacy much of the region's identity over the past two hundred years. Such longevity in the memory of misfortune, if it stems from the dimensions of the catastrophe as well as from the pedagogical attention it has continued to receive, may also be due to the religious character of the Vendée war. This character has set the event apart and distinguished even the hatred of which it has been the target. Bordeaux, Marseilles, Caen, and Normandy rose for the Girondins; Lyons fought under the banner of royalism; but the Vendean people asked to be given back their priests and their Church. In opposition the Convention placed the armies of the Republic under the command of sans-culottes, terrorists, and de-Christianizers. Thus, even though it was never the ambition of the Revolution to root out Christianity—Robespierre, and before him the Constituent Assembly, made this perfectly clear—circumstances nevertheless brought a Catholic people face to face with a republican people in the Vendée. For that reason this war aptly epitomizes the depth of the conflict that arose in the history of France between religious tradition and the revolutionary foundation of democracy.

François Furet

EVENTS

FURTHER READING

Bois, Paul. *Paysans de l'ouest. Des structures économiques et sociales aux options politiques depuis l'époque révolutionnaire dans la Sarthe.* Le Mans, Paris, and The Hague, 1960; abridged edition Paris, 1971.

Chassin, Charles-Louis. *La Vendée patriote, 1793–1800,* 4 vols. Paris, 1893–1895.

——— *Les pacifications de l'ouest, 1794–1800,* 3 vols. Paris, 1896–1899.

Dubreuil, Léon. *Histoire des insurrections de l'ouest,* 2 vols. Paris, 1929.

Gabory, Emile. *La Révolution et la Vendée d'après des documents inédits,* 3 vols. Paris, 1925; reprinted 1941.

Hacquet, Father Pierre-François. *Mémoires des missions des Monfortains dans l'ouest, 1740–1779: Contribution à la sociologie religieuse historique.* Fontenay-le-Comte, 1964.

La Rochejacquelein, Marie-Louise-Victorienne de Donnissan, marquise de Lescure, later marquise de. *Mémoires.* Paris, 1815.

Michelet, Jules. *Histoire de la Révolution française,* book 8, chap. 2; book 10, chap.5; book 11, chaps. 5, 6; book 16, chaps. 1, 2.

Pérouas, Father Louis. *Le diocèse de La Rochelle de 1648 à 1724.* Paris, 1964.

Petitfrère, Claude. *La Vendée et les Vendéens.* Paris, 1981.

Siegfried, André. *Tableau politique de la France de l'ouest sous la Troisième République.* Paris, 1913.

Tilly, Charles. *The Vendée.* Cambridge, Mass., 1964.

RELATED TOPICS

Ancien Régime	Civil Constitution of the Clergy	Michelet
Chouannerie	Counterrevolution	Terror

ACTORS

2

BABEUF

In the historiography of the French Revolution, Babeuf occupies a much larger place than his actual role warrants. He was not a member of any of the revolutionary assemblies. He played no role in any of the great "days" that altered the course of events. He did not appear in the limelight until quite late, under the Directory, as the leader of a conspiracy that aimed to overthrow, in the name of the people, the bourgeois government that had been created in the Year III. But the conspiracy was short-lived, for word of the plot leaked out. The conspirators were arrested without public protest, and Babeuf was condemned to death and guillotined in May 1797.

If historians have made Babeuf into one of the great heroes of the popular actions that were the very soul of the Revolution, it is not because his plot failed, nor even because martyrdom has magnified the failure. Rather, it is because his stillborn conspiracy involved not only belated followers of Robespierre but also some of the first activists to flaunt the communist ideal. Babeuf not only represents the last remnants of the popular agitation of the Year II, he also stands for a radical critique of property and an unprecedented form of political organization. Hence the disproportion between the relatively minor episode of which Babeuf was the center and the ideas he is supposed to have bequeathed to the nineteenth and twentieth centuries. His importance in the history of the French Revolution comes from the belief that he pointed the way toward another revolution.

Setting the tone for all future interpretations of Babeuf was one of his coconspirators, an Italian by the name of Filippo Buonarroti, who survived the trial of 1797 and lived to write a book published during the Restoration and entitled *Conspiracy for Equality, Known as the Babeuf Conspiracy.* In it, this Tuscan intellectual sought to go beyond Babeuf in order to establish a Babouvist tradition. In 1845 Marx himself described Babeuf as an ancestor in these classic lines from *The Holy Family:* "The revolutionary movement, which began in the Social Circle in 1789 and whose principal leaders as it evolved were Leclerc and Roux, briefly succumbed at the time of the Babeuf conspiracy, which gave rise to the communist idea—an idea Babeuf's friend Buonarroti brought back to France after the revolution of 1830. When all its consequences have been fully developed, this idea emerges as the principle of the modern world." Given this handsome epitaph, it is hardly surprising that twentieth-century communist historiography has been careful to lay wreaths on Babeuf's grave.

Babeuf therefore has two fates, depending upon whether attention is focused on the revolutionary activist or the political writer. He was born in

1760 into a poor family in Picardy and while still quite young found employment as a scribe thanks to his fine hand. He found himself suddenly the head of the family when his father died in 1780, and two years later he married. He was a loving, affectionate father to his two children, like so many other late eighteenth-century readers of *Emile*. An autodidact, he lifted himself out of poverty by dint of his own considerable energies and established himself as a keeper of land records in Roye, still in Picardy. In this capacity he maintained registers of feudal dues paid to various seigneuries in the area, an ideal position from which to observe the social and legal problems of rural life under the Ancien Régime. We know something about his thinking at that time from a correspondence that developed after he submitted a paper to the Academy of Arras. Babeuf exchanged letters with the Academy's secretary, Dubois de Fosseux, an enlightened notable with a passion for agriculture. Babeuf appears to have been a man of encyclopedic curiosity, which his correspondent encouraged. Agricultural questions were his special interest. Though not especially original, Babeuf's thinking reflects the spirit of the times, a compound of reformist optimism and obsessive concern with "social happiness." Here Babeuf no doubt developed his taste for radical change, which given his youth and occupation might have taken less literary form.

Then came the Revolution, in which Babeuf was unable to carve out a role for himself prior to the Directory. Since the Constituent Assembly was dominated by the elite of the Ancien Régime, that inability is hardly surprising. Babeuf was an enthusiastic observer of the events of the summer of 1789, and he played a very modest role in the night of August 4, when he joyfully celebrated the abolition of feudalism, which of course meant the sacrifice of his profession as recorder of feudal dues. His correspondence from this period contains a fine passage, noted by Jaurès, in which Babeuf comments on the Revolution's first incidents of violence (in July) and the murder of Councillor Foulon and his son-in-law, Bertier de Sauvigny, the intendant of Paris: "The masters, instead of disciplining us, have turned us into barbarians, because they are barbarians themselves. They reap, and will continue to reap, what they have sown."

Upon returning to Roye in October, he placed his passion for writing at the disposal of the local revolutionary authorities. On a local level he played a role similar to that of Marat in Paris: the uncompromising champion of the weak and the poor, of the "passive" citizens against the aristocrats and their accomplices in the Assembly, from Lafayette to Barnave. Twice imprisoned and twice liberated, after 1792 he quite naturally moved from the role of sans-culotte militant to that of sans-culotte administrator, initially with the General Council of the Somme département and later with the Directory of the Montdidier district. There he committed an act of forgery (on a deed to national properties for the benefit of a fellow sans-culotte) and was forced to flee to Paris in February 1793 to avoid twenty years in irons. Friends found him a place in the Ministry of Supply, but his enemies from Picardy located him that autumn and once again he was imprisoned. He was paroled after only six months, however, in July 1794, just a few days after the fall of Robespierre. In short, his career resembled that of countless other sans-culottes, moving from militant action in the cause of equality to a series of positions in the revolutionary bureaucracy. Only repeated brushes with the law and prison distinguished him from the rest and hindered his progress.

Was his slow progress the reason why Babeuf enthusiastically welcomed 9 Thermidor and the end of the Terror? This peculiar episode is hard to square with the rest of his political career. No doubt Babeuf was influenced by the sudden change of climate, as fear of the guillotine evaporated in the months following Robespierre's downfall. Always one to oversimplify, Babeuf went so far in his condemnation of "Maximilien the exterminator" that he wrote a short pamphlet at the time of Carrier's trial in which he argued that the secret purpose of the Robespierrist Terror was to reduce the size of the population so as to ensure an adequate supply of food.

In the fall, however, he executed a full about-face, founding a newspaper called *La tribune du peuple* (*The Tribune of the People*), which condemned the Thermidorian bourgeoisie in the egalitarian accents of 1793. Before long he was once again a Robespierrist, so much so that by February 1795 he was back in prison for "inciting rebellion, murder, and dissolution of the national representative body." It was in prison—initially in Paris, then in Plessis and Arras, where he was transferred—that the core of the future Conspiracy of Equals was born. It consisted of "ex-Terrorists" and "neo-Terrorists" among the prisoners: Germain, Bodson, Debon, and Buonarroti. The last, scion of an important Pisan family and an intellectual steeped in the philosophy of the Enlightenment, was a loyal Robespierrist who became a naturalized French citizen in 1793. The future historian of Babouvism may have played a key role in rethinking the group's doctrine. In October, following the royalist insurrection of Vendémiaire, an amnesty was declared for all republicans, and Babeuf was again freed from prison, now as *Gracchus* Babeuf, having adopted the first name of the famous Roman as a way of proclaiming his belief in an egalitarian division of all land and property. This became the new banner of his newspaper as well as of his political action.

In the difficult winter of 1795–96, that action found support among those nostalgic for 1793: one-time followers of Hébert, Marat, and Robespierre now reconciled by misfortune and in search of a popular platform on which to mount an opposition to the nascent Directory. Such people could be found in the entourage of Amar, a former conventionnel famous for his role in the Committee of General Security, as well as in the clubs, the most active of which was the Club of the Pantheon, slowly radicalized by the influence of Germain, Buonarroti, and Darthé, one of the most extreme terrorists of the heroic era. By autumn what emerged from these groups and these men was the idea that direct, clandestine action was needed to rouse the public from its apathy. After the Directory ordered the Club of the Pantheon shut down in February, the conspirators formed a Secret Directory of Public Safety with seven members. The directors included communists like Babeuf; Debon, the author of a lost work on the injustice of property rights; and the gentle publicist Sylvain Maréchal, author of the *Manifesto of Equals*, who had somehow strayed into this tragic menagerie. Also represented were neo-Robespierrists, veterans of more heroic times, such as Antonelle, who under the Ancien Régime had been a marquis noted for his wit, but who became a Jacobin while remaining a libertine and served as a deputy in the Legislative Assembly and a juror on the Revolutionary Tribunal; Félix Le Peletier, brother of the martyr of 1793 and a wealthy banker who may have provided the group with funds; Darthé; and last but not least, Buonarroti, the very embodiment of the transition from Robespierrism to Babouvism. This Secret Directory recruited agents who agreed to strike when the signal was given, one in each arrondissement (district of Paris) and army corps. In the provinces the conspirators counted on the support of a number of nostalgic conventionnels. The group's program and rallying cry embraced the Constitution of 1793 (the second constitution, that of the Montagnards) coupled with a return to popular sovereignty. What other schemes they may have hatched are known only to the conspirators.

Unfortunately for the conspirators, the other Directory—the real one—was aware of the plot. Barras knew the whole story from informers and through contacts with his former allies. But he did nothing, for after Vendémiaire he was more afraid of the royalists than of the sans-culottes, crushed during Germinal and Prairial. In any case he was a past master of the "wait and see" approach. Carnot also had detailed knowledge of the plot from Grisel, one of the conspirators who betrayed the others in exchange for cash. As a former member of the Committee of Public Safety, Carnot was eager to make amends for his past by persecuting the Equals. With the support of Letourneur and La Révellière and the acquiescence of Reubell he led the Directory's actions against the terrorists and "levelers." Carnot's influence persuaded a segment of the bourgeoisie that the Babeuf plot represented a serious threat.

The conspirators were rounded up by the police on 21 Floréal (May 11, 1796). Of those who were carted off, the public knew only the names of the former conventionnels: Drouet (who had played a key role at Varennes), Robert Lindet, Vadier, and Amar. People looked upon the episode as marking the downfall of yet another terrorist faction, Jacobinism's last gasp. Less well known, the actual members of the Conspiracy of Equals were overshadowed by memories of 1793. Nevertheless, in the Vendôme trial held the following year, of the sixty-five indicted individuals who chose to deny the plot in spite of the evidence, only Babeuf and Darthé were sentenced to death and executed. Seven were sentenced to deportation (Buonarroti among them), and all the rest were acquitted. The verdict tells us something about the solidarity that existed among former members of the Convention.

From the ashes of the Babeuf conspiracy rose the history of Babouvism, enshrined in the book published in 1828 by Buonarroti, the survivor of so many political battles. Written more than thirty years after the events, the book has all the usual problems of an eyewitness account, particularly the kind of eyewitness account composed long after the fact. How accurate are the old Italian militant's account and analysis of the facts? Was he not perhaps tempted to set forth his own ideas in place of Babeuf's? Some Italian historians have proceeded on the assumption that it was Buonarroti who originated many of the tenets of Babeuf's doctrine while both men were imprisoned in Paris in the Year IV, in which case his exposition of that doctrine must be accepted as definitive even after a quarter of a century. What came to be called Babouvism was in fact a collective effort. The problem of ascertaining responsibility for any particular aspect of the doctrine therefore remains open.

More generally, the problem is to determine which elements of Babouvism merely drew upon Jacobin or "republican" ideas widely shared since the Year II and which other elements represented radically new contributions to the history of ideas and political traditions. Even historians who share an admiration of revolutionary egalitarianism differ on this crucial point. Mathiez stressed the neo-Robespierrist character of the Babouvist movement in terms of both its social recruitment (largely bourgeois) and its ideas. After World War II historians following the example of Georges Lefebvre have tended to emphasize the more properly communist convictions of Babeuf and his friends, in contrast to their neo-Robespierrist allies. This is true, for example, of the work of Maurice Dommanget and of the Soviet historian V. M. Daline. Both sets of historians cite persuasive sources, and their arguments are not incompatible.

The conspirators' fundamental idea was that the meaning of the French Revolution lay in the idea of equality, this being the law of nature and therefore one of man's primary needs. History—one long saga of inequality—had run counter to this idea or imperative. In this we see the extraordinary influence of Rousseau on the revolutionary cast of mind. The *Manifesto*, for example, states: "Let the arts perish if need be, provided that we are left with real equality." Of course this is the simplified Rousseau of the two *Discourses*, simpler even—if such a thing can be believed—than the Rousseau of the *Social Contract*. For Babeuf and his friends the goal was to reestablish the state of nature within society. This is the key tenet of the *Manifesto of Equals* written by Sylvain Maréchal in the spring of 1794 and accepted in one of the very first meetings of the Secret Directory as the charter of the conspiracy: "We intend from now on to live and die as equals, just as we were born. We want true equality or death: that is what we must have."

The Revolution had recognized the goal but had been unable to attain it. Buonarroti's book sets forth the reasons for this failure, but the idea is implicit in all the 1795 texts and was the basis of the bond between Babouvists and neo-Robespierrists. Buonarroti argues that the Revolution was initially led astray by aristocrats whom he characterizes as believers in English political economy and selfish individualism. But the second Constitution of 1793 (adopted after the defeat of the Girondins) and Robespierre's revolutionary government gave power back to the people and restored equality—unfortunately not for long, however, because 9 Thermidor brought the enemy back to power. Babouvism was thus an early attempt at a Robespierrist history of the Revolution critical of both 1789 and Thermidor—a historical interpretation destined for an illustrious future. In Year IV, however, this view was no more than a timetable for revolutionary action, to judge by the words of the *Manifesto of Equals:* "The French Revolution is only the forerunner of another, far greater, far more solemn revolution, which will be the last."

Which one? What is it that can make equality "real"? The elimination of private property. In this respect, Babeuf's contribution appears to have been crucial, given that his correspondence from before 1789 bears witness to an already developed interest in a sweeping plan of social reorganization based on equalization of wealth. The one-time keeper of feudal land records at Roye was not a great mind, and all his life he remained more of an ideologue than a philosopher. He was a naive and sentimental autodidact, an admirer of Rousseau and Mably who advocated the division of large farms for the benefit of the poor and who, in letters written in 1787 to Dubois de Fosseux, offered impassioned commentary on a work concerning ways of eradicating poverty. His *Cadastre perpétuel,* published in 1789, treats the same central question. During the revolutionary years Babeuf abandoned the idea of an "agrarian law" providing for equal distribution of land to individuals and adopted instead that of communal land ownership and elimination of private property: the fruits of the earth were to be distributed equally among citizens, all of whom were to be called upon to play an equal role in their production. Such distributive agrarian communism was by no means a novelty in the eighteenth century's warehouse of utopian ideas. What was new about Babeuf's use of the idea was that he presented it as the core of a revolutionary program. Without any doubt this marks communism's first entry into the public arena.

One final distinctive feature of the Conspiracy has to do with its conception of politics, which owed more to Jacobinism than to the Enlightenment. In 1794–1795 Babeuf and his friends took as their rallying cry the slogan "Back to the Montagnard Constitution of 1793." They admired this constitution for its advocacy of direct democracy (through the submission of all laws to primary assemblies), although they privately criticized it for guaranteeing the rights of property. Yet beyond all the praise for the united and indivisible will of the people, we find, just as in the case of the Jacobins—and to an even greater degree, if such a thing is conceivable—a justification of dictatorship: in this case the dictatorship of the only true interpreters of the people's sovereign will, the purest of the revolutionaries, namely, the Equals themselves. Babeuf shared with the Jacobins an exorbitant belief in the power of political authorities to change society and enforce strict egalitarian standards. In Buonarroti's version, the distribution of property was supposed to be supervised by magistrates who for an indefinite period of time were to be appointed by the Secret Directory. The Conspiracy of Equals thus welcomed the revolutionary tradition of political voluntarism. Most Babouvist documents revealingly drop the term *liberty* in favor of *equality.*

Much of what was supposed to follow upon the success of the conspiracy can be found in its concrete preparations. Babeuf borrowed his concept of political action from Marat and the Hébertists: the people, having been subjugated and deceived (by another plot, a wicked conspiracy of the wealthy), could be freed from its chains only by a clandestine minority organized like a military unit and determined to rule against all opposition through a dictatorship established in the name and for the benefit of the people for an unspecified period of time. Surely this view reflects the inability of the conspirators to rouse the masses from their apathy and to recreate, under the very different conditions of Year IV, the climate of the great days of the Revolution. But it also tells us a great deal more. Revolutionary faith knows no greater extreme than the conviction that everything must bend before the political will. Babouvism was the last resurgence of Jacobin extremism and no doubt the only doctrine to incorporate at the theoretical level the egalitarian passions of the day, but in the Conspiracy of Equals it embodied the new theory of a revolutionary putsch, so crucial to understanding the history of the nineteenth and twentieth centuries. Here, too, began not only the history of the secret societies that played such an important role in European politics after the Treaty of Vienna but also the whole Russian revolutionary tradition from populism to bolshevism.

François Furet

FURTHER READING

WORKS BY BABEUF

Correspondance de Babeuf avec l'Académie d'Arras, ed. Marcel Reinhard. Paris, 1961.
Textes choisis, introduction and notes by Claude Mazauric. Paris, 1965.

RELATED WORKS

Andrews, Richard M. "Réflexions sur la Conjuration des Egaux," *Annales ESC,* January–February 1974.
Babeuf et les problèmes du babouvisme. International colloquium held at Stockholm, August 21, 1960, with a preface by Albert Soboul. Paris, 1963.
Buonarroti, Filippo Michele. *Conspiration de l'Egalité dite de Babeuf, suivie du procès auquel elle donna lieu, et des pièces justificatives, etc.,* reprint, with a preface by Georges Lefebvre. Paris, 1957.
Daline, Victor M. *Gracchus Babeuf à la veille et pendant la grande Révolution française (1785–1794),* trans. Jean Champenois. Moscow, 1976 (orig. pub. Moscow, 1963).
Dommanget, Maurice. *Babeuf et la Conjuration des Egaux.* Paris, pamphlet in the series "Histoire des doctrines socialistes—les idées et les faits," 1922.
Galante Garrone, Alessandro. *Buonarroti e Babeuf.* Turin, 1948.
Legrand, Robert. *Babeuf et ses compagnons de route.* Paris, 1981.

RELATED TOPICS

Carnot	Marx	Robespierre
Equality	*Maximum*	Rousseau

BARNAVE

B orn in Grenoble like Stendhal but a century earlier, Barnave too might
have become an impassioned yet rational writer. He was in any event a
young man of the sort Stendhal liked: elegant, gifted, amiable, while concealing beneath his suave exterior a clinical view of the world. The son of an
avocat in the Parlement of Dauphiné and of a beautiful, aristocratic mother,
raised with care and affection in a society of Protestant notables, he made his
debut at the bar in 1781, at the age of twenty. His curiosity ranged well beyond the bounds of his profession, however, and his ambitions were greater
than any career could satisfy. He had read and studied the classics as well as
the philosophy of his own day, both French and English, and his youthful
notes attest to a mind familiar with both the pleasures of the imagination and
the savor of rational argument. Despite his talent, the success he enjoyed, and
the promise of a secure future, he dreamed of something else. Sometimes his
dreams were of greatness, either in literature or politics—he did not care
which. Other times he swore that he would never be anyone's fool in a century
that was all tinsel. Yet this very century would welcome him with open arms.

In Dauphiné the Revolution began early, a year before anywhere else,
with protests arising out of attempts by Lamoignon and Brienne to break the
parlements' opposition to their policies with the edicts of May 1788. On June
7, a market day in Grenoble, a mob pried up stones from the streets, took to
the roofs, and bombarded the king's troops with rocks and tiles. Barnave had
already thrown himself into the fray by writing, in great haste, an attack on
the king's ministers entitled "Spirit of the Edicts Registered by Military Force
at the Parlement of Grenoble on May 10, 1788," in which he called upon the
king to convoke the Estates General. Dauphiné did not await permission from
Louis XVI before convoking its own Provincial Estates. On June 14 an illegal
Assembly of the Three Orders gathered in Grenoble and took it upon itself
to convoke the Estates of Dauphiné, at the same time approving what was in
effect a signal innovation, namely, that the number of deputies of the Third
Estate would be equal to the number of deputies of the clergy and nobility
combined. On July 21 at Vizille the three orders sat together, made decisions
together, and together called for convoking the Estates General, establishing
new rights for the Third Estate, and restoring the kingdom's unity. Mounier
was responsible for the text of the resolution, but Barnave closely followed
his lead and was an active, passionate, and visible presence. In the following
month the king capitulated, clearing the way for elections to choose the deputies who would go to Versailles. Very early in 1789, at Romans, Barnave was

elected second after Mounier to represent the Third Estate of Grenoble in the Estates General.

He wasted no time establishing his presence as a man to be reckoned with in Versailles, where he took a prominent part in the very first debates on the allocation of power. He showed himself to be one of the best orators in the assembly, a speaker capable of improvising an argument without losing the thread while nearly everyone else read speeches written out ahead of time. His eloquence was of a highly intellectual kind, much given to rational demonstration and, compared with Mirabeau's, less intuitive, less inspired: in Mirabeau's words, there was "no divinity in him." But, unlike that elder statesman, the deputy from Grenoble had no scandalous past to live down, and his speeches had a charm and freshness in tune with the times, an almost ingenuous tone in which one catches some of the same accents as in the young man's private notebooks. Barnave lacked moderation, but he had style.

He quickly parted company with Mounier, voting on June 17 in support of a motion bestowing the name "National Assembly" upon the deputies of the Third Estate. Throughout 1789 he could be found participating in every battle on the side of the "patriots." He was a man in the public eye, one of the omnipresent, popular heroes of the Revolution. This was surely the happiest period of his life: at the age of twenty-eight, glory was his, and his role on the great stage of history had brought deep contentment to his troubled soul. In the Assembly on July 23 he let drop an unfortunate remark—unfortunate but not unforgivable, for he was portraying not so much his own exalted state of mind as the violent temper of the times. This was the day after Foullon and Bertier had been murdered by a Paris crowd. Lally-Tollendal had attempted to work on the emotions of his colleagues by describing the dreadful circumstances surrounding the murders. Barnave responded: "Gentlemen, there are those who would attempt to elicit our sympathies in favor of the blood spilt yesterday in Paris. Was that blood therefore so pure?" An inept, demagogic argument, to be sure, yet one that captured an idea shared by many at the time, that blame for the violence of the Revolution should be laid at the door of the Ancien Régime.

In any case, Barnave's remark gives us some idea of the depth of his revolutionary passions, which can also be gauged by his break with Mounier. The first signs of tension appeared in July, and by late August or early September the debate over the Constitution and the king's veto power had consummated the break between the two leaders. In the Assembly Barnave found new allies, men of roughly his own age and as committed as he was to the "patriotic" cause even though they came from the nobility: Adrien Duport, ex-councillor in the Parlement of Paris, and Alexandre de Lameth, a young colonel schooled in the American Revolution. All three were scions of prominent families, and they soon came to be known as the "triumvirate," an appellation indicative of a generational solidarity born of revolutionary commitment. The triumvirate is an excellent symbol for the new society that was just coming into being upon the ruins of the old society of orders. All three men gave unstintingly of themselves in order to destroy the Ancien Régime, and all three were staunch supporters of the common folk of town and countryside: Duport was the author of the famous decree of August 4. But once the Revolution had been made, and made as radically as possible, they intended to determine its course, because they believed themselves to be the most qualified to guide it. In attempting to achieve this impossible or at any rate premature goal, they, like so many others, came to grief, and the Revolution continued on without them.

A change came over Barnave's political life in 1790, as little by little the identity of the enemy changed; now the danger was not so much aristocratic reaction as escalating democratic demands. His political development followed a zigzag course, and it would take a detailed, day-by-day commentary on the debates in the Assembly to illustrate in full the role played by shifting allegiances, intrigues, and tactical maneuvers. In March, yielding to the influence of the Lameth brothers, who were deeply involved in trade with the colonies, Barnave argued in favor of maintaining the status quo in the "islands," a position that put him, the great champion of the rights of man, in danger of being seen as a stooge of the plantation owners. In May, however, he regained some of his popularity with the left by attacking Mirabeau for his concessions to the king concerning the power to make war and peace. By October he stood at the height of his career, having been elected president of the Assembly before the age of thirty. But once again the colonial debate was the order of the day, and once again Barnave argued the case of the white colonists against the free mulattoes and black slaves. As a result he was denounced, not only by Marat, who denounced everybody, but also in an open letter written by Brissot, who refused to forgive Barnave's sacrifice of his principles over the colonial question. Early in 1791 Barnave regained some of the ground he had lost by delivering a series of uncompromising speeches on the priests' oath and the right of emigration, but his passionate enthusiasm for the Revolution, the secret of his success in 1789, was long since gone.

Mirabeau's death on April 2, 1791, left Barnave and his allies in a prominent position. This early stage of the Revolution is marked by the inability of the Constituent Assembly's leadership to reach agreement on the principles of the constitutional monarchy they wished to establish. Mirabeau detested the triumvirate, and the triumvirs returned his enmity in kind; and both they and Mirabeau hated Lafayette, the third center of power in the Assembly. Yet Mirabeau shared the ideas of Barnave and his friends: they wanted a strong monarchy limited by an Assembly, a king who had declared his independence of the aristocracy, and suffrage based on property qualifications broad enough to embrace the entire middle class. The substance of Mirabeau's secret advice to Louis XVI from the middle of 1790 until his death was to accept these propositions. In the summer of 1791 Barnave, Duport, and Alexandre de Lameth offered the king the same advice, also in secret. With the death of their rival they may, naively, have supposed that they were close to achieving their goal, but instead they were obliged to pay the price that premature death spared Mirabeau from paying in person.

The Varennes episode clarified the new situation. Having fled Paris, the king was arrested in Varennes, a village in Lorraine, and brought back to the capital. The Assembly designated three of its members—La Tour-Maubourg, Pétion, and Barnave—to ride out to meet the lugubrious procession. Barnave traveled in the royal berlin, and one can only imagine what this strange, prolonged journey must have been like, with the celebrated representative of the people riding face to face with the distraught royal couple being returned to the Tuileries in the midst of a nation up in arms. One need not speculate that Barnave was in love with the queen to suppose that he was moved by the unfortunate turn of events and that it altered his thinking about the Revolution. In the previous month he had been defeated twice in the Assembly, first on the question of the political rights of free mulattoes (once more the colonial affair, his perennial albatross) and later on the eligibility of members of the Constituent Assembly for reelection to the next Assembly. Overnight France would find itself deprived of all its political leaders, he felt. And what if the constitutional monarchy also found itself without a king?

Barnave concluded that the king must be saved in order to save the Constitution and preserve order. This was his last great public battle. Paris was in turmoil. The clubs demanded that Louis XVI be brought to trial. Condorcet called for a republic. And Barnave, speaking to the Assembly on July 15, said: "Are we going to end the Revolution, or are we going to begin anew? . . . For those who may wish to go further, what other 'night of August 4', can there be but laws against property?" In the summer of 1791 he and his allies therefore advocated restoring the king to his throne (to that end pretending to believe the fiction that he had been "abducted" from Paris); they also made themselves the champions of public order, in opposition to the Paris clubs, and of a revised Constitution, signed, sealed, and delivered. But Barnave's apparent triumph was in fact a hasty patch job, threatened on all sides. He had lost what remained of his popularity when he sanctioned repressive measures against a popular demonstration on the Champ de Mars on July 17. He had abandoned the Jacobins to Robespierre when he founded the Feuillants. He had been no more able than Mirabeau or Lafayette to gain the confidence of the royal couple, unwilling to forgive and forget. Having been leader of the Assembly for one summer, he was ineligible for reelection. But the central reason for his failure was that France in that summer was still the France of 1789: the propertied class was not yet mobilized by the threat from below. In the Assembly the royalists looked on with glee as Robespierre ticked off the crimes of which he suspected Barnave: the hour of the *juste milieu* had not yet come.

For three months, from the close of the Assembly until Christmas, the former deputy, once more a private citizen, engaged in a pathetic and silly correspondence with the queen, in which he asked her to help convert the old monarchy into a revolutionary institution. Meanwhile, the queen continued to place her trust in her own people: Fersen, Mercy-Argenteau, and her brother the emperor. Barnave had wisdom enough not to press for war, but he was now a man without influence. He returned to Grenoble in the final days of the year, and there he would remain, for reasons not clear from his correspondence but among which we may suspect the volume of abuse he had received, the turn of events in Paris, and the desire to examine his thoughts in private. He worked, he read, he took care of his property, and he commanded the National Guard at Saint-Egrève, the location of his family home. But among the papers seized at the Tuileries on August 10 was a "Project of the Committee of Ministers in Concert with Messrs. Alexandre Lameth and Barnave." That was enough for the Legislative Assembly to return an indictment against Barnave on August 15.

He was arrested three days later and spent the rest of his life in prison, at first in Dauphiné, where he continued working and writing for more than a year in the hope that the authorities would forget about him. But in early November of 1793 he was transferred to Paris, hastily tried by the Revolutionary Tribunal on the twenty-seventh, and executed on the twenty-ninth.

***

At his death he left a collection of papers, notes, and letters as well as a detailed outline of a book; four volumes of these materials were published in 1843 under the supervision of Bérenger de la Drôme, peer of France and member of the Institute. Barnave's sister later turned his papers over to the Grenoble Municipal Library, where they can still be consulted today. As a result, specialists have been able to criticize the editing of the 1843 edition: Bérenger de la Drôme actually added some documents and cut others. At present no scholarly edition of Barnave's papers exists. Only his *Introduction to the French Revolution* is available. (The title, incidentally, is not his; he only wrote the word "Introduction" at the top of the manuscript.)

For a book written by someone who played such an intimate role in the events he describes, the most surprising thing about the *Introduction* is its aloofness. Barnave looks back from a great height on the history he has just made. This is even more surprising in light of the fact that the author had only recently been disavowed by the Revolution, and now found himself abandoned, threatened, and already in prison. Like Condorcet's *Esquisse*, Barnave's *Introduction* was the work of a man on the brink of death and with no illusions about his fate. Both works were composed hastily and left unfinished. Barnave's in particular is short, peremptory, devoid of titles and chapter headings, and without stylistic embellishment; it is not so much a book as the skeleton of a book. But the most striking contrast between the two works is in their tone. Whereas Condorcet was painting a fresco of the human spirit imbued with anthropological optimism, Barnave was setting forth the laws that governed the behavior of the revolutionaries without their knowledge, as if he himself had played no role in the events he described. Condorcet remained the man he had always been; Barnave contemplated, with patrician detachment, the man he once was.

There is another explanation for Barnave's divided self. The French Revolution was made in the name of natural right, and the men of 1789 intended to establish a new society based on abstract reason. Three years later, Barnave, defeated and held prisoner, proposed a different cause: the logic of history. The most original thing about his manuscript is this substitution of the laws of history for the rights of nature. Indeed, Barnave was so prescient that he was able to think of the Revolution as already complete, even though it was still a long way from having run its course. Perhaps this anticipation was a way of achieving in thought what he had been unable to bring about as a member of the Constituent Assembly in the summer of 1791: an end to the Revolution consistent with its true nature, and specifically a victory of the "middle class." In any case, Barnave's thinking was so different from that of any of the other revolutionaries about their roles that it marks a radical shift in the interpretation of the event. For his political blunders Barnave paid with an early death, but his manuscript, published posthumously, ensured his intellectual survival in the nineteenth and twentieth centuries.

To understand Barnave's influence one has only to open Jaurès' *Histoire socialiste*. What the leader of the socialists discovered in the work of the leader of the Feuillants was not the dry husk of speeches exhumed from the *Moniteur*, full of platitudes about the sovereignty of the nation and representative government; it was history, and what is more, history close to the kind that Jaurès himself was writing, for he saw in it a line of interpretation which anticipated that of Marx. Barnave saw a connection between the Revolution on the one hand and economic progress and the growth of capital on the other, and in this analysis Jaurès detected a genealogical ancestor of Marxism. Barnave was an unfinished Marx, the Marx of the bourgeois revolution. The idea is not absurd in that it marks an intellectual affinity (although Marx never read Barnave), but crudely handled it has led too many commentators since Jaurès to read the *Introduction* in the light of the Marx it supposedly anticipates. Methodologically, it is preferable to interpret an author in the light of what preceded rather than what followed his work. And there is no mystery about the vast reading that went into the construction of Barnave's work, for he left ample notes in his papers: the most important influences were French philosophers, especially Montesquieu, and the thinkers of the Scottish Enlightenment, primarily Adam Smith—as it happens, the same thinkers whom Marx would study so intently half a century later.

From Montesquieu, his favorite author, Barnave derived his historical relativism, along with the idea that it is more important to study the sources of power, the conditions that make it possible and the forces that underlie it, than to examine the question of its legitimacy. From Scottish philosophy he derived his view of European history as dominated by man's relation to nature, by the growth of the population and progress in the arts and commerce culminating in a prosperous and civilized modern society—what the Scots called a "commercial society"—dominated by "movable wealth." In this society the power of democracy replaced that of aristocracy. The whole structure of this model shows how far Barnave was from Rousseau. In his notes he attacks Rousseau for his abstraction, for his idea of the state of nature, and for the arrogance of his reasoning, while Barnave himself raises the banner of observation and empiricism—themes that can be found in some of his speeches from the summer of 1791, in which he is in some ways looking back on 1789. To be sure, his vision of history simply substitutes one philosophy for another. Yet he renounces the ambition to reconstruct society in the light of reason and based on the belief that the purposes of the will and the motives of action can be made perfectly transparent. No longer does he ascribe to revolution the purpose of bringing the political into line with the social. Man can participate in history not as a conscious actor but as an intelligent observer, provided he accepts the lessons of experience rather than tries to bend reality to his will.

The history of men in society is therefore a dialectic between the "social state" and the "political state," between the substance and the form of power. Barnave preserved Montesquieu's use of the Aristotelian classification of polities as democratic, aristocratic, or monarchical, but he attempted to link these categories to the historical evolution of societies. Monarchy, he argued, depends on the existence of a powerful army, aristocracy on landed property, and democracy on public opinion. In the beginning man lived in democracy. Knowing nothing of property, he lived in independence and equality. Barnave thus transformed Rousseau's state of nature into a kind of rudimentary society. Later, man settled in one place and evolved the notion of property in land. The population increased, leading in some places to aristocratic rule, in others to the rule of one person, or, monarchy. Ultimately, however, progress in the arts, the growth of movable wealth, and the development of public opinion restored democracy, but at a higher level than before.

Barnave's conceptualization of history is not rigidly mechanical. It has room for other causal mechanisms, such as a country's size or climate. (Here, of course, he was following Montesquieu.) It also has room for specific factors that may impede the operation of general causes in such a way as to yield a bewildering variety of political regimes. For example, the commercial spirit tends to foster freedom and democracy, yet in some republics it may have the effect of bringing extraordinary wealth to a few individuals, with the result that those republics (Barnave has in mind the United Provinces) come to be governed by a bourgeois aristocracy, admittedly an aristocracy of a kind very different from a landed aristocracy. Or again, a commercial republic may be driven to expand its territory, thus requiring a strong army, the maintenance of which may conflict with the commercial spirit that led to the need for expansion in the first place. Even if foreign policy requires a large standing army, its existence may threaten stability at home (as in ancient Carthage or modern Venice).

For obvious reasons the heart of Barnave's brief work is devoted to the evolution of French society, first from feudalism to absolute monarchy and then from absolute monarchy to the Revolution. The feudal regime marked the rule of a landed aristocracy, military and sacerdotal, which controlled three sources of power: the land, the army, and public opinion. Nascent democracy was just strong enough to support the prince against the aristocracy by backing his efforts to tax landed wealth. Soon, however, the growth of movable wealth rendered democracy strong enough not to govern on its own but to enable the prince to triumph, thus ushering in the age of absolute monarchy.

The absolute monarchy represented a state of equilibrium between aristocracy and democracy. The king broke the power of the nobles by drawing upon the strength—and the cash—of the people. Hence the power of the absolute monarchy arose out of a situation in which the contradictory powers of land and capital canceled each other out. It rested not on production but on the army. Absolutism was peculiar to an era when "the government, having emerged from feudalism, was proceeding toward a new form, not yet developed; when the aristocracy had ceased to be tyrannical but before the prince had become a despot or the people free; an era dominated by royal power limited by the memory of the nobles' power and by opinion, the prelude to the people's power." In this superb definition, which anticipates not only Marx but more notably historians like Augustin Thierry and Guizot, Barnave reveals his understanding of the provisional, fragile nature of monarchy, which he sees as an unstable form of government apt to evolve in a variety of ways ranging from despotism to popular government and not excluding the Feuillant parliamentarian's ideal, "free and limited" monarchy. Unlike aristocracy and democracy, which are comparatively stable, monarchy is constantly torn by the conflict between those two cardinal principles. On this point Barnave is clearly at odds with his master, Montesquieu, who admired the French monarchy and all that it had inherited from its feudal past: "M. de Montesquieu seems to me to have made a government of what is merely a precarious state, a stage of transition between two more definite forms of government. He portrayed the situation in which he saw a number of European states at the time he was writing, without considering whether that state could endure, given that it was founded on a power of opinion for which a base no longer existed and that monarchy would soon need to find other limits and other props. Montesquieu's monarchy was on its way to either military despotism or organized monarchy."

Did "organized monarchy" mean the British crown? No. The Barnave of 1792 lent no support to the claim that had been raised against him in the summer of 1789 by the monarchiens in the debate over how to organize the new government. England was an island without an army, a commercial kingdom in which the House of Commons had nothing to fear from the House of Lords, whereas in France the equivalent of that upper house would have held both people and king in its power. In Britain, moreover, the democratic revolution had come a century earlier than in France, hence it had been religious rather than philosophical in character. The revolution in France had been a long time coming but no less necessary than the English Revolution; the way had been cleared by absolutism, the crushing of the aristocracy, the rise of commercial wealth and popular power, and the philosophy of the Enlightenment. The Revolutionary War in America had served as prelude. By 1789 the king's ineptness, the court's blindness, and Necker's indecision had let power slip into the hands of the people. In general Barnave argues that the Revolution was necessary, but at the end of his manuscript he considers the possibility that events might have taken a different and perhaps better course: "What might have been done by the government was done without it and against it. The communes, tired of so much inaction and sensing the support of popular opinion, organized and in so doing declared that they represented the nation. From then on they were the only power, and from then on the fate of the revolution was almost a foregone conclusion."

Why "almost?" In the Bérenger edition, the hundred-odd pages devoted to the philosophy of European history are followed by a more topical analysis of the work of the Constituent Assembly and a consideration of what went wrong in the Legislative Assembly. Barnave emphasizes the decision to make members of the Constituent Assembly ineligible for reelection to its successor body, a measure approved at Robespierre's urging and over Barnave's objections in 1791. This provision, the result of a coalition born of lassitude, self-interest, and calculation, ensured that the benches of the Legislative Assembly would be filled with fantasists who quickly succumbed to the manipulative machinations of the Paris clubs.

Barnave was particularly inclined to stress the ineligibility provision because he was unwilling to accept the idea that little was left of the work of the Constituent Assembly in which he had played so large a part. He was familiar with the objections to and criticisms of that work, and from his writing we gather that to some extent he shared the critics' views because he shared the spirit that motivated them, namely, the wish to create free institutions and a balance of powers as described by Montesquieu. But could such a balance have been achieved by the Constitution of 1789 as revised in 1791? Barnave in his writings revives the debate of September 1789 concerning the validity of the English example in the French revolutionary context, in a sense resuming his dialogue with his old compatriot Mounier. In the summer of 1789, he argues, there was absolutely no prospect of establishing an upper house, which inevitably would have raised fears of a restoration of the aristocracy. Other criticisms strike him as resting on firmer ground: that insufficient power was given to the executive, and that property was underrepresented in the National Assembly despite efforts to remedy the situation through revisions to the Constitution in the summer of 1791.

To these charges the one-time Feuillant deputy replied that what was at issue was not so much the measures adopted by the legislature as the general shift in attitudes. "On this point and many others," he wrote, "people have totally confused the effects of the revolutionary situation with those of the constitution." For one thing, the king, on whom the Paris clubs looked with unremitting suspicion, was never able to exercise the powers accorded to him. For another, so many aristocrats emigrated or turned their backs on the new regime that property was never able to present a powerful, united front against the demagogues and the forces they unleashed.

Thus, in pondering the current situation in France, Barnave contributed a new idea to the philosophy of history: that of a "revolutionary state," a mode of transition from one regime to another, a perilous passage between past and future during which men exerted even less control over the course of events than usual. The regime that governed France in 1791 had not had time to strike deep roots, and it was obliged to contend with both the resistance of the aristocracy and the ever more insistent demands of the demagogues. Its constitution, though marked by the tumultuous circumstances of its birth, was not a bad one, but it was never put into practice. The men who drafted it were evicted from power en masse in order to make room for new men inexperienced in the business of government, a new wave of theoreticians at the mercy of the Parisian demagogues. As a result the "revolutionary state" gained ground and the "constitutional state" receded, while the Legislative Assembly used the war to create the conditions for a second revolution. "Having returned home," Barnave wrote in June of 1792, "I ask myself if it might not have been better if I had never left." But this melancholy thought soon gave way to a reflection on the necessity of progress: "A moment's reflection is enough to convince me, however, that whatever happens we cannot cease to be free, and that the principal abuses that we destroyed will never recur. How many misfortunes one would have to endure to erase the memory of such benefits!"

This thought is a good epitaph for a man who died at age thirty-two, having spent the final year of his life like a hero of antiquity, reflecting on the force of circumstances rather than the wickedness of men. From this stoic final year came a meditation on the course of European history that makes one more sorry for the books Barnave did not write than for the career he did not enjoy. Sainte-Beuve, true to form, was the first to understand this. Listen to him describe Napoleon paying his respects to the memory of Barnave: "The Consul, who had given orders that Barnave's statue be placed alongside Vergniaud's in the great staircase of the Senatorial Palace, would have seen to it that the man himself, had he lived, would climb the rungs of power. He would have been named Count Barnave under the Empire. He would have aged honorably, albeit in awareness that his ardor was diminishing and with the sparkle gone from his eyes."

François Furet

Further Reading

WORKS BY BARNAVE

Introduction à la Révolution française, ed. and with a preface by Fernand Rude, Cahier des Annales 15. Paris, 1960.

Marie-Antoinette et Barnave, correspondance secrète (juillet 1791–janvier 1792), ed. Alma Söderhjelm. Paris, 1934.

Oeuvres, ed. Alphonse-Marc-Marcellin-Thomas Bérenger de la Drôme, 4 vols. Paris, 1843. The first volume contains the *Introduction à la Révolution française*.

On Barnave's papers, preserved in the Grenoble Library (U 5216), and the preparation of the Bérenger edition of his works, see François Vermale, "Manuscrits et éditions des oeuvres de Barnave," *Annales historiques de la Révolution française*, vol. 15, 1938, 75–77.

RELATED WORKS

Bradby, Eliza Dorothy. *The Life of Barnave*, 2 vols. Oxford, 1915.

Chevallier, Jean-Jacques. *Barnave ou les deux faces de la Révolution, 1761–1793*. Paris, 1936.

Chill, Emmanuel. *Power, Property and History: Barnave's Introduction to the French Revolution and Other Writings*. New York, 1971. Includes an English translation of the *Introduction* and some of Barnave's notes, together with a substantial preface (74 pages) entitled "Barnave as Philosophical Historian."

Michon, Georges. *Essai sur l'histoire du parti feuillant*, vol. 1, *Adrien Duport;* vol. 2, *Correspondance inédite de Barnave en 1792*. Paris, 1924.

Sainte-Beuve, Charles-Augustin. "Oeuvres de Barnave," *Causeries de lundi*, vol. 2, 1950.

Related Topics

CARNOT

C arnot's early years were typical of a generation that would soon be swallowed up in the din of the Revolution. Born in 1753, the son of a notary settled near Dijon, he had done brilliantly as a student at the Royal School of Engineering in Mézières. A military engineer with a passion for mathematics and mechanics, he was earnest and industrious in the performance of his professional duties but showed little enthusiasm for the work and was soon disappointed by the limited prospects of a military career. The reforms of 1776 and 1781, which put obstacles in the way of promotion for officers without an aristocratic pedigree, put an end to whatever remained of Carnot's interest in a monotonous and inglorious profession.

Too provincial to share the enthusiasm of the Parisian salons for the American Revolution, he identified wholeheartedly with his contemporaries' passion for literature and literary celebrity. On the eve of the Revolution he enjoyed a modest renown owing to his scientific works, his election to the academies of Arras and Dijon, and minor poems in honor of Bacchus to which the honorable members of the Rosati Society of Arras, among them Robespierre, were obliged on occasion to listen. He also took an enthusiastic part in the strategic debates that were all the rage in the army in those days, winning for himself a reputation as an old-fashioned eccentric for his impassioned defense of Vauban's defensive tactics and of Montalembert's fantastic "perpendicular fortifications."

Despite these healthy occupations, Carnot missed the opportunity offered by the convocation of the Estates General; he was in prison at the time in the wake of a scandalous love affair. Soon freed, he pleaded his case to various authorities, describing himself as a victim of both ministerial despotism and military hierarchy in tones of outrage that estranged him even further from the corridors of power, where several of his colleagues were launched on brilliant careers.

His marriage in May 1791 brought him back into politics. In marrying the sister-in-law of his brother, who like himself was an officer in the Engineers, he joined a family of notables well established in the Pas-de-Calais and shortly thereafter became president of the Club of Aire, this time determined to make a success of his new "career." In September 1791 both Carnot brothers were elected to serve as deputies in the Legislative Assembly.

In that body and later in the Convention, to which he was reelected in September 1792, Carnot was shrewd enough to hew closely to a tortuous and evolving political line. Upon arriving in Paris he had been a staunch defender of the Constitution and the king, but by the spring of 1792 he was close to the Girondins. After August 10 he sat on the benches of the Mountain, though he never joined the Jacobin Club. A stalwart supporter of whoever held power, he was instinctively suspicious of the populist demagogy and plebeian, anti-elitist spirit that animated the most extreme of the Jacobins. Toward the end of 1792 he clashed violently with Pache, the minister of war, and his Hébertist protégés. Having flown at one time or another every color in the political spectrum, he earned a reputation for fickleness. Though the appellation was no doubt deserved, it fails to take account of a crucial aspect of Carnot's personality: a poor speaker and mediocre tactician, he was not at his best in the public arena. But left to himself in an office or out in the field, he had no equal. He was a bureaucrat rather than a politician, with unstinting faith in the accomplished fact and the lawfully established power, too timorous to make any decision that might compromise his position or his future but implacable when it came to carrying out a policy not of his own devising.

In the Legislative Assembly Carnot had been somewhat overshadowed by his brother, but in the Convention he stood out. He undertook several liaison missions with the army, first in the Pyrenees and later in the north, and prepared reports on the annexations and on the dispatch of commissars to the provinces—reports that drew a good deal of attention and earned him a reputation for efficiency and hostility to extremists. With this reputation in mind the Committee of Public Safety called upon his services on August 4, 1793. Away on another mission at the time, he hurried back to Paris and took up his new post on the eleventh. The worsening military situation following the loss in July of fortresses in Mainz and Valenciennes justified the choice of an undisputed expert in military affairs. At Barère's urging Carnot and his compatriot and colleague Prieur (of the Côte d'Or) were elected members of the Committee. Barère's motives were in part political, aimed at reestablishing the Committee's political balance, which had been compromised by the expulsion of the Dantonists on July 10 and the nomination of Robespierre on July 27. By pressing for the election of two relatively neutral deputies, Barère hoped to strengthen his hand and thwart the hegemonic designs of the three Robespierrist members.

Like the Committee's other "experts," Carnot could thank his special talents for preserving him from the inquisition led by Robespierre, who had little knowledge of things military, although he was not entirely immune to interference from Saint-Just and Billaud-Varenne, men with greater ambitions in matters of war. Carnot also had to cope with the Hébertists at the Ministry of War, with whom he was obliged to share power—not without frequent conflict. His fierce hatred of the Hébertist faction very likely determined his position within the Committee: without the support of the Robespierrist trio, he could not have survived repeated onslaughts from Bouchotte and his entourage. After the September Days of 1793, which inaugurated the Terror, a campaign was mounted against him and his circle of clients, composed of relatives, friends, and officeholders in the Ancien Régime. The attack was partially successful, and Carnot was forced to accede to the sacking of numerous protégés. As a result, he joined forces with Robespierre and supported every step toward greater centralization under the Terror. But the Jacobin leader pursued a political goal, while Carnot's aims were more prosaic: to eliminate his enemies and add to his own power.

It is therefore misleading to ask what responsibility he must bear for the policies of the Terror: an efficient administrator, a bureaucrat without ideology, Carnot condemned the Hébertists much as he had denounced the pre-insurrectional activities of the clubs and sections in 1792. He served the Terror as he had served the monarchy and as he would later serve under the Directory, the Consulate, the first Restoration, and the Hundred Days, withholding protest until he felt that his capacities were being underestimated. A champion of the state, he supported any policy that aimed to strengthen it and weaken its enemies. His scruples did not prevent him from signing decrees ordering "the extermination of the brigands of the Vendée" or the suppression of opposition in Lyons and Toulon, and if the liquidation of the Hébertists must have pleased him no end, he also countersigned the order to arrest Danton.

In April 1794 Carnot achieved his objective of virtually total control of military affairs. On the first of that month he presented to the Convention a decree breaking up the Executive Council into twelve committees, six of them under his authority. Now he was free to turn his thoughts to the great northern offensive that he had long favored.

While pursuing his political goals Carnot made impressive gains in other areas, primarily in reorganizing the army. Although he was never able to overcome the "principle of amalgamation" to establish a system in which new recruits would be incorporated into existing units, the system of old regiments and volunteer battalions had created tremendous disorder, which he managed to reduce by creating eleven combined armies with a unified command structure. Deployed along France's frontiers, these units were operational by the beginning of 1794. In his insistence on tightening discipline, he now approved the passive obedience he had previously condemned, and he steadfastly fought to stanch the flow of deserters.

Then, on January 30, 1794, he described the way in which this new army was to be used in his "General System of Operations for the Next Campaign," which set forth the principles of mass warfare with its need for rapid troop movements and dynamic leadership. Repudiating his youthful admiration for Vauban and "civilized" warfare, Carnot now taught that soldiers ought to "profess hatred and contempt" for the enemy and "exterminate [him] down to the last soldier" as "long as terror is the order of the day at home." In April 1794 he voiced his astonishment: "Why are fleeing enemy troops not cut to pieces? . . . Only the dead do not return." This exaltation of devastation, this nationalism of the narrowest kind, explains the nineteenth century's admiration of Carnot.

For the resumption of operations in the spring of 1794 Carnot envisioned using plans that had been elaborated two years earlier: a quick march across Belgium was to lead to the capture of Ostende, thereby cutting off all communication between England and the continent. Ultimately, more for political than for strategic reasons, only part of this plan was used. Worried about Carnot's control over military affairs, Robespierre, with decisive support from Saint-Just, won agreement that the armies of the Moselle and the Ardennes, which Carnot needed if his plan was to succeed, would be concentrated on the banks of the Rhine. The complement of an eastern offensive to the northern offensive would restrict Carnot's authority as well as limit the credit he could claim in case his forces alone achieved victory.

But even that victory was to elude him. It was won instead at Fleurus (on June 26, 1794) by his rivals Jourdan and Saint-Just, Carnot having vested all his hopes in Pichegru. The battle for influence revealed internal dissension within the Committee. Fleurus served only to poison the atmosphere, with Saint-Just accusing Carnot of incompetence and lack of patriotism. Threatened with loss of control over the conduct of the war, Carnot chose sides, much as he had done in September 1793 against the Hébertists: he played a discreet though probably crucial role in the preparations for 9 Thermidor.

After resigning from the Committee of Public Safety on October 6, 1794, he was reelected on November 5 only to be ousted permanently on March 5, 1795. He carried on with military policies intended to consolidate the victories of the previous summer while working on the diplomatic front to prepare for peace negotiations. But conditions had become almost intolerable for him, and on March 5 he was expelled from the Committee. Since Thermidor Carnot had been obliged to justify his past actions. If he supported his indicted former colleagues Barère, Collot, and Billaud, it was to distinguish them from an alleged Robespierrist "majority" (oddly composed of just three members), at whose door Carnot laid blame for the Terror; the rest of the Committee, he insisted, had done much to improve the military situation. Thus the survivors were credited with all the positive achievements of the Committee, while its negative actions were blamed on the dead. Yet his spirited defense of Barère and Billaud did not go unnoticed, and during the "days" of Prairial (May 1795) he was approached by the insurgents. Cautious as ever, he spurned their advances, but he was nevertheless compromised, and only his reputation as the "architect of victory" saved him.

Following a brief retreat into prudent silence, however, he reemerged at the end of the session (October 1795), no doubt to remind the electors of his existence before they convened. But there was little enthusiasm for the repentant terrorist, and only one département, the Sarthe, included his name on its principal list, while twelve others mentioned him in their supplementary lists.

At this point a new phase of Carnot's political career began. On November 4, 1795, after declining the post of minister of war, he was elected to the Directory along with Letourneur, a former officer in the Engineers and his only ally, as well as Barras, Reubell, and La Révellière-Lépeaux. Neighbors in private life as well as partners in public, these men, so different in character and political background, lost no time before commencing to flay one another mercilessly. Barras suffered from "love of money," Reubell from "a mania for respect," and Carnot from a desire to live in peace with his family as a rentier of the Revolution. At this point Carnot, certain of his authority in military matters, believed that he had reached the peak of his career, but he did not see that the new army, which owed its existence to him more than to any other individual, was more and more beyond the control of the divided and not very credible civilian authorities. If the army had saved the Republic in Year II, it had since acquired a dangerous autonomy. In Germinal, Year III, the army put down a popular uprising, and in Vendémiaire, Year IV, it quelled a royalist insurgency. The civilian authorities were still answerable to the army, which exerted growing influence over political life.

Carnot was soon to learn this sad lesson. The waltz of the generals that had characterized the period from 1792 to 1794 was now over. The general staff at the head of each army, no longer hesitating to countermand civilian orders or even to usurp the role of the civilian authorities, signed truces and armistices on their own initiative, as Jourdan and Pichegru had done with Austria and as Hoche did with the Vendée insurgents. The planned offensive on the Rhine and in Italy was left virtually to the discretion of the generals. On the Rhine the offensive slowed and seemed headed for failure, whereas in Italy, Bonaparte, buoyed by his spectacular successes, went well beyond the plan authorized by Carnot. Confident of his powers, he refused to share his command with Kellermann and entered into negotiations with the Italian states, and the Directory had no choice but to give in. Late in 1796 Carnot decided to open talks with Austria, but in February of the following year, Bonaparte, with the support of Barras and Reubell, "torpedoed" these negotiations by resuming the offensive, this time in the direction of Rome. In the end it was Bonaparte who, in April 1797, signed the Treaty of Leoben with Austria, leaving the Directory to accept the fait accompli.

The divorce between the army and the civilian authorities stemmed in large part from the Directory's inability to quell Jacobin and royalist temptations, make firm decisions, or restore normalcy. Innumerable conflicts arose among the five directors, each of whom intrigued to protect himself against the intrigues of the others.

With Carnot's election to the Directory, his relatives and friends returned to government service. The new director could rely on Bénezech and Faypoult, both officers in the Engineers, and Cochon, who was appointed minister of police in April 1796. In allying himself with Cochon, Carnot demonstrated that he had chosen a moderate line. In the minority within the Directory, he had refused the advances of the neo-Jacobins, now regrouped in the Pantheon Club, and thus had abandoned those who demanded that the Constitution of June 1793 be enforced. But it was the Babeuf conspiracy that would demonstrate the degree to which Carnot had become a conservative.

Babouvist propaganda, particularly directed at the army and the police, did not fail to point out how Père Duchesne had aimed to influence military opinion in 1793. Carnot, a bureaucrat who believed that the talented should rule, had always been hostile to "maximalist" movements promoting plebeian, egalitarian, anti-elitist ideas, the rule of force, and antiparliamentarian sentiments. Men like Vadier, Amar, and Drouet, who had been the mentors of the Hébertists, were still at work behind the new "anarchists."

Beyond the Babeuf conspiracy, Carnot and Cochon aimed to liquidate the last bastions of Jacobinism. In May 1796, after an impending plot was opportunely denounced by an informer, the Pantheon Club was closed. In September the sweep of the Grenelle camp signalled the beginning of a wave of repression and a series of purges. Throughout the political reorientation that followed Carnot played the leading role, not hesitating even to have contacts with avowed royalists such as General Willot, the "white Jacobin," on whom he relied to carry out harsh repressive measures in the south.

As he steadfastly pursued Jacobinism into its last strongholds, Carnot declared, in a speech delivered on May 10, 1796, that his aim was to prevent a return of the "anarchy" of 1793 and to consolidate the Constitution of Year III. In exhorting his fellow citizens to rally round a text that would finally put an end to six years of political convulsions, he hoped to gather a legalist majority against the proponents of "exceptionalism" and "public safety." But this strategy had no foundation and no future. What could the center envisioned by Carnot be other than a narrow, self-interested circle of the Directory's clients? To attack the Jacobins—was this not to fall into the clutches of the royalists, whose influence with the voters had already been demonstrated by the elections of October 1795? In any case, Carnot had played into the hands of the Clichy Club in the Babouvist affair and its sequel. The by-elections of Germinal, Year V (April 1797) confirmed the unlikelihood of a consensus in the center; the royalists triumphed in the electoral assemblies, so that the councils now posed a direct threat to the very existence of the Directory.

With Letourneur eliminated from the Directory by lot, Carnot, more isolated than ever, resolutely joined the royalist side to oppose Reubell, who wanted to nullify the Germinal elections. In choosing this course, he implicitly conceded that the councils could elect a royalist Director and thus left it to a heterogeneous coalition of monarchists and moderates to decide the nation's political fate. He was victorious over his colleagues, and on May 26, 1797, Barthélemy joined the Directory.

His colleagues immediately began sharpening their swords. Carnot, wishing to remain in his position but without assuming responsibility for the crisis, remained suicidally inactive throughout the summer of 1797. He refused to heed the counsel of his friends, who urged him to strike first, and denounced the monarchist party for needlessly provoking his enemies (August 10, 1797). He remained passive in July when Hoche ordered his troops into the "forbidden perimeter" that protected the capital. By not acting, he allowed Barras and Reubell to act instead. On September 4, 1797, Augereau, dispatched by Bonaparte, carried out the coup: Barthélemy was arrested, but Carnot, warned in time, was able to flee.

Amnestied after 18 Brumaire, Carnot returned to France. After a brief stint as minister of police in 1800, he held a seat on the Tribunate, but his opposition to the Empire forced him to return to his scientific work, for which exile had rekindled his enthusiasm. After the first Restoration, which he supported though not without reservations, he enthusiastically welcomed the return of the emperor and accepted the post of minister of the interior, in which he hoped once again to play an important role. In that position he championed a neo-Jacobin policy, twenty-three years after the fact conceiving a new version of the "fatherland in danger" scenario. Napoleon's abdication put a sudden end to his dreams. He nevertheless tried in every way he could to prevent the return of Louis XVIII. As an elected member of the Government Commission he favored resistance under the banner of the king of Rome. The others on the Commission left him to his illusions, and only too late, after the unconditional surrender, did he understand that he had been duped by the wily Fouché.

This time the curtain would really fall on the political career of a man who, in order to satisfy his ambition, pride, and conceit, was ready to serve any regime but who, owing to the rigidity of his character and his lack of political instinct, had been unable to hitch his star to the wagon of the Empire, for all its generous dispensing of sinecures. Carnot sought not so much high office as high responsibilities, and he steadfastly refused the minor role that the Emperor, who held him in low esteem, was willing to offer. Carnot did not give his support to the Empire until after the return from Elba, when he convinced himself that Napoleon would finally be forced to turn to the savior of Year II, the "architect of victory." Blinded by the illusion of a return to power, Carnot this time could do nothing to mitigate the consequences of his mistake. When the Bourbons returned, he was obliged to leave France for a permanent exile.

Patrice Gueniffey

FURTHER READING

Carnot, Lazare. *Correspondance générale*, ed. Etienne Charavay, 3 vols. Paris, 1892–1897.

Charnay, Jean-Pierre. *Lazare Carnot: Révolution et mathématiques*, 2 vols. Paris, 1984 (contains a selection of Carnot's writings).

Reinhard, Marcel. *Le grand Carnot, 1753–1823*, 2 vols. Paris, 1950–1952.

RELATED TOPICS

CONDORCET

In 1789, the marquis de Condorcet was, as Sainte-Beuve remarked, one of the most serious ornaments of the Ancien Régime. Principal heir of the philosophes, distinguished among the forty immortals of the Académie Française, he symbolized the capture of that body by the Enlightenment and epitomized the claim of men of letters, in an enlightened monarchy, to direct public opinion and to speak for the nation before the throne. Celebrated mathematician, perpetual secretary of the Académie Royale des Sciences— and thereby principal spokesman for institutionalized science in France, indeed throughout Europe—he embodied the convergence between the values and interests of organized science and those of the reforming state, a convergence that was one of the most marked features of Louis XVI's reign. The rationalization of social and political life through the elaboration of scientific principles and the application of mathematical analysis, the transformation of a society of orders and estates into a nation of citizens with rights equal before the law, the redemption of monarchical power through enlightened administration and rational public deliberation: such was his ideal, such the program for which he worked and argued under the Ancien Régime. He had calculated the probabilities of political stability in France, along with the chances for progressive social reform through the institutions of the monarchy. But the calling of the Estates General represented a critical failure for his calculations. It was one of many such failures to be experienced by this rationalist in politics, the last of the philosophes, who found himself unexpectedly caught up in a revolution.

First failure, the Revolution of 1789. Condorcet did not want the convocation of the Estates General. On the contrary, he was convinced that parlementary demands for this assembly, while they spoke the language of liberty, were part of a reactionary and anarchical program designed chiefly to sabotage the government's policy of administrative and fiscal reform, together with its plans for national regeneration through the institution of provincial assemblies. Although critical of the modifications imposed by the first Assembly of Notables upon the project for the provincial assemblies, he still believed in the summer of 1788 that Brienne's program would introduce peaceful, rational change, while the calling of an antiquated assembly of estates would lead to interminable disputes in a twilight of reason, a war of corporate claims fueled by the babble of historical texts. Thus his contributions to the great debate over the calling of the Estates General consisted of several pamphlets arguing against the convocation of that assembly, and a lengthy "Essai sur la constitution et les fonctions des assemblées provinciales" ("Essay on the Constitution and Function of Provincial Assemblies"). This complicated treatise was devoted to the technical intricacies and political implications of organizing a hierarchy of provincial assemblies representing the rational interests of *citoyens propriétaires,* assemblies that would create the basis for a unitary national assembly composed of "representatives of the citizens, chosen by themselves" (*Oeuvres,* VIII, p. 234).

In all this debate, Condorcet was true to the inspiration of his principal political mentor, Turgot, whose *Mémoire sur les municipalités* had offered an entire program for the rational representation of social interests and the administrative regeneration of the monarchy through the creation of assemblies of property owners organized without distinction of order or estate. Indeed, it was to the problem of representation that lay at the heart of Turgot's project that Condorcet had devoted his most substantial scientific treatise—the work that he regarded as his greatest intellectual achievement—the *Essai sur l'application de l'analyse à la probabilité des décisions rendues à la pluralité des voix* (Essay on the Application of Analysis to the Probability of Decisions Rendered by a Plurality of Votes), published in 1785. In the most general terms, this work was intended to demonstrate the conviction, shared by Turgot and Condorcet, that the moral and political sciences could acquire all the precision and certainty of the physical sciences. Condorcet developed this claim by combining a Humean analysis of belief with the mathematical theory of probability then being brought to fruition by Laplace. Since the calculus of probabilities provided a sure means of estimating the reliability of our (always probable) opinions and expectations, he argued, the application of this calculus to social and political affairs would yield a rational science of conduct in which the contingencies of human life and action would be finally subjected to mathematical rule.

More particularly, however, the *Essai* was intended to answer the fundamental problem of representation: on what grounds can it be justifiable to subject citizens to decisions that have not been directly and unanimously voted by all, decisions that may well seem contrary to their personal opinions and interests? Condorcet found the answer to this question in a mathematical guarantee: "a very high probability of such a decision is the only reasonable and just grounds on which one may require them to submit in this way" (*Essai,* p. xvii). The terms of this solution should be emphasized, for they are central to Condorcet's thinking. Since politics was, in his view, a matter not of will but of reason, collective decisions should not express arbitrary preferences, but the voters' judgment of the truth of the propositions set before them; a majority vote was justified only if a proposition declared to be true by the greater number was more likely to be true than one so declared by the lesser number. Thus the problem of representation was not how the decision of a representative body could arrive at the general will (a problem that Rousseau had declared insoluble) but how it could be sufficiently guaranteed to express the public reason. Condorcet argued mathematically that such a guarantee (that is, a sufficiently high probability of the truth of decisions taken by a representative body) could be reached where the great majority of voters in a society was at least enlightened enough to choose its representatives among a rationally competent elite, but it could be reached only by specifying precise procedural rules for collective decision making and by requiring majorities that vary in proportion to the importance of the issue to be decided. Many of the complex provisions he proposed for the organization of the provincial assemblies (as for his later constitutional plan) were dictated by the mathematical considerations of this earlier work.

By the time the "Essai sur la constitution et les fonctions des assemblées provinciales" was published, at the end of 1788, it had already been left behind by events. The transformation of the monarchy was to be effected not by administrative reason but through the conflict of political wills. Full of apprehension, Condorcet attempted to avert impending disaster by bombarding the public with pamphlets explaining the rights of man and the principles of rational politics. Although he participated in drawing up the liberal *cahiers* of the nobility in Mantes and Paris, he was not elected by the members of his order. Others were to preside over the improbable transformation of the Estates General into a unitary assembly representing a nation of citizens. Condorcet, the theorist of representation, had to wait for election until the creation of the new municipality of Paris in July 1789.

***

Second failure, the Revolution of August 10. Within the municipality of Paris, Condorcet played a conspicuous part in efforts to maintain order and calm as the Revolution threatened, with the October Days, to drift into anarchy. Outside the municipality, with Sieyès, he was one of the principal organizers of the Société de 1789, founded early in 1790 to counter the more radical influence of the Jacobins by articulating and propagating the truths of a rational social art—"that science for which all the others labor." The society appealed to the liberal elite of the Ancien Régime, those who had embraced the principles of 1789 but now wished to bring the Revolution to an orderly close under their enlightened guidance.

In 1791, convinced by the flight to Varennes that the king's continued presence would breed anarchy and disorder rather than prevent it, Condorcet broke dramatically with his friends among this elite and declared himself in favor of a republic. When he entered the Legislative Assembly, it was with new allies among the Brissotins. With them, he pressed for the French declaration of war against Austria as the only means of exorcising the foreign threat that was supporting counterrevolutionary hopes and sustaining the king in his resistance to the Constitution. With them, he flirted with the threat of popular insurrection as a means of intimidating the monarch and forcing the Assembly to take more decisive action against him. But this strategy backfired: when the insurrection came, it was directed as much against the divided and indecisive Assembly as it was against the obdurate monarch. On August 9, 1792, Condorcet found himself drafting, on behalf of the National Assembly, an address to the French people regarding the exercise of the right of sovereignty and the principles of representative government. This philosophical lecture on the obligation of the people to respect the laws under a representative constitution had not even reached the press before the people of Paris took the exercise of sovereignty directly into their own hands. Once again, the advocate of rational politics was too late to avert the assertion of revolutionary will.

Among the casualties of the failure of the Legislative Assembly was the project proposed by Condorcet on behalf of its Committee on Public Instruction in April 1792. True to the inspiration of Turgot and the physiocrats, and drawing on the arguments of Condorcet's own earlier *Mémoires sur l'instruction publique,* it offered a plan of public instruction for an enlightened and individualistic modern society that was quite different from the communal education advocated by those who admired the civic virtue of the ancient republics. In this liberal and progressive society, individuals would remain free and equal in the enjoyment of their natural rights while functionally differentiated by profession and occupation, socially differentiated by wealth and expertise, and politically differentiated in the allocation and fulfillment of political responsibilities. Such a society was to be achieved through the creation of a hierarchical system of public instruction independently directed and controlled by men of knowledge, acting as the custodians of public enlightenment and the guardians of public freedom. An enlightened people is a free people, Condorcet argued, because "truth is the enemy of power and of those who exercise it. The more widespread it is, the less hope they can have of deceiving men. The more strength it acquires, the less need societies have of government" (*Oeuvres,* VII, p. 421). With the spread of enlightenment through public instruction, power would wither away and social and political conduct would express the informed choices of free individuals in a representative system of government. The conditions would be created, in short, for a politics both rational and democratic.

Its discussion postponed in April 1792, Condorcet's report on public instruction was never seriously taken up by the Legislative Assembly. Although a plan based on it was offered to the Convention by a new Committee on Public Discussion, its fundamental conception and principal provisions were attacked as contrary to equality and republican virtue, an insidious effort to replace the corporate tyranny of priests with that of an aristocracy of savants. Only after the Terror, when the Thermidorians recovered the Enlightenment discourse of the social, renewing the sources from which Condorcet had drawn the principal inspiration for this plan, did the Convention turn to its combination of individualism, liberalism, and scientific elitism as the basis for the educational legislation of Year III.

***

Third failure, the Revolution of June 2, 1793. For Condorcet, the fundamental problem facing the Convention was to rescue the principles of representation and constitutionality from the implications of the insurrection of

August 10, 1792. It was to vindicate these principles that he argued with the Girondins for a trial of Louis XVI that would substitute the rule of law for the assertion of revolutionary will. And it was with the aim of bringing the Revolution to a close on the basis of these principles that he drafted, on behalf of the constitutional committee of the Convention, the so-called Girondin Constitution. Indeed, this constitution was conceived as an elaborate solution to the essential problem posed by the revolution of August 10: how could the representative body be made responsible to the national will without permitting a portion of the population to usurp the right to speak in the name of all?

Condorcet's solution to this problem rested on the extensive political role he gave to primary assemblies. In his constitutional scheme, they would have the power to elect not only the National Assembly but the council of ministers; they would accept or reject constitutional amendments or decide other issues submitted to popular referendum; and they could initiate demands for legislative action or for a constitutional convention. To ensure that deliberations of the primary assemblies would express the rational will of the entire people, questions would be logically reduced to a series of unambiguous propositions requiring a simple yes or no vote, submitted to each primary assembly in exactly the same form, and decided without any prior discussion. These procedures, Condorcet argued, would allow for short meetings attended by peaceful and industrious citizens, leaving no opportunities for a minority of extremists to seize control of the proceedings.

In all this planning, Condorcet's central concern (and the most profound concern of his allies among the Girondins) was to eliminate what he perceived as the most pressing threat to representative government: the claims of the Parisian crowd to exercise the direct right of popular sovereignty by force of insurrection. Diverting that threat required an elaborate mechanism that would simultaneously legitimate protest and prevent revolutions by giving citizens "the facility to make [protests] in a legal and peaceful form" (*Oeuvres*, X, p. 612). The process could be initiated whenever fifty citizens demanded a meeting of the primary assembly in their locality to consider whether the Legislative Assembly should address a particular issue. That primary assembly could call for the convocation of all the primary assemblies in the arrondissement, which could call for the convocation of all the primary assemblies in the département, which could call upon the Legislative Assembly to decide whether to take up the issue. If the Assembly refused, its decision would automatically be submitted for ratification to primary assemblies throughout the republic; and in the case of a negative vote, the legislature would be dissolved and new elections held. The same mechanism could also be used to demand a constitutional convention at any time, thereby creating the possibility for constitutional revision whenever circumstances and popular judgment required. "The claims of the various divisions of the territory would have an equal authority, since they would be led with equal force, with all the force of law, to consult the universality of the people. There would be no pretext for movements, since a movement could only be of a part against the whole, whose decision it would clearly be trying to prevent or thwart" (*Oeuvres*, XII, p. 353). The problem of insurrection would thus be solved constitutionally by providing for permanent, legal revolution.

One knows the fate of this plan, as of its author. Presented in February 1793 in a report as intricate as it was lengthy, Condorcet's constitutional proposals fell hostage to the struggle between the Girondins and the Jacobins until the popular insurrection of June 2, 1793, assured the latter's control of the Convention. It was from the Mountain, as Marat had said, that a new constitution would come. The Jacobins now lost no time in introducing their own constitutional plan, which was hastily adopted by the Assembly. Condemned for his protest against these events, Condorcet slipped into hiding to avoid arrest. Characteristically, his last publication before his flight was a *Tableau général de la science qui a pour objet l'application du calcul aux sciences politiques et morales* (General Portrait of the Science Whose Purpose Is the Application of the Calculus to the Political and Moral Sciences), a futile effort to popularize the conception of a mathematical social art, at once rational and democratic, whose diffusion would "destroy this empire usurped by rhetoric over reason, by passions over truth, by active ignorance over enlightenment" (*Oeuvres*, I, pp. 542–543). As before, the politics of reason had failed before the assertion of revolutionary will.

Nothing illustrates more clearly than the frustrations of Condorcet's political career the growing incompatibility within revolutionary discourse between, on the one hand, the rationalist discourse of the social that found its roots in the physiocrats and the Scottish school and, on the other, the voluntarist discourse of political will that found its principal source in Rousseau's reworking of classical republicanism and the theory of absolute sovereignty. Condorcet's fundamental goal was the redemption of power through reason, his concern less with the location of sovereign will than with its dissolution into the free choices of rational individuals in an enlightened society. But before 1789 the enlightened monarchy was too weak, and after 1789 the sovereign nation insufficiently enlightened, to realize his hopes. Neither under the Ancien Régime nor in the Revolution had the philosophe/mathematician been able to square the political circle.

Historical consolation, the idea of progress. Frustrated in all his political efforts, unable to transform revolutionary will into the ideal of rational consensus under the guidance of an enlightened elite, Condorcet fell back in hiding upon the enlightened philosophy that had provided his deepest inspiration. He had long planned a historical demonstration of the progressive ability of mankind to control its own destiny through the power of reason and the elaboration of a rational social art. Now the composition of this historical picture of the progress of the human mind offered consolation for present defeats in the assurance of a rational future, as in the contemplation of "the human race, freed from all its chains, rescued from the empire of chance and from the power of the enemies of progress, and marching with a firm and sure tread on the road to truth, virtue, and happiness" (*Oeuvres* VI, p. 276).

The celebrated *Esquisse d'un tableau historique des progrès de l'esprit humain* (Outline of a Historical Portrait of the Progress of the Human Spirit) was but the introduction to a much more extended work on this topic, substantial sections of which were completed before Condorcet left his hiding place in March 1794 only to be arrested on the outskirts of Paris, near Bourg-Egalité (Bourg-la-Reine), where he was found dead in his cell two days later.

This bitter and obscure death, at the height of the Terror, was quickly followed by historical resurrection. After Thermidor, Condorcet became the epitome of a political alternative to Robespierre that was nevertheless revolutionary and republican. He had been one of the earliest among the revolutionary leaders to declare the need for a republic in France. But his was a philosophical republicanism that could be embraced as antithetical in every respect to the assumptions and excesses of the reign of virtue, his an enlightenment philosophy of social progress celebrating the scientific reason, individual rights, and representative government that marked the advance of modern civilization over the classical republican model of the ancients implicated in the Terror. Inaugurating a cult of Condorcet that was to be sustained throughout its existence as the principal journal of the liberal republicanism of the post-Thermidorian period, the *Décade* (10 Nivôse, Year III, or December 30, 1794) dwelt in detail on the circumstances of a death the news of which would have shocked the whole of Europe had it not been suppressed by those "vile and ferocious tyrants who were at that time making all bow before their scepter of iron." With the posthumous publication of the *Esquisse d'un tableau historique des progrès de l'esprit humain* early in 1795, that work was seized upon as at once the philosophical testament of the Enlightenment and the political chapbook of the post-Thermidorian period. On 13 Germinal, Year III (April 2, 1795), following the proposal of Daunou speaking for the Committee on Public Instruction, the Convention voted to purchase 3,000 copies of the *Esquisse* for distribution throughout France. "This is a classic work, a gift to your republican schools from an unfortunate philosopher. The perfection of the social state is described herein as the goal most worthy of the human spirit. And your pupils, by studying the history of the sciences and arts in this book, will learn above all to cherish liberty, to detest and defeat all tyrannies," Daunou proclaimed.

This tribute on behalf of the Committee on Public Instruction was to be followed by a more enduring one. With its hierarchical system of instruction crowned by an Institut National, the comprehensive educational law finally adopted by the Convention on 3 Brumaire, Year IV (October 25, 1795), clearly drew its inspiration from Condorcet. And the Institut National, in its turn, now became the principal intellectual and institutional home of his disciples among the Ideologues. Under their direction, the new Class of Moral and Political Sciences of the Institut served as a laboratory for the development of the philosophe's idea of a rational social science grounded on the analysis of sensations and ideas no less than as a center for the diffusion of that idea in France and elsewhere—most notably, in the latter case, to the English radicals.

After the closing of the Class of Moral and Political Sciences by Bonaparte in 1803, the spirit of Condorcet continued to preside over the gatherings of the republican remnant in the salon of Mme. Condorcet at Auteuil. One of the most frequent members of that salon, Benjamin Constant, drew on the *philosophe*'s inspiration not only in his ideas about education and human perfectibility, but—more fundamentally—for his characterization of the profound differences separating the liberty of the moderns from that of the ancients. In the succession of works cut from his *Principes de politique*, Constant consistently turned to Condorcet's *Mémoires sur l'instruction publique* for proof of his claim that the ancients knew nothing of modern civil liberty, based as it was on a conception of individual rights completely alien to their conception of citizenship. From Constant on, modern liberalism has owed much to Condorcet's philosophy of liberty and progress.

Nor was his philosophical legacy neglected in other intellectual efforts to bring the Revolution to a close. It became a fertile source, too, for those who sought in the project of a positive science of social organization a very different solution to the conflicts introduced by the revolutionary events into European society. Both Saint-Simon and Comte invoked Condorcet as their principal precursor in the effort to establish a positive social science; both claimed to be rewriting his *Esquisse d'un tableau historique des progrès de l'esprit humain* in a manner more consistent with what they saw as his fundamental insight into the nature of the historical progress upon which a scientific politics must henceforth rest. But the insight they attributed to the *Esquisse* was, in essence, a serious misreading of it; and their efforts to rewrite this work involved a profound transformation of the idea of progress as Condorcet had conceived it.

Condorcet cast the idea of progress as a warrant to free politics from history; for Saint-Simon and Comte, it became the warrant for the subordination of politics to history. The aim of the *Esquisse* was to show how "by dint of time and effort, [man] has been able to enrich his mind with new truths, perfect his intelligence, extend his faculties, and learn to make better use of them both for his own well-being and for the happiness of all" (*Oeuvres*, VI, p. 283). In it, Condorcet finds proof of the expanding power of a rational politics—grounded in the principles of the rights of man that he regards as the first truths of social science—to shape an open future in the service of human liberty and welfare. The only law in his history is the law of increasing reason and freedom. Saint-Simon and Comte, on the contrary, found human progress governed by laws of historical development that men were powerless to affect, and whose unfolding a scientific politics could do no more than facilitate. In their thinking, Condorcet's philosophy of progress was recast in the light of the organic view of society elaborated by Bonald and Maistre; the epochs into which he had rather arbitrarily divided his cumulative, unilinear view of the progress of the human mind gave way to a necessary succession of closed and hierarchical social systems, separated by the inevitable periods of crisis that occurred as one gave way to another. On this basis, Comte's positive philosophy announced the emergence of a new organic age in which science would serve as the new spiritual power, and sentiments of hierarchy and subordination would necessarily be inculcated in the guise of a new positivist religion. There was little room in such a conception for Condorcet's ideas for a comprehensive system of public instruction that would render individuals free and independent in the exercise of their rights through the spread of scientific reasoning. Nor did it allow for his vision of a mathematical science of social conduct in an open society, that is, for individual and collective choices made rational through the application of the calculus of probabilities; repudiated by Comte, Condorcet's *mathématique sociale* (though cultivated by such mathematicians as Laplace, Poisson, and Quételet) was to be generally neglected until our own day. In rewriting the *Esquisse* in more systematic terms, Comte arrived at a conception of social science fundamentally antithetical to that of the philosophe he claimed as his principal precursor.

In conclusion, at least one other aspect of Condorcet's intellectual succession is worth mentioning here. Jules Ferry was greeted with applause when, in 1870, surveying the new system of education appropriate to the scientific age, he found it formulated "with great precision of theory and detail" by "its prophet, its apostle, its master . . . one of the greatest philosophes to honor the eighteenth century and humanity . . . a man who combined philosophical conviction and incomparable intellectual power with belief in the republic carried to the point of martyrdom: I am speaking of Condorcet" (*Discours et opinions,* ed. Robiquet, I, p. 291). The philosophe offered a powerful symbol for the convictions of the men of the Third Republic, whose republicanism, scientism, secularism, and anti-clericalism were to be enshrined in Ferry's educational legislation. And through that legislation, indeed, generations of Frenchmen, in their turn, became his heirs.

Keith M. Baker

FURTHER READING

WORKS BY CONDORCET

Condorcet: Mathématique et société, ed. Roshdi Rashed. Paris, 1975.
Essai sur l'application de l'analyse à la probabilité des décisions rendues à la pluralité des voix. Paris, 1785.
Oeuvres, ed. François Arago and Arthur Condorcet-O'Connor, 12 vols. Paris, 1847–1849.

RELATED WORKS

Baker, Keith Michael. *Condorcet: From Natural Philosophy to Social Mathematics.* Chicago, 1975.
Cahen, Léon. *Condorcet et la Révolution française.* Paris, 1904.
Reichardt, Rolf. *Reform und Revolution bei Condorcet: Ein Beitrag zur späten Aufklärung in Frankreich.* Bonn, 1973.

RELATED TOPICS

Constant	Enlightenment	Physiocrats	Sieyès	Suffrage
Constitution	Girondins	Republic	Sovereignty	

DANTON

D anton, like Robespierre and Marat, was a creation of the Revolution. He emerged unheralded out of the great event itself. Despite the diligence of his biographers in scouring his youth for early signs of future greatness, it is hard to see in their portraits of the young Danton a man with his course firmly set on the Revolution to come. He was born in 1759, at Arcis-sur-Aube, into a family of minor court officials only recently risen from the peasantry. Educated by the Oratorians, he had been a fair student who had gone on to become a legal clerk in Paris and then an *avocat*. On the eve of the Revolution he was a modest attorney, less impoverished than his adversaries claimed (in order to call attention to the suddenness and alleged impropriety of his later wealth) but less prosperous than his supporters maintained. His library contained a copy of the *Encyclopédie*, between volumes of Plutarch and Beccaria, but such a possession was almost obligatory at the time and does not prove that he imbibed great quantities of Diderot. For his first case he had had to defend a shepherd against a noble lord, but what enlightened attorney in those days could not boast of such a case? Nothing in this background suffices to account for Danton's commitment to the Revolution.

Mme. Roland, who hated him, was right when she described him as a man "born in his section." We have the corroborating testimony of Laveaux, who, on July 13, 1789, to his great stupefaction saw his colleague Danton, previously "mild-mannered, modest, and quiet," climb onto a table and exhort his fellow citizens to riot. That episode marks Danton's entry into the public arena, and it was thus as a street agitator that he began his revolutionary career. He gained further experience in this line as leader of the Cordeliers, the *district* of his quarter. Throughout 1790 this revolutionary avant-garde waged war on "municipal despotism" and Bailly, who had led the way at the Jeu de Paume. It was a guerrilla war, more harassment than all-out combat, and because of it Danton, repeatedly elected president of the district, earned an arrest warrant. At the same time he developed a talent for oratory that Thibaudeau described as prodigious. He enjoyed a growing reputation as a popular spokesman, a "Mirabeau of the gutter."

Like Mirabeau, Danton was a prominent "face" and a profoundly theatrical personality. His was a formidable presence. Atlas, Hercules, Cyclops— contemporaries could never quite settle on an apt word for the "athletic form" with which he somewhat boastfully acknowledged nature had provided him. He was a mass of contradictions: Mme. Roland saw a "repulsive and atrocious" face with "a look of great joviality," a killer without ferocity, a hedonist without lust, a terrorist without principles, a parvenu without greed, a frenetic idler, a tender giant. It was Danton's genius to inspire a portrait in antitheses. Last but not least, he was intimately involved in all the dramatic crises of the Revolution. His was a "nature" to which the Revolution gave not just a mission but an identity.

Like Robespierre, Danton in effect was granted the power to embody the Revolution. A legend, an ideological and political polemic, soon grew up around him as dedicated Dantonists set about appealing the verdict on Danton rendered by Saint-Just and Robespierre. Indeed, the verdict had been rendered before the case was even argued. Hence the posthumous defense of Danton is also an indictment of his judges, and inevitably it becomes a comparison of Robespierre and Danton. This comparison, endlessly repeated, is one of the commonplaces of revolutionary historiography. Robespierre has been compared to Danton as virtue to vice, incorruptibility to venality, industriousness to indolence, faith to cynicism—so goes the version of the Robespierrists, whom Michelet calls the "Catholico-Robespierrists," pleased to "Septembrize the memory of unbelievers." But one might equally well contrast the two men as sickly to strong, suspicious to generous, feminine to masculine (or more accurately, female to male), abstract to concrete, written to oral, deadly systematizer to lively improviser—such is the Dantonist version.

Mathiez called the Danton legend a late embellishment, a poor business of scholars laying flowers on a grave, or in this case on an image invented out of whole cloth by the men of the Third Republic. But Danton's image was already complete in the time of the Romantics. When Michelet, in the opening pages of his *History of the Revolution,* first shows us Danton and Desmoulins, he says that "they will follow us, they will dog our steps," because "the comedy and the tragedy of the Revolution are in them or in no one." Though at times in the course of his work Michelet is forced to concede that his luminous heroes were temporarily eclipsed, he nevertheless persists in casting them as the embodiment of the Revolution, its "true practical genius, its fundamental force and substance." But what was this genius? "Action, as an ancient said. What else? Action. And again, action." Michelet is of course paraphrasing Danton's famous call for audacity: *"De l'audace. Encore de l'audace. Toujours de l'audace"*—a call that Quinet, in turn, who had learned from Baudot to admire the "sovereign of the Revolution," saw as "the motto of an entire nation."

Nor were Romantic fiction and theater immune to Danton's appeal. Hugo, who imagines a dialogue among Marat, Robespierre, and Danton in a hovel in the Cordeliers district, attributes this decisive rejoinder to Danton: "I was there on July 14, I was there on October 6, I was there on June 20, and I was responsible for August 10." And Büchner has him say: "On the Champ de Mars I declared war on royalty. I toppled the monarchy on August 10, I killed the king on January 21, and I threw down his head as a challenge to other kings." For the Romantics Danton was a man upon whom played the dramatic shadow of death, a man whose voice could be electrified by "sudden impulses of the soul," whose strength both engendered and epitomized the Revolution's absolutely unprecedented *journées.*

Is there any truth to all this? On July 14: not a trace of Danton. No one saw him at the storming of the Bastille. He was seen *beforehand,* haranguing the troops at the Cordeliers on the thirteenth, and *afterward,* on the night of the fifteenth, leading the same troops to the fortress to arrest a Fayettist governor, released shortly thereafter. *Before* the fact he had drafted the Cordelier poster calling Paris to arms, and *after* the fact he thanked Louis XVI for returning to his people. On April 18, 1791, the day the king attempted to reach Saint-Cloud, Danton did play a part, but again after the fact: he lectured the Jacobins on the day's lessons. On July 17 he was not present at the Champ de Mars, but he had been there the night *before,* delivering, along with Brissot, a petition of vaguely Orleanist hue calling upon the Assembly to accept the king's abdication; the day *after,* moreover, he found it prudent to flee Paris. On the night of August 10 he was seen making a brief tour of his section and another brief appearance at the Hôtel-de-Ville. Saint-Just would later charge: "You were absent on that terrible night." *Beforehand,* however, he had indicated to the *fédérés* how they should proceed, and in the sanctuary of his own section he had sought and won passage of the celebrated declaration that abolished the distinction between "active" and "passive" citizens and invoked the danger to the fatherland as the ultimate ground of political equality. *Afterward,* however, he became minister of justice, the position that established his reputation as the man responsible for August 10, and the Girondin government certainly saw him as such. He enjoyed good relations with the Insurrectional Committee, which confirmed him as an alternate, and that fact alone might suffice to cast him as an insurrectionary. Condorcet came close to awarding him the title; the ministry, he judged, needed a "man who, through his influence, might contain the wretched instruments of a useful, glorious, and necessary Revolution." Danton did indeed become a minister—as Camille Desmoulins said, "thanks to the cannon"—but it was a cannon to which he was content to listen from a distance. Forget the Romantic legend. Danton arranged and set the stage for events in which he did not take part: "I set the stage for August 10," he told the Revolutionary Tribunal. In return, the *journées,* especially August 10, made him. It was that day in particular that marked a great watershed in the life of Danton; beforehand he was a mere neighborhood agitator, afterward a leader of the Revolution.

By portraying Danton as a leader, the mythmakers aimed to single him out. As Mathiez put it, the positivist school decided "to elect itself a precursor in the unbuttoned hedonist of the Cordeliers" and to portray Danton as the son of Diderot. Of the three rival philosophies that dominated the eighteenth century, Comte detested Voltaire's (the throne without the altar) and Rousseau's (the altar without the throne) but revered the school of the *Encyclopedia* for both its radical emancipation (neither altar nor throne) and its relativist attitude, "relative" in the positivist lexicon meaning that no absolute value was ascribed to the present, which always had to be interpreted in light of the future. The philosophy of the *Encyclopedia* was of course still immature, for while theology was dead, positivism had not yet been born. Nevertheless, it produced two heroes: one a theorist, Condorcet, the other a practitioner, Danton. Hence the third volume of the *Système de philosophie positive* contains unexpected praise of those ten months during which the "organic tendency" of the French Revolution reigned supreme. During this phase the Revolution substituted its own institutions for those of royalty, repudiated theology and attempted to found its own religion, forged a single nation around the concept of "public safety," and instituted a civil government capable of securing order without compromising liberty. During the entirety of this brief period Danton was the soul of the Revolution, for he alone had grasped the fact that a transitional regime requires a transitional—and "naked"—dictatorship. With the advent of the antiprogressive Robespierre, however, the revolutionary tide began to recede.

Let us begin by eliminating all the dubious hagiography from this portrait traced by Comte and later embellished by Robinet and Laffitte. Was Danton the soul of the republican movement under Louis XVI? There are grounds for thinking otherwise. Danton's statements to the Jacobin Club (concerning "the royal individual, who can no longer be king since he is an imbecile"), as well as the petition he and Brissot drafted for the Champ de Mars, are ambiguous: was he taking a step toward the Republic or toward the duc d'Orléans? And Danton's attitude during the king's trial did nothing to dispel the ambiguity. Did he, moreover, favor the cult of Reason, as the positivists, who detested Robespierre's cult of the Supreme Being, wished to believe? It seems unlikely. True, there is his superb response to the Revolutionary Tribunal: "My home? Tomorrow in Nothingness." Yet one must not overlook his rather Voltairean pronouncements on priests—a consolation to an uneducated people—or the fact that he supported Robespierre's policy of moderation. The positivist Dantonists reply, "It was all a question of circumstances." But that avowal is precisely the point: on the question of religion as in the matter of the Republic, Danton's only convictions were those that suited the circumstances.

The positivists' strongest argument remains, however: namely, that Danton was the one person who understood "the transitional character of the social situation" and who unflinchingly argued that a revolutionary situation was an extraordinary one that demanded extraordinary measures. Accordingly, Danton's truly revolutionary *journées* were March 8–11, 1793, when, upon his return from Belgium, he urged deputies to go personally to the Paris sections to recruit new troops. It was during this period that he backed Robespierre's call for a strong government and opposed the Girondins by calling for the creation of a revolutionary tribunal because he "saw no middle ground" between it and the ordinary institutions of justice. It was then too that he suggested the deputies choose ministers from among their own ranks, a proposal the Convention did not heed; on April 6 it created the Committee of Public Safety, but the Committee's responsibility was to "oversee" the actions of the Executive Council, not to replace it. The following summer Danton made another attempt when he lent his support to a law authorizing the Committee of Public Safety to issue arrest warrants and suggested that the

Committee be made into a provisional government "until such time" as the Constitution could be put into effect. In this neglect of principles the positivists recognize and venerate the "relativist" attitude. Danton, moreover, gave an excellent definition of himself in a phrase that seems to have been intended to describe Robespierre: "It is impossible to make the Revolution geometrically."

Danton's political program in 1793 was based on repudiation of the separation of powers and dismissal of the Constituent Assembly's wariness of executive power. He dreamed of a strong government that would not only carry out the laws but exhort and guide the nation, and whose ministers, chosen from the ranks of the Assembly itself, would be jointly responsible to the Assembly for every decision. He proposed an innovation: the brief tenure of the Committee of Public Safety, just one month, a proposal that made it possible for the majority of the moment to control the executive. Hence Danton has sometimes been seen as the inventor of the French-style parliamentary regime, with a government drawn from the legislature yet at the same time distinct and invested with genuine powers of its own. Nevertheless, Auguste Comte insisted on portraying him as the instigator of a dictatorship "comparable to that of Louis XI, Richelieu, Cromwell, or even Frederick II." Viewed in this light, Danton made only one real mistake, for which neither Comte nor Jaurès forgave him: his failure to accept the consequences of his own views, views that would seem to have required that he embrace the personal dictatorship and accept membership on the Committee of Public Safety.

But the fault lay not so much with Danton as with the role invented for him by the positivists, who saw his actions as much more consistent than they actually were. Obedient to the force of circumstances, heedless of the legitimacy of numbers, never at a loss to justify an insurrection, the Danton of 1793 was indeed a man who sought to stabilize the Revolution by strengthening the government, establishing the Revolutionary Tribunal, centralizing authority, relying on military justice, and devoting little thought to the problem of creating enduring institutions. But his "repudiation of metaphysics" was not a product of systematic thought. In his first appearances before the Convention he had argued for the opposite position by declaring, for example, that ministers should not be chosen by the deputies even in case of resignation. Danton used force, but he never made a principle of it or offered a theory of dictatorship. In short, he does not deserve the place Comte made for him in the "glorious phalanx of Western dictators."

Comte's use of the word "dictatorship" was very special, and it proved embarrassing to those who wished to sweeten Danton's reputation. Republican Dantonists soon abandoned the whole idea, thus reducing the Danton created by the positivists to a mere opportunist. From Comte's portrait of his hero the republicans took only those traits that suited the temper of the times—of the period, that is, after France's humiliation at the hands of Prussia in 1870, when the republicans, after much hard struggle, finally conquered the Republic. For academic Dantonists, Aulard foremost among them, Danton became a precursor of Gambetta. He was portrayed as a champion of public education on the basis of a rather uninspiring speech on free—

but not compulsory—schooling. Above all, he was seen as the defender of the endangered fatherland, who sought to mobilize the nation's energies to combat the enemy. The historians of the 1880s saw only the Danton of the tragic period after the invasion of August 1792, the man who opposed retreat beyond the Loire and who organized the recruitment of 30,000 men. He was more the minister of defense than the minister of justice, even though the latter was his official title. They also remembered the Danton of the spring of 1793, who after his return from Belgium stepped up the recruitment effort, this time seeking 300,000 men, and who that summer raised the levy to 400,000 and won the vote on the Revolutionary Army. In these situations Danton's oratory worked wonders. His enthusiasm was contagious: "While it is good to make laws with maturity, war can be waged well only with enthusiasm." He had a natural gift for bellicose metaphor, and an ingenious, affecting way of using the present indicative—the tense and mood of miracles—to transform wishes into realities by the magic of language: "All are in motion, all are astir, all are burning to fight." Danton himself predicted that posterity would be astonished by the contagious quality of his language, which had the power to cause a "general commotion," a sudden "national fever." Oddly, the stereotype of Danton contained in Third Republic textbooks is therefore probably the image that comes closest to the truth. Danton's eloquence worked miracles because the least threat to the fatherland brought the orator to his feet.

The simplicity of this image succumbed, however, to the reprise of Danton's trial at the hands of Robespierrist historians. Laponneraye, Buchez, and Roux began the job; they relied on the indictment that Saint-Just drew up on charges supplied by Robespierre. But not one of the three ever thought of filling in the blanks left by Danton's accusers. That job was left to Mathiez, occupying the chair of Fouquier-Tinville (the revolutionary prosecutor); the historian added a lengthy list of new charges to the prosecutor's indictment. He tirelessly scrutinized Danton's accounts, clocked every minute of his time—including those moments when he discreetly chose "withdrawal," as Saint-Just put it—catalogued his suspicious friends, vilified the hedonist and womanizer, and bequeathed to revolutionary historiography some of its poorest arguments. One of them was recently developed by Frédéric Bluche: that in the case of Danton, the Revolutionary Tribunal's inherent wickedness actually resulted in a certain justice. The whole issue of Danton's venality stems from this determination of the Robespierrists to try Danton yet again before the bar of history. And so also stems the far more important issue of whether Danton's whole policy is contained in his venality.

As to the question of venality, Danton's contemporaries were in no doubt. Today there is still less doubt, even after discounting the obviously dubious testimony of enemies such as Brissot and Bertrand de Moleville as well as the suppositions of Mathiez, for whom, as for Camille Desmoulins, "powerful clues" were enough to convict. Not only did Danton very quickly pay off the debt he contracted to purchase his office of *avocat;* he also purchased national properties (for cash, not availing himself of the clause permitting payment in twelve annual installments) and, being a shrewd Champenois peasant, continually added to his holdings throughout the Revolution. Where did the money come from? Was it from the court, as a letter from Mirabeau would seem to suggest? (Of all the documents this is probably the most damaging, because Mirabeau, who knew a thing or two about corruption, indicated no moral judgment.) The possibility cannot be dismissed out of hand, since Danton surely did want to save the life of Louis XVI. Or was it from the duc d'Orléans? Again, it is possible, since the petition of the Champ de Mars would propose that Louis XVI be replaced "by constitutional means," thus holding out the prospect of a regency. Or, again, was it from the shady financial dealings of friends involved in the Compagnie des Indes affair? Or did Danton perhaps help himself from public coffers? Whenever he was required to render an accounting, as when he quit the ministry of justice or after his return from Belgium, his defense was meager: citing the extraordinary circumstances, he admitted to "having no legal receipts." This nonchalant attitude toward finances stayed with him; he had always viewed passing out money by the handful as a useful way of furthering the revolutionary cause, and it is probable that he did not exclude himself from the government's bounty. Hence there is little doubt about the verdict, and it would be of no historical interest had not Robespierrist historians portrayed Danton's venality as the source of all his policies, foreign and domestic.

Danton's foreign policy is generally associated with a very definite idea of France: that of a country stretching from the Rhine to the Pyrenees, the Alps to the Atlantic, its people burning with desire to identify with the Revolution and free themselves from the tyranny of kings. This conviction, of which Jaurès praised the "admirable clarity," is evident in a speech delivered on September 28, 1792: "We have the right to say to other nations, you shall have no more kings." It also inspired another speech on January 31, 1793, on the annexation of Belgium: "I say that those who wish to raise fears about extending the Republic too far do so in vain. Its boundaries have been marked out by nature." If the "clarity" of Danton's conviction later became somewhat clouded—and Jaurès no doubt exaggerated that clarity in the first place, because Danton had been uncertain of the need for war—it was because Danton had not foreseen the defeat of Dumouriez, from whom he was the last to withdraw his confidence, nor the fact that the Revolution was not strong enough to withstand military defeat. Once that fact became clear to him, in April 1793, when he was a member of the first Committee of Public Safety, he repudiated interventionism and convinced the Convention to abandon the war of propaganda and, implicitly, to permit negotiations. Does this reversal prove, as Mathiez argues, that he had abandoned hope of victory and morally accepted defeat? If so, then one would have to concede that an audacious policy of defense was incompatible with a policy of negotiations and deny that realism required any politician always to seek peace but never to talk about it. There were of course hesitations and contradictions in Danton's policies. (He helped to provoke war with England but worked to reconcile that country with France.) But the same hesitations and contradictions can be found in the policies of the Committee of Public Safety. There are no grounds for linking them to the money passed around by disreputable agents and traitors. The Dantonists, accused of naïveté by Mathiez, have always pointed out that there is no evidence that any of the money probably received by Danton affected any of his decisions. On this point, at least, they are right: Danton's alleged services to the counterrevolution are invisible.

We come now to the most interesting question, the crucial issue in the trial of Danton: namely, the charge of "indulgence" toward the enemies of the Revolution, which has sometimes been used as a pretext for honoring Danton, to the great dismay of the Dantonists, determined to exonerate their hero of "the infamous honor of clemency." There are two ways of looking at Danton's alleged indulgence: as the final chapter of his life's story (an illustration of the rule that all the revolutionaries turned moderate at the end), proof that he belonged briefly to a suspect "faction" of which Desmoulins was the spokesman but which included various corrupt individuals, such as Chabot and Basire, compromised by the scandal of the Compagnie des Indes; or else as a reflection of deeply rooted aspects of his personality.

There is no dearth of good arguments to support the contention that Danton's indulgence was a product of circumstances. By this point he had become a well-to-do bourgeois and the happily married husband of a young and innocent woman. He was, it is alleged, keen to save his shady friends and personally ready for a rest. In short, the hero was tired. Suddenly, therefore, he turned lenient, and the change was of course striking, since his reputation until this point was hardly one of lenience. He was the man who had created the Revolutionary Tribunal. He presented himself before the bar of history "with September's blood on his hands," as Louis Blanc put it, and he had indeed been taunted on the floor of the Convention with shouts of "September, September!" Today, however, we know that Danton did not organize the massacres. His account of them was as dully conventional as Roland's: "Let us draw a religious veil over all those events." Later he held firmly to the Montagnard theory that an organized Terror would be less costly than an unorganized one: "Let us be terrible in order to dispense the people from being so." Yet he did not lift a finger to stop the carnage, probably because he was convinced that what already had been done was irreparable. Therein perhaps lies the true secret of Danton's behavior, and that conviction was probably also the reason for his attitude toward the expulsion of the Girondins from the Convention. Because of this penchant for acquiescing in the inevitable, it is hard to make him out as an "indulgent" personality. He himself said that it was better to "offend liberty than to give our enemies the slightest hope."

One can argue, however, that the Terror was merely a brief episode in the life of a man who by nature was indulgent and whose policy reflected this tendency well before the "indulgent faction" realized that its hour had struck. In support of this view, one can cite cases in which Danton exhibited leniency even as he was giving in to what he believed to be irresistible circumstances: for example, he saved Duport's life in September. He also favored exploring all possible avenues of conciliation, as he showed with Dumouriez: "I have tried every possible way to persuade this man to accept the correct principles once again." Or, again, in the dispute between the Girondins and the Montagnards, he attempted to avoid an irrevocable break by calling for moderation and reconciliation to the very end, or at any rate until he became exasperated by the acrimony of the Girondins. Levasseur later reported that the break came as a terrible surprise to the Mountain because Danton had worked so assiduously to reconcile the two parties to the dispute. Additional evidence for Danton's indulgence includes his statement on the compensation of priests and his decision not to choose deputies to be sent on missions to the provinces "as a function of their sitting on one side or another of the hall." Even after the dramatic meeting of the Convention on April 1, 1793, when the Girondins questioned his alliance with Dumouriez and he broke with them for good, he did not seek revenge. He rejected the petition of the Halle-aux-Blés section, which wanted Roland arrested and brought to trial, and he urged the Convention not to embark on a sea of "calumny and error." After the transformation of the Convention on June 2, Danton accepted the Montagnard interpretation of the event but introduced a measure granting a twenty-four-hour grace period to "administrators who might have gone astray." A thousand similar declarations make it possible to portray Danton as a man less preoccupied with "seizing traitors than with seizing arms," as Jaurès put it. In this he differed markedly from Desmoulins: the latter used indulgence as a weapon against the Hébertists, but Danton ordered Vincent and Ronsin set free.

Was he merely a more flexible politician? Yes, but there was also something else. Danton was apparently incapable of viewing "factions" and "conspiracies" as indiscriminately as Marat and Robespierre. "I tell you, the conspiracies alleged to exist in this Assembly just are not there." And "no faction can exist in a Republic." When charges of dictatorship were bandied about in September 1792, he protested against "a vague and indefinite allegation, which ought to be claimed by the person who made it," namely, Lasource. Danton was willing to allow that there were individual conspirators, and it did not bother him if their heads rolled for specific crimes, but he did not assemble those conspirators into one abstract conspiracy. Finally, there was one aspect of his personality which by itself would be enough to establish his "indulgence": he was perfectly willing to believe that some people wished to live without regard to the exigencies of politics; he refused to regard their traditionalism as wickedness. He tirelessly repeated that some men "are not born with revolutionary blood in their veins but should not therefore be treated as criminals." He recognized a silent majority that "loves liberty but is afraid of storms." Should ardent patriots expel from their ranks "those whose souls are less diligent in the pursuit of liberty but who cherish it no less than themselves"? Should this moderate element be treated as an enemy because "it often condemns energy, which it generally believes to be misguided or dangerous"? Danton's answer was no more in doubt in 1792 or 1793 than during the brief period of alleged "indulgence." His language was always the same: that people should have the right to live without giving a thought to the fact that they happened to be in the midst of a revolution.

It is touching to see a man of such energy willing to absolve those who had none. Note that even in his most violent declarations tolerance is never dismissed. With a subtlety born of hatred Saint-Just understood him well: "All your exordiums began with thunder, but in the end you struck a compromise between falsehood and truth." Danton's speeches were indeed a strange pas de deux of audacity and moderation. To cite just one example, consider the speech on Dumouriez's treason. Danton did not call for dissolution of the Convention (moderation), but he did argue that no one who had not had the audacity to say, "A king must die," could legitimately claim to represent the nation. He continued: "Let us insist that all who did not vote for death admit that they are cowards" (audacious but inconsequential). Then he asked that the Convention "purge itself" (audacity), but "without division" (moderation). And to conclude: "We want to appear deliberate and cool," that is, moderate in judgment, "but if you dare to raise your head again, you will be annihilated" (audacity). The logic of this curious speech seems to be, "Hold me back or I may do something I will regret."

There is a temptation to blame Danton's indulgence on some inner weakness of the giant. Saint-Just said: "Your robust frame seems to have disguised the flaws in your advice." This weakness is also supposed to account for his lack of perseverance, of what Sorel called "the dull, steady throb of will," and to explain his abrupt withdrawals to Arcis-sur-Aube, his resignation from the Ministry of Justice, his lack of presence in the summer of 1793—in short, all the times when his glory was eclipsed. Yet it is possible to view Danton's indulgence in a more favorable light. As Condorcet was well aware, the man was incapable of resentment: "Danton has one very precious quality that ordinary men never have: he does not hate or fear intelligence or talent or virtue." Not only was Danton himself two men in one; he explicitly believed that all men have the right to two lives and that a man's private proclivities are no business of the public authorities. (In this respect his portrait of Dumouriez prefigured Jaurès'.) More than Mirabeau and Condorcet, Danton with every thought and fiber of his being protested the Jacobin assimilation of the private to the public. In this protest he lived up to his legend —and Robespierre and Saint-Just were not mistaken in their choice of an enemy.

Mona Ozouf

FURTHER READING

WORKS BY DANTON

Discours: Choix de textes, ed. Pierre-Jean Jouve and Frédéric Dilisheim. Freiburg, 1944.

RELATED WORKS

Comte, Auguste. *Cours de philosophie,* vol. 4. Paris, 1830–1842.

Dubost, Antonin. *Danton et la politique contemporaine.* Versailles, 1877.

Madelin, Louis. *Danton.* Paris, 1914.

Mirkine-Guetzévitch, Boris. "Le parlementarisme de la Convention," *Revue du droit public et de la science politique,* 1935.

Wendel, Hermann. *Danton.* Paris, 1932.

RELATED TOPICS

Blanc	Louis XVI	Paris Commune
Buchez	Marat	Revolutionary *Journées*
Committee of Public Safety	Michelet	Robespierre
Condorcet	Mirabeau	Terror
Enlightenment	Natural Borders	

LAFAYETTE

On July 29, 1830, Lafayette was chosen by acclamation to head the Paris National Guard. Forty-one years earlier, almost to the day, on July 15, 1789, he had received the same homage from a victorious insurrection. He was then not yet thirty-two years old; now he was seventy-three. One of the last heroes of 1789 still alive, was he not being honored as a symbol, a bearer of hope? Much was omitted in an unvarnished attempt at hagiography: he was portrayed as having come through the political convulsions of the turn of the century without once having wavered in his allegiance to liberal ideas or to constitutional monarchy, now made possible by the fall of the last of the Bourbons. From his involvement in the American Revolution to his opposition under the Restoration, he embodied loyalty to the great principles of 1789. A representative figure of the *juste milieu,* the "furies of Jacobinism" had forced him into exile, and the European monarchies had thrown him into prison. His return to France after 18 Brumaire marked the beginning of a tenacious silence of fifteen years. In celebrating him, the men of 1830 could claim as their own the heritage of 1789 without 1793 or Brumaire. This artificial Lafayette was a kaleidoscope of clichés: the hero of two worlds, the triumphant idol of 1789, the prisoner of Olmütz, the silent opponent of the Empire. His legend drew on the period before as well as after the Revolution. Nothing was left of the general, the politician who for three years, from 1789 to 1792, threw himself wholeheartedly into political combat. Perhaps the rebirth of his extraordinary popularity would have been impossible had the failure of his ambition not been relegated to the shadows.

The man has drawn few eulogies. According to Michelet, he was a "mediocre idol" whom the Revolution lifted far above what his meager talents deserved. Many of Lafayette's contemporaries shared that opinion. When the Jacobins accused him of Caesarism, Brissot's retort was that "Cromwell had character, but Lafayette has none." After the king's flight, Danton maliciously asked him whether he was a traitor or simply stupid. Mirabeau was curter still when, in one of his notes to the court, he skewered "the imbecility of his character, the timidity of his soul, and the small size of his head." Michelet was willing to concede that he was a man of great courage and chivalry, but such generosity coupled with such mediocrity made him a prime instrument for manipulation of every sort. Mme. de Staël, on the other hand, rejected the "reproach of stupidity" against Lafayette and preferred to see him as a man whose convictions were unshakable, no matter what the cost. But was not his only conviction his "love of glory" and "popular favor," as he himself acknowledged in his *Memoirs?* Even Mme. de Staël was compelled to note his "wish to please in salons" as well as his "love of popularity, his soul's favorite passion."

A controversial character, Lafayette was not noted for his qualities as a thinker. He wrote little: a "Memoir to the King" in April 1790, a few pages pompously entitled *On the Royal Democracy of 1789 and the Republicanism of the True Constitutionals* in 1799, and, at a later date, annotations to the works of Mounier and Malouet, the *Memoirs* of Mme. Roland, and the book of Thiers. His own *Memoirs* are nothing but a disorderly compendium of his papers. He mentions the few principles that guided him through life but has little of note to say about them. His only "work" was a Declaration of Rights read to the Constituent Assembly on July 11, 1789, but largely inspired by the text drafted by Jefferson in 1776 for the state of Virginia.

Nevertheless, the mediocrity of the man should not be allowed to obscure all that the personage stood for. Heir to a prestigious name and a vast fortune, which, after his parents' premature death, left him to dispose of an annual income of 120,000 livres, he might easily have become a dissipated young noble pursuing an undistinguished military career. In 1774, at the age of seventeen, he started down just this path: he married a Noailles, joined the dragoons with the rank of captain, and assiduously frequented the court and the queen's entourage. But his correspondence with his wife reveals a very different man, who repudiated the future that tradition and his milieu held in store: although he makes only veiled allusions to a marriage that weighed on him, he rails constantly against the monotony of military life and the futility of the court.

It was from across the Atlantic that sounds of the epic events he dreamed of reached him and promised deliverance from the "inglorious life" to which he believed himself condemned "among persons most strongly opposed to [his] way of thinking" (letter of May 30, 1777). From July 1776 on, French public opinion favored the American insurgents. Lafayette was swayed too, but for him armchair enthusiasm was not enough, and in May 1777 he embarked for America after a series of swashbuckling adventures. While he had set out to win glory on the field of battle, the "American spirit" impressed itself upon his mind and made him a champion of the cause, turning this young and prestigious scion of the French nobility into a central figure of liberal and reformist thought in the decade prior to the Revolution. As early as his first visit to America (1777–1778) he became an enthusiastic supporter of equal rights and a champion of the civic spirit demonstrated by American citizens: "Republican relations charm me," he wrote. He sensed that he was witnessing an event that transcended the borders of America; on several occasions he wrote friends that the future of Europe was being decided here.

After his return to France in 1782, he may have used his prestige to hasten the triumph of the principles that had recently carried the day at Yorktown, or he simply may have played the role expected of the "hero of two worlds." In any case, he gave freely of himself, with an alacrity that provoked the irony of Lacretelle. He traveled in Prussia and later in France, where he agitated in favor of civil rights for Protestants; he became a Freemason, succumbed to the vogue for Mesmerism, and during a visit to the United States in 1784 did his best to export "animal magnetism." He made innumerable statements against slavery and acquired a plantation in Cayenne in order to conduct an experiment in emancipation. In this wholehearted enthusiasm there was something more than a rather silly snobbery. No doubt Lafayette did his utmost to maintain his popularity in the salons. In his correspondence we see him avidly casting about for causes to champion. In 1785 he deplored the fact that he could do nothing for Ireland or Holland. The following year he asked Washington not to forget him in case of war with Spain: "A visit to Mexico City or New Orleans would be most agreeable," he wrote. Yet like many enlightened men of his generation he helped disseminate new ideas outside the traditional networks. He was not a mercenary. In 1786 he criticized the revolt in Peru, noting that "this people is a long way from the ideas that guide a sensible revolution." Ultimately his whole credo lay in the Revolution, to which he devoted himself with an extraordinary perseverance that earned the praise of Mme. de Staël.

Lafayette perceived the first glimmerings of this "sensible revolution" in the Assembly of Notables, to which he was invited. Convinced that its failure would make it necessary to convoke the Estates General, he called for this convocation on several occasions. Not content with ringing declarations, he plunged into action by assuming a leading role in the "patriotic" party and taking part in the activities of the Committee of Thirty, which issued instructions and coordinated action. Along with Lauzun, Beauharnais, La Rochefoucauld, Mirabeau, and many other liberal nobles, he was at the point of combat, demanding that a weakened monarchy grant the nobility the political role of which absolutism had deprived it.

The violent incidents that accompanied the parliamentary agitation of 1788 did not frighten him. In October 1787, when he diagnosed the situation for his friend Washington, he was optimistic; he noted the contrast between the formal organization of power, which he characterized as "Oriental," and "general liberty," which he saw as manifested horizontally in French society. He concluded that "all these ingredients combined will lead [us] gradually, without major upheaval, to an independent representation, hence to a diminution of royal authority." Such a constitutional monarchy would be a permanent point of reference in his coming years' political activities. This devotion to an ideal shared by most of the men of 1789 may not have made Lafayette a theoretician, nor did it make him a strategist; faced with a choice of means, he showed himself to be incapable of adapting to an evolving political situation that, after the first few weeks, outstripped his ability to evaluate it.

His difficulty in winning election to the Estates General attests to a fragile popularity, limited to the capital. In the assembly of the nobility of the Riom *sénéchaussée*, two other deputies won by larger margins: the comte de Langhac, *sénéchal* and president of the assembly, was elected with 382 votes out of 397 cast; the marquis de Laqueuille, received 212 of 393 votes. Lafayette, receiving only 198 of 393 votes, just barely won an absolute majority. The man had enemies, a fact little appreciated at Versailles, where his past commitments led to his being suspected of demagogy. Elsewhere his popularity, seen as excessive, soon aroused anxieties. In July 1789 he reaped the benefits: on the thirteenth the Constituent Assembly chose him as its vice-president, and on the fifteenth in Paris he was unanimously proclaimed commander of the "bourgeois guard," with decisive help from his friend Moreau de Saint-Méry. This "election" actually reinforced the popularity that it claimed to consecrate, since no other vote had provided a true measure of its extent. On July 17, accompanied by the mayor, Bailly, Lafayette welcomed Louis XVI to the capital, to which the king had come, as Jefferson said, to "make amends." On that day Lafayette was truly the king of Paris!

During those weeks, however, the capital was a city at the boil, a city to which calm returned only with difficulty, and an abyss soon opened up between the role Lafayette wished to play and the one imposed on him by his duties. In the districts the general staff of the National Guard was soon accused of wishing to repress the popular movement of July, yet the Guard's interventions only partly reassured the "respectable" segment of society. On several occasions Lafayette was forced to give way to menacing crowds, as on July 22 when his courageous intervention had been unable to prevent the lynching of Foullon. The court suspected him of secretly encouraging persistent disorders in the hope of obliging a monarch in difficulty to turn to him for support.

Despite the violence and misunderstandings, Lafayette's popularity remained substantial. He sustained it, for example, when he refused the compensation offered him by the municipal council and in so doing drew the rage of Brissot, who, in *Le patriote français*, saw in this apparent generosity toward the public treasury a demagogic maneuver intended to curry favor with the crowd. Powerful in the capital, Lafayette was much less influential at Versailles, where he seldom appeared. In August 1789 he attempted to insinuate himself as mediator between the monarchiens and the "left" in the Assembly, divided over the question of the royal veto. But his attempt failed after fruitless discussions. The accusation of double-dealing that was leveled against him was rooted in his speculating on strengthening his political influence in the Assembly and with the king by maintaining the capital of confidence still vested in him in Paris.

For Lafayette, as for the other members of the first revolutionary generation, the October days of 1789 were a genuinely traumatic experience, which in Michelet's words created a "crowd of royalists." Throughout those dramatic hours Lafayette's attitude was ambiguous, a sign that it was impossible to be sure of anyone's ability to contain the popular violence. On October 5, perhaps before he had measured the extraordinarily serious nature of the movement just getting underway, he resisted for nearly six hours the insistence of his own national guardsmen that he lead them personally to Versailles, and he ultimately gave in only when he understood that Paris would judge him by his decision. After reaching the château, where rioters and guardsmen were fraternizing, he at no time attempted to prevent the assault, as evidenced by the weak guard he posted for the night around the castle walls. But the next day it was he who saved the royal couple by appearing on the balcony of the castle and persuading the crowd to acclaim the monarch, yet in conditions so humiliating for Louis XVI that the Parisian general became an object of revilement in the court.

Unlike the monarchiens, for whom October 6 dashed all hope of seeing the Revolution root itself in an alliance between the nation and the king, Lafayette did not retire, perhaps because he did not fully appreciate the consequences of that fateful day. He was obstinate—some called it perseverant—and he believed that his personal ambition and political goals were not compromised. Perhaps he even believed that his chances had improved, now that the king had been brought back to Paris and placed under the protection—the guard?—of his troops. During the winter of 1789–90 he criticized those who had chosen to retire or emigrate. To Mounier, for example, he wrote: "You left; that was a great mistake." To the marquis de Bouillé he repeated that it was necessary to "rebuild the executive power," to reestablish "a strong measure" of it in order to put an end to "anarchy" and secure "a constitutional liberty." At the same time there could be no question of challenging the achievements of 1789, and he wrote Bouillé that it was necessary to "rebuild the machine in the sense of the Revolution," adding by way of persuasion that "the king is imbued with this truth." But Louis XVI did not heed the counsels of Lafayette, who was awaiting his moment.

Lafayette believed himself to be strong and indispensable, in which faith he resembled all the leading spokesmen of the Constituent Assembly. All, from Mirabeau to Barnave, shared the same political ideal, but motivated by personal ambition and by the prospect of becoming the king's sole recourse in difficult circumstances, they squandered their chances for success through relentless competition and endlessly vacillated between the poise that occasionally united them in moments of crisis and the double-dealing which alone could make one of them stand out from his rivals. Thus, at the end of 1789 Lafayette rejected an alliance, proposed by Mirabeau, whereby the great orator actually hoped to neutralize his troublesome rival. In the spring of 1790 he ostensibly moved away from the Jacobins, where the "triumvirs" were going strong, and founded the Society of 1789 in conjunction with Sieyès and Bailly. But his tenacity, his efforts to impose himself as the leader of the party of moderation, could not hide his growing isolation. Mirabeau clearly understood what was artificial in Lafayette's popularity. In his secret note of September 10, 1790, he said he was waiting for the day when through political miscalculation Lafayette "would mortally wound himself."

On July 14, 1790, he was, according to his biographers, "at the zenith of his glory." One might equally well say that on that day the idol began to crumble. Acclaimed by the provinces, he was the laughing-stock of the Paris press. Loustalot wrote that "slaves wearing the uniforms of the various départements . . . kissed Lafayette's hands, thighs, and boots." He added: "If there had been an election, one would have feared that popular folly might bestow upon his horse the same honors with which Caligula rewarded his."

The day after his day of glory Lafayette committed the irreparable mistake that would bring him down, by seeking to obtain through terror the stabilization that no one had been able to impose through politics. Since the October days the Revolution had run away with itself to the point where it seemed to pose a threat to the very foundations of social order. To all who now strove to restore the authority of the state, the army symbolized the extreme gravity of the situation. Mutinies erupted; clubs spread revolutionary ideas in the garrisons; committees of soldiers, challenging hierarchy and discipline, sought to apply to the military the principles that had just turned civilian society upside down. At the beginning of August 1790 several regiments stationed in Nancy rebelled, demanding back pay and the right to oversee the administrative activities of the general staff. On August 8, informed of these new incidents, Lafayette wrote to Bouillé: "It seems to me, my dear cousin, that we ought to strike an impressive blow for the whole army and by an example of severity put an end to the general disarray that lies ahead." Acting in concert, the two generals ordered line troops and "reliable" National Guard battalions to converge on Nancy. On August 31, after a veritable battle, order was brutally restored: several mutineers belonging to the Swiss regiment of Châteauvieux were executed, and others were condemned to the galleys by court martial.

The choice of means could not have been more impolitic: Lafayette handed the Jacobins a weapon to use against him. He became a traitor, while in the eyes of the "party of order" credit for the operation went to the man who carried it out, the marquis de Bouillé, whose star was on the rise in the summer of 1790 and who was infinitely more credible as a "last resort" than the Parisian general, intoxicated by illusions of his own strength. Over the following months Lafayette became entangled in the contradictions of his not very coherent policy, which in any case reflected outdated and unrealizable goals. He squandered his capital of popularity and exposed his flank to Jacobin attacks through several demonstrations of loyalty to the royal couple, yet he was never able to persuade the king to rally, under his aegis, to the side of the Revolution. Lafayette clung to his ambitions in the teeth of the evidence, since it was at this point that the king's escape became the avowed aim of the queen and the émigré contingent.

Over the next few months several incidents showed that Lafayette's position was becoming increasingly delicate. At the beginning of 1791 he was the target of the court, which could not forgive him for the attitude of the National Guard in the murky Vincennes affair (February 28, 1791). Later, Lafayette would maintain that the march from the faubourg Saint-Antoine to the château had been "organized" in order to force the Guard to leave Paris long enough for partisans of the king to seize the Tuileries. Upon their return to the capital Lafayette's troops had unceremoniously expelled the "knights of the dagger." The Jacobins, on the other hand, suspected him of having arranged the whole affair in concert with the court in order to justify subsequent repressive action against the most seditious Paris sections.

Two months later the club attacked him once again, this time on suspicion that he had ordered, to no avail, the use of force in order to allow the royal family to leave for Saint-Cloud, where the king was to have celebrated

Easter (April 17, 1791). According to the Jacobins, Lafayette had at worst cooperated in an attempted escape and at best attempted to point up the monarch's loss of liberty.

This affair was to have unfortunate consequences, skillfully exploited by Lafayette's enemies. Censured by the municipal council for indulgence toward the king, he resigned on April 21. That same night, twenty-three of the sixty battalions of the National Guard asked him to remain at his post. When he seemed to hesitate, forty battalions approached him again, whereupon Lafayette gave in and withdrew his resignation. Was this simply an emotional reaction? Nothing could be less certain; perhaps he had wished to test the loyalty of his troops, some of which had failed him on April 17. The trap slammed shut: a general, whose authority derived solely from the law, had accepted a personal oath of allegiance. Indeed, several battalions had sworn "an inviolable oath of loyalty and unlimited confidence" in him and had even expelled those who refused to participate. By not disavowing this plebiscite, Lafayette became its accomplice.

His enemies then began accusing him of planning to cross the Rubicon, though some of these charges actually dated back to earlier times. As early as June 1790 Mirabeau described Lafayette to the king in these terms: "He is going to have himself made supreme general" and "accept de facto dictatorship." If his ambition were not bridled, he would end up as "the most absolute, the most redoubtable of dictators." These words no doubt owed something to the orator's vindictiveness, but in the spring of 1791 it was no longer a question of personal resentment. The accusations converged, stirred up debate among the Jacobins, and were ultimately confirmed during the crisis of the regime in the summer of 1791.

At a time when Lafayette had to answer for the king in the eyes of the nation, the flight of Louis XVI on June 21, 1791, was a veritable slap in the face. It seems that he was in fact shrewdly circumvented and knew nothing of all the preparations for the escape. Indeed, it is not very likely that the royal entourage would have confided in him. This occasion in any case offered an excellent opportunity to destroy Lafayette's tottering political credibility once and for all. Finally, the initial plan, to which Lafayette might ultimately have given his assent, had been profoundly altered: the military force placed under Bouillé's command had been reduced to the point where Austrian assistance would have been indispensable in any attempt to reconquer the homeland. To that recourse Lafayette could never have agreed.

On June 21 Lafayette proposed the idea, immediately adopted by the Assembly, that the king had not fled but had been abducted. Even more instrumental in saving him, however, was his willingness to accept the alliance proposed by the triumvirate, thanks to which the offensive launched against him at the Jacobin Club by Danton failed, despite his incoherent explanations followed by his blunt refusal to appear in his own defense. In spite of the hostility and skepticism of some members of the society, Lameth closed down the club, provoking the furor of Marat (June 28). Lafayette used this reprieve for one more attempt at winning approval of his "system." Faithful to his double game, he humiliated the king after his return to the Tuileries by zealously organizing the surveillance of a monarch whom he was at the same time helping to prop up through his participation in the drafting of the famous decree of July 15, which called for amnesty.

The fusillade on the Champ de Mars (July 17, 1791) was the response to the split between the Jacobins and the Feuillants, which the night before had wrecked the scaffolding erected by the Constituents in the hope of saving their work. In its results the seventeenth of July was a repeat of the Nancy affair, even if Lafayette's responsibility remains problematic; he was present on the Champ de Mars, prancing back and forth at the head of his troops, but there is no certainty that he gave the order to open fire on the petitioners. The important thing, however, is not whether or not he was responsible for the massacre but rather the fact that he was held responsible. Desmoulins denounced him as another Charles IX, and the Jacobins led a campaign against him. This time the divorce between the capital and the general it adulated was consummated. As if to sanction his collapse, his mandates came to an end: the Constituent Assembly disbanded at the end of September 1791; the next month he was obliged to relinquish command of the National Guard, the general staff having been discharged. In November he received undeniable evidence of his defeat: in the municipal elections, running against Pétion, he obtained only 3,000 of the 11,000 votes cast.

Rejected by the capital, he lingered on the political scene for another year before disappearing entirely. Already, however, he had ceased to be master of his fate. Previously Lafayette, however maladroitly, had shown himself steadfastly loyal to the Constitution. His personal ambition surely drove him to seek the highest responsibilities, perhaps even the post of prime minister, but he was prepared, as he proved abundantly, to wait until the king understood that only through him could the throne and the Revolution be reconciled. Yet hostile propaganda would attempt to portray this convinced legalist as a seditious threat. After he was named commander of the army of the Center, Danton, on December 14, 1791, sought to unmask him before the Jacobins: "The wish to be named mayor of Paris was a ruse; his real role is the one he is playing now." Charges proliferated as war drew near and again as preparations were made to honor the victims of 1790, the soldiers of Châteauvieux. His past, the positions he had occupied, the coups of 1790 and 1791, and the plebiscite after the Saint-Cloud incident all fostered suspicions of Caesarism.

In the spring of 1792 it was widely believed that Lafayette was waiting until the moment was ripe to launch a civil war. Accused in the Jacobin Club of being Lafayette's accomplice, Brissot, in a speech to the Jacobins on April 25, 1792, raised the fundamental issue. He began by dismissing the charge of collusion, denying that the alleged traitor possessed the slightest credibility. Then, after noting the continual calls for vigilance against the threat of an imminent coup d'état, he observed: "You who think you see in Lafayette another Cromwell know neither Lafayette nor your century nor the French people." Was not sacrificing an insignificant general to popular persecution in fact a way of concealing the identity of the true instigators of the coup d'état already in the works? The threat was not the sword, but the word: "For orators, gentlemen, are another class of enemy, far more dangerous for the people," said Brissot. But Lafayette conscientiously played the role expected of him. For nearly seven weeks he behaved like a seditious general, fueling efforts by extreme radicals to tighten the screws and bring the political crisis to a head. Lafayette ceased to have any real substance and became in a sense a figure in Jacobin discourse, living proof that a plot existed.

The final act came on June 16, 1792. Lafayette sent two letters, one to the Legislative Assembly, the other to the king. In the first he repeated his devotion to liberty and the Constitution and urged the legislature to strike his enemies with legal arms, although between the lines was an implied threat in Lafayette's assertion that he respected the representatives but "even more the people whose Constitution is the supreme will." The letter to the king was less prudent. Once again, he offered his aid and this time clearly offered his sword "to defend him against the plots of the rebels and the enterprises of the seditious." On June 28, 1792, after the riot of June 20, he at last took action and crossed the Rubicon, but alone. Appearing at the bar of the Legislative Assembly without authorization, he "beseeched" the Assembly to prosecute the instigators of June 20 and take measures against the "Jacobite sect"—as the enemies of the Jacobins referred to them at that time—and he insisted on respect for his authority and for that of the king. As in his letter of June 16, the humble tone was meant to convey a threat: "Finally, I dare beseech you . . . to assure the army that no harm will come to the Constitution from within." A majority of the Assembly approved Lafayette as the result of a speech by Ramond, who waxed so lyrical that Saladin interrupted him: "I ask Monsieur Ramond if he is delivering Monsieur Lafayette's funeral oration."

In effect, a moribund legislature, having surrendered to a riot, seemed out of fear to be applauding a defunct general. That same night Lafayette attempted unsuccessfully to rally the National Guard behind him. Shortly thereafter, he went to see the king, who dismissed him. When he returned to the army the following day, his effigy was burned in Paris.

After the tenth of August and the fall of the throne, he made one last attempt to rally his troops. Disavowed and indicted on August 18, he, too, was obliged to flee on the night of August 19–20. Five years in prison awaited him on the other side of the border. But after a long spell of amnesia, a second youth also lay in store: "The Austrians did him the essential favor of arresting him, and in doing so they rehabilitated him" (Michelet).

Patrice Gueniffey

FURTHER READING

WORKS BY LAFAYETTE

Mémoires, correspondance et manuscrits . . . publiés par sa famille, 6 vols. Paris, 1837–1838.

RELATED WORKS

Bardoux, Agénor. *La jeunessse de Lafayette, 1757–1792.* Paris, 1892.

——— *Les dernières années de Lafayette, 1792–1834.* Paris, 1893.

Gottschalk, Louis R. *Lafayette Comes to America.* Chicago, 1937.

——— *Lafayette and the Close of the American Revolution.* Chicago, 1942.

——— *Lafayette between the American and the French Revolution (1783–1789).* Chicago, n.d.

Gottschalk, Louis R., and Margaret Maddox. *Lafayette in the French Revolution,* vol. 1, *Through the October Days.* Chicago, 1969.

——— *Lafayette in the French Revolution,* vol. 2, *From the October Days through the Federation.* Chicago, 1973.

RELATED TOPICS

American Revolution
Danton
Feuillants
Jacobinism

Louis XVI
Michelet
Mirabeau
Monarchiens

Revolutionary Assemblies
Sieyès
Staël

LOUIS XVI

L ouis XVI was king of France by his birth and by his death. But between the heir to the throne and the sovereign-martyr historians have had difficulty distinguishing the role of France's last absolute monarch in the series of events that swept away the Ancien Régime and with it the oldest monarchy in Europe. They have been able to portray him sometimes as a wise and enlightened king, eager to preserve the crown's patrimony by bringing about necessary changes, sometimes as a weak and imprudent sovereign, a prisoner of court intrigue, a skillful navigator with no effect on the course of events. There are political reasons for such contradictory judgments, since the unfortunate Louis XVI was caught up in the forefront of the great controversy between the Ancien Régime and the Revolution, but there also remains a great deal of uncertainty about the king's personality.

This uncertainty was evident quite early. While Louis XVI left very few written texts, hundreds upon hundreds of commentaries by contemporaries on his character have survived. These were products of the court and its courtiers, nearly all superficial and more often than not mean spirited, as the rules of the genre required. As dauphin and youthful king he paid the price for what he lacked in charm and assurance, awkwardly filling a symbolic role tailor-made for Louis XIV and which had already proved burdensome to young Louis's grandfather. Over the course of his reign he was slowly tarnished by the queen's unpopularity and portrayed in scurrilous broadsides as filling the unfortunate role of second fiddle and indulgent husband. What was already being called "public opinion" was no more benevolent than the court's and dealt the king even more serious blows, for while the viciousness of Versailles was part and parcel of French court society, the ferocity of Paris destroyed the royal image. From 1789 on the Revolution immured the former absolute monarch in almost total solitude: without court, without friends, cut off from his people in the midst of Paris, he was held prisoner first in the Tuileries and later in the Temple. The confidential letters written to him in 1790 and 1791 by Mirabeau, who had become his secret adviser, survive as pathetic witness to the king's moral and political isolation: they are a correspondence in monologue, letters in a bottle tossed into the sea, which paint the portrait of their sender, never of their recipient. Imprisonment, judgment, and martyrdom add a final touch of mystery to this royal tragedy. Mediocre as a defendant before the Convention, heroic as a victim facing the guillotine, Louis XVI died as a king without having defended the institution of the monarchy. The hagiography that followed his death is some consolation for the insults to his memory that preceded it, although it adds nothing to our knowledge of the kind of man he was. Hence the historian must hew as close to the facts as possible in recounting his life, leaving to the reader's imagination great latitude for interpretation.

⁂

The future Louis XVI was the third son of the dauphin, himself the son of Louis XV. The dauphin's first marriage had been to Maria-Theresa of Spain, who died in childbirth at age twenty, leaving him inconsolable. He remarried very quickly, taking Marie-Josèphe of Saxony for his second wife in 1747. Though he did not love her, he at least gave her many children: first a daughter, who died very young; then Louis-Joseph, duc de Bourgogne, born in 1751; Marie-Joseph, duc d'Aquitaine, born in 1753 (and dead the following year); and then, in 1754, the child who would become Louis XVI, who received the title of duc de Berry. His birth was followed by that of two younger brothers, who would also reign but over postrevolutionary France between 1814 and 1830: Louis Stanislas, comte de Provence, born in 1755, and Charles-Philippe, comte d'Artois, in 1757. The last two additions to the family were Marie-Adélaïde Clotilde in 1759, and in 1764 Elisabeth-Philippine-Marie-Hélène, who would become Mme. Elisabeth and share her brother's captivity in the prison of the Temple.

What made the duc de Berry heir to the throne, in this vast family not immune to the curse of high infant mortality, was the death of his elder brother the duc de Bourgogne in 1761 at the age of ten. His father, the heir apparent, died in 1765. Hence at age eleven the future Louis XVI knew his fate: he would be king of France.

This hereditary devolution wrought by the hand of God disrupted what had appeared to be God's plan: death claimed the child who had seemed in every way destined for the throne in favor of one who had exhibited only commonplace inclinations. As much as Bourgogne was vivacious, charming, adulated, precociously authoritarian, and congenitally a king, Berry was withdrawn, solitary, and graceless. The grief of his parents and of his grandfather—"papa-king" he called him—brought him no additional affection. His younger brothers, Provence and Artois, became the favorites. In a word, the future Louis XVI was the family outcast.

In addition to this psychological disgrace, young Berry probably suffered from being his father's heir, a circumstance that estranged him from his grandfather and thus from the métier of king. Berry's father, the dauphin, had all his life been denied a political role or even so much as a political apprenticeship. Under Louis XV the royal family had in effect taken a standard story from the bourgeois repertory and set it in the court of France. On one side stood the king and his mistress Mme. de Pompadour, who reigned over Versailles and even, if we are to believe her enemies, over royal policy: she was the protectress of Choiseul's "philosophical" party and of the Austrian alliance. On the other side was the queen, Marie Leszczyńska, sick and aging yet fortified by the offended loyalty of her children, guardians of morality and religion.

The dauphin chose his mother's side, and he became the symbol and the hope of the "devout" party, the man of the Jesuits, the implacable adversary of Choiseul and the Austrian policy. A stocky man, almost obese, intellectually lazy, torn in the Bourbon manner between sensuality and devotion, the dauphin was carefully kept out of affairs of state by Louis XV. He never forgot the respect he owed his father, yet he was a living reproach and a potential rival. He died too soon to reign—nine years before his father—but he took sufficient care with his children's education to prepare them for their future role, as though he knew that this time the throne of France would skip not two generations but only one.

When he died in 1765, the duc de La Vauguyon, the royal preceptor, retained responsibility for the new dauphin, and the course of studies remained unchanged. It was a strict regimen, and the pupil was diligent enough, though his work may not have warranted the excessive praise that has been heaped on him by historians bent on rehabilitation. The curriculum was not particularly innovative: the lessons and "conversations" prepared for the instruction of the future king remained a mixture of religion, morality, and humanities, upon which the shadow of Fénelon bestowed an air of unreality and the ponderous duke a modicum of grandiloquence. As for the student, I see nothing in the assignments he prepared for his tutor beyond a docile and insipid mind, which repeated back exactly what was pounded into it. The style, at times elegant, is more interesting than the form, which is always banal: from these pastorals on paternal monarchy and superficial commentaries on *Télémaque* or "the politics derived from Holy Scripture" the future king learned neither how to make an argument nor how to run a state.

The great event, and the greatest failure, of his youth was his marriage, arranged in 1768 through the influence of Choiseul's party and therefore to an Austrian princess, the youngest daughter of Maria-Theresa, the archduchess Marie Antoinette. The wedding was celebrated in 1770, when the dauphin was sixteen and his bride fifteen. For seven years, until the summer of 1777, he was unable to consummate the marriage. For seven years the court of Versailles, Paris, the kingdom, and foreign courts treated this fiasco as either a problem of state or an object of ridicule, the one not excluding the other. When Louis XVI became king in 1774, he was the butt of this European vaudeville.

He was not, strictly speaking, impotent, like his brother Provence, but incapable of ejaculating and in any case little inclined to the love of women. One imagines that this anomaly must have intrigued his libidinous grandfather, quite apart from the damage it did to the future of the kingdom. Indeed, it may have stemmed in part from a repudiation of the cynical and blasé old king, then in the hands of *la du Barry;* young Louis, that is, may have internalized his father's legacy. The Bourbons, thanks to Louis XVI, would end in virtue but without reaping its rewards, since virtue in this case began in ridicule. In the end it appears that it was a discussion with his brother-in-law Joseph, who traveled incognito to France in the spring of 1777, that finally enabled Louis XVI to overcome his inhibition. In August news of the event traveled in correspondence between the courts of Europe, and confirmation came the following year in the form of the queen's pregnancy. The future emperor of Austria—with perhaps the additional aid of a minor operation (the matter remains in doubt)—had resolved the affair within the family, but not even he could erase the memory from the public mind, much less from the minds of the royal couple.

Thus the young man, still an adolescent, who acceded to the throne on May 10, 1774, with the passing of Louis XV after a reign of fifty-nine years, was a man long accustomed to solitude, which the exercise of power would only accentuate. It was this that made his personality "undecipherable" to contemporaries, as Marie Antoinette remarked in her letters to her mother.

When he became king of France at the age of twenty, Louis XVI was a somewhat gauche young man, already plump, with a full face, a Bourbon nose, and a nearsighted gaze not without sweetness. Michelet emphasizes the Germanic descent (through his mother, daughter of the elector of Saxony) of this stout, slow-moving, thick-blooded prince who ate and drank to excess. But these traits might equally well have come from his father, the dauphin, son of Louis XV and Marie Leszczyńska. Contemporary accounts of the young king repeatedly mention not only his lack of grace but also his difficulty in communicating or even reacting. Without conversation or distinction, he had common sense but limited intelligence. In this respect our best source is the journal he kept of his daily activities, in which he noted, along with news of the hunt, his meals, interviews, and family events. This daily diary never betrays the slightest emotion, the least personal commentary: it reveals a soul without strong feelings, a mind sluggish for lack of exercise.

By contrast, what a prodigy he was when it came to physical exertion! The energy he so jealously husbanded in his contacts with men and relations with women was expended on his passion, hunting. He paid meticulous attention to the maintenance of forests and animals, knew the hounds and the men who tended them, and several times each week spent long hours hunting deer, a typically Bourbon pastime from which he emerged exhausted and happy, with the evening set aside for stories of the afternoon's exploits. Another characteristic hobby of this solitary and rather arid man was a kind of manual labor: locksmithing. Louis XVI had a small forge installed above his apartment, in which with modest talent he fabricated locks and keys. From there it was but one flight up to his belvedere, from which he could observe by telescope everything happening in the gardens of Versailles. Some days he roamed the castle's attics and chased stray cats.

It is easy to see how historians could have taken this ultimately rather mediocre personage and turned him into either a hero or an incompetent, a martyr or a criminal, depending on where they focused their attention: the depiction of a simple, honorable man, ill suited to the role he was obliged to play and the historical destiny that awaited him, could equally well arouse indignation at fate's injustice or provoke an indictment of the king's imprudence. His qualities as a private individual hardly make him the ideal monarch to incarnate the twilight of French royalty: he was too serious, too faithful to his duties, too frugal, too chaste, and in his final hour too courageous. Yet through his visceral attachment to tradition, the adolescent who spent his youth in the skirts of Mesdames Tantes and in the shadow of the devout party stood as the symbol of a monarchy that no longer suited either the man or the times.

Michelet, as usual, grasped the essential point: for him this monarchy made in the image of God was the quintessential evil of the Ancien Régime. He understood that Louis XVI was not a very good emblem of the monarchy's end, for he was too scrupulous, too unpretentious, and also too "national" (owing to the war against England and on behalf of American independence). He was paying, in fact, for his grandfather, the depraved old king, the man of the Deer Park and of Austria. For Michelet the drama of the French monarchy was played out under Louis XV, and by the time his grandson ascended the throne, it was too late: the monarchy was already dead.

There is something profound in this insight, which explains where the true failure of Louis XVI actually lies: not so much in his day-to-day policy, domestic or foreign, which had its great moments, as in his inability to revive for any length of time the great expiring body of the old monarchy. The new king was anointed at Rheims in 1775, just as his predecessors had been, but by that time the only coronation was that of opinion. He had it for a moment, thanks to his youth, his good will, the return of the parlements, and Turgot; but too quickly he allowed his popularity to become mired in the unpopularity of the court and the queen. Already, before the Revolution, even his virtues had become targets: this frugal sovereign had endured the "affair of the necklace"; this reformist monarch embodied everything that was old-fashioned; this moral king was married to a loose woman. It was not simply a matter of the frivolity of Marie Antoinette, a princess without much education, not well liked, a foreign queen without roots, without support, and a providential target of satirists. The authority that was lacking was his.

Not that his reign had been static. The contrary was true. The spirit of the times had shaped the modern face of the old monarchy, namely the centralized state, run by intendants and by Versailles bureaucrats. But the progress made in modernizing the kingdom could be controlled by the government only by forging a new contract with society and with public opinion, and that required the end of absolute monarchy à la Louis XIV. If Louis XVI inherited a power too contested to remain an absolute king, he was for that very reason too weak to lead his kingdom toward something else. He supported Turgot during the first two years of his reign only to abandon him to the aristocratic cabal. Shortly thereafter he, rather tactlessly, called Necker a Protestant banker and never could accept his idea of a monarchy "in the English style." But since he was also wary of the clans at court—the petty intrigues of his brother Provence, the ambitions of his cousin Orléans, the queen's clients, and so on—and since he had no esteem for an aristocracy without a public spirit, there existed no recourse in his eyes other than to the traditional exercise of power, as it had been taught him and as he had known it all his life.

This "absolute monarchy" maintained in the absence of an absolute, or even strong, power makes his reign look somewhat chaotic, as king, queen, ministers, Versailles clans, Paris, and public opinion interfered constantly.

Things did not go badly at first, with the keynote struck by the American war, over which Louis XVI hesitated at first before ultimately giving in to Vergennes. But that war aggravated the systemic crisis, of which the deficit was only the most obvious sign. The act by which Louis XVI finally precipitated the revolutionary crisis, early in 1787, was typical of him: by convoking the Assembly of Notables (to solicit its advice) he was consulting his subjects, but by means of an ancient canonical procedure. The same can be said of the Estates General, called the following year. To sample opinion the monarchy resorted to an institution that it found in its tradition. But it transformed that institution just enough to turn it into the first act of the Revolution.

For a good example of this mechanism, which illustrates the mixture of naiveté and traditionalism in Louis XVI and his counselors, one can do no better than consider the Estates General. The institution was an ancient one, but it had not been used since 1614, and as always in the Ancien Régime its rules were uncertain. The nobility and the court insisted on a strict separation of the three orders of the realm, each meeting and deliberating individually. The Third Estate, and, more generally, "enlightened" opinion—that is, opinion period, the spirit of the times—would have preferred a single assembly and double the number of deputies from the nonprivileged order. Louis XVI's "decision," if it can be called a decision, was typical. He left it up to Necker, who had returned to public life more through force of circumstance than by deliberate choice, not only to double the size of the Third Estate but also to organize a genuine election by universal suffrage of all subjects who were neither clergy nor nobles. Yet at the same time he commanded the two privileged orders to cling more jealously than ever to their privilege of distinct election and separate deliberation, thus surrendering completely to the other side and nullifying the concessions made to what was already being called the national party. This contradictory, explosive compromise epitomizes Louis XVI: he was wary enough of the aristocracy to reinforce the Third Estate, but he was so utterly incapable of conceiving of anything other than aristocratic society that he could not even imagine rebuilding the monarchy on a different foundation. At the very moment when he was attempting to reinforce his authority over the divided orders of the realm, he yielded a crucial trump card to what would become the nation by granting it its first parliamentary representation and a ready-made scapegoat in the form of two isolated, oligarchic corps.

At this point began the unhappiest period of his life, since the French Revolution defined itself in opposition to the Ancien Régime, indiscriminately condemning and destroying absolute monarchy and aristocratic society, the twin pillars of the political tradition within which the king had been raised and between which he was never able to appreciate the difference. His last public act made with full authority came on June 23, 1789, when he appeared before the Assembly in an attempt to halt the transfer of sovereignty just enacted by its ultimate beneficiaries, the deputies of the Third Estate. The two declarations he commanded to be read that day indicate just how far he was ready to bend tradition: he could accept a monarchy controlled by the Estates General but not a new society. At its inception this program may have opened the door to the future, but fifteen years later it put an end to all negotiation. In July Louis XVI was already a defeated man; in October he was a hostage, a prisoner of Paris, in the guise of a constitutional monarch. The Assembly left only his person after destroying his symbol and his power. He was condemned, in his rare public appearances, to the lie that kept hope alive.

The history of his hostility to the Revolution is not very difficult to reconstruct. He was obliged to bow down before Paris on July 17, forced to recognize the faits accomplis. He detested the decrees of August 4–11, which destroyed the only society he could imagine; for a long time he refused to approve them. He was horrified by the violence of the crowd, which he confronted directly, along with the queen, on the morning of October 6. At the Tuileries, a stone's throw from the Assembly, under surveillance by Lafayette's National Guard and the activists in the clubs, he was no longer even free to come and go as he pleased. The hunter-king had become the prey. The monarchy paid a heavy price for its escape to Versailles a century earlier: it had taken root in exile, and the people brought it back to Paris only to die. Last but not least of all the blows, the Assembly despoiled the Church of its property in the fall and in July 1790 approved the Civil Constitution of the Clergy, which was soon followed by a law obliging priests to swear an oath of loyalty to the Constitution. Now it was not only Louis XVI's political tradition that was under attack but also his religious conscience: at stake was his salvation.

The compromise between royalty and Revolution dreamed of by so many revolutionary leaders, Mirabeau foremost among them, was therefore never seriously explored. From the great orator's "secret notes" to the court we can see in broad outline what form such a compromise might have taken. On the part of the revolutionaries it would have involved a moderation of the Revolution, to be accomplished by playing off the provinces against Paris and giving the royal executive power its full due. On the part of the king it would have meant accepting the new society born on August 4, which, as Mirabeau tirelessly explained to his correspondent, was more favorable than the old society to the exercise of a strong executive power because the corps of the Ancien Régime had been destroyed.

The first part of this program could never have been implemented. The Constituent Assembly could never have offered the king of the Ancien Régime anything more than limited power without genuine content. Mirabeau's argument, while philosophically profound, could have no immediate effect. In any event it had very little chance of being heard. Neither Louis XVI nor Marie Antoinette could conceive of the monarchy prospering on the ruins of aristocratic society. To judge by the efforts that Mirabeau made, against all hope, to convince the queen even more than the king—"the king has only one man," he said, "his wife"—one begins to think that the misfortunes of the monarchy increased Marie Antoinette's power within the family circle, which no doubt made the policy of the Tuileries more resolute but perhaps also less coolheaded.

It would be wrong, however, to think of that policy as focused purely and simply on the aristocracy, the émigrés, and the counterrevolution on the borders. Louis XVI continued, now as in the past, to be wary of his brothers and their confederates. Marie Antoinette's letters of 1790–1791 are full of recriminations against the politics of the émigrés (although she urged her friends to emigrate). The queen's suspicions of the court nobility remained intact, while all Paris imagined her at the émigrés' feet. In the royal couple absolutist tradition survived the catastrophe that the Revolution represented for both monarchy and nobility. If the idea of temporarily fleeing the kingdom took shape late in 1790, it was not in order to join the emigration but to seize the initiative and recapture authority with the help of diplomatic mediation from Europe and a hoped-for waning of revolutionary ardor in Paris. If it loomed larger that spring, it was because on April 18 Louis XVI was prevented by the crowd from leaving the Tuileries to spend Easter at Saint-Cloud as he did every year. He wished to regain not only his political and religious freedom but also his freedom of movement.

The poorly executed escape attempt that came to grief in Varennes on June 20 offered instead the spectacle of a king isolated in the midst of his people; more than ever he was a captive. It also inaugurated a secret negotiation between the royal family and the moderate revolutionaries, in which Barnave took the place of Mirabeau and Marie Antoinette that of Louis XVI. This conspiracy had no more likelihood of succeeding than the previous one, and it failed for the same reasons. The solemn acceptance of the Constitution by Louis XVI in September 1791, three months after Varennes, was merely a demonstration of the king's inconstancy and duplicity—or, if we take him at his word, of his wish to gain time without resorting to a foreign invasion, a remedy worse than the disease. This was in fact what he wrote just after the charade in the Assembly to his two brothers, who were all for war and dreamed of nothing but military reconquest: "These foreign troops," he wrote in allusion to the hypothetical restorers of his authority, "will not be able to remain in the kingdom, and once they are gone how will one govern if the insubordination begins anew? And how can that be avoided, if the mind of the nation is not changed?" This was followed by a diagnosis more realistic than the one that preceded Varennes and which once again shows some judgment: "I know that my émigré subjects congratulate themselves on a great change in people's minds. For a long time I thought that it was coming, but today I am disillusioned. The nation loves the Constitution, because this word reminds the inferior class of the people only of the independence in which it has lived for two years, and reminds the class above of equality. . . . The *bas peuple* sees that it is reckoned with; the bourgeois sees nothing above. Amour-propre is satisfied; this new ecstasy has blotted out memory of any other." Whence his conduct: "I have therefore preferred peace to war, because it seemed to me at once more virtuous and more useful. I have been reunited with the people, because that was the only way to win it back, and, given a choice between two systems, I have preferred that which accused me neither before my people nor before my conscience. . . . I commiserate with the nobility, with the clergy, with all the victims of the Revolution; but when my duty joins with their interests, should I expect from them only sentiments unworthy of them and of me?"

But in addition to this shrewdly temporizing Louis XVI, who remained more hostile than ever to the émigrés—those intriguing courtiers transformed into swashbuckling crusaders—there was also a sovereign whose sole remaining card was pressure from the monarchies of Europe against France, even at the risk of war. To no avail Marie Antoinette recommended and beseeched (through Mallet du Pan in particular) the princes of Europe, and above all her brother the emperor, to draw a careful distinction between this pressure, this possibility of war on the one hand and the cause of the émigrés and French internal affairs on the other. In so doing she indicated that the royal couple understood the magnitude of the risk, though they did not appreciate the inevitability of failure. Against the advice of their counselors, against Barnave, who (of all people) reminded the queen of the nature of her dignity, Louis XVI in December 1791 turned more bellicose. If he wanted this war, his enemies also wanted it, but for opposite reasons. And as they had foreseen, it was the king whom the war would sweep away. Treason became the new name for his duplicity.

At that point the story of Louis XVI entered its final phase, during which he lost all influence over events yet continued to exhibit through all misfortune and right up to the scaffold the placid courage that was one of the traits of his character and that he also derived from the certitudes of tradition and of his religious faith: courage on June 20 in the face of riot; courage on August 10, the day the monarchy fell; courage in the Temple prison, where the fallen king remained an attentive and serene head of the family. About his trial, seen from his side, there is little to say, since he remained silent, refusing to discuss even the most incontestable evidence, such as the contents of the iron chest. For this I see two explanations, one religious, the other political. Like his father, the dauphin, like his mother, like his aunts, Louis XVI spent the final months of his life in spiritual meditation and hope, comforted by a refractory priest introduced to him by his defender Malesherbes, the abbé Edgeworth de Firmont. With a death sentence hanging over him, he was already in another world.

What in any case would he have had to say to the Convention and its judges? He recognized no relation of justice between them and himself. To him it made no difference whether he was judged as the king of the old France or of the Constitution of 1791. For him to be king was to be justice and the law. Those who constituted this makeshift tribunal had usurped his role, his sovereignty, his majesty: now they wished to do away with the witness. Paradoxically, Saint-Just and Robespierre shared the same thought, but in reverse: if they argued in favor of executing the king without trial and without legal grounds, it was because his crime, patent and proved beyond a shadow of a doubt, was simply to have been king. By restoring sovereignty to the people, the Revolution simultaneously spelled doom for the man who had usurped that sovereignty for so long.

Thus the execution of January 21, implicit in the logic of the Revolution, was accepted by Louis as a sacrifice and endured with simple heroism. Contrary to what the regicides had feared and the royalists had hoped, it was not followed by any particular manifestation of emotion or indignation on the part of the public. In March came the Vendean insurrection, which inscribed the king's name on its banners but did not grow out of loyalty to the king. Later, in the nineteenth century, neither the royalist nor the legitimist tradition was able to make a popular legend of the royal martyr of 1793, for all his exemplary qualities. In contrast to what had happened in seventeenth-century England, in France the Revolution killed not only the king but also the monarchy. Perhaps the real question to ask, following Michelet, is whether the monarchy had not died some time before: before January 21, before Varennes, before 1789, and even before the accession of Louis XVI. That would have made his reign an almost impossible enterprise, terminated by tragedy.

François Furet

FURTHER READING

Falloux, Count Alfred-Frédéric-Pierre de. *Louis XVI*. Paris, 1840.
Faure, Edgar. *La disgrâce de Turgot*. Paris, 1961.
Fay, Bernard. *Louis XVI ou la fin d'un monde*. Paris, 1955.
Girault de Coursac, Pierette. *L'éducation d'un roi: Louis XVI*. Paris, 1972.
Veri, Joseph-Alphonse, abbé de. *Journal*, 2 vols., published by Baron Jehan de Witte, preface by Pierre de Nolhac. Paris, 1928–1930.

RELATED TOPICS

Ancien Régime	Emigrés	Michelet
Aristocracy	Estates General	Mirabeau
Barnave	King's Trial	Necker
Civil Constitution of the Clergy	Lafayette	Robespierre
Counterrevolution	Marie Antoinette	Varennes

MARAT

The historiography of the French Revolution has had Dantonists. It always has Robespierrists. But it has few Maratists. In the revolutionary portrait gallery Marat occupies the place of the fanatic. He had the physique for it ("To a painter of massacres Marat's head would be of immense interest," said John Moore on a journey through France in September 1792), as well as the behavior (histrionic and exhibitionistic) and rhetoric (full of calls for riot and massacre). His function in the Revolution, Camille Desmoulins was certain, was to put a check on the popular imagination: "Beyond what Marat proposes there can be only frenzy and extravagance."

Marat's unique destiny also stems from a death that combined all the characteristics needed to gain a permanent place in collective memory: a celebrated man, ugly and sick, struck down by a beautiful woman in the bloom of youth; a man who clamored for the heads of others but who was known as the "friend of the people," whose murderer gained access to him by means of a petition, a circumstance most apt, as Augustin Robespierre remarked, to "de-Maratize Marat." A bloody man who died a bloody death: what an extraordinary image of the martyred executioner.

He was also a man whose case, opened by the Girondins in April 1793, was argued well before his death. Apart from Louis XVI, Marat was the only person whose fate the Revolution deemed worthy of a roll-call vote; hence we know how every member of the Convention voted, and we also know the words with which they justified those votes. For nine hours deputy after deputy paraded to the podium, revealing the whole spectrum of "opinions" regarding Marat, from patriotic virtue to frenzied madness: the range of views through which posterity has ever since continued to sift was quickly defined.

These views, moreover, are striking for their extremity: he was a "streetcorner Caligula" to Chateaubriand, a "functionary of ruin" to Victor Hugo, a "king of the Huns" to Louis Blanc; it was Marat's genius to inspire caricature. For Nodier he was "the one creature who made me understand the meaning of hatred." Every interpreter of Marat has felt the need to account for this singularity: to counterrevolutionaries he stands for the singular madness of the Revolution itself; to champions of the Revolution he is a singular aberration. With Marat, therefore, one always comes back to the same two questions: If he was a singular personage, to what did he owe his singularity? And can that singularity be considered emblematic of the Revolution as a whole?

*
**

244

MARAT

There are at least three ways of rationalizing Marat's uniqueness: as great sufferer, great victim of persecution, and great visionary. Each of the three possible portraits yields a type of intelligibility: biopsychological in the first case, sociopsychological in the second, political-cultural in the third.

The interpretation of Marat in terms of illness—the inflammatory skin disease which has given rise to an immense medical literature and which explains the bathtub and the turban—was a providential theme for counterrevolutionary historiography, which borrowed it from Michelet. Struck by his discovery that "strange maladies correspond to extreme situations," Michelet had called for a pathology of the Terror. His wish was granted, moreover, for historians since Taine have identified Marat's enigmatic disease with the Jacobin malady itself, his madness with the revolutionary neurosis, the fever of the masses corresponding to the fever of the man. Intended to dispose of both Marat and the Revolution by reducing political upheaval to individual disorder, this superficial argument has been totally discredited by its excesses. Yet it is not clear that Marat makes sense without introducing the theme of morbidity. His illness can be treated as a cause: physical irritation may have inclined Marat toward violence, as he himself confessed. Or it can be treated as effect: whether contracted in the course of a life of obligatory hiding in "tunnels that had eaten away his soul" (as the charitable Danton suggested) or the price he paid for political overexertion (as Marat, who was good at exploiting his illness for effect, maintained), the disease would in either case be an allegory for the life. The frequency of morbid metaphors in his prose, the anthropological pessimism that caused him to view the French people as too corrupt and diseased to make use of the liberty that had come their way, might lend substance to such an interpretation. But then Marat's suffering would be a consequence of his life, not of his body—a sociopsychological rather than a biological explanation.

To the social psychologist Marat is the very type of the frustrated intellectual who becomes a hotheaded revolutionary in the depths of the intellectual sewer where, according to Robert Darnton, the Jacobin determination to liquidate the aristocracy of the mind was born. Marat's violence, we are told, stemmed from his life as pariah: a child plucked early from the bosom of his family, a man without a country, a physician without a diploma, a scholar without intellectual recognition to whose work the academies responded with indifference or skepticism despite his obsequiously diligent efforts to win their esteem and gain entry into their precincts. Yet Darnton's account of Marat's objective frustration is open to challenge. Gottschalk has shown that in England Marat was hardly a pariah but a "gentleman of considerable standing." Daniel Roche, convinced that Marat's scholarly ambitions were far from mediocre or limited, weighs Voltaire's sarcasm against Diderot's respect and notes that Marat received the plaudits of at least one academy, that of Rouen. Gérard Walter points out that Marat's subversive tone remains the same whether he is comfortable or penniless. At bottom it hardly matters though. Nothing is more alien to a sense of frustration than the attempt to measure its "objective" justification: the passion of *ressentiment* never wants for rationalizations. To all who experienced such feelings, the Revolution made an unprecedented promise: the ability to avenge slights received or imagined and thereby to avenge humanity. It was indeed as such that Marat hailed the Revolution: therein lies one key to the man, but it tells us nothing about what set him apart.

Did his uniqueness lie in a remarkable capacity to foresee the Revolution's future? It is worth pausing a moment to delve a bit more deeply into this question, for there is more than one way to anticipate, and different interpreters have ascribed every possible way to Marat. One is to have predicted the coming of the Revolution before the event itself, and a careful selection of citations from Marat's prerevolutionary writings might support the contention that he did make such a prediction, while a different selection might refute it. (To take just one example, one sentence in *Chains of Slavery*—"The murder of a prince is nothing more than a simple assassination"—in which Marat seems to have foreseen the coming regicide, is often singled out, without mention of the fact that the very next sentence is, "God forbid that I should diminish the horror this crime must inspire.") Another manner of prediction is to have discerned in the Revolution itself future revolutions or their sequels. This second interpretation has several variants: Marxist, leftist, and reactionary.

Was Marat a precursor of socialism? Jaurès thought so, as did Mathiez and Vovelle. Lending support to this interpretation is Marat's reflection on the rights of man, "beautiful rights altered, mutilated, truncated, and even destroyed by subsequent decrees," along with his anticipation of the distinction between formal rights and real rights, quite evident in his vehement plea on behalf of the passive citizen, wickedly ignored in spite of the Declaration of Rights. There is also his awareness of "the influence of wealth over the laws" and his presentiment that the people, "having smashed the yoke of the nobility, may well smash the yoke of opulence." All these predictions explain the constant support for Marat, after his indictment in January 1790, from the radical district of the Cordeliers and buttress Jaurès' argument that it was "thanks to Marat that the proletariat became aware to some degree that it formed a class."

"To some degree": this caveat was cast aside by Mathiez. Where Jaurès saw the appeal to the proletarians as an episodic reaction of despair, Mathiez saw a deliberate, self-conscious act: "Marat's whole effort was to inspire a class consciousness in the proletarians." Marat's writings, however, do not warrant such a sweeping assertion. Those of his texts written prior to the Revolution contain the commonplaces of his intellectual milieu (including praise of religion as guarantor of morality and limited monarchy). In his revolutionary writings he continued to make similar statements, at least until mid-1791. As late as March 1793 Marat stated his view that the agrarian law was a "disastrous doctrine" and recalled that he had "moaned a hundred times that exaggerated principles of equality would lead us to this fatal outcome." Marat no doubt set to music the lament of "those who have nothing against those who have everything." But he saw no system capable of saving these "damned of the earth."

Another way of portraying Marat is as a forerunner of leftism. His statements are scoured for hostility to all forms of representation (but Marat drew upon Rousseau as well as upon what was for him the repulsive experience of English politics); for his consistent preference for voting by raised hands (and even, in the king's trial, his insistence that every vote be recorded in a "special register," signed by the person casting the ballot); for his sense that the Revolution was interminable and never truly won; for his praxis, predicated on the belief that the revolutionary must swim among the people as a fish swims in water; and for his preference for the masses over the "apparatus." Finally, and especially for Massin, whose biography typifies this line of interpretation, there is Marat's "correct" appreciation of violence. Massin even sees this "correctness" as the sign of Marat's superiority over Robespierre, hopelessly tangled up in respect for law. For Massin, therefore, Marat is the founder of one of the traditions of the French workers' movement.

Once again, this coherence is obtained at the cost of a deliberate simplification of Marat's words and roles, which were in fact largely dependent on circumstances: the "appeal to the people," which ought to have been attractive to an enemy of representation, met with hostility from Marat on the grounds that it was improper to turn farmers into politicians by taking them away from their plows—a surprising argument from a "grass-roots" political leader. Furthermore, he was not a leader but a follower of a popular movement that grew up independent of him: wholly preoccupied in the winter of 1793 with the king's trial and the struggle with the Girondins, Marat was slow to realize the significance of Jacques Roux's attack on hoarders. In short, this man of the avant-garde at times lagged far behind events.

The final portrait of an anticipatory Marat belongs to the literature of the counterrevolution, which skewers Marat's proposal of himself as dictator, already evident in *Appeal to the Nation,* written in England in 1790, but most prominent in the wake of Varennes. Mathiez himself takes up this theme in attempting to demonstrate that Marat wanted a dictatorship not as a continuation of the Revolution but as a temporary expedient, to be maintained just long enough to crush the defeated class once and for all. But Marat's call for dictatorship was hardly an anticipation: it had to do with both a personal fantasy and a woefully outdated vision of a tribunate, a combination of war with justice. If others among his contemporaries played the game of "If I were the lawmaker," Marat played "If I were the tribune of the people." In his imagination he granted himself "the support of public might" and the privilege of punishing the guilty. For him, however, this dream was circumstantial and sporadic. Here as elsewhere he indiscriminately mingled conservatism with radicalism, and so his uniqueness cannot be ascribed to any theory that he held.

Did he at least play an effective role in the Revolution? Even if we give up the notion that he suffered a particularly unfortunate fate or produced a singularly advanced philosophy, it might still be possible to relate Marat's exceptional violence to events that he experienced. It is clear, however, that his violence was not a violence of action: Marat's actual participation in the revolutionary *journées* remains doubtful. His role on July 14, 1789, was a subsequent literary embellishment of the facts. The only evidence that he took part in the events of August 10 is a document written on August 9 in which he suggests that the royal family be held hostage, words whose impact is hard to evaluate and which he had uttered a hundred times before. The September massacres, with which his name is associated in a sort of automatic reflex, are generally blamed on him because of this injunction delivered on August 19— "Put to the sword all the prisoners of the Abbey, particularly the Swiss"—and because he signed the circular of September 3 exhorting the provinces to follow Paris' example. As Caron has shown beyond a doubt, it is always Marat's words, whether before or after the event, that furnish evidence of his responsibility. By contrast, his participation in the proscription of the Girondins is more solidly established. (Michelet and Esquiros, backed up by Aulard, see Marat as the organizer of June 2: "He issued pardons and sentences," Michelet wrote. "Kings did the same.") He did in fact obtain the first abolition of the Committee of Twelve, thwart the compromise proposed by Barère, and revise the proscription list. Yet on the crucial day he did not appear at the Jacobins but went instead to the Convention, where he contributed several insignificant speeches to the debate. On all the great days of the Revolution Marat was absent. To interpret those days as the fruit of his writings is to accept his own megalomaniac logic: Marat wanted to be the man whose pen was equivalent to an army of 100,000 soldiers and who had only to set words down on paper. His central belief was that words and actions were identical, so that to deny him the right to speak was in his eyes tantamount to counter-revolution.

*
**

This brings us closer than anything in his thought or actions to what was exceptional in Marat's character. Marat had invented for himself a role with a bright future—that of the journalist correcting and shaping public opinion—and identified himself with his newspaper to such a degree that his life during the Revolution became confounded with his paper's: public when it was published, underground when it was proscribed. And for this *Ami du peuple* that was his life he invented a language: therein lay his originality.

Originality, first of all, as a chronicler of the Revolution: no day in the Revolution's past found grace in his eyes, no day in its future seemed to hold anything good in store. His pessimism about the past was the product of a rhetorical trick, a mechanical way of using "only" to deflate any enthusiasm. The night of August 4? It came to pass "only" because castles were burned. The Federation? Such euphoria could "only" be accounted for by the frivolity of the French. June 20? What had been accomplished was "only" "pulling a red cap over Louis XVI's ears." August 10 was "only" an abrupt about-face by the most putrid of deputies. As for the future, every one of its days was conjured up out of an imagination filled with woe. The *Ami du peuple* was full of "frightful mysteries unveiled," "infernal plots," and dire prognostications. (Jaurès, perceptive as always, sensed that Marat was in tune with the popular imagination.) Marat tirelessly predicted the departure of the king's aunts, the desertion of Lafayette, the corruption of Mirabeau, the flight to Varennes, the treason of Dumouriez. And since all these things actually came to pass, it was easy enough for readers of the paper to point to Marat's extraordinary prescience and for Marat to congratulate himself: "More than three hundred accurate predictions prove that I know how to judge men and things." In light of these successes, the predictions that failed to come true obviously did not count.

The prophet of woe, in whom Mathiez saw "a marvelous psychologist," derived his consistent view of things from a monotonous interpretation of the Revolution's ills and a repetitious vision of the proper remedies. That interpretation revolved around a vast conspiracy hatched against the Revolution by the privileged classes, the favored ministers, the divine Motié, the infamous Riquetti: everyone and no one. Despite the violence of the language, Marat displayed a kind of indifference toward those whom he cast as conspirators. They served mainly to prove that he was not one of them and to guarantee the purity and integrity of his words.

If the misfortunes of the day were due to so predictable a cause, there was only one remedy: a purge. At one time or another Marat called for the heads of the fugitive Capets, or for "600 well-chosen heads," or for the "200,000 heads" for which the Girondins would not forgive him. The important thing, however, was not the number of heads, for this was in any case ridiculously small compared with the number of victims of despotism: one of Marat's constant themes was the need to "shed drops of blood" so as to avoid spilling torrents, to punish "a few individuals" so as to save a host of wretches. This sacrificial logic, by which violence was conjured away, was contagious. Robespierre was not above using what Marat called "a very simple calculus," and despite his distaste for exhibition also imitated Marat by portraying himself as a man near death and ready to avoid bloodshed by sacrificing his own life.

One senses how Marat, this solitary figure of the Revolution, could at times have seemed to be its incarnation. The *Ami du peuple* not only disseminated the philosophy of conspiracy that is inseparable from Jacobinism but also invented the language of the Terror. Central to that language was an obsession with visibility. For Marat the absolute evil was not so much the hostility of the counterrevolutionaries as the obstinacy of the people in not seeing it. The French were purblind: sometimes because the tinsel of "vanities" dazzled them, other times because they were asleep. The two besetting national sins were gullibility—the illusion of seeing where there was nothing to be seen—and lethargy—seeing nothing when vision was needed. And the great crime was to prey on these weaknesses, as did the "Brissotins" or Pétion "the opium supplier" or "Roland the soporific." Between the slumberers and the scoundrels there was only Marat, in the solitary role of sentinel of the people, watchdog of the Revolution, who, while everyone else slept, tirelessly fingered the guilty. Only he saw clearly, ripped away veils, and drove out traitors who "feared nothing so much as the luminous writings of patriotic writers." Marat was the eye of the people.

Here Marat touched a sensitive chord in the revolutionary imagination, haunted by its obsession with vigilance and surveillance, its banners festooned with radiant eyes. This vigilance, more than hatred, was the reason for Marat's denunciations. Félix Le Peletier said it best: "Marat was great above all because he reversed the most deeply rooted prejudice that ever existed, a prejudice that caused shame and infamy to be heaped on anyone who denounced a traitor. Denunciation is the mother of all virtues, just as surveillance is the most reliable guarantee of the people's happiness and liberty." Denunciation for Marat was simply pointing to the truth, an act that immediately removed all blinders and broke all spells. So immediate was its effect that proof was unnecessary; all that was needed was induction, always trustworthy for "the observer who knows the springs of the human passions." Obviously, therefore, Marat's accusations were irrefutable. In May 1791 he wrote Desmoulins that to judge men he had no need "of positive, clear, precise facts. For me, their inaction or silence on great occasions is often enough."

This rhetoric without argument, breathless and full of vengeful injunctions ("arrest," "inspect," "impale," "flay," and so on), makes the *Ami du peuple* resemble a frantic monologue, so repetitious that it all blurs into a single issue in which a single idea is hammered home by a single man—a man alone. Marat proudly insisted on his solitude ("the only man to have seen clearly"), sensed it and heightened it when he could (when the Gironde attacked him during the session of February 26, 1793, he challenged Thirion, the only deputy who rose in his defense), and never for a moment thought of doing anything to end it. What could he do? He had no use for dialogue with a fundamentally cowardly, imbecile, stupid, blind people or for the consoling idea of posterity. For "the experience of the fathers is lost on their sons, and every individual, starting from the same point of ignorance, instructs himself only at his own expense." It was the Girondin attack that gave substance to this lonely man, as Dubois-Crancé clearly understood, just as it was Charlotte Corday's knife that called forth Maratists and inaugurated the cult of Marat.

That is why Marat's role in the French Revolution is both exemplary and peripheral. That it was peripheral is shown by the difficulty the men of the Revolution had in making a place for Marat and by their propensity to consider him as an extreme limit beyond which it was impossible to go; it is evident too in the difficulty historians have faced in trying to turn him into a hero, and in the fact that he was less a revolutionary actor than a revolutionary speaker: "I took part in public affairs only through my writings." Yet for that very reason he was exemplary: an emblematic figure of the journalist in the service of the people, the embodiment of that new and decisive power, public opinion; and also the trumpet of the deepest fears in the popular imagination—of famine, poisoned bread, and conspiracy. And finally, as Thiers realized, he was the expression of this dreadful thought, "a thought that revolutions repeat to themselves every day as dangers mount, yet which they never avow, the destruction of all their enemies." To have tirelessly shouted out that hidden truth: therein lay Marat's true singularity.

Mona Ozouf

MARAT

FURTHER READING

WORKS BY MARAT

Les pamphlets de Marat, ed. Charles Vellay. Paris, 1911.
Textes choisis, ed. Michel Vovelle. Paris, 1963.

RELATED WORKS

Bonnet, Jean-Claude, et al. *La mort de Marat.* Paris, 1986.
Caron, Pierre. *Les massacres de Septembre.* Paris, 1935.
Darnton, Robert. *The Literary Underground of the Old Regime.* Cambridge, Mass., 1982.
Gottschalk, Louis R. *Jean-Paul Marat: A Study in Radicalism.* New York, 1927.
Huet, Marie-Hélène. *Rehearsing the Revolution: The Staging of Marat's Death, 1793–1797,* trans. Robert Hurley. Berkeley, 1982.
Massin, Jean. *Marat.* Paris, 1960.
Walter, Gérard. *Marat.* Paris, 1933.

RELATED TOPICS

Blanc	Girondins	Jaurès	Michelet	Taine
Danton	Jacobinism	King's Trial	Robespierre	Terror

MARIE ANTOINETTE

"Calumny had dogged the queen even before partisan spirit caused truth to vanish from the face of the earth. For this there was a depressing and simple cause, namely, that she was the happiest of women. Marie Antoinette, the happiest! Alas! Such was her fate, and so deplorable is man's state now, that the spectacle of brilliant prosperity survives as nothing more than a somber forecast." It was in August 1793, two months before the queen ended her days on the scaffold, that Mme. de Staël thus summed up the career of Marie Antoinette in her highly apologetic *Reflections on the Trial of the Queen*. In this work she did more than express, magnificently, one woman's compassion for another. She put her finger on the secret of a life that could and should have been merely mediocre, but that the great issues of the age transformed into a heroic destiny. Most of all she states quite clearly what, far more than misfortune, made this life important and unwittingly exemplary: public and private were mixed to a degree never before seen so close to the throne of France, and it was the good fortune of the private woman that brought on the misfortune of the queen. Thus, during Marie Antoinette's own lifetime Staël stated themes that for two centuries have sustained a profuse, indiscreet, and repetitious literature. Was she good? Was she wicked? The queen's case is endlessly reargued, though little new information has come to light. Her fabulous biography is examined, her love affairs are enumerated, her pleasures and pains recounted. Writers pretend to weigh scrupulously what must remain ambiguous in any intimate experience; they invent reasons for hating or loving this woman who died long ago. In all this verbose literature few works have even tried let alone succeeded in doing what Stefan Zweig did in a still memorable book, namely, to understand the queen's life in its context.

She was born on November 2, 1755, the youngest daughter of Empress Maria-Theresa and Francis of Lorraine, during the period preceding the great reversal of European alliances that would decide her fate. The following year Austria and France reached an understanding in response to what was deemed a threatening rapprochement between Prussia and England. The new international alignment enticed Louis XV into the disastrous adventure of the Seven Years' War, from which France emerged exhausted (leaving its new ally apparently unchagrined) and stripped of most of its colonies. Weakened in Europe, the king had no choice but to strengthen further the ties that bound him to the house of Hapsburg, despite the anti-Austrian polemic unleashed by the Treaty of Paris (1763), which left cruel traces. The architect of this policy was the king's adviser, Choiseul. A need was felt to cement the alliance through a royal marriage. One idea was to marry an Austrian princess to the aging king. Later it was proposed that one of Louis XV's daughters be married to Emperor Joseph, for the second time a widower. Neither sovereign exhibited much haste in settling the matter. Choiseul and Kaunitz then fell back on an easier solution, and one that seemed to hold a riper promise for the future: they made preliminary arrangements for the marriage of Archduchess Marie Antoinette to the duc de Berry, the grandson of Louis XV, whose father's death in 1766 had just made him dauphin of France.

On that date the marriage was set in principle, but the business was more complicated than it might appear. The father of the future Louis XVI had been one of the most obstinate adversaries of Choiseul and his Austrian policy. The new dauphin's mother, Marie-Josèphe of Saxony, did all she could to delay a marriage that she did not like. Yet it was not her delaying tactics that for four years postponed conclusion of the marvelous bargain but rather an endless diplomatic ballet in both courts as each sovereign tried to derive maximum advantage from a situation that was not yet definitively settled. From the French standpoint this marriage was the best way of controlling a frequently inconvenient ally. On the Austrian side the French marriage was envisioned as one element—an essential one, to be sure—in a grand matrimonial policy in which Maria-Theresa simultaneously married off two of her other daughters, Maria-Emily and Maria-Carolina, one to the child prince of Parma, the other to the king of Naples. In this determined strategy, designed both to reinforce the Hapsburg position in Europe and to strengthen the empire's resistance to forces that threatened to break it apart, Marie Antoinette, the last born, was only a pawn. But she was a brilliantly played pawn, and in the end the empress extracted from Louis XV an official letter, dated June 1769, asking for the hand of the little archduchess in the name of the dauphin. The contract could then be signed. After a marriage by proxy in Vienna the young girl left her family and her homeland to be "delivered" in great pomp to her new country. The ceremony, the last great ritual of this type under the Ancien Régime, took place on the Rhine, near Strasbourg, on May 8, 1770. Eight days later the newlyweds were united at Versailles.

The new dauphine was fifteen years old, which, given the customs of the day, was by no means remarkable. But this adolescent was not prepared for her task, to say the least, and this is astonishing, since she had probably figured in her mother's complex calculations from the moment of her birth. She grew up almost uneducated and never received even the most rudimentary intellectual training. She was lively but superficial: such was the diagnosis rapidly formulated by the abbé de Vermond, who was dispatched from Paris to Vienna in 1768 to attempt to repair the deficiencies in the princess's education, and who would remain her companion for most of her life. "She understood me quite well when I presented very clear ideas to her. Her judgment was nearly always correct, but I could not accustom her to delve deeply into a subject even though I sensed that she was capable of it." Whatever this neglected education may say about the princess's personal qualities, it also gives us an idea of the difference that existed at the time between the courts of Vienna and Versailles. In the one a future queen was expected to exhibit moral qualities and piety, to be a fertile mother, and to show strict obedience to the instructions of her own mother, who had placed her where she was in order to advance her parent's projects with unswerving loyalty. In the other people awaited her debut with interest but without indulgence: how would she make her way and establish her place in the midst of the rivalries and conflicts that rent the court? Had she been better prepared, would Marie Antoinette have gone about her business with greater skill? Of course it is impossible to say, but there is reason to think that the world she had just entered would in any case have presented her with insoluble problems.

She did not arrive empty-handed, however. The empress had seen to it that she was accompanied by a mentor, her ambassador, the comte de Mercy-Argenteau, who was simultaneously a counselor, a confidant, and a spy. He was the man who kept Vienna informed of the young woman's actions and of the success of this political placement, and his correspondence with Maria-Theresa and later with Joseph II remains one of our best sources of information. Behind Marie Antoinette, as well as above her, was her imperious and obtrusive mother, who until her death in November 1780 brought to bear on her daughter all the pressure she could muster. The empress judged, rebuked, and commanded. This aging woman, quite without illusions, knew better than anyone just how precarious her grand design was, yet she continued to run things with an iron hand. As a vade mecum she gave her daughter a set of religious and political precepts that Marie Antoinette was ordered to reread once a month. During the ten years that mother and daughter corresponded, the mother interfered in every aspect of her daughter's life: in the marital problems of the young royal couple, in Marie Antoinette's friendships, in Versailles gossip, and in the foreign policy of France. She did so with a bluntness and brutality that doubtless played no small part in the constant accusations of irresponsibility against the dauphine and later the queen. And she stood aside only to make room for her son Joseph, whose visit to Versailles in 1777 seems to have turned the court against this indiscreet Austrian presence.

The wife of France's future king was assigned a threefold mission. In all three areas she fared badly, though the fault cannot always be laid at her door alone. Yet as early as the 1770s these unfortunate experiences gave rise to a dark legend about Marie Antoinette, which would follow her for the rest of her life. The exact content of this legend was subject to revision, and its tone could be more or less violent, but the basic themes had been established once and for all.

The first theme was of course that of a marriage not consummated until 1777 and a pregnancy that did not come until 1778. None of the blame was hers. It was wholly Louis's, whose moderate interest in love left him feeling no particular urgency about diagnosing and then repairing a minor physiological problem. But when such a problem afflicted a king and a queen, it could hardly remain private for long. The deficient virility and alleged impotence of Louis XV's heir apparent were soon matters of public debate of the most humiliating sort imaginable. For the aging king and for the empress and her son the concern was primarily dynastic and political. The royal line had to be perpetuated, and a child was essential in order to put a durable seal on the alliance between France and Austria. All three were therefore concerned that an immediate solution be found, whatever form it might take. For Louis's brothers, Provence and Artois, this prolonged failure raised great hopes of a change in the order of succession to the throne. Hence it comes as no surprise to find them at the center of most of the rumors that circulated both at court and in the city.

The rumors were in fact the heart of the matter. The misfortunes of the royal couple had all tongues wagging. Every snippet of information was avidly received and dissected. Spies were set to watch the royal bed and report on every minute of the young couple's existence. There was also much mockery, for what was an affair of state became a crude comedy. Marie Antoinette, plunged into torment, often struggled clumsily. In 1775 she permitted herself to speak of her husband in terms so hurtful that she was immediately reprimanded most harshly by Maria-Theresa, and there is every reason to think that this was not an isolated occurrence. By behaving in this way she also opened herself up to every kind of slander. A child finally came of this marriage at the end of 1778. Unfortunately it was a daughter, Marie-Thérèse, the future Mme. Royale, an inadequate reward for such a long period of waiting. It was another three years before a dauphin was born, in 1781, then another son and a last daughter in 1785 and 1786. In a sense these offspring, for some of whom an unhappy future lay in store, came too late. The damage had already been done. Louis XVI's intimate relations with his wife had become an object of public derision that would not cease. Who could believe that this pretty queen could accept the condition imposed on her by her oafish husband's timidity and lack of ardor? Since the king was impotent, the queen must be wanton. By the mid-1770s people were convinced that she had found consolation for the disappointments of her marriage, and talk of a latter-day Messalina emanated from the court itself.

At court she simultaneously faced a second set of difficulties. Versailles in the final years of Louis XV was torn by rivalry among various coteries. To her credit Marie Antoinette seems to have possessed a grace that initially won her sympathy, including that of the old king. But this alone was not enough to enable her to find her way in a complex and changeable situation. Though her mother, the empress, ordered her to remain aloof from the factions that were tearing one another apart, there came a time when she had to choose allies. Hers was truly a hopeless predicament. The dauphine felt nothing but hostility for Mme. du Barry, the mistress who shamelessly reigned over the last years of Louis XV and through him acted as regent of France in all but name. She therefore opposed the king's mistress by pretending to ignore her and allied herself with the king's daughters, who wished to put an end to their father's debauch. Superimposed on this conflict of individuals and influences, however, was a second conflict in which the sides were reversed. It was of

course quite natural for Marie Antoinette to find herself in the camp of Choiseul, the architect of France's Austrian policy and the man who had brought
about her marriage and who was in fact truly devoted to her as a friend. In
the enemy camp she discovered, however, a diverse alliance that embraced,
pell-mell, Mme. du Barry, Mesdames Tantes, and her own husband, the dauphin, who had adopted his father's anti-Austrian sentiments. Choiseul's disgrace in December 1770 did not put an end to these tensions; for a long time
the exiled minister nursed hopes of returning to power, and the dauphine,
loyal in friendship, continued to support him and his plans. She even managed to cause a scandal by meeting him at Rheims during the celebration of
Louis XVI's anointment. At no time does she seem to have been capable of
finding her way in the political labyrinth of the court. Usually she gives the
impression of having been manipulated by Choiseul's coterie or by others.
The king's brothers had their own strategy, as did his cousin Orléans. Marie
Antoinette intervened inappropriately and allowed herself to be drawn into
compromising affairs such as the Guines scandal. Mercy, who kept Maria-
Theresa apprised of her daughter's chaotic activities, was a harsh judge of
this blundering amateurism, which in the end won nothing but enemies:
"People manage to prick her vanity, to irritate her, to blacken those who for
good reason want to resist her desires. It all takes place during races and
other amusements." Behind these maneuvers, which formed the court's daily
fare, there was no political project but only an ill-considered passive engagement that gave credence to the notion that this foreigner wanted to have a
party of her own.

This brings us to a third set of blunders for which Marie Antoinette
cannot bear the entire blame but whose cumulative impact formed the subject
of one of the leading chapters in her black legend. Despite the decision that
she be formally naturalized when she entered France in the spring of 1770,
the dauphine was criticized for having remained in her heart *l'Autrichienne*.
Her mother's relentless pressure was no doubt responsible for this reputation.
Even though Maria-Theresa advised her daughter to stay out of French politics, she also constantly reminded her that she was a German and urged her
to intervene with the king and his ministers in defense of the empire's interests. In her very first year in France, had not Mercy encouraged the hope that
"Madame la Dauphine will certainly govern her husband the prince" owing
to what he was already calling the latter's "state of nonchalance"? Instructions
accordingly came from Vienna ordering her to push for certain decisions and
choices. The empress, who insisted on being informed of everything, wanted
to influence Maurepas's choice of ministers, especially his nomination for the
post of minister of foreign affairs in 1774. Then in 1778 she urged the queen
to make "good use of her influence over the king" to shape France's position
in the matter of the Bavarian succession: "I have need . . . of all your feelings
for me, your house, and your fatherland." This incessant appeal to foreign
loyalties, however much it may have been warranted by ties of blood, ultimately became common knowledge, and the court, in which anti-Austrian
sentiment remained strong, took a dim view of the matter. Adverse judgment
grew even more severe in the 1780s as Joseph II continued to encourage his

sister's interventions. Marie Antoinette, a dutiful daughter, obeyed. She did so with a naiveté and "frivolity" that Mercy continually deplored, usually to no avail. Nor were her attempts to intervene fruitful, since Louis XVI seems to have decided quite early to keep his wife out of his decisions. It made no difference. The queen talked too much and invited ministers in the hope of swaying their views, and people were convinced that she served a cause other than that of France.

*
**

By the end of the 1770s the principal features of the portrait were therefore fixed. Thereafter their aspect would harden as the queen, well before the Revolution, became the object of a veritable propaganda campaign. After 1789 they gave rise to resentment of incredible violence, expressed primarily in an abundant pamphlet literature. Not only did the dimensions of the criticism change but also the stakes. Yet the basic repertoire of themes was never altered. For two decades the same obligatory points remained: the queen was a foreigner; she was an ambitious woman who sought to take advantage of Louis XVI's weakness; and last but not least she was a woman, and as a result of the royal couple's initial disappointments was openly identified with a sexuality that people were ready to believe capable of every kind of excess. These three themes were intertwined and mutually reinforced one another, as in the *Historical Essays on the Life of M.-A. of Austria, Queen of France,* one of the first satirical attacks on her, first published in London in 1781 (and reprinted with great success in 1789): "Antoinette had long planned to become pregnant. This was the key point in the instructions given her in Vienna by the shrewd empress, her mother. She allowed her august husband to squander all his resources on that purpose; they were as scanty as they were useless. She was therefore obliged to resort to a lover." In other words, *l'Autrichienne* was set on the path of vice by her own mother for her own political purposes. These accusations were repeated constantly. We hear echoes of them not only in the trial of 1793 but also in the brief for the defense written two months earlier by Mme. de Staël, who attempted to refute the charges point by point. They are also present in the perfidious apology written anonymously by the comte de Provence, the future Louis XVIII, in his *Historical Reflections on M.-A.* in 1798.

Such consistency poses a problem. Like all rumors, the legend of Marie Antoinette was based on a few facts along with many details that were merely plausible. Facts and details were freely reworked to fit the legend's own logic. Of the many lovers the queen was supposed to have had there is not the least shred of evidence apart from her long, discreet, and complicated relationship with Fersen. But her imprudent behavior in the early years and the fact that she and the king made an odd couple rendered all the reports credible. Hence it was as if the lovers really did exist. Beyond the lust in which she was ostensibly mired there were charges of greed and vindictive cruelty, seemingly confirmed in most spectacular fashion by the murky "affair of the necklace" in 1785–1786, even if the queen was implicated in spite of herself and never fully appreciated what was at stake. The plot, worthy of scandalmongering fiction, exposed the leading figures of the court to public view, and naturally the queen had a place among them. The victim of machinations, she was held after Rohan's acquittal to have been their instigator. Of her desire to intervene in public affairs she gave the most tangible proof in the final years of the monarchy, as perils mounted and the outcome of the crisis was increasingly in doubt. She went about it in her own way, disorganized, maladroit, but more imperious than in the past. She attempted to have her say about the selection of ministers: it was she, backing the wishes of the notables, who obtained Calonne's dismissal, and it was she too who secured the choice of Brienne, a friend of the abbé de Vermond, instead of Necker as *contrôleur général*. More and more she participated in ministerial committees, and it was predicted that she would soon join the King's Council. When she was obliged to accept Brienne's dismissal, she again played a role in the recall of Necker, to whom Mercy-Argenteau was sent as an intermediary in August 1788. Her activities were feverish and known to everyone outside the court. Yet they did not make Marie Antoinette politically shrewd—far from it. In a situation that grew worse from day to day, she seems never to have grasped the changing stakes. As always, she prodded those around her whenever the opportunity arose. For the rest, she invariably recommended a policy of firmness that may have reflected nothing more than her exasperation with the vacillation of the king and his ministers. Taken together, all these things do not add up to a policy.

Whether established or invented, the allegations against the queen would probably not have sufficed to make her as important a figure as she became had they not served a larger purpose. How did it come about that Marie Antoinette, for so long a mediocre personage, was ultimately enshrined in mythology as one of history's great criminals: "Blacker than Agrippina / Whose crimes were unheard of / Lewder than Messalina / More barbarous than the Medicis?" Without realizing it she became the embodiment of the blackest image of royalty.

That image was double, moreover, and contradictory, both arrogant and vile, and it emerged from two conflicting sets of charges. On the one hand, here was a queen who presumed to act as king instead of contenting herself with the usual maternal and charitable functions of the sovereign's wife. Her intolerable ambition placed her in the line of royal mistresses who took advantage of the apathy of Louis XV, and she pointed up the inadequacies of Louis XVI. Yet this queen was not even capable of being a queen. She sought to escape the public arena in which for more than a century the monarchical spectacle had obligatorily been staged. Marie Antoinette did much to restore the luster of Versailles and to keep the elite of the European nobility there. Before long, however, she began to insist on having a private life away from the court and among friends of her own choosing. Louis XV had dragged his boredom and his pleasures from castle to retreat, and it was in fact with him, at midcentury, that the long process of privatization of the royal person began, a process that did so much to alienate the people from its king in the opinion of the marquis d'Argenson, one of the first to comprehend it.

Mme. de Campan, who at least suspected it, observed: "Kings have no interior. Queens have neither *cabinets* nor boudoirs. This is a truth that cannot be instilled in them too strongly."

This fundamental truth was one that Marie Antoinette wished to ignore. In her first years in France she thought she could lead the life of a private individual, whirling from party to ball to theater, and most of the gossip concerning her stemmed from this attempt. After 1779 she had apartments fixed up for herself and attempted to protect some kind of intimacy. But this was of course the Trianon, whose sumptuous simplicity stood poles apart from Versailles: an entirely private space, freed from the encumbering weight of etiquette, ruled by a woman, where the king himself was only a guest; a place where nature eschewed the orderly transparency of the park and whose shrewdly arranged disorder seemed to symbolize the licentiousness of a small group that liberated itself from the self-imposed constraints of court society. In such a space everything became possible in the eyes of those who were not admitted (or were no longer admitted). The favor the queen accorded to her confidants, male and female, was not in itself a new thing. But under these new conditions having intimates somehow seemed shameful, and it was widely assumed that these men and women had to be the lovers of the insatiable queen. She was rumored to be a lesbian, and her whims became "uterine furors." As early as 1775 Marie Antoinette confessed to her mother that a growing number of satirical songs "very liberally" ascribed to her "both tastes, for women and for lovers." Among the former were rumored to be the princesse de Lamballe and later, especially, the comtesse Jules de Polignac, upon whom she lavished spectacular kindnesses until the mid-1780s. Among the men there was not only the comte d'Artois, the king's brash brother, "Charlot" to this "Toinette," but also the whole party of Choiseul and soon all the men she invited to the Trianon. The "royal menagerie," the "stinking and ferocious animals" on whose heads the broadsides set a price from the very first days of the Revolution, faithful friends and simple bit players—all were included. Through them and with them the queen, in the eyes of the public, had done irreparable damage to the virtues of royalty, and in turn she saw herself dragged down into a self-made vortex of destruction.

In a century that set such high value on the feminine virtues while at the same time reinventing the values of private life, Marie Antoinette seems to have stood as a kind of counterexample. The public disapproved of her for attempting to impose a way of life, and she was maligned because she was a woman. But this judgment calls for correction. For one thing the queen, who by all indications was well aware of what she represented, lived so imprudently for so long that the only possible explanation is that she did not realize what she was doing. Yet she did know much if not all of what was being said about her, and on occasion it caused her pain. She never seems to have drawn any lessons from it, however. Still more important, her unhappy experience reminds us that until 1789, and perhaps even longer, queens were not entitled to be women like other women. The evil legend that attached itself to her name is like a negative image of what an exemplary sovereign should have been, and she was criticized for not identifying with the queenly ideal. In an ironic paradox the fate of Marie Antoinette, which did so much to degrade the collective perception of royal individuals in the final years of the Ancien Régime, at the same time demonstrates that the strength of monarchical values remained intact, for she was severely criticized for her failure to live up to them.

*
**

The Revolution helped dramatize this portrait but added no really new features. The silence that greeted the queen's passage during the opening ceremony of the Estates General simply confirmed an already long-standing hatred, which the people of Paris had demonstrated on several occasions since the mid-1780s, in quite striking contrast to the sympathy that for a long time continued to be shown to Louis XVI. In return, Marie Antoinette favored a hard line from the beginning. In the aftermath of June 17, along with Artois and Provence, she joined with those urging the king to opt for confrontation by refusing the compromises proposed by Necker. She still thought it possible to dismiss the deputies and call in the army to regain control of the situation. All witnesses agree that she repeatedly attempted to influence the king to take a more intransigent course. She did not succeed, and in any case between June and October first the Assembly and then Paris forced the sovereigns to make a series of concessions that soon rendered such bravado illusory. After July 14 the first wave of emigration created a vacuum around the royal couple. Not only Artois but also the Polignacs and the abbé de Vermond fled, leaving the king and queen in a deserted palace from which they would emerge only when forced to return to the Tuileries.

Marie Antoinette's hostility to the Revolution never wavered, nor did she ever signal a readiness to compromise. While uncertainty as to the king's true feelings remained for some time, the queen was classed among the staunchest adversaries of the new regime. Whenever the aristocratic plot or, later, the "Austrian committee" was mentioned, she was presumed to be at the center of the alleged maneuvers. On October 1, 1789, when a banquet in honor of the regiment of Flanders turned into a loyalist demonstration (and, rumor soon had it, an orgy as well), the queen once again became the first target of accusation. And when the women of Paris marched on Versailles in October, they uttered threats of tremendous violence against her. Throughout these weeks it is true that the queen exhibited an "imprudence" (Sagnac) that gave clear evidence of her decision to ignore the political situation and act as if nothing had changed. On Saint Louis's Day did she not see fit to receive the representatives of Paris in majesty and give haughty display of her displeasure? She also let it be known that she had been "enchanted" by the banquet of October 1. Such foolish thrusts could do nothing to alter fate, but they quickly cast the queen in the role of a vehement enemy of the Revolution.

Once the sovereigns were held under surveillance in Paris, only three choices remained: attempt to negotiate with the men newly come to power, flee, or solicit help from other European powers. On all three points Marie

260

Antoinette's options and decisions were not very different from those of Louis XVI. But far more than he, she displayed a resolve and at times a courage quite unlike her amateurish improvisations of years past. She showed courage on October 5 when she refused to take refuge at Rambouillet, and again when she ignored the advice of all who urged her to flee, in particular Fersen, and chose to stand and fight. She detested the crowd and held it in contempt, but she was not afraid of it, for which she was even rewarded with an occasional public success, yet to no avail. As for her will, many agreed with Mirabeau that "the king has only one man: his wife." She felt nothing but contempt for the new men and had no intention of bargaining with them on the fundamental issues. Nevertheless, it was she who negotiated, with surprising authority, with the corrupt tribune in the summer of 1790. It is perhaps in her unlikely secret correspondence with Barnave, from shortly after the abortive flight to Varennes until the beginning of 1792, that the change in her style and tone is most noticeable. Marie Antoinette was certainly guilty of duplicity. She was playing for time. Nevertheless she displayed a capacity to follow an intrigue and discuss an argument as well as to dissimulate. More than that, it was she who taught her temporary partners a lesson in determination when she found them too cautious for her taste: "I confess quite frankly that I was unable to find in this proceeding on their part either the character or the desire for the public good that I used to be pleased to find in them" (October 21, 1791).

These were desperate attempts to regain control of a situation over which the queen was in even less of a position than anyone else to claim mastery. As the Revolution turned more and more radical, any attempt at accommodation became illusory, even as all hope of a political restoration favorable to the monarchy vanished. Well before the Varennes disaster escape appeared to be an inappropriate solution as long as the sovereigns wished to set themselves apart from the émigrés, even if they included the king's own brothers. The latter, moreover, did not make things any easier, and the queen complained openly of their ambiguous initiatives and suspect loyalism. Flight would have made sense only if it had been the first phase of a plan to reconquer the kingdom with the aid not of the émigrés but of the courts of Europe. The queen, in her correspondence with Mercy-Argenteau in April 1791, called for just such graduated political pressure, counting more on rising discontent within France than on armed intervention by outside forces, which could be used only as a last resort. Yet despite their declarations the European powers were in anything but a hurry to intervene, even from afar, in French affairs. Contacts under way since the autumn of 1790 led to nothing, and neither Joseph II nor his successor, Leopold II, also a brother of Marie Antoinette, did anything: their reasoning was that of international politics, and the weakening of France served their interests. Hence the queen's appeals remained without effect. The Austrian princess no doubt believed that she was entitled to expect whatever she wanted from the family policy that had placed her where she was, but she underestimated the importance of raison d'état and national self-interest. When war was finally declared in April 1792 the situation seemed clear. But it was too late. The queen could wish disaster on the troops of the Revolution; she could even contribute to their defeat by actively engaging in treason. But she could not influence the outcome of the battle, much less anticipate or control the domestic consequences of a conflict which within a few months would bring down the monarchy and leave the dethroned sovereigns accused criminals.

In any case the queen's fate had long since been decided by public opinion. In the very first years of the Revolution an abundant pamphlet literature had made her its target. It began not in 1789 but, as we saw earlier, in the 1770s, with several periods of particularly high intensity, such as the campaign of obscene Christmas carols that affected her so strongly in 1781 as well as the aftermath of the "affair of the necklace." Much of this material was prepared, usually in London, by professional satirists with mysterious connections to the French police: Thévenau de Morande, Pelleport (who was probably linked to Brissot), and in France itself the police official Goupil were the best known of them. It was they who created the basic repertoire of themes used in all later productions. With the Revolution, however, the dimensions and significance of the phenomenon changed. The pamphlets were now published in France (complete with invented references that make it difficult today to reconstruct the history of publication). Their numbers increased greatly. Printed on bad paper, often no more than eight or sixteen pages, sold at low prices, they were offered for sale on a wide market (through used-book dealers and hawkers), in contrast to the final years of the Ancien Régime when the primary audience for such literature was probably the court and the city. Fragile and perishable, these texts have not been well preserved. From the collection that it is possible to reconstruct today, however, it appears that there was a disparity between the actual political situation and the situation as portrayed in the pamphlets. It was in 1790, the "happy year," that Marie Antoinette became the leading lady of the satirists, at a time when the political journalists were still ignoring her and Hébert's *Père Duchesne* had yet to take up the refrain. The themes were not really new, but the criticism had turned harsh. The libertine had become a whore; the schemer was now thirsty for the blood of her fellow citizens; the Austrian openly proclaimed her obsession with betraying the Revolution. The writing turned more violent in anticipation of a "popular" audience, to which it pandered to the point of caricature. Most important of all, pornography became a means of political expression. By indulgently detailing the alleged debauchery of the queen and her "menagerie," the pamphlets spoke the classic double language of obscenity and moral instruction. They also offer a glimpse of their enigmatic central figure: woman as enemy of the Revolution. The incredible verbal frenzy, the proliferation of metaphors for which the body of Marie Antoinette provided the pretext, suggests that beyond the queen it was the female sex that was the target in an age that burned incense to mothers but did not always know what to make of citoyennes.

In an ironic paradox this literature was unleashed at a time when Marie Antoinette, who had devoted so much ingenuity to inventing the rules of a kind of private life at the Trianon, was forced by circumstances to retire there. From the end of 1789 to 1793 the circle around the royal family shrank steadily, and its life became increasingly domestic. This final role may have been forced on the queen, but she seems to have embraced it with conviction.

When she testified at her trial that in going to Varennes she had done nothing but follow her husband and children; when she answered her accusers, "I was merely the wife of Louis XVI and . . . I had no choice but to accede to his wishes"; and finally, when she placed her son's happiness above all other hopes, there is no reason to doubt her sincerity or to see it, for example, as a flight from her responsibilities. The queen—the woman rigid in misfortune whom David captured in a cruel sketch on her way to the scaffold—adopted in the face of circumstances a sort of familial and Christian heroism that echoed, albeit in a different key, the saintly resignation of Louis XVI. This final and unexpected maternal image seemed threatening enough to her adversaries that Hébert, during her trial, hazarded one last—and quite shocking—attack by introducing testimony from her eight-year-old son accusing her of incestuous games.

The trial itself is of interest only in that it brought together all the features of this collective portrait. It had neither the scope nor the significance of Louis XVI's trial. In December 1792 the secretary of the Committee on Legislation had announced that it would be held, and then Robespierre followed suit, but events precipitated the proceedings. In the summer of 1793 the Convention faced three urgent needs. In Michelet's blunt language they were: "To kill the queen, to kill the Girondins, and to beat the Austrians." Preceded by lengthy interrogations, the case was dispatched in two days by the Revolutionary Tribunal (October 14–16, 1793). Forty witnesses repeated the traditional accusations: treason, squandering of public funds, and immorality, as well as specific charges concerning Marie Antoinette's role at the time of Varennes, on August 10, and in clumsy attempts to arrange her escape from the Temple and the Conciergerie. Old resentments resurfaced, in particular the affair of the guards' banquet in October 1789, coupled with new insinuations concerning private crimes. It was a thoroughly undistinguished affair, as the judges complacently listened to witnesses and evidence. The confused debate, in which the fallen queen displayed undeniable skill, never got off the ground. This was because her trial, unlike the king's, involved no major political issue. It was left to Fouquier-Tinville to make something out of the whole confused mess. This he was able to do. He skillfully summed up the counts of the indictment, the well-founded charges along with the baseless ones, and painted one last mythological portrait of a queen "fertile in intrigues of every sort . . . so perverse and so familiar with every kind of crime," who, "from the beginning of her sojourn in France, has been the scourge and bloodsucker of the French people." The life that ended on October 16 on the Place de la Révolution had long since been eclipsed by the legend of Marie Antoinette.

Jacques Revel

FURTHER READING

Correspondance entre Maria Theresa et Marie-Antoinette, ed. Georges Girard. Paris, 1933.

Correspondance secrète du comte de Mercy-Argenteau avec l'empereur Joseph II et le prince de Kaunitz, 2 vols., ed. Alfred d'Arneth and Jules Flammermont. Paris, 1889–1891.

Correspondance secrète entre Maria Theresa et le comte de Mercy-Argenteau, 3 vols., ed. Alfred d'Arneth and Auguste Geffroy. Paris, 1874.

Fersen et Marie-Antoinette: Correspondance et journal intime inédits du comte Axel de Fersen, ed. Alma Söderhjelm. Paris, 1930.

Lettres de Marie-Antoinette: Recueil des lettres authentiques de la reine, 2 vols., ed. Maxime de La Rocheterie and Gaston du Frexne, marquis de Beaucourt. Paris, 1895–1896.

Marie-Antoinette et Barnave, correspondance secrète (juillet 1791–janvier 1792), ed. Alma Söderhjelm. Paris, 1934.

Tourneux, Maurice. *Marie-Antoinette devant l'histoire: Essai bibliographique.* Paris, 1895.

Walter, Gérard. *Marie-Antoinette.* Paris, 1948.

Zweig, Stefan. *Marie-Antoinette.* Paris, 1933 (original edition: *Marie-Antoinette: Bildnis eines mittleren Charackters,* Leipzig, 1932).

RELATED TOPICS

Barnave	Hébertists	Mirabeau	Staël
Emigrés	Louis XVI	Necker	Varennes

MIRABEAU

M irabeau had two lives, one under the Ancien Régime, the other with the French Revolution. The first was a failure, though it did show flashes of genius. The second covered him with glory, despite certain unmentionable episodes. Of the most despised offspring of the old nobility the Revolution made the most brilliant personage of the Constituent Assembly. Yet Mirabeau's talent and character did not so much change as find employment; thus there is no better illustration of the shift that took place in 1789 than this life, upon which that famous year belatedly bestowed its meaning.

At that time Mirabeau was already forty years old; his life had been one of family feuds and lovers' quarrels, prisons and exiles, great scandals and minor literature. He was born into a well-known family of the Provençal nobility, the son of a celebrated marquis whose passions included agronomy and political economy and who had been a friend of the physiocrats and the author of heavy didactic tomes. Yet this "friend of mankind" was not exactly an affectionate father. Since his son was not the kind who makes a father sleep easy, the family chronicle was a typical saga of the Ancien Régime, filled with *lettres de cachet* rather than sentiment. The philanthropic marquis and the future leader of the Revolution reserved the philosophy of the age for public use.

The son was admittedly a volcano. While still quite young he abandoned his regiment, piled up debts, compromised wives (including his own), slept with his sister, and pummeled his rivals. The marquis went to court many times, obtained proscriptions, and had his son locked up in the Château d'If outside Marseilles and later exiled to Joux in the snowy Juras, from which Mirabeau escaped the following year (1776), after a series of escapades worthy of a western, sharing his saddle with the young wife of the old president of the Cour des Comptes of Dôle, Sophie de Mounier. He took refuge in Holland, where his angry father and the French king's police had him arrested and sent to the dungeon of Vincennes (1777), where he remained until 1780. Then followed long years of legal wrangling with his father and wife. The comte de Mirabeau's experience of the Ancien Régime was thus without parallel. His future colleagues in the Constituent Assembly were lawyers, judges, and magistrates. He had been a defendant, a convict, a litigant.

Apart from women, debts, and courtroom affairs, Mirabeau had one constant occupation: writing. The son of an indefatigable penman, Mirabeau inherited the passion of his father and persecutor. Like his father, the son hoped to conquer glory with his pen rather than his sword as a writer, philosopher, and benefactor of humanity. In 1772, at age twenty-three, he wrote an *Essay on Despotism,* and subsequently, as he moved from prison to prison and exile to exile, from the Château d'If to the dungeon of Vincennes by way of Joux and Amsterdam, he composed a series of essays on the most diverse subjects, yet always concerned if not with self-justification then with the edification or utility of the public: works about his family, about the salt marshes of Franche-Comté, about *lettres de cachet* and state prisons, and even *Advice to the Hessians,* urging them not to fight the American rebels under the English flag, to say nothing of all his translations of Latin poets, his pornographic works, and his minor historical novels—works that he wrote in order to live but that afforded him only a poor living.

Mirabeau's private life was unusually disorderly, but the disorder of his literary production was typical of the late eighteenth century, littered with the intellectual small change left by philosophy's destruction of a world. Great works and great ideas were just beginning to reach a broad public, served up to it by fluent scribblers with a "nose" for the market. Mirabeau was continually proposing new ideas for publication. For a long time he dreamed of putting together an encyclopedia of knowledge, and later he envisioned a collection of works devoted to the leading European states. The magnitude of the change wrought by the eighteenth century can be gauged by the fact that what had been a somewhat extravagant mania for writing in the father had become mere conformism in the son. As a writer the father was an eccentric; the son was like all the rest. Though a count, Mirabeau shared the ambitions of the ardent young commoners of his generation: to make a name for himself through his books. The society that Balzac would later describe already flourished on the ruins of the old world of privilege by birth, well before the great thunderclap. What else did Barnave, Brissot, Desmoulins, and Saint-Just want? All imagined but one road to notoriety: writing. All continued to be obsessed with "King" Voltaire. Since literature had assumed a political function, it was hardly surprising that it would appear to the generations of the 1770s and 1780s as the royal road to glory. When careers in politics became available, these ambitious young men took to that path as naturally as they had taken to literature.

In the meantime Mirabeau sold his pen—and that of others—without much in the way of scruples. In the final years of the Ancien Régime this hard-pressed aristocrat was manipulated by the leaders of the day, publishing on behalf of Calonne, against Necker, for the stockjobber Panchaud, against his rivals, a series of compositions often written by others, especially his Genevan friend Clavière and the young Brissot. He poured his literary ambitions into *La monarchie prussienne,* a vast four-volume historical and statistical compilation in honor of the great Frederick and decidedly in keeping with the spirit of the times, an honorable if unoriginal work. The principal author was an officer of engineers, a professor at Brunswick, Major Mauvillon, whose work Mirabeau shamelessly appropriated. But when the book appeared, in 1787, after the failure of the Assembly of Notables, history at last opened up a new field to this miserably wasted genius, a field in which he would finally flourish.

*
**

Mirabeau bungled everything, yet fate would smile on him. This dissipated, inconsistent, unfaithful, venal man managed to grasp the opportunity of a lifetime: to become the voice of the new nation. In 1788 the king's ministers asked him for help against the parlements, which had given the signal for rebellion. Like everyone else, the royal ministers knew that Mirabeau's pen was for sale, and in any case how could this inveterate litigant, who had suffered so much at the hands of the men in wigs and robes and who had fought all his life against the "parlementary aristocracy," pass up this golden opportunity for revenge? Yet he did just that, flatly turning down the chance to settle a personal score on the grounds, as he explained to the minister Montmorin in a letter dated April 18, 1788, that the stakes now were far greater:

> Disregarding whatever personal risks I may be taking in drawing upon myself the implacable hatred of the corporate bodies not yet laid low, which will devour a good many enemies before being put down, or, rather—to put it plainly—who will never be put down so long as one goes on attacking them without the support of the nation, is this really the moment to effect the denunciation before France of an *aristocracy of magistrates,* a moment in which the king has not deigned to denounce that aristocracy himself? Today, can one usefully serve the government while wearing its livery? Is this the moment to do battle for authority, a moment in which some have not been afraid to impute to the king an argument that will resound through France, and from which it follows, in good logic, that *the will of the monarch alone makes the law?* Can anyone believe that those who set forth such principles want in good faith to see the Estates General meet and are preparing for that meeting? It has been my honor to tell you, monsieur le Comte, and I have repeated it to monsieur le Garde des sceaux [the Keeper of the Seals]: *I shall never make war on the parlements except in the presence of the nation.*

The hired propagandist was no more. The great Mirabeau had just found himself, being one of the first to grasp—a year before the meeting of the Estates General at Versailles—the immensity of the event that was about to take place and the change that had occurred in the rules of the game. What he called the "nation" was democracy: a radical shift in sovereignty. He would become the man of this new era. And if he clashed once again with his own kind, the nobles of Provence, during the electoral campaign, at least he had found his true colors. Thus on April 6 he was elected deputy of the Third Estate of Aix-en-Provence. Rejected by his own order, he was consequently even more a deputy of the nation.

This was a role that from the first he filled eminently, more so than any of his colleagues. He was the most visible, the most powerful, the most brilliant of all. He possessed strength, inventiveness, and an instinct for decisiveness and action. "All eyes," wrote Michelet when recounting the first session of the Estates General, "were on Mirabeau. His abundant mane and leonine head, powerfully ugly, were astonishing, almost frightening. Nobody could take their eyes off him. . . . Everyone sensed in him the great voice of France." And Victor Hugo wrote:

> When he was forty, there rose up around him in France a great anarchy of ideas, to which societies that have outlived their time are susceptible. In these circum-

stances Mirabeau was the despot. . . . It was he who, silent until then, shouted on June 23, 1789, to M. de Brézé: "Go tell *your master* . . ." *Your master!* The king of France was being declared a foreigner. A frontier was being drawn between the throne and the people. It was the Revolution that let out this cry. No one would have dared to admit it before Mirabeau. It is given only to great men to utter the decisive words of an epoch." (*Sur Mirabeau*)

What gave such force to his rhetoric? What was it that made him, in such a short time, the most symbolic figure of the Revolution? It was the mystery of his oratorical talent and the quickness of his wit, but to some extent a reinvestment of his past in the new age also played a part.

Despite the tumult and misery of his life, he was among those intellectually best prepared for the coming events. At a time when Saint-Just was still writing poetry for ladies and Robespierre was still fawning in the salons of Arras, Mirabeau, having tussled with the Ancien Régime, was one of the few to have foreseen its fall and imagined its aftermath. He lacked the legal skills of the jurists who filled the Assembly, yet he enjoyed the advantage of having been legally deprived of his rights and having endured the arbitrariness of authority. His stormy past had equipped him to face the tempest that now descended on the nation.

Nevertheless, neither his works alone, nor his adventures or talent or even his persecution, suffice to explain the power of incarnation with which the events of 1789 invested him. He benefitted from a further and probably capital source of prestige: the comte de Mirabeau was a noble. Déclassé to be sure, as marginal as anyone could be, but noble: nothing in his life could erase what had been fixed beforehand by his birth.

Among other revolutionary figures one would search in vain for a similar mix of birth and bohemianism. Many of the leaders of 1789 were nobles—Lafayette, the Lameths, Talleyrand—yet a liberal noble was not a déclassé noble but quite the opposite: liberty was the common property of the bourgeoisie and the aristocracy. As for the bohemian life, lord knows it was well represented in the French Revolution, but in 1789 its time had yet to come. When that time did come, in 1792, birth became a curse. In 1789, amid the chaos of events, France was still groping toward the formation of an "English-style" elite, combining the liberal nobility with the enlightened bourgeoisie of the Third Estate. In English history such a fusion took place over several centuries, but now the old kingdom was forced to accept it all at once, and in the midst of popular tumult. Who could speak for the new elite before the still young "nation"? Who was both enough of a democrat and enough of an aristocrat to lower the flag of tradition before the flag of the Revolution? Mirabeau was the only noble sufficiently déclassé, and the only déclassé sufficiently noble, to join the past with what was happening now.

From this providentially mixed background he drew, with the skill of a great musician, unforgettable tones: he was "the very voice of the Revolution" (Michelet). Never mind that he did not write his speeches himself but usually relied on his "workshop" (Clavière and Etienne Dumont in particular); never mind that his knowledge of the technical subjects on which he sometimes spoke was superficial. All his life he had plundered the works of others, and the Revolution did not alter his habits. What it brought him was its genius: its aggressiveness, inventiveness, intuition, and histrionics. Sieyès was the Revolution's thinker, Mirabeau its artist. He seized upon other people's words and ideas and added to them what he called the *trait,* that touch which transformed the ordinary into the virtuoso. To a Constituent Assembly full of intelligent and capable men he offered imagination. This voluminous writer, this amateur, this restless soul discovered the strange power to incarnate the Revolution and poured his formidable energy into it: popularity was the new rule of democracy.

*
* *

It was the same Mirabeau who in 1790 signed a secret accord with the court, through his friend the comte de La Marck, himself a friend of Mercy-Argenteau, one-time ambassador of Maria-Theresa to Paris—the queen's Austrian connection. Mirabeau would advise the royal family. In exchange his debts (more than 200,000 livres) would be paid, and he was to receive 6,000 livres per month plus 300 for a copyist. Finally, he was promised a million more when the Assembly disbanded.

The soldier of fortune in Mirabeau survived the extraordinary change in his circumstances. His loose ways, female entanglements, and need for money found a thousand new opportunities after his success in public life. At last he could spend freely, keep an open table, and surround himself with a court that was a revenge for his life. But he lived on credit, cashing in on his political credit to obtain financial credit. The accord with the court wiped away his debts and reassured him as to his future. From now on his habits and excesses would be paid for by the king's money. This led to charges of corruption, already in the air at the time and crystalized two years later in Jacobin propaganda, when his secret correspondence with the court was discovered in the iron chest from the Tuileries. In the present century Jacobin academics, who always disliked Mirabeau for his women, debts, ideas, and genius, have taken an even more virtuous line in condemning his double-dealing.

Yet his case, already argued by Sainte-Beuve, is not difficult to win. The customs of the day were different from our own. In that time, which resembled the Ancien Régime in so many of its characteristics and mores, those who served the king were always compensated with money and rewards, which did not detract from the dignity of the position or the role but actually constituted recognition of it. Mirabeau was even more a part of that tradition because he passionately wished to be in public what he was in secret: a minister of the king of France. As early as 1781, when he was released from Vincennes, that was his plan: "I need fifteen or twenty more years, and with strength I shall have them. When I am no longer fit for love, I will have no further business here, unless I become a minister." In this typical career of an eighteenth-century aristocrat—first women, then politics—the Revolution provided the means. He spared himself no intrigue, he neglected none of his connections to advance his candidacy: he saw Necker; he made overtures to the court; he established contact with the Orléans party; he maintained connections with the Jacobins. But everyone knew his past and was suspicious of his intentions. The royal household detested everything he stood for. The Assembly was jealous of his talent and his popularity: in November 1789 it opposed him by voting that no deputy could be a minister of the king.

He therefore became the king's secret minister, an unequal bargain which deprived him of the publicity of office and made the king's commitment a matter of caprice. In fact the royal family paid him more in order to sound his depths than to follow his advice. It paid others as well. By contrast, he treated this clandestine bargain as the kingdom's highest magistracy. A glance at the notes he periodically sent Louis XVI and Marie Antoinette reveals that in drafting them he believed he was still presiding over what was left of the King's Council. On February 3, 1791, concerning the journey of Mesdames (Louis XVI's aunts) to Rome, he wrote these words, which are a portrait in miniature: "I would certainly have offered my opinion in the Council that . . ."

If he took this somewhat pathetic post so seriously, and if he was so loath to regard it as a financial expedient—he who was so cynical about other men—it was not only because it offered him a chance to avenge his youth, this position that would have impressed his father, but above all because it enabled him to defend his ideas. By giving him direct access to Louis XVI and Marie Antoinette it gave him hope of furthering his noblest ambition, which was to reconcile the Revolution with the monarchy in order to safeguard liberty. His friend La Marck, who knew how the story turned out because it was he who served as intermediary with Marie Antoinette, aptly summed up his role: "He accepted payment only for holding his own opinion."

Mirabeau's conviction stemmed from the fact that in his eyes the Revolution had already fulfilled its purpose in 1789, having established on the one hand the sovereignty of the people and on the other hand a society of citizens equal before the law. The appropriation of constituent power by the deputies in the name of the nation in June and July and the decrees of August 4–11 that put an end to feudalism: these were the achievements of the Revolution, and they were irreversible. The Revolution may have done away with divine-right monarchy, but it was by no means incompatible with a modernized monarchy; in fact the existence of a society composed of equal individuals, in contrast to the old society of corps, was actually a change favorable to the exercise of a strong royal power. (Richelieu would have liked this idea, Mirabeau wrote to Louis XVI.) Such power was all the more necessary because the regime established by the Constituent Assembly and justified in theory by Sieyès, with its representative assembly, risked alienating the national sovereignty to a new parliamentary aristocracy. In his speeches, particularly from September 1789 on, and hence well before he entered the service of Louis XVI, Mirabeau continually pointed out that a strong king was the safeguard of the nation in the face of an assembly charged with making the law. Furthermore, such a king was a figure of the national history, anchored in the depths of the ages, uniting past with present and rooting modern democracy in traditional authority. Mirabeau was Chateaubriand thirty years before his time: his idea was to "nationalize" the monarchy.

MIRABEAU

What was it that this great actor in his double role sought to accomplish with the king and in the Assembly? First of all, to separate the royal family from the dead end, the hopeless policy of counterrevolution. Then to persuade the Constituent Assembly to adopt a balance of powers and what Mirabeau called a good constitution. At court he pleaded in favor of the Revolution, or at any rate for that part of it that was irreversible. In the Assembly he pleaded on behalf of the king, or at any rate for maintaining royal authority in the name of the nation. It is true that, placed in the untenable position of incarnating the Revolution and supporting royal power at a time when the Revolution relegated the king to the past and the king repudiated the Revolution, he did not always have his genius under control. In the same Assembly, facing the violent attacks of the counterrevolutionary right, he sometimes went beyond the limits he had set for himself and sought to replenish his reserves of popularity with a flourish of revolutionary rhetoric. In his notes to the king he sometimes became bogged down in minor intrigues and allowed his hatred of Lafayette to carry him away. Fundamentally, however, he remained the freest spirit of the age, precisely because he was familiar with both camps and was the only man to be in both at once. If he was—perhaps—the greatest man of the Revolution, it was because he was able to be its incarnation without losing his identity: the "treason" of the comte de Mirabeau was his dialogue with himself.

When he died on April 2, 1791, on the eve of Varennes, his great project was already limping. The king was less reconciled to the Revolution than ever, and the Revolution less willing than ever to share power with the king. The failure of the Feuillant stabilization in the aftermath of Varennes was also Mirabeau's failure—but without Mirabeau. Had he lived, the course of events would probably have been no different, for it was just too difficult to remake both the old monarchy and the new democratic idea only two years after 1789. Even if the Revolution had dared to change kings—how many of its leaders thought of the duc d'Orléans!—it is not certain or even probable that it would have been able to carry Mirabeau's project through to completion: in these years of popular effervescence, every effort to transform events into institutions collapsed like a sand castle before the evening tide.

Mirabeau's project is nevertheless important to the extent that it was the most coherent and precocious expression of the dream of "halting the Revolution," which would obsess all the leaders who looked on while power raced out of control. Who among them, from Mirabeau to Bonaparte, did not share this dream? Who did not attempt to use the fragile equilibrium of forces to establish durable institutions? After Mirabeau came the turn of Barnave and the Feuillants, then the Girondins, then Danton, and finally Robespierre, who, lacking a king—in other words, without history—chose the Supreme Being for his ally. Ultimately, after the failure of the Thermidorian Republic, it was Bonaparte who became the instrument of Mirabeau's project, a king of the Revolution. But the price to be paid was more than Mirabeau would have stood for: liberty.

François Furet

271

Further reading

WORKS BY MIRABEAU

Correspondance entre le comte de Mirabeau et le comte de La Marck pendant les années 1789, 1790 et 1791, 3 vols. Paris, 1851. Reprinted (and ed. Guy Chaussinand-Nogaret). Paris, 1986.

Discours, edited, introduced, and annotated by François Furet. Paris, 1973.

RELATED WORKS

Dumont, Etienne. *Souvenirs sur Mirabeau et sur les deux premières assemblées législatives.* Paris, 1832.

Hugo, Victor. *Sur Mirabeau.* Paris, 1834.

Loménie, Louis de. *Les Mirabeau: Nouvelles études sur la société française au XVIIIe siècle.* Paris, 1889–1891.

Les Mirabeau et leur temps. Proceedings of the Colloquium of Aix-en-Provence, December 1966. Paris, 1968.

Sainte-Beuve, Charles-Augustin. "Des mémoires de Mirabeau et de l'étude de M. Victor Hugo à ce sujet," *Portraits contemporains, February 1834.*

——— "Mirabeau et Sophie" and "Correspondance entre Mirabeau et le comte de La Marck, 1789–1791," *Causeries du lundi,* vol. 4, 1851.

Related topics

Ancien Régime	Feuillants	Necker
Aristocracy	Girondins	Physiocrats
Barnave	Jacobinism	Revolutionary Assemblies
Constitution	Lafayette	Robespierre
Counterrevolution	Louis XVI	Sieyès
Democracy	Marie Antoinette	Tocqueville
Département	Michelet	Voltaire
Enlightenment	Nation	

NAPOLEON BONAPARTE

The French Revolution had no use for the elderly, and not even Napoleon Bonaparte, its greatest and perhaps its only hero, was an exception to this rule. In contrast to the American Revolution, whose aging leaders, consecrated by the role they had played and respected by all citizens, were transformed into Fathers of the Country, the French Revolution was a theater that used up its heroes and cut them down in their prime, transforming those left alive into survivors and its vanquishers into bourgeois. For a few years, however, it had its Washington in Bonaparte—but a Washington who was thirty years old. Ten years later he was a king, and a few years after that, a defeated, captive king. Not even he had been able to master the course of events for long. The moment his power became hereditary it cut itself off from its source; he embarked upon a course different from that of the Revolution, and the fortunes of war reasserted their rights. By attempting to root his reign in the law of monarchy, the emperor deprived it of both its magic and its necessity.

In order to understand him, to bring him into clearer focus, we may therefore begin by asking why this Corsican, this Italian, this foreigner—Buonaparte, as the dowagers of the Restoration called him—became so profoundly a part of the history of France. And the answer is that he was chosen by the Revolution, from which he received his strange power not only to embody the new nation (a power that others before him, most notably Mirabeau and Robespierre, had possessed) but also to fulfill its destiny. Of this fate he was so well aware that on Saint Helena he would hark back to these beginnings as to an obsession, not so much in order to turn the origin of his power into a posthumous propaganda weapon (which it nevertheless became) as from a need to remember what was at least explicable in this most extraordinary of lives.

He had been born at the right time, twenty years prior to 1789, but on an out-of-the-way island that had only recently—and unwillingly—become French. Napoleon was the second son of Charles Bonaparte and Laetitia Ramolini, parents of twelve children in all, of whom eight survived, five boys and three girls. They were a Corsican family, a tribe under parental authority and speaking Corsican like everyone else on the island. They came from the marginal "nobility" of Ajaccio, eking out a living from vineyards and olive trees. The family patriarch had the clever idea of throwing in his lot with the

French, thus abandoning his friend Paoli and the cause of independence. He thus became one of the beneficiaries of the edicts of 1776, which stipulated that scions of impoverished noblemen were entitled to a free education in the royal military academies. The two eldest boys obtained these scholarships, which enabled them to look forward to a career similar to that of so many of their compatriots since that time: from rural township between sea and scrub to a lifetime of public service on the continent. Napoleon studied at Brienne (1779–1784), where he received a good education, although Stendhal later deplored its governmental character: "Had he been educated in a school independent of the government, he might have studied Hume and Montesquieu; he might have understood the strength that public opinion bestows upon government" (*Life of Napoleon,* chap. 1). Perhaps. But at Brienne's military school he learned to speak French—though without ever entirely losing his Italian accent; he also studied history, with which he filled his solitary days, and mathematics, for which he demonstrated a gift. In 1784 he was admitted to the Ecole Militaire, and in 1785 he graduated forty-second in a class of fifty-eight and was assigned as a sublieutenant of artillery to the regiment of La Fère. Ségur and Taine attribute the following judgment to his history teacher: "Corsican in character and nationality, this young man will go far if circumstances permit."

The "circumstances" of his youth and his first posts were the final flickers of the Ancien Régime. Napoleon remained a stranger to the life and passions of the age; education's effects are often delayed. "Corsican in character," he was typically moody, somewhat rough around the edges, and lacking in worldly experience. And "Corsican in nationality," he took the island to be the framework of his world, and he would join the cause of Paoli, which his father had abandoned. His garrison duty was interrupted by lengthy stays in Corsica. He had yet to make his rendezvous with France, and even after the Revolution it was a long time coming. Nothing linked him to the losing side in 1789, but neither was there any sign of anything more than modest enthusiasm for the victors. He continued to spend the better part of his time in Corsica. As late as the spring of 1792, if his Brienne classmate Bourrienne is to be believed, he was contemptuous of Louis XVI for not having ordered his troops to fire on the rioters of June 20. This is one of the rare glimpses we have of him between 1789 and 1793. When, somewhat later, the cannon roared at Valmy, Napoleon was once again awaiting the boat that would take him back to Corsica. Paradoxically, it was the victory of Paoli's insurrection in April 1793 that would break this powerful tie to his native island. The Bonaparte tribe, marked down as pro-French, was banished. Headed by a handsome widow flanked by pretty daughters and ambitious sons, the family disembarked with all their belongings at Marseilles.

Napoleon was *already* twenty-four. (In three years people would say, "He's only twenty-seven!") He was a captain of artillery but still had done nothing. His encounter with the new France, like everything else in his life, came about by chance, but at a time—the summer of 1793—when the true partisans of the Revolution, those willing to burn their bridges behind them, were being singled out from their more tepid comrades. It was then that

Napoleon became not only a Montagnard but a Robespierrist. In August he authored a broadside against the Federalists, who had brought civil war to the south. An unoriginal text, it consists of a discussion among a soldier, a man from Nîmes, a merchant from Marseilles, and a manufacturer from Montpellier concerning the Federalist uprising in Marseilles, for which the soldier pleads the cause of "public safety." Despite the work's lack of originality, it is an important document because it marks the moment at which the Corsican artillery captain joined the history of the Revolution and thereby—carrying a Jacobin passport—entered the history of France.

What in those terrible months did this young officer find so much to his liking? Probably that which accorded with his temperament and tastes: the government's energy, worthy of the ancients; its unlimited authority; and also the fact that careers were open to talents, that military men were honored if they were victorious, and that a young officer might hope for equal treatment in a profession still encumbered by particles and prejudices. By serving the Montagnard dictatorship, which in Marseilles wore the visage of a Corsican compatriot, Saliceti, Napoleon served both his predilections and his interests. When, following his advice, Toulon was recaptured from the English on December 17, he was promoted to brigadier general; in February 1794, he became commander of artillery in the army in Italy in the offensive against the Austrians.

When the Thermidorians sidelined him temporarily and even imprisoned him for several weeks, they confirmed his reputation as a Robespierrist general. Yet in spite of appearances Thermidor carried the Revolution forward, and in the following year it provided him with an opportunity for a spectacular comeback on the occasion of 13 Vendémiaire (October 5) 1795. If Toulon was the first phase of his marriage with revolutionary France, this was the second. It was Barras who put Napoleon back in the saddle—Barras, that staunch defender of the Republic, who ordered its troops to fire on the young *muscadins* leading the insurgency against the Convention. There was also a more civilized aspect to Barras' patronage: Bonaparte became a minor figure in Paris's newly reconstituted high society.

That society was an amalgam of the revolutionary *nomenklatura* with the monied elite; the former had survived long enough to celebrate the return of the latter. A modern alliance between power and finance supplanted the Robespierrist utopia of a virtuous republic. The time had come to mix business with pleasure, and over it all presided Barras, former viscount and ex-Terrorist now ensconced in a court worthy of the late Roman Empire. In this environment the young general cut a peculiar figure: emaciated, taciturn, his youthful face devoured by his huge eyes, he had a full head of hair that hung down to his shoulders like "the ears of a dog." His marriage to Josephine tells us a great deal about what drew him to this society. The story can be recounted as a farce: in marrying a half-impoverished denizen of the demimonde whom Barras had placed in his bed, Bonaparte believed he was marrying a wealthy aristocratic heiress. Yet it can also be told in colors less lurid but no less true: the burning passion he felt for Josephine, fanned by all that the name Beauharnais evoked, was the product not so much of vulgar *arri-*

visme as of all the childhood humiliations that his union with her erased. The minor noble from Corsica was critical of the bourgeoisie, to which he would never belong, yet he shared its deepest collective sentiment, its love-hate relationship with the aristocracy: that peculiarly French passion for equality, the unwitting legacy of the Ancien Régime, which can be temporarily assuaged only by acquiring recognized, guaranteed superiority over one's neighbor and "equal." Later, Stendhal, like Napoleon, would refer to this passion as "vanity." In marrying a Beauharnais, little Bonaparte became a naturalized citizen of France.

His vanity, however, was sustained by an imagination that was anything but bourgeois, or at any rate more than just bourgeois—although the words that he spoke to his brother at Notre Dame on the day of his anointment—"Joseph! If only our father could see us now!"—might well have been those of a character in Balzac. Yet the success that so amazed the man who earned it was not a question of money or power. It can be compared only to the empire of Charlemagne or the triumph of Caesar. The Bonaparte of 1796 had inherited from his many predecessors—Mirabeau, Lafayette, Brissot, Danton, Robespierre, and so many others—the ambition of governing the Revolution. But from the outset, the dreamy, clever Mediterranean had one advantage over the rest: he came from the outside at a time when the political program of the Revolution was exhausted, and he could impose upon it an agenda of his own choosing. Like the others he was a champion of equality, but to the nation's glory he lent the powerful luster of his personal genius.

Within the space of a few months, between spring and autumn, he would emerge from Italy as the arbiter of France's political future. Italy had been in his dreams since the campaign of 1794. To some extent it was his country, it spoke his language, and it offered the ideal arena in which to join his two fatherlands in victory. His plan had been ready for a long time: to drive a wedge between the Piedmontese and the Austrians by means of a quick offensive, thus obliging the monarchy of Turin to agree to peace or even to enter an alliance with the French, after which victory he would drive the Austrians out of Lombardy. The first phase of the plan was executed in two weeks, but the second ran into difficulty, for when Bonaparte took Milan in the middle of May the Austrian army was still intact and would continue to cause trouble until November. But the French commander had given an impressive demonstration of his tactical prowess, which relied on rapid troop movements and coordinated attacks, and he did not wait for others to sing his praises. No one had more fully grasped the fact that the reign of the well-born had ended and that of public opinion begun. In his victory communiqués Napoleon revealed a real genius for publicity.

He was not yet king of France, but as of May he became king of poor, defeated, plundered, ransomed Italy, which he made over as though it were his by patrimonial right. He lived in the Montebello palace in Milan, more like a sovereign than a general of the Republic, surrounded by a court, protected by strict etiquette, and already ensconced in omnipotence. Josephine, false as ever, accompanied by one of her lovers, joined him. Napoleon's brothers and sisters had preceded her, trading on his victories and avid for honors and profits, liberally helping themselves to whatever they could get. This Balzacian side of his life as a parvenu was destined to continue unabated. Napoleon tolerated and even encouraged these sordid activities, provided they originated with him. These indulgences were the perquisites of glory, prizes to be given to those who served him. But already distinguished from his most famous generals by their acquiescence in his superiority, conferring as an equal with the Directory, on which he imposed his views thanks to his power over public opinion, and receiving republican France's most eminent thinkers and scientists, he belonged to another world. He had conceived an idea of what his life could be, of what he was now sure it would be: "Fate will not resist my will," as he would later put it, in what might be a definition of modern happiness.

Of the things he said at Montebello, already recorded by numerous attentive witnesses, the most interesting is this confidence: "What I have done up to now is still nothing. I am only at the beginning of my career. Do you think that I have triumphed in Italy only to make the reputations of the lawyers of the Directory, the Carnots and Barrasses? And do you suppose that it was in order to establish a republic? What an idea! A republic of thirty million people! With our customs and our vices! Is such a thing possible? It is a chimera of which the French have become enamored, but it, too, will pass, like so many other things. They need their glory, the satisfactions of vanity. But they understand nothing of liberty." This declaration is far more than an avowal of ambition, which by this point was evident anyway. We hear echoes of what Napoleon had learned from the literature of the day about the impossibility of a republic in a large country, a judgment reinforced by a pessimistic assessment of Thermidorian society, whose citizens exhibited the opposite of republican virtues. Slaves to self-interest and pleasure, their great passion was "vanity": individual vanity, which demanded "perks," the petty gradations of status and prestige upon which egalitarian societies thrive; and collective vanity, jealously protective of the glory of the nation and the grandeur of the new France. Let the government satisfy these passions and it would not have to worry about liberty any more than the French people did. Formulated at a very early date, this philosophy of power enabled the commander-in-chief of the army of Italy to shape his plans to flatter the nation's passions—a simple, almost simplistic, yet masterly strategy, a formula for revolutionary dictatorship based not on virtue but on self-interest.

A lengthy peregrination in Egypt still stood between Bonaparte and power, but he bided his time brilliantly in anticipation of what was to come. Even before this undertaking, in 1797, on 18 Fructidor, the army of Italy had saved the Directory, but its commander-in-chief had wisely delegated Augerau for the purpose, thereby managing both to avoid working for a discredited government and to keep clear of the renewal of terror that followed the coup d'état. Young as he was, he exhibited all the caution of a wizened politician, aged by his participation in the battles of the Revolution. The subsequent Egyptian expedition was an exercise in image-building. Ill-conceived but executed with great panache, this useless foray served no purpose but to magnify Napoleon's glory. The man who abandoned his army in almost clandestine fashion on August 22, 1799, added the Pyramids to his list of victories. When he reached Fréjus on October 9, time had in effect worked in his favor. He was acclaimed by the public, and even the politicians offered him the reins of power—on their own terms, to be sure, but without the means to enforce those terms. Paris theaters interrupted performances to announce his arrival. On October 27 municipal officials in Pontarlier informed the directors that "the news of Bonaparte's arrival so electrified republicans that a number of them shed tears."

Napoleon's landing at Fréjus threw all Paris's plans into turmoil by introducing a joker into the deck, a joker that Sieyès had not anticipated: the popularity of a hero. From the moment he returned Bonaparte had the upper hand over his associates, for in a crowd of notables he was "the people." Well-conceived but executed in panic, 18 Brumaire enjoyed the nation's blessing before the fact.

*
**

Now began the happiest period of Napoleon's life: his marriage to the Revolution. The Republic persisted, with the general holding the supreme office of first consul, in accordance with the public's wish. Stendhal, who had come to Paris as an adolescent from his native Grenoble in November 1799, learned of the coup d'état at Nemours on the day after it took place: "We heard the news in the evening. I understood little of what it meant, and I was delighted that young General Bonaparte had made himself king of France" (*La vie de Henry Brulard,* chap. 35). Revolutionary France was indeed under the spell of the new sovereign, who was its son and had saved it from the danger of a restoration: anything royal about him came from his being the hero of the Republic. France had finally found the republican monarchy toward which it had been groping since 1789.

The "citizen consul" at age thirty was physically at his most prepossessing, less sallow than the general of the Italian campaign but not yet the plump emperor to come. He lived amid the clamor of his fame and the fever of governmental work, the two passions of his daily life, and even devoted a little of his time to recreation and amusement: this was the heyday of Malmaison, as recounted by Junot's wife, the future duchesse d'Abrantès. Bonaparte as yet had no court and lived among his aides-de-camp and generals, above them but not cut off from them. Josephine had at last understood that she had accidentally picked the winning number, and the two of them, in the very uniqueness of their fate, exemplify the uncertainties of life in the new society. Insignificant bystanders during the Revolution, the courtesan from the islands and the little soldier from Corsica ultimately came to embody landlord France. The public, having chosen its leader, discovered that in style and habit he exhibited all the requisite attributes of republican simplicity and civilian government. The first consul partook of none of the foolish customs of the Bourbons: he ate quickly, always wore the same clothes and old hats, and wasted no time in court ceremonies. He worked and made decisions.

Such, at any rate, was the public image that he so cleverly created, and at the time it was also the truth. Consul Napoleon combined the qualities of a republican hero and bourgeois monarch with tendencies in his personality that were already despotic and uncontrollable. He himself had a clear understanding of the conditions that had brought him to power and of the civilian nature of his dictatorship: "I govern not as a general but because the nation believes that I have the civilian qualities necessary to govern. If it did not have this opinion, the government could not stand. I knew full well what I was doing when, as general of the army, I accepted the position of member of the Institute. I was sure of being understood by even the lowliest drummer. Nothing about present conditions can be deduced from centuries of barbarism. We are thirty million people united by enlightenment, property, and commerce. Three or four hundred thousand troops are nothing compared with that mass" (May 1802, to the Council of State). Enlightenment, property, commerce: a definition of the nation that might have been put forward by Necker, Sieyès, or Benjamin Constant, who had learned it from the philosophes— except that none of the three had been in a position to deal with the instability and civil conflict likely to result from the application of that definition. Napoleon saw himself as the heir and symbol of this tradition, its long-sought champion, and there was a whole bourgeois side of him that was well suited to this role: he believed in the sanctity of property, the idea of marriage and the family, women in the home, order in the streets, and careers open to talent. To all this prosaic legacy of 1789 he lent his flamboyant genius, while at the same time subjecting it to a kind of Corsican exaggeration, injecting the new France with a dose of the patriarchal spirit. In doing so he responded in two ways to the wishes of the nation. With an epic revolution barely behind them, the French were not ready for a less brilliant leader. But tired of the revolutionary agenda and jealously guarding what they had acquired, they wanted guarantees for the safety of property and the preservation of law and order. At once revolutionary and conservative, a rural and petit-bourgeois nation awaited Bonaparte's Civil Code. It spontaneously supported the program he set forth in 1800 to the Council of State: "We have finished the romance of the Revolution. Now we must begin its history, looking only for what is real and possible in the application of principles and not what is speculative and hypothetical. To pursue a different course today would be to philosophize, not to govern."

A dictatorship of public opinion intended to consolidate the Revolution, the Consulate was thus also, in Bonaparte's mind, the "beginning" of its history. The revolutionary "romance" had been written by the intellectuals who had led it before him and who had explored its "speculative" side. Napoleon surely had in mind Robespierre and his Republic of Virtue, but he was probably also thinking of other leaders as well, from the Constituent Assembly to the Institute—Sieyès, for example, his temporary ally in Brumaire and the champion of the "perfect Constitution." To begin the real history of the Revolution was to treat in terms of practical reason problems with which his predecessors had dealt as metaphysicians, and to establish a modern state on a foundation of experience and realism. This was the other side of the Consulate, which Bonaparte used to modify the model of despotism to suit the new postrevolutionary society. As early as 1790, Mirabeau, in his secret correspondence with the king, had attempted to convince poor Louis XVI of the wisdom of such a course: why, he wrote in substance, do you balk at accepting the new state of things? Instead of mourning the loss of aristocratic society, with its nobility, parlements, and privileged corps that constantly hindered your authority, take advantage of its demise to root the monarchy in the new society by becoming the head of the nation.

While the king of the Ancien Régime had not heeded or even heard this advice, the new sovereign possessed all the qualities required to put it into practice. He was by temperament a thousand times more authoritarian than the former king, and he governed a society that had become more than ever a society of equal individuals, relatively defenseless against the power of the state. In contrast to 1790, moreover, the revolutionary tide had by this time been ebbing for several years, and as it waned it became possible to see that the idea of absolute power remained intact, as potent as ever, the monarchy's legacy to the new democracy. The sovereignty of the people had replaced the sovereignty of the monarch, but sovereignty itself remained unlimited in extent and indivisible by its very nature. The consular monarchy thus incorporated three elements that combined to make it more powerful than any previous monarchy. First, it reigned over isolated individuals, deprived of the right to assemble but guaranteed equality. Second, it derived its authority from the people and was thus rid of that divine scrutiny that had served as a brake on the power of the king. And third, it unwittingly derived part of its power from the absolutist tradition—unwittingly, because France remained profoundly convinced that it had broken all ties with the past, of which the war, the émigrés, and the brothers of Louis XVI were all reminders. But the first consul understood, for on several occasions he said that his power derived in part from the history of France and the habits of the nation.

Such was the foundation upon which Napoleon was to erect his most enduring achievement, the modern French state. The Civil Code and much of the work of legal unification and new legislation were already underway before he came to power and could have been finished without him in much the same fashion. But the new structure of government bore his stamp. He drew liberally on tradition: on Cartesian rationalism as applied to politics, on enlightened despotism, on the body of laws born of the interminable conflicts between the state and the corporations under the Ancien Régime, and on established customs and attitudes. But he also left his mark, at once Corsican and military, on the new system, in its tendency to value order and authority above all human needs and in its very structure, so well adapted to his principal passion: undivided rule.

The administration, Napoleon believed, is the nervous system of government. It should run by itself, a well-regulated organ whose function is to convey the will of the center to the extremities: "I have made all my ministries so easy that they can be staffed by anyone possessing the necessary loyalty, zeal, energy, and industriousness. . . . The prefectures were admirably well organized and yielded excellent results. Forty million people were spurred to do the same thing at the same time, and with the aid of these local centers of activity, the extremities moved as quickly as the heart itself" (Council of State, 1806, Molé). Thus centralization not only permitted the unified and ubiquitous application of rational power, it also allowed the state to rely on agents whose only qualities were "industriousness" and "loyalty." Every prefect became a "miniature emperor" in his own département, but the prefect's power had nothing to do with his merit or personality; he was merely the representative of the central government.

Although Bonaparte on occasion liked to raise the "public safety" argument, that the dictatorship and the suppression of local liberties were due to the war, it is difficult to take him at his word, so much do his designs bear the unmistakable imprint of his education and character. The strong point of the system was also its weak point: himself. To make the government work he employed all the resources of his charismatic yet realistic genius. He was capable of mastering numerous subjects in a short time, pleased by the variety of experience offered by the work of government, aware of the value of detail and knowledge of the terrain, and excited by the possibility of controlling everything by knowing all, as on the battlefield. He "was involved in everything," according to Chateaubriand. "His mind was never at rest. His ideas were in perpetual motion. Impetuous by nature, he proceeded not in a steady, straightforward fashion but by fits and starts. He threw himself upon the world and shook it" (*Mémoires d'outre-tombe*, chap. 24, p. 6). But this very energy carried within it the seeds of its own corruption, and implicit in the ambition to exert absolute authority was the possibility of a degradation of authority into tyranny. And such corruption, such degradation were quickly evident in the first consul. No one carried out his orders with sufficient haste; no one ever obeyed fully enough. In a country where fawning was a national pastime, flattery wreaked havoc on a character that constantly elicited it, and was soon intoxicated by it. Thus the famous charming smile was joined by an impatience with contradiction, a dark and violent energy, outbursts of anger, and a crudeness of insult for which Bonaparte soon became noted. Following a very French dialectic, the same man who apotheosized the abstract sovereignty of the state was also the man who weakened that sovereignty by acting as though it were embodied solely in himself. Napoleon was the Louis XIV of the democratic state.

Yet his possessive passion never blinded him to the point where he confused public with private. Temperament aside, his extraordinary ascent by itself would account for his tendency to regard all that he acquired, including the Republic, as his patrimony. Nevertheless, he remained first and foremost the heir of the Revolution, since the administrative state that he created in opposition to local powers was established upon the universality of law. Though in later years he resorted increasingly to arbitrary actions and established a nobility that owed its titles to the state, the source of his power over the nation remained the fact that he was the chosen embodiment of popular sovereignty, its instrument for making and enforcing laws that were to be the same for all. In this sense he was the ultimate incarnation of that crisis of political representation that was the essence of the Revolution. And he resolved that crisis by becoming the people's sole representative; he diluted the effects of universal suffrage by filtering it through restricted electoral lists, and he dominated the legislature by fragmenting the responsibilities of the assemblies. Yet he—and the administration that was nothing but an extension of him—remained the symbols of a new state, based on the consent of its equal citizens and embodying the general interest.

It was this public image that the people approved, and their approval enabled Napoleon to restore order and reconcile a nation divided by the Revolution. Ex-Constituents, ex-Girondins, ex-Terrorists, and of course ex-Thermidorians worked in his administration and served as his state councillors, magistrates, prefects, and military commissars, and in thousands upon thousands of other government employments. Even émigrés returned, many to the same two careers in which their their ancestors had distinguished themselves, careers now expanded and democratized yet somehow more brilliant than ever: the government and the army. No one needed to teach them how to be courtiers. The Consulate was a cornucopia of patronage, and Bonaparte played on a national scale one of the king's great roles at court: handing out rewards, honors, and jobs. He had more to distribute than any king had ever had, because he was the founder of the modern state. He therefore had not only to flatter the "vanity" of the nation but also to supply the needs of a vast administration and an immense army. More than any king in history he banked on the national passion for "position." This democratic transformation of noble values was the Corsican aristocrat's final secret. In a way it restored to the nation the aristocratic legacy that the Revolution had attempted to abolish and thus brought the reinforcement of the past to the hero of modern politics.

One last achievement seems to have rooted his work in the age: he bound the Church to his success. The Concordat of 1801 bears the mark of his genius: an intelligent use of a position of strength tempered by a revival of tradition and a bourgeois philosophy of religion. To a Catholic Church violently deprived of its history and its possessions by the Revolution he restored not its property, now in the hands of new lords, but its unity and status, in exchange for even more strict submission to the civil authorities than in the days of the kings. The Church he dealt with was of course no longer the powerful corporation it had been under the Ancien Régime, with its myriad ties to aristocratic society. Napoleon could therefore afford to restore its position without restoring its former power, in fact using it as a kind of buttress to his own power. This strategy his old friends from the Institute failed to understand, for they remained as staunchly anticlerical as in the halcyon days of the Directory, and they reproached Napoleon for the Concordat. But he was a man for naked political calculation, unencumbered by futile passions inherited from the Revolution. Nevertheless, his thoughts on religion were shaped in part by a very French bourgeois wisdom that owed more to Voltaire than to Machiavelli and that would continue to shape conservative policy throughout the nineteenth century: "Deprive the people of their faith and you will be left with nothing but highway robbers" (Council of State, 1805, Marquiset).

Such was Bonaparte, first consul, son and king of the Revolution, product of an event that the French cherished as part of their national heritage and therefore wished to enjoy in peace. A self-made dictator, he enthroned equality at his side. The best way to understand the chemistry that wedded him to the French people is to look at the years that followed 18 Brumaire. When he was able to offer the nation a triumphant peace with Europe, as he did at Amiens (1802), his triumph over public opinion seemed complete and unshakable.

Yet the man who gave France the Civil Code was also the most improbable of bourgeois rulers. If it was not as a general that he governed France, it was indeed as a general that he conquered public opinion. His dictatorship, born of the war, managed to control the war for only a few months.

So the great question is, "Could the dictatorship have endured?" So deeply was it rooted and so easily had it taken hold that it is tempting to answer "yes." What is more, the only French regimes since 1789 not to be overthrown from within have been the First and Second Empires. But the fact that the First Empire was born with the resumption of war in 1803 and collapsed slightly more than ten years later in military defeat is likely to suggest to the historian that what actually happened was in fact inevitable, and that the fate of Napoleon was linked to an interminable war that one day he was bound to lose.

Again we must give the Revolution its due. For the war was yet another legacy of the Revolution and of its conflict with Europe, which began in 1792–1793 and to which a complex of interests, hopes, and passions became attached over the ensuing decade. The revolutionary spirit was rekindled with the volunteers of Year I and the *levée en masse*. Within the army, discipline had been maintained ever since by the heroic defenders of the threatened Republic: neither 9 Thermidor nor 18 Brumaire seriously disturbed this republican institution, and if the army intervened on 18 Fructidor it was to save the Republic from royalist machinations. It was never seriously threatened by any of the major cleavages on the domestic front. The army and the future were one: it was the training ground for future leaders and the reward of talent. But it was more than that: it was an army created in the image of the new nation, the sans-culotte having matured to become the soldier.

The army, as old as the Revolution itself, became the bearer of French messianism as popular passions waned at home. After 9 Thermidor, after Vendémiaire, Year III, the syndicate of regicides that governed the Republic was all the more dependent on the war because it had disarmed the faubourgs of Paris; the only way to wrest the Terror from the control of the sans-culottes was to keep up the war with royalist Europe. There can be no doubt that the French public received the news of the peace of Amiens with joy. But this welcome was the result of a misunderstanding. The public interpreted first Lunéville and then Amiens as signs of triumph implying that Europe and England at last recognized the "great nation" and its universal mission. But this was not the case.

In December—the treaty of Amiens had been signed in March—at the news that the comte d'Artois, "wearing an order of a monarchy that England no longer recognizes," had reviewed a regiment, Bonaparte asked Talleyrand to represent to London "that our dignity, and we daresay the honor of the British government, demands that the princes be expelled from England, or that, if they are to be shown hospitality, they not be suffered to wear any order of a monarchy that England no longer recognizes; that to permit them to do so is a continual insult to the French people; [and] that the time of tranquillity has arrived in Europe." But this "tranquillity" was so poorly established that as soon as the war resumed it was England that hired assassins to act on behalf of the Bourbons against the usurper in Paris. On the morning of the duc d'Enghien's execution, Napoleon therefore declared: "I shall never agree to peace with England until she agrees to return the Bourbons as Louis XIV returned the Stuarts, because their presence in England will always be dangerous for France." On that March 21, 1804, the consul joined the regicide camp in spectacular fashion. What he expressed in dynastic terms—at bottom speaking the same language as those who wished to kill him—was merely another way of stating the popular conviction that there would never be peace between the Republic and the kings of Europe.

Nevertheless, the interminable war against the Ancien Régime, the war that carried him to the imperial throne (1804), also transformed his republican principate into a personal reign, inextricably bound up with his character and destiny. With the coronation of 1804, when his domination of the Revolution turned into a monarchy, it plainly ceased to be a matter of means and ends. When Napoleon became a hereditary monarch, he reached the height of his independence from revolutionary France, but never was he more dependent upon what can only be called his star. The great question was what he would do now that the revolutionary torrent that had brought him to the throne had subsided. His domestic policies daily revealed with increasing clarity the corruption of his domineering character by the exercise of absolute power, by his mania to control everything and make every decision, by his overestimation of his luck and his strength, and by his development of a police state of which Louis XIV could never even have dreamed. Yet the French, prisoners of his glory even more than of his police, had no alternative political future to offer: the Bourbons would bring back the nobles, and the Republic would bring back either Terror or disorder. The fate of the Empire would be decided outside its borders, which is to say, by the mystery of its intentions and the fortunes of war.

What did he want, this imposing and accidental heir to a unique moment in the fortunes of the nation? It is easier to say what he had, which at least explains his vast superiority over each of his adversaries taken individually. He was the master of a centralized and efficient modern state and able to mobilize all its resources to maximum advantage. He was the leader of an egalitarian society that recruited government officials and military officers from every stratum. In other words, he had no technological secrets—those belonged to England—but a social secret: an eighteenth-century nation and army liberated by the convulsion of revolution and rationalized by his enlightened despotism. Even more important, however, was another secret: his genius for action and what can only be called, for want of a better word, his

star: for if the Revolution could never clearly define its war aims—Danton
had his, and Carnot his, and Sieyès his—neither could he. He had studied
war, he had experienced it, he was born of it, and it never ceased to shape his
life. Condemned never to be compelled to make peace or even to lose an
important battle, he continued to up the ante with each new round. In this
respect Bonaparte as Charlemagne was the same man as Bonaparte the consul, a man obsessed with his own unique adventure. Though his army became
increasingly a professional army, though he married a daughter of the Hapsburgs, though he dreamed of a universal empire, he remained the plaything
of chance. The moment he surrendered his sword in 1814, his son and heir
vanished from the world stage along with himself. Ultimately only his administrative reorganization of France was solid, or, what comes to the same thing,
necessary. This internal structure was his bourgeois achievement. The rest of
his life was an incomparable improvisation, which remade the face of Europe
but ultimately left France with the same borders it had in 1789.

Yet his final adventure, the most insane of his life, showed that even the
Empire, a regime without tradition and dependent solely on battlefield victory, could be restored, just as the monarchy had been the year before. The
Hundred Days were extraordinary theater: no sooner had the legitimate king
regained his throne than the imperial usurper was restored in turn, as though
a few triumphant years could outweigh the possession of the throne by one
family for centuries. The truth is that the triumphant march in March 1815
from Gulf Juan to the Tuileries resurrected not so much Napoleon as the
Little Corporal, not so much the Empire as the Revolution. It crystallized a
popular sentiment that combined Jacobin egalitarianism and the glory of the
tricolor with a tinge of revolutionary souvenirs and national nostalgia, a formula that was destined to enjoy a long career in nineteenth-century French
politics. The Emperor's final appearance on the world stage cost France
dearly; but in this hopeless venture, soon to end at Waterloo, Napoleon rediscovered a little of his youthful popularity along with something of the spirit
of the army of Italy. Ultimately the English, by locking him up at the other
end of the world, provided him with a final, tailor-made cell in which the
cause of liberty could share his misfortune; the ultras, the *chambre introuvable*,
and the White Terror would do the rest. When, from Saint Helena, he dictated his "Memorial" to his loyal supporters, the defeated Napoleon once
again became the soldier of the triumphant Revolution. Thus he erected his
own monument in the nation's collective memory, and there the nation would
indeed worship him.

To this encounter between a man and a people, so brief yet so difficult
to forget—its memory would endure for nearly a century—there was no
more penetrating witness than Chateaubriand, and on Bonaparte's tomb
there is no better epitaph than his, composed in the inglorious days of the
Orleanist monarchy:

> Daily experience makes plain that the French are instinctively attracted to power.
> They have no use for liberty; equality is their only idol. But there are secret ties
> between equality and despotism. On these two counts Napoleon drew his strength
> from the heart of the French, a people militarily inclined toward force but dem-
> ocratically enamored of leveling. Risen to the throne, he seated the people there

beside him. A proletarian king, he humiliated kings and nobles in his antechambers. He leveled ranks not by lowering but by raising them. Lowering would have been more pleasing to plebeian envy, but lifting was more flattering to its pride. French vanity also swelled at the superiority that Bonaparte gave us over the rest of Europe. Another source of Napoleon's popularity was the affliction of his last days. After his death, the more people learned of his sufferings on Saint Helena, the more they softened toward him. They forgot his tyranny and remembered that first he defeated our enemies, and then having drawn them into France he defended us against them. We imagine that he could save us today from the shame into which we have fallen: his renown was brought back to us by his misfortune; his glory has benefited from his misery.

François Furet

FURTHER READING

Bainville, Jacques. *Napoléon*. Paris, 1931.
Bergeron, Louis. *L'épisode napoléonien: Aspects intérieurs, 1799–1815*, vol. 4 of *La nouvelle histoire de la France contemporaine*. Paris, 1972.
Chateaubriand, François-René. *Mémoires d'outre-tombe*, pts. 2 and 3, ed. Maurice Levaillant, 4 vols. Paris, 1948–1949.
Faure, Elie. *Napoléon*. Paris, 1921.
Lefebvre, Georges. *Napoléon*. Paris, 1947.
Masson, Fréderic. *Napoléon et sa famille*, 9 vols. Paris, 1897–1907.
Sorel, Albert. *L'Europe et la Révolution française*, 8 vols. Paris, 1885–1904.
Stendhal [Beyle, Marie Henri]. *Napoléon*. Paris, 1825.

RELATED TOPICS

Army	Centralization	Coups d'Etat	Mirabeau
Carnot	Civil Code	Italian Campaign	Sieyès

NECKER

Necker has against him the unconditional proscription that attaches to the memory of the vanquished. His reputation suffers, moreover, from the fatal handicap of moderation. Radical adversaries are of incalculable assistance in defining and legitimizing one's own positions. Maistrians need Robespierrists and vice versa. "The spirit of temperance," by contrast, disturbs and confuses these mirror identifications, while at the same time seeming not quite equal to the grandeur of events. Necker himself admirably describes the torment of the public man who sought measure "in times of trouble and agitation," "in the midst of all the passions without being in favor of any one," sustained only by "the uncertain probability of future judgments or by the muffled and trembling voice of the decent people of one's own time." He explains that since such men are seen as "overtaken by the accelerated motion of the passions, since they are also seen as behind the times in relation to new and systematic ideas, people disdain the workings of their minds, and even their characters are accused of being weak." With bitter dignity he concludes: "Nevertheless, it also takes courage to remain loyal to moderate opinions" (*Oeuvres complètes, RF*, 1, pp. 322–323). Indeed, he has never recovered from a charge of inconsistency, which takes two forms: he is accused by some of unwittingly wrecking the monarchical tradition, by others of irresolutely defending a lost cause.

His reputation had reached the highest pinnacle before it collapsed in a single year, from August 1789 to September 1790, into the abyss of posthumous failure and disgrace. A man for difficult situations, he faced an impossible task. In 1776, a few months before the fall of Turgot, it had taken the most dire circumstances for control of French royal finances to be given to a foreigner, the resident minister of the Republic of Geneva in Paris, who had no title but his success as a banker and who, moreover, was not only a Protestant but also linked, through his wife's salon, to the Encyclopedists. Financing the war in America demanded an expert in credit. But Necker was unable to transform the administrative reform that the Treasury's distress had made possible into a political opening. His startling *Account to the King* of January 1781 caused a sensation and stirred controversy. But his attempt to alter the spirit of French institutions by making "for the first time affairs of state the business of all" proved abortive. In May came disgrace. Thereafter Necker had all the leisure he needed to draft his appeal to the nation "to understand and scrutinize the public administration," a document upon which he had hoped relations between the prince and his subjects might be based; this became his great treatise *On the Administration of the Finances of*

France (1784). One of his most powerful political ideas arose out of his exceptionally sharp awareness of the power of public opinion and of the need to enlist its support in order to govern. Add to this his fatalistic view of property and its consequences, the basis of an interventionist doctrine that made him an opponent of the "laisser faire, laisser passer" of the physiocrats, along with his sense *Of the Importance of Religious Opinions* (the title of a work that he published in 1788, during his retirement) in the functioning of a free society, and you have the basic kernel of his thought. The bankruptcy of the royal Treasury brought him back to public life in August 1788 and made him the most important minister in the government. He was obliged to preside over the convocation of the Estates General promised by his predecessor. With that began a dreadful match in which, caught between the hostility of the court and the clamor of the people, he fruitlessly attempted to save the monarchy from itself.

At first he fared rather well. He committed himself to doubling the representation of the Third Estate and promoted a remarkably liberal set of electoral rules. Things went sour when the Estates met, conflict erupted among the orders, and the deputies proclaimed themselves the National Assembly on June 17. The conciliatory line recommended by Necker was disavowed by the king, who took the part of the privileged orders in his declaration of June 23. Necker submitted his resignation, but it was rejected. He was finally dismissed on July 11, with orders to leave France in secret. The proposed royal coup fizzled, however, in the face of the Parisian insurrection. Necker was recalled, and it was then that he committed the greatest blunder of his life by agreeing to accept a power that was impossible to wield. He sensed this but allowed himself to be taken in by the public favor to which he attached so much importance. "I am returning to France as a victim of the esteem with which I have been honored," he wrote just before setting out. "It seems to me that I am about to plunge into a pit." His return was triumphant. His popularity was at its height. A year later his resignation was greeted with widespread indifference, for public opinion had turned against him and he had been discredited in the eyes of all. His reformism was too bold for the aristocratic party and too timid for the patriots. Even his financial expertise, which for a time had enabled him to maintain a measure of control over the Assembly, ultimately paled, having been made to seem like narrow, old-fashioned orthodoxy once the miracle solution of the assignat began to shimmer in all its seductive splendor. His only mistake, said one deputy on August 2, 1790, with a benevolent condescension that only called attention to the way in which yesterday's miracle worker had been rendered superfluous, was to have clung to "ideas consistent with a long experience that prevented him from rising to the height of the new conceptions." Moreover, if any man could have governed the Revolution, it is clear that Necker had neither the right profile nor the right stuff. He lacked the talent for manipulating people and the intuition to sense the passions that moved them; nor did he possess the quick will or the firm resolve that guide the leaders of nations in cataclysmic times. A cautious, analytical man who placed too much confidence in the resources of analysis and the authority of intelligence, he lacked the means to confront the destructive and violent side of politics.

The minister's weaknesses were the author's strengths. He gives a marvelous account of a situation he was unable to master. His uninterrupted commentary on the course of the Revolution through Brumaire and the Constitution of Year VIII, which unjustly fell victim to the discredit of the government, ranks among the most pertinent and profound of contemporary critical observations. It is contained in three works: *On Executive Power in Large States* (1792), *On the French Revolution* (1796), and *Last Views on Politics and Finance* (1802). (A fourth work, *On the Administration of M. Necker, by Himself*, which dates from May 1791, was an apology written in midcrisis and presented an interpretation that would be developed in the later works.) This commentary was neither solemn proclamation nor prophetic pronouncement but rigorous, closely argued analysis of the role of a political practitioner preoccupied with the problem of *means* of government as opposed to actors obsessed with the problem of *principles*. And owing to this realistic acuity, indeed because of its very limits, it is one of the most enlightening of all works on the political experiment that was the essence of the Revolution.

In retirement Necker was not always accurately informed. More than that, his powerful common sense barred him from comprehending the essential and very real issues at stake in that "abstraction of general ideas" whose functional unsuitability he exposed better than anyone else. In this respect he exhibits a blindness that mirrors the blindness of the revolutionaries themselves concerning the impracticality of their constructions. Since, moreover, we know today that the history of democracy would prove to be the history of the slow and painful conversion of those same "general ideas" into "active maxims," we are entitled to condemn both sides with equal justice. In what sense is it true that "the French Revolution is over"? In precisely this sense: that after two centuries of accommodation of democratic principles to the inexorable constraints of the political order and to the functional needs of society, we can unreservedly welcome the abstract ideals of liberty, equality, and popular sovereignty while at the same time doing full justice to the cogency of the pragmatic criticisms of a man like Necker. In this we can claim no special merit. What has happened is that in the meantime the abyss that initially separated the two orders of reality has disappeared. From a distance Necker's words illuminate like no other the original depth and tragic existence of that gap.

From book to book Necker's reflection was guided by the series of constitutions: the Constitution of 1791, the Constitution of Year III, and the Constitution of Year VIII. (Necker warns us that he removed from his 1796 book the pages concerning the Constitution of 1793, rendered irrelevant by the march of events.) His central problem, the touchstone to which his analysis constantly returns, is governability. A special place must be reserved, however, for his retrospective reflections on the origins of the Revolution, which form the first section of the work entitled *On the French Revolution*. Their purpose is largely one of self-justification. The former minister sets out to explain and defend his policy, but in so doing he manages, through small touches in his narrative of events, to paint a rather striking portrait of the forces in contention on the eve of 1789 and of the irresistible influence of circumstances. On one side stood a unique combination of despotism and confusion in the form of the existing royal administration and the lack of awareness of the situation in the king's entourage, what Necker calls "the negligence with which they considered both the great changes that had taken place in France over the past two centuries and the singularity of the present age" (*RF*, 1, p. 252). Primary responsibility, before the "popular" party took over and before "the people had learned in one day," with the fall of the Bastille, "that supreme power lay in the union of wills" (*RF*, 1, p. 233), belonged without a doubt to the short-sighted intransigence of the privileged orders. "When history is free to raise its voice," he sums up, "it will ask the first two orders, especially the nobility, to account for an inflexibility that caused the scepter of opinion to pass into the hands of the Third Estate. It will reproach them for having sought to obtain everything through courage and stubbornness rather than by making, at an opportune moment, the sacrifices demanded by the authority of circumstances and the imperious law of necessity" (*RF*, 1, pp. 249–250). Necker's whole analysis is in fact designed to demonstrate that the goal toward which he was working, and which determined his conduct, was attainable: "One would have today in France the government of England, and the government of England perfected, if the king, the nobility, and the Third Estate had each desired it at a certain moment, and had been able to will it all together at one time" (*RF*, 1, p. 312).

The great word was spoken: the Constitution of England. This was the model that should have been adopted, at least as a point of departure, not in order to follow it servilely but in order to bring to it "all the amendments made advisable by reason and experience" (*Oeuvres complètes, PE,* p. 316). In the English Constitution the fundamental political problem was if not fully resolved then at least provided with a relatively satisfactory solution: the marriage of efficiency with liberty. "It is in the formation of obedience," wrote Necker, "it is in the combination of means in order to secure general subordination without despotism and without tyranny, that all political science and all the difficulty of social organization lie" (*PE*, p. 19). That one could now obtain such submission without brutal coercion was an "almost mysterious" thing, which must be looked upon as the most difficult achievement of the constitutional art. Necker's fascination with the secret of obedience without violence is the true heart of his thought. But rather than base its work on an existing example, the Constituent Assembly made a fatal choice: to follow the path of abstract reconstruction. It chose to guide its action by abstract principles. Necker lacked words harsh enough to assail the constructivist ambitions of the National Assembly. In 1796 he summed up his complaints in these terms: "A youthful taste for new things, a glorious desire for originality, a vain and pusillanimous distaste for imitation of any kind, and finally a credulous confidence in figures traced by theory and a thoughtless contempt for realities etched by experience" (*RF*, 1, p. 299). This was Necker's limitation: he failed to perceive the psychology of other actors in the drama, and he was blind to the objective factors that might have given such persuasive force to the illusion of the blank slate. He did not see the intrinsic power in the idea of the sovereignty of the nation; he could not conceive of its dynamic effectiveness. In addition, he suffered from the ordinary prejudice as to the political incapacity of that part of the population "wholly occupied in earning its subsistence through continual labor," which made him radically insensitive to what was profound in the aspiration to equality.

In a word, he had no sense of the causes, yet he was acutely aware of the effects. Thus he was able to explain clearly, and immediately, the contradiction that sapped the Constitution of 1791, which its authors had hoped would endure for all eternity. Monarchic in its title, it was "republican in its forms," and, Necker added, "despotic in its means of execution" (*PE*, p. 449). "It was a mistake that will be remembered forever," he said again in 1796, "for an assembly of lawmakers to have attempted to maintain monarchical government in France, to have deemed it most appropriate to a nation of twenty-five million souls, and to have believed that it was realizing that idea by placing a king at the head of a democratic constitution" (*RF*, 1, p. 261). But this inconsistency, crucial as it was, was itself only the fruit of a more general error of method. The Constituent Assembly had been caught in the trap of mistaking the logical order of things for the real order, which was actually the reverse. Hence it dealt with the executive branch of government last when it did not "overlook it absolutely," whereas "this branch, though apparently second in the political organization, plays the essential role" (*PE*, p. 17).

The objection is far-reaching. It goes to the heart of the modern theory of legitimacy. Think of Locke's famous formula, "There can exist only one unique supreme power, the legislative power, to which all others are and should be subordinate." In the logic of representative government, sovereignty is concentrated in the legislative body, of which the executive power is merely the instrument. Necker, by challenging that order on grounds of social efficiency, put his finger on the central contradiction, which for more than a century and a half would make it impossible to achieve stable representative government where "representative" was understood to mean "parliamentary." In the abstract the executive branch exists only to enforce the laws elaborated by the representatives, but in practice the executive is the primary power, "the driving force of a government. It represents in the political system that mysterious power which in the moral man combines action with will" (*PE*, p. 15). It "forms the cornerstone of the political edifice." Because the "political metaphysicians" of the Constituent Assembly neglected this essential constraint, they deprived the monarch of the eminence and authority necessary to discharge his duties as supreme head of the executive branch. Not only did they unduly limit his real prerogatives (and Necker endeavors to show, through comparison with both the English and the American constitutions, his constant reference, that the United States, republican as it was, "has given the government means of action much more powerful and respectable than we have given the government in France," *PE*, p. 357). But, what is in the final analysis even more serious, the Constituent Assembly undermined the symbolic preeminence of the monarch, "the imposing character of dignity necessary to his action." To command is "to dominate the imagination" (*PE*, p. 197). The efficacy of power depends crucially on the force of representation: "He must have his reasonable authority and his magical influence; he must act as nature acts, through visible means and an unfathomable superiority" (*PE*, p. 19). This is indeed the price of liberty, for whatever cannot be obtained by spontaneous submission must be gained by effective coercion.

Necker again treats this theme at length in his book *On the French Revolution*, of which it forms the principal subject if the work is seen in the light of its culminating "Reflections on Equality." Liberty is unthinkable unless the existence of a symbolic hierarchy makes it possible to dispense with actual violence. Political wisdom in a genuinely liberal regime consists in "availing oneself of the conventional grandeur of this political being, of his external splendor, of his hold over opinion and over imagination itself, in order to establish a moral authority apt to facilitate the action of government, apt to maintain public order without continual recourse to acts of violence and tyrannical means" (*RF*, 1, p. 344). In a related idea, the monarch's majesty has as its necessary complement "differences of status, rank, and fortune," gradations "that inculcate the sentiments of respect and obedience" (*RF*, 2, p. 349). Therein lay the ultimate contradiction of the Constitution of 1791: to have presumed "that a throne could remain standing if battered by waves of equality" (*RF*, 1, p. 292). Remove this instinctive bulwark of authority and you must replace it with the machinery of coercion: "All means of force become necessary to the government in a large state when no gradation of rank disposes minds toward respect and subordination" (*RF*, 2, pp. 399–400). For having thought that "authority was created by the law's commandment," and for having neglected, in addition, the primary necessity of the active branch of government, the revolutionaries were condemned to watch their government lurch from ineffectiveness in its regular operations to brutality in exceptional situations. The dissolution of the bonds of obligation naturally inherent in the pyramid of ranks resulted in the rule of naked force: "The reign of violence and the reign of equality are closely related" (*RF*, 2, p. 399). For the same reason Necker rejects the common association of liberty with equality: they are allied "only through abstractions. . . . In reality, introduced together on a vast stage, [they] will be in constant opposition" (*RF*, 2, p. 401).

In the final analysis, Necker's vision of politics is based on a religious view of the world. Hierarchy is rooted in the nature of things: "Everything proclaims to us that the ideas of preeminence and superiority are inextricably intertwined with the spirit of creation" (*RF*, 2, p. 376). The lawmaker's task is to put "inequalities in harmony," thanks to which the social order participates as if by resonance in the divine economy, while the adjunct of faiths "diminishes the task of governments." Therein lies the interesting originality of his position: the most extreme liberalism possible, one might say, within a coherent religious understanding of the world. It made him exquisitely sensitive to the immense phenomenon heralded and propelled by the Revolution: the exorbitant expansion of the sphere of power implicit in the uprooting of the religious structure of dependency. By what other means than despotism could 25 million men be contained when no traditional bonds remained to

hold them together? And—as it was prettily put—what a tremendous increase in power when authority ceased to consist of anything else. The representative reconstitution of public power was thus reflected first of all in a
formidable expansion of that power:

> This representative system, through a sort of metaphysical sleight-of-hand, is in
> our day proclaimed to yield something like an exact impression of individual
> wills, a likeness so good that a small number of elected deputies may reasonably
> and legitimately dispose of the persons and property of an entire nation; that
> they may do so indefinitely and in the same way as that nation would be entitled
> to do if all the individuals of which it is composed were consulted one by one.
> What abuse of the word *representative!* . . . There is, it seems to me, no greater
> proof of the degree to which the French nation is still in its political infancy than
> its respectful adherence to an unprecedented servitude.   (*RF,* 2, p. 167)

Over the long term, and not without costly upheavals, these fears of an abyss
of domination "of which no one has yet measured the nature or extent"
proved unfounded. It has turned out to be possible to obtain, without violence, unity in a multitude of equals within a large state, as well as to prevent
a usurpation of authority by the new "aristocracy" (the word is Necker's) introduced by the electoral system. Yet it is infinitely enlightening to be able to
see, with the eyes of a man whose rare combination of conservatism and
openness made him a privileged witness, the unsettling discovery of the problem at a time when no one was yet in a position to say whether or not it had a
solution.

 The radicality of the revolutionary movement's principles stand out in
his perception in remarkable relief, and the less well he understands those
principles, the more evident their radicalism. He has a powerful passage, for
example, on the differences in strategic significance between the American
and French declarations of rights. He is wrong to impute this to a misappre-
hension, but he is profoundly perceptive when it comes to the difference between, on the one hand, the French need for refoundation ex nihilo and
institutional universalism and, on the other hand, the generally pragmatic
approach of the Americans. Because it appeared in the preamble to the
United States Constitution, Necker says,

> we looked upon this declaration as the beginning, in some sense, of the political
> nature [of the Americans], whereas it was rather the distillate and the result.
> Their continental situation, the nature of their foreign relations, their mores,
> their habits, and the limits of their wealth, all those great circumstances that de-
> termine the genius of a nation, existed before their declaration of rights. Thus
> their profession of faith arose, as all words should, out of concrete circumstances
> and a just harmony with the absolute empire of realities. Our legislators, however,
> have looked upon this declaration of rights as the efficient cause of the liberty of
> the Americans and as a universal principle of regeneration equally well suited to
> all nations.   (*PE,* p. 320)

He has no difficulty, moreover, in showing how all the elements that ensure
that the American Constitution will work are missing from the Constitution
of 1791. His objection concerning the means accorded the executive was men-

tioned earlier. He also lays stress on the way in which a narrow understanding of equality led the French to reject the idea of a bicameral legislature, and in which a doctrinaire view of the separation of powers led to "setting the powers at war with one another even before they were created." He also calls attention to the inconsistency of opting for an extensive elective system while rejecting the federal counterweight adopted by the Americans in the name of the unity and indivisibility of the kingdom. "England in its unity, America in its system of federation, offer two fine models of government," Necker concludes. "England teaches us how a hereditary monarchy can be maintained without inspiring distrust in the friends of liberty; America, how a vast continent can be subjected to republican forms without causing anxiety in the friends of public order" (*PE*, p. 362). These are virtues of which the French Constitution—"uncertain as to its ends, confused as to its principles, unsteady as to its course, an imperfect combination of governments and political ideas of every kind" (*PE*, p. 449)—is sadly deprived.

It was these principles, assumed in their plenitude and rigor, independent of and beyond what reality could bear by way of transcription, that constituted the grandeur of the Revolution and would propagate its influence. To this Necker's mind was of too positive a cast to be sensitive, at least initially; distance would modify his views somewhat. But there was another aspect regarding which his powers of realistic description worked wonders: the tragic lack of executive power, which grew out of the ambition and radicalism of the plan to establish a new society grounded in universality. He was a peerless analyst of the experience of impotence that was also part of the revolutionary experiment: impotence to equip a democracy determined to ignore existing forms and to eschew the aid of examples; impotence to equip oneself with adequate instruments, substantive incarnations, and stable institutions, resulting in deviations and correctives that only aggravated the problem. His systematic dissections of the measures taken by the government at times endowed him with rather remarkable powers of prediction, especially in his 1792 book, in which an analysis of the choices made in the Constitution and of the dynamic set in motion by the National Assembly led to a forecast of various ways in which events might evolve: toward a precarious, vestigial monarchy grafted onto a body "so democratic" that it would take very little "to complete France's metamorphosis into a republic" (*PE*, p. 386); toward a gathering of "all forms of power into the hands of the nation's elected officials"; or, finally, toward widespread disillusionment once people noticed, as they were bound to do quite soon, that their lot had not changed and that "the price of bread and the wage scale were not in the power of [their representatives]" (*PE*, p. 591).

Necker had previously criticized at length the division of responsibilities between the legislative and executive branches and the relation between the two. The Convention had represented an extreme form of the tendency, which he denounced at the time, to favor concentration of all powers within a legislature itself reduced to a single chamber, the better to mark its preeminence. The Constitution of Year III, which veered to the opposite extreme, offered an occasion to level a further blast at his favorite targets: the systematic spirit and abstraction of politics. The concern to repudiate the structure of government proposed by the Convention had led lawmakers to the other extreme, "complete and absolute separation of the two primary authorities, the one that makes the laws and the other that supervises and directs their execution" (*RF*, 2, p. 122). Once again, the practical sense of "combinations and relations" was to be preferred to the false rigor of paper designs. In 1792, in opposition to the rigid doctrine of separation and balance of powers, Necker stressed that it was "bonds more than checks, proportions more than distances, conventions more than vigilance, which contribute to the harmony of governments" (*PE*, p. 68). Four years later he repeated the point with even greater force: "One must seek to establish a constitutional link between the executive power and the legislative power. One must believe that their prudent association and ingenious intertwining will always be the best guarantee of mutual circumspection and effective oversight" (*RF*, 2, p. 133). In the absence of such coherence in the division of responsibilities, "either order or liberty" would be in peril—and sooner rather than later. Indeed it did not take long before Necker's detailed diagnosis of the fatal flaws in the new Constitution was abundantly confirmed by the facts.

Two years before his death Necker took up his pen for what he knew would be the last time, as is evident from the title of his book: *Last Views on Politics and Finance*. The work is astonishing for the openmindedness it reveals in its elderly author. The man who had always been a champion of the English government yielded to the march of history. Convinced "that a series of unprecedented events has made France into a new world," he shed his old prejudice and attempted to put forward his own plan for a "republic one and indivisible, subject insofar as possible to the laws of equality," yet still a republic capable of normal operations, unlike the immature attempts at republican government that had been tried to date, or worse yet, the dictatorial travesty established by the Constitution of Year VIII. That Constitution met with no more approval in Necker's eyes than the previous ones. He saw quite clearly that it was merely a transitional camouflage. It had "by itself no support. None of the authorities of which it is composed can oversee or offer support to the others, and the independence of the primary power has been prepared in every way" (*Oeuvres complètes, DV*, p. 5). It was in fact a "bourgeois oligarchy ranged around a master, in which only the name of republic has been preserved" (*DV*, p. 33). Soon it would be necessary to choose between the truth of dictatorship and the republican disguise. Whence the book's strategy: a discreet appeal to Bonaparte to establish the republic at last on a firm foundation.

Necker finally decided to make this proposal openly, not without fear and trembling at the difficulty of the task: "The union of order, liberty, and equality in a *government one and indivisible* must be considered the great work in politics; and if the problem can be resolved in a vast country, history offers no example of it" (*DV*, p. 84). In 1792 he had declared that a republic in a large country was impossible without the support of a federal system like that of the American government. Since experience had apparently shown that the French nation would very definitely remain one and indivisible, Necker attempted in 1802 to dispense with the federal system. His Constitution provided for two chambers with equal powers, elected for terms of five and ten years, respectively, by *censitaire* suffrage (with a relatively modest *cens*, or property qualification, set at payment of 12 francs in taxes for electors and 200 francs for eligibility for office), and, in a tribute to the Revolution's general repugnance at the idea of a replacement for the king, a collective executive of seven members. Necker made no secret of his private preferences, which continued to be for moderate monarchy, a choice justified by an argument that never wavered: "The advantage of such a government, its particular merit, is that it enlists all the corps and all the powers in maintaining the existing harmony" (*DV*, p. 229). The problem was simply that in France its time had passed, "so much do minds shun every kind of fiction" (*DV*, p. 243). Its symbolic underpinnings, those "prerogatives of respect" to which he had once assigned such an important role, had been destroyed for good. As early as 1792 Necker had issued a warning to those who believed in the possibility of a "return, pure and simple, of an old government long since undermined by public opinion." And further: "A despotism of twenty years and the most terrible tyranny would not be enough to carry out this plan" (*PE*, p. 591). Ten years later it was the very principle of royalty that seemed to him to have been damaged beyond repair: not even Bonaparte, he noted without illusions, could succeed now "in establishing a moderate hereditary monarchy." He could, however, do what not even the Convention itself had been able to do at the height of its power, "when the supreme authority was entirely in the hands of men impassioned by the most total equality": "Lay the foundations of a republic that would enjoy both respect and strength and that would withstand the test of time" (*DV*, p. 258).

Is there any reason to think that the sick old man who wrote these lines at what he believed to be a crucial moment nursed many illusions about either the man Napoleon or his brief's chances for success? It is highly unlikely. Still, it was worth one final try to alter the course of a history that had long since eluded his grasp. Perhaps no other destiny better illustrates, without the illumination of death and on a stage no larger than Necker's tranquil gray study, the scale of the revolutionary tragedy, for in it we see the futile clash of a reasonable man with reason in history, which is to say, with the unreason of events.

Marcel Gauchet

FURTHER READING

WORKS BY NECKER

Oeuvres complètes. Paris, 1820–1821. Vol. 8: *Du pouvoir exécutif dans les grands états* (cited as *PE*). Vols. 9 and 10: *De la Révolution française* (cited as *RF*, 1 and 2). Vol. 11: *Dernières vues de politique et de finances* (cited as *DV*).

ON NECKER'S POLITICAL CAREER

Egret, Jean. *Necker, ministre de Louis XVI, 1776–1790.* Paris, 1975.

ON HIS THOUGHT IN GENERAL

Grange, Henri. *Les idées de Necker.* Paris, 1974.

RELATED TOPICS

Ancien Régime	Equality	Louis XVI
Constitution	Estates General	Napoleon Bonaparte
Democracy	Liberty	Rights of Man

ROBESPIERRE

How was it possible for the "lawyer from Arras" to become, within the space of a few weeks, the "absolute master of France"? The question that tormented Necker in 1797 is banal: revolutions commonly bestow extraordinary fates on ordinary lives. Most of the actors in the French Revolution could be subjected to the same inquiry. In defense of the former minister, however, one might say that none of them wedded his era as Robespierre did, none merged with it to the point where his death became the conclusion of countless histories of the Revolution. The death of Robespierre was also the death of the Revolution, whereas for others the Revolution that ground them under continued after they were gone. Robespierre gave of himself totally in defeat as well as in victory, while his adversaries climbed over the corpses of their predecessors apparently without ever dreaming that their turn would come, exhibiting in the end what Cochin called the "same naive stupor when the tide swept over them." In Thermidor Robespierre was not caught by surprise. His death hovered on the horizon of every speech he made: "I know the fate that lies in store for me," he said in 1791. Marat's death heralded his own: "The honors of the dagger are also reserved for me. . . . My downfall draws near with great strides." A "premature death" is the price that the "virtuous man" must pay, he wrote in his celebrated dedication to Rousseau. Tirelessly he rang all the changes on the theme of virtue persecuted and crime ineluctably triumphant—ineluctably but temporarily, for if both "the good and the wicked disappear from the earth," they do so "under different conditions." Doomed to an imminent death at the hand of the enemies he saw posted on his path, Robespierre left it to posterity to judge—and to justify—his sacrifice for the "good of his fellow man."

Robespierre's words reflect not so much experience of life as a tested rhetoric well attuned to the conformism of the man. A lawyer in 1781, he prospered in the shadow of his protectors at the bishopric of Arras. In 1783 he won his greatest success, championing the cause of persecuted science with a skillful defense of lightning rods—a defense, incidentally, of which he was not the author. That made no difference, however, for he took credit for his victory with great satisfaction, savoring his new notoriety. Society received him in its salons. The Academy of Arras opened its doors to him. He was appreciated in circles that Marat described, with a little envy and a great deal of justice, as "assemblies formed by the vanity of self-important little men who sought to play a role and by the boredom of petty amateurs who had no idea how to kill time." What better description could one give of the lackluster but respectable existence into which Robespierre threw himself with energetic diligence? For him, respectability was constraint and rigidity, hatred of all spontaneity: disorder in dress or emotions, vulgarity of expression, and, more generally, any form of indecency or exhibition horrified him. The vigor and debauch of Mirabeau and Danton provoked revulsion in this desperately proper and, as Büchner would say, "unbearably honest" man.

Behind this unruffled front lay a total absence of passion. One of his teachers said of him, "Stubbornly occupied with adorning his mind, he seemed unaware that his heart too needed care." He was surrounded, however, by women, beginning with his sister Charlotte, prepared to do anything to keep her adored brother by her side, ready even to fight like a harpy when the female Duplay coterie succeeded in sequestering this eternal "big brother" in 1791. His alleged fiancées were nothing more than female correspondents to whom he sent insipid poems celebrating the purity of his sentiments, or, more prosaically, a copy of his latest brief. He was chaste by choice and might have sighed like Julie: "I want to be chaste, because that is the primary virtue, which nourishes all the others."

The Revolution did not change the provincial lawyer, whose manners Robespierre preserved until he came to power. Nothing could make him give up his rigid schedule or meticulous appearance. When the Convention filled with sans-culottes and Phrygian caps, he continued to wear a tie and powdered wig. Yet this was the man in whom the spirit of the Revolution was made flesh. Seeing the Jacobin people behind the orator, Michelet observed that "it was more than a man who spoke." But he was simply stating a fact, without explaining the reasons for this strange power of incarnation, an enigma that will never be fully unraveled. Perhaps this power can be ascribed in part to Robespierre's personality: beyond the reach of passion, he was fully available to virtue. Having eliminated in himself all distinction between private and public, between love of self and love of country, he had completed the cycle of "regeneration" that would become the center of his politics: he came to the Revolution a citizen while others remained subjects. His words gained strength from his personal experience of virtue. Robespierre perfected ideological discourse in the highest degree because he was himself ideology incarnate.

It was in the aftermath of his "triumph" in the lightning rod affair that he found employment for his talents and worked out a strategy, rejecting both the ordinary means and the ordinary ends of political action. At first sight the case seems commonplace: Robespierre had to defend a rope maker accused of theft by a monk anxious to cover up his own prevarications. Robespierre easily won his case, but, refusing to settle for mere vindication, demanded financial reparations for his client, to that end drafting a vehement brief in which he denounced inequalities before the law and fulminated against the dubious morals of monks. Rights mocked and vice triumphant: the tones of the future conventionnel are already audible here. People began to speak of him as the "upholder of the wretched, avenger of innocence." Unmoved by his devotion, his colleagues at the bar denounced the "infamous libel" that Robespierre, contrary to all custom, had had printed before the case was judged. Without a moment's hesitation he attacked the prejudices of his profession and waxed indignant over the persecution to which he was being subjected. In a series of conflicts he turned his back on all that might have served either his career as a lawyer or his political future, at a time when the ferment preceding the convocation of the Estates General might have made it advisable to cultivate whatever contacts one had that might prove useful: he shunned the Academy and turned away from the high clergy and notables. Placed on the blacklist, he soon felt the consequences: in 1788 he pleaded the same number of cases as when he had begun his career in 1782, while his colleagues had doubled or even tripled their caseloads. But Robespierre turned defeat and isolation into victory and popularity: the bishopric did not forgive him for his accusations, but the curés became his propagandists. The elite of the Third Estate rejected him, but the poorest guild in Arras, that of the *savetiers-mineurs,* chose him as its deputy.

In Robespierre's political apprenticeship practical experience was a major component; and when the Estates General met, his course was set. Fortified by his convictions and his experience of political combat, he arrived in Versailles with a very sure political judgment that enabled him quickly to take the measure of the contending parties and evaluate his chances of playing a role when the moment was ripe.

All of Robespierre is in this early experience. From Arras to Versailles, where he represented the Third Estate of the province of Artois, he remained faithful to a single strategy: the uncompromising repudiation of duplicity erected into a political art. He sacrificed everything to transparency, immolating all personal interest on the altar of that "imperious sentiment" that had made him wed the cause of the people. He rejected any possibility of coexistence between fidelity to ideas and the parallel pursuit of a legitimate ambition: "I am not the defender of the people," he admonished Brissot. "I am of the people, I have never been anything else, I do not wish to be anything else. I despise anyone presumptuous enough to wish to be anything more." Harassed by the Girondins in 1792, he thundered: "In taking this podium to respond to the charge against me, I am defending not my own cause but the public cause." On 8 Thermidor he reminded his enemies that their denunciations "are not an insult to an individual but an insult to an invincible nation that tames and punishes kings." Robespierre was himself *peuple;* the cause of the one was also the cause of the other. His honesty was incontestable, and by 1790 he was known to all as "the Incorruptible." Sharp-tongued and far too human to understand a man hailed as a "living commentary on the Declaration of Rights," Roederer suspected some affectation in this cult of transparency: "He would have paid someone to offer him gold in order to say that he had refused it." But Robespierre, "that little god in a magnificent void," preached only to the converted, like Saint-Just, who wrote with ardor that he knew him only as one knows "God, through his miracles." Unwittingly he came close to the truth: dead to himself, Robespierre was all action, and in his case one might almost have "deduced his existence from his acts," as Kierkegaard said of God.

All action—but what kind of action? In the Constituent Assembly he did not participate in the work of any committee and took no part in legislative debate per se. He systematically resigned the judicial posts to which he was called on several occasions by the electors of Paris and Versailles. In renouncing one of these mandates he invoked the mission that was his: "To defend the cause of humanity, of liberty, as a citizen and as a man, before the tribunal of the universe and of posterity." He was already a judge in the Assembly. Repository and guardian of the people's rights, he judged legislative acts in the light of these "simple and incontestable principles." He was the Assembly's censor, "the vigilant sentinel who cannot be taken by surprise," and the Jacobins of Marseilles saw in him "the only rival of the Roman Fabricius," of whom it was said that "it is easier to sway the sun from its course than to make Fabricius stray from the path of honor." Anchored in the world of principles, Robespierre did not act. In him immobility became action, and he stood as a fixed point in the tumult of the Revolution, which turned everything upside down and swept men away.

He soon measured the irresistible power of the revolutionary dynamic and the futility of efforts to restrain it. One after another all the party leaders had attempted to control the course of events by becoming advisers of a phantom monarch whose authority they themselves had destroyed. "Cruel and ingenious sophists," said Robespierre to all who wished to end the Revolution, "you will be swept along like helpless insects." He allowed them to compromise themselves, to destroy themselves one by one, gaining stature with each and every downfall and "betrayal." While his adversaries gazed upward toward an empty space, he cast his eyes downward, toward the people, which filled the entire stage. "Stop slandering the people," he protested, paraphrasing Rousseau, "by constantly portraying it as unworthy of enjoying its rights, wicked, barbarous, and corrupt! It is you who are unjust and corrupt; it is the people that is good, patient, and generous." Robespierre never missed an opportunity to celebrate the generosity of "the people," as for example when he wrote these words about the July 1789 massacres: "M. Foullon was hanged yesterday by decree of the people." Nor did he pass up any occasion to stigmatize his colleagues' criminal intentions, as when he embarked, almost alone, on a relentless campaign against the *censitaire* suffrage.

A "sophist" according to Baudot, a "vile incendiary" according to Duquesnoy, this man who shrewdly blended sincerity with demagoguery compelled the attention if not always the respect of his colleagues. Mirabeau said: "He will go far; he believes everything he says." Robespierre was not, as Aulard maintains, "the unwitting laughingstock and stuffed shirt of the Assembly." He was its termite. In the space of a few months he acquired a surprising political influence precisely because the Assembly disapproved of his words or refused to listen to them. No matter. He was addressing not his colleagues but public opinion, speaking to the galleries: "What is remarkable," wrote the editor of *Babillard* in regard to Robespierre's speeches, "is that they are always known in advance, and that the opinions of this famous deputy enjoy prodigious success in all the taverns of the capital before being uttered in the nation's senate." The hostility that he was obliged to confront in the Assembly increased his popularity outside it.

His efforts were focused primarily on the Society of Jacobins. In March 1790 he was already its president, but he still had to reckon with powerful rivals such as Mirabeau and later the triumvirs. In order to strengthen his position he entered into constant relations with certain affiliated clubs and did not disdain to frequent Paris clubs less concerned with legality than were the Jacobins. From these investments in radicalism he reaped the benefits at the Jacobin Club. Little by little the gallery became *his* gallery, the public *his* public. The crowd arranged, the adversaries in the audience carefully identified, Robespierre could make his appearance at the rostrum. Although he could not yet demand a place on the podium, as he would do after August 10, he called the tune, signaled for applause or "murmurs," and monopolized the platform for hours at a time. As early as the spring of 1791 Louvet charged him with seeking to establish the "despotism of opinion." If he was master in the Jacobin assembly, however, access to the Committee of Correspondence—the society's veritable executive body—was for a long time denied him. It was the king's flight to Varennes on June 20, 1791, which, by provoking a split with the Club's moderate element, swept away the last obstacles between Robespierre and total domination of the Jacobins. The reconquest of initially hesitant affiliates, "regeneration," and purge made the society that emerged from the summer crisis of 1791 an organization freed from the National Assembly's domination, a counterpower over which Robespierre henceforth reigned alone.

With virtuoso skill Robespierre moved back and forth between the Assembly and the Jacobins, the rue Saint-Honoré and the Salle du Manège. In the Assembly he pulled all the strings of parliamentary tactics, in the Club he availed himself of every means of manipulation. Of course he was not the only shrewd tactician. Seventeen eighty-nine had produced others just as formidable and tenacious. Some, such as Mirabeau and Barnave, were also brilliant orators, a talent Robespierre lacked. In Baudot's word he was a *discoureur*, a speechifier, but of a very particular kind, whose language was that of preaching and inquisition. Tireless in his denunciation of intrigue and conspiracy, he might be compared to Marat. But in the imprecations of the "ami du peuple" there was something rudimentary that made him far inferior to Robespierre. Robespierre's suspicions and denunciations were not the product of a pathological instinct but a political masterstroke. "Do not slander distrust," he once said. "Whatever you may say about it, it is the guardian of the people's rights; it is to the profound sentiment of liberty what jealousy is to love." Coming from him the parallel is amusing, yet it has the merit of defining quite accurately the task that Robespierre assigned himself. When others proposed or acted, he examined and scrutinized, searching for the intention hidden behind their acts. His role was not to do or even to will but to discern, to bring to light what others wished to hide. The conspiracy was *here*, omnipresent, in even the most apparently patriotic initiatives, behind the evidence of proclaimed intentions. In this systematic suspicion there was at times great lucidity: when Brissot pushed for war and won the backing of public opinion, Robespierre denounced the Girondin leader's self-interested motives with great lucidity. In late 1793, when he set himself against the cult of Reason and its Hébertist champions, he rightly attacked the base ambitions of those unscrupulous self-promoters. But with him suspicion was not isolated but a general and permanent condition. Every action—and most of all any action that seemed to further the Revolution—was legitimately suspect, a priori the product of a double motive. Approval or disapproval could come only after Robespierre, and Robespierre alone, had penetrated to the truth, he being the only person to have rid himself of every vestige of duplicity and double language: "I have just impugned the entire National Assembly," he said on June 21, 1791, full of confidence in himself. "I defy the Assembly to do the same to me."

Through such universal suspicion the Revolution lost all certainty. Reality was not truth but in fact masked the truth; it was opacity. What could be seen was not what really existed: reality was a lie. If the facts were deceiving, the words that expressed those facts were no less so: "Let them stop talking so much about the constitution," he exclaimed in October 1789. "Words have only lulled us to sleep." What was needed was liberation from words: "How good-naturedly we are still duped by words," he declared in Pluviôse, Year II. Words did not have the meaning ordinarily ascribed to them and might just as well signify the opposite, as Robespierre demonstrated in his great speech on 17 Pluviôse: "He who exhorted France to conquer the world had no other purpose but to exhort tyrants to conquer France. The hypocrite stranger who for the past five years has proclaimed Paris the capital of the globe was simply translating into a different jargon the anathemata of the vile federalists who wished to see Paris destroyed. To preach atheism is only a way of absolving superstition and indicting philosophy, and to declare war on Divinity is only a diversion to benefit royalty." By exposing the artifices in the lying "jargon" of the people's enemies, Robespierre ripped the mask from words and from reality.

This demystifying discourse was the work of a great illusionist. One searches Robespierre's speeches in vain for Danton's excesses, Mirabeau's lapidary phrases, or Barnave's sense of improvisation. There is evidently little to arouse enthusiasm in these diligently prepared speeches, exempt from vulgarity as well as facility and attentive, as Garat emphasizes in his *Memoirs*, to "forms of language that have elegance, nobility, and luster." Robespierre incessantly recycled his copy: "He needed a rut," Aulard wrote. "It pleased him to be in one, to follow it to the end, and to extend it further every day. That is the reason for his endless repetition, his verbosity, his returning to the same themes, each time more fully developed." His speeches were interminable and could ultimately tire even the most favorably disposed listeners. As one of his colleagues in the Academy of Arras put it:

> Robespierre, toujours le même
> Contre les préjugés dirigeant son effort
> Toujours intéressant, comme à son but il court
> Et combien, sans ma montre, il m'aurait semblé plus court.
>
> (Robespierre, always the same
> Against prejudices making great strides
> Always interesting, as he hastens toward his goal
> How much shorter it would have seemed without my watch.)

To his adversaries his speeches were compounded of "insignificant chatter" and "eternal repetition."

Yet this monotonous rhetoric stirred the enthusiasm of the Jacobin audience: "It was no longer applause," wrote Louvet, "but convulsive stamping. It was a religious enthusiasm, a holy furor." The rhythm of the incantation mattered more than the rigor of the argument. Though the latter might be weak, the magic worked on the public nonetheless. With rhetoric Robespierre led his audience out of concrete times and concrete realities. As Aulard rightly said, he "practiced with predilection . . . all modes of diction that awaken in the listener vague feelings, a vague admiration, a vague terror, a vague hope. He made the tyranny of uncertainty weigh on people's minds." Periphrasis and insinuation were de rigueur when it came to denouncing the traitors who still opposed making good on the promise of a radiant future. Robespierre never named the supposed conspirators implicated in the plot that he incessantly denounced, invariably reborn each time it was defeated. People undoubtedly awaited revelations and arrests, but he was a master of the art of suspense and equivocation: "The moment to unmask the traitors will come," he said on April 23, 1792. "But first the seeds that are being sown today must sprout," and in the meantime the evildoers will "do themselves in through their own excesses." And the "evildoers" would succumb to the power of this rhetoric by hastening—through blunder or blindness—to make amends, even though the Jacobin leader had carefully avoided naming them. Robespierre's part in the preparation and execution of the decisive purges has often been questioned. Very likely he played no role at all, for his job was not to liquidate those whom he had induced to unmask themselves; he halted precisely at the moment when, suspicion having been sown, judgment was virtually pronounced. Traitors must be "hurled back" into "nothingness," he said on May 28, 1793, to the Convention, only to add, on the following day at the Jacobin Club in the plaintive tone that he liked so well: "It is not up to me to indicate these measures, not I who am consumed by a slow fever and above all by the fever of patriotism. I have said that at this moment I have no further duties."

"I have said": Robespierre spoke as a master. Excluding debate and contradiction, he delivered a monologue and expressed outrage at any interruption. On September 25, 1792, interrupted and harassed, he shouted: "I feel that it is irritating for me always to be interrupted. . . . Well, then, I shall leave and force you to listen to me." In March 1792 at the Jacobins he said: "No, gentlemen, you will not silence my voice. There is no agenda that can smother this truth." From the truth there was no appeal; it was uttered in the form of an injunction. "Whoever does not want and does not counsel this discharge is a traitor," he threatened in June 1791, when the issue was whether to discharge noble officers, and immediately the society echoed his sentiments even though a moment before it had appeared to be divided.

Terror lay in this magisterium of speech, which Robespierre developed to the full. His rhetorical art was not merely one weapon among others in the political arsenal: his oratory terrorized and, as Claude Lefort has shown, annihilated all other oratory. He concluded his speech following the controversial arrest of Danton with these words: "Furthermore, the debate that has just begun is a danger to the fatherland. Already it is a criminal attack on liberty!"

Armed with the truth, Robespierre dispelled the shadows of reality and ripped away the veil of language. Through him confusion became order, obscurity became clarity: he unmasked, united, and divided—divided in order to unite and rally the people against its enemies.

It was by confronting the hostility of the Assembly that "the Incorruptible" took charge of the Jacobins; it was by becoming the master of the Jacobins that he was ultimately able to take charge of the Assembly. On June 16, 1791, Robespierre delivered the speech that established his reputation once and for all, brilliantly winning approval of a bill making incumbent deputies ineligible for reelection to the next legislature. His argument was most shrewd, mingling self-congratulation with flattery and threat. By declaring himself ready to renounce the honor of a new mandate, Robespierre invited the other deputies to follow his lead: a heavy sacrifice, he averred, knowing full well that his colleagues were in a hurry to return home and certain that they would hasten to embrace so noble an alibi to justify a less noble retreat. Should they desire to remain in politics, a threat was at hand to temper their zeal: "How weak efforts at slander will be, if they cannot reproach a single one of those who erected [the Constitution] with having wished to profit from the credit his mission established with his constituents to prolong his power." No one missed his meaning, and the Constituent Assembly voted to approve the bill. On that day Robespierre began his long march. By eliminating from the new legislature the whole class of political men who had been gaining experience in public affairs since 1789, while he himself continued to honor the indefinite mandate conferred upon him by the Jacobins, he struck a fatal blow to the weak and controversial Constitution, now deprived of the support of those who had created it. In his final speech as a deputy he was able to say: "I do not think the Revolution is over."

In the conquest of power, his ultimate objective in everything he did, Robespierre took a long-term view: "Before starting out," he wrote, "you must know where you want to end up and what routes you must take." There is no better maxim to illustrate the skill, perseverance, and tenacity with which he pursued his adversaries. Within three months the fate of the triumvirs was decided: on June 16, 1791, they were wounded; after Varennes and the split with the Feuillants, they were close to death; and during September in the Assembly Robespierre delivered the coup de grâce. With Brissot and the Girondins the pace was not so quick. Having grown up like Robespierre in the Jacobins, supported by the press and enjoying tremendous prestige in many départements, they were able to hold out for eighteen months. The confrontation, which began at the Jacobin Club in December 1791, when Robespierre opposed Brissot's prowar policy, ended in the Convention when charges were brought against the Girondins on June 2, 1793.

That decisive victory was consecrated when Robespierre joined the Committee of Public Safety on July 27. This marked a radical change in attitude on the part of a man who had always shunned responsibilities that might limit his freedom of action. He could have stuck with that strategy and refused a seat on the committee while making his views known through Couthon and Saint-Just. Why this change of heart? Robespierre did not belatedly discover a talent for administration. Things had changed since the days of the Constituent Assembly. Political power was fragmented, divided up among Convention, Jacobins, Commune, sections, and now the committees. At the same time, the vital center had shifted: since September 1792 debates were no longer held at the Jacobins. The Club was content to approve decisions made outside its precincts. The *journée* of June 2 presaged the reining in of the Commune and sections, which were too unreliable, too susceptible to radical sirens or else "gangrenous" with "moderatism." Paralyzed, the Convention held its peace, and when in September 1793 it attempted to appoint a new Committee of Public Safety, Robespierre rightly put it in its place: "If you do not believe in its zeal, then destroy this instrument. . . . But first examine the situation." Henceforth the action was all in the committees, the end result of a slow shift from the grass roots to the summit.

Robespierre closely followed this evolution. From 1789 until his election to the Convention in September 1792, he defended above all else the principles of direct democracy. The Rousseauist argument that it was impossible for the body politic to be represented without alienating its sovereignty enabled him to claim that the people's sections enjoyed an unlimited right of recall. But after 1792 times changed, and so did Robespierre's language: the disciple repudiated the master and adopted the rhetoric of representation. On August 27, 1792, he was still in favor of allowing the primary assemblies to override decisions of the secondary assemblies; but, elected on September 5, he changed his mind on September 9! In the Convention he subsequently opposed all attempts to codify the powers of the lowest-level assemblies over those whom they elected. Because of these continual changes, any attempt to present a coherent portrait of Robespierrist ideology is doomed to failure. In 1789 he had borrowed his arguments against the royal veto from Sieyès, at that time the most radical and influential member of the Constituent Assembly. From Varennes until August 10 he defended the Constitution that he more than anyone else had condemned to failure and showed himself to be the most determined adversary of the republicans, but no sooner was the insurrection victorious than he adopted the opposite point of view.

His social views were no more consistent. When he proposed limiting property rights in April 1793, it was primarily in order to distinguish his position from the Girondin declaration of rights at a time when the Jacobins and the Commune were mobilizing against "factious" deputies. A year later the decrees passed in Ventôse were used to force the sections to accept the liquidation of the Hébertists while offering them less costly compensation. In return Robespierre spoke out in protest against social turmoil, behind which he invariably saw the hand of the counterrevolution. He vituperated against the agents of "aristocracy" who "roamed the streets offering the image of indigence and famine" and attacked "scoundrels disguised beneath the respectable cloak of poverty." In the Constituent Assembly he never once intervened in the debate on the Le Chapelier Law. Caution is therefore in order when judging the repeated use of expressions such as "opulent farmers" or "selfish bourgeois" on the one hand and "respectable pauper" or "virtuous peasant" on the other. Such epithets, along with other insults such as "federalist" or "aristocrat," do not refer to any objective reality but belong to the vocabulary of politics. The people to which Robespierre dedicated his life took to the streets to call for the heads of conspirators but never to clamor for bread. The common denominator of his "social ideas," shared moreover with most of his contemporaries, was his literary ignorance of the real people. "A peculiar thing about these classically educated men," Quinet wrote, "is that the crowd's blind passions seemed to them of foreign inspiration, so little did they share the temperament of the masses. . . . No orator in the world spoke a language less popular, more educated, more studied, than Robespierre or Saint-Just. Anyone who attempted to speak the language of the people was immediately and naturally odious to them, for that language seemed to undermine the Republic."

Robespierre's genius was to be always in tune with the times. Had he allowed himself to be hemmed in by a coherent and finished system, he would have been obliged to give up speaking in the name of the people. Thus he could be a monarchist on August 9, 1792, and a republican on August 11 without contradiction or gross opportunism. The reversal, sudden though it may have been, was legitimate, since the sovereign people had spoken on August 10. All definite ideas concerning law, institutions, or the form of the government were overshadowed by the strategic imperative.

On June 2, 1793, the bond between Robespierre and the people was modified in a decisive fashion. All difference of opinion having been banished from the Convention, unanimity now reigned supreme; hence there was no further reason for the sovereign people and the Convention to be at odds: the representatives were at last worthy of their constituents. The *journée* of June 2 was the last face-to-face confrontation between the street and the Assembly, the people and its representatives, since the former would supposedly sit from now on in the latter. After June 2 Robespierre could identify the people with the Convention and thus dispose of the dualism operative since 1789; he could set aside his critique of representation in favor of a defense of the legitimacy and prerogatives of a humbled Assembly, deprived of any real power to make decisions. The people, it was assumed, now wanted what the Convention wanted, and the Convention wanted what Robespierre and the Committee of Public Safety dictated. Between the autumn of 1793 and the spring of 1794 Robespierre left his stamp on the unfinished process of restoring the state: the Convention was muzzled, the organization of the popular movement was dismantled, the clubs were transformed into cogs in the bureaucratic machinery, and local autonomy was destroyed. All that had originated at the base and periphery was transferred to the summit and center.

Robespierre succeeded, incompletely to be sure, where his predecessors had failed: in "fixing" the Revolution, as Duport put it, or "freezing" it, in the words of Saint-Just. "Stabilizing" it might be more appropriate, since Robespierre never envisioned the situation as one in which the Revolution was over, the problem being one of preventing a return to the past. His project was indeed one of closure, of how to "substitute all the virtues and all the miracles of the Republic for all the vices and all the foolishness of the monarchy." The political revolution was in fact complete: with the republic proclaimed and universal suffrage instituted, the fundamental principles of 1789 had become reality. Yet at the same time everything remained to be done: "It is not an empty word that makes the Republic," he wrote at the end of 1792, "it is the character of its citizens." Politically republican, France was morally still a monarchy, for the Revolution continued to partake of the world it had destroyed: "We have built the temple of liberty with hands still bruised by the irons of despotism." Robespierre occupied precisely that interval when the memory of what had been lost still filled the present. The Revolution had to be rescued from the past by elevating "the people incessantly to the height of its rights and destinies," or, in other words, by amputating everything that drew it downward into that "putrid abyss," the "abjection of the individual ego." Here, the necessary interval of regeneration is indefinitely prolonged, and Robespierre makes no secret of the need to struggle constantly against "intriguers who scheme to replace other intriguers." Each purge presaged still further proscriptions: when on 18 Floréal he proposed establishing a civic cult to mark the beginning of a new era, he asked at the same time for punishment of the conspirators. On 8 Thermidor he offered a fraternal hand to the "good men" sitting in the Convention and promised a "final purge." On 11 Germinal he said: "The number of the guilty is not so large." And no doubt he was correct, but it was a small number repeated ad infinitum.

Maintaining an equal distance from all factions, both those that wished to see the Revolution renewed (Hébertists) and those that wished to see it regress (Dantonists), Robespierre took it upon himself to postpone indefinitely the end of an endless revolution. He played a decisive role in determining the course of events with speeches such as those he delivered on 5 Nivôse and 17 Pluviôse to systematize and legitimate the Terror. He was also one of those most responsible for the Terror, thanks to his tireless involvement in police matters both in the Committee of Public Safety and in the Bureau of General Police, which remained under his direct supervision even during his supposed retirement in Messidor.

In Thermidor, in order to relieve himself of all responsibility, he attempted with manifest bad faith to blame the excesses of the Terror on the Machiavellianism of his enemies. In fact the Terror escaped his control because no one could control it. The product of a perverted faith in the power of the will, it fed on the illusion that spawned it. What is more, its daily operations required an apparatus and gave rise to specific practices and to a routine; it relied on a multitude of agents, both functionaries without scruples and declassed individuals whose special skills were indispensable. All these people thrived on the Terror and resisted any slowing of the deadly work by which it lived. During this somber period Robespierre's interventions—whether out of hypocrisy or naiveté—reveal a desire to close the ever-widening gap between the justification of the Terror and its reality: on the one hand the emanation of virtue, on the other a criminal practice that made it possible to gratify the passions it pretended to repress. "In perfidious hands," he said, apparently forgetting that no executioner has clean hands, "all the remedies for our ills become poisons" and a danger to liberty! Already we see the confusion of values, the inversion of the meaning of words. Having said that all terrorism begins as deviation, Robespierre was obliged, as on 18 Floréal, to ascribe utmost importance to the principle of terror because the Terror was so obviously contrary to all principle. In order to remain ostensibly in conformity with its principle, the Terror had to be turned against its own agents: Robespierre obtained the recall of the bloodiest proconsuls and had the others placed under surveillance by agents such as Jullien. In the first few months of 1794 some minor officials were prosecuted and a few were guillotined, setting the stage for the elimination of still bigger fish, who, feeling themselves threatened, in turn conspired against Robespierre.

The decree of 18 Floréal instituting a system of civic festivals in honor of the Supreme Being came at a critical moment that blurred its significance: following the elimination of the factions, this law seemed to mark the end of an era; preceding a period of heightened violence, it seemed to be laying the groundwork for another.

The festival staged on 20 Prairial to inaugurate this new cult had brought a genuine sigh of relief. An observer as lucid as Mallet du Pan, at this time a refugee in Berne, reported in his *Memoirs* "the extraordinary impression" that this event had created abroad: "People believed that Robespierre was going to close the abyss of the Revolution." After the frenzy of de-Christianization the singular tone of the 18 Floréal speech did indeed seem to mark a change of direction, if not a complete reversal. Robespierre had no intention of resurrecting the Church, restoring one iota of the temporal authority of which it had been deprived, or reestablishing the link between religious opinion and the political power of religion that the Enlightenment critique had destroyed.

An enemy of superstition, Robespierre shared the religious sentiments of his century: he believed in the God of nature, close to mankind, ready to assist those in need, and still a source of "eternal principles in which human weakness can find the strength it needs to make the leap to virtue." At the same time he accepted the Rousseauist critique of the rational proofs of God's existence: the Supreme Being is accessible not through reason but through intuition, or through the heart once liberated from the shackles of the senses and the passions. On 18 Floréal he exhorted his colleagues to rise above present circumstances, to look into themselves in order to "heed in the silence of the passions the voice of wisdom and the modesty it inspires"—an intimate experience "limited," in the words of Rousseau, "to purely inner worship of the supreme God and to the eternal duties of morality." Reason even stands as an obstacle on the road to truth; it proceeds by way of emulation of the passions, whereas truth depends on victory over the passions. Robespierre was thus able to oppose the instinctive moral sentiment of the people to the corruption of the philosophers' "metaphysical spirit." Drawing a parallel between the impressive progress of the sciences and arts in the physical sphere and the "stupidity" in which his contemporaries found themselves in the moral sphere, he rejected the rationalist optimism of his century and opposed civilization to happiness just as Rousseau had done when he praised "the happy ignorance in which wisdom had placed us." To deny reason the capacity to make men aware of the "profound truths" that each of them carries in his heart was also to contradict the role usually ascribed to the Enlightenment as one of the sources of the Revolution. Progress in knowledge had done nothing to reduce the power of kings, Robespierre observed, and he went on to accuse the philosophes of having been "proud in their writings and assiduous in antechambers," of having been relentless in their attacks on superstition and morality the better to spare the throne, and finally, of having debased the character of citizens so as to leave them more than ever subjugated to the power of the prince. His unmodulated indictment sees one vast conspiracy against truth and liberty ranging from the Encyclopedists to the coterie of baron d'Holbach and the de-Christianizers of Year II. Yet he was also forced, in order to explain the revolutionary explosion, to admit that "human reason has for a long time been on the march against royalty," threatening the despotism of kings "even when it seems to cherish it."

If superstition and "philosophy" were the usual props of despotism, atheism was the surest way of returning to it. "Never was there a state that religion did not serve as foundation," wrote Rousseau. Robespierre echoed those words on 18 Floréal: "The unique foundation of civil society is morality." By preaching nothingness, atheists deprived man of the certainty of future reparations or punishment; they erased the distinction between good and evil, in the end depriving man of everything that "enlarges his being and lifts his heart." Atheism—"a species of practical philosophy, which, by reducing egoism to a system . . . [and] confusing the destiny of the good with the wicked, leaves between them no other difference but the uncertain favors of fortune, no other arbiter but the right of the strongest or cleverest"—threatened to dissolve the social bond. Religion, by contrast, holds society together. In the moral order, Robespierre explained, it supplants pain, which, "without the belated help of reasoning," guides choices in the physical order by impressing "upon souls the idea of a sanction given to the precepts of morality by a power superior to man." A "constant recall to justice," the cult of the Supreme Being was useful, and it would continue to be useful even if it were merely a fiction. By degrees Robespierre shifted from the religion of man to the religion of the citizen, from the truth of religious sentiment to the efficiency of a social police.

The question, in other words, was whether the purpose of civil religion is to create the kind of people required by the new institutions or simply to give laws a power they would not have without the support of morality. After criticizing unbelief and immorality, Robespierre hastens to make clear that he does not wish to proscribe "any philosophical opinion in particular" and that he wants to maintain the principle of freedom of religion that was reaffirmed on 18 Frimaire. He thus appears to distinguish between what each individual *may* believe as an individual and what he or she *must* believe as a citizen. This avowed tolerance, however, is neither coherent nor liberal. As early as June 1793, while the Convention debated the Declaration of Rights, Robespierre vainly opposed passage of a bill guaranteeing freedom of religion, warning his colleagues of the danger that counterrevolutionary intrigues might flourish in the shadow of religious freedom. On 18 Floréal, using the same argument, he obtained passage of a bill authorizing repression of "disturbances of which any religion whatsoever may be the occasion or cause." From then on a vague threat hung over the principle proclaimed in other contexts.

More to the point, the liberal distinction between private and civil faith was due solely to Robespierre's realism, evident for example in his warnings not to interfere with opinions consecrated by time. The diversity of beliefs would resolve itself, he argued: "To lead men back to the pure cult of the Supreme Being is to strike a deadly blow against fanaticism. All fictions disappear before the truth, and all follies fall before reason. Without coercion, without persecution, all sects must merge themselves into the universal religion of nature." But the unrealistic assumption that the commandments of all religions will always be compatible renders the idea of a gradual fusion under the sole banner of truth quite obviously illusory. Born in benighted minds, "superstition" must inevitably give way. Truth is one, and not all opinions are equally legitimate: the conscience of the individual is itself only when it is *right*—that is, when it is exercised in the silence of the passions—at which time it is spontaneously in contact with the universal consciousness. Everything else, Robespierre emphasizes, is "fanaticism" and "superstition." Despite merely formal precautions, the project is nothing other than to purge the individual of what distinguishes him from the civic body and saddle him with a yoke of state dogma that determines what both public and private conscience ought to be, so as to lead the citizen to identify with the operation whereby he is incorporated into the totality. Morality, which has hitherto been a part of the private sphere, now separates out and crystallizes as a morality of state: "What does this mysterious science of politics and legislation come down to," said Robespierre, if not "the application to the behavior of peoples of the trivial notions of probity that everyone is forced to adopt for his private conduct"?

Robespierre was no doubt the first to believe not only in the realization of this utopia but also in the possibility of halting the Revolution by decree. The public's enthusiasm was short-lived, however: on 22 Prairial a law was passed reforming the procedures of the Revolutionary Tribunal, dispensing with evidence and defense, and inaugurating a period during which the Terror raced ever more wildly out of control. Was this merely an unfortunate coincidence? In fact the backdrop to the ceremony of 20 Prairial was not destined to replace the guillotine, and there are similarities between the two decrees that cannot be coincidental. The support and guide of the virtuous, the Supreme Being was also apt to become the source of that moral force needed by judges who "do their duty, . . . live without fear, and act without remorse," as Couthon said on 22 Prairial. A simple principle for distinguishing between good and evil, a justification for punishment, the Supreme Being was the instrument that enabled revolutionary justice to recognize and to strike the enemies of the fatherland, governed only by "the conscience of the jurors, enlightened by love of country." Far from heralding the end of the Revolution, the new civic cult provided the Terror with moral underpinnings, with a legitimacy made indispensable by the disappearance—aided by the elimination of factions and the victories of the military—of any credible criterion for singling out wrongdoers.

ACTORS

The speech of 18 Floréal was Robespierre's first genuine "action" and the prologue to his downfall. He had never been so powerful, obliging the Convention to adhere to a policy of generalized terror, or so isolated—by what his speech contained in the way of threats directed toward an Assembly that had welcomed the abjurations and ordered the closing of the churches. Robespierre overestimated his authority in the Convention: reigning thanks to the silence of his colleagues, to the artificial unanimity imposed on June 2, confirmed by Danton's death, and perpetuated by the seventy-three Girondins saved from the guillotine in order to serve as hostages, he became in turn the hostage of the very same indulgent silence. He delivered his monologue, received his applause, and believed himself all-powerful. But all it took was for the conventionnels to regain their voice, and Robespierre, deprived of the support of those who had carried him in triumph three years earlier, suddenly appeared terribly vulnerable and defenseless. His error was to have believed that time was on his side. Having spent the entire month of Messidor preparing for the inevitable confrontation, polishing his indictment, he had allowed his enemies time to regroup.

Had Robespierre emerged victorious from the test of strength on 9 Thermidor, a few additional tumbrils would have made their way to the scaffold. But he lost, and the Terror was dealt a death blow. On 9 Thermidor, by liquidating Robespierre and his henchmen, the Terrorists whom he himself had chosen as his target put an end to the Terror, at least in its most brutal form.

Patrice Gueniffey

FURTHER READING

WORKS BY ROBESPIERRE

Oeuvres complètes, 10 vols., ed. E. Déprez et al. Paris, 1910–1967.
Textes choisis, with an introduction by Jean Poperen, 2 vols. Paris, 1974.

RELATED WORKS

Aulard, Alphonse. *Les orateurs de la Constituante.* Paris, 1882, pp. 512–540.
——— *Les orateurs de la Législative et de la Convention.* Paris, 1886, pp. 354–422.
Baczko, Bronislaw. "Robespierre-roi ou comment sortir de la Terreur," *Le débat,* March–May 1986.
Fleischmann, Hector. *Robespierre et les femmes.* Paris, 1909.
Furet, François. *Penser la Révolution française.* Paris, 1978, esp. pp. 80–87.
Jaume, Lucien. "Robespierre: Une politique au nom de l'Etre Suprême," in François Châtelet et al., eds., *Dictionnaire des oeuvres politiques.* Paris, 1986.
Lefort, Claude. "La Terreur révolutionnaire," *Passé présent,* no. 2, 1983, 11–43.
Walter, Gérard. *Robespierre,* 2 vols. Paris, 1961.

RELATED TOPICS

Committee of Public Safety
Enlightenment
Girondins
Hébertists

Jacobinism
Marat
Necker
Quinet

Revolutionary Assemblies
Revolutionary Religion
Rousseau
Terror

SIEYÈS

"My protector consoles himself with the master stroke he failed to pull off. His lack of success certainly causes him less pain than it does me. If the thing had gone as he had hoped, I would have become *everything* instead of which I am *nothing*." "I no more believe in those people's promises than in the predictions of the almanac. But I have the appearance of believing, because I can do no better" (Bastid, *Sieyès et sa pensée*, pp. 35–36, 39). There was nothing exceptional, in the privileged society of the Ancien Régime, in these protestations of the young provincial, Emmanuel-Joseph Sieyès, to a father avid to see returns on his investment in the education of a brilliant son, nothing exceptional in these frustrations of an ambitious commoner dependent for advancement on the uncertainties of aristocratic patronage or in this disenchantment of a cleric to whom the church offered no more than a means of satisfying "the passion to have an estate" (p. 42). What was exceptional was that their author would find a moment and a language to give the experience of such frustrations a political force, to transform the individual ambition of a "nothing" to become "everything" into a collective demand for the reconstitution of social and political order, to focus social resentments through the political laser of revolution. The frontier between the privileged and the unprivileged was only one of many social cleavages that existed at the end of the Ancien Régime. In late 1788 and early 1789, for reasons more political than social, it became the issue upon which the very constitution of social and political order was seen to hinge. More powerfully and persuasively than any other, the abbé Sieyès articulated the inescapable necessity of deciding this issue by an act of political will—of a political will that could only be that of the nation. All that was to follow was made possible by this definition of the revolutionary moment. It was a rhetorical act that made the ambitious abbé, still but a canon of Chartres, the first and most profound theorist of the French Revolution.

Though later events were to reveal his feebleness in spoken debate, Sieyès emerged at the end of 1788 as a master of the written word. For this disciple of Condillac, inspired by the ambition to create a rational science of politics through the creation of an exact and precise system of signs, no target was more vulnerable to ridicule than the lexicon of privilege his early pamphlets attacked with unerring rhetorical skill, no task more pressing in a world where "language had outlived the thing" (*Qu'est-ce que le Tiers Etat?* p. 194) than to reconstitute public order through the articulation of a new political language philosophically grounded in the nature of things. To read the principal pamphlets he contributed to the debate over the forms of the convocation of the Estates General—the *Essai sur les privilèges,* the *Vues sur les moyens*

313

d'exécution dont les représentants de la France pourront disposer en 1789 (*Views on the Executive Resources That Will Be Available to the Representatives of France in 1789*), and, above all, *Qu'est-ce que le Tiers-Etat?*—is to follow the creation of revolutionary discourse itself. This discourse did not take shape whole, as it were, behind the backs of the articulate French public; it emerged in the context of a generalized consciousness of political crisis, and it took on meaning in relation to the problems and possibilities of a particular political situation. Nor did it have a single univocal source. The language that gave explosive force to the events that destroyed the old order was a radical political invention, but its elements were derived from many sources. It follows from the process of bricolage by which it was created that revolutionary discourse necessarily contained tensions, inconsistencies, and ambiguities within it. Much of the subsequent political history of the French Revolution can be understood only in the light of that fact.

To understand Sieyès' part in the creation of the revolutionary discourse, it is necessary to see it in relation to the principal political discourses that the Ancien Régime offered to the political actors engaged in its last great crisis. Taken together, these discourses represent the disaggregation of the attributes traditionally bound together in the concept of monarchical authority and their reconceptualization as the basis of competing definitions (or attempted redefinitions) of the nature of the body politic. According to the traditional language of absolutism, as is well known, monarchical authority was characterized as the exercise of justice, according to which each receives his due in a hierarchical society of orders and estates; justice is given effect by the royal will, which is in turn preserved from arbitrariness by reason and counsel. In the course of the political contestations of the last decades of the Ancien Régime, however, this cluster of attributes seems increasingly to separate into three strands of discourse, each characterized by the analytical priority it gives to one or another of the traditional terms.

The discourse of justice remains the prevailing language (though not of course the exclusive one) of the parlementary constitutionalism that became so important in focusing the attack on ministerial despotism in the 1750s and afterward. In this discourse, justice is opposed to will in the same way as the lawful and constituted is opposed to the arbitrary and contingent. It finds its clearest expression in arguments for a traditional constitution as old as the monarchy, a historically constituted order of things that both defines and limits royal power, and in the opposition between government conducted according to regular legal forms and government emanating from the arbitrary will of a monarch or his agents. In the great debate over representation in 1788 and 1789, the discourse of justice sustains the claims for the traditional separation of the three orders in the Estates General, and for restriction of the deputies to the binding mandates of their constituents.

In contrast, the discourse of will becomes the central feature of thinking about the nature of public life that is couched in explicitly political, rather than in judicial/constitutional terms. In this discourse—as in the writings of Rousseau or Mably, for example, which find a major source of inspiration in the tradition of classical republicanism—will is opposed to will; liberty appears as the active expression of a general political will; despotism occurs through the exercise of any will that is individual or particular, rather than collective or general. If, in 1788 and 1789, this discourse sustained arguments for the sovereignty of the national will, it also offered serious obstacles to the theory of representation, which had been condemned by Rousseau as incompatible with the idea of the general will.

The discourse of will can in turn be distinguished from a third discourse, a discourse of reason most clearly evident in the social theory of the physiocrats and in the administrative program of the ministers of Louis XVI. In the terms of this discourse, public life must be reconceptualized on the basis of reason and nature, political will must yield to enlightened understanding of the natural and essential order of societies, and the language of political will must give way to a rational discourse of the social. Thus, in contrast to the discourse of will that appealed to the model of the ancient city-states, the discourse of reason was a discourse of modernity, a discourse that emphasized the growth of civilization and the progress of civil society. At the end of the Ancien Régime, this discourse sustained reforming arguments for greater administrative uniformity, civil rights, and fiscal equality, and it sustained the representation of social interests through the participation of property owners in the rational conduct of local government by provincial assemblies.

The elaboration, competition, and interpenetration of these three discourses defined the political culture that emerged in France in the latter part of the eighteenth century and provided the ideological elements for the creation of revolutionary discourse itself. And it is in relationship to them that one can clarify the process by which the revolutionary language took form in the writings of Sieyès. To do so, one must begin with the celebrated parlementary declaration of September 25, 1788, whose insistence that the Estates General "be regularly convoked and composed in accordance with the form observed in 1614" opened the revolutionary debate proper. That declaration (which was no more than a reiteration and further specification of a clause in the Declaration of Fundamental Laws issued by the Parlement of Paris on May 3, 1788) was prompted by the desire to insist upon regular legal forms as a bulwark against arbitrary and despotic ministerial intervention in the organization and deliberations of the Estates General. It found its logic within the discourse of justice elaborated by the parlements in the course of several decades of confrontation with ministerial despotism. And its implications for the organization of the Estates General according to the traditional forms were characteristically defended, during the political debates to which it gave rise in the last months of 1788, in a language that appealed to the legitimacy of a historically constituted order of things.

It was against such an appeal that Sieyès argued most powerfully in the *Vues sur les moyens*. Written during the summer of 1788 (doubtless in response to the royal declaration of July 5, which called for historical researches relating to the calling of the Estates General), this pamphlet offered a bitter indictment of the "*extase gothique*" which led so many authors to "rummage in all the archives" in order to discover "in miserable traditions, tissues of illogic and lies, laws to restore the public order." Imprescriptible rights, Sieyès argued, could not depend upon chance historical discoveries in "a few ill-conceived notebooks, written with the hand of servitude"; nor would the principles of the social art be revealed in "inept drafts from the Middle Ages." Powerless to contain arbitrary power, such researches could lead only to empty quarrels among the representatives of the nation.

Thus it is hardly surprising that we find little trace in *Qu'est-ce que le Tiers Etat?* of the traditional discourse of justice. Indeed the corrosion of the juridical appeal to tradition and historical precedent, which Sieyès repudiates as an already discredited language resuscitated by the privileged orders to defend their interests, is one of the most striking features of this pamphlet. For Sieyès, as for Mably, French history is the political story of oppression, usurpation, and expropriation rather than the juridical story of the evolution and continuity of legal-constitutional forms. As a result of this analysis, precedent is reduced to the intolerable right of conquest, and the only admissible appeal to history is to return to that zero point—"the year before the conquest" (*Qu'est-ce que le Tiers Etat?* p. 128)—at which the nation is restored to its true political identity and recovers the opportunity for a new and unambiguous assertion of its political will. Sieyès introduces into revolutionary discourse a conception of political action as occurring in a new moment in time that is simultaneously a point of rupture with the past. Unlike the Machiavellian "moment" described by John Pocock, which presents a challenge to stabilize the existence of the political order within and against the flow of time, the Sieyèsian moment invites an assertion of political will that will break out of history entirely.

What, then, are the principles according to which this new age is to be inaugurated? Sieyès seems, in effect, to answer this question in two quite different languages. At times, he falls back upon the resources of a rational discourse of the social, which substitutes a vision of the progress of enlightened, civil society for the arbitrariness and vicissitudes of the political past: "Above all, let us not become discouraged because we see nothing in history that corresponds to our position. The true science of the social state is not very old. Men built cottages for a long time before they were in a position to erect palaces." But he also resorts at critical points to the very different language of a discourse of will, according to which "the nation exists before everything else; it is at the origin of everything else. Its will is always legal; it is the law itself." Sieyès claims for the Third Estate a complex blend of competing social and political discourses, a blend that explains many of the ambiguities of the revolutionary language that began to take form in his writing.

It has long been known that Sieyès' thinking was shaped by an extended early confrontation with the ideas of Quesnay and the physiocrats, on the one hand, and with Adam Smith and the Scottish school on the other. Thus, in considering political questions, he frequently resorts to a discourse of the social in which the nature of production and wealth, the implications of the division of labor, and the reorganization of society according to the self-evident principles of a rational social art form principal themes. This is the principal idiom of the *Essai sur les privilèges* (published in November 1788) in which the arguments for social hierarchy offered by the privileged are repudiated as incompatible with the free relations of exchange in civil society ("there is no subordination, but rather a continual exchange"), true honor is shown to derive not from royal favor but from the free market of public esteem (that "moral currency"), and privilege is denounced as a species of begging in which "the privileged swallow up capital and individuals; and everything is inevitably destined for privileged sterility."

This is also the language to which Sieyès appeals at the very beginning of *Qu'est-ce que le Tiers Etat?* when he enumerates the categories of useful and productive activity upon which social life depends; in thus grounding social existence on the active encounter of human industry with physical nature, he not only excludes the privileged from the social order by the very act of definition, but in doing so he also utterly negates the cultural foundations of the Ancien Régime as a corporate order structured according to a logic of spiritual differentiation and hierarchization. It is the language in which he goes on to praise Calonne's proposals for provincial assemblies as attempting to institute a true national representation expressing a "real" order of relations based on property rather than a "personal" order based on status. (These proposals were in contrast to those introduced by Brienne, which had retained the traditional distinction among estates, thereby incidentally offering the abbé an important political education as a clerical deputy to the assembly of Orléanais in 1787.)

It is the language in which he describes the long process of social development—"the revolution effected by time and the force of events"—which has destroyed feudal society by fostering the growth of commerce and industry, thereby rendering the Third Estate "the national reality" and the aristocracy nothing but a shadow of its former monstrosity. And it is equally the language in which he demands that the Third Estate now choose its own representatives from the "*available* classes" within it, those who have "a manner of well-being" necessary to secure education and enlightenment and to interest themselves in public affairs.

Yet at the same time as he drew upon the discourse of the social in his claims for the representation of the Third Estate, Sieyès also freed the idea of representation itself from the constraints that had been so powerfully imprinted upon it within this discourse during the last decades of the Ancien Régime, most notably in the campaign for the creation of provincial assemblies. Limited by physiocratic notions that landed property was the only basis for the true expression of social interests, representation was also restricted in this campaign to an administrative summons to rational participation in the conduct of local government. In repudiating the physiocratic argument for landed property as the exclusive source of wealth, a repudiation found also in his early fragments on economic theory (today in the Archives Nationales), Sieyès also undermined the argument that land alone offered a basis for the rational expression of social interests. More fundamentally, however, he freed the practice of representation from administrative constraints by assimilating it into the basic social principle of the division of labor. A note among his papers inscribes the idea of liberty within a theory of society and social progress in which "representation" and "the division of labor" appear as interchangeable categories in what Sieyès presents as his "representative order": "To secure representation or allow oneself to be represented is the only source of civil prosperity. . . . To multiply our means/powers to satisfy our needs; to enjoy more, to work less—therein lies the natural increase of liberty in the social state. Now, such progress in liberty ensues naturally upon the establishment of *representative labor.*"

While Sieyès offers no immediate extrapolation from what he here calls "representative labor" to political representation, the connection seems clearly implied; indeed, it becomes quite explicit in his other political writings, as in the speech of October 2, 1789, which justifies representative government on the grounds that the division of labor "is appropriate to political labors as to all forms of productive labor." While the distinction between active and passive citizens is an obvious expression of this way of thinking, it is not the most important one. More fundamentally, by assimilating representation into the division of labor in this way, Sieyès liberated the idea of representation quite decisively from the constraints placed upon it in prerevolutionary social and political theory. Representation, at once a principle and a consequence of liberty, ceased to be an administrative device on the one hand, or a poor substitute for direct democracy on the other, and became an integral expression of the very principle to which civil society owed its autonomous existence.

Yet if Sieyès frequently falls back upon a discourse of the social in his definition of the nation and his conception of representation, this discourse coexists in his writings with a more explicitly political discourse that seems to owe its principal inspiration to Rousseau. Thus, to a definition of society as a productive entity satisfying the various needs and interests of its members through the application of the principle of the division of labor, *Qu'est-ce que le Tiers Etat?* adds a political definition of the nation as a unitary body of citizens exercising an inalienable common will. "A political society can only consist of a collection of associates. A nation cannot decide that it will be the nation or that it will be so in only one way. For that would mean that it was not so in any other way. Similarly, a nation cannot decide that its will will cease to be its common will." In this discourse, the nation is the ultimate political reality, upon whose identity all else depends.

This conception of the nation has several crucial implications. The first, inherent in the definition of the nation as a body of associates living under a common law, involves the status of citizenship as a relation of equality and universality, and the exclusion of the privileged as representing an *imperium in imperio* necessarily outside the political order. Thus the privileged orders are defined as out of the nation according to a political logic of citizenship, by way of which they cannot be equal; similarly they have been excluded from the nation according to a social logic of productive activity, by way of which they cannot be useful.

The second implication, inherent in the definition of the nation as possessing an inalienable and unitary common will, involves a repudiation of the

language of an ancient constitution and a fundamental law upholding claims
for the traditional organization of the Estates General. Because the will of the
nation is the unitary common will of a body of citizens, it cannot be expressed
through a representative body that is organized by order and estate: "The
general will . . . cannot be *one* so long as you allow three orders and three
representations to remain." Thus a unitary political will requires expression
in a unitary representative body; indeed, in a complex modern society, it can
barely be said to exist without it.

This link between a unitary representation and a unitary national will—
crucial to the elaboration of the revolutionary ideology—was a point upon
which Sieyès (tardily elected deputy of the Third Estate of Paris, after several
rebuffs from electors of his own order) was to insist throughout the debates
that transformed the Estates General into a National Assembly and subsequently laid down the principles of the new constitutional order. Yet it was
also a problematic link. For if the theory and practice of representation were
perfectly consistent with the social theory of the division of labor in a complex
modern society, they were less clearly and immediately compatible with the
political theory of a unitary and inalienable general will.

In the *Social Contract,* of course, Rousseau had decried representation
as a feudal practice inconsistent with the exercise of the general will; and
while he had allowed for representation in drawing up his constitution for
Poland, he had also insisted that popular sovereignty be guaranteed by a *mandat impératif* binding deputies strictly to respect the explicitly stated will of
their electors. Interestingly enough, this latter argument brought the theory
of the general will into convergence with the traditional constitutional practice of representation of the Ancien Régime, according to which the binding
mandate was an essentially conservative device to protect communities from
arbitrary demands placed by an absolute monarch upon the deputies to the
Estates General. In itself, the convergence is suggestive of the conservative
social assumptions underlying Rousseau's notion of the general will, and of
their incompatibility with the far more dynamic conception of society implied
in Sieyès' discourse on the social. But more important, the convergence of
general will and representation reveals the problematic issue faced by revolutionary theorists in legitimating what in effect became a revolution of the
deputies carried out in the name of national sovereignty. As a defense of a
traditional society against arbitrariness, the binding mandate was quite incompatible with a revolutionary assertion of national sovereignty on behalf of
a body of citizens exercising a unitary common will. Not surprisingly, then,
the repudiation of the mandate was a crucial step in the effective transformation of the Estates General into a National Assembly during the spring of
1789, and a central element in the fusion of the concept of the general will
with the theory of representation accomplished in the crucial constitutional
debates that followed upon the Declaration of the Rights of Man and of the
Citizen.

During the early debates over the binding mandate, in July 1789, Sieyès
consistently argued that no further action on this issue was necessary because

the question had already been decided by the creation of a National Assembly on June 17, 1789—an act that, in declaring the representative body of the nation "one and indivisible" (following the script set forth in *Qu'est-ce que le Tiers Etat?*), had claimed for that body alone the right "to interpret and present the general will of the nation." But he made his thinking on this point more explicit during the constitutional debates of early September 1789, when the argument for the royal veto (also justified as a device permitting an appeal to the general will of the nation against the particular will of its representative body) was added to that of the binding mandate to threaten the claims of the National Assembly to express the national will. Elected "immediately" by his *bailliage* but "mediately" by "the totality of *bailliages*," Sieyès argued in his speech of September 7, "every deputy represents the entire nation." Because the will of his immediate electors is necessarily a particular will in relation to that of the nation as a whole, an individual deputy can never be bound by that particular will in his capacity as representative of the nation. Nor can a decision of the representative body, once assembled, be subject to an appeal to the general will, which in a populous nation could only take the form of a vote by primary assemblies that would "fragment France into an infinity of petty democracies, which would then be linked only by the bonds of a general confederation." Thus reversing the Rousseauian opposition between representation and the general will, Sieyès insisted that national sovereignty could find expression in France only in the unity of the representative body: "The people can speak, can act only through its representatives."

Speak, act. Yet another repudiation of Rousseau was implied in these words. For the theory of the general will required that each individual in an assembly of citizens think his own thoughts, free of the partial interests that might emerge in the process of communication with others; hence the formula of the *Discours sur l'économie politique*—"public deliberation is one thing, the general will is another." Nothing was more foreign to the thinking of Sieyès than this formula. According to his general theory of the division of labor, representation was justified on the grounds that it permitted the majority of men (who were nothing more than "laboring machines" occupied with their daily labor) to confer active exercise of their right to participate in legislation upon the minority whom leisure, education, and enlightenment rendered "far more capable than themselves of discovering the general interest and interpreting their own wishes in this regard." But representatives chosen for their enlightenment could not make enlightened decisions unless they were free to deliberate in a manner unconstrained by the prior wills of those who had elected them. Thus slipping from the discourse of will to the discourse of reason, Sieyès found in the latter yet another argument against the binding mandate. "When a meeting is held, it is for the purpose of deliberation, of finding out other people's opinions, of taking advantage of their complementary enlightenment, of contrasting particular wills, of modifying them, of reconciling them, and finally of obtaining a decision supported by a plurality. . . . Beyond a shadow of a doubt, the deputies are in the National Assembly not to announce the already formed will of their direct constituents but to deliberate and vote freely in accordance with their *current* opinion, shaped by such enlightenment as the Assembly may bring to each of its members."

In this way, Sieyès disengaged the idea of a unitary general will from the communal dream of direct democracy and reconciled it with the practice of representation as an expression of the division of labor in a populous modern society. At the same time, he freed the concept of representation from the restrictions placed upon it in prerevolutionary thinking (within both the discourse of the social and the discourse of will), thereby locating the exercise of the sovereign general will not in the dispersed primary assemblies of the nation but in the representative body that alone constituted the nation as a whole. While the resulting conception of "representative sovereignty" was an ingenious invention, however, it was far from a stable one; and the tensions it introduced into revolutionary discourse did much to structure the meaning of subsequent events. In the course of the Revolution, the language of the general will constantly subverted the language of representation. The failure of the Constitution of 1791, which gave institutional form to the ambiguous synthesis between representation and national sovereignty effected by the National Assembly in 1789, was a clear symptom of the instability of that synthesis; the emergence of the Terror was the overwhelming expression of its collapse.

Sieyès himself, no less than others, had laid the basis for the subversion of principles of constitutionality in the name of the general will that was implied in the Terror. For it was a fundamental implication of the political definition of the nation offered in *Qu'est-ce que le Tiers Etat?* that the nation's sovereignty exists independent of all constitutional forms: "However a nation may will, it is enough that it does will; all forms are good, and its will is always the supreme law. A nation is independent of any form." Against the arguments of the privileged in favor of a fundamental law and an ancient constitution, Sieyès was obliged to maintain that there can be no constitutional arrangements not directly and immediately dependent upon the inalienable general will of the nation: "The national will, on the contrary, needs only its reality in order to be, at all times, legal. It is the origin of all legality. Not only is the nation not subject to a constitution; it *cannot* be subject to one, it *must* not be subject to one, which is also equivalent to saying that it is not so subject." The consequences of this argument are immense. For in repudiating claims for a traditional constitution, Sieyès had also undermined the capacity of any constitutional arrangement to withstand the subversive effects of the principle of national sovereignty.

How then to save constitutionalism and representative government from subversion in the name of general will? This challenge, in effect, was the problem faced by the Thermidorians in drawing up the Constitution of the Year III. And, although for personal reasons he remained aloof from the committee charged to write that constitution, it was also the problem that Sieyès (having survived the Terror to return to the Convention after the fall of Robespierre) addressed in his most important speech of this period, on 2 Thermidor of that year. To resolve it, Sieyès now sought to give clear priority to a rational discourse of the social over the discourse of political will. "Woe unto men, woe unto peoples who think they know what they want, when all they do is want. Nothing is easier than wanting." Reiterating his conviction that "everything in the social state is representation," he argued that just as in civil society an individual was freer the more others worked for him, so in politics it was "an extremely harmful error" to maintain that "the people should delegate only those powers that it cannot exercise itself." Danger lay not in the delegation of powers, but in their concentration in a single body— whether in a single representative body, or in the nation as a whole. To avoid the former, it was necessary to divide political functions precisely among a number of bodies in a way that would ensure "*l'unité d'action*" without risking "*l'action unique*." The dispersion of powers upon which Sieyès now insisted not only divided legislative and executive functions; it separated the responsibility for proposing laws from that of deciding upon them, thereby preventing any exercise of "spontaneous wills" by a representative assembly. Furthermore, to safeguard against any infringement upon this division of powers, Sieyès argued that it should be overseen by a special jury with authority to decide on charges of constitutional violation.

But it was not enough to prevent the concentration of power in a representative body acting in the name of national sovereignty. It was also necessary, Sieyès now insisted, to repudiate an exaggerated notion of national sovereignty itself, a notion that had been infected by the royal superstition of absolute and unlimited power and sustained by mistaken (but clearly Rousseauian) conceptions of the social contract. In creating political society, individuals neither transferred all their rights to the community, nor conferred upon it the sum of their individual powers. On the contrary, they retained their rights and placed in common only as little power as was necessary to maintain those rights. "The sovereignty of the people is not unlimited, and many systems approved and honored, including the one to which people are today persuaded they owe the greatest obligations, will seem mere monkish conceptions, poor plans for *re-total* rather than republic, equally disastrous for liberty, and ruinous for public as well as private affairs." Like Benjamin Constant, who also reverted to a discourse of the social as the basis for a new political liberalism, Sieyès now saw the Terror as the logical fruit of Rousseauian arguments.

If the Constitution of Year III did not precisely follow the details of Sieyès' proposals, it expressed a shared impulse to safeguard representative government while containing the implications of the theory of national sovereignty. One knows with what results. In the circumstances of the Directory, as it proved increasingly difficult to preserve "*l'unité d'action*" without "*l'action unique*," this recent advocate of a jury to safeguard the Constitution soon found himself participating in the coups d'état of 18 Fructidor, 22 Floréal, and 30 Prairial, and presiding over the transfer of power to Napoleon Bonaparte on 18 Brumaire. It is one of the great ironies of the French Revolution that the theorist whose script opened the revolutionary drama also brought it to a close.

Keith M. Baker

Further reading

WORKS BY SIEYÈS

Ecrits politiques, ed. Roberto Zapperi. Paris, 1985.

Qu'est-ce que le Tiers Etat? ed. Roberto Zapperi. Geneva, 1970.

Vues sur les moyens d'exécution dont les représentants de la France pourront disposer en 1789 (1788?). N.p., n.d.

RELATED WORKS

Baker, Keith Michael, ed. *The French Revolution and the Creation of Modern Political Culture,* vol 1, *The Political Culture of the Old Regime.* Oxford, 1987. See Baker's essay "Representation" and Bronislaw Baczko's essay "Le contrat social des Français: Sieyès et Rousseau."

Bastid, Paul. *Sieyès et sa pensée.* Paris, 1970.

Manin, Bernard. "Volonté générale ou délibération? Esquisse d'une théorie de la délibération politique," *Le débat,* January 1985.

Related topics

Constant	Democracy	Physiocrats	Sovereignty
Constitution	Estates General	Revolutionary Assemblies	Terror
Coups d'Etat	Nation	Rousseau	

EMIGRÉS

I n the aftermath of the taking of the Bastille and during the first years of the Revolution, tens of thousands of French men and women left their homes in wave after wave and crossed the borders. Some left the country out of open hostility to the principles of the new regime; others were afraid; still others simply allowed themselves to be caught up in the circumstances surrounding so radical a change. The rhythm of the exodus was dictated by the logic of the revolutionary phenomenon itself: as the ideal of unanimity implicit in the "general will" was realized through expulsion, one after another, of all who sought to impede its progress—absolutists, monarchiens, liberals, Girondins—the moment came for emigration. From England to Germany, from Switzerland to Russia, from Spain to Scandinavia, there was no country without its colony of French emigrants, including even the New World, which welcomed the most enterprising of the lot.

The Revolution soon came to look upon those who had deserted their country as implacable foes, and after a period of toleration it passed a series of increasingly repressive laws. Emigration was an exceedingly diverse phenomenon, but the Paris authorities in their legislation and propaganda placed it in the same class as the alleged aristocratic plot and conspiracy with foreign powers. The émigrés were destined to become one of the symbols of the past that the Revolution hoped to eradicate: their intrigues, their programs of restoration, their mere existence made them the very embodiment of nostalgia for the Ancien Régime.

There was also a less symbolic, more materialistic reason for the persistent hostility of revolutionary France toward the émigrés, a hostility that actually outlived the Terror and the Jacobin government. The émigrés' property had been confiscated and sold, and the prospect of their return from exile had become a nightmare to buyers of "national properties" who had hitched their wagon to the star of the Revolution and feared that their rights of ownership would be challenged.

Nor did the Restoration calm the contradictory passions that the figure of the émigré continued to arouse. Some viewed the émigrés as the only people who had demonstrated loyalty to the legitimate sovereign, while others saw them as implacable enemies who had renounced the French nation in fact and in law.

In considering the issue of emigration in broad outline, the first question that arises is just how many people left France during the Revolution. The "General List in Alphabetical Order of Emigrés from throughout the Republic," kept from the spring of 1792 until it was terminated by Bonaparte in 1800, includes the names of 145,000 émigrés but is not very credible: it lists names of people who did not emigrate and omits others who did. The first author to study the question in depth was Donald Greer (*The Incidence of the Emigration during the French Revolution*). By combining numerous local lists, more accurate than the so-called General List, with records of indemnities paid to the émigrés in 1825 he was able to pare the latter list down to around 129,000 names, to which one must add a number of émigrés who did not appear on any list, hard to pin down but estimated to have been between twenty and thirty thousand, for a grand total of 150,000 to 160,000 persons.

This is a large number, but not extraordinary, given that it amounts to just 0.6 percent of a population estimated at 26 million. In 1685, moreover, France had experienced an earlier emigration following the revocation of the Edict of Nantes, whose demographic effects were more dramatic and more durable. The historical importance and significance of the emigration that began in 1789 cannot be measured in statistical terms, however. Linked to the revolutionary process, it was above all a sign of two kinds of impotence: that of the Ancien Régime aristocracy, incapable of formulating an effective policy to react to the crisis of the French monarchy, and that of the liberal forces, incapable of establishing an English-style constitutional government. This twofold impotence in turn points up the sovereign omnipotence of the "general will." In this sense the comparison between the two great emigrations in modern French history has been used chiefly as a way of denouncing the absolutism of the Revolution. This was true not only of Taine but also of Michelet, who compared the laws against émigrés with Louis XIV's laws against Protestants. Taine, in his *Origines de la France contemporaine* (*La Révolution*, book 2, chap. 3), remarks: "One hundred thousand Frenchmen driven out at the end of the seventeenth century; one hundred twenty thousand Frenchmen driven out at the end of the eighteenth century—that is how intolerant democracy completed the work of intolerant monarchy."

A second question, statistical in nature, concerns the social composition of this mass of exiles. The symbolic charge associated with the phenomenon of emigration has made it difficult to give an objective evaluation by accrediting the legend that the emigration was essentially aristocratic or at any rate composed primarily of members of the Ancien Régime's privileged classes. In fact all classes of French society were involved. According to Greer's calculations the distribution was as follows: clergy, 25.2 percent; nobility, 16.8 percent; grande bourgeoisie, 11.1 percent; petite bourgeoisie, 6.2 percent; workers, 14.3 percent; peasants, 19.4 percent; unidentified, 7 percent. Thus, the two privileged orders account for 42 percent of the total, whereas the Third Estate represents 51 percent. Of course these comprehensive totals present too general a picture and are apt to cause confusion. In fact the emigration was anything but uniform in either its temporal or its geographic aspect. Not all émigrés left at once; wave followed wave over a period of several years. Only after 9 Thermidor did the intensity begin to diminish. Still, for all the complexity of the many episodes in this collective flight, two principal waves stand out: one before the fall of the monarchy, the other after.

Before 1792 the emigration was essentially aristocratic. The political character of this early exodus is obvious: these nobles left voluntarily in order to demonstrate their hostility to the Revolution. The early exiles were in no doubt about the legitimacy of organizing militarily in foreign countries and even accepting service in foreign armies. Louis XVI publicly disapproved of the mass emigration of the aristocracy (partly because he was forced to do so by circumstances, partly because it worried him to see a rival court growing in size abroad). But once his brothers had proclaimed their crusade against the Revolution, the enemies of the new regime, critical of the king's "weakness," saw their place as being in Koblenz or Worms at the side of the émigré princes. Some years later the vicomte de Bonald would claim legitimacy for the movement as a whole on grounds of a higher patriotism: "The emigration, obligatory for some, was legitimate for all. The soil is not the fatherland of the civilized man. . . . The civilized man recognizes the fatherland only in the laws that regulate society, in the order that reigns within it, in the powers that govern it, in the religion preached in it, and for him his country cannot always be his fatherland" (*De l'émigration*, in *Mélanges littéraires, politiques, et philosophiques*). This idea of extraterritorial loyalties and allegiances fit in quite well with the cosmopolitanism of French nobles, who considered themselves more the compatriots of foreign aristocrats than the fellow citizens of other Frenchmen.

The comte d'Artois openly deserted France on July 17, 1789. With him went many noble families: the prince de Condé, the Polignacs, the Rohans, the Contis, and the duc de Bourbon. This "joyous" emigration, motivated by "honor," was soon followed by a "timorous" emigration in the aftermath of the summer's disorders and the October days. The march on Versailles provoked the first wave: nobles, officials, and prelates quit the country. The failure of the monarchien party led to the departure of certain moderate deputies, including Mounier and Lally-Tollendal. In 1790 the pace of emigration accelerated in the wake of decrees abolishing feudalism, eliminating the parlements, and expropriating the property of the clergy, along with increasing insubordination in the armed forces. Above all, however, it was the abortive escape attempt and the king's arrest in Varennes that precipitated the move to abandon French soil. In 1791, moreover, military men were among those most inclined to emigrate: this was the year in which the prince de Condé established his headquarters in Worms and the army of the princes was organized. The signal was given for desertion on a large scale, and by the end of the year nearly 6,000 officers, some three-quarters of the royal army, had sought refuge abroad.

In this first phase of the Revolution the French government took no steps to discourage emigration. The borders were open, and anyone could leave the country without great difficulty. The Assembly was reluctant to pass laws infringing liberty, as is evident from the February 28, 1791, debate on the right to emigrate, during which Mirabeau scornfully attacked and succeeded in defeating a law aimed at curtailing the right to cross the border in peacetime. Michelet, discussing this debate, observed that the principle of justice had not yet given way to the principle of public safety. Early anti-emigration measures such as the law of August 6, 1791 (nullified in September by the Constitution) were cast in extremely indulgent terms. The bill of November 9, 1791, which imposed a sentence of death on any émigré who did not return to France by the end of the year, was much harsher, but a royal veto prevented it from becoming law. It was not until the eve of the war, on April 8, 1792, that the Legislative Assembly passed the first major law against émigrés. It provided for confiscation (but not yet sale) of the property of any person who left France after July 1, 1789, and did not return in one month's time.

The fall of the monarchy, followed by the war, the beginnings of the Terror, and the increasingly dire consequences of the policy of public safety, resulted in a new wave of emigration. The laws quickly became more harsh: in August 1792 the first properties of exiles were sold; on October 25 exiles were banished "in perpetuity" and sentenced to death; on November 15 a grace period of fifteen days was granted to those who wished to return to France. Finally, between March 28 and April 5, 1793, a comprehensive code was approved defining the "crime of emigration in time of war" and confirming the death penalty for any émigré who fell into the hands of the Republic.

The very nature of the emigration changed after the crucial month of August 1792. The exodus continued despite the more repressive laws. Its magnitude actually increased, and it became more and more chaotic. Greer's statistics show that nearly twice as many émigrés left the country after 1792 as before, but whereas aristocrats were more numerous in the initial phase, the later exodus drew on all classes of French society. This time people were fleeing from events. The intensity of the exodus, moreover, was linked to circumstances that varied considerably from place to place. It was provoked sometimes by episodes of insurrection, other times by terrorist reactions or foreign invasions. The Girondins and their friends left in June and July of 1793, fearing reprisals in the wake of the federalist revolt. The people of Toulon fled en masse in December 1793 when the republican army arrived to quell rebellion in the city. Many people in western France, where civil war was raging, took refuge abroad. But above all it was foreign invasions that caused enormous waves of emigration, as in Bas-Rhin following the advance and then retreat of the Austrian army in 1793: more than 20,000 people emigrated, most of them peasants, a far higher number than was recorded in any other département. In addition, 1792 was the year of the priests' departure. The king had refused to approve the first law calling for the deportation of refractory priests on May 27, 1792. But on August 26, after the fall of the monarchy, refractory priests were faced with a dilemma: either leave France or be deported. Many swelled the ranks of the émigrés.

The unwilling participants in this second emigration were not enemies of the Revolution. They came, rather, from the parties that had supported it and encouraged its radicalization. Hence they refused to be regarded as part of the counterrevolution, with which they continued to engage in a lively polemic. "One must distinguish between voluntary emigration and forced emigration," wrote Mme. de Staël, an illustrious representative of this second wave, for whom—following the example of the ultras, who measured monarchical purity by the earliness of their date of exile—the year 1792 was the true dividing line of patriotism. "In 1791," she added, "the system of emigration was false and damnable, because a handful of Frenchmen were lost among all the bayonets of Europe. There were, moreover, still many ways of coming to an understanding in France, among ourselves. Very worthy men were at the head of the government, political errors could have been repaired, and judicial murders had not yet been committed. . . . In 1791 the aristocrats' party deserted the nation in fact and in law" (*Considérations sur les principaux événements de la Révolution française,* Paris, 1818, part 3, chap. 1).

Historical judgment has always been rather severe, and rightly so, concerning the political action of the émigrés, or rather, more precisely, of the counterrevolutionary emigration led by the king's two brothers. Everything that was done to influence the course of events in France had disastrous results. The comte d'Artois first set up a counterrevolutionary committee in Turin. Calonne, who came from London, provided the political brains of the operation, which pursued three objectives: to organize the king's escape, to provoke insurrections in France, and to persuade other European sovereigns to intervene. But one after another the attempts to make Louis XVI leave France in secrecy ended in failure, culminating in the catastrophe of Varennes. The insurrections organized in several regions (Languedoc, Rhone Valley) produced no significant results. Nor did pressure on Emperor Leopold II yield the hoped-for results: Europe was indifferent to if not accepting of what was going on in France and had no intention of intervening. The émigré princes' lack of discipline was also worrisome. What is more, relations between the émigré nobles and the king of France were always difficult (and the king, in September 1791, had sworn an oath of allegiance to the Constitution, depriving his brothers' actions of all legitimacy). Thus, the émigrés' plans were nursed in political isolation.

Beyond political impotence, the emigration suffered from a rather pathetic sense of futility. With headquarters at Koblenz in the Rhineland (where the comte de Provence joined his brother and assumed control of the émigré forces), the noble officers of the émigré army attempted to revive the manners of the Ancien Régime, exaggerated to the point of caricature, so that all that was left was the unadulterated narcissism of the court and the puerilities of etiquette, whose rules were all the more scrupulously respected because the world that had given birth to them had disappeared. Nor did this spectacle of gallantry and intrigue lack for favorites who wielded exorbitant power, among them Mme. de Balbi and Mme. de Polastron, mistresses, respectively, of the comte de Provence and the comte d'Artois.

Preparation for war continued to be the émigrés' true objective. Yet their military efforts hardly added to their glory. The prince de Condé had organized an army in Worms. Koblenz was the bivouac of what was called the "princes' army." Both were composed of the many officers and few soldiers who had deserted France. After war broke out, the émigré armies asked to participate in the campaign under the command of the duke of Brunswick, but it cannot be said that their efforts were particularly notable. The only combat in which they took part, the assault on Thionville, was a failure, and after the defeat at Valmy the campaign ended in polemic and recrimination between the émigrés and the Austro-Prussian army. The emperor then ordered the émigré troops to disperse, because he held them responsible for the defeat.

The comte de Provence, the comte d'Artois, and their most faithful supporters thereupon began a long odyssey across Europe, an odyssey that would not end before 1814 and the Restoration. The comte de Provence, who at first proclaimed himself regent and then king of France under the name Louis XVIII, was an embarrassment to the courts of Europe, which were threatened by the armies of the Revolution. He was therefore condemned to wander from place to place, availing himself of the precarious hospitality of the Prussians, Venetians, Austrians, Russians, and finally the English. Abrupt changes in the course of the Revolution and above all the insurrections that erupted in France fostered illusions, but these were short-lived. The comte de Provence tried in vain to reach insurgent Toulon. In Vendée no real contact was ever established with the rebels owing to the émigrés' deep misunderstanding of the Vendean movement. In 1795 came a final failure: an attempt by émigré forces to land at Quiberon with the support of the English fleet ended in defeat and a massacre of the counterrevolutionaries. Meanwhile, the comte d'Artois, having landed with English help on the Isle of Yeu off the coast of Vendée, was unable, after much delay, to persuade himself to come to the aid of the rebels. He was obliged to return ingloriously to London, where he was awaited by his implacable creditors.

Faced with such dismal results, even the most moderate of the king's champions showed no mercy: "One of the laws of the French Revolution," wrote Joseph de Maistre in his *Considérations sur la France,* "was that the émigrés could not attack it without doing damage to themselves and were totally excluded from the work that was being accomplished. . . . Everything they tried was marred by impotence and futility" (chap. 10, p. 3). For Maistre, this futility only confirmed the "moral degradation of the nobility," the principal cause of the crisis of the monarchy.

The ultras' political program of total restoration was unrealistic. They refused at any price to lower themselves by negotiating with revolutionary France. The most extremist émigré elements always dreamed, in Tocqueville's words, of "an Ancien Régime even more odious than the one that had been destroyed." Among the émigrés there were of course less extremist positions, held in particular by former members of the Constituent Assembly, as well as by various representatives of liberalism who little by little swelled the émigré ranks. The legitimist party was already divided into two factions: a radical one led by the comte d'Artois, and a more moderate one led by Louis XVIII. Both persisted until the Restoration. Among the monarchiens, moreover, a more profound analysis was developed of the Ancien Régime's crisis, the causes of the Revolution, and the monarchy's needed reforms. During the period of emigration the old debate about the "constitution" of the kingdom of France continued, and proponents of constitutional monarchy such as Mounier, Lally-Tollendal, Montlosier, Malouet, and Mallet du Pan contributed on several occasions (most notably in 1796 and 1799) to animated discussions in opposition to the idea of a straightforward return to absolutism.

What is certain is that with so many contradictory pressures impinging on Louis XVIII, it was impossible to define any clear doctrine of sovereignty, as would become apparent in 1815.

*
**

After the fall of Robespierre the emigration was more or less over. There were a few brief spurts—in October 1795 after the royalist defeat in the *journée* of 13 Vendémiaire, and again in September 1797, after the coup d'état of 18 Fructidor—but now with the end of the great exodus came the problem of return.

The law providing the death penalty for émigrés remained in force under the Directory, but a circular of 30 Pluviôse, Year IV, made it possible for a person to request that his name be stricken from the notorious list. The fortress was now breached, and under the Thermidorians an underground return began. This still involved only isolated individuals and was subject to the discretion of the police and dependent on the vagaries of French internal politics, but the number of returnees soon grew to impressive proportions. The ultras disapproved of those who wished to return, but after long years of absence nostalgia had become unbearable for many. Feelings for the "fatherland" rose in people's breasts, the opposite of the cosmopolitan feelings associated with departure. "The fashion is now for going back, as it was previously for leaving," noted Neuilly in his *Souvenirs*.

The return of the émigrés was the result of Bonaparte's policy. The first consul was in favor of striking names from the list and had encouraged the return of former members of the Constituent Assembly: Lafayette, the Lameth brothers, the vicomte de Noailles, and the ducs de La Rochefoucauld-Liancourt were among the first to return. But the policy of national reconciliation—after the Concordat of 1801, which had put an end to the hostility between France and the Church by authorizing the return of exiled priests—culminated in a general amnesty for émigrés, promulgated in the form of the senatus-consult of April 26, 1802 (6 Floréal, Year X). Though this was a measure that did nothing to flatter the pride of the émigrés ("a rather disdainful gesture of clemency" Napoleon called it), the amnesty was the signal to return for nearly all who still remained abroad. Only diehards and very loyal partisans of the king stayed away until the Restoration, but they now represented a tiny minority.

If the amnesty of 1802 gave the émigrés back their homeland, it did nothing to restore their fortunes, confiscated by the revolutionary government and for the most part sold off. The senatus-consult of 6 Floréal provided for restoring unsold properties to their former owners but in no way challenged the new property statutes, thus leaving the reparation of damages to chance. The "national properties" issue is one of the best illustrations of the inability of partisans of restoration simply to erase the work of the Revolution. Louis XVIII gradually abandoned his initially uncompromising position on this delicate point. At first he wished simply to declare the confiscation and sale of the national properties null and void, but he was forced to adopt a more flexible view and ultimately to reverse his initial policy to the advantage of the new owners, to whom the charter solemnly guaranteed possession of their purchases ("All properties are inviolable, not excepting those called national, there being no difference in law between these and any others"). The émigrés felt betrayed, but public opinion was against them. Henceforth an abyss separated the émigrés from the new society. Intransigent legitimists were consequently destined to remain in opposition, at odds with both the Revolution and the Restoration.

The final act of pacification came only in 1825, under Charles X, when a measure of indemnification of former owners of nationalized properties was approved (the so-called *milliard des émigrés*, or "émigrés' billion"). But once again the bill was not accepted for what it was: an opportunity to let bygones be bygones. Instead it became the pretext for a very violent clash between the two parties that had been vying with each other for the past thirty years: the party of revolution and the party of counterrevolution. The bill submitted by the ministry, which argued that the émigrés had been dispossessed unjustly but legally, in fact raised a question of principle: if the Revolution was a violent and arbitrary act, as the Restoration implicitly contended, then all the measures it had adopted ought to be considered null and void, and the émigrés, expropriated in fact, were still owners in law (and if they were to accept an indemnity it would be out of pure generosity on their part): this was the position of the ultras. This bill was opposed by Benjamin Constant, who argued that the émigrés deserved no indemnification. By leaving voluntarily, they had displayed not loyalty but treasonous behavior toward the sovereign and the nation: the king had in fact ordered nobles not to emigrate. "By disobeying the orders of the king, by deserting the majority that obeyed those orders, the émigrés exercised what has been called the right of resistance" (*Ecrits et discours politiques,* Paris, 1964, vol. 2). But the time for partisan confrontation was past, and the ministers' conciliatory bill, moderate rather than partisan, ultimately carried, settling the question of emigration once and for all.

Massimo Boffa

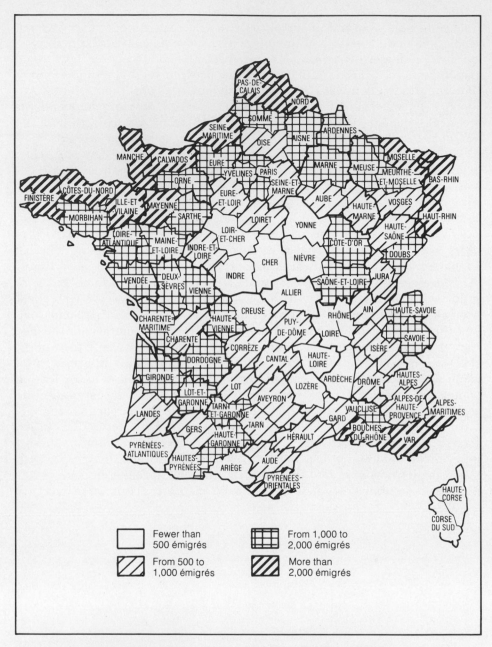

EMIGRATION, 1789–1799, BY DÉPARTEMENT

Note: This map reflects administrative boundaries as they currently exist in France. Since the Revolution the names and boundaries of certain départements have changed slightly.

STATISTICAL BREAKDOWN OF THE EMIGRATION.

Département	Clergy Number	Clergy %	Nobility Number	Nobility %	Grande bourgeoisie Number	Grande bourgeoisie %	Middle bourgeoisie Number	Middle bourgeoisie %	Artisans and workers Number	Artisans and workers %	Peasants Number	Peasants %	Unidentified Number	Unidentified %	Total
Ain															660
Aisne	368	32.50	329	29.25	105	9.25	62	5.50	141	12.50	44	4.00	79	7.00	1,128
Allier	70	20.50	128	37.75	59	17.25	3	1.00	7	2.00	4	1.25	69	20.25	340
Alpes, Basses-	205	40.50	119	23.25	57	11.25	9	1.75	22	4.25	2	0.25	96	18.75	510
Alpes, Hautes-	39	37.25	39	37.25	13	12.25	0	0.00	0	0.00	0	0.00	14	13.25	105
Alpes-Maritimes															3,000
Ardèche	122	27.00	184	40.75	49	10.75	4	1.00	14	3.25	7	1.50	71	15.75	451
Ardennes	339	28.25	251	21.00	128	10.50	56	4.50	170	14.25	173	14.50	84	7.00	1,201
Ariège	277	57.75	54	11.50	29	6.00	4	1.00	59	12.50	35	7.25	22	4.50	480
Aube	157	21.50	229	31.50	133	18.25	53	7.25	36	5.00	80	11.00	40	5.50	728
Aude	507	66.75	125	16.25	19	2.50	4	0.50	14	2.00	4	0.50	86	11.25	759
Aveyron	274	46.00	177	29.50	19	3.25	5	0.75	12	2.00	13	2.50	97	16.25	597
Bouches-du-Rhône	480	9.25	360	7.00	2,049	40.00	945	18.50	819	16.00	472	9.25	0	0.00	5,125
Calvados	114	38.75	75	25.50	10	3.50	9	3.00	36	12.25	42	14.25	8	2.75	2,080
Cantal	402	56.75	241	34.00	37	5.75	4	0.50	11	1.50	1	0.25	13	1.75	709
Charente	173	27.25	191	30.25	25	4.00	5	0.75	5	0.75	0	0.00	234	37.00	633
Charente-Inférieure															1,335
Cher	92	38.50	102	42.75	27	11.25	1	0.50	3	1.25	0	0.00	14	5.75	239
Corrèze	316	39.25	236	29.25	104	13.00	4	0.50	19	2.25	43	5.25	85	10.25	807
Corse (Dép. de Liamone)	4	9.25	29	67.25	6	14.00	0	0.00	2	4.75	0	0.00	2	4.75	43
Côte-d'Or	346	19.50	449	25.25	424	23.75	136	7.50	150	8.50	46	2.50	230	13.00	1,781
Côtes-du-Nord															2,575
Creuse	135	48.25	101	36.00	8	3.00	0	0.00	1	0.25	9	3.25	26	9.25	280
Dordogne															2,000
Doubs	521	27.00	216	11.75	88	4.50	39	2.00	294	15.25	684	35.50	88	4.50	1,930
Drôme															632
Eure	52	24.50	40	19.00	15	7.00	12	5.75	23	11.00	41	19.50	28	13.25	1,112
Eure-et-Loir															760

Département	Clergy		Nobility		Grande bourgeoisie		Middle bourgeoisie		Artisans and workers		Peasants		Unidentified		Total
	Number	%	Number	%	Number	%	Number	%	Number	%	Number	%	Number	%	
Finistère															2,086
Gard	336	52.75	68	10.75	78	12.50	14	2.25	31	4.75	20	3.00	91	14.25	638
Garonne, Haute-	525	45.50	300	26.00	92	8.00	21	1.75	65	5.50	6	0.50	148	12.75	1,157
Gers	262	43.00	197	32.25	51	8.25	4	0.75	22	3.50	14	2.25	61	10.00	611
Gironde	331	28.00	360	30.25	196	16.50	53	4.50	79	6.75	34	3.75	133	11.25	1,186
Hérault	338	51.25	81	12.25	94	14.25	34	5.25	37	5.50	29	4.50	46	7.00	659
Ille-et-Vilaine	758	36.25	793	38.50	43	2.00	30	1.50	71	3.50	71	3.50	306	14.75	2,072
Indre	57	20.50	117	42.25	39	14.00	6	2.25	7	2.50	3	1.00	48	17.50	227
Indre-et-Loire	285	51.75	160	29.00	24	4.50	6	1.00	4	0.75	2	0.50	70	12.75	551
Isère	320	50.75	142	22.50	50	8.00	4	0.50	2	0.25	0	0.00	114	18.00	632
Jura	131	30.25	138	32.00	87	20.00	2	0.50	20	4.50	2	0.50	53	12.25	910
Landes	383	65.25	119	20.25	32	5.50	3	0.50	4	0.75	4	0.75	41	7.00	586
Loir-et-Cher	111	29.00	137	35.50	47	12.50	3	0.75	5	1.25	0	0.00	82	21.25	385
Loire															105
Loire, Haute-	110	40.50	85	31.50	17	6.25	3	1.00	10	3.75	23	8.50	23	8.50	271
Loire-Inférieure															1,750
Loiret															520
Lot	130	22.75	187	33.00	65	11.50	12	2.00	19	3.25	7	1.25	149	26.25	569
Lot-et-Garonne															1,610
Lozère	209	61.75	59	17.50	21	6.25	4	1.25	7	2.00	22	6.50	16	4.75	338
Maine-et-Loire	609	37.00	483	29.50	109	6.75	34	2.00	152	9.25	235	14.25	21	1.25	1,643
Manche	812	40.50	394	19.50	83	4.25	24	1.25	239	12.00	358	17.75	95	4.75	2,005
Marne	350	33.75	269	25.75	110	10.50	33	3.25	43	4.25	65	6.25	170	16.25	1,040
Marne, Haute-	283	37.25	189	25.00	97	12.75	31	4.00	47	6.25	21	2.75	91	12.00	759
Mayenne	589	18.25	294	9.00	25	0.75	100	3.00	628	19.25	1,454	44.75	163	5.00	3,253
Meurthe	519	33.50	292	19.00	186	12.00	11	0.75	150	9.75	386	25.00	0	0.00	1,544
Meuse	488	29.75	594	36.25	266	16.25	47	2.75	151	9.25	37	2.25	57	3.50	1,640
Mont-Blanc (Savoie)	1,033	57.25	349	19.25	283	15.50	55	3.00	37	2.00	16	1.00	33	2.00	1,806
Morbihan	741	54.75	136	10.00	97	7.25	66	4.75	108	8.00	145	10.75	60	4.50	1,353

	No.	%	No.	%	No.	%	No.	%	No.	%	No.	%	No.	%	Total
Moselle	982	25.50	697	18.25	480	12.50	263	6.75	614	16.50	791	20.50	0	0.00	3,827
Nièvre	123	35.75	183	53.25	11	3.25	0	0.00	5	1.50	3	0.75	19	5.50	344
Nord	738	28.00	374	14.50	436	16.50	188	7.25	277	10.50	600	22.75	22	0.75	2,635
Oise	238	32.50	162	22.00	142	19.50	7	1.00	25	3.50	6	0.75	152	20.75	732
Orne	267	47.25	97	17.25	101	18.00	19	3.25	22	4.00	39	7.00	19	3.25	1,870
Pas-de-Calais															2,260
Puy-de-Dôme															840
Pyrénées, Basses-	137	30.50	66	14.75	27	6.00	16	3.50	45	10.00	25	5.50	133	29.75	449
Pyrénées, Hautes-	228	58.50	50	12.75	15	3.75	5	1.25	4	1.00	34	8.75	55	14.00	391
Pyrénées-Orientales	482	12.50	252	6.50	385	10.00	209	5.50	431	11.25	1,677	43.50	418	10.75	3,854
Rhin, Bas-	936	4.50	499	2.50	993	5.00	2,113	10.25	6,051	29.50	9,601	46.75	317	1.50	20,510
Rhin, Haut-	855	31.25	323	11.75	224	8.25	93	3.25	686	25.00	407	14.75	158	5.75	2,746
Rhône	98	29.50	91	27.50	111	33.50	13	4.00	10	3.00	1	0.00	8	2.50	332
Saône-et-Loire	437	41.50	375	35.75	144	13.50	25	2.50	27	2.50	13	1.25	31	3.00	1,052
Saône, Haute-	443	49.75	219	24.75	136	15.25	12	1.25	41	4.75	20	2.25	18	2.00	889
Sarthe	95	20.00	115	24.25	87	18.25	9	2.00	59	12.50	97	20.50	12	2.50	1,090
Seine	462	22.25	942	45.50	93	4.50	9	0.50	16	0.75	0	0.00	547	26.50	2,069
Seine-et-Marne	177	28.50	166	26.75	50	8.00	14	2.25	7	1.00	7	1.00	202	32.50	623
Seine-et-Oise															1,598
Seine-Inférieure	335	38.75	290	33.50	74	8.25	31	3.50	29	3.25	16	2.00	90	10.50	2,038
Sèvres, Deux-	169	33.00	235	46.00	45	8.75	10	2.00	20	4.00	32	6.25	0	0.00	1,200
Somme	666	51.75	221	17.25	142	11.00	54	4.25	32	2.50	71	5.50	100	7.75	1,286
Tarn	546	64.50	131	15.50	20	2.25	6	0.75	29	3.50	12	1.50	102	12.00	846
Var	335	6.50	374	7.00	1131	21.25	808	15.25	1,407	26.25	535	10.00	741	14.00	5,331
Vaucluse	311	24.50	223	17.50	196	15.25	107	8.50	227	17.75	33	2.50	178	14.00	1,275
Vendée	500	43.75	409	35.75	21	1.75	23	2.00	62	5.50	127	11.25	0	0.00	1,142
Vienne															1,710
Vienne, Haute-															1,165
Vosges	204	36.00	156	27.50	56	10.00	9	1.50	23	4.00	99	17.50	20	3.50	567
Yonne	129	27.25	163	34.50	76	16.00	14	3.00	28	6.00	10	2.25	52	11.00	472
Total no./Average %	24,596	25.25	16,431	16.75	10,792	11.00	6,012	6.25	13,953	14.25	18,910	19.50	6,851	7.00	129,099

Actors

Further reading

Baldensperger, Fernand. *Le mouvement des idées dans l'émigration française, 1789–1815.* Paris, 1924.

Castries, René de. *La vie quotidienne des émigrés.* Paris, 1966.

Daudet, Ernest. *Histoire de l'émigration pendant la Révolution française.* Paris, 1905.

Forneron, Henri. *Histoire générale des émigrés pendant la Révolution française.* Paris, 1884.

Gain, André. *La Restauration et les biens des émigrés.* Nancy, 1929.

Greer, Donald. *The Incidence of the Emigration during the French Revolution.* Cambridge, 1951.

Vidalenc, Jean. *Les émigrés français.* Caen, 1963.

Related topics

Aristocracy
Civil Constitution of the Clergy
Constant
Counterrevolution
Lafayette
Louis XVI

Maistre
Michelet
Mirabeau
Monarchiens
Napoleon Bonaparte
National Properties

Staël
Taine
Tocqueville
Varennes
Vendée

ENRAGÉS

The very name "the enragés" underscores the discredit that attached, during the Revolution and throughout the nineteenth century, to this extreme left-wing movement, which Albert Mathiez for no good reason characterized as "socialist." Michelet failed to do the group justice. Jaurès at least recognized that it was a spontaneous movement, and Mathiez (writing in 1927) shed some light on the motives of its leaders, particularly Jacques Roux. Since that time historians have argued about the group's program. Daniel Guérin thought it contained the core of a proletarian revolutionary strategy. Albert Soboul on the whole underestimated its influence. Maurice Dommanget portrayed the "red priest" Jacques Roux as a model popular leader in a revolution initiated by the bourgeoisie.

Essentially the enragés were three men—the abbé Jacques Roux, the postal clerk Varlet, and the errant Leclerc—and a woman, the actress Claire Lacombe, who, by founding the Society of Revolutionary Republicans, gave the movement a feminine (but not feminist) dimension.

Varlet came from a well-to-do family. At the time of his trial, which was conducted by his section (the Rights of Man Section) in Brumaire of Year II, his annual income was 5,800 livres, including both income from his properties and his salary as a postal clerk. Orphaned at an early age, he had been a good student at the Collège d'Harcourt. The Revolution captivated him: he did not miss a single session of the Constituent Assembly, and he soon began writing revolutionary pamphlets. But it was not until the king's attempted escape to Varennes that Varlet's talents as an orator and leader of men were revealed (at the Palais Royal). After the "fusillade" on the Champ de Mars, he drafted and circulated a petition against Louis XVI. Under the Legislative Assembly he continued to wage war on the king and other "traitors," above all Lafayette, of whom he wrote that "he was and always will be a scoundrel." On August 6, 1792, speaking for his section, he presented a petition to the Legislative Assembly demanding that the king be deposed. After August 10 he was named an elector. He soon displayed distrust of representative government. From the start of the Convention he made no secret of his low opinion of deputies, even Montagnard deputies. He preferred direct universal suffrage to the existing two-tiered electoral system, and he wanted representatives to be bound by a strict mandate from their constituents, who he thought should have the power to recall at any time those whom they elected. On December 9, 1792, he said: "We cannot help feeling the same distrust even toward those to whom we gave our votes." With this antiparliamentarism went an ambition to alleviate social inequality and to "prevent financial manipulators and monopolists from expanding their private fortunes at the public's expense." Varlet called for nationalization of profits stemming from monopoly and hoarding. But he was no dreamer. The anti-Girondin insurrection of May 31, 1793, owed much to his talent as a leader of men.

Jacques Roux, the most detested of the enragé leaders, belonged to a different generation, yet he too came from a relatively well-to-do family. A native of Saint-Cibard de Pronsac in the diocese of Angoulême and son of an infantry lieutenant who became an assessor in the marquisate of Pronsac, Jacques settled on a career in the Church while still very young. After studying at the Angoulême seminary, he was tonsured in 1767 at age fifteen and was immediately offered a canonry in Pronsac. This was a comfortable living reserved for the children of local luminaries. For a while he taught at the Angoulême seminary, but in 1785 he moved to the diocese of Saintes, where he was offered first one and then another parish. It was there that he learned of the events of July 1789. Later, in a polemic with Marat, he wrote: "I rebelled against the usurpations of the nobility and the hypocrisy of the old clergy." The only text by him that has survived from this period is a celebration of the taking of the Bastille and a eulogy of Louis XVI. He was subsequently removed from his parish and placed under interdict by the Church hierarchy, apparently after participating in an antifeudal peasant movement. Early in 1791 he went to Paris, where he took an oath to support the Civil Constitution of the Clergy on January 16. Since he was under interdict at the time, he was not actually authorized to take the oath. At Saint-Sulpice, however, no one was about to quibble over the qualifications of priests who volunteered their support to the new regime.

"Prohibited from performing the sacred functions of the priesthood by the vicars-general of Saintes only to be declared the *apostle* of the Revolution . . . I am ready to give every last drop of my blood to a Revolution that has already altered the fate of the human race by making men *equal* among themselves as they are for all eternity before *God*." The italicized words indicate themes that would remain fundamental to Roux's thinking for the rest of his life. Named vicar of Saint-Nicolas des Champs, he became active in the Gravilliers section, frequented the Club des Cordeliers, and formed a temporary association with Marat, who stayed at his home in March 1792. His sermons reveal how his thoughts turned more and more to terrorism. On March 17, 1792, he exclaimed:

> Disarm tepid and suspect citizens! Put a price on the head of émigré conspirators! . . . Hold the wives and children of these traitors hostage! Let them answer for the events of the war, which the race of nobles and priests has unleashed at home and abroad. Chain them up and let them be the first to be exposed to the fire of the enemy, or rather of the murderers the enemy has recruited. Let the homes of the cowards who surrendered our fortresses be razed and demolished. . . . Above all, remember that England saved itself only by making the scaffolds run red with the blood of treacherous and false kings.

It comes as no surprise that the selfsame Jacques Roux later led Louis XVI to the scaffold and terrified the women of his section by describing in gory detail the king's severed head. In priests brought up in the tradition of the League and imbued with the spirit of the Old Testament, a thirst for impure blood was not uncommon.

The "red priest" was a friend of the common man. His influence steadily expanded from his own Gravilliers section to the neighboring Temple and Observatoire sections. To the very end he counted numerous artisans among his loyal friends, as is evident from the occupations of his codefendants: we find a tavern keeper, a cobbler, and a carpenter. He addressed his appeals to women. On August 28, 1792, he wrote a friend: "Victory is inevitable if the women join with the sans-culottes." He had a genuine feeling for the common folk, to judge by his liaison with the widow Petit, a linen worker, and his adoption of a fourteen-year-old orphan.

In the spring of 1793, in response to his appeals, a young actress, Claire Lacombe, formed the Society of Revolutionary Republicans, which began meeting in the middle of May in the Jacobins' library. The members of the society were indignant about the high cost of living, the scarcity of necessities, and the wretched conditions in which they lived. On May 19 Claire Lacombe, acting in conjunction with the Cordeliers, sent a petition to the Jacobins: "Do something about stockjobbers, hoarders, and selfish merchants. A dreadful conspiracy has been mounted to kill the poor by driving prices sky high. At the center of the plot is a merchant aristocracy, an insolent caste that wants to put itself in a class with royalty. . . . Exterminate the scoundrels." From words she quickly moved to deeds: on May 26 she spotted another woman, the Girondin Théroigne de Méricourt, on the benches of the Convention and began to beat her savagely with a whip. She would have killed her if Marat had not intervened.

On the eve of the May insurrection Théophile Leclerc joined the enragés. Although he was not originally from Lyons, it was there that he established his reputation as a politician. Born in Montbrison in 1771, he too came from a moderately well-to-do bourgeois background. His father was an engineer employed by the Ponts et Chaussées (the royal administration of bridges and highways). But he had lived a life on the fringes of society. He sailed for Martinique in 1790, joined the revolutionary party, was thrown into the brig of a ship in the harbor of Fort de France, returned to Lorient in July 1791, and subsequently served, until February 1792, with the first battalion of Morbihan volunteers. After a brief stay in Paris, where he distinguished himself by delivering a memorable speech to the Jacobins in which he attacked Louis XVI and the "modern-day Brunhild," he went to Lyons, where he joined Chalier in the so-called Central Club. Shortly before May 31 he returned to Paris and was named a member of the insurrectional committee. He was popular among revolutionary women and married one of them, Pauline Léon. But he was no gentler a soul than the other enragé leaders. He was of the opinion that the June 2 insurrection had not gone far enough and called for the execution of the expelled Girondins: "Why are you afraid of a few drops of blood?"

Despite differences of age and background, the biographies of all four enragé leaders are in many respects similar. From the time of Etienne Marcel to the Commune of 1871, the clergy and middle class have always provided the common folk with spokesmen and leaders drawn to the oppressed and at odds with their own class. The Revolution added certain new elements to this tradition. Perhaps the best expression of popular suspicions of the wealthy elite is to be found in Jacques Roux's speech of June 25, 1793, after the expulsion of the Girondins from the Convention: "Who among you deputies of the Mountain has visited the third to ninth stories of the houses of this revolutionary city? Had you done so, you would have been moved by the tears and moans of a vast population without bread or clothing, reduced to this state of distress and misfortune by stockjobbing and hoarding, because the laws have been cruel to the poor, because they were made by the rich and for the rich."

For the "patriots of 1789" (as well as 1793), this radical protest movement represented a threat to a revolution that depended on an alliance between rulers and people. On July 4, 1793, Marat, "the friend of the people," wrote: "Varlet may be nothing but a brainless intriguer, but little Leclerc appears to be a very clever rogue," and Jacques Roux was greedy, hypocritical, and self-seeking. Robespierre attacked Roux at the Jacobin Club: "I say that those who go around preaching against the Mountain and against the Convention are the only enemies of the people. . . . Do you suppose that a priest who, in concert with the Austrians, denounces the finest patriots can possibly have pure motives or legitimate intentions?" Here we witness a clash between two cultures, two sensibilities.

The enragés were active from February until September 1793. Paris was short of supplies, particularly of soap, sugar, and foodstuffs normally imported from the Caribbean islands. In the midst of this economic crisis, the sans-culottes were prepared to follow men and women who seemed to offer two magic remedies: price regulation through the so-called *maximum* and an end to monetary speculation. The political program reflected these economic demands, calling for expulsion of the Girondin deputies and punishment of financial manipulators. Countless petitions repeated Jacques Roux's platform: "Demand the death penalty for those who are hoarding food supplies and those who, through commerce in currency and fabrication of coinage worth less than its natural value, are discrediting the assignat." Disturbances erupted on February 25. At first around Les Halles and subsequently throughout central Paris, women went from grocery to grocery setting maximum prices on soap, sugar, and candles. Roux pleaded their cause: "It seems to me that the grocers are merely restoring to the people what they took through overcharges." Initially the Montagnards were extremely reluctant to respond to these demands. They shared the Girondins' belief in the free market, as Robespierre stated in no uncertain terms on February 25: "I do not say that the people is guilty. I do not say that these acts are a crime. But when the people rises, should it not have a goal worthy of it? Will it concern itself with trivial commodities?"

ENRAGÉS

In a speech to the Convention Marat too spoke forcefully against price controls. To petitioners who came on February 12, 1793, to demand, in threatening fashion, price controls on all foodstuffs, he gave a vehement reply: "The measures for restoring plenty that have just been proposed from the floor are so outrageous, so bizarre, so subversive of rational order, and so obviously likely to end free commerce in grain and stir up trouble in the Republic, that I am surprised to hear them from the mouths of men who pretend to be reasonable and free citizens, friends of justice and peace. . . . I demand that those who have wasted the Convention's time in this manner be prosecuted for disturbing the peace."

Between early March and late May the situation changed. The Montagnards, in search of sans-culotte support in their battle with the Girondins, reluctantly gave in on several of the sans-culottes' demands. Jean Bon Saint-André wrote to Barère: "It is imperative that you allow the poor man to live if you want his help in completing the Revolution." On April 24 Robespierre proposed adding four articles limiting property rights to the Declaration of the Rights of Man. Subsequently the Convention approved the creation of a Revolutionary Tribunal and committees of surveillance (March 11 and 21); decreed that assignats must be accepted as legal tender at a fixed value (April 11); and set a maximum price on grain and flour (May 4). It had no intention, however, of leaving the political initiative to the enragés. When Varlet attempted an insurrection on March 9 and 10, he was disavowed by the Commune and the Jacobins. And when disturbances began again in Paris toward the end of April, the authorities were able to put them down.

The final battle between the Gironde and the Mountain (the *journées* of May 31 and June 2), provoked by the Girondins, was actually arbitrated by the sans-culottes and won by the enragés, yet in the end these two groups were the major losers in an insurrection that fell short of the goals they had set for themselves. Disturbances continued throughout the month of June. The September Days and subsequent repressive measures finished off the enragés. The Society of Revolutionary Republicans was dissolved, and Claire Lacombe was imprisoned twice, as were Varlet and Leclerc. Jacques Roux committed suicide during his trial. Despite efforts by the Hébertists to take up the cause, the end of the enragés also spelled the end of popular influence on the revolutionary government and ultimately the end of the sectional movement.

Denis Richet

ACTORS

FURTHER READING

Dommanget, Maurice. *Jacques Roux (le curé rouge) et le manifeste des "Enragés."* Paris, 1948.

Guérin, Daniel. *La lutte de classes sous la Première République: Bourgeois et "bras nus" (1793–1797)*, 2 vols. Paris, 1946 (second edition, 1968).

Mathiez, Albert. *La vie chère et le mouvement social sous la Terreur.* Paris, 1927 (reprinted in 2 vols., 1973).

Soboul, Albert. *Les sans-culottes parisiens en l'an II: Histoire politique et sociale des sections de Paris, 2 juin 1793–9 thermidor an II.* La Roche-sur-Yon, 1958. Reprinted Paris, 1958, and 1962 with the subtitle *Mouvement populaire et gouvernement révolutionnaire.*

RELATED TOPICS

Civil Constitution of the Clergy
Girondins
Lafayette

Marat
Maximum
Montagnards

Robespierre
Sans-culottes

342

FEUILLANTS

On July 16, 1791, one month after the king's flight and on the eve of the fusillade on the Champ de Mars, the most moderate members of the Jacobin Club walked out. The so-called triumvirs—Barnave, Duport, and Lameth—as well as nearly all the Jacobins who were also deputies met in the nearby church of the convent of Feuillants, adjacent to the Salle du Manège. They were joined by certain leading figures of the constitutional party, most notably Le Chapelier, the founder of the Breton Club, as well as friends of Lafayette such as Aimery and La Tour-Maubourg, who after Varennes had thrown their support to the triumvirs. These dissidents did not really intend to found a new society to rival the old but, as Barnave later wrote, "to transfer to the Feuillants the Society of Friends of the Constitution of which they had been the original founders." They drafted new constitutions, attempted to enlist the support of affiliated provincial clubs, and established a newspaper. Their program was summed up in a lapidary phrase of Faydel's: "Punctilious adherence to the Constitution."

In short this was a split, not a purge. Like the monarchiens two years earlier, the Feuillants formed a "party" in order to protect not only a policy but a conception of power. They also suffered from the ingenuous belief—which would prove fatal to them as it did later to the Girondins—that a maneuver would be enough to "end the Revolution." Their goal was to neutralize the intransigent royalists by enlisting the support of the moderate right; to isolate, on the left, the democrats from the majority of patriotic deputies; to undermine Jacobin influence; and ultimately to do away with the revolutionary societies that threatened the legitimacy and independence of the National Assembly. By quitting en masse, the dissidents could drape themselves in legality as defenders of the Constitution, at that time inseparable from the Revolution. This maneuver was destined to fail, however: on the right, the proponents of constitutional monarchy did not respond to the appeal; on the left, the most determined Jacobins were quick to react to the shock; and the court, out of either indifference or paralysis, stood idly by.

The Feuillants' failure was not simply that of a misconceived strategy, however. It was even more a consequence of inept tactics: the group attempted to create a political lobby but out of legalistic concerns refused to adopt the necessary means (working behind the scenes, pressure, intimidation, elimination of the opposition). They declined to take up the arms from which their power derived, choosing instead to bide their time—lulled by the naive conviction that the Jacobin movement would soon vanish. They did not understand that political power in the summer of 1791 depended not on legality but on revolutionary legitimacy; that the Varennes episode had driven a wedge betweeen the two; and that legitimacy had deserted the Salle du Manège and from now on lay with the detested clubs.

It was Robespierre's good fortune and chief resource that he grasped this crucial ideological shift and became not only its interpreter but ultimately its symbol. Having chosen to remain in the Jacobins along with Pétion, Buzot, and a handful of loyal members, he endured the trial first as victim, then as vanquisher. In this the genius of the tactician combined with the acute intelligence of the political theorist who sensed that the future of the Revolution lay in its sudden new direction. He won his victory not, as Barnave supposed, by means of "the terror of pikes and lampoons" but through his ingenious mastery of a particular form of political discourse, which within a few weeks would persuade old allies bewildered by the actions of the Feuillants to return to the Jacobin fold. Robespierre had long since catalogued all the forms of revolutionary legitimacy: a discourse that remained unwavering yet adapted itself to changing circumstances; a rhetoric that established virtue as an instrument of purification; a storehouse of symbols, representations, and emblems. In the Feuillant crisis, however, he immediately saw that legitimacy lay above all in a sacred place, which for the country had become the temple of patriotism and the civic spirit. There the abstract figure of the sovereign individual was reinvented every day and the marriage of the Revolution with the people was celebrated. The Feuillants had therefore banished themselves from the Revolution merely by crossing the street.

Robespierre still had to get the message out. The memorandum he sent to the affiliated clubs in the provinces was a masterpiece. In the first place, it indicated that the members who had left the Jacobins had twice been invited "to rejoin the mother society" and twice turned a deaf ear to the appeal, thus making the Feuillants seem guilty of desertion. Robespierre describes the dissidents, now outside Jacobin protection, as miserable wretches vulnerable to all sorts of contagious influences. Indeed many—and here the tone becomes one of distress—have already engaged in rather unpatriotic activities: "They sent us their regulations concerning admission to the new society. We would have accepted them gladly if they had not excluded all except active citizens and sons of active citizens. Imbued with a patriotism not allied with any particular view, we did not wish to oblige ourselves to reject the Constitution's strongest supporters, the most honorable class of humanity, merely because it was their misfortune not to pay a certain sum in taxes." These words were not without audacity, in view of the fact that the Jacobins continued to collect membership dues much higher than the *cens* and would cease to do so only after the fall of the monarchy.

After the requisite homage to the civic spirit of the poorer classes came the assignment of blame: first there were the instigators of the exodus, and then there were the followers, not shrewd enough to detect the factional tactics behind the maneuver. "We blamed this decision not on the majority of the Feuillant Club, which fully shares our sentiments, but on a few individuals, who for a short time were able to influence its thinking." Because patriotism remained the virtue of the mother society alone, the dissidents were faced with a stark choice: either return to the fold or persist in error. "We were all counting on an imminent return of the friends of liberty. We were already assured of this advantage by the appearance, in our assemblies, of some members of the National Assembly. We know that many others have remained with the Feuillants only to counterbalance the unfortunate influence of the factious." Revolutionary legitimacy was thus intimately associated with a consecrated locale, the meeting place of the Jacobins. In conclusion, Robespierre exhorted all good citizens to keep a sharp eye out for false friends of the fatherland—to ferret them out, denounce them, isolate them. A powerful writer, he invoked the threat of a conspiracy to reestablish the unity of the Jacobin movement and, through it, of the sovereign people. Rarely has a polemical text so effectively resolved a struggle for power whose outcome had seemed to be determined by sheer numbers. The Feuillants were defeated at a time when their triumph appeared beyond doubt. They lost because they were unable to bring their resources to bear where they were needed most: with the affiliated societies in the provinces, which one after another gave their approval to the Incorruptible's arguments. Initially they advocated reconciliation, but later, disconcerted by the inconsistency of Feuillant propaganda, they quietly and naturally returned to the Jacobin fold. There is no more eloquent testimony to the magnitude of Robespierre's success than this admonition to the Feuillants from the Société de Saint-Germain:

> The Jacobin Society, in its letter, swears to abide faithfully by the decrees of the Assembly, so that in our eyes its actions are fully justified. Through submission and obedience the citizen acquires the right to reason about the law, to compare its advantages and disadvantages. He who executes a law is a much more reliable judge of its advantages and disadvantages than the lawmaker himself. . . . All the intelligence in the realm is not concentrated in the Assembly. Representatives would therefore be wise not to disdain the reflections of citizens. Note the circumstances under which citizens have expressed the opinion that you characterize as a crime. . . . Why do we not see, on the list that you sent, the names Pétion, Robespierre, and Buzot, whom the people have always regarded as the most zealous defenders of their interests? Why do we see instead names that figured in the Society of '89? If many of you sympathize with them, one of two things must be true: either their patriotism has greatly increased, or yours has greatly diminished. Where do things stand if the moderates of '89 are the patriots of today?

*
**

As the Feuillants saw it, the split that took place in the summer of 1791 was supposed to have altered the thinking of a whole segment of the patriotic party. Since springtime many members of the Constituent Assembly had reached the conclusion that the Revolution was nearly complete. In order to establish a reconciliation with the king and enshrine the achievements of the Revolution in a constitutional monarchy, it was necessary to mark an end. This was Mirabeau's ambition, the meaning of his commitment to the Revolution and of his secret relations with the court. As the months passed, however, the great orator of the Constituent Assembly became increasingly isolated. His enemies in the Assembly waited for him to make a false step. From the galleries the people monitored his every move. The Jacobins nullified his influence by applauding his speeches without following his recommendations. And the king paid him but did not heed his advice. When he died on April 2, it was old adversaries, the triumvirs, who claimed his political legacy. When they too found their way to the court at the Tuileries and attempted to formulate a plan for restructuring the government, they had no intention of rejecting the spirit of 1789. Indeed, they attempted to revive that spirit in order to save a revolution that was increasingly in jeopardy, threatened by "democratic" pressures, popular unrest, and the growing influence of extraparliamentary organizations. For the triumvirs and their friends the crucial thing was to prevent the Constituent Assembly from moving toward a republic, to prevent the passion for equality from threatening liberty, property, social unity, and governmental continuity. Their program was to restore the authority of government, silence the democrats, and revise the Constitution so as to increase the king's powers and raise the *cens*. While they still appeared to control a majority in the Assembly, they had already begun to lose control of the patriotic party. By favoring elimination of "passive citizens" from the National Guard (April 27, 1791), remaining silent during the debate on the right to petition and post bills, opposing the political emancipation of the blacks (May 11–15, 1791), the triumvirs exhausted their popularity within the space of a few months.

In the early days of the Revolution that popularity was immense. The triumvirs had met in the Assembly and soon discovered that their talents were complementary: "Duport thought about what had to be done, Barnave said it, and A. de Lameth did it." Barnave was the most illustrious of the three, Duport the most powerful. The Revolution found him ready to fill a great role. Founder and leading spirit of the Society of Thirty, he became an influential member of several committees: research, constitution, criminal law, and taxes. He played a decisive role in all the crucial debates: on combining the three orders, abolishing the "feudal regime" (especially in the drafting of the decrees that gave the sanction of law to the night of August 4), the Declaration of Rights, and the nationalization of Church property, to name a few. This noble scion of the parlementary aristocracy showed no indulgence toward the Ancien Régime. A reader of Rousseau and the physiocrats and an admirer of Montesquieu and Beccaria, he came to Versailles with a mature plan of judicial reform, and events offered him an opportunity to put it into effect. He not only laid the foundations of a new system of justice but better than anyone else pointed out what obstacles remained to be overcome: how to ensure order without limiting rights, how to keep the peace without infringing on individual liberties, and how to make the punishment fit the crime. He was the author of a powerful brief against the death penalty as well as one of the most determined champions of emancipation for the Jews: to deny them citizenship, he warned in December 1789, would be to confound the status quo with the law, prejudice with justice.

FEUILLANTS

But not even a man who had been the voice of the Revolution, like Barnave, or the thinker, like Duport, could determine its course. As it had done before, the Revolution overtook and passed those who had blazed its trail. Once again the triumvirs were overwhelmed by the patriotic press, denounced in the popular societies, and discredited with the Jacobins, over whom Robespierre increased his authority, which ultimately gained him new influence in the Assembly. On April 7, taking advantage of a discussion of ministerial responsibility, he secured passage of a law providing that no member of this or subsequent assemblies could be promoted to the position of minister, a measure aimed squarely at the triumvirs.

Within the patriotic movement a duel began between two now irreconcilable visions of the Revolution. The future Feuillants knew full well that if they wished to enshrine the principles of 1789 in law, it was not enough to have destroyed absolutism and aristocratic society. They would also have to deal with the question of popular sovereignty and establish a clear distinction between the powers of the elected Assembly, which alone was empowered to make law, and those of the various societies that had set themselves up as guardians of the revolutionary spirit. The clubs continued to speak in the name of the people, as if they were regularly constituted deliberative bodies. On May 9, 1791, Le Chapelier, speaking for the constitutional committee, proposed a sweeping indictment of the sections and clubs in response to a challenge that had been laid down by Robespierre two days earlier. The central issue of the conflict was now on the table: Where would revolutionary legitimacy lie, with the Assembly or with the clubs?

The real test of strength came a week later, however, over the question of whether members of the Constituent Assembly should be eligible for reelection to the subsequent legislature. The triumvirs along with the constitutional committee and its secretary, Thouret, believed that they should be. But the Assembly as a whole was far from unanimous. One deputy suggested: "It would be honorable for the Assembly to approve this article by acclamation." Another replied: "Anything approved by acclamation is never honorable." The stormy debate turned into a duel to the death between Duport and Robespierre that consummated the split in the patriotic party. Robespierre launched the attack with a memorable speech in which he revealed a previously unsuspected talent for oratorical improvisation. It was inappropriate, he argued, that the powers of future legislatures be fixed by the very same people who might be called to exercise them. The Assembly could demonstrate its disinterest and eliminate the ambiguity in the situation by opting in favor of noneligibility for reelection. The deputy from Arras received an ovation from the members and gallery, was applauded in the press, and was backed by those Jacobins who were not deputies and wished to be elected to subsequent assemblies. He was also supported by the right, which hoped to weaken the Constitution by eliminating its authors from government. Robespierre realized, as Michelet would later write, that "for both extremes, the Jacobins and the aristocrats, the common enemy to be destroyed was the Constitution, along with the Constitutionals, the natural fathers and defenders of that not very robust infant." Now that he had gained control of the revolutionary movement, he "was not afraid to close the *official* Assembly, in the name of principle, so as to tighten his control over the one *active, effective* Assembly, the great guiding club. . . . Having advised his adversaries to make a mild philosophical retreat, he himself knew just where he wanted to go, right to the true center of the movement." His motion carried almost unanimously. Thus Robespierre effectively nullified the revision of the Constitution in advance by paralyzing those who were in the best position to implement it.

Resigned, Duport replied the next day with a speech whose somber eloquence already assumed ominous accents:

> By degrees, gentlemen, you are being led down a path that leads to veritable and total social disorganization. For some time others have been seeking to inspire in you I am not sure what mania for simple principles. For those behind these ideas, the well-calculated effect is to weaken or destroy all the springs of government: not the abuses—you have gloriously eliminated those—but the salutary and conservative action. Indeed, the fact is that they want to change the form of government entirely. . . . The real danger, gentlemen, is still hidden beneath the cloud of opinion but is already profound and extensive: it is the exaggeration of public ideas, their deviation and lack of a common center, a national interest to hold them together and unite them. One more step and the government will no longer be viable, or else it will be totally concentrated in the executive power alone. For in the distance I see despotism smiling at our petty ways, our petty views, our petty passions, upon which it quietly rests its hopes. [Applause] What they call the Revolution is done. Men will no longer obey the old despots. But if we are not careful, they are ready to fashion themselves new ones, whose power, more recent and more popular, would be a thousand times more dangerous.

Though Robespierre was never named, it became more and more apparent as the speech progressed that he was its target. Duport spoke of men "who rejected principles when what was needed was to establish them [and who exaggerated them] when what was needed was to limit their scope . . . who passed without transition from pusillanimity to enthusiasm because opinion stood at that temperature on the thermometer . . . who assumed no personal responsibility, for it was no responsibility to have fought against all that was reasonable and to have remained continuously in a chair of natural law." In this ostensibly collective portrait no one had any difficulty recognizing the Incorruptible. Duport thus showed himself to have been one of the first—and most profound—exegetes of Robespierrism. His memorable speech revealed what the moderates considered to be inevitable in the Revolution.

The Feuillants would make one final effort, however, to determine the outcome of the Revolution once and for all with the revision of the Constitution. Paradoxically, they enjoyed a brief second wind thanks to the king's flight and the fears it aroused in the Assembly. They achieved undeniable success on the three fundamental questions: the king's authority, limitation of suffrage, and national constitutional conventions. Faced with calls to depose the king, they managed to save both his person and his prerogatives. But in order to ensure the longevity of a constitutional monarchy and protect it from popular pressure, they sought to limit participation in public life to that segment of society whose interests, income, and culture depended on maintaining civil peace. Barnave justified his call for a higher *cens* in these terms: "If it is true that in an established Constitution all honest men, all who want prosperity and peace, have essentially the same interests, then the goal is to place the common interest in the hands of those who present the necessary guarantees to convince everyone that that interest will be adequately protected and defended" (August 11, 1791).

It was also necessary to make sure that such harmony would not be threatened by political crises that might place the Constitution in jeopardy. Jacobins and moderates alike favored an amendment process that would make it possible to improve the Constitution and prevent insurrections, but they differed as to the manner in which constitutional conventions should be called. The Jacobins preferred regular or special constitutional assemblies convoked by popular initiative. The moderates wanted to reserve the power to convoke constitutional assemblies to the legislature. The latter view prevailed.

The Feuillants thus won the parliamentary battle. But they lost a more important battle: the Revolution chose the radical rather than the moderate course and proceeded without them. Excluded from the legislature, eliminated from the Jacobin apparatus, they carried on a rear-guard action out of the public eye, abandoning democratic debate in favor of behind-the-scenes negotiations and intrigues reminiscent of politics under the Ancien Régime. Yet their resources in the period just after the Constituent Assembly disbanded were far from negligible. The Feuillant Club was still in operation. The moderate press was unstinting in its support. The Feuillants controlled the administrative apparatus in Paris and the provinces. And above all, they could count on roughly half the deputies in the new Legislative Assembly. But what good was a parliamentary majority when the focus of revolutionary politics had moved elsewhere? Impressive as the moderate coalition was, it remained, in Barnave's words, without "any principle of motion," without unity or force. The Feuillants were paralyzed and their resources rendered inoperative by the illusion that the Constitution could serve as a rampart of the Revolution if only the king would abandon his misgivings and agree to become a constitutional leader. The illusion was only compounded by the fact that Louis XVI, passive, distrustful, and worst of all powerless, neither could nor would grant the moderates what he had already refused to Mirabeau. Almost a year before August 10 the weakness of the Feuillants thus revealed the flaws in the institutions created by the Revolution in its Constituent Assembly phase.

The Feuillants looked on as helpless spectators as their society crumbled (December 1791). Power went to the Girondins, the embodiment of everything the Feuillants detested: the Republic and the war. Then came the outbreak of hostilities with Austria in April 1792. In this sequence of events that would culminate with the fall of the monarchy, the Feuillants—neutralized, dispersed, and demoralized—once again preceded their adversaries by leaving the scene before being forced to do so by exile or the guillotine.

They were the Revolution's last moderates.

Ran Halévi

FURTHER READING

Aulard, Alphonse. *La Société des Jacobins: Recueil de documents pour l'histoire du Club des Jacobins de Paris,* 6 vols. Paris, 1889–1897.

Barnave, Antoine-Pierre-Joseph-Marie. *De la Révolution et de la Constitution.* Text established and annotated by Patrice Gueniffey. Preface by François Furet. Forthcoming, 1988.

Lameth, Alexandre de. *Histoire de l'Assemblée Constituante,* 2 vols. Paris, 1828–1829.

Lameth, Théodore de. *Mémoires.* Paris, 1813.

Michon, Georges. *Essai sur l'histoire du parti feuillant: Adrien Duport.* Paris, 1924.

RELATED TOPICS

Barnave
Clubs and Popular Societies
Constitution
Jacobinism

Louis XVI
Michelet
Mirabeau
Monarchiens

Revolutionary Assemblies
Robespierre

GIRONDINS

The Girondins had a late baptism. In the revolutionary lexicon there was a Mountain well before there was a Gironde. When Dulaure, in the first issue of the *Thermomètre du jour*, attempted to draw the "physiognomy" of the National Convention and described its parties as "still unstable aggregations of men," he singled out a "Mountain" standing at one extremity on the left, but no Gironde. He cited "Brissotins," "Rolandists," and "Girondists," three denominations for a single group, bound together, according to Dulaure, by the horror of the September massacres. Dulaure's uncertainty attests to a still unsettled terminology. A few months later, during the trial of the Girondins, Billaud-Varenne in assailing the defendants still called them simply "leaders of the right wing." Robespierre referred to them nebulously as "*the* faction." Only Amar, in his indictment, hammered at the "*Girondin* faction."

Do not imagine modern, organized political parties, and do not assume that revolutionary assemblies were divided into two camps with clear boundaries. In the Legislative Assembly future Girondins and future Montagnards had jointly fought the Feuillants and had worked together to vanquish royal authority. Patriots' hearts in those days beat for both "the vigorous Robespierre and the wise Pétion," whom Mme. Roland celebrated in the same sentence. In the Convention newly elected provincial deputies looked on incredulously as those who had battled side by side against despotism and aristocracy now ripped one another apart. In their eyes this was an unnatural confrontation, neither the first nor the last to divide the revolutionary camp, but this time past patching up. Historians in turn have made a particularly dramatic story of this clash, no doubt because it revealed what Sainte-Beuve called a critical line of demarcation within the Revolution and dealt a first blow to the representatives of the nation. The scandal of this split accounts for the persistent efforts to explain it: the struggle between the Girondins and the Montagnards has become a classic problem of revolutionary historiography.

Among the explanations proposed, some have been socioeconomic, others generational, still others ideological. The Girondins have been described as wealthier than their adversaries, older, educated in rival collèges, familiar with different milieus, and nourished on Voltaire rather than Rousseau. No matter which of these accounts is chosen, one senses that the point is to suppress the scandal of a fratricidal struggle by ascribing its origins not to the Revolution itself, nor to the struggle for power that it touched off, but to the development of a preexisting structure. If the elimination of the Gironde by the Mountain was the necessary culmination of a conflict between classes or ideas, a clash between two segments of the bourgeoisie distinguished by their incomes or their theories, then the human waste of the French Revolution seems less terrifying and the lessons of the conflict seem more clear: its meaning is then to have brought about the victory of the *moyenne bourgeoisie* over the *haute bourgeoisie*.

Such interpretations are predicated on a precise identification: out of the nebulous "Brissotins," "Buzotins," and "Girondists" described by Dulaure can one put together a homogeneous group of Girondins? All recent historiography of the Gironde has been absorbed by this question of identity. Detailed enumerations have contributed decisively to knowledge of the Girondins yet still have not made it absolutely clear what the members of the group had in common.

Nothing was less expected than the *journée* of June 2, 1793, when rioters in Paris, continuing a partly unsuccessful demonstration begun two nights earlier, threatened the Convention with cannon and persuaded it to expel twenty-two "factious" deputies, something the sans-culottes had been demanding since the king's trial and the moderates had predicted a thousand times before the fact. Once the Convention had glumly and ingloriously agreed to this mutilation, however, it was essential that the sans-culottes be given the satisfaction of a trial, for fear of yet another *journée*. It was this trial, held in the summer and fall of 1793, that fabricated a Girondin group. From Barère's interventions on June 6 through those of Saint-Just and Billaud-Varenne, and culminating in Amar's indictment on October 3, the number of Girondin conspirators continued to grow: Amar named forty-six conspirators, whereas Saint-Just had named only nine (plus five suspects). If we add to this list of forty-six "factious" deputies those who in one way or another protested the coup of June 2, we arrive at a figure of 140 Girondins. This simple method can be criticized, however, on the grounds that it makes no sense to identify as Girondins those whom the Mountain chose to expel (to have incurred the opprobrium of the Montagnards was not a criterion of membership in any group) or those who protested the coup d'état. In theory it is possible that a deputy may have deplored or been outraged by the amputation of a wing of the Assembly without thereby demonstrating pro-Girondin sympathies.

Over the past twenty years historians, for the most part British and American, have endeavored to refine this preliminary identification, attempting to develop a series of snapshots of the Convention by studying successive votes (roll-call votes on the questions of the king's guilt in January and Marat's guilt in April, and the vote to reinstate the Girondin investigative committee, the so-called Committee of Twelve, in May). This work has led to revision of the number of 140 Girondins, sometimes upward, sometimes downward: Jacqueline Chaumié counts 137, Michael Sydenham favors a figure as high as 200. The most accurate tally has been given by Alison Patrick. From Sydenham's work she arrives at a figure of 58 members of the Girondin "inner circle" (Sydenham had put the number at 60), reconstructed through study of Brissot's personal relations; to this number she adds the 94 deputies who voiced protests after June 2, 8 deputies who offered their assistance to the federalist revolt, and finally those who in some way manifested their opposition to the Terror. When all the counting has been done and redone, we end up with 178 Girondins.

These counts, notwithstanding the polemics that have divided their authors, are all generous to the Girondins, because they include not only the inner circle but also those who voted with the Gironde. But to include them is to expand the Girondin nebula as well as to dilute the Girondin identity: the longest list, that of Sydenham, is thus used, not surprisingly, to support the thesis that the Gironde did not exist. By contrast, in order to argue that the Girondins were a cohesive group, the membership must be limited to the authentic inner circle. Patrice Higonnet takes this tack; he accepts Michelet's judgment that deputies in the Convention were neither Girondin nor Montagnard and refuses to count as Girondins anyone who did not frequent the salons of the inner circle. In this narrow sense one is left with a handful of some 60 Girondins.

How can one choose between the two interpretations? Strictly speaking, the only deputies who can be called Girondins were those who represented the Gironde in the Legislative Assembly: Ducos, Gensonné, Grangeneuve, Guadet, and Vergniaud, all young lawyers and merchants linked by memories of a militant youth (together they had founded the Society of Jacobins of Bordeaux) and by admiration for the eldest and most brilliant of the group, Vergniaud. In addition, Gensonné was connected with Dumouriez, and Guadet and Gensonné had ties to the Roland household; all were linked to Brissot through the cause of black emancipation. The very nicknames pinned on them by their enemies—"Brissotins," "Buzotins," "Rolandins"—attest eloquently to the importance here of personal affinities. Barbaroux and his Marseilles contingent soon swelled the ranks of this small band, which extended its influence and network of contacts through political battles in the Legislative Assembly. These men gathered in the salons of Mme. Dodun and Mme. Roland as well as in the Club de la Réunion and the Valazé Committee, the latter being the most likely place where they might have discussed strategy for the Assembly and planned joint actions. These ephemeral salons, which, though not precisely contemporaneous, were nevertheless quite jealous of one another, could not have been all that the Jacobin imagination made them out to be: shadowy dens of intrigue in which Girondin policy was concocted. Still, these sumptuous gatherings, dominated by brilliant and beautiful women, instigators of so many friendships and enmities and well satisfied to play, through the men they seduced, their part on a great stage, contributed not a little to the Girondins' reputation for cunning, deviousness, and clandestinity. Patriots were repelled by the odor of the Ancien Régime, which hovered in the air and with which it was easy to contrast the austerity of the Jacobins. It is plausible to assume that the salons, held at regular intervals and graced with frequent appearances of illustrious guests, especially Brissot and Gensonné, gave reality and consistency to the inner circle of the Girondins.

But did they for that reason give consistency to the Girondins' political line? Contrary to what Higonnet suggests, it is not clear that the coherence of the Girondins is to be looked for within this select circle. Sydenham's most interesting contribution is to have shown that this small group, whose fate depended on its ability to arouse and enlist sympathies and whose cohesiveness seems at first sight to warrant belief in a firm Girondin "line," was in fact much more divided in its votes than was the larger circle of sympathizers. In the roll-call votes during the king's trial the larger group was more consistently inclined toward clemency than the inner circle, where severity had almost as many adherents as indulgence: Barbaroux, Ducos, Vergniaud, Gensonné, Isnard, and Lasource ultimately voted in favor of severity. The inner group was again divided in April 1793 in the roll-call vote on Marat: of the thirteen "pure" Girondins present, only five voted against Marat. Were these discordances due to the powerful personalities that composed the inner circle, more individualistic than their followers and in some cases—Vergniaud's, for example—quite impervious to influence? If so, then one must give up the hypothesis that the group agreed in advance on a strategy aimed at attaining common goals. And one must revise the widely accepted view that the Girondins were more "visible" than their adversaries and therefore easier to attack through a group trial. The lack of coherence on crucial occasions within the more narrowly defined Girondin group therefore suggests a need to reconsider the major charges against them. It also forces us to ask whether the source of Girondin unity ought not to be located, paradoxically enough, outside the inner circle in what I have called the Girondin nebula, or perhaps even outside the Assembly, in the circles, newspapers, brochures, and other places where the group displayed the fruits of its intellectual labors.

Along with the number of the accused, the charges against the Girondins grew continually over the course of their trial. Barère referred in his speech, still evasive, to the political cunning of the Gironde, to "carefully crafted plots of moderatism." Saint-Just's theme was again "the mysterious and political faction," but he added the charge that all these crafty skills had been employed in the service of royalty. Saint-Just also mentioned the Girondins' exploitation of provincial sentiments, though he did not yet charge them with a conscious project of "federalism." The charge of having sought deliberately to stir up rebellion in the provinces was Billaud-Varenne's personal contribution to the debate. To these allegations Amar's report added a note of asperity and a further charge (destined to enjoy a great future), namely, an incorrect assessment of the "moment": the Girondins had called for a Republic too soon, a charge directed primarily at Brissot and the "premature" petition of the Champ de Mars. Furthermore, throughout the trial, whose escalation also reflected that summer's escalating events (the federalist insurrection and the murder of Marat), the Girondins were seen primarily as "Brissotins." The indictment was constructed so as to place Brissot at the center. Admittedly, Brissot, who had been a freelance journalist and perhaps even a police spy, and who had served everyone at once—Lafayette, the duc d'Orléans, Clavière—had gained a reputation as one who played the Revolution as though it were a casino.

If we neglect the charge of "factionalism"—an all-purpose accusation freely bandied about by the Jacobins—the Montagnard indictment comes down to just two counts: royalism and federalism. The historical literature has sometimes merely repeated these, sometimes added further charges of its own. On the whole the Girondins have not been well served by historians, including the one (Lamartine) who passed as their acolyte. As early as 1835 Sainte-Beuve warned of the "theoretical immolation that some wish to make of the Protestant and corrupt Gironde to Catholic and pure Robespierre." Even for Michelet, who acquitted the Girondins of relations with Louis XVI, Lafayette, and Dumouriez, did not believe in their federalism, and held their declaration of war on all kings to be a "title to eternal glory," something was missing in the Girondins: "the divine fire of the Revolution." Though innocent of the charges against them, they were guilty for not having known how to incarnate the Revolution. Among them there was neither a Danton nor a Robespierre. Their Brissot was pretentious, agitated, and garrulous, a man of expedients and chimeras. Their Vergniaud was an absentminded idealist intermittently shaken by the rage of the weak.

Three new counts were therefore added to the indictment: ill-considered recourse to revolutionary violence, mindless warmongering, and self-interest. The first of these complaints was stated in its classic form by Quinet: by supporting the *journée* of June 20, 1792, by allowing the mob of petitioners to parade before the deputies, the Girondins countenanced the first violation of the rights of representatives. When the sorcerer's apprentices themselves were swept away the following June by an identical crowd, gathered at the doors of the Convention "armed with the very memory," it was only justice being done. The second complaint was dealt with equally severely by Jaurès and Albert Sorel: the Girondins had hoped through war to secure not the triumph of the Revolution but their own personal power. The bitterness of Jaurès' account comes from the futility of a war that circumstances in no way required. Sorel's, by contrast, is inspired by the ineffectiveness of the Gironde, which, having preached war, proved incapable of waging it. Both emphasized the Girondins' lack of seriousness: they did not understand that by calling for war they had imprudently linked their fate to the army's fortunes. The third complaint, not so much political as social, developed a theme first stated by Louis Blanc: the Girondins were champions of liberty, the Montagnards of equality. In Mathiez's view, the struggle between the two factions expressed and symbolized a class struggle: closely allied with commerce and manufacturing interests, the Girondins wished above all to end the Revolution in order to protect their interests and defend their property. Thus the charge of self-interest was added to an already lengthy indictment.

It was the question of war that revealed the split (visible in the Jacobins before the Assembly) in the patriotic party, which for a long time hesitated between Robespierre and Brissot. Brissot, who had been elected to the Legislative Assembly with great difficulty, burned with passion to root out both his royalist and Feuillant adversaries. (The Brissotin party had defined itself in the battle against Barnave as the philanthropic party of friends of blacks.) Hoping to eliminate both obstacles at once, Brissot in December 1791 hit upon the idea of an indirect war: by waging war on a distant enemy, he could attack the infinitely more detestable enemy at home. The war was probably meant to destroy Koblenz: despite the anti-émigré laws passed at the behest of the Girondins, the exodus had only grown worse since Varennes. But the primary purposes of the war were to root out the Feuillants, confound the king, and provide Brissot with the opportunity to play a major role. The only requirements were that the war must be short-lived and remain Continental, so as not to compromise the prosperity of the ports. Brissot, invoking his reputation, based on his travels abroad, as an international expert, guaranteed that these conditions would be met. In this way he sought—successfully—to transform a modest conflict with the bishop-electors of Trier and Mainz into a crusade on behalf of universal liberty, a blitzkrieg to free peoples from their kings.

Brissot, who carried "his triumphant army to all neighboring nations," everywhere installed "municipalities" without firing a shot, and shouted immodestly that his thought was sublime, "as if fate were being decided by rhetorical figures," presented Robespierre with a golden opportunity to portray the irresponsible utopian in an unforgettable sketch of his character. Though enduringly emblematic, the confrontation between Brissot and Robespierre has nevertheless obscured the issue of the Gironde's warmongering. It has left the impression that the Gironde defined itself through war, and that the war had pitted a blind Girondin party against a lucid Montagnard party. The first idea contains a measure of truth: by urging war, the Gironde bound its fate to the vagaries of combat, so much so that its popularity waxed and waned with the armies' victory and defeat, and the party did not survive the series of reverses that came in the spring of 1793 or the treason of Dumouriez, Brissot's friend, for which the Girondins bore the full measure of blame. The second idea, however, cannot stand up to scrutiny: some Girondins were only late supporters of the idea of war (Guadet and Gensonné), others were hesitant (Debry and Lasource), and still others were suspicious and wanted assurances that the offensive would be limited (Fauchet). On the other side Robespierre stood alone. The charge of warmongering is therefore accurate, but it does not single out a Girondin group: the hawkish strategy was common to the whole patriotic left, with which Brissot's universal Republic struck a responsive chord.

The war proved to be a trap, however, which snapped shut on the Girondins. The battle with the Feuillants had cast them in the role of adversaries of constitutional monarchy, almost specialists in tweaking the nose of the court. But with war as their objective they inevitably had to come to an understanding with the Fayettists and with Narbonne, the king's minister. They consequently encountered a first wave of suspicion of royalism, and Robespierre exploited the situation. The second wave was provoked by their association with the government in April 1792, in the person of Clavière and Roland and later Servan, in what was misleadingly called the "Girondin ministry," compounded by the first military reverses. When the king dismissed their ministers in June, they returned to their old tactic of intimidating royalty, as evidenced by their actions on June 20 and by Vergniaud's violent attack on July 3; no sooner did they adopt this tactic, however, than they sought to enter into negotiations with the court over their return to government. The *journée* of August 10, which brought them back into the ministry, did not dispel the suspicions that were heightened by their delaying tactics in the king's trial: the *appelants*, as those who favored appealing the verdict against the king to the people were called, now had the support of all the conservative forces. The Montagnard charge of Girondin royalism is a red herring, but in this period the party was, in Michelet's phrase, "royalized" in spite of itself.

The same ambiguity characterized the Girondins' relation to legality. They are often portrayed as champions of law (sometimes to praise them, sometimes to attack their concern with formal freedoms), yet Quinet saw them as apprentice incendiaries, and Louis Blanc described them as a party of violence. In fact everything in this regard was a matter of timing. Varennes had convinced Mme. Roland of the necessity of a "regeneration by blood," and in April 1792 Brissot called for "great betrayals." No strangers to the Jacobin obsession with a plot, the Girondins contributed to that obsession. They did not initiate the *journée* of June 20, but they did take advantage of it, even if Vergniaud and Isnard did hasten to save the king from harm. They laid the groundwork for August 10 and at times claimed that it was a specifically Girondin *journée*. Even September 1792 did not immediately push the Girondins over to the side of the law. Confronted with the massacres, they reacted with shame and horror, just like the rest of the political class, and in their newspapers and statements they sought to set the events in context (the massacres were a response to the monsters of Koblenz and the perjury of Louis XVI) and diminish their magnitude (the perpetrators had implemented a rough popular justice by attempting to distinguish "correctly" between the innocent and the guilty). The desire to erase all memory of the monstrous event as quickly as possible dictated this quasiacceptance of illegality. It was short-lived, however, for within a few weeks, still reeling from the shock, the Girondins had gone over to the side of legalism, support for which grew among them over the winter and spring of 1793 along with their fear of Paris and of sans-culotte agitation. Was this a definitive conversion, so that henceforth one can identify the Girondins with respect for law? Not at all: their attack on Marat in April 1793 made short shrift of the representative principle: "But the monster was a deputy," one of them said in a moment of scruple. Having rejoined the revolutionary assemblies after Thermidor, most of them assented to the coup of 18 Fructidor in order to save the Republic. So Quinet was right: their acceptance of illegality was a question of timing. But what is legalism when subordinated to opportunism?

By contrast, the federalism for which they have been criticized seems to have been their most persistent idea and was likely the genuine basis of their unity. Yet if one takes the word "federalism" in a theoretical sense, the Montagnard accusation could not have been farther from the truth: the Girondins never ceased to believe in the sovereignty of the Convention and the unity of the Republic; Condorcet's abortive Constitution, though it sought to establish an equilibrium between Paris and the provinces, was in no sense "federalist"; and only Buzot showed sympathy for the American model. Nothing could be closer to the truth, however, if by federalism one means hatred of Paris and reliance on the départements: it was Mme. Roland who first proposed the idea of convoking the départemental guard, and it was the Girondins who inspired the départemental petitions against Paris. From the king's trial to the indictment of Marat, the Girondins compulsively displayed this hatred on numerous occasions. It inspired the obsessive denunciations by which they gradually isolated themselves from the rest of the Convention, the petitions to moderates to recapture the Paris sections, and the ultimate battles against the Commune in May.

At first these moves appeared to meet with success: on May 18, on the basis of Guadet's denunciation of the Paris authorities, the Girondins secured the appointment of an investigative committee whose members were loyal to them. On May 24 Hébert and Varlet were arrested. The next day Isnard pronounced his notorious curses. In this context—a struggle to the death against the Parisian authorities—the appeal to the provinces was less an end than a means. The heart of the problem was the Girondins' encounter with a rival power; this was the true origin of the conflict. ("No longer did the whole of the enlightened universe belong to these infatuated minds," as Jaurès put it.) Against those who robbed them, as Sainte-Beuve would say in his portrait of Mme. Roland, of "that central stage upon which one encountered at every step the nourishment of intelligence and the excitement of glory," the Girondins exhibited an indefatigable and suicidal zeal. This explains why the Gironde, in opposition to the Paris that it abhorred, sought the support of a moderate bourgeoisie favorable to economic liberty, hostile to taxation, and frightened by the escalating egalitarian demands of the sans-culottes. Roland had always inveighed against the taxers and predicted that regulation of grain prices would simply cause the markets to disappear. Nevertheless, the economic liberalism of the Gironde was not the fruit of an "inflexible dogmatism," as Jaurès maintained. It coexisted with a protectionist position on foreign trade. Compromise was possible: during the economic crisis of spring 1792 Fauchet had proposed tempering freedom of commerce with some state controls. Furthermore, the economic analysis of the Girondins was shared by the entire Convention, which continually rejected calls for taxation in the name of the principle of private property. Robespierre, however, who was the first to support a state-controlled economy, shared Vergniaud's position in February 1793. Economic and social views thus did not single out a Girondin group except for the period of a few weeks (the month of May) that separated the Mountain's unenthusiastic embrace of sans-culotterie from the Gironde's exclusion.

Thus, if we follow the history of the Girondins in this way, we see the Revolution's major conflict in its proper context. It became a legend not just because the Girondins sang as they mounted the scaffold in November but also because the clash between the Gironde and the Mountain was a clash between powerful personalities: on the question of war Robespierre rose alone in opposition to Brissot; in the king's trial Robespierre and Saint-Just alone argued for the impossibility of judging the king; again, it was Robespierre alone in the economic crisis of the spring of 1793; against Guadet and Brissot, who at the Jacobin Club celebrated Condorcet's collaboration with Voltaire and d'Alembert and derided Providence, it was again Robespierre who replied by branding all those great men with an indelible mark of infamy—they had been tormenters of Rousseau. This final skirmish was typical, moreover, for it established the image of the Girondins as anticlericals— a most dubious proposition when one knows their ties to the constitutional clergy. One senses that in the ineradicable struggle for control of the Convention, party leaders availed themselves of every opportunity to promote and rekindle confrontation.

Was the Girondin identity totally diluted as a result? The idea that best united them was one that they had taken from their Feuillant adversaries: that of ending the Revolution, which inspired all their actions after August 10, 1792. Expelled from the Jacobins in October, Brissot responded that two of the three necessary revolutions—one against despotism, the other against monarchy—had been completed, leaving the third, which was to quell anarchy. Vergniaud in March 1793 divided the Convention into two groups: one wished to "sustain the effervescence of the Revolution" because it believed it to be—Vergniaud was equitable—"indispensable to the energy of our defense"; while the other, to which he belonged, believed that the time had come "to halt the revolutionary movement."

The Girondins did not merely spread this well-worn idea to their sympathizers, who were more strongly in favor of it than the Girondins themselves, as shown by their votes for clemency toward Louis XVI and severity toward Marat. It was the idea of ending the Revolution that attached the nebulous sympathies of the larger group to the inner circle and that explains how, just four days before their downfall, the Girondins still had enough support in the Convention to win reinstatement of the Committee of Twelve. The most recent study, which uses sophisticated methods to revise all previous estimates from Sydenham to Patrick, shows that in the last two roll-call votes—against Marat and for reinstatement of the Twelve—a homogeneous Girondin group stands out much more clearly than in the votes connected with the king's trial; this group acted in concert and in these instances clearly differentiated itself from the Plain. If the Girondin faction existed, it was surely on the occasion of these two votes, which admittedly came in a radicalized political climate and whose content lent itself to what was not yet party discipline but something very much like it.

Finally, the idea of preventing a revolutionary resurgence was expressed more clearly outside the assemblies, in the Girondins' writings rather than in their votes. If their politics were incoherent, their editorial policy was remarkably consistent. Through their newspapers (*La feuille villageoise, La sentinelle, La chronique du mois*), presses (primarily that of the *Cercle Social*), brochures, pamphlets, and satires they were able to wield what Baudot called "all the trumpets of Renown." They placed their talents as publicists in the service of a firm anti-Jacobin policy. They presented themselves as champions of an enlightened, rational politics as opposed to the irrational impulses of the Jacobin multitude. They exaggerated their consistency by antedating their republicanism and opposition to the Jacobins. To be sure, the Montagnards helped shape the intellectual identity of the Girondins by branding them "men of the quill." But the Girondins themselves pitched in. And after Thermidor it was as an "underground colony of patriotic orators and republican philosophers" that Chénier called them to resume their places on the benches of the Convention.

*
**

It remains to be seen whether this political unity can be explained by what preceded it—that is, whether the geographical or social or generational makeup of the Girondin group prefigured and predicted its expulsion by the Montagnards.

These hypotheses have motivated many scholars and contributed to knowledge of the group. Geographic unity? A glance at the Girondin map shows that certain regions were strongly represented. These were not necessarily the wealthiest: some very poor départements (Morbihan, Hautes-Alpes) are found together with some prosperous ones (Seine-Inférieure, Gironde, Bouches-du-Rhône). Broadly speaking, Girondin France favored the southern and western portions of the country, and the great port cities played an important part: the geography is the same as for the federalist insurrection. Generational unity? This was a period in which most politicians were young men, and on the average the Girondins were older than their adversaries, belying the notion that they were a brilliant and irresponsible group of youths, a reputation that has become attached to their memory. Socioeconomic unity? This has been the most controversial point since Mathiez attempted to interpret the conflict between the Girondins and the Montagnards as a class struggle between two segments of the bourgeoisie. But close scrutiny has revealed more of an identity than an antinomy. Nobles are found on both sides of the conflict. Men on both sides purchased national properties. Patrice Higonnet recently added an interesting item to the debate by showing that the leading conventionnels of both the right and the left were relatively wealthy. Their followers on both sides were men of more modest means, a highly homogeneous intellectual petty bourgeoisie. If "Gironde" and "Mountain" are used to describe a climate rather than a group, therefore, the partisans of both sides are interchangeable. If attention is focused on the Girondin inner circle, we find a somewhat more socially mobile and urban group with somewhat closer relations to commerce and manufacturing interests than their Montagnard counterparts. But, Higonnet concludes, these are "subtle differences."

Are these subtle differences sufficient to justify the contention that the political was determined by the social? For Mathiez this was self-evident: the Girondins defended their class interests. Economic and social antagonism preceded the political conflict and made it inevitable. Georges Lefebvre was closer to the position of Jaurès, who said of the Girondins that apart from any question of economic determinism there are "groups bound together by passion." Lefebvre believed that what was initially a political conflict later took on a "social coloration." The latter was thus a consequence, not a cause. Albert Soboul combined Mathiez with Lefebvre without apparent awareness of the impediments to such a marriage of interpretations: "Beyond the political aspects of the conflict loom, as usual, the social motivations that were one of its essential causes." Here, "beyond" points to a social conflict that was a terminal efflorescence of the political. "Essential cause," however, indicates the primacy of the social. "As usual" tips us off to the fact that the question will not be dealt with.

It is in any case unrealistic to rely on a concept of causality that makes it necessary to link political opinions so unstable and so dependent on the revolutionary situation to far more stable factors such as wealth or social position. How can the class interests of the Montagnards explain why, having argued after Varennes in favor of the contention that the king was a citizen, they changed their tack a year later at the time of the king's trial? How can one explain why Girondins such as Ducos and Boyer-Fonfrède, who owned property in Santo Domingo, actively supported a revolt of the black population that threatened to cost them their fortunes? And how can one account for the fact that the socialist idea came of age in the *Cercle Social,* filled with Girondins identified as champions of the industrial and commercial bourgeoisie? The road that goes from the social to the political, rough enough in ordinary times, became totally impassable during the Revolution.

It must be concluded, therefore, that the conflict was largely dependent on the vagaries of the Revolution. Even the Girondin idea of ending the Revolution, so often judged to be emblematic of their regressive politics, must be seen in light of the situation that existed at the time it was proposed; it was characteristic more of a moment than of a faith. Levasseur acknowledged in his memoirs that he and his Montagnard colleagues had committed an injustice against the Girondins: "Whatever hitched itself to the chariot of the Revolution in order to hold it back was the same in our eyes. What is more, this error was so natural that the Girondins fell into a similar one in regard to the Constitutionals."

Mona Ozouf

ACTORS

FURTHER READING

Darnton, Robert. "A Spy in Grub Street," in *The Literary Underground of the Old Regime*. Cambridge, Mass., 1982.

Di Padova, Theodore. "The Question of Girondin Motives: A Response to Sydenham," *French Historical Studies,* vol. 9, 1976, 432–447.

Higonnet, Patrice. "The Social and Cultural Antecedents of Revolutionary Discontinuity: Montagnards and Girondins," *English Historical Review,* 1985.

Kates, Gary. *The Cercle Social, the Girondins, and the French Revolution*. Princeton, 1984.

Lamartine, Alphonse de. *Histoire des Girondins*. Paris, 1984 (reprint).

Lewis-Beck, Michael, Anne Hildreth, and Alan Spitzer. "Was There a Girondist Faction in the National Convention (1792–1793)?" To appear in *French Historical Studies,* spring 1988.

Patrick, Alison. "Political Divisions in the French National Convention, 1792–1793," *Journal of Modern History,* vol. 41, 1969, 421–474.

――― *The Men of the First French Republic: Political Alignments in the National Convention of 1792*. Baltimore, 1972.

Proceedings of the Colloquium "Girondins et Montagnards," Paris, Société des Etudes Robespierristes, 1980.

Sydenham, Michael John. *The Girondins*. London, 1961.

RELATED TOPICS

Condorcet
Federalism
Feuillants
Jaurès

King's Trial
Lafayette
Marat
Michelet

Montagnards
Quinet
Revolutionary Assemblies
Revolutionary *Journées*

Wille,
*Portrait of Danton
on His Way to Execution.*
Musée Carnavalet, Paris.

Danton (Alexandre Koubitzky) in Abel Gance's *Napoleon*.

Bust of Marat.
Musée Carnavalet, Paris.

Marat (Antonin Artaud)
in his bathtub in
Abel Gance's *Napoleon.*

Delaroche,
*The Girondins
on Their Way
to Execution.* 1793.
Musée Carnavalet, Paris.

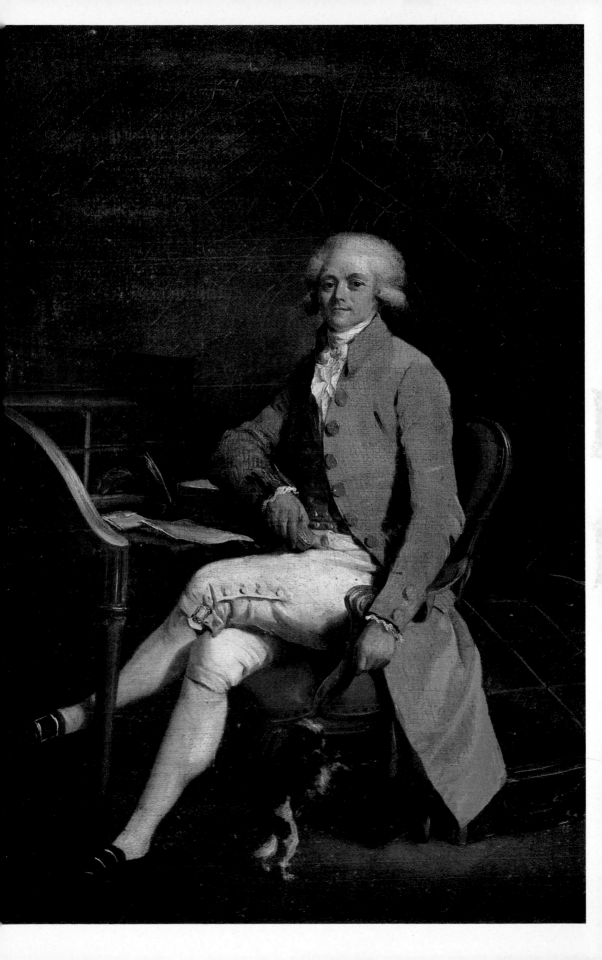

Le petit Condé piquant Des Deux L'autriche
Sur. Lequel il Est Monté

Retour d'un Emigré

Revolutionary Patrol.
Musée Carnavalet, Paris.

...igration: Four
...ricatures. 1792–1793.

...e Prince of Condé.
...sée Carnavalet, Paris.

...e Return of an Emigré.
...sée Carnavalet, Paris.

...risian Sans-culotte.
...sée Carnavalet, Paris.

...ober 16, 1793:
...e Furies on the Steps
...aint-Roch.
...sée Carnavalet, Paris.

Ronot,
...e Last Montagnards. 1882.
...ée de la Révolution Française,
Vizille.

Bacler d'Albe, *General Bonaparte in Milan in Year V: Head of the Army of Italy*. Château de Malmaison.

HÉBERTISTS

I s Hébertism a useful name? As Georges Lefebvre pointed out, Hébert was never the leader of a party, and it was only later that the term "Hébertist" was applied to the ultrarevolutionary tendency represented in 1793–1794 by the group known at the time as Cordeliers. Revolutionary historiography has not been kind to this group, and particularly to Hébert. In describing the Paris Commune on August 10, 1792, Michelet spoke of "weasels with pointy snouts ideally adapted for sniffing blood," a species typified by two men: "Chaumette, a medical student and journalist, and Hébert, a ticket seller at sideshows and writer of ditties before he achieved a terrible celebrity under the name Père Duchesne," that is, as the editor of a newspaper that common people "used to toss down every morning like a shot of bad brandy." Jaurès, who was so sensitive about the memory of Jacques Roux and the enragés, wrote that "the Hébertist party had neither a social program nor a religious program nor military tactics nor an administrative system nor vigor nor humanity" and "represented nothing but a desire for more blood, unrestrained martial administration, and exhausting warfare." For Jaurès, who was thinking of *Père Duchesne* (sometimes spelled Duchêne), "Hébertism wore a saber and a belligerent mustache" and "was the first appearance, in demagogic form, of militarism in the French Revolution." It embodied a popular form of militaristic chauvinism that would join with other, similar currents during the Empire. Furthermore, when Jaurès comes to the Cordeliers' attempted coup in Ventôse, Year II (March 1794), he describes a party "led by a man as inconsistent, as mediocre in both intelligence and feeling, as fickle and cowardly as Hébert." More recently some historians have been just as extreme in expressing opposite judgments.

Sound historical method requires, however, that we distinguish carefully between the newspaper *Père Duchesne*, its editor Hébert, and the Club des Cordeliers, which was far from a monolithic political party. Originally Père Duchesne was a familiar and beloved if acid-tongued character of eighteenth-century popular theater, who appeared in the company of Mère Duchesne, Jean Bart, and Les Poissardes (The Fishwives). Their vulgar, sexual language lent itself to revolutionary uses, and not only the press but also the theater seized the opportunity. In 1788 Père Duchesne appeared in a comic carnival tale. In 1789 he figured in two comedies that played in fairground and boulevard theaters. In the end, however, it was the press that really adopted the name. A recent study of twelve periodicals and forty-two separate articles entitled "Père Duchesne" has pinpointed three distinct types of Duchesne literature: one right wing, one Fayettist, and one left wing. Hébert's newspaper, which first appeared in September 1790 and continued publication until February 1794, was not only the longest-lived of all but also the only one to exert any influence on the Paris sans-culottes. In the words of Albert Soboul, "It was, as much and perhaps even more than Marat's *Ami du peuple*, both the voice and the guide of the popular masses." After Marat's assassination on July 13, 1793, the enragés and Hébertists fought over his legacy, but the efforts of Jacques Roux and Leclerc (the enragé leaders) were in vain. Hébert's *Père Duchesne* became the newspaper of the masses, particularly after Hébert's friend Vincent saw to it that it was distributed to soldiers in the army.

Hébert the man was quite different from his newspaper's hero. In a sense he was a man who had come down in society. The son of a master goldsmith, born into a middle-class family in Alençon in 1747, he had had a tumultuous youth. After an unfortunate episode that resulted in a jail sentence, he found himself in Paris in 1780, where he spent the next eleven years in poverty, misery, and humiliation. Unlike the leading journalists of the Revolution's early years, Hébert did not participate in the great outpouring of emotion that occurred in 1789. He was an obscure ticket taker at the Théâtre des Variétés. In 1790 he ventured into journalism with an article entitled "Abbé Maury's Little Fast." Then he started *Père Duchesne*. In early 1791 the paper attacked Lafayette, Mirabeau, the moderates, and the king. Hébert joined the Club des Cordeliers in March 1791 and signed the Champ de Mars petition after the king's flight to Varennes. After the insurrection of August 10, 1792, he was elected to the Commune's general council and was subsequently appointed deputy to Chaumette, the Commune's prosecutor. He failed, however, to win election as a deputy to the Convention, and the Convention in turn refused to appoint him minister of the interior. He found his true place in the Cordeliers, of which he was one of the most respected leaders. He always felt a certain resentment toward the men of 1789 who had gone on to become government leaders.

Other members of the Cordelier Club also distinguished themselves. Chaumette was another leader who had made his mark on August 10 and who was beloved by the sans-culottes for his simplicity of language and dress. Hanriot was a former customs clerk who became commander in chief of the National Guard and played a key role on June 2, 1793. The offices of the Ministry of War were staffed by members of the Cordeliers, two of whom— Vincent and Ronsin—gained particular prominence. The former was secretary general of the ministry and an influential figure in the Club des Cordeliers. The son of a prison guard, he believed that the Revolution ought to provide an opportunity for those excluded from the elite under the Ancien Régime. In September 1793 a sweeping purge provided him with an occasion to fill the offices of his ministry with sans-culottes. Ronsin had enlisted in the army in 1786 at the age of seventeen, only to quit four years later to enter the theater. He does not figure in the history of the Revolution until after August 10. He served first as a *commissaire* with the executive council, then held the post of *ordonnateur* with the army of Belgium, and later became the director of an office in the war ministry. In March 1793 he went to fight in the Vendée and appointed himself general. Recalled to Paris, he was named in September to head the Revolutionary Army sent to reconquer Lyons, surrounded by a group of ambitious young men for whom the Republic's troubles provided a golden opportunity.

These men had various sympathizers and opportunistic allies. Some belonged to the Paris Commune, whose mayor, Pache, was for a long time considered to have been one of them, although it now appears that he was only a cautious sympathizer. Other allies were found in the Convention itself, where in September 1793 Collot d'Herbois and Billaud-Varenne were chosen to sit on the Committee of Public Safety thanks to the influence of the Cordeliers. Broadly speaking, the Cordelier program had three fundamental points (which were pressed, however, only when circumstances permitted). First, for the Cordeliers the revolutionary war was a crusade for liberty. From this came the group's "militaristic" outlook, which was denounced by Jaurès. Second, the Cordeliers backed the ultraterrorist policies that had been pursued in Lyons and Nevers by government representatives but that had run into opposition in Paris from the more cautious Montagnards. Finally, the Cordeliers promoted de-Christianization, which shocked Robespierre.

Above all, these latecomers to the Revolution experienced a kind of generational conflict with the patriots of 1789, with whom they also competed for jobs. Robespierre was not wrong when he said, "You want our positions." They aimed to use popular discontent to gain power. But hadn't the Montagnards done the same on June 2? And what about the enragés, who raised even greater demands? For a period of somewhat less than a year the Cordeliers steered a careful course between the two.

The Cordelier movement can be divided into three phases: before June 2, 1793, from June to September, and from September 1793 to February or March 1794.

Prior to June 2 Hébert and the Commune had been hostile to demands for price controls and ultraterrorist measures as expressed in petitions by the sans-culottes backed by the enragés. On February 25 and 26 laundresses demonstrated against grocers to protest the high price of soap. Jacques Roux defended the demonstrators, but Pache did everything in his power to halt the disturbances. The Commune's general council blamed all the turmoil on Roux, and Hébert accepted the Jacobin interpretation that the trouble had been fomented by aristocrats disguised as sans-culottes and Brissotins. "Former marquis dressed as coalmen and wigmakers and countesses disguised as fishwives—the very ones who shouted 'Mercy!' the day Capet lost his taste for wine—have fanned out into the faubourgs, warehouses, and markets to stir up rebellion and looting. . . . Parisians, know your real enemies! The Brissotins and Rolandins are doing you more harm than the hoarders. Beat the daylights out of them and I tell you it will all be over. Do it!" (*Père Duchesne*, no. 219). The tactics behind this declaration are clear: to stem the popular movement against the high cost of supplies and support the Montagnards in their fight to eliminate the Girondins from the Convention. After the first defeats in Belgium, when Varlet on March 9 and 10 urged the sections to join an insurrection, the Commune refused to go along. Neither Chaumette nor Hébert, much less Pache, wished to see an insurrection that might drive both the Mountain and the Plain into the arms of the Gironde. *Père Duchesne* continued its campaign against the enragés, whom it lumped together with émigrés and traitors: "They're the ones, damn it, who on hearing people moan about the high cost of goods dressed as workers and infiltrated the faubourgs and marketplaces to advise the sans-culottes to loot warehouses and shops."

It was hard to maintain such tactics for long, however. In April and May, as pressure from the sans-culottes increased and the Mountain and Plain offered concessions (which became the first steps toward the Terror), the Commune and the Cordeliers, though still in doubt concerning what to do about high prices, lent their support to the revolutionary movement that was developing in the sections. To be sure, on the eve of May 31, after Hébert, arrested along with Varlet, had been freed, the Cordeliers had no desire to see the insurrection planned by the insurrectional committee of the Evêché proceed without control from above. Hébert and Chaumette did everything they could to moderate the movement. They could not issue orders, however, since they were not the ones who had proposed the insurrection; that was the work of Varlet and Jacques Roux. Nevertheless, it was Hanriot and his gunners who determined the outcome on June 2.

Was that outcome truly a victory? The Montagnards did succeed in eliminating the Girondins from the Convention, but it was not in order to turn that body over to the ultrarevolutionaries. Furthermore, until the assassination of Marat on July 13, the Cordeliers, worried about the enragés on their left, pursued a tactic of reconciliation with the Montagnard Convention. A glance at the contents of *Père Duchesne* confirms the continuity of this ambiguous political line. Hébert sought to reassure wealthy property owners: "The sans-culottes have nothing against the property of the rich." The paper also called for abiding by the people's wish to punish its enemies, disarm those suspected of opposing the Revolution, purge the bureaus of government, and take steps against the Girondins expelled from the Convention on June 2. At the same time, however, Hébert refuted the enragés' arguments and attacked their demands for price controls: "Where are these so-called hoarders? In Paris? No, damn it, in the leading commercial cities. So you damn well ought to go looking for them there, and not in Paris, where there are only retailers. The millionaires of Bordeaux and Marseilles don't give a damn if you loot one of their boats on the Seine when their warehouses and ships are groaning with merchandise." In an odd way this anticipates later French populist movements such as the Poujadists of the 1950s, but with a curious twist: here Paris is the city of the humble and the provinces are the stronghold of the rich. On June 9, when Varlet's section called for the *maximum général* (universal price and wage controls) and a law against hoarders, Hébert and Chaumette rejected the demand on the grounds that it might well prevent the Convention from getting down to its essential mission, that of drafting a new constitution. Neither the "soap riots" of June 25–28 nor the petition that Jacques Roux submitted to the Convention altered this line. On June 30 twelve Jacobin delegates went to the Cordeliers to disavow Roux's petition, and the Cordelier leaders came down hard on the priest from Gravilliers: "Your petition," said Chaumette, "is a clarion call for looting and for a revolution in ownership." Collot d'Herbois later recounted the events of that day: "You should have seen Hébert examine that hypocrite priest's face by the light of truth's torch, which melted away his mask of filthy mud." It is difficult to see Hébert as the "leader of the sans-culottes."

Marat's murder triggered a war of succession between Roux and Leclerc on the one hand and Hébert on the other. Roux, seemingly oblivious to Marat's vehement attacks on him, published *"L'ami du peuple," by Marat's Ghost.* Leclerc and the Society of Revolutionary Republicans invoked Marat's name. But it was Hébert who most openly claimed Marat's legacy. Before the Commune on July 13 he shouted: "If I thought I counted for anything, I would tell you that every day I receive letters containing the most serious threats." And on July 21 he told the Jacobins: "If a successor to Marat is needed, if a second victim is required, he is ready and resigned to his fate: I am that victim."

Hébert won the battle. With the demise of Marat's paper (*Publiciste de la République française*), *Père Duchesne* was the only great popular newspaper that remained, and it had the backing of the Cordeliers, which had decided to make a shrine of the embalmed remains of the "ami du peuple." Yet Marat's legacy inevitably deformed the propaganda and political tactics of the Cordeliers. From July to early September *Père Duchesne* and the Cordelier leaders adhered as closely as possible to the sans-culotte line, calling for further terrorist measures, massive recruitment of troops, price controls, and laws against hoarders. "Let every citizen who can walk arm himself with pick or saber or skewer or scythe and make the German bear dance the Carmagnole. And let our wives and daughters boil oil and burn sulfur to rain down on any soldier of despotism who may dare to enter our cities." And further: "Let the Convention declare eternal war on hoarders." *Père Duchesne* broadened the definition of the "suspect" to include "all the brutes who until now have lived exclusively on the misfortunes of others": wholesalers, hoarders, and other wealthy parasites. This required a new view of government. On August 1 Hébert withdrew his support of Montagnard policy. From that point on *Père Duchesne* relentlessly attacked the government as "a new clique of scoundrels and intriguers who are attempting to take the place of the Brissotins and lead the Convention down the garden path." Despite concessions by the Convention (which voted in favor of the *levée en masse,* mass recruitment, on August 23), preparations for a new revolutionary *journée* were under way. At the end of August *Père Duchesne* adopted slogans for which it had vehemently reproached the enragés in the past: "Merchants have no fatherland, damn it! They supported the Revolution as long as they thought it would be useful to them. They lent the sans-culottes a hand to destroy the nobility and the parlements, but only so that they themselves could take the place of the aristocrats." On September 4 the rioters invaded the Hôtel-de-Ville. Chaumette and Hébert in extremis joined in planning the insurrection. (News of Toulon's surrender to the English had arrived on September 2.) Listen to Hébert: "Let the people go tomorrow en masse to the Convention. Let them surround it, as they did on August 10, September 2, and May 31." Hébert himself took no part in the action on the fifth, but on the fourth Chaumette had emphasized the social orientation of the movement: "I, too, have been poor, so I know what the poor are like. Now we have open warfare of the rich against the poor. They want to crush us. Well, we must stop them and crush them ourselves. We have the power." On September 5 armed sections surrounded the Convention, prodding Pache and Chaumette at their head, calling for the creation of a Revolutionary Army, the arrest of suspects, and the purge of the revolutionary committees. On all these points the Convention gave in. But it retained the one essential thing: power. Shortly thereafter the enragés were rendered harmless. That left the Cordeliers, whose pressure succeeded only in winning Billaud-Varenne and Collot d'Herbois places on the Committee of Public Safety. These men proved not to be very reliable allies and abandoned the Cordeliers on the eve of their downfall.

September 5, 1793, had two contradictory consequences. On the one hand, the *journée* made it possible to give a definitive structure to the revolutionary government—a wartime dictatorship, which was what the sans-culottes initially wanted. But for that very reason it increased the means available to the Committee of Public Safety to eliminate what Robespierre called "factions": a "moderate" wing, of which Danton and Camille Desmoulins, especially the latter, would become the spokesmen (and whose newspaper, *Le vieux cordelier,* was beginning to establish itself as a serious rival to *Père Duchesne*), and the Cordelier group itself, which continued to do battle. This was a "war on two fronts," but for the men of the Committee of Public Safety, especially Robespierre, the two fronts were not equal. From the end of November 1793 until mid-January 1794 Robespierre relied on Danton and the new moderates to combat ultrarevolutionary "exaggeration." Not until both enemies had made tactical errors did he move against the two simultaneously.

Neither *Père Duchesne* nor the Cordelier leaders ended their campaign after the September Days. They actually accentuated their criticisms, taking advantage of continued tension in sans-culottes ranks. Not content simply to press for all-out repression, they openly attacked the Montagnards. "Why the hell aren't certain of the new-style Montagnards, who a few months ago were yapping like mongrels amid the toads of the Swamp, considered to be suspects?" These "new Brissotins" had to be purged from the Convention. As Danton and his friends, and especially Desmoulins, began to show greater "indulgence," Hébert thundered—in vain, because the attacks on the Hébertist leaders resulted in the arrest, on December 17, of Vincent, Ronsin, and Héron (an agent of the Committee of General Security). The majority's "left wing" reacted, however. Returning from Lyons on December 21, Collot d'Herbois praised Ronsin and denounced indulgence. The liberation of Vincent and Ronsin on February 2 (14 Pluviôse, Year II) seemed to be a success. But the food crisis in Ventôse (February-March 1794) encouraged the Hébertists to broaden their attacks. On 12 Ventôse Ronsin spoke of insurrection. On the fourteenth (March 4) the Cordeliers veiled the Rights of Man. Preparations for a new and "holy" insurrection were under way. Collot d'Herbois made one last attempt at compromise, but to no avail: it was vehemently rejected by Ronsin. The end had come. Abandoned by Pache, Chaumette, Hanriot, and Bouchotte, the Cordelier leaders were arrested on the night of 23–24 Ventôse (March 3–4). In keeping with the usual practice, genuine militants such as Hébert, Vincent, Ronsin, and Momoro were lumped together with more or less suspect foreigners. Chaumette, spared at first, was taken in a second group along with Hébert's widow.

The trial in Germinal was decisive, far more than that of Danton and Desmoulins, legend to the contrary notwithstanding. It was the prelude to Thermidor and the return to bourgeois liberalism. The Commune of Paris had its membership replenished and its structure bureaucratized; the popular societies were gradually eliminated. As Michelet saw clearly, "the genius of Paris disappeared with its Commune."

Denis Richet

FURTHER READING

Herleaut, General Auguste-Philippe. *Le Colonel Bouchotte, ministre de la guerre en l'an II*. Paris, 1946.
——— *Le général rouge Ronsin (1751–1794): La Vendée, l'armée révolutionnaire parisienne*. Paris, 1956.
Jacob, Louis. *Hébert le Père Duchesne, chef des sans-culottes*. Paris, 1960.
Soboul, Albert. *Les sans-culottes parisiens en l'an II: Histoire politique et sociale des sections de Paris, 2 juin 1793–9 thermidor an II*. La Roche-sur-Yon, 1958. Reprinted Paris, 1958, and 1962 with the subtitle *Mouvement populaire et gouvernement révolutionnaire*.
——— "Hébert," introduction to the reprinting of *Père Duchesne (1790–1794)*, 10 vols. Paris, 1970. Reprinted in Albert Soboul, *Portraits de révolutionnaires*, Paris, 1986.
Walter, Gérard. *Hébert et le Père Duchesne*. Paris, 1946.

RELATED TOPICS

Committee of Public Safety	*Maximum*	Revolutionary *Journées*
De-Christianization	Michelet	Robespierre
Enragés	Montagnards	Sans-culottes
Jaurès	Paris Commune	Terror
Marat	Revolutionary Government	

Monarchiens

O f all the revolutionary parties the monarchiens were the first to take the stage and the first to leave it. No sooner did they organize than they were defeated: in August 1789, when the party was born, it was already swamped by the left wing of the Assembly, viewed with suspicion by the galleries, denounced by the patriotic press and the orators of the Palais-Royal, and worst of all transcended by the event that had momentarily lifted it up and that would soon sweep it away in the whirlwind of the October Days. The monarchiens were the embodiment of a particular moment in French history, that brief interlude in the spring and summer of 1789 when the Revolution had left the Ancien Régime behind but had yet to abolish it entirely. The party's political fate is entirely comprised within that interval: the monarchiens were at once the authors and ramparts of the revolution of the Third Estate, its symbol and its first scapegoat. They lent it the imperious voice of public opinion, even as they brandished the monarchy's deeds of ownership.

In contrast to Sieyès, whom they feared, and unlike Mirabeau, whom they suspected, the monarchiens did not speak the language of democracy and expressed something other than the Revolution. Nation, king, law: in content as well as form, the monarchien project, modeled on the English Constitution, embodied the reformist spirit of an age known for its enlightened schemes. These voices, which denounced abuses and clamored for a constitution, which never compromised on the issues of deliberation in common and voting by head, drew most of their inspiration and ideas from the legacy of the Enlightenment. There they found, along with an invincible distrust of any kind of political upheaval, the fundamental values of progress and tolerance, as well as the ambition to carry out a deliberate reform of institutions and men under the aegis of an enlightened monarch, who would remain on the throne as the best possible guarantor of national regeneration. This determination to reconcile the rights of princes with the rights of man would be shattered by the Constituent Assembly's Revolution. The failures that marked the monarchiens' unhappy itinerary gradually lifted the veil that had lain over a devastated political culture. The Ancien Régime had outlived its time, and there remained no possibility of appealing to the past as the foundation of political legitimacy. The monarchiens' real weakness was their failure to understand this change, much less to accept it; they had hoped to build, as Barnave later put it, "with bricks that had just been smashed," and they remained wedded to an intangible project while everything around them was being turned upside down.

The history of the monarchiens is first of all the history of a man: Jean-Joseph Mounier, born in 1758, the son of a Grenoble cloth merchant. A lawyer and later a royal judge, he became in the spring of 1788 the leader and symbol of Dauphiné's revolt against the edicts of Lamoignon and Brienne aimed at quelling the opposition of the parlements. "Passionately reasonable," as Mme. de Staël would call him, and firm to the point of brutality, he had neither Barnave's graceful style nor Mirabeau's magical eloquence but rather a strength and consistency that made his voice irresistibly influential.

On June 14, during an illegal meeting of the three orders in Grenoble, he succeeded in persuading nobles and lawyers to join in a unanimous denunciation of "ministerial despotism." At this gathering it was announced that there would soon be a meeting of the Estates of Dauphiné, in which the size of the Third Estate had already been doubled. This declaration, followed by an intense campaign to influence public opinion, cleared the way for the even more celebrated assembly at Vizille. Here, in a major innovation, the three orders met together in one chamber and with a single voice called for restoration of the parlements, reestablishment of the Provincial Estates, and above all the convocation of the Estates General, which had the right to approve proposed new taxes. In the resounding statement drafted by Mounier, the three orders also declared themselves ready, if necessary, to relinquish their provincial privileges in order to take part in a national assembly.

Vizille thus bequeathed to the Revolution not only unanimity in opposition to absolutism but also the collective ambition of the Third Estate, soon to be incarnated by the monarchiens: namely, to substitute citizenship for the prerogatives of birth and to establish a constitution consecrating the liberties of citizens and guaranteeing the powers of the nation as well as the monarch—a constitution that would not rebuild atop old ruins but rather marry the progress of civilization to the legacy of the past. That is why Mounier was so persistent in arguing for the Third Estate's minimal yet extremely important demands: doubling its representation, deliberating in common, and voting by head. He expressed these demands at Romans as well as in memoirs and petitions that he sent everywhere, including Versailles, where he arrived as the first elected representative of the Third Estate of Dauphiné, already enjoying a national renown.

In conferences of conciliation with the privileged orders the keynote was set: the Third Estate had neither the right nor the power to negotiate with a segment of the body politic that which belonged to the nation as a whole. For Mounier as well as for Sieyès, there was no middle ground between paralysis of the Estates and surrender of the privileged. Yet the common ground between the two men was also the ground on which they divided. Sieyès envisaged the conflict in terms of conquest. Mounier, rigid as he was, saw no way out other than consensus: the merging of the three orders must be agreed to by the nobility and the clergy, not obtained by force. While Sieyès urged the commons to "cut the cable" and declare themselves the National Assembly, the legalistic Mounier preferred a more cautious formula: "Legitimate Assembly of the representatives of the major part of the nation, acting in the absence of the minor part." He rejected any hasty initiative that might carry the commons beyond the limits of their charge: to claim that the Third Estate was the nation would be a rash provocation of the clergy and the nobility, a challenge to royal authority, and an affront to their constituents.

This view was shared by Malouet, also destined to become a spokesman of the future monarchien party. "We cannot renounce the principle that the Estates General are indivisible," he warned, "but we cannot and should not declare that we represent them by ourselves." This sentence sums up the dilemma of the Third Estate: it could not simply accept the forms of previous Estates, yet neither could it summarily dispense with those forms and adopt a new constitution. If the commons settled for a debatable legitimacy, they ran the risk of being reduced to impotence: their strength would become weakness and their decrees would never possess "the august character of law."

The commons circumvented the dilemma. On June 17 they formed a National Assembly, the sole body capable of "interpreting and presenting the general will of the nation." In so doing they destroyed the Ancien Régime and created a new power, independent of the king. Deliberation in common and voting by head were therefore recognized. But with the triumph of his ideas Mounier also met with his first political defeat, for the price of victory was a revolution he would have preferred to avoid, but which the nobility by its refusal and the king by his delaying tactics made inevitable and which the left wing of the patriotic party already hoped to carry on to further victories. Mounier found himself caught between the court's wish to regain the upper hand and the now uncontrollable dynamic of events, against which this serious but unbending man could do no more than raise immutable principles. If Mirabeau became a past master of the political game, Mounier never mastered or even understood it. He invoked the force of law at a time when the power of words and the law of numbers were already in control, winning victories of which others would reap the fruits.

Nothing illustrates this paradox more clearly than the aftermath of the Constituent Assembly's Revolution. On June 20, in the memorable session at the Tennis Court, Mounier, who had already incurred the suspicion of the patriots, briefly regained his popularity by denouncing, in a speech that remains famous, any attempt to interrupt the Estates by an authoritarian act; it was he who invited the deputies to swear an oath not to disband. He reacted with equal vigor to the royal declaration of June 23, nothing less than a *lit de justice*, a summary judgment commanding the three orders to continue their separate deliberations.

On June 27, however, the court gave in, and this was all it took to revive the divisions within the patriotic party and set Mounier once again at odds with the movement. The revolution of June did not give him back his popularity. It did, however, increase his political influence by bringing the three orders together. On June 24 a majority of the clergy rejoined the National Assembly. The next day forty-seven noble deputies also arrived, among them all the nobles elected from Dauphiné. The core of the future monarchien party was thus reunited. Within it we can identify three distinct groups. First, around Mounier, the Dauphinois delegation was once again intact. If Barnave was already keeping his distance, others—the archbishop of Vienne, the comte de Virieu, the marquis de Blacons—remained loyal to a fault. A second group consisted of members of the privileged classes who had been won over by the idea of reforms: the bishop of Langres, La Luzerne, and the spokesmen for the liberal nobility such as Lezay-Marnésia, deputy for Lons-le-Saulnier, and Clermont-Tonnerre and Lally-Tollendal, both representing the capital and both brilliant, eloquent, and respected orators.

The third group consisted of deputies from the Third Estate, including Bergasse and Malouet, different in almost every respect. In the midst of Enlightenment France Nicolas Bergasse had dedicated himself to the dark cult of animal magnetism, over which he had already broken a few lances with absolutism. It was not until the eve of the Revolution, however, that this celebrated lawyer abandoned the Mesmerists' tubs for politics. He published one after another two strident pamphlets attacking the ministers and the privileged. In them he denounced "the sad chaos of feudal government" and called for an alliance of the throne and the Third Estate against the aristocracy. "The law, the people, the king": as the Ancien Régime came to an end, Bergasse hit upon a credo that he never saw fit to change.

If Bergasse and Malouet shared certain ideas, Malouet nevertheless belonged to another world. This formal naval intendant of Toulon and brilliant Ancien Régime administrator, the first man to be elected deputy from the *sénéchaussée* of Riom, was the most lucid of the monarchiens. He was also by far the most unpopular, too close to Necker for the aristocrats and too aristocratic for the patriots: "He invariably gave off the *ministerial odor*," in the cruel words of one of his colleagues. More equitable, Mme. de Staël, who paid tribute to his intelligence and integrity, nevertheless saw him as a man unfit for modern government, a man who preferred to dispose of issues without dealing with people and who was too certain that he was right to "think sufficiently about how to induce others to share his conviction." Aware of the new sovereignty of public opinion, Malouet noted with alarm the old monarchy's lack of courage. Before the elections to the Estates General he urged Necker and Montmorin to respect the wishes of the public in order to contain their effects. "Obliged to invoke the counsels and aid of the nation," he wrote them, "you can no longer proceed without it. From its strength you must draw your own. But your wisdom must govern its strength. If you allow it to act without a leader and without restraint, you will be crushed." In Versailles the distance between Malouet and Mounier owed less to divergence of their views than to incompatibility of their temperaments. Only later did they become friends, when tested by their first political defeats.

Malouet understood at once that the revolution of June was irreversible. He was also one of the few people to appreciate how much the event owed to the royal capitulation of June 27: "When the Assembly, in its first transports of delirium, dared to nullify its oaths and its mandates and declare itself free of the instructions that we had received from our constituents, the king was justified, or should I say obligated, to send us back to our *bailliages* to report to those who had sent us and who certainly would not have approved of our having erected an authority independent of that which they had bestowed upon us." Thus by nullifying the strict mandate, Louis XVI consecrated the revolution of the Third Estate in the name of the Ancien Régime that it unwittingly helped to end.

***

If the monarchiens were unable to foresee the end of the regime, they did at last try to discern its future. For them the Revolution was complete. What remained was to moderate its passions, reconcile it with the monarchy, stabilize it with a constitution, and regulate its operation. The monarchien project was born at precisely that moment when political debate shifted from what had just been abolished to what one wished to erect in its place. That project therefore originated well before the group that would lay claim to it. Unlike the Breton Club, the monarchien party was not—and would never be—a "machine" for producing consensus. Rather, it was a political consensus that produced the monarchien party, a solidarity created not by birth, rank, or interest but by the ambition to imagine what a just accord between monarchy and liberty might look like. Before the monarchiens formed a "coalition," they had shared a similar idea of political order, a common distrust of democracy, and a desire to draw on the English example of a free government based on inherited rights, guaranteed not by the substitution of one absolute sovereignty for another but by redefining the balance of powers. And they proposed to do all this without raising the question of the basis of political legitimacy.

This "oversight," which they took from their reading of Montesquieu, placed them to one side of the revolutionary movement from the beginning. After June 1789 it was no longer possible to discuss power without discussing the foundations of its legitimacy. The constitutional debate, for which the monarchiens fought so hard, could not have begun without a revolution, and the Revolution was above all a question of sovereignty. Before the monarchiens even existed as a party, they had therefore been eliminated from the debate over the new constitution of the kingdom as a result of having failed to understand the stakes.

Nevertheless, they ardently committed themselves to the constitutional process. On July 6 the Assembly formed a committee to establish the plan of a new constitution. It was to consist of thirty *bureaux*, each of which was to appoint a *commissaire*. Mounier, elected by the eighth bureau over Sieyès, became the leading figure in this committee, which also included his friends Lally-Tollendal, Bergasse, Virieu, and Clermont-Tonnerre. On July 9 he submitted a widely applauded first report, which displayed unshakable faith in royal authority and invincible opposition to arbitrary government but which was also characterized by its refusal to start with a clean slate and by its conviction that the French "are not a new people recently emerged from the forests in order to form an association but a great society of 24 million men . . . for whom the principles of the veritable Monarchy will always be sacred." This proposal touched on all the key questions: the extent of royal prerogatives, the forms and modes of representation, legislative priorities, and above all the usefulness of including a Declaration of the Rights of Man as a preamble to the Constitution. Mounier, hesitant, agreed to this only on condition that the two texts not be separated. In order to avoid a proliferation of extreme interpretations of abstract ideas, the Declaration must be "short, simple, and precise," and its final form ought not to be set until examination of all the articles of the Constitution had been completed. As for the constitutional debate itself, Mounier and his friends wanted it to be carried out in the bureaus, where it would be immune to pressure from the galleries. This point aroused considerable protest. The patriots proposed entrusting the constitutional plan to a new committee of eight elected members. This motion ultimately carried. Mounier, Lally, Bergasse, and Clermont-Tonnerre were all included in the new committee, along with Talleyrand, Champion de Cicé, and two avowed enemies of the monarchiens, Le Chapelier and Sieyès. Drafting of the text of the Constitution did not take place in the bureaus, which soon became bogged down, but in plenary sessions of the Assembly, which now met twice daily. This was a severe setback, and it was not long before the monarchiens felt its effects.

It was a harbinger of other defeats to come over the next few weeks. Caught between two equally redoubtable "factions"—the royal entourage and the "popular" party—the monarchiens watched their prestige as orators wane and their rhetoric lose its effectiveness. Consider what happened after Necker was dismissed on July 11. Although the monarchiens indignantly denounced the engineers of this intrigue, they also stubbornly insisted on the need to maintain unfailing respect for royal authority, regardless of the circumstances. This plea was jeered by the Assembly. A few days later the break with Barnave was complete. For Mounier's former disciple, the revolution of the Third Estate, the discredit of the court, and the taking of the Bastille had shaken the old edifice and rendered obsolete any thought of transaction "between a power that was everything and a power that had ceased to be." Except for the monarchiens, "all elements of the revolutionary party accepted the need for a total reconstitution." The spirit of Vizille and Romans was dead. The monarchien committee was born, a desperate coalition intended to turn back what had become an irresistible movement.

In mid-August Mounier published his *Considerations on Governments, and Principally on That Which Is Suited to France,* which passed for the party's manifesto. Although the Ancien Régime had ceased to be, despotism could still exist: what had been the despotism of one man was now the work of a multitude in a kingdom in the grip of anarchy. The only way to avoid the peril was to save the king's authority from usurpation by the legislature and above all to guarantee the king's prerogative. A monarch stripped of his influence "would be absolutely nothing more than a subaltern magistrate or a simple general. The government would then be not monarchical but republican." For the time being the patriots were not demanding that much, but one may ask whether the Revolution was not already faced with this alternative in the autumn of 1789.

*
**

To break with tradition and make the democratic abstraction the sole criterion of political reason was now the Revolution's central ambition, its message, or, as Burke might say, its lie. This message took shape in the great debates of July through September, which consummated the monarchiens' defeat.

The first issue was the Declaration of the Rights of Man and of the Citizen. Begun in July and renewed in August, this debate revealed the magnitude of the abyss that already separated the victors of June from their former allies. The monarchiens feared that the Assembly would prove impervious to the wisdom of age and experience; they believed that it was dangerous to formulate rights in the abstract, leaving them subject to constant interpretation and distortion, particularly when those rights were offered to a people so long deprived of political experience. Malouet observed that too great a disparity between natural rights and positive rights was an expedient all the more hazardous because the former were invariably reshaped by the latter: indeed it was through the dialectic of principle and law that natural man became a citizen. "Why, then, begin by transporting him onto a high mountaintop and showing him his limitless empire, when he will only have to descend to where limits impinge upon his every step?" Accordingly, the monarchiens vehemently opposed Sieyès' proposal, which they deemed "enigmatic and perfidious," "too metaphysical and too obscure," drawn "almost entirely from the *Social Contract*." Mounier's counterproposal insisted on the necessary separation of powers, deliberately omitted all reference to the periodic national conventions that Sieyès had called for, and hedged freedom of the press with a thousand precautions. It enshrined freedom of conscience but did not explicitly recognize the freedom of any non-Catholic denominations.

This verson was received coolly by the Assembly, and another proposal was selected as the basis for discussion. Although the final draft of the Declaration was, but for subtle differences in tone, identical to Mounier's text, the political benefit was reaped by others. In the end Mounier's ideas prevailed, but not his politics.

No sooner had the monarchiens recovered from this ordeal than they found themselves involved once more in the crucial debate over the royal sanction and the bicameral legislature. As early as February 1789 Mounier in his *New Observations on the Estates General of France* had accorded the king full executive power and an absolute veto over ordinary laws passed by the national legislature. "When the Constitution has been formed, in order to preclude any changes prejudicial to the rights of the Throne, it must be stipulated that no law may take effect without the approval of the royal authority and that refusal by the Prince nullifies any resolution." The future deputy from Dauphiné also argued in favor of bicameralism: a Chamber of Representatives to be elected by all orders and an Upper Chamber, composed of ex officio members and others elected from the clergy and the nobility but without discrimination as to rank within those two orders.

On August 31 Lally-Tollendal and Mounier, speaking for the Constitutional Committee, set forth the principles and organizational modalities of the legislative power. These two reports vigorously stated the monarchiens' policy, their theory of a balance of powers, and their determination to stabilize a revolution whose future they could already see was fraught with unpredictable dangers. Paris was still in turmoil, and for some days the Palais-Royal sought to stir up opinion against the royal sanction. With this climate of agitation, threat, and suspicion hanging over the Assembly, the monarchiens hoped to secure passage of their proposed constitution as quickly as possible: their aim was to grant the king an absolute veto over decisions of the legislature and to set alongside the Assembly of elected representatives a senate composed of independent landowners appointed for life by the king upon nomination by the provincial assemblies. All power, Lally explained, potentially leads to abuse of power: hence limits must be established to prevent such abuse. That is why three powers were needed, for "a single power would necessarily end by devouring everything. Two would fight until one had crushed the other. But three will maintain one another in a perfect equilibrium if they are combined in such a way that when two struggle, the third, having an equal interest in preserving both of the others, will join the one that is oppressed in combatting the oppressor to restore peace among all."

Lally, like Mounier, believed that this argument was ironclad. Neither suspected as they mounted the rostrum that they were about to read their political last testament. The deputies dismissed the case they presented. Many of them doubted that the king could refuse to approve the general will once it had been voiced by the nation's legitimate representatives. This was also the opinion not only of Necker but also of Malouet. In early September Necker presented to the King's Council a "Report on the Royal Sanction," in which he argued in favor of a suspensive veto on grounds not of principle but of opportunity. If the veto carried by a small majority, he warned, a "dangerous commotion" might result, the mere threat of which might prevent the king from making use of it.

In fact the first minister of finance showed that he was a far better politician than the uncompromising proponents of the absolute veto. In a country in turmoil, faced with the machinations of the "popular" party, he was afraid that the bicameral legislature and unlimited veto would lead to a general uprising. To this Mounier is supposed to have replied, in a phrase that sums him up, "One must not purchase peace by sacrificing royal authority and the people's interest." If the deputies in their vast majority were unmoved by this judgment, it was because the very notion of an absolute veto left them cold.

Malouet did not believe in it either, but he drew different conclusions. Like his monarchien friends he was willing to grant the monarch, as guarantor of the wishes and interests of the people, the right to make sure that the laws were indeed in conformity with the general will, to prevent abuse of power by the legislature, and thus to protect the integrity of the nation's sovereignty. Unlike Necker, who did not challenge the legitimacy of the absolute veto but withheld his support for pragmatic reasons, and unlike the monarchiens, who saw it as an untouchable royal prerogative, Malouet recognized that any veto must by definition be suspensive. Nevertheless, he concluded in favor of the unlimited sanction. In this case the principles of the law took precedence over the pragmatics of government, with that tinge of rigidity that was so much a part of the monarchien manner and that ultimately did them in.

On September 10 a final vote in the Assembly settled the question of the two chambers: 89 votes for, 849 against, with 122 abstentions. This over-whelming vote presaged the passage of the suspensive veto the following day (673 votes for, 325 against, 11 abstentions).

To compound this double defeat, which apparently surprised the mo-narchiens more than anyone else, they then committed a fatal tactical error. Having been rebuked so dramatically, Mounier, Lally, and Bergasse, soon fol-lowed by Clermont-Tonnerre, all resigned from the Constitutional Committee.

They did not acknowledge defeat, however. Hope remained alive until the October Days and the king's forced return to Paris. The crisis spelled the dissolution of the monarchien committee and ended the brief revolutionary careers of Bergasse, Lally-Tollendal, and Mounier, who presided over the As-sembly during the dramatic Days. He resigned his chair on October 8 and started back to Dauphiné. (On November 15 he also resigned as deputy.) His return home, which his enemies attributed to fear, actually signified his re-fusal to compromise in any way with the course taken by the Revolution. He was moved as much by personal instinct as by political resolve, hoping to regain his freedom of speech and action, which had been compromised by violence, pressure, and threats, as well as to exhort the provinces to prevent the Revolution from sinking into anarchy and possibly even civil war.

For Mounier the October Days destroyed the fragile political equilib-rium established by the Constituent Assembly. When the court was forced to return to Paris and the king was held prisoner in his capital, the legislature, organ of the general will, remained silent or indifferent in the face of the crowd's demands: these outrages violated the principles of the Revolution and exposed it to every kind of excess.

Mounier met with further disappointments after returning home. The Dauphinois showed little inclination to oppose the capital and were too at-tached to the National Assembly to accept its dissolution (something that Mounier always denied planning, despite his enemies' assertions that he had). Even his friends judged his plan too risky and, worse yet, inopportune. The crisis was nearly over, and the king was too weak to do without the Assembly. To be sure, the latter, whether out of calculation or cowardice, had been un-able to defend the authority of the monarchy. But it alone could still restore it, whereas a call for dissolution and rebellion risked hastening the collapse. The fate of the Revolution would be played out in the Salle du Manège in Paris. Lafayette begged Mounier to return. Other appeals followed, less con-fident but no less urgent. "We cannot do good," wrote Virieu. "Let us prevent evil. We cannot prevent great evils, let us save ourselves from minor ones."

Whether out of pride or clairvoyance, Mounier rejected any form of compromise. The conduct of the debate that would lead to nationalization of clerical property (on November 2) confirmed him in his pessimism: the Rev-olution no longer derived from a philosophical principle or constitutional project; it had become a political passion, a question of power whose outcome no one could now predict.

Ran Halévi

Further reading

WORKS BY THE MONARCHIENS

For speeches, see the fundamental *Archives parlementaires*, series 1, vols. 8–9. Paris, 1875–1877.

Lally-Tollendal, Thomas-Arthur, baron de Tollendal, comte de Lally, known as. *Mémoire . . . ou second lettre à ses commettants.* Paris, 1790.

Malouet, Pierre-Victor, baron. *Mémoires*, 2 vols. Paris, 1868.

Mounier, Jean-Joseph. *Considérations sur les gouvernements, et principalement sur celui qui convient à la France.* Paris, 1789.

———*Exposé de ma conduite dans l'Assemblée Nationale et motifs de mon retour en Dauphiné,* followed by *Faits relatifs à la dernière insurrection* and *Observations sur les motifs de mon départ.* Paris, 1789.

——— *Nouvelles observations sur les Etats Généraux de France.* N.p., 1789.

RELATED WORKS

Du Bus, Charles. *Stanislas de Clermont-Tonnerre et l'échec de la révolution monarchique.* Paris, 1931.

Egret, Jean. *La Révolution des notables: Mounier et les monarchiens, 1789.* Paris, 1950.

Related topics

Barnave	Louis XVI	Revolutionary Assemblies
Constitution	Montesquieu	Rights of Man
Estates General	Necker	Sieyès

MONTAGNARDS

T he word "Mountain," Ferdinand Brunot tells us, was not simply an allusion to the upper benches of the Convention. The dominant position chosen by certain deputies was not enough to start people talking of a Mountain, for there was also a "Mountain" on the right side of the chamber. But there, we know from Dulaure, the upper benches "did not bear this name," at least not at the very beginning of the Convention. Memories of the Legislative Assembly were still sufficiently vivid that no one was keen to sit on the right: that had been the side of the aristocrats, while the left was for the "friends of Liberty." In the Convention, therefore, "Robespierrists" and "Maratists" first colonized the upper benches on the left side and then gradually all the upper benches, where they were soon joined, Baudot indicates, by all who were possessed of a lively imagination and a rebellious spirit. Deputies of more sober temperament took seats on the "slopes," while nonentities headed for the Swamp. At first sight nothing seems less important than this topography. Yet nothing binds a group more tightly than sitting on the same benches. Dulaure, who from the very first days of the Convention observed this still hesitant political geography, deplored the gregarious and crude morality that was its result and as a way of avoiding it suggested "changing places frequently."

These eyewitness acounts also make us realize how fluid the situation was in the first days of the Assembly. When deputations arrived at the Convention, they were neither Girondin nor Montagnard, and often it was départemental solidarity that determined where newcomers would sit. Although it took a while before the word "Gironde" took hold, "Mountain" was soon in common use by both enemies and sympathizers (in January 1793 the Lyons Society of Jacobins observed that votes should be weighed rather than counted and that a "patriot of the Mountain" was worth 100,000 Brissotins). One aim of the Gironde's strategy in the months preceding its downfall was to associate the Mountain—both the word and the thing—with "faction." This was the meaning of Gensonné's famous apostrophe on January 2, 1793, during the king's trial: "What! You do not form a faction, yet you call yourself deputies of the Mountain, [as if] to recall the Asian tyrant who is known to history only by the horde of assassins he dragged about in his wake." This was the meaning, too, of the countless petitions that came to the Convention from municipalities and départements indicating the "pain" that good citizens felt at the nicknames "Plain" and "Mountain" and begging the Convention to renounce them, sometimes courteously ("in the temple of Laws there should be neither Plain nor Mountain"), sometimes aggressively ("Equality, no more

Mountain!"). Not even petitions emanating from the popular societies sympathetic to the left side of the chamber resigned themselves easily to the divisive word. Of course they expressed the hope that "the unshakeable Mountain would fill the Swamp" but still conveyed a clear wish ("that the ground on which you live be as unified as yourselves from now on") and a clearly defined purpose: "That one no longer be obliged to study the geography of the Convention in order to find out what spirit animates it."

Despite these hesitations, despite the irony with which moderates used the word, it began to turn up in positive metaphors in the spring of 1793. To criticisms directed at a word that smelled of faction, the deputies of the upper benches responded by invoking necessity. Before the citizens of Saint-Flour in April 1793 a representative by the name of Lacoste pointed out that it was idle to regret that the Convention was not united. Could they be united with the local aristocrats? "It is impossible for the Mountain to descend to the Plain or for the Plain to climb the Mountain." In this speech we find an early mention of the phrase "holy Mountain," laying the groundwork for the metaphors and images that would occupy an increasingly important space in patriotic society speeches after May 31, 1793. Many were biblical images: the Mountain was "Sinai." It was born of the "Flood" that "divided the world into plains and mountains." From its volcanic summit came thunder, lightning, lava, and flames capable of terrorizing the enemies of the Revolution, for this blazing judicial mountain was the image most often used to evoke the Terror. Plaster mountains bristling with cardboard rocks began to crop up everywhere in the urban scenery erected for republican festivals. Any city that contained a hill, no matter how modest, emulated Quimper, which ambitiously baptized its hill Montagne-sur-Odet. A glance at the memoirs of Montagnard deputies is enough to gauge the degree to which this imagery and the ingenuous axiomatics of altitude that underlay it maintained its hold on the mind.

Thermidor, however, had appeared to be fatal to both. Although for a few weeks after Robespierre's downfall the popular societies continued to entreat "true Montagnards" and "patriots of the Mountain" ("Mountain of Sinai! Thunder! Explode! Give a new edge to the axe of the nation!"), fewer and fewer voices were raised to recall the glories of the Mountain, and those that were raised sounded increasingly desperate. Vadier in September 1794 still dared to tell the Jacobins that the Mountain had "saved liberty on August 10, May 31, and 9 Thermidor." But the last date tells the story: 9 Thermidor was indeed the work of Montagnards, but paradoxically it condemned the Mountain as a whole. Well aware of this, Vadier observed melancholically: "Since people began to say there was no more Mountain, they have begun to undermine the foundations of the Republic." Enjoying the fiction of a newfound unity, the deputies no longer wished to hear of the Convention, and the Mountain once again became a faction.

Yet it was in these dark days that the Montagnard legend began its subterranean growth. Thermidor severed the Montagnard achievement from the politics and personality of Robespierre (as is shown by both Babeuf's diary and Soubrany's correspondence). Freed from this burdensome paternity, the memory of the Mountain was transmitted by Babouvism to the secret societies of the Restoration and the July Monarchy. The latter circulated portraits of the brave Montagnards and kept alive the religion of the Constitution of 1793, which had stipulated that all laws be subject to the scrutiny of primary assemblies and therefore seemed to hold out the promise of direct democracy, which, Levasseur said, "beneath the ice of age caused the stoic Buonarroti's heart to beat" and which the whole century invoked as the breviary of democracy. Ballanche and Hugo dramatized and magnified the image of the "old conventionnel," who was always a Montagnard, always a regicide, as if no one could have been a conventionnel who did not sit on the benches of the Mountain. Esquiros and Louis Blanc brought the Montagnard legend to a peak of perfection (the world, according to Esquiros, "is still radiant with the luster of their dictatorship and their battles"), and even historians not initially favorable to the Montagnards, such as Lamartine, could conclude that they had been vanquished by their virtues. When 1848 came, the representatives of left-wing sentiment naturally called themselves the party of the Mountain, a party which, different as it was from the Mountain of 1793, most notably because it was not terrorist, terrified respectable folk nonetheless.

There were three main features of the Montagnard legend as it existed in the nineteenth century. First, there was the energy of those who defined themselves as "boiling patriots," which caused them to send representatives from Paris on missions to the provinces and to recruit battalions of volunteers of every ilk to fight the Vendeans, impose the *maximum,* and galvanize the army. This epic of national enthusiasm was so powerful that it was capable of attracting historians who hated Jacobinism, such as Michelet, or who were reluctant to admit the Terror, such as Louis Blanc. Hence it is not difficult to understand how it was able at times to make people forget the Terror or accept it as a necessary ingredient of success. The Mountain then became an allegory for historical necessity. It was seen as a group consisting of those members of the Convention who understood, as Esquiros put it, that once one embraced the Revolution, "it had to be accepted whole, entire, in its logic, and accompanied by all the conditions necessary to establish and perpetuate it."

This heroic Mountain, fully imbued with a sense of the inevitable, was also blessed with foresight. The Constitution of 1793 had laid down the principle that society must provide its least fortunate citizens with the means of subsistence, either by offering them work or, if they could not work, by securing them the means to live. By institutionalizing the state's debt to the poor, equipping a powerful government with the means to manage the economy, placing "equality" above "liberty," and inventing (according to Louis Blanc) the idea of fraternity, the Mountain therefore expressed the true meaning of the French Revolution. For nineteenth-century socialists the true grandeur of the Revolution was, as Sylvain Maréchal put it, as "the forerunner of another, more complete revolution, which will be the last."

Finally, the Mountain was seen as the very embodiment of national unity and the Montagnards as the champions of a France "one and indivisible," as nineteenth-century republicans religiously repeated. In the prisons of 1848 a rumor mysteriously spread that "the one and indivisible has arrived."

The war effort was central to this image, and so was the struggle against Girondin federalism (even if that was a political fiction). One senses, moreover, how much the legendary portrait of the Montagnards was constructed as an antithesis of the Girondin image. The Girondins' delaying tactics, hesitant policies, and reputation for hedonism were contrasted with the austere determination of the Montagnards. Girondin individualism was contrasted with the Montagnards' generous sense of community. Girondin feeling for diversity was contrasted with the Montagnard religion of unity. This rhetoric of antitheses was immensely successful. The image that transformed the adolescence of Vallès (after which he "dreamed of nothing but rebellion") was an engraving he had seen in a bookseller's shop in Saint-Etienne of men in the dress of conventionnels swearing to die for their endangered fatherland and for "the one and indivisible." This religion of sacrifice preached by "men of serious mien," which shook the young Vallès "more than all the promises of Paradise," was the heart of a memory of the Montagnards that, according to Esquiros, blazed through the century "like a column of fire." That such a flamboyant fate lay in store for a group of parliamentarians in bourgeois dress is what we must try to comprehend.

Before attempting to unravel the various strands of this fascination, we must pause for a moment to examine the composition of the group. Who chose to sit in the highest rows of the Salle du Manège? Why did deputies go to the Mountain, and how many were there? When the Convention first met, Levasseur tells us, new deputies were unaware that there were two camps. For these novices, going to the Mountain may have been simply a matter of sitting next to people they already knew, other deputies from the same département. Or they may have been attempting to demonstrate their independence of mind. These choices may appear to be mutually exclusive, yet Thibaudeau made both at the same time. The Girondin contention that the Mountain was a unified and coherent group, from the beginning favorable to the Paris Commune and guilty of having if not fomented then at least approved the September massacres, is totally unjust. It takes a very subtle observer indeed to make out, in the Assembly's early days, the contours of a Montagnard group that only gradually assumed its identity.

Some months earlier, Girondins and Montagnards alike had all been meeting at the Jacobin Club, which had been the scene of the clash between Robespierre and Brissot over the question of war. It was within the Club itself, at the very time the September massacres were taking place, that the Parisian deputies were chosen in an election influenced by both the time and the place. If Brissot, Kersaint, and Condorcet had been able to hold Paris seats in the Legislative Assembly, the city now excluded them and gave victory to the Montagnard trinity (Robespierre, Danton, and Marat), its luster heightened by an almost all radical deputation. A month later those Girondin leaders not expelled from the Jacobins quit the Club voluntarily. This does not mean, however, that Jacobins and Montagnards were one and the same. There were

Montagnards, such as Carnot, who scrupulously avoided the Club. Thibaudeau, who made a point of never going there because he deemed it incompatible with the dignity of a legislator "to go to a meeting whose only right was to submit petitions, note its opinions, accept them wholesale, and then draft the decrees of the Convention," observes, however, that his abstention was seen as an anomaly. This is a sign not of compulsory membership but at least of extreme proximity. Although the Montagnards were initially little inclined to grant Paris the right to oversee and intervene in the affairs of the Convention, they were still less willing to admit that granting such a right would pose a major threat to the Revolution. In their eyes a much greater threat lay in the appeal to local governments (still thought to be under the influence of the aristocracy) and the use of départemental forces. Thus there arose a first split, as a result of which the Montagnards seemed to swing toward the side of Paris, and they were soon hounded in the Assembly as so-called *Septembriseurs*. For the Girondins this charge seemed to be a godsend, ammunition for use in a war of position; but contrary to their expectation their attempt to use it only forced initially indifferent deputies firmly into the Montagnard fold.

In this prehistory of the group the king's trial was a fundamental event. Choices made during the trial bound those who made them for a long time to come. It is remarkable, in particular, that although individual Girondins voted in very different ways, the Girondins as a group were already firmly branded with the dubious reputation of having wished for clemency and remembered for having proposed an appeal to the people that the Montagnards deemed irresponsible. It was therefore inevitable that the latter, whose votes had been far more homogeneous, were subsequently firmly linked to the somber decision in favor of regicide. Not all the regicides were Montagnards, but all the Montagnards were regicides. The shared conviction that the king's death was the only conceivable solution was to prove decisive for the group's cohesiveness and for its destiny. Since members of committees were chosen after the trial from the ranks of the regicides, as were most *représentants en mission* to the provinces, one can say that the government of the Convention was Montagnard well before May 31. Furthermore, the number of Montagnards was, as Alison Patrick has shown and as recent studies at the University of Iowa have confirmed, far greater than the Girondin legend made it out: far from a feeble faction and therefore all the more impudent and noisy, the Mountain was by the winter of 1793 a substantial group comprising some forty percent of the Convention. With the support of sympathizers, the group was therefore able to prevail in certain crucial votes.

Forty percent is an approximate figure, and historians have attempted to make it more precise; but in a situation where political parties did not exist or their contours varied in response to events, scholars have been compelled to establish their own criteria of membership. Some, including Alison Patrick, have proposed a high estimate: 302 Montagnards, a figure obtained by adding to the 142 members identifiable because they frequented the Jacobin Club 73 others who, though not Jacobins, sat with the Mountain and 87 deputies who, having sometimes voted with the left prior to June 1793, became supporters of the Montagnard Convention thereafter. A lower estimate is also possible. Françoise Brunel puts the number of Montagnards at just 258, counting only those whose votes in 1793 were totally consistent. In order to be counted as a Montagnard in her estimate a deputy must *never* have cast a moderate vote in 1793. This estimate is more rigorous than the previous one, but the other is probably a closer approximation to a shifting reality. It takes better account of the fact that group affiliation was still an uncertain business and makes room for the idiosyncrasies of individuals who, though generally favorable to the Mountain, could nevertheless regard Marat as a dangerous fanatic or deem it more politic to spare the life of Louis XVI than to execute him. In any case, while these scholars deserve credit for using the only serious criterion for discrimination available, namely, the records of roll-call votes, their results must be set in context, for they tend to present an image of a stable group when in fact the membership of the Mountain changed constantly as the weeks went by. Some Montagnards—Lindet, Jean Bon Saint-André—were tempted for a time by the Gironde. Others—such as Couthon—wished to avoid as long as possible being enlisted in either the party of *exagérés* or the party of the *subtils*. Finally, the Plain—which Robespierre would later describe as "pure"—was throughout this period a breeding ground for the Mountain. In this respect the crucial moment was March 1793: faced with the Vendean insurrection and the threat of foreign invasion, some deputies who were not Robespierrists and still less Maratists decided to vote with the Mountain in support of revolutionary measures. Barère was both an example and the theorist of this tendency, in which, according to Baudot, a sense of necessity played a decisive role. Many deputies were convinced that when a "revolutionary" measure was passed—even one as detestable and detested as the Convention's acquiescence in its own mutilation on May 31—the consequences had to be accepted: acceptance of what seemed inevitable was the key ingredient of the Mountain's triumph.

Events therefore played a large part in deciding the political roles of deputies who initially formed a quite homogeneous group. Was this true to such a degree that today's attempts at classification are pointless? The attempt to distinguish between Montagnards and Girondins on the basis of social and occupational criteria has engaged many historians without yielding convincing results. Two rather surprising features differentiate the group portrait of the Montagnards from that of the Girondins. First of all, the Montagnards were—despite the reputation of the Gironde as a group of brilliant youths—on the average younger than their fraternal enemies, and the youngest of them were also the most activist. This confirms an observation made by Garat, who said that youth was one factor influencing political decisions, for a man went to the Mountain as he would go to war, when "age makes one more likely to serve the Republic in the armies than in the sanctuary of the laws." But these young men had already completed a political apprenticeship: forty percent of them, for example, had been members of the Legislative Assembly. Alison Patrick found that the more political experience a deputy had upon arriving at the Convention, the more likely he was to join the Mountain; thus the archetypal Montagnard was not a Parisian rhymester like Fabre d'Eglantine but a provincial legislator like Couthon.

*
* *

Let us return now to the Mountain en bloc and the traits that earned it its prestige among historians. The first of these is the heroic energy that it displayed, "the political strength," as Garat put it, "needed by a nation assailed on all sides." The first series of "revolutionary" measures dates from the spring of 1793, following Dumouriez's disappointments and amid concern over the Vendean insurrection. These measures were proposed by Barère, an unmistakable sign of the rapprochement under way between the Plain and the Mountain. Their aim was to strike at émigrés and suspects and at the same time to calm the clubs and sections. On March 11 the Convention (anxious to organize the repression itself so as to avoid further massacres) created a Revolutionary Tribunal and stiffened the anti-émigré laws. On March 21 it instituted communal surveillance committees. Representatives, endowed with unlimited powers, were dispatched on missions to the provinces and, later, the armies. Finally, on April 6, the first Committee of Public Safety was instituted to coordinate the government's actions. Taken together these measures suggest an image, destined to enjoy a bright future, of a nation determined to put an end to a domestic and foreign coalition by means of an almost superhuman effort, in a situation in which people had no choice but to conquer or die.

Did all this energy come from the Montagnards alone? The first emergency measures, including the Revolutionary Tribunal, were passed unanimously by the Convention, Girondins included. If they were seen as specifically Montagnard measures, it was because their execution—arrests of suspects and purges of reputedly tepid local administrations—was primarily the work of Montagnard deputies. In what proved to be a fatal calculation on the part of the Gironde, the *représentants en mission* were recruited chiefly among deputies of the Mountain, which between March and June dispatched nearly three times as many members to the provinces and the armies as all other groups combined. In September 1793 the Girondins were out of the picture, and since the second series of measures out of which the revolutionary government would emerge was right in line with the first, most historians (with a few exceptions, such as Albert Sorel) have bestowed on the Mountain the honor of having saved the country. In the terrible summer of 1793 the Convention made the Terror the order of the day, reorganized the Revolutionary Tribunal, ordered mass recruitment, and passed the Law of Suspects. The decree of Frimaire, Year II, completed the edifice of the Montagnard dictatorship, now supported by the propaganda of the Jacobin Clubs and by an obedient press, which conducted a strenuous campaign to unify the nation around the concept of public safety. The first result of this effort was to win the support of the army, for, as Roger Dupuy has shown (suggesting the need for modification of the received view that the Montagnards' efficient pragmatism was in every way at odds with the Girondins' dreamy lack of realism), the army, in the hope of a radicalization that would lead to the dismissal of noble officers, played a decisive role in the Mountain's victory by offering its assistance in the crucial task of expelling moderates from the popular societies.

The Mountain's admirers have one obvious point in their favor: the effort to make the government more effective and mobilize the nation achieved its goal. By the autumn of 1793 its fruits were visible everywhere. The "federalist" revolt was crushed. Lyons was finished. Toulon was recaptured. The Vendean army was cut to pieces in December. The foreign armies were held at bay outside French territory. The Committee of Public Safety had lived up to its name. The Mountain had found its heroes, and the victories so aptly demonstrated the usefulness of the measures adopted that the Terror ceased to seem like a monstrous exception. It was absolved by some; others found additional reasons to admire it. The Montagnard episode thus gave birth to a new type of hero: the ruler who rules despotically in the name of liberty, the general who makes war while hating it, the Terrorist who uses the guillotine without loving it, all united by their acceptance of necessity. Thus, as Esquiros later put it, "the regrets and complaints engendered by the Terror must fall before these words, as sharp and unyielding as an axe: it was necessary."

To this portrait of Terrorists not fond of the Terror one might add that of price setters who, as Saint-Just said, disliked "violent laws on commerce." The second part of the apology for the Mountain is the progress it made in bringing about a revolution in favor of equality for which its adversaries showed little concern. Louis Blanc stated this argument in its classic form, basing his view on both the terms of the Montagnard Constitution and the realities of its economic policy.

A product of circumstances, quickly drafted, quickly brought to the floor, immediately adopted (and immediately suspended as well), the Constitution of the summer of 1793 was a document whose very existence was an illustration of Montagnard efficiency as opposed to Girondin delays. Louis Blanc contrasts the two constitutions in terms of passion. In the one proposed by the Girondins, interminably long and interminably debated, there was, he said, "not a single heartbeat." In the Montagnard proposal, so laconic and yet so expeditious, he discovered "the breath of Jean-Jacques." A more debatable comparison can scarcely be imagined. In many respects the Girondin Constitution, which accepted direct election to all offices, was more democratic than the Montagnard, which provided for indirect election of functionaries, administrators, and the Executive Council. With respect to egalitarianism, the Montagnard Constitution fell far short of the Declaration of Rights, for which Robespierre had secured the acclamation of the Jacobins in April. There Robespierre had defined property as the right of each individual to dispose of the *portion* of wealth defined by law. In the Constitution, however, there is no mention of a "portion" of wealth, and there are no limits on property, which is defined as the right to dispose of one's wealth "as one sees fit." Still, the Montagnard Constitution specifies "communal happiness" (and not individual liberty) as a prerequisite of all social organization. It also proclaims a right to work and to public assistance. In the eyes of Philippeaux its superiority consisted "in the help promised from the pocketbook of the rich to poor families that lived on the fruits of the father's daily labor." It could be read as a promise to go beyond bourgeois liberalism, granted by the bourgeois Montagnards under pressure of circumstances and as required by the logic of their alliance with sans-culotterie.

The same can be said of the Mountain's economic policy. The Montagnard deputies were as much under the sway of physiocratic liberalism as the rest of the Convention, and they repudiated that heritage only under the powerful pressure of popular discontent and in furtherance of a political strategy. On the issue of property the Montagnards were profoundly united. In the very first days of the Convention Danton had proposed proclaiming that "all territorial properties would be maintained without exception." In February 1793 they condemned the enragé-inspired riot in favor of price controls. In March they voted with other deputies to approve the death penalty for those who propagandized in favor of land reform. Two months later the exigencies of their struggle with the Gironde caused them to give in to pressure from the galleries and proclaim the first *maximum,* or price ceiling on grains. The sans-culotte *journée* of September 5 forced them to proclaim a second *maximum.* Nevertheless, now that they were left alone to deal with what Robespierre called the "phantom" of the agrarian law, they approved, on September 21, yet another decree concerning the preservation of properties. To the end they continued to oppose land reform, in which respect they differed little from the Girondins. To the end they followed Robespierre, who held that equality of ownership was a "chimera." Baudot aptly summed up their policy: "We wished to apply to politics the equality that the Gospel accords to Christians. We did not on that account want equality of property or the agrarian law, because nowhere does the Gospel say that one must share one's wealth with one's neighbor. But it does say everywhere that one must help one's neighbor in his needs."

How could this hesitant policy, forced on the Mountain by popular pressure and always marked by reluctance, have been taken for a vigorous and deliberate effort to establish an egalitarian economy? First of all because of the interest in social welfare. That charity should be a matter of state and that taxes should provide a common reserve had been a principle of the Constituent Assembly. The Mountain borrowed this theme and acccentuated its compulsory aspect: "The rich man," said Lakanal, "is worthy of his political rights only insofar as he is the father of the poor man." The assertion that every man has a right to subsistence, with the implication that the rich should be taxed and the poor protected, is remembered as the emblem of Montagnard policy, which culminated in Ventôse, Year II, with laws passed in order to defuse Cordelier agitation. The decree concerning the confiscation of suspects' property and the indemnification of indigents found an inspired sponsor in Saint-Just: "The wretched are the powers of the earth. They have the right to speak as masters to governments that neglect them." This is what has survived of the Montagnards' economic policy and what has given war-

rant to its "socialist" interpretation. In light of this powerful image it ultimately matters little that the Montagnards adopted only a part of the sans-
culotte program, rejected price controls on meat, and dismissed the idea of a
special jury to judge hoarders, or that, unable to enforce the *maximum,* they
settled for simply nationalizing the grain trade. Memories of the harvest
stored in the communal warehouse, token of a Montagnard communism of
consumption, were enshrined by Babouvism and transmitted to posterity.

In places, however, the Montagnard *représentants en mission* carried out
this policy with greater daring. Well before Ventôse some of them had initiated a vigorous social policy, which they then radicalized. Availing themselves
of the very elastic definition of "suspects" and resorting to inquisition and
repression, some, such as Saint-Just in Strasbourg and Bo and Chabot in the
Tarn and Aveyron, prosecuted hoarders and monopolists, to say nothing of
the merely "selfish" and "indifferent," levied special taxes on wealthy people
found lacking in civic spirit, and organized a sort of municipal collectivism.
Some, like Lakanal, convinced that the noblest role a man can play in this
world is that of "defender of the poor," set up a system of public assistance
offering medical care and work to the poor. These representatives frequently
confronted the Convention with what they had already done. Laplanche, for
example, upon his return from Loir-et-Cher, said: "I had no instructions
from the Committee of Public Safety, but I thought that I had better act in a
revolutionary manner. Everywhere I made terror the order of the day. I taxed
the rich and the aristocrats, not arbitrarily but upon advice of people I met."
Thus, Montagnard practice helped to forge an image of the Mountain more
radical than it actually was. Obliged to resort to price controls in order to feed
the cities, drawing arguments in favor of state intervention from circumstances alone, and convinced that, if citizens were obliged to abandon their
property and a fortiori the production thereof to serve "the most urgent social need," they must always be indemnified, the Mountain never ceased to
look upon property as the foundation of the social order. It did of course
develop a moral rhetoric attacking the selfishness of the rich, yet it never
relinquished the dream of a nation of small, independent owners, owing
nothing to anyone, living frugally and virtuously on their individual plots and
in their utopian cottages.

That leaves one final trait of Montagnard grandeur, which won the
heart of Michelet despite his doubts about Jacobinism: that of having placed
the unity of the nation above everything else, of having overcome threats of
secession and fragmentation, of having called for and maintained the unity
of the people and its representatives. Here the gap between legend and reality is widest, for while the Montagnards never ceased to celebrate unity (between the "healthy part" of the Convention and the healthy mass of the governed), the facts contradict their rhetoric. When the sans-culottes pressed for
more radical measures, they soon discovered the Mountain's political heterogeneity and were quick to denounce what *Père Duchesne* called "two-faced
Montagnards" sitting on the same benches as the Montagnards who were
"good sans-culottes." Buchez and Roux later expanded on this theme, de-
ploring the fact that the word "Mountain," "one of the most disastrous words

in revolutionary language," applied to both honest men and scoundrels. The Mountain's heterogeneity manifested itself, moreover, as discord within the Committee of Public Safety. Most significant of all, the Mountain took it upon itself to search out the ever-renascent factions within its bosom and to expel them, something the Gironde had never done. In this respect 9 Thermidor was by no means an exception to the rule: the Mountain simply purged itself of one more faction, and the Plain, at first hesitant, finally came around and supported what was initially a settling of scores among Montagnards.

In the collective imagination, however, 9 Thermidor seemed to sound the death knell of the Mountain as a source of national unity because it brought down Robespierre, and Robespierre had wielded the rhetoric of unity and filled the role of unifier in an exemplary fashion—the rhetoric of unity because for him the purge, always natural and necessary and directed only against the wicked, was the chosen instrument of "imperishable unity" among patriots; and the role of unifier because, as François Furet has shown, although Robespierre was brought to power by the coup of the Paris sections against the Convention, he never ceased to be the man of the Convention. "He is the people in the sections, the people at the Jacobins, the people in the national representation," mythically reconciling antagonistic principles in his person and singlehandedly guaranteeing the unity of power and the people.

***

After Thermidor, when this symbolic unity died, how many Montagnards remained, how many of those who were now ironically rebaptized "Cretans" and who, as Soubrany wrote, had the courage "to climb back up the Mountain?" And it did indeed take courage, because, he continued, to ask for the floor from the height of the Mountain was to risk being stricken from the list of speakers. In Vendémiaire, after the Jacobin Club was closed, only two voices dared to ask for a roll-call vote. In order to gauge the number of loyal Montagnards who remained, Françoise Brunel suggests adding to the fifty deputies who supported Lecointre's motion for a roll-call vote on 12 Germinal, Year III (Lecointre had been among the Committee's accusers in Thermidor but had quickly been repulsed by the magnitude of the reaction), the seventy-four deputies arrested after Thermidor and again after the riots of Germinal and Prairial. There is some overlap between the two lists, so the numbers cannot simply be added together; one arrives at a figure of roughly one hundred "last Montagnards."

The historical misfortune of these loyalists, these "ardent patriots determined to give their lives for their principles," was the occurrence of two riots that gave them an opportunity to manifest their existence. On 12 Germinal, Year III, a mob of women and malcontents invaded the Convention demanding bread and the Constitution of 1793. The mob's leader, Van Eck, harangued the Mountain in terms that showed that the people, as Levasseur remarked, had not ceased to recognize it as the home of its natural leaders: "And you, Holy Mountain, you have fought so much for the Republic, the

390

men of July 14, August 10, and May 31 call upon you in this moment." Despite efforts by Montagnard orators to persuade the crowd to evacuate the hall, the Thermidorians seized upon this heaven-sent pretext to issue warrants for the arrest of a group of Montagnard deputies and to send Barère, Billaud-Varenne, and Collot d'Herbois off to exile in Guiana. A few weeks later Prairial repeated Germinal, but the second riot, triggered by the collapse of the assignat, abolition of the *maximum*, and soaring prices, seems to have been more thoroughly prepared, if Buonarroti's statements on the matter are to be believed. Nevertheless, the riot bore the usual earmarks of an old-fashioned popular disturbance. The crowd was made up of women and children, and once it invaded the Convention it resorted to the standard tactics of revolutionary violence: deputies insulted, debates ridiculed. To top it all off, the deputy Féraud was guillotined, the last head to fall in the Revolution. The novelty this time was in the behavior of the Montagnard deputies: with the support of the galleries they secured passage of motions including the release of the deputies and militants arrested in Germinal and—Romme's obsession—a single kind of bread for all. This participation led to their downfall: the Convention issued warrants for the arrest of another group of deputies, and a military commission handed down seventy-six sentences, including thirty-six death sentences. On 29 Prairial six Montagnard deputies attempted suicide (some successfully) before going to the scaffold. This collective suicide marked the end of the Mountain. Even in the Jacobin renaissance that followed the coup d'état of Fructidor, Year V, it was no longer a political force.

But this historical end was a legendary beginning. On the one hand, the exemplary death of those whom Quinet baptized "the last of the Romans" and to whom Michelet promised eternal glory furnished the Revolution with a final sublime scene, adding a crowning touch to the portrait of republican heroism. Celebrated by Baudot, Choudieu, and Levasseur, the memory of the last Montagnards was soon taken up by Babouvist propaganda. In the Vendôme trial Babeuf glorified the "disastrous but honorable" days of the spring of Year III, the last days of the Revolution in which "the people and its loyal delegates" stood side by side: "O Gracchi! Glorious martyrs! Intrepid champions of Holy Equality!"

The personalities of the men who were the heroes of these last Days did much to round out and fortify the epic legend of the Mountain. Romme's role was particularly important. Through his work in the Convention Romme was the man responsible for *l'instruction publique,* the calendar, the anthology of noble deeds, and the regeneration of mankind through republican institutions: the embodiment of the Mountain as educator. Through his actions as a *représentant en mission* in Charente and Dordogne, he had demonstrated his devotion to a state-controlled economy and had seen to it that the same "bread of equality" was distributed to rich and poor alike. He was the author of a Declaration of Rights that portrayed labor and not just capital as the source of property: the embodiment of an egalitarian Mountain. Finally, because he preached the "religion of laws" and never engaged in denunciation or exclusion, he was also the embodiment of a legalist Mountain. Romme and his friends, the "martyrs of Prairial," thus worked the miracle of lending a semblance of reality to the most improbable of all images: that of a Mountain without factions, miraculously dissociated from the memory of the Terror.

Mona Ozouf

FURTHER READING

Actes of the conference "Girondins et Montagnards." Paris, 1980. Cited below as CGM.

Baczko, Bronislaw, "L'expérience thermidorienne," in Colin Lucas, ed., *The French Revolution and the Creation of Modern Political Culture*, vol. 2, *The Political Culture of the French Revolution*. Oxford, 1988.

Baudot, Marc-Antoine. *Notes historiques sur la Convention Nationale, le Directoire, l'Empire et l'exil des votants*. Paris, 1985.

Brunel, Françoise. "Les députés Montagnards," in CGM.

——— "Les derniers Montagnards et l'unité révolutionnaire," in CGM.

Dulaure, Jacques-Antoine. *Physionomie de la Convention Nationale*. Paris, 1793.

Dupuy, Roger. "Du pseudo-fédéralisme breton au pseudo-fédéralisme parisien: Révolution et structures," in CGM.

Esquiros, Alphonse. *Histoire des Montagnards*, 2 vols. Paris, 1847.

Galante Garonne, Alessandro. *Gilbert Romme: Histoire d'un révolutionnaire, 1750–1795*. Paris, 1971.

Garat, Dominique-Joseph. *Mémoires*. Paris, 1862.

Higonnet, Patrice. "The Social and Cultural Antecedents of Revolutionary Discontinuity: Montagnards and Girondins," *English Historical Review*, July 1985.

Levasseur de La Sarthe, René. *Mémoires*, 4 vols. Paris, 1829–1831.

Lewis-Beck, Michael, Anne Hildreth, and Alan Spitzer. "Was There a Girondist Faction in the National Convention (1792–1793)?" *French Historical Studies*, Spring 1988.

Patrick, Alison. *The Men of the First French Republic: Political Alignments in the National Convention of 1792*. Baltimore, 1972.

Thibaudeau, Antoine-Clair. *Mémoires sur la Convention et le Directoire*, 2 vols. Paris, 1824.

RELATED TOPICS

Babeuf
Clubs and Popular Societies
Constitution
Equality
Girondins
Jacobinism
King's Trial

Paris Commune
Revolutionary Assemblies
Revolutionary Government
Revolutionary *Journées*
Robespierre
Terror

SANS-CULOTTES

Before 1789 Paris had its *petit peuple*. In Year III the capital seems to have been teeming with what the political mythology of the day baptized *buveurs de sang* (blood-drinkers), harbingers of the nineteenth century's pairing of *classes laborieuses/classes dangereuses*. The sans-culotte's existence was therefore very brief, from 1792 to 1795. The classical period of the phenomenon was still more ephemeral: from the spring of 1793 to the halting of de-Christianization in November of the same year. (Claire Lacombe was briefly detained in September 1793, and the Society of Revolutionary Republicans was dissolved on October 30. The enragé Jacques Roux committed suicide in February 1794.) This brief summary makes it quite clear that the sans-culotte must be seen in two different contexts: Parisian and revolutionary, social and political.

In one sense sans-culottism should be seen in relation to the political radicalization of Jacobinism (the fall of the monarchy, the king's death sentence, the populist turn in Montagnard policy in the spring of 1793, the fall of the Gironde in May–June, the death of Marat, the political-military crisis of July and August with Terror the order of the day). Celebration of these famous days would soon become a key element of the sans-culotte myth.

A second line of force was generated within the movement itself, a consequence of the social and cultural condition in which the common people of Paris lived, in quartiers whose diversity needs to be emphasized. (The faubourgs, for example, were less antireligious than the central quartiers.)

In answer to the question, "What is a sans-culotte?" a May 1793 document invoked social criteria: "He is a person who always travels on foot . . . and who lives very simply with his wife and children, if he has any, on the fifth or sixth story." Yet the same question could also be answered in entirely political terms. Listen to Brutus Magnier, who "said that he understood [by the term sans-culotte] the victors of the Bastille, of August 10, and of May 31, especially the latter two."

This political identification claims our attention all the more because the social situation of the Parisian sans-culottes is quantitatively uncertain: most of the documents vanished in the 1871 fire at the Hôtel-de-Ville. (Of the 6,000 members of the revolutionary army, only 280 dossiers have survived.) Furthermore, the surviving documents were often the work of the police and are therefore difficult to interpret. The aggressive—and artificially populist—biography of the sans-culotte of Year II has little in common with the sketchy answers he may have been obliged to give to soften *réacteur* judges and policemen.

Broadly speaking, let us assume nevertheless that the sans-culottes were fairly representative of the Parisian population. They were not marginals, as Taine and other conservative nineteenth-century historians made them out. A quarter of the *commissaires civils* of the sections were rentiers. Among these functionaries of the sections there were more shopkeepers than artisans. True, the militants, as well as the members of the revolutionary committees, were of more modest background: twelve percent were wage-earners, eight percent were domestics, and forty-two percent were artisans. In September 1793, on a motion by Danton and Barère, all were granted indemnities in order to allow them to attend the general assemblies of the forty-eight sections. The typical sans-culotte was neither a worker in the Gobelins factory nor an indigent living in a boarding house but an artisan, journeyman, or owner of a small business.

His cultural identity was both more novel and less ambiguous. Oddly enough, the sans-culotte's sensibility is more sharply defined than is his economic situation.

For Robespierre, the true revolutionary, the great Jacobin legislator, was a solitary figure. Cato, Brutus, and Socrates, the great martyrs and suicides of antiquity, were his models for Jacobin action. The sans-culotte, on the other hand, was gregarious. He lived among and for others, at least in principle. The sans-culotte orator never failed to present himself as the spokesman for a group, a committee, or an assembly, for his section or quartier. The Girondin Vergniaud rightly said of these "anarchists" (whom he detested) that "they came close to overthrowing the Republic by making every section believe that sovereignty resided within its bosom." Rhetorically, moreover, this line was often crossed. The sans-culotte orator's tactic was to portray at the same time the people and his own quartier, the capital and the Great Nation. Deaths of friends could not go unpunished. The massacre on the Champ de Mars was the vengeance of the bourgeoisie. For some, the September massacres would be a sort of popular counter-vengeance. In April 1793, when the Convention insisted that petitions be signed individually by each petitioner, the Gravilliers section objected that this principle would destroy "the fraternal unity that prevails among good citizens [and] is not suited to our system of government, which calls upon all citizens without distinction to perform civic functions." Instead the section advocated the collective petition: "In these difficult moments, rather than seek to divide citizen from citizen, it is essential and in the interest of all to band together to form an impregnable rampart."

Fraternity was the first principle of the popular *Weltanschauung*. Revealingly, the first popular society called itself the "Fraternal Society of Patriots of Both Sexes." There were countless moments of enthusiasm, of "republican joy." Members of sans-culotte societies liked to exchange "fraternal kisses." Group singing—of *La Carmagnole* or "the hymn of the Marseillais"—was an integral part of sans-culotte ritual. It was also important to express one's allegiance to the group through the wearing of distinctive clothing, made immortal by engravings, caricatures, and the noble art of the anti-academician David. The sans-culotte wore pantaloons (of necessity, since as the name implies he did not wear breeches), along with a carmagnole, suspenders, sabots, a red cap, and a tricolor cockade.

This fraternal vocation meant that for sans-culottes, the autonomy of the individual, of the private as opposed to the public, was necessarily limited: "The patriot has no personal life," the Fontaine-Grenelle section explained to the popular society of Auxerre. "He relates everything to the common mass: his joys, his feelings of pain, everything is poured into the bosom of his brothers, and therein lies the source of the publicity that distinguishes fraternal, i.e., republican, government." It was therefore obvious that voting and debate ought to be public: "No secret ballot in which the cabal triumphs." When members of another section found themselves in difficulty, it seemed entirely justifiable to come to their aid by mounting a friendly invasion of a general assembly. The sans-culotte spoke fraternally to every citizen, male or female. He aimed to be simple, frugal, affable, and accessible. His language, which was often excessively rhetorical and at times echoed the tones of prerevolutionary corporatism, was meant to be bluff and direct, clear and distinct. For the sans-culotte, use of the familiar *tu* was a political act.

It was hard for the sans-culotte to believe that a man could be moral in public and dishonest in private. Mirabeau was supposed to be a counterexample. Civility was a political and social continuum. The sans-culotte was a moralist. Politics as he understood it involved not a simple interplay of interests but a moralization of the political and a politicization of the citizen: "In order to be an honest man," the French republican explained to the citizen of Philadelphia, "you have to be a good son, good husband, and good father. In a word, you must combine all the public and private virtues. . . . Only then will you arrive at the true definition of patriotism." The rich man and even the noble are harmful not by dint of fortune or birth alone but rather because of their character, antisocial and corrupted by money, and because of their exercise of domination.

The fraternal sans-culotte deemed himself perfectly justified in feeling implacable hatred toward his antithesis, the "aristocrat," the epitome of selfishness and pride. For the sans-culotte, to be "haughty and proud" or to speak "with irony" was an offense worthy of arrest. The aristocrat, having chosen to live outside the social pact as demonstrated by his decision to leave the country, merited hatred and persecution. The sans-culotte was a unanimist, who saw the fundamental and characteristic perversity of the aristocrat as the reason for his sectarian rejection of the popular will, embodied in sans-culotterie. The aristocrat was not fully human. The sans-culotte frequently portrayed him as having the features of a monster or an animal: hydra, vulture, virus, or schizophrenic, two-headed monster. The unity of sans-culotterie signified the victory of the just.

For the sans-culotte, society was a whole, represented by a single, indivisible republican state. This Parisian did not desire equality of ownership, even if he believed that the state and society ought to grant every citizen the means to live. Yet without being truly in favor of equal distribution of wealth, he scorned money. Gold was for him an object of suspicion. The assignment of a compulsory exchange value to the assignat seemed natural to him, as did the struggle against the black market. For sans-culottes in the Jardin-des-Plantes section, it was essential to "fix at an invariable level the prices of the most necessary supplies, the wages of workers, the profits of enterprise, and the margins of commerce."

The sans-culottes' vision of the social world was one of complementarity and fraternity. The sans-culotte sought not so much to overthrow the social order as to make it more just: "Have a government that places the people above its meager resources and the rich man beneath his means. The balance will be just right." Transposed into the key of the Ancien Régime, this theme implied membership in a corps, conservatism, formalism, proceduralism, and traditionalism. In the revolutionary context it signified republicanism, fraternity, and even universalism.

The political flowering of the popular movement led, moreover, to a notable development of its communitarian aims. From political equality spokesmen moved rapidly to the theme of equality of enjoyment. Before long they were also proposing state aid for mothers, rent control, and confiscation of agricultural produce. This development makes a sharp contrast with the extreme individualism of the Le Chapelier Law and with the neutral social role of the state as envisioned by the Feuillants.

The moralistic, unanimist aspect of the sans-culotte sensibility had important consequences. To mobilize the sans-culotte politically, momentary indignation (over a political betrayal or a food crisis) was more important than the enemy's tactical weakness. Babeuf recognized this when he later organized his Conspiracy of Equals, led by a secret committee prepared to strike when the time was ripe. The sans-culotte had a hard time understanding the delegation of power. His instinct impelled him toward direct, violent action. The pike was the symbol of the militant on the march. The sections' cannons were the fetishistic symbol of their sovereignty. From such a state of mind it was often but a short step to legal terrorism: "'Is there guillotine today?' 'Yes,' replied a candid patriot, 'for there is always treason.'" The carpenter Richer expressed the widely shared opinion "that we will have bread only by spilling blood. Under the Reign of Terror there was no shortage."

Explaining the deep reasons for the rise of sans-culotterie in Year II is one of the thorniest problems in the history of the Revolution. In one sense, the emergence of the sans-culotte was, as Marx explained, merely a reflection of the radicalization of the bourgeois revolution. It was thanks to the struggle that led to the downfall of the monarchy in August 1792 that the sans-culottes truly entered into history. For Marx, sans-culotterie was essentially the reserve army of a hard-pressed bourgeoisie. The execution of the king in January 1793, coupled with the economic crisis in the spring of that year and the divisions within the patriotic party, suddenly increased the influence of popular militants. The expulsion of the Girondins in May–June 1793, willed by the Mountain but accomplished by the people, was a veritable triumph for the sans-culottes. September 5 was the high point of this political evolution. Its chief accomplishments were the *maximum,* or price controls, and the creation of an urban people's militia, the revolutionary army, as well as the surprising launching of a popular women's movement, associated with the actress Claire Lacombe and with Pauline Léon, the wife of the enragé Leclerc. For the first time in history, women gathered independently in order to carry on their own autonomous political action. This movement was all the more astonishing in that Chaumette and Robespierre, the Jacobins and the Hébertists, were for the most part violently antifeminist.

For some authors (notably Richard Cobb), ideas and ideology played a negligible part in the sans-culotte episode of the Year II. For Soboul and Rudé, on the other hand, the flareup in the spring of 1793 cannot be explained without taking into account, at least indirectly, the work of the publicists and even of certain philosophes, especially Jean-Jacques Rousseau, whose life the sans-culottes regarded as exemplary. Of the 200 Parisian revolutionaries arrested in July 1791 on orders of Bailly and Lafayette, nearly all of whom would be sans-culotte militants two years later, eighty percent could read and write. Certain sans-culottes, in any case, were fully conscious of their place in history: "*Au grand Sir Constance il faut un grand Caracter*" ("the great circumstance needs a great character"), one of them wrote. In my view, the ideologization of the popular movement in the form of Babouvism in 1795 was an accentuation rather than a diversion of the popular movement of Year II.

The historiographic problem of the relative importance of ideology in shaping the nature of sans-culottism is all the more important because it probably relates to another aspect of the movement, namely, its internal structure. For Richard Andrews there was indeed a sans-culotte ideology, but it was a doctrine one of whose functions was to permit the manipulation of the Parisian popular masses by small militant oligarchies.

Each of the forty-eight Paris sections comprised roughly 12,000 to 25,000 inhabitants (of whom 1,600 to 6,000, or from one-tenth to one-third of the total, were indigents on relief). At times *Père Duchesne* may have had as many as 200,000 readers. The sectional battalions numbered around 100,000 men, and Paris in 1793 sent 80,000 men to the front. The number of sans-culotte militants was far smaller. The popular societies of the sections rarely numbered more than 400 members. After Germinal and Prairial, Year III, the indictment of 6,000 persons was enough to break the back of the Parisian popular movement. Only five to ten percent of the eligible Parisians actively participated in the life of the sections. Richard Andrews goes so far as to speak of a "sans-culotte oligarchy."

The institutional apparatus of the sections included only 3,000 to 4,000 persons, and these sans-culotte "functionaries" are a phenomenon unto themselves. Andrews spends a great deal of time on the important example of sectional *juges de paix* (assisted by *assesseurs*), who, though elected, had backgrounds as legal officials under the Ancien Régime. Thus, it is important to distinguish between the popular base of sans-culotterie and its (literate) elite of paid functionaries. Also included under this head are the *commissaires de police* and their secretary-bailiffs, as well as members of the *comités civils*, those important personages who managed the capital's supplies. Initially elected, they too received salaries after January 1794, and before long they were incorporated into the Jacobin state apparatus.

Seen in this dualist light, sans-culottism becomes, to modify Soboul's phrase, an ideologized revolutionary democracy rather than a truly popular manifestation.

In cooperation with the Convention, the sections governed Paris from the summer of 1793 until the fall of Hébert. Yet contrary to what the enragés and friends of Hébert no doubt assumed, sans-culotterie proved to be impotent without the critical support of bourgeois Jacobinism. Much weaker than they seemed at first sight, the sans-culotte masses were helpless to prevent their leaders' defeat in the period from November 1793 to March 1794. They were equally defenseless after Thermidor, during the terrible winter of what Richard Cobb most aptly called "the great murder year."

The analysis of this sudden collapse of sans-culotterie naturally reflects the ideological options available to modern historiography. For the empiricists, fatigue is a sufficient explanation. "The people are tired," explained the Incorruptible. Less nobly, Jacob Clique confessed: "I am embittered by misfortune. I am the father of three young children, and penniless, so that my daily labor must provide for the existence of five people. I have done almost no work in the harsh winter we have just endured." Thousands of sans-culottes set out for Vendée or for the eastern frontiers. The movement fell apart.

Soboul's Marxist explanation, highly schematic and harshly criticized by Richard Cobb and Richard Andrews, is of a very different order, focusing on the heterogeneous nature of the sans-culotte movement: not being a class movement with a uniform social base, sans-culottism could not succeed.

Owing to certain of its cultural features, its tolerance of physical violence, its inflated rhetoric, and its refusal of all economic modernization, sans-culottism was certainly a backward-looking movement. Yet in its consciousness of specific social roots, its politicized social goals, and its partial tolerance of a feminist movement, the revolutionary popular movement of Year II was a forerunner of the nineteenth-century workers' movement. Of this heritage the revolutionaries of 1848 and 1871 were fully aware.

Patrice Higonnet

Further reading

Andrews, Richard Mowery. "Social Structure, Political Elites and Ideology in Revolutionary Paris, 1792–1793: A Critical Evaluation of Albert Soboul's *Les sans-culottes parisiens en l'an II*," *Journal of Social History*, vol. 19, no. 1, Fall 1985.

Cobb, Richard. *The Police and the People: French Popular Protest, 1789–1820*. London, 1970.

Markov, Walter M., and Albert Soboul, eds. *Die Sansculotten von Paris: Dokumente zur Geschichte der Volksbewegung, 1793–1794*. East Berlin, 1957.

Rose, R. B. *The Making of the Sans-Culottes: Democratic Ideas and Institutions in Paris, 1789–1792*. Manchester, 1983.

Soboul, Albert. *Les sans-culottes parisiens en l'an II: Histoire politique et sociale des sections de Paris, 2 juin 1793–9 thermidor an II*. La Roche-sur-Yon, 1958. Reprinted Paris, 1958, and 1962 with the subtitle *Mouvement populaire et gouvernement révolutionnaire*.

Sonenscher, Michael. "The Sans-Culottes of the Year II: Rethinking the Language of Labor in Revolutionary France." *Social History*, vol. 9, October 1984, 301–328.

Williams, Gwyn. *Artisans and Sans-Culottes: Popular Movements in France and Britain during the French Revolution*. New York, 1969.

Related topics

Aristocracy
Babeuf
Clubs and Popular Societies
Danton
Enragés
Fraternity
Hébertists
Jacobinism
Marx
Maximum
Robespierre
Rousseau
Terror

THERMIDORIANS

T hermidor, Thermidorian: words with many meanings. Thermidor is, first of all, the name of a month in the revolutionary calendar. In the annals of the Revolution this name has become synonymous with 9 Thermidor, the date of the fall of Robespierre and his acolytes. For certain historians, this date has taken on a symbolic value: it supposedly divides the history of the Revolution into two parts, or even marks the end of the Revolution as such. Thermidor (or the Thermidorian period) is also used in a broader sense to refer to the period from 9 Thermidor, Year II, to 4 Brumaire, Year IV, the date on which the Convention ceased to exist. The phrase "Thermidorian Convention" is used to distinguish this period from the Assembly's earlier activity. Consequently, "Thermidorians" are those conventionnels who took part in the conspiracy that toppled Robespierre, as well as others—conventionnels, politicians, ideologues, and what have you—who later approved "the tyrant's downfall." This entire fifteen-month period (or at least its latter part) is seen fairly frequently as a time of reaction, whence the consecrated expression "Thermidorian reaction."

Not only is the vocabulary confused; so are the phenomena themselves. During the Thermidorian period and under the Directory, the anniversary of 9 Thermidor was solemnly commemorated as a "joyful revolution." Subsequently, however, celebrating the event would have been unthinkable. Thermidor was destined to become memorable in a different way: like certain other words that originated in the revolutionary period, such as Jacobinism and Bonapartism, it came to denote a "formative event" for revolutionary ideologies that used the French Revolution as a historical reference and theoretical model. After the death of Lenin, for example, Trotskyists used the word "Thermidor" and its derivatives to name, and indeed to explain, Stalin's rise to power. The October Revolution, they argued, had met its Thermidor; the Stalinists were Thermidorians, that is, former revolutionaries who had "degenerated" into profiteers of revolution and who consequently became its gravediggers (in which respect they differed from ordinary counterrevolutionaries, the inveterate "class enemies" of the Revolution). The Trotskyist interpretation of Thermidor is the best known, but every revolution of the nineteenth and twentieth centuries has had to face the specter of a Thermidor, that is, a moment when some one-time revolutionaries themselves turn against the revolution, breaking its spirit. Note in passing that the term "Thermidorism" never caught on; Thermidor was not seen as a doctrine, nor was it identified with a stage of the Revolution or a political practice.

This essay is concerned with the political experience that gave this fifteen-month period its unity and distinctive character. The experience was an important one for the political culture of the Revolution, even though it did not grow out of a political or ideological program that preceded the event. It is interesting primarily because of the political problems the Thermidorians had to face and the ways in which they responded to them. Those problems, all interrelated, form a remarkably coherent system, an integral part of the political experience of the Revolution. Finally Thermidor has a unique role as a "formative event," a symbol and myth in the revolutionary tradition.

*
**

On 10 Thermidor France awoke anti-Robespierrist. The fall of Robespierre and the consequent end of the Terror were welcomed with approval and even enthusiasm throughout the country: so goes the history books' cliché. Some eight hundred petitions of congratulation addressed to the Convention after 9 Thermidor seem to confirm that cliché. All express unanimous support for the Convention, the "sole rallying center," from the entire country: constituted authorities, popular societies, military units, and so on. These petitions outdo one another in denunciation, as grandiloquent as it is repetitive, of Robespierre ("new Catiline," "new Cromwell," "scoundrel"), as well as in exaltation of the Convention, the "fathers of the country" who are called upon to "remain at their posts." These clichés and stereotypes inevitably suggest a common model. And one need not look far: the Convention's appeals and session minutes were quite obviously the primary source of inspiration. The petitions were like an echo chamber that reflected back the Convention's own words. Their standardized language points up the conditions that made such remarkable unanimity possible. They were in effect speaking the stereotyped language of Year II, the same language, but for a few epithets, that had been used to condemn previous "conspirators," the Dantons and Héberts, as well as to exalt the "sacred person" of Robespierre. Whatever real relief may have been felt at the news of the "tyrant's downfall," the petitions bear witness to the uniformization of political language and behavior that occurred during the Terror, to the obligatory unanimity of that period, and to the conformism adopted as norm and model of political conduct. The messages to the Convention thus reproduced the fundamental ambiguity inherent in the referential event itself, 9 Thermidor. The "tyrant's downfall" marked a point of no return with respect to the Terror. Beyond that significance, however, it was an event in search of its own meaning. Was 9 Thermidor, the "revolution made by the Convention," a self-contained episode that put an end to "tyranny," or was it merely an initial act, inevitably destined to lead to other acts in which its implications ultimately came to pass?

"Down with the tyrant!" the unanimous cry in the Convention on 9 Thermidor, was at once a slogan and a specific objective, which enabled the deputies to move quickly and to overlook political differences among those still unaware that they were in the process of becoming "Thermidorians." On 9 Thermidor Robespierre was cast as the tyrant and his "reign" identified with tyranny. Very quickly, however, voices were raised to denounce the Ter-

401

ror as a multifarious phenomenon that went far beyond the person and power of Robespierre himself. The term "system," used sporadically at first, came to be firmly associated with the term "Terror." The Terror was not simply a group of men in power; it was denounced by Tallien as a system of power based on fear. To denounce the Terror as a system and demand its dismantlement was certainly to embark upon an exciting and impassioned political debate about the Revolution's past and future. But it was above all to engage in a political conflict and struggle over a range of issues: To what extent should the Terror be dismantled and its consequences repaired? How should this reparation be done? Against whom should the effort be directed, and who should guide it? All these questions were in turn related to the central question: Who would hold power after 9 Thermidor?

After 9 Thermidor there was of course room in the political spectrum not only for denunciation of the Terror but also for escalation of anti-Robespierrist and antiterrorist attacks. Political divisions that developed among the Thermidorians inevitably harked back to this lost unity. Hence it was impossible to emerge from the Terror without giving rise to new sources of violence. The five or six months immediately following 9 Thermidor are of particular interest for students of the political problems and mechanisms engendered by a situation of this kind. During this period, forces external to the Revolution played a relatively limited role. The traditional counterrevolutionary forces, most notably the émigrés, were still too frightened by the Terror to show their hand, particularly since in many cases they were slow to grasp the importance of the event. Consequently, the period is almost a laboratory for study of the processes by which the legacy of the Terror—political, institutional, and symbolic—disintegrated, along with the impact of that disintegration on revolutionary imagination and symbolism. To begin emerging from the Terror was to expand the sphere of liberty, but it was also to subject the political arena thus liberated to divisions and conflicts of its own. Still, the end of the Terror did not necessarily alter the mechanisms and principles of revolutionary politics; rather, it adapted them to novel tasks.

The contradictions and paradoxes inherent in the dismantling of the "system of Terror" revealed themselves one after another. The institutions inherited from the Terror were as much as possible patched up. The decree of 7 Fructidor, Year II, maintained the "revolutionary government" but reorganized the committees and shifted their responsibilities. (In particular, the powers of the Committee of Public Safety were curtailed and reassigned to the Committee of General Security and the Committee on Legislation.) Committee members were replaced. Freedom of the press was dramatically increased: new newspapers and dozens of brochures enjoyed enormous success, attacking with ever mounting violence the "Robespierrist rump." No one dared to challenge the principle of freedom of the press, but the Convention was not yet ready to declare it "unlimited," as Fréron demanded—Fréron, along with Tallien, having become the symbol of the "political chameleon," the former Terrorist who had changed his stripes. There was nothing new about political turncoats, of course, and the Revolution had known others. The fact that after 9 Thermidor such maneuvers again became possible is further evidence of the freeing up of the mechanisms of politics. Yet the change in direction was so sudden that it surprised people and aroused suspicion. Those who became "turncoats on the scaffold" still reeked of their recent past when they denounced the Terror and persecuted "Terrorists" and "*buveurs de sang*" (blood-drinkers). Nevertheless, they posed the problem of responsibility for the Terror, especially for former members of the governmental committees. Once that question arose, it could not be wished away, and it came up repeatedly wherever the Terror had done its damage, which is to say, throughout the country, at the level of both the central government and each revolutionary committee.

In the aftermath of 9 Thermidor the victors recalled the old slogan, "Terror the order of the day!" and countered with the new slogan, "Justice the order of the day!" Thus they held out the promise of a new era—a promise easier made than kept. Beyond the rhetoric of "justice" there were in fact difficult and unavoidable problems: What to do with the legacy of the Terror, and in particular with the prisoners held in jail as a result of laws passed by the Convention itself? What to do with the political figures of Year II who were inextricably associated with the Terror? The Convention was slow to appreciate the magnitude of these problems, despite the fact that they were related by an inexorable political logic. It formulated its answers not in relation to an overall project but on a case-by-case basis. Yet those partial and partisan responses, hesitant and tortuous as they may have been, did result in a fairly clear choice that was both political and emotional: the Thermidorian government decided on revenge as the way to put the Terror behind it.

The release of prisoners was in itself a dramatic and complex problem. After 9 Thermidor the gates of the prisons were more than slightly ajar, and the victims of the Terror, once freed, called for vengeance against those who had denounced and oppressed them. The Convention had not yet decided on an amnesty. Nevertheless, the law of 22 Prairial was abolished. Arbitrarily held prisoners were released in a chaotic manner, often as a result of personal requests to committee members, but in large numbers: in five days, from 18 to 23 Thermidor, the Committee of General Security ordered the release of 478 prisoners in Paris. In the départements the release policy depended on local circumstances and especially on the political attitudes of the *représentants en mission*, who were gradually replaced. Even more than the Terror itself, the dismantlement of the Terror was a policy carried out on the local level. The release of prisoners provoked growing anxieties among Jacobins in the popular societies, who had served as the political personnel of the Terror. Not only were "aristocrats" and "suspects" released, but "patriots" themselves came under attack and were persecuted. They were denounced as "Robespierrists," "*buveurs de sang*," "Terrorists," and "cannibals." A whole new vocabulary of accusation quickly came into use. Toward the end of Year II the Convention was besieged by dozens of petitions calling for an end to the "persecution of patriots" and for "energetic" opposition to the aristocracy and moderatism now "rearing their heads" once more. The Jacobin Club became the focal point of these alarms, which it communicated to its affiliated societies. Yet this wave of petitions provoked a reaction in the form of appeals to keep "justice the order of the day," to repair the consequences of the Terror, and to punish the Terrorists. The "war of petitions" of the fall of 1795 gives some idea of the distance traveled in the space of just a few months. Those with different political views now dared to clash publicly, and the Convention's increasing division was an incontrovertible sign of political liberalization. Nevertheless, the issues raised by political differences, the passions they aroused, and the mounting desire for revenge presaged a coming political confrontation over the dismantlement of the Terror.

The policy best suited to the collective passions of the day was quite simply one of revenge. It was also the policy best adapted to the mechanisms of exclusion put in place by the workings of revolutionary politics. From one stage to the next, the Revolution transmitted the language and the myth of its fundamental unity, but at the same time it reproduced its basic political regulatory mechanism: the exclusion of political adversaries as "factions," as enemies of the unity of the nation, the people, the Republic, or what have you. The image and symbolism of unity were used constantly, throughout the Revolution, as a weapon of political combat, a principle legitimizing exclusion of the adversary. In this respect 9 Thermidor was in no sense innovative. The emergence from the Terror was accomplished by excluding "Terrorists" and "Jacobins." Repression was justified by invoking unitary principles and values, by insisting that unity had to be achieved in opposition to the "factious" and to the "successors of Robespierre." The great innovation of the period, however, was the return of the vanquished—specifically, the surviving members of the Gironde. For the first time a revolutionary assembly had repented of its exclusions, and it did so in the name not of "indulgence" but of "justice." To be sure, the Convention was scarcely willing to recognize its own responsibility. Even those who had condemned the Girondins now presented themselves as victims of the "tyrant" and the "rebel Commune." Nevertheless, the seventy-five deputies who had signed the protests against the *journées* of May 31 and June 2 were the first to be called back (18 Frimaire, Year III, or December 8, 1794). Those who had been declared outlaws and who had managed to hide were recalled later (on 18 Ventôse, or March 8, 1795). Simultaneously, the Convention rescinded the decree by which it had established a commemorative holiday on May 31. The return of the Girondins was thus a gesture intended to unify all "good citizens" and put an end to "suspicions."

The experiences and memories of the Terror did less to unify, however, than to stir conflicts and arouse suspicions. It was the language of suspicion that best expressed the hatreds and fears bequeathed by the Terror. The release of prisoners, the sudden change in the political situation, and the first "persecutions of patriots" created a climate of insecurity and fear among Jacobins and militant minorities who had been thrust to the center of the political stage and who were now being asked to account for their actions. Hatred was directed toward "Terrorists" and others deemed guilty simply for having participated in a government now judged to be reprehensible. Last but not least, there was fear of a return of the Terror and of further massacres, a fear stirred up by the press, by anti-Jacobin pamphlets, and by countless rumors. These fears and suspicions combined to arouse desires for revenge, individual as well as collective, against the "scoundrels" and "cutthroats," looters and thieves, and ignorant and insolent men who had monopolized all the jobs and who dreamed of only one thing: regaining the upper hand vis-à-vis "honest men."

It is impossible to overstate the impact on public opinion, on the collective fears mentioned above, and on the desire for revenge, of the great political trials involving those held responsible for the Terror, particularly Carrier and the revolutionary committee of Nantes (the latter tried on 25 Vendémiaire, Year III, or October 16, 1794, and the former on 26 Frimaire, Year III, or December 16, 1794). For two months the attention of all France was focused on the revelations issuing from the courtroom of the Revolutionary Tribunal. The trial, which ranged far beyond the ostensible charges against the defendants, was actually transformed into a trial of the Terror, indeed of the Revolution itself. All the fears and fantasies that the Terror had both engendered and repressed now returned to the surface. The trial first exhibited terrifying images of the "Great Terror": the drownings at Nantes, the arbitrary executions, the gunning down of Vendean prisoners—crimes epitomized in the image of the bloody Loire, the river brimming with corpses. In addition, the trial also dramatized the "Little Terror," the terror in everyday life: an entire city subjected to the arbitrary power and exactions of a handful of sans-culotte militants, some of them rather shady characters of dubious background, who put their revolutionary zeal to work oppressing honest folk. The two Terrors—the "Great" and the "Small"—reflected each other in countless ways, as in a hall of mirrors: all those who had had to endure the chicanery and blackmail of the revolutionary committees and popular societies could identify with the horrors revealed in the Paris trial and could *almost* imagine themselves in the place of the drowned victims of Nantes. The trial ultimately demonstrated the responsibility of the Convention: Carrier continually leveled a finger of accusation, proving that he had acted with the tacit approval of the Convention, which he had kept informed of the role in the punishment of suspects that had been assigned to the "revolutionary river." Carrier's trial provided the basis for the Terror's dark legend, which discredited the heroic image of the men of Year II, branded all who participated as criminals, and baptized militant minorities with names such as "*buveurs de sang*," "cannibals," and "vandals." Carrier, abandoned by the Convention and condemned by nearly unanimous vote, was executed. Above all, the trial was the death warrant of the Jacobins (who had dared neither to defend Carrier openly nor to condemn him severely) and led to the closing of the club (22 Brumaire, Year III, or November 12, 1794), an action fraught with symbolic importance. In the closing of the club as well as in the destruction of symbols associated with Year II, the so-called *jeunesse dorée* played an important part: these youthful shock troops, manipulated by the committees, dominated such public places as squares, cafés, and theaters, where they hunted down "Jacobins" and "vandals." The Jacobins made the painful discovery that the power of their rhetoric, in which they so fervently believed, had rested largely on the fact that in Year II theirs had been the rhetoric of power. Deprived of the support of power, left vulnerable to attacks by organized groups who used their control of the streets against the Jacobins as the Jacobins had once used it against others, ideologically disoriented and shorn of their triumphal symbolism, the Jacobins could do nothing to stem their decline. They became the prime victims of anti-Terrorist vengeance.

The Thermidorian government was thus swallowed up in the politics of legal revenge, where "legal" means contained within limits set by justice. The verbal violence of the calls for vengeance suggested the fragility of such restrictions, however. The policy of revenge reflected the emotional needs of the moment. By stirring unbridled passions of revenge, it inevitably initiated a new cycle of violence. But it offered no answer to the central political problem stemming from the condemnation of the "system of Terror": What space was to be created for politics and institutions after the Terror? The response could only be formulated in constitutional terms. Hence the question, "How do we put the Terror behind us?" necessarily led to another question: "How do we end the Revolution?"

Theoretically the Republic had a Constitution. It had been drafted hastily in June 1793, after the fall of the Girondins, and its adoption was solemnly celebrated during the festival of August 10. That night, the text was just as solemnly enclosed in an "ark of cedarwood" and deposited in the hall of the Convention. Enforcement of the Constitution was postponed, however, until peace returned, and as of 9 Thermidor it had never been put into effect. The document was open to challenge on two grounds: the conditions under which it had been drafted and approved, and the nature of its contents. In the first few months after Thermidor, however, the Constitution bothered no one, and it was left tranquilly in its "ark." It was not until the winter and spring of Year III that it became an unavoidable obstacle to dismantling the Terror and defining the politics of the post-Terror period. In effect, the Montagnard and Jacobin deputies, as well as the sans-culotte militants, those who had constituted the political personnel of the Terror, continued to insist on application of the Constitution as a means of pressuring the Convention's committees and majority. Applying the Constitution thus became a far-reaching political symbol, an indirect way of contesting the antiterrorist policy, demanding the liberation of "persecuted patriots," resurrecting the Jacobin societies, and condemning the purges and the denigration of the symbolic legacy of Year II. The fixation on the Constitution also reflected the political weakness of the whole campaign, whose instigators continually invoked the fundamental event of this whole period, the "revolution of 9 Thermidor." Paradoxically, it was therefore in the name of the "true meaning of 9 Thermidor" that opponents rejected its inevitable consequences and demanded the "democratic Constitution of 1793."

The conflict daily grew more bitter, and the issue could not be left unresolved. The *journées* of the spring of Year III—12 Germinal and especially 1–2 Prairial—not only accelerated the resolution of the crisis but ended it in a particularly brutal way. The rebellious crowd that forced its way into the

Convention with shouts of "Bread and the Constitution of 1793!" gave the Assembly proof, if any was needed, that dismantling the Terror and abolishing the Constitution of 1793 were merely two aspects of a single problem. The Prairial days were not simply a Thermidorian phenomenon. Inextricably intertwining the archaic and the modern, they illustrated a common feature of revolutionary mentalities and political cultures. In a crisis brought on by grave shortages of food, a new version of an old rumor spread: that the famine was the result of a conspiracy. This time it was not the royal government but the Convention that was accused of hiding grain in order to starve the people and in particular to strike at its vital core, the children. The plan of the riot, the movements of the sections, and the rallying cry were all worked out by sans-culottes (mainly in the Paris prisons) and were part of a political strategy of confrontation with the government over the way out of the Terror. But once the Convention had been entered, there was no controlling the crowd, which had no notion of this strategy. It entertained itself with gratuitous and unbridled acts of violence. After cutting off the head of the deputy Féraud, impaling it on a pike, and planting it in front of the chairman of the Assembly, the crowd behaved in an almost carnivalesque manner. It pushed deputies out of their seats, took their places, and parodied their behavior. The revolutionary *journée* was consequently drained of its political substance; the initial plan was overshadowed by the crowd's own ritual of violence. The Prairial days were in a sense revolutionary *journées* turned upside down. They sounded the death knell for all the heroic, militant imagery of the "people on the march." The incarnation of direct democracy, they revealed the vulnerability and fleeting, historically limited character of sans-culottism.

The Prairial revolt ended in failure and brutal repression. It did not fundamentally alter the political problems to be resolved, but it did entail many grave consequences for the remainder of the Thermidorian political experiment: a resurgence of fear of a possible return of the Terror; a brutal settling of scores among conventionnels (particularly with what remained of the Mountain); a dramatic intensification of the vengeance against the "Terrorists," which went so far as to include lynchings; and irrevocable doom for the Constitution of 1793, judged to be both illegal and terrorist.

The word "reaction," as well as its derivatives *réacteur* and *réactionnaire* (both meaning "reactionary"), did not really enter the political vocabulary until the end of the Thermidorian period, as if people only then began to feel the need for a specific word to describe the sequence of events and capture its meaning. (As in the case of the words "revolution" and "progress," the political lexicon borrowed the term "reaction" from mechanics, extending to the moral realm the proper sense of a movement in response to an earlier movement, a counteraction.) After the royalist revolt of 13 Vendémiaire, Year IV (October 5, 1795), was crushed, the term "reaction" gained a permanent place in political discourse, particularly in the official vocabulary, while at the same time it took on multiple meanings. The government used the word exclusively to refer to the perversion of the initial Thermidorian goal of ending the Terror, or even the deliberate subversion of that aim by forces hostile to the Revolution. Thus, the lynchings and massacres of "Terrorist" prisoners in

Lyons (February–May 1795) were denounced as a "reaction," as were the massacres of "Jacobins" and *"buveurs de sang"* in the Midi (in particular, the massacre of more than 100 "Terrorists" at Fort Saint-Jean in Marseilles on June 5, 1795). The hesitation as to the meaning to give to the term "reaction" reflects discomfort with the facts, events, and tendencies that, taken together, constituted a novel and disconcerting political phenomenon, but whose outlines remained ambiguous and boundaries uncertain. It might be said that reaction began when the antiterrorist revenge overstepped its legal limits, turned arbitrary, and therefore cast doubt on the Republic and its institutions. It is easy, however, to demonstrate the apologetic, not to say hypocritical, character of all the distinctions intended to absolve the Convention of responsibility for encouraging and fostering the "reaction." The choice of legal revenge as the political response to the problems raised by the dismantlement of the Terror was one fraught with peril, with an inherent risk of escalation in the intensity of the repression. To be sure, neither the Convention nor its governmental committees themselves organized the massacres. Nevertheless, the excesses that went along with the policy of legal and systematic repression of the *buveurs de sang* were predictable and inevitable. Furthermore, in certain cases, most notably that of Marseilles, the *représentants en mission* acted as overt accomplices in the massacres. Hence it was not far-fetched to accuse the Thermidorians of being "reactionaries" or even thinly disguised counterrevolutionaries. Former Jacobin and sans-culotte militants, persecuted, arrested, confined to their homes, did not hesitate to raise the charge, and Jacobin historians have followed suit. For them, the "reaction" was not a mere episode but something like an all-encompassing system of government, the epitome of all that had taken place in the political realm since 9 Thermidor.

The Thermidorian political experience was not limited to the various manifestations of reaction, however. The spasms of violence were irregular and were not encouraged by the governmental system, in contrast to the Terror, when violence was erected into a system. The immediate effect of the Prairial crisis was an increase in the intensity of the "reaction," but it also hastened the search for positive, institutional solutions to the problems that arose in the first months of the experiment. Both the strength and the weakness of Thermidorian policy lay in the fact that it was defined primarily in negative terms: neither Terror nor monarchy. The formula was vague enough to answer to the needs of the moment on 9 Thermidor but too vague to define a more durable and coherent policy. Early in Year III, as the Convention's policy suffered from its increasingly ad hoc character, the need for such coherence was more and more acutely felt. A new constitution would have both to draw the lessons of the past and to formulate a project for the future. It would not only have to complete the Thermidorian political experiment but, more broadly, cap the extraordinarily complex and contradictory history of six years of revolution.

The new constitution was supposed to define the principles and institutions of a liberal, representative republic and therefore terminate the Revolution. It would also have to meet two requirements of the Thermidorian Convention: both to preserve the Republic and to prevent any possibility of a return of the Terror. It would therefore have to take its inspiration from the founding principles of 1789, while drawing the inescapable lessons of the Terror. In that way it could determine the true meaning of 9 Thermidor. To end the Revolution: neither the project nor the slogan was new, of course. Both had cropped up periodically at various stages of the Revolution, in terms vague enough to reflect quite opposite political tendencies and projects, from moderate to extremist. For some (monarchiens, Feuillants, certain Girondins), ending the Revolution meant putting an end to illicit actions and seditious demands, the Revolution already having attained its objectives. For others (enragés, Hébertists, certain Jacobins), ending the Revolution was merely a call to continued action: an occasion, not to say pretext, for asserting the will to effect more radical political change, to push the movement toward its ultimate goal, which could only be full realization of the great revolutionary promise. In 1795 the Thermidorian Convention left no doubt about its intentions: the Revolution could not be ended by fulfilling all the hopes and promises it had engendered. Disillusionment or, if you prefer, bitter realism presided over the drafting of the Constitution. To end the Revolution was to establish the Republic as a state of laws on solid and durable foundations and thus to protect it against the return of its own past, against the Terror and a demagogy that simultaneously invoked the indefinite promise of the Revolution and the unlimited sovereignty of the people.

In 1795 the awareness of confronting an unprecedented task was curiously reminiscent of the state of mind that animated the first great constitutional debate in the summer and autumn of 1789. Nevertheless, in six years the terms in which the problem of drafting a constitution for France was posed had changed radically, and this change can in some ways serve as a measure of the evolution of political culture and attitudes.

In 1789 the accent was placed on a radical rejection of the past. In 1795 the Revolution carried with it an unavoidable past of its own, which it could not jettison. It was obsessed, moreover, with memories of the immediate past: the Terror. The sense of having lived through a corrosive and destructive time was repeatedly alluded to in the constitutional debate. In contrast to the symbols it admired, the Revolution was not a fountain of youth. It aged and caused people to age. In 1789 the idea of a radical break with the past and the determination to create something entirely new and original went hand in hand with the affirmation of the nation's unlimited sovereignty. Since its will was in no way limited when it promulgated the laws by which it lived, the nation could and should exercise its constituent power to the full, without impediment of any kind. In Year III the sovereignty of the nation was still recognized as the foundation of the republic. It was commonly acknowledged, however, that that sovereignty could only be conceived of as limited in certain ways. The dogma of unlimited popular sovereignty had been used to legitimate the Terror and its ravages—the tyranny exercised in the name of the "people on the march" by an ignorant rabble claiming to act in the name of direct democracy. The representative system therefore limited popular sovereignty. It protected inalienable individual liberties against the risks and dangers of their nullification by a so-called general will and consequently by a government that might claim unlimited powers by invoking that will. The representative system made it necessary to think of politics as a specialized activity, entrusted to enlightened, competent individuals possessing the necessary time and means to devote themselves to the job. Only in this way could the common interest be identified, and it was up to the representatives, not the represented, to formulate the general will. A specifically French version of liberalism, which sought to reconcile de facto inequality with equality before the law and popular sovereignty with the power of enlightened elites, was thus elaborated as a reaction to the Terror and as a conclusion of Thermidor. The establishment of a "democracy of talents" may thus be seen, in constitutional terms, as a response to two concerns. To prevent any resumption of the Revolution, it set up the institutional machinery necessary to maintain control over the political system; and it united all citizens through recognition of their civil equality while at the same time making sure that France would enjoy "government of the nation by the best."

Without analyzing the Constitution of Year III, we can call attention to two promises or hopes fostered by the invention of a new political space: order in stability and progress through education. After years in which permanent upheaval became the rule, the Convention in its final days conceived the utopia of a republican order capable of establishing a stable and durable framework for communal life and of resisting violent change by means of intrinsic mechanisms of self-preservation. Historians have often criticized these institutional mechanisms on the grounds that they produced paralysis, ultimately leading to 18 Brumaire. Be that as it may, the fundamental political phenomenon must be looked for elsewhere. For all its institutional and legal sophistication, France was nevertheless a democracy at a very rudimentary stage of historical development. In this respect, the Constitution of Year III is especially indicative of the limits of the political and social imagination of the entire revolutionary period, precisely because of all the accumulated precautions. It conceived of the political space at best in terms of a balance of powers and the exercise of sovereignty. It was never able to conceive of or imagine that space as necessarily divided by opposing political tendencies, hence inevitably contradictory and in conflict. In this sense the Constitution of Year III remained the prisoner of the revolutionary mythology of the unified nation and of political life as the expression of that unity. The Thermidorian Convention did not accept political pluralism, not even as a necessary evil. It therefore did not seek to invent mechanisms by which such pluralism could function. When public opinion, which of course changed from election to election, got too far out of step with the government in power, the only remedy was a coup d'état, and the end of the story is well known.

The determination to leave the Terror behind, along with the need to carry out the new policy, made it necessary to redefine social alliances. The Thermidorians quite naturally turned to the "owners," the well-to-do, the buyers of national properties (whose title was guaranteed by the Constitution), and notables—a social strategy that complemented the decision to revitalize manufacturing and commerce laid low by the Terror. In a broader sense, they returned to the ideas and principles of the Enlightenment, revised and adjusted as a result of the experiences of the Revolution. Thus, they developed a model of a republic governed by the "best," the most enlightened men, the owners of property that gave them a stake in the republican order. And they established a regime based on property qualifications of two kinds: wealth and education. The Constitution in fact stipulated that, starting in Year XII, children could not be inscribed on the civic rolls unless "they prove that they know how to read and write and practice a mechanical profession." This project demonstrated the influence of specifically cultural factors on political and social choices. On the one hand, it still breathed fear at the prospect of a return of the "rabble" and the "vandals," the ignorant folk who presumed to govern without being able to read or write. Only education, to be enforced by making the acquisition of a minimum of culture a prerequisite for the enjoyment of civil rights, could protect the people from itself and preclude the return of "vandalism." On the other hand, the education policy grew out of a hope, to which it gave new substance: the Enlightenment had been a source of the Revolution, and now it was up to the Enlightenment to end it. The trials the nation had endured were not in vain. Ultimately France would be a country of enlightened individuals as well as citizens, or, if you will, a country in which citizens were citizens because they were enlightened. The government consequently assigned itself an educational mission, to give effective support to the arts, the sciences, and the schools, and in particular to train new elites. Daunou, in his *Report on the Organization of Public Instruction*, came as close as anyone to summing up the pedagogical dreams and symbols of the Thermidorians: an enlightened republic that would return to the very sources of the Revolution, and a triumphant enlightenment that would bring the revolutionary ordeal to a close.

Daunou's report was both a manifesto and a promise: the Revolution and the Republic were joined in the imagination as two symbolic figures, at once complementary and opposed. There could be no legitimate power without the sovereignty that resided in the universality of citizens, and no citizens without a state that offered them access to both enlightenment and politics and which, if need be, would know how to protect the people from the reawakening of the people's own demons. The fate of the conventionnels, their own subsequent careers, is perhaps the best illustration of the degree to which the Thermidorians identified with an image of politics as a professional specialty in the service of the state. The Thermidorian Convention ended its labors with the notorious decree ensuring that two-thirds of its members would be reelected to the next legislature. Historians have all too often seen in this measure only the "base intention" of wanting to hold on to power at any price. The reality was more complex, however: eighty percent of the conventionnels who survived the Convention never returned to their prior activities; six percent would serve Bonaparte. Beyond the charges of opportunism, more justifiable in some cases than in others, we are witnessing the emergence of a new social type: the revolutionary who went on to make a career of state or bureaucratic service as regimes came and went.

We are now in a position to reconsider the significance of Thermidor as a "formative event." If Thermidor became such a formative event for the revolutionary mythologies of the nineteenth and twentieth centuries, if every subsequent revolution was haunted by the specter of a possible Thermidor, it was not because the French Revolution was, as some have alleged, betrayed, murdered, destroyed, or what have you on 9 Thermidor, Year II. The debate over who "really" buried the Revolution—Girondins or Dantonists, Jacobins or Thermidorians, corrupt directors or the first consul, and so on—is as interminable as it is sterile. It reflects and reproduces the revolutionary myth. Like all myths, the myth of the murdered Revolution at once betrays and obscures its own truth. It portrays a Revolution nipped in the bud, betrayed, killed before it had a chance to keep its promises. In other words, it presents a myth of the Revolution's eternal youth. The Thermidorian period compromised and destroyed this imagery. Thermidorian rhetoric is full of metaphors of fatigue, of the erosion of revolutionary mythology by time; every year of the Revolution counted as a century. Which caused the Revolution to age more, which did more to dispel its myths and illusions: the sixteen months of the Terror or the fifteen months of the Thermidorian period? The drownings at Nantes, or the exposure of the truth about those masssacres during the trial of Carrier? The Thermidorian moment is noteworthy for having exposed the Revolution's fatigue and aging. It was a moment of disillusionment for revolutionary ideals and symbols, a time when the Revolution was forced to accept the weight of its past and acknowledge that it would not keep all its initial promises. It was above all the moment when those who had inspired it and participated in it declared that they did not wish to begin its history anew or relive their experience.

Bronislaw Baczko

FURTHER READING

Baczko, Bronislaw. "Robespierre-roi ou comment sortir de la Terreur," *Le débat,* March–May 1986.

Brunel, Françoise. "Sur l'historiographie de la réaction thermidorienne," *Annales historiques de la Révolution française,* 1979.

Cobb, Richard. *The Police and the People: French Popular Protest 1789–1820.* London, 1970.

Lefebvre, Georges. *Les Thermidoriens.* Thirteenth edition. Paris, 1951.

Mathiez, Albert. *La réaction thermidorienne.* Paris, 1929.

Ozouf, Mona. *L'école de la France.* Paris, 1984, "Thermidor ou le travail de l'oubli."

Tonnesson, Kare D. *La défaite des sans-culottes: Mouvement populaire et réaction bourgeoise en l'an III.* Oslo, 1959.

RELATED TOPICS

Committee of Public Safety
Constitution
Coups d'Etat
Enlightenment
Girondins

Jacobinism
Napoleon Bonaparte
Revolutionary Assemblies
Revolutionary *Journées*

Robespierre
Sans-culottes
Sovereignty
Terror

INSTITUTIONS
AND CREATIONS

3

ARMY

From the outset the revolutionaries lived in fear of attack, since they recognized that they had thrown down a formidable challenge to the old order in Europe. By 1791 the pressure for war had become acute, with Brissot, among others, arguing that the Revolution could either be expansionist or be destroyed. The Declaration of Pillnitz and the Brunswick Manifesto served only to enflame popular passions and to increase national neuroses. From 1792, when hostilities were declared against Austria, until Napoleon's coup d'état in Brumaire, France was involved in almost constant war against the other great powers of Europe, a war that was costly in men and materials and that distorted much of France's domestic achievement. It was unavoidable, too, that such a war would quickly become politicized and identified as an integral part of the revolutionary polity.

The Revolution, of course, inherited an army, the line army of the Ancien Régime. It was not disbanded, and until military reforms were implemented, it remained France's principal means of defense. But to many people it was a most unsatisfactory body with which to protect the Revolution. It was recruited locally through the old provincial regiments, which the revolutionaries quickly identified with privilege and the old order. The men who served in the ranks did so less from a burning sense of duty than out of misery and desperation; morale was low, army discipline was imposed by savage corporal penalties, and the ordinary soldier was denied any civil rights or liberties. In contrast, the officer corps was composed of nobles—the Ségur Ordinance of 1781 had demanded that all officers must be able to prove four quarterings of nobility—and office was frequently venal. The army was relatively small, and in times of emergency it was supplemented by the imposition of militia service, an invidious and unequal burden on the population, which had been the subject of numerous complaints in the *cahiers de doléances*. It was, in short, an army whose basic structures seemed to undermine the very ideals to which the Revolution aspired. More practical objections were also raised. At the Bastille many of the troops showed their true feelings when they defied military discipline to join forces with the crowd. In 1789 and 1790 the army faced repeated instances of mutiny, most memorably at Nancy, by men who looked to the Revolution to throw off the tyranny of their officers. Many of these officers were among the first to emigrate, abandoning their posts and joining their families abroad rather than betray their church or their king. Between 1791 and December 1792 the line army lost around a third of its officers through resignation or political emigration. Dumouriez may have been the most notorious military émigré, but he was only one of many.

Army reform resulted not just from a doctrinaire desire to create a pliant tool of the state, but from a wide range of competing pressures. The mutiny at Nancy in 1790 administered as great a shock to the old system as did Dumouriez's defection, and though it was savagely repressed, its implications were not lost on those in government. Reforms followed in rapid succession. Cruel and humiliating punishments were abolished. The officer grades were filled on the basis of merit rather than for reasons of social precedence. The king's dependence on foreign mercenaries was ended. The distinction between the line and the militia was abolished, as was the practice of pressganging, which had helped to make the military widely feared in the towns and villages of Ancien Régime France. The provincial attachments of individual regiments were abandoned, and men were called upon to serve France, the nation, the *patrie*. In other words, an attempt was made to transform the old line regiments into a truly national army in which Frenchmen would be proud to serve as a duty, as part of the obligation implied by the fact of citizenship.

These reforms in themselves went some way to improve the morale of the troops, but the revolutionaries could not be content with piecemeal change. An army that would march across Europe carrying the message of emancipation that was the French Revolution had to be well-suited to that task, politically as well as militarily. And though the troops inherited from the royal army of 1789 were often well-trained and skilled in the military arts of the day, the suspicion remained that they lacked the political will that this new kind of warfare necessarily implied. It was not just that they might desert the colors or slink back home at the end of each campaign season. It was rather that every Frenchman retained an image of the eighteenth-century soldier, cowed and beaten into submission, returning to his village a broken man, without family or trade or means of support, condemned to eke out the rest of his days in the local poorhouse or *maison de charité*. The new political order required a new kind of army, recruited in a very different way and from a much wider cross-section of the population. Hence the insistence of the Assembly on the voluntary principle and the impassioned call in 1791 and 1792 for *volontaires* who would selflessly offer their services, and if necessary their lives, to save their country from its enemies. To the delight of local administrators, young Frenchmen came forward in large numbers, especially in response to the first *appel* in 1791, when France was still at peace with her neighbors and when any possible conflict promised to be short and glorious. In contrast, the recruitment for the old line regiments fell away. There was something carefree and heroic about the image of the volunteer in the first glad days of the Revolution. They were honored by their fellow-countrymen, promised favors when they returned in triumph to their communes, and offered privileges denied to the *culs blancs* of the line. They even had the right to return home if their personal affairs demanded it, and their engagement lasted for no more than a single campaigning season. A decree of 28 December 1791 was quite specific on this point: "All citizens accepted into the volunteer battalions of the national guards shall be free to resign at the end of each campaign. . . . The campaign shall be deemed ended on the first of December of each year."

The creation of regiments of volunteers separate from the line regiments and enjoying privileges denied to the line troops could not help stirring up tensions and jealousies. If the line soldiers prided themselves on their technical skills and despised the amateurism of the new recruits, the volunteers emphasized their political commitment to the Revolution and dismissed the regular troops as mere mercenaries. Such divisions poisoned relations within the army and made cooperation between the different units difficult to achieve. It was to resolve this problem that Dubois-Crancé introduced the most sweeping organizational reform of the period—the law of the *amalgame* of February 21, 1793, a highly contentious piece of legislation that encountered fierce opposition, especially from the Gironde. The *amalgame* ended the duality within the army by merging two battalions of volunteers with one regular battalion to form a new unit, the demi-brigade. It ended differences in the pay, discipline and uniform of the two forces. It introduced the principle of election for junior officers and noncommissioned officers, with only a third of the positions to be filled by seniority. Within the new demi-brigade, it was believed, cooperation would be possible among all the soldiery, the regulars educating the volunteers in military technique, the volunteers communicating in return their political and civic awareness. Delayed for some months because of the immediate dangers of the war, the law was finally implemented during the winter months of 1793–94, and though scorned by many contemporaries for its raw idealism, it played a vital part in molding the revolutionary armies into an effective and victorious military force.

Rather more idealistic was the idea that a long and costly war could be fought by voluntary inscription alone. The initial law calling for volunteers had asked for men aged between eighteen and forty, and in succeeding years the pool of potential recruits remained substantially unchanged. The mass of real enthusiasts had already joined up in 1791, with the result that in 1792 enrollment dipped considerably. The war unleashed against the Austrians did not result in the kind of easy victories that the optimists had dreamed of; wounded and soldiers began to filter back into French villages; letters from the front told the full horror of military life, the blood and wails of the dying as well as the failure of supply and the sheer boredom of army routine. Men who had been prepared to make a grand patriotic gesture recoiled at the idea of a prolonged period of service. Hence by 1793 the government found itself forced to resort to some form of compulsion if the regiments were to be filled. Though the language of voluntarism was carefully maintained, the two great recruitments of 1793—the "*levée* of 300,000" of February and the "*levée en masse*" of the following autumn—involved designation and constraint. In the spring of 1793 the government was desperate for men. Need took precedence over the principle, and little attempt was made to lay down the modes of procedure to be adopted. The levy was simply fixed, by département, in accordance with population, and it was left to individual communes to decide how best to implement it. Their duty was to provide bodies for the regiments, and all men aged between eighteen and forty who were unmarried or were widowers without children were placed in a state of permanent requisition. The recruitment exercise worked in the sense that the generals were provided with the infantrymen they required, but it left a corrosive sense of bitterness in many parts of the community. The *levée en masse,* which was carried out by ballot and which—alone of the recruitment exercises of this period—did not allow for the replacement of those with the money to buy themselves out, may still have been resented, especially in rural areas. But it was regarded as being less unfair and less divisive, and for that reason it was more calmly received by the population at large.

In spite of the rhetoric, it should not be imagined that the Revolution had achieved a totally equitable method of recruitment. In practice the level of sacrifice varied considerably. Towns still gave more than the countryside, artisans more than peasants. Young men aged eighteen to twenty-two formed the bulk of the recruits. Throughout most of the Revolution, replacement favored the rich, and the exemptions offered to officials caused widespread resentment. Most significantly, the demands of the army varied enormously from year to year. If the numbers raised in 1793 seemed quite dreadfully large, no systematic large-scale recruitment was enacted in the years that followed until the introduction of annual conscription in 1799. The men who were unlucky enough to draw the hated *billet noir* in 1793 still formed the backbone of the army five years later; they could be forgiven for thinking that they were being expected to pay an inordinate share of the government's *impôt de sang* (blood tax). The introduction of annual conscription under the Loi Jourdan in Year VI formed the basis of the huge armies of the First Empire. It could impose a heavy drain on manpower, particularly in agricultural villages, but conscription of this kind, involving the examination of each class as it came of age, at least had the advantage of being understood by the population and seemed relatively fair. The revolutionaries, with their dependence on balloting and on the *scrutin épuratoire,* never achieved that degree of standardization or of administrative sophistication. The *scrutin,* which involved the villages' voting for patriotic young men to march on their behalf, was open to the grossest abuse, while balloting reminded many villages of the worst excesses of the old *milice.* During the 1790s, the Revolution never really succeeded in persuading the mass of the population, at least in the countryside, that military service was a sacred obligation of citizenship or an acceptable *rite de passage* for the young.

Where it did succeed was in creating a new kind of army, quite different from the armies of the eighteenth century. As officers it employed men of proven ability, many of them noncommissioned officers in the old line regiments, who could now hope to see their services rewarded by rapid promotion and responsibility. Social background no longer formed an obstacle to advancement, though for the more important commands political loyalty was paramount. Youth was rewarded, and brilliant young officers, like Hoche or Bonaparte himself, rose rapidly to the very highest positions in the army. Generals were appointed directly by the government, often on political criteria, whereas the junior officers were elected by their men. As Saint-Just explained, "the right of electing the generals belongs to the entire community." To foreigners this seemed a recipe for chaos, yet it was this system that provided France with its greatest victories and that endowed the army with leaders of distinction like Marceau and Hoche, Kléber and Jourdan. Within the armies it produced a new unity of purpose, in that the officers no longer found themselves cut off from the troops they commanded by stultifying and unbreachable divisions of the Ancien Régime. The officer cadres now came from a commendably wide range of social backgrounds—men of middle-class origin accounted for around a third of the officers in the army of Year II and in no sense can be said to have exercised a dominant role—and this new openness played a significant part in molding the army into a truly national institution.

The creation of the revolutionary army was not, of course, achieved painlessly. Its sheer size proved a source of difficulty, from both military and administrative standpoints. For the army which emerged from the reforms of 1793 and the Year II was by eighteenth-century standards enormous. In 1757, during the Seven Years' War, France had fielded two armies, respectively 99,000 and 24,000 strong. In contrast, the purpose of the revolutionary conscription was to raise total manpower to some three-quarters of a million, the strength deemed necessary to save *la patrie en danger.* In the years that followed that number dropped dramatically, to less than half a million by Fructidor, Year III, and to 326,000 by the end of Year VI. Nonetheless, the fact remains that revolutionary France continued throughout the war years to rely on mass armies, and this reliance in turn raised problems of supply, of discipline, and of control. It also necessitated the adoption of new tactics, quite different from the tight, well-rehearsed battle formations of the eighteenth century.

Military tactics had to be adjusted to fit the character of the military itself. Early setbacks, indeed, can be ascribed largely to a failure to recognize that traditional warfare could not be successfully pursued with the enthusiastic but largely untrained infantry at the Revolution's disposal. In this early period too much importance was attached to political conviction and moral rectitude, as though these qualities alone could win battles. Armies were asked to defend too lengthy frontiers and were dispersed too indiscriminately across wide areas of territory. And the French columns were often shown to be cumbersome and unmaneuverable. By the winter of Year II, however, tactics were being reexamined and soldiers instructed more professionally in the art of warfare. Generals laid new emphasis on speed of maneuver, so that large areas could be protected while still allowing for the rapid concentration of force at critical points on the battlefield. The flanks of the army were trained to turn quickly and break up the enemy ranks. Above all, *la tactique de masse* was evolved into a military doctrine. The Committee of Public Safety put this very concisely in a letter of October 8, 1793: "The time has come to strike decisive blows, and that requires mass action. A single action of this kind makes up for and brings about all the rest. It does more than all detail actions. There is no reason for pride at beating the enemy in various positions with equal or inferior forces. That is a chivalrous honor that is not suited to our system, and with this mistaken notion of honor we are perpetuating the war indefinitely." In short, the revolutionary armies were developing a military strategy that was consistent with the mass of young recruits that they had at their disposal. They were making their own distinctive contribution to the evolution of modern battlefield tactics.

The revolutionaries relied heavily on infantry, though with significant support from the artillery; cavalry played a much lesser part than in traditional eighteenth-century wars. They laid great emphasis, too, on the value of offense and on the tactics of surprise. "Take the offensive, always be on the offensive," wrote the Committee on 8 Prairial, Year II; "Attack so as not to be attacked yourself." This aggressive approach goes far to explain the newfound success of republican arms during 1793 and Year II. This was the period when the fortunes of the war were most clearly transformed, when the French seized the initiative from their opponents and won a formidable reputation as soldiers. Characteristically they engaged in hand-to-hand combat, and their weapon was the *arme blanche,* the bayonet. As John Lynn has shown, the cult of the bayonet came close to being a military doctrine in its own right, but the tactical system that emerged in these months amounted to very much more than a simple dependence on one weapon. However tempting it may be to discuss French successes in terms of morale and political conviction, high motivation alone cannot explain the rapid transformation in French fortunes. In Lynn's words, "French battlefield performance also depended on at least three other factors: a force structure consistent with the resources of revolutionary France; an adequate degree of technical expertise, which could be gained only by training; and a tactical system that exploited the full range of techniques suited to the men and weapons of the era. Infantry achieved dominance because it met these criteria." Historians, dazzled by the rhetoric of the revolutionary leaders, have perhaps been too ready to explain the success of the armies in nonmilitary terms. The political appointees to high command and the newly promoted noncommissioned officers who found themselves in charge of the demi-brigades were often highly innovative soldiers. Victory was also the result of the rapid emergence of a new sense of professionalism.

Politics, of course, was never irrelevant. The conduct of the war was one of the most important tasks allotted to the great committees, and they interpreted their role in a highly interventionist manner. Deputies on mission went to the armies just as they went to the departments to oversee the conduct of the war and to ensure that political instructions were carried into effect. *Commissaires des guerres* maintained a political presence within the battalions themselves. Even in battle, military authority was not clearly distinguished from political control, and deputies could and did overrule commanding officers when they believed that circumstances merited it. When, for instance, generals lost battles or committed their troops to hopeless causes, they might find themselves subject to political sanction—to reprimand, dismissal, and even criminal charges. In the Nord, for instance, three commanding officers, Luckner, Custine, and Houchard, were tried and guillotined for their military failures in the period between 1791 and 1794. Incompetent generals could be replaced at the head of the armies by political commissars whose experience of war was based on debate in the Club or the Convention. Dugommier, a Jacobin deputy sent on mission to the army of the eastern Pyrenees, resolved the problem of poor leadership by taking over the command himself and exercising it with such flair that he succeeded in reversing French fortunes along the treacherous Spanish frontier. In an age when careers were suddenly thrown open to talent, there was no reason why ambitious men should not excel in both military and political spheres, and politicians never quite lost their fear of treason and counterrevolution from a depoliticized officer class. Besides, a politically aware army was seen as a source of military strength and conviction. Saint-Just, one of the most active of the deputies on mission to the armies, was in no doubt that political responsibility was essential to the effectiveness of the battalions as fighting units. For, he argued, "the troops . . . are exhibiting a loyalty to the nation that cannot be denied, and it is this loyalty, allied with the professionalism of the career soldier, that constitutes the army's true strength."

Whereas other armies made every effort to root out political opinions from their ranks, the Republic consciously set about politicizing its soldiers. They were, after all, citizens, and as citizens they enjoyed political liberties. They could vote, they could take part in demonstrations, they could form clubs within the army or join civilian clubs in the towns and cities where they were garrisoned. Newspapers were distributed to the troops to help foster their political education—not only papers, like the *Soirée du camp,* designed specifically for the military, but also the *Bulletin de la Convention Nationale* and a selection of the more political newssheets of the day. Bulk orders of newspapers—some seven and a half million copies in all—were bought for the armies, and every effort was made to ensure that the men were made aware of the major political issues of the day. In the army of the North, for instance, copies of *Père Duchesne* were widely circulated, as well as numerous patriotic tracts and songsheets. Political harangues helped motivate the soldiers on the eve of battle, and patriotic festivals were used to project politics in a vivid and visual manner. Discipline—imposed by military courts-martial—also contained a strong element of political morality, concentrating on those crimes that were deemed to destroy the confidence and viability of an army, crimes like pillage and insubordination, desertion to the enemy on foreign soil, the expression of unpatriotic or counterrevolutionary opinion. *Propos inciviques,* widely defined to include virtually any criticism of the Revolution and its leaders, were not tolerated from soldiers any more than they were in civilian society. In all these different ways—by example and deterrence and through the direct intervention by the political arm in the affairs of the army—the Revolution sought to create soldiers who would be sufficiently politicized to believe in the cause for which they were fighting. Sometimes, of course, it did more, creating within the army cells of Hébertists and enragés whose egalitarian zeal far outstripped that of the political leadership in Paris. In many of the northern towns, like Lille and Cambrai, militants from the garrison imposed their radical views on the local Jacobin clubs and helped turn them into hotbeds of extremism. Later, under the Directory, the armies would become havens for Jacobin politicians threatened with retribution following the closure of the club and the purge of its members.

Problems, of course, remained. Despite severe penalties, pillage and looting remained the scourge of many of the French battalions. When they were fighting on foreign territory, soldiers considered that booty was a legitimate reward, and it was often difficult to dissuade them from seeking the same benefits when they were stationed on French soil. Pillage was all the more attractive, indeed, in that pay was often months in arrears, while the assignats that the government issued to those on its payroll were widely refused by farmers and innkeepers. The supplying of the armies with food and clothing, weapons and ammunition, was another problem that often seemed beyond the capacities of revolutionary administration, and the troops, hungry and damp and ill-armed, could easily become resentful. Boredom and deprivation sapped their energies. Homesickness—the dreaded *nostalgie* diagnosed by army surgeons in troops stationed far from their native *pays*—caused sickness and lethargy and even, in extreme cases, death. Soldiers felt abandoned and cheated, especially when they heard that their wives and children were not receiving the pensions they had been promised by the state. And discontent could often lead to desertion—not, in most cases, to join the enemy, but simply to return to the familiar and comprehensible lifestyle of the farm or the *atelier*. Government propaganda painted a rosy picture of volunteers burning with enthusiasm for a cause in which they deeply believed. Such idealism did exist, especially during the Jacobin months when politicization was most widespread. But the letters sent home by revolutionary soldiers often tell a different story, of young men torn from their communities by the draft and forced into uniform to fight for a cause they barely understood. Village boys from the Pyrenees or the Massif Central were not always ready for the heady talk of citizenship and equality, and the day-to-day reality of soldiering often seemed far removed from the heroic language of the recruiting sergeant.

It would be perverse to linger too long on such shortcomings, many of which were common to all armies at the time. The achievement of the Revolution was real enough—in creating a new and integrated army structure; in breaking down the old traditions of provincialism and social precedence; in establishing a precarious harmony between soldiers and citizens. All these fields demanded political will as well as military prescience, and that will was not lacking. In its efforts to look after its soldiers and their dependents, in its schemes for pensions for widows and orphans, and in the reform of the *Invalides,* the Revolution also showed commendable imagination. As for the armies themselves, they soon abandoned the extremes of Jacobin politicization and stressed skill and training rather than patriotism. By the time of the Italian campaign they bore little resemblance to the volunteer battalions that had fought the early battles like Valmy or Jemmapes. They were much more sophisticated, much more professional in their approach to soldiering. Already they formed the basis on which Napoleon would build his vast military ambitions.

Alan Forrest

ARMY

FURTHER READING

Bertaud, Jean-Paul. *La révolution armée: Les soldats-citoyens et la Révolution française.* Paris, 1979.

—— *La vie quotidienne des soldats de la Révolution, 1789–1799.* Paris, 1985.

Corvisier, André. *L'armée française de la fin du XVIIe siècle au ministère de Choiseul: Le soldat,* 2 vols. Paris, 1964.

Forrest, Alan. *The French Revolution and the Poor.* Oxford, 1968.

Godechot, Jacques. *Les institutions de la France sous la Révolution et l'Empire.* Paris, 1968.

Gross, Jean-Pierre. *Saint-Just: Sa politique et ses missions.* Paris, 1976.

Lynn, John Albert. *The Bayonets of the Republic: Motivation and Tactics in the Army of Revolutionary France, 1791–1794.* Champaign, 1984.

Meynier, Albert. "L'armée en France sous la Révolution et le premier Empire," *Revue d'études militaires,* 1932.

Reinhard, Marcel. "Nostalgie et service militaire pendant la Révolution," *Annales historiques de la Révolution française,* 1958.

Scott, Samuel F. *The Response of the Royal Army to the French Revolution: The Role and Development of the Line Army, 1787–1793.* Oxford, 1978.

Soboul, Albert. *Les soldats de l'an II.* Paris, 1959.

RELATED TOPICS

Committee of Public Safety	Hébertists	Nation
Emigrés	Italian Campaign	Natural Borders
Enragés	Napoleon Bonaparte	

ASSIGNATS

I nnovations in terminology are never entirely innocent. A hint of the tortuous fate that lay in store for the word *assignat,* which all of France would learn in December 1789 and use for several years thereafter, can perhaps be gleaned from the ambiguity surrounding its inception. The highly technical *Encyclopédie des finances* (1784) mentions only the word *assignation,* meaning a "note or rescription ordering a treasury official (*comptable*) to pay a certain sum within a fixed period." The assignat was something else entirely: in the ancient language of southern France's legal code, the word *assigner* meant to establish an annuity or dowry by immobilizing certain funds (the assignat) as security against future payment. Thus an *assignation* was simply a promissory note, a provisional monetary sign, whereas an *assignat* represented real wealth, a concrete, certified guarantee of future payment. By describing what was in fact an *assignation* as an *assignat,* the Constituent Assembly was engaging in a subtle play on words. This semantic shift presaged what lay ahead, all the way up to the final collapse in 1796. A symbol of the new system of state finance, the assignat was so much the emblem of the Revolution that two centuries later scholars are still arguing over which of the two led the other to disaster.

When first introduced in December 1789, the assignat was conceived as nothing more than a modest and temporary treasury instrument. To pay off a short-term debt to the Caisse d'Escompte, the government was authorized by the Constituent Assembly to sell properties formerly owned by crown and clergy and recently nationalized for the sum of 400 million livres. The Assembly did not wish to establish a national bank, which, as in England, would have lent the king and his ministers not only the technical advice but also the political support of leading capitalists. Therefore another way had to be found to reimburse the Caisse d'Escompte quickly and to make use of funds anticipated from the sale of national properties (*biens nationaux*) without tying up too much cash in the various transactions. The device chosen was the "original" assignat, a series of notes issued by the Treasury starting in January 1790. Notes bearing five percent interest were issued in denominations of 200, 300, and 1,000 livres (which naturally restricted their use to the well-to-do). They were to be used as the preferred means of payment for national properties; in this way they would be returned to the Caisse de l'Extraordinaire, which would in turn reimburse the Caisse d'Escompte in the spring of

1791 after the first sales of national properties, so that eventually all the notes would be retired. In other words, the assignats constituted a compulsory (but not expropriatory) loan to the government by its creditors, a simple rescheduling of the government's debt. Nothing could have been more commonplace. Ever since the reign of Louis XIV financiers in Paris and other large cities had become accustomed to using rescriptions issued by the *receveurs généraux* (state tax collectors) and notes issued by the Farm against anticipated tax receipts, which were circulated and used as paper money by those well versed in the arcana of the system. The new assignat seemed even more secure than those forms of government paper, indeed as good as gold, and for the first few months the new paper retained its nominal value. Had not the Lecouteulx family, shareholders in the Caisse d'Escompte and importers of Spanish silver, obtained the position of Caissier de l'Extraordinaire for one of their own? Paradoxically, it was the initial solidity of the assignat that led to its collapse.

In the summer of 1790 three difficulties combined to create a very serious situation. The state Treasury, in crisis since 1788, now found itself seriously short of cash, since the old taxes were no longer being collected and receipts from the new ones had not yet begun to flow into public coffers. The amount of debt for which payment was due had been augmented considerably by the need to reimburse the enormous sums invested in public offices eliminated by the Revolution. Finally, doubts about the further course of the Revolution encouraged monetary speculation of every sort. The Comité des Monnaies, created in September by the Constituent Assembly, considered demonetizing gold and adopting a silver standard. In the circumstances it was tempting to regard all the national properties as alienable and to issue 800 million livres in new assignats. This would be enough to pay off the bulk of the debt due immediately and would considerably reduce the pressure on metal.

Debate on the issue occupied the Constituent Assembly during the month of September 1790. (Necker had resigned on the fourth.) The result was a decision to issue a "second" assignat, this time in the form of non-interest-bearing notes declared by the government to be legal tender. This currency issue has been the subject of countless works of French financial history. The Assembly's debates have often been cited and its arguments repeated as recently as 1926; they remain of enduring interest for the simple reason that, beyond the political motives of the orators, they raise a fundamental issue. Given that France, like England, had reached the point where a paper currency was needed, was it possible for the government to organize the issuance of such a currency by itself, without the aid of banking and commercial interests? The settled opinion of the Ancien Régime, chastened by its experience with John Law, was that the answer was no, and therefore that there should be no paper money, or at any rate very little. No was also the answer of Necker and the bankers, who would finally obtain satisfaction in 1800 with the creation of the first, quasi-independent Bank of France (which survived until 1806). But yes was the answer of the optimistic eulogists of a "regenerated" nation presumed ready to pledge all its wealth to ensure the success of its policies. Yes was also the answer of the technocrats of the Ministry of Finance and the Treasury, who never doubted their own skills or their ability to dominate events. One of the most typical of this group, Anson, former *premier commis des impositions* and *receveur général* who became a member of the Constituent Assembly and secretary of its Finance Committee, gave his approval as a technical expert to the plan supported by Mirabeau and opposed by Talleyrand and Dupont de Nemours.

The central issue of the debate was not the elimination of interest payments (which in any case had already been reduced in April to three percent). All participants were well aware that the value of the national properties, which was put at somewhere between 2 and 3 billion livres, considerably exceeded the total face value of the notes to be issued, and indeed was greater than the total debt. The real issue was monetary. Speakers could point to the recent example of American paper money, which had suffered substantial devaluation despite the commitments of Congress. There were also lessons to be drawn from the Calonne reform, which had encountered serious psychological and technical difficulties in the relatively simple matter of attempting to alter the relation between gold and silver. The problem was clearly stated by a number of deputies: What ratio would the market establish between existing money, metal, and the new paper money? Talleyrand argued:

> In reality there is at present only one dominant currency, namely, silver. If you circulate paper, it will be paper. You will, I grant, command that this paper not lose its value. But you will not be able to prevent silver from gaining in value, and that will be tantamount to the same thing. You will ensure that an assignat of 1,000 livres must be accepted as payment for the sum of 1,000 livres. But you will never be able to force anyone to give 1,000 livres in écus for an assignat of 1,000 livres. And because of that the whole system will collapse.

In response to this forecast of inflation, rising prices, and devaluation, Mirabeau offered two arguments inspired by the optimists in the ministries. First: "Why will the assignats lose value against metal? Because metal is absolutely necessary, because, scarce as our assignats may be, hard currency is even scarcer. See to it that there is less need to exchange one for the other. Create smaller assignats and you will not drive silver out. You will bring it closer to parity, and its scarcity will then be a less pressing matter." Mirabeau's second argument was that England, inferior to France in size, population, and wealth, nevertheless circulated far more paper: "If we raised the amount of paper money in circulation even to two billion, we would still have far less of it than those wealthy islanders." And even if French paper were to disappear, there would still be "fields, estates, properties of the greatest value, whereas the English national paper rests solely on the prestige of credit. . . . England prospers, despite the immensity of its debt, by means of a sign of opinion, a useless simulacrum of wealth."

In rereading these debates, we are struck by the excellent arguments on both sides. The outcome could only have been determined by a political fact: the success or failure of the Revolution. Twenty-five years later England triumphed decisively over France, not because it had adhered slavishly to economic orthodoxy but because it had been willing to risk massive indebtedness and widespread circulation of fixed-denomination paper currency. What proved possible even in the circumstances of a calamitous world war might have seemed even more plausible in September 1790, before peace had been compromised and the only issue in dispute was whether the sale of the national properties would succeed: "The assignats," Montesquiou maintained, "will establish a bond between all private interests and the general interest. Even the adversaries [of the assignat] will become landowners and citizens through the Revolution and for the Revolution."

The issue was decided by a vote of 518 to 423, and a currency based on the assignat was established. It became unpatriotic to question its usefulness, for to do so would have been tantamount to questioning the capacity of the nation to make wise use of its wealth and liberty. Yet awful truths were insinuated on both sides: "This operation must be of considerable benefit to the people," said *Les révolutions de Paris*, "since so many of its natural enemies have spared neither pain nor effort to prevent it." To which Dupont de Nemours replied: "The assignats are good for the wealthy, who have many debts to pay to the poor. They would rather give paper than écus and would prefer even more to sell their wheat and their wine for twice what they are worth." In these declarations there is more politics than sound thinking, which in itself is a powerful argument in the pessimists' favor.

Meanwhile, the assignat had a part to play in the sale of national properties, which began in earnest in November 1790. Prices ran considerably higher than estimated. Was this because buyers were counting on a progressive devaluation of the paper they used to make their payments? In that event the prescribed method of payment—in annual installments—would have yielded very good bargains over the long term. Shrewd purchasers may have anticipated this outcome, thereby heightening competition and driving up prices. Very likely this was the case, even if the Constituent Assembly preferred to use the higher prices as an argument for issuing still more assignats. In June 1791 authorization was given to issue 100 million livres in notes of 5 livres and, later, on the eve of the king's flight, 480 million in larger notes. Facts—a crisis of confidence and a monetary crisis—thereafter proved more powerful than arguments, although for a time words served to camouflage the gravity of the situation.

There was a crisis of confidence at the very summit, since by this point it had become clear that Louis XVI would never be a sincere supporter of the Constitution. More surprisingly, however, there was also a crisis of confidence on the part of taxpayers in the institutions they had just created. Although taxes were now lawfully levied and the fiscal system had been revamped in accordance with the taxpayers' preferences, landowners nevertheless stubbornly refused to pay their due despite the pathetic pleas of the fiscal authorities and successive assemblies. Thus one major argument in favor of paper money, that based on a supposed natural solidarity between the nation and its government, collapsed. At the same time the deficit grew larger than ever, so that the issuance of additional paper currency seemed the only way to cope with it.

The crisis in hard currency confirmed Talleyrand's pessimistic prognostications: the value not just of silver but also of gold and copper rose with even the slightest depreciation in the value of paper. For buyers there was always an advantage to paying in paper rather than metal, which disparity not only led to higher prices for goods and services but also literally drove out hard currency. This occurred throughout France, and the situation was further exacerbated by the export of hard currency by émigrés. By 1791 a host of convenience tokens, patriotic notes, and sight drafts had entered circulation. Employers in Paris and other large cities attempted to foist these on their workers, but farmers were reluctant to accept them in payment for food. Once again it was tempting to take the cause of the ill for its cure and to issue small notes to replace the missing coin.

Faced with such pressing needs, the Legislative Assembly took a surprisingly long time before resigning itself to further issues of assignats: an issue of 750 million livres was approved in December 1791, 400 million of which was in notes of 5 livres. In January 1792 another milestone was passed with the issuance of 300 million livres' worth of notes in denominations of 10, 15, 25, and 50 sous. This time the intention was indeed that the assignat should entirely take the place of hidden and exported metal coin. In view of the internal difficulties the government faced and the recent declaration of war, the new notes were immediately discounted by up to forty percent. Further issues were made discreetly between April and July, raising the total amount of paper in circulation at the time of Louis XVI's fall to approximately 3.2 billion. In other words, the constitutional revolution had used up the entire value of the originally confiscated national properties. The assemblies dominated by the former Third Estate had placed in circulation notes with a theoretical value equal to all the hard currency in circulation under the Ancien Régime and equivalent to the value of the property confiscated from the king and clergy. But yet another career lay in store for the assignat, this one quite unanticipated by its creators: it became the fiduciary currency of the Republic. In November 1792 Saint-Just was not terribly optimistic about the young Republic's finances: "I no longer see anything in the State but misery, pride, and paper." Worse yet, France had just embarked on a war against England, mistress of the seas, and Spain, mistress of the silver supply. After the death of Louis XVI it would have to contend not only with those two powers (something that had not happened for a long time) but with the states of the Continent as well. A European war meant troops to equip and pay, preferably with hard currency. The Convention's only hope of emerging victorious from circumstances such as these was by means of "misery, pride, and paper." Between the fall of the king and the fall of Robespierre, approximately 11 billion livres' worth of paper was issued: 3.237 billion in the last four months of 1792, 3.686 billion in 1793, and 4.190 billion in 1794. Of this total, 1.44 billion was in notes of 10 to 50 sous.

The need to produce such vast numbers of banknotes led to some interesting developments, particularly on the technical side: authenticating signatures were now written by machine rather than by hand; engraved steel plates were used for the first time; and the first note-numbering machine (numbering 1 to 9,999 with 10 assignats per sheet) was invented in 1793. The search for old rags to manufacture the special paper needed for notes took some rather picturesque turns in 1794. On several occasions workers in paper mills, closely watched and greatly exploited, attempted to rebel against the infernal pace of work. After several strikes had been brutally put down, the government was compelled to go so far as to deny paper workers the right to enlist in the army.

Nearly as much energy went into the manufacture of counterfeit assignats. Before 1794 most of this counterfeiting activity was French. But by then the harshness of anticounterfeiting measures, the difficulty of the work, the scarcity of raw materials, and the depreciation of paper currency had discouraged most domestic counterfeiters. Abroad, however, the fabrication of false assignats flourished as late as 1796 under the auspices of governments at war with France. During the Quiberon landing (July 1795) several billions' worth of assignats printed in London were seized. In the face of so many practical difficulties, it is rather remarkable that the Convention, and primarily Cambon and Ramel, its leading specialists on the subject, managed to adhere steadfastly to certain fundamental principles.

Amortization first and foremost: the rule laid down by the Constituent Assembly, that assignats once used to purchase a national property were to be burned, was never violated, a fact facilitated after January 1793 by the absorption of the Caisse de l'Extraordinaire into the National Treasury. In 1793 some 881 million livres in assignats were destroyed, and 2 billion more in 1794, according to official reports. Thus the initial theoretical connection between the monetary symbol and its backing in real wealth was preserved in spite of innumerable difficulties.

This link was reaffirmed with each new issue, albeit at the price of some dubious and rather optimistic evaluations. It was never the intention of the Convention to turn the assignat into pure paper currency without any connection to the real property and land on which it was based: the words "Mortgaged on the National Estates" were inscribed on every note from 1791 to 1795. Forced by the lack of hard currency to issue ever greater amounts of paper, the Convention was thus also obliged to nationalize ever more properties: the belongings of émigrés were sequestered in 1792, followed by possessions of relatives of émigrés (November 1793), and properties belonging to citizens of enemy countries and to the clergy and nobility of Belgium and the Palatinate (1794). Thus it was always possible to proclaim a rough equivalence between the number of assignats in circulation and the value of the underlying wealth. In February 1793 Cambon put the value of the assets on hand at 4.6 billion; in December 1794 Johannot mentioned a figure of 15 billion.

A third and related principle was also respected: the assignat continued to be the preferred instrument for acquiring national properties. Here, at least, its depreciation made people happy. It has been shown that in the majority of purchases made in 1793 and 1794, the value ultimately paid ranged from five to fifteen percent of the apparent purchase price set at the time of auction and from ten to twenty-five percent of the real price. With numerous and contradictory laws designed first to promote sales and then to slow their frenetic pace, the Convention provided shrewd manipulators with endless opportunities to fulfill their ambitions in real estate at small cost. From this the government hoped at least to reap political benefits even at the undoubted cost to the state in losses on the confiscated capital. Only after Thermidor was this calculation openly avowed, not without a certain impudence, by the two partners in the transaction, the government and the buyers.

Yet even as the assignat accomplished its primary mission, to serve as the instrument of a vast and revolutionary transfer of wealth, it was also used as money. It therefore suffered from the usual problems of money in a country at war and with a disorganized economy. The measures taken first by the Convention and later by the Committee of Public Safety were hampered by one insuperable difficulty: when metal is scarce and dear and paper abundant and depreciated, but both are legal tender, what can the authorities do to manage the situation?

One thing they could try was deflation: this was the meaning of the demonetization, in July 1793, of assignats bearing the king's picture, although it is true that their value subsequently began to appreciate dangerously relative to that of "republican" assignats. Hundred-livre Louis XVI notes ceased to be legal tender and could henceforth be used only for payment of taxes and purchase of national properties. By this act the Republic not only made a political statement but simultaneously withdrew assignats worth approximately 600 million livres from circulation. Yet the effect seems to have been to accelerate rather than restrain inflation.

Another option was to control prices. In May 1793 a so-called *maximum*, or ceiling price, was set on grains and flours, and in September it was extended to other commodities. To enforce this measure the government was obliged to assert full control over domestic and foreign trade. Among innumerable adverse consequences, including scarcity of food, the measure had little effect on the value of paper: depreciated to fifty percent of face value at the beginning of the Terror, it had risen to just sixty-five percent by Thermidor.

Still another option was to proscribe precious metals: "Let us debase gold and silver, let us drag those gods of monarchy through the mud," cried Fouché in October 1793 after confiscating metal coins in the Nièvre. Throughout France zealous local patriots forced citizens to exchange precious metals for assignats in the early months of Year II. Viewed with some suspicion from Paris, this practice might have led to total demonetization of metal or limitation of its use to certain foreign transactions only. Cambon suggested as much in a report that was not debated (December 1793), but whose main effect was probably to encourage further hoarding of gold and silver.

It must be said, however, that these measures to protect the assignat, and the Terror on which they depended, enabled the Convention to put a million men in arms and to hold out until the summer of 1794 and the Revolution's first battlefield successes. Furthermore, the Committee of Public Safety was able to pay its domestic political overseers at the rate of 3 devalued livres per day (600 million in one year). Above all, those who engaged in supplying the army and navy and in trading with neutrals—the only economic activity that was able to continue—reaped fabulous profits, relative to which the depreciation of paper money was of quite secondary importance. Years later Ramel observed: "The assignats made the Revolution. They toppled the throne and founded the Republic."

Because the assignat had proved to be a relatively effective monetary instrument in a time of crisis, the third and final phase of its existence, post-Thermidor, was particularly dramatic. How could such a valued "republican" instrument be done away with? And how, in particular, could the Treasury resolve to forgo pleasures described by Necker with deadly irony: "Those were good times for the Administration, when with an unlimited sum of banknotes one could not only satisfy every need known to man and then some but still have cash on hand at the day and hour of one's choosing. It was enough to assign some to work in the paper mills, others in the mint, still others in the engraver's and printer's shops, and the needs of the Public Treasury would be met."

*
**

In 1795 several contradictory tendencies collided, with dire consequences for the assignat. One was monetary in nature. Since the Treasury could apparently no longer make do without paper, the Thermidorians in January 1795 authorized a new issue of bills totaling 7 billion livres by May and 30 billion by the end of the year. To be sure, the astonishing rate of depreciation affected the real value of these notes. Nevertheless, notes issued in 1795 accounted for more than three-quarters of all assignats ever printed.

This continued prominence of paper currency coincided with a new flow of metal. Inaugurated by the rapid resumption of trade in precious metals and continued by the reopening of the Bourse, the thaw was hastened in May by the Treaty of The Hague, which raised hopes of payment of cash indemnities by the Netherlands. When peace with Spain followed in July, moreover, it was clear that the previous flow of American gold and silver, interrupted for the past three years, would now resume. In August, just before dispersing, the Convention therefore indulged itself by defining a new monetary unit, the franc, set to represent a value of five grams of silver—a rate that remained in force until 1928. Yet there was a certain mystification in this, for the word "franc" engraved on the new Hercules coin of 5 francs obviously did not have the same meaning, or in any case the same value, when printed on an assignat. So much was obvious to every bearer, assignee, or creditor holding government notes: the assignat declined from ten percent of its nominal value in January to six percent in April to three percent in June. The resurgence of metal raised prices and caused the value of paper to drop. Would good money drive out the bad since the bad seemed good for nothing?

What was the assignat actually worth? At this point another contradiction came into play, this one of a political nature. Even though the Convention in January doubled its members' pay in response to inflation, and even though growing numbers of voices and pamphlets called for making the assi-

433

gnat a commodity whose value would henceforth be determined by the market, there remained a powerful political impediment to decisive action. The liberals, led by Johannot, got what they wanted in most areas except for the "floating assignat." To allow the market to determine the value of the assignat, Lindet argued, would be "to make the Nation guilty of bank fraud, to declare that a monetary token that it had issued at one value would now be accepted only for a smaller value. . . . It is fraud to repudiate a note that has been given to a creditor. . . . Whoever wishes the Republic to commit fraud wishes for its shame and ruin." After innumerable debates a rough compromise was worked out, and payments and receipts once again appreciated, but not enough to compensate for the market's free fall. In a final twist of the logic of state control, the devaluation was simply adjusted to coincide with those aspects of the situation for which the state assumed responsibility, the assignat's date of issuance and the increase on that date of the total amount of paper in circulation. Neither this devaluation of approximately five-sixths nor the "law that makes the value of money variable without saying when the variation will end" (Marion) could be regarded as having permanently resolved the problem.

At this point the third contradiction came into play. In order to reduce the circulation of paper, it would theoretically have been enough to accelerate the sale of national properties. But by this point no one had any idea what those properties were worth. Every imaginable scheme for fixing their value in a manner that would prove profitable to the buyer had already been thought of, such schemes having been used, for example, to ensure the success of the voluntary loan of Year II. But the bearer of assignats might still hope to hit upon an even more complex and profitable system than any yet tried, and his hopes would not have been misplaced: on May 31, 1795, a law was passed authorizing any individual to purchase national property without a public auction provided that he pay in assignats seventy-five times the property's annual revenue in 1790. In other words, capital goods were being sold at four times earnings, nothing less than an outright gift. There was a tremendous rush of buyers, soon halted by the repeal of the disastrous and inept law. The auction system was reinstated, and of course the fall in the value of the assignat only accelerated. "Past Sèvres you cannot find so much as a glass of water for assignats." Only the capital, where annuities, wages, and public contracts resulted in large cash flows, was capable of sustaining a market in assignats, which came to be known as "Paris paper." And of course this encouraged market rigging, which flourished in all its forms.

In the first months of the Directory the return of silver, the resumption of free commercial transactions, and the tenacious hopes of peace with England rekindled the ambitions of some Ancien Régime financiers—those who were left alive. In partnership with men who had made their fortunes under the Republic, Lecouteulx de Canteleu did not hesitate to refloat his old proposal for a national bank, which would discount bills and issue its own notes. The plan was thwarted by the Anciens in March 1796. Two months later, under strictly private auspices, the Caisse des Comptes Courants was created, and this became the training ground for those who would run the Bank of

France under the Consulate. It was left to the state to retire its paper on its own and to the Directory to overcome the contradictions that had inhibited the Convention in its final days—a difficult task, since five hundred conventionnels had joined the ranks of the new councils. A few spectacular measures notwithstanding, the attitude of the authorities in the face of the assignat's agony was hardly one of coherence or candor.

Ramel first attempted to retire the circulating paper through a forced loan of 600 million livres in hard currency; payment could be made in assignats, accepted at one percent of their face value, so that theoretically this loan could have retired 60 billion in assignats, more than there were in circulation. The government had to settle for 8 billion, however, which would not have been too bad except that new issues also rose sharply at about the same time (January 1796). Dire measures were called for: the burins, molds, and plates used to manufacture the assignats were therefore destroyed. This was possibly the last great revolutionary festival (February 19), and there was something particularly absurd about it since a new paper currency was issued at the same time: the *mandat territorial*.

This note was indeed "territorial" in the sense that it could be used to purchase national properties without auction at the assessed valuation. Hence it should have been equivalent to silver, marking a return to the practices of 1790. But it had been ineptly linked to the assignat, since the law provided for exchange of one note for the other at the rate of 30 francs-assignats to 1 franc-*mandat*. The real value of the assignat was at this point 0.25 percent of its nominal value. Hence 100 francs in assignats were worth only 25 centimes, and 100 francs in *mandats* were actually worth just thirty times as much, or 7.5 francs. This was enough to cause a depreciation in the value of the *mandat*, a problem soon compounded by failure to control the amounts issued. At these prices it was in any case advantageous to buy national properties, and there was a run on these, similar to the one in May 1795, from March 18 to May 18, 1796, while the Treasury, its back to the wall, feverishly issued "promises of *mandats*." By summer it became necessary to put an end to the fiction that the *mandat* was equivalent to silver and to devalue it to one-eighth face value; at the same time the price of wheat was adopted as the standard of exchange. After six years the arguments of Dupont de Nemours triumphed at last: "Finally," he wrote, "the legislature is beginning to emerge from the labyrinth into which it was led by those who want money always to be on the move so that they can engage in their perpetual manipulations of the market. We are just pulling into port. . . . Land, land!"

This was to prove a somewhat optimistic view, since for the next ten years the Treasury would rely on the plunder of Italy by the army, on the Belgian national properties, on various international financial maneuvers, and finally on the self-interested favors of the leading military suppliers. But paper currency was indeed dead, and the rest of the story of how Ramel and his Compagnie Dijon in the winter of 1796 managed to "nail down" the value of paper at one percent of face value and then to eliminate it from the public coffers belongs as much to the realm of colorful anecdote as to the history of finance.

⁎

It was four and a half years from the time John Law established his Banque Générale until the government ceased to back its notes, a period slightly longer than the lifetime of the assignat. But the resemblance between the two periods went beyond even the darkest prognostications heard by the Constituent Assembly in 1790. In both cases the causes of the disaster were the same: injudicious imitation of England and unwarranted presumption by the government. England had a bank independent of the government whose paper was backed by the profits of an international commerce second to none. Even if Paris, Lyons, and other large French ports were home to numerous sophisticated merchants and financiers needful of and well versed in the use of commercial paper, the overall condition of the French economy at the end as well as the beginning of the eighteenth century, and especially in time of war, did not warrant large-scale issuance of paper currency. Any sudden and massive infusion of money into the economy could therefore have had no other result than to fuel inflation.

As for the presumption of the government, for which the blame must be shared by agents of the Treasury and members of the various assemblies, it was a legacy of centuries of monarchy during which it had been an accepted practice for the sovereign to meddle at will with the rules of the monetary game. Since the Revolution made it possible to link this age-old practice to a huge base in real property as well as to the patriotic tumult of the times, it was all but inevitable that every possible manipulation would be attempted. The outcome was all the more predictable in that the assignat also served the self-interest of a few tens of thousands of shrewd manipulators, reluctant taxpayers, and fortunate purchasers of national properties: it made accomplices of the Revolution's last friends. The assignat would not have survived as long as it did had it not been—for those few at least—a very good deal.

Michel Bruguière

FURTHER READING

Aftalion, Florian. *L'économie de la Révolution française*. Paris, 1987.
Encyclopédie méthodique: Finances, 3 vols. Paris, 1784.
Lafaurie, Jean. *Les assignats et les papiers-monnaies émis par l'etat au XVIIIe siècle*. Paris, 1981.
Marion, Marcel. *Histoire financière de la France*, vols. 2–4. Paris, 1919–1925.
Say, Léon. *Dictionnaire des finances*, 2 vols. Paris, 1889–1894.

RELATED TOPICS

Maximum   Mirabeau   National Properties   Necker   Taxes

CIVIL CODE

"Having trod for a long time on the ruins, we must now erect the great edifice of civil legislation: an edifice simple in its structure, majestic in its proportions, great by virtue of its very simplicity, and all the more solid in that, not being built on the shifting sands of theory, it will rise upon the firm ground of the laws of nature and the virgin soil of the Republic." On August 9, 1793, when Cambacérès, speaking for the Convention's Committee on Legislation, presented to his colleagues a proposed new legal code upon which work had begun three years earlier under the Constitutent Assembly, he could not possibly imagine that eleven years later an ex-Jacobin general would become for posterity the "author" and sponsor of the Civil Code. Was he aware that in attemting to set forth a compilation of "simple, clear laws in conformity with the Constitution" and common to all French citizens, he was fulfilling one of the monarchy's oldest dreams? From Charles VI to Charles VII and Louis XI, sovereigns responding to the wishes of the Estates General of 1484 and of Parlement had continually promised the nation a published compilation of its customary laws—a delicate, complex undertaking that had begun to bear fruit only in the sixteenth century. To publish and thus attempt to stabilize the diverse body of French customary law was but a first step toward the unification of civil law demanded first by the Third Estate and later by all three orders in the Estates General of Orleans (1560), Blois (1576), and Paris (1614).

Ordinances concerning birth, death, and marriage certificates were promulgated as early as the end of the sixteenth century, but it was not until Louis XIV personally presided over meetings of the commission charged with drafting a new legal code that the codification of France's civil laws was placed on the political agenda. This premature plan did not succeed, owing in part to quibbles and obstacles put in its way by the parlements, but it did encourage political theorists and jurists to think about standardizing the legal code. This led to the so-called d'Aguesseau ordinances on donations (1731), wills (1735), and entails (1745). Although these new laws surely favored a formal unification of the relevant codes and perhaps practices relating to inheritances, the diversity of French law, a product of the mingling of Roman, canonical, feudal, and customary traditions, persisted.

From the *cahiers de doléances* is it possible—making all due allowance for the varying degrees and levels to which particular cahiers were representative—to form a precise idea of the general state of opinion on the question of legal unification? Quantitative analysis yields some interesting results:

437

slightly less than half of the *cahiers* from the *bailliage* level mention a need for new legal codes or reform of existing civil or criminal law. (The *bailliage* was an administrative district under the monarchy.) The proportion drops to slightly less than one-quarter in a sample of a thousand *cahiers* from the primary level, and some of these pertain to a single code, law, or custom. Hence it is somewhat misleading to assume that there was a powerful current of opinion in favor of a unified legal code. Although the drafters of the cahiers were eloquent and specific about seigneurial power and the laws of property, they were oddly silent about the subjects that would divide legislators for some fifteen years: vital records, marriage, divorce, illegitimate children, paternal authority, donations, and inheritances. Their silence does not indicate lack of interest in these matters. It can be assumed that the majority favored maintaining current practices and wished only to correct obvious abuses and circumscribe and unify judicial procedures. These ambiguities would lead to serious misunderstandings between 1789 and 1794. The typical Frenchman was familiar with the traditions governing marriage and inheritance in his own region and favored a uniform national code only if the rule that was applied to the whole nation was that of his own parish, valley, or province.

This defense of family, community, corporate, and municipal values drew criticism from the philosophes and physiocrats, who favored and gave currency to universal principles from which first reformers and later revolutionaries drew their inspiration. Legal scholars and philosophers almost unanimously criticized the patchwork of legal systems in France and urged a standardization and simplification of the more than 360 customary codes still in force. D'Aguesseau and Linguet found themselves in agreement on this score with Turgot, Quesnay, and Dupont de Nemours, as well as Voltaire, Diderot, Rousseau, Mably, and most of the Encyclopedists. "What is a law," Diderot asked, "whose local justice and authority, limited now by a mountain, now by a stream, vanish for any subject of the state who crosses that stream or mountain?" And Voltaire wrote: "In a single province in Europe, between the Alps and the Pyrenees, there are more than 140 minor peoples who call themselves compatriots but who are really as much strangers to one another as the citizen of Tonkin is to the citizen of Cochin China." In all this concert of praise for uniformity one dissonant voice stood out: Montesquieu's. Convinced that customary laws were various and changeable because they reflected life itself with all its diversity of geography, economics, and social situations, he held that the principle of difference ought to be respected and that a careful effort should be made to determine "which cases require uniformity and which require differences. . . . If citizens obey the laws, what difference does it make if they obey the same law," the principle of uniformity being an idea that "sometimes grips great minds but infallibly assails small ones." This intellectual controversy, ignored by the vast majority, sustained much of the debate over French law from the time of the Constituent Assembly to that of the Corps Législatif and the Council of State. Differences as to whether the laws were universal and rational or pragmatic and empirical were inevitably reinforced by the ambiguity of such concepts as liberty, equality, and "laicity" (separation of church and state), which were used in the fight against "despotism," whether of religious, political, social, or juridical origin.

In matters of civil law, however, there existed a consensus among intellectuals and other members of the elite concerning numerous fundamental questions: abolition of the old system of land tenure and aristocratic control of land ownership; secularization of vital records; marriage, which Voltaire called "a civil legal contract that the Roman Catholics have made into a sacrament"; and divorce. This apparently united front broke down, however, as soon as there was a question of the respective rights of husband and wife in marriage, for example, or the role of the head of the family, or paternal authority. Although a majority agreed that some limitation in the duration and scope of paternal authority was necessary, there was no national consensus on such basic issues as the regulation of marriage, the right to make a will, or the ability to favor or disinherit a child. In the matter of inheritance laws, for example, France in 1789 was influenced by three great legal traditions: the customary, the Roman, and the feudal. Inheritance was different in a region governed by customary law from what it was in one governed by written law. In the west and through much of Champagne there was a preference for equal—or "perfect," as it was called—division of estates, while in the Paris basin, Flanders, and some other parts of Champagne estates were equally divided after exclusion of those children who had received marriage portions. In areas subject to written law from Saintonge to Bresse and including Limousin, southern Auvergne, and the Lyonnais, as well as in regions where unequal inheritance was the custom (Auvergne, Artois, Lorraine, Burgundy, Nivernais), the usual practice was to select a privileged heir and divide the estate unequally on the grounds, for example, that the rights of male and female heirs were different.

Even before the Revolution, then, there were problems in the areas of property law and the relation between the state and the family. The evolving intellectual and political situation hardened attitudes, however, and heightened differences over the very concept of law. The notion that over and above positive law there is a prior natural law according to which individuals are governed by reason and passion and that the legal code itself plays only a secondary role was now opposed by theorists who advocated an active role for the state, which they portrayed as the embodiment of historical reason. For the good of society the state complemented natural law by creating positive laws. Many revolutionaries believed that civil laws were superior to natural law and radicalized their views accordingly. Convinced that their fellow citizens had, in Montesquieu's words, "renounced their natural independence in order to live under political laws" and "renounced the natural community of property in order to live under civil laws," they did not hesitate to derive the rights of liberty and property from the law itself, and they entrusted the state with the mission of guaranteeing those rights through legislation. This ideological shift, later reinforced by the circumstances of political struggle, may have caused the Revolution to go farther in its reforms than most people wished. Given the variety of opinion and the diversity of local and regional legal systems, it was no easy matter to fashion and impose a single Civil Code for a divided and supposedly individualistic nation; it took clear-sighted political determination and favorable circumstances to win acceptance of the notion that the public good outweighs the private.

*
**

A majority of representatives came to the Constituent Assembly with the intention of unifying France's civil laws. On July 5, 1790, they decided to begin work on a General Code. The public insisted that priority be given to reform of the criminal code, however, and this work was completed in 1791. But the main objective, as stated in the Constitution of 1791, was to establish a uniform civil code throughout France; this project was perpetuated under the Legislative Assembly. The public was consulted on the reforms, but the Legislative Assembly became bogged down in endless debates over the relation between the old law and the new principles. On September 20, 1792, the day it disbanded, the Assembly passed a law transferring responsibility for registering births, deaths, and marriages from the religious to the secular authorities and legalizing divorce. It is impossible to overstate the significance of these steps, which initially had much greater impact than the Constituent Assembly's often inconsistent efforts to dismantle the feudal system of land tenure. Yet the same Constituent Assembly had raised pertinent questions about paternal authority, the scope of the marriage contract, wills, and equal division of estates. Among the prominent deputies who contributed to the discussion were Cazalès, Saint-Martin, Merlin de Douai, Mirabeau, Tronchet, Dupont de Nemours, Pétion, and Robespierre, and their reports later proved invaluable in the lengthy process of drafting the Civil Code.

There can be no doubt, however, that it was the Convention's Committee on Legislation that was chiefly responsible for the unification of French civil law. Minutes of its sessions show the broad scope, high intellectual quality, and efficiency of the work it accomplished under the chairmanship of Cambacérès. There were four subcommittees: one dealing with vital records, family matters, marriage contracts, inheritances, illegitimate children, and adoption; another with donations, entails, and wills; a third with contracts and mortgages; and a fourth with "vestiges of feudalism." The Committee, filled with jurists and lawyers, naturally availed itself of works by experts in the law of the Ancien Régime. It also took advantage of the increasingly radical climate of the Revolution to press for legal unification. A first proposed code was produced very quickly and presented by Cambacérès on August 9, 1793. All the civil laws of France were reduced to just 719 articles, which sought not to anticipate every possible case but to establish unity and equality as fundamental principles of law. Only certain sections of this proposal were approved by the Convention, however, which wanted a shorter document to work with. A year later, on September 9, 1794, the Committee on Legislation presented a second proposal, whose 297 articles were intended to "establish the civil order and found the moral order." The citizen's relation to society having been settled by a "very popular constitution," the pressing need now was to complete the work by fixing "relations of citizens among themselves in accordance with the same principles approved by reason and guaranteed by liberty." Both proposals shared one goal: to make the new laws, the new civil code, the "palladium of the Republic." But only ten articles from the second proposal were passed by the Convention, for the deputies' thinking changed as fast as the political situation. A third proposal, once again presented by Cambacérès, was not finished until June 1796, under the Directory. It contained much of the 1793 proposal together with some additional material— some 1,104 articles in all—and, as a remarkable digest of the work of many years, would be drawn upon heavily by future legislators. Once again, however, political circumstances did not favor serious discussion of the project as a whole. This was also the fate of the next reform proposal, submitted by Jacqueminot on December 21, 1799. For all the persistence of politicians and jurists and all the powers of the revolutionary government, the Revolution failed to achieve what had been one of the monarchy's main objectives. By decree of the consuls on August 12, 1800 (24 Thermidor, Year VIII), it was decided to begin work on yet another revision, which proved to be the last.

This rapid overview should not be allowed to give the impression that the revolutionary assemblies were powerless and incapable of achieving their aims in the area of legal reform. Everything possible was done to hasten completion of the work: public debates were held, reports were written, committees were established, campaigns were waged in the press. The astonishing thing is that despite the frantic agitation of these years so much was accomplished in matters of difficult detail. Indeed, by the time the second proposed reform was submitted, the broad outlines of the future Civil Code were already firmly established and were never again tampered with: "Three things are necessary and sufficient for man to live in society: he must be master of his person, he must have belongings to meet his needs, and he must be permitted to dispose of his person and belongings as his own interest dictates. Therefore all civil laws can be reduced to rights of liberty, property, and contract." Not only did these become the principles on which future legislative action was based; but those who drafted the final version of the Civil Code were able to avail themselves of the work of their predecessors, including some of the most far-reaching reforms in all of French history.

Between 1789 and 1796 the Revolution drastically altered, if it did not abolish, the feudal system of land tenure; it transformed the relations between church and state; it imposed the Civil Constitution of the Clergy and nationalized ecclesiastical properties. In the realm of family law the secularization of vital records "struck at the very heart of social life" and "changed the basis of life itself," as Jaurès was the first to note. Other innovations included secularization of marriage, legalization of divorce, a new attitude toward illegitimacy and adoption, and curtailment of paternal authority. All these changes marked a sharp break with feudal, canonical, and Roman law; yet some were based on the more egalitarian forms of customary law found, for example, in Anjou, Rheims, and Touraine. These customs were hailed as "national" laws as opposed to the "alien" laws of the Romans, yet they were transformed beyond recognition by incorporation into the new code. In the area of inheritance, for example, feudal privileges accorded to male heirs and eldest sons were abolished, and unequal division of estates of intestate decedents was prohibited. Soon thereafter, the right to make wills was eliminated and strict equality established among heirs.

Of course, revolutionary legislators were sometimes carried away by ideological zeal, going beyond the wishes of the people and neglecting social and cultural traditions. But if one will grant that their mission was to establish a "revolutionary" legal code for the admittedly utopian purpose of leveling statuses and fortunes and increasing the number of smallholders (hence the new regime's base of support), their accomplishment was enormous. The Directory and Consulate eliminated their greatest excesses: overliberal divorce procedures, compulsory equality between heirs (something that half of rural France rejected out of hand), and above all the decision to make all laws retroactive from Nivôse, Year II, to July 14, 1789. Nevertheless, the Revolution did establish individual liberty and secularization of civil life as fundamental and durable principles of French law. The legal structure that emerged from the Revolution, though known by the unfortunate name of "interim law," was actually an amalgam of Roman law, customary law, and innovations introduced by the Assembly. It was the raw material out of which eventually came the Civil Code. The whole process took more than ten years, and much of the credit must go to the Convention for its bold decision to unify the laws of the nation in accordance with the wishes of the majority. Yet we must be careful not to forget that the goals pursued were often ambiguous or contradictory. The Convention's ambition was greater than its achievement, however; ultimately it adopted not a new legal code but only particular laws, which at least had the beneficial effect of adapting the old French legal system to the new political situation.

*
**

If a new Civil Code was finally adopted in 1804, it was the result of a fortunate combination of factors: Bonaparte's determination to mark the end of the Revolution and the restoration of civil peace by completing work begun earlier; the adoption of new legislative procedures; and the drafters' wish, backed by the first consul, to achieve a compromise between the old legal tradition and the novelties introduced by the Revolution. Recent historiography, much of it hostile to Napoleon, has perhaps underestimated the role of the Civil Code's author (his paternity having been officially recognized by a law of 1807). "My true glory is not to have won forty battles; Waterloo will efface the memory of any number of victories. What nothing will efface, what will live eternally, is my Civil Code." When he wrote these words on Saint Helena, Napoleon could not have foreseen the fate of "his" Code. Still in force in France two hundred years later, it has also inspired legal codes in many other countries (among them the Netherlands, Italy, Rumania, Portugal, Spain, Bolivia, Chile, Argentina, and Egypt) and has left traces in the laws of countries conquered by Napoleon and forced to accept the "benefits" of the Napoleonic Code. Like the German Civil Code of 1846, the French

Civil Code of 1804 has often been imitated and even copied. The Charters of 1814 and 1830 may have withdrawn the epithet "Napoleonic," but a decree of 1852 restored it "for the sake of historical truth." In any case, the "Civil Code of the French" has ever since been attributed, both in France and elsewhere, to the emperor. There is no point trying to gauge how much time Bonaparte actually spent with the Committee on Legislation or the Council of State. The important thing was his determination to further the enterprise by declaring on 24 Frimaire, Year VIII, that "the Revolution is over." He consistently included legal reform in his plans for a new government that would be authoritarian in nature yet an authentic heir of the Revolution. When the final project was disapproved by the Tribunate and consequently rejected by the Corps Législatif, Napoleon decided to halt further preliminaries and, with the consular message of 12 Nivôse, Year X, to force the assemblies "to suffer with a shortage of laws." He then forced the Senate to consent to a purge of the Tribunate, beginning with the expulsion of the "Ideologues," who were fighting to preserve the achievements of the Convention. He also modified the Tribunate's procedures and created a special council, chaired by himself and responsible for reviewing all texts prior to submission to the Council of State. All these steps cleared the way for the accomplishment of the "great design."

Thus, political determination played an important part in bringing the Civil Code to fruition. The intelligence and professionalism of the Code's drafters were also crucial. With the appointment of Bigot-Préameneu, Malleville, Portalis, and Tronchet to the Consular Commission on 24 Thermidor, Year VIII (August 14, 1800), the balance of power was shifted significantly toward those who favored basing the new code on the old written law; Tronchet was virtually the only member of the Commission to favor customary law, and even he was a moderate on the issue. A few Jacobin ideologues and a handful of staunch enemies of Napoleon's dictatorship in the three assemblies did manage to slow the first phase of the work, but the other principal drafters—Cambacérès, Berlier, Boulay de la Meurthe, Emmery, Galli, Réal, Thibaudeau, and Treilhard—shared the views of the four commissioners. All lawyers, nine of whom had held high judgeships and most of whom had participated in the revolutionary assemblies, these were learned men, well versed in Roman as well as French law, and familiar with the disparity between theory and practice. Without Bonaparte's determination and the drafters' great learning and skill, the project never would have been carried through to completion; for most lawyers remained hesitant about the reforms, and the legislative issues involved were extremely complex.

A fairly accurate picture of the variety of lawyers' and judges' views on reform can be gleaned from a survey of responses to the first consul's August 1800 proposal for a new code by the Tribunaux d'Appel and Cour de Cassation (two types of appellate court). The members of the Cour de Cassation, for the most part Paris magistrates, indicated their agreement with most of the proposal except for the section concerning the laws of inheritance. Like many legal scholars, they favored equal partition of estates, either because this principle was enshrined in customary law or because it accorded with the egalitarianism promoted by the Revolution. Most of the Tribunaux d'Appel were situated in regions of France governed by customary law and therefore shared this view. By contrast, appellate courts in regions governed by written law (with the exception of Lyons and Grenoble) saw clearly that the drafters of the new Code wished to introduce a compromise by reinstating the right to make a will and favor one heir over others. Indeed, they wished to go even further by reestablishing the right to disinherit and to choose a preferential heir. In short, the responses simply reflected the existing diversity of French law. The reformers were encouraged to strike a balance between sharply divergent cultural traditions, especially in regard to questions of inheritance, which became the focus of controversy.

The plan for drafting and winning approval of the new Code was complex. After the Consular Commission had completed a draft, it was to be sent to the appellate courts for examination. Then the draft, together with the opinions of the appellate courts, was to be submitted to the Council of State and examined by its legislative subcommittee. After debate in general assemblies, the draft proposal was to be submitted to the Tribunate for preliminary examination, then presented to the Corps Législatif, then resubmitted to the Tribunate for formal approval and a final report to the Corps Législatif, followed by debate and a vote.

Like the Edict of Nantes and the Concordat, the Civil Code was both a charter for society and a way of quelling social conflict. Everything possible was done to preserve France's three legal traditions: customary, written, and revolutionary. "Many laws and political customs of the Ancien Régime disappeared suddenly in 1789 only to resurface a few years later, just as rivers sometimes plunge underground only to reappear a little farther on in a different channel." Tocqueville meant these words to apply to the Revolution, but they are also an apt description of the history of the Civil Code.

Consider, for example, the lengthy argument developed by Portalis in his speech presenting the proposal to the legislature. His case rests on three main points. The first involves the relation between law and jurisprudence: "No matter how complete a code may appear, the magistrate is soon confronted with a thousand unanticipated questions. . . . The purpose of the law is to set forth broad views, general maxims of law. . . . It is up to the magistrate and the legal expert (*jurisconsulte*) to guide their application" and to develop case law as a "true supplement to legislation. Strictly speaking, a people's code is not made but develops over time." The second point was the relation of family to society: "Our purpose has been to establish a link between customs and laws and to foster the family spirit which, for all that may be said against it, has done so much to promote civic spirit. . . . Good fathers, good husbands, and good sons make good citizens." The third and final point was that the new Code was a compromise: "What we have done, if I may put it this way, was to strike a bargain between written law and customary law wherever we found it possible to reconcile the provisions of one with those of the other or to modify the provisions of one in light of the other without destroying the unity of the system or violating its general spirit."

Thus, a spirit of compromise or "bargain" was absolutely central. But

444

the lawmakers also wished to create a unified legal code applicable to the nation as a whole and to establish the principle that the law has only one source: the state. The drafters sought to provide a law whose mission would be to "govern" family and social relations and to establish the clearest possible dividing lines between the spheres of politics, morality, religion, and law.

The Civil Code that was promulgated on March 21, 1804, contains 2,281 articles grouped together in thirty-six laws. Legal historians have differed as to its meaning ever since: some emphasize its continuity with earlier French law, while others see the new Code as the bible of contemporary bourgeois France. At the center of the controversy is the question of what it means to "filter" old traditions, to pick and choose selectively among them. It is interesting to examine Portalis' argument in this light to see how well it captures the reality of the text. In the area of property law the drafters were concerned mainly with property in land as opposed to movable wealth. The Revolution's abolition of feudal tenures was reaffirmed. Property, it was said, had "founded human societies" and was not responsible for inequality among men; hence ownership consisted in the "right to enjoy things and dispose of them in the most absolute fashion." This was a view of property ideally suited to a nation of peasant landowners. Yet too many subsequent commentators have attempted to portray it as one particularly favorable to the development of industrial and finance capitalism.

Following Philippe Sagnac, many legal historians have taken a harsh view of the Code's treatment of family law. In contrast to the Revolution, which allegedly had fostered equality and brotherly love and had liberated women and illegitimate children, the Civil Code reaffirmed paternal authority and established a model of the family based on the state.

Note, however, that the Revolution's legacy in three particularly important areas was left intact: vital records, marriage, and divorce. Divorce was no longer considered a natural complement to marriage, however, and of the seven grounds for divorce specified by the Law of 1792 only three were retained in the Civil Code: adultery, "excess" (*excès*), and grievous insult. Although divorce by mutual consent was maintained after lengthy debate, there is no doubt that the stricter regulations served to make divorce a relatively rare phenomenon. The Code's drafters were far more reactionary in regard to paternal authority and the status of women. Nearly all the *patria potestas* of the old law was restored to the father, with only two provisos: paternal authority was now of limited duration, and fathers were no longer authorized to disinherit children as a "corrective" measure. No longer were illegitimate children considered legal heirs; bastards were now viewed as outcasts from both family and society. Bonaparte was adamant that bastards not be accorded the legal right to present evidence of paternity in court. "Society," he said, "has nothing to gain by recognizing bastards." Adoption was permitted provided the adoptee had reached the age of majority and the adopting parent was childless and past "the age at which society welcomes marriage."

Without a doubt it was the status of women that suffered most from the adoption of the Civil Code. The principle of equality of husband and wife had long since vanished, having been stricken from the third proposal of

1796. Not only Bonaparte but also the vast majority of drafters, legislators, and jurists believed that woman was weak, fickle, frivolous, and in need of protection, while man was "free because he is stronger." Inequities in the old legal tradition were thus aggravated. Women were excluded from managing the couple's joint property and not allowed to sign important administrative or legal documents. They could not sell their own property. At best they retained only a limited right to engage in contracts. Made virtual wards of their husbands, to whom they owed absolute obedience, women were treated as inferiors even in matters of infidelity and divorce.

Nevertheless, compromise was the order of the day when it came to matrimonial law and the laws of inheritance. Although marriage contracts were allowed, two different systems for handling property in marriage peacefully coexisted: separate property (*régime dotal*) and community property. The Convention's misguided efforts to impose equal division of estates receded as legislators showed greater respect for different cultural traditions and a willingness to restore personal choice in bequests. Many historians have been led astray, however, by a tradition according to which the supposedly egalitarian Code led to the breaking up of farms and a decline in the birth rate; they have not paid sufficient attention to the shrewdness of the lawmakers. By stressing the principle of equipartition the Code's drafters satisfied the proponents of customary law. Yet they also recognized the testator's right to increase the share of designated heirs. At the same time they sought to put a damper on the litigiousness of colegatees oblivious to the harm they might inflict. They limited an heir's ability to sell a share of undivided property by reviving the *retrait lignager,* or right of entail accorded to the colegatees, to whom the property would revert on the death of the buyer. Although they advised against division of inherited property, they nevertheless authorized physical subdivision. However contradictory these measures may appear, they enabled family heads to continue, with the help of the notary, to select a favored heir, just as they had always done in areas governed by written law.

Montesquieu, forgotten by a Revolution bent on imposing uniformity, thus prevailed over Rousseau and Robespierre. There was indeed one law, but it was full of subtleties. Bretons could continue to divide their estates equally, while Basques could indulge their penchant for inequality. Innumerable regional variations on the theme of inheritance were preserved. Was this a victory for legalism over philosophy? Was it a return to Roman law undertaken as a corrective to the legislative excesses of the Convention, unduly influenced by customary law? Was it a translation of the rights of man into the language of law or an attempt to define the individual in terms of his relation to property? Was it a glorious synthesis of order with liberty or a rule book for paternalistic bourgeois society? Celebrated by many, and first and foremost by nineteenth-century law professors and schoolteachers, the Code was vilified by the conservative right for establishing equality in inheritance and tampering with the traditional law of the family. It was accused sometimes of embodying the philosophical ideas of the Revolution, sometimes of sacrificing those ideas to triumphant bourgeois individualism. Socialists and later communists attacked the Code as a monument to the idea that property is a natural right and blamed it for worsening the lot of the working man and having failed to foresee the future development of industry and capitalism. Libertarians disliked the Code for having expanded the role of the state in such areas as the registration of births and deaths and the regulation of marriage. These implacable critics do not always avoid anachronism, at times projecting their views of twentieth-century society back into the minds of the Code's drafters. They are right, however, on one important point. Earlier law, both customary and written, generally stated what it was desirable to do in a particular situation given that one shared in a particular cultural tradition. The Civil Code stated *the law*, setting firm limits that must never be transgressed. It established a dialectic of prohibition that rested on two principles: the notion of public order and the concept of proper behavior. In the hands of the state, bourgeois society, and its judges, this proved a very flexible instrument.

Did the Code absorb the legal traditions that preceded it? This question, which figured in debates throughout the nineteenth century, now seems settled. I would not want to suggest that Louis XVIII was the best analyst of the Civil Code, but his estimate of its merits was fairly accurate, even if he was discreetly silent about the contribution of the Revolution and more than a little calculating in his decision to accept the work of so many years: "The new Code, which in large part contains nothing more than the ancient ordinances and customs of the kingdom, will remain in force, except for those of its provisions at variance with the dogmas of religion." Oddly enough, the king's judgment was sounder than that of the great German scholar Karl von Savigny. The latter was engaged at the time in a fierce struggle with Thibaut and other proponents of a new civil code for Germany that would go beyond traditional customary laws. He therefore staunchly defended the idea that law is a historical construct against the champions of natural law, while failing, as he later conceded, to take account of the Code's embrace of and compromise with tradition. Henri Klimrath, who brought the historical school of legal studies to France and was a founder of the sociology of law, reacted against the excesses of the "exegetical school," which attempted to study the Code in isolation from its historical roots. His judgment of the drafters' work was far more measured than Savigny's: "They forever eliminated from our laws the few vestiges of feudalism that the monarchy had not yet eliminated, but which public opinion had long repudiated and the Revolution had only recently destroyed. For the rest, they limited themselves, as one may put it, to mere changes in wording, respecting established customs and occasionally rejecting arbitrary, tyrannical innovations that the interim legislation had tried without success." Yet certain revolutionary measures in favor of individual liberty were maintained, as was the separation of law from religion. The lawmakers eliminated chiefly those elements of family law that in their judgment were not yet approved by a national consensus. It would take nearly a century for the Revolution's thinking about illegitimate children and married women to find its way back into law, and nearly a century more to incorporate the Convention's ideas about divorce by mutual consent, guardianship, matrimonial property, and inheritance. What greater tribute could there be to the wisdom of the Civil Code, that remarkable legal and historical compromise, and to the modernity of the Revolution's civil legislation?

Joseph Goy

FURTHER READING

Arnaud, André-Jean. *Essai d'analyse structurale du Code Civil français: La règle du jeu dans la paix bourgeoise.* Paris, 1973.

Carbonnier, Jean. "Le Code Civil," in Pierre Nora, ed., *Les lieux de mémoire,* vol. 2, *La nation.* Paris, 1986.

Esmein, Adrien. *Précis élémentaire de l'histoire du droit français de 1789 à 1814.* Paris, 1911.

Fenet, P.-Antoine. *Recueil complet des travaux préparatoires du Code Civil,* 15 vols. Paris, 1836.

Locré, Jean-Guillaume. *Législation civile, commerciale, et criminelle de la France,* 31 vols. Paris, 1827–1832.

Ourliac, Paul, and Jacques de Malafosse. *Histoire du droit privé,* 3 vols. Paris, 1967.

Sagnac, Philippe. *La législation civile de la Révolution française, 1789–1804.* Paris, 1898.

RELATED TOPICS

Enlightenment   Napoleon Bonaparte   Tocqueville
Feudalism   Physiocrats   Voltaire
Montesquieu   Revolutionary Assemblies

CIVIL CONSTITUTION OF THE CLERGY

P assed in June 1790, the Civil Constitution of the Clergy was the Constituent Assembly's attempt to turn the Church of France into a temporal institution. This raised two issues: what would be the relation between church and state in the new France, and what would be the relation of the French Church to the Pope? The passage of the Civil Constitution thus marks a crucial date in the political and religious history of the Revolution. The vote finalized the divorce between the Revolution and Catholic tradition, a divorce that polarized public opinion and provided the counterrevolution with its first troops.

Its origins can be traced back to the summer of 1789. The Catholic Church was the chief victim of the reforms enacted in the summer and autumn. On August 4 it was stripped of its "feudal rights," but in return it was supposed to be reimbursed as provided for by common law. More onerous was the subsequent elimination of the tithe, this time without indemnity, a decision at variance with the rule followed in the abolition of all other dues. This exception scandalized Sieyès, the champion of equality before the law, but was justified by Mirabeau: if the tithe was too much to pay for the public services rendered by the Church (poor relief and education), then the nation was entitled to do away with it.

But the worst was yet to come. The Church would be obliged to make up the government's deficit, the original reason for which the Estates General had been convoked. On November 2, 1789, the Assembly, acting at the behest of Talleyrand, bishop of Autun, placed the property of the clergy "at the disposal of the nation" for use in paying off the national debt. Once again the grounds given for the action invoked the notion of public service: the Church did not truly own its property but merely enjoyed the benefits thereof for the purpose of discharging certain functions, responsibility for which could be withdrawn from it and reassigned to other institutions. Nor was the confiscation of church property unprecedented in European history: the English crown and German princes had done the same thing in the name of Protestantism, and, more recently, Joseph II, Louis XVI's brother-in-law, had acted in the name of enlightened despotism. In France, the men of 1789, who were not especially anticlerical and, taken as a group, by no means antireligious, killed two birds with one stone: they solved the problem of the public debt by stripping one of the Ancien Régime's privileged orders of its possessions.

Having done that, they were caught up in a series of possibly unforeseen yet inevitable consequences. If, for instance, the Church was now merely a corporation subject to regulation by the civil authorities, what was the status of corporations existing within the Church, such as the conventual orders, and what was to be done about them? In February 1790 the Assembly's Ecclesiastical Committee approved a decree that the law no longer recognized monastic vows and authorized anyone who wished to leave a monastery or convent to do so. During the debate the bishop of Nancy moved that the Assembly recognize Catholicism as the national religion, but the motion was tabled. Discussion then turned to the question of who would administer the church properties "placed at the disposal of the nation." The atmosphere was tense, stormy at times, particularly when the Assembly once again refused to recognize Catholicism as the national religion, and the outcome was that church properties were turned over to the new administrations that had just been set up in the départements and districts. The moment of truth had come, and the apparent unity of the previous autumn was at an end.

At that time a majority of the clergy and its flock had supported the "patriotic" cause. Neither the elimination of the tithe nor the vote of November 2 had put much of a damper on the general enthusiasm or raised the issue of church-state relations. The clergy continued to play the role it had assumed the previous spring in the convocation of the three orders, and in any case it had profited from the Revolution: in the impassioned climate of early 1790, the Assembly had approved a maintenance budget for the Catholic Church that promised an improvement in living standards for most parish priests. Even such high-ranking dignitaries as Boisgelin, the archbishop of Aix, and Champion de Cicé, the archbishop of Bordeaux, who were more administrators than pastors, found it relatively easy to enter into negotiations with the government because that is what church dignitaries had learned to do under the Ancien Régime. Though unenthusiastic about the new government's principles, they had no difficulty recognizing in it the same temporal sovereignty they once had found in the king, now transferred to the people.

Among the jurists of the Third Estate the Gallican spirit was of course strengthened by memories of the parlements' struggles against the papal bull Unigenitus as well as by Jansenist tradition. In these circles hostility to Rome and to any form of papal intervention was widespread, and this was coupled with a determination not to accept any appellate authority over Assembly decrees whether in temporal or spiritual matters. Thus, the Revolution and the Church of France shared the view that national sovereignty took precedence over Rome, but that very agreement could also become an issue in a conflict over the extent of the Church's authority versus that of the Pope. The declaration, in February, that monastic vows were not legally binding had offered a glimpse of what lay in store. The monarchy had issued countless decrees in the eighteenth century regulating the religious orders, but they had left the principle of monastic vows intact. So the question was whether or not the Assembly's vote constituted an unacceptable infringement of spiritual by temporal authority.

Two other key factors heightened the Assembly's risks in moving little by little toward radical changes in the government's regulation of the Church. There were growing signs of resentment of the state's interference with religious tradition, for example in the Cévennes, where not coincidentally Catholics had to contend with a large Protestant minority and the Revolution had awakened old memories of the Wars of Religion. July 1789 had been greeted with unanimous enthusiasm, but by November the specter of renewed religious struggle had brought the defeated aristocracy its first popular support. On April 13 a motion by Dom Gerle—a Carthusian whom Michelet called an "ardent patriot but a no less devoted Catholic"—that Catholicism be declared the national religion was again rejected, touching off disturbances in the area around Nîmes. A strong, prudent, yet firm Protestant bourgeoisie suddenly found itself confronting a Catholic plebs aroused by demagogues and seemingly dredged up from the depths of the sixteenth century.

The second important factor was of course the attitude of the Pope. Born an aristocrat, a priest of narrow views, accustomed to luxury, Pius VI was no mean representative of Roman tradition. The Revolution was something of which he could scarcely conceive. His hostility to the new spirit was fully formed long before the night of August 4, when he lost the *annates,* dues paid to Rome when an ecclesiastical benefice went vacant. In the summer of 1789 the events in France had stirred up trouble among his subjects in Avignon and, to a lesser degree, in the Comtat: the Revolution threatened the Holy See not just through the Church of France but also through papal possessions in French territory. On March 29, 1790, on advice of elderly Cardinal de Bernis, the French ambassador (who in advising the pontiff violated his instructions), Pius VI condemned, in a secret consistory, the principles embodied in the Declaration of the Rights of Man. Conflict continued to smolder, but it had not yet erupted into the open.

In Paris a break with Rome was not considered imminent or even inevitable. Neither the members of the Assembly's Ecclesiastical Committee, which in February and March pondered a plan for reorganizing the Church of France, nor even the prelates of that Church, no great friends of the Roman Curia, anticipated the bitterness of the coming struggle. Historians such as Pressensé and Mathiez, though very different politically, agree that to contemporaries the troubles were unpredictable and unforeseen. The Civil Constitution of the Clergy was not the work of dedicated anticlericals out to destroy the Catholic Church. Nor did it suddenly arouse the holy ire of the French episcopate. Although it was indeed the point at which the Revolution and the Church parted company and became implacable enemies, in the spring of 1790 no one yet knew that this would be the case. The Constituent Assembly's decree gradually drew it deeper and deeper into a controversy whose consequences it never deliberately intended.

Perhaps that is why the parliamentary debate of mid-May to mid-July 1790 out of which the Civil Constitution was born strikes most historians as disappointing: it seems not quite equal to issues whose magnitude the future would reveal. "The debate was neither clever nor deep," according to Michelet, who noted only one important idea, put forward by Camus, a Jansenist and one of the leaders of the Ecclesiastical Committee: "We are a National Convention. We surely have the power to change religion. But we will not use it." For Michelet, these words of the Paris deputy offered a momentary glimpse of his dream: the revolutionary religion whose time he thought had come but which was never to be. The thought, no sooner proposed than withdrawn, also revealed the Assembly's timidity in spiritual matters: like the kings who preceded it, the Assembly's one obsession was sovereignty. The debate, though long and meticulous, revealed a sort of intellectual exhaustion when it came to the great question of the new principles' relation to the old religion. It was a debate among politicians, jurists, and lawyers that pitted an etiolated, subjugated, almost secularized Catholicism against a Revolution clinging to its new power, which it conceived on the model of the old absolutism.

The proposed bill contained four titles. The first substituted new religious districts (*circonscriptions*), based on the new division of France into eighty-three départements, for the old subdivisions. The number of bishoprics was accordingly reduced from 130 to 83, together with 10 metropolitan districts. Clerical nomenclature was simplified and rationalized through elimination of traditional titles and offices such as prebendaries, canonries, abbeys, chapters, and so on. From now on, episcopal power was to be collegial, each bishop being required to consult a permanent council of vicars in the fulfillment of his responsibilities. Article 5 of title 1 stipulated that the Church of France was in no way subject to any foreign bishop or metropolitan, including that of Rome. Title 2, in an even greater innovation, substituted election for the traditional canonical procedures used for filling vacancies in the Church. All electors were entitled to participate in the voting, which was required for the selection of bishops as well as parish priests. As employees of the state, bishops and priests were required to swear an oath of allegiance to the Constitution. Title 3 established a schedule of clerical salaries and provided for significant cuts compared with traditional levels. Title 4 required clergymen to reside in the places they were supposed to serve, a regulation to be enforced by municipal governments.

The religious order was thus based on the civil order, the structure of the Church on that of the state under a sovereign constitution that derived its legitimacy from popular election. Ties to the papacy were severed. The French Church was now entirely dependent on the temporal authorities.

Against these sweeping reforms the opposition, led by Boisgelin, argued that the state had no competence in spiritual matters. On May 29, early in the debate, the archbishop of Aix contended that the traditional rules of ecclesiastical discipline could be modified only with the joint approval of both spiritual and temporal authorities. A bill that tampered with such basic Christian traditions as the power of bishops and the selection of priests would have to be approved by a national council of the Church of France and by the head of the Universal Church.

The first response to this argument came the next day from Treilhard, a deputy for Paris. He extended to the Church the Revolution's condemnation of the Ancien Régime. The misdeeds and abuses for which it was responsible were subject to judgment by the civil authorities and none other. He thus signaled at once that the Church would be made to pay dearly not for religion as such but for its intimate involvement in the old order, its collusion with yesterday's powers. And who defended the spirit of Christianity better than the Ecclesiastical Committee, whose decision that priests be chosen by election moved the Church closer to its origins? Furthermore, there were no grounds for challenging the sovereign state's absolute power over church discipline, for the whole tradition of the monarchy dictated otherwise. This argument was developed further by Camus on May 31, who invoked the traditions of both early Christianity and French public law to bestow upon the Committee's draft the twin blessings of charity and necessity: "Submission to the sovereign authority of the nation is not only an obligation of necessity but also a duty of charity. Let the pastors of our century be imbued with the principles that motivated those of the Church's early centuries . . . and religion in France will be pure as it was then in Africa." Represented by the one-time advocate of the clergy, the Jansenist party took its revenge for the humiliation and persecution it had suffered at the hands of the Church, abetted by the monarchy, since the papal bull Unigenitus.

The discussion of the articles of the proposed Constitution, which began on June 1, was interminable and dull, frequently interrupted by debates on other pending legislation. At the urging of Abbé Grégoire, article 5, title 1, was changed to reserve the rights of the Pope. After this, the two most hotly debated points were the election of priests and compensation of curates (who wished to maintain the endowment of cures through the income on certain small properties). In mid-June, however, the Ecclesiastical Committee voted to approve its draft in more or less its original form. The bill was adopted on July 12.

Despite the great changes that the new law made to the Church's organizational structure, it was not unacceptable to a Church that the kings of France had accustomed to the brute supremacy of the temporal authorities. Not long before, the Church in Austria had been forced by Joseph II to submit to comparable reforms. A majority of bishops had expressed reservations about the Civil Constitution, but the bulk of the clergy was prepared to accept it. The prelates, unwilling to heighten suspicions that attached to them by virtue of their aristocratic names, and, in any case, doubtful about the compatibility of the reform with canon law, warily acquiesced. On advice of Champion de Cicé and Boisgelin, Louis XVI, hesitant as usual, signed the decree.

The debate, however, had revealed one paramount condition that had to be satisfied before the Church could accept a reform such as this, drafted and approved by the state: namely, the approval of some spiritual authority. The Constituent Assembly had rejected the idea of a national council. That left the Pope, now wrestling with the Avignon affair and less and less inclined to distinguish between spiritual and temporal in his condemnation of the Revolution. Prudently concerned about both the situation in Avignon and the position of the French bishops, he did not condemn the Civil Constitution until March 10, 1791, but his opposition was known by the summer of 1790. Free use was made of the fact, particularly by one interested party, the indefatigable Bernis.

Catholic France was aroused well before its priests. Mobilized by intolerance and intrigue, Catholics were also alarmed by all the changes in the law affecting Protestants and Jews and indignant that the Assembly had refused to recognize Catholicism as the "national" religion, which would have maintained something of its privileged position. Intolerance had reared its head where it was most deeply rooted, namely, in partly Protestant southern cities such as Nîmes, Uzès, and Montauban. In Nîmes in mid-June, even as the Assembly debated the Civil Constitution, civil war raged for several days, and Catholic forces suffered defeat and massacre.

By the end of the summer the situation had grown worse throughout France. The Civil Constitution had been published in the départements, where it enjoyed the sometimes belligerent support of the administrations elected the previous spring. The clubs and popular societies agitated in favor of immediate application of the law. In the meantime Catholic opinion turned increasingly hostile. Those bishops who were members of the Assembly broke their silence on October 30 by publishing an "Exposition of the Principles of the Civil Constitution of the Clergy," a detailed refutation of the bill passed in July. At this point, with violence still rare but the calm clearly precarious, the Constituent Assembly chose to move forward. On November 26 it issued a decree allowing serving priests two months to take an oath to the Constitution, hence also to the Civil Constitution of the Clergy that was part of it. This was the signal that touched off the schism.

A third of the ecclesiastical members of the Assembly took the oath in January 1791. Only seven bishops "swore the oath" (the phrase was *jurer le serment* rather than *prêter le serment*), and, of those, three swore *in partibus*. But what the Assembly did was now beside the point; what mattered was the country. The publication of the decree of November 26 followed by the ceremonial oath-taking in January triggered demonstrations both for and against the Civil Constitution. The disturbances were particularly grave in places where the populace supported a priest's refusal to take the oath or called for such refusal. In Paris it was the opposite, however: popular pressure was brought to bear on hesitant or recalcitrant priests to force them to take the fateful step. On one Sunday when oath-takings were scheduled, a large crowd entered Saint-Sulpice and threatened the obdurate curate, who fled to cries of "the oath or the gallows." But in Alsace, the Massif Central, and especially in the Catholic highlands of Velay and Rouergue as well as in western France, particularly the rectangular region that would become the center of armed insurrection in the Vendée in 1793, large crowds opposed the swearing of the oath, and in many cases it was the local authorities—mayors and municipal officials—who were forced to capitulate. These disturbances have been subjected to systematic analysis by an American historian, Timothy Tackett, who has succeeded in showing how the whole affair touched something fundamental at the heart of French social life: the parish community. Accordingly, it is not at all easy to determine in any particular case how much the reaction reflected the curate's personality and how much the religious attitudes of the parishioners. Nevertheless, it is clear that the refusal to take the oath was the first sign of popular resistance to the Revolution, and therefore it is important to understand how such refusals were distributed geographically.

Resistance was so powerful and so widespread that the Constituent Assembly was soon forced to pull in its horns. After, in effect, opting for intransigence on January 4, 1791, it compromised on January 23, authorizing refractory priests who had not been replaced to remain in their parishes (and in any case guaranteeing them a small pension). On May 7 it passed a "tolerance decree," giving force of law to a measure taken in Paris by the administration of the Paris département authorizing refractory priests to celebrate mass in "constitutional" churches. This quelled the disturbances for a while but did nothing to improve the situation, merely acknowledging the political and religious impasse into which the Civil Constitution had led the Revolution. By early summer the Pope's opposition to the text was obvious to all, and all ambiguity was eliminated from the situation of the "ecclesiastical public functionaries": all refractory priests already had been or soon would be replaced. Yet they remained in their villages and neighborhoods, and the Assembly, determined to stabilize the situation, was finally forced to accept the existence of two churches, only one of which was in conformity with the law. The Constituent Assembly's aim had been to call a halt to the Revolution, but instead it provided the counterrevolution with leaders and troops.

Over the past quarter-century numerous historians have sought to adduce social or socioeconomic explanations of the rural counterrevolution, but their findings have proved either negative or tenuous. The regions and social groups that rose in rebellion against the Revolution in 1793 were no more favorable to the Ancien Régime in 1789 than the rest. *Cahiers de doléances* from the Vendée and Chouan territory were as hostile to feudal dues as other texts drafted on behalf of rural communities throughout France. Nor can the peasant counterrevolution be blamed on particularly severe antagonism between town and country or bourgeois and peasantry. Dramatic as that opposition was during the war in the Vendée, it was quite widespread and assumed a variety of guises. In Quercy and Rouergue, for example, peasants continued to fight well after August 4, 1789, for abolition without indemnity of seigneurial dues, thus challenging the authority of the new urban administrations. Yet Quercy and Rouergue did not rise against the dictatorship of Paris and the cities in 1793. Farther north, in Lozère, an insurrection did begin around this time, however. In any event, wherever the arrogance of the new rulers of the towns proved more unbearable than the paternal exactions of the nobility, hostility between town and country was perhaps more political than social.

The religious element, it seems, cannot be reduced to some other set of factors for interpreting the counterrevolution. Clearly, however, the religious element was immediately transformed into a political issue because both the monarchy and the Revolution had turned the Catholic Church into an auxiliary of the state. The crisis of the oath was simply a more bitter and far more widespread reprise of other episodes in the history of relations between the state (the now deposed monarchy) and the Jansenist clergy, such as the "affair of the *billets de confession*." In 1791 the whole Catholic Church paid a heavy price for its pact with absolutism, for Jansenism's revenge, carried out in the name of Gallicanism, only accentuated the Church's subordination to the state. Now all priests were called upon to choose between Paris and Rome, between a universal church and a national one, between inner conviction and governmental authority. And beyond the priests, in some cases standing shoulder to shoulder with them, millions of the faithful understood and embraced this dilemma, inextricably religious and political.

An idea of the depth of the conflict can be gained from its duration. Broadly speaking, religious practice in mid-twentieth-century France correlates with politics: where religion is strong, so is the right wing. And the distribution of religious practices is roughly correlated with the distribution of parishes in which priests refused to take the oath in 1791. Thus there has been an enduring political dichotomy in France between clericals and anticlericals, illustrating the depth of the controversy that erupted in 1791. Catholic tradition has been a more durable and effective source of ideas and passions than loyalty to the monarchy. In their different ways both Michelet and Quinet criticized the Revolution for having battled the Church without eradicating the faith. Michelet would have liked the Revolution to have become its own religion. Quinet would have liked it to have invented a new religion in harmony with the spirit of liberty. But could it have done so? In the late eighteenth century the Reformation was already too far in the past to permit the establishment of a home-grown Protestant sect, yet the Jansenist battles and the Gallican heritage remained too fresh in memory to permit the establishment of a secular cult independent of the state. From this dual impasse was born an anti-Catholic revolutionary culture imbued with all the intolerance of the Catholic spirit.

François Furet

Fᴜʀᴛʜᴇʀ ʀᴇᴀᴅɪɴɢ

La Gorce, Pierre de. *Histoire religieuse de la Révolution française,* 5 vols. Paris, 1909–1923.

Latreille, André. *L'Eglise Catholique et la Révolution française,* 2 vols. Paris, 1946–1950.

Leflon, Jean (canon). *La crise révolutionnaire, 1789–1846,* vol. 20 of *L'histoire de l'Eglise depuis les origines jusqu'à nos jours,* ed. Augustin Flèche and Victor Martin. Paris, 1951.

Mathiez, Albert. *Rome et le clergé français sous la Constituante.* Paris, 1911.

Pressensé, Edmond de. *L'Eglise et la Révolution française: Histoire des relations de l'Eglise et de l'état de 1789 à 1814.* Paris, 1820.

Quinet, Edgar. *Le Christianisme et la Révolution française.* Paris, 1845; reprinted with revisions by Patrice Vermeren, Paris, 1984.

Tackett, Timothy. *Religion, Revolution and Regional Culture in Eighteenth-Century France: The Ecclesiastical Oath of 1791.* Princeton, 1985.

Van Kley, Dale. "The Jansenist Constitutional Legacy in the French Prerevolution," *Historical Reflections,* vol. 13, 1986.

Rᴇʟᴀᴛᴇᴅ ᴛᴏᴘɪᴄꜱ

Counterrevolution
De-Christianization
Louis XVI
Michelet

Mirabeau
National Properties
Quinet
Revolutionary Assemblies

Revolutionary Religion
Sieyès
Tocqueville

CLUBS AND
POPULAR SOCIETIES

For a long time the history of Jacobinism overshadowed that of the revolutionary societies. Seldom have the same historians been interested in both of these emblematic participants in the Revolution. The questions asked about the Jacobins are generally different from those asked about the societies, and different historiographical controversies have arisen about the two subjects. Yet both are parts of a single history, and neither can be understood without reference to the other. The historian is faced with two realities. On the one hand, a body of sacred yet infinitely malleable beliefs, an imperious if ambiguous rhetoric that permanently influenced the Revolution's understanding of itself: national sovereignty, the will of the people, public safety. Notions such as these soon became the supreme arbiter of revolutionary legitimacy—its instrument and voice. On the other hand, the Jacobin *machine*, as Michelet called it, a tightly knit network of political societies that proliferated in France between 1789 and Year III: patriotic clubs, Amis de la Constitution, correspondence committees, popular and fraternal societies, village societies, youth societies, women's societies, soldiers' societies, foreigners' societies, and many others.

Estimates of the magnitude of the phenomenon vary with the author and method. Michelet, and later Aulard, put the number of societies at about 1,000. Augustin Cochin counted no fewer than 44,000 (roughly the number of communes in Year II). Crane Brinton estimated between 5,000 and 8,000, and Louis de Cardenal found slightly more than 3,000. More recently, Jean Boutier and Philippe Boutry (upon whose work we shall rely in what follows) put at 5,500 the number of communes (villages, towns, and cities) with a political society of some kind between 1789 and Year III. Not surprisingly, such societies were found throughout urban France. Less predictably, the map shows that their distribution coincided with the distribution of what have been called "democratic social forms" (*sociabilité démocratique*) in the Ancien Régime: densest in northern, northwestern, and southwestern France as well as in Ile-de-France, Aquitaine, and eastern Provence; sparsest in the *bocage* of Normandy, inland Brittany, the Vendée, the Vosges, Meurthe-et-Moselle, Alsace, Champagne, Berry, the Bourbonnais, and portions of the Massif Central. One also finds the same contrast between rural and urban France and between coastal and inland areas in both cases.

As schools of political culture, the revolutionary societies quickly developed into a laboratory for experimenting with the language, practices, and imagery of direct democracy: identification of the individual with the citizen, egalitarian rhetoric, consensus rule, and the reign of opinion. By "opinion" we mean a system for organizing and legitimating power based not on tradition but on formal rules, obligations, and procedures.

This widespread and routine exercise of sovereignty by an inexperienced yet energetic group was described by Michelet as a "powerful lever," proof of patriotic virtue at a time when the Revolution was most seriously threatened. Few writers, however, have paid attention to the internal dynamics of this type of organization, much less to the kinds of ideological production that it fosters. Little has been said about the ambiguous relations between ideas and political action, between imagery and the organization of power, between egalitarian rhetoric and the practice of equality.

Revolutionary historiography has been torn between two approaches that rarely intersect. One group of historians has been content to turn out countless monographs reconstructing with varying degrees of success the endless variety of Jacobin politics, yet without delving very deeply into the ideological dimension of Jacobin views. More traditional historians (both legitimist and Jacobin) have systematically reduced the history of the revolutionary societies to that of the Montagnard dictatorship.

Augustin Cochin (1876–1916) is notable for having combined these two approaches. His thesis, presented many decades ago but unenthusiastically received and soon abandoned, was never tested by systematic research. Yet it offers a most sound and fruitful approach to the study of Jacobinism, its origins, evolution, and genealogy. Cochin's fierce hostility to the Revolution and modern democracy, his defective scholarship, and his sometimes faulty hypotheses in no way detract from the value of his intuition. He is the only historian since Michelet to attend not only to Jacobin ideology but also to the sociological conditions and mechanisms that made it possible to win unanimous support for an extremist doctrine. From the meetings of the "mother-society" (that is, the Jacobin Club of Paris) the will of the people was supposed to emerge: that, in short, was the ideology of the Jacobins. Without the support of the nation, made manifest by unanimous acclamation, no action was justifiable or explicable. Yet the unique will of the people was open to interpretation and distortion of many kinds. By definition the will of the people brooked no minority opposition, no genuine debate, no divided opinion. Accordingly, periodic purges were carried out to maintain the Club's unanimity, and through it the unity of the people. The purges were both a political weapon and a governmental instrument. No one not in a position of power could "represent" the nation, and by using that power it became possible to eliminate, in the nation's name, any discordant voice. With each new crisis, Jacobinism, like prerevolutionary Freemasonry, pointed up just how difficult it was to conceive of everyday democratic practice in terms other than unanimity, as opposed to the chaos and conflict born of the clash of selfish private interests. All dissidence was necessarily deemed suspect or illegal, hence reprehensible. The language of democracy masked these difficulties, and constant insistence on transparency and obsessive fears of conspiracy served to justify Jacobin practice.

In all of this there was a kind of continuity from the Ancien Régime to the Revolution that has sometimes gone unnoticed. The birthplace of this "ideological practice" was the society that the Revolution was supposed to have abolished, in which one finds early democratic social forms embodied in literary circles and societies, reading groups, and especially Masonic lodges. We call these social forms democratic not because they sought to abolish monarchy and establish universal suffrage but because they were in many ways incompatible with the organic imagery of a society of orders and corporations. Democratic sociability rested on an often purely formal principle of social equality. This represented a fundamental ideological shift: a change not necessarily in the real society to which it referred, which remained quite diverse, but in the discourse that flowed from what came to be seen as an infallible and imperious moral principle. The new social forms were democratic because they invoked no authority other than the common will of individual group members. Prerevolutionary Freemasonry is undoubtedly the most fully developed, highly structured, and widely spread example of this indirectly political (not to say directly apolitical) model. A half century before the Revolution it unwittingly demonstrated the limits of the corporatist imagery of the old society. In place of an organic solidarity based on common origins or shared interests, the new model substituted fraternity as both a value and a rallying cry. In Freemasonry all legitimacy depended on the structure of power. It was a legitimacy based not on a body of doctrine, on a law, or even in most cases on written norms (statutes, regulations, or constitutions), but on a man's capacity to act as spokesman for a group by dint of his political acumen, consecrated by election (regardless of the manner in which the votes might have been obtained).

To be sure, the men involved in "societies of thought" were not necessarily the same ones who joined revolutionary societies. The environment had changed, and people's concerns became less intellectual and speculative and more political. Nevertheless, one finds surprising continuity in such routine practices as procedures for admission, deliberation, election, and expulsion. In Lille, Bergerac, Tulle, Perpignan, and Le Gers, a clear line of descent can be traced from the Masonic lodges to the revolutionary clubs. Initially certain regulations of the latter were not based on the model of the Paris Jacobin Club but were transcribed almost verbatim from Masonic ritual. The Jacobin Club in Castres descended from a local literary society established in 1783; hence it was only natural for it to record its minutes in the same register used by its predecessor.

The old and the new organs of democratic sociability were similar both ideologically and sociologically. They provide us with a way to answer certain key questions about the Jacobin phenomenon: Where did it come from, why did it prove so powerful, and how did it develop under the Terror?

Most historians of Jacobinism seem to be unaware of the genealogy we have traced. For them the Jacobin Club grew out of the Breton Club that was formed in Versailles on the eve of the meeting of the Estates General. Notwithstanding a few obscure passages, the history of the Breton Club is well known. The forty-four deputies of the Third Estate from Brittany decided to hold a regular "provincial chamber," a decision that owed as much to the political determination of certain deputies as to the confusion of some others. The aim was both to champion the cause of the Third Estate and to defend the prerogatives of Brittany. It reflected a desire for reform as much as an attachment to the privileges of the Ancien Régime. The determined deputies included Le Chapelier, Lanjuinais, and Glezen, *avocats* at the bar of Rennes, who first learned the art of politics in their battles with the parlement and nobility of Brittany. They had come to Versailles intent on pressing the two key demands of the Third Estate: joint deliberation of all three orders and voting by head rather than by estate. Among the more confused deputies were those representing less agitated districts; for example, Palasne de Champeaux felt as if he had "fallen from the sky into a country and state of affairs about which we have not the slightest idea." The provincial loyalties that united this and many other delegations were reinforced by the decision of Brittany's nobles not to take part in the Estates General. They owed even more, perhaps, to the constituents' insistence, recorded in the *cahiers de doléances,* "to carefully preserve Brittany's rights and concessions." Initially, therefore, the Breton Club reflected both tradition and innovation, both the specific rights of corporations and communities and *the* right of the nation, both the Ancien Régime and the Revolution.

The vocation of the Breton Club was neither to elaborate nor even to "represent" a body of doctrine but to produce unanimity. On May 15, La Ville Le Roulx, deputy for Hennebont, wrote his constituents that it had been agreed that "questions proposed in the Estates General would be proposed the very same day in the Assembly of Brittany, and that the dominant opinion would be moved by one member of the Assembly and seconded by the rest, on the principle that all views would always be directed toward the general good in general affairs. As for the affairs of the province, a similar resolution in our common interest will be taken in time."

Unlike the monarchiens, who from the first meeting of the Estates General held a very clear idea of what form the "regeneration of France" ought to take, the Bretons were merely reacting to events. Opening the Club to other "patriotic" deputies and a few liberal aristocrats did not change its fundamental character, which was that of a pressure group caught in the thick of events and united not so much by ideological cohesiveness as by the intransigence of its adversaries. Even the Club's spectacular contribution to the abolition of privileges on the night of August 4 was primarily a response to an improvised initiative on the part of a few high nobles in the face of peasant insurrections.

From May to October, the Breton Club's politics were determined by circumstances. The Club was not attempting to realize a plan or model but sought only to enlist support, intimidate adversaries, and "build a consensus." For proof, consider one striking passage from the memoirs of Abbé Grégoire concerning the *séance royale* of June 23. The Breton Club, informed of the court's intentions, discussed what to do the night before: "The first resolution was to remain in the hall in spite of the king's prohibition. It was agreed that prior to the opening of the session, we would circulate among our colleagues to inform them of what was about to take place before their very eyes and explain why they must oppose it. Someone objected, however, that the votes of 12 or 15 people could not decide the behavior of 1,200 deputies. He was told that phraseology could work wonders. We would say, 'This is what the court is going to do, and *it has been decided* that the patriots will take such and such measures in response.' *It has been decided* could signify 400 just as well as 10. This expedient worked."

In the absence of a political strategy the Club counted on parliamentary discipline; lacking a definition of the general will, it relied on singling out its adversaries. An exasperated Sieyès confided to Etienne Dumont: "I will not have anything more to do with those people. Theirs is a caveman's politics. They propose murder as an expedient." Although the Breton Club did not survive the October Days, it left as its legacy some key features of the newly emerging Jacobinism, features that were soon developed, amplified, and institutionalized in the new association known as the Amis de la Constitution (Friends of the Constitution).

Soon after its formation the new Club boasted 200 members. Before long its rolls had swelled to 400 and by December to more than 1,000. Membership was no longer restricted to members of the Constituent Assembly. A deputy from Brittany wrote to one of his constituents: "People from outside the National Assembly covet the honor of being allowed to pay this society the tribute of their ideas, and societies in some of the kingdom's leading cities have already requested the favor of being granted affiliation and engaging in correspondence."

Until the end of 1789, however, the Jacobins had only a modest base in the provinces: affiliated clubs could be found in some twenty cities. There was also a parallel structure of partially organized "patriotic clubs." Descended from the "societies of thought" of the Ancien Régime or formed spontaneously in the first months of the Revolution, these functioned autonomously and in many cases knew nothing about the Amis de la Constitution. Before long the Paris Jacobins sought to organize these scattered but active groups. They sent countless printed copies of their constitution to other societies in the hope of attracting new members and exerting leadership over a movement whose political significance they immediately grasped. This campaign was strongly supported by the patriotic press and, after October 1790, by the *Journal des Sociétés des Amis de la Constitution,* founded by Choderlos de Laclos, which kept the public informed of the work of the Amis, reported on new affiliations, and above all stressed the urgent need to coordinate the defense of the Revolution, the Nation, and the Constitution under one banner and one organ.

These efforts quickly bore fruit. By the spring of 1790, 50 cities had affiliated clubs. By May the number was 66; by June, 91; by September, 152; and by December it had reached 276. The spread of Jacobin influence was chaotic but steady, and it is not always easy to determine whether a particular club was founded more because of local initiative or Parisian influence, old social patterns or revolutionary commitments, collective forces or personal ambitions. Nevertheless, the clear correlation between the growth of Jacobin affiliates and the progress of the Revolution suggests that after 1790, at any rate, it was the impact of events that mattered most.

The most striking example of such a correlation can be seen in connection with the crisis of the constitutional oath, which gave a tremendous impetus to the spread of Jacobinism in the first few weeks of 1791. The refractory priests (those who refused to take the oath to support the Civil Constitution of the Clergy) now abandoned the Revolution in large numbers; but many priests did take the oath, and their authority was enhanced because they became intellectual and physical symbols of resistance to the old order. In a France divided between proponents and adversaries of the Civil Constitution, the clubs became emblems of patriotism, places where people swore to uphold the decrees of the National Assembly and to remain vigilant against counterrevolutionary plots and cabals. Between December 1790 and March 1791 the number of clubs almost doubled, from 276 to 543. The pace of foundations accelerated: there were 650 clubs by April, 745 on the eve of the king's attempted escape, 833 immediately after his return, and nearly 1,000 when the Constituent Assembly disbanded.

Although the Jacobin Club in Paris was in favor of this expansion, it sought to regulate it. Its blessing was not bestowed lightly: it was accorded to only one society per commune and usually required the recommendation of a deputy or a member of the Paris Club. These two requirements prevented or at least impeded any attempt to alter the internal power structure of the Jacobin movement, and they probably account for the remarkable stability and apparent cohesiveness of the movement up to the time of the Feuillant crisis: dissidence and scissions were as rare in the Jacobin movement as they were common in prerevolutionary Freemasonry (the Masons having permitted more than one lodge in a city). Direct controls were augmented by indirect ones: several provincial clubs accepted affiliates with or without the authorization of Paris, expanding Jacobin influence still further.

An analysis of the social background of Jacobins in Paris as well as the provinces under both the Constituent Assembly and the Convention reveals a prevalence of the Third Estate's elite: merchants, magistrates, government officials, physicians, rentiers, and—at least until the crisis of the oath—many members of the clergy. In other words, the Jacobins were, socially speaking, quite similar to the members of prerevolutionary democratic societies. An even more surprising aspect of the social composition of the Jacobin clubs is how many exhibited a desire to achieve social homogeneity. When "passive citizens" were excluded from municipal elections in January-February 1790, they were also excluded from the Sociétés des Amis de la Constitution. Very few peasants were admitted. Despite the institutionalization of equality, notables of the Third Estate were reluctant to rub elbows with small shopkeepers and artisans. To prevent such "debasement" they established openly discriminatory regulations or set dues so high as to discourage applications. Those prevented by such measures from joining existing clubs attempted to form their own societies: they account for about twenty percent of the Jacobin membership before the Terror.

Jacobin ambivalence toward equality was especially noticeable in connection with the sale of national properties, in which Jacobins played an active role. Peasants and sans-culottes were discriminated against and did not share in the profits. Furthermore, the campaign mounted by the Amis des Noirs (Friends of the Blacks) to abolish slavery does not seem to have found much support among the Friends of the Constitution. As a result of pressure on the latter from certain cities with an interest in maintaining slavery, egalitarian principles were discreetly deemphasized in favor of predictions of disorder and appeals to economic interest. Grégoire's call in February 1790 for extending political rights to people of color did find some support, however, though it was far from unanimous.

The political activities of the clubs were confined mainly to the municipal and district level, though occasionally extending as high as the département. Relations between the clubs and the urban corporations elected in January and February 1790 were not always cordial. Certain municipal councils wanted to believe that the Revolution was over and feared that any patriotic demonstration might rekindle it. Others, convinced that the elections had vested legitimate authority in them, had little use for Jacobin attempts to interfere in their affairs. Many societies suffered bitter disappointments—but not for long. In November half the municipal officeholders were replaced, and the Jacobins were able to regain control of numerous town halls. Within a year, however, the tide had turned again in elections to the Legislative Assembly: Jacobin influence in the Assembly was drastically curtailed, despite a campaign of unprecedented vigor. Thus the spectacular growth in the size of the Jacobin movement did not immediately translate into increased political influence.

The king's attempted escape in June 1791 marked a major turning point. From the outset the queen had been the object of much of the Jacobins' hatred, while the king had been granted the benefit of the doubt. But his flight suddenly and dramatically changed all that, even if it did not lead to immediate calls for the establishment of a republic. The Friends of the Constitution refrained from going that far; yet they were compelled to reconsider the basis of a political consensus whose fragility had been revealed by the king's flight. In the ensuing disarray we detect perhaps the earliest sign of a new direction in the history of Jacobinism.

The Jacobin movement was unified administratively but not ideologically, and one is struck by the persistence of diversity up to 1793 in the activities of the clubs, which were greatly influenced by local circumstances. In 1790 some provincial affiliates corresponded with both the Jacobin Club and the Society of 1789, founded by ex-Jacobins who had quit the Club in order to combat its influence. In the spring of 1792, while Brissot and Robespierre were fighting for control of the Jacobin Club in Paris, provincial affiliates, seemingly unconcerned by the outcome of this fateful struggle, continued to heap praise on both men. Michael Kennedy has shown that affiliated clubs preferred to get their information from newspapers that reported on parliamentary debates rather than from the militant press, which paid more attention to the ins and outs of Paris politics, or even from the newspaper that Deflers had founded for the purpose of reporting on the meetings of the Paris Jacobins.

Aware of the impossibility of obliging the affiliates to hew closely to an ever-changing political line, the Paris Jacobins concentrated their efforts on maintaining the movement's organizational unity. Until after the fall of the Girondins the Club made no effort to establish its own newspaper. It relied on others to report more or less accurately on its deliberations. Nor did the Paris Club always choose the local society most closely aligned with its own political views as its affiliate. In Bordeaux, for example, the local Friends of the Constitution remained the official Jacobin affiliate until 1793, even though it had been moving steadily toward a more conservative position. The rival National Club, which systematically followed the line of the Paris Jacobins in the hope of being accepted as an affiliate, succeeded only after its rival publicly broke with the Paris group.

The effects of this ambivalence were most obvious during elections. In each département the clubs freely chose which candidates they would support, often with decisive influence on the outcome, and the Paris Club made no attempt to intervene. In the September 1792 elections to the supposedly Jacobin Convention, the Paris Club controlled the Paris vote; but in the provinces its affiliates contributed to the triumph of the Girondins, whose prestige was so great at the time that Paris could not openly combat them without jeopardizing the movement's organizational foundations.

In response to the circulars sent out by the Paris Jacobins, countless petitions converged on Paris, seeming proof of the influence of the affiliated societies on Jacobin opinion. In fact, however, there was no genuine communication between center and periphery. As Michelet noted, the purpose of the circulars was not to set themes or provoke debate but to demand support for every change in the Jacobin line. The responses from the provinces yielded a formal consensus, but they also reflected the underlying diversity of the movement. Unanimity stemmed not from the "unification of Enlightenment with interest," as the rules of the society laid down, nor from a synthesis of varied opinions, but from the elimination of heterodox views. Slogans and strategies were elaborated in secret by the Correspondence Committee. The support of the affiliates was "fabricated" so as to allow the leaders in Paris to present themselves as spokesmen for popular opinion and, by invoking widespread support, to impose their views on the sometimes reluctant Jacobin Assembly.

This practice differentiated the Jacobin movement from other societies that were established to oppose its influence. The Society of 1789, founded by Sieyès, was never anything more than an academy that staged banquets at which the celebrated abbé as well as Lafayette and Condorcet searched in vain for support with which to rival the Jacobins' power over the Assembly. In

April 1790 the monarchiens created the Society of Friends of the Monarchical Constitution, whose name alone gives an adequate idea of the ambitions of its founders. With no real audience or network of correspondents and lacking any sort of apparatus to impose an orthodoxy, this group quickly became the target of Jacobin attacks; in March 1791 it was closed by the police in the wake of several violent incidents.

The Jacobin movement remained remarkably cohesive until the scission of July 1791. Its unity was based in part on support for the decrees of the National Assembly: in deliberating what laws ought to be made, the Jacobins agreed to accept those that had already been passed. But this consensus was seriously shaken by the flight of Louis XVI to Varennes, which brought the Jacobins to a crossroads. They did not immediately call for the establishment of a republic, however. After passage of the decree of July 15, 1791, which established the fiction of the king's "abduction," it was not so much the nature of the regime that was in question as it was the nature of the relation between the Society of Friends of the Constitution and the nation's deputies. For the first time the Jacobins continued, even after passage, to oppose a decree that they deemed contrary to the "principles of the Society." Between the vote of July 15 and the fusillade on the Champ de Mars of July 17, a new Jacobinism was born.

The birth was not without difficulties. Hostile to the radicalization of the Club, four-fifths of its members abandoned the regular Jacobin meeting place, a chapel on the rue Saint-Honoré, for the Convent of the Feuillants. The seceding group therefore came to be known as the Feuillants. In a circular sent immediately to the provinces, the Feuillants sought to justify their break with those who dared to protest a decree passed by the Assembly. They seemed in no doubt that they would emerge victorious from the dispute. Within two months, however, the minority faction—the Jacobins—had succeeded in gaining the confidence of nearly all the affiliates.

In the first few weeks the Feuillants received approval from some seventy clubs, while the Jacobins were backed by somewhere in the neighborhood of fifty. The vast majority of affiliates refused to take sides, however, and advocated reconciliation. This hesitation soon gave way to support for the Jacobins as one provincial club after another abandoned the Feuillants. The shift, still barely discernible at the end of July, had become irreversible by the end of August.

The Feuillants had shown astonishing irresolution, neglecting their correspondence at a time when their views needed to be publicized as widely as possible. By contrast, the Jacobins staked their all on gaining the allegiance of the affiliates. They sent circular after circular, dispatched agents to the clubs closest to Paris, made use of a supportive "patriotic" press, and shrewdly exploited the popularity and reputation of the "virtuous" Pétion and the "incorruptible" Robespierre.

By stressing the loyalty of those two deputies to what Pétion called liberty's "first asylum," the minority sought to win recognition as the uncontested heir of the Society of Friends of the Constitution. The Jacobins understood the symbolic importance of their meeting place as proof of that continuity, and on two occasions Robespierre thwarted belated efforts by the Feuillants to take back the hall and the Society's archives. Michelet wrote: "This was no ordinary hall that one could abandon without serious consequence. The proof that the Feuillants were not politicians is that they failed to grasp this fact."

Yet to win the support of the provincial clubs it was not enough for the minority to include the phrase *séante aux Jacobins* (meeting at the Jacobins) in their letterhead. They had to persuade people of their fidelity to the statutes of the Society and refute their adversaries' charges. By ignoring reality they scored a decisive victory. On July 18 Robespierre sent a circular to the affiliates to counter Feuillant propaganda and delay any decision. With shrewd rhetoric he proclaimed the Jacobins' undying devotion not to the constitution that the Assembly was about to revise but, more subtly, to the principles on which a constitution ought to be based. It was not the loyal minority that had abandoned the Club's historic mission but those who had walked out of the rue Saint-Honoré because they had been led astray *temporarily* by a handful of intriguers. Robespierre cleverly shifted blame for the schism to the Feuillants, and by declaring himself ready to absolve those who repented of their error he isolated the triumvirs, for such magnanimity seemed to accord with the affiliates' wish for a reconciliation. By contrast, the Feuillants, overly confident of their strength, haughtily rejected several conciliatory overtures from the Jacobins, thereby displeasing the provincial clubs and playing into the Jacobins' hands.

After the crisis of the summer of 1791, the Jacobin Club remained for the majority of societies the birthplace and bulwark of the constitution. Despite this apparent continuity, however, the Society of Friends of the Constitution experienced a profound mutation.

Despite the loss of much of its membership, the Society allowed itself to be further purged by a committee that included all who would emerge as leaders of the "regenerated" club, from Robespierre to Brissot. To make up for the defections and eliminate the more moderate affiliates, the Paris Club accepted new affiliations in the provinces and encouraged provincial clubs to create a network of contacts: "These will be your branches, and you will be their trunk, just as we are the center of all the affiliated societies," was the way one circular put it. That autumn the Jacobin movement was able to boast of some 1,000 affiliated societies, a figure that remained relatively constant until the downfall of the Girondins, which was followed by a second wave of expansion.

The reorganized Society abandoned its original function as an auxiliary to the Assembly and set itself up as an autonomous body, the champion of the people's rights. No longer a mere "thinking society," it had become an instrument of power. The most visible sign of this change was the decision, taken on October 12, 1791, to admit the public to meetings. In a speech defending popular societies on September 28, Brissot had enumerated the tasks that the Jacobins faced: they would continue, as before, to discuss "laws to be passed" and to encourage parliamentary discipline; they would also begin to monitor the execution of the laws by subjecting the conduct of public officials to the strict censure of the "tribunal of public opinion." Above all, the clubs, as instruments of the will of the people, reserved the right to denounce evil laws and seek "means to obtain [their] repeal."

Three months earlier such a speech would have been inconceivable to any Jacobin. But it would have been approved by innumerable fraternal societies that had formed within the Paris sections in 1790 in a move to circumvent restrictions on their autonomy imposed by the municipal law of May 21. These societies had applauded Robespierre's campaign against the silver *marc* and later, in July 1791, had hailed speakers calling for the establishment of a republic. Now, in September 1791, the Jacobins found themselves moving closer to the position of these Paris societies. Proponents of a second revolution thus found themselves equipped with a powerful central organization backed by hundreds of subsidiaries. Sixteen of these fraternal societies became affiliates of the Jacobins, who incorporated into their statutes this regulation from the Club des Cordeliers: "To denounce before the tribunal of public opinion abuses committed by the various authorities and infringements of any kind upon the rights of man."

Having concluded its work, the Constituent Assembly foresaw the probable consequences of these developments. On September 29, 1791, Le Chapelier, preoccupied by a question that he had treated earlier in his report on the right of petition on May 9, directly confronted the question of the clubs' right to intervene in public affairs. His clear target was the Jacobins, who since Varennes had openly condemned the moderate policy of the parliamentary majority. Pointing out that he had been one of the founders of the Society of Friends of the Constitution, he proposed a distinction based on circumstances: though useful in making the Revolution, the societies were dangerous when the Revolution was "ended"; the time had come to apply the Constitution and obey the law. In this way he was able to pay his respects to the societies for their past role yet insist that they served no useful purpose in the present.

He further argued that the societies were incompatible with the concept of sovereignty that the Revolution itself had engendered. In the terms of the Constitution there was no place for "intermediate bodies" invested with public authority and standing between the individual and the sovereign Assembly to which power had been delegated. This was the way in which the Revolution was to avoid the factionalism of parties. The societies were something like modern parties: though lacking official status, they, like the Assembly itself, constantly claimed to voice the will of the people. Though comparable in many ways to the abolished corporations, they refused to accept the status of *private* associations of citizens and sought instead to usurp positions of public authority.

The Constituent Assembly passed a decree embodying Le Chapelier's recommendation that the societies be prohibited from assuming "any form of political existence whatsoever." That very night Robespierre reassured the Jacobins that there was no need to pay any attention to this decree: the power acquired by the clubs since Varennes negated any attempt to limit their sphere of action by legal means. The Assembly's passage of the decree was not so much a declaration of war against the societies as a confession of weakness. In the coming months the Legislative Assembly would continually be challenged by these guardians of the revolutionary spirit, who within a year succeeded in bringing about a crisis that proved fatal to the work of the Constituent Assembly, for even if it is impossible to be absolutely certain that the Jacobins were responsible for what happened on August 10, 1792, there is no doubt that they were the principal beneficiaries of that day's events.

*
**

After the Convention convened for the first time on September 21, 1792, the face of the Paris Jacobin Club changed dramatically: Brissot's expulsion in October ended the impassioned debates that had agitated the Club periodically since its inception. From now on Brissot and Robespierre would confront each other in the Assembly; the Club gave up its leading role and instead supported the actions of its leaders, who in September had been elected deputies for the capital. The Jacobins were no longer a counter-assembly; their purpose was rather to support the Convention's most radical minority, now proclaimed to be the incarnation of popular sovereignty. Many provincial clubs, still close to the Girondins, did not back this new policy, and few followed the example of Marseilles, which supported even the most extreme proposals of the mother-society. In the winter of 1792–93 the authority of the Paris Club over its affiliates was in doubt, pending the outcome of the battle under way within the Convention itself.

The expulsion of the Girondins on June 2, 1793, paved the way for the political unification of the Jacobin movement, although the willingness of most of the clubs to support this *journée* cannot be regarded as convincing proof of unity. For example, the Cognac Club, which had jeered Marat in November 1792, condemned the Paris Commune in April 1793 but approved June 2 as a reflex response. Yet in August a radical minority split with a moderate majority, moved to a different hall, and founded a new society. During the summer of 1793 most of the societies were purged and some were even stricken from the rolls of affiliates; by October 1793 the number of affiliates in correspondence with the mother-society declined to just 793, a solid core on which to base future expansion.

Beginning in 1793 the goal of political unity, previously unattainable, was achieved through purges. In March and April 1793 a purge was carried out in Paris by an appointed rather than elected committee, because Robespierre insisted that "the Society has many enemies within its own ranks who have reason to fear the severity of certain members and who may therefore attempt to eliminate them." This initial purge signaled others to come on May 31 and afterward. In July Robespierre again denounced the "Austrian moles" plotting within the Club, and in Frimaire launched a new purge that had not been completed when 9 Thermidor arrived. In addition to these successive purges, which rid the Club of "factions," there were also expulsions of individual members.

In the provinces purges were encouraged by agents from Paris. The troublesome Foix Club, for example, which had been stricken from the list of affiliates in the spring of 1792, was purged for the first time in April 1793, again in Brumaire (at which time it took on a Hébertist hue), and finally in Germinal, when the deputy Chauchon-Rousseau dissolved it only to found a new club purged of the most "extremist" members of the old.

As Louis de Cardenal has observed, the history of the popular societies in late 1793 can be told in terms of their relations with the *représentants en mission* dispatched to the provinces by the government in Paris. Called upon to lend support to these officials, the societies depended on them for their very existence and were often granted extensive powers. In the autumn of 1793 the popular societies thus became the key instrument of the *personal* policies of the most extremist *représentants*, such as Carrier, Javogues, and Laplanche. The societies provided the agents needed to carry out terrorist measures and zealously pursued a program of de-Christianization, showing a certain willingness to push the Revolution forward and offering quite a cool reception to representatives sent by the Committee of Public Safety in 1794 to put an end to the machinations of the "proconsuls." No doubt the clubs had few means of circumventing the then absolute authority of the Committee, but by holding on to some of the powers that had been delegated to them they sought to regain some of the influence and autonomy they had lost as a result of the political unification of the summer of 1793. In Prairial, Chauchon-Rousseau wrote: "I observe that the popular societies regret having lost the extraordinary authority that the circumstances of last year compelled the Convention to grant them. Several are engaged in reprehensible actions to maintain an authority that the revolutionary government is no longer willing to permit."

This was plainly the case in Paris, where the sectional societies, which had played a prominent part in the preparations for May 31, were unwilling by the end of 1793 to relinquish their political role and were showing increasing restiveness under Jacobin authority. In early 1794 they welcomed, against the wishes of the Committee of Public Safety, the Hébertists' attempt to avail themselves of popular enthusiasm as in the great "days" of 1792 and 1793. The failure of the Hébertists, coupled with tightening of controls over the societies in the spring of 1794, is indicative of a metamorphosis in the societies' role: they had become a cog in the machinery of government, a substitute for the absent people. As Crane Brinton has shown, the proliferation of popular societies in this period was by no means a consequence of renewed popular enthusiasm for the Revolution. On the contrary, militancy in urban areas had declined considerably; new societies sprang up in smaller cities and towns previously unaffected by the phenomenon. Thus the network that was established throughout the country was in many ways an artificial one, its growth guided by Paris.

The societies no longer generated popular will; they approved government directives and lent the government "popular" support. By this time they were no longer allowed the least ideological latitude. Their only option was to join the terrorist "proconsuls" in attempting to provoke the government into even harsher measures. The decree of 14 Frimaire on the organization of the revolutionary government stripped the societies of their autonomy, prohibiting any direct contact between one society and another, such as that which had occurred in October 1793 with the convening of a Congress of Popular Societies of Southern France in Marseilles. From now on the societies were official institutions subordinate to the Convention. The decree of 14 Frimaire further specified that they were "to be arsenals of public opinion," but the content of that opinion was to be determined exclusively by the Convention, which would take care to indicate which "targets it should strike."

Responsibilities of many kinds were assigned to the popular societies by the Convention's representatives. A directive of the Committee of Public Safety stated that in each commune there should be one society to "rekindle the public spirit, protect the people, and watch out for anyone who might do it harm." The societies monitored execution of the laws, prodded officials deemed timorous, and denounced and hunted down persons suspected of disloyalty to the Revolution: former nobles, priests in hiding, citizens who violated the "law of the maximum." They encouraged enlistment and supported the war effort. The public, however, often proved, if not recalcitrant, then at least apt to exhibit devotion to the fatherland more through words and promises than through actions. Accordingly, as Mandoul has shown in his study of the Carcassonne Club, the clubs' "rekindling" of the public spirit often verged on coercion. The same can be said of efforts to enforce acceptance of the new calendar and the ten-day week, in which some clubs proved more successful than others. As Mandoul points out, the revolutionary government looked upon the popular societies as representing, if not the cities themselves, at least the republican elements in the cities: "Any citizen who was not a member of a popular society was virtually an enemy of the government." One is reminded of Tallien's judgment of the Terror: "The country was divided into two classes: those who sowed fear and those who were afraid."

A substitute for and prefiguration of a people not yet ready for republican institutions, the popular societies logically constituted the electorate of a regime without elections. During the summer of 1793 they assisted the *représentants en mission* in their purge of local authorities and advised them on the choice of "candidates" for vacant posts. In Pluviôse, Year II, the *représentants* were ordered to nominate schoolteachers "on advice of the popular societies." In fact, however, the societies usually played a merely formal role. In Quimper, for example, the local authorities were removed from office in October 1793. The popular society was convened and heard Guermeur, *commissaire* of the Executive Council, propose "candidates" for a list that was then narrowed down by Jullien, an agent of the Committee of Public Safety. It comes as no surprise to discover that the society unanimously approved the choice made by the two envoys from Paris.

*
**

On 9 Thermidor, a year after having slain "the hydra of federalism," the Jacobins greeted the fall of the "bloodsucker" Robespierre with equal enthusiasm. Despite this immediate reaction, the very existence of the clubs was threatened, for they had been closely associated with the inception and operation of the Terror they now condemned.

With the opening of the prisons and the return to the political arena of many who had been banished through five years of upheaval, calls for revenge against those responsible for the Terror and for dismantling its apparatus became irresistible. The revival of genuine political debate doomed a form of association whose characteristic feature had been to dissolve all debate, all plurality of opinion, in an artificially created unanimity. By October 1794 the handwriting was on the wall for the Jacobin movement. Affiliation and correspondence between societies were prohibited. Then, on November 12, the Jacobin Club of Paris was closed. Many provincial clubs deemed it prudent to disband, and the decree of August 23, 1795, which ordered the dissolution of all the popular societies, merely closed a chapter that had already come to an end.

Patrice Gueniffey and Ran Halévi

FURTHER READING

GENERAL WORKS

Brinton, Crane. *The Jacobins: An Essay in the New History.* New York, 1930.

Soboul, Albert. *Les sans-culottes parisiens en l'an II: Histoire politique et sociale des sections de Paris, 2 juin 1793–9 thermidor an II.* La Roche-sur-Yon, 1958. Reprinted Paris, 1958, and 1962 with the subtitle *Mouvement populaire et gouvernement révolutionnaire.*

Walter, Gérard. *Histoire des Jacobins.* Paris, 1946.

ON THE JACOBIN CLUB OF PARIS

Aulard, Alphonse. *La Société des Jacobins: Recueil de documents pour l'histoire du Club des Jacobins de Paris,* 6 vols. Paris, 1889–1897.

ON THE PROVINCIAL CLUBS

Boutier, Jean, and Philippe Boutry. "La diffusion des sociétés politiques en France (1789–An III): Une enquête nationale," *Annales historiques de la Révolution française,* no. 266, September–October 1986, 365–398.

Cardenal, Louis de. *La province pendant la Révolution: Histoire des clubs jacobins (1789–1795).* Paris, 1929.

Kennedy, Michael L. *The Jacobin Club of Marseille (1790–1794).* Ithaca, 1973.

———— *The Jacobin Clubs in the French Revolution: The First Years.* Princeton, 1982.

Labroue, Henri. *La société populaire de Bergerac pendant la Révolution.* Paris, 1915.

Mandoul, J. "Le Club des Jacobins de Carcassonne," *La Révolution française,* vol. 47, 1904, 409–435.

ON THE INTERPRETATION OF JACOBINISM AND ITS ORIGINS

Cochin, Augustin. *L'esprit du jacobinisme.* (A nearly complete reprint of *Les sociétés de pensée et la démocratie: Etudes d'histoire révolutionnaire.* Paris, 1921.) With an introduction by Jean Baechler. Paris, 1979.

Furet, François. *Penser la Révolution française.* Paris, 1978.

Halévi, Ran. "Les origines intellectuelles de la Révolution française," *Le débat,* January–March 1986.

ON OTHER REVOLUTIONARY CLUBS IN PARIS

Cardenal, Louis de. *Les clubs contre-révolutionnaires.* Paris, 1895.

Mathiez, Albert. *Le Club des Cordeliers pendant la crise de Varennes.* Paris, 1910.

RELATED TOPICS

Civil Constitution of the Clergy
Democracy
Elections
Equality
Estates General
Feuillants
Jacobinism

Monarchiens
Public Spirit
Revolutionary Assemblies
Revolutionary Government
Robespierre
Sieyès
Sovereignty

COMMITTEE OF PUBLIC SAFETY

Public safety (*salut public*): the connection between the two words is not obvious. To authors of contemporary dictionaries public meant the opposite of private, that is, everything of concern to an entire people. The 1694 edition of the *Dictionnaire de l'Académie Française* mentions "public interest, public authority, public utility, public treasury, public revenues." Only in Furetière's dictionary do we find the two words linked: "The public safety is always preferable to that of private individuals. If you attack this power, there is no safety for you, no asylum, no place of grace" (1684). *Salut* in French means salvation, an eminently Christian and individual value, and what is clear from these definitions is that the word was secularized by extending it to the collectivity. The great *Encyclopédie* of d'Alembert and Diderot spoke only of the "public good" and the "public interest," which it contrasted in the traditional manner with private interests. Not until the sixth edition (1823) of the *Dictionnaire de l'Académie* is the phrase *salut public* mentioned without comment. At the time of the Revolution there can be no doubt that a Christian vision of salvation was fused with a political experience that dated back several centuries.

That experience, wholly secular and influenced by quattrocento Italy, had two baptismal names: necessity and *raison d'état*. By the 1630s it was generally agreed that extraordinary circumstances at home or abroad could compel rulers to have recourse to extraordinary measures, including temporary suspension of the liberties and property rights of their subjects. Cardin Le Bret wrote: "It seems to me that a distinction must be made between different times, because if it is in order to meet pressing needs essential to the public good, I dare say that resistance to the edicts would be pure disobedience. *Necessitas omnem legem frangit.*" Giovanni Botero's *Della ragione di Stato*, printed in Turin in 1589, was twice translated into French (1598 and 1607). It was highly influential not only in "libertine" circles but also among men of government. Richelieu in October 1642 was clear about the use of extraordinary measures: "The government and security of great states require precautions that dispense with the forms observed in the course of ordinary justice." Speaking of kings, Louis XIV dictated these lines, even more illuminating than Richelieu's: "What they seem to be doing against the common law is most commonly based on reason of state, which is the first of all laws yet the least known and most obscure to those who do not govern." The monarchy bequeathed to the Revolution not the word but the concept. As Michelet wrote, "the Revolution, become queen, upon entering the Tuileries found this ancient item of royal furniture and immediately made use of it, smashing it over the heads of the kings who had used it previously." But there were two differences between the revolutionaries' actions and those of the old monarchy. Violations of property rights under the monarchy had been more apparent than real. Decisions by the *chambres de justice* intended to force financial agents accused of extorting and accepting bribes to make amends had never had serious consequences. When property was confiscated, families were generally indemnified. When the vast holdings of the connétable de Bourbon were joined to the crown, the king generously compensated the family, particularly the Montpensiers. Royal justice was not a matter of "Off with their heads." Another difference was in duration. Extraordinary measures were limited to certain individuals and to brief periods of time. It was an innovation of the revolutionary government to suspend the Constitution of 1793, passed by the legislature but never put into effect, for an indefinite period. Discontinuity within continuity: such was the Revolution.

*
**

On July 14, 1789, patriot deputies such as Barnave, Robespierre, and others argued that circumstances justified the people's violence: a nation cannot be governed in a time of revolution as in a time of peace. The principle of revolutionary government was thus stated, and with clearly antiseigneurial overtones. Speaking of the victims of July 14, Barnave cried: "Was that blood so pure then?" Purity of the blood, a concept that had shaped people's ideas for several centuries, was thus challenged or, rather, turned upside down: the pure blood of the seventeenth century became the impure blood of the *Marseillaise*. The notion of public safety was placed on the agenda by the war and the first defeats suffered by French forces, in 1792. On July 11 the Legislative Assembly proclaimed that the fatherland was in danger. All administrative bodies and municipal administrations were required to remain in permanent session. Volunteers were called to form new battalions. The insurrection of August 10 gave new life to the movement. Huguenin, a member of the Paris Commune, notified the Assembly that the Commune did not recognize it as "judge of the extraordinary measures to which it had been compelled by necessity and resistance to oppression." On September 2 Paris learned that Verdun was under siege. Danton delivered his famous speech: "All are in motion, all are astir, all are burning to fight. . . . The tocsin that is sounding is not a signal of alarm, it is a signal to charge the enemies of the fatherland. In order to defeat them, gentlemen, we need audacity, more audacity, and then still more audacity, and France is saved." But Danton was still working to mobilize the energies of the nation against foreign enemies alone.

The situation was totally transformed between the beginning of March and the end of May 1793. The Convention's approval of extraordinary measures signaled the advent of the revolutionary government. Its best theorist was not a Montagnard but a centrist deputy, Barère, who, yielding to the necessities of the moment, threw his support to the Mountain. Barère had previously voted with the Girondins out of distrust of the Montagnard leaders, but he approved the revolutionary measures advocated by Robespierre. In a major speech on March 18 he stated the three axioms of the moment. In extraordinary times one does not govern by normal methods; revolutionary means must therefore be accepted. The bourgeoisie must preserve its alliance with the popular classes, even if it must pay for that alliance with economic and political concessions. The Convention must, however, remain in control of that alliance and take the initiative in instituting revolutionary measures that might otherwise be dictated by the street. Subsequently, various laws were passed by the Convention, including one establishing a Revolutionary Tribunal. Marat summed up the significance of these measures: "It is through violence that liberty must be established, and the time has come to arrange for a temporary despotism of liberty in order to crush the despotism of kings."

On April 6 the Committee of General Defense was replaced by a Committee of Public Safety, which was to have secret deliberations and full executive powers. The Girondins denounced the Committee as a form of dictatorship. Yet seven of the nine members designated by the Convention were centrists (including Barère). Only Danton and Delacroix represented the Mountain.

Danton, damaged by the defeats of the summer of 1793 and attacked by Marat, who declared war on the "comité de perte publique," asked the Convention to remove him on July 10. Reelected in spite of himself on September 6, he refused to serve. Jean Jaurès was right to emphasize the danger inherent in this refusal to serve by such a powerful figure and obvious choice for minister. (The recent film by Wajda sheds little light on Danton's strengths and even less on his weaknesses.) Danton removed himself from a world he had lost.

Of the fourteen members of the Committee of Public Safety, the Convention reelected seven: three "centrists" (Barère, Lindet, and Gasparin), and four Montagnards chosen in May (Saint-Just, Couthon, Jean Bon Saint-André, and Hérault de Séchelles). It added two other deputies from the Mountain, Thuriot (a friend of Danton) and Prieur of the Marne. A few days later (August 14), Carnot and Prieur of the Côte d'Or also joined. Robespierre had replaced Gasparin on July 27. This was the Great Committee of Year II, whose membership was completed in September with the addition, under pressure from the Hébertists, of Collot d'Herbois and Billaud-Varenne and the removal of Hérault de Séchelles, who was later executed in April 1794. These men, united by youth (the eldest was forty-seven, the youngest twenty-six) and training in government and administrative service, were hard workers. Public safety was an apostolate. When the *levée en masse* was approved on August 29, Barère expressed, in a style not lacking in beauty, the goal that all the committee members shared despite their differences: "From this moment until the last enemy has been driven from the territory of the Republic, all French people are in a permanent state of requisition for military service. Young men will go to combat; married men will make arms and carry supplies; women will make tents and uniforms and serve in the hospitals; children will shred old rags, and the elderly will be carried into the public squares to stir the courage of our fighting men and preach hatred of kings and unity of the Republic." Two centuries earlier, in August 1589, the priests of Paris had issued a similar appeal to youths, women, and the elderly, in the name not of the Fatherland and the Republic but of God and the City. The mental mechanism was the same: a general and revolutionary mobilization.

One bridge had yet to be crossed: legitimation of the extraordinary measures. On June 24 the Convention had approved a "hasty and temporary constitution of circumstance." Was it applicable in this time of trial for the Republic? It was necessary to generalize the exceptional, suspend the Constitution, organize a republican government. On October 10, 1793, Saint-Just addressed the Convention: "The laws are revolutionary; those who carry them out are not. In the circumstances in which the Republic finds itself, the Constitution cannot be established. . . . It would become a guarantee of attacks on liberty because it would lack the violence necessary to repress them. It is impossible for revolutionary laws to be carried out if the government itself is not revolutionarily constituted." Thus began the Terror, the wartime dictatorship, the government of economic controls, and the dissension that culminated in the great trials of the spring of 1794. The extraordinary became ordinary.

The ninth of Thermidor put an end to this centralization of power. On a motion by Merlin de Thionville (on the eleventh) the Convention voted to replace a quarter of the committees' membership every month and to make outgoing members ineligible for reelection the next month. Henceforth the Committee of Public Safety was in theory only one committee among others, responsible solely for foreign and military affairs. But this was a fiction, and until the Directory the Committee embodied the reality of the Revolution.

Over the long term the notion of public safety has played a unifying role with respect to public opinion on the right as well as the left. The connection is not difficult to understand. Anti-German feeling in 1871 and even more in the period 1914–1918 drew on memories of the armies of Coburg. Fostered by elementary school and university teaching, the idea of a connection between the policies of Louis XIV and the Convention became a sort of fundamental dogma of the national identity. This can be seen quite clearly in the work of Lavisse, as well as in the speeches Clemenceau delivered at the height of battle.

Of greater importance was the appropriation of the "public safety" legacy by Charles Maurras and his friends. On several occasions (in articles reprinted in his *Dictionnaire politique et critique*) the founder of fundamentalist nationalism indicated his devotion to 1793 and rejection of 1789. "The heavy burden, the duty and honor of public safety, falls on us monarchists and no others. I have no fear in thus borrowing from the vocabulary of the Revolution one of its few meaningful phrases. . . . That phrase spurred all that was courageous, honorable, and patriotic in the French Revolution: resistance to the foreigner. Under the Restoration a minister of the king thanked the Committee of Public Safety for having saved the integrity of France. Public safety has ever since been a leading idea of conscientious nationalists, by which I mean those who are royalists. Leave it to others to revive the disastrous utopias of 1789. If it is absolutely necessary to find inspiration in the history of our great crisis, we prefer to go to 1793. After all, Danton was carrying on the work of Henri IV, Louis XI, and Philip Augustus, even if he was carrying it on wretchedly. A Roland or Lafayette could only disrupt the state or diminish it" (*Le soleil,* March 17, 1900). And in 1913 he wrote: "We are not for the sovereignty of public safety" (*L'action française,* May 19, 1913). Léon de Montesquiou reprinted articles from *L'action française* in a book entitled *Le salut public,* published in 1901: "One should say not sovereignty of the people but sovereignty of the people's interest, sovereignty of public safety." He added, "Our individualism stems from that of the Revolution; our collectivism has its roots in absolute monarchy." This *cartel des oui* had a long life. If General de Gaulle did not (so far as I know) use the expression "public safety," it was because he was above all intent on restoring some form of legitimacy. But those who organized the coup d'état in Algiers in 1958 were not afraid to revive this ghost.

Denis Richet

FURTHER READING

Botero, Giovanni. *Raison et gouvernement d'estat, en dix livres,* trans. (from the fourth Italian printing) Gabriel Chapys. Paris, 1599.
Bouloiseau, Marc. *Le Comité de Salut Public.* Second edition. Paris, 1968.
Le Bret, Cardin. *Oeuvres.* Paris, 1635.
Maurras, Charles. *Dictionnaire politique et critique.* Paris, 1932.
Montesquiou, Léon de. *Le salut public.* Paris, 1901.

RELATED TOPICS

Barnave	Danton	Michelet
Carnot	Revolutionary Government	Robespierre
Constitution	Marat	Terror

CONSTITUTION

B etween revolution and constitution there was, at the beginning, a fundamental link. Barely had it declared itself representative of the sovereign nation than the National Assembly, insisting that it was "called upon to fix the constitution of the realm, carry out regeneration of the public order, and maintain the true principles of monarchy," swore in the Tennis Court Oath to remain assembled "until the constitution of the realm is established and consolidated on a firm foundation." With this bold act of defiance against royal authority, a dramatic condensation of several decades' protests against arbitrary government and ministerial despotism, the Assembly defined the achievement of a settled constitutional order as the essential purpose of its revolutionary actions. Yet the task of "fixing" the French constitution was to prove an extraordinarily problematic one. Unlike the American Revolution, which effectively translated the assertion of revolutionary will into the establishment of a stable constitutional order, the French Revolution opened a widening gap between revolution and constitution, effectively resisting successive efforts to bring the revolutionary movement to its constitutional completion. It is impossible in these brief pages to follow the vicissitudes of that entire series of constitutions drafted, adopted, suspended, implemented, and subverted in France during the decade separating the Tennis Court Oath from the moment in 1799 when Napoleon Bonaparte, laying yet another constitution before the French people, once again declared the French Revolution ended. Instead, this article considers the uncertainty of the idea of constitution on the eve of the Revolution, the radical definition that the theorists of 1789 gave to the term, and the implications of this definition for the revolutionary dynamic.

What did it mean to "fix" the constitution of the realm? Despite the resolution with which it was taken, the Tennis Court Oath was not without its ambiguities. Certainly, it announced an end to despotic government, the substitution of a stable and predictable legal order for the disorder and uncertainty resulting from the tyrannical exercise of arbitrary will. But since a constitution was by definition something fixed and stable, the phrase *fixer la constitution* was a pleonasm, rather like talking of rounding a circle. If there was a constitution of the realm, it was fixed by definition; if it was not fixed, it was of necessity not a constitution. Thus to speak of "fixing" the constitution in this way left an essential problem: did it imply the existence of a constitution to be preserved and defended, or the absence of a constitution still to be created? On this question, the deputies to the Estates General remained divided, as did the *cahiers* they brought to Versailles. In referring to a constitution in the weeks preceding the Tennis Court Oath, deputies of the nobility, disagreeing among themselves, had used such verbs as *établir, rétablir, maintenir, se donner;* those of the Third Estate such verbs as *asseoir, donner poser* [*les bases*], *faire, faire entrer dans.* In relationship to these terms, however, the *fixer* of the Tennis Court Oath remained relatively unfixed: it could be understood equally well in the conservative sense of *rétablir* or *maintenir* (implying the existence of a constitution to be preserved and strengthened) or in the more radical sense of *établir, se donner,* or *faire* (implying the absence of a constitution that still remained to be created).

Thus the Tennis Court Oath left undecided, and for the National Assembly still to resolve, the central political question of the prerevolutionary decades: the existence, or nonexistence, of a traditional constitution of the monarchy. The issue had been clearly joined since the constitutional conflicts of the 1750s and 1760s, when parlementary theorists, following the lead of the redoubtable Le Paige in his *Lettres historiques,* had countered ministerial despotism by an appeal to the existence of a traditional monarchical constitution in which the arbitrary exercise of royal authority was prevented by fundamental laws and by the juridical responsibility of the magistrates for the registration and verification of royal edicts. In contesting this view, no voice was more powerful than that of Mably, whose historical refutation of parlementary theory exploded all claims to the existence of an enduring constitutional order, and revealed instead a domain of instability and revolutions alternating between anarchy and despotism. The lesson of this account of French history became explicit in the second volume of Mably's *Observations sur l'histoire de France,* completed in the context of the Maupeou coup and published at the height of the prerevolutionary debate over the convocation of the Estates General: the French lacked a constitution because they had yet to exercise the sustained political will necessary to fix the form of their political existence and preserve their liberty.

The political debate joined by Le Paige and Mably echoed throughout the prerevolutionary pamphlets, as the conflicts over the nature and limitations of royal power that forced the calling of the Estates General were intensified by new contestations over the mode of composition and the procedures of that body. In this new debate, political passions were fueled by yet another ambiguity still remaining in eighteenth-century uses of the term "constitution." For those who now insisted that France still lacked a constitution tended to emphasize the need for a settled order of government limiting the arbitrary exercise of power, while those who appealed to an established constitution used the term to include the necessary existence of a social order constituted by the division of orders and estates (and hence their separate and equal representation in the Estates General). Sieyès played on this ambiguity very effectively in *Qu'est-ce que le Tiers Etat?* "Six months ago . . . there was only one cry in France: we had no constitution, and we asked to create one. Today we not only have a constitution, but, if we believe the privileged, it contains two excellent and impregnable provisions. The first is the division of citizens by orders; the second is the equality of influence of each order in the formation of the national will."

What then was a constitution? Throughout the eighteenth century, the dictionaries hesitated between two general senses of the term. The first emphasized the activity of institution and establishment, as in the original use of the term in Roman and canon law to mean the laws and ordinances of emperors or popes, kings or ecclesiastical superiors, or an act like the constitution of a rente or dowry. The second emphasized the order of existence of an entity, its arrangement, mode of being, or disposition, as in the constitution of the world or the constitution of the human body. Apart from the usages deriving from Roman law, specifically political definitions of the term appeared relatively late in the laggard dictionaries. But this same ambiguity between institution and order also reappeared among the political writers upon whom the dictionaries were eventually to draw. Montesquieu, adopting English usage, gave the term "constitution" a new centrality in eighteenth-century political understanding, but he did so by emphasizing its reference to the order of existence of an entity—its arrangement, mode of being, or disposition—rather than to an act of establishment or institution that brought it into being. With *De l'esprit des lois*, "constitution" stood as the modern equivalent of the Aristotelian *politeia*, the indispensable term to describe the fundamental order of a state, the mode of political existence of a nation or people, the essential disposition of the elements or powers composing a form of government. With Montesquieu, too, England became the *locus classicus* of constitutional discussion, the test case for an ideal of a political order as a fixed, enduring structure (stable though not necessarily fixed in writing) in which the forms and functions of the constituent parts were clearly delimited and distributed for the preservation of liberty. In this respect, Montesquieu's analysis of English government—subsequently reworked by such authors as Delolme, Blackstone, and John Adams—was to provide a powerful model for the constitutional committee appointed by the National Assembly in 1789.

But could such a model be imitated? Could one nation indeed adopt a version of another's constitution? Such questions required a shift in the semantic register of the term "constitution" from its meaning as an existing order to its meaning as an act of institution or establishment. Their answers required further clarification of the relationship between the idea of the constitution of a state, the constitution of a people, society or nation, and the constitution of a government: notions that Montesquieu had continued to invoke quite indiscriminately. In both these respects, the essential arguments came from the theorists of the school of *droit naturel*, most notably Vattel and (in this respect) Rousseau.

In his *Droit des gens* (1758) Vattel offered a clear definition of a constitution as the form of government instituted by a society or nation to secure the advantages of political association, from which it followed that "the nation has every right to form its own constitution, to maintain it, to perfect it, and to regulate as it wishes everything that has to do with government, and no one may justly prevent it from doing so." This language soon appeared in other influential works, including the Swiss edition of the *Encyclopédie* edited by Barthélemy de Félice, and the section of the *Encyclopédie méthodique* devoted to political economy and diplomacy, edited by Jean-Nicolas Demeunier (later to play an active part in the constitutional debates of the National Assembly). But a far more radical elaboration upon Vattel's argument occurs in Rousseau's *Social Contract,* with its insistence on the theory of the general will and its fundamental distinction between sovereignty and government.

Rejecting the naturalistic implications of the traditional analogy between the constitution of the human body and the constitution of the state, the *Social Contract* emphasizes that if the former is the work of nature, the latter is the work of art. It is a political contrivance entirely contingent upon the will of the nation, an act of institution by which a sovereign people creates its particular form of government. Nor is this act of institution adequately accomplished once and for all. The constitution once fixed by the decision of "the people assembled," Rousseau argues, the sovereign body must nevertheless reassemble at regular intervals to manifest its force and presence. At such moments, in the immediate presence of the supreme political being, the effects of the constitution are suspended: "The moment the people is legitimately assembled in sovereign body, all jurisdiction of the government ceases: the executive power is suspended, and the person of the last citizen is as sacred and inviolable as that of the first magistrate, because the represented is found, there is no longer a representative." It followed from this argument that the constitution of the state depends not only on an original act of institution but on a perpetual reaffirmation of that act. Since "there is no fundamental law in the state that cannot be revoked, not even the social pact," the constitution remains in force only as the direct expression of the general will.

The implications of this radical voluntarism were made abundantly clear by Sieyès in *Qu'est-ce que le Tiers Etat?* Sieyès destroyed the traditional meaning of "constitution" in the sense of a necessarily existing social and political order inherent in the very nature of things, and gave powerful force to its meaning in the sense of the institution of a government. In repudiating the arguments of the privileged for a traditional constitution, Sieyès posited the existence of the nation as an ultimate political reality, immediately present, and prior to any constitutional form. "The nation exists before anything else. It is at the origin of everything else. Its will is always legal; it is the law itself." This political reality being the case, it was impossible to suppose the nation bound by existing social or political arrangements in the name of a prior constitution. "A nation is independent of any form. And however it may will, it is enough that its will appear for all positive law to end before it as before the source and the supreme master of all positive law." Powerful words against those who would defend a traditional constitution of the French monarchy, but no less dangerous for those who would establish a new constitution on secure foundations. The revolutionaries were to find that the implications of the conception of national sovereignty required to destroy an old order could not be contained in defense of the new. Sieyès inscribed a conceptual space between revolution and constitution, even before either had been achieved.

*
**

CONSTITUTION

A constitution to be restored or a constitution to be created? The division over this matter, found in the mandates the deputies had brought to Versailles, was made clear to the Assembly by Clermont-Tonnerre, reporting on behalf of its constitutional committee, on July 27, 1789. "Our constituents want regeneration of the state. But some expected that it would come about through simple reform of abuses and reestablishment of a constitution that has existed for fourteen centuries. . . . Others have looked upon the existing social regime as so defective that they demanded a new constitution, and, with the exception of the monarchical government and forms, which every Frenchman cherishes and respects in his heart . . . they have given you all the powers necessary to create a constitution." Following a strategy proposed by Mounier, the committee sought to minimize these differences by emphasizing on the one hand the traditional devotion of the French to the monarchy as their historically chosen form of government, while on the other pointing to general recognition of the need to perfect the work of history through the institution of a fixed order of government in which the powers would be clearly separated and limited.

This same effort to find a middle ground between competing views also expressed itself in the committee's thinking on the question of a declaration of rights. Clermont-Tonnerre, reporting on the *cahiers,* stated that the demand for such a declaration was the only difference "between the *cahiers* that desire a new constitution and those that call only for reestablishment of what they regard as the existing constitution." Accordingly, the committee proposed a declaration that would precede the constitution in the form of a preamble but would not be published separately; it sought thereby to satisfy demands for a declaration of rights while placating those who feared the consequences of following the American example by enunciating abstract principles of liberty and equality. But when, in the restless early days of August, the Assembly finally came to discuss whether a declaration of rights should precede the constitution, the committee's effort at compromise began its slow but dramatic process of erosion. The debate over the necessity for a declaration of rights drew the line between those who would return to first principles and those who preferred to turn immediately to the "positive law appropriate to a great people, united for fifteen centuries." When, the very day of August 4, the Assembly decided almost unanimously that the constitution would indeed be preceded by a declaration of rights, it took a decisive first step away from the idea of a constitution to be preserved and towards that of a constitution to be created. Furthermore, after the deliberations set in train by the events of the night of August 4, the deputies moved rapidly to draw up a Declaration of the Rights of Man and of the Citizen before turning to the constitution itself. The Assembly would start its constitutional work from first principles.

But what principles? Three articles of the Declaration bore most directly on the task of "fixing" the French constitution. But none was without its ambiguities; nor were they necessarily compatible one with another. The sixteenth, "any society in which rights are not guaranteed and powers are not separated in a definite manner has no constitution," gave moderate expression to the fundamental prerevolutionary concern to limit the arbitrary exercise of power through the legal protection of rights and the clear separation of powers. If it implied that France had hitherto lacked a constitution in the full sense of the term, it was also consistent with the constitutional committee's proposals to build the ramparts of liberty upon the historical foundations of the ancient monarchy, following the example of the English model. But since it left open the precise definition of the powers to be separated and of the nature of their separation, it was no less compatible with the Rousseauian notion of the division between the legislative and the executive power as a fundamental condition for the exercise of the general will. This latter interpretation, furthermore, was encouraged by the explicitly Rousseauian principle of the sixth article of the Declaration: "The law is the expression of the general will."

Nothing would seem clearer from this latter article than the need to create a constitution that would ensure the direct expression of the general will. But the article presented difficulties in this respect by adding that "all citizens have the right to participate personally or through their representatives in its formation." How then was this statement of the idea of the general will to be understood, if it admitted the possibility of representation so emphatically denied by Rousseau? Nor was ambiguity on this point dispelled by the less than emphatic declaration of the principle of national sovereignty in article 3 of the Declaration: "The source [*principe*] of all sovereignty resides essentially in the nation. No corps and no individual man exercises authority that does not emanate expressly from it." To assert that the "source" of all sovereignty resided in the nation was not necessarily equivalent to saying that the exercise of sovereignty inhered directly in the nation as such, as Adrien Duquesnoy remarked in his journal: "Article 3 provides that the source of all sovereignty resides in the nation. That is not correct. It should have said: 'All sovereignty resides in the nation.' Indeed, it is clear that if the nation possesses only the source of sovereignty, then there is a sovereignty that is not the nation's and that only emanates from its sovereignty, which is both dangerous and false." The formulation accepted by the Assembly glossed over the considerable difference between the strong, Rousseauian version of the principle of national sovereignty embraced by its more radical members and the weaker one espoused by the moderates led by Mounier (whose language article 3 adopted).

Thus when, in late August and early September 1789, the deputies finally turned to debate the preliminary constitutional articles proposed by its committee, fundamental issues remained unresolved. The Assembly had endorsed the principles of national sovereignty and the general will, but the understanding of these principles remained far from clear; it had defined a constitution as an instrument for the separation of powers, while leaving the precise nature of that separation still undetermined. Furthermore, it had not yet resolved the ambiguity of whether it was "fixing" the French constitution by tempering an existing monarchy or creating a new one on the basis of first principles. Discussing the first constitutional article proposed by the committee—"The French government is a monarchical government"—the deputies found themselves passionately divided not only over the nature of the government that was to be called monarchical in France, but over the nature of their action in making such a statement. For some, it remained true that "when they were sent to the Estates General, they were not told: you will make a new constitution, but you will regenerate the old one. You will not say that you are erecting our government into a monarchical state, but you will confirm our old monarchy." Others insisted that they had been sent, as representatives of a sovereign nation, to exercise the full extent of its constituent power, "to make the constitution." In the famous debates over the royal veto, these issues were finally resolved. Pressed by the protagonists of national sovereignty in the Rousseauian mode, the spokesmen for the constitutional committee lost the middle ground they had sought to maintain since the Assembly's earliest debates on this question. The idea that France possessed a traditional form of government providing at least the elements of a constitution—whose principles could now be reaffirmed, perfected, and fixed in a written document—was finally rejected in favor of a conception of the constitution as created anew by an act of sovereign national will and instituted in accordance with abstract principles of political right. In the process, the ideological dynamic that was to drive subsequent revolutionary events—the insoluble problem of instituting and maintaining a form of government in direct, immediate, and constant relationship to the general will—was given its force.

During these debates, the principal spokesmen for the constitutional committee, Lally-Tollendal and Mounier, sought to hold a middle ground between history and philosophy. To their minds, the revolution meant the regeneration of an existing political order through the destruction of abuses, not the construction of a radically new order of things. They saw the idea that the Assembly had been charged, as a national convention, to exercise the right of the French people to decide its constitution *de novo* as the purest metaphysical nonsense. Such a notion required the absurd conception of the nation as a society existing prior to government, prior to laws, prior to magistrates. Nothing was more alien to their thinking than the idea of the revolution as a new founding moment in which all existing institutions were suspended before the general will; nor could they imagine it as a zero point in time at which society existed prior to, and independent of, its form of government. The National Assembly, they insisted, had been convoked by a king whose authority preceded its own; its members had been enjoined by their mandates to act, in concert with the crown, to preserve the monarchy from degeneration into despotism. Thus the monarch existed and possessed a power anterior to the constitution, and must necessarily remain a party to its establishment: "Being an interested party to the provisions of the constitution, responsible for making certain that they are respected, and possessing a prior power that it must regulate and not destroy, it is necessary that he sign and ratify it." Furthermore, Mounier argued, while the king could not refuse any constitution whatsoever, he could demand changes before giving his consent to the document proposed by the Assembly, thus giving him a historical title to a kind of suspensive royal veto over its establishment as a constitution.

If the committee spokesmen defended their proposals as grounded in the nature of the monarchical government the nation had chosen historically and now charged its deputies to affirm, however, they also justified those proposals as perfecting this inherited form of government in the light of historical experience and practical reason. In their eyes, experience was represented above all by the example of England, clarified by a side glance at recent constitutional choices in America; reason was represented by the arguments of Montesquieu, Blackstone, and Delolme on the one hand, Adams and Livingstone on the other. Taken together, these prototypes suggested that power must necessarily be divided to avoid arbitrariness and abuse; passions must be limited one by another; interests counterbalanced. And they suggested that no power was more dangerous than that of a unitary legislative assembly, which would be constantly subject to passion and caprice, and never bound to respect its own deliberations from one moment to the next. Hence the necessity of a distribution and balance of powers achieved by the existence of a strong executive authority, united in the person of the monarch, and a divided legislative power, shared among the monarch and two houses of representatives. The key to this system was the preservation of an absolute royal veto in matters of legislation. Without it, there would be no guaranteee of a balance between the executive and the legislative power, and no means of resolving disputes between the senate and the house of representatives. Without it, as Mounier maintained, the king would be not an integral part of the legislative body but merely "a magistrate under its orders. . . . The government would be no longer monarchical but republican."

Revealing words. For at the heart of the committee's proposals there lay a profound concern to limit the implications of the principle of national sovereignty announced in the Declaration of the Rights of Man. "I know that the source of sovereignty resides in the nation," Mounier acknowledged. "But to be the source of sovereignty and to exercise sovereignty are very different things." For the committee spokesmen, sovereign power found its source and justification in the nation, and must necessarily be exercised for the benefit of the nation; but it could not be exercised by the nation directly, or in a unitary manner. They saw the balance of powers guaranteed by an absolute royal veto as ensuring government in the interests of the people while preventing the arbitrariness inherent in the tyranny of the multitude. In the last analysis, while they appealed occasionally to the language of the general will, they could only imagine the general will as the end result of a balancing of particular wills. They lacked the fundamental assumption underlying that idea in its Rousseauian formulation, the postulate of a unitary will inhering in the nation by definition, prior to all government.

Nothing seemed more misguided to the principal opponents of the committee's proposals—men like Salle and Pétion, Grégoire, Rabaut Saint-Etienne and Sieyès—than this retreat from the principle of national sovereignty to the language of passions and interests, and of the balance and counterbalance of powers. To call them Rousseauians is not to claim that they invoked Rousseau at every point; explicit references to the citizen of Geneva were rare in these debates. Nor is it to assert that they followed the specific arguments of the *Social Contract* in every particular; according to such a criterion, Rousseau himself could hardly be counted a Rousseauian, since when faced with immediate political problems (as in the *Considérations sur le gouvernement de Pologne*) he himself modified particular arguments—most notably in the matter of representation. But Mounier was not entirely wrong in claiming that opposition to the proposals of the constitutional committee derived from the fact that "we are blindly invoking the maxims of a philosopher who believed that the English were free only when they appointed their representatives, who believed representation to be a kind of servitude." The most telling opponents of the model of the English constitution were Rousseauian in the sense (and to the extent) that they cast the constitutional problems facing the National Assembly in terms of a strong version of the language of the general will. They were Rousseauian in the sense that they demanded the institution of a constitution *de novo*, as a direct expression of the sovereignty of the general will. They were Rousseauian in the sense that they saw the purpose of such a constitution to be ensuring the continuing exercise of national sovereignty on the basis of the general will. And, with the important exception of Sieyès who in this respect drew upon a very different language, they were Rousseauian too in the sense that they saw the relationship between the general will and the practice of representation (unavoidable in a large state) as an essentially problematic one—to which the suspensive royal veto could provide a solution.

Opposition to the proposals of the constitutional committee rested, above all, on giving article 3 of the Declaration of the Rights of Man and Citizen its full Rousseauian meaning. "While granting the principle that sovereignty resides in the nation," Salle insisted, the defenders of the absolute royal veto "take refuge behind the idea that public utility, more imperious than the principle, requires that it be changed; what is more, that it is useful to act on behalf of the French people, because it is not a new people; that it is accustomed to being ruled." For Salle, on the contrary, the French were no longer slaves grown old in their bonds, but a people regenerated through the very act of revolution; they required only good laws to make this regeneration permanent. "The French are today all that they can be." Others among the Rousseauians were convinced that good laws were still necessary to transform subjects into citizens. But whatever their view on this point, it followed from their conception of the revolutionary moment that the idea of requiring any form of royal consent to the constitution was palpably absurd. As a constituted power, the monarchy was to be created anew by the constitution and was not a historical party to its creation—which could only be the work of the National Assembly acting as a constitutional convention endowed by its electors with the constituent power to institute *de novo*. "Charged by our mandates to rejuvenate the constitution or to create a new one on the ruins of the old," Grégoire proclaimed, "we are now exercising the constituent power."

From the perspective of this revolutionary moment, then, little was to be learned from that historical compromise between particular interests that was the English constitution. Having belatedly recovered their liberty, the French now had an advantage denied to the English in their slow search for freedom: that of ordering all the parts of their constitution simultaneously.

Philosophical principles, not historical experience, were to be the touchstone of this moment of political choice. "The history that is all too often invoked is an arsenal where each person finds weapons of every kind," Grégoire insisted. "The multiplicity of facts frequently does not bolster a principle but only demonstrates its violation." And of all these principles, the sovereignty of the general will of the nation was the most fundamental.

For the Rousseauians, national sovereignty did not mean merely that the nation was the ultimate source of all power, but that this power resided directly and inalienably in the general will. Rabaut spoke for many in identifying the two consequences of this strong version of the principle of national sovereignty. The first was the substitution of the Rousseauian dichotomy between sovereign legislative power and delegated executive authority for the balance of powers exemplified in the English model: "What [the sovereign] delegates is execution; what it keeps is legislation." The second was the insistence on the need for a unitary legislature as the logical expression of a unitary sovereign will. "The sovereign is a unitary and simple thing, since it is the collection of all without excepting a single one: hence the legislative power is unified and simple. And if the sovereign cannot be divided, legislative power cannot be divided." But this easy equation between a unitary legislature and a unitary national will concealed the fundamental problem posed for the Rousseauians by the necessity of representation in a populous nation: that of assuring (despite the argument of the *Social Contract*) that an elected legislature would indeed express the general will rather than its own corporate interests. Forced to acknowledge that "the decisions of the representatives of the nation may not always be those of the nation itself and that they may be mistaken," the principal Rousseauians in the Assembly opted for the idea of a suspensive royal veto. Understood not as the act of a co-legislator, but as a specific charge laid upon the king in his capacity as executive, the suspensive veto would function as an appeal to the people in cases where the king suspected that the will of the legislature was not identical to the general will. It therefore became the key to the revolutionary reconciliation of national sovereignty and representative government. Fully consistent with "the nature of a government in which sovereignty can only be exercised by proxies," Salle argued, "this right conserves the people's sovereignty without any disadvantage."

Understood in this sense, then, the suspensive veto was simply a mechanism to permit a direct appeal to the people in the primary assemblies—conceived as the ultimate expression of the general will—against the particular will of the representative body. It reflected at once the Rousseauians' acceptance of the necessity for representation in a large state and their continuing distrust of it. But was such a direct appeal to the people feasible? Powerful arguments against it came not only from Mounier, but from none other than Sieyès, the theorist who had perhaps done more than any other to interject Rousseauian notions of national sovereignty into the Assembly's debates. Sieyès was a passionate opponent of any kind of royal veto, be it absolute or suspensive. And he based his opposition to the suspensive veto precisely on the grounds of the incompatibilty of the idea of an appeal to the people with the principle of national sovereignty and the practice of representation.

Because the will of the electors in a *bailliage* is necessarily a particular will in relation to the will of the nation as a whole, Sieyès insisted, it follows that a deputy can never be bound by that particular will in his capacity as representative of the nation. This argument destroyed the case for the suspensive veto by insisting that the legislative decisions of the representatives of the nation could in no way be appealed to the sum of the *bailliages,* understood as constituting the body of the nation as a whole. "I know that by dint of distinctions on the one hand, confusion on the other, some have managed to consider the national wish as if it could be anything other than the wish of the nation's representatives," Sieyès maintained: "As if the nation could speak other than through its representatives. Here false principles become extremely dangerous." Given that direct democracy was impossible in a nation as populous in France, an appeal to the people would necessarily take the form of an appeal to an aggregate of particular communities, rather than to a common body of citizens. The effect would be "nothing less than cutting up, chopping up, tearing up France into an infinity of petty democracies, which would then be united only by the bonds of a general confederation." If France was to remain a single political body possessed of a unitary general will, that will could find expression only in the national assembly. "The people or nation can have only one voice, that of the national legislature. . . . The expression *appeal to the people* is therefore bad, for all that it is uttered in impolitic fashion. The people, I repeat, in a country that is not a democracy (and France cannot possibly be one), the people can speak and act only through its representatives."

In this respect, Sieyès—the only consistent theorist of representation in the assembly—went far beyond the more conventionally Rousseauian view of representative government as, in essence, a *pis aller*—an unavoidable alternative to democracy imposed by the imperious law of numbers in a populous state. In his conception, the unitary character of the general will necessarily implied not merely that the latter could only be expressed in a unitary national assembly, but that it could not even be considered to exist outside that assembly. At the same time, drawing upon a very different language, he also saw the practice of representation as a natural consequence of the division of labor in modern society, a device for the political application of the enlightenment that was one of the benefits of social progress. Since it was a necessary feature of modern society that the great majority of men could be no more than "laboring machines" occupied with their daily labor, it was in the interests of this majority to entrust the work of legislation to those with greater leisure, education and enlightenment, "far more capable than they themselves of knowing the general interest and interpreting their own will in this respect." For Sieyès, this emphasis on differential enlightenment as an essential feature of the theory of representation made the idea of an appeal to the people essentially incoherent. Representatives chosen to exercise a social function on the basis of their superior enlightenment could not make rational decisions if they were constrained to follow the wills of those who had elected them; nor should their enlightened formulation of the general will be appealed back to the sum of the ill-informed and particular wills in the primary assemblies.

Thus the constitutional debates of late August and early September 1789 presented the deputies with three principal choices. They could opt for the perfected historical constitution offered by the spokesmen for the constitutional committee, in which royal authority and national representation were to form mutually limiting principles in a complex system of the balance of powers. Or they could institute the radically new constitution offered by the Rousseauians on the basis of the principle of national sovereignty, with its radical division between a unitary legislative assembly and the subordinate executive authority placed in the crown, and its emphasis on the suspensive veto as the key to the reconciliation of the theory of the general will with the practice of representation. Or they could implement the variant upon that new constitution proposed by Sieyès, a constitution also instituted *de novo* by an act of national sovereignty, but one that placed ultimate expression of the general will not in an appeal to the will of the people in the primary assemblies but in the rational deliberation of the unitary representative body. In the stormy votes of mid-September that concluded these fundamental and impassioned debates, Sieyès' arguments against the suspensive veto proved to be no more compelling than Mounier's for the absolute veto. The Assembly repudiated the constitutional committee's recommendations for a dispersion and balance of powers maintained by an absolute royal veto, in favor of a unitary legislative body, a subordinate executive authority exercised by the crown, and a suspensive royal veto. The consequences of these decisions for the nature and dynamics of the French Revolution were momentous.

A first implication of these constitutional choices of mid-September 1789 was that the Assembly opted for the radical, Rousseauian definition of the constitution as a formal organization of the organs and functions of government created *de novo* by an act of sovereign will. If, indeed, there was any remaining doubt on that matter, it was soon dispelled by the events of the October Days, which definitively resolved the issue of whether a form of royal consent was necessary for the constitution itself. Pressed by the Assembly on October 1 to accept the Declaration of Rights and the constitutional articles so far decided, Louis XVI replied on October 5 by according his "accession"—not his "acceptance"—only on the strict condition that the constitution, once completed, would preserve the full force of executive power in the hands of the monarch. This conditional response proved less than satisfactory—even "ambiguous and insidious"—to many deputies, who argued that in reserving the possibility that the king might subsequently modify or refuse—hence even destroy—the constitution, it threatened to subvert liberty, restore despotism, and annihilate the very principle of national sovereignty. "The king's response is destructive not only of the whole constitution but, even more, of the national right to have a constitution," insisted Robespierre;

"He who can impose a condition on a constitution has the right to prevent that constitution. He is placing his will above the nation's right." Pétion in his turn reiterated the supremacy of the constituent over the constituted power by repudiating any lingering notion of the constitution as a reciprocal pact between king and nation: "They say that there is a social contract between the king and the nation. I deny the principle. The king cannot govern according to laws presented to him by the nation." Convinced by these arguments, the Assembly voted—immediately before a deputation of women marching from Paris appeared in its midst—to require the king to give the constitutional articles his "pure and simple assent." Carried to the château, with the women's demand for bread, by a combined deputation of representatives and marchers, the Assembly's demand was accepted by Louis XVI that very evening, under the threat of popular violence. Though it took almost two years for the Constituent Assembly to complete its work, the essence of the constitutional revolution was accomplished. Louis XVI, his new designation decided by the Assembly three days later, became not only "by the grace of God," but "by the constitutional law of the state, king of the French." From fixing the forms of a traditional monarchical constitution, the Constituent Assembly had moved to the decisive act of creating a constitutional monarchy instituted and organized on the basis of the principle of national sovereignty.

But if a constitution could be created anew in accordance with the principle of national sovereignty, could it not also be abolished and replaced on the same basis? And if popular action could force the acceptance of constitutional principles in the name of the nation, could it not also force their revision or repudiation once accepted? This possibility was a principal concern of a majority of the deputies almost two years later when, in the antipopular mood that prevailed in the months following the king's flight to Varennes and the Champ de Mars Massacre, the Assembly decided upon the forms for subsequent constitutional change. While the Assembly declared in the Constitution of 1791 that "the nation has the imprescriptible right to change its constitution," it also added a fateful "nevertheless" limiting this right to revision of particular constitutional articles "whose drawbacks had been revealed by experience"—and that only after three successive legislatures had agreed on the necessity for such action, and only by an assembly of revision composed of the fourth legislature augmented with additional members for this purpose. When it came to the need for constitutional change, the general will in such a matter was to be expressed, only under certain conditions, by the legislative body itself. Having unleashed the principle of national sovereignty, the National Assembly now faced the difficulties of containing it.

These difficulties were to be exacerbated by a second implication of the Assembly's decisions of mid-September 1789. For while accepting in effect the principle that they were instituting a constitution by an act of sovereign will, the deputies at the same time repudiated Sieyès' arguments for a constitution that would henceforth locate the expression of national sovereignty unambiguously in the representative body of the nation. They thereby opted, in effect, for the most unstable of the three choices with which they were presented—

the problematic combination of the Rousseauian principle of the inalienable sovereignty of the general will with the practice of representation. The suspensive royal veto was meant to close the gap between sovereignty and representation by allowing for an ultimate appeal to the people. In practice, by multiplying competing claims to express the general will, it simply exacerbated the problem it was meant to resolve.

Thus when the Constitution of 1791 was finally adopted, it embodied a fundamental contradiction, and a recipe for constitutional impasse. To safeguard national sovereignty from the dangers of representation, it permitted the monarch to veto legislative decrees—hence paralyze the Assembly— for the duration of two legislatures. But to protect the Constitution itself from the dangers of popular action in the name of national sovereignty, it required the assembly to delay constitutional revision for the duration of three legislatures. These provisions lay at the heart of the conflict between the principles of constitutionality and national sovereignty that occurred in the weeks preceding the revolution of August 10, 1792.

As a result of the veto, the Constitution of 1791, as Brissot remarked, could function only under "a revolutionary king." Thus, once it appeared in the spring of 1792 that Louis XVI's exercise of the veto was frustrating rather than upholding the sovereign will of the nation, not only the monarch but the Constitution itself was under siege. As growing popular demands for the king's suspension or deposition appealed to the principle of national sovereignty, so were they denounced in the Assembly as subversive of a constitution that made no explicit provision for such circumstances. The Constitution, the deputies insisted, could only be saved by constitutional means; but they were unable to agree on any such means. And as they dithered, so popular demands for action against the king were followed by demands for immediate action to change the Constitution—demands that also required repudiation of the restrictive provisions regarding constitutional revision established under the Constitution of 1791. Denouncing these provisions in the Assembly on July 25, 1792, as one more example of the truth that "no people on earth has ever been able to delegate its sovereignty for a moment without those to whom they delegated it trying to put them in chains," Isnard followed Chabot in maintaining that "the French people will always have the incontestable right to change its constitution when it deems it appropriate to do so." On August 4, a famous address of the Mauconseil section, declaring the impossibility of saving liberty by constitutional means, announced that the Constitution itself could no longer be considered an expression of the general will. Following the logic of such arguments, a petition opened for signatures on the Champ de Mars declared the nullity of all acts taken by the Constituent Assembly after the flight to Varennes, and appealed from the Constitution of 1791 to the principles of the Declaration of the Rights of Man. Presented to the Assembly on 6 July, this petition called for the deposition of the king, the election of a constitutional convention, and a program of revolutionary mobilization—all on the grounds that "the fatherland is in danger, the Revolution is starting again." The destruction of the Constitution of 1791 on August 10, 1792, was but the logical consequence of this call to renew the Revolution.

CONSTITUTION

With the overthrow of the monarchy, French government became radically provisional—long before the Convention formally declared on October 10, 1793, that the government would remain "revolutionary until peace" returned. The revolutionary reassertion of national sovereignty on August 10, 1792, reopened the conceptual space between revolution and constitution—a space that the Constituent Assembly had been anxious to seal when, in concluding its deliberations less than a year earlier, it declared both the Revolution and the Constitution complete. Within this space the Terror would find its form, to be followed by the vicissitudes of the many efforts to bring the Revolution once again to its constitutional completion.

This consideration suggests a third and final implication of the constitutional decisions taken by the National Assembly in mid-September 1789. To the extent that the Assembly's acceptance of the suspensive veto implied a repudiation of Sieyès' arguments for a theory of representation based on the division of labor, the Assembly was in effect discarding a discourse of the social, grounded on the notion of the differential distribution of reason, functions, and interests in modern civil society, in favor of a discourse of the political grounded on the theory of a unitary general will. In the most general terms, it was opting for the language of political will rather than of social reason, of unity rather than of difference, of civic virtue rather than of commerce, of absolute sovereignty rather than of the rights of man. Which is to say that, in the long run, it was opting for the Terror.

Keith M. Baker

FURTHER READING

Carcassonne, Elie. *Montesquieu et le problème de la constitution française au XVIIIe siècle.* Paris, 1927.

Duclos, Pierre. *La notion de Constitution dans l'oeuvre de l'Assemblée Constituante de 1789.* Paris, 1932.

Egret, Jean. *La révolution des notables: Mounier et les monarchiens, 1789.* Paris, 1950.

Lemaire, André. *Les lois fondamentales de la monarchie française d'après les théoriciens de l'Ancien Régime.* Paris, 1907.

Valensise, Marina. "La constitution française," in K. M. Baker, ed., *The French Revolution and the Creation of Modern Political Culture,* vol. 1, *The Political Culture of the Old Regime.* Oxford, 1987.

RELATED TOPICS

American Revolution   Revolutionary Assemblies   Sieyès
Estates General   Rights of Man   Sovereignty
Montesquieu   Robespierre
Napoleon Bonaparte   Rousseau

DÉPARTEMENT

For two centuries the département has been the fundamental administrative subdivision of the French government. Notwithstanding its longevity, it has also been, for that whole length of time, the center of a vast controversy. The administrative reorganization envisioned early in the Revolution was carried out quite quickly. The plan, conceived on the night of August 4, 1789, was put into operation on September 7. By February 26 of the following year boundaries of départements and districts had been fixed and capitals chosen. None of these decisions was carved in stone, however; many were soon modified. The Montagnards and, later, the imperial administration sought to create a different kind of département, better adapted to the needs of centralized government. Not surprisingly, the significance of the département has been interpreted in many different ways.

Was reform quick because it was easy or because it was ruthless? Burke was the first to call attention to its surgical aspect: "It was the first time that men had ever carved up their own country in so barbarous a fashion." Tocqueville countered, however, that the surgery had not been performed on living flesh: "They were only cutting up the dead." To him it was surprising that anyone should be surprised at the speed with which the operation was carried out.

Continuity or change? There had long been ample sentiment in favor of some reform along these lines. Many eighteenth-century thinkers, especially physiocrats, had called for change. Certain *cahiers de doléances* included calls for redistricting among their grievances. The very structure of the provincial assemblies of 1787 had influenced the revolutionary reformers. And even the word *département* was not new. The complexity of the Ancien Régime's administrative structure had long been attacked as an impediment to rational administration. Yet to judge by the way in which the reorganization was perceived by those whom it affected, it seems clear that it was deemed a radical break with the past, "a plan without parallel since Antiquity." One new départemental official, a native of Calvados, even remarked on November 16, 1790, that he and his colleagues were like "captains sailing uncharted waters."

Was the département an abstract and dangerous invention or a reflection of reality? A vast regionalist literature, much of it hostile to the Revolution, has devoted a great deal of energy to describing the new districts as a mere political and administrative convenience, empty shells without soul or substance. By contrast, writers favorable to the départements have argued that the new départements had genuine identities of their own. Did the départements promote national unity, or did they become focal points around

494

which regional identities could be forged? Powerful arguments support both positions.

*
**

Precisely what was at issue? The reform was partly opportunistic, as Sieyès candidly acknowledged: after the night of August 4, it became necessary to exert some control over the formation of municipal governments, a process that had been proceeding in a state of virtual anarchy. Later in August Sieyès called for a "plan for municipalities and provinces" in order to prevent the kingdom from "fragmenting into a multitude of small states disguised as a republic." No one at the time favored maintaining the status quo. Inspired by the works of Sieyès and the personality of Thouret, a constitutional committee set to work and on September 29, 1789, submitted a plan that remains notorious to this day for its egregious regularity: eighty-one square départements (together with eighteen unincorporated zones), each divided into nine cantons. It was nothing less than a surgical remedy for the existing "gothic" hodge-podge of dioceses, *bailliages*, governments, and *généralités*.

Sieyès' initial call for a plan embracing *both* municipalities and provinces refutes the allegation that the reform was designed to destroy the provinces. The provinces were not mentioned in Sieyès' or Thouret's early texts, and when the "provincialist" counterattack began, the committee's response was quite moderate: the new subdivisions were described as a direct consequence of the abolition of the old legal and administrative units on the night of August 4. The old arrangements were said to have reflected the aims of a despotic regime: to divide and thus to rule tyrannically. The purpose of the new plan was precisely the opposite. There was, Thouret insisted, no intention of destroying the provinces. It was never a matter of "revolutionary abstraction" unable to tolerate the rich variety of provincial life. Yet it was in such terms that nineteenth-century writers with an agenda of their own sought to recast the debate.

But was the committee's silence on the question of the provinces a camouflage? The committee had every reason to conceal its plans from deputies who after all were representatives of their *bailliages*. By the same token, the provincialists could not, in August 1789, appear to be defending corporations and special interests. The political circumstances helped cloud the debate. Yet as Brette has shown, the provincial concept was quite vague. Two definitions coexisted. On the one hand, the province was portrayed as a natural and cultural unit with its own unique spirit. On the other hand, it was a nexus of special interests. The provincialists liked to invoke, in rather vague, general terms, the spirit of local culture, whereas the committee preferred to denounce the mean-spiritedness of local special interests. The crux of the matter was whether the former invariably engendered the latter. The provincialists refused even to consider the question. The committee may have believed that the answer was yes, but it did not say so openly. Most deputies agreed with Malouet that one had nothing to do with the other and that the committee's plan was designed to stamp out local selfishness but not local spirit, that mysterious amalgam of a "multitude" of individual spirits. Since this multitude was assumed rather than analyzed, however, the idea that each province had its own particular physiognomy, which nineteenth-century regionalists endeavored tenderly to reconstruct, had little influence on a debate dominated by political issues of the moment.

The political goal was to complete the job begun on August 4. Many historians have portrayed France under the Ancien Régime as a chaotic, incoherent collection of overlapping ecclesiastical, judicial, and fiscal subdivisions, whose respective powers and jurisdictions were continually matters of dispute, as illustrated in particular by the difficulties attending the convocation of the Estates General. The physiocrats had stressed the inconvenience of the old system, but they were concerned mainly with estimating revenues and assessing taxes. Looked at in this way, the départements were a simple, rational substitute for the old patchwork. Curiously, however, simplification was not a major issue in the debate, nor was it much mentioned in the *cahiers de doléances*. To be sure, Thouret conceded that the "old divisions" represented an embarrassing confusion, but for him the crucial issue was that "they could not be usefully or properly adapted to the representative order."

This was indeed the issue stressed explicitly by both Thouret and Sieyès. Since it was impossible to have representatives chosen by the entire electorate, some division of the territory into electoral districts was necessary. Thus the département was merely, in Sieyès' words, a new form of *bailliage*. But behind this seemingly modest change lurked great stakes. In an earlier text, Sieyès had noted that once representative assemblies were established throughout the country, they would provide, in the form "of reason and interest associated with the national interest, a powerful counter" to longstanding claims of the so-called *pays d'Etat*, provinces with their own provincial estates (which enjoyed a range of special privileges under the Ancien Régime). Although Sieyès deemed it prudent to characterize the département as a mere electoral division for the purposes of the debate, he fully anticipated that over the course of time its significance would "extend to all the forms of public power."

It is not surprising, therefore, that the debate quickly moved beyond the question of the département as an electoral unit. In Thouret's mind the shift was connected with the abandonment of the strict mandate. In order for deputies to see themselves as representatives of the nation rather than of their *bailliages,* they had to be helped to overcome the understandable loyalty they felt to their constituents. As Rabaut Saint-Etienne observed, that loyalty was a sticking point, because many regarded it as a point of honor. In this painful transformation, made imperative by the need for national regeneration, the département was to be the instrument. The mention of the fateful word "regeneration" shows how quickly debate became radicalized in the first few weeks of the Revolution. The subject of the debate seemed to be highly technical: the number and boundaries of certain administrative subdivisions. Yet discussion quickly turned to issues of equality, the relation between history and nature, and the meaning of regeneration.

How many départements were to be created? The committee—Thouret, Target, Démeunier, and Rabaut Saint-Etienne—suggested a number around eighty. The provincialists—Pison du Galland and Martin de Besançon—suggested a far smaller number, designed to coincide with the old provinces. Mirabeau advocated a far greater number, for he wanted a large number of units of intermediate size (large "communes" or districts under the committee's original plan). Underlying this issue of number was a dispute over the definition of equality. The committee, in keeping with physiocratic tradition, wanted to define equality in terms of surface area—"square leagues"—which Condorcet described as a powerful antidote to "differences in climate, production, opinion, and spirit." The desire to divide the country into units of equal size explains the geometrical fixation of these early plans with their square boundaries. Although these utopian proposals were quickly abandoned, they were used to ridicule the work of the committee. By contrast, Mirabeau favored a demographic definition of equality. He argued that population density was the truest indicator of prosperity: "What are six square leagues without inhabitants?" Despite the success of Mirabeau's speech, which forced a compromise, the territorial plan ultimately prevailed. In its favor was the fact that space was a neutral quantity, malleable at will, whereas "population," for Mirabeau the key factor, varied constantly. By choosing territories of equal size, all had an equal chance of future success, despite differences in their current population.

Mirabeau had proposed creating 120 départements. Would this larger number really have made it easier to equalize populations rather than acreage? It seems unlikely, for Mirabeau was concerned not only with the number but also with the process of drawing boundaries. He favored respecting frontiers established by both nature and habit. Thouret had no difficulty showing that to establish units of equal population and fiscal contribution would require just as much tampering with existing boundaries as would his plan—a prospect that he, for one, did not find "so distressing." The euphemism is revealing. Once again, a seemingly technical debate over drawing boundaries actually hinged on a philosophical question, the relation of the part to the whole, of the local to the national. It is clear from the debate that special interests were seen from the first as illegitimate. Those who invoked them were forced to argue that the only way of formulating the general interest was to start with particular interests and proceed by degrees toward generality. This played into the hands of the committee, hostile to local claims. If local interests triumphed (as they would if the strict mandate prevailed), deputies could hardly call themselves deputies: "We would not be a National Assembly because we would not have wished to be one," Thouret triumphantly concluded.

Finally, the debate dramatized the conflict between nature and artifice, or, as Barnave put it, between genius and custom: "The committee has sacrificed too much to genius and not enough to custom." Was compromise on this score possible? Although eventually the committee reluctantly gave in, it resisted at first on the grounds that compromise was incompatible with the spirit of the Revolution: when reason and utility favored one plan over the other, why give any weight to the imperfections of the old system, however venerable? When it came to "reconstructing and regenerating the state, things ought not to be done by halves," said Thouret.

Thus the parliamentary debate suggests that the reform involved more change than continuity. Even the provincialists no longer dared invoke history, privilege, and tradition in defense of their views. They were forced to argue that geography in some vague way creates a unique local "personality." Both they and their adversaries shared the view that the structure of government and the unity of the nation were somehow related.

***

Nothing very radical emerged from this debate, however. Despite Thouret's rejection of compromise, many signs of it can be seen in the division of the territory and the organization of the départemental administrations.

In the first place, although the Assembly chose to divide the territory in such a way as to equalize area rather than population, it compromised by making the number of representatives and the amount of taxation proportional to population. The geometrical plan was rejected. As far as possible the Assembly sought to respect existing provincial boundaries in drawing new frontiers, and when this was not possible it proceeded cautiously. Even when an old province had to be divided in two to create a new département, as in the case of Indre, the Assembly drew the new boundaries along existing divisions between *généralités,* duchies, and dioceses. It did not break up parishes, now rebaptized communes. In choosing names for the new départements, it sought to use the names of oceans, mountains, rivers, and other geographical designations in order to avoid arbitrariness.

In other words, the provincialists had made their objections heard. Even though provinces had "new representative and administrative divisions," they were still "provinces with the same names as before." The final boundaries were not drawn solely with straightedge and compass; geographical considerations played a part. Attention was paid, as Mirabeau had wished, to "age-old constellations of mores, customs, products, and language." The initial plan, obsessed with rational design, had paid little heed to the traditional hierarchy of cities, but the committee, in bitter negotiations with the cities, was forced to correct its mistake, which had been predicated upon a desire to ensure that no citizen lived more than a day's journey by horseback from a *chef-lieu* (cantonal or départemental seat).

After all the compromises were made, can it be said that the Constituent Assembly took adequate account of local realities? Did it recognize genuine local interests, or did it simply regard the département as a cog in the machinery of centralized government?

The Constituent Assembly established two départemental institutions. The départemental or General Council was an elected, deliberative body whose function was to approve public works and expenditures. Its members were elected for two years by a secondary electoral assembly consisting of from 300 to 600 electors, who met in the départemental seat. They were chosen by primary assemblies, which gathered in each cantonal seat (the canton being a purely electoral subdivision). Thus elections were a two-stage process, a victory for Duport, Mirabeau, Barnave, and Pétion over the three-stage process initially proposed by the committee. The other institution was the Départemental Directory, whose eight members were appointed by the Council. Its responsibilities included schools, prisons, church maintenance, highways and canals, poor relief, and agricultural assistance. The king was represented by a *procureur général syndic*, but even this representative of the central government was *elected* by the secondary assemblies.

A durable historiographical tradition holds that the Constituent Assembly thus created a small, autonomous republic in each département, thereby providing France with a decentralized regime. In favor of this view is first of all the fact that all départemental offices were elective; not a single official was not ultimately subject to the sanction of the ballot box. Furthermore, all intermediate authorities between the départemental administrations and the supreme executive were eliminated. Memories of the hated intendants, outsiders who reigned over provincial life, played an important part in this decision; the abolition of the office of intendant on December 10, 1789, had been greeted with applause in the Assembly. Distrust of royal power was also important. Both government officials and those whom they administered insisted that local authorities should be close to the people for the sake of efficiency. When, for example, there was a question whether départemental officials should be chosen by eligible electors in all départements or only in the département in which the official would serve, the Assembly opted for the latter in order to avoid having officials foisted on local regimes by the central authorities.

Despite such evidence, which demonstrates the Assembly's concern for local issues and desire to expand political participation, regionalists have argued that the département was actually an instrument of centralization. They contend that in fact the départements could do very little on their own, because decrees of the General Council became law only when confirmed by the king. Furthermore, the hierarchy of assemblies—commune subject to département subject to king—was intended primarily to ensure that decisions would flow smoothly from the center to the periphery. Like the administrators of the monarchy, the revolutionaries dreamed of controlling the entire country from Paris.

What made such divergent interpretations possible? In fact, the département was two-faced. Subdivisions and procedures were indeed standardized. In this sense, the département was an instrument of centralization. On the other hand, local political life was enriched by the advent of representative democracy. In this sense, the reform was an instrument of decentralization, and the département as envisioned by the Constituent Assembly was the forerunner of the département created by the Third Republic: a place where prefects, representing the central government, engaged in constant negotiations with local interests. But the Constituent Assembly was not aware of this duality. It envisioned a world in which special interests were invariably subsumed in the general interest. The desire, as Thouret put it, to "dispatch all affairs pertaining to special interests as quickly and carefully as possible" was in no sense an admission that special interests were private, individual affairs. There was no mention in the debate of specific needs peculiar to each locality. Narrow local views were "good only under despotism." Now that tyranny was overthrown, there must of course be enough administrative units to encourage political activity, yet individual units must not be allowed to represent special interests and must be encouraged instead to contribute to the national interest.

Thus, the Constituent Assembly created a département that was more "deconcentrated" than truly decentralized. It was the agent of the central government, but it was also the administrator of local interests. In fact, it maintained two distinct budgets. Part of the reason for the département's durability was that these contradictory functions allowed room for negotiation and permitted the local authorities to adapt to changing circumstances. During the decade of the Revolution the département proved its flexibility, filling the needs of both centralization and decentralization as circumstances required. The federalist crisis of 1793, which profoundly altered the nature of the départements, would not have been possible without them.

Who were the men elected by the départemental assemblies? Taine described them as a "rabble of insignificant men drawn from the dregs of society." Yet there were among them landowners, lawyers, and prominent citizens, and as a group they were far from devoid of talent. After August 10—an event they greeted unenthusiastically—many were replaced; yet the Convention's decision to introduce universal suffrage did not profoundly alter the social composition of the councils, whose new members were drawn from the same segments of society as the old ones. When Montagnard representatives were forced to deal with these moderate local officials, they were astonished to recognize in them the old "parlementary haughtiness." Throughout the winter of 1793 the départemental assemblies attempted to put together an armed force; after June 2, some sixty of them protested the Commune's violence. The Convention forced many to resign and compelled the assemblies to comply with its wishes. The Law of 14 Frimaire, Year II, altered the structure of local government by eliminating the General Councils and *procureurs syndics* and limiting the powers of the Départemental Directory; local elections were also abolished, and the government's agents were made responsible for filling council vacancies. After Thermidor the powers of the local authorities were gradually—but not totally—restored. The General Council was not reinstituted, and the départements were assigned to monitor the activities of lower echelons of government. The Constitution of Year III took even greater care to ensure obedience to the central authorities, providing for a *commissaire* appointed by the government to be dispatched to each département. This official, offspring of the national agents of Year II more than of the elected *procureurs syndics* (and of course precursor of the imperial prefects), symbolizes the growing centralization of government in the revolutionary period.

This was intended as a response to "federalism," yet federalism had shown no consistent regional orientation in its demands. The federalist revolt had been carried out in the name of the départements, but taken together and regarded as homogeneous, not as heterogeneous provinces. Hatred of Paris, evident in all the sources, was by no means tantamount to repudiation of centralized government. Indeed, there is considerable evidence that the insurrectionaries were keen to find a new center of government outside Paris. Nowhere were the rights of individual provinces mentioned. Thomas Paine was correct when he wrote to Danton on May 31, 1793: "The danger of a break between Paris and the départements is increasing daily." Note the plural: *départements*—not this or that département. Paradoxically, regionalism played no part in the Girondin insurrection. This can be interpreted as a sign that the département had by this time been accepted, or at any rate that the people of France had reconciled themselves to the new reality. Maurice Agulhon points out that the Vendée so dear to royalist enemies of the Revolution was the name of a département, not a province. And what better proof of the département's astonishing success than this anecdote, recounted by Pétion: in the carriage that brought Louis XVI back from Varennes, the king amused himself by repeating the names of the départements through which the procession passed.

Does all this suggest that the département quickly took on an identity of its own? Resistance was strong. During the debates on the Constitution of Year I, Saint-Just was still remembering the "ten thousand deputies who came to the Constituent Assembly from every corner of France demanding a local seat of government." The provinces were mobilized, and from that mobilization flowed a huge volume of briefs, petitions, and affidavits in support of the claims of this or that town or city to be named a district or départemental capital or be chosen as the site of a courthouse.

These sources tell us a great deal about how provincials conceived of geography. Here, feelings of attachment to a province (particularly the *pays d'Etat*) were more candidly expressed than in the Assembly debates. Charges of abstraction and "geometrism" were also more violent, coming as they did from men who knew the lay of the land and the meaning of the verb "to hike." They suggested that the Assembly's planners visit their mountainous provinces, dotted with swamps and devoured by moors. They pointed out that some regions had better roads and better weather than others, and they called attention to the resulting inequalities in money spent and time wasted in dealing with the authorities. Yet the bulk of the protests reveal not so much a provincial spirit as a local spirit. Reflected in them were the sentiments of urban communities, each with an identity of its own. Each of these communities insisted on its ancient privileges and demanded new ones, dredging up old quarrels with rival cities as to which enjoyed precedence over the other. Their arguments adhered to no particular set of principles: sometimes they were historical, sometimes geographical, sometimes linguistic, sometimes demographic. Opportunism even went so far as to permit some cities to raise against the Assembly the argument of the general interest, which the Assembly itself had declared to be paramount. There was an enormous outpouring of communal chauvinism, and the Assembly took all these protests seriously enough to suggest in some cases that two cities share the honor of being named *chef-lieu,* an expedient that was rejected in 1791. Goslin said that such "alternation" had proved unsatisfactory in practice and had been agreed to in the first place only as a concession to the cities' demands.

All of this gives some idea of the magnitude of the change wrought by the Revolution. Each community recalled the privileges it had won over many years and expressed its hopes and fears concerning the new structure of government. The protests do reveal a deep-seated local spirit, but they do not suggest that resistance was shaped by anything like a "regional identity." The division of the country into départements encouraged not broad views but proliferation of local differences. One sign of the new spirit was the advent of a new category of literature: books about travels in "the départements of France." Another was the requirement that *commissaires* submit reports to Paris describing the state of mind of the local populace. The département became the new frame of reference, and within its relatively narrow borders the usual terms for characterizing geographical regions were deployed: north/south, plains/mountains, closed field/open field. Differences continued to exist but on a smaller scale. Later, imperial prefects were urged to describe their départements as if they were autonomous territories, and those who proved insufficiently sensitive to the particularities of their locality were ordered by Chaptal to discuss its principal distinguishing features. Meticulous observation and description of such differences gave rise to a kind of "départemental patriotism." This was a gauge of the reformers' success in achieving their goal: to sap the regions of their ability to mobilize resistance to the central government, which (it was hoped) would embody the unified will of the nation in a unique social contract.

Ironically, however, even the minor differences between départements could be politicized. The most important element in the *commissaire*'s report was the assessment of the political situation. As the Revolution proceeded from one phase to the next, the départements received grades, some good, some bad, some healthy, some diseased. Local officials learned the rudiments of electoral sociology. Supposed to be homogeneous and to serve the cause of unity, the départements actually exhibited the invincible heterogeneity of French political attitudes, everlastingly associated with the very soil out of which they grew. The implementation of a politics of topography thus revealed the topography of politics.

Mona Ozouf

Département

Further reading

Among innumerable monographs on the formation of the départements, see Louis Boivin-Champeaux, *La Révolution dans le département de l'Eure* (Evreux, 1895); René Hennequin, *La formation du département de l'Aisne* (Soissons, 1911); and above all Henri Mettrier, *La formation du département de la Haute-Marne en 1790* (Clermont, 1911).

Agulhon, Maurice. "Conscience nationale et conscience régionale en France de 1815 à nos jours," in J. C. Boogman and G. N. Van der Platt, eds., *Federalism: History and Current Significance of a Form of Government*. The Hague, 1980.

——— "Plaidoyer pour les Jacobins: La gauche, l'état et la région dans la tradition historique française," *Le débat*, June 1981.

Berlet, Charles. *Les provinces au 18e siècle et leur division en départements*. Paris, 1913.

Brette, Armand. *Les limites en 1789*. Paris, 1907.

Ferron, H. de. "L'organisation départementale et la constitution de 1789," *Nouvelle revue historique du droit français*, 1877.

Grémion, Pierre. "Régionalisation, régionalisme, municipalisation sous la Ve Républi-que," *Le débat*, November 1981.

Lebègue, Ernest. *La vie et l'oeuvre d'un constituant: Thouret, 1746–1794*. Paris, 1910.

Mage, Georges. *La division de la France en départements*. Toulouse, 1924.

Ozouf-Marignier, Marie-Vic. *La représentation du territoire français à la fin du XVIIIe siècle d'après les travaux sur la formation des départements*. Paris, 1987.

Related topics

Barnave	Estates General	Revolutionary Assemblies
Burke	Federalism	Sieyès
Centralization	Mirabeau	Taine
Condorcet	Night of August 4	Tocqueville
Democracy	Physiocrats	Vendée
Elections	Regeneration	

MAXIMUM

I n the context of the French Revolution the word *maximum* refers to legislation with which the Convention attempted to regulate economic life by imposing price controls first on goods and a short while later on wages. This legislation contradicted the convictions of all the leaders of the Revolution, who, in economic matters, were liberals, including the Montagnards. Although the Montagnards did break with the physiocratic orthodoxy of *laisser faire, laisser passer* in 1793, that break was for political reasons. Furthermore, the fact that the two most important stages in the passage of this regulatory legislation came in April–May and September 1793 shows fairly clearly that the laws on the *maximum* were part of the process of establishing the "revolutionary government."

On the ruins of the Ancien Régime, the Constituent Assembly had established internal free trade (while ensuring that protectionism was preserved on the borders): a radical transformation in an old monarchy accustomed to meticulous state regulation, particularly of the "grain trade." But by the end of the Assembly's mandate, in 1791, clouds had gathered over this new system of nonintervention. Assignats had already lost a third of their nominal value (and twice as much on the foreign exchange market), metal currency was disappearing from circulation, prices were rising, and the political crisis (Varennes) heightened suspicion, hoarding, and stockpiling. By this point the problem had become what it would remain: more political than economic. Rising prices, that old sign of the people's misery, resulted not so much from a disastrous harvest as from widespread anticipation of crises to come. Historians have perhaps not adequately noted that when the Revolution freed the economy from state controls, it multiplied the reasons why the state might be blamed for misfortune and poverty; if sovereignty now belonged to the people, how could the sovereign be indifferent to the people's woes? How could democracy, having instituted equality, do less than the monarchy had done?

In this gap between expectations and everyday reality, popular discontent welled up—discontent unconsciously magnified by memories of monarchical regulation. The spring of 1792 saw the massing of proletarian armies, backing the demand for price controls, in the countryside west and south of Paris. Put down by départemental administrations, these economically based disturbances flared up again in various places and often forced local authorities to institute regulatory measures similar to those employed by the Ancien Régime. War accelerated the inflation, peasants were increasingly reluctant to sell their products on a volatile market, and since August 10 the sans-culottes had reigned in Paris, where in September they forced a sale of grain at a fixed price for military purposes. The movement spread that autumn, especially south of the Perche and throughout Beauce, but repression reestablished order, and the Convention, urged on by the Girondins, repealed September's regulatory legislation.

The "social question" remained open, however, and it was at the heart of the conflict between the Gironde and the Mountain. Not for theoretical reasons: both groups shared the same liberal philosophy in economic matters, and both registered their fundamental disapproval of the spreading call that fall for an "agrarian law." They had no liking for such demagogic attacks on private property, attacks often led by rural priests. But the Girondins fulminated, while the Montagnards kept quiet and looked ahead: a remarkable difference in behavior that stemmed from the differences in their respective political strategies. The Girondins hoped to counter Paris by courting the bourgeoisie and the "interests," old and new, and in their appeals we see the inception of a theme destined for a great future in French politics, that of the "red peril." The Montagnards sought to seize power with the support of the *petit peuple* of Paris. They were the champions of "public safety" and of national unity against the invader, and their obsession with the aristocratic plot tied them to the sans-culottes. A figure such as Marat illustrates what there was in common between a parliamentary bourgeoisie like the Mountain and the artisans and others of similar station who filled the Paris sections.

Nevertheless, in February 1793, the conflict between the Montagnards and the price-fixers was still raging. The popular movement had chosen independent leaders, the enragés Varlet and Jacques Roux—a hothead born to wealth and a demagogic priest. The Mountain, led by Marat and supported by the Jacobins, condemned and combatted the riot by the price-fixers. Two months later, however, the Montagnards, faced with the growing power of the movement and the need to defeat the Girondins, changed sides. This coerced compromise resulted in the law, establishing the *maximum* on grains, that was approved by the Convention on May 4 after impassioned debate and under constant pressure from the galleries, besieged by activists organized in "delegations." Mathiez, the author of the most comprehensive study of the question, cannot bring himself to believe that the Assembly succumbed to the influence of the street. Nevertheless, the debate was a kind of dress rehearsal for June 2, which dealt the final blow to the Girondins.

The law of May 4, by establishing a ceiling price on grains in each département based on the average price over the past six months, led, as was only to be expected, to a series of measures to control the grain trade and punish infractions: declarations, inventories, inspections, administrative licenses, and penalties for those who refused to comply. Enforcement of this law was in any case a long and difficult process. It was also uneven, being left to the discretion, more reluctant than zealous, of local and départemental administrations. In the short term the result was that the "average price" varied sufficiently between départements that grain flowed out of some and into others. The logic of the new system was not so much regulation as requisition and Terror.

What is more, the *maximum* on grains did not quell the escalating egalitarian demands of the enragés but gave them a new lease on life. In the months that followed, Jacques Roux put the Convention in a position where it had no choice but to approve a general *maximum* on prices, only to retreat in the face of a counterattack by Robespierre and Marat. In July the offensive resumed, aided by the death of the "Friend of the People" and the seriousness of the situation: extraordinary danger, extraordinary means. Paris was short of bread, owing to the chaotic arrival of shipments from the rural départements. The Convention tried to buy time in July by passing a law, recommended the night before by Collot d'Herbois, against hoarding: this law required merchants to declare, within a week, how much of the most necessary food items they held in their possession and opened the door to a legal inquisition by the revolutionary police.

At this point the Assembly hoped, as a countervailing measure, to rescind the law of May 4, whose harmful nature had been underscored by countless criticisms emanating from the provinces. Yet once again political logic prevailed over economic rationality: the agitation of the Paris sections and the centralized mobilization of national resources compelled the deputies and the Committee of Public Safety to move toward a state-controlled economy based on requisitions and controls. Robespierre defeated Jacques Roux, but at the cost of adopting his program. In August a series of decrees gave the authorities almost full discretionary power over the production and transport of grains, as well as providing drastic punishments for fraud, with the inevitable bonus promised for denunciations. "Storehouses of plenty" were to be established to stockpile the grain requisitioned by the districts. By this point any notion of rescinding the legislation of May 4 had become unrealistic. Mass conscription, approved on August 24, vastly increased the number of mouths to be fed by the state. And the sans-culotte *journée* of September 5 compelled the Convention to radicalize its entire policy, including economic measures. This shift led to the laws of September 11 and 29, which instituted the general *maximum*.

The text of the eleventh, which endured slightly longer than the revolutionary government itself (remaining in force until the fall of 1794), set a nationwide *maximum* on grain and fodder prices and set very specific conditions of purchase. Non-harvesters could buy only in their own commune, and regions with a grain shortfall could be supplied only upon requisition by the district. The grain trade became a monopoly of the administration, and recalcitrant peasants joined the vast category of "suspects" defined by the law of September 17.

The decree of September 29, debated since the 22nd, was a matter of intense controversy, with the debate once again subject to pressure from the gallery and from delegations representing the Commune and the sections. Certain Montagnards, such as Thuriot, took up the Girondin argument about the necessity of freedom of commerce. The Convention, however, ultimately voted to impose price controls on all essential supplies. The *maximum* on tobacco, salt, and soap was uniform throughout France, as was that on grains. The price ceiling on other basic items was set at one-third above the market price in 1790, the actual price to be established on a district-by-district basis. The wage ceiling, a natural complement to the system of price-fixing, was somewhat higher, fifty percent above the 1790 level, to be established by each municipality. All these price schedules were to be prepared within the week.

This absurd measure, which would have required armies of regulators, inspectors, and enforcers, to say nothing of warehousemen, lacked only one thing to complete its impeccable logic, namely, a central authority. This oversight was repaired in October, with the creation of a Commission des Subsistances, whose responsibility included all of French commerce, foreign and domestic. Its mission was to make sure that the people and the armies were fed by requisition and redistribution from district to district, by grain imports, and by export of manufactured goods. This vast program, which transfigured the old administrative logic of the monarchy through an infusion of egalitarian language, was entrusted to three revolutionary militants: Raisson, an important supplier of Paris pubs; Brunet, a member of a family of Montpellier merchants, brother-in-law of Aigoin, a commissaire in the Treasury, and an associate of Cambon, who took charge of French finances under the Convention; and Goujon, *procureur général syndic* of Seine-et-Oise, replaced soon thereafter by one Jouenneault, probably the brother of the unscrupulous conventionnel. As Michel Bruguière has shown, these relatively unknown names illustrate the presence of a bourgeois administration of revolutionary policy at the height of the terrorist dictatorship.

This administration never had any power, domestically at any rate, other than that of the Terror and its secular arm, the revolutionary army and the envoys dispatched by the Committee of Public Safety. The system established by legislation immediately engendered its opposite: withholding of merchandise, illegal stockpiling, fraud, and black marketeering. It provoked resistance among manufacturers, merchants, and shopkeepers, as well as peasants, who had little incentive to bring their harvest to market. The state-controlled economy launched a parallel economy, along with penury for the majority. At the end of October, Albitte, a member of the Convention dispatched to Lyons, reported his impressions to the Committee of Public Safety: "Everywhere I saw people searching for bread, which in many places is in short supply, and what little they find they eat, though it is very bad. Three times I myself could find none to eat in the inns or even in the postmaster's home. The *maximum* on grain, the greed of the farmer, the malevolence of aristocrats and egoists, and the huge requirements of the army are to blame. . . . Nearly everywhere I found a shortage of the things most necessary to life, markets deserted and empty, and many shops closed."

This testimony from a Montagnard deputy explains why the Convention, throughout the autumn, repeatedly attempted to patch up its two major laws of September with additional decrees that sought in vain to accommodate the interests of agriculture and commerce—in vain because the Convention's authority over the country depended in large part on coercion and fear and because the spirit of the *maximum* was not economic rationality but terror. Sans-culottes filled the ranks of the revolutionary army and staffed the system of inquisition and repression. Montagnard deputies tried to outdo them, as evidenced by the example of Saint-Just and his famous mission to Alsace on 3 Nivôse: "The criminal tribunal of the département of Bas-Rhin is hereby ordered to raze the house of anyone convicted of stockjobbing or selling at a price above the *maximum*." Will and requisition might feed the army, but they could do little about the reality of domestic trade.

It would be a mistake, however, to think of the economic dictatorship, on the evidence of terrorist rhetoric, as having been more centralized than it actually was. There were two reasons for this lack of centrality. First, the *maximum* was actually enforced only for grains, that is, for bread: what had been the obsession of the Contrôle Générale became the obsession of the Commission des Subsistances and was all the more acute because now it was necessary to feed not only the people but also the armies. With this mission accomplished for better or worse through threats and requisitions, peasants were allowed to sell poultry (but not cattle) and produce pretty much as they wished. Furthermore, the *maximum* on grains—in other words, cheap bread—was popular at least among the *petit peuple* of the cities, whereas price ceilings on other goods affected the shopkeepers and artisans among whom the sans-culottes were recruited.

The second reason was that local situations varied widely, something one tends to lose sight of if one approaches the history of the Revolution by way of the speeches and decrees published in the *Moniteur*. The Convention's economic policy—apart from foreign trade, which was controlled by the Commission des Subsistances—was in the hands of local administrations, the communes and above all the districts (since the départements were suspected of moderatism and kept at arm's length by the revolutionary government). Implementation of the proposed regulations was impeded by technical obstacles such as slow transportation, in many cases aggravated by a shortage of horses; in some places it met with fanatical support, in others with passive resistance, depending on the loyalties prevailing in a particular town or canton or on accidents of the local situation. The price *maximum*, especially in the bakeries, was better controlled in Paris than the wage *maximum*, since the Paris Commune was dominated first by enragés and later by Hébertists; in the rest of the country the opposite was more likely to be the case. Policies to restrict consumption were always municipal. Each city, supplied by the efforts of its district, regulated distribution as it saw fit. Paris established a bread ration card, but only a few other cities followed suit. Finally, the various *représentants en mission* sent to the provinces by the Convention were not consistent in enforcing repressive measures; the likelihood that they would be obedient to the legislation emanating from Paris varied with the fear they inspired and the proximity of the revolutionary army.

Finally, the *maximum* system never ceased to be governed by the logic responsible for its existence. It was not established to resolve an exceptional economic situation but was the product of an escalation of egalitarian demands of which the Montagnards somewhat reluctantly became the sponsors. Hence even before the fall of Robespierre, the liquidation of Hébertism at the end of March 1794 dealt the system a first blow. At the moment when Hébert and his friends were guillotined, Paris was in the throes of a dramatic shortage: here was yet another reason to accentuate an evolution that began in February with the reform of the Commission des Subsistances, now divided into two sections while its actual role was curtailed. The Committee of Public Safety did not repudiate the *maximum*, of which a general schedule had just been published, but it attenuated its impact on its suppliers by granting increases or bonuses. As for retail trade, elimination of the hoarding inspectors cut back the inspection machinery to the point where little by little the parallel market began to prosper. The abolition of the revolutionary army on 7 Germinal (March 27, 1794) had a similar effect. Finally, the Committee once again authorized the export of foodstuffs in order to incorporate international high commerce into its strategy.

As for the *maximum* on wages, the Committee continued to enforce the ceiling, since the state factories were themselves the largest employers in the Republic. Had it abandoned the ceiling set by law, it would have added additional inflationary pressure to the economic cycle. In many places, however, wage-earners obtained increases in spite of the law or, especially in the country, demanded payment in kind. Inflation continued to threaten their precarious standard of living, and the final months of Robespierrist dictatorship were marked by growing signs of worker discontent. On the night of 10 Thermidor (July 28), as the procession conveying Robespierre and his friends to the guillotine passed by, the fickle crowd insulted the latest victims of the Terror, and the common folk were heard to cry: "To hell with the *maximum!*"

The *maximum* was indeed abolished at the end of December, in the context of a general dismantlement of the revolutionary government. Foreign trade, currency exchange, and banking regained their freedom, and the government substituted contractors for state economic controls. It did, however, retain the right to requisition food if needed to keep the market and army supplied. Nevertheless, the main thing, the return to uncontrolled prices, involved the Thermidorian Convention in a different but no less difficult cycle of problems: a plummeting assignat, a collapse of foreign exchange, scarcity and high cost of metal currency and merchandise, rationing by wealth, and misery of the populace. A new history was beginning, one in which the revolutionary bourgeoisie simultaneously discovered its convictions and its interests.

The interval of the *maximum* and of the state-controlled economy continued to loom large in memory. Its extraordinary character and its association with the war and "public safety" proved less durable than the intention it embodied: to protect the small man, the poor man, and perhaps even more to strike at the rich man. What did it matter that it had given rise to a largely inefficient, costly, and tyrannical bureaucracy? What counted was that it displayed within the Revolution the ambition to transcend the Revolution by seeking to extend the principle of equality to the actual conditions in which people lived. Once the stomping feet of 9 Thermidor celebrating the end of the Terror had fallen silent, the memory of the *maximum* pointed the way to a socialist interpretation of Robespierrism or, what comes to the same thing, a socialist critique of the French Revolution: Babeuf's time had come.

François Furet

FURTHER READING

Bruguière, Michel. *Gestionnaires et profiteurs de la Révolution.* Paris, 1986.

Calvet, Henri. *L'accaparement à Paris sous la Terreur: Essai sur l'application de la loi du 26 juillet 1793.* Paris, 1933.

Commission des subsistances de l'an II: Procès-verbaux et actes, ed. Pierre Caron. Paris, 1925.

Guérin, Daniel. *La lutte des classes sous la première République: Bourgeois et "bras nus" (1793–1797),* 2 vols. Paris, 1946; second edition, 1968.

Mathiez, Albert. *La vie chère et le mouvement social sous la Terreur.* Paris, 1927; reprinted in 2 vols., 1973.

RELATED TOPICS

Assignats	Girondins	Sans-culottes
Babeuf	Marat	Terror
Enragés	Montagnards	
Equality	Revolutionary Government	

NATIONAL
PROPERTIES

O n November 2, 1789, by a vote 568 to 346 with 40 abstentions, the
Constituent Assembly approved a bill proposed by Mirabeau:

1. That all ecclesiastical properties are at the disposal of the Nation, which un-
dertakes to provide in an appropriate manner funds to meet the expenses of the
Church, stipends for its ministers, and relief for the poor. . . .

2. That . . . no parish shall be allowed less than 1,200 livres per annum excluding
the costs of maintaining lodging and dependent grounds.

This "bold expropriation," as Jaurès called it, should not be confused with a
long series of later measures (beginning December 19, 1789) designed to turn
the clergy's wealth in real estate into cash through the sale of properties and
the issuance of assignats. It was, however, related to the earlier abolition of
the tithe (in August 1789). The reform of the clergy's status was also a separate issue, dealt with later, in appearance at least, through the Civil Constitution of the Clergy (1790). Over the period that extends from the Constituent Assembly to the Directory the manner in which the national properties
were sold changed in many ways, details of which can be found in books on
the history and institutions of the Revolution. Here I shall concentrate instead on the debate prior to the decree of November 2, as well as on a later
debate—this one among historians rather than deputies—over the long-term
social and economic implications of this momentous event.

Jaurès notes that "while the Church put up only weak resistance to the
abolition of the tithe, it fiercely resisted nationalization of its real estate." In
order to win a majority in the Assembly, therefore, proponents of nationalization were obliged to present a rather amusing argument. It was most rigorously stated by Talleyrand, the bishop of Autun, and its chief purpose was
to alleviate fears that what happened to the Church's property might one day
happen to the property of ordinary private citizens as well. "The clergy," Talleyrand argued, "is not an owner like other owners, because it enjoys but may
not dispose of properties given it not for the benefit of individuals but for the
performance of certain functions." Hence there was nothing immoral in allowing "the Nation" (that is, the state) to terminate the Church's title, provided that in so doing it offered "a decent subsistence to members of the
clergy, agreed to maintain temples, hospitals, charity workshops, and educational establishments," and pledged not to spend revenues beyond what was

required to discharge these functions—"except in times of general calamity" when confronted with "extreme needs." Nor was Talleyrand above resorting to theological subtleties, for he pointed out that the Church consisted not just of the clergy but of all the faithful, hence that it was merely another name for "the Nation" itself.

Thouret, a lawyer and deputy of the Third Estate from Rouen, bolstered this case with expert legal arguments. He drew a distinction "between real persons, actual living individuals, and corporations (*corps*) that . . . constitute moral and fictive persons. . . . Individuals exist independent of the law. . . . By contrast, corporations exist only by virtue of the law, [which] has unlimited authority over all that pertains to them, indeed over their very existence. . . . Thus the law, having created corporations, can also abolish them. Of this there are hundreds of examples." Under these conditions "revocation of the faculty granted to corporations to possess property in land cannot be construed as spoliation."

The principal opponent of the proposal was abbé Maury, the king's chaplain and a spokesman for the aristocrats, who emigrated and was named a cardinal in 1794 but who later rallied to the side of Napoleon. (Made archbishop of Paris in 1810 at the height of the conflict between the Pope and the emperor, he would be challenged by his chapter because he had not received the papal investiture.) He took a resolutely demagogic stance—as the Church had done before in the time of the League: so said Jaurès, who denounced Maury as Drumont's earliest inspirer. It was Jaurès' view that by using the Church's property to pay off the state's debts, the Assembly was simply "transferring the Church's revenues primarily into the hands of legions of rentiers, bourgeois lenders, and capitalists." In Maury's language this meant that the wealth of the nation was to be sacrificed to the self-interest of usurers, stockjobbers, and other speculators and that the sweat of the provinces would go to feed the appetites of the capital.

Of course the clergy itself was deeply divided: to some parish priests it was all one whether they received benefices from the Church or salaries from the state, and such humble clergymen found themselves at odds with prelates whose luxurious ways they considered scandalous. It was hard to persuade such priests that no less a figure than Charles de Talleyrand-Périgord himself was about to deliver France and the Church into the hands of the Jews. Many of them joined with Le Chapelier and especially Mirabeau in laying the Middle Ages to rest on November 2. The former emphasized the need to root out "all these ideas of corporations and orders that are constantly springing up." The latter, in a country where style has always counted as much as content, was shrewd enough to draft his motion in such a way that its central theme was the Assembly's request to the Church that it place its property "at the disposal of the Nation." He thus avoided the word "expropriation," which Maury would have seized as a red flag to wave before the revolutionary bourgeoisie. Such shrewdness was necessary: "Had there not been nearly two hundred noble deputies among the ranks of the émigrés," Jaurès observes, the outcome of the vote might well have been in doubt. For the socialist historian "this great day" was "surely the most decisive of the Revolution," fostering "a vast revolutionary solidarity" among citizens ranging "from bankers and wealthy shippers in Nantes and Bordeaux to Paris shopkeepers and peasant landowners," all of whom approved of the nationalization of what had been the property of the Church.

The history of the nationalization as it is usually told has two great themes: one economic, the other social. Under the heading of economics, the confiscated properties served as backing for a new paper currency, the assignat. The ensuing inflation bought political triumph (financing the war and consolidating the Revolution) but at the price of severe disruption of the economy and of the daily lives of those who depended on it. Under the heading of social history, the secularization of clerical properties, followed by the confiscation of the possessions of émigrés (termed "second-round properties" to distinguish them from the "first-round properties" taken from the clergy), meant that vast quantities of once settled wealth suddenly flooded the market, offering ripe prospects to buyers drawn from all segments of society. Although perhaps no more than ten or twenty percent of the confiscated properties actually changed hands (mainly real estate), even this much represented a huge volume compared with the normal volume of transactions in periods of stability, and the nature of the shift in capital was such as to alter profoundly the social distribution of wealth, and hence the structure and values of society itself.

Probably the most surprising aspect of the whole business was the diversity of its beneficiaries. Benefits were substantial, albeit uneven and inconsistent, but the overall effect was to make French society more stable. It is important to consider this effect from two standpoints, focusing first on the relation between town and country, second on social and occupational differences among those who gained from the sales.

A good place to begin is with an excellent recent study by Jean-Claude Farcy: *Les paysans beaucerons de la fin de l'Ancien Régime au lendemain de la première guerre mondiale* (1985). Farcy shows that in the Beauce region nobles purchased the largest of the confiscated properties (accounting for thirteen percent of the total): "Already well established in the Beauce, the nobility strengthened its hold on the land early in the Revolution, benefiting quite handsomely from the sale of national properties." The nobles in question resided mainly in the cities. Among those owning property of more than 1,000 hectares at the beginning of the nineteenth century, thirteen were Parisians (with 26,000 hectares in all) and twelve were from Orléans (12,400 hectares); nearly half of all major landowners were nobles.

The rentier bourgeoisie purchased fourteen percent of the national properties sold. But the biggest winners were farmers (just under twenty-five percent) and the commercial bourgeoisie (just over twenty-five percent). The figures thus show that the rich got richer but that smallholders also extended their holdings, and some previously landless individuals were at last able to join the propertied class. The trend toward concentration of property, pronounced throughout the eighteenth century, was halted, and a limited yet relatively important democratization of land owning partially satisfied the intense desire for land among proletarianized peasants. Still, it must be emphasized that the gain was only by comparison with the past; peasants remained dissatisfied—a fact often cited in interpretations of the insurrection in the Vendée—because they felt that wealthy city folk had snapped up more than their share of the pie. In the Chartres district sixty-four percent of the clergy's properties were purchased by townsfolk; elsewhere the proportion was as low as forty percent. Parisians added substantially to their holdings. Louis Baron, secretary to the king and tax collector for Franche-Comté, acquired 724 hectares. And let us not speak of the Parisian bankers.

Nevertheless, many properties were acquired by vineyardists and modest agricultural laborers. In central Beauce one laborer in ten was able to purchase a plot of land. During the Consulate the prefect of Seine-et-Oise observed: "The man who had nothing he could call his own has become a landowner. His style of life has changed to match his newfound wealth. The day laborer who could not afford to buy, having become a scarcer commodity than before, has been able to demand higher wages. . . . The hired man has been clever enough to take advantage of the shortage of hands to sell his services more dear."

Some sharecroppers purchased their farms. The most prosperous "bought large amounts of the clergy's properties, taking advantage of an ideal opportunity to transform themselves into a landed bourgeoisie." Peasants formed partnerships among themselves or joined with notaries and bourgeois from Chartres to buy large farms that were then broken up into smaller plots.

The commercial bourgeoisie could be found in the countryside as well as in the town, a good example being the millers of the Eure or Etampes valleys. Big merchants in the towns bought national properties to use as collateral for loans, to enhance their power and social position, or to use as warehouses or, on occasion, factory sites. Between 1790 and 1805 some eighty-two entrepreneurs in the cotton trade purchased first-round properties throughout France, according to Serge Chassagne (*La naissance de l'industrie cotonnière en France,* 1986).

The Revolution thus spelled an end to the concentration of landed wealth in France, but it also slowed improvements in the farming of that land. Was the nationalization responsible for blocking a capitalist revolution in French agriculture? The answer appears to be no, on two counts. First, as Farcy has shown, the most prosperous farmers abandoned the eighteenth-century reliance on extensive cultivation, which had been linked to the growing concentration of land, in favor of more intensive agriculture: fields were no longer allowed to lie fallow; artificial pastures were created; and both the quality and quantity of the sheep flock were improved by the introduction of merinos and crossbreeding of existing flocks with good merino stock (between roughly 1786 and 1800). By the end of the Empire more than two-thirds of the flock in the Beauce had been replaced. Livestock provided fertilizer for the soil, thereby increasing grain yields enough to cover ground rents. Second, despite longstanding beliefs to the contrary, it is not true that peasant smallholders were a tenuous, backward group. Peasants with small plots did aspire to acquire land enough to ensure them independence, and many bought small lots of properties confiscated from émigrés in Years II and III. These acquisitions, together with opportunities made available to rural folk by certain protoindustrial forms of work organization, did ensure that people remained on the land who might otherwise have left much sooner for industrial work in the cities. This slowed the rural exodus, so that one does not find the rapid increase in the ratio of urban to rural population that is so characteristic of industrialization in countries other than France. Nevertheless, recent studies (see Ronald Hubscher, *Annales ESC,* January–March 1985) of small- to medium-sized and multifamily farms in nineteenth-century France suggest that the Revolution resulted in changes in family structure, inheritance, and pooling of incomes that enabled families to compete quite well, keep up with progress in agricultural methods, and specialize as necessary to meet the demands of the market.

Other recent work has altered our picture of the period. Christian Bonnet, in his study of the Bouches-du-Rhône, has discerned a tendency for large properties to be broken up as a result of peasant demand for new plots. In the Arles region, for example, which Michel Vovelle terms "a huge expanse of large or even very large estates," large properties owned by the Order of Malta and the Benedictines were subdivided, apparently resulting in economic calamity: livestock herds disappeared, leading to a shortage of fertilizer, which reduced yields. Although the number of small landowners increased, the hopes of the vast majority of peasants were frustrated. Those who profited most from the sales were the most prosperous farmers, along with lawyers, doctors, notaries, and merchants. In Marseilles fifty-nine percent of the land sold went to people in commerce, with manufacturers among the major purchasers. For example, twenty-two soap makers acquired urban lands and built a factory, ending worries that their leases would not be renewed and they would have to move their operations to a new location.

Guy Lemarchand, in *La fin du féodalisme* (1985), has found that in the Cany district 3,370 hectares of first-round national properties were sold to 682 buyers, and 1,759 hectares of second-round properties were divided among 357 buyers. "All told, 47.5 percent of the total land area was sold in lots of more than 30 hectares to 4.3 percent of the buyers, chiefly prosperous farmers together with a few townsfolk from Rouen, Le Havre, and Saint-Valéry. Still, significant numers of small plots were bought by relatively modest peasants living in the communes where the land was located: 76.5 percent of the buyers purchased 22.03 percent of the land in lots of 5 hectares or less." So the rich became richer, while the poor remained hungry for land. Nevertheless, more people owned land than ever before: "Probably for the first time in centuries, the proportion of the land owned by peasants increased, while the classes that had been privileged before the Revolution suffered some significant blows."

A large proportion of the national properties was acquired by merchants, a fact whose long-term consequences for the evolution of the society, the economy, and popular attitudes have been interpreted in many contradictory ways. Some commentators treat it as an early sign of France's reluctance to embrace a modern capitalist economy in which capital naturally flows into the most productive investments. Others see it as yet another triumph of a social system based on ground rents. Still others regard it as a sign that France's reactionary elite chose to bury its wealth in the ground rather than put it to work. The reality was surely more complex than these simplistic views would allow. To be sure, the rising bourgeoisie continued to feel the pull of a persistent ideal: that of the gentleman who lived on his rents without working. The view that finance and commerce were merely a means of acquiring wealth, a "purgatory" to be endured in order to gain access to a more honorable social status, remained firmly rooted in France, despite the existence of numerous commercial and manufacturing dynasties in the eighteenth and nineteenth centuries—dynasties whose members were proud of the economic role they played and conscious of the prestige they derived from continued success. But during the Revolution and afterward, in the time of Napoleon, there were also many other reasons why men of commerce found it attractive to invest in land.

Some of these reasons were political. After 1789 the view of social hierarchy and political participation that prevailed in France made it necessary for the merchant to establish himself as a landowner if he wished to play a political role. More than one merchant bought large amounts of national properties out of a desire to gain prominence and be recognized as a natural political leader. Such a decision could lead to a career in the government or legislature just as easily as to retirement in idle comfort.

Economic and military factors also played a part. Commercial firms engaged in maritime trade or doing business with colonial plantations were forced to invest in land as long as the war continued. When peace finally returned, two possible courses of action presented themselves. Money temporarily invested in land could be reinvested in commerce: the Begouëns of Le Havre did so with great success. Or livestock raising or wine making might be deemed more profitable under the conditions prevailing in the new international marketplace: many merchants in Maine and Languedoc came to just this conclusion.

In making such a decision structural factors played an important part. Many mercantile and even manufacturing operations had been built around rural properties, which were not distinct from or antagonistic to but an integral part of the business. For a long time availability of long-term loans or lines of credit depended on the ability to provide collateral. Gérando, eulogizing Scipion Perier at the Society to Encourage National Industry in 1821, remarked: "It is always useful for a great commercial house to call upon a base of landed wealth to secure its credit." In the same eulogy Gérando shrewdly analyzed the diverse nature of the operations conducted by these businesses: "Especially nowadays it is a great advantage to combine industrial production with banking operations. In this way a business can sell the output of its own factories; it can better ensure the flow of raw materials and supplies; and it can always find a lucrative use for its capital. The leading firms in the capital are a fine example of this principle. This view was shared by Scipion Perier." The trading firm that owned its own farms could assure itself of a steady source of supply on favorable terms. Bordeaux wine merchants owned their own vineyards, for example, many of them acquired at the time of the confiscations. And property in the Charente played an integral part in the operations of the Depont firm, as Robert Forster has described. Farm revenues were seen as providing a steady source of income, safe from unpredictable and severe fluctuations in exchange rates. Such considerations may well have numbered among the more important reasons why Paris bankers so avidly acquired land—not only châteaux and parks but also large farms yielding significant quantities of grain—which enabled them to supplant the old nobility of court and Parlement as the dominant presence in the country around the capital.

There is one aspect of the history of the national properties about which scholars have had little to say, namely, its effects on urban growth and transformation, given the fact that urban real estate (buildings as well as land) was affected by nationalization. Paris offers the most striking example. According to an estimate made in December 1795, first-round properties (confiscated from the Church and the crown) made up more than one-eighth of the total area of the city and were valued at more than 100 million livres tournois at 1790 prices. This estimate is corroborated by another document (National Archives F 19 863), which puts the annual revenue from ecclesiastical property in Paris at 3 million livres (including 2.3 million from abbeys, priories, and other communities and more than 0.5 million from chapters).

Ecclesiastical properties existed in all sections of old Paris as well as in the suburbs. Frequently they posed an obstacle to urban renewal plans, despite the fact that, in the second half of the eighteenth century, many orders had attempted to raise cash by leasing properties for long periods to speculator-developers. This was especially true of the northern and northwestern outskirts of Paris, as has been shown by the remarkable work of Jeanne Pronteau. The so-called Artists' Plan, drawn up at the behest of the Convention, presumably took account of this new state of affairs. For the first time it became possible to envision laying out new streets, establishing open spaces, and making improvements for which a need had long been felt. But by 1815 few of these plans had actually been carried out. Sales of ecclesiastical properties were slow, and many remained untouched. Social and political conditions were hardly favorable to urban development, and there was in any case a slowing of the boom that had occupied the last thirty years of the Ancien Régime.

The real impact of the nationalizations on the cities is therefore to be found elsewhere: buyers amassed reserves of wealth that could later be turned into cash. In this acquisition of land certain groups of speculators played a key role: bankers and wholesalers, notaries, and tycoons from neutral foreign powers such as Denmark and above all the United States. (The New Yorkers Parker, Thayer, and Harrisson figured prominently in these transactions.) In the very chic first arrondissement (under the old numbering system, equivalent to today's eighth arrondissement) properties were bought by Michel the younger (a banker); Delpont, Bodin, and Cerfbeer (government contractors); Pérignon (a notary); Mosselmann, Danloux-Dumesnil, and Decrétot (wholesale traders and manufacturers); and Lecordier (an exchange agent).

Plans to modernize the capital were also slowed by the decision early in Year IV to halt the sale of properties associated with hospitals and to set aside certain of the nationalized properties for government use, as well as by the nationalization of the city's estates in 1793. In some respects the venerable aspect of certain districts of the city was preserved by the new uses: the government, for example, took over what had been aristocratic houses. The Elysée Palace on the Right Bank is a good example, while the Faubourg Saint-Germain on the Left Bank became the "Ministry District." Meanwhile, celebrated speculators snapped up properties abandoned by émigré aristocrats: Bandelier-Béfort, for example, bought the Hôtel de Beauharnais, and other notable acquisitions were made by Vans, Parker, and Lanchère. In 1811 the Hôtel Matignon (today the office of France's prime minister), once the property of Honoré Grimaldi, the prince of Monaco, was selected for use by high-ranking dignitaries after a long and complicated history in which Talleyrand had a hand; later it was acquired for a short time by the Galliéras. The Quai Malaquais, Quai Voltaire, rue de l'Université, and rue de Grenelle were taken over by the military, the Legion of Honor (Hôtel de Salm), and the ministries of the Interior, Police, Foreign Relations, and Religion.

In 1789 the Revolution was able to count on the support of those who had benefited through the acquisition of national properties, but at the same time nationalization earned it the enmity of the Church and the impoverished nobility. Nevertheless, the decision to sell the national properties was one of the few to be approved by a genuine consensus, and it was of course of great benefit to the state. In the end, "aristocrats" and clergy also profited from this vast redistribution of wealth, along with wealthy commoners and others of more modest station who were at last able to acquire land of their own.

Louis Bergeron

FURTHER READING

Bois, Paul. *Paysans de l'Ouest: Des structures économiques et sociales aux options politiques depuis l'époque révolutionnaire dans la Sarthe.* Le Mans, Paris, and The Hague, 1960; abridged edition, Paris, 1971. See pt. 2, chap. 13, sec. 2.

Bournisien, Charles. "La vente des biens nationaux," *Revue historique*, vol. 99, 1908, 244–266; vol. 100, 1909, 15–46.

Lefebvre, Georges. "La vente des biens nationaux" (1922), in Lefebvre, *Etudes sur la Révolution française.* Paris, 1954; reprinted 1963. Pp. 307–337 (with extensive bibliography).

———— *Les paysans du Nord pendant la Révolution française.* Paris, 1924; reprinted 1972. Pt. 2, chap. 2.

Marion, Marcel. *La vente des biens nationaux pendant la Révolution.* Paris, 1908.

RELATED TOPICS

Assignats
Civil Constitution of the Clergy
Emigrés

Jaurès
Mirabeau

PARIS COMMUNE

The principal result of the *journée* of August 10, 1792, was not so much the fall of the monarchy as the sudden emergence of the rebellious Paris Commune. The attack on the Tuileries put an end to the crisis begun by the king's flight to Varennes. But the seizure of the Hôtel-de-Ville, the seat of the Paris municipal government, opened a new chapter in the history of the Revolution. More than ever before, the country's legal authorities would have to reckon with the people of Paris, who raised a challenge to the legitimacy of the government. While rebellious battalions were still forming up, twenty-eight of forty-eight of the city's sections, acting at the behest of the Quinze-Vingts, delegated *commissaires* with "unlimited powers to save the fatherland" to meet at the Maison Commune.

Before August 10, administration of the capital had initially been entrusted to a number of assemblies created during the summer of 1789. In May 1790 a law provided for regular election of municipal authorities, who proved to be representatives of the first generation of revolutionaries, concerned mainly with halting recurrent disturbances and shoring up the new institutions. Elections late in 1791 proved crucial: Pétion succeeded Bailly as mayor, Jacobins and Cordeliers made a discreet entry into the city council, and the authority of the principal magistrates was seriously undermined. These changes partially explain why the legal authorities proved so easy to topple on August 10. The violence of the insurrection impressed most municipal leaders with the need for a prudent retreat, especially since their real authority had largely collapsed in the weeks prior to the rebellion of the sections. In effect, the Commune of August 10 had been in existence since July 26, meeting in ad hoc assemblies created by the sections to draft petitions calling for the removal of the king.

This situation was not entirely unprecedented. Before May 1790 there had been a series of skirmishes between parallel assemblies in the districts, which claimed to represent the "true commune," and the legal authorities, suggesting that control of the capital, the seat of the legislature, was an essential objective on the road to power. What had been an effective barricade on that road was overcome on August 10, and nothing more stood between the people and its representatives, Paris and the state.

The Commune, which managed to hold the legitimate government in check for many long weeks, was composed of Paris radicals of every sort. Most, particularly those involved in preparations for the insurrection of August 10, were activist leaders of their respective sections, such as Huguenin, Pâris, and Truchon. Alongside them were many Jacobins, the best known of whom would be elected to the Convention three weeks later: Robespierre, Léonard Bourdon, Billaud-Varenne, Fabre d'Eglantine, Tallien, and Laignelot. Other Jacobins, such as J.-J. Lubin and Arthur, continued to play a leading role in the Commune until Thermidor. Future Hébertists, from Père Duchesne to Pache and Vincent, were also represented, as was the Orleanist Choderlos de Laclos, whose presence accounts for the Commune's support, in September, of Philippe-Egalité's election to the Convention. Also, despite Roland's opposition to the Commune, several of his friends were members, including Restout, in charge of the Garde-Meuble, the future mayor Chambon, and the journalist Louvet. More surprising was the presence of the former Feuillant André Chénier. Thus the Commune was a composite group, but it was destined to lose much of its diversity after Jacobin sympathizers gained both the chairmanship and the secretaryship of the municipal council and imposed the Club's discipline.

The Commune of August 10 did not suddenly materialize out of thin air. Some sans-culottes had held office since 1790, a few even since 1789. For local activists August 10 was a chance for collective advancement. Massive purges had left many positions unfilled. Revenge was possible: Malbeste-Champertois, for example, had been sacked as battalion commander for his district in 1790, but on August 10 he was able to take back what was rightfully "his," winning election to the département as well as the Commune. Théophile Mandar, previously a professional troublemaker and one of the very few republicans in the very moderate Temple section, was suddenly thrust to the fore. Most of the men elected in August reaped the dividends of reputations earned in earlier battles: Juste-Concedieu, who had made a name for himself as the reformer of the Mont-de-Piété, became "boss" of the Arsenal section. The lawyer Pépin-Desgrouettes, who had gained notoriety as the defender of artisans and workers in the faubourgs, of sturdy Les Halles laborers, and even of the Périer brothers, availed himself of the first opportunity to assume much-desired responsibilities. On the whole, Commune members were a fair cross section of working-class Paris, together with a few well-known orators from the clubs and one or two unsavory characters, such as Méhée and Boursault.

Brought to power by force of arms, the Commune was able to exploit its capital of terror. Within a few days, opponents were purged from the sections and the départemental council, the National Guard was reformed, and the press muzzled. By August 11 the Commune was in control of Paris and ready to confront the weakened legal government. The Legislative Assembly proved quite docile, however, and simply converted the Commune's decrees into law while renouncing its own decisions. Although the Assembly had decided to "lodge" the royal family at the Ministry of Justice, the Commune, simply by making its wishes known, persuaded the deputies to incarcerate the king at the Temple instead. On August 17, in much the same fashion, the Assembly overruled token opposition and voted to try the "conspirators" of August 10. The Commune sought to achieve several objectives through several weeks' harassment of the deputies. It served as the "military wing" of the

Jacobins in their battle for power with the Brissotins. At the same time it consolidated its position as the uncontested leader of the insurrection by eliminating any possibility of militant opposition in the sections. (Not without occasional hostility, however: here and there, people took umbrage at its power.) It had little room for maneuver. Tension had to be kept high to preclude any movement toward "moderation," yet the capital's day-to-day problems had to be dealt with, so that before long the Commune found itself behaving like any governmental agency.

By the end of August the Legislative Assembly felt strong enough to attempt a mild counteroffensive: it challenged the sacking and replacement of members of the départemental council. Several sections simultaneously recalled the *commissaires* appointed on August 10 on the grounds that an authority established in the midst of a violent crisis should not be perpetuated once order was reestablished. With this backing, the Assembly issued an order on August 30 that the Commune be replaced, but when the current incumbents made a menacing appearance in the hall the order was effectively nullified. The next day Tallien, the assistant prosecutor, appeared to point out that the municipal council "had issued no important order that was not preceded or followed by a decree" of the Legislative Assembly. The Assembly could not order the Commune to disband unless it was willing to attack those from whom it derived its legitimacy, "the people who made the revolution of July 14 and who consolidated it on August 10." As long as the air remained full of shrewdly planted rumors of conspiracy and treason, the Commune remained invulnerable. The apocalyptic proclamation of September 2 calling Parisians to arms to repel an alleged invader demonstrated that the Commune was willing to sow panic to stifle the least sign of opposition.

Were the prison massacres part of this strategy of provocation? Some observers, determined to find the Commune guilty of high crimes, stress the reorganization of its Surveillance Committee, which Marat joined at the end of August, and the circular of September 3, which urged the provinces to follow the lead of the capital. Others, equally determined to exonerate the Commune, emphasize attempts by members of the municipal council to halt the executions, supposedly thwarted by unnamed executioners. By way of evidence for the prosecution, it is worth noting that the dubious independence of the Maratist committee enabled the Commune to keep clear of a bloody operation while silencing its terrified adversaries and thus increasing its power. In the end, however, the continuing massacres diminished the Commune's influence. The Legislative Assembly, slow to react, emerged from the affair stronger than before, as the public's revulsion against the excessive violence grew steadily. Afterward, for a time, sentiment in the sections tended to favor "security of persons and property." Deprived of the support of a part of its militant base, the Commune entered a long period of decline. Other factors were at work besides the desire for a restoration of order, which, as persistent disorders demonstrated, the Commune was unable to achieve. Radicals in the sections had enlisted in the army, clearing the way for the return of many who had abandoned the political arena after August 10. In addition, the Convention was about to convene, and it was imperative that the city remain relatively calm so as not to isolate further a Paris delegation already under fire from provincial deputies.

Forced to take the defensive, the Commune responded boldly. On September 18 it launched an investigation of its own Surveillance Committee, effectively throwing it to the wolves. On September 25 it similarly abandoned the *commissaires* who had represented it in the départements, going so far as to say to the Convention: "If they exceeded their authority, it is up to you to punish them." Thus scapegoats were chosen to bear the blame for past excesses. Yet even this was not enough. Several incidents in October and November 1792 showed that the Commune remained vulnerable. When it attempted to correspond directly with other municipalities, there was a hue and cry in the Convention, which accused the Commune of attempting to usurp the rightful role of the government, once more exceeding its authority. The November elections were followed by still more impassioned debate.

The moment of truth had come. Taking advantage of the changing political situation in the sections, the Legislative Assembly just before disbanding had ordered new municipal elections. In a difficult situation the Commune attempted to shore up its position by decreeing that primary assemblies would proceed by voice vote. But the Girondin members of the Convention, backed by moderates like Cambon, always hostile to Parisian pretensions, prevailed in their insistence upon secret balloting. The first results confirmed the Commune's fears. On October 15, 1792, Pétion, sent to the Convention the previous month by the département of Eure-et-Loir, was reelected mayor of Paris by an overwhelming majority. The meaning of this was clear in light of the innumerable insults to which the Commune had subjected him since August 10: by confirming Pétion in a post that he had occupied for a year, the electorate was disavowing the Commune. Compelled to choose between the mayor's office and his post as deputy, however, Pétion opted for the latter. Thereafter, it took no fewer than four rounds of balloting to reach a decision. The candidates supported by the Jacobins—Hérault de Séchelles, Antonelle, and ultimately Lhuillier—were all beaten, and finally, at the end of November, it was Chambon, a moderate close to the Gironde, who was elected. Then the Jacobins failed again in new elections to the municipal council: of 288 incumbents, only 45 were reelected. Even more remarkable, 28 municipal magistrates who held their posts before August 10 now withdrew. The final elections, notable for a low turnout, proved more favorable to the radicals: Chaumette was elected prosecutor and Hébert and Réal assistants.

Under Chambon's administration the Commune abandoned its once prominent political role and confined itself essentially to police and administrative chores, and above all to the ever more urgent problem of supplying the city's basic needs. Chambon's resignation early in 1793, after the execution of Louis XVI, disrupted this fragile equilibrium. The mayor's resignation came not a moment too soon: Pache, elected minister of war four months earlier, had been removed from office, and on February 14 he was elected mayor of Paris.

renet, *Louis XVI Swears Allegiance to the Constitution on the Altar of the Fatherland.* Musée des Beaux-Arts, Quimper.

Monsiau, *The Abolition of Slavery Proclaimed to the Convention on 16 Pluviôse, Year II*. Musée Carnavalet, Paris.

National Assembly, Session of September 14, 1791: The King's Speech. Bibliothèque Nationale, Paris.

Patriotic Priest
Taking the Civic Oath
in Good Faith.
Engraving.
Musée de l'Arsenal, Paris.

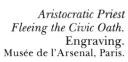

Aristocratic Priest
Fleeing the Civic Oath.
Engraving.
Musée de l'Arsenal, Paris.

essieurs les Noirs. Bibliothèque Nationale, Paris.

Revolutionary Calendar, Ventôse.
Musée Carnavalet, Paris.

Revolutionary Calendar, Vendémiaire.
Musée Carnavalet, Paris.

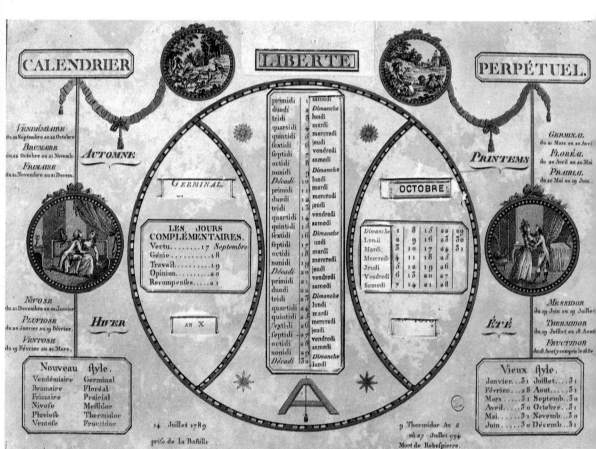

Revolutionary Calendar. Musée Carnavalet, Paris.

...cession of the Goddess Reason.
...iothèque Nationale, Paris.

Béricourt,
...ascarade of the Common People.
Watercolor.
Bibliothèque Nationale, Paris.

Demachy, *Festival of the Supreme Being, June 8, 1794.* Musée Carnavalet, Paris.

Meeting of the Jacobins, January 1792. Engraving. Bibliothèque Nationale, Paris.

Revolutionary Committee: The Arrest of Several Members. Musée Carnavalet, Paris.

Duplessis, *The Maximum*. Musée Carnavalet, Paris.

Central Committee of Public Safety of the Year II. Bibliothèque Nationale, Paris.

The new mayor was one of the most enigmatic figures of the Revolution. Once a collaborator of Necker's, Pache was late in entering politics. In 1792 he had joined his close friend Roland at the Ministry of the Interior, where he proved an efficient assistant, purging the ministry of its moderates after August 10 and establishing a "bureau of the public spirit" that served as something like a press office through which the minister sought to influence public opinion. After his resignation Roland did not forget Pache's excellent service, and the Girondins saw to it that he was named minister of war. Their hopes for him had been high, and their disappointment was no doubt equally great; for Pache quickly abandoned them and allied himself with extremist elements, filling offices in the ministry with Hébertist militants. What makes Pache a mysterious figure, however, was not this shift in loyalties—a commonplace of the revolutionary period—but the immunity he seems to have enjoyed in spite of it. Though accused many times of involvement in conspiracies and even of plotting to make himself "Great Judge" or dictator, he was never seriously threatened, much less tried. Père Duchesne and Babeuf lost their heads, but Pache emerged from the Revolution unscathed.

Upon taking up his new post as mayor, he found a situation that had been restored more or less to normal. Prosecution of those responsible for the September massacres had been halted; the *fédérés* who had congregated in Paris as a kind of praetorian guard had dispersed; the outcome of the king's trial had weakened the moderates' hand. The predictable hostility of the municipal council elected in November was soon overcome. The November elections had in any case been provisional, and new ones were held early in 1793, with results less favorable to the moderates. Votes of nomination and censure continued until July 1793, and Pache had every reason to be pleased with the outcome: 111 of the 144 men who had been members of the council at the end of 1792 were replaced. Nevertheless, the Commune of 1793 was very different from its counterpart in 1792, not only in its composition but also in its internal power structure. In 1792 the mayor was a mere figurehead without real authority. In 1793, however, all important decisions were made at the top by a small group consisting of Pache, Chaumette, and Hébert and only then submitted to the council for formal approval. This concentration of authority was coupled with relative autonomy from the Jacobin Club, proof that the Hébertist leaders of the Commune were in fact following their own agenda. If their chief ambition was still to gain power, they could no longer hope to do so by mounting a frontal assault on the Convention as they had done the year before against the Legislative Assembly. The battle was now being waged within the Convention itself, where Paris was represented by a delegation of deputies. The Commune was obliged to reckon with this new reality, and it had no hope of ruling without forging at least a tactical alliance with the Jacobin deputies, who needed help to defeat the Girondin opposition.

From the riots of February 25, 1793, to the disturbances of March 10, the Commune demonstrated that it could quell the violence of a movement that originated outside it by assuming leadership, shifting the issue from food and other basic needs to the more stable categories of politics, and stamping out isolated attempts to radicalize the protest. Temporarily powerless to halt the looting, the Commune mobilized the citizens of Paris by issuing a proclamation on March 8 concerning the military reverses suffered by the French army, which it deliberately exaggerated (just as it had done in August 1792). Then, claiming to interpret the wishes of its mobilized citizenry, it called upon the Convention to vote on certain terrorist decrees. With the principle of a Revolutionary Tribunal approved on March 9, there was no great difficulty thwarting the efforts of the enragé Varlet to turn the debate back to the question of food supplies. The Commune emerged from this episode even stronger than before. Vergniaud expressed his satisfaction, and Garat spoke at length in praise of Mayor Pache. Not only had the Commune reestablished order; even more, it demonstrated that it would be a key player in the final confrontation between the Jacobin and Girondin deputies.

The Jacobins gave the signal: on April 5, the Club approved a petition to the départements requesting that they recall all deputies who in the king's trial had voted in favor of allowing an appeal to the people. The Commune followed up, but only after an incident in which it showed some signs of independence: on April 1 it had agreed to support an insurrectional committee formed at the Evêché, but it had been forced to back down in the face of intense opposition from the Jacobins, who disapproved of any initiative that had not received their prior consent. Having accepted this discipline, the Commune on April 15 submitted to the Convention a petition demanding that the twenty-two leading Girondin deputies be expelled. The background of this petition clearly shows how the general will was "manufactured" by a small committee. Drafted by an informal assembly of *commissaires* from the sections, the petition was then submitted to the latter for approval. Paradoxically, only thirty-five of forty-eight sections offered their support. That was enough, however, for the petition to be characterized as expressing the "wishes of Paris." When a fair portion of the Convention reacted with indignation, however, the Commune decided that the wisest course would be to make certain its own troops were in line by insisting that members of the municipal council countersign the document, even though, the night before, the petition had been announced as the work of the sections and the Commune. It seems clear that the municipal council had been kept in the dark, since a week later nearly half of its members still had not signed.

After an insurrectional committee—this time duly approved—met at the Evêché on May 16, the Commune called for a meeting of the sections' revolutionary committees at the same place, ostensibly to consider two issues: a compulsory loan and recruiting an army to send to the Vendée. The coexistence of the two committees allowed the Commune to take part in preparations for the insurrection, yet be able to claim innocence if anything went wrong. Thus, after one of the committees demanded on May 20 that the twenty-two Girondins be not merely expelled but executed, Pache appeared twice before the Convention to assure the deputies that the Commune was in no way responsible and in fact condemned the move. This overt extremism actually revealed the existence of a more radical group lurking about the fringes of the quasi-official organizations meeting at the Evêché. At the same time the Commune had to contend with a movement that had arisen in the sections in support of the threatened deputies. Force had to be used to expel opponents from the compromised sections. Arrests were made, but the support of the sections was still not assured. On May 26 the Commune attempted to organize a demonstration to call for the release of Hébert, who had been arrested two days earlier, but it was able to mobilize only sixteen sections.

In such an uncertain situation quick action was of the essence. On May 26 Robespierre made his famous speech to the Jacobins calling for an "insurrection" of "patriotic" deputies against their allegedly treasonous colleagues. He made no reference to pressure from the street: that aspect of the movement—the organization of "popular" pressure—was the responsibility of the Commune. The Commune dithered, meanwhile, because it knew that the outcome of such an unspontaneous uprising was very much in doubt and that the sections were divided. On May 28 Robespierre was obliged to step into the breach, and in no uncertain terms he urged the Commune to commit itself to the success of the operation and make sure things did not get out of hand: "If the Commune does not join with the people and forge a close alliance with it, it will be violating the most important of its obligations. It will no longer deserve the reputation it has enjoyed until now of being a friend of the people." In no doubt as to the threat that hung over it, the Commune decided to act: on May 30 Dobsent was dispatched to the Evêché. There he took control of the small central committee that had been organized and placed it under the command of the municipality. By the morning of May 31 the Commune was firmly in control of the movement. Efficiently aided by Hanriot, the Commune kept its part of the bargain: during the *journée* of May 31 and its sequel of June 2 it was able to provide a menacing mob that could be manipulated at will, because in fact it was not a mob but a disciplined force of shock troops.

With the Jacobins in control in the Convention, the Commune restored order in the streets. The Evêché committee was abolished and calls for "further insurrection" were resisted. Disturbances persisted for several more weeks, sustained by the enragés, who exploited the fact that the question of food supplies was once again the order of the day. A response was not long in coming. After intervention by the Jacobins, Jacques Roux was expelled from the Cordeliers on June 30 and the next day was censured by the Commune, of which he was a member. Late in August the Commune went back on the offensive and ordered him arrested, but it was only after the September "days" that a decisive blow could be struck against the enragés: with Roux imprisoned in Sainte-Pélagie, Varlet and Leclerc quickly removed themselves from the scene.

The disturbances of September 4 and 5, 1793, proved that the Commune was still powerful, able to rival the influence of even the most extreme of the extremists and seize leadership of popular demonstrations while refocusing demands from the social realm to the political one. It experienced a brief moment of difficulty on September 4, when a crowd laid siege to the Hôtel-de-Ville, but it pretended to resign itself to the situation and on the fifth led the rioters to the Convention, where the crowd most opportunely seemed to forget its demands of the night before, following what by now was a well-orchestrated scenario for dealing with such emergencies. But the chief beneficiary of this new demonstration of the Commune's strength was the government and its committees. Collot d'Herbois, at this point close to the Hébertists, was elected to the Committee of Public Safety as a concession to the rioters. Thus "Hébertism" found a place in the government, but not the Hébertists! In the wake of June 2, the September events and their aftermath dealt a fatal blow to the Commune, which soon bore the consequences of the strengthening of the central government at the expense of all the quasi-official bodies that owed their legitimacy to the insurrection of August 1792. After June 2 there were ominous signs of what lay ahead. Bouchotte, the minister of war, was nearly fired later in June, and the Commune was forced to use all its influence to keep him in his job. In August it became clear that there would be no quid pro quo for the services rendered on May 31: Hébert had been overwhelmingly defeated in the voting for the position of minister of the interior. From that moment on, the Commune was doomed. By February 1793 it had become an instrument of the Jacobins in the Convention, used to terrorize their political enemies. But once the Terror was officially the order of the day, the Constitution suspended, and the government declared "revolutionary until peace returns," the Commune became useless, and because it was politically valueless it was also dangerous (for it might be tempted to try some risky venture).

Faced with the erosion of its authority, the Commune became involved, slowly and cautiously at first but later enthusiastically, in the de-Christianization campaign that culminated in November 1793 and was over by December. It staged the abjuration of Bishop Gobel on November 23 and closed the churches of Paris. The roots of this episode were many; its proximate causes are still unknown. For the Commune it was a gamble on the future direction of the Revolution, a bet that it would turn more radical and assure the Commune's victory over Robespierre and the Convention. On November 21, however, the Incorruptible cracked down hard and forced the Commune's leaders to beat an inglorious retreat.

The rout had already begun. A short while earlier, on October 10, 1793, all officially constituted bodies had been declared subordinate to the Committee of Public Safety, and on the twenty-sixth the election of new municipal councils had been postponed indefinitely. Placed under surveillance, the Commune also had lost control of one essential cog in its machine: the revolutionary committees, which it had turned into veritable executive agencies for manipulating the sectional assemblies. On September 17 it was decreed that the committees would henceforth report directly to the Committee of General Security, bypassing the municipal authorities, who attempted to resist but in vain. The decree of December 4 effectively destroyed the Commune by eliminating the important post of prosecutor and replacing it with a "national agent" appointed by the Committee of Public Safety and subject to its exclusive authority. Chaumette became nothing but a go-between linking the Committee to a Commune that was little by little being cut down to size.

Between December 1793 and March 14, 1794, the Commune lay low and allowed less prominent activists to take the lead while it attempted to reestablish a network of sectional clubs and through them its own base of support, which the terrorist decrees had demolished. The Commune was itself divided. With the Hébertist leadership weakened, the municipal council, which for the past year had allowed Pache, Chaumette, and Hébert to carry on pretty much as they pleased, reasserted its independence in order to protect its own political future. After the arrest of Vincent and Ronsin in December, the leaders of the Commune, aware of the council's ambivalence, abandoned the Hôtel-de-Ville and began meeting at the Club des Cordeliers. The Commune was no longer the ideal instrument with which to provoke an uprising in Paris in order to bring pressure to bear on the Convention.

After the collapse of an abortive conspiracy the Hébertists were arrested on March 14, 1794, without causing much of a stir. The Commune did nothing. Could it have reacted? Would the people of Paris still have taken to the streets? The answer is by no means certain. Hanriot and Pache were spared. The latter, arrested on May 10, was conveniently "forgotten" in prison. Hanriot served the Robespierrist municipality with as much zeal as he had served the Hébertist one, but the second time around he did not escape so handily.

Under Payan, who was named national agent, discipline was strict. Forty members of the municipal council were purged, and Lescot-Fleuriot was named mayor of Paris by the central government. This short-lived municipal government was a docile auxiliary of the Committee of Public Safety, but it was in no sense the heir of the insurgents of 1792: the bond between Paris and its Commune had been broken. In 1793 and afterward, the Commune had surely done more for the ambitions of its leaders than for the people of Paris, but whenever the leaders called, the people responded. On June 2 the Convention had been surrounded by 100,000 demonstrators. When the Hébertists were eliminated, however, the Commune's charisma evaporated; its legend was at an end.

On 9 Thermidor Hanriot was able to turn out only 3,400 men to defend the Hôtel-de-Ville, and the Commune's calls for an insurrection to save Robespierre and his codefendants were heeded by only nineteen sections. The Gravilliers section, always a bastion of radicalism in the past, even provided Barras with troops to arrest the proscribed deputies. Disavowed by the people, isolated, and finally defeated, the members of the Commune, some of whom had held their positions without interruption since August 1792, would pay with their lives for their splendid illusions about the past: three-quarters of them went to the guillotine. In the end the capital condemned those who had altered the course of the Revolution begun by the municipal uprising of July 1789.

From August 1792 to 9 Thermidor the Commune had been a symbol of the great days of the Revolution, an incarnation of direct democracy, an ever-present menace looming over the elected Assembly, and a constant battleground for ambitious politicians and revolutionists. It had welded the sectional movement into a potent force, and, using it as an instrument, the Jacobins had been able to seize power in September 1792 and later, after May

527

31, 1793, to achieve unchallenged domination. The Commune had also created a powerful administrative apparatus, which had achieved great things on a daily basis despite the inexperience of most of its employees.

Apart from its political battles, the Commune was responsible for managing the everyday affairs of the largest city in France, fortunately with the aid of the old *corps municipal,* which survived August 10. Experienced men such as Bidermann in the Relief Office and Cousin and Garin in the Supply Office stayed at their posts while battles raged around them. The Commune's task became more and more difficult, particularly when it came to maintaining the supply of food: to meet popular demands, it was forced to sell grain for less than it paid suppliers outside the city. In October 1792 it admitted that it had run up a deficit of two million francs and with difficulty received a subsidy from the Convention, which was not unhappy to see the Commune in trouble. The situation remained tenuous: in early December 1792 the municipal storehouses contained only a four-day reserve of flour. Yet owing to its origins and its rhetoric the Commune could not take unpopular measures, and it was therefore compelled to juggle its precarious finances to meet the inescapable daily need for food. By succeeding as well as it did, the Commune avoided serious social unrest, and it was able to redirect popular discontent into the political sphere to its own advantage.

The Commune also served as a buffer protecting the legislature itself. At every demonstration the crowd respected the boundaries set for it and waited patiently for the representatives of the people to satisfy its demands. It was not until Prairial, Year III, by which time the Commune no longer existed, that the "populace" invaded the hall, threatened and insulted deputies, and cut off the head of Féraud. From 1792 to 1794 the Commune had orchestrated the disorders and kept things from getting out of hand while sagely funneling the rage of the populace into the struggle for political power.

Patrice Gueniffey

FURTHER READING

Braesch, Frédéric. *La Commune du dix août 1792: Etude sur l'histoire de Paris du 20 juin au 2 décembre 1792.* Paris, 1911.
Caron, Pierre. *Les massacres de septembre.* Paris, 1935.
Genty, Maurice. *Paris, 1789–1795: L'apprentissage de la citoyenneté.* Paris, 1987.
Procès-verbaux de la Commune de Paris, 1792–1793. Paris, 1894.

RELATED TOPICS

De-Christianization	Marat	Sans-culottes
Girondins	Revolutionary Government	Terror
Hébertists	Revolutionary *Journées*	
Jacobinism	Robespierre	

REVOLUTIONARY ASSEMBLIES

Furetière's eighteenth-century *Dictionary* defines an *assemblée* as "a joining together of a number of people in a specific place for a specific purpose; for example, *Assemblée du Clergé, Assemblée des Etats, assemblée illicite, clandestine.*" Prerevolutionary France was indeed familiar with assemblies of all three kinds. With the contract of Poissy (1560) the king had granted the clergy the privilege of gathering in assembly once every five years. The so-called *pays d'Etats,* regions of France that retained their Provincial Estates, held annual assemblies whose principal function was to pay the king the amount he claimed as his due in taxes—although not without haggling. But when the king wished to consult with all of his provinces, he had two ways of proceeding, which were in fact more similar than the formal differences between them might lead one to believe: the *assemblées des notables* and the Estates General. The assemblies of notables enabled the monarch to achieve a certain consensus when faced with a decision of fundamental importance, yet without resorting to the cumbersome and complex electoral procedures required to convoke the Estates General. In 1506, when Louis XII desired approval of his decision to break off his daughter's engagement to the future Emperor Charles V; in 1527, when François I resolved not to keep promises he had made in the Treaty of Madrid; in 1560, to examine the statute on Protestants; in 1596 in Rouen; and again in 1627–1628 in Paris, assemblies of notables were convoked. But between 1628 and 1787 no such assemblies were held. The last Estates General prior to 1789 was in 1614. To contemporaries the differences between the two types of assembly were less striking than they seem to us. Although delegates were chosen by different means (nomination for the assemblies of notables, election for the Estates General), the three orders (clergy, nobility, and Third Estate) were represented in both, and groundwork for the meetings was laid either through open letters or *cahiers de doléances,* formal grievances submitted to the king by the various estates.

From these ancient institutions the Revolution was born. From the moment Calonne announced in February 1787 that an assembly of notables would be held, the response throughout the country was swift and enthusiastic. People saw it as the possible beginning of a system of representative government, harking back all the way to the ancient Carolingian *champs de mars* and *champs de mai.* A chronicler wrote: "The great news of the day is the convocation of a national assembly, which is creating quite a sensation. We are as admiring as we are grateful to see the monarch calling the nation to his side." Louis XVI was compared to Charlemagne. Never mind the misconception involved in thinking of 144 persons, most of whom were nobles, as representatives of the nation. The image was more revolutionary than the reality. When the Assembly of Notables failed to resolve the crisis, demands for a convocation of the Estates General became all the more urgent.

The creation of provincial assemblies, an idea of Calonne's that Loménie de Brienne expanded with the assignment of new responsibilities (edict of June 17, 1788), was either too much or too little. The first revolutionary assembly was held at Vizille in Dauphiné on July 21, 1788. Dominated by the Third Estate, the assembly of Vizille demanded that the representation of that estate be doubled and voting by head instituted. On August 8 Brienne announced the convocation of the Estates General but made no reference to these demands. With a "council minute" dated December 27 Necker agreed to a doubling of the representation of the Third Estate but pointed out that tradition dictated voting by estate rather than by head. This was precisely the crucial issue, however: voting by estate ensured that conservatives—the clergy and nobility combined—would hold a majority, whereas voting by head raised the possibility that the bourgeoisie would be able to act in concert with allies among the lower-ranking clergy and liberal nobility. On May 5, 1789, the Estates met at the Palace of Versailles in the Salle des Menus Plaisirs. Conflict smoldered for a month before the Third Estate took the first steps toward revolution: on June 10 it invited the other two estates to join with it in verifying the credentials of all the deputies. On June 20 the deputies, upon finding the Salle des Menus Plaisirs closed, repaired to the Jeu de Paume (Tennis Court) and took the famous oath: "The National Assembly, in consideration of the fact that it was called upon to establish the Constitution of the Realm . . . decrees that all members of this Assembly shall take an oath never to disband, and to meet wherever circumstances may require, until such time as the Constitution of the Realm is established and settled upon solid foundations." On June 23 Louis XVI issued a solemn order to the assembly to disband and to deliberate separately by estates. The assembly refused and declined to rescind its previous decrees: "Orders cannot be issued to the assembled nation." On June 27, yielding to the evidence, the king issued an invitation to "his loyal clergy and his loyal nobility." And thus in response to the revolutionary initiative of the deputies of the Third Estate was born the National Constituent Assembly, the first of the Revolution's three great assemblies.

***

It is hard to say precisely when the Constituent Assembly was born. Was it on May 5, June 17, or June 20? In any case it lasted for more than two years, until September 30, 1791. It is easier to ascertain the social and occupational backgrounds of its members than to state with certainty how many there were at any given moment. As time went by, some deputies—clergymen, nobles, and bourgeois—emigrated, in effect renouncing membership. Emigration came in waves, with a first peak after July 14, a second after the October Days of 1789, and another after the king's attempt to flee, which ended in failure at Varennes in June 1791. Yet these great waves should not obscure the fact that there were quieter but steadier ripples of emigration all along, something of a constant trickle.

As for the social composition, the inequalities are striking. The three orders represented were the same as in 1614: clergy, nobility, and Third Estate. There were only forty-six bishops among the clergy, the bulk of the estate being made up of lower-ranking clergymen, primarily parish priests. Among the nobility, nearly two-thirds were from middling to minor provincial aristocracy. The large contingent of deputies from the Third Estate included no peasants, artisans, or workers, just as in 1614. Hence it represented the "bourgeoisie"; but what bourgeoisie? Along with merchants and rentiers, the majority consisted of men of the law. The provinces tapped their leading orators: Mounier and Barnave represented Dauphiné and the assembly of Vizille, Touret and Bouzot stood for Normandy, Lanjuinais and Le Chapelier for Brittany. Eloquent speakers such as Robespierre from Arras and Rabaut Saint-Etienne from Nîmes helped hasten the transformation of the Estates General into the Constituent Assembly. Paris bowed to the prestige of the academician Bailly. All of these men were financially well off, experienced, and mature. All deferred to some extent to the priority of the liberal nobility. Incidentally, two members of the first two orders were elected to the ranks of the third: abbé Sieyès in Paris and the vicomte de Mirabeau in Provence. A revolution of lawyers, if you will, but lawyers invested with the prestige of the nobility.

The differences in these first months of the Constituent Assembly were not so much social as political. In assuming the leadership of the "patriotic" party, Lafayette, Duport, and Alexandre de Lameth lent it the aura of their prestige. Lafayette's role was particularly important, for he was the "Hero of Two Continents" as well as a member of the Assembly of Notables which in 1788 had called for the convocation of a national assembly, and for nearly a year he had been the idol of the crowds. Of the fifty-four presidents of the Constituent Assembly, thirty-three belonged to the nobility. Among the presidents of the Jacobin Club, which was founded in December 1789 by "patriotic" deputies meeting on the rue Saint-Honoré, were not only illustrious commoners but also such aristocrats as the duc d'Aiguillon, Alexandre de Beauharnais, and Victor de Broglie. Thus in late 1789 and throughout 1790 the liberal nobility played an important role. But the deputies who asserted themselves most forcefully in June and July 1789 and who became the leaders of the patriotic party were men of the Third Estate such as Bailly, Barnave, Mounier, Le Chapelier, and Malouet. Opposing the patriotic party was an "aristocratic" party known as the "blacks" (from the color of the queen's cockade). From the beginning this group, led by Cazalès and abbé Maury (primarily the latter, who constantly drew the ire and sarcasm of the democratic press), steadfastly defended the system that had existed prior to the Revolution and refused all concession or compromise.

The unity of the patriotic party broke down in debates that arose after the Assembly had voted on its two most significant accomplishments: the elimination of feudal dues (decrees of August 4 and 11) and the Declaration of the Rights of Man (approved on August 26). In the meantime, however, the deputies had been grappling with the problem of how to organize the government, and it was this issue that caused the first factional split within the patriotic party, and indeed the first sign of dissension within the revolutionary camp. A right wing led by Mounier, Malouet, Clermont-Tonnerre, and Lally-Tollendal and supported by the Necker government wanted to give the king an absolute veto over laws proposed by the Assembly and, further, to adopt a new constitution based on an English-style bicameral legislature with an elected assembly and a hereditary senate. Known as monarchiens, this group shared many of the views of the royal court. By contrast, Duport, Barnave, and Lameth rejected the royal veto and refused to divide the Assembly's power. Despite Lafayette's attempts at mediation, by the end of August the split between the two factions was irrevocable. In the Assembly the monarchiens were reduced to minority status when the deputies voted on September 2 to grant the king a suspensive veto in exchange for a promise that royal approval would be forthcoming for the Assembly's August decrees, and when the proposal to institute a second chamber was defeated by a vote of 849 to 89 (with 100 abstentions). After the October Days a number of monarchiens withdrew from the Assembly altogether, including Mounier, who returned to his native Dauphiné and later emigrated. Others, including Malouet and Clermont-Tonnerre, formed the core of a resistance group within the Assembly, by now meeting in Paris at the Salle du Manège. The historical importance of the monarchiens was greater than the failure of their proposals might suggest. In various forms under various regimes their guiding idea—that of a conservative government led by aristocrats—would endure for a long time, at least until the Burgraves of 1849 and, later, the so-called *république des ducs*. In the short term, however, the monarchiens' break with the left did not win them immediate acceptance by the "blacks" or "aristocrats," for the monarchiens were reluctant to join the emigration.

Buoyed by its new-found majority position in the Assembly, the patriotic party, led by such nobles as Montmorency, Talleyrand-Périgord, and two La Rochefoucaulds but strengthened by the quiet committee work of its bourgeois lawyers, soon began to move away from the two men who had once been its idols: Mirabeau and Lafayette. Mirabeau's talents as an orator had made him one of the Estates General's leading spokesmen. But as early as October 1789 his venal instincts drew him more and more into the orbit of the court. In May 1790 he joined the side of the king in exchange for payment of his debts and a monthly stipend of 6,000 livres. When his treachery was exposed, Mirabeau was discredited, and after his death on April 2, 1791, a pamphlet was sold in the streets of Paris detailing "the high treason of the comte de Mirabeau." As for Lafayette, in the first few months of 1790 his popularity had been immense. Albert Mathiez somewhat misleadingly called him the "mayor of the palace," while Georges Lefebvre dubbed 1790 "the year of Lafayette." True, but by autumn he was making everyone unhappy, both the court (where opposition to him had been stirred up by Mirabeau) and the left, which suspected him of indulging the aristocracy. As a result, leadership of the Assembly's left wing gradually passed to a triumvirate consisting of Alexandre de Lameth, representing the *noblesse d'épée*, Duport, representing the *noblesse de robe*, and Barnave, a lawyer and the cleverest of the three. Supported by the Jacobin Club, of which they were active members, these patriotic deputies were able to accomplish a good deal in just under two years.

The patriotic party was nevertheless headed for a further split. The first signs of tension begin to appear in the spring of 1791 over the issue of the colonies (especially Santo Domingo) and above all over insistent calls to the deputies to forge ahead with the Revolution, calls encouraged by the press and the clubs. A "Tory" party was coming into existence behind Barnave and Duport, and on May 17 the latter set forth the key points of its program: "The Revolution is over. It must be established and protected by combating all excess. Equality must be restricted, liberty reduced, and opinion settled. The Government must be strong, solid, and stable." The king's flight to Varennes precipitated a break. On the grounds that property had to be defended, Barnave supported the fiction that the king had been "abducted." "Are we going to end the Revolution? Are we going to start it over? You have made all men equal before the law. You have consecrated civil and political liberty. You have claimed for the State all that had been robbed from the sovereignty of the people. Any further step would be harmful and frightening. Another step toward equality means the destruction of property." On July 16 virtually all the Jacobin deputies abandoned the Jacobin Club and moved into the convent of the Feuillants, also on rue Saint-Honoré. In the provinces 45 affiliated clubs sided with the Feuillants (as the seceding faction came to be known), while 26 remained loyal to the Jacobins. More than 150 declared themselves in favor of unity, but unity was no longer possible. The Constituent Assembly was obliged to make way for new deputies. Robespierre had secured approval of a resolution that none of the current members would be eligible for reelection to the next Assembly, which was to meet on October 1, 1791. "We have reached the end of the Revolution," the Constituent Assembly proclaimed before disbanding. It mistook its wish for reality.

The new Legislative Assembly had only a short life, divided into two unequal phases. Between October 1791 and August 10, 1792, it discharged its legislative function to the full, though not without internal dissension and external threats. Essentially it gambled on the possibility of coexisting with the king. After August 10, however, it barely limped along until the first meeting of the Convention on September 20.

From the beginning power in France was not divided but diverted into two parallel streams, one of which flowed through the Legislative Assembly, the other through the clubs, to which many of the deputies belonged. Those who had been members of the old Constituent Assembly but who were at odds with the new Legislative Assembly made their influence felt through the clubs. The new deputies, who had held important posts in their départements, districts, and municipalities, came to Paris and joined one or another of the various clubs. One hundred thirty-six chose the Jacobins, 260 the Feuillants. But a majority of more than 300 refused to join either of the two great factions formed by the July split in what had been the patriotic party. This group, like that which later came to be known as the Plain or the Swamp (*Marais*), remained faithful to the principles of 1789 and continued to defend the achievements of the Revolution's first phase. But those achievements were threatened by the court, by the machinations of those around Louis XVI, and by revolutionary pressures from below. Both Louis XVI and the vast majority of deputies wanted war, and a declaration of war was passed on April 20, 1792, with only seven deputies voting against it. But news of the first defeats sparked the insurrection of August 10, an uprising carried out despite the opposition of the Assembly, which had come to be suspected of "moderatism" by the Paris sections and provincial federations. This altered the balance of power both within the legislative body and outside it. The king was reduced to political irrelevance.

In his place the Assembly bestowed executive power on a council of six, of whom only Danton seemed capable of bridging the gulf between the Assembly and the Paris Commune. In any case the Assembly was already doomed, for on August 10, under the prodding of pikes, its members had approved the election of a national convention by universal suffrage. Right and centrist deputies soon vanished from their benches. The political landscape changed dramatically. Having tried in vain to mobilize their provincial supporters, the Feuillants were left without real power. Lafayette turned to the Austrians for refuge but was arrested and imprisoned for several years. Hopes for a great liberal party, for all that they were consonant with the temper of the times, evaporated. Nothing was capable of bridging the chasm between counterrevolution and "democratic" revolution. The latter, as it happens, was embodied in a new center of power, the Commune of Paris, offspring of the insurrectional committee of August 10. Only 248 members were left in the Assembly: shopkeepers, artisans, relatively unimportant members of the legal profession, and functionaries. In the Commune the former actor Collot d'Herbois and the former Oratorian Tallien were receiving a rapid education in politics. Despite the apparent duality of power, with the Assembly and Commune sitting jointly, the only real power belonged to the latter. These six weeks witnessed what historians call "the first Terror": France was invaded; in September there were massacres; and on September 20, the very day that the Legislative Assembly gave way to the Convention, Valmy was recaptured.

*
**

Why a "Convention"? The word, borrowed from English, had been made famous by the Constitutional Convention in America. It designated an assembly invested with power of two kinds: to establish a new constitution (in which respect this was a new constituent assembly) and temporarily to assume sovereign power. Hence this was both a legislative assembly and a source of executive power. Election by universal suffrage was a myth. Only a minority participated in the elections. Men of the right, ranging from "aristocrats" to Feuillants—all those who had been enemies of the Revolution on August

10—were excluded (or excluded themselves). The "passives," those whose right to vote had been eliminated by the Constitution of 1791, either did not know that their right to vote had been restored or were afraid to exercise it. The elections were dominated by men who had gained prominence in the wake of the Revolution, ranging from local and provincial government officials to members of the two previous national assemblies; most of those elected were drawn from this group. Of 749 deputies elected on September 20, nearly 400 had sat in district or département assemblies, 96 had been members of the Constituent Assembly, and 89 of the Legislative Assembly. The Revolution may have devoured certain of its children, but it was an incredibly fertile mother. And it was remarkably steady: amid factional dispute and division it proceeded for the most part along its charted course, from which it diverged only when necessary to skirt the gathering storm. When Sieyès was asked what his role had been during the Terror, he was right to respond: "We survived."

At the end of September 1792 the political lines were still not sharply drawn. Some one hundred deputies who belonged to the Jacobin Club would find themselves at loggerheads in the coming months. That is hardly surprising: except in Paris, where supporters of the August 10 Commune were in control, those elected ranged over the whole spectrum of democratic revolutionaries from future Girondins to future Montagnards. Very soon, however, differences of sensibility and strategy began to emerge. The Brissotins or Girondins, who had dominated the previous assembly, were the best known of the factions and—I am tempted to write—the most elected: Carra seven times, Brissot three times, Condorcet twice. Again, Paris was the exception. Its contingent of deputies included not only Robespierre and Danton but the entire leadership of the Commune: the poet Fabre d'Eglantine, the actor Collot d'Herbois, the professor Billaud-Varenne, and the journalist Camille Desmoulins. Also included were Marat, for all his reluctance, and, despite the opposition of Robespierre, Philippe-Egalité (as the former duc d'Orléans now styled himself). The Girondins dominated the assembly. Champions of revolutionary war, they were heeded because of their undeniable oratorical talents, to which they added the luster of youth and the attractiveness of a certain premature Romanticism. They seduced an assembly in which they did not hold a true majority. Indeed, the majority belonged to an unorganized but powerful group that would persist throughout the Convention, the so-called Plain, dubbed the Swamp by its detractors. Its leaders—Barère, Cambon, Sieyès—supported the Girondins in their defense of property and liberty but split with them over the need to take exceptional measures in order to protect a revolution thought to be in danger from its enemies. Some one hundred deputies backed the Paris delegation: this group came to be known as the Mountain. But it too was divided. Danton cast himself in the role of ardent champion of republican unity, but the Girondins rejected the olive branch he offered them and crushed the Paris Commune and its deputies. From then on it was open warfare.

Like all classical tragedies, the Convention was a drama in three acts. Two dates stand out: June 2, 1793, and 9 Thermidor, Year II (July 27, 1794).

This is not the place to describe all the scenes of violence and tumult and all the ins and outs of an assembly that was the longest and perhaps the richest in the whole history of the Revolution. I shall confine myself to the broad outlines of the story.

Before June 2 the Girondins controlled the Convention. But the king's trial, the spring defeats, the revolt in the Vendée, and the demands of the Parisian sans-culottes stemming from the crisis forced the Convention to approve exceptional measures that were in fact the first steps toward the Reign of Terror. At the same time an open struggle for power was raging between the Girondins and the Montagnards (as the deputies of the Mountain were known).

Dumouriez's treason provoked a violent reaction among the Montagnards. Danton proclaimed: "There is no more truce between the Mountain, the patriots who urged the tyrant's death, and the cowards who, in attempting to save him, have slandered us throughout France." Those "cowards" were the so-called *appelants,* that is, members of the Convention who insisted that the verdict against Louis XVI be "appealed" to the people. On April 5 Marat demanded their recall. The Girondins issued a call to arms to the worried bourgeoisie: "Your property is threatened yet you close your eyes to the danger." (The words were Pétion's.) On May 25 Isnard threatened to destroy Paris, thus triggering the insurrection of June 2. For two reasons . this was a date of the utmost importance in the history of the Convention. Twenty-nine Girondin deputies were indicted. Seventy-five others signed a protest and were excluded from the assembly. Others quit their benches and returned to the provinces in the hope of fomenting a "federalist" uprising, which proved ephemeral and inconsequential. They were beaten before they began. The Convention, however, had been deprived of a significant proportion of its deputies, setting a terrible precedent that would haunt the body until its final days. Much later, the Montagnard deputy Levasseur wrote in his *Memoirs:* "Yes, the Gironde was republican. . . . Yes, its expulsion was unfortunate."

June 2 inaugurated the second—Montagnard—phase of the Convention, which lasted more than a year. It saw the organization of a revolutionary government, the Reign of Terror, and a series of purges of its membership as a result of the great trials of Germinal and Prairial. Yet—mark this well—the extraordinary dictatorship exercised by the Committee of Public Safety under the leadership of Robespierre, Saint-Just, and Couthon was desired, approved, and accepted by the Convention and its majority, the Plain. Robespierre never sought to control the assembly by any means other than the persuasive power of his voice. Far from being a "dictator," he was the first great parliamentary leader. This was the reason for his passivity on the eve of 9 Thermidor, following his liberation by the forces of the Commune: he was not a rioter but a parliamentarian.

The Convention outlived Robespierre by fifteen months. During this "Thermidorian" period, and despite its crises and reversals (including the persecution of one-time Terrorists, the return of the Girondins, and the end of the state-controlled economy), the Convention kept faith with the main thrust of the Revolution. The Plain now replaced the Girondins and Montagnards, even welcoming reformed Montagnards into its ranks. Men like Sieyès and Cambacérès, at long last breaking their prudent silence, were now free to speak and act. A new constitution was approved on 5 Fructidor, Year III (August 22, 1795). With a Declaration of Rights and a Declaration of Duties in its preamble, this document revived the ideals of 1789 while incorporating the lessons learned between 1792 and 1794. Its chief concern was to establish impregnable defenses around the principle of representative government. Boissy d'Anglas said: "When insurrection is general, it needs no apology; when it is partial, it is always guilty." The fundamental principle of the reorganization of government was that there should be no sovereign power. What about the sovereignty of the people? Sieyès declared: "This word took on such colossal proportions in the imagination only because in the minds of the French people, still filled with royal superstitions, it seemed necessary to endow it with the whole legacy of pompous attributes and absolute powers that have lent their luster to usurped sovereignties." Here is an open affirmation of nothing less than a true liberalism. Concretely, legislative power was divided between two chambers: a Council of Five Hundred, which possessed the power to initiate legislation, and a Council of Seniors (Anciens), which transformed the proposals of the other chamber into law. And so the Directory was born, but the history of its councils is not part of the history of revolutionary assemblies. The Convention, which decapitated a king and drove power into the streets, in its last meeting (on 4 Brumaire, or October 26, 1795) may have rebaptized the Place de la Révolution the Place de la Concorde, but it had yet to complete its mission of exorcising the past.

Denis Richet

FURTHER READING

For a concise account of the current state of knowledge about the French Revolution, see François Furet and Denis Richet, *La Révolution française*, 2 vols. Paris, 1963–1965. New edition in 1 vol. 1973, also in 1979, 1986.

RELATED TOPICS

Ancien Régime
Barnave
Clubs and Popular Societies
Danton
Elections
Emigrés
Estates General
Federalism

Feuillants
Girondins
Jacobinism
Lafayette
Louis XVI
Marat
Mirabeau
Monarchiens

Montagnards
Necker
Paris Commune
Robespierre
Sieyès
Sovereignty
Suffrage

REVOLUTIONARY CALENDAR

I n contrast to the Revolution's division of territorial space—which remains unchanged even today—the revolutionary division of time did not survive the Revolution: adopted by the Convention on October 5, 1793, the calendar was abolished on January 1, 1806. Furthermore, while the new map dates from the very beginning of the Revolution, the new calendar did not emerge until the Terror.

The only attempt to revise the calendar prior to the Revolution was that of Sylvain Maréchal in 1788. As late as June 1793 Sieyès, who wished to fill the republican year with specially tailored festivals, stopped short of altering the calendar itself: "The time has not yet come to change the way we divide up the year. Our customs and our countless entanglements with the customs of neighboring peoples and previous centuries constitute a mass too great to push aside." Sieyès' reluctance derived from his keen awareness of the educational importance of continuity and the pervasive influence of the calendar.

Why, then, was the decision taken only a few weeks later to interfere with that "great mass" and attempt to "revolutionize time"? The most widely accepted hypothesis is that the political situation made this a propitious moment: the calendar reform came when popular and government-sponsored de-Christianization were briefly allied. But this hypothesis is inadequate, for the new calendar survived not only Robespierre's decision to call a halt to the de-Christianization policy but also the reaction of 9 Thermidor. This suggests that it was a product of more than just temporary circumstances.

The substance of the calendar reform—the time periods, the choice of labels, the rhythm marked by festivals—has received little attention from historians, notwithstanding a certain nostalgia for the beautiful names dreamed up by Fabre d'Eglantine. Most have seen it as a reflection of the revolutionary sensibility's bucolic genius, so out of keeping with a time of terror. Richard Cobb points out that 4 Germinal, the day on which the Hébertists were put to death, was dedicated to tulips; 14 Germinal, when the Dantonists went to the scaffold, was the day of the beech; and the Law on Suspects was passed on the day of chamomile. Such condescending irony is encouraged, to be sure, by the patent failure of calendar reform. One must be quite naive and willing to swallow whatever the revolutionaries themselves said, however, to write, as Serge Bianchi does, that "the calendar did not bother peasants because it was based on the products of the soil." Such a view hardly stands up to scrutiny: a veritable ocean of texts attests to popular opposition to the new way of reckoning days and seasons.

The calendar reform was thus an extremely ambitious project whose effects were short-lived. It grew out of a specific political situation but in many ways transcended the circumstances of its inception. Its contents, though incongruous, were nevertheless emblematic of revolutionary regeneration. In short, the revolutionary calendar was full of contradictions.

*
**

The new calendar was inaugurated before it was institutionalized. As early as July 15, 1789, the day after the fall of the Bastille, people began dating documents "the second day of freedom." People thus experienced the new way of reckoning time before they rationalized it. Bastille Day became the first day of Year I of freedom. Yet the feeling that the new year begins on the first of January remained powerful enough even in the minds of the revolutionaries that a proposal was made to begin Year II on January 1, 1790. The difficulty of adjusting to changes in the calendar is illustrated by what took place at a meeting of the Legislative Assembly on January 2, 1792. The deputies declined to approve a calendar in which the new year would begin on July 14, for this would have been in "contradiction with the year commonly accepted in Europe." Hence July 14 to December 31 was to be counted as an entire year. January 1, 1792, became not Year III, as logic would suggest, but Year IV of liberty. The problem with this system was that August 10 introduced a new complication. This being the date that was supposed to have inaugurated the age of equality, Year I of equality would also be Year IV of liberty. (Some issues of the *Moniteur* actually bear both dates.) In September this became Year I of the Republic. On January 1, 1793, this Year I prematurely became Year II, causing still further bewilderment.

As the difficulties mounted, so did calls for a clarification of the system. On August 17, 1790, Lalande proposed making the date of historical regeneration coincide with that of natural regeneration by defining the beginning of the era of liberty as April 1, 1789, a little before the fact. After September 1792 the Convention received numerous petitions suggesting that the year begin on September 21. A few days before January 1, 1793—which could be regarded variously as the first day of Year IV of liberty, Year II of equality, or Year II of the Republic—the Convention took the fateful step suggested by Sieyès: it assigned its Committee on Public Instruction to prepare "as soon as possible" a report on "the advantages to accrue to France from bringing the common era into harmony with the republican era." Unfortunately the report remained nine months in gestation, and the modest initial aim—to achieve "harmony" between the two modes of reckoning—was rejected by the Committee. Going beyond its charter, it proposed that the Convention dispense with January's New Year's Day (in fact reconfirmed by a decree of January 2, 1793) and start the year on September 22, and further, that the old calendar be thrown out and replaced with a new one of its own devising.

The Committee's report was issued in September 1793, which suggests a de-Christianizing intention behind these recommendations. The calendar's contents did indeed reflect anticlerical aims. But the Committee was not a monolith. Anticlericals such as Fabre d'Eglantine and Marie-Joseph Chénier sat on it alongside scholars such as Monge and Lakanal. What is more, work on the report had been in progress since December 1792. The radicalism in the Committee's proposals has more to do with what happened in the terrible year 1793 and how these events changed the conception of revolutionary time. Before 1793 it was possible to think of the Revolution as a time of regeneration—dazzling, prodigious, and spontaneous—which blurred awareness of an interval between the beginning of the Revolution and its effects. But as incident followed incident, that ugly interval grew longer and longer, and there were increasing signs of deviation and degeneration. People suddenly became aware of time as duration, an expanse filled with obstacles to the Revolution's project of renewal. As the *Anti-fédéraliste* wrote in Brumaire of Year II, the great discovery of 1793 was that "there are among us new men not stunned by the Revolution and who, by a lucky coincidence, are made for the new order of things. But there are also false patriots in our midst, corrupting the very seeds of virtue." This awareness of internal and external obstacles to the Revolution constituted a new reality, to which the republican calendar—that instrument of a new regeneration that had not affected everyone—attempted to respond. According to its inventors, the new calendar could help remedy this situation by achieving four objectives: rationalization, commemoration (of the rupture), purgation, and replacement.

Rationalization was the first explicit objective of the plan presented to the Convention on September 20, 1793, by Romme, speaking for the Committee. He linked the report to far-reaching reforms intended to eliminate "diversity and inconsistency in weights and measures." Accurate measures of time were also needed. Romme gleefully noted "errors" in the Julian calendar: its year was eleven seconds too long, amounting to an error of ten days over six centuries. As for the Gregorian calendar, a book by Nicolas Boulanger had popularized critical assessments of Gregory VII's work: the year was again too long, and dates of holy days varied (a fact that Michelet would stress in defending the superiority of the republican calendar). The new calendar was notable for adopting the same decimal system employed in the new system of weights and measures. This system was thought to have a basis in nature, since men count with ten fingers. There were to be ten months of equal length, divided into "weeks" of ten ten-hour days. First, of course, the clockmakers would have to manufacture decimal watches and clocks (which to this day remain priceless antiques). Because of the determination to make all months as well as all years equal in length, Romme was forced to resort to the annoying expedient of tacking five extra days on to the end of each year and providing for an intercalary year, whose timing, which he hoped to set at fixed intervals, caused him much trouble. Nevertheless, he believed that the new calendar was simpler and more economical than the old: significantly, the number of nonworking holidays was reduced from fifty-six to thirty-two, a reform long advocated by eighteenth-century economists.

Apart from the intellectual challenge of rationalizing the calendar, Romme infused it with emotional and political content, thus enabling the new system to fulfill its essential function: to commemorate the Revolution as a new historical beginning, a discontinuity in time. When everything else had changed, how could people go on using the old calendar? The aim was to establish unambiguously that the republican era was not the age of monarchy. To make this point absolutely clear, September 22, 1792—the day the Republic was proclaimed—was chosen as the first day of Year I. In the debate that followed, some deputies suggested not having any beginning. All calculations should be extended into the past, so that one could say, for example, that Lysippus lived in the twenty-first century before the republican era rather than in the fourth century before Jesus Christ. In this way the old era could be "harmonized" with the new. This had actually been the Committee's charge. But "retrospective computation" was of little interest compared with the regenerative virtues of starting afresh. Fabre d'Eglantine said it best: "We can no longer count years during which the kings oppressed us as a time in which we lived."

Romme, however, was quick to acknowledge that both nature and history had claims to establishing the calendar's beginning. As it happens, September 22, 1792, is also the autumnal equinox. What a miraculous coincidence between nature and the Revolution, as Romme never tired of pointing out: "equality of day and night was marked in the sky" on the same day that "civil and moral equality were proclaimed by the representatives of the people." The idea of simultaneity proved persuasive, and September 22, that doubly fateful day, was chosen as the beginning of the "era of the French [people]."

Whatever anti-Christian purposes the calendar may have served appear to have been of secondary importance compared with the two primary objectives of rationalization and commemoration. But once a new calendar was adopted, it had to be filled in, and inevitably that had anti-Christian consequences. The old calendar was essentially a martyrology, as earlier reformers had understood: Sylvain Maréchal had wanted to create a "martyrology of Liberty." One anonymous "calendar of the Frankish people" included a preamble expressing outrage that the calendar of Christian Rome did not include Socrates or Phocion or any other hero of humanity. Everyone wanted to rid the calendar of "fantastic objects" and afflicting images of Christian martyrs. Yet the anticlerical republican calendar paid explicit homage to the genius of Catholic pedagogy with its wonderfully sensuous imagery. When Romme's nomenclature was rejected and Fabre d'Eglantine presented his own proposal, he was quick to state his admiration for those who had been shrewd enough to associate All Souls' with mournful November and to use the splendor of Corpus Christi to redirect toward the Church the attention of youths diverted by the arrival of spring. The priests had created a "talisman" (the word is Romme's), which could only be opposed by another talisman.

This part of the project was obviously the most difficult. To achieve the fourth objective the deputies had to resolve contradictions inherent in the central symbols and emblems of the Revolution. Would the new calendar be a calendar of history or of nature? Of the French or of all mankind? A definitive masterpiece, never to be revised, or an open-ended work, ready to receive future additions? Each of these issues provoked considerable debate.

History or nature? Romme had decided in favor of history, indeed of revolutionary history, having drawn all of his nomenclature from "our Revolution." He envisioned the calendar as a huge narrative of the Revolution, encompassing all its events in a single year. Among the names of the months were Bastille (June 19–July 18), an obvious reminder of July 14, 1789; People (July 19–August 17), in commemoration of August 10, 1792; Mountain; and Republic. Other months' names were more emblematic: Unity, Fraternity, Liberty. As for the "epagomenous" days (those five or six troublesome days tacked on to the end of the year in order to preserve the sacrosanct equality of the months), they were to be named after the ages of man, in honor of biological rather than historical time.

But Romme's calendar, which condensed the history of the Revolution in sometimes bewildering, sometimes predictable ways, was too bizarre to convince the Assembly. On October 5, 1793, it approved Romme's report but rejected his nomenclature and voiced its approval of the ordinal nomenclature favored by egalitarians such as Duhem. Unfortunately this seemed awkward to apply in practice: the very next day, October 6, would have to be denominated the fifteenth day of the second year. The Assembly therefore sent the Committee back to work. Its new secretary, Fabre d'Eglantine, then submitted his agricultural calendar, which won the Assembly's approval. It was Fabre who conceived the wonderful names of the months, with their three-letter endings and sonorities evocative of the seasons; who consecrated each *décadi* (tenth day of the decade, or ten-day week) to a different agricultural implement and each *quintidi* (fifth day of the decade) to a different domestic animal; and who filled the rest of the days with a "fragrant herb garden" in opposition to the "disgusting ossuary" of the priests. The calendar of nature thus triumphed over the calendar of history: in Fabre's calendar there were neither heroes nor martyrs, and he explicitly voiced fears of a cult of personality. The moral virtues were relegated to the "epagomenous" days, rebaptized the *sans-culottides*. Fabre knew full well that the peasant's only book was his almanac, and that with his calendar every French child would be enrolled in a course in rural economy.

The loser in this debate was the Revolution, reference to which was dropped from the new nomenclature. On October 5 the Assembly rejected the revolutionary terms "level," "cap," and "Republic" as names of days. There was a good argument for dropping from the calendar the names of the Revolution's great men and important dates (which had begun to coalesce in people's minds): the desire to create a calendar that was not simply French and could plausibly claim universality. On October 5 Bentabole put it this way: "When Mohammed gave his people a new era, it was to set them apart from other peoples. Our aim is the opposite of that impostor's: we want to unite all peoples through fraternity." But Bentabole's argument collapsed in the face of the need to establish a boundary between what came before the Revolution and what came after. The names in the calendar would not make explicit reference to the Revolution, but by its very existence that calendar would recount the rupture the Revolution introduced into the history of France.

A third area of controversy was the question whether the calendar should be, as Romme's was, a definitive creation, designed to remind every citizen every day of the events of a now completed Revolution, or should remain open to additions and amendments. Romme's whole proposal was colored by the idea that the calendar should be immutable. But certain conventionnels such as Duhem were convinced that the Revolution had not yet exhausted its creative potential; they were not persuaded that it had "reached the term indicated by philosophy" and completed "all its memorable epochs," and they had no desire to imitate the Pope by producing a calendar so filled with names that there was no room to add a single saint. They preferred to leave the question of nomenclature open. If they were not heeded, it was because most deputies were increasingly suspicious of further developments in the Revolution, the most recent ones having become tragically repetitious rather than inventive.

The Convention's ultimate choices were quite consistent. It settled on a French calendar rather than a universal one, because commemorating the beginning of the Revolution was essential. It chose a fixed calendar rather than an open one, because rationalization was imperative. And since it needed a talisman, since even the priests had, in Fabre's words, made their idols consistent only by "casting Saint John as the distributor of the harvest and Saint Mark as the protector of the vine," it chose a calendar based on nature rather than history.

These three decisions met with varying degrees of success. The most easily accomplished goal was that of commemorating the beginning of the Revolution—despite the obstacle posed by the tenacity of New Year's Day. Rationalization was a more complex affair. Romme argued that the intercalary days could be arranged to come every four years. But Delambre soon called the attention of Lalande and Laplace to the thorny problem of "sextile years." If the year was set to begin at midnight on the day of the true autumnal equinox, sextile years would not follow regularly at four year intervals. Three times a century—and worse yet, at irregular intervals—the interval between sextile years would be five rather than four years. The wisest course would be to give up the equinox as a marker. Romme, who was suddenly confronted with the fact that irregularity might be "in conformity with the principles of astronomy," did not accept this conclusion, however, and went back to work. Rather than allow the sextile day to be determined automatically by the equinox, he suggested that certain corrections be made (once every four hundred years and once every thirty-six centuries), demonstrating how determined he was to cling to a regular pattern of intercalation. Yet the issue raised by Delambre encouraged later resistance to the calendar and provided Laplace with a decisive argument for returning to the Gregorian calendar (on 15 Fructidor, Year XIII).

*
**

The third purpose of the new calendar, to provide France with a substitute for the Christian calendar, was the most difficult of all to fulfill and the one that ultimately settled its fate.

From the first the reformed calendar relied on coercion to gain acceptance. The Convention's executive commission ordered government officials to take their day of rest only on *décadi,* which was also the day on which post offices, theaters, fairs, and markets were required to close. Printers of almanacs and calendars were permitted to "print old hours, minutes, and seconds" on their wares alongside the new decimal times, but this was only a provisional measure until the new calendar "had come into customary use." A long period of repressive measures followed.

After Thermidor the calendar, to no one's surprise, became a target of the reactionaries. Lanjuinais wrote a vindictive pamphlet denouncing the calendar of the "tyrants" who had dared to change "times and days." Petitions to the Convention called for elimination of the new calendar, and some deputies announced that it would soon be burned. In this period pikes, the familiar *tu,* red revolutionary caps, artificial mountains, the ever-vigilant "eye of surveillance" on banners, and busts of Marat all disappeared from the scene. Yet the calendar, with the support of such authoritative figures as La Réveillière-Lépeaux, survived. Successive assemblies continued to approve both the principle of the new calendar and the repressive measures needed to enforce it.

Especially after 18 Fructidor, in the neo-Jacobin atmosphere of Year VI, there was a new flurry of peremptory decrees reminding journalists of the need to use republican dates in their articles and ordering municipal officials to schedule markets and fairs on dates close to the old dates but avoiding Christian holidays. People who leased property were required to use the "calendar of liberty" in dating the period of the lease. It may at first seem paradoxical that the revolutionary calendar survived when so much other revolutionary baggage disappeared, but in reality there is nothing surprising about it. As Bronislaw Baczko has shown, to renounce the calendar was to acknowledge that the events of the Revolution could be undone: this a regicide Assembly could not tolerate.

There was invention as well as repression. An effort was made in Year VI to give new life to republican institutions, and one of the most interesting episodes involved the great debate in the month of Messidor concerning the failure of *décadi* to dethrone Sunday. Here the penalties for nonobservance of *décadi* are less interesting than the pathetic attempts to make it an attractive day of rest. It was proposed that, in addition to allowing time for reading the text of new laws—always good for excitement—this day would be appropriate for announcing "discoveries useful to the arts" and "new methods" of

544

agriculture. In order to involve women this was to be the day for publishing announcements of births, marriages, and adoptions of foundlings. The day was also set aside for communal commemorations, always more vivid than the great national festivals. Dancing and games were not to be neglected. All these measures were summed up, however, in one imperious declaration: "People of France, abjure thy servile errors and make use of thy calendar."

Obviously this shows how attached people remained to their traditional Sundays. Bonnaire, who in Year VI submitted on behalf of the Committees of Public Instruction and Republican Institutions a long report on the *décadi* festivals, called upon his colleagues to have the courage to confirm what he had found in the provinces, namely, "that people detest our national festivals and that we have managed in the end to drive the people away, when there is nothing so brilliant as our spectacles and public promenades on religious holidays." This observation is confirmed by thousands of others, among them this report by the cantonal commissioner of Selles-sur-Cher, drafted on 4 Germinal, Year VII: "Sundays and Catholic holidays, even if there are ten in a row, have for some time been celebrated with as much pomp and splendor as before. The same cannot be said of *décadi*, which is observed by only a small handful of citizens. The first to disobey the law are the wives of public officials, who dress up on the holidays of the old calendar and abstain from work more religiously than anyone else." If even government officials were reluctant to heed the republican calendar, what could one expect of other rural folk?

What these local officials have to say about their efforts to persuade citizens to accept the republican revision of time suggests nothing less than a peasant rebellion geared to the Christian calendar, which the revolutionaries, following Romme's lead, deemed a discredited institution. The enforcement measures themselves all focused on the high points of the liturgical calendar: Christmas, Easter, and Lent, when people deserted their jobs, and All Saints', when they were more openly disobedient, knowing full well that the commissioners would hesitate to violate the sanctity of the dead. Desperate officials actually encountered an even deeper source of resistance, older, more exhibitionistic, more likely to lead to riot: a still vital popular calendar whose high points were the spring planting, Saint John's summer festival, and carnival. This posed an even more formidable obstacle to reform than the Christian calendar, which after all had itself been a product of historical developments and might therefore have been vulnerable if only the Revolution could have dealt with its promoters, primarily the refractory priests. Here were revolutionaries who had hoped by decree to fix the beginning of eternity at a specific point in time—the date of the Revolution—now forced to confront another eternity stretching not forward in time but backward into the dim past, which survived without benefit of institutional support.

The surprising thing is not that the revolutionary calendar disappeared but that its demise took so long. The first premonitory symptom was the abolition, in Year VIII, of all the revolutionary festivals except for July 14 and 1 Vendémiaire. The second came in Germinal, Year X, with the law on organized religion: by establishing Sunday as the day of rest for government employees, it struck a mortal blow at *décadi,* restored legality to the week, and indirectly reestablished the Gregorian calendar. The third and final blow came on 15 Fructidor, Year XIII: Laplace separated the calendar reform from the reform of weights and measures and condemned the calendar on grounds that would have infuriated Romme: its "irrational" system of intercalation and its national rather than universal character.

*
**

As Hannah Arendt observed, the abandonment of the revolutionary calendar deprived the Revolution of its extraordinary character and restored it to the process of history. Yet even that abandonment revealed something of the profound inner logic of the calendar reform. In the debates of Year X and Year XIII Romme's work was praised in spite of everything. What a shame that France could not keep an instrument based on "simple and convenient ideas," compared with which the Gregorian calendar was full of flaws. The day would perhaps come when "a new calendar could be constructed for all Europe, for the commercial as well as the political world, from the remains of the one which France is now abandoning so as not to be left alone in the midst of Europe." Regnaud d'Angély and Mounier confidently looked forward to that day: the reformers of the future would find their work already done. The hope of a new life based on a new calendar was not really dead.

By now it should be clear that the purposes of the reviled calendar were more than just anticlerical. The dream of a new man, so central to revolutionary thought, presupposed freeing the old man from his moorings in order to make him a citizen and then surrounding him with a dense network of luminous images, disciplining rituals, and instructive habits. In order to make this positive pedagogy possible, time had to be restructured in such a way that the regular occurrence of special days with their attendant emotions would forge new habits. The republican calendar was thus conceived as an instrument, whose content was to have engendered the new loyalties of the citizen and whose form was to have been a "mold" to shape an obedient nation.

Mona Ozouf

FURTHER READING

Arendt, Hannah. *Between Past and Future: Eight Exercises in Political Thought.* Revised edition, New York, 1968.

Baczko, Bronislaw. *Lumières de l'utopie.* Paris, 1981.

——— "Le calendrier républicain," in Pierre Nora, ed., *Les lieux de mémoire,* vol. 1, *La République.* Paris, 1984.

Boulanger, Nicolas-Antoine. *L'antiquité dévoilée par ses usages.* Amsterdam, 1766.

Friguglietti, James. "The Social and Religious Consequences of the French Revolutionary Calendar." Doctoral dissertation, Harvard University, 1968.

Procès-verbaux du Comité d'Instruction publique de la Convention Nationale, published by James Guillaume, 6 vols. Paris, 1891–1907.

Romme, Gilbert. *Rapport sur l'ère de la République fait à la Convention Nationale dans la séance du 20 septembre de l'an II de la République.* Paris, 1793.

RELATED TOPICS

De-Christianization   Sieyès

REVOLUTIONARY GOVERNMENT

Before historians took up the term "revolutionary government," it was the men of 1793 themselves who applied it to the various institutions and mechanisms of power that constituted public authority in France between the autumn of 1793 and Thermidor (July) 1794. In those days the word "government" had a wider meaning than it has now: it referred not only to the apparatus of power but to a type of political, and to a certain extent social, regime. Montesquieu, for example, contrasted the "feudal government" with the "political government" of monarchy. In 1793 the term "revolutionary government" was therefore intended to connote the unprecedented nature of the state and its relations with society. The adjective meant that the legitimacy of public authority stemmed not from a constitution or from law but from conformity with the Revolution.

Listen to Saint-Just speaking to the Convention on October 10, 1793: "The laws are revolutionary; those who execute them are not. . . . Under the circumstances in which the Republic finds itself, the Constitution cannot be established. . . . It would be used to justify attacks on liberty, because it would lack the violence necessary to put them down. . . . It is impossible for revolutionary laws to be executed if the government itself is not revolutionarily constituted."

What does this mean? The contrast between Revolution and Constitution was a new element in revolutionary history and ideas. The men of 1789 never conceived what they were doing in these terms, for it was in the nature of the Ancien Régime that it had no constitution, and it was the Constitutent Assembly's raison d'être to provide it with one in order to put an end to arbitrary rule. The Assembly disbanded in September 1791, however, without completing work on the document that was to have been the fruit of its efforts. Less than a year later, on August 10, 1792, the Legislative Assembly deposed the king, and the work of writing a constitution had to begin anew. For this reason a second constituent assembly, this one known as the Convention, was elected, and from its labors came not one but two constitutions—not a good sign. Condorcet submitted a draft constitution in early spring, but it was set aside when the Girondins were expelled from the Convention on June 2. The Montagnard constitution was approved on June 24, with a new Declaration of Rights as its preamble. It was based on a National Assembly elected by universal suffrage, with laws subject to the direct control of the people through primary assemblies. This constitution was a product of circumstances, hastily drafted and debated, and its application was put off till better times.

Thus, the month of June 1793 was the moment when the Revolution began to conceive of its role and purpose in a new way, officially abandoning the idea of establishing a republic of laws. This abandonment was implicit in the Convention's capitulation to the insurgent Paris sections on June 2: having been forced to expel a part of its membership, the national representative body was no longer consistent with the will of the people. The change became explicit when application of the new Constitution was postponed, and Saint-Just, in October, was merely reporting the obvious. What is interesting about his way of putting it is the attempt to appropriate the concept of law for the benefit of the Revolution by suggesting that there was a temporary conflict between the law and the Constitution. To do this, Saint-Just shifts from the notion of law to that of applying the law. He links the idea of "revolutionary laws" (issuing from a revolutionary but illegal government, the post–June 2 Convention) to the idea of "aconstitutional power." In effect, the existence of a "revolutionarily constituted" government—in other words, a government constituted in violation of the Constitution—is the prerequisite for application of the "revolutionary laws." The notion of law is thus deprived of meaning, for it is no longer universal; it no longer guarantees the same rights to each and every individual. Instead, it was argued that circumstances required the use of arbitrary violence against the enemies of liberty, that is, of the Revolution. This was tantamount to a renunciation of the great achievement of 1789: equal individual rights based on a written constitution. This renunciation is the distinguishing feature of the second period of the French Revolution, which began on August 10. The Revolution's raison d'être is no longer to establish a new law of the land. Its logic has become tautological: the Revolution exists because its government is "revolutionary."

It was all a product of circumstances. As Edgar Quinet noticed, the men of 1793 unwittingly resurrected a common argument of legal scholars under the absolute monarchy: the imperative of public safety. Ancien Régime jurists had used this argument to justify "extraordinary" measures (usually additional fiscal levies). The men of 1793 used it more broadly to justify a new type of regime. It is true, moreover, that the situation in the summer and early fall of 1793 was dramatic. French territory had been invaded on several fronts: in the north, along the Rhine, in the Alpine valleys, and in the south. The federalist revolt, born of conflict between Montagnards and Girondins, was essentially over by August, but Lyons was not recaptured from the royalists until October and Toulon until December. The insurgent Vendée had defied the Convention throughout the summer, winning victory after victory. And the peasant insurrection was halted but not wiped out on October 17 at Cholet.

The circumstances therefore fostered the idea of "public safety" and all that it implied about the need for exceptional measures. Yet the circumstances alone are not enough to account for the form and nature of the revolutionary government. Any national emergency creates a unique political situation, but to explain the kind of regime that grows out of such an emergency requires something more: account must be taken of the day's ideas, passions, and conflicts. Under the Ancien Régime the idea of public safety was used to justify the king's absolute authority. Under the Revolution it was used to justify a dictatorship exercised in the people's name. Both regimes grew out of comparable situations, or perhaps one should say that both relied on identical pretexts. Both put utility ahead of law and accepted arbitrary power as the price of efficiency. Yet they were also very different, because they existed in different political universes, separated from each other by the chasm of 1789.

Here I shall concentrate on the political universe of the Revolution, leaving it to the reader to pursue the parallel with the Ancien Régime. The call for a dictatorship to combat the enemies of the Revolution was as old as the Revolution itself, which is to say that it was heard well before 1793. It was Marat's obsession in the summer of 1789, for example, as well as the key to his popularity, given that *L'ami du peuple,* which first appeared in early September, was a sounding board for popular sentiment. The idea of a dictatorship to protect the weak from the strong was a more or less conscious outgrowth of absolutist tradition. But it also had a punitive component, which was associated with the feeling that the enemies of the Revolution were particularly powerful and all the more fearsome because hidden: the "aristocratic plot" was the diabolical counterpart of the will of the people. Ultimately this feeling was perhaps the most basic expression of a debased version of Rousseau's philosophy, according to which the sovereignty of the people could be expressed only through a single, indivisible body in full command of all public authority. From this belief stemmed the seemingly paradoxical possibility of a dictatorship exercised by the National Assembly, as well as the no less paradoxical if diametrically opposite demand that dictatorship be exercised through the direct democracy of the sections and clubs. The concept of a "revolutionary government" was thus rooted in ideas and passions that predated the whole question of "public safety" and would survive the return to normalcy.

That concept took shape gradually over the course of 1793 in response to both the national emergency and popular pressure. It all began in the spring. Economic distress, bad news from the front, and the struggle between the Gironde and the Mountain created a climate of riot and escalating demands. The sans-culottes besieged the Convention with complaints and calls for action. On March 11 came a call for a revolutionary tribunal to judge "suspects" and on March 21 another call for committees of surveillance to identify those suspects. Also on March 11 the Convention dispatched representatives to the départements, officially for the purpose of hastening the recruitment of 300,000 new troops but in fact wielding very broad powers. On April 9 additional agents were dispatched to the armies with unlimited powers. Most important of all, on April 6 the Committee of General Defense was replaced by a Committee of Public Safety (not fully staffed until May), whose responsibility was to monitor and guide the Executive Council of Ministers. This committee soon became the true executive branch of the revolutionary government. Marat answered the protests of the Girondins: "Liberty must be established through violence, and the time has come when we must temporarily establish the despotism of liberty in order to crush the despotism of kings." The Mountain formed an alliance with the sans-culottes to defeat the Gironde in the Convention. The Montagnards also made economic concessions to their allies, in April stipulating that assignats must be accepted as legal tender at officially fixed values and in May setting price controls on grain and flour and levying a compulsory billion-franc loan on the rich.

Phase two began that summer, after the defeat of the Girondins. On July 10 a new Committee of Public Safety was chosen, and it became the focal point of governmental action. Danton quit, perhaps as a calculated maneuver, perhaps because he was tired, perhaps both. The Convention reelected seven of the fourteen members of the original committee: three deputies of the Plain (Barère, Lindet, and Gasparin) and four Montagnards originally elected in late May (Saint-Just, Couthon, Bon Saint-André, and Hérault de Séchelles). Two additional Montagnard deputies were added: Thuriot and Prieur of the Marne. On July 24 Gasparin resigned, and on July 27 he was replaced by Robespierre. On August 14 Carnot and Prieur of the Côte d'Or were added. Finally on September 6 the sans-culottes forced the committee to include Collot d'Herbois and Billaud-Varenne. Thuriot resigned on September 20. With the exception of Hérault de Séchelles, who would be arrested, tried, and executed along with Danton and the Dantonists on April 5, 1794, this was the committee—the Great Committee, reelected by the Convention month after month—that would govern France for the next year, until 9 Thermidor (July 17, 1794). This was the central organ of the "revolutionary government."

Activists in the sections and clubs continued to make trouble, however. Enragés, Cordeliers, and Hébertists rivaled one another in egalitarian and persecutorial zeal, all vying for the legacy of Marat, who had been assassinated in July. The two great sans-culottist issues were price controls and terror, and the shortage of supplies only added to their appeal. On July 26 the Convention approved a bill proposed by Billaud-Varenne and Collot d'Herbois providing the death penalty for hoarders and placing the most vital food supplies under municipal control. On August 1 the Assembly, acting on a report prepared by Barère, sent Marie Antoinette to the Revolutionary Tribunal and decided to issue warrants for the arrest of all foreigners not resident in France prior to July 14, 1789; it also voted to confiscate the property of all outlawed Girondins. On August 23 came the order for mass recruitment of troops. Disturbances continued, however, climaxing on September 5, when the armed sections surrounded the Convention, as they had done on June 2, to demand the creation of a revolutionary army of the interior, the arrest of suspects, and a purge of the committees.

This was probably the crucial period in the formation of the revolutionary government. The Convention gave ground but retained control over events. It made "Terror the order of the day" on September 5, elected Collot d'Herbois and Billaud-Varenne to the Committee of Public Safety on the sixth, created the Revolutionary Army on the ninth, set price controls on grain and flour on the eleventh (and on all wages and prices on the twenty-ninth), reorganized the Revolutionary Tribunal on the fourteenth, passed the Law on Suspects on the seventeenth, and on the twentieth made local revolutionary committees responsible for preparing lists of suspects. At the same time, however, it ordered the arrest of the leaders of the enragés: having endorsed their program, the Convention had deprived them of the source of their strength. Thus the revolutionary government was the result of a progressive but rapid institutionalization, by the Convention, of the principal demands of the sectional movement. Such a course was dictated by the logic of Montagnard policy, for the Mountain had needed the sans-culottes to defeat the Gironde in the spring of 1793 and wished to keep them as allies but without giving up any important powers. By maintaining a vestige of a deliberative body in the Convention, the Montagnards kept intact their link to the original source of the Revolution's legitimacy while meeting the demands made in the name of direct democracy by the innumerable de facto powers that ruled the streets of Paris. Saint-Just caused this de facto balance of power to be enshrined in law on October 10, though his rhetoric did nothing to diminish the law's illogicality. Nevertheless, its first article did set a time limit: "The provisional government of France is revolutionary until peace is restored."

The institutions, structure, and procedures of the new government were codified in the Law of 14 Frimaire (December 4), which merely consecrated the centralized dictatorship that had gradually developed under the Terror. Debate, led off by Billaud-Varenne, lasted for eleven days. Its purpose was to simplify the system and perfect its "intermediate cogs." At the center was the Convention, whose right arm, the Committee of Public Safety, wielded immense powers: it interpreted the Assembly's decrees and determined how they would be enforced; it exerted direct authority over all departments of state and their functionaries (even the ministries were eliminated in April 1794); it had control over all diplomatic and military activity; and it appointed generals and the members of other committees, subject to ratification by the Convention. The Committee was responsible for the conduct of the war, for maintaining law and order, and for supplying the needs of the population. And finally, the Paris Commune, notorious bastion of sans-culotte power, was placed under the Committee's control and thus neutralized.

In the provinces the Committee governed through the districts (bypassing départemental authorities suspected of federalist sympathies), municipalities, and revolutionary committees, which were charged with enforcing all public safety measures. For the purpose of liaison with these local authorities it chose, in addition to the *représentants en mission* dispatched to the provinces, a corps of "national agents," who were chosen locally in "purgative elections" (that is, elections in which only local activists were permitted to vote) and then empowered by the Convention. Authority was actually less centralized than it appeared on paper. The revolutionary government, like its absolutist predecessors, had to contend with slow communications and ingrained habits and attitudes. To overcome these problems it relied on an immense effort of propaganda and education, ranging from the introduction of the revolutionary calendar on October 5 to articles published in hundreds of Montagnard newspapers throughout the country. In this the Jacobin Club played a major role, calling upon its many provincial affiliates. The revolutionary government required ideological orthodoxy and could not tolerate a diversity of opinion.

It governed in part through fear: the death penalty loomed large in the eyes of civil servants and citizens alike. At the apex of the machinery of terror was the Committee of General Security, the second most powerful organ of government, which consisted of twelve members elected monthly by the Convention and responsible for security, surveillance, and law and order, with jurisdiction over both military and civilian authorities. For this it employed a large number of people. Little by little it created a network of local revolutionary committees and attempted to enforce the Law of Suspects by sorting through countless reports of denunciations and arrests that filtered up from the local authorities. Indictments and prisoners were sent to the Revolutionary Tribunal. Reorganized in September, the Tribunal began its work in earnest in October, hastily trying a large number of cases. As a general rule, in cases involving civil conflict the *représentants en mission* ordered that they be tried by ad hoc judicial committees rather than by the regular criminal courts. Prosecution of the Revolution's enemies was entrusted to these ad hoc committees in Lyons, Marseilles, Nîmes, Toulouse, and throughout western France. Thus, throughout much of the country, the revolutionary government suspended the rights of man for reasons of state.

Finally, the Committee of Public Safety had full authority to regulate the economy. As far as state finances were concerned, this power was more theoretical than actual, because the financial administration created by the Constituent Assembly and largely staffed by financial experts from the Ancien Régime remained much the same as it had been under the monarchy. Throughout this period it was controlled by Cambon, chairman of the Convention's Finance Committee. But when it came to the economy proper, the Committee of Public Safety was obsessed, as the kings had been, with the need to feed the population, that of Paris above all, in order to prevent riots. The Committee therefore set up a new administration under the control of the Subsistence Commission on October 22. Headed by three "patriots" and armed with the General Maximum law establishing broad powers to control prices, this bureaucratic apparatus was responsible for regulating production, transportation, and consumption. Its many departments specialized in such matters as foreign purchases, domestic requisitions, price controls, and supplies for Paris and the army, as well as recent advances in agriculture, forestry, mining, and so forth. These were grouped into three major divisions employing approximately five hundred people. The Commission adopted statistical and regulatory methods similar to those employed by the old Contrôle Général. Despite the Terror and the prosecution of "hoarders," however, the attempt to control prices, monitor production, and secure necessary supplies by state requisition was met, by people in every class of society, with widespread fraud and deception.

The revolutionary government resurrected the centralizing and regulatory tradition of the state that had been briefly interrupted by the Constituent Assembly, leading to a huge increase in the number of government jobs of which the revolutionaries themselves were the chief beneficiaries. In 1791 there were only 670 official ministerial positions (roughly the same number as in the final years of the Ancien Régime), but by the beginning of 1794 there were 3,000 and by the end of that year the number had risen to 5,000. (The events of 9 Thermidor did nothing to halt the increase.) Sans-culottes not serving with the army staffed the police, the Ministry of War, and the Subsistence Commission. It was in this period that the word *bureau* first began to be used in connection with these government departments. But even as Robespierre and Saint-Just were attacking this nascent "bureaucracy" for constituting a barrier between constituents and their representatives, the two leaders' policies were increasing the number, influence, and responsibilities of government offices. The revolutionary government's political rhetoric was at odds with its sociological reality.

That rhetoric is essential, however, for understanding the forces and passions that determined the relation between this period and the rest of the Revolution. Paradoxically, the regime of Year II fully realized what was perhaps the Revolution's leading principle, namely, the absolute and indivisible sovereignty of a unique assembly chosen by universal suffrage and supposed to represent the general will: in short, Rousseau's theory was modified (or distorted) so as to accommodate representative government. I say "paradoxically" because the post–June 2 Convention was not the Convention chosen by universal suffrage, and the "revolutionary government" was a political concept patched together under pressure from proponents of direct democracy. Yet I also say "fully realized," because the Convention was the unique center of government, and the Committee of Public Safety, the true organ of dictatorship, was not a distinct executive power but simply a committee of the Convention, a part of that body and therefore identified with it. It was no accident that Billaud-Varenne, in his introductory report of 28 Brumaire (November 16), criticized the Constituent Assembly's provision for a distinct executive branch as criminal. Precisely when the Revolution seemed farthest from its original goal of founding a society based on the universality of law, it was also most faithful to its idea of sovereignty, an indication that 1789 and 1793 are to be contrasted in some ways, identified in others. In Year II the power of the people was finally established. It rested on a pyramid of equivalences: the people equals the Convention, the Convention equals the Committee of Public Safety, and, within a short time, the Committee equals Robespierre. The purpose of the Terror and the theme of civic virtue was to keep this series of abstractions from falling apart.

The most elaborate "theory" of the revolutionary government was probably contained in the report presented to the Convention by Robespierre on 5 Nivôse, Year II (December 25, 1793) on behalf of the Committee of Public Safety. A novel form of power never anticipated and therefore never studied by "political writers," the revolutionary government differed from constitutional government, Robespierre said, in that the rules that governed it were "less standardized and less strict," a euphemistic way of saying that it existed outside the law. It was, however, a prelude to the rule of law, for its purpose was to "institute" the nation against the opposition of its enemies, on whom it waged a war for freedom: "The purpose of constitutional government is to preserve the Republic; that of revolutionary government is to found it."

What did Robespierre mean by "found?" He meant, first of all, to maintain its existence in the face of both foreign enemies and domestic "factions." Robespierre thus echoed the old idea that the greatest risk to popular sovereignty was usurpation of power by special interests. In the winter of 1793–94 this notion was used to justify the first measures against the Indulgents and Hébertists. What determined the dividing line between "the people" and "the factions," between good and evil? The answer: "Love of the fatherland and of truth." Ultimately, therefore, political life was to be judged by a moral criterion; if the French people identified with the Convention, it was not so much because of the law as because of the "character" of the Assembly's action.

The temporary suspension of law, including the rights of man, was thus justified not only by the needs of public safety but by the higher need to found a society based on civic virtue. From the Ancien Régime the Revolution had inherited corrupt individuals, and this had perverted its own actions. Before it could establish a government of laws, it had to regenerate each and every participant in the new social contract. For Rousseau the transition from individual to citizen was a difficult, almost impossible task. For Robespierre it became the meaning of the Revolution, thanks to the radical action of the revolutionary government.

The revolutionary government was therefore a product of both special circumstances and a particular political culture. Judgment depends on whether one chooses to focus on the circumstances or the culture.

Many neo-Jacobin historians in both this century and the last were fervent admirers of the revolutionary government. They took the view that the political system of Year II was simply a response to the situation of extreme peril in which France found itself. War normally leads to increased governmental powers. The war that was raging in Europe in 1793 was especially likely to have this effect because France had had no true executive since 1789 and its government had been largely decentralized by the Constituent Assembly's efforts to reform the administration. The invasion of French territory by foreign enemies, coupled with the civil war being fought in more than one province at home, made it imperative that the central government strongly reassert its authority.

According to this view, the dictatorship was thus a product of circumstances, an expedient forced on the Revolution by its enemies and not an inherent part of the revolutionary phenomenon, whose true purpose was to bring liberty to France. Indeed, the ultimate justification of the dictatorship was that it achieved its goal, in the end saving France from both invasion and civil war. The revolutionary government established itself between the early spring and late summer of 1793, at a time when the nation's distress was greatest, and by the end of the year it was triumphant almost everywhere. Lyons and Toulon were recaptured in the fall; the Vendean army was cut to pieces in December; the foreign invaders were repelled. On September 8, a combined English and Hanoverian army under the command of General Freytas was defeated at Hondschoote, alleviating the pressure on Dunkirk. Less than a month later, victory in the battle of Wattignies delivered Maubeuge, which had been threatened by Coburg. In November the army of the Moselle under Hoche distinguished itself by turning back the Austro-Prussian threat to Alsace. These military successes were accompanied by "Terror in the armies." General Houchard, the victor at Hondschoote, was guillotined for having failed to cut off the retreating English forces. Chancel, commander of the Maubeuge garrison, met the same fate for his failure to take part in the battle of Wattignies. The Committee of Public Safety incontrovertibly established civilian supremacy over the military, with Carnot in charge of the northern frontier and Saint-Just and Le Bas overseeing operations in Strasbourg.

It is therefore understandable that the revolutionary government was credited with having saved France from invasion and civil war. It was there, and its policies succeeded. But that does not prove that another policy, such as that of the Girondins, might not have achieved the same end at smaller cost. Ultimately, the illogical claim that the victories of Year II were due to the government's "revolutionary" character rests on a confusion denounced long ago by Benjamin Constant in a brochure published in May 1797 ("On the Effects of the Terror"). It is one thing to credit the government, led by the Committee of Public Safety, with regaining control of the situation. It is quite another thing to argue that the Terror was indispensable to its efforts to regain control. The Terror, which sowed fear everywhere and struck at people in every class of society, did nothing to enhance the devotion of republicans to their fatherland, a devotion that already existed. The Terror in fact inaugurated a vicious circle of repression and rebellion: "The Terror caused the revolt of Lyons, the départemental insurrection, and the war in the Vendée. And in order to regain control of Lyons, end the coalition of the départements, and end the war in the Vendée, it took terror. Yet without terror Lyons would not have risen, the départements would not have joined forces, and the Vendée would not have proclaimed Louis XVII king" (Benjamin Constant).

Nevertheless, those who believe that "circumstances" were responsible for the revolutionary government generally take its effectiveness for granted. They are drawn to the republican rhetoric of "conquer or die." Although they admit that the revolutionary government was nothing but a bloody improvisation, they insist that it was extraordinarily efficient. For two centuries the French left has been filled with admirers, who base their enthusiasm not so much on the government's actual performance as on what Mona Ozouf has called "the French propensity to conjure up images of threats to the homeland, the fatherland in danger, and the miracles wrought by great power." The revolutionary government is one of the great sources of French political imagery, at once democratic, popular, dictatorial, and national.

That government's most outspoken champions are those who see it as a precursor of socialism: a circumstantial and provisional regime, to be sure, but one that exercised its dictatorial powers on behalf of the poor and against the wealthy bourgeoisie and that attempted to recreate true community upon the ruins of 1789-style individualism. This was Babeuf's interpretation of Year II, first proposed in Year IV and since then transmitted from generation to generation by Buonarroti's book. In one form or another it was taken up by Saint-Simon, Buchez, Esquiros, Louis Blanc, and countless lesser-known writers, who have made the dictatorship a necessity not simply of war but—much more than that—of justice and equality. They used the revolutionary government to express their contempt for law and formal democratic procedures as well as their hatred of the bourgeoisie, the market, and the power of money. Long before Marx, long before there was even a working class, the socialist idea thus took root in France in the form of reflection on the revolutionary government. Patriotic memories served to embellish the idea of class struggle.

It is even easier to succumb to romantic images of national energy, however, if the necessary and admirable revolutionary dictatorship can somehow be separated from the detestable and dreadful Terror. This was the line taken by many nineteenth-century republican historians, obsessed with the relation between revolutionary government, the Terror, and Robespierrism. Michelet, for example, loved the Mountain but hated the Jacobins. The great heroes of the war that saved the fatherland belonged to the former: Carnot, Cambon, Lindet, and the two Prieurs. The Jacobin Club's only contribution was the ideological orchestration of the Terror, led by the high priest Robespierre. By contrast, Louis Blanc looks upon Robespierre as a hero, but he sees a distinction between the work of the Committee of Public Safety, which saved the nation, and the Terror, which was the crime of the Hébertists. True, he has more reasons than Michelet to admire the wartime dictatorship, because as a good socialist he sees it as the precursor of the powerful modern state, protector of the poor and administrator of the economy. He does not, however, count the Terror among the measures necessary to save France. For that we must await Albert Mathiez and other twentieth-century communist historians, who celebrate the guillotine as it was celebrated in 1793, as an indispensable element in the victory of the fatherland and the establishment of an egalitarian society.

At the opposite extreme, historians more concerned with liberty than equality, such as the liberals of the Restoration period, reject both the revolutionary government and the Terror as the two faces of an illegal regime imposed on the nation by an illiterate rabble. Mignet nevertheless cites extenuating circumstances and is willing to be lenient because the government was so short-lived. Guizot, who in the early 1820s wrote his admirable polemics against the ultras, stresses the role of aristocratic resistance in provoking the terrorist measures of 1792–1794. But that only makes him all the more critical of the revolutionary government, a regime so lawless that he dubs it "anarchist."

For the liberals, the revolutionary dictatorship that rode roughshod over rights of man proclaimed to be sacred in 1789 was the result of an unwarranted extension of public sovereignty into the realm of individual liberties. Benjamin Constant, followed in this respect by Guizot, blamed this philosophical and political error on the nefarious influence of the *Social Contract* and the exorbitant powers imputed to the general will. Other writers, more libertarian than liberal, offered another interpretation of what they too regarded as an extreme form of domination of society by the state. Proudhon, the champion of "socialism through self-management," and Quinet, a republican exiled by Napoleon III, saw the Robespierrist Republic as a resurrection of monarchical despotism using the same "public safety" pretext so often invoked by the Bourbons. Both liberals and libertarians agreed that the revolutionary government had accomplished precisely the opposite of what the Revolution of 1789 had intended. Instead of founding liberty on law, the Revolution established a dictatorship in the absence of law.

If, however, one takes the view that the terrorist state of 1793 was merely the logical continuation of the Revolution itself, then the revolutionary government is to blame not for violating the principles of 1789 but for putting them into practice. The paradox of counterrevolutionary historiography lies in its use of the Jacobin dictatorship to discredit the Rights of Man. Joseph de Maistre, for example, admits that it was the ferocious energy of the men of the Terror that saved France, but, he says, the most detestable nature of their effort should reveal to even the blindest observer just how awful the Revolution was throughout its duration.

Thus the debate over the nature and causes of the revolutionary government has for two hundred years included a debate about the unity of the Revolution itself. Counterrevolutionary tradition condemns the Revolution in toto; Jacobin, socialist, and communist historiography celebrates it all; republicans generally cite circumstances to absolve it of blame. Opposing these monolithic views are the authors who refuse to see the course of the Revolution from August 10, 1792, to 9 Thermidor (1794) as an episode in the saga of liberty and the Rights of Man. The liberals exalt 1789 and revile or regret 1793. Or, what comes to the same thing, they approve the outcome of the Revolution but disapprove the process. The political writers most passionate about liberty, such as Quinet, go so far as to exclude the dicatorship of 1793 from the Revolution's heritage, characterizing it instead as a revival of the Ancien Régime. Divided into two diametrically opposed periods—one heady with liberty, the other despotic—the French Revolution has been, since the time of Tocqueville, the focus of reflection on the ambiguity of modern democracy.

François Furet

FURTHER READING

Aulard, Alphonse. *Histoire politique de la Révolution française: Origines et développement de la démocratie et de la république (1789–1804)*, pt. 2, chap. 5. Paris, 1901.

Cobb, Richard. *Les armées révolutionnaires, instrument de la Terreur dans les départements Avril 1793 – Floréal an II*, 2 vols. Paris and The Hague, 1961–1963.

Guérin, Daniel. *La lutte des classes sous la Première République: Bourgeois et "bras nus" (1793–1797)*, 2 vols. Paris, 1946. Second edition, 1968.

Lefebvre, Georges. "Le Gouvernement Révolutionnaire." Mimeographed course notes. Centre de Documentation Universitaire, Paris, 1947.

Palmer, Robert. R. *Twelve Who Ruled: The Committee of Public Safety during the Terror.* Princeton, 1941.

Soboul, Albert. *Les sans-culottes parisiens en l'an II: Histoire politique et sociale des sections de Paris, 2 juin 1793 – 9 thermidor an II*. La Roche-sur-Yon, 1958. Reprinted Paris, 1958, and 1962 with the subtitle *Mouvement populaire et gouvernement révolutionnaire*.

Wallon, Henri. *Les représentants en mission et la justice révolutionnaire dans les départements en l'an II*, 5 vols. Paris, 1889–1890.

RELATED TOPICS

Babeuf

Blanc

Buchez

Carnot

Centralization

Committee of Public Safety

Condorcet

Constant

Constitution

Danton

Enragés

Girondins

Guizot

Hébertists

Jacobinism

Maistre

Maximum

Michelet

Montagnards

Montesquieu

Paris Commune

Quinet

Regeneration

Revolutionary Assemblies

Robespierre

Rousseau

Sans-culottes

Sovereignty

Terror

Tocqueville

REVOLUTIONARY RELIGION

T he title is "Revolutionary Religion," but it might easily have been "Religion of the Revolution" or "Revolutionary Religions." In such a title everything is problematic: the connection between the noun and the adjective, the choice of the singular, and even the certificate of existence that it seems to bestow on revolutionary religion. Camus proudly proclaimed: "Surely we have the power to change religion." Should we take him literally and believe that there was indeed a revolutionary religion other than in the wishes, or illusions, of the men of the Revolution?

Indeed, if it were found that the Revolution peremptorily relegated religion to the realm of private belief, then it might be argued that the noun and the adjective stand in violent contradiction. Or, if one agreed with Tocqueville that "religion [had] found itself temporarily enmeshed in the powers that democracy overthrew," then it might make sense to maintain that all the historical strangenesss of the Revolution can be accounted for by the divorce between religion and democracy. Between religion and the Revolution, then, there was a conflict of principles and a relation of mutual exclusion. Christian historiography of the Church and the Revolution has a predilection for this theme: it recognizes no religious content in the cults of the Revolution and insists on a doctrinal antagonism between religion (in the singular) and revolutionary religions (in the plural).

This plural brings us to the old quarrel between Aulard and Mathiez. Aulard preferred to speak of revolutionary religion only in the plural, or better yet, to speak of religions of the Revolution, because in his eyes the revolutionary cults were simple expedients for the national defense, sects that met a series of political needs and were implemented by rival political groups. Thus, the Hébertist cult of Reason was supplanted by a Robespierrist cult of the Supreme Being. In other words, the revolutionary cults were artificial creations, at once the object of political confrontation and its means. Aulard does not credit these cults with any religious content, nor does he believe that they were related to any collective need or to the revolutionary project as a whole. For him, there was no revolutionary religion.

All these points were specifically challenged by Mathiez. Where Aulard saw artificiality, Mathiez saw spontaneous creation: revolutionary religion was a late flowering of eighteenth-century philosophy. Where Aulard saw pluralism, Mathiez saw unity: the revolutionary cults must be apprehended as a global effort. And finally, where Aulard distinguished between the social and political aspects of the religious, Mathiez, much influenced by his reading of Durkheim, argued that the two were closely intertwined. From Durkheim, Mathiez took the definition of religion as a universal phenomenon, invariable in its essence despite the multiplicity of its particular manifestations, "an integral system of beliefs and practices pertaining to sacred things, that is, distinctive, taboo objects," a set of constraints that integrated the individual into society. These characteristics, ascribed to the revolutionary cults, were unified and dignified as social religion. When Mathiez read in Durkehim that religion was "life taken seriously," he may well have imagined how fervently his favorite hero, Robespierre, would have subscribed to this definition. Hence for him there was indeed a revolutionary religion.

Although theatricalized for purposes of polemic, the gap between Aulard and Mathiez can be reduced. The logic of Aulard's argument causes him to exaggerate the differences among the various revolutionary cults. In fact, he notes many mutual influences between the cult of Reason and that of the Supreme Being, which must therefore be assumed to have achieved some independence from the antagonistic groups of political leaders that created them, and he therefore recognizes that there was greater unity than he had initially assumed. Nor does Mathiez, for his part, deny that the cults were in part an artificial creation. If revolutionary religion was a substitute religion, men were responsible for making the substitution, and Mathiez honors them for having made the attempt. Rather than speak of revolutionary religion, it would be better to say that the Revolution imagined and instituted a religion. But then, Mathiez's opinion to the contrary notwithstanding, what one has is an external relation between the Revolution and religion: the Revolution *had* its religion.

This relation can be viewed—as Mathiez views it—as a success, or it can be viewed as a failure, as it has been by a whole historiographical tradition that runs from Constant to Quinet by way of Fourier. Constant set the tone by pointing out, in an oft-repeated phrase, that "even the most minor saint in the most obscure hamlet had the upper hand against all the authority arrayed in battle against it." The failure that Constant attributed to the omnipotence of habit, Fourier blamed on the impotence of the revolutionaries' imagination: they underestimated the resilience of the Catholic Church, had nothing to offer in opposition to it, and lacked the noble courage of heresy. Quinet wedded the two interpretations: from Constant he borrowed the theme of defeat, from Fourier the diagnosis of timidity and the strategic interpretation of religion. He, too, believed that there was "a great blow to be struck in religious matters." And that "great blow" would have been to substitute another religion for Catholicism. Quinet's contempt for the miserable symbols invented by the revolutionary cults is therefore ambiguous. He judges the actual powerlessness of the revolutionaries against their theoretical power. Like Camus, he believes that it was possible for them to change religion. Hence he speaks not so much of a revolutionary religion—for here the political remains separate from the religious—as of a religion *of the* Revolution.

Michelet could not accept the artificialism implicit in Quinet's view. If the French Revolution adopted no church, Michelet countered, it was because it was itself a church. The critique of revolutionary symbols he simply shrugged off, convinced that in the Church of the Revolution "faith is everything, form is nothing." The inability of the Revolution to give itself a different foundation was more than compensated by its ability to serve as its own foundation: a relation of identity is in this case superior to a relation of exteriority. The Revolution did not need to invent a new faith because it was that faith—at least until the day when the men of the Revolution "descended from justice to salvation, from its positive to its negative idea," for never "was a new faith founded on a negative idea." Until that disastrous turning point in revolutionary history, however, religion and Revolution went together, and it was redundant to speak of revolutionary religion.

Revolutionary religion? Must we see this expression as inadequate, even scandalous? Should we replace it, as Aulard did, by the plural: revolutionary cults? Or as Mathiez did on the one hand, Fourier and Quinet on the other, by the unity of a religion of the Revolution, successful for the former, a failure for the latter? Or again, as Michelet suggested, by a revolution-religion?

*
**

The first revolutionary religion was quite simply the Christian religion, and in particular the Catholic religion. The federative holidays had embodied an alliance of religious fervor with revolutionary fervor. They had combined the *Te Deum* with the civic oath. They had seen newborns brought to the altar of the fatherland beneath an archway of swords raised up by national guardsmen, whereupon tricolor cockades were fastened to the infants' diapers and a double baptism was celebrated, at once Catholic and revolutionary. They had heard priests deliver sermons that were also orders of the day. The Gallican Church, which played a central role in these ceremonies, celebrated the kinship of the Revolution and the Gospel, or again, as Fauchet wrote, "the accord between religion and liberty." In these early years of the Revolution, a thousand speeches, sermons, pamphlets, and patriotic prayers bear witness to an effort to popularize the notion that the message of Christianity was consonant with that of patriotism, either by drawing an explicit parallel between the commandments of the Constitution and those of the Gospel (both "recommend the sweet fraternity and holy equality of the children of God," the curé of Coutances affirmed in October 1790) or by exalting the image of a patriotic Jesus or, again, in the most audacious texts, by redefining the kingdom of God. Far from being purely spiritual, that kingdom obliged men while still living on earth to institute a perfect equality of rights and perhaps even common ownership of property, a practice of which the early Church had set a holy example.

The Civil Constitution of the Clergy sent out shock waves that shattered this communion of hearts: the first division dates from autumn 1790 and the oath. Patriotic and religious ceremonies continued to be held in common, however, until the summer of 1791, which marks a second cleavage. It was during this summer that the king fled to Varennes. In a posthumously published text Mirabeau recommended excluding from patriotic ceremonies a

Christian religion whose austerity precluded dancing, singing, and profane plays. Voltaire's enshrinement in the Pantheon was not only the first revolutionary festival without religious participation but also a demonstration with an anticlerical tone, against which constitutional priests protested.

As clouds gathered over the Legislative Assembly, the divorce between religion and civism was consummated. One still found curés pondering the "accord between religion and cults under a free nation," but like de Moy they did so in order to express their desire to ban clerical garb, prohibit priestly celibacy, and require civil burial in which death would be treated as an eternal sleep. The "universal Church" now became that of the political societies, which Lanthenas urged to form a federation in 1792, and it was from this new church that "patriotic missionaries" set forth to preach the cult of Reason and the Law. The crucial step was taken after the tenth of August: on September 20, 1792, acting in response to the chaos in the recording of vital statistics (records of births, baptisms, and deaths) caused by the refusal of the faithful to receive the sacraments from priests who had taken the oath to the Constitution, the deputies of the Legislative Assembly declared that such records would henceforth be kept by the secular authorities, and for good measure they legalized divorce. For the priests this move spelled the end of one of their traditional functions, and for everyone it meant a break with the past. It also marked the beginning of the constitutional clergy's desertion of the revolutionary camp.

A further step toward a replacement cult came from the départements and the creative energy of certain *représentants en mission,* often former men of the cloth. Despite the freedom of worship proclaimed by the Constitution of Year I, the representatives availed themselves of the room for initiative afforded by the suspension of the Constitution until peacetime to prohibit Sunday services (André Dumont in the Somme), to exhort priests to marry (Fouché in Nièvre), and almost everywhere to launch an offensive of vandalism against what contemporaries called the "external signs" of religion: crosses, calvaries, statues of saints on church facades. (And since the financial woes of the day encouraged finding new sources of precious metals, the churches' interior treasures were not respected, either.) Paris at first had misgivings; even Hébert, even Chaumette, even the sans-culottes, even the Commune were slow to follow the movement, in which people recognized the handiwork of certain foreign revolutionaries, such as Anacharsis Cloots and Pereira, with influence in Hébertist circles. In the midst of scenes of pillage— the most symbolic being the breaking of the Holy Ampulla at Rheims—and the burlesque processions that accompanied them there emerged a substitute cult, the first to assume the role that Catholicism had played in public life, the first to pretend to the title of revolutionary cult. In any case, it was the first of a series of attempts to which some grant and others refuse the dignity of being called a revolutionary religion.

*
**

Of all the revolutionary cults, the cult of Reason has been most decried by historians, who have seen it at worst as a permanent orgy and at best as a "crude caricature of Catholic ceremonies." The term "cult of Reason" admittedly encompasses a variety of very different elements: the dedication of churches to Reason, offerings of silver, recantation of oaths by priests, the cult of martyrs of Liberty, the grotesque processions of the de-Christianizers. It was a multifarious phenomenon, marked by disorderliness and ostentation: "a religion for the eyes and ears," Fourier called it. The fusion of all these elements in an instituted ceremony was quite sporadic; on the de-Christianizers' day of triumph, November 7, 1793, when the Convention received the treasures taken from the churches of Nièvre by Fouché and heard the abjuration of the bishop of Paris, the département and the Commune decided that on the following Sunday the civic festival of liberty that was originally to be held at the Palais Royal would instead be transferred to Notre Dame. This masque was to celebrate "the triumph that Reason has just won over the prejudices of eighteen centuries." The same play was produced in the provinces, with a certain freedom in making additions. Nearly everywhere, however, the central plot involved a woman triumphant over fanaticism, whose luminous unveiling caused shadows and monsters to flee, by relying on the simple stagecraft of appearance and disappearance. This play was the heart of what would later be called the "cult of Reason."

Few standards regulated use of this appellation, for it was not entirely a cult, nor was it a cult of "Reason." It was not a cult because the festival of Reason had a profoundly theatrical character. Its motif and staging were taken from an opera libretto. As in the theater, it could be "restaged," and in fact it was restaged before the Convention. It was confined to the inside of the church (not so much out of anticlerical provocation as because of the rigors of the season). Finally, just as in the theater, a female star was needed, a star who heightened the artificiality of the whole production, as Quinet perceptively noted: "The actress removed her divinity an hour later." Nothing in this production, which in many cases required a good deal in the way of technical ingenuity, suggests a cult: no prayer of any kind was directed toward the woman who was its dazzling centerpiece.

Was it, moreover, a cult *of Reason?* Historians of the late nineteenth century took an interest in this "cult," which they interpreted as a harbinger of the triumph of free thought. But they found that the Reason celebrated was without any principle: in some cases it was indeed reason, but in others it was liberty or nature (Chénier's hymn hailed it as "Liberty, daughter of Nature") and in still others victory; the festival was not well characterized and went by a variety of names (festival of mores, festival of virtue), in addition to which it sometimes involved invocations of the Supreme Being, prayers that were almost a contradiction in terms. Hence it would be unwise to take too systematic a view of the festival of Reason. It caused such a scandal among historians not because of its message or imagery but because of the militant de-Christianizing that often went with it: scenes of pillage, mocking processions, and iconoclastic commandos from the revolutionary army. The whole occasion, owing in part to the absence of any national program, was rather plastic.

This plasticity was not the case with the cult that succeeded it: the cult of the Supreme Being. To contrast this movement with the cult of Reason is particularly easy, since its creators themselves made the comparison. It is enough to note that the bonfire that consumed cassocks and skull caps in the festival of Reason now burned an allegory of atheism. (In Paris it was Robespierre himself who lit the flames.) Once again, however, we must be careful not to overestimate the importance of the auto-da-fé that was at the center of the ceremony: the essence of the festival was a procession of elderly men, mothers, young women, and children, punctuated by stations and accompanied by hymns, bouquets tossed heavenward in homage to the "Great Director," and prayers of gratitude to the Supreme Being. This festival, in other words, had all the earmarks of a cult. Here there were not spectators but celebrants, not an audience but a people. And finally, since David's script was used everywhere, the ceremony, which was performed throughout France, allowed little room for local initiative.

For historians, considerations of this ceremony have always figured in interpretations of Robespierre's personal policy. It was Robespierre who, on 1 Frimaire, Year II, took the first steps to halt de-Christianization. On 18 Frimaire it was again following an intervention by Robespierre that the Convention confirmed the principle of freedom of worship. ("On that day," wrote an indignant Quinet, "Robespierre and the Committee of Public Safety reaped the glory of saving the counterrevolution and declaring it inviolable; on that day they did more for the old religion than Saints Dominic and Torquemada.") On 18 Floréal it was Robespierre who read the important report on republican principles (which specified the calendar of regenerated ceremonies, distributed over the entire year, the first example being the festival of the Supreme Being). Again it was Robespierre, by chance chairman of the Convention on the day of the festival, who figured as its leading light and seemed to occupy the role of pontiff. And finally it was with Robespierre's downfall that the cult of the Supreme Being was abolished. These are reasons enough for associating the new cult with Robespierre's personality and destiny.

Some historians, including Aulard, have seen the cult as the expression of a deeply mystical soul and a truly religious project. Others have seen it as a ruse: for some, such as Daniel Guérin, an evil ruse designed to preserve established wealth on a newly shored-up foundation of social order; for others, such as Mathiez, a well-meaning ruse designed to reconcile the Revolution with Catholicism. The cult of the Supreme Being therefore invariably raises the same question for historians: was it the invention of a believer or the contrivance of a strategist?

Judging someone's sincerity is always a ticklish business, and in any case there is no need to choose between these two interpretations, both of which are supported by strong arguments. There is no need to assume any special penchant for mysticism in Robespierre (Charles Ledré, for example, speaks of Robespierre's "mystical crisis" in Floréal) to account for his belief in the Supreme Being. This outdoor cult, with its dramatic staging of a natural religion liberated from the narrowness of the sanctuary and the presence of priests and thus "purged" of both superstition and atheism, is not evidence for any very personal powers of imagination on Robespierre's part; the entire intellectual elite of the eighteenth century dreamed of and wished for nothing else. True, Robespierre brought to it the faith and force of a particular temperament: his instinct for respectability, which was the source of his distaste for masquerade and exhibition.

Taking this deistic cult seriously and subscribing to it personally obviously did not prevent Robespierre from ascribing to it a particular purpose, namely, to restore order to the sphere of religious and moral ideas. The Floréal report is studded with verbs of establishment and completion: it is a question of "attaching" morality to eternal moorings, of "settling" law and prosperity, of "founding" order on a basis of justice. In short, the issue is one of ending the Revolution by establishing a state religion.

Neither the goal—ending the Revolution—nor the means—republican ceremony as a means of social integration and conservation—make Robespierre particularly deserving of either admiration or vituperation. He relied on an old argument of the Enlightenment—that religions are useful for holding the people in check—and expanded on a commonplace of revolutionary thought. Bear in mind, moreover, that the festival of the Supreme Being was part of a global plan to establish civic ceremonies, a plan drawn up by the Committee on Public Instruction under the supervision of Mathieu. Robespierre relied heavily on this plan and retained what was essential in it. And do not forget that enlightened opinion approved of the ceremony, contemporaries drew from it comforting feelings of conformity, and it met with success.

There is, however, a distinctively Robespierrist stamp on both the Floréal speech and the festival of the Supreme Being, namely, in the new cult's relation to the Terror. That relation has often been described as one of pure coincidence in time and space: in Paris the guillotine coexisted with the bouquets of the Supreme Being (which has scandalized many historians, some because of the guillotine, others because of the Supreme Being, still others because of the glaring contrast between the utopian festival and the instrument of death). Furthermore, the festival was held within two days of the passage of the dreadful laws of Prairial. In fact, this conjunction was much more than mere coincidence: there was a logical connection deliberately intended by Robespierre. The Floréal report shows this intent clearly by establishing a peremptory connection between imperatives that appear to have little in common: "Establish a tranquil life on immutable foundations of justice and revive public morality" (in other words, create a state religion), and "hurl thunderbolts at the heads of the guilty and rain lightning on your enemies" (in other words, make war and pursue the Terror). The link between the two sets of imperatives is clear. It would not have been easy to win acceptance of the Terror if people had believed that a blind force struck randomly at virtue as well as crime and that posterity held no compensation—in short, to gain acceptance from people who believed in "Chaumette's depressing doctrines." It was even less easy to accept personal responsibility for the Terror. In order to win acceptance of this necessity and erase any sign of personal responsibility, what better warrant, what better shelter than providence? The

Supreme Being was thus by no means an incongruous fantasy but the best way of supporting the Terror with the prop of orthodoxy.

Might this state religion, which sank with Thermidor, have been *the* revolutionary religion? It is difficult to say that it was not. But there is an indication that in one respect, at least, it was found wanting: in the petitions of congratulation that came to Robespierre from towns and villages, many expressed regret that the hymns and invocations specified in the official program included no prayers intended to obtain the *protection* of the Supreme Being—a sign that this bookish religion, in which there was indeed no way of calling upon the Supreme Being for help, offered rather meager nourishment to the religious sensibility.

The final attempt to create a revolutionary cult, which bore the unappealing name of "theophilanthropy," was both similar to and different from the cult of the Supreme Being. The new cult differed from its predecessor in that it did not have the official approval of the regime—the Directory and the councils remembered Robespierre only too well—although it did for a time enjoy its protection. The cult of theophilanthropy, which held its first solemn meeting on 26 Nivôse, Year IV, would remain a private affair, the creation of a small group of men formed by Masonry and led by a tireless bookseller by the name of Chemin, the organizer of the new cult, inventor of its rites, and writer of its handbooks. He was joined by Valentin Haüy, with his choir of blind young men, along with Dupont de Nemours, Bernardin de Saint-Pierre, and the director La Révellière-Lépeaux, an enthusiastic supporter of the new religion. Despite the efforts of these men, and despite a core group of militants—defrocked priests, journalists, and booksellers who won adherents to the cult in the provinces, particularly in central France—theophilanthropy suffered because it failed to receive a warm reception from the directors and councils. To various proposals to institute a state religion they responded as Talot did in Messidor, Year IV: "We are not the creators of a new cult," a phrase that bespoke renunciation of a great revolutionary ambition. With such a background of disillusionment, it is easy to understand why the anti-Jacobin turn taken by the government in Floréal, Year VI, permanently put an end to theophilanthropy.

Yet this new cult, like that of the Supreme Being which preceded it, was one in which all eighteenth-century deism could have recognized itself. Theophilanthropy believed in the possibility of an accord between the morality of the gospels and republican morality and at times held that its true founder was "Jesus, the philosopher of Judaea." It saw itself as a purified cult, without priests—to be replaced by fathers of families—without emblems, without images, and without statues, as a return to the simplicity of the beginning (the theophilanthropists had almost decided to call themselves "primitive Christians"). It also incorporated the theme of religion's social utility. Religious ceremonies were indispensable for bringing solemnity to the great occasions of an individual's life—birth, marriage, death—because without rites life degenerates into insignificance. Furthermore, only such ceremonies were capable of instilling a sense of duty in simple minds. The educated man can practice the social virtues as a result of "rational choice," but according to La

Révellière-Lépeaux, in yet another melancholy assessment, "that is not true of a people." Chemin went even further: "A large group of men that recognized no God and believed that their crimes would be buried forever in the grave would soon become a herd of ferocious animals."

Thus theophilanthropy comprised a range of austere and edifying ceremonies and was doomed to failure because it refused the aid of the imagination. It was far too "reasonable," Fourier wrote, for a people that wanted a cult "that would propel it into enthusiasm." In delivering "the great blow" of which the men of the Revolution had dreamed it was no more successful than its predecessors.

Having made our way from one cult to another, can we now say whether there was ultimately one or more than one? Was Aulard or Mathiez correct? It is easy to understand why a history of political events like Aulard's placed the accent on the successive attempts and the multiplicity of cults. But if one focuses on the content, then Mathiez's account is more pertinent: regularity overshadows singularity. For all their disagreements, the rival groups shared two beliefs: that morality is the basis of religion, and that laws make mores. It is actually rather astonishing to observe the collective instinct that impelled the revolutionaries, once the break with Catholicism occurred, to imagine, in terms of an identical model, the ceremonial of ages, family, and friendship in which Renan saw an "Eden of happy bourgeois, amusing themselves in squadrons, believing by decree": a unified world view, in fact, but not enough to convince us that it was a religion.

*
* *

Where, then, is revolutionary religion to be found? One might still look for it on the fringes of the official cults or, as Michelet suggested, in the revolutionary spirit itself.

The summer and autumn of 1793 saw, amid waves of emotion triggered by the death of Marat, a proliferation of funerals, apotheoses, and inaugurations of busts. This memorializing may be interpreted as emulation on the part of sections and popular societies. Or it may be seen, as Albert Soboul saw it, as a genuine cult: the irrational religiosity of the popular crowds found nourishment here. The interpretation of these ceremonies as a true cult is based on well-known facts to which counterrevolutionary historians have called attention: Marat's heart placed in a vessel and hung from the roof of the Cordeliers; psalms (*O cor Marat, O cor Jesus*); prayers and catechisms. But it is a long way from such facts to the inference that Marat, and soon Chalier and Le Peletier as well, were perceived and invoked as saints. This interpretation is based not so much on acts (touching or kissing busts of the "revolutionary saints" or ascribing therapeutic powers to them remained extremely rare occurrences) as on texts, which are repeatedly cited. But the "martyr" of liberty, to use the revolutionary language, was simply a hero: the religious component was absorbed into the vocabulary and imagery of a quite human heroism, which placed Marat along with Brutus, Lycurgus, Rousseau, and Voltaire in a moral Pantheon in which Jesus also figured as an "honorable victim of the Judaic aristocracy." Similarly, Marat was called "immortal," but immortality in the language of the Revolution was not so much a hope as a symbol of survival in collective memory (as "Pantheonization" clearly demonstrated). Catechism and gospels were in any case ways for the revolutionaries to take advantage of a traditional form; simply because one catechism proposed that "we shall have no other god but Marat" and the women of the Society of Republican Revolutionaries swore that they would give their children no "other gospel than the collection of his works," it does not follow that there was a true devotion. In the homage that was paid to the revolutionary saints of 1793, one can no doubt find signs of emotional identification, but the cult lacked the essential thing, which is the request for sacred protection. These saints were not intercessors. Once again, a rudimentary revolutionary cult can be discerned, but not a revolutionary religion.

That leaves the reinterpretation of the Revolution itself as the spirit of Christianity rediscovered and reinvested. Esquiros wrote: "Some modern writers regard democracy as the necessary development of Christian ideas. For them, the French Revolution grew out of the Gospel, or should I say, it was the Gospel itself incarnated in an act." This interpretation, which makes inescapable the conclusion that there was indeed a revolutionary religion, found its most striking imagery and most powerful arguments in the work of Michelet. According to Michelet, the Revolution was a religion because it was at once regeneration and foundation: its sacred character was the same as that of baptism. The Revolution was a religion because "it ignored space and time." The Revolution was a religion because it dramatized the relation of each individual to humanity and—a most important point for Michelet—returned women and children to public life. The Revolution was a religion because it detached the individual from himself and worked tirelessly to relate him to his fellow man, through federations and civic banquets, and to the fatherland, the new expression of collective unity, which the citizen, in an endless ritual of oaths, swore to defend and for which he promised to die.

If we forget about the revolutionary cults, was Michelet right that there was a religion consubstantial with the Revolution? If one defines revolutionary religion as a reinvestment of the sentiment of the sacred in the fatherland and humanity, then one must say "yes." The revolutionary cults in no sense attempted to eliminate the sacred. Once the tragic, dolorous, somber aspects of Catholicism had been eliminated, the inventors of those cults worked hard to find common ground on which to pitch their ceremonies. That common ground was the revelation of a homogeneous humanity present in yet transcending each and every individual. It was necessary, Robespierre said, to "inspire in man a religious respect for man," and, Cabanis added, to give him a "sublime idea of the dignity of his existence." Jesus himself was defined as a "sublime man." The revolutionaries constantly invoked the humanity in man to justify the sacrifice of the individual to the whole, a central tenet of the revolutionary religion.

And yet if one believes that religion requires the designation of a different order of being, a different kind of place, an extraordinary state, then there was no revolutionary religion. The organizers of the revolutionary ceremonies, who sanctified biological and social bonds, were unable to imagine anything transcending man other than man himself. Their pathetic attempt to solemnize what Constant called the "private affections" through the publicity of ceremony is the best indication there is of the weakening of the collective bond and the increasing retreat into privacy: "revolutionary religion" was the harbinger and symbol of a society without religious support.

Mona Ozouf

FURTHER READING

Aulard, Alphonse. *Le culte de la Raison et le culte de l'Etre Suprême (1793–1794): Essai historique*. Paris, 1892.

Bowman, Franck-Paul. *Le Christ romantique, 1789: Le sans-culotte de Nazareth*. Geneva, 1973.

Latreille, André, et al. *Histoire du catholicisme en France*, vol. 3. Paris, 1962.

Ledré, Charles. *L'Eglise de France sous la Révolution*. Paris, 1949.

Lefort, Claude. "La Terreur révolutionnaire," in *Essais sur le politique, XIXe–XX siècle*. Paris, 1986.

Mathiez, Albert. *Les origines des cultes révolutionnaires (1789–1792)*. Paris, 1904.

——— *La théophilanthropie et le culte décadaire, 1796–1801: Essai sur l'histoire religieuse de la Révolution*. Paris, 1904.

McManners, John. *The French Revolution and the Church*. London, 1969.

Menozzi, Daniele. *Letture politiche di Gesù: Dall'ancien regime all rivoluzione*. Brescia, 1973.

Soboul, Albert. "Sentiment religieux et cultes populaires," *Annales historiques de la Révolution française*, 1956.

RELATED TOPICS

Civil Constitution of the Clergy
Constant
De-Christianization
Enlightenment
Federation

Hébertists
Marat
Michelet
Mirabeau
Quinet

Robespierre
Terror
Tocqueville
Vandalism

SUFFRAGE

S uffrage was the object of numerous debates and confrontations, both inside and outside the assemblies, during the Revolution. What limits
would there be on political participation by citizens? What would be the composition of the electorate? As early as 1789 these questions were essential.
The answers provided by successive assemblies are not in themselves sufficient to characterize the political regimes with which the Revolution experi-
mented, but they do underscore the values, aspirations, and justifications of
those regimes.

By transferring to the nation the source of a sovereignty previously
held by the king on extrasocial grounds, the Revolution placed the suffrage
at the center of the new political order; it became the essential means of instituting and legitimating public authority. Along with this purpose went a
new definition: suffrage was an attribute of citizenship, which, abandoning
organic representations of society, was now defined in terms of equal individuals. Thanks to the individuation and equalization of voting, to majority rule,
and to the secret ballot, citizens could genuinely assent to the authority that
was to be exercised over them. At the same time, the suffrage severed the
political from the social; it nullified social diversity in a unified body politic,
thus preventing any one social group from identifying itself with power. A
voter was no longer an actual, socially identifiable human being; he became
an abstraction, a citizen whose autonomy and equivalence were specified by
law. Power having been instituted by all, either "immediately or through their
representatives," the suffrage was a generator of consensus—a guarantee of
peaceful politics. It was with much bitterness, moreover, that the Constituent
Assembly, the heir to a century of enlightenment, discovered that the suffrage
was powerless to eliminate all "archaic" and violent forms of political action.

Did the establishment of a *censitaire* electoral regime (that is, one based
on property qualifications) in 1789 and again in 1795 destroy the coherence
of a political system based on universal consent? In order to understand the
fundamental yet limited role ascribed to suffrage, we must consider several
factors, among which the representative principle should be regarded as essential.

The representative system meant denying the people immediate exercise of their sovereignty. Ideally, direct popular sovereignty would have been
preferable, of course, but it was not practical except in societies of limited
extent, whose limited needs and simple interests permitted all citizens to devote themselves fully to public affairs. In large, socially and economically complex states, and in societies based on equality of rights rather than servitude,

the principle of division of labor justified the institution of a system of representation to deal with affairs common to many citizens. Elected representatives were more than just mediators made necessary by circumstances, however; the general will was not the sum of individual wills. Only the common interests of individuals entered into the formation of the general will; private interests were excluded. Through their deliberations the representatives performed the *labor* necessary to arrive at a formulation of the general will. Representation unified a diverse nation; it was the nation assembled. Outside it there were only individuals.

The representative system gave the suffrage its importance, for it was through the vote that citizens participated in the formulation of the general will, by choosing those who would be responsible to speak for, and in the name of, the nation; yet representation also defined the limits of suffrage. The suffrage, necessary in one respect, was sufficient in another; it named those who would temporarily hold authority, but it also implied the citizens' consent to the use made of that authority by their elected representatives. Elections permitted a choice but allowed for no control, and the Constituent Assembly would resolutely oppose any proposal to extend the scope of suffrage on the grounds that the deliberative character of the representative assembly required that deputies be totally free from influence of any kind by their constituents. The legislation passed in 1789–1790 is very precise in this respect; it limited the exercise of the suffrage to elections only and prohibited elective assemblies from deliberating or limiting the powers of those whom they elected: in voting the electors exhausted their powers. Once the votes were counted, the representative ceased to be in the power of his constituents and became the representative of the undivided totality of electoral districts, that is, of the nation as a whole. Sieyès wrote: "All cantons mutually authorize and commit one another to conduct this by-election, which for that very reason is supposed to be the work of the entire community." Each canton, as well as each voter, represented the nation in the electoral system: the voter did not exercise a right by voting but rather performed a function entrusted to him by the nation. Limited suffrage made sense and was justifiable only in relation to the doctrine of voting as function; to that extent it was compatible with Article 6 of the Declaration of the Rights of Man, concerning the right of every citizen to participate in the formulation of the law, since with some sleight of hand every vote cast was supposed to express the wishes of the nation as a whole.

Sieyès thus distinguished between universal rights, which were "passive" because they belonged to every member of the association, and political rights, which were "active" because they were bestowed by the nation to be exercised in the interest of society as a whole. The suffrage was a public function, "to which no one has a right, which the society dispenses as prescribed by its interest" (Barnave, August 1791). The aptitude for exercising political rights was to be measured in terms of utility.

Until 1792 the organization of the electorate was governed by three main principles: a voter must be a full-fledged citizen, whose citizenship was not impaired by bankruptcy or indictment; he must possess independence of judgment; and finally he must have an "interest in the public establishment," that is, in good government of men and things. Pursuant to the second of these conditions, anyone, such as a minor, a woman, or a domestic servant, whose will was presumed to depend on that of another person, was excluded from the suffrage. With the exception of domestics, who were granted civil rights under the Constitution of 1793, these groups would remain excluded from voting throughout the Revolution, although on rare occasions there were those, including Condorcet and Sieyès, who argued in favor of female suffrage. The third condition was that the exercise of the nation's powers was to be entrusted to those whose private interest was linked to public prosperity. Active citizens must have an "interest" in the public good, all the more so the higher they rose on the ladder of responsibility. Was it reasonable to assume, the Constituent Assembly asked, that those who owned nothing and had no stake in anything would vote for laws to preserve property and the social order? This qualification of "interest" was the whole purpose of the *censitaire* decrees, among which we may include the condition of a year's residence in the same canton, a relatively restrictive measure in a country that at the time counted a rather large "floating" population.

Agreement concerning these reasons for disqualification from voting was reached fairly easily. The same cannot be said, however, for the precise qualifications associated with the *censitaire* regime. At the end of 1789 there were, broadly speaking, two opposing positions in the debate, between which the Constituent Assembly sought to strike a compromise.

Inherited from the century of the Enlightenment and the physiocrats, the figure of the citizen-owner, prosperous, educated, at leisure, was strongly present in the political imagination of 1789 as a guarantee of aptitude to weigh the interests of the nation, presumptive evidence in favor of balanced judgment. As late as 1795 Boissy d'Anglas presented this model as the most effective possible barrier against any return of the anarchy of Year II. Condorcet had long since associated citizenship with "rights over a portion of the territory." Several deputies in the Constituent Assembly, such as Dupont de Nemours and Cazalès, asked that the suffrage be limited exclusively to landowners, and Cazalès even argued that merchants, preoccupied solely with their profits and without national roots, ought to be excluded.

Sentiment in favor of a government of talent in the Assembly was a forerunner of the position championed in the following century by liberals and "doctrinaires": Barère, for example, argued that "industry and the arts" ought not to be excluded, for in them lay the true source of the nation's prosperity. More systematic, Barnave in 1791 expounded an early version of a theory that would be developed in his book published in 1793, namely, that a leading role in the suffrage ought to be reserved for the "middling" citizen of society, for the producer of movable wealth, who had an interest in "free government" and therefore offered the soundest possible foundation for the political system.

In opting for an electoral system based on *compulsory* tax payments, the Constituent Assembly, seeking to reconcile Cazalès' traditionalism with Barnave's modernism, staked out a position distinct from both these opposing schools of thought. Access to the ballot box was denied to anyone who did not pay a direct tax equivalent to three days' labor (between 1 livre 10 sous and 3 livres); to serve as an elector in the second stage of elections the required tax payment was the equivalent of ten days' labor (5 to 10 livres); and finally, to serve as deputy, one had to own property and pay a tax equal to one silver marc (more than 53 livres). One-third of all citizens were thus excluded from the electorate in 1791. Sixty percent of the "active citizens" met the criterion for the primary *cens*, but fewer than twenty percent satisfied the very restrictive requirement of the *marc d'argent*.

The system functioned poorly from the outset. The administrative vacuum that existed in the first few months of 1790, along with fiscal disorder, created insuperable difficulties, which forced the Assembly to make compromises and issue exemptions. In the Committee on the Constitution, the future Feuillants even encouraged petitions aimed at abrogating the *marc d'argent*. In August 1791 the Constituent Assembly undertook to revise the system almost completely: the property clause and the *marc d'argent* were eliminated, and any active citizen could be elected to the legislature. On the other hand, the intermediate *cens* for second-stage electors was sharply increased (to between 15 and 65 livres in tax payments, depending on the circumstances). This reorganization was in line with Barnave's proposal: second-stage electors were required to meet particularly stringent requirements, since they were the ones who made the crucial decisions. By requiring a fairly high *cens* for them, the hope was to obtain some guarantee against bad choices. Eligibility, however, was no longer to be subject to any conditions of wealth, the only requirement being the ability to distinguish between citizens on the basis of "their virtues and talents." The rigid, hierarchical system of 1789 thus gave way in 1791 to a more flexible arrangement that combined a selective structure with the principle that every citizen should be eligible for any public office.

Was the *cens* contrary to the Declaration of Rights? The very same article of the preamble to the Constitution of 1791 both gave constitutional value to the Declaration, by stipulating that the legislature could pass no law contrary to its provisions, and gave the legislature the power to define the content of, and thus set limits to, rights set forth in the Declaration only in the abstract. To that extent, no law duly approved by the representatives of the nation could be declared void on grounds of incompatibility with the Declaration. Nevertheless, it was obvious to many people that the *cens* was incompatible with the principle of equality of rights; they deliberately ignored the two distinctions drawn by the Constituent Assembly, between rights and their exercise and between civil rights and political "rights."

Paradoxically, the *cens* was based on equality, even though it created an undeniable inequality: it grew out of a tension between the principle of equality and actual inequality. By establishing a minimal distinction, the *cens* preserved the principle from the negative effects of an abstract equality implemented without taking actual conditions into account: Barnave observed, for example, that to admit "poverty" into the electorate was ipso facto to place "opulence" at the head of the state. Indiscriminate recruitment resulting

574

from an equality of principle would inevitably increase the influence of actual inequalities. In 1788 Condorcet also argued that by means of a moderate *cens* political life should be organized in such a way as to create the *possibility* of equality, in order to prevent a disastrous collusion, through abstract equality, between the richest and poorest citizens, between those who have no interests and those in whom private interest outweighs every other consideration. Under these conditions, universal suffrage would inevitably lead to manipulation and a patron-client system. Yet as the obsession with this probable collusion shows, to reject universal suffrage in 1789 was also to favor the progressivism and reformist spirit of the elites over the society's egalitarian and perhaps conservative tendencies, there being no proof whatsoever that the latter had been profoundly affected by the "shock" of 1789.

The *cens* was deceptive in that it seemed to consecrate the power of a "fiscal aristocracy"—quite a broad group, moreover. By itself, however, the *cens* did not give access to suffrage: one still had to have one's name inscribed on the electoral lists and take the civic oath—in other words, one had to clearly demonstrate one's intention to take part in political life. It was a volunteer system rather than a regime in which all citizens who paid the required minimum tax were automatically inscribed. To be sure, this aspect of the system was not the result of deliberate design, since the Assembly had rejected Sieyès' proposal to make the suffrage dependent on a modest voluntary contribution distinct from normal taxes. Nevertheless, when the Constituent Assembly authorized citizens, regardless of their fiscal status, to pay the required patriotic contribution of their own free will, it in effect opted for a voluntary system. Still more concretely, the fiscal reform then in progress, by diminishing indirect taxes and increasing direct ones, was supposed to lead to a rapid and marked increase in the number of active citizens. In addition, the *censitaire* regime was conceived with expansion in mind: here we see the influence of the century's optimism and rationalism, in the deep-seated conviction that good laws, combined with the effects of public education and economic progress, would soon "increase the number of citizens and decrease the size of the common populace" (Condorcet).

The limited *censitaire* suffrage reflects a concern with prudence, a desire to remove political power from the influence of the amorphous and manipulable "multitude." Yet it was not a reaction against the egalitarian dynamic unleashed in 1789. On the contrary, that dynamic made it possible to define the *censitaire* suffrage as a prelude to universal suffrage.

Universal suffrage, and still more the abolition of conditions on eligibility, were major elements in the radicalization of revolutionary demands. On those demands Robespierre built his astonishing popularity, and the fraternal societies prospered. Later, the Jacobins used the same demands to cement their alliance with the most radical of the sectional militants, and the mobilization that preceded the tenth of August was based in part on the theme of civic equality. The importance of these issues in the political debate is evidence of an especially strong sense—if not the reality—of injustice. It is even rather surprising to note the disproportion between the demands and the almost universal indifference to the institution of suffrage: a 1791 statistic indicates that of 1,600 citizens recognized as active in the Luxembourg section, barely 800 were inscribed on the voter lists and fewer than 400 participated in the elections. Furthermore, all signs are that after the establishment of universal suffrage in August 1792, the former passive citizens did not avail themselves of their newfound right to vote.

The opposition to the *cens* clearly demonstrated the tactical use that could be made of the general principles set forth in the Declaration of Rights to deny legitimacy to the positive laws passed by the Assembly. In April 1791, for example, Robespierre denounced the *censitaire* decrees for being contrary to rights solemnly proclaimed in 1789; by destroying natural equality through inequality in the exercise of political rights and by limiting freedom of choice, the Assembly purportedly violated the principles whose preservation was supposed to be the purpose of all positive legislation. For Robespierre, the Constituent Assembly had no choice but to repeal a law that, having been passed on the basis of such specious arguments as the (illusory) sovereignty of a nation distinct from its constitutive elements or the distinction between civil and political rights, was "null and void."

Radical discourse was not content to condemn an injustice that could be repaired easily. It struck in two ways at the very heart of the representative system. First, it was argued that only universal suffrage would make it possible to associate the entire nation with the institution of political power. Second, limiting the suffrage was said to be destructive of the sovereignty of the nation because it permitted the nation to be robbed of its rights for the benefit of "parliamentary despotism."

The first argument challenged the representativity of the legislature in the *censitaire* system. With property qualifications, deputies represented the active citizens, not the nation. Not without reason, some critics pointed out that the distinction between active and passive citizens threatened to exclude a segment of society from political life and therefore represented a danger to civil peace by threatening to weaken the consensus upon which representative government depended. From a political standpoint, this situation, further aggravated by the system of indirect elections, tended to legitimize the efforts by the clubs and societies to establish themselves as agencies to monitor the work of a representative body only too likely to betray the interests and desires of a nation not allowed to participate fully in its selection. From 1790 to 1792 the campaign against the *censitaire* system played a powerful part in substituting "public opinion," as expressed in the clubs, for the suffrage as the means by which power was legitimated.

In December 1789 an article in *Révolutions de Paris*, after alluding to the incompatibility between the *cens* and the Rights of Man, pointed out that the new electoral legislation "did not destroy national liberty, because by excluding most of the French people [from the legislature], it did not deprive them of the ability to contribute to the ratification of the laws." Indeed, it was laws limiting the exercise of the suffrage to elections alone that destroyed the national sovereignty. The principal issue was the control of the legislature's actions, their sanction by the people, and not the election of deputies, which in the end could be seen as a minor or even subsidiary aspect of the exercise of the suffrage.

The insurrection of August 10, 1792, by spelling the end of the Constitution of 1791, laid the groundwork for extension of the suffrage in two ways: on that very day universal suffrage was instituted, and on September 21 the Convention declared that "there can be no constitution that is not accepted by the people."

For Aulard, these two decrees marked the victory of the democratic spirit in the Revolution. Unfortunately, such enthusiasm must be tempered by noting the limits of the universal suffrage of 1792: citizens over the age of twenty-one (rather than twenty-five, as required until then) were granted the right to vote provided they could give proof of one year's residence in the same canton and of income sufficient to prove that they "lived on the fruits of their labor," a requirement that was tantamount to excluding non-taxpayers. In addition, perpetuation of the system of indirect elections probably nullified much of what people expected from universal suffrage. Subsequent constitutional proposals ostensibly favored true universal male suffrage, yet while Condorcet in February 1793 made direct election by the people an imperative rule, the Constitution approved in June reestablished indirect elections for nomination of public functionaries and even instituted a three-stage election for the Executive Council. Since this text was postponed *sine die* in October 1793, the legislation approved in August 1792 would remain in force until the plebiscite of Year III.

In conformity with the decree of September 21, 1792, the primary assemblies were called upon in July 1793 to vote on the Constitution, but none of the broader systems envisioned in 1793 was put into practice. Here again, Condorcet's proposal was the most ambitious; it specified that through the suffrage citizens could disapprove laws deemed contrary to individual rights; vote on the articles of the Constitution itself, on petitions for its amendment, and on questions of general interest submitted to referendum by the legislature; and, finally, initiate legislation. Thus incorporating a threefold power to institute, sanction, and to a lesser extent initiate, the suffrage in Condorcet's plan occupied a central place in a very extensive democracy, in which the powers retained by the nation for direct exercise greatly exceeded the powers it delegated. Setting the terms of an almost ideal democracy, Condorcet's plan depended on rationalist axioms: the viability of the whole structure required each voter to conform to the model of *homo suffragans* previously proposed by the philosophe.

More pragmatic, the text passed after the fall of the Girondins eliminated any reference to a supposed right of legislative initiative and preserved only the negative right of the primary assemblies to disapprove laws "proposed" by the legislature. Less ambitious than the February proposal, the Constitution of 1793 seemed to make the promises of the summer of 1792 concrete. A closer examination shows that this fulfillment was by no means the case, however. In the February proposal the primary assemblies were the pillars of the political order, and Condorcet was determined to guarantee strict equality among the elementary sections of the nation. In the June text, however, a superior authority, irreducible to any organization, dominated all institutions and largely negated the power of the primary assemblies: that undefined, torrential, and uncontrollable constituent power was the "sovereign people" in the sections. The sovereign had the last word in judging the delegates elected by the primary assemblies. The "people," as it manifested itself through insurrection, and as distinct from the primary assemblies that voiced their opinions through the suffrage, was the supreme source and ultimate arbiter of legitimacy. The assemblies elected the deputies, but the "people" could at any moment oppose its veto! Under such conditions, what remained of the suffrage, other than a provisional mode of legitimation whose results could be nullified by the "will of the people" or even, as specified by an article in the Declaration of 1793, by the will of only a "portion" of the people? The Constitution of 1793, far from being the inaccessible ideal of the revolutionaries of Year II, was instead, quite concretely, the fruit of a duality between institutional legitimacy and popular legitimacy, a duality that on June 2, 1793, made it possible to expel, in the name of the will of the sovereign people, a portion of the representative body elected by universal suffrage.

The Constitution of June 1793 was the work of the most determined partisans of universal suffrage. By consecrating the means that had gained their victory in 1792, they revealed the limits of their democratic convictions. The campaign in favor of an optimal extension of the suffrage culminated in its absolute devaluation, as the indeterminate will of an undefined people was invoked to overrule the legally determined wishes of a plurality of citizens. In this sense, when the revolutionary government of Year II substituted facts for laws, it did not repudiate the spirit of the Constitution: it was rather the undisguised confirmation of that spirit.

Subsequent changes in the suffrage confirmed the wreck of an institution that had been one of the major conquests of 1789.

Once the torment of Year II was over, the Thermidorians again faced the same problem as the Constituent Assembly—how to reconcile the principle of popular sovereignty with institutional stability—but with the advantage of having drawn the lesson of the excesses of 1793. In Messidor, Year III, Boissy d'Anglas characterized the spirit in which the future Constitution would have to be drafted, one that would "courageously protect against the illusory principles of an absolute democracy and an unlimited equality, which are undeniably the most dangerous reefs that true liberty must face." In regard to suffrage, the Constitution of Year III largely adopted the provisions of the "revised" text of 1791, except that the right to vote was granted to anyone who paid any amount of direct tax. One new clause illustrates the desire to erect obstacles against a possible return of the Terror. Against the "vandals" of 1793, characterized by youth and ignorance, the conventionnels on the one hand raised the age of eligibility and on the other hand stipulated that as of Year XII no citizen could be inscribed on the list of voters unless he could prove that he knew how to read and write. Of course by the time Year XII came around, France had yet another system of government, and this article was never enforced.

Could the failure of 1792 be overcome? The final defeat of the sectional movement in Prairial and the dismantling of the popular societies had made it possible to do away with the machinery by which the "sovereign people" had for six long years waged war on the institutions of government. The principal obstacle to normalization was removed. Nevertheless, by Fructidor of Year V it was clear that the Constitution approved two years earlier had failed to achieve its goal; legitimacy remained dependent on the outcome of the struggle for power. The fate of the suffrage during the Directory period is a flagrant example: for the political actors, the verdict of the ballot box was legitimate only to the extent that the wishes of the electorate conformed to their own interests, in this instance the political survival of the "*conventionelle* caste." The suffrage was supposed to provide the machinery whereby the group in power could be confirmed by plebiscite. Conservative tendencies in the electorate threatened the *juste milieu* line of the Directory. With each new election the discredited government, which included both former Terrorists and representatives of the "silent majority" of Year II, was exposed to the rebuke of the electorate. In Fructidor, Year V, and again in Prairial, Year VI, the Directory showed how little store it set by suffrage by overturning elections that went counter to governmental directives. In 1799 a pro-government newspaper summed up the government's point of view this way: "The executive Directory, which does not like royalists any more than anarchists, will know how to put things in order."

The repeated failures of the suffrage cannot be reduced to a single cause. In the first period of the Revolution, it failed when challenged by a parallel mode of legitimation that enforced the verdict of the streets over that of the ballot box. Under the Directory, the situation was the reverse: the suffrage held an honored place among the nation's institutions, but this maturity resulted in a new failure, with the ballot box this time thwarted by the power of the government. In 1795 as in 1792, the suffrage sowed seeds of instability, at first because it was not yet strong enough to hold sway, and later because it was strong enough and held the key to the political future.

One may blame the frequency of elections, with annual election of a third of the deputies leading to changes of majority little conducive to coherent governmental action. But frequent elections were of no small importance to the functioning of the electoral system; they were one important means of forcing power back to its source. In reaction against a monarchical absolutism perhaps more imaginary than real, everything possible had been done since 1789 to hold the arbitrariness of power in check and to ensure the preponderance of civil society over the state, in granting the former all that was taken away from the latter. No doubt the representative system as conceived in 1789 tended toward a government by assembly, in which the assembly held all the powers supposed to belong to the nation. But the biennial reelection of the legislature limited the dangers associated with this new omnipotence by ensuring uninterrupted communication between society and its representatives. For its part, the Constituent Assembly sought relentlessly to reduce the responsibilities and decision-making powers of the king, the nation's unelected executive, to the point of stripping him of all genuine authority. Conversely, it was the fiction of the "sovereign people" that, by invalidating the suffrage, served as the agency by which the government freed itself from the oversight of civil society in 1793. In the autumn of 1793 the suffrage was thus the first victim of the dual process of administrative centralization and reinforcement of the executive (in the form of the Committee of Public Safety), a process that began at that time in opposition to the profoundly liberal impulse of 1789. After the Terror, the Constitution of 1795 marked an undeniable return to the spirit of 1789, but the directorial period shows on the contrary that the tendencies of 1793 toward emancipation of the executive as well as diminished influence of citizens on the state continued.

The coup d'état of 18 Brumaire put an end to all these ambiguities, and the Constitution promulgated shortly thereafter, in part following the plan proposed by Sieyès, abolished elections. The electorate, once again recruited on the basis of universal suffrage, was supposed to serve a dual function: maintain the "civic tablet" of electors and choose "candidates" (with each round reducing the list to one-tenth its previous size) who would be inscribed on the communal, départemental, and national lists. For Sieyès, this was a way of preserving the representative principle, according to which no person could exercise authority without the consent of the nation. "Confidence comes from below," he wrote at that time, and added: "Power comes from above." He thus extended to the political authorities what he had envisioned in 1789 for public functionaries. In Year VIII, however, he would have liked to bestow the right to conduct elections for the nation on a "great elector," but the Constitution attributed that role to the conservative Senate, which was made responsible for filling all government posts from a list of "candidates" designated by the people. Beyond a doubt the suffrage had been drained of all substance. The dismantlement of the suffrage was the price to be paid for the reinforcement, this time decisive, of the executive.

Patrice Gueniffey

Further reading

Few works have been devoted to study of the suffrage in the French Revolution. Many items pertinent to the analysis may be found, however, in François-Victor-Alphonse Aulard, *Histoire politique de la Révolution française,* Paris, 1901. The legal aspects were explored in depth by the legal scholars of the Third Republic, especially R. Carré de Malberg, *Contribution à la théorie générale de l'Etat,* 2 vols., Paris, 1920–1922; reprinted, 2 vols., Paris, 1962. See also Eugène Pierre, *Traité de droit politique, électoral et parlementaire,* Paris, 1893; Albert Lheure, *De l'influence de la fortune sur la capacité politique,* Paris, 1900; Maurice Gras, *Du suffrage politique censitaire en France et en Belgique,* Montpellier, 1910. Recently, the problem of the suffrage in a later period but one still influenced by the revolutionary experience has been studied in a most interesting fashion by Pierre Rosanvallon, *Le moment Guizot,* Paris, 1985.

Related topics

Barnave	Equality	Rights of Man
Clubs and Popular Societies	Nation	Sieyès
Condorcet	Physiocrats	Sovereignty
Democracy	Public Spirit	
Elections	Revolutionary Assemblies	

Taxes

From a modern viewpoint, taxation can be defined as an ongoing, obligatory contribution levied on private wealth to support public services. In the Ancien Régime, however, the permanent, compulsory, and public character of taxation was still being formulated. Only during the Revolution was this definition of taxation, as well as the institutional apparatus necessary to sustain it, fully developed. According to the medieval tradition, the monarch had no ongoing right to tax his subjects. Taxes were regarded as temporary and exceptional expedients levied in times of emergency, usually war. In times of peace, the king was supposed to "live from his own" (*vivre du sien*), that is, to support himself from fees, feudal and seigneurial dues, and other "ordinary" revenues derived from the royal domain. If additional revenues were necessary, he might obtain voluntary gifts and subsidies by bargaining with his vassals or towns.

During the chronic warfare of the fifteenth and sixteenth centuries, the idea that the king had the right to collect a limited number of permanent levies began to receive general acceptance. The new and hence "extraordinary" taxes of the king included the direct tax on non-noble persons or property called the royal *taille;* the gabelle, requiring subjects to purchase specified amounts of salt; the excises or *aides,* primarily on wine and liquors but also on paper, playing cards, and other commodities; and the royal export duties termed *traites.* By the mid-1500s, these ongoing taxes were being reclassified as part of the king's "ordinary" revenues and, owing to a combination of repression and negotiation with the elite, no longer required the consent of a representative body like the Estates General.

The permanent and compulsory nature of royal taxes thus came to rest upon a compromise with influential groups. Obligatory taxes were, in theory, to fall upon the servile, unprivileged members of society, while the crown was to guarantee the "liberties" and privileges, including fiscal exemptions, of various provinces, orders, and corps. Since the *taille* had originally been a tax levied by seigneurs on their subjects, payment of this tax, in particular, symbolized baseness and dishonor. The "public" services performed by royal taxation, furthermore, were not clearly distinguished from the private, patrimonial wealth of the king. Although most taxes were destined for such national concerns as the defense of the country, they also supported the king's household as well as gifts and pensions to the aristocracy. Secrecy in matters of finance was regarded as the king's right, since he, like any noble, enjoyed the freedom of conducting his financial affairs in private.

The financial weakness of the absolute monarchy, a result of its inability to service its debts, led to its collapse in 1789. Scholars have offered several reasons for the monarchy's inability to generate sufficient revenues. The first emphasizes the inequitable distribution of the tax burden upon those least able to pay and the resistance of the privileged elite to the government's program for reform. The government was unable to increase taxes because the lower classes, especially the peasants, were economically exhausted while influential groups obstinately defended their immunities. A second perspective stresses the inefficient administrative apparatus of the royal government, including the lack of a budget and the loss of royal revenues to tax collectors who supported their private business ventures from a public service. A third viewpoint emphasizes the fiscal underside of the monarchy, that is, how the crown's financial expedients and patterns of borrowing, far from rationalizing society, actually reinforced the hierarchical and corporate structure of the Ancien Régime. Because the royal government relied for loans upon privileged intermediate groups like provincial estates and tax farmers, it was able to reform neither the administration nor the tax structure.

To what degree the lower classes were exhausted by taxation is difficult to determine, because the precise burden of royal taxation at the time of the Revolution is unknown. Several estimates, however, have been made based on the incidence of formal taxation reported to the central government. These estimates are usually divided into direct taxes (*impositions*) placed upon persons, income, or property, and indirect taxes (*perceptions*) assessed during the production, sale, or circulation of goods. The most important direct taxes included the royal *taille* and its supplement, the *taillon* and *quartiers d'hiver* used to support troops; the *capitation*, established in 1695, which assessed individuals according to their position in twenty-two professional and status groups called *états*; the *dixième*, a ten-percent tax on revenue imposed during wartime between 1710 and 1749, and its successor, the *vingtième*, a five percent levy on revenue. After 1756 the *vingtième* was doubled, and in the periods 1760–1764 and 1782–1786 it was tripled. Usually paid in service, rather than in money, was the royal *corvée*, which was extended into many areas after 1730 and obligated peasants within five to ten miles of royal highways (routes) to furnish labor or animals to build and maintain roads. Necker estimated the value of this service at 20 million livres.

The major indirect taxes comprised the *traites*, the *aides*, the *gabelle*, and the government monopoly on tobacco. Frequently also classified as indirect taxes were the *droits domaniaux*, including revenues derived both from the royal domain proper and from a variety of far more recent stamp duties (*timbre*) and registry fees (the *contrôle, insinuation*, and *centième denier*, for example). Finally, the royal government placed surtaxes, *sol pour livre*, on most of the taxes it collected. By the late eighteenth century there were four *sols pour livre* (twenty percent) on the *capitation* and first *vingtième*, and ten sols pour livre (fifty percent) on all indirect taxes collected by the company of tax farmers known as the Farmers General (*Fermiers Généraux*).

From 1725 to 1789, the monarchy's tax revenues rose by a factor of 2.6, from 180 to 472 million, but when the rise in population, prices, and production are taken into account, there appears to have been no significant real increase in the weight of formal taxation before the Revolution. A fairly standard estimate of the tax burden per head in 1788 is 18 livres per head, between 10 to 11 livres in indirect taxes and 7 to 8 in direct. The weight of formal taxation in France, it appears, was probably no heavier, and perhaps even lighter, than that in Great Britain. According to these statistics, the crisis of the Ancien Régime was a result not of too much but too little taxation.

One problem with these estimates of the per capita tax burden is that they rely on the monarchy's revenues as reported to the central government and exclude regional, local, and ecclesiastical taxes. Since, as will be discussed shortly, the monarchy used disguised forms of taxation through privileged intermediaries to support itself, estimates based solely on formal government taxation may well underestimate the burden of royal taxation as a whole.

A second question that nationwide calculations of the tax burden are unable to address is that of the distribution of the tax burden across the geographical and social spectrum. The task of analyzing the social incidence of taxation is complicated enormously by the wide variety of privileges in the Ancien Régime. Legal inequality was built into the structure of French taxation not only vertically as one moved along the social scale but also territorially. It was rare for any one social group, even the nobility, to enjoy uniform tax exemptions across France. In the *pays de taille réelle*, exemption from the *taille* was based upon the classification of the land as noble or non-noble property, regardless of the status of the owner. In the *pays de taille personnelle*, exemptions were based upon the status of the individual; nobility, officeholding, or membership in a privileged city (*ville franche*) all conferred some form of immunity.

Regional disparity was also rampant in the assessment of the salt tax, excises, and customs. To assess the salt tax, for example, France was divided into no fewer than six regions, the region of the *grandes gabelles* paying the highest rate but with some provinces enjoying total exemption. Within the provinces that were members of the customs region known as the Five Great Farms, goods paid virtually no customs duty (*traites*) as they circulated, but commercial relations among the provinces falling outside this area were governed by over two dozen local tariffs. Once again, nobles, officeholders, and bourgeois citizens of privileged cities usually enjoyed at least partial immunity from the salt tax and excises on alcoholic beverages.

Local variations, administrative arrangements, urban privileges, ownership of government offices, and noble or clerical status thus were all factors influencing the degree of legal escape from taxation. Overall, it appears that a variety of influential social groups in France, and not simply the nobility, transferred down to the lower classes a disproportionate share of the tax burden.

During the eighteenth century the government was gradually cutting back, or trying to cut back, the legal role played by privilege in the tax system. The *taille* was the most overtly discriminatory direct tax, since nobles, clergy, and many cities were exempt. While in 1725 this tax constituted about twenty-five percent of the total royal receipts, by 1788 it had fallen to only about fifteen percent. In contrast to the *taille*, the *capitation* assessed the privileged elite according to their *état,* and the *dixième* and *vingtième* were placed on the revenues of all groups, including the privileged.

How successful the egalitarian program of the monarchy was is a matter of debate. It is often pointed out that in many regions the *capitation* was transformed into a supplement to the *taille,* and that favoritism and connections allowed at least some members of the elite to evade their fair share of the tax on revenues. While such practices deprived the royal treasury of revenues, avoidance of a tax like the *vingtième* cannot be equated with immunity from taxes by legal right. The government's program toward privileged groups led them, in turn, to demand participation in the government, a demand that the monarchy was loath to consider.

The constitutional struggles provoked by direct taxation led the monarchy to resort heavily to indirect taxes, in particular to surtaxes on taxes collected by the Farmers General. By the end of the eighteenth century, indirect taxes (including the *droits domaniaux*) formed well over half of the monarchy's tax revenues. The monarchy's reliance on indirect taxes challenges the view that the taxpayers of the Ancien Régime were primarily peasants. Although peasants paid these taxes, in particular the *gabelle,* the brunt of the indirect tax burden fell upon cities, the centers of exchange and consumption. In fact, as Necker's figures indicate, urban inhabitants may have paid more per head in taxes than their rural counterparts. The most striking example is the city of Paris, which, with an average tax of around 140 livres per head, was the most highly taxed region in France. Because most indirect taxes fell upon necessities, and a variety of privileged corporate groups held at least partial exemptions to these levies, this form of taxation struck the urban poor most heavily.

As the case of Marseilles illustrates more specifically, it was not simply the weight of taxation, but its unequal social incidence combined with a process of politicization that made taxes an explosive issue. Before the Revolution, Marseilles paid a relatively small amount, only about 18 livres per head for all taxes, both royal and local. Nonetheless, the tax structure of this city was among the most regressive in France. The municipal government had the privilege of transforming all royal taxes, including direct taxes on revenues like the *vingtième,* into indirect taxes falling on grain, wine, and other necessities. After the Seven Years' War, local conflict between the oligarchic town council and the rest of the urban elite over the town's finances made the regressive nature of indirect taxation a political issue. In March 1789, a time of escalating grain prices and elections to the Estates General, the people of Marseilles staged the first municipal revolution, four months before the storming of the Bastille. The revolt was an assault on the city's regressive taxes and closed political system. The crowd sacked the home of the director of the city's tax farms, and the new municipal government not only abolished the city's indirect taxes on wine and flour, but made it a crime of treason and *lèse-patrie* to reimpose any taxes on the foodstuffs of the poor.

Thus it was not the tax burden as such but the political hostility generated by a regressive system of taxation—and a privileged, oligarchic local government that refused to reform it—that led to revolution in Marseilles.

Historians have suggested that this pattern held true for much of France: not the weight of taxation but the arbitrariness, inequitable distribution, and inability to reform the system provoked deep hatred of the tax structure. A crucial question thus becomes the failure of the monarchy to reform the tax system before the Revolution.

The fundamental weakness of the absolute monarchy, it may be argued, was political; the crown wished to rule without the consent of the privileged elite. From this desire for royal political autonomy stemmed two interrelated financial problems: the inability to tax privileged groups without provoking constitutional battles and, owing to the secrecy of royal finance and arbitrary repudiations of royal debts, the incapacity of the king to generate credit in his own name at reasonable rates of interest.

The rising costs of war during the eighteenth century laid bare the financial contradictions upon which absolutism rested. The War of the Austrian Succesion, the Seven Years' War, and the American War, the last costing between 1,000 and 1,300 million livres, made it imperative to rationalize the system of taxation. The tripling of the *vingtième* during the Seven Years' War and again after the American War, and finally Calonne's proposal for a land tax (*subvention territoriale*) falling on all privileged groups, are all testimony to the government's desire to tap the wealth of privileged groups by taxation. This demand, however, provoked an escalating and unresolvable constitutional conflict, in which privileged groups demanded the right to consent to taxes and to audit the government accounts before paying any new levies. The political impasse, generated by both the monarchy's desire to remain absolute and the elite's to protect its privileges, was one reason for the failure of reform.

A second reason, also related to the refusal of the monarchy to share power with the elite, was the lack of public credit. Since taxation never met the expenses of war, governments had always resorted to borrowing and other financial expedients to meet their obligations. During the eighteenth century, however, the reliance on credit escalated. France financed twenty-eight percent of the War of the Austrian Succession, sixty-five percent of the Seven Years' War, and ninety-one percent of the American War by loans. In England, the corresponding percentages were eighty-five percent, eighty-one percent, and one hundred percent. Although it was only about a third the size and population of France, England humiliated France in the Seven Years' War largely because it could mobilize credit readily through the Bank of England. Since the British budget was published and submitted to the Parliament each year and the Parliament stood behind the Bank of England, credit was far more "public" in England than in France, where secrecy in royal finances still reigned. By the mid-eighteenth century, confidence in the British bank allowed the English government to borrow at between three and four percent; by contrast, the French government relied on a variety of long and short-term loans at five to ten percent, averaging a little over six percent.

As important as the rate of interest, however, was the effect of royal borrowing upon the corporate organization of the old regime. Because of prior historical developments, including repudiations of debts by the crown, all financial operations in France went through privileged intermediate bodies including municipal governments, the clergy, provincial estates, and tax farmers. In addition to direct loans from these institutions, the crown resorted to a variety of fiscal expedients and disguised loans, in particular the sale of offices in the judiciary, the guilds, and the administration. Thus, at the same time that the monarchy was attempting to undermine tax exemptions and rationalize administration, it was forced to rely upon loans and other subsidies from privileged intermediate bodies. As a result, corporate groups gained a financial stranglehold over the monarchy from below, for they were able to negotiate for the right to maintain their various privileges, including tax exemptions and independent administrative networks, in return for credit. The consequence was that the monarchy locked into place a number of closed, hierarchical, and semi-autonomous forms of political authority and social status. This irreconcilable contradiction—privilege in return for loans, but greater equality as the basis for taxation—made fiscal reform structurally impossible.

Several examples illustrate this process. The corporate groups that collected the king's taxes, first of all, were also bankers of the crown. In the provinces with the status of *pays d'états,* provincial estates controlled the collection of most taxes for the king. In the area of the the *pays d'élection,* the Receivers General of Finance remitted to the royal treasury the direct taxes gathered by parish collectors. The bulk of the indirect taxes were collected by the Farmers General.

Viewed as agents of tax collection, the corps of Receivers General and Farmers General are often indicted for their unwieldiness, harmful administrative autonomy, and high cost to the monarchy. The Receivers General, for example, had virtually no bureaucratic relationship to the central government. Each receiver had his own set of accounts, his own treasury (*caisse*), and the freedom to mix his own private business affairs with those of the state. Because the government had no way to transfer surpluses from one *caisse* to another, or even to know immediately when such surpluses existed, it ended up borrowing short-term funds and paying unnecessary interest.

The monarchy was unable to reform this system, however, because the Receivers and Farmers General had become a major source of credit for the government. The Farmers General, for example, advanced funds to the government in return for interest deducted from the price of future leases. They also issued short-term notes (*billets des fermes*) to the public on their own private credit, notes which were, however, indirectly secured by tax revenue in a future lease.

In addition, most of the financiers involved in tax collection or disbursement held venal, or purchased, offices, a kind of loan. The initial purchaser paid the government a sum (the *finance*) for the office, on which the government then paid *gages,* or interest. A very common type of forced loan was the *augmentation des gages,* by which the government obliged officeholders to raise the capital invested in their offices—capital on which the king then paid interest. The government could not suppress the offices unless it could reimburse the officeholders' capital investment, a difficult task when, in 1788, offices in the corps of Receivers General alone totalled 65,399,000 livres.

A probing of other privileged bodies reveals a similar fiscal underside of the corporate regime. In the decades before the Revolution, the provincial estates frequently loaned the government money. The government had multiplied the number of venal offices in the guilds, judicial courts, and administration, and had shaken down the elite through various *augmentations des gages*. By 1789 the capital invested in the ennobling offices of the king's secretaries (*secrétaires du roi*) alone represented about 76 million livres. These offices played no administrative function; they were simply a credit device that brought the crown critically needed money at low interest rates and gave society a flock of new nobles ready to defend their fiscal exemptions.

Cities, meanwhile, were called upon to buy up venal offices in their town councils, to have their privileges confirmed for a price, and after 1758 to pay the king subsidies (*dons gratuits*) that became permanent in all but name. To pay for these financial obligations, urban governments borrowed the necessary funds. Cities also contracted debts when they were required to perform such work for the monarchy as building royal roads, constructing barracks, and housing intendants. Urban debts were secured by indirect municipal taxes called *octrois,* which, in spite of their local nature, were often created to support the tasks of the central state. In 1787, for example, of the 24 livres per head of the *octrois* collected in Lille, at least 11 livres were used for expenditures incurred by royal demand rather than by municipal needs. These *octrois* were recorded only in Lille's accounts and were never reported to agents of the royal treasury. Thus, the case of Lille suggests that formal estimates of the royal tax burden that exclude local taxes underestimate the real weight of royal taxation in France.

Overall, royal ministers may have denounced the vexing privileges—of cities, provinces, tax farmers, and nobles—that stymied reform in France, but seen from below it is evident that the end of privilege also spelled the end of traditional methods of financing the absolute state. The Ancien Régime did not die from a lack of absolutism, that is, the inability of a reform-minded government to force privileged groups to accept increased taxation. It died from its inability to extricate itself from a structure of credit backed by privileges that were incompatible with a rationalized tax base. A centralized, easily mobilized system of public credit depended on confidence, something absolute monarchy did not readily inspire. The use of absolute power to suppress the parlements, as Maupeou did, or to renege on financial obligations, as Terray did, simply made the elite less willing to invest its money in the state. The basic thrust of Necker's program of reform, by contrast, was not absolutist but designed to generate confidence and stimulate investment by sharing knowledge within the elite, including publishing the accounts of the king and establishing provincial assemblies. Through these reforms and others designed to make tax collection more efficient and less costly, Necker attempted to begin to distance the monarchy from its traditional dependence upon privileged intermediaries. His fall from power left France with the huge debts of the American War, and these debts were multiplied by his successors. By 1787, around 285 million livres, well over half the monarchy's annual revenue of 472 million livres, was destined for debt service. Overall the crown's expenditures exceeded its revenues by 161 million livres.

Constitutional struggle between the parlements and the king continued to preclude tax increases, while the economic depression of the late 1780s decreased tax revenues and dried up the short-term credit of the tax farmers and other financiers. No longer able to tap the short-term credit of its tax officials in order to tide it over, the monarchy in August 1788 effectively admitted to bankruptcy.

The revolutionary solution to the fiscal problems of the Ancien Régime entailed a complete redefinition of the basis of public power and civil society. The permanent, compulsory, and public nature of taxation and, for that matter of credit, was accepted on the new theoretical grounds of the "social contract." The state and its taxes were permanent not because the passage of time and tradition gave them legitimacy but because the people had agreed to live within a civil society. The people became, in fact, sovereign. Taxes were compulsory for everyone in society, including those who had formerly been privileged, because everyone benefited equally from the protection afforded by the state. Taxes became truly public forms of property, and no longer mixtures of public revenue and royal patrimony, because the representatives of the people consented to taxes, openly scrutinized budgets, and controlled the disbursement of revenues. The venality of offices, by which public services had become inextricably entwined with individual social status and property, was abolished, a measure that paved the way for a rational bureaucratic system of tax collection and administration. Thus profound theoretical, institutional, and political transformations lay behind the declaration of Lavie to the National Assembly in 1792: "We only made the Revolution to become the masters of taxation."

Gail Bossenga

FURTHER READING

Behrens, C. B. A. "Nobles, Privileges, and Taxes in France at the End of the Ancien Regime," *Economic History Review,* 2d ser., no. 3, 1963, 451–475. See also the debate with G. J. Cavanaugh in the *French Historical Studies,* vol. 8, 1974, 681–692, and vol. 9, 1976, 521–531.

Bien, David. "The Secretaires du Roi: Absolutism, Corps, and Privilege under the Ancien Regime," in Ernst Hinrichs et al., eds., *Vom Ancien Regime Zu Französischen Revolution.* Göttingen, 1978.

Bosher, John F. *French Finances, 1770–1795: From Business to Bureaucracy.* Cambridge, 1970.

Bossenga, Gail. "City and State: An Urban Perspective on the Origins of the French Revolution," in Keith Baker, ed., *The Political Culture of the Old Regime.* Oxford, 1987.

Harris, Robert D. *Necker: Reform Statesman of the Ancien Regime.* Berkeley, 1979.

Hincker, François. *Les français devant l'impôt sous l'Ancien Régime.* Paris, 1971.

Marion, Marcel. *Histoire financière de la France depuis 1715,* 6 vols. Paris, 1914.

Mathias, Peter, and Patrick O'Brien, "Taxation in Britain and France, 1715–1810: A Comparison of the Social and Economic Incidence of Taxes Collected for the Central Governments." *Journal of European Economic History,* vol. 3, 1976, 601–650.

Matthews, George T. *The Royal General Farms in Eighteenth-Century France.* New York, 1958.

Morinea, Michel. "Budgets de l'état et gestion des finances royales en France au dix-huitième siècle," *Revue historique,* no. 264, 1980, 289–336.

Riley, James C. *The Seven Years' War and the Old Regime in France: The Economic and Financial Toll.* Princeton, 1986.

RELATED TOPICS

Centralization   Feudal System   Necker

IDEAS

4

AMERICAN REVOLUTION

The history of the relations between the two great revolutions of the late eighteenth century, the French and the American, admirably illustrates one of their major features: contemporaries very quickly achieved a keen understanding of the issues of the day and therefore rapidly developed forms of interpretation that have dominated debate ever since. Thus the simplest way to understand the complex relations linking the two traditions born in this period is probably to begin with the way in which the French Revolution was received by the actors of 1776 and, conversely, with the way in which the comparison between France and America was used to clarify revolutionary thinking in France.

One of the first effects of the French Revolution on the English-speaking world was to point up the ambiguity of the English and American Revolutions by putting an end to liberal unity. Liberals were divided over 1789 even though they had previously been united in defense of the American rebels. In 1776 Burke had defended the American Revolution, as had the Unitarian minister Price and the American publicist Paine, both of whom became his adversaries during the French Revolution. Those on both sides believed, not without reason, that their fundamental attitudes had not changed, and all supported their positions by comparing France with America. For Burke, the American Revolution was the legitimate offspring of England's Glorious Revolution. It defended, against Parliament itself, the principles (such as "No taxation without representation") from which its strength derived; it also drew on a long experience of liberty, which gave its demands a *conservative* rather than a *subversive* character. In every respect it was therefore opposed to the "metaphysical" spirit of the French Revolution, whose assertion of transcendent "rights of man" had the potential to destroy the European social order. By contrast, for Paine, the defense of the French Revolution (in *The Rights of Man,* his response to Burke's *Reflections*) was a continuation of the battle he had waged in 1776 on behalf of the American Revolution in his celebrated pamphlet *Common Sense;* it was from America that the French had learned, with Lafayette, to love liberty. In hindsight the French Revolution thus confirmed Paine's "radical" interpretation of the American insurrection: that the defense of liberty could not take the form of preservation of the English Constitution (an incoherent compromise among democracy, aristocracy, and monarchy) but must opt instead for popular sovereignty, and that the American Revolution was legitimate only because peoples have a fundamental right to rid themselves of rulers whom they judge to have violated their rights.

For Burke and Paine, who grew up in the English tradition, it was first of all the meaning of that tradition that was at issue in 1789. Yet in many respects their controversy anticipates more purely *American* debates, such as the one that pitted the supporters of Jefferson against those of John Adams in the 1800 election campaign. Friedrich Gentz, a German disciple of Burke, had some time earlier published an essay giving systematic form to Burke's ideas, in order to show that the French Revolution was an unprecedented event, wholly incommensurate with the American Revolution, which had sought only to combat abuses in order to preserve rights that American citizens had long enjoyed as British subjects. This book was translated into English by John Quincy Adams in order to discredit Jefferson, who was suspected of sympathy for French ideas. Thus the notion of a radical opposition between the two revolutions was not unknown to certain of the American republic's founding fathers, but it was only one point of view within American political debate. By contrast, in the Jeffersonian camp, developments in the French Revolution (from the Terror to the Empire) were criticized, but the criticisms were aimed more at the *actions* of the French (their imprudence, hastiness, and even fanaticism) than at their principles; though moderate in its actions, the American Revolution was no less radical than the French in its principles.

On the French side there was no less ambivalence in attitudes toward the American experience. Before 1789 the American Revolution was perceived by most philosophes (with the significant exception of Voltaire) as a triumph of reason, but many saw it as oddly moderate because of its loyalty to the "gothic" system of common law and to archaic institutions such as bicameralism. Accordingly, men like Mirabeau, Turgot, and Condorcet were soon disappointed—well before the Constitutional Convention in Philadelphia—by the constitutional labors of the Americans.

The case was put most clearly by Turgot in his letter to Dr. Price (March 1778). He observed that most of the American state constitutions took their inspiration from the English system of checks and balances and the separation of powers. Now, there was every reason for such a system in the English Constitution, where the problem was to place a brake on royal power, but there was no reason for it in a regime based on the equality of all its citizens. Turgot and his friend Condorcet therefore proposed a powerful critique of two institutions that would later become fundamental parts of the federal constitution: the Senate and the "strong executive." Dividing the national representation between two houses contradicted the principle of national unity. (Indeed, it presupposed the existence of an aristocracy.) Furthermore, the power of the executive must necessarily be limited wherever *law* ruled and the government remained confined within its proper sphere. For a major part of enlightened French opinion, the American experience thus seemed from the first insufficiently radical, unduly influenced by English tradition. Care must be taken, however, not to misinterpret the social meaning of this opposition: hostile to the "aristocratic" elements in American institutions, Turgot also criticized the Americans for underestimating the importance of the only "natural" distinction (based on ownership of land). At the source of the critiques of both philosophes and physiocrats was a peculiar combination of radical political rationalism with certain traditions of European absolutism. Condorcet and Turgot had supported the French monarchy's efforts at rationalization (most notably in the areas of administrative and financial reform) to the extent that those efforts were opposed to the "gothic" or aristocratic heritage; and it was the opposition between enlightenment and tradition more than the limitation of sovereignty that they deemed the most pertinent criterion for distinguishing between political regimes. Conversely, for them, rationalization of society by itself offered sufficient guarantees of liberty, which was identified with the rule of law (in the sense of general rules). The same ambiguous attitude toward the American experience is evident in the debates of the Constituent Assembly: on the one hand, the American example was still invoked to show that a free regime could be the result of a deliberate, voluntary project of social regeneration and did not necessarily have to emerge out of a history as chaotic as England's; on the other hand, those who, like Lafayette, cited the American experience as an argument in favor of a second house or a powerful executive found themselves lumped together with the admirers of the English regime.

On the American side, suspicion of the French Revolution never reached the point of total and complete rejection of revolutionary principles, while on the French side enthusiasm for the American precedent was usually accompanied by a very firm rejection of American constitutional theories, a rejection not unrelated to the close bonds between the Revolution and absolutist mores. It would turn out that neither revolutionary tradition was ever able to overcome this double paradox. Conversely, it is impossible to understand the relations between the two revolutions if one is content merely to contrast American moderation with French radicalism (whether to deplore the absence of a true liberal tradition in France or, on the contrary, to argue that only the French experience is worthy of being called a revolution). In the final analysis, whatever the differences between the two movements, the affinities are more important, as has been shown by historians who, like Palmer, speak of the "age of *the* democratic revolution." In America there was indeed an *internal* political conflict, which, even if it lacked the bloody character of French conflict, did give rise to a substantial emigration. Furthermore, the history of the American Revolution, from the Philadelphia debates to the Jefferson-Hamilton conflict, can be interpreted, just as much as the history of the French Revolution, in terms of the distinction between "antique" liberty (civic virtue) and "modern" liberty (individual liberty and the enjoyment of prosperity promoted by the development of commerce and industry). Finally, while the American Revolution was born of a national conflict, it, too, affirmed universal principles in its Declaration of Independence.

In comparing the constitutional principles of the two revolutions, care must be taken not to underestimate the importance of the political problem faced by the American rebels, a problem very different from the one faced by the Constituent Assembly in France.

The Americans, as writers since Tocqueville have repeatedly noted, were born free, in the sense that they enjoyed the "rights of the English" without a powerful domestic aristocracy. Despite the long diatribe against George III in the Declaration of Independence, the major conflict was not so much between the Americans and the crown as between the Americans and the British Parliament, against which the rebels raised the classic cry, "No taxation without representation." They were able to protest only by appealing to a theory of representation different from that held by Parliament. In the eyes of the English, Parliament could legitimately tax the colonies because they were by law fully represented in a Parliament that had been duly elected under English law, even though the colonies were not able to elect their own representatives. British laws and taxes obliged the Americans no less legitimately than any other British subjects, some of whom, as residents of large cities, were not electors, since the purpose of representation was not to defend the interests of some segment of society but to discover the common interest. Conversely, in refusing to pay taxes approved by the British Parliament, the rebels inevitably insisted that representatives in some degree respond to the wishes of their constituents and thereby opened the way to a concept of *explicit* representation of interests, while assuming, at least implicitly, that a conflict of interest was always possible between citizens and Parliament.

France faced the opposite problem: there it was a question of *creating* a representative regime by making the Assembly that emerged out of the Estates General a legislative rather than a merely consultative body. In order to effect this change, it was necessary first to abandon the old doctrine according to which the delegates were bound by the strict mandate of their constituents, a mandate whose purpose was to deprive them of all decision-making power; logically this doctrine led to a theory of representation that was, all things considered, fairly close to the one rejected by the American rebels.

This difference in the initial situation no doubt gave rise to one of the paradoxical traits that distinguished the French revolutionary spirit from American radicalism: the French, much closer to Rousseau in their conception of the general will, were also in some ways much less suspicious of the mechanisms of representation.

Bernard Bailyn's careful study of revolutionary pamphlet literature has demonstrated the existence of a strong radical, even "republican" current in America, which interpreted classical liberal themes in a very particular way. The dominant theme of this literature concerned the inevitable *corruption* of those in power; as developed by Machiavelli's "republican" interpreters this argument and the pessimistic view of man on which it was based led to a demand for control of the governors by the governed. Civic virtue is here founded, at least in part, on interest properly understood. Since governors are naturally impelled to abuse their power, participation in public affairs is the best assurance of protection for the governed. At the outset of the revolution, these themes were easily incorporated into an apology for "mixed government" of the sort exemplified by the English Constitution, considered as a system for the limitation of royal and aristocratic power. Later (particularly in the work of Paine) they took on a very different democratic meaning, once it was stipulated that the monarchical or aristocratic element could and should be eliminated from the government (and not simply limited). By the time the federal constitution came to incorporate ideas already accepted in most state constitutions, however, a "liberal" interpretation of revolutionary principles was reinstated in the system of checks and balances, which again assumed a fundamentally pessimistic view of human nature. Thus the central problem of the American Revolution was how to combine two elements that were perceived as fundamentally heterogeneous: government (necessary for repression of antisocial forces and unity of collective action) was instituted for the purpose of defending the rights of security and liberty, but liberty itself was a limitation on the action of government.

Despite certain resemblances between the Declaration of Independence and the Declaration of the Rights of Man, the inspiration of the majority of French Constituents (and particularly of Sieyès) turned out to be quite different: it was based on a synthesis, at first sight rather surprising, of the idea of representation with the Rousseauist doctrine of the general will. Sieyès' defense of representative government was based not only on contingent factors (the impossibility of popular sovereignty in a large state) but also on a positive conception of liberty; distinguishing between "civil rights" and "political rights," he defined liberty in terms of the security and enjoyment of individual rights (rather than in terms of participation in sovereignty), and he held that liberty was in fact extended, not reduced, by representation, which, being a consequence of the division of labor, liberated citizens from tasks that could be carried out by others. Yet this essentially liberal doctrine was from the first combined with a very different line of reasoning: the primacy of the law, or "expression of the general will," which was formulated with the cooperation of all citizens and therefore was superior to any other source of right and incompatible with any form of "partial association," stood between the individual and the sovereign. It was in this way that the Revolution forged its link with Rousseau, from whom it borrowed its legicentrism, its rejection of any notion of a "fundamental law" superior to the will of the sovereign, and its distrust of "factions" (while at the same time it renounced absence of representation and identification of the people with the sovereign—things that in Rousseau's eyes had been guarantees of liberty). This ambiguity persisted throughout the revolutionary period; Robespierre never renounced representative legitimacy, and the Thermidorians never renounced the primacy of law.

Thus the two revolutions grew out of very different experiences, which led to the formation of two institutional logics at odds on many points. Where the French held that factions could be neutralized only through submission to the general will, the Americans sought (with the authors of *The Federalist*) to tame factions by assigning them a limited but explicitly recognized place in the institutional framework. Separation of powers, which led the Americans to stress the importance of the judiciary, seemed to the French to require absolute primacy of the legislature, the sole guarantor of liberty but also the sole judge of all matters impinging on it.

*
**

By now the artificial nature of certain traditional debates on the relations between the two revolutions should be clear: for example, the debate early in this century between Boutmy, a Frenchman, and Jellinek, an Austrian legal scholar, on the relation between the Declaration of the Rights of Man of 1789 and the various American declarations. There is no doubt, as Jellinek points out, that the members of the Constituent Assembly were inspired by the American example, from which they borrowed certain ideas stemming from an already long liberal and Protestant tradition, and that the French Declaration should be seen as a successor to the long series of "bills of rights" found first in English and then in American history. On the other hand, it is equally certain, as Boutmy maintained, that the Americans themselves owed a great deal to the philosophy of the Enlightenment, hence to French sources. Furthermore, while the two principal declarations had different objects (in one case to legitimate American independence in the opinion of mankind, in the other to set forth in a systematic way the "natural, inalienable, and sacred rights of man"), both laid claim to universality. At a deeper level, however, what distinguishes the two declarations is the status they ascribe to law, a difference that proceeds from a fundamental divergence as to the conditions of liberty and the scope of natural rights.

The Declaration of Independence begins with the natural law instituted by God, who endows men with "inalienable rights," the protection of which constitutes the purpose of governments. Governments therefore cease to be legitimate if they lose sight of those rights, but conversely they are presumed legitimate so long as they respect them. By contrast, the French declaration begins with the natural rights of individuals, whose defense no longer depends on a mere limitation imposed from outside but on the participation of citizens in the making of the laws, which are therefore placed on the same plane as individual rights (article 6: "All citizens have the right to participate personally or through their representatives in the formulation of the law"). Hence the principle of national sovereignty poses a challenge to the legitimacy of all established governments, since governments exist only by the will of the nation. What usually remains implicit and subordinate to natural law in the American declarations (the consent of the governed, the right of the people to modify the political order) therefore occupies center stage in the French declaration and implies a universal requirement for regeneration of the political order.

The real originality of the Declaration of the Rights of Man lies in this shift in liberal doctrine, which not only undermined the old order but in certain respects presaged some of the less liberal aspects of the Revolution. For one thing, the Declaration threatened all established governments by asserting the absolute superiority of natural rights over the social order and by insisting that all authority emanate expressly from the nation (article 3). For another, it made positive law responsible for determining in almost sovereign fashion the conditions under which "inalienable rights" would be guaranteed, so that those rights were from the outset subordinated to the legislature's idea of what public order required (articles 4, 10, and 11).

This paradox, which Burke was the first to notice, is a major theme of one line of liberal criticism of the French Revolution and of classical comparisons between it and the American Revolution. The moderation of the Americans is explained by their fidelity to the doctrine of natural law, while the French are denounced for veering from individualistic anarchism to statist despotism. Nevertheless, this divergence should not be allowed to obscure the similarities between the two traditions in terms of doctrinal logic. The French doctrine is in fact interesting for the way in which it points up the ambiguities in the Declaration of Independence; once it is conceded that a nation has the right to alter or abolish a government that fails to live up to its natural purpose, it must also be acknowledged that the people in the final analysis are sovereign, since they have the right to judge when such a failure has occurred and, in such a case, to proceed by "organizing [government's] powers in such form as to them shall seem most likely to effect their Safety and Happiness." In other words, even before 1789, when it was a question of founding a durable political regime, the principle of popular sovereignty took precedence over natural law even in America, as can be seen in *The Federalist*. Yet it remains true, as Hannah Arendt pointed out, that the American tradition is based on a new relation between the body politic and fundamental rights, in that it is assumed that the body politic is organized before its limits are defined (those limits being fixed by amendments to the Constitution), whereas the French tradition invoked a prepolitical principle (the "rights of man") while remaining suspicious of the idea of a fundamental law.

For Hannah Arendt (who was nevertheless looking for "the lost treasure of modern revolutions"), the raising of the "social question" in the French Revolution was associated with the French insistence on the rights of man, antipolitical in that such an insistence tended to "reduce politics to nature": "The perplexities of the Rights of Man are manifold, and Burke's famous argument against them is neither obsolete nor 'reactionary.' . . . The new body politic was supposed to rest upon man's natural rights, upon his rights insofar as he is nothing but a natural being, upon his right to 'food, dress, and the reproduction of the species,' that is, upon his right to the necessities of life. . . . The Ancien Régime stood accused of having deprived its subjects of these rights—the rights of life and nature rather than the rights of freedom and citizenship" *(On Revolution*, pp. 104–105).

What is interesting about this analysis is, first of all, the demonstration that the raising of the "social question" in the French Revolution did not reflect a more "egalitarian" outlook than that of the American Revolution but rather a new perception of the problem of poverty, according to which pity became a public passion. In fact, equality was a major theme of the Declaration of Independence ("All men are created equal"). What struck Americans who knew Europe well was the notion that the extreme inequality existing there constituted a major obstacle to the establishment of liberty, while conversely the relative equality prevailing in America, along with the absence of pauperism, was the best guarantee of the Republic's survival (Arendt, *On Revolution,* pp. 95–103). It was in this respect, Arendt believed, that the French Revolution anticipated all subsequent revolutions. If it ceased to give priority to liberty, it was not because it overestimated the value of equality but because it yielded to necessity by giving priority to vital needs (*On Revolution,* p. 84).

The difference between the two revolutions emerges perhaps even more clearly when one compares the importance in each of the distinction between the "liberty of the ancients" and the "liberty of the moderns." In the United States the debate (between Jefferson and Hamilton, epitomizing the conflict between republicans and federalists) essentially concerned the effects of commerce and industry on the citizenry. Jefferson marshaled the classical arguments of republican "Machiavellianism" to place stress on the dangers to liberty from increasing inequality, political centralization, and excessive development of industry, insofar as these things increased the personal dependence of citizens while reducing their influence on public decisions. Hamilton, for his part, situated himself in the tradition of Hume: for him the problem was to derive the maximum advantage from the selfish passions by making them contribute to the increase of the nation's wealth and power. Both parties to the debate shared a common conception of man, however, hence their goals were limited to questions of political organization rather than human nature. In France, by contrast, the same themes, traditional at least since Montesquieu, took on new significance owing to the importance of the social question, the radical opposition between "nature" and aristocratic or bourgeois civility, and, ultimately, the virtually limitless character of political demands: the sans-culottes' goal was not merely equality but transcendence of poverty, "corruption" being not so much a political term as a moral characterization, so that regeneration became a task without end.

*
**

The absence or relatively low level of "pauperism" in America was only one aspect of a more general difference between it and other western countries in the eighteenth century: namely, the relative "equality of conditions" that existed in America, where the virtual nonexistence of an aristocracy was even more important than economic equality. Since Tocqueville it has been widely acknowledged that this fact—that Americans were "born free"—is one of the keys to American history because it explains the peaceful nature of democracy there. In the United States (as opposed to France) the "democratic" spirit was constructive rather than destructive; it was not confused with the "revolutionary spirit." In contemporary historiography this theme has been developed with particular flair by Louis Hartz, who sets forth what has become the standard theory of "American exceptionalism." For Hartz (who, unlike more recent historians, believes that Locke was the source of the American political tradition), American democracy was distinguished by having been an almost "natural" phenomenon owing to the lack of any experience with feudalism. American society has had neither a great revolutionary tradition nor a great reactionary tradition ("because it lacks Robespierre, it also lacks Maistre; because it lacks Sidney, it lacks Charles II"), and subsequently it has also lacked a major socialist movement (Hartz, *The Liberal Tradition*, pp. 6–14). Although this interpretation may underestimate the importance of "radical" elements in the American political tradition, it does point up one essential feature: in the absence of any actual experience of aristocracy, reactionary thought was never able to portray the return to a pre-egalitarian world as a plausible alternative to democracy, and the thinkers most hostile to democratic logic (such as Fitzhugh and Calhoun, theorists of the Old South's "peculiar institution") lacked the coherence of a Maistre or a Bonald. Conversely, the French political tradition was dominated by the conflict between Ancien Régime and Revolution, even though the Revolution took on many key elements of the "absolutist" tradition (administrative centralization, sovereignty, subordinate role of the judiciary, special legal status of functionaries, and so on).

Here again, in the most extreme situations some affinity between the two revolutionary traditions must be acknowledged, as is shown by the example of the American Civil War, perhaps the only real tragedy in American history. Slavery stood in flagrant contradiction to the principles of the Declaration of Independence, which had affirmed the universality of equality and liberty. As the institution of slavery took on central importance in southern society, southern theorists gradually came to deny the principles of the Enlightenment. Both sides in the slavery debate produced arguments that ranged well beyond the traditional framework of American political thought. The abolitionist side invoked not only constitutional guarantees of liberty but rights of man existing prior to society, which took on the same "subversive" character they had had for contemporaries of the French Revolution. By contrast, on the proslavery side the principles of the Declaration were sharply restricted (limited to defense of the rights of free men) or even repudiated. For the most rigorously logical champions of the South, the Declaration of Independence was full of "meretricious and inconsistent generalities," and Jefferson's ideas came from "that sentimental French philosophy so widespread at the time, which subsequently produced such bloody consequences" (Choate and Hammond, cited by Carl Becker). Hence while the abolitionists ultimately came to attack the Constitution as a "pact with the devil" (Garrison), their adversaries defended it largely with arguments inspired by Burke and intended to counteract the influence of "abstract" humanitarian principles that everyone believed were in some way connected with the principles of the French Revolution. What was at stake, then, among other things, was the relation between the two revolutions: the Civil War and Reconstruction settled the issue in favor of "abstract principles," using means worthy of the Convention.

*
**

Throughout the nineteenth century, fluctuating French opinion in regard to the United States accurately reflected a widespread feeling at the time that there was something ambiguous about the American Revolution. For traditionalists like Maistre, the American Revolution was merely a temporary aberration, since it rested on the abstract principles of Enlightenment philosophy. On the republican side there was admiration for the first great modern republic, which had offered refuge to French liberals in reactionary times, and this attitude was often coupled with a certain idealization of American equality. But this admiration was tempered by important reservations, which not only reflected American debates (the controversy over virtue versus commerce in the debate between republicans and federalists, slavery and the race issue) but also pointed up the persistent differences between the two revolutionary traditions (the French republicans never accepted federalism or bicameralism). Simultaneously, among liberals, the "American School" stood out more and more clearly from the "Anglophile" current. For the latter, the American Revolution was merely the sequel to the English Revolution, whose socially "moderate" character it shared. For friends of America such as Tocqueville and Laboulaye, America had developed from a radically new principle (the democratic principle), which it shared with the French Revolution, although America had been spared the excesses of the "revolutionary spirit" (Tocqueville) and spared from the doctrinal errors in its own Constitution (Laboulaye). With the rise of various forms of socialism and the experience first of the Revolution of 1848 and then of the Second Empire, the Americanophile current acquired a durable identity; firmly liberal and antiauthoritarian, the friends of the United States saw themselves as democrats but were suspicious of socialism, which in their eyes was a distortion of the democratic spirit and was linked, in the case of France, to the absolutist tradition.

If the French have had doubts about the American system, Americans have often found themselves perplexed by the French political tradition, which to them seems both extremist and archaic. From this perplexity stems a line of argument still very much alive in American political science today, according to which the best thing that could happen to France would be for its political and social system to move closer to that of the United States. Conversely, on the French side, although such a rapprochement has to a certain extent already occurred (most notably in institutions and politics), there remains a sense of a profound difference of spirit between the two nations, evident chiefly in culture and mores. It is up to the reader to decide how much of these attitudes stems from the difference between the two revolutionary traditions and how much from the contrast between "American exceptionalism" and the French experience with aristocracy and the Ancien Régime.

Philippe Raynaud

FURTHER READING

Arendt, Hannah. *On Revolution*. New York, 1963.

Bailyn, Bernard. *The Ideological Origins of the American Revolution*. Cambridge, 1966.

Becker, Carl. *The Declaration of Independence: A Study in the History of Political Ideas*. New York, 1922.

Buel, Richard, Jr. *Securing the Revolution: Ideology in American Politics*. Ithaca, 1972.

Hartz, Louis. *The Liberal Tradition in America: An Interpretation of American Political Thought since the Revolution*. New York, 1955.

Palmer, Robert R. *The Age of the Democratic Revolution: A Political History of Europe and America, 1760–1800*, 2 vols. Princeton, 1959–1964.

Rémond, René. *Les Etats-Unis devant l'opinion française, 1815–1852*, 2 vols. Paris, 1962.

Wood, Gordon S. *The Creation of the American Republic, 1776–1787*. New York, 1972.

RELATED TOPICS

Burke	Enlightenment	Maistre	Rousseau
Condorcet	Equality	Nation	Sieyès
Constitution	Lafayette	Revolution and Europe, The	Sovereignty
Democracy	Liberty	Rights of Man	Tocqueville

ANCIEN RÉGIME

The notion of the Ancien Régime is inextricably linked to the French Revolution. It is the Revolution's inverted image, its bad side, its negation: not only that which preceded the Revolution but that in opposition to which the Revolution defined itself as repudiation, rupture, and new beginning. In French the phrase *ancien régime* forms an indissoluble pair with the word *révolution,* and this differentiates the French idea of revolution from the English. The English Revolution of the mid-seventeenth century overthrew the monarchy, but only in the name of the traditional Constitution. It was not within the ambition of even its most outspoken champions and egalitarian proponents to establish a radically new society upon a basis of regenerated humanity; their idea was rather to *restore* a social order that had been betrayed, a promise that had been forgotten. Somewhat later, just prior to the events in France, rebels in America rose against English tyranny in the name of the English Constitution. How could such rebels have had an "old regime"—they who had fled Europe a century earlier in order to rid themselves of monarchy, aristocracy, and established church? Tocqueville would later draw a contrast between democracy in America, established in the New World from the first days of European colonization, and French revolutionary democracy, which was compelled to overthrow a preexisting aristocratic order. Comparable in nature and principle, the two experiments in democracy differed in that one was obliged to confront the existence of an "old regime" while the other was not, the Ancien Régime being in Tocqueville's view the sine qua non of "revolution."

Nineteenth-century Frenchmen continued to be obsessed with the violent shift from Ancien Régime to Revolution that defined France as a political collectivity. They formed a nation so dramatically divided that it could not love in its entirety a history with which it nevertheless remained obsessed, a nation that, if it loved the Revolution, detested the Ancien Régime, and if it mourned the Ancien Régime, hated the Revolution. Even those who wished to repair the fabric that history had rent found it hard not to feel that the damage was irreparable. Chateaubriand sought to reconcile the old monarchy with the new democracy, yet his work thrived on his irrepressible sense that the old world was gone forever and a new age had begun.

In French culture this sentiment was and is so powerful that it has established the Ancien Régime as an almost palpable reality, an idea accepted by all and treated as though it required no further comment. Even the curriculum of historical studies in French universities is defined by this canonical watershed: "modern" history begins with the Renaissance and ends in 1789, and "contemporary" history begins in 1815. Between the two blocks thus defined lies the no-man's-land of the Revolution: the Ancien Régime's death certificate, duly signed by the professors, fixes the moment of transition between the two eras as 1789.

This tells us when the revolutionary rift occurred, but it hardly defines the substance of what went before. If the Ancien Régime died in 1789, when had it been born? The Revolution indiscriminately used the phrase to denounce both feudalism and monarchy, both the Middle Ages and the bureaucratic regime of the seventeenth and eighteenth centuries. Does it follow from this that the revolutionaries meant to reject the whole prior history of France? Or to repudiate the whole history of mankind as a history of corruption? Whenever one attempts to erect a historical watershed and to argue that what went before was radically different from what came after, epistemological problems arise. To these the concept of the Ancien Régime adds ambiguities arising out of its extraordinary political success. The simplest way to reduce those ambiguities is to reexamine the conditions under which the concept was first evolved.

The expression *Ancien Régime* was already used in a number of *cahiers de doléances,* or compilations of local grievances, but in a rather limited and specific sense. For example, in the *cahier* submitted by the clergy in the *sénéchaussée* of Carcassonne, we read that "the old regime of voting by orders is therefore the most advantageous." When a *cahier* wished to express the idea of a sweeping, overall change, it contrasted the old "order of things" with the new (see the *cahiers* of the Third Estate of Amiens and of the nobility of Paris *intramuros*).

The word *régime* was thus initially limited in scope to a sector of the administration. On March 17, 1789, a prospectus for a work entitled "L'Impôt abonné" ("Taxes by Subscription"), published as a supplement to the *Journal de Paris,* referred to the "abuses of the Ancien Régime" and contrasted them with the proposed new system. On August 11, following the celebrated debates that had begun on the night of the fourth, the National Assembly voted to "destroy completely the feudal regime." By that it meant, as the body of the decree makes clear, not only what remained of feudal property and the fief contract but tithes, the sale of offices, and the system of privileges granted to various individuals and corporations—in short, the entire corporate structure of society. An orator did indeed speak on August 4 of a "new regime" in discussing the scope of the reforms, but no one had as yet used the term "Ancien Régime" to refer to the past in its entirety. No doubt this was because nothing was yet settled concerning the Constitution of the realm. Furthermore, article 17 of the decree of August 11 "solemnly proclaims King Louis XVI the Restorer of French liberty." This formulation indicates not just that royal sovereignty still had a hold on men's minds but also that liberty had deep roots in the nation's history, since the king was said to have "restored" it. In both respects this proposition ran counter to the notion that the "Ancien Régime" was something to be wiped off the face of the earth.

Nevertheless, the expression came into wider use, though it was still far from commonplace, when toward the end of August the deputies took up the question of how the government should be organized: Should there be one chamber or two, should the king have veto power, and where should sovereignty reside? Orators had previously referred to the "feudal regime" or the "old Constitution," but now they were increasingly likely to affix the word *ancien* to the word *régime* in discussing matters of power and its legitimacy. As a result, the noun "regime" acquired a political as opposed to a social connotation. On September 1 the duc de Liancourt spoke of "monarchical government" as having always been the government of France, "even before the kings had shaken off the yoke of custom that required them to consult the people concerning the formation of the laws. If the representatives of the nation received from it the power to abolish this Ancien Régime, the National Assembly can no doubt reduce that regime to naught; but if our mandates grant us only the capacity to restore it, we would be violating those mandates if we were to assume that we possess the power to destroy it." The duke, who like the monarchiens wished to see sovereignty divided in the English fashion between the king and two chambers, defended the royal veto as an essential element of monarchy. He naturally favored the second of his two hypotheses, but his own words placed the first on the table, and it was destined to win an easy victory over the arguments of the monarchiens. With them went what the orator of September 1 had called "monarchical government" or "the Ancien Régime," now replaced by a unicameral Assembly endowed with indivisible sovereignty and a king transformed into the kingdom's supreme functionary.

Thus the Revolution did not wait until it had dethroned the monarch (which it did only on August 10, 1792) to use him as a foil in defining the "Ancien Régime." As early as September 1789 the Assembly diluted what for Liancourt was the "essence" of monarchy by denying the king co-sovereignty and reducing Louis XVI to a subordinate role as head of the executive branch. On October 5 and 6, moreover, the people would render even that role largely illusory. Things were actually less clear-cut than this summary would suggest. Many deputies, Mirabeau foremost among them, continued to draw a contrast between, for example, the young American Republic, where it had been possible to create entirely new institutions, and the old kingdom of France, where it had been necessary to rescue hereditary monarchy from the disarray of the past. In the end, however, no compromise was necessary. The rout of the monarchiens signaled the end of the monarchical tradition and thus laid the groundwork for the new concept of an "Ancien Régime."

A dictionary published by Chantreau early in 1790 gives an idea of how far the phrase and the idea had progressed. The purpose of the work was to "aid in the understanding of words added to our language since the Revolution and of new meanings attached to certain old words." In it we find this definition of *régime:* "In politics, it is equivalent to administration, to government. The Ancien Régime is the old administration, that which functioned prior to the Revolution, and the new regime is that which has been adopted since that time and from which true patriots expect their good fortune, but which spells despair for those drone insects who used to feed on the abuses

authorized by the old regime." By this point, apparently, Revolution and Ancien Régime were firmly established as antagonists. The disappearance of the
Ancien Régime is credited with having brought good fortune to France's new
citizens. The noun "regime" had insinuated itself as a substitute for the old
word "government," commonly used in eighteenth-century political philosophy in a sense far broader than it has today. "Patriots" could now simultaneously denounce both the "monarchical constitution" and the "feudal regime," for "regime" referred indiscriminately to both the old society and the
old "government."

The Constituent Assembly, having "destroyed everything" to begin
with, soon came to feel that it had subsequently "reconstructed everything."
Talleyrand used these very words in his address to the nation of February 11,
1790, in which he summarized and celebrated the accomplishments of that
legislative body. Under the heading of things destroyed were the absolute
monarchy, the Estates General, the system of orders and privileges, and feudalism. Among the things reconstructed were the sovereignty of the nation,
embodied in the Assembly; citizenship; a new division of the kingdom; the
basis of a just system of representation; and equality before the law. Having
contrasted the new "edifice" point by point with the old, the bishop of Autun
cited the fundamental principle on which the whole structure was based,
namely, the Rights of Man: "Ignored and insulted for centuries, the Rights
of Man have been reestablished for all mankind."

Thus the ultimate justification for the abolition of the Ancien Régime
lay in the philosophy of natural law. The overall significance of the Assembly's
reforms stemmed from its desire to base the new social contract upon the
inalienable rights of individuals, and especially upon the foremost of those
rights, liberty. Ultimately, it was this sharp break with the principles of the old
society that established both the philosophical ground and the radical meaning of the term "Ancien Régime." Implicitly it described a contrast between
the old social order, thought to be justified by a hierarchy that reflected the
will of God, and the new, based upon a social contract among free individuals
who had chosen to form a community in order to preserve their "rights." The
Revolution marks the point at which the transition from old to new was consummated, negating all those centuries during which the rights of man were
"ignored and insulted." In his address to the nation on February 11, 1790,
Talleyrand did not go so far as to invoke the "state of nature" referred to in
contemporary philosophical works. He spoke only of "reestablishing" a principle that had long been trampled underfoot. How long? That he did not say,
and his silence, reinforced by the allusion to "all mankind," is a fairly clear
indication that his condemnation of the past, like Rousseau's, was directed at
the continuous corruption of human nature by history.

Applied at first to monarchical government, the notion of the Ancien
Régime soon took on a wide range of social, political, and philosophical connotations. In September it was used to designate, and repudiate, the old "constitution of the realm." Soon thereafter it came to imply condemnation of the
feudal regime, abolished on August 11, followed fifteen days later by the vote
on the Declaration of Rights: a cascade of events and decisions that wrested

the old kingdom from the grip of the past and unified the new nation around the idea of a fresh start. Bizarre as it may seem in light of the inevitable continuity of any nation's historical existence, the idea that society could be made over starting with a clean slate drew considerable power from the people's revolt against inequality and the elite's faith in the philosophy of the Enlightenment.

Yet that power was tempered by the role accorded to Louis XVI in the new Constitution. It was as though this man, who had only yesterday been king but who, having been rehabilitated by the Revolution, was now being tapped for quite a different role, remained in spite of everything a bridge between the French people and their history. But this fragile fiction, already strained by the October Days of 1789, collapsed with the king's flight to Varennes (June 1791). Before quitting the Tuileries, Louis XVI had left on his desk a public disavowal of the revolutionary laws he had been compelled to sign, and even without this his departure stood as eloquent testimony to his true sentiments. The majority of deputies, pretending to believe that the king had been abducted, could have restored him to the throne, but the public had already made up its mind to sever the final tie between the Ancien Régime and the Revolution. Robespierre, as always, understood the public's mind and voiced its sentiments, leading the parliamentary fight that summer against the Feuillants' attempt to patch things up and make a place—not just a token position but a place of honor—for Louis XVI in their revised Constitution. And a year later, on July 29, 1792, it was again Robespierre who told the Jacobins that the government of the Revolution is "a monstrous mixture of the old regime and the new."

On August 10 that monster was slain, and in the following month the Convention, in its first meeting, proclaimed the Republic. The last constraint on the revolutionary use of the term "Ancien Régime" was thereby lifted. Increasingly it came to denote anything antagonistic to the Revolution; the Ancien Régime became the Revolution's antithesis. Hence its meaning and even its chronological limits remained quite fuzzy. The captive Louis XVI was its symbol par excellence. There was now ample reason to expand the malediction to include not only all that had preceded 1789 but also those three years, from 1789 until August 10, 1792, during which the Revolution had haggled with the king over the shape of a constitutional monarchy. Year I in the new time began with the Republic on September 21, 1792, but Louis XVI was not judged and executed until December 1792–January 1793. Yet the role that he had assumed was not eliminated but put to other uses. The Ancien Régime was like a stage, upon which yesterday's revolutionaries were made to tread alongside yesterday's counterrevolutionaries: émigrés with Girondins, Marie Antoinette with her regicide cousin the duc d'Orléans, Desmoulins, Danton, and Hébert, and the whole show a mere curtain raiser for the ultimate appearance of Robespierre, whom the Thermidorians would accuse of attempting to restore the crown for his own benefit.

At no time was the meaning of "Ancien Régime" in the revolutionary lexicon broader or vaguer than it was then. The phrase had come to denote any manifestation of resistance or even mere inertia in the face of the collective effort to establish a new order for the common good. No longer did the Ancien Régime mean simply feudal society as opposed to the new society of free individuals. Nor did it refer to just the chaotic old system of disparate institutions that stifled the rule of law, nor to the despotism of kings as opposed to the republic of citizens. It also implied a range of habits of mind, customs, and mores that impeded progress toward the republican goal of creating a new man. The old regime was conceived as a kind of residue, a survival of the past that made it impossible to reap the full benefits of the present. Besides the constant political threat posed by the creatures of the "Ancien Régime," the aristocrats and their accomplices within the Revolution, there was also the less visible but still formidable danger of "old-regime prejudices." What use were good laws if custom and prejudice prevented them from bearing fruit?

The problem had been raised much earlier, at the time of the first Constitution. Consider, for example, the following quotation from the *Dictionary of the French Constitution and Government* published in late 1791 by P. N. Gautier: "If a Revolution in our laws has restored our rights, in order to preserve them there must also be a revolution in our mores. Having shaken off the irons of slavery, we have yet to shake off those of habit. Our condition has changed, but our character has remained the same. Let us hasten to rid ourselves of everything in that character that still derives from our former servitude." After 1792, however, the pace of the Revolution accelerated, and ideas like this were advanced as arguments to justify its chaotic course. The repeated crises that had impeded the progress of the Revolution were due, it was argued, to the persistent presence of the past, which had proved quite difficult to eradicate. If the Revolution was the protagonist in a drama, the Ancien Régime was the antagonist, which lurked not only in the shadows of conspiracy but also in the dark recesses of memory, ever present, ever ready to wield sword or idea against the revolutionary enemy, ready even to mobilize the forces of ignorance. For the Revolution encountered no obstacles, only adversaries. Inventing modern politics, it imagined a world compounded of hostile intentions and desires. The Ancien Régime was not simply a curse, it was the enemy. Against the fledgling new world the Ancien Régime mobilized the forces of opposition.

In modern French political history the idea of the Ancien Régime has enjoyed the same brilliant career as that of the Revolution, because the two are inseparable. It continues to exert a powerful hold on people's minds, most commonly as a symbol of rejection, of repudiation of the old world of nobility and absolute monarchy, generally seen as having ruled in conjunction with the Church. Such sentiments were common among the nineteenth-century bourgeoisie and peasantry. Those who had acquired clerical and noble properties during the Revolution naturally feared a return of the Ancien Régime, and the intensity of that fear increased whenever such a return seemed imminent, as it did, for example, during the Restoration at the time of the *chambre introuvable* (1816) and later, after 1820, when the ultraroyalists returned to power. With time such fears abated, yet they were periodically rekindled by republican politicians up to the eve of World War II. Even today, the Ancien Régime, the era of noble landlords and the tithe, remains a vivid image in the mind of the French peasant.

In the twentieth century, however, the formula has been used for the most part outside the historical context in which it was born, simply as a negative for revolution and social progress. It evokes an image of the past as a time of oppression and inequality, evils that are to be abolished by revolutionary action (as in the well-known couplet of the "Internationale"). Thus it contributes to the vision of radical social change that is of course part of the post-Jacobin heritage of left-wing extremist culture. Instead of lords and nobles, today's leftists denounce "divine-right capitalists" and "old-regime politicians."

The idea also belongs to the history of scholarship, for it has never ceased to arouse the passions of historians. It was Burke's primary target as early as 1790. The Whig parliamentarian was astonished by the revolutionaries' radical rejection of the monarchical past. He knew full well that the Ancien Régime had not provided the Estates General with a proper constitution—for him, obviously, a constitution modeled on that of England. Yet in spite of absolutism the foundations for such a constitution had indeed been laid. The structure had only to be completed, and that was precisely what the Estates General had initially tried to do, its efforts culminating in the royal *séance* of June 23. Burke in effect interpreted Louis XVI's speech that day as a blueprint for an English-style monarchy. Instead, however, the French had pursued the abstract notion of "pure democracy," dismissing the experience of centuries and renouncing the national patrimony. They had attempted to "set themselves up in business with no capital."

Why this insistence on starting with a clean slate? To this question Burke had no answer, except perhaps in his remarks on the social composition of the Assembly, which he saw as having been deserted by the kingdom's elites and dominated by pettifogging lawyers of modest social background. Burke's facts are dubious. Even worse, they have little or no explanatory value. For if it is true that the "Ancien Régime" had provided France with institutions and a "government" that had at least some good in them, and that the Revolution, insofar as it was in any way useful, was complete by June of 1789, then why did men previously so empirical and reasonable suddenly become so blind? If for Burke the characteristic folly of the Revolution was its repudiation of the past, his ultimate interpretation is of a theological type: the Revolution, he insists, was an arrogant rebellion by man against an order willed by God.

Burke's critique, so fertile a source of inspiration for counterrevolutionary thinkers, posed a fundamental question for French liberals as well. What did it mean that the price of liberty in France was revolution and therefore suspension of the rule of law? What was the nature of that period between the Ancien Régime and the Revolution in which French liberty was born? What made Burke's question even more urgent was that history seemed to bear out his pessimistic assessment: the Revolution, having failed to establish the rule of law, veered toward dictatorship and arbitrary rule in the Reign of Terror. It is no mystery why Burke was one commentator on the Revolution with whom Thermidorian intellectuals liked to argue. If only the Revolution could be ended by instituting the rule of law, they argued, then Burke's criticisms would effectively be refuted. Hence they drew a sharp distinction between the Republic and the Terror and attempted to restore the dignity of the Revolution of 1789, which they said had brought liberty to France. In Constant's brochures of 1796 and 1797 ("De la force du gouvernement et de la nécessité de s'y rallier" and "Des réactions politiques"), for example, Burke is rarely cited but constantly argued with and refuted. The Directory's young and brilliant spokesman drew a sharp contrast between the "age of privilege" (which he also called the "era of heredity" to underscore his point that social rank was then determined by birth) and the age of equality before the common law, the fulfillment of the idea of man's universality. What Burke described as an inevitable condition of society in general—the fortuitous "sedimentation" of property, status, and prejudice over the course of centuries—was for Constant simply the "Ancien Régime." What 1789 revealed was how the idea of equality had secretly gnawed away at the vast body of settled opinion and unchallenged hierarchy: the Revolution marked the triumph of law, which was also the triumph of reason.

Fifteen or twenty years later, the Restoration had changed the nature of the question. By dating the Charter of 1814 from the nineteenth year of his reign, Louis XVIII attempted to abolish a discontinuity that seemed incompatible with the legitimacy of the monarchy. But this act of exorcism was not enough to erase either his supporters' nostalgia for the Ancien Régime or his adversaries' nostalgia for the Revolution. The problem for proponents of the Charter, however, was to restore what the Revolution had destroyed, namely, the continuity of French history, and to establish a single, unbroken tradition of liberty extending back before and continuing on beyond 1789. On the ultraroyalist side, Chateaubriand clung to the two worlds out of which the fabric of his existence had been woven: an aristocrat loyal to his king, he remained convinced that the spirit of 1789 could not be undone. He discovered antecedents for that spirit in the preabsolutist monarchy, in the rather elusive era that he dubbed the "monarchy of Estates," situated somewhere between the time of feudalism and the end of the Valois dynasty, during which royal power was protected from the temptations of despotism by an aristocracy jealous of its rights and zealous in its defense of liberty. Transplanted to the early nineteenth century after the agony of the Revolution, that monarchy ought indeed to restore the Church, religion, and morality, but it must also compromise with the times by accepting civil equality and modern society; it must reckon with the new importance of the bourgeoisie and join in the evolution of ideas and customs rather than imprison itself in the past. "Representative government," established and organized by the

Charter, was thus a new symbol designed to replace both the Ancien Régime and the Revolution by restoring to Louis XVI's brother history's undivided legacy.

About the same time Mme. de Staël confronted the same problem, but she came to it from a very different world. Daughter of Necker, the hero of the spring of 1789, a Protestant, involved in the Revolution up to 1792, a republican under the Directory, she was in no way attached to the Ancien Régime. Yet like Chateaubriand she was opposed to imperial despotism and wished to reconcile monarchy with liberty under the Charter of 1814. Her *Considerations on the French Revolution* (published a year after her death in 1818) can be read as yet another response to Burke, a systematic attempt to link 1789 to the history of France and thus diminish the magnitude of the revolutionary chasm. If a "constitutional" monarchy did indeed exist before the absolute monarchy, between the fourteenth and sixteenth centuries, then it was liberty that was old and despotism that was new. Hence "the revolution of 1789 had no other aim than to regularize limits that have existed in France at all times" but that the absolutist monarchs tended to forget. Like the English Revolution of the seventeenth century, and like 1814, 1789 had been a restoration.

Yet the interesting point is that neither Chateaubriand among the ultras nor Staël among the liberals managed to bridge the gap between Ancien Régime and Revolution. The assassination of the duc de Berry in 1820 revived all the old animosities between the two camps and inaugurated a lengthy period of ultraroyalist rule, during which the Ancien Régime was more than ever inseparable from the restored monarchy. Chateaubriand, enshrined in literary glory, neglected politics, while the heirs of Staël gave liberal thought a freshly revolutionary turn: if the ultras wished to go back to the Ancien Régime, then liberals would revisit 1789. For Guizot at this stage in the evolution of his thinking, that famous year marked the date of the Third Estate's decisive victory over the nobility. By attempting to reverse the judgment of history, the ultras exposed themselves to a second rout. Once again the Ancien Régime and the Revolution would pit one nation against another.

In this sense the Revolution of July 1830 represented a reprise of 1789, and for the second time it put an end, if not to the Ancien Régime, then to its ghost. But the replay of the inaugural event only burned its component elements even more deeply into the French political imagination: Louis Philippe, the son of a regicide who became king of the wealthy bourgeoisie, proved no more successful than the brothers of Louis XVI had been at reuniting the memory of the nation around his bastard reign, though he certainly tried. The Ancien Régime remained as vivid as ever in political imagery and even more in historiography, celebrated by legitimists and denounced by republicans. It was kept alive not so much by the threat of a return of aristocratic society as by denunciation of monarchy in the name of the Republic. It was as though the nineteenth century was destined to reproduce the political-semantic shift that had marked the course of the Revolution itself. Among many examples, none is more revealing than the case of Michelet, Orleanist in 1830 and republican ten years later. No one had more thoroughly internalized the revolutionary rift than Michelet, or more sharply contrasted Ancien Régime and Revolution, divine right and the rights of man, arbitrary rule and the rule of law, misery and fraternity. In all the hateful legacy consigned to oblivion by the Revolution of 1789, it was the monarchy that played the central role and assumed responsibility for the evils of the past—so much so that Michelet, for whom nothing rated higher than the festival of the Federation and who was none too fond of the Jacobins, nevertheless chose to cast the judgment of Louis XVI as the Revolution's moment of truth.

This vision of an Ancien Régime symbolized by and embodied in the monarch stands in sharp contrast to another no less celebrated but completely different vision, that of Tocqueville. Both Michelet and Tocqueville suffered the same fate of "internal exile" under the Second Empire, but unlike the republican historian the philosopher of "democracy" had little interest in the question of monarchy versus republic that so stirred the passions of his contemporaries.

Tocqueville's passions were roused by something quite different. For him, the idea of a radical break between what went before and what came after, in terms of which the Revolution had defined itself, was itself the product of a history that encompassed both the Ancien Régime and the Revolution: the supplanting of civil society by an administrative state. His history of the Ancien Régime traces the ineluctable growth of centralized government and its effects on the whole of society. In this way he discerns a chronology in which local political life, once dominated by the aristocracy, was gradually taken over by agencies of the central government. Instead of dialogue between lords and local communities, France came to be ruled by administrative fiat, reducing both aristocracy and communes to political irrelevance. Born in the late fifteenth and first half of the sixteenth century, the centralized state did not truly come into its own until the reign of Louis XIV, but it had not yet finished growing. Tocqueville analyzes centralized government as it existed in the eighteenth century, when it had acquired two characteristics that would ultimately lead to its downfall: on the one hand, it had stifled all participation by society in decisions affecting the general interest and had reduced the French to equality under its stewardship, while, on the other hand, the sale of public offices and privileges, made necessary by the government's financial needs, led to a more rigid social structure, indeed to a veritable caste system. The Ancien Régime was thus a world in which the administrative monarchy simultaneously sowed seeds of aristocracy and democracy.

In the absence of regular political institutions the resulting conflict could not be discussed and resolved; so it was treated instead in literary and philosophical terms by intellectuals, who took the place of a political class. It was they who slowly developed the radicalism that would become the Revolution. Lacking any real experience of the world and given to abstract generalizations, the philosophes remade the world not according to tradition but according to reason. Their denunciations of the "abuses" of feudalism and despotism later became the rallying cries of the Revolution. Thus the idea of wiping the slate clean itself grew out of the history of this Ancien Régime. An essential element of the revolutionary consciousness, it was a powerful goad to action, yet it was also an illusion: for the Revolution, which was brought about by the action of the administrative state on the old society, ended with that state in a position of unchallenged power over modern society. Bonaparte realized the dream of Louis XIV. Together the Ancien Régime and the Revolution deprived modern France of its taste for liberty and perhaps even robbed the word of its meaning.

It is not difficult to understand why this Tocquevillian attempt to reconcile the two antagonistic symbols of French history met with little success in the political arena. True, it made history's legacy whole and reestablished its continuity, but it did so in such a pessimistic way that after the collapse of the Second Empire republicans found it useless for their pedagogical purposes. Tocqueville proposed a wicked Ancien Régime followed by a wicked Revolution; what the republicans needed was a laudable Revolution preceded by an Ancien Régime in which the state could at the very least be plausibly portrayed as the enemy of aristocracy and inequality and founder of the French nation. For this they turned to the Orleanist historians—Mignet, Thiers, and Guizot—rather than to Tocqueville.

Somewhat more mysterious is the indifference that historians exhibited for more than a century toward a work that today dominates our thinking about the question of the Ancien Régime. That indifference can probably be accounted for by one rather odd fact about Tocqueville's analysis: it reveals the same factors at work prior to the celebrated eruption as afterward. If democratic individualism and administrative centralization were as much products of absolute monarchy as of the Revolution, the dividing line between the history of France before 1789 and the history after 1789 is somewhat obscured, and the term "Ancien Régime" itself is reduced to little more than a name belatedly attached to the first subversion of aristocratic society by absolutism. Hence the Ancien Régime's only legacy to the revolution that led to the triumph of democracy was a revolutionary disposition latent in thought and culture, from which the notion of a *tabula rasa* ultimately emerged as a radical condemnation of the present.

Tocqueville's Ancien Régime is therefore a historical object that must be studied on two levels: first as a product of the transformation of aristocratic society by a centralized administrative monarchy, and second through the strange way in which the men of the late eighteenth century conceptualized their past in order to reject it. In order to understand 1789, these two levels of analysis must be combined. The radically new character that the Revolution wished to give to its enterprise was itself a consequence of what preceded it.

Nearly a century and a half after its formulation this idea continues to point the way to new areas of historical research. Counterrevolutionary historians, drawn to Tocqueville by his tone of disillusionment, cannot accept his indictment of the monarchic legacy, while admirers of the Revolution, liberals as well as socialists, can at least agree that the Revolution marks the inception of democracy. Vague yet powerful, the concept of the Ancien Régime has managed, through two hundred years of French history, to preserve its freshness.

François Furet

FURTHER READING

Goubert, Pierre. *L'Ancien Régime,* 2 vols. Paris, 1969.

Tocqueville, Alexis de. *L'Ancien Régime et la Révolution.* Paris, 1856. Reprinted as vol. 2 of *Oeuvres complètes,* Paris, 1952.

Venturino, Diego. "La formation de l'idée d'Ancien Régime," in Colin Lucas, ed., *The French Revolution and the Creation of Modern Political Culture,* vol. 2, *The Political Culture of the French Revolution.* Oxford, 1988.

RELATED TOPICS

American Revolution	Guizot	Rights of Man
Burke	Liberty	Robespierre
Centralization	Louis XVI	Staël
Constant	Michelet	Thermidorians
Equality	Monarchiens	Tocqueville
Feudal System	Night of August 4	
Feuillants	Revolution	

ARISTOCRACY

W hat are we to understand by "aristocracy"? The meanings vary, and the term, often used loosely, was made looser in the Revolution. Strictly speaking, political thought since Aristotle has defined aristocracy (according to Robert's dictionary) as a "form of government in which sovereign power belongs to a small number of persons, especially to a hereditary class." Such a narrow definition, applied to France—which has had sovereign kings and a sovereign people but never a sovereign aristocracy—would leave us with nothing to write about. Other definitions, such as an "aristocracy of talent," are too broad. So is the group implicit in the expression *aristocrates à la lanterne* (aristocrats to the gallows), which was applied to any opponent or alleged opponent of the Revolution. By that time the very efficacy of the word, its capacity for political mobilization, had made it useless for objective social description. In a perhaps somewhat arbitrary fashion I shall concentrate on the nobility, though I am fully aware that the French nobility only partially fits the classical definition, in that it was a "hereditary class."

Inheritance of privileged status was in fact the hallmark of the nobility, which isolated it from the rest of society and bestowed unity on a group otherwise diverse with respect to wealth, occupation, and culture. The possession of privileges extended well beyond the nobility, since many commoners—administrators, magistrates, and even cobblers—also had them. But the privileges of commoners were never more than temporary and personal, associated with an office, a purchased right or monopoly, or simply a place of residence. Unlike the privileges of nobles, those of non-nobles could always be revoked by the king (if he reimbursed their costs), and up to a point they were separate from the individual, disposable properties that could be sold to others or lost by moving from one place to another. For nobles, by contrast, the essence of nobility and its distinctive privileges were inherent in the person. Once acquired, nobility was intrinsic and permanent, transmissible only to one's children, and that without the slightest difficulty, without even requiring an appearance before a notary.

For two centuries, characterizations of the Ancien Régime nobility have inspired generalizations that form a thicket of truths and half-truths. The oldest of them, and probably the most common in the nineteenth century, was based on a moral condemnation. The eighteenth-century nobility was supposed to have been licentious, self-indulgent, frivolous, arrogant, lazy, unproductive—in short, totally different from the honest and upright bourgeois whose solid interest in work and moral integrity made the new order. For persons sensitive to the pain of others, this view was comforting, for as we

616

know now, the eighteenth-century nobility was marching inexorably toward disaster—its destruction as an order. Certain nobles were destined for the guillotine; many more lost their property, and thousands fled into exile. It is reassuring to think that they somehow deserved their fate, that they brought it on themselves. Moralists had written persuasive books on the subject: luxury and licentiousness among Rome's patricians had caused the fall of the Empire, they said, and the hypocrisy and venality of the Roman clergy had brought on the Reformation. It was hardly surprising, therefore, that latter-day moralists should have blamed the French Revolution on the moral bankruptcy of an elite. For them, *Les liaisons dangereuses* was a work of ethnography, a clinical description of a corrupt and dying world.

Yet corruption is not enough to characterize a nobility whose personal morality was no different from that of other social groups. In the 1830s the comte d'Allonville, who could still remember what life was like before the Revolution, claimed that he had known a morality that was at least decent, crimes less frequent than in other milieus, mothers who did what was expected of them, and adults who were solicitous and careful in treating the young. The sexual habits of nobles do not appear to have been very different from those of bourgeois. True, noble arrogance is frequently attested. The royal pages at Versailles amused themselves by spitting on bourgeois from the balcony of the Opera and by marching through the city in close ranks, pushing people into the garbage-filled streets. Such examples could no doubt be multiplied, but it should be noted that we know about these particular episodes from records that detail the discipline the pages received. Condescension notwithstanding, personal relations between nobles and commoners were generally relaxed and reasonably good. In provincial and Parisian academies the noble third mingled easily with the non-noble two-thirds, and the rapid spread of Masonic lodges prior to the Revolution provided other opportunities to negate the pretensions of birth. Over the course of the century even dress became simpler. No admirer of aristocrats, Babeuf observed on the eve of the Revolution that for some time it had been impossible to distinguish between a great lord and his inferiors on the basis of appearance. At home, where the number of liveried male lackeys and the pomp of their appearance had once been matters of rivalry among aristocrats, relations with servants seem to have evolved much as they did in bourgeois homes. Domestic service had become an increasingly female occupation over the course of the century, and servants' chores tended to be limited to the kitchen, cleaning, and child care. In short, aristocratic and bourgeois codes of morality and styles of life were more similar than different, although nobles were wealthier on the average and therefore able to acquire more of the good things in life.

What about the criticism, so vehement in 1789 and afterward, that the aristocracy was unproductive, even parasitic? Again, distinctions must be drawn. Of two hundred thousand noble individuals, roughly forty thousand were adult males capable of holding a job. At least a quarter of them served as officers in the army and navy. One out of twelve or fourteen was a magistrate in a sovereign court or in the upper levels of the royal administration. Others were bishops or vicars general. Guy Richard has found more than a

thousand involved in commerce and industry. They were important in sea-
ports, where privateering and the colonial trade occupied many, as well as in
the mining, iron manufacturing, textile, and paper industries. Uncounted
and little studied, some lesser nobles were glassmakers or—especially in Brittany and Provence—active in local commerce. They held posts in finance
alongside commoners. Many more nobles than one might think held positions
in municipal administration or the low-level clergy. Some even served, in violation of regulations, as simple soldiers rather than officers in the army. There
may have been a high rate of idleness among the poorest nobles, the roughly
one-fifth with annual incomes below 1,000 livres. But idleness was then an
involuntary choice, and a good majority of nobles did lead productive lives.

But reality and its perception are two totally different things. The fact
that most nobles were active did not protect them from the charge that, as a
class, they were idle and useless. Tocqueville and Sieyès would have agreed
on this if nothing else, and the charge was widely believed at the time of the
Revolution. How did such a conviction arise if nobles were generally active?
Perhaps it was because the tasks to which they devoted themselves were remote and increasingly carried on in institutions where they could be observed
only by professional colleagues. What struck the vast numbers of peasants,
villagers, artisans, and shopkeepers about the nobles in their vicinity was not
their work but their privileges. In the village nobles played little or no role in
daily affairs and in meeting vital needs. Those who might have counted for
something were far away, and those close at hand were not a fair sample of
the class, for they included its poorest, apparently greediest, and certainly
least powerful members. The absence of specific functions for nobles in local
government and their failure to serve as mediators between individuals,
groups, communities, and the expanding state inevitably calls to mind
Tocqueville, in whose view the responsibility for this sad state of affairs belonged to the royal administration, which for a century had worked to destroy
the nobility as an aristocracy and transform it into a caste. Expanding rapidly
from the time of Richelieu, the state exploited to the full the fatal bargain it
had struck with aristocrats in the fifteenth century. For it was then that nobles,
yielding to temptation, had committed their original sin. They had traded
liberty and power for privileges. In return for surrendering to the state their
ancient right to participate in government and decision making on both the
local and national level, they had received privileges and exemptions without
obligations. Thus the nobles bought peace, but at too heavy a price. Suffering
under the illusion that they were free because they paid no taxes and the state
left them alone, they scarcely noticed that by no longer governing they had
lost true liberty. From that moment on, the nobility steadily retreated into
political isolation and irrelevance.

The king then dealt with the people directly, his power unmediated by
vassals. Tocqueville's story, told in rich detail, traces the long conditioning of
the French into habits of dependence on the ever more intrusive state. Free
men who had once acted spontaneously and independently to meet their own
needs and solve their own problems were now obliged to await the approval
and orders of a higher authority before doing anything. There was no longer

any room for an independent nobility, no longer any role for nobles as such. Gradually the state filled the expanding space increasingly called public and became thereby the sole object for hope and fear, for praise or blame by individuals in good times and bad. Sadly but inevitably, the nobles lost touch with the population. No common interests held the different groups together—local tasks belonged to the state, and resistance to its fiscal incursions ceased to interest nobles, who paid no taxes. Lacking any function to legitimate its special status and distinctions, the nobility became vulnerable. Among the people, the idea of equality was born simultaneously with hatred of privilege. Why believe that a nobleman was different from anyone else, since everyone was equal before the state—equal in being excluded from power? The inegalitarian regime, though inscribed in law, had become anachronistic and therefore had to disappear. The king himself suggested as much in the preambles to his fiscal edicts, and the government regularly insisted that fiscal privileges were unfair, a terrible burden to be borne by a hard-working and overtaxed people. Hence, Tocqueville argues, it was hardly surprising that when the Revolution came, the nobility was generally deemed useless and idle and therefore detested.

This brief summary does not, of course, do full justice to Tocqueville's analysis. Rather than consider that analysis in full detail, let us examine certain aspects of the nobility to which Tocqueville devoted less attention. Consider first the idea that the nobility was exclusively or primarily a landed elite. The material interests of a "feudal" nobility—that is, a social group whose unity derives from an agrarian power based on a common type of economic domination—have in recent years been a subject of lively debate. Does the mere fact that many nobles owned fiefs constitute a class interest? Seigneurial dues, which varied widely from region to region, apparently accounted for only a very small portion of the nobility's income. Nor were feudal revenues exclusively monopolized by nobles: some fiefs belonged to bourgeois, and many nobles had none. The feudal regime obviously included exemption from taxes, but the economic significance of that exemption is somewhat ambiguous. The law concerning the *taille* (tallage) limited its exemption to 120 or 125 hectares, and numerous officeholders and bourgeois also profited from it. New taxes created in the eighteenth century to supplement the *taille* did not exempt nobles, and on the whole it is likely that the nobility paid more direct taxes than the underassessed inhabitants of the cities. During the Revolution, the committees responsible for restructuring the tax system estimated that, all told, exemptions cost the state 30 million livres annually. The nobles' share of those exemptions was not more than half, and the 15 million additional livres that the nobility ought to have paid, though not negligible, would have barely made a dent in a state deficit that was approaching 150 million in 1789.

The nobles' financial stake in the land had little to do with feudalism and much to do with modern ground rents, something quite familiar to capitalists. As landowners, nobles had benefited from the growth of the rural population after the middle of the century. Malthusian pressures and growing competition for access to land drove up the price of grain and, with it, ground rents, to the advantage of larger landowners and the detriment of most peasants. This development was of course good for many nobles. Their advantage would have been more decisive had they owned more land. It is known, however, that the nobility actually owned only twenty-five to thirty percent of the land, the rest being divided among the clergy (perhaps ten percent), the bourgeoisie (twenty percent), and the peasants themselves. Demographic growth was therefore no more profitable to nobles than to ordinary bourgeois or wealthy peasants. That fact did not improve anyone's opinion of them, however. But growing hostility to the nobility stemmed not so much from feudal and institutional factors as from demographic and economic ones, that is, from impersonal, modern causes. Nobles, moreover, were but one of several groups constituting the agrarian regime that weighed so heavily on many peasants.

These details can easily mask a crucial point, however. The striking thing is how little the French nobility was attached to the soil. A comparison will help to make this clear. In a sense, the French aristocracy was the least "feudal" aristocracy in Europe—to use "feudal" in its loosest, broadest sense. In France no law, no custom, no social ambition required a noble to own land in order to enjoy his special status. The system was totally different from that of England, for example, where the rural elite defined itself almost entirely in terms of landholding. There, some twenty thousand families of "mere gentlemen" or better formed a group comparable to the French nobility in both prestige and percentage of the total population. On the English side of the Channel, however, this elite owned not twenty-five or thirty but eighty percent of the land. Owning land—lots of it—was an indispensable prerequisite for the status of gentleman. More than sixty percent of the French nobility would not have qualified to belong to the English elite. Rural England may be pictured as a vast checkerboard of indivisible estates, any one of which would have seemed quite large to most French nobles. The great landowners might own several of these, but even the most insignificant member of the elite had to own one such estate to gain or maintain his status. Lack of land put one out of the game. In eastern Europe, too, the connection between elites or service nobilities and land was also very close, though for different reasons. There, extensive estates and servile labor were the sole source of wealth that sustained nobles in the almost permanent, unremunerated state service that defined their status. Fortunately for them, in these regions of low population density, land was relatively abundant, for they had no opportunity to make the kinds of investments on which many French nobles counted to supplement their income: offices, loans to individuals and the state, urban property, and sometimes commerce. Thus in France, the nobility, without being an Italian or Rhenish patriciate, relied less on land than did many other elites.

Of course tradition, ideology, devotion to a native region or family tradition, or need for a place to escape the summer heat led nobles to maintain or acquire an estate or modest property. And some nobles owned vast properties and worked diligently to enlarge them. It must be recognized, however, that landed property was not the essence of the French nobility. In fact, the fundamental condition of the nobility was precisely that of having no limits: it could define itself at will, or, rather, in accordance with the king's will, for kings made nobles. Though some with vivid imaginations dreamed of ancestors emerging from the Germanic forests or galloping as conquerors alongside the king, most were well aware of their family background. They carefully preserved the royal parchments recalling or confirming the status that had been granted them. But with the growth of the modern state, and especially of the costs of the administration, the army, and the completely revamped navy, the nobility quickly became an important financial resource for the monarchy. Incapable of collecting enough taxes to cope with the chronic shortage of funds and at times unable even to borrow in a normal manner, the French state as early as the fifteenth century gradually transformed what had been old privileges into purchasable commodities and invented new ones. Although nobility was but one part of a wider order of privilege including monopolies, offices, and dues of bewildering variety, trophies that ambitious men sought for themselves and their posterity, it was a particularly important and coveted one. In short, the state discovered that nobility could be turned into a source of profit.

Several conditions had to be met before that profit could be realized, however. First of all the dividing line between the classes had to be sharpened. By giving a very precise definition of the status of noble, the state singled out a group of people just below that line who might pay for the privilege of crossing it. The state also had to guarantee that it alone could confer nobility and that no one could usurp it as in the past. New mechanisms of access to the Second Estate had to be put in place. Gradually the sale for cash of letters of nobility, a practice common from the sixteenth century on, gave way to sale of offices that conferred nobility on their holders. This practice proved most useful. Offices represented a kind of capital that kings could create at will and sell for much more than letters of nobility. Passed from person to person, each office could, it is true, confer nobility upon several individuals. But for the king the transfer fees were lucrative, and, even more important, the ambitious buyers, whether individuals or groups, were rich and vulnerable to the demands of the state, which from time to time forced them to make involuntary loans. At intervals, usually during wartime, they were asked to invest additional funds in new offices. In the end the offices were locked into a system of royal borrowing. Having come to represent a sum of capital too large for the state to reimburse, they remained until 1789 an institutional fixture of the monarchy.

In the seventeenth and early eighteenth century, offices were created in waves. Seemingly moribund institutions took on new life. At a time when the work load declined, the bureaus of finance grew from four or five offices apiece around 1600 to twenty-eight in the eighteenth century. After 1715 there were eight hundred ennobling but otherwise functionless offices in the chancelleries, along with an equal number of redundant offices in the sovereign courts. All told, there were more than four thousand offices of this type in the eighteenth century, and wealthy commoners made effective use of this royal road to nobility. The chancelleries alone, which created ten new nobles annually at the beginning of the seventeenth century and twenty at the end, reached an all-time peak of fifty in 1730 and remained at that level until 1789. The *chambres des comptes, cours des aides, bureaux des finances,* sovereign and superior council, and even several parlements all recruited their officials largely among the bourgeoisie. In the last fifteen years of the Ancien Régime, no fewer than twenty-two hundred commoners acquired offices that would have ennobled their descendants had the Revolution not intervened. In short, the last sixty years of the monarchy were the golden age of ennoblement. It is hardly astonishing, then, that in the minds of some there seemed to be no limit to the expansion of the nobility in France, unlike in other European countries, where the supply of land served as a brake.

Probably most of the men who gained access to the nobility in this way would have seemed perfectly worthy to anyone who knew them. But to those who did not know them personally, who saw in them only a type, their rise was a disaster, a symptom of a deeper disease afflicting French society. They personified what was wrong: the operation of money in a France that many people condemned for its excessive luxury, for the topheavy growth of its court and cities, for a commercial spirit based on the principle of selfishness and encouraged by an inefficient and wasteful state. Most of those who were ennobled were thought to have enriched themselves at the expense of the state through profits on finance, and it was quite apparent that they held useless offices. Lacking virtue, they nevertheless purchased honor. This widespread hostility to practices that made nobility a commodity was evident in 1789, and the *cahiers* of the nobles and of the Third Estate joined in expressing a common wish: nobility should be a reward for merit and never sold to individuals whose only merit was money. But the impoverished state's only response to this current of public opinion was to impose, in 1771, a new fee on commoners who purchased offices and to require a similar fee from those ennobled since 1715 in order to confirm their status. The state thus ratified past practice and committed itself to continuing on the same course.

Having stripped the nobility of its local and political functions, the state seemed also to have cheapened a status that it no longer needed for governing. This degradation played a part in the subsequent fate of the nobility by triggering an apparent "aristocratic reaction," which had a disastrous effect on public opinion. Though actually directed against the ennobled, this reaction offended commoners. Non-nobles could hardly have been expected to understand that the famous Ségur ordinance of 1781 requiring four generations of paternal nobility in order to be an officer did not concern them. After all, bourgeois seldom served in the army, and their purely tacit exclusion had never previously been challenged. Once made explicit, however, it became a matter of controversy. From the army's standpoint, however, the requirement of genealogical proofs was an aspect of reform. It would close the officer corps to those who arrived, freshly signed letters of nobility in hand, attracted exclusively by the prestige of the uniform and the status of an officer. Coming from families without a military tradition, accustomed to independence, money, and luxury, such recruits would have been impossible to assimilate. A strict genealogical criterion was the only way to eliminate them. Many parlements, especially in cities and regions where ennoblement had been very rapid, imposed similar restrictions for analogous professional reasons. But the new men of the Third Estate knew nothing of these tactical maneuvers by which some nobles sought to exclude other nobles; outsiders saw these tactics as fresh and gratuitous acts of harassment directed against themselves. The whole business of genealogical proofs entered the public consciousness in the 1780s and crystallized the hostility of ordinary bourgeois who had never dreamed of becoming either lieutenants or magistrates.

*
* *

The hostility of commoners toward nobles therefore had fairly clear sources, but a problem remains. Why, with all its advantages, was the nobility unable to defend itself better in the Revolution? In the end it was more successful at resisting the crown, at fighting what many considered royal despotism, than at protecting its own status. Oddly enough, the nobility, even in the minds of nobles, was less than the sum of its parts. During the Revolution, and despite the theories of Montesquieu, few nobles displayed much ability to defend nobility effectively. Resistance to revolutionary principles, when it existed, was confined to individuals, isolated groups, or regions, and, worse yet, it came too late. In the end probably about twenty percent of adult male nobles voted with their feet and fled the Revolution, but the vast majority who did so departed only in 1791 and 1792. The ending of privileges in August 1789 and the destruction of the noble estate itself in June 1790 had left most nobles grumbling but quiet, still willing to make their peace with the new order as individuals. If the very existence of the nobility had been the overriding issue, the emigration would have begun sooner and involved more people. How can we explain the nobility's behavior? Failure of nerve? Intimidation and fear? Perhaps some of each, but far more important was the evolution of institutions and ideas that had already fragmented the nobility before 1789 and changed the way that status was embedded in its thinking.

It is the evolution of ideas that needs investigating. Not all nobles responded to the Revolution in the same way, but most apparently accepted or could live with many of its principles: individualism, representative institutions, constitutionalism, the end of tax exemptions. What caused trouble, but not immediately, was the issue of equality, particularly as it affected the social composition of institutions.

For many nobles who were doing serious work, it was almost self-evident that recruitment by birth, sons succeeding fathers, was a good thing. In general, they thought it preferable to recruit "from inside," within families in which tradition was well established, a sentiment that accorded well with the new views of the Enlightenment, according to which an individual's basic disposition depends on conditioning through education. In this perspective the formation of a caste in accordance with professional traditions made sense, so that at the beginning of the Revolution nobles were prepared to defend their program of exclusion with a good conscience. In this they were determined, and they were also potential counterrevolutionaries. Accustomed before 1789 to challenge the acceptance of the recently ennobled on grounds of nonprofessionalism, many aristocrats did not hesitate to resist the revolutionaries who were attempting to democratize institutions and open careers to all.

This explanation of aristocratic responses to the Revolution rests on an assumption, namely, that the concerns and even the identities of many nobles in 1789 were increasingly professional. That brings us to the particular form that the socialization of the nobility took in the eighteenth century. At the origin of the process was a profound sense, derived from the Enlightenment, of the dignity of useful labor. The idea, known earlier to mercantilists, spread everywhere. It was particularly visible in the new culture's choice of enemies: monks, who did nothing useful and spent all their time in prayer; bachelors, who shunned social commitment; hacks, who turned out gutter literature; scholars, who indulged in idle speculation; unproductive financiers; courtiers, whose role was purely decorative. For some, all these people were "aristocrats." Benedictines scrambled for teaching posts, and pages from Versailles sought berths in the infantry rather than return home. Enrollments in law schools doubled. It was as though occupation had replaced rank at the core of personal identity, giving rise to new feelings of guilt: those who remained idle increasingly felt the need to conceal their idleness. The idea of work, once "bourgeois," was no longer the monopoly of a single class. Central to the ideology of the sans-culottes during the Revolution, it was no less crucial in the minds of nobles. Students at the Royal Military School constantly heard administrators, including the minister of war, insist that birth without a useful occupation was worthless and that an idle noble was a disgrace. In numerous contexts a puritanical language of emulation, merit, and talent came to the fore.

In this climate of new ideas many members of the nobility felt impelled to take on new roles, to be active and, by their own lights, useful in one way or another. But how? As Tocqueville pointed out, one way was now closed. It was too late to contemplate a reform that would have transformed this fragmented nobility into a true political class on the British model. Though perhaps conceivable in the mid-seventeenth century, such a solution had been foreclosed by the state's destruction of ancient customs and associations. It was also too late to take part in local decisions: networks of relations that had developed over a long period of time no longer existed, and it had become second nature for the nobility to avoid involvement in community affairs. The only new role the nobility could hope to find in society was bureaucratic and professional and consistent with the aims of the state. Nobles could be functionaries of the administration, officers in the army, magistrates, or financiers. Even those who remained in commerce sought to legitimate their activity by purchasing offices and by pointing out the utility of commerce to the state.

This return to an active life had two dramatic consequences that weakened the nobility's capacity to defend its rank and status. The order became increasingly fragmented along professional lines, and this fragmentation allowed new groups, often suspicious and resentful of one another, to appear. The great debate over the nature of nobility (circa 1750) brought these conflicts and inner tensions into the open. Montesquieu, in *L'esprit des lois,* idealized the role of nobles, magistrates intermediate between the king and the people, jointly bulwarks of monarchy and guarantors of liberty: a justification for the *noblesse de robe.* Then came abbé Coyer with his plea on behalf of the commercial nobility, a new branch stemming primarily from the *anoblis,* the ennobled. Next came the turn of the chevalier d'Arcq, who extolled a selfless military nobility uncontaminated by money and civilian values generally. Still other voices were raised in the clergy: increasingly sensitive to the perceived threat from the philosophes, the parlements, and the secularizing state, some aristocratic bishops attempted to define the independence of the Church and their own role within it. Only the administrative nobility, secure in real power, remained silent. From all these sometimes acrimonious disputes and their institutional aftermath emerged the image of a multitude of nobilities, more like diverse professions than parts of a single social class.

All this suggests a need to reconsider the view that nobles formed a common front united behind a single ideology embodied in Montesquieu and the parlements. This supposed unity did not manifest itself where one might expect to find it: in the elections to the Estates General, only one in twelve noble deputies was a member of a sovereign court. The nobility probably entered the Revolution more divided than before. To have imagined it as a corps capable of being integrated as an order into the new constitutional regime of 1789 was, in retrospect, an enormous miscalculation stemming from a failure to perceive the realities of the day.

Nobility of individuals—individual rank and status—was defended much more strongly than nobility as an order. In this respect nobles knew what they were fighting for. But in a context of general hostility to the Revolution, they could do battle only on terms that ensured in advance they would be defeated. Unwilling to assert ancient privileges, most stressed the continuing importance of nobility as a rank and distinction. Ranks and distinctions were necessary, they argued, to the functioning of institutions and professions. There is no better illustration of this than the at first puzzling case of Guibert. The leader of a movement to reform the army, he welcomed nearly everything the Revolution brought: the Constitution, representation, individual rights, and the end of fiscal privileges. He even rejoiced in the fusion of the three estates into one. Yet a year earlier the same Guibert had tightened the genealogical requirements for the rank of officer, and as late as December 1789 he was still calling for preservation of nobility. Against democrats he argued that armies, unlike civil societies, are not made for equality and that one cannot expect merchants, magistrates, and priests to show an aptitude for command. Discipline, subordination, and obedience required social distance, which reinforced differences of military rank, and for that nobility was irreplaceable. Guibert went on to explain how dignities and distinctions bolstered the authority that even a constitutional regime must have. Nobility, by conferring consideration on public service, elevates an otherwise lethargic people above its purely private interests. Nobility, considered purely as a rank, cost the nation nothing; it even saved money by instilling a sense of duty that impelled nobles to accept poorly remunerated service.

Guibert was speaking for the army, but other institutions aroused similar sentiments. Nevertheless, there was nothing heroic or mysterious about the nobility invoked here, nothing that was not within the reach of many commoners as well. Although professionalized nobles used the good old words, virtue and honor, to define themselves, they altered their meaning. They used them to mean work, acquisition of practical experience, and unflagging attention to dull routine. In professions undergoing modernization, only experience mattered. These were terms that commoners could understand. If experience and fitness for the job were all that counted, many nonnobles could claim the right to hold these same positions. Veterans of the legal profession knew more about law and procedure than young noble magistrates; older curés could argue that they were in a better position to carry out the Church's spiritual mission than were aristocratic bishops; and so on. Why, once within the framework of professions and institutions, give priority to the accident of birth? Professionals, whether noble or common, detested any intrusion by frivolous amateurs. But when non-noble professionals were excluded by nobles whose status reflected nothing other than a grade in a bureaucratic hierarchy, the commoners were prepared to respond to Sieyès' call. Whence the paradox of a nobility simultaneously improving and detested.

The Ancien Régime thus incorporated a nobility that was neither an aristocracy in the classical sense of a governing oligarchy, as in Venice, nor a participant in the government, as in England. Largely independent of the land, the French nobility was constituted by its relation to the state. But that relation, which had defined it ever since the advent of absolutism, had also deprived it of political power. The most remarkable aspect of its social existence was therefore its character as a class of individuals possessing personal hereditary status by right of birth and under royal guarantee. Notwithstanding efforts made in the eighteenth century to link that status to a specific social function, nobles were unable to shed the image of costly and useless privilege of which they were the quintessential embodiment. Even the efforts they made in this direction produced the opposite of the desired result. The existence of a strong reformist current within the aristocracy only reinforced the idea of a birthright that was condemned by the prevailing opinion of the age.

The great observer of all these changes was Sieyès, who at the end of 1788 wrote and published two books in rapid succession: *Essai sur les privilèges* and *Qu'est-ce que le Tiers Etat?* (the latter published in January 1789). The first, and shorter, work defined privileges as legal monstrosities, in contradiction with the universality of law, alien to the natural order of the societies from which they benefited as outsiders. Privileges belonged to the aristocrat, or in any case the aristocrat embodied the very essence of privilege, because of heredity. The birthright turned what ought to have been nothing more than a reward for a particular merit into a durable and essential inequality, contrary to the universal rights of individuals. Aristocratic society was not a society but a mere relation of power. *Qu'est-ce que le Tiers Etat?* extended and systematized this argument in preparation for the impending meeting of the Estates General. Sieyès, a great reader of the physiocrats and of Adam Smith, excluded the nobility from the nation on grounds of social uselessness: all the active roles in the society were filled, or could be filled, by the Third Estate. Invoking Locke, Sieyès reinforced the exclusion of the nobility on grounds of natural law. A nation, he argued, is "a body of associates living under a common law and represented in the same legislature." The nobility stood outside this association, since by definition it stood outside the common law. But this alien body had come to dominate the nation. In a crucial paragraph of the second chapter, the abbé denounced the aristocratic usurpation, the true face of absolutism: "It is a great error to think that France has lived under a monarchical regime. Remove from your annals a few years of Louis XI, of Richelieu, and a few moments of Louis XIV in which one sees nothing but pure despotism, and you would think you were reading the history of a court aristocracy. It is the court that has reigned, and not the monarch." Thus Sieyès anticipated the definition of the Ancien Régime—aristocratic usurpation under cover of the monarch and through the spectacle of the court—and marked out the course of the Revolution in advance by reclaiming the nation's rights in civil equality and constitutive sovereignty.

The genius of the vicar general of Chartres lay not only in his having anticipated events, predicted the transformation of the assembly of the Third Estate into the National Assembly, and published the program of the Revolution at the very beginning of 1789. It lay even more in his having been the first to produce a body of ideas that foreshadowed what would become the principal source of revolutionary activism: hatred of the aristocracy carried to the point of reading the nobility out of the social contract. The force of this feeling, for which scarcely any equivalent is to be found in the *cahiers de doléances,* on the whole far more moderate, is one of the keys to the political passions that would characterize the Revolution. As for the idea of exclusion, there could have been no more fitting inaugural for the policies of the Revolution: the new and sovereign nation did not define itself in relation to other nations, through combat with its foreign enemies. Its defining boundary lay within itself, in the political expulsion of a group of Frenchmen who had usurped its rights. Sieyès, as Bernard Manin put it, opened the Pandora's box of the Revolution. For him, the enemy was still defined in legal terms by the notion of privilege. Yet it was he who introduced into the democratic, revolutionary imagination the idea of an undefined domestic enemy, lurking within the nation, altering its nature and undermining its foundations. Furthermore, the aristocratic emigration that began in July 1789 was not enough to limit that image to the role assigned to it by the abbé. In the French Revolution the Ancien Régime never died; it kept on giving birth to "aristocratic plots," thus offering patriots the opportunity to redefine the nation and the people in opposition to the "aristocracy." After the aristocracy of birth came the aristocracy of wealth. After the aristocracy of the monarchiens came the aristocracy of the Feuillants, the Girondins, the Dantonists, the Robespierrists—an endless and murderous list in which the aristocracy was nothing other than the defeated political enemy.

IDEAS

What is paradoxical about the idea of aristocracy in the French Revolution is that it was very quickly defeated and destroyed as a principle of social organization yet constantly returned as the ghost of inequality and as a decisive issue in political struggles. "Feudal" society, more accurately a society of orders and corps, was abolished by the decrees of August 4 and 11, 1789, and the nobility was eliminated in June 1790. The Constituent Assembly based civil equality on a radical individualism, which can be interpreted as a repudiation of a society based on privileged orders. Yet "aristocracy" survived its abolition as the inverted image of democracy: Ancien Régime versus Revolution, inequality versus equality, factions versus the people. Under the monarchy the idea of aristocracy never corresponded to the reality. Under the Revolution it gave rise to a formidable egalitarian dynamic. There is a hidden causal link between these two facts of the French eighteenth century, a link on which Tocqueville remains the most profound commentator.

David D. Bien

FURTHER READING

Bien, David. D. "La réaction aristocratique avant 1789: L'exemple de l'armée," *Annales ESC*, 1974, 23–48 and 505–534.

Chaussinand-Nogaret, Guy. *La noblesse au XVIIIe siècle*. Paris, 1976.

Higonnet, Patrice. *Class, Ideology, and the Rights of Nobles during the French Revolution*. Oxford, 1981.

Meyer, Jean. *La noblesse bretonne au XVIIIe siècle*, 2 vols. Paris, 1966. Abridged edition, Paris, 1972.

Sieyès, Emmanuel. *Essai sur les privilèges* (1788) and *Qu'est-ce que le Tiers Etat?* (1789), reprinted Paris, 1982.

Tocqueville, Alexis de. *L'Ancien Régime et la Révolution française*, 2 vols. Paris, 1856. Reprinted as vol. 2 of *Oeuvres complètes*, Paris, 1952.

RELATED TOPICS

Ancien Régime	Enlightenment	Montesquieu	Taxes
Army	Equality	Necker	Tocqueville
Babeuf	Estates General	Night of August 4	
Emigrés	Feudal System	Sieyès	

CENTRALIZATION

For Tocqueville centralization was the thread that wove the monarchy and the Consulate into a single national history—a history of a centralized government, of a monarchy that treated the French people as its ward and destroyed traditional society even as it unified it into one nation. Centralization was a "product of the Ancien Régime" that survived the Revolution because it suited the new society. Tocqueville enumerated its component parts: a unique central organ of government, the King's Council ("All matters ultimately come before it, and from it emanates the impetus that is communicated to everything else"); intendants and subdelegates dispatched to rule the provinces; "secondary" agencies unable to act on their own without permission of the central authorities; and the use of special courts to try cases in which the administration had an interest. "It [centralization] had only to cut down whatever had risen around it in order to appear as we see it now." Since the intendants were the sole agents of the will of the government, the Finance Ministry (*Contrôle Générale des Finances*) under which they served became a key organ of government.

This image of a centralized monarchy organized around the King's Council and the finance ministry long dominated a historiographical tradition that relied primarily on the writings of royal "jurists" and apologists as well as on the works of their adversaries. The distinction between governmental centralization and administrative centralization, which Tocqueville used in *Democracy in America* to account for differences between England and the United States on the one hand and France on the other, was blurred in his *Ancien Régime and the Revolution*. Governmental centralization was inherent in the logic of western political development, whereas administrative centralization was symptomatic of a state that came into being by differentiating itself from civil society. In Tocqueville's *Ancien Régime,* centralization and "state-ization" go hand in hand. The analysis overstates the importance of a form of government in which the state dominates civil society, a situation symbolized by the intendants (and later the prefects).

The eighteenth-century intendants helped to create a system of administrative courts and claims bureaus that encroached on the traditional province of the sovereign courts and ordinary tribunals. When the Cour des Aides of Montpellier complained in 1734 of certain actions of the intendant of Languedoc, d'Aguesseau responded that administrative matters could "hardly be entrusted to the many hands of a company" but must "be guided by one and the same spirit." To apologists of monarchy it was essential that the king, as universal judge, have the right to arrogate to himself jurisdiction over certain cases. This right had been invoked most recently when the King's Council intervened in certain financial affairs as well as in religious matters associated with the papal bull *Unigenitus*. In the eighteenth century, however, the extraordinary character of such proceedings was increasingly overlooked. A decisive step toward regularizing royal interventions was taken on June 28, 1738, when d'Aguesseau issued a regulation governing judicial procedures conducted by the King's Council. This ascription of judicial functions to the Council prefigured the administrative courts of the nineteenth century, even though the operation of the Council's Extraordinary Committees was not strictly determined by the modern dichotomy between public and private: the king continued to assume jurisdiction over numerous private cases, particularly when it was necessary to hush up scandal.

The Constituent Assembly, influenced by royal jurists and haunted by memories of parlementary obstruction, approved the Law of August 16–24, 1790, which solemnly affirmed the separation of the administration from the judiciary. Yet the Revolution never really established a system of administrative courts: the administration was at once deliberative body, executive, and judge. Not until Year VIII were administrative courts established that were distinct from the administration as such: the Council of State and the Prefecture Councils. In fact the jurisdictions of these bodies still overlapped with those of the ordinary courts, and it was not until the early Third Republic that the administrative courts acquired their autonomy. The state, hidden behind its laws, proclaimed itself external and superior to society; the idea of "public authority" justified state intervention, and the idea of public service justified its exorbitant character.

In the eighteenth century, the intendant—"the Council's provincial eye," as one intendant put it in 1781—saw his responsibilities, which had never been clearly defined, broadened in economic and social matters. Two-thirds of all intendancies at the time coincided with the older fiscal subdivisions known as *généralités*. The rest either were located in outlying areas or covered extensive territory in provinces that had retained their provincial estates. Assisting the intendants in their work were general subdelegates of two types: those who were appointed by the intendant and those who were commissioned by the king. The latter were professional administrators, while the former represented a primitive application of the idea, widely adopted later on, of recruiting prominent local citizens to assist the government in its work.

At the same time, as shown by the example of Bertrand de Molleville, who served as intendant of Brittany from 1784 to 1788, their staffs grew in size and their assistants came more and more to resemble bureaucrats. Yet the system was not nearly as efficient as its neat organization chart might suggest. Everything depended on the circumstances and the personality of the intendant. The intendant was much like the prefect as portrayed by Pierre Grémion: a mediator, a negotiator who steered a course between local and national powers. The colossus had feet of clay, and the very nature of monarchy made his power all the more fragile. According to Tocqueville, it was the monarchy that stripped the nobility of its local political power and thus laid the groundwork for egalitarianism. Hence the shift that undermined absolute monarchy occurred before the Revolution: by 1787 centralization and its attendant "cultural revolution" had done their work. Now the intendants, whom Malesherbes had denounced in his 1775 remonstrances as "stiflers of the municipal spirit," found themselves rivaled by provincial and municipal assemblies.

The creation of such assemblies had been anticipated in numerous eighteenth-century works, most notably the well-known "Memoirs on the Establishment of Municipalities in France," which Dupont de Nemours prepared for Turgot. But it was left to Necker, anxious to strengthen public support for the monarchy and more sensitive than Turgot to the need to enlist the aid of economic interest groups, to attempt the experiment. In 1778 he submitted a memorandum to Louis XVI in which he argued that a more broadly based administration would be preferable to the strict hierarchy of the intendant system. Although the primary target appeared to be the intendants, Necker's plan also would have bypassed opposition in the parlements, which claimed to be representative bodies. The provincial assemblies preserved the traditional distinction among the three orders but instituted voting by head and doubled the representation of the Third Estate, composed of deputies from the cities and rural landowners.

In 1787 Calonne, who was critical of Necker's plan for its failure to provide for any intermediate echelon of government, presented a gathering of notables in Versailles with a new plan, which provided for three levels of assembly in each *généralité:* parish assemblies as set forth in the memorandum of 1775; district assemblies embracing deputies from thirty parishes, who would be responsible for distributing the tax burden among the parishes and for making proposals to the third and highest echelon, the provincial assemblies. The last were to be composed of deputies from the district assemblies with no distinction as to order, and their responsibilities would include distribution of taxation, public works, poor relief, and submission of proposals to the government. Between sessions an interim commission would fill a caretaker role.

Calonne's intentions as explained to Louis XVI in November 1786 were quite clear: "to hear the wishes of taxpaying landowners . . . [and] to limit them to enlightening the administration through consultative deliberations without giving them, or allowing them to claim, the right to administer themselves." The intendant would be entitled to admission to all sessions of the provincial assembly, would be informed of all deliberations, and would countersign all expenditures. In no sense was Calonne's proposal a plan for decentralizing the administration of the realm.

After lengthy negotiations conducted by Calonne's successor, Loménie de Brienne, an edict creating the provincial and municipal assemblies was finally published in June 1787. The new system was to be established only in provinces without provincial estates. Voting by head was to be permitted and the representation of the Third Estate was to be doubled, but the chair was reserved for members of the privileged orders. Assemblies were to be responsible for distributing the tax burden among communities, planning public works, and informing the government of their wishes. They were to be represented by a *procureur syndic*. The edict included regulations governing relations between the assemblies and the intendant. The intendant alone determined which instructions to pass on to the assemblies and was required to be present when community accounts were examined. He could authorize expenditures up to 500 livres; beyond that amount the Council's consent was required. Thus the intendant was not as powerless as Tocqueville believed. For all his concern about the dangers of despotism inherent in eighteenth-century reforms, he underestimated the intendant's influence and failed to see how frequently the assemblies were forced to seek his approval. Renouvin was right to say that there was no decentralization.

The reform was actually begun in only seventeen of the intended twenty-six *généralités*. Renouvin has studied the difficulties that were encountered: nearly half of the deputies of the Third Estate were drawn from the privileged orders, and many elections were postponed. On October 15, 1788, Necker decided to suspend the reform measures, and from then on everything depended on the Estates General.

*
**

Centralization involves much more than the mere geographical organization of power. An exhaustive catalogue of all the legislation and practical reforms that flowed from the need to adapt indivisible sovereignty to the emergent new society cannot be attempted here. Let us, then, concentrate on three key events: the decrees of December 14 and 22, 1789, which laid down the essential features of the new structure of government; the reform of Frimaire, Year II (December 4, 1793), which established the revolutionary government; and the transformation of that government in Year III.

After the political revolution of June 17, the dismantling of the old society of orders in August, and the successes of September, the Constituent Assembly, encouraged by victories won with the help of municipal rebellions and rural uprisings but also worried by the continuing unrest, set out to reshape French institutions. The new territorial organization necessitated by the abolition of privileges drew on earlier reforms attempted under the monarchy. Each département was to have a general council elected for two years. Between sessions governmental functions were to be carried on by a directory with the power to issue decrees and by a *procureur général syndic* elected for four years, a sort of prosecutor charged with enforcing the laws. The same organizational model was to be followed in each district, and each *municipalité*—one in each parish—was to comprise a council, municipal officers and an elected mayor and prosecutor representing the king and his taxpayers, that is, the public interest as against the private. The councils' regulatory authority was to be fairly extensive, especially in the economic sphere, and they would also be empowered to summon the army and declare martial law.

There is an established historiographic tradition of describing this legislation as an attempt at decentralization—a theory based on the expanded responsibilities of local bodies with both legislative and executive authority,

the reduced administrative oversight, the elimination of intermediary echelons, and above all the election of local representatives. Taine, for example,
held that the Constitution of 1791 "almost annihilated" central power; the
law merely organized disorganization, and power slipped from the top to the
bottom of the hierarchy. The département, said Taine, was a small independent republic, a "little state that lives independently." For Aulard it inaugurated a "kind of administrative anarchy." Mathiez joined with Taine in opposition to Jaurès: this "most sweeping of decentralizations ... far from
consolidating the new order shook and nearly toppled it," as a result of which
destruction it took nothing less than the centralization effected by the Jacobins to save France. More temperate, Jaurès notes that, while there was indeed a lack of coordination between local and central authorities, owing to
the Constituent Assembly's fear of making the local powers subject to the
executive—that is, the king—the system probably saved the country from the
counterrevolutionary machinations of the court. For Jaurès, whose criticism
was surely aimed at Tocqueville, the system attests to the confidence of the
Constituent Assembly and the absence of class struggle, for otherwise it
would have been unthinkable to turn local power over, unchecked, to a populace of artisans and peasants. Not only did the new arrangement turn up a
supply of new administrators who would prove staunch supporters of the
Revolution; it also helped to educate the people in the ways of republican
government. In this respect the Varennes episode is revealing.

Those who see the reform as hastening the abolition of pluralistic
France stress the subordination of local authorities to the executive, the leveling rationality implicit in egalitarian ideology, and the many facets of the
administrative structure. It is true that the Constituent Assembly attempted
to unify the country and that the structure of the administration would influence the organization of the courts and, even more important, the churches.
The Civil Constitution of the Clergy, by unilaterally establishing ecclesiastical
districts that coincided with administrative ones and by causing upheaval in
the ecclesiastical hierarchy, drove the Church, progenitor and rival of the
state, into the counterrevolutionary camp; thus it deprived the Revolution of
a ready-made bureaucracy of trained missionaries that the revolutionaries
could have used much as Louis XIV had used his clergy. What is more, the
Church emerged from the revolutionary crisis more centralized than ever but
also more subservient to the Pope, whose power over his bishops and,
through them, parish priests was similar to Bonaparte's over his prefects and,
through them, local mayors.

To judge by parliamentary debates, several issues were of primary concern to the Constituent Assembly. First, the criteria for determining how the
administration would be divided: the choice of territorial criteria was a radical
one. Second, the subordination of local administrations to the executive. The
deputies' great fear was that whoever was charged with effecting the liaison
between the executive and the local administration would in effect become a
kind of intendant. On November 23 Target pointed out that the power of the
executive would be limited and that the Assembly would be represented by
an interim commission even when it was not in session, hence the king should

be able to convey his orders to the administrative assemblies. The problem for the Constituent Assembly was how to arrange for communication between the center, which stood for rationality, and the periphery without relying on intermediaries. Michelet saw the Constituent Assembly as a "head without arms" that equipped itself with "44,000 hands," a jibe all the more apt in that the département was not yet the Janus that it later became—the place where the central bureaucracy met and negotiated with prominent locals—and because the Revolution in this phase (Constituent Assembly) was carried forward by municipal enthusiasm. Michelet also hit the nail on the head when he described the decree of December 14, 1789, as a recognition of the existing state of affairs rather than the implementation of a systematic plan.

But there were elections, because Thouret, former *procureur syndic* of the provincial assembly of Rouen met Sieyès, the champion of political representation. The new territorial subdivisions were as much electoral as administrative units, even though the Assembly, which shared Sieyès' mistrust of local special interests, readily agreed that local administrators would not be representatives of the nation. The most far-sighted of the deputies realized after the fact how serious the consequences of this ambiguous measure would prove to be.

The elections mandated by the laws of 1789 took place in 1790. The powers of the départements may have been vague, but those of municipal officials were clearly spelled out, as were their obligations. Alison Patrick insists that only limited decentralization took place between 1789 and 1792. The Constituent Assembly's primary concern was to establish new institutions quickly in order to head off trouble. Local administrators were left to organize their departments on their own. Communication being poor, the new institutions had no choice but to function independently, like it or not. Queries to Paris often went unanswered, and local administrations, forced to work out their own priorities, ultimately consulted one another in an attempt to remedy the acute shortage of information. This had never been done under the Ancien Régime, and the innovation helped to create an illusion of federalism, which, along with the disappearance of the corporations, would prove to be a royal gift to Robespierre and his Jacobins.

Mounting perils (foreign wars, civil wars, and popular unrest) compelled the regime to centralize; to defend the Revolution, the old coercive machinery was resurrected. In 1793 the Mountain, which made up in authority what it lacked in unity, won out over the Girondins, who were accused of "federalism." After October 1793 the Committee of Public Safety institutionalized centralized rule for two reasons: it wanted to coordinate the various political, administrative, military, and economic decisions taken the month before, and it wanted to combat and ultimately destroy institutions created by provincial activists. A united and indivisible Republic also implied that the Convention, and the Convention alone, must govern.

At first it attempted to rule through officials dispatched to the provinces. The Constituent Assembly had shown the way on two occasions, at the time of the Nancy affair and again when the king attempted to flee to Varennes. The Legislative Assembly in its battle against the executive had followed suit by sending deputies to border areas, army units, and disturbed regions, and the Convention had permitted these officials to remain in place until their missions were completed. In March 1793 the Convention sent representatives to the départements for the purpose of recruiting 300,000 troops. A number of factors—the Vendée insurrection; the hostility of certain provinces and large cities to the June 2 Paris coup; the war and mass recruitment (*levée en masse*); the growing economic demands of the populace and ensuing legislation establishing the *maximum,* or ceiling price on various goods; pressure from parapolitical and paramilitary organizations; and the growing need to rely upon municipal governments, in theory elected by universal suffrage in November 1792, to exercise their police authority—made the politicians of the Mountain keenly aware of the need for a strong central government to overcome their many adversaries.

The government's offensive was launched in October 1793, at a time when the Vendée insurrection and popular unrest seemed temporarily subdued. It would continue through the period of de-Christianization and the demise of the factions, up to the crushing of the Paris Commune, the recall of officials on mission in the provinces, and the inauguration of the Great Terror. In his report on the Vendée of October 1, 1793, Barère ascribed France's woes to the proliferation of centers of decision making: "Our ability to strike at the brigands depends largely on our ability to strike simultaneously, repeatedly, and with one purpose." On October 10, after hearing Saint-Just, the Convention decreed that the government would remain revolutionary until the conclusion of a peace treaty, and that the executive council, ministers, generals, and official agencies would all be subordinate to the Committee of Public Safety. During the same session it was decided that, in order to enforce the *maximum* on grain prices and regulate wartime supplies, it would be wise to establish a production schedule for each district and a needs schedule for each département so that whatever amounts were necessary could be requisitioned. Finally, it was also decided that the difficult problem of the revolutionary armies would be resolved by the Committee of Public Safety.

Next came the Billaud-Varenne report (November 18), prelude to the Law of December 4, which Aulard called a "kind of wartime constitution." Albert Mathiez characterized this law as substituting for a "chaotic and sporadic centralization that had developed at random, as the situation required, an orderly and permanent centralization." Effective as the measure was, it was still a hastily patched-together expedient, a response to friction between the Convention's representatives and agents sent by the ministries, the Paris Commune, and the sections. Billaud's fear was the same as Robespierre's on December 25: that special interests would usurp the people's sovereignty. It was time to be done with the Constituent Assembly's "Machiavellian plan" to establish two centers of government, the legislative and the executive. The "head of the monster" might have been chopped off with the execution of the king, but "the trunk is still alive." In this case the trunk was those "vampires of liberty," the authorities in the départements, more than fifty of which had protested against June 2. The remedy was to make sure that all power flowed "from the center to the circumference" and to establish "legislative centrality." A machine with too many cogs and levers only absorbed the energies of the government or, by diverting them from their proper ends, created "legal anarchy." Hence "the sword of Damocles must hang over the whole apparatus from now on." Government, Saint-Just said, must be "laconic."

With this decree the Convention became "the sole and central mover of the government," alone endowed with the right to interpret the law. To publicize that law, a legislative bulletin was established. In January 1794 Barère drew the logical consequences in his proposal to "revolutionize the language," that is, to impose the language of the center on the rest of France, on the grounds that "the light that is conveyed at great expense to the extremity of France is extinguished upon arrival, because the laws are not understood." Henceforth "the vigorous accent of liberty and equality" would be the same from the Pyrenees to the Vosges.

The Law of December 4 profoundly altered the pyramid that the Constituent Assembly had constructed: the départements were supplanted by the districts, which posed less of a threat to the Convention. Too small to be powerful, too enmeshed in rivalry to join together, they had "only just enough power to enforce the law" and would be kept under direct surveillance by the Convention. The départemental councils and *procureurs syndics* disappeared. All that was left were administrators whose responsibilities were diminished and who were prohibited from traveling about their districts. The district and communal prosecutors were replaced by "national agents," drawn from their ranks but only after a purge by representatives *en mission* of the Convention, which appointed the new agents. They were obliged to report on their activities every ten days. Unlike the administrators, they were allowed to travel from place to place and constituted the only stable local authorities, since the chairman and secretary of the district directory, as well as those of the revolutionary and surveillance committees, had to be replaced every fifteen days. The revolutionary army was abolished, and meetings of popular societies and revolutionary committees were prohibited. Only limited authority was delegated by the *représentants en mission*.

"This law," Michelet says, "wanted what all France wanted: to promote unity of purpose and eliminate petty tyrants." But, he adds, "the destruction of départemental federalism left communal federalism intact and with it a local tyranny so oppressive and troublesome that France returned to being a monarchy for another sixty years." Both the revolutionary committees and their rivals, the municipal authorities, were charged with enforcing "revolutionary laws," albeit under the supervision of national agents. Of the latter, who were supposed to monitor these activities and report on any dereliction of duty, many had been *procureurs syndics:* the whole structure rested on their shoulders, yet they were subject to pressure from below as well as from their superiors (committees of the Assembly or its local representatives). They therefore usually proceeded with caution and were content merely to record sales of national properties and expulsions of priests.

On December 29, 1793, the Convention sent fifty-eight deputies to the provinces with a broad mandate. With the fall of the factions and the transformation of the Paris Commune into a docile bureaucracy, the Committee of Public Safety faced no further open opposition and wielded uncontested power. On April 1, 1794, the Executive Council was abolished and replaced by twelve executive committees attached (with the exception of the Finance Committee) to the Committee of Public Safety. On April 16 it was decreed at the behest of Saint-Just that persons suspected of conspiracy would no longer be tried in Paris, and on May 8 the revolutionary tribunals and commissions created by the representatives were abolished. Henceforth the Terror would be closely controlled by the Committee of Public Safety. Yet the Committee never obtained obedience comparable to that which Napoleon obtained from his prefects: the representatives it dispatched, pleading local circumstances, did not always carry out the Committee's orders and in some cases openly violated them, especially in matters of de-Christianization and price-fixing.

In general the period after 9 Thermidor witnessed the dismantling of the revolutionary government. Yet the Thermidorians and Girondins who returned to power were no less centralist than the deposed Jacobins. Although they diminished the concentration of power in some ways, they never challenged the principle of centralization. In fact, they perfected it; the state bureaucracy grew considerably under the Directory. On August 24, 1794, executive responsibilities were divided among sixteen committees. The Committee on Legislation became a veritable ministry of the interior. These committees were no longer subordinate to the Committee of Public Safety, but centralized government was maintained: local authorities remained strictly subordinate to the central power. The départements only gradually regained their powers. On September 8 the départemental administrations were authorized to correspond with the Committee on Legislation. Twenty days later, the Convention decided to fill vacant offices in the département of Paris and ordered its representatives in the other départements to fill vacancies there; if there was no representative *en mission*, the département's deputy was to submit a list to the Convention, which would then make the nominations. (On March 4, 1795, this responsibility was delegated to the Committee on Legislation.) The Girondins, now recalled to the Convention, obtained a decree on April 16, 1795, restoring to the départemental administrations the powers they held prior to May 31, 1793, and reestablishing the *procureurs généraux syndics* and directories. They were still to be appointed, however, by the representatives *en mission* or by its Committee on Legislation.

The Constitution of Year III (August 22, 1795) and the "two-thirds decree" also contributed to centralization. The districts were eliminated, and the cantons became the basis of a new standardized municipal organization. Municipal administrations were placed under the départemental administrations, which were placed under the ministries. At each level of the hierarchy, administrators could cancel decisions taken at lower levels and suspend or fire subordinate administrators, but only after confirmation by the Directory. The latter could also intervene directly and replace dismissed personnel with men of its own choosing until the next elections. Last but not least, a provision of Condorcet's proposed 1793 Constitution was resurrected: the Directory was to name a *commissaire* to serve at its pleasure and monitor local conformity with the law. The *commissaires* were generally former *procureurs syndics,* mayors, or members of the Convention, and it is remarkable how many of them endured in their posts through subsequent coups d'état and purges, especially after 18 Fructidor, Year V. To members of the Convention who opposed this institution, Louvet pleaded the cause of republican unity, and Daunou carried the day by arguing that the aim was no longer, as it had been under the Constituent Assembly, to disorganize the royal government but to organize the republican one. Removals from office, annulment of elections, deportations, and coups d'état proved effective instruments of centralization in the hands of the shrewdest directors. Once again it was Daunou who delivered the fatal blow in 1800: in the debate on the Law of 28 Pluviôse, Year VIII (which gave centralized government a modern look by eliminating election of officials and collegial administration), he argued in favor of Bonaparte's proposal on the grounds that it would be dangerous not to adopt it. The Brumairiens had understood the lesson of the Revolution as summed up by Sieyès: power comes from above and confidence from below.

As Barnave feared, it was left to a general to establish the principle of strict obedience on which centralized bureaucracy rests. The state administration outlives all governments and must function "independent of the merits of the workman." Anyone who knows how to grasp what Tocqueville termed the "crank" of the administration can run the government. Napoleon, "by constructing this powerful hierarchy . . . made revolution easier but also less destructive." For Tocqueville, administrative centralization and the omnipotence of Paris together were largely responsible for the political instability of France in the nineteenth century.

Relations between Paris and the kings of France were always ambiguous. Royal power "amplified local power" and allowed the city to thrive. In 1789 France found a master in Paris, no longer content merely to hold the king in check but determined to go for mate, as it did in July and October 1789, again on August 10, 1792, and later, in July 1830 and February 1848. In 1789 Paris became a département: for Dupont de Nemours this was a way of making the city "not merely accidentally but constitutionally the capital of the kingdom" and "one of the principal elements of the state organization." The revolutionaries saw clearly what was at stake, as Mirabeau and later Robespierre indicated. Barnave lucidly observed that one could not both "establish unity and repudiate the influence of the capital. But that influence is a constant source of revolutions." Robespierre, who knew a thing or two on that score, took precautions, but the Thermidorians reaped the benefits by responding to Parisian riots with a coup d'état, another way of seizing power at the center. Warily mindful of "80,000 Parisians," they demoted Paris from capital of France to "département de la Seine." Nothing demonstrates more clearly the triumph of centralization—that convenient instrument of government—than the endless succession of French governments that have fallen to a Paris riot or a coup d'état. Even Charles X's "ultras" chose to seize the state rather than take Bonald's advice to go back to a society of "communities." Local society no longer had any identity but that given it by the political and administrative system. Although the state is indeed the winner in this saga, it was not until the Third Republic that universal suffrage demonstrated how thoroughly centralization had been tamed, when it deprived Paris of its dictatorship over the provinces. The combination of centralization with universal suffrage created a new kind of power, in which prominent local figures served as contact points between state and civil society.

Taine could therefore comment ironically on the talent of Treilhard, Merlin de Douai, and Cambacérès for joining "despotic tradition to tyrannical innovation" while emphasizing that the France that was thus born was "possible, real, and durable"—a polemical way of saying that centralization, as Tocqueville saw, linked the old regime to the new but also became, with the advent of universal suffrage, the bulwark and prerequisite of social order in an egalitarian society.

Yann Fauchois

FURTHER READING

Antoine, Michel. "La monarchie absolue," in Keith Baker, ed., *The French Revolution and the Creation of Modern Political Culture*, vol. 1, *The Political Culture of the Old Regime.* Oxford, 1987.

Barnave, Antoine-Pierre-Joseph-Marie. "Réflexions politiques," in *Oeuvres*, vol. 2, published by Alphonse-Marc-Marcelin-Thomas Bérenger de la Drôme. Paris, 1843.

Bordes, Maurice. *L'administration provinciale et municipale en France au XVIIIe siècle.* Paris, 1972.

Grémion, Pierre. *Le pouvoir périphérique.* Paris, 1976.

Le Roy Ladurie, Emmanuel. "La monarchie française classique," *Commentaire*, Fall 1984.

Patrick, Alison. "The Centre and the Periphery: French Revolutionary Local Government, 1789–92," in Colin Lucas, ed., *The French Revolution and the Creation of Modern Political Culture*, vol. 2, *The Political Culture of the French Revolution.* Oxford, 1988.

Peuchet, Jacques. *La police et les municipalités*, vols. 9–10 of *L'encyclopédie méthodique.* Paris, 1789–1791.

Renouvin, Pierre. *Les assembléees provinciales de 1787.* Paris, 1921.

Tocqueville, Alexis de. *L'Ancien Régime et la Révolution,* 2 vols. Paris, 1856. Reprinted as vol. 2 of *Oeuvres complètes,* Paris, 1952.

RELATED TOPICS

Ancien Régime

Barnave

Civil Constitution of the Clergy

Coups d'Etat

Département

Federalism

Jaurès

Michelet

Necker

Revolutionary Government

Sieyès

Taine

Thermidorians

Tocqueville

COUNTER-REVOLUTION

I n 1797 Joseph de Maistre wrote: "The reestablishment of the monarchy, which is called *Counterrevolution,* will be not a *contrary revolution,* but the *contrary of the Revolution.*" Such was the program, not to say the myth, with which the adversaries of the new regime born in 1789 introduced themselves. Their triumph was not supposed to be a reaction of the kind that frightened Benjamin Constant, as violent, blind, and anachronistic as the Jacobin methods of government had been; rather, it was supposed to be a simple return to the stability, prosperity, and mildness of life under the Ancien Régime. This reassuring myth was based on a surgical view of the revolutionary phenomenon, which was diagnosed as an obscure ailment that afflicted an otherwise healthy body and which therefore had to be cut out in order for the patient to get well. In short, the Revolution was viewed as a harmful interlude, a gaping void suddenly opened in the history of France, which had to be closed in order to restore continuity.

This persistent, mythical core of the counterrevolutionary vision gradually eroded, for it was powerless to cope with the more dynamic imperatives of politics and incapable of producing a more realistic analysis of the crisis of the Ancien Régime and its internal contradictions. Nevertheless, over the next century the rational kernel of this repudiation of the principles of 1789 formed the basis of a sustained critique of a world built on the "rights of man." The polemical image of a revolution that had emerged out of the void and was destined to return there was not simply naive. It was in fact an inverted image of the myth that the Revolution offered of itself: did not the patriotic party view the Revolution as the absolute inception of the reign of liberty, based on new rational principles, after centuries of despotism? Was its destiny not to rescue France from its own past?

The men who came afterward and who wished to quell the conflicts stirred up by opposing factions, seeking to reconcile what the Revolution had achieved with tradition, opinion with custom, and liberty with order, were naturally compelled to take account of the objections raised by these adversaries of modernity, not only to refute them but also, in some cases, to incorporate them into their own views. While keeping faith with their basic inspiration, the heirs of the counterrevolution ultimately moved a considerable distance from its origins and exerted a noticeable influence on various currents of thought from political romanticism to moderate liberalism and social Catholicism.

*

Destined to grow more complex with time, the idea of the counter-revolution was from its inception neither simple nor one-dimensional. In fact the word does not denote a homogeneous phenomenon, for it applies to doctrines and tendencies ranging from the most uncompromising apology for absolutism to a more moderate range of Continental opinion drawn together by refusal of the democratic principles of 1789. If the dividing line between Revolution and counterrevolution is clearly perceptible in the extreme elements in both camps, it becomes more subtle when the focus is expanded to include intermediate political tendencies, particularly the liberal, which was ambiguous by its very nature and within which "revolutionary" and "counter-revolutionary" arguments coexisted.

The counterrevolution was not defined by hostility to reform of the monarchy in 1789. In fact nearly all of French society agreed on the need for reform, including the privileged orders. Until the end of 1789 those who would become the leading exponents of counterrevolutionary doctrine—Burke, Mallet du Pan, Maistre, Bonald—approvingly followed developments in Paris, hoping that they would lead to a reform of the monarchy resulting in a limitation of absolutism. Initially, moreover, even those who opposed innovation were more resistant to the process of reform than truly engaged in a counterrevolution. The program of Louis XVI, set forth in his speech of June 23, defined the limits of the monarchy's willingness to tolerate reform: concessions were made to liberal demands (in regard to freedom of the press, individual liberties, and so on), and fiscal but not legal equality was instituted; the hierarchy of aristocratic society was maintained. This excessively timid program, to which the monarchy gave its approval on the eve of the catastrophe, for a long time remained the manifesto of the restorationist party. Louis XVIII summed it up thus from exile: "The Ancien Régime minus the abuses." The definitive crisis developed elsewhere: what caused the shift from mere resistance to outright counterrevolution was the rapid metamorphosis of "political representation," which transformed the Third Estate, a component of the Ancien Régime, into the National Assembly, that is, into a sovereign body that set itself the task of remaking the foundations of French society.

Over the course of 1789 the democratic drift of the Revolution became increasingly clear. Immediately after the taking of the Bastille the emigration of aristocrats began, with the comte d'Artois and the prince de Condé leading the way, but it was not until September that the opposition front broadened considerably when the Assembly lost its moderate wing, defeated in the debate over the veto and the second chamber. This defeat marked the failure of the attempt to guide the Revolution toward an English-style constitutional monarchy, which had served as a model for many eighteenth-century reformers. Within a few months the monarchiens—Mounier, Lally-Tollendal, and their friends—had joined the exodus, following the "ultra" princes into emigration.

Once generals were recruited, the hard core of the counterrevolution settled first in Turin, under the command of the comte d'Artois, later in Koblenz, where in 1791 the comte de Provence replaced his brother as the leader of the legitimist emigration, and finally in Worms, where the prince de Condé organized his army. These actions proved relatively ineffective, however. The king's flight ended in fiasco; the insurrections that the committee of Turin attempted to stir up in Lyons, Valence, and Poitou resulted in nothing more than sporadic disturbances, while efforts to involve the European powers for a long time bore no fruit; and finally, when war did break out, the émigré princes' army reaped no glory from the 1792 campaign.

The sequel was consistent with this debut. In fact the real threat to the Revolution did not come from the plots of exiles scattered all over Europe and obliged to wander from country to country, nor from the spy rings and military adventures such as the landing at Quiberon. Much more serious were insurrections in Vendée and southeastern France (Lyons, Marseilles, and Toulon), because these grew out of the internal dynamic of events and erupted at a time when the religious policies of the Paris government and the extreme radicalism of the Jacobins enabled the counterrevolution to enlist the popular troops that it had previously lacked.

The attempt to bring about a lawful restoration of the monarchy after 9 Thermidor, thwarted by the "two-thirds decree" and the abortive uprising on 13 Vendémiaire, was somewhat less unrealistic given the weaknesses of the Thermidorian regime. Yet despite those weaknesses the counterrevolution never posed a credible threat. Torn internally by polemics between absolutists and constitutionals, weakened by Bonaparte's policy of national reconciliation, it spent itself in ill-advised attempts to force the situation to a head, either under the illusion of a restoration in the English manner with Pichegru or Napoleon himself in the role of Monck or, more simply, in the hope that ultimately the international situation would bring down the Paris government. When the European coalition finally restored the Bourbons to the French throne in 1814, the Restoration was not a military vindication of the principles of the old world, safeguarded in exile, over those of the new world, temporarily defeated: in order to reign, the legitimate sovereign had to compromise with the "illegitimate" interests that the Revolution had created in the interim.

Ineffective as far as short-term politics, the counterrevolution achieved its most durable results in the realm of thought. It elaborated a systematic doctrine whose influence would be felt throughout the nineteenth century, in which it explained its hostility to the modern world to which the Revolution had given birth. This was a radical and precocious hostility that did not wait for events before making its presence known. As early as 1790, apparently the Revolution's happiest year, Edmund Burke delivered a summary condemnation in his *Reflections*. For him the real drama had taken place in the summer of 1789; the rest would be no more than an epilogue. For those who rejected it, the Revolution had been ill from birth. Not even the work of Joseph de Maistre, who wrote some years later, contains any indication of a real analysis of the episodes that drove the Revolution off course: from the death of the king to the Terror and the war, those events were for him nothing but the fatal consequences of the original act of rebellion contained in the Declaration of the Rights of Man. The classic question, posed by the Thermidorians and bequeathed to the liberals, was how the liberty of 1789 could have led to the despotism of 1793; for the counterrevolutionaries the question did not even arise, for they saw nothing but a necessary relation of cause and effect.

Burke wrote that the French Revolution was the most stupefying event in the history of the world: before 1789 no one had ever dared start with a clean slate and remake society from top to bottom on the basis of purely rational principles such as "rights of man" and "popular sovereignty." In the previous century England too had had a revolution, but then the aim had been not to establish a totally new society but to restore a violated legality. That is why it had attained its goal of bestowing on the nation liberties of which it had temporarily been robbed. Unlike their French counterparts, the representatives of the English nation in 1688 had not availed themselves of their abstract power to overturn the laws of the kingdom but had instead acted judiciously and with respect for tradition. They had resisted and deposed the sovereign, but their revolution had been a passive one, a temporarily necessary means of maintaining order, not destroying it. By contrasting a "good" revolution with a "bad" one, Burke was the first to introduce a comparison with the English experience into the debate over the French Revolution. His basic question—why the revolution in England had succeeded in establishing free institutions while the one in France initiated decades of instability—soon became a commonplace of liberal historiography from Mme. de Staël to Guizot, although these writers sought to avoid the polemical conclusions reached by the Whig conservative.

Could France have followed the English example by "restoring" historical rights contained in its "ancient constitution," thereby giving liberty roots in tradition? Burke answered in the affirmative: "You [that is, the French] might . . . have profited of our example and have given to your recovered freedom a correspondent dignity. Your privileges, though discontinued, were not lost to memory. Your constitution, it is true, whilst you were out of possession, suffered waste and dilapidation; but you possessed in some parts the walls and, in all, the foundations of a noble and venerable castle." Burke described the former powers of the aristocracy, the parlements, and the intermediate bodies, which, had they been reestablished, might have counterbalanced and tempered the absolute sovereignty of the monarch. "You had all these advantages in your ancient states, but you chose to act as if you had never been molded into civil society and had everything to begin anew. You began ill, because you began by despising everything that belonged to you" (*Reflections on the Revolution in France*, ed. Thomas H. D. Mahoney, New York, 1955, pp. 39–40).

Burke's position was of course based on a rigorous legal and antispeculative conception: society is a natural order independent of individual wills. Human creations and political institutions gain legitimacy slowly and spontaneously, as the experiences of generations are sifted and empirically selected. No assembly can decree a liberty not already present in the mores of a people. But Burke's judgment of the French Revolution also contains an optimistic interpretation of the Ancien Régime. The "ancient constitution" of the kingdom of France, the tradition of balance of powers, which according to Burke had survived the tabula rasa of absolutism and ought to have guided the course of a "good" revolution in the early months of 1789, was actually a very mysterious thing and certainly a highly controversial one: not even jurists could agree whether France was or was not a "constituted" nation. "France has been governed by customs, often by caprices, but never by laws," Mme. de Staël wrote in 1818, summing up this uncertainty. Tocqueville answered Burke's arguments directly, criticizing him for having given an idealized image of the Ancien Régime: "Burke had little notion of the condition in which the monarchy for which he mourned had left us vis-à-vis our new masters." He also attacked Burke for neglecting the "revolution" accomplished by absolutism, which had eliminated the old liberties associated with aristocratic prerogatives, creating a vacuum around the sovereign. In short, Burke failed to recognize, according to Tocqueville, that the absolute democracy of the Revolution was the daughter of absolute monarchy. Nevertheless, Burke had uncovered a problem that French liberalism found difficult to deal with: lacking a positive tradition of liberty to adopt as a reference, French liberalism was never able to be "traditionalist" like English liberalism. French liberals were compelled, moreover, to recognize that liberty had a birth date, and they therefore needed to explain precisely how it had developed in French history. Benjamin Constant and Mme. de Staël, both admirers of English institutions, both influenced by Burke's critique, proposed an evolutionary concept of social order involving a succession of eras (feudalism, monarchy, representative government) as a way of conceptualizing both what was new about 1789 and what was historically necessary.

The debate over the Ancien Régime was not all there was to counterrevolutionary thought, however. Underlying that thought was a more essential insight: that the Revolution's negation of historical time was inseparable from the advent of democracy. The abstract universalism of its principles severed the ties between the monarchy's subjects and national institutions on the one hand and historical memory on the other. Sieyès wrote that "the nation is a corporation of partners," that is, a collection of equal individuals endowed with natural rights who freely choose to associate with one another in the name of a shared human identity. This egalitarian, voluntarist idea, which formed the basis of the new conception of representation proclaimed by the Revolution, required that social bonds be worked out in abstraction from individuals' concrete conditions and solely on the basis of the humanity in everyone.

The enemies of the Revolution attacked precisely this "geometric spirit," which they saw as an integral part of democracy. Instead they proposed recognizing the real differences that distinguish one person from another. They did not deny that the nation ought to be "represented," but that representation, they argued, ought to be nothing other than the sum of the nation's corporate interests, the direct expression of the social, which was also the natural, constitution. The nation is not a voluntary association of citizens: people are already integrated at birth into a body of rules sanctioned by time, which they learn to respect. Society, like language, preexists the individual, who can do nothing about its arbitrariness. Louis de Bonald wrote: "Man can no more give a constitution to religious or political society than he can give weight to bodies or extent to matter." Thus the counterrevolutionaries radically rejected the natural-law conception of a pact that binds the power of the sovereign to the popular will, so dear to eighteenth-century philosophy. In fact, contrary to the belief of those who took society to be the result of a convention, nothing prior to it even existed. Joseph de Maistre wrote: "Properly speaking, *man* never knew a time prior to society, because before political societies were formed, man was not entirely man." Society is a natural and transcendent order, directly created by God. Even when (as in the case of Burke, who belonged to the Lockean and contractualist Whig tradition) counterrevolutionary thought used the categories of natural law, these were given a conservative twist. "Society is certainly contractual in essence," Burke wrote. But the social contract, whose origins were lost in time immemorial, remained morally beyond the reach of individuals, because it bound each person to all preceding and subsequent generations; the people as presently constituted were only one link in the uninterrupted chain of civilization. Society was quite simply an organic community: "As eternal value, society joins the lower strata to the upper and the visible world to the invisible." It was not in the power of man's will to make sudden innovations, not so much because of a transcendent bond, as the "theocrats" argued, but because of a reason immanent in the course of history itself, an unconscious reason that expressed itself in the form of habits, inertia, and even in the prejudices that shaped the wisdom of a people.

Whether theocratic or traditionalist, counterrevolutionary thought formulated a critique of democracy that served throughout the nineteenth century as a model for authors of both the right and the left who attempted to refute what they took to be illusory "rights of man." In reality, said both Edmund Burke and Joseph de Maistre, man does not exist, but only concrete men. Equality is an abstraction, inequality a reality, and a regime that proclaims all men to be equal is nothing but a lie: the critique of "formal" democracy, from the romantics to Marx, Taine, and so many others, was rooted in this early rejection of the universal values proclaimed by the French Revolution. For counterrevolutionaries, the rights of man and democracy were not merely a lie but a nihilist aberration. By endowing individuals with absolute sovereignty exercised in accordance with the law of numbers—in other words, majority rule—this aberration produced an illusion of omnipotence in modern man, suggesting that the possibilities of action were unlimited and that man could do whatever he wished or whatever served his interest. This opened the way to relativism: so long as the majority wished, nothing was forbidden. To view individuals in purely rational and quantitative terms was, moreover, a destructive factor at work in the moral as well as the aesthetic sphere. All the stratagems and artifices by which the civilized man sought to conceal the defects of his nature were dismissed as vulgar superfluities. So that the world might be laid bare in the name of truth, an end was decreed to taste, elegance, chivalry, and courtly ceremony. (In one of his invectives against rationalist philosophy, Burke wrote that in the new order of things a king was nothing but a man, a queen nothing but a woman, and a woman nothing but an animal, and not of the proudest species.) Beneath the critique of egalitarianism lay a distaste for the materialism of bourgeois society and for the egalitarian power of money.

The two major currents of counterrevolutionary thought—the traditionalist, represented by Burke, and the "theocratic," represented by Bonald and Maistre—though united in their rejection of the Revolution, ultimately took divergent historical forms and influenced the development of political thought in France in different ways. It was primarily in the form of the theocratic doctrine that the counterrevolution influenced first the "ultra" party during the Restoration and later, after 1830, the legitimists. To be sure, it is impossible to distinguish sharply between the two positions, since both were antirationalist and antivoluntarist, and both were based on a pessimistic conception of human nature, upon which foundation a whole edifice of political doctrine was erected. But Burke's antihumanism led to a strictly immanentist notion of history: his sense of human fragility and divine omnipotence was transformed into a positive confidence in the constructive work of time and in the collaboration of generations. This was the foundation on which civilization was constructed—that noble, worthy ornament that concealed the poverty of human nature.

In the theocratic position these "Burkean" themes were integrated into a tragic view of the human condition as irrevocably determined by man's fall and original sin. An apparently senseless spectacle, history—with its bloody wars, gratuitous violence, and unpredictable, inexplicable reversals—was the very symbol of the vanity of any effort on man's part to take control of his destiny. The results were invariably a long way from the intentions, the will was always disappointed, and men never knew what they were doing. Chaotic as this spectacle was, an even grander metaphysical drama was being played out in the wings, according to Maistre: divine providence was simply working out its unfathomable designs, making use of the most vile and painful instruments. In such a conception (whether primarily of a historical order as in Maistre or of a social order as in Bonald), politics lost its autonomy and became a derivative form whose truth lay in the religious sphere. It was therefore only logical that in the search for the causes of the Revolution 1789 would be seen as the last link in a chain of guilt whose immediate predecessor was the Protestant Reformation, which proclaimed the principle of free examination and destroyed the principle of authority. The indictment presented by Bonald and Maistre had its rightful place in Catholic apologetics. Both authors shared a concern to restore an intrinsically dogmatic religion that contained within itself the principle of authority, at once religious and political.

Lutheran Reform and French Revolution: these were the two historical crises to which theocratic thought attempted to give a response that would embrace the whole "metaphysical" range of the modernist challenge, and do so more successfully than the absolutist principle had managed. Absolutism ultimately proved to be an unsuitable solution to the problem raised by Protestantism: its historic role had been none other than to "neutralize" religious conflicts and set itself up as an autonomous secular power. Mutatis mutandis, it was this same "neutral" behavior that the theocrats saw in the doctrinaires' attempt to reconcile the Revolution with tradition. Instead of reconciliation, they proposed a view of the world as the theater of a mortal struggle between good and evil, in which neutrality was out of place. Indeed this insistence on the will, on an ineluctable metaphysical choice, makes clear the distance between theocratic thought and the traditionalists' praise of history's spontaneous creativity. The theocrats wanted a committed government, a government that deliberately went against the tide and offered itself as a conscious instrument of the divine order. To Burke's still ardent concern for liberties they added an obsession with authority. Whereas the Englishman was an adversary of democracy, the theocrats were the last champions of an absolutist conception of sovereignty, henceforth embodied—in a changing Europe—exclusively in the infallible power of the Pope.

Inevitably, however, this will to effect a restoration was destined to appear to contemporaries as "human" and "abstract" as the activism of the constitutionals or the Jacobins. The theocratic counterrevolutionaries were never able to overcome this paradox. How, indeed, could anyone have reconciled their apology for the tranquil and impersonal work of time with their call for all-out combat to alter the course of events? During the Restoration this paradox became more glaring than ever with the "ultra" party. In any case, the impasse of the counterrevolutionary position had long been evident to those who, having endured the trauma of the Revolution, had no wish to repeat the experience in reverse. In 1814 Benjamin Constant wrote: "The authority that would attempt today to reestablish feudalism, serfdom, religious intolerance, the Inquisition, and torture—that authority would claim in vain to wish for nothing more than to reinstate ancient institutions. Those ancient institutions would only be absurd and somber novelties." The truth is that the counterrevolutionaries did not aspire to halt the Revolution; in spite of the myth that they themselves proposed, it was a contrary revolution that they hoped to witness.

Massimo Boffa

IDEAS

FURTHER READING

Baldensperger, Fernard. *Le mouvement des idées dans l'émigration française, 1789–1815,* Paris, 1924.

Beik, Paul Harold. *The French Revolution Seen from the Right: Social Theories in Motion, 1789–1799.* Philadelphia, 1956.

Godechot, Jacques. *La contre-révolution: Doctrine et action.* Paris, 1961.

Madelin, Louis. *La contre-révolution sous la Révolution, 1789–1815.* Paris, 1935.

Omodeo, Adolfo. *La cultura francese nell'età della Restaurazione.* Milan, 1946.

Rémond, René. *Les droites en France.* Paris, 1982.

Rials, Stéphane. *Révolution et contre-révolution au XIXe siècle.* Paris, 1987.

Schmitt, Carl. *Politische Romantik.* Munich and Leipzig, 1919. Second edition, enlarged, 1925.

Vingtrinier, Emmaneul. *La contre-révolution, première période, 1789–1791,* 2 vols. Paris, 1924–1925.

RELATED TOPICS

Ancien Régime	Constant	Monarchiens	Staël
Burke	Emigrés	Revolution	Tocqueville
Chouannerie	Maistre	Sieyès	Vendée

DEMOCRACY

T he French Revolution has been viewed since the nineteenth century as
a major step in the formation of modern democracy, meaning not just
a type of *political* regime, combining political representation with universal
suffrage, but also a type of *social* regime, devoid of hereditary status inequalities and stressing egalitarian values. As it unfolded, the Revolution revealed
for the first time some of the tensions inherent in contemporary democracies:
between representative government and "direct democracy," between equality
of rights and demands for "real" equality, and between individual rights and
the sovereignty of the general will. Any analysis of democracy in the Revolution inevitably touches on crucial political issues, and there is always a danger
of lapsing into polemic or anachronism. Perhaps the simplest way of avoiding
these pitfalls is to ask first what democracy could have meant to the men and
women of 1789 and then how the Revolution affected their idea of democracy.

*
**

To an enlightened Frenchman of the late eighteenth century, the term
"democracy" referred first of all to a specific type of political regime. According to the article "Democracy," written by the chevalier de Jaucourt, in the
Encyclopédie, a democracy was "one of the basic forms of government, in
which the people as a body enjoys sovereignty." For Montesquieu, democracy
was one of the two forms of republic (the other being aristocracy). Most philosophes associated democracy with the small cities of the ancient world—an
age that was gone forever. It seemed impracticable in a large state like France,
in which the complexity of social relations, the vastness of the territory, and
the number of citizens all seemed to rule out any form of collective deliberation by the entire nation in matters of public interest. In some respects, moreover, the French Enlightenment was an "elitist" movement: the goal of the
philosophes was to establish the sovereignty of Reason, and this aim was
coupled with a certain wariness of the people's judgment, so easily clouded
by "prejudice." Yet democracy was also seen as an eminently rational regime,
which, because it preserved natural equality, was not only morally superior
but also practically advantageous; the citizens being the lawmakers, they were
inclined to respect laws that they had themselves made, presumably in conformity with their own interests. Furthermore, the Enlightenment's critique
of inequality and tradition furnished no basis upon which to erect a stable

hierarchy, for it presupposed the universality of human reason, an essentially egalitarian principle.

Among the authors whose works the revolutionaries might have known, Rousseau was of course particularly important. Yet while the drafters of the Declaration of the Rights of Man and the Constitution were close to him on certain key points, they also accepted the principle of representative government, which Rousseau, in the *Social Contract,* called illegitimate.

Rousseau's contribution to political theory was the distinction between *popular sovereignty,* which strictly speaking pertains only to legislative activity, and *democracy,* which is a form of government, that is, a way of organizing executive power. True, the *Social Contract* does express reservations about democratic government: "If there were a nation of gods, it would govern itself democratically." But contrary to a common misunderstanding, Rousseau was criticizing not the people's capacity to make laws but the corruption that ineluctably follows when the people enters the sphere of government, for then its will ceases to be general and concerns itself with "particular objects" (*Social Contract,* book 3, chap. 4; see also book 2, chap. 4). Rousseau's concept of democracy was based chiefly on the doctrine of the general will. It assumed popular sovereignty (the people as a whole alone being capable of expressing the general will) and repudiated representative government (the will cannot be represented), but it imposed strict limits on the sovereign's activities (genuine in its source, the sovereign will is also general in its object). Rousseau was therefore wary of democratic government, of a regime in which government and sovereign are one: "If it were possible for the sovereign, considered as such, to wield executive power, then right and fact would be so confused that it would no longer be possible to say what was law and what was not, and the body politic, thus denatured, would soon fall victim to the violence against which it was instituted" (*Social Contract,* book 3, chap. 16). This was not Rousseau's final word on democracy, however: the Roman people, "almost as often magistrate as citizen, offers the example of a quasi-democratic yet prosperous government" (book 3, chap. 12). For both Rousseau and Machiavelli, moreover, the instability and division inherent in democracy were sometimes signs of political health: "A little agitation imparts energy to the soul, and what makes the race prosper is not so much peace as liberty" (book 3, chap. 10).

These excerpts are enough to remind us of the distance between Rousseau's thinking and that of the Constituent Assembly. The majority of deputies, whether they drew their inspiration from the physiocrats or Adam Smith, sought first of all to guarantee the *security* of persons and property. They accepted representative government because for them liberty meant individual autonomy rather than participation. (Initially, moreover, the Assembly attempted to enhance the importance of the representative by denying that he was bound by the mandate of his electors.) Furthermore, as Carré de Malberg has shown, the deputies' conception of the relations between the sovereign and the government was not the same as Rousseau's. The latter prescribed precise limits for the sovereignty of the law; the sovereign should make only a small number of laws, all concerning general issues. By contrast, the Constitution of 1791 set no limits to the power of the legislature other than those that it set for itself: "Whatever was decided by the legislative body in legislative form was law and deserved the name of law . . . regardless of its nature or content" (Carré de Malberg, *La loi*, p. 24).

The distinction between the "sovereignty of the nation" as envisioned by the Constituent Assembly and Rousseau's concept of "popular sovereignty" should not be exaggerated, however. For Sieyès himself, democracy and representative government were both legitimate, but only the latter was suited to modern society, with its expanded commerce and division of labor. In both regimes citizens were supposed to take part in making the law—directly in the case of democracy, through "mediate cooperation" in the case of representative government, which (it was argued) therefore allowed for "participation-liberty." The same doctrine, which contains key elements of Rousseau's concept of liberty ("obedience to the law that one has given oneself"), is also found in the Declaration of the Rights of Man and in fact accounts for the particular importance that document attaches to the idea of law: "The law is the expression of the general will. All citizens have the right to participate personally, or through their representatives, in its formation."

Paradoxically, Sieyès' doctrine also turns out to be faithful to one of Rousseau's essential ideas even when the two men seem farthest apart: namely, in Sieyès' argument against strict mandates, which Rousseau saw as the only possible remedy for the evils of representation. The constituents' mandates to the deputies of the Estates General had been set aside, not only by radicals in the Third Estate but by the king himself, in order to allow the deputies to represent the nation effectively (Avril, "Origines de la représentation parlementaire," p. 624). Sieyès added a more profound theoretical argument: he bestowed upon the nation's representatives characteristics of the general will that Rousseau had ascribed only to the mass of the people. Like Rousseau's citizen, Sieyès' "representative" was not supposed to consider the interests of any particular group of electors. His only wish was to be the "wish of the nation," and his function was to represent, not the will of one segment of the population, but the general will. (On this question, see R. Carré de Malberg, *Contribution à la théorie générale*, II, pp. 212–256.)

Incomplete as this fidelity to Rousseau may have been, it was nevertheless undeniable, and it explains why the revolutionaries immediately ruled out any notion of government that involved representation and conciliation of competing interests and chose instead to emphasize the abstract notion of equality. Most striking was the decision to abolish privileges, a decision that within a few days destroyed the hierarchical and corporate structure of the Ancien Régime. As a consequence of such measures, however, the Revolution invariably had difficulty when it came to ascribing any legitimacy whatsoever to dissent. Organized minorities quickly came to be seen as "partial associations," factions standing between particular wills and the general will. Revolutionary doctrine therefore seemed to authorize if not require proscription of minorities, and this suppression proved to be one of the more tragic aspects of the Revolution.

In the eyes of contemporaries, moreover, the French Revolution was seen at first as having far more potential than the English or American revolutions for "democracy." It extended the suffrage much further than England had done, and it cast doubt on the legitimacy of all existing European governments by recognizing only those that respected the Rights of Man (which precluded hereditary-status inequalities and insisted upon the sovereignty of the general will). Under these conditions it is not hard to understand why explicitly "democratic" issues soon gained prominence in political debate. The democrats' demands went far beyond mere guarantees of individual liberty or equality before the law.

In constitutional debate in the revolutionary period, this democratic dynamic was overpowered by a dialectic of popular sovereignty and representation, a dialectic that was itself influenced by the "unanimist" logic of the general will. Out of these debates came two distinct political traditions: one running from the Convention to the Third Republic, the other from Sieyès to the liberals of the nineteenth century.

The first tradition looked upon the law as the expression of the general will, although it rejected Rousseau's limits on the sovereignty of the legislature and his strictures against representative government. "Republican" heirs of these views have always rejected any attempt to limit the power of the legislature, whether by constitutional restrictions or referendum. (Their attitude also accounts for the continuing hostility in France today to anything that resembles American-style lobbying.) The sovereignty of the nation can also be interpreted in a liberal sense, however: that is, as hostile to the omnipotence of the "representatives." (This interpretation was no doubt what Sieyès had in mind when he defended, after Thermidor, the proposal to create a "constitutional jury" responsible for passing on the constitutionality of the laws.) Nevertheless, liberal aspects of revolutionary thinking had little real impact until "revolutionary legicentrism" was ultimately abandoned, and that change did not come about until the advent of the Fifth Republic.

The evolution from the Constituent Assembly to the Convention can be interpreted in part as a consequence of elaborating the democratic aspects of revolutionary doctrine. On August 10, 1791, Robespierre, attacking ambiguities in the then prevalent view, had refused to regard the delegation of authority as a sacrosanct principle of the constitution. Somewhat later, under the Convention, the conflict between the Assembly and the king, along with the intervention of the "people" of Paris, led to debate over two proposed constitutions, which, though quite different from one another, both rejected the doctrine of 1791 by questioning the distinction between "active" and "passive" citizens and by expanding the electors' control over their representatives. Condorcet, the principal drafter of the so-called Girondin Constitution, sought above all to strike a compromise between the needs of representative government (which requires that representatives be allowed some freedom of action) and the demands of democracy by establishing a careful distinction between those powers that the nation "retained" and those that it "delegated." The Montagnard Constitution, the conditions of whose adoption are well known, manifested identical concerns, in addition to which it indicated a wish to concentrate the national will in the national government at the expense of the primary assemblies. (Saint-Just even proposed that all deputies be elected by the nation at large, and it was only for technical reasons that his proposal was rejected.) Both sides felt that the survival of democracy depended on the regeneration of the people, and gradually this project took on greater importance than the constitution itself. Nor can it be said that the Girondins were always more moderate than the Montagnards when it came to what Mona Ozouf has called the "formation of the new man."

Beyond questions of political tactics, the two constitutions stemmed from very different philosophies, the nature of which is revealed by other Convention debates such as the one over education. Condorcet's starting point was the classic problem of the Enlightenment; for him, the question was how to establish conditions under which a rational politics could flourish and the body politic naturally be led to make rational decisions. Top priority in his draft constitution was therefore assigned to the organization of public debate. (One side effect was to complicate decision-making procedures to the point where the constitution probably would have been unworkable.) The primary purpose of education was to spread "enlightenment" and thus create citizens capable of thinking for themselves. For the Montagnard Lepeletier de Saint-Fargeau (whose proposal was presented after his death by Robespierre), the primary purpose of state education was to negate the effects of existing inequalities by taking children out of their family environments and instilling "patriotic" and egalitarian sentiments in them through communal living, festivals, and so on. Similarly, the Montagnards proposed a structure of government that emphasized the need to unify the national will above that of organizing collective deliberation.

Beyond the constitutional question, the Convention debates raised the new issue of "virtue," which was destined to take on tremendous importance in the period of Jacobin domination. Of course the whole question of public virtue had long intellectual and political roots: the cult of civic virtue drew upon a theme from Montesquieu, who himself drew inspiration from Machiavelli; through Jefferson the notion also influenced the American Revolution. But Robespierre added a sentimental and moralistic interpretation of civic virtue that increased its scope to unprecedented proportions, until it all but swallowed up the very idea of democracy. For political thinkers in the Machiavellian tradition, republican civic virtue might have radical *political* consequences, but its *anthropological* significance was limited, since it derived from a fairly pessimistic view of human nature. For them the challenge was not to repress the passions and the interests but to create an order in which citizens would recognize immediately that their interests depended on the interests of the city. Therefore, despite the constant danger that the body politic's adherence to principle might flag, political participation was always the ultimate guarantee of survival, and "virtue" was more a political than a moral disposition. By contrast, for the Jacobins, the very legitimacy of the popular will depended on the virtue of those who inspired it. If that will was virtuous, however, then there was no domain to which it could not be applied. Beyond the law and the general will, Robespierre appealed repeatedly to the principles that ought to guide the Republic. Those principles were neither legal nor political but simply expressed the happy confluence of morality and the people in the person of the Incorruptible.

*
**

In the whole history of French democracy no period arouses more impassioned debate than that of Jacobin rule, which was also a time of sansculotte agitation. For pro-Robespierre historians (such as Mathiez and to a lesser extent Lefebvre), the period that began on June 2, 1793, with the expulsion of the Girondins from the Convention was, despite the Terror, a period of decisive progress for democracy. It sealed an alliance between the popular movement and the most radical segment of the bourgeoisie and marked a first step toward social democracy (with the *maximum*, or price ceiling, introduced on certain supplies and experiments undertaken with a state-controlled economy). For Mathiez, Robespierre's ultimate failure ended "the democratic republic for a century" (*La Révolution française*, III, p. 223). By contrast, for the liberals, this was the most tragic period of the Revolution, an era that discredited political liberty for a long time to come and established a prototype for modern despotism. The debate, which has now been raging for a long time, is often linked with another, between two groups of Marxist historians, for whom the question is whether "direct democracy" as practiced by the sans-culottes was, as Daniel Guérin argues, a precursor of proletarian revolution in a process of "permanent revolution," or, as Albert Soboul suggests, more simply a matter of popular support for the Montagnard "bourgeoisie," support that proved politically expedient but had little prospect of inaugurating durable social change.

This is not the place to resolve such intricate questions, so I shall limit myself to a few remarks intended to set those questions in their proper context. First, as François Furet and Denis Richet have pointed out, the political and social program of the Montagnard dictatorship offered little in the way of innovation; poor relief, public education, and universal suffrage were ideas shared by all members of the Convention, including the Brissotins (*La Révolution française*, 1973, pp. 205–206). The alliance between the popular movement and the bourgeoisie was always tenuous, as is shown by the hostility of many sans-culottes to the *maximum*, which froze wages as well as prices. Mathiez, Robespierre's greatest champion, has masterfully shown that the terrorist government and its state-controlled economy were "profoundly at odds with the ideas, tendencies, and aspirations of a society passionately attached to the liberty it had just conquered" (*La vie chère*, II, p. 245). Indeed, Mathiez often portrays the Jacobin dictatorship as a premature attempt at democratization, a "memorable example of the limits of the human will when faced with the resistance of things" (*La Révolution française*, III, p. 223). Mathiez also notes that "the most stringent laws are powerless to change human nature and the social order at one stroke." Thus, Mathiez's admiration for his hero does not prevent him from implicitly acknowledging the validity of one of the liberals' critiques of Jacobin "voluntarism"—namely, that its "abstract" character was ill adapted to society as it actually was and that it was responsible in large part for the recourse to terror and, ultimately, for the Jacobins' failure. Rereading Mathiez's *La vie chère et le mouvement social sous la Terreur,* it is easy to put one's finger on the central enigma of Year II. Clearly there was a close connection between, on the one hand, the disparagement of private interests in the name of revolutionary equality and the general will and, on the other hand, the choice of an antiliberal economic policy (which was also largely improvised and chaotic). At the same time, this policy of "regulation and price controls" was very much in line with the long-standing traditions of the Ancien Régime, even if it assumed "an entirely different character" under the Revolution. In Mathiez's words, "it was no longer an act of charity but was seen as the reprisal of a party, as an act of vengeance and spoliation" (*La Révolution française,* II, p. 245). Thus, Jacobin social policy, which was of course inseparable from the Terror, clearly exhibited what liberals since Tocqueville have regarded as the Revolution's chief originality: its ability to wed revolutionary radicalism to absolutist political tradition.

From a strictly political point of view, the government of Year II poses a similar problem, that of the relation between direct democracy and national representation. Jacobin historians sometimes minimize the importance of this question in order to emphasize the complex relations between the sans-culottes and the committees of Public Safety and General Security. Neverthe-less, as Furet and Richet point out, "the reality of 1793 . . . was parliamentar-ianism" (*La Révolution française,* 1973, p. 208), and despite pressure from the street the Convention remained the center of power. The "despotism of lib-erty" was a complex affair involving not only the committees and the sans-culottes but also the Convention and the Jacobins, and the fundamental con-flict between those who favored representative government and those who advocated direct democracy was never overcome. This conflict, Furet tells us, accounts for Robespierre's special role: "Brought to power by the antiparlia-mentary riots of May 31–June 2, he remained a man of the Convention. Adored by the Paris sections, he ordered them to remain silent. He succeeded because, having established himself at the summit of a pyramid of equiva-lences that he daily promised to maintain, he alone embodied a mythical rec-onciliation between direct democracy and the principle of representation. He stood for the people in the sections, at the Jacobin Club, and in the National Assembly" (Furet, *Marx et la Révolution française,* p. 86).

This is the background against which the direct democracy of the Paris sections must be viewed. Note, as Michelet also observed, that by 1793 the popular revolution was dead, and the activism of the sections and the Jacobins contrasted sharply with the lack of interest in public affairs exhibited by the bulk of the population. (The Convention itself had been elected in balloting for which the turnout was very low.) Hence it is wrong to see the sans-culottes as a simple continuation of democratic opposition to representative govern-ment. Like the Jacobins, the sans-culottes were actually obsessed with una-nimity, virtue, and the conviction of "traitors," and although they were fre-quently in more or less open conflict with the more moderate elements in the Convention, they had no alternative program to propose in regard to either social policy or institutional structure. That is not to say that "revolutionary democracy" was an archaic resurgence or that the factors underlying the movement were the same as those underlying popular unrest in earlier periods. Deeply influenced by the Revolution's insistence upon popular sovereignty and the general will as opposed to special interests, the democratic movement also embodied the concerns of actual men as opposed to "abstract" principles. What is more, the movement initially portrayed itself as a movement to *radicalize* the Revolution's own demands. It is this aspect of its history that accounts for its later prestige. Because the sectional movement looked beyond the Rights of Man to discover the social question, it became possible later on to portray it as the harbinger of *another* revolution.

* * *

The idea that there was a deep connection between the French Revolution and the irresistible rise of "democracy" was surely one of the central themes of French thought in the nineteenth century, a period in which the interpretation of the Revolution was intertwined with contemporary political debates.

The "republican" interpretation, seeking to claim the legacy of the Revolution for itself, insisted that the principles of 1789 remained vital and current. Among historians Michelet was probably the ablest of the republicans. He made the "people" the hero of his *Histoire de la Révolution française,* in which he treated the Revolution as the embodiment of an idea: it was both the negation of the Ancien Régime, accomplished through a struggle against privilege, and the affirmation of human liberty, accomplished through struggle against liberty's opposite, Christianity. As the work of the people, the Revolution established law in opposition to arbitrary tyranny and privilege. Democracy embodied the triumph of law and equality. Bear in mind, however, that while many republicans indiscriminately admired Danton, Robespierre, and Bonaparte, they were far from unanimous in their judgment of certain aspects of the revolutionary process, particularly the Terror. Justified by some as a product of "circumstances" (and generally regarded as a form of government *no longer* necessary), the Jacobin Terror was seen by Edgar Quinet, for example, as a survival of absolutism, and by Michelet as the price to be paid for the people's disenchantment with the Revolution. The orthodox republican view of the history of the Revolution—"the Revolution is one"—did not really crystallize before the advent of the Third Republic.

Though more "advanced" than the liberals, the republicans are nevertheless not to be confused with the "socialists," who, even if they were "democrats," always regarded the social question as more important than political democracy and universal suffrage. (Even Michelet declared his hostility to this "socialism.") In fact, the socialist movement's attitude toward the Revolution was ambiguous from the start. Its principal instigator, Saint-Simon, offered a critique of the Revolution and of Enlightenment philosophy that oddly enough owed a great deal to counterrevolutionary thought. Saint-Simon accused the intellectuals and "lawyers" who dominated the Revolution of suf-

656

fering from abstract thought. His intellectual goal was to reveal the hidden factors that caused the upheavals of the late eighteenth century, namely, the development of industry and the growing division of labor. His practical goals were more social than political and included a call for a new "spiritual power," a departure from the Enlightenment's "critical" attitude toward religion. On the other hand, it was during the Revolution that the "social question" originated. The more radical of the revolutionaries could be seen as precursors of the socialist movement; a continuous tradition linked some of the more "advanced" democrats to nascent socialism. Yet the socialist movement was itself divided, for it reproduced within itself some of the tensions of the Revolution. Louis Blanc defended the legacy of Robespierre, which advocated social democracy based on representative government, terror no longer being needed, while Blanqui looked to the Committee of Public Safety as the model for a revolutionary dictatorship. Proudhon and the anarchists viewed the Jacobin experiment as the height of political mystification and alienation and advocated the multifarious creativity of "association" as a remedy. These divisions persisted up to the time of the Paris Commune. Marx owed much of his prestige to his seeming ability to combine all these heterogeneous elements into a grand synthesis (though to be sure he too hesitated to choose among several interpretations of the Revolution).

For the liberals, the problem was to separate the results of the Revolution from the revolutionary process, at once despotic and anarchical. Initially, therefore, they concentrated on a critique of Rousseau's doctrine, which they took to be the origin of the Revolution's supposed democratic deviation. This analysis remains the best known part of the work of Constant and Guizot, but it is not the most important contribution of liberal thought. Tocqueville (borrowing a distinction already found in the work of Royer-Collard) identified two aspects of democracy. He conceded that political liberty does not automatically bring about equality of condition, but unlike the conservative liberals he argued that a democratic political regime was the best guarantee of liberty. There is more to his political theory than the distinction between the French "revolutionary spirit" and the peaceful "democratic spirit" of England and the United States. Tocqueville always acknowledged the grandeur of 1789, and he saw that the very moderation of American politics might lead to a decline of the civic spirit. Perhaps the best way to conclude this essay is to recall what he wrote during the dark days of the July Monarchy:

> Dare I say it in the midst of the ruins that surround me? What I fear most for the generations to come is not revolution. If citizens continue to shut themselves up in the ever narrower circle of their petty domestic interests and confine their restless activities to that small sphere, one can imagine them at length becoming insensible to those great and powerful public emotions that agitate nations but also develop and rejuvenate them. . . . People think that new societies change their appearance from day to day, but my fear is that they may end up too invariably attached to the same institutions, the same prejudices, and the same mores, with the result that the human race will stagnate and its growth be limited; that its mind will be eternally preoccupied with itself, without producing new ideas;

that man will exhaust his energies in petty actions, solitary and sterile; and that mankind, though ceaselessly in motion, will cease to advance. (*De la démocratie en Amérique*, Gallimard edition, book 2, p. 260)

Philippe Raynaud

FURTHER READING

Avril, Pierre. "Les origines de la représentation parlementaire," *Commentaire*, Summer 1985.

Carré de Malberg, Raymond. *Contribution à la théorie générale de l'état*, 2 vols. Paris, 1920–1922. Reprinted, 2 vols., Paris, 1962.

—— *La loi, expression de la volonté générale*. Paris, 1931. Reprinted Paris, 1984.

Cochin, Augustin. *L'esprit du jacobinisme*. Virtually complete reprint of *Les sociétés de pensée et la démocratie: Etudes d'histoire révolutionnaire*, Paris, 1921. Introduction by Jean Baechler, with supplementary texts. Paris, 1979.

Furet, François. *Penser la Révolution française*. Paris, 1978.

—— *Marx et la Révolution française*, followed by texts of Karl Marx collected, introduced, and edited by Lucien Calvié. Paris, 1986.

—— *La gauche et la Révolution française au milieu du XIXe siècle: Edgar Quinet et la question du jacobinisme (1865–1870)*, texts introduced by Marina Valensise. Paris, 1986. Contains selected texts of Alphonse Peyrat, Jules Ferry, Emile Ollivier, Louis Blanc, Edgar Quinet, Jules Michelet.

Furet, François, and Denis Richet. *La Révolution française*, 2 vols. Paris, 1963–1965. Reprinted in 1 vol., 1973, 1979, 1986.

Guérin, Daniel. *La lutte de classes sous la Première République: Bourgeois et "bras nus" (1793–1797)*, 2 vols. Paris, 1946. Second edition, 1968.

Mathiez, Albert. *La Révolution française*, 3 vols. Paris, 1922–1927. Reprinted 1933–1939.

—— *La vie chère et le mouvement social sous la Terreur*. Paris, 1927. Reprinted in 2 vols., 1973.

Nicolet, Claude. *L'idée républicaine en France*. Paris, 1982.

Soboul, Albert. *Les sans-culottes parisiens en l'an II: Histoire politique et sociale des sections de Paris, 2 juin 1793–9 thermidor an II*. La Roche-sur-Yon, 1958. Reprinted Paris, 1958, 1962.

RELATED TOPICS

Constitution	Liberty	Robespierre	Sovereignty
Equality	Republic	Rousseau	Suffrage
Jacobinism	Rights of Man	Sieyès	Tocqueville

ENLIGHTENMENT

O n July 11, 1791, Voltaire's remains were solemnly transferred to the
Pantheon (formerly the Eglise Sainte-Geneviève). The staging was
grandiose: the sarcophagus was carried by an enormous chariot in the ancient
style, surrounded by young pupils of the academies dressed in Roman costume. Houdon's statue of Voltaire was carried on a litter in a long procession
that included "the citizens of the faubourg Saint-Antoine armed with pikes."
This "Pantheonization," which made a powerful impression, was a high point
in the history of the Revolution's festivals. The ceremony preceded by just
two days the occasion of a double commemoration, of the taking of the Bastille and of the Federation of 1790. Celebrated in a tense climate, three weeks
after the flight to Varennes, it portrayed in images the profound unity between two struggles for liberty, one by the "enlightened century," the other by
the "regenerated Nation." Three years later, on 20 Vendémiaire, Year III (October 11, 1794), the Pantheon received the remains of Rousseau. That ceremony was the culmination of a complex history: the transfer, conceived during the Terror, was not carried out until after 9 Thermidor. Twenty days
earlier Marat had been Pantheonized. (During the same ceremony the ashes
of Mirabeau, the first revolutionary leader to be taken into the Pantheon,
were removed.) Hence the festival in honor of Rousseau became in a sense a
demonstration against Marat: the memory of the man who had called for "a
hundred thousand heads" was contrasted with the image of Jean-Jacques, the
friend of nature, sensitive soul, and wise legislator, who had called for a city
of liberty and justice.

Beyond the fact that the two ceremonies took place in similar circumstances and were both exploited for political ends, they also shared a common
symbolic meaning: through them the Revolution paid homage to its precursors and inspirers. Speeches, ritual, and symbolic language in both ceremonies forcefully emphasized the link between the Revolution and the "enlightened century" embodied by Voltaire and Rousseau: the regenerated Nation
identified with the "great man," whose renown, glory, and merit lay not in
birth, hereditary titles, and military exploits but in services rendered to humanity.

The two ceremonies epitomized and set in images a twinned conception
of the Revolution and the Enlightenment, each reflecting the other. By claiming to have taken place under the auspices of the "enlightened century," the
Revolution created a past for itself and enhanced its legitimacy. It put an end
to long centuries of darkness, tyranny, and prejudice. It laid claim to a tradition—that of the flourishing of letters and the clamor for liberty—which,

though relatively brief, was rich with promise. It thereby gave itself an identity and a continuity. Whatever the vicissitudes of its own history, it could always look to its origins for its ultimate justification. Return to those origins could thus provide a constant source of rejuvenation and greatness.

Along with the imagery of the Revolution there was also an imagery of the Enlightenment. (Or, rather, of the "enlightened century," the "century of reason." The term *Lumières,* the equivalent of *Aufklärung* in German and Enlightenment in English, had only recently come into use. In the rest of this essay I shall use it for the sake of convenience, even at the risk of a certain anachronism.) To lay Rousseau to rest for all eternity alongside Voltaire was to effect a reconciliation, to overlook the differences, disputes, and conflicts that had separated the two men during their lifetime and judge them to be of secondary importance compared with the fundamental unity of the Enlightenment, a common source of ideas, values, and formative models. It was also to propose an ideal image of the Enlightenment as a continuous whole whose ultimate purpose, to lay the groundwork for the Revolution, unified a succession of individuals and generations. In paying homage to the Enlightenment, the Revolution in a sense called Voltaire and Rousseau and all the rest to witness the work it had accomplished, supposedly to find in it their own ideas, their message.

The Pantheonizations of Voltaire and Rousseau were only the high points in the diffusion of this double imagery of Revolution and Enlightenment. As a result of being repeated and reworked in countless speeches, ceremonies, and allegories, that imagery became a commonplace, a figure of rhetoric, capable even of reconciling revolutionaries and counterrevolutionaries. Both Robespierre and Maistre could agree that the Enlightenment had given birth to the Revolution—Robespierre so as to exalt both mother and child, Maistre to denounce both. The revolutionary period bequeathed this imagery to its historians, and it has been adapted and amplified through much subsequent historiography.

As one moves from this overarching imagery to more specific questions, however, the metaphors become increasingly problematic, giving rise to three much-discussed sets of questions: Did the Enlightenment herald the Revolution, and were the "philosophes" its precursors? Did Enlightenment ideas and values stir revolutionary passions in 1789 and thus exacerbate the political crisis? Finally, did divergences among the various philosophes influence political attitudes, especially differences between radicals and moderates, during the Revolution? These questions really need to be rephrased, for the very terms in which they are posed reflect a concern to establish convergence between two finalities, that of the Enlightenment and that of the Revolution. I do not share that concern: my chief interest is in the political culture and outlook of the revolutionary period as they relate to the legacy of the Enlightenment. It is exclusively from this standpoint that I shall discuss the problem of the Revolution's cultural origins as well as that of the function of Enlightenment ideas in triggering the Revolution and its political conflicts. It is nevertheless worth pausing a moment to consider the traditional questions, if only because historians have been interested in them for so long.

Did the philosophes call for revolution? Were they precursors of the Revolution, hence responsible for it? Such questions were already being asked during the revolutionary period itself, and frequently they were answered in the affirmative. As evidence people cited "prophetic" texts such as these celebrated sentences of Rousseau: "We are drawing close to a state of crisis and a century of revolutions. I hold it to be impossible that the great monarchies have long to live. All have shone brilliantly, and any state that shines is in its decline." Louis-Sébastien Mercier, in his book *On Jean-Jacques Rousseau Considered as One of the First Authors of the Revolution* (1791), never tired of demonstrating, over hundreds of pages, that the works of Rousseau heralded the Revolution and formulated its program in advance. Nor did Mercier hesitate to cite his own utopian novel, *The Year 2440* (1770), to argue in all modesty that he had foreseen the unfolding of revolutionary events beginning with the taking of the Bastille. On the counterrevolutionary side, the abbé Barruel, a Jesuit, also expounded the theme of the philosophes' responsibility. In his *Memoirs for Use in the History of Jacobinism* he set forth in three large volumes the idea that a plot by philosophes and Masons lay at the origin of the Revolution. With the aid of citations from Voltaire, Rousseau, Diderot, the *Encyclopedia,* and the like, he demonstrated that a conspiracy aimed at overthrowing the social order had existed since the middle of the eighteenth century; the philosophes were its leaders, and the Masonic lodges (particularly the Illuminati of Bavaria) constituted a network of subversion. Criticism of religion and clergy, family and morality, nobility and throne had long served the plotters as tools with which to undermine society and prepare for the frontal assault that finally came in 1789.

These two attempts to ascertain the paternity of the Revolution, opposed as they are ideologically, indicate that for contemporaries the Revolution was a surprising and at bottom incomprehensible event. To portray the revolutionary phenomenon as the fulfillment of enlightened predictions and ideas was a way of rationalizing it. (The mystical sects that proliferated at this time had no need of such secular prophecies; they simply blamed it all on the Apocalypse.) Abbé Barruel did the same thing. If portrayed as the result of a plot, the Revolution, a work of darkness, became intelligible while remaining an impenetrable mystery. The idea of a philosophical and Masonic plot was destined to enjoy a great future. On the revolutionary side, too, people tirelessly explored the ramifications of the aristocratic and clerical "plot" in order to explain the vicissitudes of the Revolution.

Writers willing to exculpate the philosophes were a far rarer species. J.-J. Mounier, the leader of the monarchiens, engaged in polemic with abbé Barruel from exile in Weimar (*De l'influence attribuée aux philosophes, franc-maçons, et illuminés sur la Révolution en France,* 1801). He showed that the plot idea was one that appealed to "lazy and superficial" minds; that the philosophes had never called for rebellion; and that their objective was by no means to overturn the social order but, on the contrary, to protect it from disaster through modernization and reform.

Mounier was surely right. The "prophecies" of the philosophes were generally mere figures of rhetoric, so many attempts to head off trouble. Enlightenment political thinkers did of course consider utopian alternatives to the existing order. But insofar as it is possible to find a common denominator to their many proposals, it was by no means a call to revolution but an exhortation to reform. Before the crisis of 1789, the ideal that loomed on the philosophes' horizon was that of a reformist state and a reformist policy, the closest approximation to which was the government of Turgot, say, or perhaps that of Joseph II.

Thus the philosophes were not "precursors" of the Revolution. In general, the concept of precursor has little explanatory value. Isn't a precursor someone who cannot state what he is supposed to think? Nevertheless, it would be difficult to overstate the importance of reformist ideas in shaping new political mentalities. A common fund of ideas and hopes, values and expectations, did more to shape a new outlook than all the specific projects for reform that accumulated over the course of the century.

Reforms were in fact thought of as practical answers to the questions that troubled the Enlightenment: how to redefine and rationalize the social order, how to change man in heart and mind. An enlightened government would bear responsibility for carrying out needed reforms. Hence to link such hopes to projects of reform was implicitly to recognize politics as the crucial agency of all social change. The very diversity and multiplicity of reform projects reflected two intertwined beliefs: that institutions and men are endlessly malleable, and that change can come about only through politics, whose transformative potential is equally unlimited. In propounding a political theory and investing their hopes in it, the philosophes created an image of power as an agency capable of applying firm, rational solutions to all social and even moral problems, and this became the source of their great interest in politics and especially the state—not just any state, but one that would become the primary means of spreading enlightenment. Such a government would make the ideas of the philosophes its own and implement them in such a way as to reform society. Generally speaking, the form that such a government was thought to take was nothing more radical than enlightened absolutism. Moderation, not to say political timidity, was perfectly compatible with utopian dreams of a different social state, one in which a redefinition of the social order would yield a happy and prosperous society. The reformist impulse combined politics and morality. The very legitimacy of government was supposed to depend on the nature of the cause it served. A reformist government would in a sense embody society's sovereign power over itself. It would challenge hierarchies whose only legitimacy lay in tradition and authorities whose only basis was prejudice. A political power invested with all these hopes, erected into a decisive agency of rationalizing innovation, and subjecting the social sphere to the critique of reason would inevitably aid in the emancipation of the individual and recognize the inalienable rights of man as the condition of its own legitimacy.

In the crisis of 1789 the ideas and images elaborated by the philosophes played a complex, varied role. The artisans of 1789 were not "revolutionaries" as we understand that word. They neither wished for nor imagined the Revolution but slipped into it unawares. To understand how this came about, it is extremely important to take account of the ideas and values bequeathed by the Enlightenment, in terms of both what they revealed and what they concealed. In 1789 the crisis of the regime had two distinct aspects: financial (the deficit, the imminent danger of state bankruptcy) and institutional (the need to redefine the responsibilities, powers, and mode of operation of the Estates General). The "patriotic" party and its "publicists," who influenced public opinion, approached these problems in terms elaborated by Montesquieu, Rousseau, and Mably and reworked by the drafters of the American state constitutions. In reading the countless brochures published when the Estates General were convoked and even more in studying the minutes of the National Assembly, especially in its early debates, one is struck by the remarkable knowledge of Enlightenment political literature on the part of the new political elites. Their spokesmen and ideologues saw the crisis and defined its issues, as well as their own and their enemies' roles, in terms of values and concepts elaborated by Enlightenment thinkers. It was in the language of the Enlightenment, and with the aid of Enlightenment images and models, that they elaborated a global interpretation of the crisis, an interpretation that opposed the rule of law to arbitrary rule, liberty to despotism, justice to privilege. The universal values involved in this interpretation compromised any attempt to take a pragmatic approach to the concrete problems that lay at the center of the conflict; they forced people to radicalize their positions and reduce all controversial issues to one, namely, the transformation of a political power that was seen as the decisive agency for remaking the social order. With the issues defined in such terms, it was easy to think of the violation of positive law as a return to prior moral values that alone had the power to bestow legitimacy.

The publicists of the patriotic party availed themselves quite freely, moreover, of the ideological and intellectual legacy of the philosophes. They drew eclectically from a wide range of authors, picking and choosing their arguments as required by the polemical needs of the moment. Growing numbers of brochures gave wide currency to a wealth of Enlightenment ideas. In addition, the first meetings of the Estates General brought "enlightened patriots" into direct contact with one another, in many cases for the first time. The result was an intense interchange of ideas and broad agreement on what actions needed to be taken. The very variety and wealth of ideas convinced these ideologues (along with a broad spectrum of newly emergent public opinion) that they were in possession of intellectual tools appropriate to the situation, sufficient to understand the crisis and cope with its consequences. In large part this was an ideological illusion, for the problems that the men of 1789 faced were not the same as those faced by the philosophes they invoked. Whereas the latter had theorized about politics and reduced it to rationality, the former confronted an unprecedented political and social phenomenon governed by a dynamic of its own and giving rise to its own conflicts and passions. Before their eyes, and with their cooperation, it became increasingly complex, difficult to master, and even frankly uncontrollable. It was precisely this singularity of the revolutionary phenomenon, its true essence, that the concepts inherited from the philosophes tended to obscure rather than illuminate.

In order to make sense of the accelerating sequence of events, people increasingly resorted to the comprehensive term "Revolution." By imperceptible degrees the Revolution began to take on a finality of its own, summed up by the phrase "national regeneration," a synonym for return to a more primitive time and for the vague promise of liberty, for a break with the disastrous past and embrace of the radiant future. For the ideologues of 1789 the constitutional power would make realities of such concepts as social contract, national sovereignty, the general will, and so on. It would immediately redefine the social order and unite reason, liberty, and justice in politics. Confidence in politics and its all-but-limitless capacities for action, along with the hopes engendered by the first revolutionary experiences, gave rise to any number of certitudes: that the Revolution possessed all the necessary intellectual and political resources to cope with and resolve any problems that might arise; that once its goal had been rationally defined, it would stick to that goal steadfastly and generate sufficient energy to ensure its accomplishment; and hence that to accelerate its pace and smash any resistance was to move closer to the Revolution's ultimate objectives. The escalation, during the summer and fall of 1789, of verbal violence—demands and threats, recriminations and promises in brochures, the press, assemblies, and so on—was not due simply to the unleashing of passions and the struggle for power. Paradoxically it was also animated by the widely shared certainty that the Revolution, by virtue of its basic principles and consequently its implicit ends, was fundamentally rational, hence controllable. In other words, radicalizing the crisis and hastening it toward its final resolution was simply the most effective way of coming quickly to a happy outcome. How illusory these certainties proved! As is well known, once the Revolution had begun, the very idea of guiding it into port, of fulfilling the hopes that it had aroused, became one source of its energy and made it more and more difficult to control.

To be sure, this radicalization encouraged by a kind of "fanaticism of reason" was opposed by more moderate tendencies which also drew on aspects of the Enlightenment: reformism, empiricism, realism. In August and September of 1789, for example, during the first constitutional debate, whose importance for subsequent events cannot be overstated, the monarchiens, proponents of a representative system based on coexistence of a bicameral Assembly with a strong royal power, simultaneously invoked the example of a liberal regime to be found in England, the continuity of French political traditions, and the authority of Locke, Voltaire, and Montesquieu, among others. These arguments were quickly dismissed in a debate that saw the patriotic party splinter and the Assembly itself divide into a right and a left. The necessary change could not be a restoration of the traditions of the past; it would have to be portrayed specifically as a revolution, a radical break. Traditions were no fetter on the liberty of the nation and no limitation on its sovereignty. Admittedly France was an old nation, but the *regenerated* French were a people that had recaptured its youth. Hence they had no need to imitate any model. They were inaugurating a new era and offering the world an example of universal significance, as the Declaration of the Rights of Man both demonstrates and proclaims.

Did differences among the philosophes on political and moral questions influence the opposition between radicals and moderates in the revolutionary period? The debate summarized above takes us straight to the heart of the question and suggests an affirmative answer. Historians have often—even to the point of cliché—sketched a contrast between two tendencies in revolutionary thought: one liberal, empiricist, and reformist, inspired by Voltaire and Montesquieu; the other dogmatic, radical, and combining popular sovereignty with revolutionary dictatorship, inspired by Rousseau. Some writers allude to two distinct phases of the Revolution: one influenced by *L'esprit des lois,* which ended in 1791, and the other marked by dictatorship and consequently, it is argued, by the influence of Rousseau.

It is obvious that the Age of Enlightenment was a time in which political philosophy flourished. Modern liberalism would not exist without the work of Montesquieu and Adam Smith, nor would modern democratic thought exist without the *Social Contract.* Nevertheless, the political theory and practice of the Revolution were in no sense the application of this or that doctrine. As we have seen, the men of 1789 made very free use of the legacy of the Enlightenment. They had to deal with novel problems, and the more aware they were of the novelty of the problems they faced, the more original was their thinking. The Declaration of the Rights of Man is explained not so much by what it borrowed—from Locke as well as Montesquieu, from Rousseau as well as the American state constitutions—as by the need to which it responded: to redefine the sphere of politics in terms of liberty and law. Consider another example, also much treated by historians: it is true that Robespierre particularly admired Rousseau and that at the height of the Terror he invoked Rousseau's work and contrasted it to that of Voltaire and the Encyclopedists. Yet one must not jump from this fact to the conclusion that the *Social Contract* contains the seeds of Jacobinism and the Terror. Furthermore, Robespierre was not the only revolutionary to refer to Rousseau. The diffuse influence of the *Social Contract* is evident in all revolutionary political thought: in Sieyès and (as Burke noted) in the work of the Constituent Assembly; in Brissot, who swore by Rousseau and no other; and in Mme. de Staël. Finally, to mention just one more example, revolutionary liberal thought was certainly molded by the works of Montesquieu and Condorcet. Its real originality, however, stems from its reflection on the Terror, that is, from its efforts to explain how it was that the Revolution, starting from the principles of 1789, could have arrived at the practices of Year II, and even more from its attempt to imagine a democratic polity equipped with institutions that would prevent any possibility of a return of the Terror. It was on the basis of experience of the Terror that Sieyès and Constant developed their critiques of unlimited popular sovereignty, hence of the *Social Contract.* In other words, the Revolution projected on the Enlightenment the shadow of its dissension and conflict. In 1799 it was difficult if not impossible to read Montesquieu and Rousseau in the same way as ten years earlier.

The Enlightenment's legacy to the Revolution was therefore both something less and something more than mere political doctrines or systems await-ing transformation from theory into fact. It was above all a certain style of thought, along with a specific set of images and expectations in which politics and morality were combined. Revolutionary educational doctrine is a good example of how that heritage survived the vagaries of the Revolution as a common fund of ideas. From the first, a pedagogical purpose was ascribed to the Revolution: to regenerate the nation and form a new people. Government after government discovered that this mission exerted an irresistible fascina-tion. The Enlightenment legacy is easily recognizable, not so much in borrow-ings from particular works as in the pedagogical enthusiasm that pervaded all Enlightenment thought and in the dream of producing new men, free of prejudice and imbued with the progress of the age. The educators of both the Enlightenment and the Revolution shared a single faith in the almost unlimited capacities of education and in the transforming energy of the Rev-olution. Pedagogy and politics were thus two ways in which the sovereign nation acted upon itself. The nation-state defined itself as an educator-state. Enlightenment had begun the Revolution; it was up to Enlightenment to end it: this idea recurred often, as a sort of maxim, in revolutionary discourse. The educational debate was all but permanent, and there were countless pro-posals for public education in service of the sovereign nation. The Revolu-tion's educational ambitions were not limited to the creation of republican educational institutions per se, designed to train the nation's new elites: the Ecole Polytechnique, Ecole Normale, and so on. The aim of making educa-tion a part of daily life helped shape the revolutionary calendar and the met-ric system of weights and measures, both institutions intended to make men think rationally and to promote the universalism of the Enlightenment.

Constant repetition of the claim that the Revolution and the Enlight-enment were necessary reflections of each other created a dual mythology: on the one hand a mythology of the Enlightenment, according to which the "enlightened century" was the parent of the Revolution, even if the spokes-men for the Enlightenment neither predicted nor desired it; on the other hand a mythology of the Revolution, according to which the Revolution, as messenger of the Enlightenment, marked the beginning of a new era in his-tory, abolished the past, and translated the most advanced ideas of the age into facts. In Lenoir's Museum of French Monuments the age that preceded and therefore presaged the Revolution was symbolized by rooms whose shad-ows were dispelled by a brilliant light.

That the Revolution was the child of its century is a truism. Contrary to the images celebrated by revolutionary mythology, however, the Enlight-enment cannot be reduced to a few great, symbolic figures, nor can eigh-teenth-century culture be limited to the Enlightenment. The Revolution surely drew upon the legacy of Voltaire and Rousseau. But it was also the heir of what is sometimes called the "vulgar Enlightenment," the mass of scandal sheets and pamphlets that dealt with the mistresses of Louis XV or the de-bauchery of the clergy, a literature whose bad taste was matched only by its verbal violence and which, in the last quarter of the century, flooded the clan-destine book market and undermined the foundations of the regime. The pamphleteers—often failed writers, sometimes failed human beings—formed a frustrated, marginalized intelligentsia that provided the Revolution with a ready reserve of potential leaders. To this teeming Grub Street, to men like Fabre d'Eglantine and Collot d'Herbois, Brissot and Hébert, the Revolution offered a chance to participate in politics and escape their marginal status. The figure of Condorcet of course symbolizes the continuity between the apex of the Enlightenment and the revolutionary period. By contrast, the figure of Marat reminds us that revolutionary culture also inherited the effects of the intellectual disintegration of the Enlightenment, of its murkier ideas, its combination of the occult and the parascientific, which in the form of movements such as Mesmerism marked the decades prior to the Revolution. A child of its century, the Revolution inherited more than just the culture of the elite. The political culture of the revolutionary period also reproduced, in its own manner, the deep structures of Ancien Régime mentalities. One of the Revolution's remarkable peculiarities, in fact, is that it incorporated a largely traditional cultural environment into a modern political framework. The Republic's good news was often transmitted through the networks of the traditional oral culture. Every abrupt change in the course of revolutionary politics awakened ancient panics and collective fears, rumors, and fantasies. Successive revolutionary governments found it all the more difficult to comprehend the resistance with which their modernizing schemes were greeted because they were convinced that they had laid their plans in the people's name and for its greater good. By way of explanation, their only recourse was to reactivate the usual opposition between a civilizing government and a people to be civilized.

Every myth contains a truth of its own. Was the Revolution, then, the heir of the Enlightenment? Of course; but it made use of its heritage as it saw fit.

Enlightenment ideas and values were a permanent point of reference in the political and ideological conflicts of the revolutionary period. But as they passed along the sinuous byways of the Revolution, those ideas and values were subject to a transmutation: cosmopolitanism became conquering nationalism, pacifism became militarism, tolerance became fanaticism, liberty became Terror. The Revolution subjected the ideas it had inherited to its own constraints, amalgamated them with its own myths, and recast them in its own molds.

Bronislaw Baczko

Fᴜʀᴛʜᴇʀ ʀᴇᴀᴅɪɴɢ

Baczko, Bronislaw, ed. *Une éducation pour la démocratie: Textes et projets de l'époque révolutionnaire.* Paris, 1982.

Cassirer, Ernst. *Die philosophie der Aufklärung.*

Darnton, Robert. *Mesmerism and the End of the Enlightenment in France.* New York, 1970.

Dérathé, Robert. *Jean-Jacques Rousseau et la science politique de son temps.* Paris, 1950.

Egret, Jean. *La pré-Révolution française.* Paris, 1956.

Mornet, Daniel. *Les origines intellectuelles de la Révolution française.* Paris, 1933.

Starobinski, Jean. *1789: Les emblèmes de la raison.* Paris, 1973.

Rᴇʟᴀᴛᴇᴅ ᴛᴏᴘɪᴄꜱ

Burke	Maistre	Regeneration	Rousseau
Condorcet	Marat	Revolution	Sieyès
Constant	Mirabeau	Rights of Man	Voltaire
Estates General	Montesquieu	Robespierre	

EQUALITY

"Although property, liberty, and equality are inseparable, they may nevertheless be held in very unequal esteem by nations, they may be very unequally distributed, and their existence may possess more or less of perfection. . . . Between equality of rights and equality in fact, and between the real and supposed superiorities to which equality of rights authorizes one to aspire, there are great gaps." Who spoke these words? Not Tocqueville or Quinet or Taine but a participant in the Revolution, Roederer, who in 1831 published a book entitled *Esprit de la Révolution* that he claimed to have written in 1815 and that was for the most part conceived after Thermidor. Roederer sensed that each of the values celebrated by the Revolution could come into conflict with the others; that the French were not equally attached to them all; and that for one, equality, they showed a preference so marked that they were prepared to pay for it with their liberty (which explains how Napoleon, the Revolution's heir, by courting equality was able to weaken liberty without opposition). Here, then, in an early formulation, is one of Tocqueville's great themes.

Like Tocqueville, Roederer had a complex idea of equality that was an unstable compound of objective evaluation and subjective appreciation. Ultimately, he believed, representations of equality mattered more during the Revolution than actual equality. "The servitudes imposed on rural property and the impediments to industry were shaken off by the people not so much because they were onerous as because they were insulting." The motor of the Revolution was thus not the quest for profit but revenge for humiliation; the Revolution was a remedy for the "sufferings of amour-propre." Again as in Tocqueville, while the Revolution may have craved equality, the society to which it gave birth was not one from which distinctions had vanished. On the contrary, the existence of a single norm exacerbated the love of distinctions, gave rise to petty and merely symbolic differences, and, though intolerable, caused them to proliferate.

Like Tocqueville and Taine after him, Roederer linked this passion for equality to the national history and psychology. He traced the roots of the Enlightenment back to the eleventh century, to the "first sounding of the tocsin by free men in cities and towns," that is, to the founding of the communes. One fact sums up the progress of Enlightenment: "the material, intellectual, and moral elevation of the common man, while *seigneurie* declined." And one cause was enough to explain it: the monarchy's assent to this first "revolution," which was therefore complete long before the other began. In 1815 the idea of a leveling, subversive monarchy, which was also examined by Montlosier

and which Augustin Thierry would soon make commonplace, was still quite
fresh. It added to revolutionary equality the ballast of a long prehistory, which
exploited and reinforced a trait in the national character, a collective predilection for emulation that was by no means inconsistent with equality but in
fact closely allied with it. It was in the soil of equal rights, which "young
Frenchmen call democracy," that infinite differentiation among individuals
flourished. By offering prodigious scope to the competition of talents, an increasingly homogeneous society thus gives rise to an increasingly heterogeneous human variety.

This remarkable text touches on most of the problems that nineteenth-
century authors debated in attempting to define the place of equality in the
French Revolution. First it dismisses the notion that the Revolution was an
inaugural event in the history of equality: equality triumphed in opinion well
before this event caused it to enter into mores. Roederer also firmly rejects
the idea that there was a moment in the Revolution when equality took on
special importance. From the beginning the Revolution belonged entirely to
equality: this was a distinctive feature, which set France apart from England.
England fostered love of "liberty through privilege." France, a "nation whose
elite was deeply wounded," made equality its exclusive passion, its justification
for infringements on liberty. Finally, Roederer touched on the endless question of the relation between formal equality and real equality. According to
him, the men of the Revolution had little use for de facto equality, which
seemed to hold out the promise that all men would ultimately be identical
and which made no special place for "superior minds." But they adored
equality of rights, which involved ranking "inherited distinctions below acquired distinctions." Roederer rejected the idea that the demand for equal
rights might lead to de facto equality. By demonstrating the open-endedness
of equal rights, he did, however, suggest that equality was by nature elusive
and eminently desirable, thus implying that a revolution that had chosen
equality for its banner could have no end.

How are we to choose between Louis Dumont's view that the eighteenth
century discovered equality only quite late and Corrado Rosso's claim that the
entire century was animated by egalitarian passion? In fact the answer depends on how one proposes to define the idea of equality.

The definition given most often, as well as the most radical, is that of
the Christian preachers, especially Bossuet, echoes of which could be heard
in eighteenth-century Jansenism. Jansenists saw the equality of the Trinity as
the true foundation of total Christian equality. This was both positive and
negative: positive because no creature needs an intermediary to enter into
relation with God; negative because, since all human beings are made out of
the same mud, their equality is one of abjection. Death, which reveals this
identical nothingness of all mankind, is therefore the great teacher of equality. "Perched on the edge of the grave," Bossuet, in the words of abbé Maury,
"humbled the inherent pride of princes and kings, which after distinguishing

them for a brief moment on earth confounds them forever in the common dust." After the Revolution Saint-Simon was thus able to argue that Bossuet had been its true teacher.

To cast the point of death as the revealer of extreme equality was obviously to show much indifference to inequalities. Part of God's plan, inequalities once established could not be eliminated without injustice, but they endured no longer than the brief compass of a human life. Compared with eternity this was nothing at all; hence inequality lost all its meaning: "Death confounds the prince and his subject: between them there is nothing other than a fragile distinction, too superficial and ephemeral to count." As for personal merits, also highly unequal, Jansenist-influenced thought was inclined to believe that salvation could not be proportional to them. Saint-Cyran had persuaded the Jansenists that a series of good or even excellent actions was as nothing unless aided by the hand of God. Without transmutation of the divine will into human will by means of grace, merit had no way to express itself. Hence nothing could be farther from Christian equality than an equality of reward according to merit. The prodigal son and the laborer of the eleventh hour were rewarded out of all proportion and beyond all logic: this irrational foundation made Christian equality the antithesis of an apportioned equality. Clearly, whatever role Christian equality may have played in countering "established grandeur," this was not the equality that the eighteenth century cherished: its hedonistic tendency carried it a long way from an anthropology of destitution.

The equality for which the century showed a predilection was that based on the presence of reason in every human individual. If man examines his conscience, he discovers the universal requirement of rationality and moral judgment. Reason fills man with a desire to combat the absurd and irrational, to work on projects compatible with reason and law and useful to the human race. The most desirable equality is therefore an equality proportioned to the services rendered to the community by the individual. The century provided a thousand illustrations of the special favor it bestowed on meritocratic equality. To take one example, La Mothe Le Vayer, replying to Arnauld and abbé Esprit—who denied that pagans possessed any virtue (or, in other words, who claimed that merit cannot exist in the absence of God)—argued that pagans could indeed epitomize the grandeur of mankind and in so doing turned an unreadable book into a best-seller. The eighteenth century saw in it the image of "true merit," reduced entirely to simple and strictly human virtues: temperance, moderation, sympathy, pity, and above all benevolence and utility. Or think of the triumph of the eulogy as literary genre over the previous century's cherished funeral oration. A funeral oration could make bold to depreciate the merits of the deceased individual, since a single good thought at the moment of death was enough for the hand of God to reverse the course of an otherwise depraved life. By contrast, the eulogy, a cumulative genre, required a patient accumulation of merits: not an instantaneous good death but an extended good life.

This meritocratic equality tolerated and even engendered inequalities and distinctions in status and reward. Yet these seemed acceptable to the majority of philosophers, who, like Voltaire, were narcissistically prepared to accept that the best places should go to the enlightened. Such inequality, as Montesquieu very aptly said, arose out of equality itself. In a democracy, he explained, if men cannot all render equal services to their country, at least all must render some service. And if—in strict proportional justice—these unequal services give rise to "distinctions," at least it is the exercise of equality that is being rewarded: "Thus rewards are born of equality even when they appear to be claimed by useful services or superior talents." In the same way, praise of a great man raises him above other individuals in admiration and respect, but these deferential sentiments actually arise out of equality, which inspires in every man the desire to emulate the great and the conviction that it is possible.

The essential point, however, is that meritocratic equality carries with it a devastating critique of privilege. It discredits what Mirabeau called the "monster" of hereditary transmission and the rigidity that it entails. Equality of merits and talents eliminates the prerogatives of birth. There is no better way to measure the critical potency of the meritocratic idea than to recall the texts that attempted to argue against it, in defense of privilege. Consider just one of these: the remonstrances of the Parlement of Paris against Turgot's edict abolishing compulsory road work, which as late as 1776, and with startling ingenuousness and assurance, illustrates the hierarchical social ranking of individuals: "It is a necessity that some command and others obey. Sovereign lords issue orders to everyone in their state; they address their orders to the great, the great to the middling, the middling to the small, and the small to the people."

Can eighteenth-century equality be defined by reference to merit alone? There was more than a mere suspicion that meritocracy might become in turn a kind of "aristocracy." Some vigorously denounced the hidden injustice of such egalitarianism, which reduced everything to the "qualities" of individuals and did not concern itself with their needs. Yet the needs of men without particular merits, without dazzling works or useful industry, were just as imperious as those of others and formed the basis of a homogeneous humanity. Good legislation could therefore be recognized not by its ability to assure equitable rewards but by its capacity to yield an "equal distribution of happiness among citizens."

With the word "happiness," so fresh in conjunction with the word "equality," one senses that the new egalitarianism was to be directed not against inequality of birth but against inequality of wealth. To the latter form of inequality there were two powerful objections. First, as d'Argenson and Mably agreed, inequality of wealth caused degeneration in individuals and before long decadence in states. Second, and more positively, only the return of relative equality could reduce the scandalous disparity between citizens and thus restore the social bond. The major virtue of equality—a classical theme—was that it healed the resentment engendered by poverty and encouraged civic participation. It therefore became the major task of good government to reestablish an equilibrium of ownership through laws on inheritance, sumptuary laws, and whatever other means might prove useful.

Equality

Whether rewarded for merit or apportioned to need—hence quite different depending on who defined it—equality nevertheless became the test of truth for eighteenth-century ideas, even those that seemed most hostile to it. Boulainvilliers, who seemed to cling so desperately to noble distinctions, was in fact thoroughly imbued with the idea of natural equality. If history had created inequalities of status on a basis of original equality, within each status group the most rigorous equality must henceforth prevail. The physiocrats, whose ideas seemed so aggressively inegalitarian because of their emphasis on property, based their system on a strict equivalence between individuals, any one of whom could be substituted for any other in their self-centered ambition to seek pleasure and avoid pain. Despite their horror of democracy, the physiocrats were the first to conceive of that homogeneous and flat society from which Tocqueville would later decipher democracy's essence. Despite the diversity of eighteenth-century theories, taken together they definitively put an end to the organicist and hierarchical conception of the world, in which respect they were all egalitarian ways of thinking.

Beyond this radicalism, however, the striking thing about the eighteenth century's attempts to resolve the problem of inequality is their moderation. To see this, consider the man who passed for the impassioned champion of egalitarianism: Mably, who saw inequality of wealth as the absolute evil. Each time he had to issue a prescription, however, Mably showed himself in favor of folk medicine. Do not suppose, he told the prince of Parma, that I am urging you to "lay a sacrilegious hand on the property of your subjects," for it was no longer possible to aspire to "Spartan equality." What hope was left, then, since "we no longer know how to be brothers?" Surely equality of rights ("Let the quality of citizen be respected by the lowliest official") and a reduction in inequality of wealth ("To banish mendicancy and excessive opulence from a state") was Mably's invariable prescription. Rousseau said the same thing: "My purpose is not to destroy private property but to confine it within narrow limits."

Such moderation is surprising coming from a man honored as the inventor of a new kind of equality, and about whom Louis Blanc said that with him "a new order of citizens presented itself, demanding its place in the world." Yet one can easily turn Rousseau into a moderate thinker by citing texts in which he celebrates proportional equality and the sacred right of property. To do so, however, would be to neglect Rousseau's capacity for subverting his own ideas. Nothing could be further from his deepest wishes than an equity according to which rewards would be distributed in proportion to merits: for merit, along with rank, power, and wealth (the latter summing up the other three), was one of the four inequalities liberally sown about society. Rousseau was simply indifferent toward, if not contemptuous of, the differences in performance that divide men. He hoped that his Emile would be made into not a magistrate, soldier, or priest, but a man, that he would be raised to encourage his resemblance to others, not to accentuate his differences. But to base equality on merit would only establish those differences. Nor should equality be based on needs, in spite of appearances. Although man's basic needs reflect the similarities of the human condition, they still do not produce unity. In view of the conflicts to which satisfaction of those needs has given rise, it is obvious that needs can divide men when they ought to be united.

Furthermore, and this is the essential point, the idea of need in Rousseau's thought is a long way from possessing a naïve immediacy: since each person in society sees himself in the mirror of his fellows, his needs include prestige, reputation, and "public esteem." This gives rise to the folly of comparison, the root of human misfortune. What Rousseau understood better than anyone else was the difficulty of finding objective criteria to define need and the impossibility of separating need from the shifting and ambiguous world of subjective representation. Envious comparison, constantly revived and never satisfied, prevents man from regarding any reward as equitable and makes the egalitarian demand limitless. As for the laws by which the good legislator corrects inequality of ownership (to which commentators on Rousseau often turn for proof of his timidity), their effect is also ambiguous: to reduce inequality is also to recognize and institutionalize it, when ideally one should try to end it. An abstract, elusive equality, exempt from all proportionality, thus became Rousseau's ideal of collective as well as individual life, while everywhere a surreptitious inequality was constantly being revived. In this respect Rousseau was profoundly in harmony with the French Revolution. The various phases of the Revolution seem to illustrate the various philosophies of the eighteenth century: at first concern with equality of rights, which opened careers to talent; later a greater concern with equality of property; and finally reconciliation with property and inequality. Yet the Revolution exhibited throughout what Rousseau had earlier perceived: the impossibility of setting limits to the passion for equality, the torment of having to compromise between limited equality and the limitless desire for equality.

Tocqueville distinguishes three stages along the way to equality of conditions: equalization of legal status, which makes all individuals equally fit to enter into contracts, to buy and sell, to marry; then equalization of political rights; and finally, equalization of the conditions of material existence. The Constituent Assembly fully accomplished the first, imperfectly accomplished the second, and did nothing about the third. Posterity's judgment of its work would therefore depend on how relations among the three forms of equality were conceived. It might see the first two as a move toward or promise of the third: one would then move from one to the other by a simple extension or intensification of one's demands. Or it might see the first two forms of equality as a self-serving ruse, either conscious or unconscious: in other words, formal equality was the means by which the Constituent Assembly preserved the status quo, a way of camouflaging actual inequality. In that case there would clearly be no way of going from the first two forms of equality, which simply reflected the selfish individualism of bourgeois society, to the third. On the contrary, social inequality would merely be the other side of political equality.

"A large clearing in the immense forest of abuses" was the way Grégoire described the work of the Constituent Assembly. On the night of August 4, when the president of the Assembly had to summarize the main points of the debate, he reeled off a litany of "suppressions," "abandonments," "destructions," and "abolitions." Also struck down were all immunities, fiscal and legal exemptions, and exonerations, these being "the object of a violent and ineradicable hatred" because the hereditary nature of these privileges seemed the height of irrationality to men imbued with the notion of meritocratic equality. Heredity had deprived the possession of privileges of "even the feeblest justification," according to Sieyès. The abolition of orders eliminated the inequalities of personal status characteristic of the Ancien Régime. The Constituent Assembly proclaimed equality with regard to taxes and punishments and free access to all public offices and administrative functions, and it reinstated Jews and Protestants as members of the national community. It combined this affirmation of homogeneity with a concern for proportionality: Mirabeau pointed out that arithmetic equality in the calculation of taxes would be inequitable. "Contributive capacity" had to be taken into account as a corrective in order to achieve "true proportion." This obsession with "just proportion," which was the essence of this century's notion of equality, can also be found in the reports of the Committee on Mendicancy and even in the debates on the division of the territory into départements, where it counterbalanced the principle of "geometrical equality."

This vast effort to root out aristocratic inequality shattered the predominance of the symbol. There is no better indication of this than the debate on the abolition of hereditary nobility, which began almost inadvertently on June 19, 1790. The obscure deputy who proposed the measure initiated a vehement argument in which positions were the reverse of what one might have expected. The abbé Maury, a commoner, defended coats of arms against the Noailles and Montmorencys, who were quite prepared to accept the sacrifice. Here the central issue was meritocratic equality: men should have no dignity, said Lameth, other than that associated "with the functions entrusted to them," no glory other than "that which they owed to their actions." And by every indication meritocratic equality triumphed, even among those opposed to the abolition of hereditary nobility. Their strongest argument, of whose future importance they had no premonition, was based on the idea of equality: "You are destroying the social rewards of the nobility," moaned Faucigny de Lucinge, "and you are preserving those of bankers and usurers." Abbé Maury himself recognized that the ideal solution would be to grant social rewards to men according to their merits, but for the time being there was no choice but to preserve the nobility, which was inextricably bound up with the monarchy. No one dared to defend emblems, even though they harmed no one. Social heterogeneity and private rights were absolutely and definitively disqualified.

Everyone, it was said, should have the same rights, the same courts, the same manner of making wills, and the same indignation with regard to discrimination of any kind, even when its purpose was one of compensation. (Rabaut protested against granting "tolerance" or "pardon" to Protestants when all they were asking for was equal rights.) Should they also have the same political rights? The Constituent Assembly had promised not only equality before the law but also equality in the making of the law, equal participation by all in the formulation of the general will. Here, however, it is clear that the Constituents violated their own principles: they introduced inequality between the representatives and the represented and, to make matters worse, established property qualifications for the right to vote.

After recognizing that all men possess in equal measure all the rights that derive from human nature, the Constituents nevertheless postponed their exercise of sovereignty, even though this represented the "ultimate degree of political perfection." There were complex reasons for this. One was among the century's commonplaces: that the modern citizen, unlike the ancient citizen, could not devote all of his time to politics. Another was borrowed, paradoxically enough, from Rousseau: that the general will is not just the sum of individual wills. Finally, there was the concern expressed by Sieyès on September 7, 1789 as to how to set limits on popular influence. While it was good for the people to be able to choose the men who would make its laws, it was not good that they should have the power to make laws themselves. Yet the Constituents knew full well that they were making it impossible for the represented to oppose the will of the representatives. At times they even feared along with Mirabeau that the people would inevitably choose its representatives from among those "most willing to sacrifice their time to the public good" and that a "de facto aristocracy" would thus be reconstituted.

This first violation of the principle of political equality was made even more glaringly obvious a little later on: the very right to elect representatives was restricted by property qualifications, which revived the old inequality between the orders. The flagrant contradiction between the Declaration of Rights and the *cens*—which according to L'Ange was nothing but a way of eliminating certain people from the social contract—was noticed and denounced by isolated voices on the Assembly's left. Clermont-Tonnerre himself, in his critical analysis of the Revolution, was sensitive to this issue: "Active citizens would cease to be equals in rights to nonactive citizens." Even more important, the clause on the *marc d'argent,* which linked eligibility for office to possession of land and a tax payment of 50-odd livres, provoked opposition across a wide spectrum from Mirabeau to Pétion. It was particularly disliked by men imbued with the notion of meritocratic equality. If the Constituent Assembly nevertheless stuck to its guns on the conditions of the *cens,* it was obviously because it was worried about both noble influence and escalating democratic demands. It was also because the Assembly feared an aristocracy of wealth less than the other kind of aristocracy. The new "aristocracy" was not a principle but a circumstance, "mobile" in its very essence, according to the marquis de Villette. Furthermore, it was possible to glimpse in the distant future, beyond the horizon of imperfect equality, the true political equality to come. Desmeuniers said that the exclusion of the poor, against which the adversaries of the *cens* protested so loudly, was "accidental" and that the goal of access to suffrage would incite them to improve their status. Before long there was discussion of extending the vote to all who were excluded: it would appear that women, "who furnish sovereigns to the greatest nations in Europe," were unjustly excluded. Must one conclude, Guyomar asked ironically, that the Declaration of the Rights of Man did not extend to women?

Thus the Constituent Assembly followed an uncertain course: it created legal equality, recoiled from political equality, and never abandoned the principle of property. Did this behavior reveal a hidden intention to grant formal equality only to deny real equality all the more effectively? Georges Lefebvre thought so. To him it seemed significant that the Constituents eliminated from the Declaration of Rights any mention of general felicity (which would have indicated the primacy of the community over individual interest). They wished, he believed, to prevent anyone from invoking equality in order to demand improvement in the lot of the disinherited, and they were determined to mark the boundary between legal equality and social equality. Yet any number of texts show that the Constituents, well aware of the problem, debated it constantly. For example, Talleyrand in his "Report on Public Instruction" conceded that amid so many actual inequalities men would have no feeling for equal rights unless education took a hand in "restoring the level." Fauchet and his friends in the constitutional Church advocated the gentle means of employing inheritance laws to restore equality among men.

There is no better indication of the close attention that the Constituent Assembly paid to the matter of transition from "formal" to "real" equality than the attitude of Clermont-Tonnerre, whose hostility to equal rights made him especially perceptive: he provides the most complete list we have of the Constituent Assembly's violations of the principle of equality. He also puts his finger on the central problem: it is all well and good to base social distinctions on "social utility" from now on, but who will be the judge of that utility, which will be used to justify inequalities? And it was again Clermont-Tonnerre who, well before the socialists, gave the best definition of formal equality: "To say that equality of rights comes down to possessing a right equal to the very unequal portion of liberty and property that belongs to each individual is [to utter] an abstraction so tenuous, so foolish, as to be absolutely pointless." So whether they denounced, like Clermont-Tonnerre, the illusion of legal equality when material equality does not exist or feared, like Delandine, that the people, taking the concept of original equality literally, might forget that it was just a "philosophical fiction" or thought, like Talleyrand, that education was the way in which the two forms of equality could be brought closer together until the differences between them vanished, the deputies of the Constituent Assembly always believed that material equality, whether they feared it or devoutly desired it, was a possible and indeed an imminent extension of formal equality.

They were, moreover, perfectly aware of the conflict that could arise between liberty and equality. Socialist historiography has portrayed them as being more concerned with liberty than with equality, always sacrificing the latter to the former. This is highly debatable; for many deputies of the Constituent Assembly, from the duc d'Aiguillon to Sieyès, equality of rights was a first principle, conditioning liberty itself. This preeminence of equality was based on the obvious generality of the law, expressed so well by Sieyès: "I envision the law as standing at the center of an immense globe. All citizens, without exception, stand at the same distance from it on the circumference and occupy equal areas." For Sieyès, men cannot be called free unless the law sets equal limits to every man's natural liberty: "A society in which one man could be more or less free than another would surely be very ill ordered and in need of reconstitution." Equality, far from being humbled by liberty, is here virtually identified with it. Arbitrariness is invariably an infringement of liberty, a hindrance to equality. The law is at once liberating and equalizing.

At times the Constituent Assembly even sacrificed liberty to equality, as the debate over equality of inheritance makes clear. Some conservatives saw the right to make a will as an essential guarantee of the right of property. A man's property rights were illusory, Cazalès argued, if he did not have the right to make a will freely. But that right was contested by Pétion, Dupont de Nemours, Mirabeau, and Lanjuinais in the name of equality: freedom to make a will, which favored concentration of wealth, seemed to them likely to produce new inequalities. They defended equality of inheritance all the more staunchly because they had linked the exercise of political power to wealth. To allow parents to give advantage to one of their children over others, Pétion argued persuasively, was to give them the power to decide who would be an active citizen and who would not, who would be eligible for parliamentary office and who would not; it was, in short, to "deprive countless citizens of their political rights." By contrast, to deprive them of that liberty was to work toward that equality of inheritance "that would attack the aristocracy even in its grave."

Thus the Constituents, attached as they were to a free and absolute right of property, envisioned a court to oversee equal partition of inheritance, which they regarded as a necessary condition for achieving equality of rights. There is no avoiding the conclusion that they were no strangers to de facto equality and that the preference they allegedly exhibited for liberty over equality was neither exclusive nor permanent. Tocqueville said that the French Revolution had only a few months for liberty, because by October 1789 it was in the grip of its central passion, equality (which was therefore by no means a Jacobin invention). One may suggest, however, that this dominant concern appeared even earlier. As early as the *Essai sur les privilèges* and *Qu'est-ce que le Tiers Etat?* Sieyès had proclaimed the supremacy of revolutionary equality, the sacrifices it required of liberty, and the indefinite nature of those sacrifices. He stressed the supremacy of equality because it was impossible to define the nation except as an association of individuals possessing equal rights, a condition without which the nation could not be regarded as one and indivisible. He affirmed its preeminence over liberty because the nation at that time excluded not only the idea of privilege but the very existence of privileged persons, who were as alien to it as foreigners. Last but not least, he envisioned the possibility of extending that exclusion without limit because the dividing line between equal citizens and strangers to the nation was an interior one whose location could be shifted at will. If exclusion were to be defined in terms not of rank and birth but of wealth, there would be new sources of division and the threat of another civil war. As early as 1792 Lequinio could write, in the pamphlet *Destroyed Prejudices*: "I no longer know either bourgeois or people in the old sense. But I know opulent classes and poor, hardworking classes. And I see and affirm that three-quarters of the opulent men still possess all the aristocracy once possessed by the nobility."

*
**

One more step in the direction of liberty, Barnave had warned after Varennes, would mean the "destruction of royalty." One more step in the direction of equality would mean the "destruction of properties." These additional steps were in fact taken by the Legislative Assembly and the Convention. They completed and extended the work of the Constituent Assembly in the areas of civil and political equality. They also took some steps in the direction of material equality, since the Convention approved equal partition of inheritance (something the Constituent Assembly had not been able to accomplish) and free division of communal property and established a welfare system. This was a long way from the division of property prophesied by Barnave, however. But the question of material equality continued to change during the Convention.

On the whole, the Convention remained hostile to the "agrarian law" that was menacingly invoked at intervals in the debates. Concerning de facto equality, which for Condorcet was "the ultimate aim of the social art," all the conventionnels were in agreement. All were convinced that corruption was inherent in excessive inequality of wealth. All believed in the same "wise laws" inspired by Montesquieu, Mably, and Rousseau as the means to reducing this inequality. In the early days of the Convention, none of them would have deemed it desirable to achieve that equality through coercion, for all had imbibed from their political readings the idea that equality in destitution is just another name for despotism. All were convinced that in a well-ordered republic, in Barère's words, "every citizen has some property." If the Convention appeared to make some progress toward de facto equality, then, it was not at all because its members had been converted to the carving up of property, which both the Girondin Constitution and the Montagnard Constitution defined in the same way.

The hierarchical relation among the different forms of equality did change, however. For some, the philanthropic requirement took priority over the meritocratic requirement. Robespierre had defined property as a manifestation of the right to exist—the foremost of man's inalienable rights. All other rights are subordinate to it, and no other right can be raised against it. If equality of property is therefore illusory, at least "everything that is indispensable for the preservation of life is a common property of the entire society," and only the surplus can be given up to "individual industry." In Robespierre's mind this conception of property did not justify intrusion by the state into the private domain (in February 1793 he was still hostile to price-fixing and requisition), but his emphasis on a minimal level of common happiness would facilitate his later support for state intervention.

Acceptance of coercion was the true dividing line in the Convention:

Vergniaud rejected it with all his might, for although he was also a partisan of "wise measures" capable of reducing excessive inequality, playing Lycurgus seemed to him only too likely to trigger civil war, in which case "that most terrible form of leveling, death, would hover over towns and countryside," spreading the equality of despair. Condorcet felt the same repugnance, though he was more prepared than Vergniaud to proceed quickly toward proportional equality, yet conscious of possible perverse effects: to mount a frontal assault on inequality would be "to open up more fertile sources of inequality, to drive men to more direct and harmful attacks." How could this hesitation be overcome and this line crossed? It is quite clear in the case of Cambon, who was just as attached to property as the two men just mentioned but who apostrophized the rich in these terms: "I want to respect your properties, but I want to bind you in spite of yourselves to the Revolution. I want you to lend your fortune to the Republic."

Robespierre's original contribution to the debate was not only to agree with Cambon that one can compel people to accept equality (a necessary but detestable and circumstantial practice) but also to affirm that one must compel people *to* equality. He deemed it essential to inculcate a taste for equality in the rich, to "force them to be honest," to correct their natural antisocial tendencies. The crucial point to understand was that "property rests on a moral principle." The rich man must not only assist the poor man but, even more important, "honor him," and for that coercion was necessary, but coercion of a very particular kind: not limited but comprehensive, not temporary but permanent, and for the purpose of creating not a state but a virtue. This modulation makes it impossible to interpret Robespierre's willingness to support price controls entirely as a political maneuver intended to win the backing of the sans-culottes. In his mind this opportunism was blessed by a unique conception of equality: not a reward for preexisting merits, talents, or even needs but a virtuous disposition to be created out of nothing. Equality thus became the object of an endless crusade, at once pedagogical and moral.

Meanwhile, sans-culotte agitation sharpened the features of the quest for equality. Without developing any views of property very different from those of the Jacobins, yet obsessed with a concern "to abolish the immense differences in happiness that have until now separated man from man," the sans-culottes applied those views in concrete fashion: looting groceries (seen as restitution of what rightfully belonged to the people), carrying out inspections, removing food from wagons at the city gates and distributing it to the crowd, and demanding that bread be made from the same flour for all—the so-called bread of equality. They also dressed identically; used the familiar *tu* as a means of education; staged carnivalesque banquets in which the rich, standing, served the poor, seated at tables; attacked emblems and marks of distinction which they called simply "the signs"; sang leveling couplets inspired by *La Carmagnole* ("Tous à la même hauteur, voilà le vrai bonheur"— "Everyone at the same level, that is true happiness"); and even destroyed bell towers, whose vertical thrust was an insult to equality. Such practices gave a vigorous look to equality sans-culotte style. They thus went far beyond the equality of opportunity with which the Revolution had wished to identify, and even far beyond equality of pleasures, suggesting instead an absolute equality of human achievement. Everything—results, success, failure, misfortune, prosperity—was "to be related to the common mass." Sans-culotte equality referred not to individual rights but to the social whole: it was not so much equality as identity.

A theory of this emancipated equality of individualism was provided under the Directory by Babeuf. In his youth he had been influenced by his reading of Mably and Rousseau. Like them, he wished that every man might have enough to live, and he suggested equally moderate solutions, such as a Caisse Nationale (National Fund) for the poor. At the beginning of the Revolution he might have subscribed fully to Tallien's definition-program: "To overburden opulence, to relieve misery, to annihilate the one with the dangerous surplus of the other—that is the whole secret of the Revolution." At the end of 1791 he was converted to what was called the "agrarian law," that is, land reform. After the Thermidorian episode, as he grew increasingly nostalgic for a Robespierrism that he had once helped to disparage, he discovered in the Montagnard Constitution the great virtue of having been based on the principle of common happiness, and he set forth the fundamental principles of Babouvism, whose major tenets were the following: to each his needs but nothing more; abolition of individual ownership; rigorous apportionment of goods in each household; and establishment of common warehouses to store vital supplies. As a corollary of this "perfect equality," exclusively proportioned to "necessity" and to "the capacity of the stomach," everywhere and always the same, meritocratic equality was disallowed, since the "capacity of brains" differed, Babeuf recalled from the *Discours sur les sciences et les arts*, only in the narcissistic illusion of the "intelligent."

Babeuf's originality lay not only in his radical critique of private property but also in his unflinching identification of the instruments of equality: a dictatorship to combat the ever-replenished ranks of the enemies of equality, to be entrusted to the "Equals"; requisition; and regimentation of society. This was a panegyric to the Terror, which accounts for the posthumous homage to Robespierre. Robespierre had understood that "a regenerator must have a grand vision; he must cut down whatever stands in his way." Babeuf's socialist posterity placed little stress on this obvious sacrifice of liberty to equality. But it retained Babeuf's vigorous protest against the hypocrisy of declaring that all men are equal only to persuade the wretched to make do with proportional equality: "We are equals, are we not? Well, then, we demand from now on to live and die as equals, just as we were born. We want true equality or death."

*
**

The time of "true equality" was already long past when Babeuf elaborated his theory. The text of the Constitution of Year III did indeed speak of equality, but only that civil equality guaranteed by the generality of the law, with no mention of common happiness. And it carefully limited political equality by imposing property qualifications that were at once more democratic (increasing the number of active citizens) and less democratic (cutting the number of electors in half) than those of 1791. The new society, which gave talent and superiority its due, completely repudiated natural equality, gave priority to meritocratic equality, and did not even wish to consider the possibility of a conflict between different types of merit: in a series of equivalences it identified what Boissy d'Anglas called the "best" with the best educated and the most "interested in preservation of the laws." In the tranquil affirmation that a "country governed by the propertied class enjoys social order," Marx saw the truth of the French Revolution at last revealed: the triumph of bourgeois interests, employed to allow social inequality to prosper under cover of the abstract equality of democracy. The latter at once camouflaged and aggravated the former. Now began the cynical reign of the propertied bourgeoisie, in which equality was a functional lie.

Had the debates of earlier assemblies and their torment over the problematic gap between the different forms of equality been forgotten entirely? Not at all, as is shown by the educational obsession of the Thermidorian Convention and the Directory. It is too simple to reduce that obsession to a determination to educate the bourgeois elites while excluding the children of common people. To be sure, it is easy to show how Thermidorian and Directorial legislation fell short of Jacobin ambitions and to point out the realism of a policy that usually (except after republican coups d'état) sacrificed the public primary schools. Nevertheless, the ambition of that legislation remained the same as Condorcet's, to reduce inequality by spreading enlightenment. When Lakanal presented his report on normal schools (actually drafted by Garat) to the Convention on 3 Brumaire, Year III, he proposed "the regeneration of human understanding in a Republic of twenty-five million men, all made equal by democracy." The school had replaced the Terror as the instrument of equality. The geographic equalization ("from the Alps to the Pyrenees") and social equalization ("children born in cottages shall have teachers as skilled as those hired at great expense to serve children born in opulence") proposed by the report would be a long-term process. Investment in education reflected the crucial fact that equality is not a state but a process of development.

The foregoing should give some idea of the originality of the word "equality" in the republican motto. Unlike fraternity, equality was not a virtue to be cultivated (except perhaps in the mind of Robespierre). Unlike liberty, which could be defined in negative terms (to be free was *not* to be constrained), equality required a positive answer to pressing questions: Equal to whom? Equal to what? Equal in what respect? We perceive the difficulty of stopping at equal rights in a society of men of unequal means, and we catch a glimpse of the fecundity of "formal" equality. Formal equality no doubt camouflaged real inequalities, but it did not protect them for long. On the contrary, it revealed that society stood in a fundamentally false position with respect to the principle on which it claimed to be based. It introduced, as Tocqueville understood so well, a source of endless upheaval into social life.

EQUALITY

The principal occupation of the nineteenth century would be to bring the reality of equality into line with its revolutionary proclamation.

Mona Ozouf

FURTHER READING

Clermont-Tonnerre, Stanislas-Marie-Adélaide, comte de. *Oeuvres complètes*. Paris, Year III.

Dumont, Louis. *Homo hierarchicus: Essai sur le système des castes*. Paris, 1967.

———— *Homo aequalis*. Paris, 1976.

Espinas, Alfred. *La philosophie sociale du XVIIIe siècle et la Révolution*. Paris, 1898.

Garaud, Marcel. *Histoire générale du droit privé français, de 1789 à 1914*, vol. 1, *La Révolution et l'égalité civile*. Paris, 1953.

Leroy, Maxime. *Les précurseurs français du socialisme de Condorcet à Proudhon*. Paris, 1948.

Lichtenberger, André. *Le socialisme et la Révolution française: Etude sur les idées socialistes en France de 1789 à 1796*. Paris, 1899.

Mably, Gabriel Bonnot, abbé de. *De l'étude de l'histoire, à Monseigneur le prince de Parme*. Maëstricht, 1778.

Roederer, Pierre-Louis. *L'esprit de la Révolution de 1789*. Paris, 1831.

Rosso, Corrado. *Mythe de l'égalité et rayonnement des Lumières*. Pisa, 1980.

Sagnac, Philippe. *La législation civile de la Révolution française, 1789–1804*. Paris, 1898.

Sieyès, Emmanuel. *Essai sur les privilèges*. N.p., 1788.

———— *Qu'est-ce que le Tiers Etat?*, ed. Roberto Zapperi. Geneva, 1970.

RELATED TOPICS

Babeuf	Liberty	Physiocrats	Sans-culottes	Tocqueville
Barnave	Mirabeau	Robespierre	Sieyès	Voltaire
Condorcet	Montesquieu	Rousseau	Suffrage	

FEUDAL SYSTEM

In modern French historiography the expression "feudal system" refers to a system of human relations which gradually established itself in western Europe after the Germanic invasions and which was based on the vassalage contract and the fief. It connotes the network of hierarchies and dependences that grew up among free, private individuals with the decay of public authority. By way of the fief, the lord and his vassal committed themselves to a mutual relation of protection and service. The "feudal system" (*féodalité*) is therefore different from "feudalism" (*féodalisme*), the dominant economic system of the same period, which was based on landed property and the rural *seigneurie*.

The word *féodalisme* is of relatively recent coinage, but the word *féodalité* is old. It had existed since the sixteenth century but was not in current usage before the eighteenth century. The *Dictionnaire de l'Académie Française* included the adverb *féodalement* in its first edition of 1694, but the noun *féodalité* is not mentioned until its fourth edition in 1762, ten years after its appearance in the *Dictionnaire de Trévoux*. In Diderot's *Encyclopedia* the word is given a strictly legal definition (the fief contract) by a specialist in the law, Boucher d'Argis. Nevertheless, its meaning had already been broadened by historians who reinvented the word to refer to Europe and especially France in the period before the modern era brought on by the progress of either absolutism or "civilization." As a result, it became one of the most widely used terms in the political vocabulary during the French Revolution, because it was one of the most negative, probably *the* most negative term for summing up all the evils of the Ancien Régime. In a sense, 1789 was a grandiose dramatization of this semantic shift.

When Boulainvilliers used the word at the beginning of the century, it had no pejorative connotation. On the contrary, it referred to a period in French history and to a political system in which the monarchy was controlled by the nobility, the descendants of the Frankish conquerors. It was based on feudal law, which had been studied systematically since the Renaissance: the fief that the vassal received from his lord was a conditional property that implied an obligation of homage and service in exchange for political rights. But Boulainvilliers used the concept only in the political sphere, to celebrate what he usually called the "feudal government," divided between the king and the nobility, and to contrast it with subsequent encroachments of absolutism on the political rights of the nobility.

Although Montesquieu does not use the term "feudalism" in books 30 and 31 of *L'esprit des lois,* he is nevertheless concerned with understanding the relation between feudal laws and the type of monarchical government that had established itself in France over the preceding centuries. For him, feudal law, a distant offshoot of the Frankish invasions, which came into being little by little as the hereditary fief supplanted gifts of land with precarious title, was the cradle of the national monarchy, a type of regime unknown in antiquity. Montesquieu saw feudal law, along with Roman law and canon law, as the third great legal system to be developed by European civilization, and the most important for the origin of the French monarchy. Initially feudal law destroyed "political government," because it distributed public authority throughout the pyramid of vassalage. It substituted "feudal monarchy" for "political monarchy." But by gradually extending its authority through the rebirth of Roman law, the evolution of mores, and the emancipation of serfs, "political government" regained its prerogatives, though no one can say just when this ascendancy occurred. And if Montesquieu regarded the French monarchy as one of the finest governments that ever had appeared on the face of the earth, part of the homage belonged to its ancestor, feudal monarchy.

This continuity was in fact the basis for Montesquieu's insistence in *L'esprit des lois* that monarchy and nobility were inseparable, and it explains why the phrase "monarchical government" in France referred to a balanced body politic in which the authority of the prince, though sovereign, was nevertheless limited by tradition, mores, dominant passions, and "the prejudice of each person and each rank." In other words, in monarchy just as in feudal government, the destinies of the king and the nobility were linked: "The most natural intermediary power is that of the nobility." The king did not share sovereignty, but if his authority was limited, the credit was due to the legacy of feudalism.

Thus Montesquieu's work contains, distinct yet intertwined, both a historical analysis of feudalism and, through it, a justification of the modern French monarchy. The analytical part, extraordinarily subtle, revived the subject. Montesquieu was the first author to characterize feudal society in terms of a combination of political sovereignty and civil property, and to see it as a novel sociopolitical system, which, starting in the tenth century, gradually evolved in response to hazard and misfortune. Thus he combines strictly juridical scholarship in feudal law—developed from the Renaissance—with the exclusively political concept of "feudal government," which for Boulainvilliers was a deliberate creation of the Frankish kings and was designed to keep faith with the spirit of elective monarchy. In this respect Montesquieu laid the groundwork not so much for polemics or politics as for history, and it is curious that the principal commentators on the last two books of *L'esprit des lois* were from the other side of the English Channel; Scottish philosophers reflected on "feudalism," a concept, encompassing the economic and social as well as the political, that they contrasted with modern "commercial society." It was through the work of Robertson, Hume, Ferguson, Smith, and Millar that the idea came back to France; it is mentioned, for example, in Barnave's posthumously published manuscript.

In eighteenth-century France, however, public opinion, even among scholars, focused primarily on Montesquieu's political conclusions and his assertion of an indissoluble bond between monarchy and nobility. In this respect, the key text—as usual all the more incisive because it was so simple, even simplistic—was again that of Boulainvilliers, published in 1727. In opposition to the liberal-aristocratic concept of monarchy, the adversaries of that birthright based on a right of conquest responded by defining *féodalité* as a usurpation of the rights of the crown: abbé Dubos saw the regalian rights as the inalienable legacy of the Roman *imperium,* transmitted to the Frankish kings through a just and lawful alliance. The most significant aspect of this debate, which raged in the first half of the century, was that the proponents of the "noble thesis" and the proponents of the "royal thesis" drew opposite conclusions from a common set of assumptions. Both camps viewed "feudal government" as a central category of French history. Both saw in it a type of regime contradictory to royal sovereignty. Both spoke of usurpation, since both were obsessed with legitimacy. If the feudal system was an extension of the conquest, then it was faithful to the origins of the nation and the monarchy was the usurper. If, on the other hand, royal authority was the point of departure, then the feudal system had usurped its titles and functions in the Middle Ages, and modern monarchy was a return to the Constitution. If Montesquieu's concept of *féodalité* was merely a product of history, Boulainvilliers's and Dubos's crystallized the passions of the nation, for already at this early date their views raised the questions of the origin and legitimacy of the nobility and of sovereign power.

This argument can be seen in the work of Mably, whose *Observations sur l'histoire de France* echoed, from the other end of the century, the observations of Boulainvilliers in *Histoire de l'ancien gouvernement en France*—a response to Boulainvilliers in his own terms. Mably dropped the Romanist thesis, which conceded too much to royal despotism, and shared with his aristocratic predecessor the idea that the history of France began with a Germanic conquest. But while Boulainvilliers grafted onto these origins a discourse on inequality, Mably drew from it a proof of equality: what the Frankish conquerors had brought to Gaul was a jealous concern for individual independence, something very like a primitive form of citizenship, in which the people assembled every year in the "fields of May" to vote on the laws. Since the time of Charlemagne—the hero of both histories and to Mably the culmination of primitive democracy—the history of France had entered on a long period of decline, marked by two long-lived usurpations, one by the feudal system, the other by despotism. The objective of the *Observations* was thus to restore the origins of that history, that is, to restore the legitimacy of government by restoring the rights, and the harmony, of the people assembled around the king. Whereas Boulainvilliers had contrasted the feudal system and absolutism, Mably linked them so as to reject both; like Boulainvilliers, he continued to think in exclusively political terms, but he turned Boulainvilliers's argument around by showing that both historical realities were equally illegitimate, hence equally detestable. This proved to be a powerful argument; its influence in the late eighteenth century can be measured by any number of brochures published in 1787, 1788, and 1789, in which the feudal system and absolute monarchy were portrayed as successive forms of usurpation of the nation's rights.

But when the two were not linked in a common condemnation, it was the feudal system that became the sole villain in the history of France. This interpretation was favored by the proponents of a powerful and enlightened monarchy responsible for the rational government of the kingdom. It can be seen in the work of Le Trosne, a physiocrat and the author of *Dissertation sur la féodalité* (1779), who argues that the turning point in the evolution of the system occurred at the moment when fiefs became hereditary: lords then became independent, and royal sovereignty disintegrated. Before long, the king, with the aid of the people, regained power, but the feudal system left hateful "remains" in society. An even more violent opponent of "feudal anarchy" was Linguet, the apostle of absolute monarchy, for whom that anarchy was but a system of might makes right, the reign of the arbitrary power of lords and barons until they were vanquished by the king backed by the people. In this version of the history of France, where royal authority was favored, the feudal system no longer represents even an illegitimate social principle: it is a non-society. We are a long way from Montesquieu!

Even as the word *féodalité* entered the realm of history and politics in the eighteenth century, its specific legal meaning continued to evolve from its original reference to the obligations of the vassalage contract through the fief. But the content of these obligations changed over time: the chain of vassalage, which linked the lowliest of vassals to the highest of suzerains, the king, disappeared with the advent of absolutism. Louis XIV called the barons and vassals to his aid for the last time in 1694. What had become gradually codified since the sixteenth century, in general treatises and customaries, under the name of "feudal law," was seigneurial law, which was essentially the definition of the dues of all kinds owed to the lord by tenants within what was called the lord's "eminent property" (as opposed to "useful property"). It made little difference whether the seigneurie was owned by a noble, a commoner (who was then obliged to pay the king a tax known as the *franc-fief*), or an ecclesiastical community. What mattered was the package of "rights" that went with it as a result of the superimposition of a "feudal" property upon an ordinary property. Those rights that entailed recognition were usually called "feudal," and the term was extended over the course of the century to dues and institutions having nothing to do with feudal law. The same phenomenon can be seen in the expansion of meaning of the term "vassal," which strictly speaking referred to a noble fief-holder but which was often applied in the eighteenth century to peasants who paid a *cens*. The reason for this broadening was that all that remained of the feudal system was the system of seigneurie, which had come to represent the whole system, this time as an integral part of absolutism.

The nature of "feudal rights" varied widely, and in the eighteenth century they still included powers of justice exercised by the lord. Generally these powers applied not to criminal but to civil cases: the numerous seigneurial courts applied customary law and local usages to settle the countless quarrels that formed the disputes of rural life. Sometimes, with the support of royal law, peasant communities triumphed over the seigneurial tribunals. At the end of the Ancien Régime, the French countryside was witness to many such triangular conflicts, and the lords did not always have the upper hand.

Even in the middle of the eighteenth century feudal rights could still include traces of the old serfdom. In the Franche-Comté, for example, some peasants were subject to mortmain; they were attached to the lord's land and lost their property and rights if they left it, and even then they remained subject to the lord's "right of pursuit," that is, they remained under his jurisdiction. But in the final century of the Ancien Régime feudal rights had mostly been transformed into dues in money or kind of one sort or another, such as ground rents, *champarts, lods et ventes,* and so on. These dues distinguished seigneurial lands from "allodial" properties, free of obligations of this kind. The denominations, as well as the importance of these dues to the lord's income, varied from region to region: in Languedoc feudal rights were practically nonexistent by the sixteenth century; in Brittany and Burgundy they were still onerous as late as the eighteenth century.

For more than a century historians have debated the question whether the burden of feudal dues increased in the decades preceding the Revolution. The idea was first proposed by Sagnac in 1898 in a thesis written in Latin (*Quomodo jura dominii aucta fuerint regnante Ludovico sixto decimo*), which was immediately criticized and has remained controversial ever since: he did not demonstrate that feudal dues increased on a national scale during the eighteenth century. True, a mathematical proof would be almost impossible, given the extraordinary variety of types of dues and local situations, which precludes an exhaustive inventory and count. To judge by available monographic studies, the reality varied not only from province to province but from seigneurie to seigneurie.

If the idea of a "feudal" (or more precisely "seigneurial") reaction seemed plausible, it was because it was deduced a posteriori from what it was supposed to explain, namely, the vehemence of antiseigneurial sentiment among the peasantry in 1789. It also drew on the prodigious efforts of eighteenth-century jurists, those Cartesians of the law, to simplify and rationalize the various customary usages, particularly in regard to seigneurial rights. Not that the so-called *feudistes,* or specialists in feudal law, challenged the basis of those rights; in fact, the main thrust of their work tended to underscore the venerable character and validity of such rights by relating the infinite variety of customs to general principles drawn from Roman law. By defining those principles with precision and eliminating contradictions, they sought to erect the diverse elements of feudal law into a coherent and intelligible system. When Dumoulin's late sixteenth-century *Traité des fiefs* was reprinted in 1773, Enlightenment jurists, led by Guyot, the most learned expert on feudal matters of the day, hailed their illustrious predecessor. This effort of several centuries to rationalize customary law eventually gave rise, in the second half of the eighteenth century, to a broad literature devoted to the revision and modernization of *terriers,* or registers recording the various seigneurial rights.

Thus revised and modernized, the idea of the feudal system only seemed more redoubtable. Its elaboration, or, rather, reelaboration, by legal scholars clearly revealed the shift that had taken place in the meaning of the word, which now referred not to what was specifically "feudal" but rather to what was more precisely "seigneurial." The weighty eighteenth-century legal tomes were scarcely interested in that aspect of the feudal system that Montesquieu and Boulainvilliers had called "feudal government." They focused not on a political but on a civil institution, a unilateral system of periodic dues and obligations to be paid to the lord, recorded in ancient contracts and falling primarily on the peasant, secondarily on the bourgeois. The political counterpart had largely disappeared, since royal power had gradually supplanted the feudal aristocracy. Where it did remain, as in the seigneurial courts, it had become pointless, deprived by time of all but its oppressive character. In all cases, the principal result of the efforts at legal and administrative reform was to have exaggerated the importance of that portion of the feudal legacy that weighed most heavily on civil society, namely, the system of rural seigneurie, which profited a class that no longer offered anything in exchange for the dues it received. Seen in this light, the question of the unpopularity of feudal rights in the late eighteenth century is independent of the question of their real weight, and it is even possible that, as Tocqueville suggested, these rights were resented all the more because they were residual: "The feudal system had remained the greatest of all our civil institutions by ceasing to be a political institution. Having been reduced to this point, it aroused even more hatred, and it has been said with truth that the destruction of some of the institutions of the Middle Ages made those that remained a hundred times more odious" (*L'Ancien Régime et la Révolution,* II, chap. 1).

In fact, the contention that the remains of the feudal system were an odious burden was a commonplace of Enlightenment philosophy before it was inscribed on the banners of the peasant insurrection. The most famous chapter in this vast saga was Voltaire's battle against the chapter of Saint-Claude in the 1770s to emancipate the last remaining serf-peasants of the Church of France. The response to Voltaire's pamphlets gives some idea of the public's surprise and indignation; the "serfs of Mont-Jura" were a regular refrain in denunciations of feudal tyranny at the end of the century. Another major episode in this connection was the publication in 1776 of a book by the physiocrat Boncerf, entitled *Les inconvénients des droits féodaux (The Disadvantages of Feudal Rights).* Criticism was leveled now in the name not of outraged humanity but rather of economic efficiency. Productive agriculture required modern forms of private property, freed of absurd "feudal" constraints. Written in a moderate, scholarly tone, the work nevertheless provoked the anger of the Paris parlement, which ordered that it be burned. But the spirit of the times, incarnated by Turgot, protected the author, and a short while later even the king was led to abolish the last remaining serfdom on royal domains (1779).

In the last two decades of what would become the Ancien Régime, the word *féodalité* thus came to stand for everything that was negative in the present age: aristocracy as opposed to equality, oppression as opposed to liberty, privilege as opposed to unity, the "gothic" tradition as opposed to reason, barbarity as opposed to civilization, anarchy as opposed to order. If feudalism became such an object of anathema, it was because it stood at the crossroads of two evolutionary processes and crystallized two sets of accumulated grievances. All the debates and writings on the subject of "feudal government" finally resulted in its radical condemnation both by proponents of absolutism and by historians of democracy from Linguet to Mably. And the attempt to revamp feudal law on a civil level was ultimately judged unacceptable by enlightened opinion. From numerous texts published prior to 1789 one gathers that, owing to the impossibility of reconciling the past with a reformed body of public and civil law or even of conceiving of the past in the light of such reform a revolution had taken place in people's minds prior to the Revolution; there is no better illustration of this impossibility than the absolute rejection of *féodalité*, understood in the sense of a social system based on pure violence, without public authority or laws. In a curious *Eloge de Montesquieu* written in 1785, Marat, already an excellent sounding board for public opinion, described feudal laws as "those bloody laws that, spreading from the forests of Germany into all of Europe, made the human race moan for so long beneath the oppression of a horde of petty tyrants."

To convince oneself that *féodalité* had already become, in the years immediately prior to the Revolution, the embodiment of the "curses of the Ancien Régime," one has only to consult the two famous pamphlets that Sieyès published in November 1788 and January 1789: *Essai sur les privilèges* and *Qu'est-ce que le Tiers Etat?* Their impact is the best measure we have of what the public made of both the word *féodalité* and the phenomenon at the culmination of this long period of semantic and political drift.

In both texts the idea of the feudal system is inseparable from the idea of privilege. As such, it is incompatible with the concept of law, which presupposes universality, hence equality of individuals before a common law. It originated in the barbarous Middle Ages, in ignorance of the true principles upon which society ought to be founded, and it resulted in the existence of an oppressive nobility, which had usurped the rights of the nation, precisely those rights that needed to be restored: "In the night of barbarism and feudalism, true relations between men could be destroyed, all nations overturned, all justice corrupted. But with the dawn of light, all the gothic absurdities must flee, and the remains of ancient ferocity must fall or be annihilated." Since it was a question of restoring to individuals their constituent rights, the abbé made sure that the privileged, who were by definition outside the social order, would be excluded from the true representative of the nation, the Third Estate: "I insist above all that attention be paid to the feudal system's countless agents. . . . All would be lost if the proxies of the feudal system were to usurp the deputation of the common order." For the vicar of Chartres, the feudal system had become almost a synonym for aristocracy and an antonym for the nation. It was the legacy against which a new social order must be reconstructed on a basis of reason and equality.

Within the space of a few months, Sieyès' doctrine had become that of the Revolution. When the deputies gathered in Versailles at the beginning of May, they carried with them the *cahiers* of their constituents, many of which in one form or another demanded abolition of feudal rights. But the first few months were taken up with the debate between the orders and the birth of the new sovereignty; the question of power took precedence over all others. Moreover, it is not certain that the deputies wished to join in any hasty liquidation of *féodalité*. When rural rebellion knocked at the Assembly's door in late July and early August, the deputies were immersed in discussion of the Declaration of the Rights of Man—yet another prerequisite, this one philosophical, to the regeneration of the old kingdom. But on the night of August 4, as the deputies weighed the risks of repression, the vicomte de Noailles and the duc d'Aiguillon proposed the abolition of feudal rights. A deputy from lower Brittany, a Landivisiau merchant by the name of Le Guen de Kerengal, set the tone of the debate, that crowning of the philosophy of the century: "The people, impatient for justice and tired of oppression, is in a hurry to destroy these titles, a monument to the barbarism of our fathers. Let us be just, gentlemen: titles have been brought before us that humiliate the human race. . . . Who among us, gentlemen, in this century of Enlightenment, would not make an expiatory bonfire of those infamous pieces of parchment, and who would not carry the torch to sacrifice them on the altar of the public good?" And further on he added: "There is no need, gentlemen, to trace the origins of those causes that led the French nation step by step into subjugation, nor to prove that only the force and violence of the great subjected us to a feudal regime. Let us follow the example of English America, composed solely of landowners who know no trace of the feudal system."

Feudalism was thus transformed into a "regime" that summed up all the past subjugation of the nation. Just as the debates of June had transferred sovereign power from the king to the Assembly, so the decrees of August 4 and 11 would revolutionize the juridical nature of civil society. The most interesting thing about the speeches uttered and decisions made during that memorable week was the collective dynamic that impelled the deputies to make a spectacular break with the past, and it was the general sentiment that that accursed past should be dubbed the "feudal regime." In this context it matters little that the abolished feudal rights were simply declared redeemable. What counts, even in those cases where feudal property was merely converted to bourgeois property, was that prosaic interests were cloaked in the idea of a detestable past and a regenerated society. On August 11 the final decree indicated that "the National Assembly entirely destroys the feudal regime." A reading of the text clearly points up the extraordinary elasticity of the definition, which included not only the vestiges of mortmain or personal servitude, seigneurial laws, and all feudal rights but also the *dîmes*—ecclesi-astical exactions that had nothing remotely to do with feudal laws. The body of the decree also abolished the sale of offices as well as privileges of all kinds, not just fiscal, in the name of equality of all before the law.

The "destruction of the feudal regime" on August 11 thus gave very wide meaning to the phrase "feudal regime," which served to denote the whole structure of the old society. The decree affected not only the relics of the rural seigneurie but also such obligations as the *dîme*, which was classed with other dues because it was seen as an exaction for the benefit of a privi-leged order, in this case the Church. The abolition also struck at institutions introduced after the feudal period, such as the sale of offices, which began in the sixteenth century. Broadly speaking, this destruction condemned a society created by absolute monarchy, hence much more recent than "feudalism." In order to build a centralized state and pay its costs, the king of France had repeatedly borrowed money from his subjects in return for his guarantee of certain privileges. These privileges were granted not to individuals but to orders, *corps,* and communities, which constituted the social fabric. By grad-ually increasing the number of special privileges, exemptions, and distinc-tions, real and honorific, the absolute monarchy had gradually created a so-ciety of castes, both in fact and in people's minds. It was to this society, in which rank no longer had anything to do with public service but was wholly embodied in the idea of social difference, that the men of 1789 ultimately applied the term *féodalité.*

The very popularity of the word in this period, as well as its indiscrim-inate use in both nominal and adjectival forms, is a sign of its central impor-tance in the revolutionaries' own conception of their actions. Along with "ar-istocracy" and "aristocrat," *féodalité* and *féodal* were contrasted with "equality" and "equal individuals" as the Ancien Régime was contrasted with what was just then coming into being. These words referred to a society characterized by hierarchy and privilege based on birth, in which the particular interests of different *corps* stood as impediments to the sovereignty of the people. By sup-pressing from top to bottom the "feudal" structure of the old society, the decree of August 11, 1789, gave the French Revolution a radical individualist character, which was seen as an indispensable prerequisite of democratic equality. "Feudalism," like aristocracy, became the negative of this new world. In this respect it matters little that it took longer to eliminate than to abolish the system: the decrees of August 1789 were supplemented by further de-crees in 1790 and 1791; feudal rights that were made redeemable were even-tually abolished without indemnity, but not until July 1793; and the owners of offices done away with in August 1789 were not reimbursed until later. In reality, however, the last word had been said at the beginning of August with the "abolition of the feudal regime." By decreeing an end to the principles of organization of the old society, the Revolution, even though it compensated the victims of its bold move with money, added to its banners a victory as radical as the reconquest of sovereignty in June and July—as radical, but easier, quicker, and more durable: for with the inception of popular sover-eignty the French embarked upon a long journey marked by abrupt changes of direction and many setbacks, while on the grave of *féodalité* they laid the foundations of modern, individualistic society for centuries to come.

François Furet

FURTHER READING

Aulard, Alphonse. *La Révolution française et le régime féodal.* Paris, 1919.
Boulainvilliers, Henri de. *Histoire de l'ancien gouvernement de la France.* The Hague and Amsterdam, 1727.
Boutruche, Robert. *Seigneurie et féodalité,* 2 vols. Paris, 1968–1970.
Burke, Peter. "Scottish Historians and the Feudal Systems: The Conceptualization of Social Change," *Studies on Voltaire and the Eighteenth Century,* vol. 191, 1980.
Doyle, William. "Was There an Aristocratic Reaction in Prerevolutionary France?" *Past and Present,* no. 57, 1972.
Forster, Robert. *The House of Saulx-Tavannes: Versailles and Burgundy, 1700–1830.* Baltimore, 1971.
Le Trosne, Guillaume-François. *De l'administration provinciale et de la réforme de l'impôt.* Basel, 1779. Contains the "Dissertation sur la féodalité."
Mably, Gabriel Bonnot, abbé de. *Observations sur l'histoire de France.* Geneva, 1765.
Mackrell, J. Q. C. *The Attack on "Feudalism" in Eighteenth-Century France.* London, 1973.
Montesquieu, Charles-Louis de. *L'esprit des lois,* 2 vols. Geneva, 1748, books 30 and 31.

RELATED TOPICS

Ancien Régime
Aristocracy
Barnave
Marat
Montesquieu
Night of August 4
Physiocrats
Sieyès
Tocqueville
Voltaire

FRATERNITY

I n the triad of abstractions that compose what Pierre Leroux calls "the holy motto of our fathers," fraternity—last and least—is the poor relation. It was the least used of the three, according to the few historians who have tried their hand at counting. It was also the last to be put into practice, according to Aulard, who says that these concepts came into use in three distinct periods: until August 10, 1792, liberty reigned triumphant; then came the turn of equality; and finally, with the Montagnard dictatorship, came the time of fraternity. Fraternity was also the concept least deeply rooted in Enlightenment thought: one could write a history of liberty or of equality in the eighteenth century; it would be less easy to write a history of fraternity. A search of the dictionaries of the day reveals that fraternity sometimes denoted relations among peoples, sometimes relations within groups, with either a Christian connotation (because "monks refer to themselves as brothers") or a Masonic connotation (because the Freemasons had made the elite familiar with "fraternal" associations). Both the Christian and Masonic senses were more symbolic than actual, however, since "the perfect friendship of the Masons no more reverses the order that God has established among the different human conditions than does the one that is supposed to unite all Christians as brothers of Jesus Christ." The egalitarian dynamic of fraternity was still weak, and the virtues of "benevolence" and "sensitivity" were more commonly invoked.

The *cahiers* exhibit a similar silence: their grievances were less concerned with fraternity than with liberty and equality. It is true that these two elder concepts could always be coupled with genitives: freedom of the press or equality of rights, for instance, which specified their meaning and intensified their use. Fraternity stood all alone. Its powerful emotional charge, emphasized by an iconography replete with birds, hearts, infants, kisses, and bouquets, made specificity unnecessary. The same emotionality also prevented any demand from being associated with fraternity and precluded any punishment for failure to live up to its requirements.

Thus there was no equivalence of status between liberty and equality on the one hand and fraternity on the other. The first two were rights, the third a moral obligation. The Declaration of Rights makes sense without the word "fraternity," which made its entry into official language through the back door, in a supplementary article to the Constitution of 1791, which envisioned fraternity as a remote product of future national holidays. Those holidays were instituted in order to "foster" fraternity, which was thought of as the goal of a long-term project to shape the civic spirit and not at all as an immediate objective. The Constitution of 1793 again ignored the idea, as did

694

Fraternity

the Charter of 1830. Not until 1848 was the threefold principle of liberty, equality, and fraternity embodied in a constitution. Prior to this belated institutionalization, it was possible to substitute other triads for the famous motto: the nation, the law, and the king in the first civic oaths, and later, after the flight to Varennes made it imperative to find another formula, the nation, liberty, and equality. Fraternity was not yet included. Outside official texts, liberty and equality also dominated, always outweighing fraternity in their presence on flags, in the names of places and people, and in planting ceremonies: whereas the tree of liberty grew in the main village square, the tree of fraternity had to make do with less significant or marginal locations—a fraternity of the frontier which thus took on another meaning.

What was the reason for the relative obscurity of fraternity? Writers such as Gérald Antoine blame it on the nebulous nature of the word, the excessive ambitions to which it gave rise, and its powerful Christian roots, which prevented it from flourishing in the atmosphere of the Revolution. Aulard blamed the heavy "left-wing" connotations of a word born at the Cordeliers and cherished by the "fraternal" societies that were the cradle of sansculotterie. J. M. Roberts, who adapted and extended Aulard's interpretation, singles out two important occasions (one in 1790, the other in 1793) when fraternity served as a way of coping with threats of disunity and social disintegration. But from its association with those violent situations, it retained an air of extremism which prevented its influence from spreading in the same way as that of liberty and equality.

*
**

In 1789 the gathering of the orders had taken place under the aegis of "fraternal union." The federations' brief moment in the sun revived the emotions of that time: in the exchange of oaths (Lafayette's on the Champ de Mars contained a promise that he would remain bound to the French people "by indissoluble bonds of fraternity"); in the ritual exchange of food and arms; in the vocabulary of speeches, which used the metaphors of a "chain" and "ties" of fraternity. Actors and oath-takers saw themselves as brothers in arms, united against the threat of brigands. In the fraternity of the federations there was thus a defensive character, stressed by the commander of the Saint-Honoré district battalion in Paris: "In your fellow men you have seen equals and, compelled by the needs of union, in those equals you have seen brothers." Here one has the sense that equality was conceived abstractly but that fraternity was practiced in the exigency of danger.

Yet this defensive character by no means precluded the possibility of extending fraternity. A simple yet certainly quite influential image was that of youths from traditionally rival villages at last mingling and "fraternizing." The most powerful image was that of the Paris Federation, which extended the local federations, and which, in itself, held the promise of still further extension, to the entire universe. Camille Desmoulins wrote: "The celebration of July 14 tends, if not to make us look upon Monsieur Capet as our equal, then at least to make us look upon all men and all peoples as brothers."

From the very first use of the term, it seems that fraternity, the ultimate goal of the Revolution, was open to interpretation.

Hence it scarcely matters that the word does not appear in legislative texts. It was present everywhere else, particularly in the sermons of patriotic priests. What better place to find justification of "the consanguinity that nature has established between the inhabitants of the earth," and consequently of fraternity, than the Christian religion? Christianity had established the consubstantiality of men with God-become-man, and hence it was able, as Fauchet and Lamourette preached, to awaken in every human individual "the most vivid and distinct feeling of identity with other men." For its part, the Revolution had made a gift to the French people of a fatherland, a society in which all men could be brothers (as Daunou defined it in September 1789), whose foundation was the evangelical precept of fraternity. This awareness of kinship between the Christian message and the Revolution was to find its fullest employment in federative ceremonies, which dramatized the abolition of differences; the priests who celebrated these ceremonies reminded their audiences that in order to create a perfect society it was necessary first to eliminate all special interests, to follow the example set by Christ of "gentle fraternity." Gentle but contagious and rousing, that is, inflammatory: the Gospel itself, Fauchet insisted in his federative sermon, aimed to "spread over the face of the earth the holy fire of universal fraternity."

From this consideration of the federative episode, one thing is quite clear: fraternity was invoked much sooner and much more frequently than is generally believed. It was related to the expansion of the law: Roederer, responsible for drawing up jury lists for the départemental tribunal of Paris, says that he chose Catholics, Protestants, and Jews in order to illustrate "the fraternity of men regardless of religion" and that he dug up the only colored person he knew in order to "consecrate the fraternity of colors." Furthermore, the place in which fraternity was invoked was first the patriotic, then the constitutional Church. Hence it is quite wrong to blame resistance to the idea of fraternity during the Revolution on its Christian origins. On the contrary, the kinship between Christianity and the Revolution explains why fraternity emerged alongside liberty and equality, completing what was perceived as another trinity.

What about the argument that the (relative) eclipse of fraternity was due to its connection with extreme situations and therefore with violence, whether real or (as in the case of the federations) largely imaginary? Those societies that officially invoked equality and liberty (such as the "Friends of Liberty and Equality" that met at the Jacobin convent) soon came to call themselves "fraternal." The custom of people greeting one another as "brothers and friends" dates, according to Aulard, from April 1791, and that of signing letters "Salut et fraternité" quickly became a part of the societies' epistolary rituals, like the use of the familiar tu, which was supposed to encourage the "inclination to fraternity." In all this there was nothing aggressive. The practice of fraternity was always seen as one that could be broadened indefinitely. The attribution of the title "French citizen" to deserving individuals—the Legislative Assembly's last inspiration prior to dispersing—shows what vitality there was in this promise of universalization. We also see it in the Jacobin period. The fact that "fraternity trees" were deliberately planted on boundaries between regions, cantons, and villages, as well as Robespierre's attack on the Constitutional Committee in 1793 on the grounds that it had deliberated for the sake of "a flock of human creatures settled in one corner of the globe" and had failed to make room for the idea that men of all countries are brothers—these were signs that fraternity was still credited with the power to shatter what Anacharsis Cloots called those "fleeting names," those "gothic labels" attached to different peoples: French, English, German. On fraternity's horizon loomed the utopian vision of "the vast city of Philadelphia."

As the Revolution progressed, however, and as it excluded more and more people, some of their own volition, others not, this dream became increasingly difficult to sustain. Three new themes entered into the evocation of fraternity with ever greater urgency. First of all, it was recognized—and had been, if only intermittently, ever since the time of the Federation—that fraternity was not for all: "Every Frenchman is today your brother, until he openly shows himself to be a traitor to the fatherland." In that "until"—intended as a threat—we already see the assumption that aristocrats, who, as Barère later said, "have no country," are excluded from fraternity. Then people began to resign themselves to the fact that fraternity was not for today. To quote Barère once more, it was always "concentrated, during the Revolution, in patriots joined by a common interest." It was a local and closed fraternity, whose natural expansiveness was deferred till a better day. No doubt a day would come when all French citizens would form "a single family," but until then it was better to be wary of deceptive and misleading manifestations of unity such as the civic meals at which "false brothers" abounded. Finally, these obstacles made it clear that fraternity would not flow spontaneously from the revolutionary well but would need to be pumped up with energetic effort. People would need to "fraternize."

Fraternization, said Sébastien Mercier in his *Néologie*, is a word that needs no definition. Every Frenchman understands it, "provided he is a patriot." Nevertheless, "fraternization" between sections referred to a very specific set of procedures, an arm in the battle against the moderates that raged in the spring of 1793, prior to the elimination of the Girondins. When progressive activists in a section wanted to get rid of lukewarm comrades, they asked activists from more robust sections for help. These last would barge into the section meeting, move for a purge, vote for expulsions, and, if need be, physically evict the losers. Some sections rebelled against these high-handed tactics; they passed resolutions prohibiting neighboring sections from sending delegations of more than four persons and stipulated that no one could come armed. But these proved to be mere delaying tactics. The troublemakers were careful, moreover, to cover their activities with signs of fraternity, kisses of peace, accolades, oaths of unity, and enthusiastic speeches in which they congratulated themselves on having subdued the "hydra of moderatism," a fanciful monster that hid the real victims of the purge. "In a free people," the men of the Marchés section declared, "there are only brothers or enemies." Fraternization was a way of effecting this division, and fraternity, the fruit of coercion, was programmed to the point where it was possible to issue orders "to fraternize once a week, by turns in every section."

Thus there was an ironic shift in the meaning of the lovely word "fraternity," illustrated by the popular expression "fraternity or death." Yet fraternity was not associated with death more often than liberty or equality, and then chiefly because it occupied the third place in the republican motto. The meaning of the connection was vague, moreover: death for whom? For those who passionately supported liberty, equality, and fraternity and who, faced with the impossibility of achieving the promised goods, preferred death to failure? Or for its enemies, those who wanted no part of the three rewards, and who therefore, so it was alleged, fully deserved to die? The phrasing of the oaths themselves makes the first interpretation more likely. The so-called Oath of Liberty and Equality, which all state functionaries were required to take in August 1792, included a pledge to preserve liberty and equality and to die, if need be, enforcing the law. In this case the phrase "or death" meant it was better to die than to live without fraternity. The meaning is close to that of "Live free or die."

Yet the phrase "fraternity or death" retained some of its aggressive connotations. To die defending fraternity was to die in combat with one's enemies. Exclusion thus constituted a fraternity of combat. As Sartre ably demonstrated, in every revolutionary group closure is indispensable to the sentiment of fraternity, and violence is inseparable from collective action. In the Revolution, that violence was directed not only against external enemies but also against internal ones: doubt, fatigue, despair, or still more simply the tendency for militancy to flag were all reasons for individuals to abandon their comrades and reclaim the liberty of each for himself. Awareness of the solvent effects of time explains the revolutionaries' obsession with oaths. Each brother in advance gave the others the right to punish him if he deserted the common cause. He thus bound himself to the now sovereign group. This was fraternity coupled with terror: terror, because the group had the right to eliminate real or potential traitors; but fraternity, because each individual recognized himself in the others and acknowledged that they might recognize themselves in him. This prisonlike conception of fraternity makes sense of all the procedures of fraternization, which arose out of the certainty that even in the midst of a revolution one could not count on man's inherent good nature, and that unless each individual kept a sharp eye on his neighbors he risked death. Here, the increase in dramatic intensity is counterbalanced by the loss in scope; the euphoric fraternity of the federations belongs to another world.

This survey of revolutionary practice shows that fraternity consisted of two contradictory components—something that twentieth-century historians, blinded by its institutionalized forms and by the emergence of the republican motto, have not always perceived. By contrast, the antagonism between these two components was central to nineteenth-century thinking about the subject. No one then considered 1790 and 1793 to be moments of comparable extremism and therefore likely to foster similar forms of fraternity. Nor did anyone regard fraternity as the weak link in the republican motto. In fact it was often considered to be more important than liberty or equality, as if it contained the meaning of the Revolution.

⁎⁎

Memories of the revolutionary shock completely transformed the intellectual climate of the nineteenth century. Historians and philosophers alike became wary of analytical intelligence and shared a faith in mysterious higher realities. They also shared the conviction that human beings are from the outset social creatures and cannot stand alone. And they shared the feeling, whose Christian origins no one denied, that mankind was united, and hence they enjoyed renewed confidence if not in Christianity then at least in the spirit of a Christianity unencumbered by clerical institutions. And finally, they shared a certainty that history revealed its promise through unfolding events. All these elements inspired philosophies of very different sorts, linked, however, by a common antipathy to individualism and fear of its bitter fruits: selfishness, competition, and class division. No longer did anyone believe that the rational calculation of interests or the spontaneous promptings of consciousness could bring about "harmony" among individuals or create "organization" or "association," to use a vocabulary that is simultaneously Saint-Simonian, Fourierist, and Comtist. Despite differences among these various doctrines, all agreed on the difficulty of reconstructing society on the basis of principles that defined individuals in terms of particular spheres of interest— the principles of 1789. All were suspicious of democratic institutions, of a Revolution that had revealed more than anything else a critical disorganization and, in Comte's words, the insurrection of the mind against the heart.

As a result, all tended to emphasize those aspects of the Revolution that could be seen as deprecating individualism and anticipating what Victor Considérant called "the great association of the human family." They were reluctant to admit that man's obligations to other men derived from a contract. They sought to root the Revolution in a principle higher than that of the contract, in a transcendence of an ethical order. Fraternity was to provide them with this principle. It was from the outset a protest against the division of humanity into either classes or races, a powerful repudiation of individualism.

No one expressed this view better than Michelet. The then widely shared horror of social division inspired his choice of fraternity as the central principle of the French Revolution: the Revolution was for him "the unanimous epoch, the holy epoch in which the entire nation, still unaware, or little aware, of class conflict, marched beneath a fraternal flag." His originality lies in his having portrayed this fraternity as an invention of the Revolution. Prior to 1789, however, the world had known fraternity of two kinds: ancient fraternity, which was limited to citizens and excluded slaves, and Christian fraternity, which included slaves and which the French Revolution simultaneously continued and contradicted. The Revolution continued Christian fraternity in the sense that it excluded no individual human being. Yet it contradicted the Christian conception in three ways. First, Christianity rooted fraternity in original sin, in the "heredity of crime," and the significance of the Revolution was precisely to have broken with the hereditary principle. Second, Christianity postponed fraternity to the other life, and the significance of the Revolution was in teaching fraternal equality "as the law here below." And third, Christianity made fraternity dependent on the arbitrariness of grace, and the significance of the Revolution was to do away with favor in all its forms. For all these reasons, the principles of 1789 cannot be derived from the Christian tradition.

Michelet's analysis guides his periodization. The great period of fraternity, in his view, was the period of the federations. For one thing, they were a new religion. For another, they abolished geographical and social divisions: "All division was ended; there was neither nobility nor bourgeoisie nor people." Michelet, in the euphoric enthusiasm inspired by the festival of the Federation, allowed himself a moment's dream: perhaps the social barriers, lowered on the day of the festival, could remain down forever. The Federation was an occasion that would never occur again, for "the proletariat of the cities, which today constitutes an enormous obstacle, did not [then] exist." By choosing the fraternity of the federations, that is, the emergence of a new religion and the disappearance of social antagonisms, as the center of the Revolution, Michelet was also taking on two groups of enemies: Catholics and socialists.

His first enemies were the Catholics, particularly those who wanted to save everything at once—Christianity, a dead system, and the Revolution, a living idea—and who thought liberty was to be found in the Gospel, "that book of resignation, of submission to the powerful." (Michelet remembered his Rousseau.) And his second enemies were the socialists, who saw in the individualism of the Enlightenment a selfish law. Michelet could not accept, could not even understand, this suspicion of subjective law in the socialist tradition: "Fraternity," he wrote in his *Journal*, "is the law above the law." Individualistic justice as he understood it was not a limit on fraternity but a prerequisite. Though subjective, it was the forerunner of fraternity, for "in order to be brothers, it is necessary to exist." What Michelet detested most was of course the conjunction in a single doctrine of both of his adversaries: the "papist socialism," of Louis Blanc or Buchez, who both traced fraternity back to Robespierre if not to Mably and did not hesitate to portray it as a product of coercion. But for Michelet, "if fraternity is written into law and made mandatory, it is no longer fraternal." For him, fraternity vanished the moment coercion entered the Revolution and revived the fraternity of slaves.

By contrast, for Louis Blanc (who nevertheless shared Michelet's admiration for the federations, cradle of the new religion) and for Buchez, the experience of fraternity was concentrated in the Montagnard dictatorship. The Girondins emphasized individual guarantees, the sovereignty of the self. (According to Louis Blanc, the striking thing about the proposed Girondin Constitution was the idea that every man was responsible for his own destiny in his own sphere and without religious support of any kind.) The Montagnards, for their part, emphasized human solidarity, which they consecrated still more by making it depend on the Supreme Being: certain that society was obliged to support its "unfortunate citizens" by securing them work and the means to exist, they understood that "the intervention of an active and just power was required wherever the weak needed protection; the poor, nourishment; or the unfortunate, salvation." For Michelet fraternity realized the law of the Enlightenment, but for Louis Blanc it challenged the formalism of that law. What did the right to move do for a paralytic? Liberty and equality could become positive only by way of fraternity or, better yet, by way of fraternization.

Louis Blanc stopped short of the fraternization of the Terror, a step easily taken by Buchez. If the direction of the Revolution was to proceed through devotion and sacrifice to fraternity, then it had no choice but to "eliminate one by one the obstacles to achieving the national goal." Was it therefore mandatory to approve "the deplorable extremes to which France was obliged to go in order to achieve its salvation?" Surely not, but the responsibility fell on the men of the Constituent Assembly, the Legislative Assembly, the Girondins, and all those who had turned a social form into an "instrument of individual appetites," thereby repudiating fraternity as a principle and a goal. On the other hand, if fraternity was an unconditionally valid ideal, how could one fail to see any progress toward realization of that ideal, whatever the cost, as a victory for humanity? How could one fail to approve of those who sacrificed the present generation to the happiness of future generations? Once one chooses the community rather than the individual as the central moral reference, the very meaning of the Terror changes.

It is striking to find men equally preoccupied with avoiding individualism and equally enamored of fraternity arriving at such different periodizations of the Revolution. Paradoxically, the one who did not conceive of fraternity as a legacy of Christianity saw it at work in the period of revolutionary syncretism. Those who did conceive of it as part of the Christian heritage associated it with the moment when the Revolution broke with Christianity. Ultimately these differences in periodization are related to two different images of fraternity. For Michelet, fraternity was the realization-transcendence of liberty and equality. For Louis Blanc and Buchez it was a protest against them. Michelet accepted the order of the republican motto as the correct order: without the prerequisites of liberty and equality there could be no fraternity. Supported on this point by Proudhon, Michelet honored the Declarations for having made the individual the source of justice, even if true justice lay in the realization of solidarity. For Louis Blanc and Buchez, fraternity was the true source of justice, because it came not from man but from God. Hence the correct order was fraternity, liberty, equality—unless one agreed with Pierre Leroux that fraternity ought to go in the middle, as the affective link between liberty and equality.

The treatment of fraternity by historians of the Revolution helps us to understand better the relation of the republican to the socialist interpretation of the Revolution in the nineteenth century. That relation could at times be one of opposition, at times one of kinship. Opposition came from two quarters. First, those who held a strictly democratic view of the Revolution, such as Etienne Vacherot, objected to the addition of the vague term "fraternity" to the republican motto, for it added nothing to the definition of democracy while raising the threat of a monastic socialism. Second, those who favored a socialist interpretation of the Revolution loved fraternity, which in their eyes challenged and contradicted individualist formalism. But there was also kinship between the republican and socialist views, for fraternity could be interpreted as a process of fermentation that tended to turn individualist law into something else: a guarantee that revolutionary law would apply to all and that the Revolution itself would continue to improve. Anyone who chose to set the two interpretations in opposition was convinced that the Revolution consisted of two antagonistic "acts," as Louis Blanc called them, "the second [of which] was only a violent and terrible yet sublime protest." Anyone who chose to stress the kinship between the two interpretations made fraternity the link that bound the diverse episodes of the Revolution together into a unified whole.

Do the texts that the Revolution devoted to fraternity allow us to choose between those interpretations? Contrary to Vacherot, fraternity was in no sense a superfluous addition. It does appear to derive from considerations of another order than liberty or equality, to belong, as Vergniaud puts it, to the realm of the supernatural rather than the natural. But fraternity is central. Even before Roland welcomed the newly elected conventionnels in September 1792 by telling them that they were about to proclaim the Republic, which was "the same thing as fraternity," Mirabeau in the summer of 1789 saw fraternity as the great revolutionary invention that divided the history of the world into two epochs, before and after: "History has all too often recounted nothing but the actions of ferocious beasts, among whom on rare occasions it recognizes heroes. We have reason to hope that with us begins the history of men, of brothers."

Contrary to Buchez, moreover, revolutionary fraternity was not seen as a repudiation of formal liberties. To be sure, Babeuf wrote that equality was a trap when it was "preached to our penniless, starving brothers" and argued that elimination of individual greed was a prerequisite to fraternity. It is striking, however, that revolutionary measures to secure social rights, such as the assistance workshops, the great work of public benevolence, and Robespierre's proposed tax for the benefit of the underprivileged, were credited not to fraternity but to equality. Article 21 of the declaration appended to the Montagnard Constitution, which defined public assistance as a sacred debt, saw such assistance as a continuation, not a critique, of individual rights. Even the Terror, in the very special meaning it gave to communal bonds of "fraternization-exclusion" forged by means of violence, was in no sense concerned with defining social rights as opposed to political ones. It was the socialists of the nineteenth century who first thought of interpreting revolutionary fraternity as a protest.

Yet that fraternity did indeed contain a principle that pointed up the existence of de facto inequality in legal equality and that held out the promise of a correction. According to Fauchet, a doctrine borrowed from a God who had fraternized with all men could not allow any individual to dominate any other, and Fauchet made it clear that he was talking not about a "tyrant" but about "a rich man, a man with pretentions in the society of his people and in his family of brothers." The word "brothers" introduces a dynamic rectification of the equality of rights. Even the distinction between active and passive citizens, so symbolic of formal law, of bourgeois law, holds out the promise of a universal law, as Jaurès was well aware. In 1790 the *Chronique de Paris* published a letter from Orry de Mauperthuy expressing resignation, owing "to the unformed nature of our societies," to the need to exclude from the franchise "a class of men, our brothers." The word "brothers" is like a magic formula: it connotes the hope that this exclusion "is not eternal but temporary." The lawyer concludes his letter: "Within a few years they will be able to sit with us." In this sense fraternity did not challenge the principle of democracy. On the contrary, it realized that principle, since it refused to imprison the individual in the concrete conditions in which he lived. It postulated the idea of humanity within the idea of individuality, added social rights to individual rights, and inscribed the social revolution in the logic of the political revolution. Revolutionary fraternity, the application of democracy to all of social life, argues for an affinity rather than an antagonism between socialism and democracy.

Mona Ozouf

FURTHER READING

Antoine, Gérard. *Liberté, égalité, fraternité ou les fluctuations d'une devise.* Paris, 1981.

Aulard, Alphonse. "La devise 'Liberté, Egalité, Fraternité,'" *Etudes et leçons sur la Révolution française,* vol. 6. 1910.

Buchez, Philippe, and Prosper-Charles Roux. *Histoire parlementaire de la Révolution française.* Prefaces to vols. 1, 25, and 26. Paris, 1834–1836.

Blanc, Louis. *Histoire de la Révolution française.* 12 vols. Paris, 1847–1862.

David, Marcel. *Fraternité et Révolution française.* Paris, 1987.

Leroux, Pierre. *De l'égalité.* Boussac, 1858.

Michelet, Jules. *Le peuple.* Paris, 1846.

———— *Journal,* ed. Paul Viallaneix, 2 vols. Paris, 1959–1962.

Roberts, John Morris. "Liberté, Egalité, Fraternité: Sources and Development of a Slogan," *Klasse en ideologie in de vrijmetserlarij: Tijschrift voor de studie van de verlichting,* (Brussels), nos. 3–4, 1976.

Vacherot, Etienne. *La démocratie.* Paris, 1860.

RELATED TOPICS

Babeuf	Buchez	Federation	Michelet	Terror
Blanc	Equality	Liberty	Mirabeau	

JACOBINISM

Before becoming a political concept or tradition or state of mind, the word "Jacobinism" evoked the history of a club whose activities, of great importance from the beginning of the Revolution, were so crucial in the period 1792–1794 that the adjective "Jacobin" was applied at the time (and has been applied ever since) to all who supported the dictatorship of public safety. The history of the Jacobins can be divided into three periods, which Michelet characterized in terms of individuals:

> There was the early Jacobinism, parliamentary and aristocratic, of Duport, Barnave, and Lameth, the Jacobinism that killed Mirabeau. There was the mixed Jacobinism of republican journalists and Orleanists—Brissot, Laclos, and so on—over whom Robespierre prevailed. And then, when this second legion somehow melted away in 1792, as its men accepted offices, administrative posts, and missions of various kinds, began the Jacobinism of 1793, that of Couthon, Saint-Just, Dumas, and the like, which consumed Robespierre and itself along with him. (*Histoire de la Révolution française*, book 9, chap. 4)

In fact, the Club faded away after Thermidor, an object of suspicion in the eyes of all the authorities; it was closed down in November 1794.

Its original purpose, when the Club first met in May and June of 1789, was to bring together for private discussions certain members of the Third Estate, initially Bretons, then other "patriots" of no particular geographical origin. The purpose of these discussions was to develop a concerted legislative strategy; in England such a practice had helped to maintain the unity of the Commons and contributed to its victory over the two privileged orders. This Breton Club, as it was then called, moved from Versailles to Paris on October 6, along with the king and the Assembly, and established its meeting place close to the Assembly in the convent of the Jacobins on rue Saint-Honoré. This was the origin of the name "Jacobins," which has become a part of history even though the Club originally was called the Society of Friends of the Constitution, and this remained its name throughout the "constituent" monarchy.

Membership dues were fairly high. Initially almost all the members of the society were deputies. Their purpose was to draft and prepare arguments in favor of proposed provisions of the Constitution of 1791. The Club selected its own members among patriotic bourgeois and liberal nobles prepared to defend the new order without reservation not only against the aristocratic party but also against the risk of escalating revolutionary pressures. Members included the cream of the patriotic party, from Mirabeau to Robespierre, from Lafayette to Pétion, and of course the triumvirs Duport, Barnave, and Alexandre de Lameth. The Club's activities were primarily parliamentary, involving prior discussion of bills to be debated before the Constituent Assembly, although a growing number of nondeputies were admitted as members (often these were future deputies, like Brissot and so many others). Very quickly the club on the rue Saint-Honoré began to serve as a unique sounding board for revolutionary politics, largely because it was at the center of a network of affiliated societies in the provinces, a network provided for under the terms of the Club's regulations: "Only a society with established ties to the National Assembly and including among its members a large number of deputies from different provinces can offer a common center to other societies that may establish themselves throughout the kingdom. It will receive their instructions and convey to them views worked out by combining Enlightenment with interest. Above all, it will convey to them the spirit of the National Assembly's decrees, in the execution of which these societies will be particularly diligent."

Thus the vocation of the Paris Club was to become a mother society. It granted authorized affiliation, for which on occasion more than one club fought in cities such as Bordeaux and Marseilles. This prerogative gave the Jacobins a power of legitimation, the first elements of a power to control. At this stage, however, the rue Saint-Honoré did not exercise any political hegemony over the provincial societies, and orders from Paris had little effect in the provinces. The Paris society would not obtain the power to control its affiliates until after the defeat of the Girondins on May 31, 1793.

Still, it arranged for the possibility of such control very early. By the end of 1790 it had accepted nearly 150 authorized affiliates, unevenly distributed throughout the country but sufficiently numerous to constitute a national network, complete with a *Journal des amis de la constitution* published by Choderlos de Laclos and responsible for communication in both directions between Paris and the provinces. In addition, the most important committee in the Club was the correspondence committee, which was in charge of relations between the mother society and its affiliates. Barnave and his friends quickly took control of this organ. By this time it was clear to everyone that power would be won and lost in Paris, but Paris also needed the support of opinion in the provinces. None of the patriot leaders of the Constituent Assembly neglected to appear at the Club, including Mirabeau, Lafayette, Barnave, and Robespierre. It was at the Jacobins on March 2, 1791, that Alexandre de Lameth destroyed Mirabeau's influence by raising charges that he had colluded with "aristocrats." And it was through the Jacobins in the first half of the same year that the triumvirs Lameth, Barnave, and Duport established their temporary power over Paris and the Revolution.

The king's flight dramatically altered the situation, however. Varennes initiated a governmental crisis that divided the Jacobins. Not that any Jacobin, even Robespierre, was yet calling for a republic. But a rival club, the Cordeliers, encouraged a Parisian movement to overthrow the king, which was harshly put down by the National Guard on July 17. The night before, the Constituent Assembly had officially restored Louis XVI to power, obliterating his attempted escape by giving official sanction to the myth that he had been abducted. By working for passage of this measure, without which all the effort since 1789 to draft a constitution would have been reduced to naught, Barnave adopted as his own the policy of Mirabeau, which he had once so bitterly combated. As a result he was forced to confront the left wing of the Jacobins, which was also the left wing of the Constituent Assembly: Robespierre and Pétion. On the day after the vote, July 16, which was also the day before the fusillade on the Champ de Mars, Barnave walked out of a meeting at the Jacobin Club, taking with him a majority of the members who were also deputies. After the split Barnave and his confederates founded their own Society of Friends of the Constitution, which met nearby at the convent of the Feuillants: different convents, different politics—more moderate and bourgeois, with the goal of ending the Revolution through law. Those who remained at the Jacobin Club, led by Robespierre, had a free hand to move the shrunken club toward an alliance with the Parisian popular movement, provided they could hold on to the network of provincial affiliates.

This they succeeded in doing during the following summer and autumn by capitalizing on the Jacobins' seniority over the Feuillants, making skillful use of the theme of union, and adopting the battle cry of universal suffrage, not previously heard among their slogans, in opposition to the *cens*. The transfer of control of the Jacobin machinery from the hands of the triumvirate to that of the left, including both deputies and activists—Robespierre, Pétion, Condorcet, Brissot—is a little-known yet decisive episode. In the first few weeks after the split, the vast majority of provincial societies sided intellectually with the Feuillants, and Barnave, in notes made a short while later, deplored the fact that the new society had proved incapable of capitalizing on that success for lack of persistence, publicity, and energy in what he called the "correspondence of the Feuillants." By contrast, "the Jacobin Club was still composed of a large number of ardent spirits, mostly journalists or pamphleteers, who staked their reputations and their lives on maintaining their club's credit and assuring its victory." Militants versus parliamentarians: this formula explains how the balance of power shifted over the course of the summer in favor of the older society, which recaptured its audience. Five hundred provincial clubs returned to its orbit, compared with fewer than one hundred for the Feuillants. This reversal was one of the major turning points in the French Revolution, and it came one year before the tenth of August, which was its consecration.

This does not mean, however, that the Jacobins at this point held all power. They had no influence on the Constituent Assembly, which revised its work one last time in a conservative direction. They were only partly successful in the legislative elections of September 1791: their candidates were crushed in Paris, and if they fared better in the provinces, they could nevertheless claim the support of only 150 deputies in the new Assembly (the Feuillants had twice that number). But the Paris society had new leaders and, more than that, a new role. It had changed from a debating society into a political machine geared up to assist a second revolution: all reference to constitutional law was abandoned in August 1791 with the debate on the national conventions.

Thereupon began a new period in the history of the Jacobins, notable for the conquest and then the exercise of power. Annual dues remained relatively high (24 livres), and recruitment, though it increased, still drew mainly on intellectual and bourgeois sources. But now the Club held public meetings, which meant that its deliberations, like those of the Assembly, were subject to harangues and insults from Parisian activists in the galleries. It consolidated its national network under the banner of universal suffrage, seeking to extend its control over opinion to popular societies that were springing up in various places. It strengthened its internal organization by adding a "committee of reports" and a "surveillance committee" to those already in existence. The most important of the Club's internal organs, however, was still the Committee of Correspondence, the heart of the Jacobin apparatus, whose membership now included, among others, Robespierre, Brissot, Carra, Desmoulins, Clavière, Collot d'Herbois, Billaud-Varenne—future Montagnards and future Girondins, future Exagérés and future Indulgents, to say nothing of Robespierrists—in short, the whole future of the Revolution, temporarily unified. The Club's primary purpose was no longer to prepare for debates in the Assembly. It now had a broader vocation: to serve as another Assembly, if need be a counterassembly. The logic of revolution gradually took precedence over the logic of Friends of the Constitution.

From this point on the Jacobin Club was as much the headquarters of the Revolution as the new Assembly, all of whose deputies were new to the national political scene. The great political debates, especially those concerning war and peace, took place just as frequently in the Jacobins' ancient convent as in the Salle du Manège, where the deputies met. At the Jacobin Club Brissot mobilized what would become the Girondin group in support of an emancipatory crusade, while Robespierre, in his hour of greatest solitude, delivered his three major speeches of December 1791 and January 1792 against the war and against his rival. Furthermore, when the war, after a disastrous start, radicalized the Revolution, it was once again the Jacobin Club that found itself in a position to unify and orchestrate the movement of the Paris sections and provincial *fédérés* to depose the king. The legalist line was abandoned once and for all in July in favor of election of a new Constituent Assembly—that is, a Convention, hence a second Revolution.

There is no written evidence that the Club played a direct role in the insurrection of August 10, although such participation, by way of a clandestine directorate, seems plausible: the presence of Jacobin militants in the events of that day is too marked for there to have been no coordination. Jacobins were also stationed at all the command posts after the fall of the Tuileries. But the society's essential contribution was to have been the crucible in which the spirit of August 10 was formed, a compound of broad suspicion and egalitarian utopianism in which we see the hallmark of Robespierrist teaching. What made the Jacobins a dominant power at the moment when the Legislative Assembly was being eclipsed was that they had found a voice—

a voice to which they gave national influence—that of the lawyer from Arras, more teacher than insurgent, but a teacher of insurrection. The spirit of the second Revolution was theirs. They chose the Paris delegation to the Convention. When that delegation was elected in September, the new Constituent Assembly inaugurated the Jacobin period of the French Revolution.

Until May 31, 1793, the Club was the scene of conflict between Girondins and Montagnards, and the provincial affiliates in most of the areas that would later be involved in the federalist revolt were still in the hands of Brissot's allies. The rue Saint-Honoré, however, was entirely controlled by Robespierre after September or October of 1792, and it stood as a sign of what the Jacobins would become in Year II: no longer just a political society but a militia that had found its general and that served the Revolution under his guidance. Rebaptized "Society of Friends of Liberty and Equality" and in control of a network of several thousand provincial clubs, the Jacobins constituted an army of 100,000 to 200,000 militants, the fundamental instrument of the Revolution's rediscovered central power, which from the end of 1791 began to lay siege to the national institutions. France in Year II had no more constitution, and the absence of fixed laws made it clear where real power lay: might made right, and power rested in what it had proved possible to organize, almost to regiment, of the national spirit of 1789.

By 1793, as Michelet saw quite clearly, the popular Revolution had been dead for a long time; the people, he wrote, "had gone home," in the cities as well as in the countryside. The time was ripe for small activist oligarchies, the last representatives of the great tide, who prospered on fear of the guillotine, fatigue with disorder, and the conservatism of the new interests. Among these oligarchies the Jacobins were the most bourgeois, the most national in scope, the best organized, and the best disciplined—infinitely stronger than all those that developed at one time or another to their left under the aegis of egalitarian or antireligious escalation. It was largely through the Jacobins and their work that the leaders of the revolutionary dictatorship were chosen, from the liquidation of the Girondins in the spring of 1793 to that of the Hébertists and Dantonists in the spring of 1794. In "purging elections" the Jacobins determined the losers in advance by denouncing them before the court of public opinion: the Girondins, for example, were in the dock from the spring of 1792 on, when they joined the ministry and thereby made themselves vulnerable to Robespierre's attacks. This "preparation" began to pay off in the fall, or six months before the Girondins' expulsion from the Convention (May 31–June 2, 1793), for Brissot was formally expelled from the Jacobins in October and a circular was sent to all the affiliated societies reconstructing his past in the light of his alleged role as a conspirator and enemy of the people. Of this document Michelet wrote: "Never before did frenzied esprit de corps, monastic fanaticism, or confraternal intoxication, stirred up behind closed doors, building by degrees, proceeding without contradiction from calumny to the limits of absurdity, come up with anything even remotely comparable" (*Histoire de la Révolution française*, book 9, chap. 3).

The expulsion of Brissot is an excellent illustration, among a hundred others one might choose, of the Club's procedures in this period of its history, of which the most profound analysis was no doubt given by Augustin Cochin, following on the work of Michelet. In this period of the Revolution, when people were being deprived of their constitutional rights, the Club became a machine for producing unanimity, a proxy for the popular will. Its orthodoxy sometimes supplanted the suffrage of the sovereign people, sometimes reinforced the results of democratic elections. At times, as on August 10, 1792, or May 31, 1793, the Jacobins encouraged and celebrated intervention by the "people" in the deliberations of their chosen representatives; they saw themselves on such occasions as the sentinels of direct democracy, guardians of the people's inalienable will. At other times, for example in the period from the fall of the Girondins to 9 Thermidor, they stood as uncompromising protectors of the Robespierrist majority in the Convention and of the indivisible sovereignty of the nation's representatives. In either case the Club's purgative function was central: "The people had lost the right to elect its magistrates on lawfully specified dates and in accordance with lawfully specified procedures. The societies assumed the right to purge the legislature lawlessly and continually" (A. Cochin, preface, *Actes du gouvernement révolutionnaire*). An unprecedented form of direct democracy was thus established, in which the Jacobins represented the revolutionary myth of the people: in other words, a people unanimous by definition and therefore subject to constant self-purification designed to eliminate enemies hidden within the body of the sovereign and thus to reestablish an imperiled unity. By definition voting was by raised hands: secrecy only favored conspiracy. Decisions therefore had to be made before the Club met, in discussions among the leaders, and ratified by the fanatic or docile troops. And the provinces followed the lead of the mother society.

In this sense the Jacobins were a far more powerful *corporation* than the Mountain, or left wing of the Convention. True, the outlines of the latter were rather fuzzy, and some Montagnard deputies did not attend meetings in the rue Saint-Honoré. Nevertheless, they shared with the Jacobins an obsesssion with public safety and were equally concerned with building an alliance between the bourgeoisie and the people, though for the most part they avoided partisan fanaticism. The Club was not just the civil army of the Revolution, its secular arm, but also its tribunal and the guardian of orthodoxy, pronouncing excommunication and in due course backing the Terror. In all these ways the identification of the Jacobin Club with Robespierre was foreordained: the lawyer from Arras had a genius for suspicion and abstraction, for tactics and ideology. Though he lacked any taste for direct action, he was unrivaled when it came to behind-the-scenes maneuvering and the propaganda of ideas. In the Jacobin Club he was in his element. In 1793 he reaped the dividends of his long-term investment in the society and his patient efforts to rebuild it in the summer of 1791. He invested his whole being in the Club, which for him was not difficult because he totally identified with it.

The history of the Jacobins from the beginning of the Convention to 9 Thermidor can therefore be written in two distinct yet related ways. One way would be to describe the role played by the society and its militants in the civilian and military policy of public safety in Paris, in the départements, and in the army; this was an essential role, in that Paris' dictatorship over the rest of the country revived the centralization of absolutist government as modified by Year II of the Revolution. The other way would be to study how the society imposed its orthodoxy on the Convention and on revolutionary opinion in general. It was in the Jacobin Club that the king was first tried, and the Gironde, and the enragés, and the Hébertists, and finally the Dantonists. The institutions of the "revolutionary government" did nothing more than enforce, through the handing down of death sentences after several months' delay, the excommunications of the Club. The sovereignty of the people, which for a long time shifted back and forth from the Convention to the Paris sections to the Commune to the Jacobins, ultimately found its most secure refuge in the Club, and for several months after the execution of the Dantonists, from April 1794 until July, it was embodied in the personal dictatorship of the Club's leader.

Robespierre's downfall on 9 Thermidor did not immediately put an end to the society. The victorious Thermidorians, though they detested Robespierre after the fact, had for the most part served him as well, and many remained firm republicans, hostile to any excessive display of "moderatism." Nevertheless, the pressure of public opinion against the Terror and those responsible for it forced the Convention to order the Paris club to be closed down on November 12, 1794. In 1795 another decree ordered that the building known as the Jacobins-Saint-Honoré be turned into a public market, to be called the Market of 9 Thermidor.

After the history of the Jacobins came the history of Jacobinism. At first Jacobinism was a memory, celebrated or detested, standing for the best and the worst of the Revolution. In 1796 Babeuf attempted to mobilize nostalgia for Year II in a conspiracy that was both communist and neo-Jacobin. In that same year Joseph de Maistre brought out his *Considérations sur la France,* which treated the Revolution as a miracle of wickedness and the Jacobins as instruments of God's punishment, rescuers—fundamentally perverse yet rescuers nonetheless—of a France at last prepared for regeneration. Thanks to Jacobinism's ability to embody what was most radical in the Revolution, and therefore to stand for the Revolution itself, it has survived for two centuries as legend, history, tradition, heritage, theory, and practice.

The semantic elasticity of the term in late twentieth-century French politics attests to the work of time. "Jacobinism" or "Jacobin" can now refer to a wide range of predilections: indivisible national sovereignty, a state role in the transformation of society, centralization of the government and bureaucracy, equality among citizens guaranteed by uniformity of the law, regeneration through education in republican schools, or simply an anxious concern for national independence. This vague range of meanings is still dominated, however, by the central figure of a sovereign and indivisible public authority with power over civil society, which is after all rather paradoxical if it is true that the history of the Jacobin Club was one of constant usurpation of the power of a Convention duly invested with the sovereignty of the people by the election of September 1792. Whatever this paradox may say about the weakness of French legal tradition and the ambiguous tyranny of historical memories, it also reflects a sort of bourgeoisification of Jacobinism, which after two centuries has gone from revolutionary patrimony to national property. Having achieved this level of historical dignity, the concept has shed its subversive character along with any semblance of a precise definition. Yet by reminding people of the virtues of a strong state promoting progress and representing the interests of the nation, it has made it possible to link the Jacobin tradition to what came before and after, and thus to stitch back together what the Revolution put asunder. By forming a bridge between the old monarchy and the Napoleonic state, the Jacobin tradition seems to have become part of the family. Thus it has been able to make room for the right while at the same time creating divisions on the left; it can please the Gaullists as well as the communists while sowing dissension among socialists.

Before it became a false beacon, however, Jacobinism in the nineteenth century was a subject of bitter political and intellectual controversy. From the Restoration to the founding of the Third Republic it was to one degree or another part of the baggage of the republican party. Its legacy remained intact: the sovereignty of the people one and indivisible; an all-powerful National Assembly elected by universal suffrage; France as a leader in the emancipation of peoples; hostility to the Catholic Church; the religion of equality; a society—secret or public as the case may be—of professional revolutionaries. But there was also the Terror, inextricably associated with the First Republic and the bloody dictatorship exercised in the name of virtue. As the crystallization of a political tradition, Jacobinism also acted like the pole of a magnet, repelling certain segments of the bourgeoisie and peasantry. If the Parisian Republic also meant the Terror, then liberty would have to seek refuge elsewhere. Such feelings go a long way toward explaining how the Orleanists were able to reap all the benefits from the July Days of 1830, before 1848 revealed to the propertied classes an offspring even more dangerous than Jacobinism, namely socialism.

The idea of socialism or communism, which crops up here and there from the Renaissance onward, in a sense received the confirmation of history from the Revolution and Babeuf. Once the idea of equality is extended to the social and economic sphere, from the citizen to the man, the critique of private property follows. The Jacobins did not follow this logic to the end, restricting themselves to advocating a limit on wealth—a timidity that Babeuf saw as the sign of their failure. Yet he kept faith with the Jacobins' central inspiration by conceiving of his conspiracy in terms of a highly organized group of partisans seizing, as in a military putsch, the centralized state machinery: the Jacobin belief in the omnipotence of politics thus led to the idea of the revolutionary party. The failure of 1796 did not prevent the Babouvist legacy from being passed on to the secret societies of the Restoration, the compost in which the socialist idea developed. Socialism, with its explicit recognition of its Jacobin ancestry, added a new feature to interpretations of the Revolution: a radical critique of 1789. For example, according to the *Histoire parlementaire de la Révolution française* (1834–1848) by Buchez, a Catholic socialist and dissident Saint-Simonian whose book served as the bible of specialists, amateurs, and militant students of the Revolution before Michelet, the Jacobins were harbingers of the socialist community of tomorrow, while 1789 and the Declaration of Rights did nothing more than establish bourgeois individualism, a barely adequate basis for creating a market but not a society.

Thus the unity of the Revolution itself was shattered by this latter-day Jacobinism and cast as a mere prefiguration of an emancipation yet to come: 1789 was relegated to the past, whereas the Jacobins represented the future. Somewhat later Louis Blanc argued that the first French Revolution belonged to Voltaire and the bourgeoisie; the second to Rousseau and the people. This was a post-Jacobin version of the Revolution which, like Buchez's, contradicted point by point the "Eighty-Nineism" of liberal historians of the Restoration such as Guizot and Thiers, who were also the political leaders of the July monarchy. In French socialism this authoritarian and statist tradition was not the only one: Proudhon, for example, opposed Jacobinism by arguing that the realization of equality depended on destruction of the state and promotion of self-management. But it was the dominant tradition and the one that in 1848 exerted the first and most powerful influence on the left, evoking memories of 1793, ghosts that were all the more frightening because they threatened not just liberty but also property. The repression of June put an end to this neo-Jacobin socialism but not to its influence on the urban working class, especially in Paris, or to the great fear that it inspired in the propertied classes and the peasantry. Continuing after June, that fear outlived its object and goes a long way toward explaining why Bonaparte's nephew was elected president on December 10, a preliminary to the coup d'état of December 2, 1851.

Under the Second Empire, a segment of the republican camp, drawing the lesson of the Second Republic's failure, sought to exorcise the ghost of the dictatorial and redistributive Republic: this was the political significance of Edgar Quinet's book on the Revolution. The support offered to the exiled historian writing on the shores of Lake Leman by the young republican lawyer Jules Ferry was quite unambiguous: the critique of Jacobinism and of the Terror was, in the eyes of this future Founding Father of the Third Republic, a prerequisite for achieving a national consensus around the republican idea. In 1871, in the wake of national humiliation born of defeat, socialist neo-Jacobinism was exhumed one last time, along with the Paris Commune and in combination with many other influences. On its ruins Jules Ferry and the "opportunist" republicans would build, with the complicity of the Orleanists, a republic that was much more the heir of 1789 than of 1793.

That is not to say, however, that nothing of the Jacobin legacy was passed on to the Third Republic. If the republicans were obliged to accept an upper house, a senate, they held fast to the idea of an all-powerful sovereign people embodied in the legislature. If they conceded a good deal to an Orleanist philosophy of special interests, they retained two of the ideas of their forebears from the rue Saint-Honoré: priority of the citizen over the private individual and the educational role of the state, hence of state-run schools, in forming the citizen. In other words, the Republic established itself, this time permanently, on an ecumenical version of the Revolution, in which the Jacobin legacy was cleansed of blood and violence but not forgotten, much less dishonored. Now tamed, the Revolution also entered the Sorbonne: Aulard, its first full professor, was the man chosen to sound this keynote.

Turning now from nineteenth-century France and its unrivaled repertory of modern political drama to the twentieth century, we discover the influence of a still more universal Jacobin legacy: the revolutionary party, that offspring of the society of the rue Saint-Honoré. This ancestry has been an obsession of the Bolsheviks ever since the 1903 split in the social-democratic workers' party from which they were born. Accordingly, the history of the Bolsheviks, and of parties of the Bolshevik type, has been the principal example in terms of which the Jacobin precedent has been interpreted in countries where communist or communist-influenced revolutions have taken place: the result is, in many respects, a rainbow of varied appearance, but when looked at from the standpoint of the nature and role of the party, it can be traced to a single source.

That source is the Jacobin Club in its prime, in the days of public safety, the triumph of the Mountain, and the reign of Robespierre. The best way to understand is to begin with Michelet, for it is this most French, indeed at times this most narrowly nationalistic historian of the Revolution who provides the most thorough analysis of what would become most universal in Jacobin democracy. Michelet does not like what he calls the Jacobin "sect"— its fanaticism, its inquisitorial spirit, its devotion to the bitter Robespierre. But he has even less liking for those who would separate it from the Revolution. For him it was the Jacobin sect that substituted itself for the sublime people of 1789—an instrumental and therefore necessary version of the Revolution in a disunited, demoralized, and imperiled nation: "In the absence of a natural association that might have given the Revolution vital unity, an artificial association was needed, a league, a conspiracy that would at least give it a kind of mechanical unity. A political machine was necessary, a great active force, a powerful lever of energy" (*Histoire de la Révolution française,* book 9, chap. 3). The Jacobins were that machine and that energy.

They were a machine that dominated the whole political process, in particular the Convention. Not only did the Club keep a close eye on the election of deputies, to the point of holding elections in Paris in the very hall in which it met; it also judged their behavior and determined in advance who would be excluded. When the Girondins were expelled from the Convention on June 2, Hanriot's cannons were only the Jacobins' secular arm. The Club determined what was true, what was just, what had to be believed—just like a church—and it forced heretics to make public confession before condemning them to *le néant* and sending them to the guillotine. If it changed its mind and contradicted itself, it still had to be believed, for it demanded faith, not reason: "Whatever changes the situation imposed, whatever deviation it required in their doctrine, [the Jacobins] asserted unity." This faith, superior to all circumstances and supposedly necessary and sufficient to overcome them, rested on the identity of the Jacobins and the will of the people, and also on the need for unflagging vigilance to guard against the multifarious aristocratic conspiracy. The Club was the avant-garde of what would soon be the Republic, once the people had been purged of its enemies and turned into equal and virtuous citizens rehabilitated by education and service to the fatherland.

Michelet is here stating two key ideas. He sees the Jacobins, first of all, as a militant oligarchy standing in the place of the people and speaking in its name, a line of analysis that was systematically pursued a half-century later by a historian of another stripe, Augustin Cochin. And that oligarchy, access to which was governed solely by its members, was itself subject to the wishes of its apparatus and leader or leaders—professional politicians, initiates, behind-the-scenes operators. This manipulation of parties by a small number of individuals behind the facade of democracy was also explored by Cochin's contemporaries Ostrogorski and Robert Michels. But the Jacobins in their prime were the prototype of a particular kind of party, in that they were not just a debating society but a temple of orthodoxy. That was the reason for the mandatory unanimity, the pathological suspicion, and the purgative elections. It was also the reason for the Club's obsessive identification with the people, for its disciplining of the people's elected representatives, and for its usurpation of the national sovereignty. Michelet, who had no liking for the Convention's capitulation on June 2, which put an end to what remained of revolutionary public law, saw this reincarnation of clerical fanaticism in the rue Saint-Honoré as a tragedy of the Revolution: a necessary tragedy, but still a tragedy.

Nevertheless, the Jacobin Club had many imitators. In the nineteenth century it was not only one of the legends of the Revolution but also one of the lessons: in every country on the continent of Europe militants joined revolutionary societies in the conviction, part of the Jacobin legacy, that their action could change the world. The era that began in 1815 with the defeat of the French Revolution had already transformed that legacy in two respects: now the societies were underground, doing their work in the darkness of clandestinity, and they were justified on grounds very different from those invoked by the Jacobins in the late eighteenth century. The Revolution had little by little transformed the Jacobins into a fanaticized ruling party, but this evolution was contrary to its principles, which rejected the very notion of a party as an aggregate of special interests standing between the will of the citizen and the sovereignty of the people. The Jacobins were an unforeseen product of the course of the Revolution before becoming, by the force of events, its avant-garde. By contrast, in nineteenth-century Europe the revolutionary party tended to be seen as a prerequisite of revolution; the control over ideas and the public will that the Jacobins had exercised only late in the day was now extended back in time to before the revolutionary event. Paradoxically (the two notions being contradictory), this belief in the demiurgic power of political action was coupled with the idea that history follows an inevitable course, which the action of the party is supposed to facilitate. Political will thus called upon the support of science. The result was an intellectual and political universe very different from that of the French Revolution, but which nevertheless drew its inspiration from that event and saw its model in the Jacobin Club.

On this still largely unexplored itinerary the major milestones were of course Marx and Lenin, the latter being the inventor of Marxism's subjectivist variant. By way of bolshevism the Jacobin party enjoyed an illustrious twentieth century.

François Furet

FURTHER READING

Aulard, Alphonse, ed. *La Société des Jacobins: Recueil de documents pour l'histoire du Club des Jacobins de Paris,* 6 vols. Paris, 1889–1897.

Brinton, Crane. *The Jacobins: An Essay in the New History.* New York, 1930.

Cochin, Augustin. *Les sociétés de pensée et la démocratie moderne.* Paris, 1921.

Kennedy, Michael L. *The Jacobin Clubs in the French Revolution: The First Years.* Princeton, 1982.

Michelet, Jules. *Histoire de la Révolution française,* book 9, chaps. 3 and 4.

RELATED TOPICS

Babeuf	Feuillants	Revolutionary Assemblies
Barnave	Girondins	Revolutionary Government
Blanc	Lafayette	Revolutionary *Journées*
Buchez	Maistre	Robespierre
Clubs and Popular Societies	Marat	Sans-culottes
Committee of Public Safety	Marx	Sovereignty
Condorcet	Michelet	Suffrage
Danton	Montagnards	Terror
Democracy	Quinet	Varennes

LIBERTY

The word "liberty," Turgot observed in 1770, "by itself constitutes the political catechism of a host of people." The eighteenth century was indeed accustomed to thinking of liberty as the touchstone of good government, Hobbes having earlier raised the question of how best to constitute the state so as to maximize the liberty of every individual. Political philosophy offered many answers, all claiming to speak in the name of liberty. Henceforth no polity could be regarded as legitimate that did not claim the consent of its members: Hobbes himself had justified submission with the argument that the best way to preserve the liberty of all was to sacrifice the liberty of each.

The Revolution, in defining itself as a rupture with an Ancien Régime woven of many kinds of servitude, made liberty at once the beginning and the end of its enterprise: the beginning, because the Revolution could not have taken place without independent individuals, cut to the divine pattern and therefore capable of determining their own fate and creating a society by an act of will; and the end, because its ultimate goal was not simply to protect individual liberty from arbitrary power but to help it flourish.

The fate of individual liberty under the Revolution is therefore paradoxical, in light of the slide into despotism that Edgar Quinet described better than anyone else: "There is in these years a miracle that one cannot find anywhere else . . . a golden age written on the threshold; but to put it into practice, there stands, on the other side of the threshold, an implacable Nemesis." At the center of every history of the Revolution is the enigma of a liberty that inaugurated an unprecedented form of despotism. Some blame the abandonment of liberty on powerful but contingent external circumstances and thus dismiss the problem without really confronting it. Others attribute despotic intentions—the ulterior motive that converts liberty to slavery—to the revolutionaries from the very first. Still others tell the story of the Revolution as a drama in two acts, illustrating two antagonistic concepts of liberty drawn from the philosophy of the age: in one, all other ethical ends are subordinated to liberty, the primary good, which can never be renounced; in the other, based on the Aristotelian tradition, human life is governed by a virtuous purpose that justifies beforehand whatever restrictions on liberty may be necessary. Indeed, the men of the Revolution did deduce right sometimes from individual sovereignty (in which case they deemed liberty more desirable than virtue), sometimes from social happiness (in which case they deemed virtue more desirable than liberty). They were also conscious of carrying out two revolutions. Listen to Cambon, speaking in the debate over the

Girondin Constitution: "We did not make the revolution of liberty; we made that of equality, rediscovered beneath the debris of a throne."

This periodization has fared so well in revolutionary historiography because of the simplicity of the design: since the revolutionaries' intellectual baggage contained two different ideas of liberty, they put them to work in two distinct revolutions. But that simple design doesn't really describe what happened at all: the representations of liberty in the century's repository were not that simple; and the phases of the Revolution were not neatly separated, consecutive moments like the rounds in a boxing match.

*
**

The political struggles of the eighteenth century were waged in the name of liberties threatened by absolutism. Liberties, in the plural, had a prestigious pedigree, celebrated by an illustrious literature from Boulainvilliers to Montesquieu. The term "liberties" referred to exemptions, immunities, and privileges enjoyed by communes, orders, universities, corps, and communities under the Ancien Régime. What appeared to guarantee these particular liberties was the division of society into intermediate corps, the hierarchy of ranks, and the multiplicity of traditions, a societal framework of which the nobility saw itself as the natural bulwark. When the provincial assemblies were created, Loménie de Brienne was still defending the separation of orders in the name of these plural liberties, which he held to be consubstantial with the French monarchy (even though the long-term consequences of that monarchy suggested something quite different): "Without this principle of distinction, the provincial assemblies would soon lead either to the liberty of republics (or, what comes to the same thing, anarchy) or to the absolute authority of despots." Between Scylla and Charybdis stretched the land of "honest liberty," in which being free meant enjoying a status that guaranteed independence and traditional protection against abuses of power. Post- and counterrevolutionary thought would make a great deal of such "concrete" liberties, which applied not to abstract states but to actual individuals integrated into vital communities.

The hotbed of these aristocratic liberties was thus diversity, which Montesquieu found in English institutions and mores. On the one hand, chronic conflict between king, Lords, and Commons, the perpetual oscillation of force and counterforce, protected individuals from arbitrary encroachment. On the other hand, the plurality of individual interests and passions that prospered in a commercial society prevented any one interest or passion from gaining supremacy. Powers, interests, and passions held one another in check, and in that impediment liberty found its opportunity. In a complicated regime where all parties were obliged to enter into "compromises, negotiations, [and] accommodations," there was no assurance that liberty would flourish, but at least one could be certain that it would not be stifled. In light of that beneficial neutralization of one power by another, it was, on the contrary, the simplicity of a regime that posed a threat to individual security.

Despite the enormous success of *L'esprit des lois,* Montesquieu's ingenious machinery of counterforces encountered a great deal of resistance in French political thought. Accepting it also implied embracing an idea more detested than any other by men who wished to establish a rational politics: that privilege, consecrated by tradition, was the instrument of liberty. The economists (whose taste for liberty Tocqueville questioned, as he questioned that of French society generally) hated the idea of counterforces and saw diversity as a source of war or paralysis. From Hobbes, whose doctrine was worked out in response to the horror of civil war, Mably and Rousseau took the idea that government is best when sovereignty is vested in a single individual, because such a regime creates unity out of the dangerous pullulation of individual opinions. Everyone believed that citizens drew their liberty not from the dust of individual statuses, nor from the dense thicket of custom, but from a unity based on identical rights and general rules. Despite individual disagreements there was general agreement on the distinction between aristocratic liberty, the "English" form of liberty that could be defined without reference to equality, and "French" liberty, based on a certainty that if reasonable individuals reflect sufficiently on the same political problem, they will all want the same thing. Thus liberty born of extreme dissimilarity was opposed to liberty born of extreme similarity of conditions.

Another important dichotomy divides eighteenth-century conceptions of liberty. Eighteenth-century definitions of liberty are generally interpreted as negative definitions: to be free is not to be prevented from pursuing chosen goals, not to be subject to constraints. Philosophers are divided on the range of constraints to be included in such a definition (Hobbes limits his to physical constraints, or impediments to action, but others include internal constraints, encompassing custom and habit). Yet all agree on one crucial point: that men's negative ends sufficed to establish the social contract. Whether it is a question of avoiding death, as for Hobbes, or hunger, as for Locke, eighteenth-century political philosophy erects its systems on the most naked and prosaic of human realities: the instinct of self-preservation. Since the liberty of each individual comes from his capacity not to pursue a positive goal but to escape coercion by others, the law's only function is to guarantee that individual independence. Good government is in no way concerned with the ends of the community: its only mission is to safeguard a neutral space. It is satisfied with preventing intrusion into a territory whose occupants live as they please. To disarm coercion is to arm liberty.

Criticism of this negative liberty, of this social bond forged out of the fear of death, flourished after the Revolution. Philosophers tirelessly denounced its consequences: selfishness, weakness, apathy toward public life. But even before the Revolution one senses such criticisms already present and active in the work of philosophers for whom liberty—that means of fulfilling human resources—entailed an involvement in public affairs and constant, direct, and intense participation in the life of the city. The ancient ideal of liberty—the image of man as a political animal whose nature can be fully realized only through public activity—rivaled the image of liberty as independence. It can be found in Mably, who believed that liberty was not secure unless the people saw to their own affairs, and in Rousseau, who defined liberty as uninterrupted participation in the general will. Both thinkers were a long way from basing liberty on the absence of impediments to desire. They saw it as dependent on the capacity to work for the common good, to which all individual independence had to be sacrificed, and argued that this positive liberty encouraged individuals, like the citizens of antiquity, to pursue goals nobler than self-interest. It was a liberty of warriors rather than a liberty of proprietors, a heroic liberty rather than a quaking liberty of self-preservation.

Liberties versus liberty; liberty rooted in complexity versus liberty unfolded in unity; liberty as pure absence of coercion versus liberty as positive activity: this series of dichotomies suggests the existence, on the eve of the Revolution, of a clear-cut antagonism between an archaic concept of liberty that postulates an objective representation of human happiness, and a modern concept comprising no such postulate. In reality, however, things were not that simple. On the one hand, some proponents of negative liberty (such as Locke) conceded that since men are creatures of God, human liberty consists in an absence of impediments to action, but action shaped by divine purpose; in other words, the content of action matters as much as the form, and the social contract is not purely negative. On the other, the champions of positive liberty did not find it easy to set aside the independent individual, with which they had begun. Rousseau continued to believe that individual desires are irrepressible. The path from one form of liberty to the other is clear; one had only to assume that it might be useful, in order to throw off constraints, for men to join together in collective action. Negative liberty then became an object of positive will.

It was easy to move back and forth between liberty born of complexity and liberty born of unity. Which was better? The complex forms, Hume wrote in a letter to Montesquieu, were subject to disruption by the "opposition of parties," and plurality then ceased to be an unalloyed good. As for the simple forms, none was as simple as it seemed: even absolute monarchy was tempered by custom, sentiment, and example, to say nothing of the fact that commerce among modern nations tended to create similarity everywhere. Hence the question of the proper form of government was one that the eighteenth century did not settle; not even Montesquieu, much less Hume, believed that one could draw a simple contrast between French subjugation and English liberty. On the other side, even Rousseau had his moments of indulgence toward the English government. Leaving aside extreme forms of government—notably, Montesquieu's despotism—all governments are capable of embracing liberty and subjugation. It was the revolutionaries who made the form of government a crucial issue; philosophy had left the debate open.

This tension between natural-law and ancient-law concepts, between liberties and liberty, between the abstract individual and the social being, was the legacy with which the Revolution was faced. Sometimes it seemed to make a definitive choice, while at other times it wavered, constantly exploring contradictory possibilities.

*
**

The Constituent Assembly, which resounded with protests against the Ancien Régime's "abuses" (the very word epitomizing the horror that violations of individual liberty inspired in the minds of the deputies), opted unambiguously for individual independence. First, it made public liberty a subordinate consideration; the aim of political association, according to article 2 of the Declaration, was to preserve man's natural and inalienable rights. Here, liberty is the primary good, prior to law, which can only be its guarantee. "The public," said Sieyès, "expresses itself poorly when it demands a law granting or authorizing freedom of the press. It is not by virtue of a law that citizens think, speak, and write, but by virtue of their natural rights." Second, in order to protect liberty, and obsessed as it was with the dispersal of power, the Assembly unanimously adopted article 16, which states that any society in which the separation of powers is not guaranteed "has no constitution." This insistence on separation of powers more than anything else reveals the Assembly's extreme distrust of the executive, whose vocation, according to Barère, was to hinder the legislative power in any way it could. This can be seen with particular clarity in the lengthy debate, lasting through two whole sessions, over the appointment of judges by the king. Despite the arguments of Maury, Mirabeau, and Cazalès, the Assembly rejected this proposal in the name of an independent magistracy and of the concept of liberty as protection: "The laws," said Roederer, "cannot protect men unless they themselves enjoy certain protection."

Rémusat, commenting in later years on the new institutions, observed that "they were all born of a negative need for protection against arbitrary rule." The Constituent Assembly set out to eliminate systematically anything that might impede free individual expression: religious orders or corporations and all private organizations in which men banded together "in the name of their so-called common interests" were seen by the deputies as erecting a much-feared screen between the individual interest and the general interest. They refused to see that in the destruction of such intermediate groups, which served to "mitigate despotism," there was, as Burke clearly understood, an opening for arbitrary government, or, as Mirabeau argued, simply for authority. Even the limited suffrage system, which eliminated the unpropertied from the body politic, illustrates the deputies' aversion to individual dependence: for them, ownership of property was the prerequisite for independence and for a claim on the title of citizen.

This powerful conviction—that protection of individual independence provided a principle sufficient to organize a society—ensured that the historic plural, "liberties," would soon be vanquished by the abstract singular, "liberty." For the Constituent Assembly, liberty was a singular, universal principle, always assumed and not needing any concrete formulation. When Grégoire spoke on September 27, 1789, in favor of the colored, he shouted: "Are they free? Prove that they aren't!" Whatever conflicted with liberty required explicit proof. There was no need, according to Sieyès, to enumerate its titles: "Otherwise liberty would be no more than a fund of abstractions, whose key the legislator had kept for himself in order to let out little bits and pieces from time to time."

Note, however, that the assertion of liberty-as-independence prior to any law was expressed primarily in opposition to the detested past, the Ancien Régime, as a guarantee against despotic tendencies in the monarchy that had had to be preserved. In relation to the present, the Revolution, things were somewhat different. Natural rights were still inalienable. But, first of all, it was left up to the legislature to judge the exercise and extent of those rights—an ambiguity that, in the absence of any higher standard, allowed considerable latitude. In addition, natural rights could be outweighed by collective necessities: "The laws of equality and liberty," Mirabeau said on June 28, 1790, "prohibit any exclusive regime, unless an overriding public interest imperiously requires the contrary." From the earliest days of the Constituent Assembly, moreover, the same Mirabeau had observed that the further the deputies proceeded with the drafting of the Declaration of Rights, the further they seemed to depart from the course they had dreamt of. Public liberty also had to be guaranteed, even if it took second place to natural rights. But the moment attention shifted from free natural man to man "bound by the civil state," it almost always became necessary to substitute "duties" for "rights." This shift led to precautionary measures, to conditions on or even violations of liberty.

The distinction between the "man of nature" and "man of the civil state" crops up at all the key points in the history of the Constituent Assembly. It can be seen in the debate on the Civil Constitution: the appropriation of clerical property was a clear violation of the right of property, which the physiocrats had declared to be essential and natural, prior to the social state. But, Barnave pointed out, although each individual, *qua* man, enjoyed total liberty, as citizen that same individual had obligations: "When society needs each person's strength and assistance, you must do all that it is your duty to do in critical times." The distinction also figured in the debate on freedom of the press; those who favored free exchange of opinions as a primary liberty protested against regulation of that liberty in the name of public order (for they were afraid of never being able to distinguish between "a regulation and the most odious inquisition"), but they lost when a new idea appeared on the scene: that there was nothing wrong with disarming the enemies of the Revolution. And the distinction came up again in the remarkably revealing debate on the freedom to emigrate, which took place in February 1791 after the departure of the king's aunts: was there a more inalienable right than the freedom to come and go, "to choose one's gods and one's friends," as Barère put it? But the same Barère stated with unmatched clarity the problem of liberty in extraordinary times: "In such times, who could doubt that the nation might temporarily suspend the natural liberty of citizens to leave the kingdom?" When Cazalès protested, Barnave, too, firmly reminded him of the vast difference between the rights of man and the rights of the citizen.

It is therefore impossible to agree with Auguste Comte's charge that the Constituent Assembly generalized the principle of liberty to the point of anarchy. The deputies very quickly gave up on the idea of a purely negative liberty. They admitted that liberty does not exist if there is no positive way of expressing it, for otherwise they would have had to concede that there was freedom under the Ancien Régime, "under the despot's brazen rod and the cenobite's frock." Duport in May 1791 declared that it was impossible to define liberty as an absolute and personal good with no relation "to our neighbors and fellow citizens." The Constituent Assembly made liberty subordinate to equality: "A society," said Sieyès, "in which one man could be more or less free than another would surely be an ill ordered society; it would cease to be free and would be in need of reconstitution." Liberty was made secondary to equality not only before the law but in the making of the law, and the Declaration contains language concerning the participation of citizens in the work of the legislature. Thus the individual was evicted from the fortress of liberty (conceived as independence) and made to take part in public life. The deputies bestowed upon the citizen the gift of a new liberty, a liberty of participation for the public good. "Public utility," that supreme good, not yet cast in the fully systematic form of "public safety," justified and absolved all violations of individualist principles by the Constituent Assembly: "The fatherland is awakening," said Barère, "the salvation of the people is becoming the supreme law. Before it the rights of man bow respectfully." Thus the Constituent Assembly did more than anticipate the Jacobin conception of liberty; the history of its own violations of principle militates against a rigid division of the Revolution into two antagonistic periods.

One cannot speak, however, of defeat of the individualist principle by the statist principle. The two grew up together, as Mirabeau knew full well: elimination of the intermediate corps left only individuals to face the state alone. The Constituents' concept of law promised two benefits: to protect the state from challenge by citizens by silencing special interests, and to protect the citizen from encroachment by the state by preventing arbitrary interventions. By invoking unchallengeable principles as the basis of citizens' claims on the state and of the state's powers of intervention, the deputies struggled valiantly to demonstrate that state power and liberty are compatible. But they remained fully aware of the difficulty of the task and continually pondered the soundness of their circumstantial case. During the debate on the liberty to emigrate, Gensonné asked whether one could reason "in the name of Salvation of the people and fatality of circumstances," these being the very terms in which the massacres of Saint Bartholomew's Day had long been justified. The minute the "conditions of liberty" were abandoned, one was lost. Continuing the argument, Darnaudet said: "A circumstantial law is being proposed. . . . Once one enters the realm of circumstances, what is needed, what is being asked for, is a dictatorship."

For all the throbbing discomforts of these debates, however, there was one balm: Rousseau. The deputies constantly reminded one another that in entering the social state the individual sacrificed his rights (but was compensated a hundredfold for what he gave up). No room was left in the social contract for rights, which ran counter to the very purpose of a social compact, namely, to set the common interest in opposition to all special interests. Hence no individual resistance to the law was thinkable, since legislation never pertained to any particular object but only to the general interest, and whatever was in the general interest was also an aspiration of every individual. Henceforth individual aspirations would be fulfilled within the state, to which it was therefore no longer possible to oppose the principle of inalienable rights.

Had the citizen lost all liberty in the process? Not if one accepts the argument that man's liberty consists precisely in his strange capacity to denature himself, to transform himself from man into citizen.

In view of these difficulties in coming to terms with the idea of liberty, Jacobinism cannot be seen as an altogether unpredictable swerve into tyranny. The Jacobins did not invent the contradictions in the Declaration of Rights but brought to a head the incompatibility between natural rights and the general will. Nor did they invent the phrases often cited to sum up those contradictions, like the famous "no liberty for the enemies of liberty." These notions already shaped the Constituent Assembly's debates. Nevertheless, it is correct to say that "circumstances"—henceforth referred to collectively as "the war," a word that conjured up the powerful image of French soil under threat or invaded by enemies—expanded and reinforced the logic of public safety. The public safety argument was expanded because the war transformed occasional adversaries of the new order, against whom one might take limited coercive measures unlikely to pose a dire threat to liberty, into traitors alien to the fatherland, ever rising from their own ashes. Exceptional circumstances that had been thought of as merely inopportune but temporary disturbances in the Revolution's course now were identified with the Revolution itself. The public safety argument was reinforced because henceforth no special interest could raise a challenge to the interest of the nation under siege without being accused of treason. Violation of principles now became the norm. The veil, once transparent, that the Constituent Assembly had been forced to draw over liberty, now became—the metaphors are Camille Desmoulin's—a shroud. The whole Revolution had become an exception, and so great was the distance between ordinary and extraordinary times that it became justifiable, for reasons of state, to suspend the rights of man. No one put it better than Robespierre: "Under the constitutional regime it is more or less sufficient to protect individuals from the abuses of public power; under the revolutionary regime the same public power is obliged to defend itself against all the factions that attack it." This defense justified every kind of coercion: censorship of press and theater, arbitrary imprisonment, expulsion of deputies from the National Convention, and even (in a measure that flew in the face of all the century's accomplishments and flouted the reform—the Constituent Assembly's crowning achievement—that had severed the administration of justice from the political authorities) refusal to present persons arrested with a written indictment since, as Robespierre phrased it, the evidence against them was "public knowledge and in the hearts of all outraged citizens."

Jacobinism thus crossed the line that the Constituent Assembly had hesitated to transgress. Not that the Jacobins had ceased to invoke individualist principles; when they defined legitimate government, they still saw it as the product of a free association of individuals defining the general will and still saw its purpose, according to the article that begins the Montagnard Constitution of Year I, as a guarantee of natural rights. But in order to counteract the newly forged unity of the enemies of the Revolution, they created the fiction of a united people wholly at one with its government. This mythical unity, the rotten fruit of Rousseauism, vital to the Jacobin regime, proved fatal to liberty as independence. The allegedly unified voice of the people and the government disguised the fact that power was in fact exercised, controlled, even seized by a governing "people" quite different from the governed one. Under this regime individuals were more radically powerless than under any other, because the constraints that bound them were supposed to emanate from themselves. Since the myth was that the people decided, opposition ceased to make sense. To have an opposition party, as in England, would according to Robespierre be proof that despotism had triumphed (since "there is opposition to patriotism"), that the majority was corrupt (since "there is opposition to the minority"). To admit that "men equally devoted to the public good could be divided" was something so far beyond the realm of possibility that, when Léonard Bourdon imprudently suggested as much, Robespierre was moved to turn against him the very word "Mountain," which in theory the Incorruptible ought to have cherished: "There should be no Mountain where a pure people reigns."

Opposition to this unified people could come, Chabot explained, from "only one party, the party of intrigue," and any explicit opposition was necessarily criminal (not only from parties but also from groups of friends, the principal charge against the Girondins having been defined as friendly conspiracy). Even implicit opposition—including mental reservations, a form of liberty-independence of which the Constituent Assembly had said no one could be deprived—was condemned as a challenge to the priority of public life over private life. Hence there was no more private sphere, no zone about which the law was silent. Even voting was public, since anyone who wished for the good of all had nothing to hide. Gone were Sundays and holidays, henceforth to be devoted to the exercise of citizenship. Gone was the possibility of retreating into privacy; as Robespierre said in his last, dramatic speech, the minute the people returned to its private abodes, "intriguers reemerged, and charlatans resumed their roles."

Since no one who shared this pessimistic view had forgotten the strength of private interests that tended to draw people back to their selfish ways, the problem was not simply to keep the people united but also to shape it, to "recreate," in Billaud-Varenne's striking formulation, "the people whom one hopes to restore to liberty." A purposeful, painstaking pedagogy thus invaded both public and private spheres. The manner of public greeting, the wearing of the cockade, dress, use of the familiar *tu*, the way to choose friends and, at Saint-Just's insistence, to end friendships: all these were matters for legislation. Liberty, far from being a prior good that had only to be declared, now became the object of the will of the legislator, who was responsible, again in Saint-Just's words, for "making men what he wants them to be." Robespierre, in making virtue the condition of liberty, as usual deserves credit for having stated the fundamental point with exemplary clarity; ethical standards, from which natural law had freed itself, reasserted their primacy. Jacobinism thus revived the old theological problem of "indifferent actions" only to conclude that there aren't any.

Instead of negative liberty, which assigns man no particular purpose, the Jacobins proposed a liberty dependent on virtuous actions. Instead of a free association of independent individuals, who exist prior to any form of society, the social bond always and everywhere took precedence over individualities. Instead of the liberty of the moderns, the Jacobins proposed the militant, committed liberty of the ancients. Their consistency must be given its due. Although they continued to invoke liberty in paradoxical and feverish terms (the "despotism of liberty"), they by no means camouflaged the reign of the extraordinary. They opposed the liberty of the constitution to the liberty of the Revolution: "The Constitution," Saint-Just said, "is the reign of triumphant and tranquil liberty. The Revolution is liberty's war against its enemies."

In the stupefied silence of the Terror, Thermidor burst forth like an explosion of liberty: the "tyrant's" fall was hailed as liberty's triumph, and the date of the event was henceforth commemorated annually as the festival of Liberty. Evidence of this explosion can be seen in the flood of brochures and broadsides as the press, in the words of Pastoret, was rescued from "its role as customs agent"; in the revival of boisterous criticism and seditious song in the streets and theaters; in the unlocking of prison gates; and in official declarations calling for restoration of the influence of letters, the freedom of commerce, and the confidence of citizens. All these things, along with the balls, the passions, the intrigue, the frivolity, the gaiety and enthusiasm for life, characterize the image of the Thermidorian Convention and the Directory as it has been fixed by history. In this latest episode the Revolution bade farewell to its unnatural effort to unify the body politic, abandoned an exhausting and heroic way of life, and restored liberty-as-independence—the security of persons and property—with a sigh of relief.

This existential relief was later elaborated intellectually in a series of repudiations and ruptures within the revolutionary legacy. There was first a rupture with Sieyès' dogma of unlimited popular sovereignty, which had attempted to protect individual liberty from the despotism of the supposedly general will by insisting that that will be interpreted not by the represented but by enlightened representatives, divided into separate bodies and monitored by a special jury; this representation was a way of instituting the kind of supralegislative authority that the Constituent Assembly had so sorely lacked. Also repudiated was the idea of a teleology leading to happiness. Without such an idea, no sacrifice of liberty was justifiable, since perfection could not be achieved in this world. The idea of a contract by which men surrendered all their rights to the community was also challenged. So was the idea that it was the mission of government to achieve liberty; the social reasserted its priority over the political.

Finally, an important distinction was introduced—which specifically bore the stamp of Benjamin Constant—between two forms of liberty. Writing during the Directory, Constant first attempted to explain the tyrannical swerve of the Revolution by suggesting an imbalance between the course of events and the state of opinion. In his view of history, drawn largely from Necker and from Scottish philosophy, public opinion explained the working of modern institutions. Public opinion had favored representative government, but in 1792 and 1793 it was pushed much further than it wished to go, to the point of instituting a republic and popular government; hence opinion had had to be restrained by terror. Once the Terror was defeated, there arose a new risk of "reaction," with the danger of restoring a form of government that would fall far short of what public opinion had wanted in 1789 or even of returning to the Ancien Régime. Admittedly this interpretation is not notable for its consistency, since "opinion" is presented sometimes in the guise of historical necessity, sometimes as a way of escaping from that necessity. But it made it possible to put a decent *juste-milieu* face on the Republic, and it deprived the Terror of the excuse of having been indispensable to the salvation of the country. Somewhat later, a few months after 18 Brumaire, Mme. de Staël in *Des circonstances actuelles* was the first to suggest that the Terror could be explained by the revolutionaries' failure to distinguish between modern liberty and ancient liberty; Constant would give this intuition a more systematic form in 1815, but he surely shared it in 1799, since he read and corrected Mme. de Staël's manuscript prior to its publication.

Distinguishing between the two forms of liberty, Constant associates each with a particular moment in history. The age of ancient liberty—the liberty of small communities in which slave labor allowed citizens to engage in full-time civic activity—was over. The age of modern liberty—a liberty suited to commercial and manufacturing societies, based on independence and allowing room for private pleasures—had begun. This distinction offered two important advantages: it made it possible to explain the failure of the revolutionaries (who mistook one era for another) while preserving the gains of 1789 (since the revolutionaries were not mistaken about principles). Revolutionary liberty failed not because its ideas were wrong but because the means used to achieve it were anachronistic. Once that anachronism was analyzed and eliminated, modern liberty would remain, an unstoppable movement, as irreversible as the Revolution itself.

It would be a mistake to conclude, however, that Thermidor unambiguously restored the negative liberty of the preceding century, free of any association with virtue. Neither existential liberation nor intellectual liberalism completely severed the Thermidorians' ties to the activist, unanimist mythology of the Revolution. They could not resign themselves to allowing complete freedom of the press, despite all the speeches about the horrors of tyranny and all the demands that liberty not be postponed any longer. They clung to a limited liberty, invoking an already much-used argument that Louvet would develop: liberty would favor the enemies of the Revolution, and furthermore, why should there be total liberty in society when no such thing existed in nature? One has the sense that these men simply could not accept full liberalization in the political sphere because they were still obsessed with the belief that a divided public opinion is inevitably deleterious. They may have wished for liberty, but they had not repudiated the image, and the hope, of a lawmaker who would have sufficient authority to unify a diverse and refractory reality.

Their solution to this dilemma is well known: education. Since it was still too early to trust in the spontaneous liberty of individuals but too late to rule by force, the only alternative was to educate people for liberty—out of which theory grew the Thermidorian era's excessive concern with education. This obsession shows that men who had just renounced the violence of the guillotine were still unable to trust in anything other than the tempered violence of education. But it also shows that they had not given up on the program they had drawn from Rousseau and the physiocrats. Despite others' advice to leave society to its own devices, they still had little faith in the free play of individual interests and continued to rely on a virtuous will to organize and discipline the social realm. In short, they continued to exhibit a trait that would survive them in French history and politics, in their continued search for a rational politics.

Mona Ozouf

FURTHER READING

Belin, Jean. *La logique d'une idée-force: L'idée d'utilité sociale pendant la Révolution française, 1789–1792*. Paris, 1939.
————— *Les démarches de la pensée sociale d'après les textes inédits de la période révolutionnaire*. Paris, 1939.
Berlin, Isaiah. *Two Concepts of Liberty*. Oxford, 1958.
Constant, Benjamin. *Des réactions politiques*. N.p., 1797. Reprinted in Constant, *Ecrits et discours politiques*, vol. 1. Paris, 1964.
Duclos, Pierre. *La notion de Constitution dans l'oeuvre de l'Assemblée Constituante de 1789*. Paris, 1932.
Manent, Pierre. *Histoire intellectuelle du libéralisme: Dix leçons*. Paris, 1987.
Martin, Kingsley. *The Rise of French Liberal Thought: A Study of Political Ideas from Bayle to Condorcet*. New York, 1954.
Sagnac, Philippe. *La législation civile de la Révolution francaise, 1789–1804*. Paris, 1898.
Skinner, Quentin. "English Liberty," lectures at the Institut Raymond-Aron, Ecole des Hautes Etudes en Sciences Sociales, Paris, spring 1987.

RELATED TOPICS

MONTESQUIEU

The Revolution is sometimes portrayed as a clash between the disciples of Montesquieu and the disciples of Rousseau, generally in order to draw the conclusion that Rousseau's influence outweighed Montesquieu's. *De l'esprit des lois* had shed light on the "necessary relations" between a people's natural situation and its history, and Montesquieu advised the "legislator" to ensure that institutions were suited to their circumstances. By contrast, the Revolution's voluntarism and determination to derive its institutions solely from principles of "what ought to be" identified it with the legacy of Rousseau. Montesquieu praised commerce because it "heals destructive prejudices," makes manners milder, and brings peace. The Revolution, particularly from 1792 to 1794, favored the austere and virtuous republic extolled by Rousseau. In addition, Montesquieu's liberalism, his support for separation of powers, is often contrasted with Rousseau's belief in indivisible sovereignty and the supremacy of the legislative power. The predominance of the legislative over the executive branch, which persisted throughout the Revolution and formed the principle of its constitutions, was, we are told, a consequence of Rousseau's influence.

This model offers a pleasing simplicity. Though valid in certain respects, it also obscures certain important points or makes them unintelligible. By simply comparing the respective strengths of two champions, as in a prize fight, one runs the risk of missing exactly how their influence worked and where it was rejected. Montesquieu no doubt played a less important role in the Revolution than Rousseau, but he did have a role, and our problem is to determine exactly what it was.

It is true that Montesquieu was in large part discredited at the beginning of the Revolution because he was seen as a writer who had justified everything, whose thought was concerned with "what is" rather than "what ought to be." This accusation was made by Mirabeau, Daunou (in the *Contrat social des français*), and even Mounier, who in September 1789 wrote: "Montesquieu's *Esprit des lois* is at this moment doing the greatest harm to liberty. Not enough attention has been paid to the fact that this writer, in seeking the spirit of institutions, always attempted to justify whatever he found established. He gave despots lessons on how to increase their power, just as he gave free peoples lessons on how to preserve themselves from servitude."

This judgment is all the more significant of the prevailing state of opinion in 1789 because it was expressed by a monarchien, a proponent of the English system that Montesquieu had praised. It explains why Mounier, unlike certain of his monarchien allies such as Lally-Tollendal and Clermont-Tonnerre, did not refer to Montesquieu in his speeches in the fall of 1789. Yet everyone in the Assembly knew, as Barnave observed, that Montesquieu was the "favorite authority" of proponents of the royal veto and the second chamber.

This critique of Montesquieu stemmed primarily from a political rationalism according to which the good is both knowable and everywhere identical. The task of the legislator is therefore to discover that good and make it a reality, not to fashion institutions suited to the circumstances in which he happens to find himself. Commenting on the passage in *L'esprit des lois* where Montesquieu criticizes the idea of uniformity in legislative matters, Condorcet wrote in 1780: "Since truth, reason, justice, the rights of men, the property interest, liberty, and security are the same everywhere, it is hard to see why all the provinces of a particular state or even all states ought not to have the same criminal laws, the same civil laws, the same commercial laws, and so on. A good law ought to be good for all men, just as a true proposition is true for all." To the legislator, Montesquieu recommended moderation; Condorcet replied: "By spirit of moderation, might not Montesquieu mean that spirit of uncertainty that for a hundred petty reasons denatures the invariable principles of justice?" Rejection of moderation was characteristic of the spirit of 1789. It was expressed in many different ways by Sieyès. Although he does not refer to Montesquieu, Sieyès' point of view is similar to that of Condorcet: in politics the truth is one. In *Qu'est-ce que le Tiers Etat?* he wrote: "Everywhere I meet moderate people who would like to proceed toward the truth one step at a time.... People are a little too ready to believe that the truth can be divided into parts and be absorbed by the mind piecemeal rather than whole. No. Usually it takes several good shocks; all the light of truth is not too much to produce those strong impressions out of which grows a passionate interest in what one has recognized as true, good, and useful."

In Montesquieu's terms, however, moderation does not mean pure relativism and neglect of the universal. *L'esprit des lois* is thoroughly imbued with a hostility to despotism that is based on reason, even if Montesquieu takes the position that despotism, too, is explicable. Furthermore, throughout the Revolution there was never a time when Montesquieu was not seen as an enemy of despotism. Marat wrote in 1789 that Montesquieu was the first "to disarm superstition ... to demand the rights of man and to attack tyranny." Surprising as it may seem, Marat also wrote in 1785 an *Eloge de Montesquieu,* and his admiration for the author of *L'esprit des lois* apparently never wavered. Other writers, including Mercier, Brissot, and Saint-Just, cited Montesquieu approvingly. Clearly, then, even during the Revolution, Montesquieu was seen not solely as an author who justified everything but also as an adversary of despotism.

The revolutionaries never managed to join both aspects of Montesquieu's project—to understand all regimes, including the despotic, by rational means and to give rational grounds for rejecting despotism—into a coherent perception of his work. At times they saw one aspect, at times the other. At a deeper level, they failed to comprehend, or refused to accept, the dominant idea of *L'esprit des lois* and the ultimate ground of the theory of moderation in making laws. According to Montesquieu, reason shows that there is one political evil (despotism) but several political goods (moderate monarchy, republican government—especially of the commercial variety— and the English regime). Political good is neither totally indeterminate (since there is an evil) nor totally determinate (since several different regimes are good); it is relatively indeterminate. In view of this relative indeterminacy, Montesquieu can advise the legislator both to adapt institutions to specific circumstances (since he may choose among several goods) and to pursue a universal goal (by opposing despotism). Montesquieu's moderation is in the final analysis rather like Aristotle's prudence: a virtue that makes it possible to work toward universal goals in a world characterized by relative indeterminacy. But for Montesquieu relative indeterminacy does not rest on the same foundation as for Aristotle: it derives not from the contingency of the material world but from the liberty of man. The consequences for action are the same for both authors, however: ordered, rational action toward universal ends is possible in an indeterminate world, because the indeterminacy of the world is only relative. The French revolutionaries, of whom Condorcet may here be taken as a representative type, rejected this prudential rationality couched in the modern form of a theory of moderation. In this opposition the Revolution marks not the triumph of reason over relativism but the victory of one form of rationality over another.

In the history of ideas the opposition between virtue and commerce is today seen as the central issue in one of the greatest controversies in eighteenth-century political thought. Some authors praised republican virtue, which demanded of individuals that they devote themselves to the public good and renounce their private interests; others saw commerce and the free play of individual interests as the foundation of a free and prosperous society. The images of Sparta and Rome were opposed to that of the commercial England that grew up in the wake of the Glorious Revolution. Montesquieu is generally numbered among the proponents of commerce. Unfortunately, this dichotomy obscures Montesquieu's relation to the French Revolution. *L'esprit des lois* was actually the first French formulation of a theory of republican virtue. Montesquieu defined virtue as "love of law and country," or, again, as that quality which demands "constant preference for the public interest over one's private interest." It is remarkable that Robespierre borrowed this definition of virtue ("love of country and its laws"), which he used repeatedly in speeches during 1793, word for word from Montesquieu. He was quite conscious, moreover, of the source. In a 1785 speech that marks one of his earliest uses of the notion of virtue, he said: "The principal source of energy in a republic, as the author of *L'esprit des lois* has shown, is virtue, that is, political virtue, which is simply love of one's country and its laws." From

Considérations sur les causes de la grandeur des Romains et de leur décadence to *L'esprit des lois,* Montesquieu was constantly fascinated by Rome. To be sure, his work also contains a critique of republican virtue, but one that is veiled by wit and ellipsis. Among the regimes that he judges to be good, moreover, there is none in which he does not observe some flaw. Not even the English are an exception to this rule. Furthermore, the imperfection of the various political goods explains their diversity: if there were a perfect solution to the political problem, it would necessarily be unique. Hence Montesquieu's work can also be read as praise of republican virtue. If one reasons in terms of the diffusion of ideas and images, there can be no doubt that Montesquieu played a role in the revolutionaries' admiration for Rome and republican virtue.

Montesquieu has long been hailed as the inventor of the theory of separation of powers, which the Declaration of Rights of 1789 consecrated in its sixteenth article. Specialists in constitutional law such as Duguit and Carré de Malberg have viewed the constitutions of 1791 and Year III as applications of Montesquieu's theory. The work of contemporary legal scholars, especially Troper, shows that one ought to say even more, namely, that the Constitution of 1793 and the Girondins' proposed constitution also embodied a form of separation of powers, in which respect they are not as different as has been said from the constitutions of 1791 and Year III. One might argue, accordingly, that with the exception of the dictatorship of public safety, the entire Revolution was, in constitutional matters, dependent on Montesquieu. But to make such a statement would be seriously misleading. Paradoxically, it is misleading not because the Revolution did not implement the principle of separation of powers or implemented it only in certain cases (in 1791 and Year III but not in 1793) but because the theory of separation of powers is not found in Montesquieu. If by separation of powers one means, as most legal scholars do, the existence of specialized *organs* of government to perform each of the three *functions* identified by Montesquieu (legislative, executive, and judicial), then it can be shown, as Eisenmann argues, that the English government as analyzed by Montesquieu did not embody the principle. The king, organ of the executive function, also participates in the legislative function through his right of veto. The House of Lords, partial organ of the legislative function, also performs judicial functions in certain cases. The legislative organ, composed essentially of the House of Commons and the House of Lords, does not have the right to "halt the executive power," but it does have "the right and must have the faculty to examine how the laws that it has made were executed." Finally, the judicial function is not performed by any organ of government. "The power to judge," Montesquieu writes, "should not be given to a permanent senate but exercised by individuals drawn from the body of the people." In this way, "the dread power of judgment, because it is not attached to a definite estate or profession, becomes as it were invisible and neutral." Thus Montesquieu does not propose a theory of functional specialization of the organs of state but something quite different, a theory according to which the legislative function is divided among three organs: the king (owing to his right of veto), the House of Lords, and the House of Commons (each house having a right of veto over resolutions approved by the other). Furthermore, Montesquieu regards it as absolutely essential that the two houses represent different social forces. The political liberty and checks of one power on another characteristic of the English regime were not, in Montesquieu's view, the result of specialization of the organs of state but rather of division of the legislative power coupled with representation in the legislature of different social forces.

Is it therefore true that the monarchiens, who favored a bicameral system and an unlimited royal veto, were the only heirs to Montesquieu in the Revolution? Certainly they were the revolutionaries among whom Montesquieu's ideas were most influential. Yet in two respects *all* the leaders of the Revolution were profoundly influenced by Montesquieu's theories.

The sixth chapter of Book Eleven of *L'esprit des lois* is a highly complex text containing a number of propositions of different significance and status. Many commentators and historians have failed to distinguish among the several themes in this celebrated chapter and thereby have rendered unintelligible the varying fortunes of these propositions during the Revolution. We must therefore attempt to unpack the different senses of separation of powers that various readers have taken from this text.

It contains, first of all, a descriptive proposition valid for all states and concerning the nature of state functions: "In every state there are three kinds of powers (*pouvoirs*): the legislative power (*puissance*), the executive power concerning things that depend on the law of nations, and the executive power concerning things that depend on civil law." Here, the term *pouvoirs* refers to functions, not organs. In despotism one organ performs all three functions, yet they remain conceptually distinct. Thus the proposition is true "in every state." The second function, which at the beginning of the chapter denotes power over foreign affairs, later shifts its meaning to become the power to execute "public resolutions" or "laws" (Montesquieu identifies the two terms), that is, executive power. The "executive power concerning things that depend on civil law" is then defined as the power to punish crimes and judge disputes between private parties, that is, judicial power. *Without exception*, the Revolution took its definition of the three state functions from Montesquieu.

One can of course show that Montesquieu had theoretical predecessors. In particular, the distinction between the three powers can be found in Locke. But in Locke the royal prerogative played an essential role. Montesquieu makes no place for a power to decide, in the absence of law, on matters that cannot be foreseen, and all the revolutionaries without exception adopted his point of view. There were debates on the issue of whether the executive organ should also take part in legislation (for example, the autumn 1789 debate on the royal veto), but the monarchiens never accepted the English theory of prerogative. No one suggested granting the executive organ the power to act in certain cases in the absence of law, because much of the Assembly distrusted the king. Yet that distrust did not prevent the monarchiens from proposing a royal veto. By contrast, the idea of a royal prerogative was totally alien to the intellectual universe of the revolutionaries, whether monarchiens or not. Obviously it is not enough to argue that the idea of a power acting in the absence of law was contrary to the most firmly established principles, so that the rejection of that idea by the French revolutionaries was merely trivial. Those principles were firmly established precisely because of the extraordinary influence that Montesquieu's definition of state functions continued to exert. Even today we reason within the framework proposed by Montesquieu. To reduce the state's functions to the promulgation of laws (by the legislative organ) and their application (by the executive and judicial organs) is a theoretical choice that is by no means self-evident, as the example of Locke makes perfectly clear. Rousseau, too, limited the state's function to the promulgation and execution of laws. He went even further than Montesquieu, since for him the judicial function was not separate and distinct from the other two. But on one crucial point he was an heir of Montesquieu: namely, that no subject is by nature outside the domain of law. When one's attention is focused exclusively on contrasting the respective influence of Rousseau and Montesquieu on the Revolution, one remains blind to the points on which those influences converged and misses the continuous line that runs from Montesquieu to the Revolution.

It is clear that the Revolution always viewed the executive organ as occupying a less important place in the hierarchy than the legislative organ. This subordination is one of the central features of the Revolution and accounts for many of its difficulties. The executive function is by nature subordinate; the executant is merely carrying out someone else's will. In legal language one says that execution is *materially* subordinate to legislation. If the organ upon which the executive function devolves has no function other than execution, it is thus necessarily in a subordinate position, as Carré de Malberg has shown. If one wishes to avoid making the executive organ subordinate, its incumbent must be given functions other than execution of the law. The definition and list of state functions that the revolutionaries borrowed from Montesquieu excluded, in particular, the idea of a function permitting action in the absence of laws. Montesquieu's influence explains in part why the revolutionaries were unable to establish a powerful executive organ. Once the avenue of the prerogative was closed, the only remaining possibility was to give the executive organ a share in the legislative function. This was what the monarchiens attempted to do by offering the king a power of veto.

Montesquieu's definition of the judicial function also played a key role in the April–May 1790 debate on the organization of justice, during which Montesquieu's name and formulations were frequently cited. The issue was whether judges would be appointed by the executive or elected by the people. The Assembly's right wing relied on Montesquieu to show that, since the judicial power was merely a subdivision of the executive power, judges ought to be chosen by the king, if need be from a list submitted by the people. The left, led at that time by Barnave, also cited Montesquieu, but in order to show that, since the three powers were distinct, judges ought not to be appointed by the executive but rather elected by the people. The Assembly ultimately voted by a bare majority in favor of election by the people ("the king shall not have the power to refuse his consent to the admission of a judge," and "electors shall present only one subject to the king").

The true interest and significance of the debate, however, lay not so much in the issue of election of judges as in the conception of the judicial function formulated for the occasion. Right and left in effect agreed on one point: the judicial power consisted solely in "applying" the laws. Roederer speaking for the left and Clermont-Tonnerre for the right explicitly cited Montesquieu. A judge must simply determine whether the case before him fell within the purview of the law; once that decision was made, he had only to apply the law. Judgment was conceived as a syllogism in which the law filled the role of the major premise, the facts of the case the minor premise, and the judgment the conclusion. In the debate of May 1790 the revolutionary conception of the judicial function was formulated for the first time and thereafter was never challenged. The final formulation was largely the fruit of a rationalist approach to judicial issues. Condorcet had explicitly formulated a theory of judgment as syllogism. On this point, however, Montesquieu was not in disagreement with the rationalist view. Indeed, Montesquieu had written of the English regime: "But if the courts should not be immutable, judgments should be, to the point where they are never more than a précis of the law." In fact, for Montesquieu, judgment "in accordance with a précis of the law" was characteristic of republican governments; in monarchies things worked differently. It was because the English regime was in his eyes close to a republic that judgment there conformed to this rule.

L'esprit des lois contained more than just a definition of the three state functions. Book Eleven set forth a second proposition, this one of normative character. In order to avoid despotism, the three functions ought not to be entrusted to the same organ. Regimes that shunned such concentration of power were not despotic, the English for one, but also monarchy for another. The monarch performed the legislative and executive functions, but since he left the judicial function "to his subjects," there was no despotism. The example of monarchy shows that, for Montesquieu, even when two functions are concentrated in a single organ there is no despotism. The principle of non-concentration is intended to guarantee that the law will not be formulated by the same authority that makes concrete decisions based on that law. Whoever takes a concrete step (whether judge or executive organ) must not be applying a rule that he himself has formulated. And he who formulates the rule should not have the power to do so solely to justify a specific decision that he wishes to take. The relation between the rule and the concrete decision should therefore be external, in order to impose a certain limit on arbitrary power. In monarchy, where legislative and executive functions are in the same hands, that externality holds only in the case of the judicial power. But that power is the most redoubtable of all, "the dreaded power to judge," because it affects individuals in their daily lives. Hence externality, even though it holds only for the judicial power, is enough to avoid despotism.

In any case, for the revolutionaries the principle of "separation of powers" signified above all non-concentration of functions, especially of legislative and executive functions. The idea that "union of powers" leads to arbitrary rule recurred constantly in Assembly debates. It can be shown that all the revolutionary constitutions, including that of 1793 (as well as the proposed Girondin Constitution), respected the principle of not concentrating all functions in a single organ. In the debates that preceded the adoption of the Constitution of 1793, virtually no orator proposed entrusting all powers to an elected Assembly. In July 1792 and again in May 1793 Robespierre insisted that legislation and execution be rigorously separated. Understood simply as non-concentration of the legislative and executive functions, the principle of separation of powers was unanimously supported by the revolutionaries.

At this point, however, a first major division can be seen. For some revolutionaries, particularly the Constituents of 1793, it was important to follow the logic of non-concentration to the end. Not only should no organ of government exercise two functions in their entirety, but no organ should exercise even part of a function primarily assigned to another. The executive organ should have no part in legislation; the legislative organ should have no part in execution. The result would be a system of functionally specialized organs, and it was such a system that was contained in both the Constitution of 1793 and the proposed Girondin Constitution. To the extent that legislative and executive functions were by nature hierarchically related, the system of functional specialization had the effect of ascribing supremacy to the legislative organ and making the executive strictly subordinate to it. The constitution proposed by the monarchiens in 1789 clearly derived from a different view. The monarchiens proposed assigning part of the legislative function to the executive organ by way of the right of veto. The king, Mounier argued, ought to be an "integral part of the legislative corps." The principle of non-concentration would still be respected, since the executive organ did not exercise all of the legislative function in addition to the executive function. Mounier made this point quite clear: "Let no one say that in granting the monarch the right to approve or reject a new law, the legislative and executive powers are joined in the same hands. Such a right is not the legislative power but only a portion of that power, since the king will not have the ability to give force of law to his private will." Therefore the veto was compatible with the principle of non-concentration, but it was not a logical consequence of that principle. It actually derived from another idea, which Mounier also discussed: "Every corporation," he said, "no matter how it is composed, seeks to increase its prerogatives. Every authority wants to increase, if no barrier is placed in the way of its ambition. . . . The people's representatives could become absolute masters of the realm if their resolutions encountered no obstacle."

*
**

The monarchiens proposed an arrangement in which the executive organ, that is, the king, would have sufficient power to resist the legislative organ, that is, the representatives of the people. They took their inspiration from another principle set forth by Montesquieu, namely, the limitation of power by power. Along with the definition of state functions and the principle of non-concentration, this limitation was Montesquieu's third lesson and the true heart of his philosophy. No doubt Montesquieu himself did not distinguish sharply among these various aspects of his thought. In order to make sense of his place in the Revolution, however, we must differentiate one from another. The monarchiens, as has often been noticed, were the only ones to accept his prescriptions in toto, including the principle of limitation of power by power. In the English regime, held up as a model in *L'esprit des lois,* this principle was put into practice in the division of the legislative function among three organs: the House of Commons, the House of Lords, and the king (through his veto). The monarchiens, who dominated the Committee on the Constitution, in the late summer of 1789 proposed a constitution inspired by the English model. At that time Montesquieu's thought played a role of considerable importance. The monarchiens' failure marked the defeat of Montesquieu's teaching taken in its totality. But it is important to understand exactly how the thinking of the Constituent Assembly in the period 1789–1791 differed from that of Montesquieu.

It is sometimes argued that the Revolution never exhibited the slightest concern with the problem of limiting power. The revolutionaries, allegedly persuaded that a power emanating from the people could not possibly be unjust or wicked, were supposedly unconcerned with limiting the power of the representatives. But this picture is inaccurate. The idea that a representative assembly could be despotic and that its power therefore had to be limited was expressed repeatedly in revolutionary debates. The difference with Montesquieu lay in the modalities of that limitation, not in the principle. This can be seen with particular clarity in the constitutional debates of the autumn of 1789. Sieyès, hostile to any kind of royal veto, including a suspensive veto, strongly criticized the monarchien project. Nevertheless he declared: "I concede that any power, whatever its nature, may extend beyond the limits prescribed for it by the constitution, and that public as well as private bodies may cease to be just toward one another." Sieyès thus recognized the existence of a danger: the encroachment of one power, possibly even that of the people's elected representatives, on the prerogatives of other powers. He nevertheless rejected the idea of a veto and proposed instead his idea of the distinction between a constituent power and a constituted power. The various organs of the state were merely constituted powers; they did not themselves establish their place in the institutional system, which was assigned to them by the constituent power (that of the assembly charged with establishing the constitution). If in the course of an ordinary legislature one of the constituted powers trespassed on the prerogatives assigned by the constitution to another organ, the constituent power would again have to be convoked to determine whether the violation had indeed taken place and if so how to remedy it. The constituted powers were therefore limited by the existence and action of another power, one of a logically superior status: namely, the constituent power that defined them and determined their limits.

In order to determine exactly what the issue was in the debate between

Sieyès and the monarchiens, we must compare this theory of the limitation of the constituted powers by the constituent power with what Mounier had to say in the same debate. "Do not think," Mounier argued, "that it will be easy to replace the royal sanction [or veto], or that by tracing the limits of the representatives' authority in the constitution it will become impossible for them to trespass. Certainly all these rules will be futile if the job of interpreting them is entrusted to the interested parties. . . . Law is an empty word if there exists no means of enforcing it." The point being made here, not without ambiguities, was the central issue of the debate. Mounier rejected the idea of limiting the various powers by appealing to another power of a logically superior status (Sieyès' constituent power), because that superior power would not be able to act as an arbiter above the parties in contention. If a dispute arose between the people's representatives and the king, it would be necessary to appeal to the people, who would thus in a sense become judge and party in the same case ("if the job of interpreting [the rules] is entrusted to the interested parties"). The monarchiens' whole purpose was to avoid this difficulty. Their aim was to design the various institutions so that they would be able to defend themselves against possible encroachments by other institutions. Respect for the constitution should come not from the problematic intervention of a power superior to the instituted organs but from the relations that were established among organs on the same logical level.

This was the meaning of Montesquieu's third prescription, which included this principle: "In order that power may not be abused, things must be arranged so that power impedes power." By this he meant that each power should be limited by another power on the same logical level (a limitation that does not imply that the different powers are equal). In England, the three key organs (king, Lords, and Commons) belonged to the same level of power. The balance that established itself among them was the result not of a higher agency but solely of the means with which the constitution endowed each of them in order to defend itself against the other two. The limitation of power was endogenous, not exogenous, with respect to the system of relations among the instituted organs. It was this view of things, and not the need to limit or divide power, that a large majority of French revolutionaries rejected.

If the objective is to ensure that the various instituted organs can limit one another, it is not enough for the constitution to distribute the various governmental functions (or, more precisely, parts of functions) among them. Those functions must be distributed in such a way as to allow the various organs to oppose one another and defend themselves. The distribution of functions (an exogenous process resulting from the action of the "legislator" or drafters of the constitution) is only a device for allowing a self-sustaining balance of power to emerge. In the absence of a guarantee by a "constitutional guardian" superior to the organs of state, this balance of power must be maintained by the social distribution of power and by cleavages already existing in society independent of political institutions. Montesquieu deems it necessary that the two houses of the legislature represent different social forces and interests.

From this point of view it is clear that the Constitution of 1791 failed to respect Montesquieu's advice. In the first place, the monarchiens failed in their effort to establish a second house. The argument that carried the day in the Assembly was not, as has sometimes been maintained, the idea that sovereignty, being indivisible by nature, could not be divided between two houses. It was rather the idea that an upper house would be tied to the existence of orders and to the "aristocracy," or that at the very least it would threaten to revive the society of orders. Foreseeing this objection, the monarchiens stipulated that the senate would not consist of nobles, and they invoked the American Senate as a counterexample. But the Committee on the Constitution was unable to reach agreement concerning the method of nominating senators and made no specific recommendations on this subject. In this absence of any concrete proposal, all who spoke in opposition to the upper house associated bicameralism with aristocracy. They argued that in England "the House of Lords is quite obviously a relic of feudalism" (Rabaut-Saint-Etienne), that the Assembly should "by establishing a single house remedy the aristocracy of orders" (Thouret), that if the Assembly created a senate, it would erect "on the ruins of this nobility, which now is no more than what it can and should be . . . the most monstrous monument to aristocracy that can possibly exist" (Lanjuinais), and finally that a senate "at this time would revive the destructive germs" of "the orders' pretensions" (Sillery).

One has the sense that the outcome of this debate turned on images and rhetoric. The position of the monarchiens was weakened by their inability to sever the perceived link between the proposed senate and the aristocracy. Their adversaries' rhetoric sought to reinforce that link. In 1789 France, the idea of different social forces inevitably conjured up images of the difference between the nobility and the Third Estate.

The monarchiens' failure on the issue of the royal veto was seemingly less clear-cut. Sieyès' opposition to any kind of veto failed to win the support of the majority, which granted the king a suspensive veto over the next two legislatures. In this result there is further proof that the crucial issue in the debate was not the question whether the legislative function should be unified or divided. It was in fact divided by the veto, if only temporarily. Yet the monarchiens—along with the rest of the Assembly—nevertheless considered approval of the suspensive veto a mark of their failure. By itself, such a veto gave the king an important right, but when seen in the light of the king's overall position, it remained an isolated right. It was not part of a comprehensive system that would have allowed the king to defend himself against the legislature; instead, it was the king's only autonomous power. In exercising the executive function in the strict sense, the king was almost totally subordinate to the legislature. He did not appoint judges or administrators, only ambassadors and officers. He was thus deprived of an important device for exerting pressure on the Assembly: in England, the crown was able to assure itself of majorities by granting posts to deputies who supported it, a form of corruption of which Montesquieu was well aware but which he refrained from condemning. In case of conflict with the legislature, the king had no power under the Constitution of 1791 other than his right of veto; he had no capacity to make a graduated response, with attendant possibilities of bargaining and negotiation. In a strategic situation, the strength of a position depends on the range of available actions. As is well known, the king of England made little use of his veto power in the eighteenth century; the ministry he appointed actually governed through its influence over the House of Commons.

Even though the Constitution of 1791 offered the king a power of veto, it therefore marked a failure of the model proposed by Montesquieu. The Constituents granted the king a legislative function, but they did not arrange for a system of relations among the powers that would have enabled the king to mount an effective opposition to the legislature. The Constituent Assembly did not follow Sieyès in his rejection of any kind of veto, but it agreed with him that there was no need to establish a balance of power among the various organs of state such that each would be able to defend itself against the others.

Montesquieu's views were even more firmly rejected in the Constitution of Year III. Once again, however, the legislature was divided. The Anciens and the Five Hundred were not designed as countervailing powers, however. They did not represent different social interests: the same electoral body chose both councils. Both were elected at the same time (article 36 of the Constitution), so there was no possibility that two successive states of the popular will could oppose each other. The drafters' objective, as shown by the debates preceding adoption of the Constitution, was to avoid investing too much power in a unicameral legislature. The division of the legislative function was deemed necessary, but the drafters conceived of it as a division of labor between two assemblies, not as a system whereby one power could "arrest" another, as Montesquieu would have it. Only the Five Hundred could propose laws; the Anciens then accepted or rejected them. Sieyès expressed the intent of this plan with the greatest clarity. In his speech of 2 Thermidor he strongly criticized the system of checks and balances, which he opposed to a system of cooperation and organized unity. In the former system, rather than separate the various functions of the representative body (formulation and approval of the laws, for instance), two different representative bodies were assigned the same functions. According to Sieyès, such a system could result only in stalemate or in de facto priority of one of the two organs over the other. He therefore proposed distinguishing among different aspects of legislative action and assigning each to a specialized organ. In an image that sheds much light on his thinking, he compared legislation to the construction of a house, in which different types of workers cooperated: "There is no unique action, but there is unity of action. Our adversaries would obtain unity of action in a different way. Confusing it, as I have said, with unique action, they want, first of all, only one type of worker engaging in all the different kinds of work. Then, discovering that there may be abuse in this accumulation of confidence and powers, what do they do? The moment the house is finished, they advise the owner to call upon a second group of masons, also jacks of all trades, to start the job all over from the ground up."

These remarks of Sieyès, along with the text of the Constitution itself, show precisely where the Revolution parted company with the thought of

Montesquieu. The issue was not the division of power, a principle accepted by the vast majority of deputies in Year III, but rather the modalities of that division. Sieyès proposed dividing power as one might divide labor. The division of labor is not intended to establish power relations among different organs but only to assign them different and complementary tasks. To deal with possible encroachments by one organ on tasks assigned to another, Sieyès proposed establishing a "constitutional jury." The various organs of government would divide the labor of government, and respect for the constitution would stem not from the actions of the organs themselves but from their common submission to a superior organ. We thus come back to the crucial problem noticed by the monarchiens in 1789: can one truly count on discovering an impartial superior power in case of conflict between the parties?

This rejection of the balanced system was characteristic of the Revolution as a whole. Rationalism played a greater role than concern for the unity of power. It seems more rational at first sight to assign a definite function to each organ than to arrange for opposition between organs. The balanced system seems "absurd." The rationalist basis for the rejection of checks and balances is clearly visible in Condorcet's writings prior to 1789. Condorcet proposed a simple and peremptory argument: "In order to refute this absurd system, we shall limit ourselves to a single observation: would a slave with two masters, often divided between themselves, cease to be a slave?" The Revolution refused to accept Montesquieu's idea that respect for universal, rational rules could be ensured by a proper organization of the conflict among different powers and interests. For Montesquieu, interests and powers never yield the rational and the universal spontaneously; they must be organized in a certain way. In this sense, voluntary, rational action by a "legislator" is indispensable. But effective rationalism, he argues, is incompatible with the will to rationalize everything. The non-rational and non-universal must be given their due.

In the final analysis, then, it is true that the Revolution turned away from the teachings of Montesquieu. On certain points, however, it owed him a great deal: the definition of the state functions and the conception of the judicial function, to name two. These points are easily missed if one is concerned only with measuring the respective influence of Rousseau and Montesquieu. Even more serious, an essential fact is obscured: Montesquieu's role was of a different nature from Rousseau's. The debate in which Montesquieu figured was a constitutional and legal one, whereas Rousseau provided the Revolution with images and slogans expressing a comprehensive vision of man and society.

Bernard Manin

Further reading

WORKS BY MONTESQUIEU
Oeuvres complètes, 3 vols. Paris, 1950–1955.

RELATED WORKS

Condorcet, Marie-Jean-Antoine-Nicolas de Caritat, marquis de. *Observations sur le vingt-neuvième livre de l'esprit des lois* (1780); *Lettres d'un bourgeois de New Haven* (1787); *Idées sur le despotisme à l'usage de ceux qui prononcent ce mot sans l'entendre* (1789); *Exposition des principes et des motifs du plan de constitution* (1793). In *Oeuvres,* ed. François Arago and Elisa Condorcet-O'Connor, 12 vols. Paris, 1847–1849.

Debate on the proposal by the Committee on the Constitution, August–September 1789, *Archives parlementaires,* vol. 15, 1883, 317–420.

Debate on the judicial order, April–May 1790, *Archives parlementaires,* vol. 8, 1875, 504–608.

Mounier, Jean-Joseph. *Considérations sur les gouvernements, et principalement sur celui qui convient à la France.* Paris, 1789. See also *Archives parlementaires,* vol. 8, 1875, 407–422.

——— *Nouvelles observations sur les Etats Généraux de France.* N.p., 1789.

Sieyès, Emmanuel. "Opinion du 2 Thermidor III," in Paul Bastid, *Les discours de Sieyès dans les débats constitutionnels de l'an III,* critical edition. Paris, 1938.

Troper, Michel. *La séparation des pouvoirs et l'histoire constitutionnelle française.* Paris, 1973.

Vile, M. J. *Constitutionalism and the Separation of Powers.* Oxford, 1967.

Related topics

Condorcet Marat Rousseau
Constitution Monarchiens Sieyès

NATION

S urely everyone agrees that it was the Revolution that gave the word "nation" its synergy and energy. It crystallized the word's three meanings: social (a body of citizens equal before the law), legal (constituent power as opposed to constituted power), and historical (a community of men united by continuity, by a common past and future). The Revolution also bestowed its own dynamism on these now inextricable features, which set the nation apart from the ambient constellation: the kingdom, which preceded it but in opposition to which it construed itself; the Republic, long informed by the shape of the regime; the state, still contaminated by monarchical mercantilism; the fatherland, with its more emotional and sentimental connotations; and finally France, whose identity was compounded not only of a long history but also of culture and will.

*
**

Speaking broadly and taking a long-range view, "nation" may be seen as a rapid crystallization, a politicization in a suddenly subverted social context and within a rapidly sanctified territorial framework, of two different but equally venerable meanings. The broader of these, religious and biblical, was transmitted by the Vulgate and the language of scholars and imbued with apostolic tradition—*gentes et nationes;* it viewed the nation as one of the great natural divisions of the human race as it emerged from the hands of the Creator. The narrower definition associated the nation with its root (*nasci,* to be born), with community in the strict sense, with family and birthplace. This was a lived as opposed to a learned understanding, which ultimately associated the nation with feeling for the *patrie,* the fatherland, that oasis of liberty in the hostile desert of the wider world. This feeling for the fatherland seemed to flourish most naturally in exile and emigration, and long after du Bellay it inspired Chateaubriand to his well-known flights of lyricism. This dual definition was already evident in the grouping of students by "nations" in thirteenth-century universities, and this was the sense of the term recorded in the seventeenth century in the first French dictionary, Jean Nicot's *Thrésor de la langue française:* "people of various nations living together in a city." Thus "nation" was an ambivalent notion, broad and scholarly yet at the same time narrow and popular, a long way from the modern meaning of the word but already incorporating the three elements that the Revolution would amalgamate because suddenly they had become both topical and necessary: a geopolitical component, neutral and plural, which assumed the coexistence of other nations in the framework of Christendom; an evangelical component, with universal and religious implications; and a physical, proximate component, duly stressed by the *Dictionnaire de l'Académie* (1694): "all the inhabitants of a single state, a single country, who live under the same laws and use the same language." This definition was quite similar to the one given by Furetière (1690), "said of a great people inhabiting a given extent of land contained within certain limits or even under a certain domination," a definition that was repeated verbatim by Trévoux in 1771.

By then, however, "nation" and to an even greater extent *patrie* had been subjected to much more thorough scrutiny by eighteenth-century thinkers, especially as a result of the controversy between Voltaire and Rousseau in the 1750s. Associated with "fatherland" were ideas of liberty, happiness, and virtue taken from memories of antiquity as well as from Bolingbroke's England (*The Idea of a Patriot King* had been published in 1738) and from a neighboring republic, the United Provinces. As a cosmopolitan, Voltaire was suspicious of the fatherland, a vehicle of nationalistic narrowness and under despotism a pure illusion: "One has a fatherland under a good king; under a wicked king one has none," he wrote in the *Dictionnaire philosophique*. Like Montesquieu, Voltaire used the world only in a descriptive sense: "the nations of northern Europe," "England, that lively and bold nation" (*Siècle de Louis XIV*, Pléiade edition, pp. 629 and 617). By contrast, Rousseau made a great deal of these two words, constantly defending the idea of a "national character" to be fostered and respected in every people. Ultimately he even suggested the need for a civic oath, such as the one he proposed that every citizen of Corsica take in his *Projet de constitution pour la Corse:* "I join my body, possessions, will, and all my strength to the Corsican Nation, so that I may belong wholly to it, myself and all that is in my power. I swear to live and die for it" (*Oeuvres complètes*, Pléiade, III, p. 913). The abbé Coyer echoed Rousseau in his *Dissertations sur le vieux mot de patrie et sur la nature du peuple* (1755), while Grimm took the part of Voltaire. In 1765 the *Encyclopédie* (vols. 11 and 12) took a synthetic, middle-of-the-road line, propounded by the chevalier de Jaucourt: "nation" is a "collective word, used to denote a considerable number of people who inhabit a certain stretch of country, enclosed within definite limits, who obey the same government" and distinguished by its "particular character." All in all this was a fairly neutral definition, and there was no "national" article, whereas *patrie* was developed at length by the same author along with its attendant notions "patriot" and "patriotism." Actually, thinking about the nation was pursued not so much by the philosophes as in the parlements and among would-be reformers of the state. The parlements opposed royal arbitrariness and the memory of absolutism in the style of Louis XIV, according to which "the Nation has no substance in France" and "resides entirely in the person of the king," the ancestral contract that associated the monarchy with the obscure power of the "nation." Meanwhile, the physiocrats and "economists" gave currency to the ideas of national consumption, national commerce, national circulation, national interest, and even national education.

Before the word "nation" could absorb the polemical and political content of "fatherland" and rapidly increase its revolutionary content, its meaning first had to crystallize; this occurred during the campaign prior to the meeting of the Estates General, with its accompanying deluge of brochures and pamphlets. That such crystallization occurred can be verified by content analysis: Eberhardt Schmitt has examined ninety-three brochures published between September 1788 and May 1789; Beatrice Hyslop has examined parish *cahiers*, and Régine Robin has studied *bailliage cahiers* for Semur-en-Auxois. The national idea made its presence felt everywhere. Great powers were attributed to the "nation assembled": to prepare a budget, to draft laws, to modify religious legislation, and even to draw up a constitution. But surely it was Sieyès in *Qu'est-ce que le Tiers Etat?* (January 1789) who formulated with unmatched brilliance and aggressiveness the basic idea on which the concept of a revolutionary nation would be erected, and according to which, "if one removed the privileged order, the nation would be not something less but something more." This was an audacious idea, which gives some measure of the depth of a historic resentment: "The Third Estate constitutes a complete nation." The boundary defining the nation lay within the national community. The idea met with stunning success, but it also included an element of exclusion in the very principle of the nation, justified civil war before the fact, and, in creating the nation, also created the national pathology.

The quasiofficial advent of the "nation" was therefore precisely contemporaneous with the very beginning of the Revolution, that is, with the meeting of the Estates General. From the moment the Estates General rejected the appellation by which it had been known for centuries and pushed beyond the limited set of issues for which it had been convoked, the rupture with what people would that summer begin calling the Ancien Régime was complete and the nation was born. The deputies of the three traditional orders had had only one mission: to resolve the financial crisis and find additional resources. The moment procedural questions concerning the verification of its powers arose and the deputies began to replace the Estates General of the old monarchy, based on a distinction between orders of unequal importance, with a homogeneous assembly of delegates elected by the population, the nation took cognizance of its own existence. This self-institution was implicit in Mirabeau's speech on June 15, 1789, concerning the naming of the Assembly: "We must constitute ourselves. On that we are all agreed. But how? In what form? Under what name? As Estates General? The word would be improper." He invoked "the principle of national representation, basic to any constitution," in proposing to his colleagues that they proclaim themselves "representatives of the French people" rather than "known and verified deputies of the French nation." When the debate ended on June 17, the deputies of course voted, on a motion by Sieyès, to renounce their original appellation and call themselves the National Assembly. As Georges Gusdorf rightly remarks, all the constitutional, legislative, and regulatory work of the assemblies of the Republic was implicit in this change of nomenclature.

These first few weeks were of great importance. Previously the national idea had inspired neither organic solidarity nor collective consciousness nor political alignment. With one stroke the new regime created a new framework of legitimacy. The transformation of the Estates General into the National Assembly sanctioned the inversion of the political scale of values by entrusting de facto sovereignty to the nation's representatives. "The clergy is not the nation," declared Rabaut Saint-Etienne, echoing Sieyès, "it is the clergy. It is an assemblage of 200,000 nobles and commoners devoted to the service of altars and religion. . . . The nobility is not the nation." The eclipse of even the "Third Estate" in turn sanctioned the disappearance of the old vocabulary and the advent of the nation, confirmed on the night of August 4 by the abolition of feudal rights and all forms of privilege. The lapidary third article of the Declaration of the Rights of Man and of the Citizen established the change of sign from negative to positive: "The principle of all sovereignty resides essentially in the Nation." Beyond the canonical texts, however, perhaps the best measure of the inroads the word had already made and of its power to attract adherents can be found in a letter unearthed by Jacques Godechot. It was written two days after the taking of the Bastille by an obscure resident of Compiègne to a lawyer in Douai and described the events that had just taken place in Paris. The writer reported the formation of a "national troop" and noted that in Paris rights had been "accepted on behalf of the nation" and that "all the troops are for the nation."

*
**

With this radical transfer of sovereignty, of the source of all power from a divine-right monarch to a National Assembly, the nation's essential structure was in place once and for all. For all that the Assembly might later nullify its powers, for all that regime succeeded regime and constitution succeeded constitution, transforming the relations between the powers and the symbols of the nation, its existence as a frame of reference and concept in terms of which people could think about their existence in common would never be challenged. Yet not a single episode of the Revolution failed to invest what Alphonse Dupront called this "resort to collective power" with a multitude of emotions. The libretto may have been in hand when the curtain rose, but it was history that supplied the music. Not a day went by in the ensuing decade without some new note or accent being added to the great national orchestration. I shall limit myself to reciting some of the principal themes.

The first was surely the cumbersome complex of ideas that attached itself to the word "foreign," and which can be derived from what one might call Sieyès' theorem. It abolished the abstract and sacred boundary, too obvious to need emphasizing, that had from time immemorial separated the king from his subjects, and established instead a multiplicity of more palpable, more concrete divisions. There were, first of all, territorial boundaries, which clearly defined a zone of sovereignty, and which accredited an idea that runs through all of nineteenth-century and even much of twentieth-century historiography, that boundaries in Ancien Régime France were vague and uncertain; such thinking also fed the myth of natural frontiers. (For a recent overview of this theme, see the contributions of Bernard Guenée and Daniel Nordman to a work I edited, *Les lieux de mémoire*, vol. 2, *La nation*.) There were

745

also legal boundaries, which clearly defined a population of individuals equal in their rights and duties over which stood an authority based not on custom or usage but on law. There was, in addition, a psychological boundary, infinitely more subtle and mobile, which made the nation a refuge, an extension of the community, a locus of identity, a symbol of membership and allegiance, and an instrument of rootedness in the earth and soil, which Danton summed up in his famous phrase, "One does not carry one's fatherland on the soles of one's shoes." The importance of this aspect cannot be overestimated, for it sharpened and deepened the potentially aggressive character of the nation. That aggressiveness turned against the king and even more against the queen the minute Louis XVI "betrayed" his oath to the Constitution and the pact by which he became a subject of the nation. It also turned against the foreign enemy in the name of "the right of peoples to decide their own fate" and by an audacious (to say the least) extrapolation of the "declaration of peace to the world" approved by the Assembly on May 22, 1790: "The French Nation renounces any intention to make war for the purpose of conquest, and it will never use its forces against the liberty of any people." Last but not least, that aggressiveness was directed against internal enemies, initially limited to aristocrats and persons of privilege as opposed to "patriots" and "nationals" but later multiplied ad infinitum by the acceleration of the revolutionary process, obsession with conspiracy, and the increasingly radical logic of revolutionary self-institution.

The nation long incorporated this divided impulse toward hostility on the one hand, fraternity on the other; and the Revolution exalted in both epic and tragic dimensions, in both its reality and its legend, each of the episodes that drew this complementary and contradictory dialectic ever more tightly together. In retrospect every date seems symbolic; passing over the great moments of July 14 and August 4, let us begin with the *journées* of October 5 and 6, which saw the king forced to return from Versailles to Paris and thus gave the nation both its heart and its center. The full meaning of the "flight" to Varennes emerges only in relation to this "repatriation." But if one absolutely must assign a date to the explosion of what Alphonse Dupront might call the "national panic," clearly it would be the crisis of August–September 1792: from the insurrection of August 10, which finally stripped the king of his remaining powers, to the policy of public safety instituted by the Paris Commune to the September massacres and the victory at Valmy, a battle whose significance was amplified by Kellermann's troops shouting "Vive la Nation!" soon followed by the proclamation of the Republic. The trial and execution of the king four months later, hailed by Robespierre as "an act of national providence," consummated the divorce of that incompatible couple, the king and the nation, leaving the nation to face alone the rigors of its destiny and the demands of its own unity.

Unity: this is the second theme that enters into the definition of the national identity. No doubt it was the most important line of force connecting the new nation to the old. Here too, however, the invocation worked in contradictory ways and performed many functions, all essential and mostly magical.

Jeaurat, *Jean-Jacques Rousseau and the Symbols of the Revolution*. Musée Carnavalet, Paris.

*Equality Holding
the Declaration of the Rights of Man.*
Engraving after J. G. Moitte.
Musée de l'Histoire Vivante, Montreuil.

Réattu, *Liberty Tours the World*. Musée Réattu, Arles.

Fraternity.
Musée Carnavalet, Paris.

Declaration of the
Rights of Man. 1789.
Musée de l'Histoire Vivante,
Montreuil.

FÉLICITÉ DE L'HUMANITÉ LIBÉRÉE

LIBERTÉ   FRATERNITÉ   ÉGALITÉ
              RÈGNE DE LA NATURE

Gérard
The Manège Invaded. Drawing.
Louvre, Paris

Revolutionary Calendar,
Year II of the Republic.
Musée Carnavalet, Paris.

Gros, *Allegory of the Republic*. Château de Versailles.

Aristocratic Elixir. Anonymous caricature.
Musée Carnavalet, Paris.

*Aristocratic Lady
Cursing the Revolution.*
Musée Carnavalet, Paris.

*The Emigrés Crossing the Rhine:
Is the Counterrevolution Nothing More Than a Caricature?*
Musée Carnavalet, Paris.

aternal Meal.
'atercolor.
bliothèque Nationale, Paris.

Freedom of the Press.
Colored print.
Private collection.

Lesueur,
Vandalist, Destroyer of the Productions of the Arts,
Mocking Costumes Fashionable before the Revolution.
Musée Carnavalet, Paris.

Pillage of the St. Lazare House, July 13, 1789.

First of all there was the association, which went unstated amidst the outburst of patriotic enthusiasm but which was nonetheless powerfully active, with the monarchy's long-term effort to unify the country, reflected in article 1, Title 2, of the Constitution of 1791: "The Kingdom is one and indivisible," a declaration that the Republic would simply adapt to its own use. With the Ancien Régime eliminated, there was a constant fear of squandering the renounced legacy along with a sudden investment of emotion in the main elements of the new edifice: "The Nation, the law, the king." The national mystique was quickly attached to the unitary symbolism of the Assembly, as well as to the Constitution, the cockade, and later the flag, the motto, the hymn, and the festival. The decisive moment in the unitary affirmation of the new national consciousness can in this case be ascribed with full confidence to the festival of the Federation on the Champ de Mars, which set the tone for Michelet's account of the Revolution as the first strictly national festival in the history of France. The very idea of "federation," as Gusdorf rightly points out, was an affirmation of the unity and homogeneity of all the country's component parts, which had previously been endowed by the vicissitudes of history with very different political and administrative statuses. The festival represented occupation of the national space, incorporation of the liberated "enclaves," and annexation of Alsace, Savoy, and Corsica to the national territory of France. It expressed the disappearance of internal boundaries, the abolition of regional disparites, and the exaltation of united France's acceptance, by mutual consent, of a freely chosen authority. The first Bastille Day had celebrated only the destruction of the Ancien Régime, symbolized by the monarchical fortress. The national festival of the Federation, held in the presence of the new constitutional king and with the active cooperation of the clergy, sealed in temporary unanimity the new alliance and the fragile concord among the reconciled people of France.

There was, first of all, the powerful unifying effect of the Revolution itself, which provoked the enthusiasm and admiration of all enlightened minds in Europe: the immense diversity of the Ancien Régime, the sedimentation of all kinds and from all ages now confounded so as to be relegated as one unit to oblivion and within a few months subjected to the appraising eye of unifying, centralizing rationality. Perhaps the best example of this geometric spirit, compounded of realism and utopia, of common sense and delirious logic, remains the debates on departmentalization as analyzed by Marie-Vic Ozouf-Marignier. An almost equally good example came two years later, however: a pair of reforms, conceived in a similar spirit yet with very different fates, the first involving weights and measures, which remains in effect to this day, the other being the republican calendar, which of course met with insuperable resistance. The striking disparity between the festive ambience, the emotional unity of the revolutionary *journées,* and the centralizing rigor, the painstaking elaboration of constitutional texts and legislative plans would remain mysterious were it not for one common denominator: the obsession with unity.

Unity, again, and most important of all, was the object of the great movement through which the nation of the philosophes, lawyers, jurists, and system builders made contact, in an ordeal of war, invasion, rebellion in the Vendée, imperiled government, and ubiquitous poverty, with the depths of the rural and peasant nation suddenly mobilized in animal response to "the fatherland in danger." It was then, with all France subject to permanent requisition, in the tragic heart of the summer of 1793, between August 20, date of the *levée en masse* (mass conscription), and September 5, when Terror became "the order of the day," that the blood of soldiers and suspects, heroism and the guillotine, sealed the wedding of the Revolution with the nation, as the nation of the Revolution rediscovered the "eternal" nation embodied in the great moments in French history. Then, in the incandescence of a nation become transcendent, all that the constant appeal to unity masked of reaction to constant threats of dislocation, to the explosion of revolutionary hyperindividualism, and to real social agony was abolished, if not for history at least in memory.

In the skein woven by the Revolution there was one final strand: the universal. Once again we must stress the twofold process that gave universality its specific character. It was not the first time that France had thought of itself as elect among nations, and it is in the nature of every nation to believe that it is unique. In this respect the revolutionary experience repeated and concentrated prior crucial moments when France had linked her identity to her liberty and her very existence to a life-and-death struggle against foreign oppression: the Crusade and the Enlightenment. The odd thing is that this time she did so under the sign of the nation and that a principle of separation, discipline, compartmentalization, individuating identification, and communitarian particularism could have been at the same time an instrument of generalization. France was not universal, though Michelet, to the great dismay of other nations, convinced her she was. But it was the one nation that had universality as part of its particularity. It was in France, in that place at that time, through these words, in this language, by these men, with these gestures and none other that universal principles were proclaimed, principles on which the Nation—a particular nation—was based. What was abstract in those principles gave them a new lease on life: "Here begins the country of liberty." The French nation with one effort amassed capital for two purposes: abstraction and exportation.

This, notwithstanding all possible historical explanations, is a mystery not easily dispelled, which points up what is most unfathomable in the capacity of the nation to mobilize and personify. The revolutionary texts, principles, and codes that set forth the axioms of nationhood were merely the strict application to the political sphere of Enlightenment ideology. But the sphere in which national consciousness and ideology developed was far larger than the political or the rational. The inadequate metaphors with which it can be described but not defined are vegetal, biological, instinctual, or religious in nature. Had they been otherwise, it would be impossible to understand how the nation founded by the Constituent Assembly on the basis of the rights of man and the right of a people to self-determination could have sustained the romantic metamorphosis that did far more than idealism and the German concept of nationhood to inspire the nationalist movement. The revolutionary nation served as a matrix for the transformation of an abstract universal into a concrete one. The inextricable mixture of what Barruel in 1798 baptized "nationalism" (which Voltaire had already lambasted without using the word) with universalistic expansionism goes a long way toward explaining the reversals in the Revolution's foreign policy: how a declaration of peace gradually came to cover a policy of occupation disguised as liberating expansion, and how an alliance with sister republics turned into a war of France against Europe that kept blood flowing for twenty years. Such were the vicissitudes of the "great Nation."

* *
*

It remains to measure the burden imposed by the Revolution on the French national model. The difficulty lay entirely with the suddenness and radicality of the shift from monarchical sovereignty to national sovereignty with all its attendant consequences.

By raising so quickly the specter of the Ancien Régime, whose disappearance was a prerequisite of national sovereignty, the nation deprived itself from the outset and as a matter of principle of eight centuries of temporal continuity, the true source of its legitimacy. To make the "Nation" the source of all power was to assume that such a thing existed. This fundamental caesura is of the utmost importance for understanding the French national model. No matter what date is chosen as the symbolic moment of the nation's founding (and, as we have seen, many dates are possible), the Revolution founded a dynamic of national continuity and unity on the negation of its own unity and continuity. This mechanism had far-reaching consequences. France comprises not two halves of one nation but two complete nations, each of which could lay claim to absolute uniqueness: the monarchical nation was ruled by an exceptionally long-lived dynasty that began with the accession of Hugh Capet in 987 and achieved full maturity in its absolutist form under Louis XIV; the revolutionary nation differed from all its predecessors of the same type, whether English, Dutch, or American, by the absolute radicalism of its principles and their suitability for export.

This national duality, no equivalent for which can be found anywhere else, has left France obsessed with its history, identity, and continuity. It has given the very word "nation" a wealth of meaning and an autonomous significance peculiar to France alone. And it is surely one of the reasons why France enjoys such a unique and central relation with its past, with its memory, or, to put it another way, with its history and with politics, which are forever charged with the mission of patching up the torn robe of the nation's past and making one nation, one history, out of two. The revolutionary creation, or recreation, has made what was "already there" for all eternity a perpetual prize, alternating between a minimal juridical existence and a maximal historical essence, its definition always uncertain. The German national problem, like the Italian, is a consequence of its geographical diversity; the Spanish of its plunge from grandeur to decadence; the English of its religious multiplicity; the French of its dual national definition.

At the same time, the second nation's inability to negate the first has made the national reality of France, historically and politically, an arena of irreducible conflict. The conflict has been fundamental between the old France and the new, between religious France and lay France, between the France of the left and the France of the right—where right and left are more than mere political orientations or groupings but forms of national identity, ways of marshaling the images of the past. These are not rival forms within a shared consensus but exclusive and antagonistic images of the nation itself. Each part of the nation, believing itself to be in sole legitimate possession of the whole, has sought to kill off the other and has been obsessed with the antagonist's alleged failure to respect the higher interests of the fatherland, especially in time of war. This has been a true civic shortcoming: the Union sacrée dispelled these fears in 1914, but the "divine surprise" of 1940 laid the reality bare.

The reason for this, and the second effect of the Revolution on the national model, is that the Revolution has tended to monopolize the national idea and focus all references to the nation on the revolutionary episode. Symbolic references first of all: it was the Revolution that produced, in record time, all the symbols of the nation: the Declaration of Rights, the flag, Bastille Day, *La Marseillaise,* the national motto—all of which, still spanking new, were quickly immersed in the dramaturgy of the Revolution. But also rhetorical formulas, references to events, a whole repertoire of gestures, and sacred institutions, beginning with the most important of all institutions, those responsible for the defense of the nation and the formation of the citizen: the army, which through amalgamation quickly acquired its national stamp, and the schools, the so-called system of national education (which quickly won out over the rival term "public instruction"). The nation's identification with the Revolution went even further: the properties confiscated from the clergy, and some of those confiscated from émigrés, were called "national" properties and redistributed to citizens. The nation also incorporated the whole visible legacy of the monarchical past: archives and monuments branded with the infamous "feudal" appellation were nevertheless saved from "vandalism" and placed under the safeguard of the nation. Even the territory of the nation was mobilized, divided up into départements turned into sanctuaries against invasion by the "enemies of liberty." Profound as this appropriation was, it was perhaps less important than the nation's appropriation by imagery and the imagination. Conversely, with the establishment of the primary school and the effort by the Third Republic to give itself roots, the whole national history was in effect reformulated in accordance with the terms, concepts, and ideals of the Revolution, which became the source of all meaning, the alpha and omega of the national adventure.

The third and still more decisive impact of the Revolution on the French model of nation building was the inevitable dialectic of the dead and the living, the articulation of two types of sovereignty, monarchical and democratic, of which Marcel Gauchet has done much to elucidate the conditions and identify the consequences.

By suddenly and without transition substituting national for monarchical sovereignty, a power derived from below for a power derived from above, an abstract, invisible, necessarily representative notion for the eminently visible authority of the king, who embodied in his person the impersonal functions of state and nation, the Revolution was not following a simple symmetry of inversion. The legacy of this abrupt change included all the inherent contradictions of monarchical power, and the whole dialectic of personal power and its impersonal exercise by which the monarchy had lived and died was simply carried over to the problem of national representation. The sudden establishment of the abstract principle of "national" sovereignty, which assumed an impersonality of power, inaugurated a long period of uncertainty as to the forms of its representation, with which the French were never comfortable and between which they could never choose, with the result that representation wavered between two possible extremes. One temptation was extreme impersonality of government; unable to exercise true control over the legislature, the people relinquished sovereignty to their deputies, with the attendant risk of parliamentary usurpation—whether carried out in the name of the people or of Enlightenment and Reason. The other temptation was extreme repersonalization of government: the people relinquished sovereignty to a providential hero, supposed to embody the profound aspirations of the popular will. Impotence or dictatorship: from government by the propertied elite as established under the limited suffrage system adopted by the Constituent Assembly to the monarchy of Napoleon, the Revolution explored the whole gamut of possible national representations and provisional symbols of the Nation.

The intrinsic inadequacy of the nation to meet its own requirements, associated with the very circumstances of its inception, accounts not only for the continuous instability of government but also for revolutionary imperialism. Again, Gauchet ("Les 'Lettres sur l'histoire de France,'" p. 292) points out that the expansionism of the revolutionary nation partakes of the same "unleashing of the national principle, the principle of the realization of the universal in the particular, in this case led astray by the return of the old means of the universal," owing to its failure to achieve equilibrium and fulfillment within itself. The war of conquest was implicit in the program of the revolutionary nation just as colonization was implicit in the program of the republican nation. The Great Nation existed because the nation *tout court* did not.

The nation's obsession with the Revolution captured the French political imagination throughout the nineteenth century, as François Furet has shown. But did the Revolution "come into port" with the founding of the Third Republic, as Furet puts it in the final sentence of his *Révolution?* If so, it was only to be outflanked on both its right and its left: on the left by socialism, on the right by Maurrassian royalism, continued in the wake of the Russian Revolution and the Depression by communism on the one hand and fascism on the other. The original riverbed of the Revolution has been overlaid in the twentieth century by a steady deposit of new silt.

Indeed, for the national model engendered by the Revolution to begin to fade, for "Sieyès' theorem" to cease to be true, and for a new national geometry to be born, it took the gradual unfolding of the second half of the twentieth century. It took the Second World War and the rise of two empires, the Soviet Union and the United States, each representing a different kind of symbiosis between Nation and Revolution. It took the Gaullist synthesis in its two major, if ambiguous, phases. In its first phase Gaullism ensured not only the reestablishment of the Republic but also a second divine surprise, France's presence in the camp of the victors. In its second phase it led the way to decolonization and equipped France for the first time with an institutional system about which a majority of citizens were more or less in agreement; but it also impeded the construction of Europe by encouraging France to cling to a traditional type of national sovereignty, masked the real reduction of French might by joining the ranks of nuclear powers, and hid the real eclipse of the revolutionary model behind the old language of grandeur—a language sufficiently ecumenical to have served Louis XIV and Danton, Bossuet and Michelet. Finally, not until France had experienced economic growth and its attendant crisis, the decline of the Communist party, the metamorphosis of a modern right wing prepared to accept the legacy of the Revolution, and the exercise of power by the left under the aegis of the Fifth Republic could the Revolution's grip on France begin to weaken and a new model begin to take shape before our eyes, as the revolutionary nation too at last heads into port.

Before the historic volcano triggered by the phenomenon, before the forces it unleashed, the hecatomb it provoked, and the sacrifices it inspired, the historian can only bow his head as before the monument of modern Tragedy itself. But the citizen joins the historian in watching it take its place in the museum of national antiquities, conscious of what he owes it yet without regrets.

Pierre Nora

FURTHER READING

Aulard, Alphonse. *Le patriotisme français de la Renaissance à la Révolution.* Paris, 1921.

Dupront, Alphonse. "Du sentiment national," in Michel François, ed., *La France et les Français.* Paris, 1972.

Furet, François. *La Révolution,* vol. 4 of *Histoire de France Hachette.* Paris, 1988.

Gauchet, Marcel. "Les 'Lettres sur l'histoire de France' d'Augustin Thierry," in Pierre Nora, ed., *Les lieux de mémoire,* vol. 2, *La nation.* Paris, 1986.

Godechot, Jacques. "Nation, patrie, nationalisme, patriotisme en France, au XVIIIe siècle," *Annales historiques de la Révolution française,* no. 206, 1971.

Gusdorf, Georges. "Le cri de Valmy," *Communications,* no. 45, *Eléments pour une histoire de la nation.* Paris, 1987.

Hyslop, Beatrice. *French Nationalism in 1789 according to the General Cahiers.* New York, 1934. Second edition, New York, 1968.

Ozouf-Marignier, Marie-Vic. *La représentation du territoire français à la fin du XVIIIe siècle d'après les travaux sur la formation des départements.* Paris, 1987.

Robin, Régine. *La société française en 1789: Semur-en-Auxois.* Paris, 1970.

Sieyès, Emmanuel. *Qu'est-ce que le Tiers Etat?* ed. Roberto Zapperi. Geneva, 1970.

RELATED TOPICS

Ancien Régime
Army
Département
Estates General
Federation
King's Trial
Mirabeau
Natural Boundaries
Physiocrats
Republic
Revolution and Europe, The
Revolutionary Assemblies
Revolutionary Calendar
Rights of Man
Rousseau
Sieyès
Voltaire

Natural Borders

For a person living in the twentieth century, a border has a precise meaning: a line separating two sovereign states and marked by customs bureaus, police officers, and passport checks. For a contemporary of François I or Louis XV, things were different. A border was a zone whose definition was sufficiently vague that residents of some border villages were able to avoid being taxed by governments on either side, sufficiently permeable that men and goods could flow across it with relative ease, and sufficiently uncertain that not even repetitive and interminable negotiations could resolve disputes over a boundary's exact location. This state of affairs was true, in particular, of France's eastern and northeastern borders. These were not "natural" boundaries but products of history, of the overlap between feudal law and de facto sovereignty and of the successful or unsuccessful strategies of sovereigns. The division of Charlemagne's empire into three parts (Treaty of Verdun, 843) had created between France and what would become the Holy Roman Empire a territory known as Lotharingia, which lay east of the Rhone and between the Meuse and the Rhine and included rich and populous areas with a promising future. Think of the Western Grand Duchy, which Philip the Good and Charles the Bold failed to make into a true state, or of today's Common Market, headquartered in Strasbourg and Brussels. But first France and then Germany became nation-states, leaving between them this vaguely defined and contested region, over which wars were fought and peace treaties signed—treaties that turned out to be nothing more than truces.

If we consult the dictionaries, we find that both Furetière's (1690) and Richelet's (1630) define *frontière* as "the extremity of a kingdom or a province, which enemies must attack directly if they wish to enter. Picardy is a 'frontier' province. The king's conquests extended and pushed back the kingdom's frontiers." There is no mention of natural frontiers or borders, about which successive editions of the *Dictionnaire de l'Académie Française* (from 1694 to 1798) were equally silent. It was conquest and annexation that allowed the monarchy to push back its "extremities." Expansion was the product not of a systematic determination but of a strategy, at once defensive and offensive. Historians have criticized Charles VIII, Louis XII, and François I for succumbing to the "Italian mirage," for giving up for a half-century the idea of improving France's northern and northeastern borders for the sake of futile conquests in Naples and Milan. (I must confess that such retrospective judgments seem to me largely out of place.) What this proves, in any case, is that there was no unified ideology of natural borders in royal policy. Bonaparte, after all, only followed the course set out by the early sixteenth-century monarchs, though he had greater success than they.

Historians in France and Germany have at times broached the subject of natural borders in the French Revolution in impassioned terms. In France the great work of Albert Sorel (whose first volume was published in 1885) raised the theme of continuity between the policy of the monarchy and that of the Revolution. "French policy was determined by geography. The national instinct suggested it even before reasons of state made it advisable. It was based on a fact: Charlemagne's empire. The history of France has been one long court case, which began with the irresolvable dispute over the emperor's legacy." In other words, geography was essential, but history was the deciding factor. In another volume Sorel laid greater stress on geography: "This policy arose out of the nature of things. Stymied by the Atlantic, the Pyrenees, the Mediterranean, and the Alps, the French monarchy could only expand toward the east and north, into Flanders and the territories that formed, at the time of the Capets' accession, Lorraine and Burgundy." Thus in 1793 and 1795 the Revolution was simply carrying on the work of many centuries. Sorel was politically conservative, but his ideas were shared by neo-Jacobin historians. Commenting on a speech of Brissot's, Albert Mathiez wrote in 1924: "Brissot embellished with a [revolutionary's] red cap the old royal policy of natural borders."

Politicians were not slow to jump on the bandwagon. In a major speech to the Chamber of Deputies on September 15, 1919, Clemenceau cited Sorel: "M. Albert Sorel . . . has clearly demonstrated what all of us instinctively knew, that the push into the Rhineland was in our ancestors' tradition. But that tradition was to create a border . . . a true border marking the limits of French territory."

Sorel, however, can claim credit only for having provided an elegant and systematic summary of ideas common to much of nineteenth-century French historiography. In 1834 Augustin Thierry had this to say in his *Récits des temps mérovingiens* (*Tales of Merovingian Times*, first published in book form in 1840): "The nation firmly and steadfastly desired nothing other than maintenance of our natural boundaries. . . . Recapturing them was an idea that never faded from view: it was profoundly national and profoundly historical. It stemmed not from the Franks, who were in a sense only a brief and superficial incident in our national history, but from the very depths of the French nation, from the primal and vital source of French nationality: independent, and later Roman, Gaul." Thierry traced this quest for the Rhine, moreover, from Louis XI ("that king of the Third Estate who seems to have anticipated the spirit of the French Revolution") to the Revolution itself ("which unfortunately went even further"). Remember, too, that the best-selling French historian of the nineteenth century (with numerous editions published between 1838 and 1856) was Henri Martin. Like Victor Duruy, Martin defended the idea of natural borders. Only the most lucid thinkers, such as Guizot and Michelet, refused to subscribe to this credo. Even Ernest Lavisse, in the conclusion to his *Histoire de France contemporaine*, echoed Sorel's theme.

IDEAS

In Germany the theme of the "French push toward the Rhine," based on the actions of Richelieu, the Treaties of Westphalia, and the revolutionary annexations, provoked a tremendous response as early as 1813. Arndt published a brochure significantly entitled *The Rhine, German River* (rather than "German border"). Later, in 1861, Janssen published his *Frankreichs Rheingelüste*, which met with considerable success. The controversy continued through the Second World War. In a book translated into French in 1941 (with a preface by F. de Brinon), the journalist Friedrich Grimm wrote: "Richelieu also followed a policy of natural borders. . . . The Pyrenees were supposed to serve as a boundary for Spain, the Alps for Italy, and the Rhine for Germany. . . . The policy of natural borders was therefore just another way of saying 'push toward the Rhine,' which for centuries had been one aspect of the traditional French policy." Is the history of natural borders the history of a myth? A closer look is needed.

It is a good idea to distinguish carefully between the policy of natural borders and the educational use of the theme in the secondary schools. In two remarkable articles (published in 1933 and 1936), Gaston Zeller demolished Albert Sorel's argument. The one passage that Sorel had ascribed to Richelieu (taken from his *Testament politique*) was an interpolation, having nothing to do with the context. The Latin passage may be translated as follows: "To restore to France the borders that nature assigned it, to identify Gaul with France and, wherever ancient Gaul existed, to reconstitute it." It was on the basis of this apocryphal text that German historiography traced the Convention's policy back to Richelieu. The annexation of Metz, Toul, and Verdun by Henri II (1552) grew out of a strategic necessity, not an ideology of borders. The same was true of Alsace (Treaties of Westphalia) and Strasbourg. In fact, as Zeller points out, the French at that time looked not to the Rhine but to the north, to the Netherlands, Flanders, and possible invasion routes. Zeller rightly concludes: "The idea of natural borders was never part of the baggage of Ancien Régime statesmen."

But was it the "history of a misconception?" As early as the fifteenth century, the idea of a border on the Rhine was defended by publicists, some of them from circles close to the throne. The theme fared especially well in two periods: around 1444, when Charles VII and the dauphin sent an army into Lorraine and Alsace (in the hope of thwarting efforts by the duke of Burgundy to reconstitute the old Lotharingia), and again after the Treaty of Cateau-Cambrésis (1559), when people began to think once more of the boundaries of ancient Gaul. In 1568 a man from Lorraine by the name of Jean Le Bon published a pamphlet, *Le Rhin au roy* (*The Rhine to the King*), expressing his preference for a Rhenish policy over an Italian one: France needed the Rhine more than the Po. "When France drinks the Rhine, all Gaul will have its fill." Yet his was an isolated voice, which found no echo. In the days of Richelieu as well as during the personal reign of Louis XIV, polemicists did not raise this issue, which was not revived until the eighteenth century, when Father Bougeant published his work on the Treaties of Westphalia.

Make no mistake about the lack of "committed" literature, however. The idea of natural borders entered public opinion in three ways. Had it not done so, it would be impossible to understand how the generation that came to power between the end of 1792 and 18 Brumaire could have had such clear views on the subject.

First, there was a scholarly historical literature, based on a critical reading of ancient texts. Such works had limited readership, to be sure, but their influence on the elite was considerable. In works from Etienne Pasquier's *Recherches de la France* to J. A. de Thou's *Histoire universelle* (which speaks of the "natural border of the Gauls") the idea of natural borders was a constant presence, though not of major importance.

Popular historical works no doubt played a more significant role. Mézeray, the royal historiographer, was surely the Henri Martin of the seventeenth and eighteenth centuries. His often reprinted *Abrégé chronologique de l'histoire de France* (1668) served as the historical bible of the cultivated public. In it one could read that "the boundaries of Gaul are fairly well known to have been the two oceans, the Rhine, the Pyrenees, and the Alps." There is no doubt that this "reconstruction" left deep traces.

Secondary-school teaching left even deeper ones. From the age of ten young pupils were confronted with Caesar's *Commentaries* on the Gallic wars. Later they were required to read Strabo, for whom the Pyrenees, the Alps, and the Rhine defined the territory of Gaul. To be sure, as commentaries on the *Commentaries* show, this notion did not occupy a central place in the curriculum. Nevertheless, it did become part of the cultural baggage of generations of young students. Neither Brissot nor Sieyès would have "invented" such an idea had they not found it ready-to-hand in their memories.

What is false is the suggestion that there was a connection between the policy of the Convention and that of the monarchy. What is true is that the theme of natural borders did exist in latent form in people's minds.

By a large majority the Constituent Assembly opposed any change in France's borders. Basically the deputies wished to continue the policy of Vergennes: "France, constituted as it is, should fear rather than seek expansion of any kind." On May 22, 1790, Montmorin, one of Louis XVI's ministers, stated the government's position: "The National Assembly declares that the French nation renounces war for the purpose of conquest and that it will never use its forces against the liberty of any people." Nevertheless, the Revolution from its inception carried with it a new conception of international law. Two specific instances made the problem concrete. The decrees of August 4, which abolished feudal rights, drew protests from German princes with "possessions" in Alsace, who demanded that the provisions of the Treaties of Westphalia be respected. The Constituent Assembly proposed to indemnify them but asserted that Alsace was French not by virtue of conquest but as a result of its voluntary membership in the Federation: this introduction of the right of a people to self-determination was an innovation. More serious was the demand by Avignon, after its uprising against the Pope in June 1790, to be incorporated into France. The Constituent Assembly was hesitant. At first it refused, but then, in September 1791, it approved the annexation. This action was a violation of principles previously in force. Meanwhile, the Legislative Assembly's declaration of war "on the king of Bohemia and Hungary" on April 20, 1792, was followed by crushing defeats. It is not surprising that the French in this period were reluctant to base territorial claims on conquest.

After Valmy, French territory was free of foreign troops, and in the autumn of 1792 the revolutionary armies took the offensive. In September Savoy and Nice were occupied without resistance. In October Custine captured Speyer and then Mainz. Early in November the conquest of Belgium got underway. At this point the Convention was faced with a formidable question: what to do with the conquered territories, since war was now being waged beyond France's 1789 boundaries. The answer depended on three factors. The thinking of officials as expressed in their speeches and writings seems to have been less firm than is often assumed: the same men who sometimes favored annexations in the name of natural borders at other times called for the creation of a protective shield of "sister republics" or for a freedom crusade. On November 26 Brissot wrote to Servant: "We cannot remain calm while Europe—all Europe—burns." The Girondin on this point agreed with the left-wing Montagnard Chaumette: "The territory that separates Paris from Petersburg and Moscow will soon be Francicized, municipalized, and Jacobinized." On November 27, however, in a letter to Dumouriez, Brissot invoked France's natural boundaries: "The French Republic should not have any boundary other than the Rhine." He also expressed his support for the idea of creating "sister republics."

In fact, the men of the temporarily triumphant Revolution were hesitant. Popular reactions, the policies of the generals, and financial constraints would force them to go further than they had originally intended. In Savoy, Montesquieu authorized the formation of an "Allobroges Convention," which by late October was calling for union with France. In Nice, a majority of whose citizens were deeply committed to Italy, Anselme supported the small Marseillaise colony, which was calling for annexation. On the Rhine, Custine encouraged the revolutionaries who had come from France to join his army. In Belgium, where Dumouriez hoped to become the leader of an independent state, none of the existing parties favored annexation. Who would pay the costs of the war? The French alone? Cambon attempted to persuade the Convention that France ought to force the conquered territories to accept the assignat. At this point the Convention definitively committed itself to a policy of annexation. On November 21 Savoy was "reunited" with France. On January 31, 1793, Nice was annexed. That same day Danton proposed the annexation of Belgium: "I say that it is pointless to fear overextending the Republic. Its boundaries have been set by nature." Carnot justified annexation on both geographical and historical grounds: "The ancient and natural boundaries of France are the Rhine, the Alps, and the Pyrenees. The parts it has lost were lost only through usurpation." On grounds of legal and diplomatic affinities, Grégoire on November 27 also invoked France's natural borders. Yet neither Danton nor Carnot nor Grégoire—nor later Robespierre—believed strongly in the realism of their declarations, as is shown by their subsequent behavior. They were impelled in part by the emotional climate (the victory of Jemmapes had marked a turning point), in part by contradictions arising out of the conquest itself—the liberating crusade was costly.

Within a few weeks, in the spring of 1793, the "natural borders" had to be abandoned. At the end of March Belgium was evacuated, followed in early April by the left bank of the Rhine: France now occupied nothing but the fortress of Mainz, which was encircled by enemy armies. The "reunited" populations did not offer a warm welcome to French troops: to be robbed and forced to accept the assignat was a heavy price to pay for liberty. No one in Belgium or on the left bank of the Rhine wanted to be French, and it was not until the spring of 1794 that the war effort mounted by the Committee of Public Safety began to bear fruit. On 9 Thermidor, when Robespierre fell, Antwerp and Liège were retaken. The offensive resumed in the fall. At the end of October the Prussians evacuated the left bank of the Rhine. Holland was conquered during the winter. Again questions arose. Did the Republic want genuine peace? Under what conditions? The two questions were related, but their significance in 1794 was not the same as it had been in 1792. The coalition was showing signs of strain. The Grand Duke of Tuscany (a Hapsburg) was prepared to negotiate with the Republic. The king of Prussia embarked on peace talks in October. Several small German states (Wurtemberg, Hesse) were prepared to withdraw their support from the emperor. Everything depended on what price the Thermidorians were willing to pay, what boundaries they were willing to accept for France. While French public opinion was unanimously in favor of peace, it was deeply divided over what conditions to accept.

The Committee of Public Safety moved cautiously. On July 16, 1794 (28 Messidor), Carnot presented his "Views on the results to be expected from the success of the present campaign," which fell far short of his earlier statements: "We could, if we so wished, plant the liberty tree on the banks of the Rhine and restore all the former territory of the Gauls to France. Attractive as this theory may be, however, it might be wise to give it up on the grounds that France can only weaken herself and sow the seeds of an endless war by expanding her territory in this way." In fact, Carnot, as well as Barthélemy (France's principal diplomatic representative), favored establishing the Meuse as the boundary rather than the Rhine. Later, Dubois-Crancé (a member of the Committee from December 5, 1794, to April 4, 1795) presented a "plan of conduct" inspired by the same idea: "As for the Rhineland territories, the Committee will form its opinion in accordance with the circumstances. It will judge whether it is wise to extend the French border only as far as the Meuse and to turn the rest of the conquered territory into two republics, which, together with the republic of Holland, would live under French rule." Sieyès himself, though often described as a champion of natural borders, wrote these revealing lines to the negotiators in The Hague in Prairial, Year III: "I also hoped that peace throughout western Europe would be the morally certain outcome of choosing the Rhine as a barrier between Germany and France. . . . But how changed I find my colleagues' thinking! If need be I shall join the majority, not without regret as I look at the map and see that handsome territory between the Meuse and the Rhine, which, being neither French nor Batavian, will remain a source of periodic war and devastation." Among political leaders only the Alsatian Reubell stubbornly clung to the Rhine boundary.

In the Convention, however, the majority pushed for identifying the Revolution with the Rhine border. For most deputies the cry "old boundaries" was the slogan of the enemies of the regime, of overt or covert royalists and counterrevolutionaries. One of the secretaries of the Committee of Public Safety wrote in September 1794 that the belief that the Republic ought to hold out for the Rhine boundary was "an opinion whose popularity is impressive and the number of whose supporters in the Convention is growing daily." There was also fear about what the army's reaction might be; to allow the neo-Jacobins a monopoly of "patriotism" was a dangerous gamble. Thus the Thermidorians, for all their lucidity, were caught in a bind: to refuse to identify the Republic with the Rhine boundary was to surrender to the counterrevolution. This quandary clarifies the contradiction between what they said in public and the instructions they issued in private, between their speeches to the Convention and their private confidences. Negotiations were conducted with Prussia in Basel and with Holland at The Hague. The negotiations with Prussia were partially successful. Under the terms of the Treaty of Basel (April 5, 1795, or 16 Germinal, Year III), Prussia recognized the French occupation of the left bank of the Rhine but "deferred the fate of these territories until a general peace [was] in effect"—a postponement of principle. On 27 Floréal Holland was obliged to accept not only the status of a protectorate but also the annexation by France of Dutch Flanders, Maestricht, and Varloo. However, on September 30 (8 Vendémiaire, Year IV), Merlin of Douai solemnly declared from the podium of the Convention the Committee of Public Safety's firm belief in the system of natural frontiers. That system was not consecrated by any vote; Merlin was calling only for the annexation of Belgium and the territory of Liège (which was approved on October 1, or 9 Vendémiaire), while using the Treaties of Basel and The Hague as a pretext for postponing the "reunion" with the Rhenish territories. He added: "It is therefore not by acts of legislation but solely by acts of diplomacy made possible by our victories and necessary by the completion of our conquests that we shall preserve this fundamental barrier." Diplomacy was not to the taste of all Conventionnels. One, the relatively obscure Eschassériaux, after alluding from the rostrum to "double-dealing Mazarin" and "bloody Richelieu," shouted: "In those days diplomacy ruled the world. That lamentable science, daughter of tyranny, usurped the rights of nature." To steer a course between realities and passions proved difficult.

Was the policy of the Directory a continuation of that of Thermidor? Many writers have held that it was. The royalists of 1795 were sure of it. "All the directors," wrote Mallet du Pan on November 8, 1795, ten days after their election, "belong to the regicide faction, which is bent on sowing chaos in Europe, on holding on to old conquests and making new ones." Indeed, the election of four former members of the Committee of Public Safety—Sieyès, Reubell, Letourneur, and La Révellière—can be seen as a victory for those who favored conquest. But the military situation had changed. At the very moment when the Convention was giving way to the Directory, defeats began to occur at an ever accelerating pace. Pichegru had been forced to retreat to Landau; Jourdan would soon be obliged to evacuate the Palatinate. It was no longer the time to dream of borders; the time had come to wage war. Carnot was once again put in charge of the war effort. But he was no longer the same man. As late as Prairial, Year IV, he had declared: "The victorious armies are pushing back our boundaries to the barriers provided by nature." But military failure, the moderatism of the Five Hundred, and the election of a new royalist "third" in Germinal, Year V (February 1797) gradually persuaded him to abandon the policy of "natural" boundaries. In the meantime he planned the campaign of 1796. But as is well known, Italy, though still a secondary theater of operations, became under Bonaparte a battlefield on which important victories were won. In Germany, by contrast, two armies, that of the Sambre and Meuse and that of the Rhine and Moselle, idle that spring, took the offensive during the summer but were pushed back throughout the fall. As a result, the commanding general of the army of Italy was able to conclude a preliminary treaty with Austrian diplomats on April 18, 1797. In the "public" articles of the treaty, Austria surrendered Belgium and the Milan region, but when it came to the left bank of the Rhine the Austrians hid behind the Imperial Diet, which they agreed would enter into discussions at Rastadt with French envoys "on the basis of the integrity of the empire."

Thus the Revolution conceded one of its essential objectives. For Bonaparte, the timing was crucial, for the German armies were about to resume their campaign. The Directory, hesitant and under threat, let him have his way. After the coup d'état of 18 Fructidor (September 4, 1797) and the removal of Carnot and Barthélemy, Bonaparte was able to sign the Treaty of Campoformio with Austria (October 17). He sacrificed Venice to Austria but did not obtain the left bank of the Rhine, whose fate still depended on a decision of the Imperial Diet. The directors were reluctant to ratify Bonaparte's treaty, but as La Révellière recognized in his *Memoirs*, "if the Directory had refused ratification, it would have alienated public opinion." The chaotic, hesitant expansionism of 1798, which aroused hostility throughout Europe, and the stalemate in the negotiations at Rastadt, made conditions ripe for a new coalition. Bonaparte's defeat at Aboukir (August 1798) brought things to a head. Austria joined Russia and England and officially resumed war with France in March 1799. Since military matters are beyond the scope of this essay, I shall say simply that by the time Bonaparte was triumphally welcomed upon his return to France, the French armies had overcome the defeats of that spring and resumed the offensive everywhere. The nation that hailed Bonaparte was therefore not, contrary to Brumairian legend, a defeated France but a triumphant one.

It is a signal contradiction that many Brumairians wished for nothing more than stability and peace. Georges Lefebvre cited an article that appeared in *La décade* in October 1799 and was attributed to Daunou, which retrospectively criticized the Convention for having declared the Republic's boundaries to be intangible, thereby initiating "endless war and the annihilation of all Frenchmen." Had they forgotten the words spoken by their hero on his return from Rastadt on December 10, 1797: "You have succeeded in organizing a great nation, whose vast territory is circumscribed only because *nature herself has set its limits*"? And how could they have believed that the man who had sacrificed the left bank of the Rhine for the sake of creating Italian protectorates would be a man of peace? With the Consulate and the Empire a different system came into being. It was not just to the Rhine but over all Europe that Napoleon intended to lead the armies of revolutionary France.

Natural borders, then, were not a political tradition but a passion, whose rudimentary sources can indeed be traced to the Ancien Régime, but to which only the Revolution gave explosive force.

Denis Richet

FURTHER READING

Grimm, Friedrich. *Das Testament Richelieus*. Berlin, 1940.

Guyot, Raymond. *Le Directoire et la paix de l'Europe, des traités de Bâle à la deuxième coalition (1795–1799)*. Paris, 1911.

Sorel, Albert. *L'Europe et la Révolution française*, vol. 1. Paris, 1885.

Zeller, Gaston. "Histoire d'une idée fausse," *Revue de synthèse*, vol. 11, February–December 1936.

——— "La monarchie d'Ancien Régime et les frontières naturelles," *Revue d'histoire moderne*, vol. 7, 1953.

RELATED TOPICS

Army

Assignats

Carnot

Committee of Public Safety

Danton

Guizot

Italian Campaign

Michelet

Napoleon Bonaparte

Nation

Night of August 4

Revolution and Europe, The

Robespierre

Sieyès

Thermidorians

Treaties of Basel and The Hague

PHYSIOCRATS

To what extent did the ideas of the physiocrats influence the men of 1789? There is no simple, comprehensive answer to this question. Although a few prominent individuals such as Dupont de Nemours might at first sight suggest the existence of a link between the "school" and the Constituent Assembly, one fact is inescapable: the members of that Assembly never ceased to display hostility toward the physiocrats. Thinking back on that period, Dupont de Nemours wrote to Jean-Baptiste Say: "The moment there was any question in the National Assembly of commerce or finances, violent invectives could be heard against the economists." The reasons for this hostility were primarily sociological and cultural. The physiocrats were seen as a closed, doctrinaire, almost esoteric group, endlessly repeating abstract, peremptory formulas. Voltaire's ironic and acerbic barbs in his *Homme aux quarante écus* had shaped the common sense of an entire generation. In 1789 even more perhaps than in the 1760s Quesnay and his disciples were never mentioned without a contemptuous reference to a "sect" or to the "economist" party.

Yet despite this rejection of individual physiocratic thinkers, was the Constituent Assembly perhaps influenced by physiocratic ideas? Rabaut Saint-Etienne suggested as much in his *Précis d'histoire de la Révolution française:*

> The economists were blamed for a mystical language, not well suited to the enunciation of simple, clear, truthful oracles . . . but we owe it to their virtuous stubbornness that Frenchmen were led to reflect on the science of government. Because they steadfastly concerned themselves for so long with the same subject, we are indebted to them for the wide currency of ideas so simple that they have become commonplace: that only freedom of industry serves posterity; that talents should be subjected to no impediment; that freedom of grain export results in an abundance of grain; and that what the farmer spends in advance of the harvest should not be taxed, but only what remains after he has been reimbursed.

Physiocratic influence in the fiscal area at first seems undeniable. When the Constituent Assembly approved the principle of a unified direct tax and rejected all taxes on consumption, it would seem to have demonstrated the inroads made by physiocratic doctrine. Consistent with their theory of the "net product," the physiocrats had always argued in favor of a modernization of the tax system of this kind. Having chosen landed property as their central figure, at once economic and political, they held that it was the only form of property on which taxes ought to be assessed. All the reform proposals of the 1780s followed the lines they had set down. Thus in 1782 the preamble of a

763

draft edict observed: "The base of taxation is the territory, whose renewable value alone can reproduce it. Whatever form the tax may take, only the territory can support and feed it." In 1787, during the great crisis of the notables, Calonne also adopted the principle of the universal territorial tax. But was this ambition to create a simplified, equitable, and economically neutral tax system by establishing a tax on land to be paid by all landowners really a legacy of the physiocrats? There is reason to doubt it. The specific contribution of the physiocrats—a single, universal tax on land—was by 1789 practically inseparable from the broad eighteenth-century liberal critique of taxes on consumption, which ever since Boisguilbert and Vauban had been accused of restraining trade and therefore impeding economic development. Although the Constituent Assembly ascribed special importance to the tax on land, it never really considered making this a unique tax; the land tax was expected to yield only 240 million livres out of a total budget of nearly 500 million. While indirect taxes were unanimously rejected, all debates on finances from the Constituent Assembly to the Directory reveal considerable indecision on fiscal matters. Furthermore, events made it possible to avoid resolution of the fundamental issue. For twenty-five years the state lived on expedients: patriotic contributions, assignats, sale of national properties, and tribute exacted from occupied countries. Such pragmatism was a long way from the rigor recommended by Quesnay. The propositions of the physiocrats had not really penetrated revolutionary society except insofar as they contained prescriptions of a generally liberal nature. As soon as one looks at the more technical details of economic and financial measures, however, one finds that little attention was paid to them. Quesnay influenced the men of 1789 only to the extent that his views were similar to those of Adam Smith and abbé Galiani, and where his views differed from theirs he had no influence. The repeated attacks on the "sect" were thus in no way contradictory with Rabaut Saint-Etienne's positive judgment of the physiocrats' role.

But the crucial point has not yet been mentioned. It was in fact in the realm of political ideas that the physiocrats played a major role by establishing the intellectual framework in terms of which the Constituent Assembly conceived citizenship.

The physiocrats' economic theory served them as a point of reference for defining the nation. In place of the traditional criterion of membership based on "incorporation" (that is, membership in a corps), they proposed an idea of social involvement based on economic factors. For them, a member of the nation was one who through his production contributed to the enrichment of society. Agriculture was the only activity that created value; hence the owners of land constituted the social class around which the social interest was constructed. Should they therefore be regarded as the only citizens? In fact the term "citizen" was not in the physiocrats' vocabulary. Landowners, Mirabeau noted in his *Théorie de l'impôt*, are "the only true—I do not say citizens, for this word comes from cities and republics—but *régnicoles* and nationals." If France was an agricultural empire, and if working the land was the heart of the modern economy, the nonagricultural professions were therefore in a sense *external* to the nation. The way in which Le Trosne envisioned this question in *De l'intérêt social* is particularly eloquent in this regard. Defining an economic ideal with autarchic overtones, he offered a territorial analysis of wealth on the basis of which he completely redefined the relations between what was inside the nation and what was outside. Merchants? "The agents of foreign commerce, whoever they may be, form a particular class scattered among nations, which by the very nature of its profession and the use of its wealth, is cosmopolitan; which makes deals anywhere it expects to make a profit without forming an attachment to any particular nation." Workers? For the most part they were "boarders maintained among us by foreigners, who may at any moment leave them to fend for themselves, in which case they will become an onerous population." Artisans? "They constitute a class which, by the nature of its work and the employment of its capital, is not attached to the territory that it inhabits and has no wealth other than its wages, which for the most part are paid by the nation itself." Manufacturers? "They are in the nation but not *of* the nation. They may transport their industry and their capital elsewhere. And they are not really taxpayers. . . . They know how to protect their wealth against taxation in all circumstances and never do anything with their money but lend it."

For the physiocrats, social involvement was governed by the relation to land. A physical bond to the soil, an obligatory and permanent residence were for them the tokens of true social integration. "Farmers," Condorcet concluded in his *Réflexions sur le commerce des blés,* "are more interested than others to make sure that the country, which they cannot leave, is governed by good laws. They should be favored in political laws by regarding them as more truly citizens than others. . . . The interest of the various classes in the general prosperity of society is inversely proportional to the ease with which they can change homeland." This was also the source of the physiocrats' critique of what they called the "city spirit." Cities were accused of destroying society from within, of ruining the economy, of spreading corruption, and of encouraging idleness. Dozens of works developed these themes from 1760 on.

The movement for the reform of the provincial assemblies, which gained strength in the late 1770s, took place in an intellectual climate dominated by physiocratic ideas, in which fiscal reform went hand in hand with a new conception of citizenship. In 1779 Le Trosne published *De l'administration provinciale et de la réforme de l'impôt,* four years after the *cour des aides* had called for convocation of the Estates General. A few months earlier Necker had already given in to diffuse pressure by authorizing a provincial assembly in Berri on an experimental basis. At least half the members were required to be landowners; thus the old logic of orders was challenged for the first time. Le Trosne's reform plan was aimed first of all at establishing the unique tax on land of which the physiocrats dreamed. But the most interesting aspect of his proposal was the system of representation he envisioned in order to implement this fiscal reform and, more generally, to help define a broad program of public works. It was a hierarchical system, a pyramid with communal assemblies at the base, district assemblies above them, provincial assemblies above them, and at the top a National Council. Only landowners could be electors, with no requirement as to the amount of property that must be owned. "The other classes of citizens," Le Trosne noted, "have no claim in view of the perfect immunity [from taxation] of their riches and labors." This was a prefiguration of the distinction between active citizens and passive citizens that Sieyès would introduce ten years later. The work that Dupont de Nemours wrote for Turgot, *Des administrations provinciales: Mémoire sur les municipalités à établir en France,* was conceived in a similar spirit. Only landowners were considered legitimate electors. "No one really belongs to a parish or village," wrote Dupont de Nemours, "who does not own real estate there. The others are only hired hands, who reside there temporarily."

Thus there is no way to appreciate the significance of the debates on the right to vote during the drafting of the Constitution of 1791 without taking account of the ideas that physiocratic literature had put into people's heads over the previous twenty years. The deputies of the Constituent Assembly simply picked up where the economic and political reflections of Quesnay, Mirabeau, and Le Trosne had left off. The figure of the landowning citizen continued to play a central role in their model of political society. That model had evolved, however, beyond the narrow "landownerism" of Quesnay's school.

Condorcet gives an idea of the direction of that evolution. In his 1788 *Essai sur la constitution des assemblées provinciales,* he still shared the "pure" physiocratic view: "Since a country is a territory circumscribed by borders, one must regard [land] owners as the only true citizens." A short while later, however, in his *Lettre d'un bourgeois de New Haven,* he conceded that "the owner of a house, by attaching his capital to the territory, has evidently identified himself in regard to both interest and social state with the owner of larger territorial holdings." Sieyès, for his part, had read extensively in the works of economists from Adam Smith to Quesnay. In 1775 he drafted a manuscript that he did not publish: *Lettres aux économistes sur leur système de politique et de morale.* Criticizing the physiocrats' theory of wealth, he indicated his support for the position of Adam Smith, declaring that wealth was produced by labor in one of its many manifestations. Accordingly, he was able to broaden the notion of the owner-citizen to the shareholder-citizen (*citoyen actionnaire*). For him the active citizen, that is, the citizen who enjoyed the right to vote, was "the true shareholder in the great social enterprise." He was a shareholder not only by virtue of his labor but even more through his contribution, in the form of a tax payment, to the functioning of what Sieyès called the "public establishment." The philosophy of social involvement on which Sieyès based his idea of the shareholder-citizen was the same philosophy in terms of which the physiocrats had defined the owner-citizen. The two figures differed only in the economic concepts with which they were associated. The point of the analysis in both cases was to distinguish individuals who are truly of society from those who are content merely to live in society. But Sieyès and the Constituent Assembly treated the question as one of differentiating between civil rights and political rights, not as Quesnay and Le Trosne did, as a matter of establishing criteria for membership in the nation itself.

That the concept of the owner-citizen was still central for the men of 1789 is also apparent in the importance they continued to attach to the relation between an individual and the land. Social involvement for them still implied some notion of stable geographical residence, as can be seen from the importance of residence among the requirements for qualifying as an elector. All whose interests were not socially fixed were to be denied the right to vote. The dangerous classes were seen as being composed of a flux of unstable individuals with no permanent roots. By contrast, a landowner was one whose private interest was so intimately intertwined with the general social interest that his situation alone equipped him to judge what was good for society as a whole. The status of landowner did not merely define an economic position; it embodied a whole system of social and moral guarantees.

Barnave's views reflect this "totalizing" approach to property as inextricably economic, moral, sociological, and political. In a major debate on the rights of the active citizen and the conditions under which those rights could be exercised (August 11, 1791), Barnave gave a speech that summed up the revolutionary conception of the owner-citizen. Electoral assemblies, he argued, ought to embody three qualities:

> First, enlightenment, and no one can deny that, speaking not of an individual but of a collection of men, a certain fortune, a definite contribution, is, up to a certain point, the token of a more careful education and a more extensive enlightenment. The second guarantee lies in interest in public affairs on the part of those whom society delegates to make its decisions, and it is obvious that such interest will be greater in those who have more extensive private interests to defend. Finally, the last guarantee lies in independence of fortune, which, by placing an individual above need, makes him more or less impervious to the means of corruption that might be employed to sway his opinion.

Where were these qualities to be found? Barnave argued first of all that they ought not to be sought in the former upper class, which too often exhibited "a private interest of ambition separate from the public interest." But, he went on, it was equally unlikely that they would be found in the class of those who, being "obliged by the insignificance of their fortune to work directly and constantly in order to provide for their needs, cannot acquire any of the enlightenment necessary to make decisions and do not have a powerful enough interest in conservation of the existing social order." He therefore called upon the middle classes, who in his view ought to constitute the center of gravity of representative government in France.

It is clear that, with Barnave, the notion of owner-citizen had evolved. Although he continued to believe that property ownership could guarantee an elector's devotion to the social interest and imperviousness to corruption, he also saw a broader significance. Ownership became a social quality, potentially separable from its legal foundation. Ultimately the word *propriétaire* (owner) can be interpreted as referring to any honest, hardworking individual concerned about maintaining the social order.

> Once the rights of all are regulated and guaranteed by an established constitution, then all men who live on their properties and all who live by honest work will share the same interest. Then there will be only two opposing interests in society: the interest of those who wish to conserve the existing state of things

because they see prosperity in property and subsistence in labor, and the interest
of those who wish to change the existing state of things because there are no
resources for them except in the alternative of revolution, because they are
people who fatten and grow, as it were, in times of trouble, as do insects in corruption.

Barnave's owner-citizen is based on a sociology of order and thus pre-
figures the nineteenth-century bourgeois. But he is more than that. He also
reflects an apparently unsurpassable view of social involvement, as if citizenship and property together formed the very substance of the modern vision
of politics. The owner-citizen of the French Revolution should not be confused with the individual property owner of English political philosophy. For
Locke, the concept of individual is virtually identical with the concept of
property. For him, property is not simply an attribute of the individual, a
possession external to his person; rather, it defines the individual. It is an
extension of his very being, his material inscription in the world, since it is
nothing but accumulated labor. Property for Locke is the individual in action,
the link between his essence and existence. A man's possession of his person
is inseparable from his possession of his goods. The individual owner is therefore not, unlike the owner-citizen, a separate and distinct social figure: he
constitutes the modern individual as such. The autonomy of the subject was
therefore conceived in terms of a territorial analogy: the individual and his
property formed a unit as intimate and sovereign as a parcel of land bounded
by a fence. Consequently, in English political theory, civil rights and political
rights were not distinct; they represented two facets of a single conception of
the individual. By contrast, in France the owner-citizen was not a mere extension of the individual of civil society. He was part of the principle for organizing the sphere of politics. He effected a mediation between civil society and
political society, a mediation made necessary by the totalizing concept of the
nation in French public law. In this sense the question of social involvement
remained open; involvement was never given, always to be constructed. That
is why the figure of the owner-citizen was such a central concept for the deputies of the Constituent Assembly.

Probably that is also why this same figure continued to serve as a point
of reference, an almost obligatory talking point, in debates from 1789 to
1791. Robespierre himself clung to it firmly. In his view property was a token
of social involvement, presumptive evidence of an individual's interest in public affairs. His argument was cast within the terms of the owner-citizen concept, and his only criticism was directed at the level of property or wealth
required to qualify as an elector or to be eligible for office. "Through a peculiar abuse of language," he said, "the rich have restricted the general idea
of property to certain objects; they have named themselves the only property
owners." Far from rejecting the reference to property, he sought instead,
rather paradoxically, to restore its purity, to strip it of the sociological value
that Barnave and Duport had given it. Although he rejected the dividing line
between rich and poor as a device for distributing political rights, he did not
really repudiate the property criterion as a matter of principle. On August
11, 1791, he observed: "I say that it is not true that one must be rich in order

to be devoted to one's fatherland. I say that it is sacred and emotional interests that attach men to their fellow men and to society. . . . Those interests are man's primordial interests: individual liberty, the pleasures of the soul, and the interest attached to even the smallest property, for one's interest in preserving one's possessions is proportional to the modesty of one's fortune." From 1789 to 1791 the immediate political issue was clear: how much of a tax contribution would be required to qualify as an active citizen? But the debates aroused by this issue, the violent clashes to which it gave rise both in the Assembly and in the streets of Paris, should not be allowed to conceal the fact that the admittedly variable status of property owner constituted the natural ground of reflection on the exercise of political rights.

The owner-citizen was the crucial link between the past and the future in regard to the conception of citizenship. It was an idea that resulted from a transformation of the conceptual legacy of the physiocrats, itself a product of grafting eighteenth-century economic concepts onto the tradition of the Estates General, according to which the right of representation was linked to the payment of a tax. In another respect, it was an idea associated with the ideal of widespread property ownership as a condition of social stability. The sale of national properties helped give substance to this idea in the collective memory of France. Taine was not wrong when he asserted: "So regardless of the great names with which the Revolution decorated itself—liberty, equality, fraternity—it was in essence a *transfer of property:* therein lay its intimate support, its permanent form, its primary motor, and its historical meaning." But Taine is right only if the accent is placed on the fact that this transfer established a political ideal as much as it reflected an economic fact. It is probably in this light that one ought to see the physiocrats' most enduring contribution to the political culture of the French Revolution. By joining the economic principles of liberalism to the structures of rural ownership, the physiocrats created a paradoxical and ambiguous framework for French political modernity. Following their lead, the men of the nineteenth century continued to believe in correcting the defects of individualistic society through the virtues of peasant rootedness.

Pierre Rosanvallon

IDEAS

FURTHER READING

Airiau, Jean. *L'opposition aux physiocrates à la fin de l'Ancien Régime: Aspects économiques et politiques d'un libéralisme éclectique.* Paris, 1965.

Cheinisse, Léon. *Les idées politiques des physiocrates.* Paris, 1914.

Esmein, Adhémar. "L'Assemblée Nationale proposée par les physiocrates," *Séances et travaux de l'Académie des Sciences Morales et Politiques,* September–October 1904, 397–420.

Fox-Genovese, Elizabeth. *The Origins of Physiocracy: Economic Revolution and Social Order in Eighteenth-Century France.* Ithaca, 1976.

Lacroix, Fernand. *Les économistes dans les assemblées politiques au temps de la Révolution.* Paris, 1907.

Schielle, Gustave. *Dupont de Nemours et l'école physiocratique.* Paris, 1888.

Vignes, J.-B. Maurice. *Histoire des doctrines sur l'impôt en France: Les causes de la Révolution française considérées par rapport aux principes de l'imposition.* Paris, 1909. Reprinted in a revised and corrected edition, Padua, 1961.

Weulerese, Georges. *Le mouvement physiocratique en France (de 1756 à 1770),* 2 vols. Paris, 1910. Reprinted Paris and The Hague, 1968.

——— *La physiocratie sous les ministères de Turgot et de Necker, 1774–1781.* Paris, 1950.

——— *La physiocratie à la fin du règne de Louis XV, 1770–1774.* Paris, 1959.

——— *La physiocratie à l'aube de la Révolution: 1781–1792.* Paris, 1984.

RELATED TOPICS

Assignats	Mirabeau	Revolutionary Assemblies	Suffrage
Barnave	National Properties	Robespierre	Taine
Condorcet	Necker	Sieyès	Taxes

PUBLIC SPIRIT

"To take the pulse of the public spirit," wrote Sébastien Mercier in *Nouveau Paris,* "demands a very subtle tact." This ironic remark is aimed at one of the most original undertakings of the Revolution, that of defining and measuring the public spirit. Mercier suggests that all the revolutionaries' pre-statistical efforts revealed less about the object under study than about the observers themselves: "They somehow managed to grasp the thermometer while consulting it and mistook the temperature of their own hands for that of the surrounding air." Public spirit was thus reduced in this sarcastic commentary to the most private opinion. The same sentiment can be found in an anonymous text published in *L'abréviateur universel:* "To talk about public spirit is obstinately to attach a common denomination to the most diverse opinions. Those who make it up out of the spirit of their own coterie pretend to ignore the fact that they are surrounded by other coteries that feed on very different illusions and that, even in the same circle, people change systems, parties, and principles every month, every *décade* [ten days in the revolutionary calendar], and often overnight." The disillusioned author—the date is Germinal, Year III—concludes that not only the investigation but the concept itself has been swept away by the torrent of revolutionary innovations: "The dictionary of the Revolution already contains words that have fallen into disuse." Did the public spirit, so firmly linked here to the revolutionary lexicon, lead a febrile but ephemeral life?

Neither "public opinion" nor "public spirit" can be found in eighteenth-century dictionaries, which always opposed the public not to the *privé* but to the *particulier.* Yet both terms can be found in the political literature of the second half of the century, in rather hazy association with "public good," "public outcry," "public murmur," "public interest," and "public love." It was the epithet that gave all these nouns their emotional charge, and that epithet was used in the singular; Condorcet pointed out to Turgot the abyss that separated the "voice of the public," a hubbub of "a hundred spiteful rumors," from the "public voice." Only the singular adjective seemed capable of rescuing opinion from menacing heterogeneity. The "contrarieties of opinion" were an old theme of political texts, and Hobbes had turned them into a horror. To believe in the goodness and rationality of the "public voice," one first had to define it in a negative way as the opposite of common opinion. Indeed, the latter was composed, Sieyès wrote, "of aggregations of men subjugated by different superstitions." Although superstitions in their own way also represented "very general and very public ideas," they in no sense constituted a public opinion. To have a true public opinion, again according to

Sieyès, one needed "a common point around which all forces can array and coordinate themselves." Public opinion, the opinion of enlightened men, was therefore not the passive, untamed, divided opinion of the multitude. Sieyès, and with him Condorcet, Necker, and Mirabeau, held firmly to this distinction, which was destined to enjoy a remarkable future. They knew that taking opinion into account would lead logically to the conclusion that one individual is just as good as another. It was this conclusion that the adjective public exorcised; the public was not a people, and public opinion was not common sense.

Who (and what) was responsible for the emergence of this public voice? Some saw it as an exotic import, an English surplus: England was at this time the country in which "the public spirit is evident at every step," if enthusiastic tourists such as abbé Coyer are to be believed. This public spirit gained a foothold in France as "public papers" from London and Leyden found their way into the country. Others saw it as the fruit of polemics that had swirled around the parlements for centuries: in tumultuous, repetitious episodes, these courts had opposed the royal authorities, which showed irritation at the magistrates' license in spreading their remonstrances among the public, while the magistrates protested that the royal authorities wished to "stifle the public voice." Still others, even more numerous, maintained that a public had existed ever since academies and other literate bodies of the elite had begun to encourage new forms of sociability in the rather utopian atmosphere of their cultivated gatherings, where strict equality was the rule. No matter what social or cultural group or political practice one associated with the birth of public opinion, however, there was general agreement that it dated precisely from the middle of the century. "Among the features that distinguish the century in which we are living from others is the methodical and serious spirit that has shaped public opinions for the past twenty years," Rousseau wrote in 1776. "Until now opinions varied without order or rule at the whim of men's passions, and those passions, clashing constantly, caused the public to embrace first one, then another, without any constant direction."

Rousseau does not deal with the question of what principle might have knitted all those wavering opinions together. Pursuing his argument, one might say that this principle was provided by opposition to absolutism: the adjective "public" always carried a polemical charge. To say that opinion had become public was to claim that a new tribunal had been instituted, as Malesherbes put it, "independent of all authorities." By this he meant independent, first, of all earthly authority, for royalty had been replaced at center stage by the immaterial authority of the public. And he also meant independent of all heavenly authority, because now the public appeared to exercise the infallible judgment of posterity, that new form of immortality available to those whom their own century had neglected. The new tribunal seemed superior to the old for several reasons. First, because of its visibility: the secrecy of royal judgment and the "law of silence" were always judged very harshly in the eighteenth century. Second, because of its impersonal nature: it seemed to promise impartiality. And third, because of the criteria by which it formed its judgments: merit took the place of birth, and the city replaced the court. For the Enlightenment, then, public opinion served as a kind of court of appeals, a second chance for those who had suffered from arbitrary judgment. The men of the Enlightenment dreamed of obtaining reparations and compensation before the court of public opinion, hopes that were renewed periodically by symbolic victories such as the rehabilitation of Calas.

Did invocation of the "public" in the second half of the eighteenth century carry sufficient weight to suggest that the modern concept of opinion as the aggregate of individual wills, a composite of dissidence and divergence whose causes and outcomes might vary, had already triumphed? Hardly, because multiplicity of opinion was still widely regarded as a misfortune. Those most determined to praise the benefits of the new tribunal found it difficult to admit that enlightened men could hold differing opinions, and they were unwilling to recognize that social life inevitably involves conflict. They were reluctant to ascribe an equal weight to each individual opinion, tally up totals, and recognize the legitimacy of the majority. Even Condorcet, who examined the logical problem of summing up individual preferences to arrive at a collective decision capable of establishing itself as the law of the majority, hesitated to ascribe any value to majority rule unless the majority's decision could simultaneously be shown to be rational: "The power of the majority over the minority cannot enforce submission when it is obviously contradictory to reason." Such a statement also marks a retreat from the idea of representation, which would give shape to division. Even late in the century, people were still sensitive to the danger that public opinion would crystallize into cabals or partisan associations. Rousseau was obviously the most vehement in his attacks on the disastrous weakening of the political bond as the result of such factions.

Thus, these prerevolutionary texts exhibit both deep agreement and serious confusion. Everyone agreed that public opinion had become the motor of history. Yet confusion stemmed from the fact that there were two ways to conceive of public opinion. One could, first of all, draw all the consequences of the individualistic and egalitarian premises on which the idea of public opinion was based, so that in the end the opinion of the public would be the sum total of a range of dissident views. But to reach such a conclusion one would have to concede that public opinion arises out of society itself; it is not under the control of political authority. Hence it can be interpreted, but it cannot be shaped at will, and therefore voluntarism is not a viable political option. The very notion of an uncontrollable yet invincible public opinion was so frightening that people were tempted to replace it with opinion of a more cohesive sort, the product of individual opinions corrected by authority. In this model, public opinion is imposed from above on corrupt, depraved individual opinions. This shaping requires vigorous efforts by an educator or legislator; it is the handiwork of the political authorities. Unfortunately, the very term "public opinion" is marred by the presence of the noun "opinion," which connotes the possibility of fragmentation of the community. People in prerevolutionary France therefore preferred the term "public spirit," which immediately conveyed the idea of unity and held out the promise of full integration in the collectivity.

IDEAS

The French Revolution exemplified both concepts of the "public," one after the other. The Revolution was indeed, as its champions described it, the moment when people stopped obeying external necessity and began conforming to the internal judgments of reason, which expressed spontaneous confidence in the diverse and heterogeneous forms of public opinion. But it was also the moment when the old dream of perfect unity between the community and its leaders made a powerful comeback, when people again began to think of individuals subsumed entirely by their roles as citizens. Jacobin texts shunned the use of "public opinion," a term too suggestive of subjectivity and liberty; the Jacobins preferred the more homogeneous and coercive term "public spirit" (or even, as Saint-Just suggested, "public conscience"). The Revolution may be interpreted as the triumph of the idea of "public spirit" over that of "public opinion," a dearly bought victory.

The history of the revolutionary press illustrates both of these stages. In the first few months of the Revolution there was an extraordinary explosion in the number of periodicals: 42 titles published between May and July 1789, and more than 250 titles in the second half of that year. In the aftermath of the Assembly of Notables, this period of growth had been preceded by a proliferation of *libelles,* or satirical journals, some of which appeared in several installments at irregular intervals and paved the way for more regular periodicals. Contributing to this development was the publication of newspapers at very low cost and with a single person managing the writing, printing, and selling. The revolutionary broadsheet, printed on poor paper and full of typographical errors, was as hasty a production as the events on which it commented and almost invariably marked by the personality of its editor, who not only signed the articles but put together the whole paper: *L'ami du peuple* is the typical example. Despite the abundance of titles and variety of formats, we glimpse some features of modern journalism, including summaries of other papers, letters to the editor, and book reviews. In some cases the work was even divided among several hands: the best example is the *Actes des apôtres,* which was put together by a team of editors.

The changes in the press began before this explosion in the number of publications, however. Jeremy Popkin has shown that journalistic language changed well before the Revolution, and that the leading revolutionary journalists, such as Brissot, Mirabeau, Carra, Gorsas, Mallet du Pan, and of course Linguet had already published in European and French gazettes and in many cases enjoyed a large and enthusiastic readership. Public opinion was at the center of political life well before the Revolution, which did not, strictly speaking, create a journalistic culture. But the Revolution did witness the emergence of a previously unknown popular journalism. Through a ruse, Mirabeau established a de facto freedom of the press: when the first issue of his *Etats Généraux* was judged scandalous and banned, he published "Letters to His Constituents" under the protection of parliamentary immunity. This response was the beginning of a period of de facto freedom, which of course

774

allowed not only the revolutionary press but also the ultra press (which exhorted people to emigrate) to flourish: *L'ami du roi* responded to *L'ami du peuple*.

In accepting this de facto freedom of the press, the revolutionaries were expressing their confidence in the free manifestation of public opinion. They saw it at this point as a revealing sign, a way of uncovering abuses. There was no way that it could be seditious; either people were unhappy, in which case sedition was a duty, or they were happy, in which case seditious writings would be met with indifference. Pétion challenged this belief in the tranquillity of the public, but in the debates on freedom of the press numerous others asserted that it was true, and this public calm clearly implied that there was no need to prohibit aristocratic pamphlets. In 1790–1791 there was still great confidence in freedom of the press, which was guaranteed in theory by the Declaration of the Rights of Man. As a result, proposed laws governing press offenses, like the bill drafted by Sieyès in January 1790, as well as the one drafted by Thouret in August 1791, were highly controversial. Thouret took the view that public officials had the same right as private individuals to protection from libel. The left in the Assembly—Robespierre, Barnave, Pétion—insisted that no such right should be granted to public men, who by virtue of their public role fell under the jurisdiction of public opinion. Their speeches introduced the idea, so important later on, that anyone who feared publicity was guilty. Thouret's proposal was finally included in the Constitution, but his repressive measures were never enforced.

Unlimited freedom of the press was therefore instituted. For a short while diversity was accepted, only to be brutally ended by the tenth of August. With the fall of the monarchy, royalist and constitutional newspapers ceased to publish. The Council and the Commune decided to parcel out their printing presses, type, and other equipment among patriotic printers. Royalist journalists were put on trial; Du Rozoi was executed for inciting civil war, and Suleau was massacred on the night of August 10. This de facto repression was institutionalized by the very restrictive law of March 29, 1793, which marked a turning point in press policy as well as in the concept of public opinion. Aristocratic newspapers were prosecuted as "poisoners." The implication was that public opinion was not "antecedent" (that is, prior to judgment) but "consequent" (that is, shaped by newspapers and other instruments). In other words, it could be manipulated, distorted, misled, and bamboozled. A multitude of counterrevolutionary publications had introduced division, making it necessary to reestablish a unified and positive public opinion.

The time for public spirit had arrived. This latest phase of the Revolution was noted for a Girondin discovery, the Bureau of Public Spirit, created on August 18, 1792, and allotted funds to subsidize the revolutionary press and distribute revolutionary papers to the départements and army units. The Girondins made use of these funds in a most partisan fashion, subsidizing their own papers (the *Courrier de Gorsas*, *Le patriote français*, and Louvet's *La sentinelle*) while denying a subsidy to Marat. But the bureau disappeared along with the king on January 21, 1793, and the Girondins' partisan spirit was later turned against them: the first signs of this turn of events came in the winter of 1793, when Girondin printers were sacked. Despite the guarantees accorded to the press by the Constitution (suspended, it is true, "until peace" returned), the Convention applied the law of March 29, stiffened by the September Law of Suspects, which made it possible to bring any journalist before the Revolutionary Tribunal and burn his writings at the foot of the scaffold. Journalists in fact paid a heavy tribute to the Terror. Meanwhile, the Committee of Public Safety subsidized Montagnard papers and ordered them to be sent free of charge to the army. In the spring of 1794 the last opposition papers—Hébert's *Père Duchesne* and Desmoulins' *Vieux Cordelier*—were branded "factional papers" and suppressed along with the factions they allegedly represented. Freedom of the press had vanished, along with any toleration of diversity. Robespierre had proclaimed the Jacobin program on April 5: "All good citizens must meet in their sections. They must *direct public opinion* more usefully than they have done until now. And they must come to the bar of the Convention to force us to arrest disloyal deputies." The whole ambition of Jacobinism was in effect to revive a unanimous civic life and restore social unity. Public spirit triumphed over public opinion, still incompletely divested of its individualistic connotations. Saint-Just would have preferred the term "public conscience," which was less intellectual and implied greater unity and a closer identification with virtue.

Thermidor unsurprisingly witnessed a new flourishing of newspapers, renewed demands for total freedom of the press, and resurgence of the old idea, developed by Jean Bon Saint-André and later cast in theoretical form by Benjamin Constant, that legislators ought to serve rather than create public opinion. Nevertheless, the freedom of the early years was not restored without modification. Between Thermidor and Brumaire raged a confused battle, marked by endless changes of position. On one side, proponents of unlimited freedom of the press—Fréron, Boissy d'Anglas—emphasized the coercive connotations of the adjective "public" in the Jacobin vocabulary ("public safety" and "public spirit" had served to justify the despotism of Fouquier-Tinville and Collot d'Herbois) and therefore argued for a return to "opinions." On the other side, men embittered by the outrages of the royalist press and worried about the rise of a new aristocracy of journalists ("They are our priests and our nobles," Louvet said) argued against unlimited freedom of the press, at least as long as the Revolution remained "open," and in favor of the public spirit, defined by Louvet as "that sacred enthusiasm, that holy love of country, that father of all immortal actions," which the royalists had nearly destroyed. The Thermidorian Convention and Directory favored the second group over the first: the Chénier Law of 12 Floréal, Year III, the law of Germinal, Year IV, and the law of 19 Fructidor, Year V, all included repressive measures intended to prevent slander of the Republic. The Directory even resurrected the Girondins' Bureau of Public Spirit; a "political bureau," composed of journalists, was chosen to distribute subsidies, prepare articles for the newspapers, and edit a *Bulletin décadaire* that would publish not only all official acts of the Republic but also bravura pieces suitable for inspiring *civisme* and virtue. Not even all these measures could muzzle the violence of the opposition papers, however. Before Brumaire it was impossible to persuade a jury to punish press offenses or to prosecute journalists. A diversity of opinions flourished in spite of all the repressive provisions of the law. Yet despite the memories of Robespierrism, despite the universal acceptance of the idea that the journalist has another role to play than that of "secretary of the government" (in Boissy d'Anglas' phrase), the revolutionaries never repudiated the concept of public spirit.

* * *

To gain a better idea of that concept, one can consult the documents compiled by François de Neufchâteau during his two terms as minister of the interior, documents that were the result of the Directory's statistical ambitions. He asked the Directory's départemental *commissaires* to prepare a report, at first *décadaire* (that is, every ten days) and later monthly, concerning harvests, schools, food supplies, and the situation in the countryside. Under each head the minister wanted his officials to paint a portrait of the "public spirit," and in order to explain what he meant by this he gave a list of the signs by which that spirit manifested itself. For example, did people stop work on *décadi* (the day of rest under the revolutionary calendar)? Who wore the cockade? Did people dress decently for weddings celebrated on *décadi*? Did people leave work on Christmas and Easter? And a very fundamental question: did conscripts heed the call? Did people shout *Vive la République!* as they marched off? In other words, the public spirit was defined in terms of attitudes toward republican institutions. The minister thus confronted his subordinates with a host of difficulties involving not only the observation but also the evaluation of the public spirit.

The most obvious problems had to do with the method of observation. The minister wanted very frequent soundings. Départements were large; hence it was necessary to rely on informants of dubious reliability. Citizens were opposed to these statistical investigations. The *commissaires* complained constantly that it was impossible to form a clear judgment. They were not really sure that there was anything to observe. The *commissaire* of the Seine observed that if, by public spirit, the minister meant mere obedience to the laws, then there was indeed a public spirit in his département. But if the minister meant a "generous spirit" or "love of the Fatherland," then it must be said that there was nothing to observe. In most of the documents produced by this investigation, the characterization of the public spirit is surprisingly repetitious and negative: "To speak of public spirit today is as if one were arguing about hen's teeth," one of them concluded on a melancholy note.

The *commissaires* were simply expressing the fact that the category of public spirit was resolutely teleological. Convinced that there was no public spirit worth observing in their cantons, and that to wait for it to well up from the source would be to wait forever, they moved from positive observation to thoughts about how the public spirit might be "formed," a theme about which they felt they could speak with some assurance: festivals, republican theater, weekend events, sending soldier-teachers out to crisscross the countryside, building roads that would make out-of-the-way places accessible to republican influences—all these were ways of fostering the development of the public spirit. In summarizing them, the *commissaires* slipped from fact to value, from observation to pious wish. Ingenuously they said: "Apathy and simplicity being the distinctive attributes of most of the residents of this area, the public spirit will always be what the men in charge of shaping it want it to be." Or again: "The public spirit needs the regenerative eye of the legislature," an elegant way of tossing the ball back into the minister's court. But the minister refused to accept these reports as the last word on the subject and continued to insist on facts and figures, so the *commissaires* were forced to note and rationalize the difference between public opinion and public spirit. If they observed and recorded diversity in the territory they were required to cover, the reason was simply that public spirit did not exist. One of them, discovering the "very judicious distinction between public spirit and opinion," commented on it thus: "Unfortunately I must tell you that the latter is the final arbiter in the département, and that the bloody vicissitudes of the political scene, the continual divergence of opinions, and all the pretentions of self-love have put man in the place of the fatherland and that there can be no public spirit where there are only opinions." If the minister still wanted his statistics, he would have them, only they would yield not a portrait of the public spirit but a typology of opinions.

Because these départemental administrators were required to perform an impossible task, they were forced to forget about the supposedly coherent public spirit and pay attention instead to the diversity of opinion, which rather than unify the community divided it into groups. They established a typology of opinions that stemmed from different times and places, opinions reflecting differences between sexes (women being more hostile than men to the public spirit), age groups (restive youth being particularly deaf to republican language), religions (the good spirit of the Protestant communes standing in sharp contrast to the deplorable spirit of the Catholic ones), and geography (republican plains versus royalist bocages). By accentuating the ideal unity of the collective consciousness, the minister paradoxically sent his most scrupulous administrators out to discover a public opinion quite the opposite of that imagined by Necker and Condorcet: diverse, fallible, irrational, and easily excited (whereas they had thought of it as indivisible, infallible, rational, and slow to form). The *commissaires* were therefore obliged to think about the social, cultural, and geographic roots of public opinion, factors that had no place in the imaginary conception of a unified public spirit. They were forced to place the accent on the social networks by which opinions were gathered, distributed, and shaped.

Finally, their reports shed light on something that was already implicit in the Enlightenment distinction between common opinion and public opinion but which now stood out with stark clarity: the antinomy between the public spirit and the life of the people. For one thing, those who played the leading roles in popular life—women, children, young people—were precisely those most dramatically devoid of public spirit. For another, the high points of popular life—fairs, pilgrimages, liturgical festivals, patronal festivals—were the low points of the public spirit. Everywhere custom triumphed over revolutionary innovations.

The *commissaires'* disillusioned conclusion was that there could be a public spirit, but only if the Revolution renounced itself. "The more I travel through the département," wrote the *commissaire* for the Nord, "the more I perceive that the public spirit is overwhelmed by religious prejudices. Give back the crucifixes, the bell towers, the Sundays, and everyone will shout, *Vive la République.*" Given these discouraging observations, it is a wonder that the minister and his administrators did not abandon the category of public spirit altogether. For them, there was no public spirit to observe, but there was at least an educable people, in whom it might be possible to form one. The public spirit continued to be thought of as a task consubstantial with the project of revolution itself, and it therefore survived, as an expectation at any rate, longer than Sébastien Mercier had supposed it would.

It took the realism of the Consulate and the Empire to put an end to the dream. Napoleon hated the "public spirit," which to him was a cliché, the password of a clique. His ministers of the interior and prefects conducted inquiries to find out whether "buyers of national properties were harasssed, public coaches were attacked, highways were infested with thieves, and communications were always secure." They completely abandoned the idea of molding people's minds and relinquished all educational ambition. What concerned them was not the activity of citizens but the tranquillity of the streets. The obsession with "public order" signed the death warrant of the "public spirit."

Mona Ozouf

F<small>URTHER</small> READING

Baker, Keith Michael. "Politics and Public Opinion under the Old Regime: Some Reflections," in Jack R. Censer and Jeremy Popkin, eds., *Press and Politics in Pre-Revolutionary France*. Berkeley, 1987.

Bourguet, Marie-Noëlle. *Déchiffrer la France: La statistique départementale à l'époque napoléonienne*. Paris, 1988.

Condorcet, Marie-Jean-Antoine-Nicolas de Caritat, marquis de. *Réflexions sur le commerce des blés*. London, 1776.

Godechot, Jacques. "La presse française sous la Révolution et l'empire," in Claude Bellanger et al., *Histoire générale de la presse française*, vol. 1. Paris, 1969.

Mercier, Louis-Sébastien. *Paris pendant la Révolution ou le nouveau Paris*. Paris, 1862.

Necker, Jacques. *De l'administration des finances de la France*. Paris, 1784.

Popkin, Jeremy. "Enlightened Reaction: The French Right Wing Press under the First Republic, 1792 to 1800." Thesis, University of California (Berkeley), 1978.

Saint-Just, Louis-Antoine de. *Rapport à la Convention sur la police générale*. Paris, 26 Germinal, Year II.

Stoll, Laurence Walter. "The Bureau Politique and the Management of the Popular Press: A Study of the Second Directory's Attempt to Develop a Directoire Ideology and Manipulate the Newspapers." Ph.D. diss., University of Wisconsin, 1975.

R<small>ELATED</small> TOPICS

Barnave	Equality	Mirabeau	Robespierre
Condorcet	Girondins	Napoleon Bonaparte	Rousseau
Constant	Jacobinism	Necker	Sieyès
Enlightenment	Marat	Rights of Man	

REGENERATION

R egeneration: the word, with its extraordinary charge of energy, crops up in the flood of brochures, broadsides, and pamphlets, many of them anonymous, that accompanied the meeting of the Estates General, as well as in works with titles such as "Letters from the Third Estate to Monsieur Necker" or "Credo of the Third Estate," which declare their belief in the "eternal life of the French monarchy, regenerated by the Estates." Even the king, in a letter urging the three orders to complete the verification of their credentials, made the enterprise of regeneration his own: ". . . the National Assembly, which I have convoked to consider, in conjunction with me, the regeneration of the kingdom." (At this point public opinion still regarded the king as "Louis XVI, regenerator," to whom it was proposed that statues be erected.) Regeneration *of the* kingdom: the expression was typical of the first days of the Revolution, when the noun "regeneration" was usually used (in the *cahiers de doléances,* for example) with a genitive that added to its freight but softened its meaning; people spoke of regeneration *of* the administration, *of* public order, *of* the state, *of* France. Soon, however, this ballast was jettisoned, and people began to speak only of regeneration, a program without limits, at once physical, political, moral, and social, which aimed for nothing less than the creation of a "new people."

At the outbreak of the Revolution the idea of a "new man" was hardly new. Images of a second birth had been at the heart of the eighteenth century's dreams. The Huron who sets foot on civilized soil, the man who is rescued from the depths of the woods, the shipwrecked sailor who lands on a lush island, the congenitally blind person whose sight is restored: all were devices for speculating on regained innocence. But these images were primarily fictions, whose purpose was to make people aware, in Morelly's words, of "the falseness of ordinary practice." The philosophes themselves, convinced that prejudice, the multifarious enemy, had made such inroads that it could be fought only by ruse, had envisioned specific improvements but never a general renewal in either ethics or politics. Only Rousseau abandoned all consideration of what was possible, and that abandonment is one of the reasons why the Revolution was all his from the beginning. It was the sudden, unprecedented character of the revolutionary rupture that blazed a trail for the idea of regeneration and made it irresistibly attractive. Even realists such as Mirabeau, who liked to point out that a "skillful farmer does not pretend that he himself gives birth to the fruits and the flowers," were carried away by the flood. While they knew that the revolutionaries could not hope to carry out all their reforms, they nevertheless maintained that the ultimate goal was to

781

reform *everything*, as if the only argument were over the timing of regeneration, not its necessity.

As to what regeneration was supposed to accomplish, the texts offered a broad spectrum of answers. The crudest ones endowed it with a sense of physical renewal: vigorous children, adolescents spared the spectacle of debauch, virtuous couples, elderly people free of infirmity. It was a new race that was about to be born, energetic and frugal. The most elaborate texts took seriously the meaning of a word that belonged to the vocabulary of theology and was defined by contemporary dictionaries as referring either to the spiritual birth of baptism or to the new life that was to follow the resurrection of all the dead. In circles associated with what would become the Constitutional Church, which welcomed the Revolution as the restoration of ancient Jerusalem and therefore as the advent of a perfect society, people hailed the "regeneration of Jesus Christ," so different from the "regeneration of Lycurgus." Lamourette, who became the constitutional bishop of Lyons, explained that Lycurgus' regeneration, being the work of a human legislator, proceeded from laws to mores. But the regeneration of Jesus Christ first changed hearts, and it was just such a true regeneration that was being accomplished by the Revolution. Even people who never dreamed, in the manner of Lamourette, of making the Revolution consubstantial with Christianity could accept the idea of the Revolution as a form of conversion—a sign of the religious dimension and singular nature of the enterprise.

Alongside "regeneration," the word "reform" soon lost its luster. On July 25, 1789, Clermont-Tonnerre pretended to give an impartial account of an opposing view but in fact discredited those who expected nothing more from regeneration than "mere reform of abuses and restoration of a constitution that has existed for fourteen centuries and that they believed could live on if only time's insults were repaired." His very language shows how insignificant such tinkering was deemed compared with the work of regeneration. It also explains why the idea of a happy restoration of the alleged ancient constitution of France, an idea so vigorous throughout the eighteenth century, was so quickly abandoned. Nothing was to be expected from the national past, whose very wealth was seen as a misfortune, not to say a curse; a past so fraught with history implied corruption and degeneration. Obviously such wealth encouraged the coexistence of disparate customs, an offense to rationality. And finally, the past bore the triple stigmata of despotism, priesthood, and feudalism. No other explanation of the Revolution's early radicalization is needed beyond the revolutionaries' inherent pessimism concerning the history of France. In that history, they believed, there was nothing worth saving, no root worth retrieving, and no guidance for the coming unprecedented adventure, which was to bring forth a new people.

This was a dream, but it was also more than a dream. During the revolutionary decade a thousand institutions and creations converged on the notion of regeneration: space was refashioned by creating new départements and time remade by creating the revolutionary calendar; places were given new names; new schools were established, and so were new festivals. These upheavals were accompanied by more modest and at first sight seemingly less significant changes such as the use of the familiar *tu* and the wearing of the cockade, which gave rise to long and highly symbolic debates. Regeneration tied all these institutions together and set the tone of the Revolution well after Thermidor; it united men thrown into disarray by the vicissitudes of the times. All were willing to be judged—and even demanded to be judged—by its success or failure. They thus expressed a boundless philosophical ambition and staked out the territory on which their adversaries, beginning with Burke, also took up their positions; they set the standard by which their trials and errors would be judged; and they inaugurated, even among themselves, an endless debate about the boundary between the possible and the impossible.

The unanimity that was achieved concerning the need for regeneration fell apart when it came to developing the means and setting a timetable for bringing it about. Over the course of the Revolution the idea of regeneration was interpreted in two very different ways. For some, regeneration was contemporary with the Revolution itself. For others, the Revolution was over, but regeneration was still to come.

For the first group, the new man sprang fully armed from the spirit of the Revolution, to which the individual simply had to abandon himself. Listen to Condorcet: "A happy event suddenly opened a vast arena to the hopes of the human race; a single instant put a century's distance between yesterday's man and today's." Condorcet spoke the language of miracle. For today's man, it was enough to turn a liberated gaze on old institutions and watch them crumble. Such magical beliefs were widely shared, and we even find traces of them in Mirabeau: "You breathed on remains that seemed inanimate. Suddenly a constitution was organized, and already it is giving off an active force. The cadaver that has been touched by liberty has risen and received a new life."

In this miraculous and energetic view of the Revolution as an unforeseen event out of which would come things never before seen or heard (an interpretation quite similar to Hannah Arendt's), it was hardly necessary to be concerned with the means of regeneration. The people that had lived through such an event, irreducible to and incomparable with anything that had gone before, was suddenly changed into a nation of heroes. In the unlikely event that these heroes should flag, they would need only to revive the sacred spirit of the Revolution's first days to recover its enthusiasm and energy. Thus Bastille Day, July 14, which commemorates a new dawn, was perceived of all the festivals imagined by the Revolution as particularly beneficial. Nor was there any need to fear that the regenerated people might subsequently degenerate: anyone who had been subjected to such a dazzling conversion was unlikely to forget what had once been revealed. Thomas Paine had already written of the American Revolution in his *Common Sense* that it was impossible to unlearn what had once been seen in the guise of plain truth.

Once the new man had arisen, there was no more need to worry about his conservation than there had been to worry about his formation.

Those who felt such confidence in the Revolution drew from it almost entirely negative conclusions. One should not make too many laws, because the Revolution accomplished its miracles by following its own natural course. One should refrain from repression, because restrictive ideas are anathema to men and women already transformed by a bedazzling regeneration. The only advice that one might give to the revitalized French was to strive for greater ambitions and loftier thoughts and to enjoy an ever expanding range of pleasures. It was almost superfluous to think of ways to endow the new man with new strengths; but if he absolutely had to be so endowed, the means should be drawn from the Revolution itself. No longer was there any need for sermons or lessons in morality, because now there was the lustrous presence of the Declaration of Rights. No longer was there any need for priests, because now fathers loved the Revolution heart and soul. And there was almost no need for schools where there were sections, clubs, and popular societies. As in the "regeneration of Jesus Christ," laws could legitimately be deduced from mores. Once the latter had been regenerated in and through the Revolution, there was scarcely any need to legislate. Here we are considering only the Revolution's liberal side, where people wagered on a liberty described by Camille Desmoulins as dispensing "goods of which it grants immediate possession to those who invoke it."

But the Revolution also had a non-liberal side, and the twofold nature of the regeneration idea shows how violently the two sides contrasted. There were, of course, those who believed that the past with which the Revolution had broken had not been totally annihilated. Of the hated and now shaken regime there remained what Grégoire called "shreds" still to be disposed of. Successful regeneration required dealing with external obstacles, with supporters of the past, people almost entirely left out of the previous description yet still there, active, industrious, and tenacious. Even more important was the need to deal with internal obstacles: bad attitudes, habits, prejudices, and above all that key trait of "ancient peoples" noted by Talleyrand, namely, their fear of innovation. Taken together, external and internal obstacles reinforced each other and delayed progress toward regeneration. Between the present, which had changed the state of things, and the future, which one hoped would change minds, lay what Mirabeau called a "space of time," a discouraging interval to be reckoned with: the new man would emerge not out of the dazzlement of a miracle but at the end of a painstaking labor.

Viewed in this way as a task, regeneration involved an initial, wholly negative phase, for each individual first had to undo the work of the past. "Undo" might mean to proscribe (frivolous entertainments, for example), to abolish (gambling and lotteries), to eliminate (jargon), or to purge (libraries). Such a task also required neutralizing regeneration's preeminent adversaries: priests, obtuse country folk, and old women, believers in an idea intolerable to revolutionaries, that truth lies only in what has endured. Such neutralization could mean exclusion and violence, for in an ironic shift in the meaning of that noble word "regeneration," a "regenerated" popular society soon came to mean a society purged of its dubious members. Once the purge was accomplished, it then became necessary, in a second phase, to surround each individual with a web of myths, rituals, and beliefs as restrictive as possible and as confining as what had gone before. Now we can see more clearly why nothing in the reconstitution of this environment seemed insignificant to men who, one might think, had more urgent things to do. New names for streets and squares, a new calendar for public time, new monuments for cities, new costumes for the people's representatives, and cockades to be pinned on the caps of the most worthy were details that could not be overlooked by men who judged that the process of regeneration was not yet complete and could come unstuck at any moment.

Clearly this meticulous and wary view of regeneration is the opposite of the view described earlier. Those who held the first view looked upon the future with suspicion, allowed individuals the means to improvise and increase their demands, and left them free to be their own teachers. Those who held the second view always assumed the invisible presence of a legislator or the hidden hand of a tutor, because they assumed that the correct regeneration was that of Lycurgus, which proceeds from laws to mores. They also lacked confidence in the work of time because they were obsessed with the fear of an accident (a chance encounter, an odd text, a disturbing event, a seditious lesson) that would somehow undo the inchoate new man.

Thus we are faced with two antinomic conceptions, two kinds of regeneration, one might even say two revolutions. The surprising thing for anyone who follows the history of these two seemingly alien ideas in the sources themselves is that they cannot be associated with different groups of political leaders or different phases of the Revolution (even if the second type of regeneration seems characteristic of the Jacobin episode). The same men who at times speak the language of miracle at other times speak the language of systematic, painstaking socialization of the new man. It is as if the French Revolution proposed two concurrent philosophies—one of liberty, the other of constraint, one of autonomy, the other of heteronomy—and was never able to choose between the two.

Confirmation of this point can be seen in the case of the schools, a case that, in this connection, is central since the discourse of regeneration was also a pedagogical discourse and all the revolutionaries invested the educational issue with enormous symbolic significance. In their eyes the school was the appointed place for turning out the more useful citizens and happier human beings promised by regeneration. To regenerate adults, rigidly fixed in their Ancien Régime habits, was far more difficult. They would require a system of adult education, of rites and festivals that were in fact known as "schools for the grown man." In children's schools, however, working with the presumably soft and malleable wax of the "newborn generation," revolutionary legislators believed they were confronted with ideal conditions, with no evil past to combat. Yet even in this ideal situation they continually alternated between a liberal and an authoritarian system as they frequently tinkered with their educational projects. In what follows I shall be concerned with those projects rather than with actual practice, since the Revolution's rapid pace made it impossible to put the plans into operation.

During the first three years of the Revolution there was no parliamentary debate on education. Speaking on behalf of the Constituent Assembly's Committee on the Constitution, however, Talleyrand did submit a report on public instruction calling for free primary education. But since the Constituent Assembly was nearing the end of its days, the report came too late to be discussed. The Legislative Assembly established a Committee on Public Instruction, whose twenty-four members labored, under the chairmanship of Condorcet, on a report that was presented on April 20 and 21, at the very moment when war was being declared on Austria. Once again events forced postponement of the debate, but Condorcet's project clearly illustrated what he believed the purposes of education to be: regeneration of the individual of course, but regeneration in the use of his natural faculties and critical spirit. Condorcet imagined teaching strictly separated from religious instruction, strictly identical for both sexes, and, at the primary level, universal. Schooling should be free but not compulsory, owing to Condorcet's hostility to coercion of any kind and to an optimism that led him to believe that education offered to all free of charge would be used by all. Finally, education for him was to be strictly independent of political authority: "Neither the French Constitution nor even the Declaration of Rights shall be presented to any class of citizens as tablets handed down from heaven that must be worshipped and believed." Any other kind of education was nothing but "a chain for the mind." Placing his hope in collective spontaneity and social need, Condorcet envisioned a day when schools as he imagined them would disappear, for "a time will come when every man will find in his own knowledge and in the rectitude of his spirit sufficient weapons to repel all the ruses of charlatanry." While waiting for that blessed day, schools would indeed be necessary, "but in working to shape these new institutions, we have constantly had to concern ourselves with hastening the happy moment when they would no longer be necessary." In Condorcet's view the school was a necessary but not a sufficient instrument of regeneration, which was an infinitely broader phenomenon than education.

Subsequent debates in the Convention (where proposals by Lanthenas and Romme were discussed in December, the latter proposal similar to Condorcet's except that Romme named the nation rather than the individual as the central concern of education) had difficulty avoiding entanglement in momentous events; the king's trial, the Vendée, the first public safety measures, and party conflict all delayed the discussion. After the fall of the Girondins and the rejection of Lanthenas' plan, Robespierre presented a proposal found among the papers of the regicide deputy Le Peletier de Saint-Fargeau, who had been assassinated on January 20, 1793, and whose proposal in every way typified the laborious conception of regeneration. It did so, first of all, by its suspicion, which stood in stark contrast to Condorcet's confidence: for Le Peletier, a child of five was already molded by family influence, and even such an innocent had already acquired wicked habits that must be rooted out. Le Peletier also favored coercion, as opposed to Condorcet's belief in liberty: his two instruments of regeneration were to be the boarding school, which created an artificial environment from which all external influences were excluded, and compulsory education, which made it illegal for any child to avoid schooling. But that was only the beginning. In addition, schools were to be governed in minute detail by a rigid schedule that left nothing to chance: not exercise or leisure or clothing or food or even sleep. Le Peletier's admiration for the Spartan model inspired this strict regime, designed to ensure that pupils would "on every day at every moment be subject to a precise rule." This constriction was the price to be paid for total regeneration, which was not complete until the student emerged from the "republican mold."

Because it was read at the Convention and defended by Robespierre, because it was conceived by a republican martyr, and because it was presented in particularly dramatic circumstances—on the day of Marat's murder and at a moment of acute national danger—Le Peletier's proposal has been seen as characteristic of the Jacobin episode, just as the painstaking, programmed regeneration it explicitly promises has been seen as inextricably intertwined with Jacobin coercion. It is true that the project was adopted by the Convention at the behest of Robespierre and that it established "houses of equality." By autumn, however, it had been stripped of its two essential aspects: boarding schools and compulsory attendance. The decrees of Brumaire, Year II, did have a coercive character, bearing the hallmark of the de-Christianizing episode of which they were a part. (Former nobles and members of the clergy were forbidden to teach.) But those decrees too were swept away barely two months later, in Frimaire, by Bouquier's quite liberal program: schools and teachers were to be chosen by families, the curriculum was free, there was no surveillance other than to make sure that nothing was taught contrary to republican laws, and the prohibition against teaching by priests was lifted. Clearly the men of the Plain, among whom ecclesiastics were numerous, recoiled before the novel figure of the teacher as agent of the state and the new priesthood that figure seemed to presage.

Was the idea that regeneration of the citizen must inevitably involve the school completely forsaken? One argument against the Le Peletier plan was family feeling, "the powerful cry of nature." Yet in the Bouquier plan that dethroned it there was also a tinge of anti-intellectualism, a wariness of the school that did not displease the Assembly's left wing. What emerged was the idea that the people had found in the Revolution itself the forms of instruction necessary to bring forth the new man. Already socialized by revolutionary practice, the new man continued to socialize himself through those schools for citizens, the popular societies. Thus liberalism reasserted its rights well before Thermidor, although there were limited experiments during the Jacobin dictatorship with regeneration through regimentation, such as the "revolutionary courses" offered in Paris to teach the art of refining saltpeter or the "School of Mars," which assembled young citizens in bivouac on the Sablons. Hence in the Jacobin episode two ways of conceiving of regeneration and education were combined.

IDEAS

After Thermidor came a new flurry of legislation, leading in the fall of 1794 to promulgation of a new educational code. The new system was intended to be coherent and complete: between the primary schools and the special schools (the Ecole Normale and Ecole Polytechnique along with the schools of health and the Conservatoire des Arts et Métiers) it established the secondary institutions known as central schools, rivals of the *collèges*, in the départemental capitals. Certain provisions in the laws establishing the special schools, particularly Normale and Polytechnique, bear earmarks of the Jacobin experience with revolutionary courses. The dream of regeneration through the schools was finally abandoned the following autumn with passage of the realistic Daunou Law. The special schools were retained, and the law paid special attention to the central schools in which the children of notables were educated, but it left the primary schools to the hazards of the local situation. The Constitution of Year III acknowledged this diminished ambition in regard to primary education: no longer calling for a minimum number of schools, it reduced curricula to a bare minimum and trusted in the good will of the community. Paid by the parents of pupils, the state teacher would find himself competing with private teachers in a growing number of ever more prosperous private schools.

Had the idea of using the school, that social microcosm, to regenerate the entire nation been definitively abandoned? Not at all, for the coup of 18 Fructidor, Year V, directed against a renascent royalism, also revived the ambition to create a republican people out of the upcoming generation. The school once again figured at the center of a cumbersome and redundant apparatus employing all the coercive methods perfected in earlier years. A whole series of measures obliging children of functionaries to attend national schools and subjecting private schools once again to surveillance and control by municipal authorities aimed at reinvigorating a public school system weakened by the Daunou Law. When administrators were asked about the situation in the schools and the state of the republican spirit in their départements and cantons, they responded as men fully aware of the difficulties of the undertaking; they had not lived through long years of revolution without discovering how attached communities were to their old schools, how reluctant peasants were to change, and how resistant custom was to law. Nevertheless, they continued to believe that the Revolution marked a discontinuity in time, to see habits as the fruit of malevolence (as Benjamin Constant understood so well), and to blame the slowness of regeneration on ill will. Despite all the disillusionment, they demonstrated the tenacity of an educational ideal that only the coup of 18 Brumaire could kill.

This fluctuating history was full of surprises. In the authoritarian as well as the liberal camp, unexpected voices made themselves heard. It was a Girondin, Dulaure, a decided adversary of Jacobin coercion, who in Messidor, Year VII, blamed the already sadly evident failure of republican institutions on the absence of system. It was a Montagnard, Duhem, who in the harshest of terms, castigating Sparta as "a convent, a community of monks," repudiated Le Peletier's Spartan utopia. And it was another Girondin, Ducos, who, in arguing for compulsory attendance and common instruction, protested that it was impossible to regenerate the mores of a corrupt people by "mild ameliorations" when what was needed were "vigorous and rapid institutions"—here the disruptive vocabulary of the miracle itself speaks in favor of state intervention. And it was a man of the Plain gone over to the Mountain, Barère, who best explained how it was possible to shift from one kind of regeneration to the other: well aware of "that very delicate interval that stands between the beginning of a Revolution and its end," he was sure that the initial outburst of enthusiasm could no longer be counted on and that it would be necessary to take "intermediate steps." But he was also certain that such steps would be suitable only "if they partake of the Revolution's quickness and share in its inherently impetuous character;" in other words, if something of the prodigious fury of the inception could still be found in this disgraced, discouraging interlude—that is, if the first regeneration continued to inspire the second.

We touch here on the heart of the relation between the French Revolution and totalitarianism, both of which seek to create a new man. Both hold out the new as a quasi-religious promise. In contrast to religion, both are willing to submit to the terrible ordeal of historical experimentation. Through analysis of the two types of regeneration and of the alternation between them we can understand how liberal principles could have coexisted with a coercive pedagogy during the Revolution. Perhaps we can also explain what secretly linked the two conceptions of regeneration; this link would be of great importance, for it would help to explain how a democratic experiment might contain within itself the seeds of a totalitarian adventure.

The first factor to consider is revolutionary time itself: over the course of an extraordinary decade the men of the Revolution discovered its rapid pace, its devilish capacity to produce disruptive, energy-sapping events, and its imperviousness to human action. To men who hoped to escape the grip of time it was devastating to be forced to recognize not only that time distorts and discolors the idea of the new but also that men can become bored with innovation itself. This encounter with time, which Lakanal had said ought to be the Republic's sole and universal teacher, affected *both* conceptions of regeneration at once. Recognition of the fact that the pace of regeneration is necessarily slow obviously proved fatal to the proponents of a miracle; the time needed to mold hearts and minds was not the time of the miraculous. But it also affected the partisans of systematic and painstaking socialization of the new man by showing that change could not come exclusively from legislative fiat. When Basire proposed a law requiring that everyone use the familiar *tu*, Thuriot countered that such an innovation should be left to time: "When reason shall have made sufficient progress, then pass this law." In this causal sequence lay the idea most unbearable to the revolutionaries, an idea that would be used against them by countless traditionalist thinkers: namely, that one cannot do time's work in its stead.

The hidden affinity between the two ideas of regeneration can also be viewed in another way, in terms of the difficulty of imagining how the old world could be used to hasten the birth of the new. If the proponents of miraculous regeneration are to be believed, that old world vanished the moment the Revolution appeared on the scene. On the other hand, the proponents of laborious regeneration believed that the old world was to be obliterated or circumvented but never used. That attitude is why the Revolution always imagined ceremonies intended to educate the "grown man" in terms of instantaneous change: crumbling castles, "slave" costumes that fell from the shoulders of the actors, hideous figures of allegory routed by the light. This simple dramaturgy of appearance and disappearance also expressed the Revolution's resistance to all thought of transformation.

Finally, what also linked the two conceptions of regeneration and made alternation possible was a sensualist philosophy, according to which human beings are changeable subjects susceptible to the flux of impressions—a philosophy that favors heteronomy over autonomy. The proponents of miraculous regeneration were probably less influenced than their counterparts by this sensualism, for they were willing to reckon with human energy and the capacity of individuals to make a fresh start. But even for them it was the *spectacle* of an irresistible revolution that converted the individual, who was therefore less autonomous than might appear at first sight. The partisans of laborious regeneration, for their part, assumed an individual so permeable to external influence that any instruction might easily be undone by counter-instruction. The most striking formulation of this doubt at the heart of sensualism, which inspired interventionist measures and left legislators panicking that they had not thought of everything, was given by Mirabeau: with appropriate means, he said, "one could arouse passion in sensitive beings for a completely absurd, unjust, and even cruel social order."

Regeneration: this key concept of revolutionary discourse enables us to comprehend fully the Revolution's difficulty, which was the same as Rousseau's. Having granted the individual his full rights, the Revolution had to find a way to bring him into step with the community, to couple absolute liberty with total obedience. It was almost inevitable that, as the Revolution unfolded, this enterprise should appear more and more desperate. At the same time the revolutionaries became increasingly obsessed with the need to create a collective spirit so powerful that it could hope to subjugate the individual spirit completely. And since the collective spirit lacked sufficient force of its own, it had to be reinforced with all the means of authority; and so coercive regeneration triumphed.

Mona Ozouf

FURTHER READING

Baczko, Bronislaw, ed. *Une éducation pour la démocratie: Textes et projets de l'époque révolutionnaire.* Paris, 1982.

Condorcet, Marie-Jean-Antoine-Nicolas de Caritat, marquis de. *Mémoires sur l'instruction publique,* in *Oeuvres,* vol. 7. Paris, 1847.

De Baecque, Antoine. "L'homme nouveau est arrivé: L'image de la régénération des Français dans la presse patriotique des débuts de la Révolution," *Dix-huitième siècle* (Paris), 1988.

Julia, Dominique. *Les trois couleurs du tableau noir.* Paris, 1981.

Procès-verbaux du comité d'instruction publique de la Convention Nationale, ed. James Guillaume, 6 vols. Paris, 1891–1907.

RELATED TOPICS

Burke	Constant	Jacobinism	Louis XVI	Robespierre
Condorcet	Estates General	Liberty	Mirabeau	Rousseau

REPUBLIC

Republic—the word is inseparable from the Revolution and its two high points: 1789, when the sovereignty of the monarch was replaced by the sovereignty of the nation, and 1792, when the monarch was deposed. In French tradition the word has retained a powerful emotional significance but a weak institutional one. In one sense it evokes images of the fatherland in danger and of the crusade for freedom: this is the Republic that is always calling upon its citizens, the Republic associated with the maxim that "Paris is Paris only when prying up its cobblestones." In another sense, however, its meaning is more neutral: it is the *res publica*, a regime eternally in search of its own identity. The term "republic" has been applied to all sorts of governments, from constitutional monarchy (the July Monarchy described itself as "the best of republics") to government by terror and coup d'état and even Caesarist dictatorship: for a short time after 1804, official French government papers bore the odd inscription, "French Republic, Napoleon Emperor." In art, images of the republic range from Rude's rude profile and the heroic bosom of "Liberty leading the people" to the innocent visage of Marianne enshrined in the tranquil lobbies of city halls across France. "Republic" is a threadbare word, endlessly repeated because it divides French men and women less than any other term. Yet it remains a magic formula that has lost none of its symbolic strength or power to mobilize.

The fundamental contradiction of the French Republic derives from its double birth. As a description of political culture it is rich with meaning, but as a political form it is empty. Most of the images that the established Republic recognized as part of its heritage—popular sovereignty, representative government, the Rights of Man, the tricolor banner, the revolutionary motto—actually originated early in the Revolution, under the constitutional monarchy, *before* the proclamation of the Republic. All these symbols of republican government existed before June 17, 1789, when the Estates General instituted itself as the National Assembly. France has known five republics, but within each of these, internal reorganizations and constitutional changes have produced a multiplicity of republican forms. The revolutionary period alone can boast of a Girondin Republic, a Montagnard Republic, a Thermidorian Republic, a Directorial Republic, a Consular Republic, and even an Imperial Republic. Following the plebiscite of 10 Frimaire, Year XIII, which made the imperial crown hereditary, François de Neufchâteau congratulated Napoleon on the results, which he said "brought the republican vessel into port."

The Republic has always been more than a regime type, however. Owing to its very political plasticity, its deep identity has always derived from its culture and tradition. There was a republican philosophy, which took its inspiration from Kantian idealism and continued to develop throughout the nineteenth century. There were a republican religion and a republican morality, inaugurated by Volney (*La loi naturelle,* 1793) and Lanthena (*Nouvelle déclaration de la morale républicaine,* 1793), which ever since have filled the libraries with catechisms. There were also a republican economics, a republican law, and a republican history; Lavisse erected a monument to the last of these (the *Histoire de France*). There was even a republican science. Thus the Republic enjoyed a fertile apprenticeship, not limited to the constitution of the concept of "republican reason" whose history Claude Nicolet has traced. The celebrated "synthesis" accomplished by the Third Republic took the form of an occupation of space, time, and mind. Through constant self-celebration the Republic made itself a part of the culture, and that celebration began and ended with exaltation of its revolutionary heritage.

The republican heritage thus falls into two parts. For France, republican government was pure experiment. The country founded a new government on an abstract principle, abruptly substituting the sovereignty of the nation for that of the monarch. The government was motivated by a powerful aspiration toward equality among citizens, tempered by recognition of the impossibility of direct democracy in a large country. Yet this principle contained no rules to guide its practical application and no internal stabilizing mechanism, nor did it have social or historical roots. The Republic was France's means of access—its only means of access—to modern political democracy. That said, it is clear how the Republic differed from the English model, in which democracy evolved under monarchy, and from the American model, in which the democratic experiment all along included a strong tradition of local representation. English democracy rested upon a history, American democracy upon a principle. French republican democracy was unique in that it derived from both a principle and a history. Hence the Republic's revolutionary heart beats with a regular rhythm: systole before August 10, 1792, when the monarchy fell, diastole after, and so on through the years that followed.

**

To judge by appearances, there was nothing republican about the constitutional monarchy established by the Constituent Assembly and respected by the Legislative Assembly. The intellectual underpinnings of the new regime had been established in the eighteenth century. It is true that, once the Republic was established, it invoked Mably and Rousseau as its spiritual ancestors. But three facts should be borne in mind. First, "the Republic," a term rarely mentioned in scholarly discussions, derived primarily from the ancient notion of the *res publica,* the community bound together by civic virtue. Second, it was believed that republican government, which is to say direct government of the people, was workable only in small political units, no larger than the cities of the ancient world or, in modern times, units like Geneva, the cities of Italy, or perhaps, at the very upper limit, the Netherlands. It was not workable in a large country of twenty-five million people with a centuries-old divine-right monarchy that remained a vital presence. Third, it was believed that the United States had succeeded in establishing a republic because it was a country without a tradition of monarchy (which made it possible to have an executive branch independent of the legislative) and because it was a federation of independent states. These beliefs were challenged by only a few proponents of direct democracy: followers of Marat and his *Ami du peuple;* the Club des Cordeliers; and François Robert, head of the Central Committee of Popular Societies, who was considered the true leader of the republican party after the publication in December 1790 of his *Républicanisme adapté à la France*. In that book he expressed his outrage at the idea that the king's person should be inviolable and sacred, argued that representatives should be bound by strict mandates from their constituents, and saw "all institutions other than Republicanism as crimes against the nation."

At that time, however, such views were distinctly in the minority. Until the king's attempt to flee, which ended at Varennes on June 21, 1791, even those who would become the most ardent champions of the Montagnard Republic proclaimed their hostility to the republican ideal. Take, for example, the Saint-Just of the *Esprit de la Révolution*. Mme. Roland observed in her memoirs: "The Jacobins go into convulsions at the mere mention of the Republic." Addressing the Assembly, Ferrières denounced "the ridiculous chimera of a French republic." Robespierre expressed his outrage: "Accuse me if you will of republicanism. I declare that I abhor any kind of government in which the factious reign." The Constituent Assembly had done all that it could to block an overtly democratic system, most notably by distinguishing between active and passive citizens and by establishing property qualifications for voting (*suffrage censitaire*). At the same time it had striven mightily to maintain some ghost of a function for the king, if only in fiction. The position of Sieyès in his speech of September 17, 1789, is quite typical of this interregnum. The idea of a republic, for Sieyès, was synonymous with the direct democracy of ancient times. The correct response to such democracy was "representative government," in which the representatives were invested with the sovereignty of the people. On the question of the proper relation between the representatives and the sovereign people, Sieyès opposed a strict mandate and favored allowing the representatives a free hand to represent the nation as a whole and not their particular constituency. However, he opposed any kind of royal veto, whether absolute or suspensive, with equal force, for the royal veto was "nothing but a *lettre de cachet* aimed against the general will. . . . I have carefully examined the arguments of those who see utility in the royal veto, looking for their reasons, however specious, and I must confess that I find none." Of course the Constitution that was ultimately adopted did grant the king a suspensive veto, but he could issue no order not countersigned by a minister, was required to swear an oath to the Constitution, and won approval of the principle of a hereditary monarchy only as a concession that accentuated the monarchy's purely decorative character.

Despite the care taken to destroy absolutism without raising the specter of direct democracy, the Constitution of 1791 bestowed its sanction upon a doctrine that contained a republican order in embryo. Auguste Comte saw this quite clearly. In his "Fragment d'article sur la Révolution" he wrote: "Let us consider only the spirit of the Constitution of 1791 as a whole. What was it in essence and by its very nature if not an introduction to the Republic? Once one failed to adopt the English constitution as a provisional measure under which one could begin to build a new social system, the advent of the Republican idea became inevitable, for this was the most widespread and deeply rooted of all political ideas" (*Ecrits de jeunesse, 1816–1828,* Paris, 1970, p. 459). The Constitution actually contains the two key tenets of what Laboulaye, in the preface to his *Questions constitutionelles* (1872), called the credo of the revolutionary school, whose determination to crush absolute monarchy distinguished it from democracies of the English type, to say nothing of the Dutch, Belgian, Swiss, and, even more, American democracies. The revolutionary credo held above all that the Assembly receives its sovereignty by delegation from the sovereign people. Since the people has but one will, there must be only one (unicameral) assembly. Its jurisdiction is unlimited. If need be it may assume judicial powers, as the Convention did when it sat in judgment of the king. The executive branch, moreover, is subordinate to the Assembly; the executive is a mere minister implementing the will of the legislature, which bestows upon it such trappings of authority as are necessary to maintain the dignity required for the exercise of its function.

This system would have been viable only if Louis XVI had been willing to accept in practice a role that was monarchical in name only. In essence the monarchy was not simply diminished but completely subverted. What happened is well known. It is striking how dramatically public opinion shifted in the space of a few weeks and how glaring the contrast was between the members of the Constituent Assembly, who desperately clung to the illusion that the king's role could be preserved, and the court, both at Versailles and in the Tuileries, where political and psychological realism were the order of the day. From the moment he reluctantly gave his approval to the decrees of August 5–11, 1789, Louis XVI's mind was bent on escape; only Necker's influence dissuaded him. He again gave his approval to the Civil Constitution of the Clergy (July 12, 1790). But three things—the decree concerning the civic oath that was forced down the throats of the clergy, the religious schism, and the Pope's condemnation of the Civil Constitution of the Clergy (March–April 1791)—finally persuaded him that he had been wrong to compromise. The flight to Varennes followed.

Thereafter, the idea of a republic, previously limited to extremists in the Club des Cordeliers, quickly gained wide acceptance. It was aided by the sudden conversion of Condorcet, who on July 12, 1791, read to the Social Circle a resounding text: "On the Republic, or, Is a King Necessary to the Preservation of Liberty?" In it he refuted point by point the well-known arguments of the "friends of royalty." This speech marked the conversion of the Enlightenment to the republican ideal. Two hundred ninety deputies denounced the decision to suspend the king temporarily from his functions as the inauguration of a dangerous "republican interim" manipulated by a party that would be headed by Lafayette. The latter publicly protested that he had been slandered but in his memoirs allowed that he had entertained republican thoughts (Brussels edition, I, pp. 369–371). At the home of his close friend La Rochefoucauld, Dupont de Nemours had already spoken in favor of the Republic, and the event, Lafayette confessed, had "republicanized" some dozen members of the Constituent Assembly, whom he classed as "politicians" and "anarchists." Thoughts of republican government were put in abeyance by the Assembly's decision on July 15 to pretend that the king had been abducted and by its refusal to bring him to trial. On July 17 there followed popular demonstrations on the Champ de Mars, which had to be put down by force. This was the true beginning of the great divide.

The Varennes crisis thus initiated a year of sham and double-dealing. Louis XVI came to the Manège and solemnly swore "to employ all the power delegated to him to carry out and uphold the Constitution." But in November the first series of Girondin decrees to issue from the Legislative Assembly renewed old doubts. The king was willing to order his brothers, the comte de Provence in particular, to return to France, and he readily agreed to request that the Elector of Trier disperse the "congregations" (*attroupements*) of émigrés on France's borders; but he refused to approve the ultimatum issued to refractory priests, which demanded that they take the oath within a week or be declared "suspect persons" and face loss of their livings. From then on the revolutionaries and the king diverged. They agreed about one thing only—the war—and that because of a misunderstanding. The Jacobins, except for Robespierre, favored war because they believed it would radicalize the Revolution, while the "committee of the Tuileries" favored a war that they believed would destroy the Revolution. Louis XVI chose a Girondin government (led by Dumouriez and Roland) hoping that it would make matters worse—and for him it did. The war (declared April 20, 1792), together with the new series of decrees that flowed from it, hastened the king's downfall by encouraging popular mobilization and strengthening the clubs and other extraparliamentary powers. Louis XVI approved the dismissal of his Constitutional Guard (May 29) but could not bring himself to sanction the deportation of refractory priests (May 27) or the calling up of 20,000 *fédérés* and volunteers to be stationed outside Paris (June 8). His refusal provoked a popular insurrection on June 20. Two irreconcilable principles confronted each other directly when the king was insulted to his face by Legendre, representative of the democratic Republic (though the offense temporarily improved the king's standing with the populace). On July 11 the Assembly solemnly proclaimed to the people that "the Fatherland is in danger," and this was seen as a denunciation of the king's weakness as well. Now the antiroyalists were joined by patriots in the provinces, popular societies, the Paris Commune, and municipalities in the east and south of France. The Brunswick manifesto, news of which reached Paris on August 3, brought matters to a head. The insurrection of August 10 ended all semblance of compromise. Yet not even the abolition of royalty, enacted by the Convention in its first public session on September 21, 1792, led to the proclamation of a new regime. The Convention merely put its stamp of approval on an already existing state of affairs when it declared the following day that its acts would henceforth be dated from "the first year of the Republic." To fill the vacuum and avoid chaos, it further declared on September 22 that the phrase "Kingdom one and indivisible" (article 1, title 2, of the Constitution of 1791) be replaced by the formula "French Republic one and indivisible."

*
**

For the rest of the Revolution, both before and after Thermidor, the Republic would bear the stamp and the burden of this inadvertent foundation. Torn between direct democracy, in whose name it had been founded, and the delegation of sovereignty to elected representatives, the Republic was unable to promulgate laws to which it could conform itself. The "revolutionary government" inaugurated a series of coups d'état.

The first, which followed the king's trial and execution, symbolizes the fate of a Revolution that had become a law and an end unto itself. Threats to the nation's survival coupled with democratic pressures from below helped bring the Republic into being, and in the tragic summer of 1793 it realized its true destiny. On September 5 it was announced that "terror is the order of the day." On October 10 it was declared that "the provisional government of France would be revolutionary until peace" returned. The decree of 14 Frimaire (December 4) definitively established the revolutionary government, which organized and coordinated the various institutions that had been created in response to circumstances over the past year: the Committee of General Security in October 1792; the Revolutionary Tribunal, first established on March 10, 1793, but not firmly in place until September; and the Committee of Public Safety, established in April but taken over by Robespierre in July, at which time its powers were expanded. In appearance all were merely ad hoc measures: "The aim of constitutional government is to preserve the Republic," Robespierre declared on October 10; "the aim of revolutionary government is to found it." In fact, however, the foundation marked the end of the Republic, the nullification of the three great principles that constitute the very essence of republican order: the separation of powers, in particular the legislative and the judicial; respect for law based on a constitution; and the integrity of national sovereignty, exercised through elected representatives.

Much ink has been spilled over the question of whether the Convention's decision to try the king and ultimately to execute him was, as Kant maintained, an illegal violation of the constitutional contract or, as Michelet argued, the inaugural act of a new national sovereignty incompatible with royal sovereignty. In any event, the king's execution established as a principle of French political life that the government could put its adversaries to death. The trial, conducted by the Assembly itself rather than by a special tribunal, served as a model for turning the entire legislative and governmental apparatus into a vast judicial machine, which it was destined to remain until the Law of 22 Prairial (June 22, 1794). Swift enforcement of revolutionary justice became the Republic's only law.

After the king's downfall, the Convention, like the Constituent Assembly that preceded it, was elected for the sole purpose of adopting a new constitution. A first constitution, proposed by Condorcet in the spring, lost out when the Girondins were expelled from the Assembly on June 2, 1793. A second, with a new Declaration of the Rights of Man as a preamble, was approved on June 24. It provided for an Assembly elected by universal suffrage and for direct popular oversight of all laws through "primary assemblies." But it was never put into effect. Thus the Republic failed to respect the rule of law and constitutional principles. National sovereignty had already been violated when the Assembly capitulated to the sections of the Paris Commune and to the ultimatum of their leader, Hanriot, who demanded that the Convention expel twenty-nine Girondin deputies. This crucial step deprived the government of *national* legitimacy and made it dependent exclusively on *popular* support, that is, in actual fact, on various surveillance committees, popular societies, and national agents in turn subject to pressures from the sections and clubs, which continued unabated until Thermidor. By making itself the defender of the Revolution, the Republic thus betrayed its three fundamental principles: separation of powers, the rule of law, and national sovereignty.

From the beginning, therefore, the Republic could be seen as an emergency government born in war and compromised by terror. Yet in the emergency it took on two traits that ensured its longevity: it became identified with the defense of France, and it rested its entire system on the enforcement of virtue. The Montagnard republic organized the first mass mobilization for the defense of the fatherland, and this defense became the source of its patriotic appeal. From Valmy to Verdun, and even in the resistance to the German occupation and the organization of a government in exile, the Republic in its darkest hours has called time and time again on this popular source of power. Even more important, Jacobin extremism has always relied on a "sublime sentiment": that the public interest outweighs all private interests. In a speech delivered on February 5, 1794, Robespierre asked: "What is the fundamental principle of democratic and popular government, the essential moving force that sustains it and drives it forward? Virtue, by which I mean the public virtue that worked so many miracles in Greece and Rome and that will yield still more astonishing miracles in republican France." On May 7, 1794, he called morality the "unique foundation of civil society." Saint-Just dreamed of a transparent society, of a perfect harmony between society and the individual, as described in his *Fragments sur les institutions républicaines*. Individual liberty was conceived in such a way as to require participation in public life. In coerced participation the Montagnards revived the ancient ideal of citizenship, which formed the basis of republican activism.

But French republicanism derived another of its essential features from the war, which fostered confusion between France's external enemies and its internal ones. This tension established a dialectic of the part versus the whole that drove the nation toward expansion and exportation of the Revolution. As in the *Social Contract,* popular sovereignty expressed itself through a unified general will rather than, as in British tradition, through a higher mode of reconciliation of private interests. Concrete application of this principle can be found, for example, in this judgment by Jaurès: "It was not unthinking acquiescence in the fait accompli that led all France to acclaim July 14 and nearly all France to ratify August 10. These things happened only because a segment of the populace used its power to defend the general will, betrayed by a handful of privileged aristocrats, courtiers, and criminals." By placing such a "betrayal" at the center of its identity, the Republic, in its Jacobin and Montagnard form, saw itself as the embodiment of a fictitious unified "people" opposed solely by the "enemies of liberty." In the absence of legal criteria for distinguishing between defenders and enemies of the Republic, the government decided. "All associations that make war on us," Robespierre would say on May 7, 1794, "rest on crime." This urge to expel all enemies from the heart of the nation was but the logical culmination of the definition given by Sieyès in *Qu'est-ce que le Tiers Etat?* (written before the start of the Revolution proper), according to which the Third Estate contained within itself all that was required to make a complete nation: "It is a strong and robust man, one of whose arms is still in chains . . . [It is] everything, but hobbled and oppressed."

At the time, this definition of the nation by exclusion of the privileged was of course based neither on social conflict nor on material interests. It was directed against an established order and intended as a principle for drafting a unified legal code. Sieyès himself backed away from the consequences derived from his premises in debates over the Constitution of Year III (July–August 1795). Nevertheless, his "model of the Third Estate," to borrow a phrase from Bernard Manin and Alain Bergougnioux, played an important part in shaping the identity of the Montagnard Republic, and Sieyès' themes, rejuvenated at different times in the nineteenth century through the infusion of nationalistic or class ideologies, ensured that the republican consensus would remain politically left-wing. Even in the twentieth century, with the Popular Front, the Resistance, the National Front, and the Common Program, the idea of the "people" has remained the heart and soul of republican ideology. The Republic needed enemies in order to define itself and steel itself for combat, and it has always lived off its adversaries. The storming of the Bastille remains one of its central symbols not only because it commemorates an inaugural act but because it is the key theme in a recurrent program.

After the fall of Robespierre (9 Thermidor or July 27, 1794) and the ensuing backlash against the Terror, the Convention returned to its original purpose, which was to establish the constitutional foundations of the Republic. French troops now controlled the whole left bank of the Rhine from Alsace to Holland, and the domestic situation was also stabilized. In the spring and summer of 1795 the Convention drafted the Constitution of Year III, intended as a replacement for the Constitution of 1793, which had never been put into effect.

The debate was dominated by Daunou and Sieyès and by a desire to exorcise the specter of the Terror, which was inextricably associated with the lawless regime—"anarchy" in the strict sense of the word—known as the dictatorship of Year II. In a speech delivered on 2 Thermidor (July 20, 1795), Sieyès was critical of the Montagnards' ascription to the people of unlimited sovereignty, like that of the king under the Ancien Régime. He proposed a special tribunal to be called the "Constitutional Jury," composed of elected judges charged with verifying the constitutionality of the laws. In general, however, his view reflected the spirit of Enlightenment rationalism, as opposed to Montesquieu's belief in a system of separate powers with checks and balances. Sieyès' system was more like the works of a clock, with each institution carefully arranged to run in harmony with all the others. Several of the former priest's propositions were not adopted, including the one on the Constitutional Jury, and he had nothing to do with the final text, which was drafted primarily by the ex-Oratorian Daunou. The idea of a bicameral assembly, rejected in September 1789, was now reinstated, but care was taken to avoid any semblance of an aristocratic upper house. The purpose was simply to divide legislative chores between two groups: the Five Hundred, charged with drafting the laws, and the Seniors (*Anciens*, all 250 of whom were required to be over forty years of age), charged with voting on them; all were to be elected by the people, with the only qualification for voting being property ownership, no matter how small the property. In keeping with republican doctrine, this bicameral legislature elected a collegial executive consisting of five directors, to be nominated by the Five Hundred and approved by the Seniors. The directors were responsible for appointing ministers and discharging the responsibilities of the executive, to be divided among them. Another typically republican feature of the Constitution was the provision for frequent elections and rapid turnover of legislators: one-third of both houses and one director were to be replaced each year.

From the first the Convention lived in fear of public opinion, which had veered sharply to the right after 9 Thermidor. The Convention had vanquished the Terror, but it was aware that it had also been the instrument of that Terror, for it had approved the king's execution and, from September 1793 to July 1794, had voted month after month to extend the term of the "Great Committee of Public Safety." Why take the risk of exposing the nascent—or renascent—Republic to an electorate that Convention members increasingly suspected of having succumbed to royalist propaganda? For that reason, the Convention in one of its last acts stipulated that two-thirds of the future members of the two assemblies under the Directory must be chosen from the present membership of the Convention. Thus, even before the new republican laws were put into effect, they were openly flouted. The Constitution of Year III was baptized on 13 Vendémaire 1795 by the suppression of a royalist riot in which young General Bonaparte, backed by Barras, made a name for himself in Paris by helping the republicans win an easy victory over reactionaries from the posher parts of town. Conventionnels therefore continued to govern France under the Directory, and five of them were actually elected directors.

The history of the Republic in Year III was thus implicit in its beginnings. On the difficulties it faced there are no better commentaries than those of Benjamin Constant and Mme. de Staël in the various works they wrote between 1796 and 1798. Both were Thermidorian republicans, loyal to the principles of 1789, hostile to the return of the Bourbons and the aristocracy, but keenly aware of the fact that the Terror and the guillotine had turned public opinion against the Republic. By 1796, when they began writing about the policies of the Directory, the Babeuf conspiracy had raised the specter of communism and thus mingled present dangers to property with memories of the Terror. Constant and Staël set out to provide the Republic of Year III with roots, based on respect for private interests and on what they called "opinion": the new consensus concerning property distribution, attitudes, and ideas, which had been created by the Revolution of 1789. The problem they faced was how to distinguish between the idea of *a* republic and the first two years of *the* Republic, how to show that the dictatorship of 1793–1794 was a throwback to the past compared with the principles laid down in 1789. The current government, the republican government of Year III, was founded not on virtue and terror but on legal guarantees of civil equality, representation of private interests, and education of the citizenry.

Yet even Constant and Staël, confronted with royalist electoral successes in the spring of 1797, supported the republican coup d'état of 18 Fructidor (September 4); three of the five directors, led by Barras, called upon the army to expel the new majority from the councils and reinstate an emergency government. This expulsion was followed by a final wave of revolutionary terror. Less than two years after the "two-thirds provision," the Thermidorians were able to remain in power only with the help of Hoche's troops—and the support of Bonaparte in Italy, who sent one of his aides, Augereau. To defend the Republic against the counterrevolutionaries and refractory priests, the Directory could no longer afford to wait for its schools to educate a new generation of citizens or for the civic struggles that it tried to promote to be played out to its advantage. It needed an ally at once: the army.

This decision to embrace the army marked a major turning point. It showed that the Republic, even if it had lost the support of the sans-culottes, whose power was broken in 1794–95, still had that of the army—in fact, the army was more staunchly supportive than ever. Since 1792 the Revolution's ambition to regenerate France had been linked with a messianic zeal to see the "great nation" liberate all mankind. The government's military strategy and territorial policy were closely associated with its war against the monarchs and aristocrats of Europe. A military career, once the private preserve of the nobility, had become an ideal avenue of advancement for the common man. The powerful social energies liberated by the Revolution were even more likely to be invested in the military after Robespierre's downfall because they no longer had a domestic outlet: at home the Revolution was all but spent, while abroad the Republic was still triumphant. The fact that through victory a man could win glory, a career, and a fortune, all at once, forged a link between the ideas of a republic and military conquest that neither Constant nor Staël had foreseen, persuaded as both were that the spirit of conquest was alien to modern society. Out of that alliance came Bonaparte, at first the hero of the Republic but ultimately its executioner.

The difference between Sieyès and Bonaparte in the Brumaire plot of Year XIII was this: Sieyès, newly elected a director, had been the first to signal the Revolution but after ten years had ceased to embody its destiny; the young Corsican general, who had been indifferent to the Revolution in 1789, was the Republic's Washington in 1799. France, however, was not the young American Republic. In choosing Bonaparte by plebiscite after 18 Brumaire, the Revolution had unwittingly given itself a new king.

* * *

After the fall of Napoleon it would take sixty years for France to adopt republican institutions permanently: the Third Republic was created in 1875–1877. As many observers have noted, the Revolution was repeatedly refought throughout the nineteenth century. In July 1830 the Paris rebels flew the republican banner, but the more conservative of them successfully enthroned the Orleans dynasty, which had been waiting its chance since 1789. The result was the "republican monarchy," which unfortunately was too monarchical and not sufficiently republican, and it too fell before the Paris barricades in February 1848. That defeat inaugurated the Second Republic, which had been in existence even less time than the first when it was likewise ended by a Bonaparte. After the downfall of Napoleon III in 1870, it was not until the Commune had been crushed and an attempt to restore the Bourbons had failed that the Third Republic was brought to the baptismal font by Thiers and Gambetta, the most liberal of the Orleanists and the most moderate of the republicans.

That the Third Republic was such a long time coming was due to the legacy of the Revolution, tirelessly reshaped by all political factions. The Republic still frightened many mid-nineteenth-century Frenchmen for a reason diagnosed by Constant and Staël at the end of the previous century: it had become indissolubly linked with memories of dictatorship and terror. Michelet said as much, as did Edgar Quinet, George Sand, Victor Hugo, and nearly everyone else. The fact that the "Constitution of 1793" was a common slogan of the republican left under the restoration and was later incorporated into socialist rhetoric did nothing to disabuse the public of the notion that republic equals Terror.

Yet the chief currents of French socialism under the Restoration and the July Monarchy flowed independent of the republican ideal; many socialists were ambivalent about, not to say hostile toward, republican principles. A distinction was drawn between political revolutions, like that of 1789 or even 1793, and social revolutions, intended to end poverty and exploitation. There followed a clear dividing line in the 1830s and 1840s between republicans associated with the *National* newspaper and a variety of socialist sects. The republicans emphasized political issues, such as expansion of the suffrage, while the socialists warned against the abstract—and by their lights illusory—notion of equality implicit in such a policy. Socialist literature was filled with critiques of the Rights of Man, while the Declaration of August 26, 1789, remained gospel to the republicans. Under the July Monarchy the Republic stood for two things: universal suffrage and secular education, independent of the Catholic Church. Republicans envisioned a civic fraternity that would overcome bourgeois individualism and transcend class divisions, but in a very different way from the socialists. Republicans were not fond of either the liberals' free market society or the socialists' "barracks society." For Michelet the symbol of the Republic was not 1793 but the festival of the Federation, which in his eyes marked its true birthdate.

The civic fraternity imagined by the republicans did manifest itself for a few days or weeks in February 1848. But the history, memories, and passions of the French people bubbled once again to the surface in the Second Republic. The bourgeoisie and the bulk of the peasantry continued to be frightened by the specter of revolution in Paris, from which emanated disorder and threats to property; the Republicans were divided between the Gironde and the Mountain. Most of the socialist sects expected nothing good to come from universal suffrage or mere "political" change. The revolution of 1848 even had its sans-culotte insurrection of the poor and unemployed: the June Days of civil war, awash in blood. But this theatrical revival had a short run: none of the circumstances that had made the "government of public safety" possible in 1793 obtained in 1848. And when a new Bonaparte appeared to take the starring role, it was not as a national military hero but, more prosaically, as a leader chosen by universal suffrage. Begun in February in fraternal reconciliation, by December the revolution of 1848 had made its way from Lamartine all the way to the Prince-President; it had wound up at the opposite extreme from where it began.

All the great families of revolutionary tradition were represented in the new government—legitimists, Orleanists, moderate republicans, progressive republicans, socialists of many stripes, and last but not least, Bonaparte—but they were more divided than ever despite the appearance of a provisional consensus around republican institutions. The situation, however, was profoundly different from what it had been at the end of the eighteenth century. France was not at war. Yet all the passionate political traditions were confronted with the same set of equations: monarchy equals Ancien Régime, republic equals uncertainty. The result was the same as it had been half a century earlier—a Bonaparte dictatorship.

The Republic had no chance until, in the wake of the failure of 1848, the Second Empire brought forth a new generation of leaders, suspicious of the rhetoric of their elders and more realistic, men for whom the Republic represented not merely the restoration of liberty but also the preservation of social interests. The Revolution receded into the past, while at the same time the Second Empire saw an acceleration of economic changes that were fast making France a wealthier, more modern nation. The centralized state and its prefects had snuffed out liberty, but they had also gradually freed peasants from dependence on local landlords, whether legitimist or Orleanist. Railroads and schools unified a population that slowly grew accustomed to universal suffrage. Young republicans such as Ferry and Gambetta, educated under the Empire, were uncompromising champions of liberty but also fully aware of economic and intellectual progress. Sons of the Revolution, they were also positivists, disciples of Auguste Comte. For them history was a science, whose secrets they had deciphered in books. The Republic they founded was based on a marriage between incompatible ideas: the principles of 1789 and the age of positivism, the Rights of Man and the "government of science."

After May 16, 1877, the vanquishers of MacMahon incorporated into the "republican synthesis" of 1875–1880 both individual autonomy—the principle of the modern world—and the need to fashion citizens who would be guided by the light of historical reason, a distant echo of the old revolutionary theme of regeneration. Whence the central importance of the school, the instrument of civic education, and the imperative that it be freed from the grip of clerical obscurantism, symbol of a bygone era. Secular education became the backbone of the new republican civilization, and the former teacher Jules Ferry its standard-bearer. Universal suffrage, at last triumphant over the dictatorship of Paris, gave the Republic the peaceful benediction of a majority of the French.

Even after its hardwon victory, the Third Republic did not enjoy real stability. Crises met and overcome tightened its grip on government. Yet despite prodigious efforts to identify itself with the nation and to shape the culture and infiltrate the society via the school, the military, and the political party apparatus, the Third Republic was never able to claim unanimous assent to its fundamental principles. The Dreyfus Affair, the riots of February 6, 1934, the Vichy regime, and a host of incidents are there to remind us of this fundamental fact. It accounts for the instinctive fear in France that republican rule might be usurped, a fear which, though it has often proved unjustified after the fact, always lurks just below the surface. Among the objects of this fear have been the communists after the Liberation, General De Gaulle in 1958, and the Algerian putschists in 1961. Constantly thrown back on itself, the French Republic has achieved equilibrium and stability only by focusing on a still fragile set of values, by slowly evolving a tradition and a frame of reference, and by gradually overcoming the various sources of resistance to its final acceptance, which in fact came about only quite recently.

It is a republic that has always been threatened internally by governmental instability, parliamentary impotence, and institutional paralysis—conditions which led two republics to disaster, one collapsing before a foreign invasion, the other in the face of the Algerian crisis. Since the end of the last century it has also had to face the external threat of the nationalist right and the revolutionary left, both of which were strengthened by World War II: the right in the form of the Gaullist Rassemblement Pour la France (RPF), the left in the form of a Stalinist communist party. The strengthened appeal of both right and left has at times shrunk the republican consensus, as in the 1947 municipal elections, when the Republic received only a third of the votes, the lowest level of support in its history. More recently, the Republic's momentum has been slowed by its very success. It has slowly but surely undergone a strange metamorphosis as a result of the greatest economic growth that France has ever known. The "glorious thirty" years of the Fifth Republic—a second French Revolution—have had the paradoxical effect of eliminating the traditional focal points of ideological and political conflict and substituting a new set of issues that have no bearing on France's identity as a republican nation: the economy, modernization, the nature of society. At the same time the political foundations of the Republic have been strengthened by the very consequences of Gaullism, which presided over this period of growth and reaped its fruits.

Curiously, the waning urgency of the republican question has itself been responsible for the recent stabilization of republican government. To achieve this stability took nothing less than the decline of the communist party and the transformation of the right by a modernist party willing to accept what the Revolution had wrought. Political parties of every stripe had to accept the central values of the Republic and the Rights of Man. Last but not least, it took a victory by the left in the elections of 1981 and the ensuing republicanization of a constitution that many believed had been designed with a single man in mind: General De Gaulle. Symbolic of all these changes has been the growing importance of the Constitutional Council, which was established by the Constitution of 1958 as the "watchdog" of the executive and which has since evolved into the guardian of the Constitution. Oddly enough, the consolidation of the Fifth Republic has been accomplished chiefly through the policies and styles of its two most notable presidents, Charles De Gaulle and François Mitterrand. In this we see the irony as well as the logic of history: with De Gaulle and Mitterrand, the monarchic republic and the republican monarchy were wedded, so that after two hundred years the Revolution finally achieved the goal it set for itself in its first few days.

Pierre Nora

FURTHER READING

Aulard, Alphonse. *Histoire politique de la Révolution française: Origines et développement de la démocratie et de la république (1789–1804).* Paris, 1901.

Furet, François. *La gauche et la Révolution française au milieu du XIXe siècle: Edgar Quinet et la question du jacobinisme (1865–1870),* texts introduced by Marina Valensise. Paris, 1986. Contains selected texts by Alphonse Peyrat, Jules Ferry, Emile Ollivier, Louis Blanc, Edgar Quinet, and Jules Michelet.

——— *La Révolution,* vol. 4 of *L'histoire de France Hachette.* Paris, 1988.

Kates, Gary. *The Cercle Social, the Girondins, and the French Revolution.* Princeton, 1985.

Manin, Bernard, and Alain Bergounioux. "L'exclu de la nation: La gauche française et son mythe de l'adversaire," *Le débat,* October 1980.

Mathiez, Albert. *Le Club des Cordeliers pendant la crise de Varennes et le massacre du Champ-de-Mars.* Paris, 1910.

Nicolet, Claude. *L'idée républicaine en France.* Paris, 1982.

Nora, Pierre, ed. *Les lieux de mémoire,* vol. 1, *La république.* Paris, 1984.

Rudelle, Odile. *La république absolue 1870–1889: Aux origines de l'instabilité constitutionelle de la France républicaine.* Paris, 1982.

Weill, Georges. *Histoire du parti républicain en France, 1814–1870.* Paris, 1928.

RELATED TOPICS

Army	Coups d'Etat	Marat	Sovereignty
Condorcet	Democracy	Revolutionary Government	Staël
Constant	Lafayette	Robespierre	
Constitution	Louis XVI	Sieyès	

REVOLUTION

T he men of the Revolution explicitly looked to the past for a prophecy of the great event they were living through. They collected texts attesting to the penetrating insight of those great authors who were supposed to have predicted the Revolution well before it occurred. This somewhat artificial search often quoted sources out of context, and its results were rather disappointing, even if the occasional text did seem to provide the proof required. No one was more eloquent in this endeavor than Mably, who in his *Droits et devoirs du citoyen* (1750) included a dialogue, destined to enjoy great success, between a Frenchman and an Englishman on the meaning of history. The Frenchman sees fate at work in all history, particularly that of France, but the English gentleman paints a history of optimism and will: the good citizen can work to make revolutions "useful to the fatherland." By way of practical advice to the Frenchman he offers a program with an uncanny ring: to loosen the grip of fate, he says, will take nothing less than convocation of the Estates General and a call for permission to remain in permanent session; amid "the general cry of approval" aroused by this meeting, it will be easy to eliminate abuses, weaken the royal prerogative, and institutionalize the nation's rights—the revolution in a nutshell.

Astonishing as Mably's text may seem, it was not really as prescient as it appeared in retrospect. For even if Mably, alone among the thinkers of the eighteenth century, portrayed the Revolution as the will of a nation anxious to recover its rights and thus held up a mirror in which the revolutionaries could recognize themselves, his text is nevertheless a compound of many themes among which eighteenth-century thought was never able to choose. Mably still used the word "revolution" in its astronomical sense (his Frenchman believed that the monarchy had reached a point of obedience that England eventually would also achieve); he still thought of revolutions as plural and continual and of men as passively caught up in a tumultuous flood of events they could never control.

In the eighteenth century the primary meaning of "revolution" was the return of previous forms of existence. According to the *Dictionnaire de Trévoux* the term was "synonymous with period." The astronomical definition was given first in all the dictionaries: revolution is the motion that brings things back to their point of departure. Applied to things human, it suggests the eternal recurrence of certain duly catalogued political forms. Modeling human revolutions on the revolutions of the planets endows them with characteristics that we have some difficulty understanding: the need for return to a prior state; irresistibility; order and regularity; passivity engendered in men destined not to make revolutions but to record their occurrence; and the absence of all novelty.

This astronomical definition, though still present even in the minds of the most advanced thinkers, as shown by the example of Mably, was nevertheless rivaled by a more common usage also reported by the dictionaries. Revolutions were vicissitudes in human life, extraordinary changes in public affairs, reversals in the fortunes of nations. Here there is no longer any suggestion of a return to the starting point; instead the term suggests the sudden, violent emergence of something new. Unpredictability takes precedence over predictability, disorder over order, the extraordinary over the ordinary.

Although the dictionaries used these two antithetical meanings without taking any particular notice of their conflicting senses or of the form, extent, or causes of revolutions, attempts were occasionally made to bridge the gap between them. In associating all changes in the world—except for "a few extraordinary blows struck, in accordance with God's will, by His hand alone"—with distinct and identifiable causes, Bossuet found a way to link extraordinary events to an invisible order. Mably, whose work abounds with "revolutions" of one kind or another, links their history—superficial and chaotic—to a more profound history, in which everything is regular and nothing truly unexpected occurs, for "the passions, by turns embittered and calmed, must prepare the ground for a revolution over a long period of time until at last the right moment arrives for it to occur." Voltaire distinguishes between dynastic revolutions, which are superficially impressive shocks, and revolutions of the human spirit or national character, which by contrast are slow, profound, imperceptible, and irresistible. If this comparison does not reconcile order with disorder, at least it sets the true revolutions apart from the rest. It remains true, however, that for the most part eighteenth-century thought failed to resolve the contradiction between visible revolutions and invisible ones.

It is remarkable that the two events that served at the time as major references—the English Revolution and the American Revolution—did not help to distinguish between competing definitions of "revolution." The Glorious Revolution of 1688 was viewed by Huguenots as a return to the past, a felicitous rediscovery of fundamental laws subverted by history, but it was also seen by partisans of absolutism as just one more revolution in a history notable for its fitful alternation between fortunate reigns and unfortunate ones. Historians of England proposed both possible interpretations of the revolution: a restoration that ended the storm and restored order, and a revolution that was implicit in the times and inaugurated a new series of disorders.

The American Revolution was far more obviously a happy event, and the role that it reserved for human will was far more impressive. For these reasons the example is all the more significant; it shows that despite characteristics of success, the two senses of "revolution" continued to be intertwined. Commentators most favorable to "the revolution of America" continued to interpret it as a restoration: having tasted English liberties, the American people had gained the ability to make a revolution, that is, to try to restore their previously held rights. But this restoration of order did not save America from the disorders of another kind of revolution; "I fear," Mably wrote, "that America will again be pushed into a hard revolution." Again we see the contrast between the concept of an orderly revolution, a return to a previous state or to tranquility, and that of a disorderly revolution, one of degradation and agitation.

What are we to make of this perpetual alternation between the two meanings of "revolution"? The eighteenth century produced a vast literature on revolutions—in England, Sweden, Spain, and the Roman Republic—so vast that it ultimately drained all historical specificity from the idea of revolution, to the point where the history of revolutions—always spoken of in the plural—became simply history. When eighteenth-century writers chose to study one revolution, they always associated it with an adjective—great, astonishing, marvelous, glorious—in order to reduce it to one particular vicissitude in a world of vicissitudes. Some portrayed revolutions as bringing irreversible changes to the lives of men in society, others as bringing reversible changes that invariably conformed to a cyclical law. But all agreed that revolutions were inevitable, and possible to describe only once they had taken place: objects of analysis, not objectives for the will. The eighteenth century ascribed no precise moral connotation to revolution. Some were good, others bad; some toppled kings from their thrones, others restored them; some bore the seeds of progress, others of regression. But men always feared them; whatever their nature, they reflected political instability and demonstrated how little control human beings have over events. All peoples are "tried" by revolutions: this was the century's last word on the subject, although a few people, Voltaire among them, began to think that revolutions might be something a people could anticipate with hope. It was a pluralist, skeptical age, unlikely to conceive the idea that men might deliberately set out to make a revolution.

The French Revolution was first of all a great spectacle that dumbfounded contemporaries. Hordes of witnesses attest to the prodigious impression it made: philosophers, journalists, English poets like Coleridge were startled to see "France in a rage raising her gigantic limbs," and German versifiers like Klopstock were amazed to see in France a smile of "blue serenity in a vast stretch of sky." Even those soonest disillusioned initially responded to the Revolution as something out of the ordinary: "What a play, what actors!" Burke wrote to Lord Charlemont. Everyone hailed it as unprecedented spectacle, its stage quickly clotted with countless actors, a whole people risen as one to root out tyranny. Once the play had been presented to the public, as in a theater, nothing would be the same. The mere fact that the Revolution had taken place and the old world had collapsed so easily led to major revisions in themes that had been put forward somewhat nonchalantly in the eighteenth century.

Restoration or inauguration? The first effect of the great spectacle was to discredit the idea that the Revolution might restore a previous social order. It is of course possible to find ambiguous texts that use the word "restoration," such as those that portray Louis XVI as a restorer of French liberties. But exactly what was it that was supposedly being restored? Not a specific era in the historical revolution of France; it is striking how quickly the idea of an ancient constitution, still a vital theme in eighteenth-century historiographic debate, was abandoned. No doubt there remained the feeling of restoring a lost connection, but it was a connection not with an earlier time but with something fundamental. The French Revolution was nourished by one powerful idea, that foundation comes only from initiation. If it was the rights of man that were being restored, and if those rights had been scorned throughout history, then all historical precedent was simultaneously discredited. Far from repairing the chain of time, the Revolution stepped outside history in search of a new world, an absolute beginning. Hannah Arendt argues that men embark on revolution with an illusion of restoration, that is, of continuity, and that it is only later that they succumb to an even more powerful illusion in regard to historical experience, the illusion of a break with the past. But even if one is willing to concede that the French Revolution nursed illusions of restoration in its earliest days, these dreams were extremely short-lived. From the first the Revolution thought of itself as breaking all historical molds.

There is no better proof of this belief than the speed with which the Revolution disposed of the English model and, more surprisingly, of the American model as well, even though Lafayette sought to celebrate its influence. (Mounier, in his speeches on the royal sanction on September 4 and 5, 1789, noted with astonishment that the Assembly cast "a scornful eye on the Constitution of England, whereas not a year ago we spoke enviously of English liberty.") As early as August 23, Rabaut Saint-Etienne conceded that if the Constituent Assembly absolutely had to imitate a preexisting model, the best was the Constitution of Pennsylvania, but he corrected himself almost immediately: "French nation, you are not made to receive examples, but to set them." The notion that the American and French revolutions were incomparable was quickly orchestrated by Condorcet, who imputed his ideas to an American citizen engaged in the academic exercise of comparing the two experiences. The object of the American Revolution had been to free the country from a foreign aristocracy, while that of the French Revolution was to throw off the yoke of a domestic aristocracy. The Americans had had only to reject taxation by men living 3,000 miles away, whereas the French had to overthrow a fiscal system under which some Frenchmen were oppressed by others. The revolution on the other side of the Atlantic had simply thrown off a tenuous bond while retaining a great deal, such as the code of criminal law, from English rule. In France the Revolution was obliged to undo very strong bonds and had nothing to preserve. Accordingly, Condorcet explained, it was necessary to return to purer, more precise, more profound principles. The French, unlike the Americans, had to declare their rights before possessing them. They had to overthrow a society, while the Americans had preserved theirs. Thus the French Revolution, unlike the American, was a refoundation not only of the body politic but also of the body social.

It was therefore an unprecedented spectacle, an absolute inauguration.

IDEAS

By declaring that this upheaval was precisely what constituted a revolution, the makers of the French Revolution discredited the plural concept of revolutions, of a host of minor changes, in order to extol the one true Revolution. In the early months of the Revolution, however, there was still a degree of uncertainty about whether to speak of revolution or revolutions. Pierre Rétat has shown that Prudhomme's paper, "Révolutions de Paris," initially published with no idea that it would become a periodical, drew its title, still influenced by the traditional definition, from its intention to report on the several upheavals that had occurred in Paris between July 11 and July 18, 1789. But when the paper continued to publish and its readers clamored for a summary of what had taken place, Prudhomme gave them one in January 1790. Entitled "Clef de *la* Révolution" ("Key of *the* Revolution"), this article amalgamated and merged several revolutions into one unlike any other, because it was "the revolution of souls and spirits." This new definition rapidly earned its patent of nobility. Henceforth only counterrevolutionaries doubted the exemplary unity and singularity of the phenomenon and persisted in viewing the French Revolution as merely "*an* upheaval that occurred in 1789," as Buée's dictionary defined it. Everywhere else the events in France—which, Robespierre later remarked, constituted the first revolution to be based on the rights of humanity—were regarded as *the* Revolution.

This unique event was also a total event. It made no sense for a nation to speak of revolution unless it had broken *all* its chains. Revolution was no longer a matter of limiting despotic power by reforming or compromising it, nor was it a question of limiting the size of the political sphere. A revolution occurred when men sought to resolve all their problems at once—political, social, and moral—and to change themselves thoroughly and completely. Thus Chateaubriand, in his *Essai sur les révolutions,* refused to use the word to refer to dynastic changes, civil wars, or "incomplete change in a temporarily insurgent nation." He reserved its use for those occasions when "the spirit of peoples changes."

Thus distinguished from isolated upheavals and political disasters, the total revolution was simultaneously associated with the universal revolution. The rights at issue in the French Revolution were not particular rights like those in the English Bill of Rights in the name of which the people of America had risen in rebellion against England. Nor did they constitute a simple definition of French liberty. The Revolution, as analyzed by Boissy d'Anglas, transcended the boundaries of its native country in at least two ways: it was the work of a whole people, not of a few, and it sought to set mankind back on its original course. Hence it held out a boundless promise, a limitless future.

The prodigious spectacle had included repulsive scenes, difficult to erase from memory. In 1791 Saint-Just, a witness who can hardly be suspected of hostility to revolution, wrote in his *Esprit de la Révolution* of his horror at the sight of a mob playing with shreds of human flesh. These disorders were expunged from the Revolution's attempts to define itself, because it wished to see itself as founding a new order. That self-definition accounts for its association with the project of making a constitution, a project that for

810

Hannah Arendt is consubstantial with the Revolution itself. A distinction needs to be made, however, between the activity of making a constitution—that is, the power the Revolution claimed for itself at its beginning and by which it emancipated itself from the chains of time—and its result, the promulgated constitution, a document subject to historical change.

This distinction between process and result is the crucial point. At its inception the French Revolution thought of itself and experienced itself as an escape from history, as Michelet was well aware: "Time no longer existed; time had perished." The discovery that the Revolution itself had a history, that it was a process extended in time, with good days and bad, surprises and deviations, was devastating to the men who had made it. Sometimes they felt the Revolution was moving too slowly, other times too fast, never just right. Things moved too slowly because as the Revolution progressed, people's actions became ensnared in webs of relations; they bogged down or were diverted and ceased to make progress toward the original goal. The passing days raised memories of the Ancien Régime, of inexpugnable habits and of men and women ill disposed toward the Revolution who had yet to be convinced or vanquished; this opposition was a self-renewing "hydra," to use the revolutionaries' own powerful image. On the other hand, things sometimes moved too quickly, as the Revolution hurtled on at breakneck speed, impossible to control. When time slowed down, the revolutionary spirit faced many obstacles that impeded its expression. When time accelerated, people were frightened by the proliferation of unforeseen events. In either case it was impossible to bring the Revolution to an end—to complete it in the first case, to halt it in the second.

Thus the discovery of revolutionary history transformed the idea of revolution. Only a few episodes in this process of transformation can be mentioned here. One was the constitutional debate of the spring and summer of 1791, a debate haunted, as expressed by Duport in May and Barnave in September, by the obsession with ending the Revolution. Starting from the premise that "what is called revolution is done," Duport voiced his fear that continually raising the stakes would in fact bring back the scheming characteristic of the Ancien Régime, because "all movement is circular, in the moral world as in the physical world"—a reversion to the old astronomical meaning. As for Barnave, no one was less willing to associate revolution with disorder; instead he saw revolutions as constant, regular effects of clearly identifiable causes and dismissed "accidental causes" as good only for determining the "era" of revolutions. The worrisome radicalization of the Revolution changed his analysis, however; he was obliged, in fact, to blame radicalization on accidents, that is, on the ambition and vanity of men to whom the Revolution had offered an unhoped-for theater, men who therefore had an interest in its continuation. The only way to stop the machine was to resolve the Constitution. It alone would make it possible to distinguish between "those who want a stable government and those who want only revolution and change because they feed on trouble as insects on corruption." This distinction spelled the end of the identification of the Revolution with the Constitution, a marriage that had been strong in 1789 because of the contrast between the Revolution, which had a constitution, and the Ancien Régime, which had none. It also spelled the end of the idea that the Revolution was a guarantee against arbitrary rule. In Barnave's mind "revolution" resumed the pejorative sense it had had in the eighteenth century, of a change from which France had everything to fear: further revolution as well as regression, rebellion as well as reaction, the one engendering the other.

The "revolution of August 10" broke the final link that tethered the Revolution to the Ancien Régime: preservation of a monarchy that the revolutionaries had felt compelled to retain because of "customs and the national wish," as Barnave put it. The new revolution required a new definition, a difficult challenge that was taken up by Condorcet, who compared the dethroning of two constitutional kings, James II and Louis XVI, in order to show that the procedure was less besmirched by irregularities in the case of the latter than in that of the former. An entire people, or at any rate a "considerable fraction of the people," strayed less from the common order of the law than a "private association of citizens" turning for aid to a foreign prince. Condorcet worked hard to circumscribe and relativize revolutionary disorder. A few months later, the word "revolution" and the adjective "revolutionary"— the latter created expressly for the French Revolution, the only revolution to "take liberty for [its] object"—inspired similar reflections. A law, he argued, was revolutionary when its aim was to maintain this revolution, that is, when it broke with the order of tranquil societies. Revolutionary law was intended not to regulate such societies but to overcome the resistance of royalists. Hence it was merely "a law of circumstance," but the qualifier, Condorcet conceded, was so ridiculous that it had had to be replaced by the adjective "revolutionary." Condorcet's tortuous argument betrays his embarrassment at revolutionary measures that were so obviously laws of exception. They could certainly be justified as laws directed against men who sought to "produce a revolution in a contrary direction," but one still ought to take note of their irregularity and shun the detestable habit of hiding behind necessity, the "excuse of tyrants." Condorcet still dreamed of ending the Revolution, but unlike Duport and Barnave he believed that the end could be achieved only by resorting temporarily to illegality.

When the revolutionary government was being established, the argument by which it was justified was not fundamentally different from Condorcet's, though the Jacobins did dispense with Condorcet's precautionary language. They contrasted revolutionary law, which they called foundational, with constitutional law, which they saw as conservative. They also gave voice to a conviction, previously singled out by Vergniaud, that the energies needed for national defense required "perpetuating for some time (*encore*) all the effervescence of the Revolution," where the word *encore* suggests that the groups that captured leadership of the Revolution one after another differed only as to the proper moment for calling the Revolution to a halt. Finally the Jacobins, too, used the word "revolutionary" tautologically to denote whatever was in conformity with the Revolution.

Between Condorcet and Saint-Just, however, a new shift occurred in the meaning of "revolution." Rather pathetically, Condorcet wanted to see revolutionary laws as nothing more than a limited renunciation of legality, all aiming toward "the time when we will no longer have to make any laws." If, with the postponement of the newly approved Constitution, Robespierre and Saint-Just removed this last safeguard against tyranny, it was because they saw the Revolution not as a prodigious spectacle that produced instantaneous conversion in all its spectators but as a strenuous labor that derived its meaning from the existence of counterrevolutionary enemies. These enemies were of a most peculiar kind. For one thing they were everywhere: inside and outside the Republic and even within the consciousness of each revolutionary, since hostility to the Revolution began with the slightest hesitation in regard to communal life or even with mere indifference. For another, they were constantly being reborn, since the moral order, Saint-Just maintained, was just like the physical order: "Abuses can disappear as moisture evaporates from the earth only to reappear before long just as moisture falls back to earth from the clouds."

The nature of the Revolution's enemies, at once as fleecy as cloud and as obdurate as stone, had at least three consequences. First, illegality was necessarily consubstantial with the Revolution, whose enemies could be defeated only through violent action, absolved in all circumstances by the idea that, in Saint-Just's words, "everything must be allowed to those who are headed in the same direction as the Revolution." This necessity accounts for Robespierre's celebrated outburst in response to Louvet's charge on November 5, 1792: "Did you want a revolution without revolution?" On that day Robespierre's point was not simply that a revolution cannot be carried out *more geometrico* and without recourse to illegality. By claiming that everything the Revolution had enacted and all the great *journées* were of necessity illegal and by identifying these things with the Revolution itself, he allowed the Revolution to be defined by illegality. The same thing can be sensed in the shift in the meaning of "revolutionary." It had already been used to characterize every energetic measure: in the spring of 1793, for instance, Barère had urged the Convention to act and declare itself a *corps révolutionnaire*. Thus "revolutionary" meant expeditious and arbitrary. The "revolutionary instrument" was the guillotine. And if, among all the rivers of France, the Loire was especially "revolutionary," it was because it had so docilely received the victims of Carrier's execution by drowning.

Second, a revolution was required within each individual, since every participant harbored within himself or herself an enemy of the Revolution. The revolutionary government, far from being merely an instrument of war and conquest, was an instrument of "transition from evil to good, corruption to decency, bad manners to good." When Saint-Just defined the Revolution in these terms in his report on law and order, he made its completion dependent on a radical transformation of hearts and minds. "Each citizen must experience and effect within himself a revolution equal to that which has changed the face of France"—this stated aim of the Lyons Surveillance Committee (November 1793) shows the degree to which "revolution" had come to mean an inward personal transformation, a conversion that was inseparably both private and public.

The third consequence follows from the other two: the enemy could not be defeated, hence the revolutionary project would never be finished. Where should the Revolution stop? Saint-Just asked the same terrible question that had been raised at one time or another by all the leaders of the Revolution. Some, like Barnave, had given precise answers. But Saint-Just's answer was to postpone that end indefinitely, for in his view the Revolution would not be over until "perfection of happiness" had been achieved. He also allowed a fatal doubt to hover over the meaning of the end: "People talk about the Revolution's high-water mark. Who will set that mark?" Implicit in this ambiguity was the idea that there will always be a Revolution to be made, that no one can fall by the wayside without "digging his own grave," that the purity of the revolutionary project must be constantly restored, and that no one is judge of that purity; in other words, there will always be a need to "revolutionize the Revolution."

At this point the Revolution had strayed as far as it ever got from the image and idea popularized at its inception: the image of the Revolution as a marvelous spectacle endowed with an irresistible power to enlist support and carry conviction, and the idea of the Revolution as the establishment of liberty through law. What remained, however, is enough to explain why the revolutionary legend has been nurtured primarily by extremist memories of the Jacobin episode. The break with the past, continually reenacted in oaths, and the mythical unity of a virtuous people constantly mobilized in the purge of "factions" constitute a simple, powerful drama, which for future revolutions became a sort of "primal scene."

After Thermidor and the downfall of "the tyrant," another revolution joined the litany of July 14, August 10, and May 31; though a little tired to take its place in this company, it was nevertheless decked out with the same euphoric adjectives that had served its predecessors: *heureuse, grande, étonnante.* Some unexpected witnesses worked to attach an inaugural meaning to it: on 18 Fructidor, Year II, Babeuf suggested "counting today not as marking five years of revolution but only one month and a few days." The first attempt to rationalize the event was to portray it as a mirror image of May 31: on that date an armed insurrection of the Commune had forced the Convention to capitulate, whereas the new revolution had seen the Convention take its vengeance on the Commune. The two days therefore balanced each other, as the Barère Report sought to show: "On May 31 the people made its revolution; on 9 Thermidor the National Convention made its. Liberty equally applauded both." This whitewash was intended to cast 9 Thermidor as "the last storm of the Revolution." It would not lead to any new outburst because it merely compensated for an old one. It was therefore reasonable to look forward to that end of revolutionary history for which all the successive leaders of the Revolution had hoped.

It was soon clear, however, that nothing was really over. The years that followed Thermidor were filled with coups d'état, alternating victories and defeats for the legislative and the executive, and sudden reversals generously covered by the name revolution, such as the bitter 18 Fructidor, which some thought worthy of the same flattering epithets that had been attached to previous *journées*. The rhetoric that accompanied these upheavals sought to efface the indecent plurality of new revolutions (primarily by presenting each of them as a return to equilibrium, the sign of a true end of the Revolution) and to camouflage their illegality. This propaganda was not enough, however, to prevent a new sense of revolutionary time from arising out of this worrisome proliferation of revolutions. No longer did "revolution" connote the instantaneity of miracle or the long and patient effort of men to recreate themselves. Instead one had the syncopated alternation of revolution with reaction, all beyond human control. In the aftermath of Thermidor the Jacobins proclaimed that after such a long period of compression one must look forward to "a powerful reaction, commensurate with the misfortunes we have had to deplore." With the division of revolutionary time between revolution and reaction and the arrival on the scene of a new set of characters—the reactionaries—the usage of the word "revolution" changed once more. The long association of the adjective "revolutionary" with exceptional emergency measures became suspect. In Year III the Committee of General Security proposed banishing it from the language of politics. The noun recovered its anarchic and plural eighteenth-century meaning. What men now remembered from the revolutionary episode was what Eschassériaux, speaking to the Council of Five Hundred, called "the ardent but passing fever of revolutions, the frightful interregnum between laws." Far from being a unique event, the Revolution was lumped together with ordinary political instability.

Throughout this dizzying period a few people nevertheless sought to save the spirit of the Revolution. Constant devoted all his energy to breaking the infernal cycle of revolution and reaction. To do so he had to distinguish between two types of revolution. When "the harmony between a people's institutions and its ideas is destroyed," revolutions are inevitable. These legitimate, reasonable revolutions are implicit in the necessary progress of the human spirit; they are not doomed to be followed by a reaction. Reaction occurs only when revolutions run wild and fail to end at the appropriate point; flawed revolutions bring on reactions, arbitrariness succeeding arbitrariness and paradoxically encouraging a further revolution. By learning how to distinguish the good revolutions from the bad, one can stabilize institutions and keep from "losing hope in liberty." What kind of revolution was the French Revolution? The question leads to a further distinction between goals and processes. The process of the French Revolution was disastrous, because the revolutionaries, obsessed with memories of antiquity, went beyond their objectives and triggered a reaction. But the goal—the substitution of an elective system for a hereditary one—is an element of human progress and must henceforth be taken into account by all. "I call [the Revolution] a happy one in spite of its excesses because I keep my eyes fixed on the results."

This was a balanced interpretation, designed to save the Revolution from its disasters and shake the fatal French belief that France "needs a master." But it was soon discredited by events, out of which came the figure of a new despot to end the Revolution. And it was neglected during the nineteenth and twentieth centuries, which preferred the Jacobin interpretation. Although the word "revolution" enjoyed a prodigious semantic career, being extended to the most incongruous of situations and to changes of the most absurd kind, its meaning remained through all these metamorphoses astonishingly faithful to that set by the Jacobin episode. Future revolutionaries took over all the Jacobins' ideas: conquest of the state apparatus, political voluntarism, and even those ideas that had been patent failures, such as the fusion of individuals in a collectivity supposedly animated by a single will and in a state of permanent mobilization. For a long time to come, people did not experience revolutions; they made *the* Revolution. From the revolutionary repertoire they chose the Convention's libretto over all others, copied its vocabulary, donned the cast-off costumes of its actors, and conceived their own history in terms of its episodes. The year 1848 had its Girondins and its Mountain. The Paris Commune had its Montagnards and, in the Blanquists, its Hébertists. And the Russian Revolution had its Chouans, its *levée en masse*, and even its Girondins, used by Lenin as an epithet with which to flay Trotsky and Bernstein. The French Revolution thus went on reproducing or parodying itself. In pondering the enigma of a revolution that became a tradition when its vocation had been to emancipate men from tradition, Tocqueville suggested that if the Revolution repeated itself, it was because it was "always the same."

What is this strange revolution, always the same yet always to be made anew? It is not exactly the French Revolution but, contained and at the same time hidden in it, another revolution, whose features Marx limned in *The Holy Family:* "The revolutionary movement, which began in 1789 at the *Cercle Social,* whose principal representatives as it evolved were Leclerc and Roux, and which temporarily succumbed in the Conspiracy of Babeuf, gave rise to the communist idea, which Buonarroti, Babeuf's friend, reintroduced in France after the Revolution of 1830. This idea, developed in all its consequences, constitutes the principle of the modern world." In reality it was not so much an idea as a promise: the promise of equality, the same promise held out by the Jacobin Revolution (to the extent that the Jacobin period can be deciphered as an anticipation of the critique of formal liberties and private property), yet a promise still to be won, for Jacobin equality was only a timid anticipation of true equality.

But according to Marx the French Revolution was not the same thing as its historical legacy, to which it cannot be reduced. Marx showed that the French revolutionary class decked out its own interests in universal trappings. Paradoxically, however, that deceptive cloak made the fiction a reality and gave the illusion a future. Future revolutionaries were able to recapture the subversive truth hidden behind the masks and use it on behalf of a new revolution, this time devoted, presumably, to real equality. Equality can never be verified, however; nature and history having sown differences everywhere, equality is a constantly disappointed, constantly revived hope, and the revolution of equality is an interminable enterprise, exportable at will in time and space and deriving its strength from its endless plasticity.

REVOLUTION

The strength of the concept of revolution comes not only from its supposedly universal validity but also, in an ambiguous way, from its ability to combine two conflicting ideas. The first, borrowed from the eighteenth-century account and also a common theme of traditionalist thought, is that the revolution is an irresistible necessity, which enables revolutionaries to justify the heroic sacrifice of individuals to the great event and to absolve in advance any crimes that may be committed. This idea is wedded, without any genuine exploration of the problems involved, to the idea that men have absolute power over their destinies. A major symbol of historicism yet at the same time an object of individual activism, an absolutely human event that nevertheless completely transcends individual human beings, the Revolution draws from these contradictory representations its extraordinary power of fascination.

Mona Ozouf

FURTHER READING

Arendt, Hannah. *On Revolution.* New York, 1963.

Baker, Keith Michael. "Revolution," in Colin Lucas, ed., *The French Revolution and the Creation of Modern Political Culture,* vol. 2, *The Political Culture of the French Revolution.* Oxford, 1988.

Boissy d'Anglas, François-Antoine. *Quelques idées sur la liberté, la Révolution, le gouvernement républicain et la Constitution française.* N.p., 1792.

Buée, Adrien-Quentin. *Nouveau dictionnaire, pour servir à l'intelligence des termes mis en vogue par la Révolution.* Paris, 1972.

Condorcet, Marie-Jean-Antoine-Nicolas de Caritat, marquis de. *Réflexions sur la Révolution de 1688 et sur celle du 10 août 1792.* N.p., n.d.

Constant, Benjamin. *Des réactions politiques* (1797), reprinted in Constant, *Ecrits et discours politiques,* ed. Olivier Pozzo di Borgo, vol. 1. Paris, 1964.

Decouflé, André-Clément. *Sociologie des révolutions.* Paris, 1968.

Ellul, Jacques. *Autopsie de la Révolution.* Paris, 1969.

Furet, François. *Penser la Révolution française.* Paris, 1978.

Goulemot, Jean-Marie. *Discours, révolutions, et histoire: Représentations de l'histoire et discours sur les révolutions de l'âge classique aux Lumières.* Paris, 1975.

Habermas, Jürgen. *Theory and Practice,* trans. John Viertel. Boston, 1973.

Mably, Gabriel Bonnot, abbé de. "Observations sur le gouvernement et les lois des Etats-Unis d'Amérique," *Oeuvres complètes,* vol. 8. London, 1789.

——— "Des droits et des devoirs du citoyen," *Oeuvres complètes,* vol. 9. London, 1789.

Rétat, Pierre. "Forme et discours d'un journal révolutionnaire: Les 'Révolutions de Paris' en 1789," in Claude Labrosse et al., eds., *L'instrument périodique: La fonction de la presse au XVIIIe siècle.* Lyons, 1986.

RELATED TOPICS

American Revolution
Ancien Régime
Babeuf
Barnave
Burke

Condorcet
Constant
Constitution
Equality
Jacobinism

Marx
Revolutionary *Journées*
Robespierre
Voltaire

RIGHTS OF MAN

"The first revolution based on the theory of the rights of humanity," as Robespierre put it in his final speech on 8 Thermidor, had considerable difficulty reaching agreement about the definition of those rights. The Declaration approved on August 26, 1789, was replaced by another in the Constitution of 1793, which was in turn replaced by a Declaration of the Rights and Duties of Man and the Citizen in the Constitution of Year III. In the eyes of history, however, the first Declaration has remained the key version, despite the criticisms to which it was immediately subjected and which were seen as telling enough to require two revisions. Being first was no doubt of some importance.

On the whole, however, justice was done, for the debate that took place in that summer of 1789 established what would continue to be the key issues in both the 1793 and 1795 versions of the Declaration. Hindsight has heightened to excess the contrast of language and intention that distinguishes bourgeois prudence from Jacobin audacity and Thermidorian fear. The options differed, but the intellectual substance was the same, and the same controversial issues were present from the beginning. Consider, for example, the famous issue of "social rights," which is supposed to have set the popular preoccupations of 1793 apart from the narrow, property-oriented liberalism of the Constituent Assembly. Nearly half of the 1789 proposals—including the most notorious and influential of all, that of Sieyès—mentioned relief for the poor and considered guaranteed employment to be among the community's fundamental obligations to its members. And what about the no less eloquent "duties" that were supposed to signify a post-Thermidorian retreat into coercion and moral preaching? These too were hotly debated in the Constituent Assembly, and though categorically rejected, the whole notion of citizens' duties nevertheless had a strong influence on the adopted text. Bear in mind, moreover, that this initial text, whose balanced periods and carefully crafted form have so often been praised, was far from having been maturely weighed; it was in fact an unfinished draft, interrupted at the beginning of the session of August 27, 1789, by unanimous agreement on the need to give priority to a more urgent task: drawing up the Constitution. Consideration of articles in addition to the seventeen already adopted, a second reading, and possible final revision of the text were postponed until "after the Constitution." In 1791 the Assembly would plead that in the meantime the "national catechism" had taken on a "sacred character" and therefore ought not to be touched. But any attempt to gauge in depth the legislature's intentions without taking account of the contingencies that limited the scope of the Declaration is doomed to error.

Looking beyond the text approved on August 26, 1789, we want to reconstruct the way in which the problem of the rights of man was posed. This formulation was *formative:* in this as in many other aspects of revolutionary political culture, later radicalization did not innovate as much as it exploited possibilities present from the beginning. The Thermidorian reaction too drew upon the same initial inspiration yet attempted to contain or defuse it. There is an intellectual unity to the revolutionary process that makes analysis of the moment of crystallization especially important. The rights of man constitute a major component of the apparatus. The distinctive features of the result become apparent only when the problem is approached in this fashion. Nor is there any other path to feel one's way through the shadowy underbrush of sources and influences. It is one thing to establish antecedents and borrowings, another to understand how they were used and for what purpose.

It is beyond doubt that the American example played a crucial role in the elaboration of the French Declaration. Quite symbolically, the first person to propose a declaration to the Assembly, as if he were the one man by nature qualified to do so, was Lafayette, the hero of American independence. He drafted his text under the scrutiny and with the advice of the author of the American Declaration of Independence, Thomas Jefferson, who at that time happened to be serving as the United States' ambassador in Paris. Others also sought out his insights. The Committee on the Constitution even requested an official consultation, which Jefferson's duties obliged him to refuse. Patriots and monarchiens met at his home on the final day of debate on the Declaration, August 26, in order to submit to his authoritative judgment their difference of opinion concerning the place of royal authority in the future organization of the government. Other veterans of the Revolutionary War such as Comte Mathieu de Montmorency joined Lafayette among the most fervent and eloquent orators in the debate. The translator of the *Constitutions of the Thirteen States of America,* the duc de La Rochefoucauld d'Enville, was a member of the Assembly, where he took the floor to remind the deputies of the American lesson concerning freedom of the press. His anthology was in the hands of all who submitted proposals, as some candidly acknowledged. Among the deputies were several other experts on American affairs, including Démeunier, who played an active role in the debate, and Dupont de Nemours. In addition to these men, who played direct and major roles, one must recognize the influence of a publicist such as Condorcet, the author of a proposal that stimulated debate from outside and the man who drafted the *cahier* of the nobility of Mantes, a rigorous analyst of the great trans-Atlantic precedents in works ranging from *De l'influence de la révolution de l'Amérique sur l'opinion et la législation de l'Europe* to *Idées sur le despotisme.*

Not only was the American model on everyone's mind; it was also explicitly or implicitly in relation to it that the members of the Constituent Assembly staked out their positions. To begin with, it offered the most advanced deputies a way of satisfying one of their most basic ambitions: to avoid the example of the English Constitution and its "gothic" sedimentation. But this does not mean that they were literally in thrall to the documents that were in their minds and before their eyes. They were acutely aware of the differences between the French and American situations. They judged those differences in light of the requirements of their own task: to give France a constitution. Should it be preceded by an explanation of its grounds and legitimate aims? For some, the difference in social conditions made it dangerous to separate the abstract statement of rights from their concrete formulation. This point was raised by Lally-Tollendal the moment Lafayette finished reading his proposal on July 11: "Think of the enormous difference between a newborn nation presenting itself to the world, a colonial people that breaks its bonds to a distant government, and an ancient, vast nation, one of the foremost in the world, which for 1400 years has possessed its own form of government" (*Archives parlementaires,* VIII, p. 222). Malouet was even more direct when he spoke on August 1. In substance he said this: if the Americans were able to "take man in the bosom of nature and present him to the world in his primitive sovereignty," it was because the relative equality that prevailed in a newly formed society "composed entirely of property owners" rendered the proclamation of theoretical equality inoffensive. "In a great empire," by contrast, "it is necessary that men whom fate has placed in a dependent condition perceive the just limits rather than the extent of natural liberty" (*Archives parlementaires,* VIII, pp. 322–323).

Others, however, without denying the gap, supported the principle yet did not accept the American texts as given. Familiarity with the source gave rise not to imitation but to emulation. The best informed openly expressed their ambition to do better. It was Montmorency who on August 1 proposed "perfecting the great example of America," claiming for "this hemisphere the advantage over the other of invoking reason more loudly and allowing it to speak a purer language" (*Le courrier de Provence,* no. 22, p. 15). And it was Rabaut Saint-Etienne who, even though he, like Lafayette, was receiving Jefferson's advice, reminded the Assembly on August 18 that "you have chosen to adopt the Declaration of Rights because your *cahiers* require you to, and your *cahiers* have spoken to you because France has had America for an example. But let no one say on that account that our Declaration must be the same." Then, like those who counseled prudence, he added: "The circumstances are not the same. [America] was breaking away from a distant metropolis. A new people destroyed everything in order to build everything anew." From this he concluded, however, that the French ought to show audacity by going further than the Americans (*Archives parlementaires,* VIII, p. 452).

The inspiration came from Sieyès. He was the source of the critiques of declarations of the American type and of the model for a better one. He presented his proposal to the Committee on the Constitution on July 20 and 21, provoking astonishment and perplexity in most deputies, enthusiasm in a resolute minority, and repugnance in a few. We know from his papers what he criticized in the American declarations: namely, their having clung to an old image of power and its limitations, an image unacceptable to a "people resuming its full sovereignty." With "that assumption, a Declaration of Rights ought to have a totally different spirit and nature. It ceases to be a concession, a transaction, a treaty condition, or a contract between two authorities. There is only *one* power, only *one* authority" (*Archives nationales*, 284 AP 5). It was not a question of enumerating prerogatives but of elucidating analytically the principles of the best possible constitution. Instead of a division into articles he therefore proposed an analytical form, while conceding to the vulgar a summary in the form of "maxims" in the style of earlier texts. The main points of this argument can be found in the statements by Montmorency and Rabaut Saint-Etienne. The innovation was more disconcerting than convincing, and the "metaphysics" in this "recognition of the ends and means of the social state drawn from man's nature" aroused fears. Nevertheless, this "enigmatic" text served as the focus of the debate.

To uncertainties concerning the wisdom of a declaration distinct from the Constitution were added questions of form and substance raised by the oracle of political science. The Assembly hesitated, all the more because the deputies' perplexity and unspoken opposition only encouraged the submission of further proposals. Some thirty of these were submitted by the deputies alone. Others outside the Assembly also became involved, including figures of no little importance: Condorcet, already mentioned, Cerutti, and Servan. The crucial debate took place from August 1 to August 4. The favorable recommendation of Champion de Cicé, Clermont-Tonnerre, and Mounier, speaking for the Committee on the Constitution, ultimately prevailed. The Constitution would be preceded by a Declaration of the Rights of Man and of the Citizen, and there would be no concomitant declaration of duties. From August 4 to August 11 the Assembly was concerned with the "abolition of the feudal regime." On August 12 a new committee of five was appointed to sift through the various proposals in circulation. The result, defended by Mirabeau on August 17, was disappointing. A maneuver by the "right" (for we have reached the time when the topographic distinction between left and right was beginning to take on meaning) resulted in a proposal drafted by one of the Assembly's bureaus being adopted as the basis of discussion. Most of this proposal vanished during the final drafting phase (August 20–26), but in the meantime it adequately filled its supporting role in this laborious gestation.

If Sieyès and his supporters were defeated, the spirit of their proposal nevertheless prevailed. Although they were unable to secure approval of the *form* they had hoped for, the *function* that they had wished to ascribe to an explicit statement of the foundations of the state did survive. There was one fundamental reason for this: the self-proclaimed National Assembly's need for legitimacy. The Assembly found itself in the position of "exercising the constituent power," whereas the "present representation," as Sieyès admitted—quite significantly at the head of his proposal—"is not rigorously in accordance with what the nature of such power requires." The Declaration would make up for this shortcoming, since the Constitution was supposed to emerge directly from the "inalienable and sacred" principles on which all societies are based, and the Assembly would limit its role to setting forth and serving those principles. This was the reason for the rather odd language of the preamble that was ultimately adopted, which was taken by way of Mirabeau's proposal from Sieyès. It has often been noted that no one enunciates the statements contained in that preamble; this was the price to be paid for ascribing the fundamental role to "simple and incontestable principles," with respect to which the Assembly served only as a modest intermediary. This was also the reason for the constraint of universality imposed on the writing. Only a "declaration of rights for all men, all times, and all countries," as Duport put it on August 18, could claim that undeniable and irresistible authority that the Constituent Assembly needed to justify its enterprise. This mooring in universality was neither the fruit of any special genius nor the mark of any specific lack of realism. It grew out of the needs of the situation. At exactly the same time the American Congress was in the process of drafting the ten amendments to the Constitution of 1787, which, when ratified in 1791, would establish the importance of "bills of rights" in the organization of societies and governments. A "strong government" having been established on the initiative of the Federalists, it was left to the Bill of Rights to mark the limits of public power and protect individuals from government encroachment. The problem of the French was of a totally different kind. To be sure, they intended to consecrate individual liberties; but they were also in the difficult position of having to establish a government in conformity with the order of individuals. This uneasy balance between the concern with foundations and the concern with protections is what distinguishes their work.

The Declaration was not only a symbolic prop but also a solution to the complex equation faced by the Constituents. They walked a narrow path: they had to establish a new government inside the old one. In other words, they had to reconcile the establishment of national legitimacy with the preservation of and respect for royal legitimacy. The signal virtue of founding a new government was that it was a roundabout way of firmly establishing the authority of the national representation without risking a confrontation with the dynastic authority. In terms of political passions, moreover, it made it possible to be radical in form while remaining moderate in practice. It satisfied the need for regeneration without directly challenging the established powers.

It was this logic, moreover, that brought about the encounter between the Revolution and the thought of Rousseau. In such a context the most naturally attractive philosophy is one that most rigorously defines the full range and preeminence of the legislative power while leaving open the possibility of a monarchical executive. The "general will" triumphed because it left room for a king while offering the most radical version of the way in which, starting with a group of individuals, collective legitimacy comes into existence. It could be accommodated, moreover, to the "national sovereignty" slowly elaborated by the absolutist state but on the verge of escaping from its original owner since its appropriation by the Assembly on June 17. The Revolution was a product of such impure conjunctions and effective interlockings. The historical legacy was projected into the philosophical schema. The general will was accepted as the dynamic translation of the sovereignty of the nation, its generality being the precise counterpart of the impersonality required by a government operating in the name of collective individuality. It not only provided an adequate camouflage for the various faces of social power but also met the most urgent of people's intensely felt needs, for dissolution of the world of dependencies and privileges. In place of organic bonds and personal command it substituted the rule of law, that is, a mode of relation between individuals in which obligation entails respect for the initial absence of any social bond. The Americans did not have simultaneously to dismantle a hierarchical society, deal with the legacy of several centuries' accumulation of public power, and establish a preeminent authority without destabilizing the formidable power already in place. All these constraining factors came together to invest Rousseauist categories with a central resolving role. The Rousseauism in question was not so much a matter of influence (presumably measured by the weight of all the volumes of the *Social Contract* in circulation compared with the mass of all the brains in France) as one of functional opportunity inherent in the specific needs of a context and an enterprise. Hence philological fidelity was not its strong point. Neglect of this freedom in the employment of references and sources accounts for the absurd quarrels of which the patriotic dispute between Jellinek and Boutmy at the beginning of this century offers a consummate example. The members of the Constituent Assembly were at the same time governed by the American example and dominated by the language of the *Social Contract* (and a few other works). But they were also a long way from the United States and were poor disciples of Rousseau. Rather than attempt to establish improbable and contradictory proof of conformity, we need to explore the rule that governed these readers' infidelities, a rule implicit in the very reasons for which they turned to the sources in question.

The debate over content arose out of the specific characteristics of the situation. The need to establish their legitimacy as representatives of the nation led the deputies to look to the first principles of all society and to invoke their authority. They were not unaware of what was at issue in this approach—quite the contrary. They were acutely conscious of the fact that they were not merely proclaiming in the abstract certain truths of nature but literally involved in rebuilding a society—a reality whose distance from the norm being asserted was hard to ignore. "Declarations of rights would not be difficult," *Le courrier de Provence* sarcastically observed, "if in declaring what ought to be one were not issuing a manifesto against what is." That difficulty was not only at the heart of all the preliminary discussions; it was also one of the principal keys to the final draft. By its very nature it was particularly acutely felt at the beginning of August 1789, at the height of the rural insurrection, the "fire in the provinces." It raised anxieties in many people and heightened the reluctance to publish the Declaration separately from the Constitution. Once this difficulty was overcome, worry shifted its ground to the tenor of a Declaration adopted under such conditions. It was not, as orator after orator repeated, a question of man in the state of nature but of the individual in the bonds of society. Hence it was not enough to speak only of his prerogatives; something also had to be said about the constraints inherent in coexistence with one's fellow man.

Conservative fears of social disorder were in this respect bolstered by the religious sensibility, which would play an important if implicit role throughout the debate. This was not just a matter of the clergy's reactionary position. It was the most progressive of the Assembly's clerical members, Grégoire, who became the most vehement advocate of man's duties. This was an authentic debate about a fundamental issue. Does existence in society imply limitations on man's natural freedom? Once again Sieyès' proposal was at the origin of the dispute. Sieyès had asserted that "man entering society does not sacrifice a part of his freedom . . . Freedom is more complete and more intact in the social order than it can be in the state known as the state of nature" (*Archives parlementaires,* VIII, p. 257). The proponents of the view that individuals have duties to balance their rights spoke up in opposition to this view. There is no social bond, they argued, without obligations that bridle man's primitive independence. Not that Sieyès was unaware of the de facto existence of such obligations. For him, however, reciprocity between individuals was sufficient to account for them: I have duties toward others to the extent that I recognize their having the same rights as myself. Hence there are in fact only rights, of which duties are simply a special case in the interpersonal sphere. In other words, it is possible to rebuild a society totally starting only with the "natural" prerogatives of its individual members. In the final analysis it was this assertion to which the proponents of duties objected. The substance of Grégoire's objection was that it is not true that duties are deduced from rights. In other words, to found a society something more is required than the rights of its members. Its functioning requires the exercise of a limiting constraint whose legitimacy is derived from other sources. Once again, it was the spirit of Sieyès' position that prevailed but not his literal formulations. The deputies chose radical individualism over the doctrine of duties. But the objection that was thrown out the door returned through the window. Though theoretically rejected, concern over what limits were to be placed on rights profoundly influenced the final draft. Henceforth rights would permanently be saddled with the ghost of duties; even before the official return of the doctrine of duties in Year III, its shadow hovered over the debate of 1793.

Full natural rights within the social state: that was what Sieyès believed needed to be secured. In particular, that implied to him a need for what would later come to be called "social" rights. In this regard it is essential that we try to rescue the ideas and intentions of the Constituent Assembly from the limits within which some interpreters have misleadingly attempted to confine them. "The advantages that can be derived from the social state," Sieyès wrote in the most unambiguous fashion,

> are not limited to complete and effective protection of individual liberty: citizens are still entitled to all the benefits of association. . . . No one is unaware of the fact that the members of society derive the greatest benefits from public properties and public works. One knows that those citizens whom misfortune has rendered unable to meet their own needs have a just right to assistance from their fellow

citizens, etc. One knows that nothing is more apt to perfect the human race, morally as well as physically, than a good system of education and public instruction. . . . Citizens in common have a right to all that the state can do in their behalf. (*Archives parlementaires,* VIII, p. 259)

It is worth citing at length from the most important and influential of the proposals of 1789, all the more so in that it was far from an exception to the rule. A dozen others made similar points. "Property must not prevent any person from surviving," stated Pison du Galland, a deputy for the Third Estate from Grenoble. "Thus, every man must be able to live on his work. Any man not able to work must be assisted." To be sure, no such provision was incorporated into the text finally adopted. There are numerous signs, however, that its absence was more circumstantial than deliberate. Had the Declaration been completed, it is quite likely that it would have contained an article on relief. In any case, the mere possibility is enough to reveal the inanity of critiques directed at the alleged monadological egoism of the bourgeois of 1789. The powerful presence of that possibility, bolstered by argument, in a Sieyès—the same Sieyès who with perfect oligarchic self-assurance introduced the distinction between active citizens and passive citizens—forces one to raise the question of the true origin of so-called social rights, which have all too conveniently been linked to the emergence of the popular movement. The claim of "citizens in common" upon "all that the state can do in their behalf" needs to be reexamined with respect to its place in the individualist universe.

The debate over the final draft (August 20–26) was dominated by lurking thoughts of the constitutional problem, which had been deliberately postponed. Its urgency was felt more and more acutely as the days went by, precipitating debate as of August 24 and resulting in adjournment on August 27. Parties began to take shape around the major outstanding question, the royal veto, the subject of negotiations in the corridors. The debate over the rights of man seemed in many respects a preliminary debate in which the moderates, led by the monarchiens, and the patriots regrouped and gauged their strength. The two parties were roughly equal, moreover, and the tactical skill of the monarchien spokesmen, Lally-Tollendal in particular, even assured them of certain advantages. Thus they were able to see to it that a rather anodine proposal, that of the "sixth bureau," was adopted as the basis of discussion. This was Sieyès rewritten in a much more moderate tone by the bishop of Nancy, and its principal quality in the eyes of its promoters may have been in its prudent omissions.

Paradoxically, however, the opposite preoccupations of the two camps finally came together in the course of drafting the final Declaration. The moderates' concern to set limits on the exercise of individual rights and the patriots' determination to "socialize" natural law, in a sense, by jointly protecting individual prerogative and the power of the nation ultimately combined, despite minor difficulties, to produce the same effect. This striking convergence was brought about essentially by the notion of *law.* The key to the mechanism can be found in article 4, proposed on August 21 by Lameth but directly inspired by Sieyès: "Liberty consists in being able to do anything that does not injure others. Thus the exercise of each man's natural rights has no limits other than those that assure other members of society enjoyment of those same rights. These limits can be determined only by the law." Sieyès' intention was to leave no room for arbitrary personal rule. The empire of law must encompass all possible relations between free and equal actors, or else it was nothing. Obviously, however, the effect of such a pronouncement was to place the liberty that had just been proclaimed under the jurisdiction of a law capable of broadening or narrowing its limits. To be sure, the next article established a symmetrical limitation on the law: "The law has the right to prohibit only those actions harmful to society" (the collective equivalent of the prohibition placed on individuals against doing harm to others). But who would be the judge of the law?

From that moment the two major difficulties that would thwart effective implementation of the rights thus proclaimed were already apparent. In the first place, there was an insurmountable tension between independence and membership. Article 2, though actually the work of Mounier, a moderate, counted resistance to oppression among man's inalienable rights, a provision ripe with consequences that attests to how strongly the deputies felt about the individual autonomy ascribed to individuals transported from the state of nature to the social state; Sieyès spoke even more vigorously about the "right to repel violence with violence." Nevertheless, a clause in article 7 significantly made use of the same word though in a different sense: "Any citizen summoned or seized in virtue of the law must obey at once; he incurs guilt by resisting." This clause had an interesting history. It too was taken from Sieyès' proposal, but it was adopted at the suggestion of Malouet, one of his most conspicuous adversaries in the monarchien camp—a clear illustration of the unnatural accord that was reached in spite of antagonistic intentions. Malouet of course saw the guarantee of authority in case of disorder. Sieyès had meant to indicate the irresistibility of power that results from general participation, each person's liberty flourishing and testing itself through the authority of all. The immediate conversion of individual independence into collective power created common ground between the ambition to deploy the rights of man in their plenitude and the conservative concern with regulating or disciplining their expression. To be sure, there were clashes over means. The most bitter conflict was over the extremely sensitive issue of religious freedom, debated on August 23. The clergy, fully mobilized, was able to obtain a restrictive formulation: "No one shall be disturbed for his opinions, even in religion, provided that their manifestation does not disturb the public order established by law." This was the major battle in the debate. But the disputes were over the particular consequences of a general measure that was not and really could not be challenged. It could have been challenged only by those who claimed unlimited liberties. For them the expression of liberty was inseparable from the affirmation of authority that extended it and served as its instrument. Hence there was no reason for them to attack the principle of oversight; more than that, victory could only have produced the opposite of the result desired, strengthening authority, so that the wish for greater independence would have increased the obligations of membership in the society. The need to translate individual autonomy into social power worked against preservation of individual rights through limitation of power. It was but a short step from the liberal inspiration to the authoritarian temptation. Thus we see why a revolution based on the theory of the rights of man failed to conceive or establish a regime to guarantee them.

The preamble to the Declaration calls for a comparison with all legislative and executive acts for any "purpose of political institution." In addition, it sets limits to the law (beyond article 5, already cited, there was article 8: "The law shall establish only strictly and obviously necessary punishments"). At the same time, it implicitly outlines an economy of powers in which there is no room for conciliating between the acts of the legislator and their foundation. Therein lay an enormous contradiction that constituted a second stumbling block to the revolutionary enterprise. Article 6: "The law is the expression of the general will. All citizens have the right to contribute to its formation personally or through their representatives." (The same formula was repeated in regard to consent to taxation: "Citizens have the right to determine the need for public contributions by themselves or through their representatives.") Article 16: "Any society in which rights are not guaranteed, or in which the separation of powers is not fixed, has no constitution." These words have taken on the innocence of timeless abstraction. But in context and in the minds of those who promoted them they had a precise significance, which the Constitution would soon attempt to make explicit: "There is no authority in France superior to that of the law. The king reigns exclusively through the law, and only in the name of the law may he demand obedience." The legislature was thus preeminent and denied anyone the right to censor its choices; the executive was strictly subordinate to the legislative branch and simply transformed the general will expressed by the latter into "particular acts," in accordance with the Rousseauist definition of government (*Social Contract*, book 3).

It was this separation of powers, strictly determined by the theory of the general will, that the Constituent Assembly had in mind when it adopted this article on its final day of deliberation. "Separation" meant complete independence of the legislative power from the monarch. This same logic accounts for the principal anomaly of the text, namely, the democratic breadth of the formula allowing for personal participation by citizens in the formulation of the general will, astonishing to say the least on the part of deputies who were preparing to establish a *censitaire* system of suffrage. Note, moreover, that the Assembly, on this point, went further than Sieyès, who while invoking the general will nevertheless explicitly stipulated that the choice of representatives ought to be limited to "citizens possessing both an interest in and a capacity for public affairs." But the draft proposed by the "sixth bureau" was even more radical than the final version: "Every citizen shall cooperate directly in the formulation of the law." Quite simply, Sieyès was in possession of a theory that gave him the assurance of having overcome Rousseau's objections to representation while incorporating all of Rousseau's contributions to political theory. His colleagues, more doubtful, preferred a formula implying a kind of equivalence between direct democracy and representative government in order to protect themselves from any possible objections at a time when they needed the support of all citizens. Here again, however, they committed themselves to a political transformation of individual rights that precluded just administration of those rights: no control was placed upon the representatives, whose usurpation of sovereignty could be corrected only by insurrection.

Thus the founding text already contained the inhibiting equation that would weigh upon the enterprise of foundation: it embodied in condensed form a concept of liberty that prevented its realization.

Marcel Gauchet

Further Reading

ON THE RECEPTION OF THE AMERICAN EXAMPLE

Echeverria, Durand. *Mirage in the West: A History of the French Image of American Society to 1815*. Princeton, 1957.

ON THE AMERICAN BILL OF RIGHTS

Rutland, Robert Allen. *The Birth of the Bill of Rights, 1776–1791*. Chapel Hill, 1955.

"CLASSIC" POLEMICS

Bouchary, M. *La déclaration des droits de l'homme et du citoyen et la constitution de 1791*. Paris, 1947.

Boutmy, Emile. "La déclaration des droits de l'homme et du citoyen et M. Jellinek," *Annales des sciences politiques*, 1902, 415–443.

"Les droits de l'homme," *Droits*, no. 2, 1985.

Jellinek, Georg. *Die Erklärung der Menschen- und Burgerrechte: Ein Beitrag zur modernen Verfassungsgeschichte*. Leipzig, 1895.

———"La déclaration des droits de l'homme et du citoyen et la constitution de 1791," *Revue du droit public et de la science politique*, 1902, 385–400.

Marcaggi, Vincent. *Les origines de la déclaration des droits de l'homme de 1789*. Paris, 1904.

Sandweg, Jürgen. *Rationales Naturrecht als Revolutionäre Praxis*. Berlin, 1973.

Walch, Emile. *La déclaration des droits de l'homme et du citoyen et l'Assemblée Constituante: Travaux préparatoires*. Paris, 1903.

Related Topics

American Revolution Lafayette Monarchiens Rousseau
Condorcet Liberty Regeneration Sieyès

Rousseau

Rousseau has often been considered the forerunner and guide of the French Revolution. Burke, Quinet, Louis Blanc, and Taine are among the countless writers who have detected signs of Jean-Jacques's powerful influence on events. Quinet, calling Rousseau the Revolution's "lawgiver," said that "he was to the Revolution as the seed is to the tree," and that the *Social Contract* was the Revolution's "book of law."

That book's author has been regarded as the man who inspired the principles put into practice after August 10, 1792, particularly the policies adopted between the defeat of the Girondins and Thermidor. The "Jacobin Republic" is generally regarded as the period of the Revolution during which Rousseau's influence was at its peak. Universal suffrage and direct democracy seemed to reflect the lessons of the *Social Contract*. The state-controlled economy of that period was held to reflect Rousseau's idea that individuals who subscribe to the social contract submit both person and property to the general will. Measures to benefit the poor were interpreted as consequences of Rousseau's critique, in the *Discourse on Inequality*, of the inequalities of wealth. According to Louis Blanc and the subsequent socialist tradition of revolutionary historiography, Rousseau's thought dominated the second phase of the Revolution. The author of the *Discourse* and the *Social Contract* is alleged to have been the originator of the idea that a just political and social order must do more than simply protect individuals and society against arbitrary rule; it must also take positive steps to benefit the least well off, over whom it exercises a "tutelary power."

Last but not least, some commentators have held that the *Social Contract* was the source of all that was authoritarian and dictatorial in Jacobin policy from June 1793 to July 1794. Benjamin Constant maintained that the Jacobin leaders took from Rousseau and Mably the idea that citizens must be "totally subjugated if the nation is to be sovereign." Taine stressed the affinity between Rousseau's idea of a democratic regime "modeled on Sparta and Rome," in which "the individual is nothing [and] the State is everything," and the Jacobins' vision of an austere, virtuous, and authoritarian republic. More recently Rousseau has been blamed in part for the Revolution's totalitarian aspects. J. L. Talmon, for example, argues that Rousseau, by asserting the existence of an "absolute, logical, and uniquely valid social order," which the political authorities must seek to institute in the teeth of whatever resistance may arise, lent credence to a belief in the omnipotence of the political will—a belief that seems to have been the guiding spirit of revolutionary absolutism, especially in the period from 1792 to 1794.

There is no doubt that the Revolution marked the moment at which a great philosophy encountered an important historical movement. For proof one has only to consider the constant praise bestowed upon Rousseau by the orators of the revolutionary assemblies long before his ashes were transferred to the Pantheon. In October 1790 a bust of Rousseau together with a copy of the *Social Contract* was placed in the hall in which the Assembly met. In December a motion was passed asking that Rousseau be awarded public honors. In August 1791 the Assembly responded to a petition by approving a new request that Rousseau be awarded "the honors bestowed upon great men by the grateful fatherland." In fact, opposition to moving Rousseau's ashes came from the marquis de Girardin, the philosopher's friend and protector, on whose property Rousseau was buried. Girardin's opposition delayed the move and forced the Assembly to vote on the issue more than once. The Convention finally acted on 25 Germinal, Year II, at the height of the Terror. In a speech delivered on 18 Floréal, Year II, on the "cult of the Supreme Being," Robespierre praised Rousseau and invoked his authority. Yet it was not until after Thermidor and the submission of the Lakanal report that the Convention gave its final approval, allowing the philosopher's ashes to be moved to the Pantheon on October 11, 1794. In 1795, during debate on the constitution, Boissy d'Anglas again extolled the "immortal author of the *Social Contract*." Toward the end of the century, however, the so-called Ideologues, a group of intellectuals close to the government then in power (and including Destutt de Tracy, Cabanis, Volney, and Degérande), criticized Rousseau for having led the Revolution astray by encouraging its experiments with egalitarianism and authoritarian rule. Roederer reports that when the first consul (Napoleon) traveled to Ermenonville in 1800, he had this to say upon visiting the room in which Rousseau had slept: "He was a madman, your Rousseau. It was he who led us into our present predicament." Thus did the man who put an end to the Revolution eulogize Rousseau's influence. Yet in doing so he apparently recognized and approved the identification of Rousseau with the events.

Until about 1795, then, the leaders of the Revolution identified with Rousseau's ideas. By itself, however, this allegiance does not prove that the *Social Contract* was the Revolution's "book of law." Nor does it prove—despite endlessly repeated claims that the Revolution sought to impose a preconception of what society ought to be—that the revolutionaries were all along inspired by a desire to put the "abstract principles" of the *Social Contract* into practice. Recent work has shown that while the *Social Contract* was not unknown, it was much less celebrated than *Emile* and especially *La nouvelle Héloïse*, one of the century's best-selling books. Prior to 1789 some thirteen editions of the *Social Contract* had been published, compared with twenty-two editions of *Emile* and fifty of *La nouvelle Héloïse*. The latter two works were regularly reprinted, moreover, whereas all the editions of the *Social Contract* appeared close to the date of the work's original publication, suggesting initial enthusiasm for the book followed by comparative indifference. Hence there are sound reasons for stating that before 1789 Rousseau's influence and notoriety had more to do with *La nouvelle Héloïse* and *Emile* than with the *Social*

Contract. However, some writers, like Barny, argue that even if the *Social Contract* was not widely circulated, it was well known prior to 1789 among those who would become leaders of the Revolution. That claim is no doubt true, but just because the work was well known does not mean that it had the impact of *La nouvelle Héloïse* or *Emile* even among this elite group. There is no reason to assume that those who would eventually become leaders of the Revolution constituted a distinctive group *beforehand,* a group with reactions and preferences distinguishable from those of the cultivated public at large. In 1789, moreover, the *Social Contract* had not been reprinted for seventeen years. Yet it appeared in four new editions in 1790, three in 1791, and thirteen between 1792 and 1795. If the book's fortunes rose after the Revolution and not before, what is suggested about the revolutionaries' attitudes toward the work?

The proposition that Rousseau's work contained the seeds of the Revolution, an idea that did no more than draw the obvious consequences and put them into practice, also serves to obscure another incontrovertible fact, namely, that up to 1791 or 1792 the Revolution's enemies invoked Rousseau's authority as freely as did its supporters. The former cited passages in which Rousseau asserted that "no sensible man" would set out to change principles and institutions established by "thirteen hundred years" of French monarchy. Violence horrified Rousseau. He wrote, for instance, that "freedom would be too dearly bought at the price of a single man's blood." The Assembly's adversaries pointed out that Rousseau approved of representative government, but only if the representatives were bound by strict mandates from their constituents. Citing Rousseau's *Considerations of the Government in Poland* in support of their position, they showed that the Assembly had gone beyond the "instructions" contained in the *cahiers de doléances* and had betrayed their spirit. Of course, citing Rousseau's work was a rhetorical device for bringing out the contradictions in the revolutionaries' own arguments: if the Assembly invoked the authority of Rousseau, then its enemies would point out how its arguments were at variance with the teachings of its avowed master. Such a tactical maneuver does not necessarily imply any real adhesion to Rousseauist principles. It does suggest, however, that for many adversaries of the Revolution it was by no means self-evident that Rousseauism and the work of the Assembly were inseparable. Nevertheless, after 1792 those who condemned the Revolution ceased to invoke Rousseau's name. Indeed, they blamed him for the Revolution's failings, thus acknowledging that their rhetorical strategy had failed. The revolutionaries, by contrast, had cited Rousseau so often that in the end they accredited the idea that they were his true heirs, an idea created in large part by the Revolution's discourse about itself. In a sense, therefore, the Revolution imposed its own meaning on Rousseau's complex thought.

Finally, the fact that Rousseau's legacy was claimed by one revolutionary leader after another creates more problems than it solves, for there were profound differences among those leaders. If the deputies of the Constituent Assembly, Robespierre, and the Thermidorians all acknowledged Rousseau as their master, what exactly was the nature of the Rousseauian heritage?

What policies was he supposed to have inspired? Those who maintain in retrospect that Rousseauism was the ancestor of the Jacobin politics of 1793 and 1794 forget that contemporaries did not immediately see it that way. Robespierre and Saint-Just eulogized Rousseau, but the transfer of his ashes to the Pantheon was arranged later by those who had just toppled the "tyrant" Robespierre, who was even accused of having delayed the ceremony out of jealousy. Such facts would be inexplicable if contemporaries had immediately associated the image of Rousseau with the dictatorship of "public safety." If successive leaders of the Revolution were able to see themselves in Rousseau, the question remains what it was that they saw.

The answer, it is often said, is that they discovered in Rousseau the principles upon which a new order could be established. The petition urging the Assembly to approve the transfer of Rousseau's ashes to the Pantheon described the philosopher as the "founder of the French Constitution" because he had demonstrated, in a systematic theory, the justice of equal rights and popular sovereignty. Yet the Constitution of 1791 established a representative system of government. Rousseau, who had forcefully condemned representative government, was proclaimed the father of a constitution that consecrated it. As mentioned above, he did accept representation provided the representatives were bound by strict mandates. But in the summer of 1789 the Constituent Assembly rejected the principle that representatives were so bound, and that decision was not challenged again during the revolutionary period. Rousseau's whole theory of the general will assumes either that there is no representation or that the representatives are strictly bound; the law must be made by all, for only then are its subjects identical with its authors, from which principle it follows that every man is free. If representatives decide in the place of the people, the central tenet of Rousseau's political theory is flouted.

Therefore it should come as no surprise that Sieyès, more lucid on this score than many of his fellow revolutionaries, was harshly critical of Rousseau in the few explicit statements he made about the philosopher. In 1793 or 1794 he described Rousseau as "a justly celebrated writer. . . . a philosopher as exquisite in sentiment as he is deficient in vision," who "in eloquent pages, rich in superfluous detail yet poor in substance, confused the *principles* of the social art with the *beginnings* of human society." For Sieyès, representative government was one of the recent discoveries of "social art." These fragmentary comments do not prove that Rousseau's ideas had no influence on Sieyès, but they do show that it was not from Rousseauism that the architect of the constitution took his inspiration. There is, moreover, an even more substantial reason for rejecting the idea that Sieyès was a disciple of Rousseau. From the *Essay on Privileges* to the law depriving nobles of citizenship (1797) Sieyès exhibited a passionate hatred of the nobility that survived every change in the politics of the Revolution. In the pamphlets he wrote in 1789, Sieyès did not merely call for the elimination of privileges; he argued that those who have enjoyed such privileges are not part of the nation, indeed that they are its *enemies*. Although it is true that Rousseau's work is, broadly speaking, a plea on behalf of equality, hostility to nobility and privilege as such (that is, to superior social status enshrined in law) is not one of its explicit central themes. In the *Discourse on Inequality* Rousseau attacks the inequalities born of private property in the name of man's natural equality. For him the key division is not between the privileged and the nonprivileged but, far more generally, between the rich and powerful on the one hand and the poor and weak on the other.

Although Rousseau's ideas about equality in general can surely be used as an argument against "aristocracy," his critique was not directed specifically against the nobility. Certainly the intention to *exclude* the privileged from the community and brand them the *enemy* was not part of Rousseau's legacy. Anti-aristocratic passion as such owed more to the state of French society than to the theories of Rousseau.

From the first meeting of the Estates General, and increasingly after the transformation of that body into the National Assembly, it was felt that the deputies embodied the "general will," a term first given currency by Rousseau, whose influence was surely responsible for the favor that idea enjoyed. The traditional view was that the Estates General conveyed the "wishes" of the people to the king. With wishes it is possible to compromise; wishes can be reckoned with and, if need be, partially granted. But if the nation expresses not its wish but its will, the only option is to carry out that will. In this sense, the view of the revolutionaries that the executive should be strictly subordinate to the legislature does exhibit Rousseau's influence. Note, however, that this influence took the form more of slogans and broad themes (such as general will and sovereignty) than of precisely articulated concepts. This lack of specificity is evident in Saint-Just's attempts to show that the Constitution of 1791 was legitimate even though it had encountered opposition and therefore could not be construed as an expression of the "will of all." In his words: "Rousseau did not tell the whole story when he described the [general] will as inalienable, irrevocable, and eternal. It must also be just and reasonable. It is no less criminal for the people to be tyrannized by themselves than to be tyrannized by others." Yet Rousseau devoted an entire chapter of the *Social Contract* to showing why the general will could not be unjust. His whole argument was intended to prove that it was impossible for a people to be tyrannized by itself. Saint-Just's misreading of Rousseau is total. Plainly he did not see some of the crucial points of the theory of the general will. This passage is also remarkable in another way. It was not from Rousseau that the future leader of the Montagnards took the idea that there was no need to take account of wills "inclined toward perversity," an argument that would be used later to justify the Jacobin dictatorship. Although one might argue that certain passages in Rousseau do suggest such a conclusion, Saint-Just would not have agreed: he in fact criticizes Rousseau for his failure to make precisely this point. In this disagreement is still further evidence that we must not overestimate the influence of Rousseau's political theories on the revolutionaries, who were ignorant of the precise content of his theoretical works. They took from Rousseau little more than the principle that all power springs from the general will.

What about direct democracy, which some revolutionary leaders clamored for and, from 1792 to 1794, put into practice? Was this the true application of Rousseau's theories? Surely Rousseau's ideas played an important role in this period. Even before 1790 a popular journalist like Loustalot or lecturer like abbé Fauchet used the *Social Contract* to show that since popular sovereignty was inalienable, citizens could not confine themselves to the role of electing representatives and allowing them to govern as they pleased. But to appreciate the extent of Rousseau's contribution, we must look at the practice of direct democracy in greater detail.

For revolutionary activists, the inalienable nature of popular sovereignty meant that laws proposed by the people's representatives ought to be submitted to the people for ratification. The *Social Contract* was often cited: "Any law that the people in person have not ratified is null and void; it is not a law." The principle of popular ratification was incorporated into the Constitution of 1793. Now, Rousseau actually points out that, while ratification of laws by the people may at first seem to conflict with the principle of popular autonomy, laws should not emanate from the citizens themselves but should be proposed exclusively by the government. In other words, the kind of democracy proposed by Rousseau was based on referendum. The revolutionaries of 1793 simply transferred to the legislature a power that Rousseau granted to the "government," that is, the executive; but the principle remained the same. It is therefore true that Rousseauism contributed one concrete and specific institution to the Revolution, namely, ratification of the laws by the people. The Constitution of 1793 was suspended shortly after it was adopted, however, so that this authentic legacy of Rousseau was never put into practice.

To revolutionary activists popular sovereignty meant that the people had the right to supervise the work of their representatives and to recall them at any time. The sans-culottes accordingly attached great importance to permanent standing committees in each section. When these were abolished in September 1793, the sans-culottes formed "sectional societies" prepared to meet as necessary to discuss the decisions of the Assembly. Leaders of the movement, justifying their insistence on permanent oversight of the legislature by reference to Rousseau, cited the slogan that "the will cannot be represented." In the view of the sans-culottes, representatives were the people's "proxies." Yet no proof exists that the forms and procedures of popular oversight derived from Rousseau. All that Rousseau said in *Considerations of the Government of Poland* was that the nation's elected representatives should be bound by the mandate of the voters. Not only did the sans-culottes not accept the idea of a strict mandate; they actually issued demands that stemmed from a very different idea of representative government. The reason that oversight had to be *constant* and recall *discretionary* was that the representatives were not thought of as conveying a precise, already formulated general will. According to the sans-culotte view, the popular will did not exist prior to the election of representatives. The people therefore had to make sure that every decision taken by their representatives conformed to their will. The procedures proposed were in a sense the counterpart of the discretionary powers implicitly accorded to the representatives. Hence it is incorrect to state, as Albert Soboul does, that "without formally accepting the theory of the strict mandate" the sans-culottes proposed procedures that amounted to the same thing. In fact, the need for constant vigilance and pressure on the legislators was a logical consequence of a concept of representation quite different from Rousseau's.

The views of the Jacobin leaders were closer to those of Rousseau. Robespierre cited Rousseau several times in his speeches. Like the sans-culottes, he, too, rejected the theory of the strict mandate, but he used Rousseau to demonstrate to the people's representatives that their will must not differ from that of the people. In reality, however, Robespierre's views were dictated by political opportunism. In the fall of 1789 he, like Sieyès, opposed the notion of invoking the will of the people over the heads of its representatives. At that time such a procedure would have strengthened the king's hand. In August 1791, during the Assembly's debates on the revision of the constitution, Robespierre invoked Rousseau and the *Social Contract* in opposition to Thouret, who argued that the people had no means to exercise its power except by delegation. At that point the tactical necessity was to combat the Feuillants. In the spring of 1793, at the height of the struggle between the Girondins and the Montagnards, Robespierre again referred to Rousseau's theory of representation. His aim then was to use popular government to crush the Girondin opposition. A few weeks later, however, after the defeat of the Girondins, Robespierre was once more championing representative government: "The people *en masse* cannot govern itself. . . . All that the people could demand was that the Convention march in step with the Revolution. It is now doing so." In February 1794, having put down the popular movement, Robespierre declared: "Democracy is not a state in which the people, meeting in continuous assembly, settles all public business on its own." In other words, Robespierre invoked Rousseauist mistrust of representative government whenever the Assembly seemed to him out of step with the Revolution. When it was in step, and when the right people were in power, his Rousseauism vanished and his emphasis on the need for representative government returned.

Clearly it was not from Rousseau that the Jacobin and sans-culotte leaders took the idea of a state-controlled economy or the design of their system of taxation and requisition. Rousseau had little to say about problems of commerce and trade, since his ideal was to limit both to the maximum possible extent. He envisioned a society composed of small, independent producers, living as far as possible on what they produced themselves. Property should be distributed as equally as possible, he said; but once constituted on that basis, respect for property rights was essential. In the *Discourse on Political Economy* he wrote: "The right of property is certainly the most sacred of all the rights of the citizen, and more important in some respects than liberty itself." To be sure, the *Discourse on Inequality* argues that the invention of property was the source of society's woes, yet in none of his prescriptive works does Rousseau suggest abolishing the rights of property or returning to the state of nature. Instead he advocates equalizing the distribution of property by controlling commerce in such a way that property, though present, does not produce its perverse effects.

In the Assembly debates over the system of taxation and requisition Rousseau's name was not mentioned, and no reference was made to his ideas. The chief argument advanced by the Jacobin leaders was that of the "right to existence." In December 1792 Robespierre declared: "The primary law of any society is that which guarantees all its members the means to exist. All other laws are subordinate to this primary one. Property was instituted and is protected only in order to establish it. It is above all in order to live that people possess properties" (Robespierre, *Oeuvres,* IX, p. 112). The notion of a right to existence was very popular among the sans-culottes. Yet it is never mentioned in any of Rousseau's works. It may be objected that it is implicit in all his writings, but his suggestion for ensuring everyone the means of subsistence is to make them all property owners. He never advocated a state-controlled economy in a country where the least fortunate citizens owned nothing.

The "right to existence" argument was also used to justify poor relief policies adopted in Year II. In April 1793 Robespierre proposed including in the declaration of rights attached to the constitution the principle that society has an obligation to "provide for the subsistence of all its members, either by procuring them work or by furnishing the means of existence to those who are not in condition to work." The declaration of rights of 1793 recognized that "public assistance is a sacred debt." Again, however, it cannot be said that the principle of *state* assistance to the poor came from Rousseau. Rousseau's aim was to make individuals independent by endowing them with property. This initiative would not suffice, however, for there would always be disabled people. Yet in *Considerations of the Government of Poland* Rousseau proposed that poor relief be provided through voluntary contributions by the wealthiest citizens, a proposal based on charity rather than on an obligation of the state. A Rousseauist policy would have been one aimed at equalizing the distribution of wealth. Such a distributive ideal did figure in the ideology of the sans-culottes, who were quick to cite the words of the *Social Contract* ("The social state is advantageous to men only so long as all are worth something and no one has too much of anything") and more receptive to Rousseau's influence than were the Jacobins. The latter vehemently rejected every proposed agrarian law, which they denounced as "a useless phantom invented by rogues to frighten imbeciles," and dismissed the idea of an imposed ceiling on wealth. Admittedly, some of their decisions reveal an intention, which can be seen as a legacy of Rousseauism, to equalize the distribution of wealth: the sale of national properties in small lots, for example, or the law making division of estates compulsory, or the decrees of Ventôse. Yet these things did not constitute the core of Jacobin economic and social policy.

What about those writers who hold that, in broad, general terms, the "dictatorship of public safety" and the "revolutionary government" were consequences of Rousseau's political theory, and especially of his conception of the social contract in which individuals alienate all their rights? They neglect one crucial fact: when the Jacobin leaders attempted to justify dictatorial rule to the Assembly, they *never* invoked the name of Rousseau or his concept of the social contract. In December 1793, in fact, Robespierre stated: "The theory of revolutionary government is as new as the revolution that produced it. Do not look for it in the books of political writers who did not foresee this revolution." Of course the "revolutionary government" and the subordination of individual rights to the general will *could* have been justified with the aid of the *Social Contract*. The fact remains that they were not. Why would Robespierre and Saint-Just have passed up the opportunity to cite Rousseau, whom they did cite on other occasions, if they believed that his authority could have been invoked on this issue?

Their silence can be understood by examining the content of their speeches on revolutionary government. They justified that government not by reference to the complex and extravagant theory of total alienation but in a far simpler way: by painting a picture, with all its train of images and passions, of the enemies with whom France was at war. Of course the Terror was not an "objective" consequence of the war and its circumstances; here, the crucial factor was the representation of reality, the mental image. In order to understand what made the dictatorship of public safety possible and acceptable in the eyes of its supporters, we must consider not the *Social Contract* but the complex of images and ideas swirling about the concepts of "war" and "the enemy."

It can be shown that the political system of the Terror was based on two things: treatment of political adversaries as enemies and a fluid definition of the word *enemy*. The government determined who was a citizen entitled to the protection of the law and who was an enemy "from whom nothing was to be given or gotten but lead." By turns the enemy was identified as the royalists, the monopolists, the enragés, the Hébertists, the moderates, and ultimately the "wicked." The Terror was in essence nothing but a system of classification whose categories were completely fluid and manipulable at will by those in power. Sieyès, though in a sense a "liberal," opened Pandora's box by branding his domestic political adversaries "the enemy." In this system Rousseau played no part. Robespierre is to be believed when he says that the revolutionary government did not originate in the books of the philosophers.

Does it follow that Rousseauism was without influence on the French Revolution? Hardly, for the Revolution was far more than a matter of anti-aristocratic passions and redefinition of the boundary between the people and its enemies. Important aspects of the revolutionary mentality bear Rousseau's stamp. His work may not have inspired any definite political methods or procedures, but it did help to mold a state of mind. Rousseau was not the Revolution's "lawgiver," but he did have dominion over a broad segment of public opinion.

He was a widely recognized authority, not so much for his political theory in the narrow sense as for his moral works. *La nouvelle Héloïse* redeemed the domestic and conjugal virtues from the world's "corruption." At Clarens happiness was born of virtue. In *Emile* he detailed a plan of "natural education" that paid heed to normal patterns of child development. Among the book's recommendations two struck a particularly responsive chord: that mothers should breast-feed their own children and that infants should not be swaddled. In 1774 Condorcet wrote: "If the bodies of children are no longer oppressed by whalebone, if their minds are no longer overburdened with moral precepts, if their first years of life are now at least free of slavery and torture, the credit belongs to Rousseau." The image of Rousseau improving upon custom, "reminding mothers of their duty" (breast-feeding), and freeing children from "barbaric" swaddling outlived the Revolution by many years, and it can be found in most of the eulogies he received while it was still in progress.

When the revolutionaries alluded to Rousseau's work of moral regeneration, however, they saw it as the precursor of the public regeneration accomplished by the Revolution. *Emile* changed the way that people reared their children, but the change was perceived as the first manifestation of the revolutionary *idea:* namely, that it is possible to reject custom, break with convention, and construct a new order more truly in harmony with nature. *Emile* lent credibility to the idea of radical change. Rousseau wrote: "Propose nothing but what is feasible, people are constantly telling me. It is as if they were saying, propose only what we are already doing, or at any rate some good that is compatible with existing evils. . . . Fathers and mothers, what is feasible is whatever you want to do." No doubt the idea that it is better to build anew rather than correct what already exists is a French tradition. But Rousseau, and *Emile* in particular, helped to establish the validity of that tradition in the moral sphere and hence, more generally, in the sphere of practice. Applied to politics, this idea left its stamp on the whole of the Revolution and was surely part of Rousseau's legacy.

If, moreover, representative government was not exactly what Rousseau had in mind, many supporters of that form of government acknowledged his authority and hailed him as the man who had laid down the principles on which the system of representation was based. It is not enough to say that they misread Rousseau. We must try to understand what made their misreading possible. First of all, they saw the system of representation as a consequence of the equality of individual wills. Since no one had the right to impose his will upon anyone else, no one could govern unless authorized to do so by his peers. An argument similar to this can be found in many writings and speeches of the time. To be sure, representative government did introduce a distinction between governors and governed, but it was not a distinction inscribed in nature. Those who governed did so not by virtue of their nature or their innate qualities (such as wisdom) but only with the consent of others who, substantially the same as themselves, were their equals. In the final analysis, then, representation was based on a presumed substantial (or natural) equality and identity between governors and governed, even if it assigned different roles and positions to each. The *Social Contract* describes a structure in which the governed *are* the governors; the two terms are the same. Nevertheless, it is clear why, from the Constituent Assembly to the Thermidorian Convention, the Revolution proclaimed itself to be Rousseau's heir: the principle that no one may govern unless authorized to do so by the people was one that all factions could support.

Much the same thing can be said about the indivisibility of sovereignty. Rousseau said: "Either the will is general or it is not. Either it is the will of the body of the people or that of only a part." It has been argued, not incorrectly, that the influence of this principle was one reason for the refusal of assembly after assembly to accept a balance of powers or system of checks and balances in any form. But what exactly was Rousseau's contribution? He was not the inventor of the idea that sovereign power is indivisible. The whole tradition of the absolute monarchy in France, in both theory and practice, was dominated by the principle that there is a single supreme power, that of the king, to which all other powers are subordinate. It was the absolute monarchy that imposed on France the idea—and not only the idea but also the reality—that sovereign power resides in *one* place and one place only. Hence it was not the idea of indivisible sovereignty that Rousseau bequeathed to the Revolution. Rather, it was the idea that the people is *one*, that it is possessed, like an individual, of a *single* will. This idea is by no means self-evident. Other thinkers have seen the people as an unstructured multitude, divided by differences of opinion and interest. By insisting more than any other theorist on the idea that the people is one (or can be made one), and by defining it as a subject with a will of its own, Rousseau beyond any doubt laid the intellectual groundwork for the Revolution and prepared people to accept its single most characteristic act: that of installing those who expressed the will of the people in the place once occupied by the king.

Although anti-aristocratic passions were not a notable feature of Rousseau's political theory, his work popularized egalitarian principles. His influence on public opinion derived in large part from his ability to flesh out those principles with concrete images. He not only theorized about equality but also dramatized it. In *Emile* he has his pupil take up carpentry, and revolutionary orators frequently evoked the image of Emile as carpenter. Beyond the work, Rousseau's life and person seemed the very incarnation of the egalitarian spirit. He was the man of the people who by genius alone had raised himself to the level of the great. Unlike Voltaire, who amassed a considerable fortune, Jean-Jacques led a simple life; he refused the pensions that would have cost him his freedom, and he was not afraid to eke out a living by copying music. He never denied his modest beginnings, and in his final years at Ermenonville he enjoyed himself in the company of peasants. Taken together, these traits made Rousseau a symbol of the humble and virtuous common man. The biographical facts were transformed by legend and took on political value. When it was proposed that eligibility for office be restricted to citizens paying taxes equivalent to one silver *marc*, Robespierre and a number of other orators invoked Rousseau's name in opposition: such a condition, they pointed out, would have excluded Jean-Jacques.

Rousseau's grip on the imaginations of the Jacobin leaders, especially that of Robespierre, derived from this same nebulous collection of images and ideas, in which politics mingled with morality and Jean-Jacques's life co-existed with his theory. In Robespierre's writings and speeches Rousseau's name is usually associated with the idea that the people is good and worthy of love. In his *Defender of the Constitution* he wrote: "I would say that it was then that I understood the great moral and political truth heralded by Jean-Jacques, that men truly love only those who love them, that only the people is good, just, and magnanimous, and that corruption and tyranny are the exclusive province of those who disdain the common man." In 1792 Robespierre had this to say to the Jacobins: "No one has given us a more accurate idea of the people than Rousseau, because no one has loved it more." Here, imagery and emotion are more important than concepts. No definite policy or institutions can be derived, however, from the idea that the people is good and worthy of love.

Imagery was also important in establishing the ideal of the austere and virtuous republic. Jacobin leaders were fascinated by images of Sparta and republican Rome, and Rousseau's work played a part in making those images attractive. But what part? The idea that the republic required virtue as well as the sacrifice of particular interests to the general interest was a commonplace of eighteenth-century political thought. Other authors, as well known to the revolutionaries as Rousseau, developed the same idea, most notably Mably but also Montesquieu. Robespierre himself associated the idea of virtue with Montesquieu. Rousseau's contribution was to use the term *virtue* in such a way as to establish a link between the classical notion of republican virtue and that of goodness. In Sparta and Rome virtue meant austere firmness of will, even hard-hearted resolve in pursuit of the public good. For Rousseau virtue also meant goodness, sensitivity, and civilized private manners. In his work, virtue wore the features of Mucius Scaevola but also of Julie. Rousseau has nothing explicit to say about the relations between these two aspects of virtue, but it is clear that their interaction was supposed to lend to Spartan virtue the charm of subjective feeling and sentiment. This charm no doubt played a crucial role in winning late-eighteenth-century adherents to the republican ideal. The combination of civilized private manners with firmness in defense of "the public safety" characterized the leaders of both the Jacobins and the sans-culottes in 1793 and 1794. For Saint-Just the "revolutionary man" embodied two traits: "He is uncompromising with the wicked, yet he is sensitive. So jealous is he of the glory of the fatherland that he does nothing precipitately. He knows that in order for the Revolution to become strong, he must be as good as others in the past were wicked. . . . Marat was gentle at home; he struck fear only into the hearts of traitors. . . . J.-J. Rousseau was revolutionary but surely not insolent." The confusion of private morality with public virtue was one aspect of the revolutionary mentality that undoubtedly owed a great deal to Rousseau.

The revolutionaries may not have followed the detailed prescriptions of the *Social Contract,* but they did draw images and general propositions about the nature of man, society, and history from it. In any case, it is wrong to conceive of the relation between thought and action as simply a matter of putting a preconceived plan into action. Lakanal was well aware of this. In a report he wrote for the legislators who were to vote on the transfer of Rousseau's ashes to the Pantheon, he observed that it was not the *Social Contract* that caused the Revolution "but in a sense the Revolution that explained the *Social Contract* to us." Rousseau's work provided the historical actors with an instrument that enabled them to name the new realities with which history confronted them and then to ponder the things they had named. Rousseau never envisioned a convocation of the Estates General, but his notion of the general will, however vague it may have been in the deputies' minds, nevertheless enabled men thrust into an unprecedented situation to understand the source from which their legitimacy derived. And those who in 1792 and 1793 repeated the slogan "the will cannot be represented" took from Rousseau a phrase with which they were able to conceptualize and justify a state of affairs that already existed, namely, the vulnerability of the Assembly to popular pressures. Once a slogan or principle was accepted, it helped determine the way in which people represented the facts, and thus influenced the decisions they reached. Words helped to define what was thinkable and possible, though they did not point the way to definite solutions.

Thus Rousseau's influence on the revolutionary mentality was exerted through a few general ideas and principles: regeneration, autonomy and unity of the people, equality, goodness, and virtue. Though more than just empty words, these ideas are compatible with more than one political position. Their very attractiveness is due in part to their vagueness. Most crucially, Rousseau embodied these ideas in immediate, accessible images. It is permissible to say, therefore, that the revolutionaries took the *inspiration* for some of their policies from Rousseau but not the technical and constitutional details of their program. What makes Rousseau's case so strange is that his writings are nevertheless full of such details. That is why so many commentators have been mistaken about the nature of his influence. Those who made the American Revolution and wrote the United States Constitution took from Montesquieu the idea of a separation of powers and a system of checks and balances. In a very different context, socialist revolutionaries put Marx's ideas to work: collective ownership of the means of production and the dictatorship of the proletariat. But Rousseau's relation to the French Revolution cannot be conceptualized in these terms. Nor can those two characteristic features of the Revolution—the redefinition of the nation to exclude the privileged and the constant redrawing of the boundary between the people and its enemies—be ascribed to Rousseau's influence.

Bernard Manin

IDEAS

FURTHER READING

WORKS BY ROUSSEAU

Oeuvres complètes, 4 vols. Paris, 1959–1969.

RELATED WORKS

Antraigues, Emmanuel-Louis-Henri de Launay, comte d'. *Mémoire sur les Etats Généraux, leurs droits et la manière de les convoquer.* 1788.

—— *Mémoire sur les mandats impératifs.* Versailles, n. d.

—— *Mémoire sur la constitution des états de la province du Languedoc.* Vivarais, n.d.

Barny, Roger. "J.-J. Rousseau dans la Révolution française, 1787–1791." Doctoral dissertation, University of Paris X, Nanterre, 1976.

Condorcet, Marie-Jean-Antoine-Nicolas de Caritat, marquis de. *Lettres d'un théologien à l'auteur du dictionnaire des trois siècles* (1774), in vol. 5 of Condorcet, *Oeuvres,* 12 vols., ed. François Arago and Arthur Condorcet-O'Connor. Paris, 1847–1849.

Lakanal, Joseph. *Rapport sur J.-J. Rousseau fait au nom du Comité d'Instruction Publique* (29 Fructidor, Year II, September 15, 1794). Paris, 1794.

MacDonald, Joan. *Rousseau and the French Revolution, 1762–1791.* London, 1965.

Mercier, Louis-Sébastien. *De Jean-Jacques Rousseau considéré comme un des premiers auteurs de la Révolution.* 2 vols. Paris, 1791.

Pétition à l'Assemblée Nationale concernant demande de la translation des cendres de J.-J. Rousseau au Panthéon français (August 27, 1791). Paris, 1791.

Robespierre, Maximilien. *Le défenseur de la Constitution,* no. 1, in Robespierre, *Oeuvres,* vol. 4. Paris, 1960–1967.

—— Speeches in *Oeuvres.* The volume numbers are indicated in parentheses: September 1789 against the royal veto (6); April 1791 on the silver *marc* (not delivered) (7); August 10, 1791 (7); January 2, 1792 (8); December 2, 1792 (9); February 25, 1793 (9); April 24, 1793 (9); May 10, 1793 (9); June 14, 1793 (9); December 25, 1793 (10); 17 Pluviôse, Year II (February 5, 1794) (10); 18 Floréal, Year II (May 7, 1794) (10).

Roussel, Jean. *J.-J. Rousseau en France après la Révolution, 1795–1830.* Paris, 1972.

Saint-Just, Louis-Antoine de. *Esprit de la Révolution et la Constitution de la France* (1791), in Saint-Just, *Oeuvres.* Paris, 1984.

—— Reports, published in *Oeuvres:* October 10, 1793; 8 Ventôse, Year II (February 26, 1794); 11 Germinal, Year II (March 31, 1794); 26 Germinal, Year II (April 15, 1794).

Sieyès, Emmanuel. Quotations on Rousseau in Charles-Augustin Sainte-Beuve, "Etude sur Sieyès," in *Causeries du lundi,* vol. 5. Third edition. Paris, 1851.

—— *Qu'est-ce que le Tiers Etat?* (1789), with "Essai sur les privilèges" (1788). Paris, 1888.

Soboul, Albert. *Les sans-culottes parisiens en l'an II: Histoire politique et sociale des sections de Paris, 2 juin 1793–9 thermidor an II.* La Roche-sur-Yon, 1958. Reprinted Paris, 1958, and 1962 with the subtitle *Mouvement populaire et gouvernement révolutionnaire.*

—— "Classes populaires et rousseauisme sous la Révolution," *Annales historiques de la Révolution française,* 1962.

—— "J.-J. Rousseau et le jacobinisme," in *Etudes sur le Contrat Social de J.-J. Rousseau.* Publications de l'Université de Dijon, no. 30. Paris, 1964.

Staël, Germaine de. *Lettres sur les ouvrages et le caractère de J.-J. Rousseau.* Paris, 1789.

Trénard, Louis. "La diffusion du *Contrat Social,*" in *Etudes sur le Contrat Social de J.-J. Rousseau* (see Soboul 1964).

R<small>ELATED</small> TOPICS

Democracy	Quinet	Revolutionary Government	Sieyès
Equality	Regeneration	Robespierre	Sovereignty
Jacobinism	Republic	Sans-culottes	Suffrage
Montesquieu			

SOVEREIGNTY

T hat the principle of national sovereignty lay at the very heart of the French Revolution need hardly be insisted upon. That this principle was created—and implemented—by transferring absolute sovereignty from the king to the nation is a truism worth repeating. And worth exploring.

Much that is crucial to revolutionary thought and action is explained by the conceptual and political difficulties inherent in claiming for the nation an idea of sovereignty progressively elaborated, on behalf of the absolute monarchy, in the two centuries since the disorders of the Wars of Religion prompted its first modern formulation by Bodin.

*
**

Like the doctrines of the monarchomachs he opposed, Bodin's theory of sovereignty drew on the conceptual possibilities inherent in an ambiguous constitutional tradition. For centuries, French constitutional theorists had insisted that the monarch was endowed with *plenitudo potestatis* as emperor in his own realm; for centuries, they had also insisted that his absolute power was limited by divine and natural law, by customary law and legal procedures, as by the constitution of the realm. The issue raised so acutely by the Wars of Religion was not whether royal power was limited, but whether a monarch could be held accountable, in respect of such limits, to any other human power. Fear of the anarchy Bodin saw as a necessary consequence of the monarchomachs' doctrine of legitimate resistance moved him to insist that the preservation of social order required the exercise of an ultimately supreme sovereign will. To be supreme, he argued, this will must necessarily be unitary. And to be unitary, it must necessarily be perpetual, indivisible (hence inalienable), and absolute: which is to say that it must be free of any conditions that would make it subject to the judgment or command of others. Sovereignty must be above the law in two senses: first, in the sense that the sovereign cannot be brought to judgment before it; and second, in the sense that prior laws cannot bind the sovereign in the free exercise of legislative will—the supreme attribute of sovereign power, which Bodin found enshrined as a principle in the traditional legal formula of the kings of France, *car tel est notre plaisir.*

"The absolute and perpetual power of a republic," sovereignty as Bodin saw it could theoretically be exercised by a prince, a ruling class, or the people as a whole. But the purpose of *Les six livres de la république* was to show that it could be effectively established and maintained only in a true monarchy. A collective sovereign power—whether comprising the many or the few—could never be assured of the unity of will, purpose, and action that was the fundamental characteristic and principal justification of sovereign authority. Unity of will could be consistently achieved only through the unity of the person found in a "prince elevated above all his subjects, whose majesty henceforth suffers no division."

While denying the right of subjects to take action to enforce limits upon the exercise of sovereignty, however, Bodin was far from repudiating the existence of any such limits. As lieutenants of God on earth, princes are subject to divine law. As holders of a constitutionally established power, they are subject to the fundamental laws governing the succession of the throne and the inalienability of the royal domain. And in the rightful exercise of their sovereignty, they are also subject to natural law, to the principles that command respect above all for the liberty and property of subjects in a particularistic social order.

That it was the essential nature of society to be composed of a multiplicity of orders and estates, communities and corporate bodies, provinces and *pays,* was a fundamental assumption of Bodin's theory, as of the theorists of monarchical sovereignty more generally. Sovereignty, the defining characteristic of a commonwealth, was that absolute and perpetual power, that unitary will, without which order and unity could not be maintained among a multiplicity of orders and estates in a particularistic, corporate society.

The idea of sovereignty took on its original force and meaning in France precisely in relation to this conception of society as an aggregate of orders and estates, communities and corporations, made one only through common subjection to a unitary sovereign power. Real legislative power, the right to make or arbitrarily modify the laws, was indeed the mark of sovereignty, but its exercise was conceivable only within the limits of a relatively constricted notion of the governmental function, whose purpose was to maintain the legitimate organization of men and things within a constituted social order. In this sense, the state was a passive entity—a social reality for preserving and maintaining proper order—rather than the active expression of a supreme legislative will. The government's function was essentially judicial: to ensure that each corporation, order, and estate received its due in light of the rights, responsibilities, and privileges defined by the traditional hierarchy.

If they shifted the emphasis within the French constitutional tradition, then, the early theorists of absolute monarchy did not abstract the doctrine of sovereignty from the religious, philosophical, and juridical assumptions inherent in this tradition. Absolute monarchy remained embedded within a metaphysical, constitutional, and juridical order, which it functioned to uphold; sovereignty remained inherently limited by the assumptions of that order, even as it was argued that the sovereign could not be called to human account in respect of such limits. Yet with the reign of Louis XIV, sovereign power began to abstract itself in a variety of ways from the juridical order that it theoretically existed to preserve. Without in any way repudiating that order, it moved to separate itself from it, to act upon it rather than merely acting within it. In modern terms, the state (as the active agency of power) began to differentiate itself from society.

Bossuet summed up this entire conception well in his *Politique tirée des propres paroles de l'Ecriture sainte* (*Policy Derived from the Words of the Holy Scripture*). That work offers a remarkable contrast to Bodin's in the extent to which it turned away from the French constitutional tradition. In Bossuet's defense of the absolute monarchy, biblical history replaced the history of the French monarchy as the privileged ground for political argument; scriptural authority replaced constitutional precedent; abstract reason replaced juridical titles. Thus disengaged from the constitutional tradition in which they had been formed, claims for monarchical sovereignty took on more expansive meanings. On the one hand, Bossuet heightened claims to the sacredness of royal power, hence its distance above the constituted social world. Of kings in the exercise of their sovereign power, it was no longer enough to say that they are the lieutenants of God: "They are gods and in some fashion partake of divine independence." On the other hand, Bossuet extended the implications of the conception of sovereignty as expressing and upholding the principle of unity in a particularistic society of orders and estates by emphasizing that social order and political unity existed only through the person, and emanated only from the will, of the prince. "A multitude of men, are made one person, when they are by one man, or one person, represented," Hobbes had argued in *The Leviathan*. "For it is the unity of the representer not the unity of the represented, that maketh the person one. And it is the representer that beareth the person, and but one person; and unity cannot otherwise be understood in multitude." For Bossuet, as for Hobbes, a people becomes one only in the act of subjection to the sovereign. The king is sovereign because the state—understood as both the abstract production and concrete expression of power—exists only in and through his individual person; his alone is a truly public person; his alone a truly public will. Such was the meaning of Bossuet's claim that "the whole state is in him, the will of all the people is encompassed in his."

This inflection within the political theory of absolutism was paralleled by changes in ceremonial representations of the monarchy. Ceremonials such as the royal entries presented the monarch as part of a juridical order constituted by a multiplicity of particularistic entities; such ceremonials emphasized the mutual definitions of crown and kingdom, the constitutional limits upon royal power. In abandoning these ceremonials for court rituals, Louis XIV proclaimed the existence of a new kind of political space emanating more directly from the person of the king. At the court, order was seen to flow immediately from the personal majesty of the monarch. From a king who represented and maintained the juridical principles of the social order (of which he remained part), emphasis shifted to a king from whom social order derived as from its very source. The king no longer entered his towns in a manner that celebrated the mutual obligations of the monarch and his subjects; instead, in celebration of the king's military successes, orders went out from the court for the singing of ceremonial Te Deums throughout the realm.

But military successes were only made possible, in their turn, by the expansion of the crown's ability to mobilize social resources in the service of the state. With the institutionalization of intendants in the provinces, as of ministers and their bureaux at Versailles; with the transformation of what had hitherto been extraordinary fiscal demands into recurring obligations of organized social life; with the introduction of new mechanisms of taxation undermining local autonomy and personal privilege; and with the substitution of centralized command for local practices of participation and consent, government in the judicial mode began to give way to government in the administrative mode. At the heart of the development of this new administrative system there lay the essential connection between warfare and social welfare, between taxation and taxability. As the yield from taxation depended upon the ability of the population to pay, so the organization of warfare depended upon the ability of the administration to produce prosperity. To mobilize social resources, government was also obliged to maximize them.

Thus it became the function of the intendants and their agents not simply to extract resources from their localities but to expand them by improving agricultural productivity, stimulating commerce and industry, initiating the construction of roads and canals, and so on: in other words, to take an active responsibility for maximizing prosperity and social welfare. By a typical displacement of goals, this relationship between ends and means, established in the seventeenth century, was reversed in the course of the eighteenth. Welfare ceased to be a means to warfare and became an end in itself. The result was a new administrative ethos that began to see government as the active and energetic use of sovereign authority to maximize social welfare, and deploy social resources, in the interests of all. Within this context, the definition of sovereignty as active legislative power, freed from the limits inherent in the traditional judicial mode of government, took on new meaning and justification. In the name of a eudemonistic conception of the general good, progressively elaborated by the Enlightenment, the sovereign could reconstitute traditional society as necessary, even transforming a realm structured by principles of hierarchy, privilege, and particularism into an integrated community of useful citizens. Sovereign power—the power of the state in the active modern sense—no longer simply upheld the social order from within; it acted upon society from without.

In the course of the eighteenth century, these developments produced profound contradictions within the political culture of the Ancien Régime. They expressed themselves in conflicts over taxation and local privileges, over issues of economic and social policy such as the control (or liberty) of the grain trade. They underlay the recurring constitutional struggles between the newer administrative elite of ministers and intendants and the older judicial elite of officers, most notably in the parlements and other sovereign courts. And they prompted the emergence of a language of opposition to absolute monarchy that conflated absolutism with arbitrariness, royal administration with "ministerial despotism."

How then was sovereign power to be reintegrated into the social order? Solutions to this problem—which dominated the political life of the Ancien Régime in its last decades—were pressed in several political languages. The first and most widespread, recovering the conceptual resources of the French constitutional tradition gradually effaced since the sixteenth century, reasserted the claims of "the nation" as a historical body endowed with a political identity and collective rights. From the 1750s onward, absolute monarchy was brought once again before the bar of historical, juridical, and constitutional argument. The historical arsenal of "the rights of the nation" was first reopened by Le Paige and other parlementary theorists from the "monuments" of French constitutional history the magistrates had continued to guard in their archives. Gradually reinforced (via the Jansenists) by conciliar arguments situating the ultimate source and exercise of sovereignty in the community as a whole, and by elements of contract theory drawn from the school of natural law, it offered the principal ideological weapons for the increasingly radical parlementary remonstrances of the 1750s and 1760s, for the anti-Maupeou pamphlets of the early 1770s, and for much of the antiministerial propaganda of the prerevolutionary period.

From a reassertion of fundamental laws as limiting the exercise of royal sovereignty, this discourse of the rights of the nation shifted to the defense of a historical constitution to which both king and nation were party, a constitution therefore subject to change only with the consent of the nation. From an insistence on the judicial forms and implications of parlementary registration, it moved to a more political justification of the magistrates' role as symbolizing the consent of the nation in matters of legislation, and finally it demanded the Estates General as the only and ultimate institutional expression of the national will. Thus sovereignty was seen as deriving ultimately from the body of the nation; its exercise was conferred by mutual contract between the king and the nation upon a monarch who exercised it subject to the limitations of that contract, including the principle of consent to legislation; it could be reclaimed by the nation in the event of noncompliance with the terms of the contract. Parlementary constitutionalism therefore offered an essentially negative, defensive conception of the sovereignty of the nation, that sovereignty understood as the ultimate limiting condition upon the exercise of royal power. But in recovering and revivifying the resources of an older constitutional tradition, parlementary constitutionalism was destined—as the authors of Louis XV's speech at the *séance de la flagellation* sensed as early as 1766—to shift the locus of political identity (and hence of sovereignty) from king to nation in profound ways. The reaffirmation of the nation as a historical and political actor (or, in arguments following the mode of Mably, of the necessity for it to remedy its historical failure as a political actor) was already clearly evident in the pamphlet literature preceding the meeting of the Estates General.

Rousseau, of course, offered a language very different from this constitutionalist discourse. Setting aside historical facts and juridical titles, he dissolved the corporate society of orders and estates that was the historical nation into a multiplicity of individuals, to be reconstituted analytically as a political community of citizens equal before the law. For Rousseau, as for Hobbes, this transformation of multiplicity into unity could be achieved only by the absolute and irrevocable submission of every individual to a single, unitary person. But Rousseau—finding no "bearable middle ground between the most austere democracy and the most perfect Hobbesianism"—located that person not in the natural person of a monarch but in the collective person of the body of citizens as a whole. Hence the form of the social contract, in which each individual gives himself to all, simultaneously acting as a member of the whole to receive each of the others.

The *Social Contract* thus transferred the sovereignty elaborated by theorists of absolute monarchy—with all its attributes—from the natural person of the king to the abstract, collective person of the people. In Rousseau's doctrine, as in that of monarchical theorists, sovereignty is indivisible and inalienable: it can be neither delegated nor represented without destroying the unity of person in which it inheres. Hence his theoretical rejection of representation, which was no less emphatic than his repudiation of absolute monarchy. Once conferred upon a monarch, or entrusted to representatives, Rousseau insisted, sovereign power is immediately particularized; it no longer exists as a general but as a particular will. We must also emphasize that in Rousseau's doctrine, as in that of monarchical theorists, while sovereign authority is absolute in the sense that it cannot be bound by other wills or prior laws, it is also limited. But it is limited not by divine law and natural law but by the logic of generality inherent in the very nature of the social contract, "proceeding from all in order to be applied to all."

In effect, then, Rousseau reintegrated sovereign power and social order by claiming sovereignty for the body of the people, understood as an abstract, collective person. Creation of the general will was the act constituting true social order; maintenance of a truly general will was the condition of continuing social existence; destruction of that will implied simultaneous dissolution of the social order. In Rousseau's political discourse, sovereignty and society were once again made consubstantial.

From this perspective, it is illuminating to compare Rousseau's arguments with those deriving from yet another discourse in which sovereign power and social order could be reintegrated: that offered by the physiocratic movement. As administrative theorists, the physiocrats and their disciples approached the growing disjunction between sovereign power and social order by seeking to transform the exercise of sovereignty into the rule of nature (hence *physiocratie*). For a juridically (now read as "artificially") constituted society of orders and estates, they sought to substitute a natural order of society based on those principles of propertied individualism that are the expression of men's true relations one to another and to the natural world. From a state as political power acting upon corporate society, they sought to arrive at a state as administrative agency deriving its authority from modern civil society, constituted as a society of property-owning individuals whose interests it would articulate and whose needs it would serve. The introduction of representation through the creation of provincial assemblies became the key to the transformation of government anticipated by such figures as Turgot, Dupont de Nemours, Condorcet, Le Trosne and, eventually, Calonne. How much easier it would be to "set a living body in motion" by eliciting the representation of social interests in provincial assemblies. Neither the corporate nation of parlementary constitutionalism, with its historically and juridically constituted rights, nor Rousseau's sovereign people constituted as an abstract, collective person, their new nation was to be a dynamic society of property holders actively pursuing individual welfare under the salutary guidance of a rational and enlightened administration, henceforth operating in perfect harmony with social needs. Ultimately, this implied a transmutation of sovereign will into the rational expression of social needs. Physiocratic theory aimed to dissolve power into society under the sign of social interest.

In the simplest terms, national sovereignty was created when the French Revolution transferred sovereign power from the crown to the nation. But which sovereignty, and which nation? The residual national sovereignty of parlementary theory could be understood essentially as the ultimate source of and limit on monarchical authority; the nation that held it was a historical actor armed with corporate rights and fundamental laws (or, according to Mably, an actor unable to impose any political order upon the continuing chaos of its own collective existence). The direct popular sovereignty of Rousseauian theory could be understood as the immediate sustaining will of any social order; the nation whose will was expressed was an abstract collective people, instituted and sustained in its existence through the operation of that will. The transmuted sovereignty of physiocratic theory could be understood as the rational expression of social interests; here, the nation took on the visage of modern civil society, an aggregate of individual social interests within the natural social order.

In fact, each of these competing discourses is to be discovered in the great pamphlet debate initiated by the government's call, on July 5, 1788, for public discussion of the forms to be followed in the convocation of the Estates General. Elements deriving from each found their way into the most powerful and influential formulation of the doctrine of national sovereignty to emerge from that debate, *Qu'est-ce que le Tiers Etat?* With this pamphlet, Sieyès took the historical nation, stripped it of the constitutionalist trappings of its residual sovereignty, and endowed it with the active, immediate sovereignty of the people in Rousseauian theory. In effect, he transformed the nation into pure political being. Bossuet had offered a metaphysical vision of kings as an awesome assembly of gods acting in an ultimate spiritual space before the immediate eye of the Almighty. Sieyès substituted a purely secular—but no less metaphysical—vision of nations as the primordial denizens of an ultimate natural order, untrammeled in the majestic exercise of their sovereign will. "One must think of the nations of the earth as individuals outside the social bond, or, as one says, in the state of nature. . . . Existing only in the natural order, their will, in order to produce its full effect, need only exhibit the natural characteristics of a will." By a dramatic inversion, the nation, created in the course of centuries by the persistent efforts of the monarchical state, now became metaphysically prior to it. The logic of *Qu'est-ce que le Tiers Etat?* threatened the entire standing order of international relations no less radically than it subverted the institutional order of the French monarchy. Once it was adopted, the history of humanity could be nothing but the story of national self-determination inflicted everywhere upon it in the two centuries since the French Revolution.

As a collective being, then, the nation was part of a natural order, prior to all history, the ground of all history. By the same token its true members were those still innocent of historical titles, those members of the Third Estate not yet disqualified by the historical accretion of privileges from membership in a common order of equal citizens. Sieyès' nation, like Rousseau's people, is an association of individual citizens equal before the law. But what is the nature of this association? It is a striking feature of *Qu'est-ce que le Tiers Etat?* that while it endows the nation with many features of Rousseau's people, most notably the unity and universality of an association of equal citizens bound together by a common will, it places no emphasis on a social contract as the explicit logical basis of its collective being. In this pamphlet, Sieyès postulates the initial existence of "a fairly large number of isolated individuals who wish to band together." This first stage in the formation of political society is therefore characterized by an exercise of individual wills: "Association is their work; they are at the source of all power." But no social contract is brought into play to specify the nature and conditions of the act of association. Instead, Sieyès simply announces that these individuals already constitute a nation by virtue of the very fact that they want to unite. This tendency to naturalize political society rather than to emphasize its contractual origins draws further strength from Sieyès' recourse, at the very beginning of *Qu'est-ce que le Tiers Etat?*, to a language much closer to the physiocrats than to Rousseau, a language in which the nation is characterized as a social and economic organization, grounded in the order of physical nature, and sustained by the production and distribution of material resources for the satisfaction of human needs.

There is very good reason for this striking elision of the central argument of the *Social Contract*. Sieyès' aim in *Qu'est-ce que le Tiers Etat?* is not to insist on the artificiality or fragility of an *être moral* created by contract, but on the essential reality of the nation and of its common will: "The national will needs only to exist in order to be legal at all times; it is the source of all legality." In Rousseau's theory, the people ceases to exist as an abstract, collective being whenever the general will ceases to operate. But Sieyès reverses this logic. The threat of the dissolution of the association, through the disappearance of the general will, into the mere aggregate of individuals from which it derived—so compelling a possibility for Rousseau—simply does not appear in his text. He does not argue that despotism and privilege have destroyed the nation through the substitution of particular wills for a general will. Nor does he argue that the French have ceased (or will cease) to be a nation the moment they acquiesce in forms of representation in the Estates General that preclude expression of the unitary and indivisible sovereign will of the entire body of citizens. Instead, he simply repudiates these forms as illegitimate, because incompatible with the reality of national identity. "A nation cannot decide that it will not be the nation." From fictive being, the nation has become primordial reality.

* *
*

Its case for national sovereignty brilliantly conceived in relation to the problems and possibilities of a specific historical moment, *Qu'est-ce que le Tiers Etat?* was a masterpiece of political rhetoric. But Sieyès was unable to control all the meanings of his pamphlet. Like any such rhetorical work, it said more—and less—than its author intended. As its leaven began to ferment in French political discourse, others were to find implications in its arguments quite different from those Sieyès had anticipated; nor could these implications be contained by his subsequent efforts to elaborate more fully upon certain aspects of his political philosophy. The principle of national sovereignty was given increasingly explicit expression in such revolutionary actions as the creation of the National Assembly, the Tennis Court Oath, the night of August 4, the Declaration of the Rights of Man, and the early Assembly debates that laid the essential basis for the creation of a constitution founded on the claim that "sovereignty is one, indivisible, inalienable, and imprescriptible. It belongs to the nation." But the constitutional implementation of this principle differed radically from that advocated by the author of *Qu'est-ce que le Tiers Etat?* And it did so in a way that already revealed the essence of the problem the revolutionaries were to encounter in their efforts to transfer sovereignty from the crown to the nation.

The manner in which the nation was to exercise its newly proclaimed sovereignty lay at the heart of the constitutional debates of late August and September 1789. The rejection of the absolute royal veto and the balance of powers proposed by Mounier and the monarchiens meant a clear repudiation of their claim (legacy of an earlier constitutionalist discourse) that the nation was the residual source of sovereignty rather than its active agent. Henceforth, sovereignty was to be understood as inhering directly and immediately in the nation. But how was the direct and immediate exercise of a unitary sovereign will to be guaranteed in a vast society where direct democracy was impossible? How was the indivisibility and inalienability of the nation's sovereignty to be sustained in the face of the necessity for representation? Sieyès argued in the Assembly debates that the national will could find its expression only in a representative assembly; only there was it possible to formulate a truly unitary will through discussion among the deputies of the entire nation, a common will free of the partial interests of a multiplicity of electoral constituencies. This was a reformulation, in terms of the theory of representation, of Rousseau's requirement that the general will be general in both its source and its object, which is to say that it would result from certain formal procedures of decision-making rather than precede them. The earlier arguments of *Qu'est-ce que le Tiers Etat?* notwithstanding, this position meant that the general will could not be understood as a primordial will existing independently of all forms; it was not a prior positive will to be transmitted from the primary assemblies to the national assembly through the device of representation. To the contrary, Sieyès now argued that a common will simply did not exist outside the national assembly: the nation (following one of the logical possibilities admitted by Hobbes) was one only in the collective person of its unitary representative body. Hence the absurdity, from his perspective, of an argument for a suspensive veto justified on the grounds that decisions of the national assembly must be continually scrutinized for the possibility of their deviation from the general will, as if such a will could exist outside the assembly.

Sovereignty

In accepting the suspensive veto, however, the Constituent Assembly opted for a very different understanding of the operation of national sovereignty, an understanding premised on the assumption that the general will did exist as a positive prior will, inhering in the body of the nation as a whole. Deputies were elected to articulate that will in the National Assembly, whose collective decisions were assumed to express it in the absence of suspicion to the contrary. But once sovereignty was held to be inherent in the body of the nation in this way, the danger of its alienation from the nation to the representative assembly—the threatening possibility that a particular will might be substituted for the real will of the nation—became ever-present. Hence the constitutional function of the king, that other "representative" of the nation (for the Constituent Assembly had not eliminated all remnants of the earlier conception of the monarch as a representative public person), in exercising the suspensive veto. It became the king's responsibility to delay acceptance, until the nation had effectively expressed itself, of any act of the legislative body that might be suspected of not conforming to the general will of the nation.

The suspensive veto was but the first of a series of attempts made during the Revolution to resolve the problem of reconciling the inalienability of national sovereignty with the practice of representation. It led, of course, to the destruction of the monarchy by a new revolution, a revolution motivated by the perception that the veto had itself been transformed, in Louis XVI's hands, into an instrument for the frustration of the general will. In place of the representative person of the king acting to safeguard the expression of the general will, the insurrection of August 10, 1792, now established the people itself, the people whose deputies were to be constantly subject to its own immediate surveillance. Popular sovereignty replaced national sovereignty as the order of the day.

As articulated in the language of the sans-culottes, popular sovereignty had several implications. Above all, it meant that sovereign power, "imprescriptible, inalienable, non-delegatable" was to be understood as inhering, directly and immediately, in the body of the citizens permanently assembled in the sections. There, its unity unimpaired by factitious distinctions between active and passive citizens, its will unimpeded by devious systems of indirect elections, the people could be found in the physicality of its existence and in the positivity of its will. At the heart of sans-culotte discourse lay the fundamental ambiguity of the political and social meanings of the term *peuple*. The people that was the sovereign was the people as political body, the entire body of citizens bound together in the unanimity of its common will. But it was also the people as social body, the people as those who labored, those whose common existence was defined by the physicality of their relation to material nature and the immediacy of their need for subsistence. In this common relation to nature, the people was consubstantial. Each member, each section, could speak for the whole. And by this common relation to nature, the people was delimited. The sans-culottes directed against the rich and idle the logic used against the privileged in *Qu'est-ce que le Tiers Etat?*: sustained as it was by its work upon physical nature, the sovereign nation comprised only those who

853

were actively and usefully engaged in that work. "And it is an obvious truth that the nation is sans-culotte and that the small number of people who hold all the wealth in their hands are not the nation; they are only the privileged, whose privilege is coming to an end," as the section of the Observatoire put it in September 1793.

This conception of inalienable popular sovereignty had several important consequences, not the least of which was the demand that legislative acts be submitted to the sanction of direct popular approval before their acceptance as law. More immediately important for revolutionary politics, it implied insistence upon the status of the deputies to the National Assembly as *mandataires* rather than as representatives. *Mandataires du peuple,* as they were reminded in countless petitions emanating from the sections, the deputies were sent to the Assembly not to decide on the people's behalf but to bear its sovereign will. And while their fidelity to that will was no longer to be guaranteed in advance by the traditional device of the binding mandate (also favored by Rousseau in the case of Poland), it was to be assured by perpetual popular surveillance. Hence the right of the people in the sections to address, control, and censure decisions of the Assembly. Hence its right to call individual deputies to account at the end of each session, or whenever such action seemed required; to revoke, dismiss, discipline, and replace unfaithful *mandataires* at will. Hence, ultimately, its right to rise in insurrection: to impose the popular will upon a divided Assembly, as on August 10, 1792; or to purge refractory deputies and restore the representative body to the unity it must necessarily possess as a reflection of that will, as on May 31–June 2, 1793.

Justified as it was by these claims, the insurrectionary action of the people of Paris therefore raised to its highest pitch the recurring revolutionary problem of the inalienability of national sovereignty. To the popular movement in Paris, as to its allies within the National Assembly, these insurrections marked the ultimate refusal of a unitary people to allow its inalienable sovereign will to be frustrated or usurped by treacherous *mandataires*. To those who denounced them from the provinces, or from within the National Assembly, the insurrections represented quite the opposite: the unlawful claim of a mere portion of the people to exercise the sovereign power belonging to the body of the nation as a whole. In either case, the problem remained the same: how to eliminate the necessity of recourse to insurrection by finding constitutional means to give particular expression to the will of the sovereign without ipso facto alienating it? This was the problem posed to the Convention by Condorcet in presenting the Girondin Constitution early in 1793; it was equally the problem posed to it by Hérault de Séchelles in presenting the Montagnard Constitution after the revolution of May 31–June 2.

The Girondin Constitution offered a solution as complex as it was thoroughgoing in its provisions for subjecting actions of the legislative body to the reasoned judgment of the entire people meeting in primary assemblies. But this project to render insurrection redundant by institutionalizing revolution on a continuing, peaceful basis gained little favor in the Convention. Saint-Just found its mechanisms for the production of the general will too tainted by Condorcet's rationalism. Robespierre, in his turn, condemned its procedures to guarantee the inalienability of popular sovereignty by constant recourse to the primary assemblies as amounting to a conspiracy to undermine that sovereignty by disgusting the people with a surfeit of democratic formalities.

The project that formed the basis of the Montagnard Constitution of 1793 was less complex in its provisions for securing the exercise of popular sovereignty. Two features stand out. It specified procedures for submission of proposed legislation to popular referendum on the demand of a proportion of the primary assemblies; and it recommended creation of a national jury (elected at the same time and in the same manner as the Legislative Assembly) to pronounce judgment on deputies accused of oppressive or unfaithful exercise of their mandate. The Convention adopted provisions for popular referendum on legislation, but it balked at the proposal for a national jury, which once again opened up all the contradictions inherent in the effort to reconcile sovereignty and representation. The national jury was repudiated on the grounds that it would diminish the authority and inhibit the proper action of the Legislative Assembly, and would introduce into the exercise of sovereignty a confusion no less dangerous than the ill-considered suspensive veto of the Constitution of 1791. How then to "guarantee the people against oppression by the legislative body?" Charged to reconsider this problem, the Committee of Public Safety offered a variation upon sans-culotte demands proposed by Robespierre: each deputy would be judged, at the end of each session, by the primary assemblies that had elected him; no deputy whose actions failed to win approval would be eligible for re-election or other public office. But this proposal, in its turn, was denounced as threatening the integrity of popular sovereignty by allowing particular sections of the people to judge deputies properly belonging to the whole. Under such a dispensation, the intriguing enemy of the nation might be honorably acquitted; its virtuous friend condemned. Would the Gironde, would the Vendée have condemned its perfidious deputies? The purged Convention thought not. It refused any portion of the people the right to "deprive the entire nation of a representative it esteemed." Short of insurrection, it seemed, no way could be found from the maze that was the problem of the inalienability of popular sovereignty. The conventionnels found consolation for theoretical defeat in a practical judgment: "The people is always there."

The people is always there. But is the people everywhere? And is everyone the people? In its troubled references to Marseilles and the Vendée, the Convention debate over the national jury pointed to yet another profound problem inherent in the concept of national/popular sovereignty. The conception of national sovereignty for which Sieyès had argued in the early debates of the Constituent Assembly required only that diverse interests be transformed into a unitary will by the deliberation of the National Assembly. But the notion of sovereignty adopted by the Constituents in accepting the suspensive veto—and intensified by the sans-culottes in their vision of the deputies as *mandataires*—required more. It required that the unity of the assembly emanate directly from the unity of the body of the nation/people. The will of the sovereign nation had to be as unitary as it was inalienable: the body of the people had to bear the same unity it sought to impose upon its deputies; difference simply could not be held to exist within it.

855

By this logic, unity was the condition of sovereignty; the nation was unanimous or it was nothing. Hence the constant aversion, throughout the revolutionary period, to any form of political activity that threatened the unity of the sovereign will by the apparent articulation of particular wills or partial interests. Hence the constant impetus to achieve unity by way of exclusion. From the very first, the Revolution constituted the nation as sovereign, one and indivisible, by excising a privileged aristocracy from its midst. But the logic of a unitary sovereign will, intensified by war and internal division, required constant elimination of difference through progressive expansion of the category of "aristocracy" and corresponding restriction of the category of "nation" or "people." Successive denunciations, purges within the popular movement, and demands for revolutionary justice against the enemies of the nation lengthened the list of distinguishing characteristics of suspects indefinitely.

In demanding a Law on Suspects, however, the sans-culottes were in effect insisting that the Convention purge the people—just as the people itself had earlier purged the Convention—of all elements of disunity. Each had to impose unity upon the other whenever it was found lacking. This was the essential logic of the Terror. It was a logic that no one articulated better than Robespierre. His speech to the Convention on May 10, 1793, offered as the essential principle of representative government that "the people is good and its delegates are corruptible; that it is in the virtue and sovereignty of the people that one must seek a preservative against the vices and despotism of the government." But this preservative against the evils of government must itself be preserved—by the government. Such was the essential argument for the Terror offered by Robespierre in his speeches to the Convention on the principles of revolutionary government (December 25, 1793) and of political morality (February 17, 1794). Popular government, he now insisted, finds its mainspring in political virtue—the virtue by which individual wills are identified with the general will. A government deprived of republican virtue can find renewal in the people; but once that virtue is lost in the people, liberty itself must perish. Clearly, it was imperative for the Convention, its committees, and its agents to sustain and intensify the political virtue of the people. Clearly, it was also imperative for them, through the determined application of that Terror which "is nothing other than prompt, severe, inflexible justice . . . an emanation of virtue," to eliminate the dissidence and disorder spread by the enemies of the people.

But how was the differentiation between the people and its enemies to be made when "the aristocracy was organizing popular societies and counter-revolutionary pride concealed its plots and its daggers beneath rags?" The fear of difference had reached the level of paranoia at which any political action or articulation must be seen as actually or potentially the expression of a subversive, immoral will.

***

Previously unimagined and unimaginable, the political experience of the Terror prompted a systematic critique of the concept of sovereignty. Sieyès, the author whose work had perhaps done more than any other to place national sovereignty at the center of revolutionary discourse, was now among the first to denounce the exaggerated implications that had been drawn from it. Sounding a retreat from sovereignty that was to become a central theme of the French liberalism that took form in the wake of the Terror, his speech of 2 Thermidor, Year III, reiterated a conception of representation as the rational application to political matters of the principle of division of labor fundamental to modern society, rather than as merely a necessary but inherently problematic substitute for the direct articulation of the general will by the people as a whole. In reclaiming the sovereignty usurped by their kings, Sieyès now argued, the French people had become contaminated with the virus of arbitrary, absolute, and unlimited power: "People seemed to say to themselves, with a sort of patriotic pride, that if the sovereignty of great kings is so powerful, so terrible, the sovereignty of a great people must be something quite different." But sovereignty was not unlimited: in creating political society, individuals did not transfer all their rights to the community, nor did they confer upon it the sum of their individual powers; on the contrary, they retained these rights, placing in common only as little power as was necessary to maintain them. Nor did politics consist in the unitary exercise of an arbitrary will: "Nothing is arbitrary in moral and social nature, any more than in physical nature." From this perspective, the concentration of sovereign power, not its alienation, became the greatest political danger; the limitation of power, its dispersion and differentiation, its transformation into the expression of reason in the service of social needs and interests, became the principal goal of the social art. Thus recapitulating the physiocratic themes of his earlier thinking, Sieyès reasserted the priority of a discourse of the social, grounded on the notion of the differential distribution of reason, functions, and interests in modern civil society, over a discourse of the political grounded on the theory of a unitary general will.

In this attitude he was followed, above all, by Benjamin Constant, whose writings gave French liberalism its classic form. As we know, Constant found the key to the Terror in a failure to recognize the essential difference between the liberty of the ancients (consisting in the collective exercise of sovereign will) and the liberty of the moderns (consisting in the security of private enjoyments). Principally responsible for that failure, in Constant's eyes, were those great admirers of classical political virtue, Rousseau and Mably. Misled by the impossible idea of recovering for modern peoples the collective sovereignty enjoyed by the ancients, the revolutionaries found themselves inevitably caught up in "that inexplicable frenzy that has been called the Reign of Terror." Two fundamental arguments were implied in this liberal reflection upon the Terror: a critique of the principle of popular sovereignty as founded on the theory of the general will; and an assertion of the essential separation to be maintained between state and society. Constant did not dispute the claim that legitimate government must depend upon the general will, understood in the broad sense as the common consent of the governed; but he did deny a view of the general will that issued in the exercise of unlimited sovereign power. The greatest error of the proponents of collective sovereignty, he argued, had been to direct their attacks against the holders of absolute power, not against that power itself. Instead of seeking to destroy it, they thought only of transferring it to the people as a whole: "It was a scourge; they considered it a conquest. They afflicted all society with it." They were correct in arguing that no individual or group has the right to subject the rest to his particular will; but they were wrong to suggest that society as a whole exercises an unlimited sovereignty over its members.

In Constant's analysis, it was because Rousseau sensed the danger of the monstrous power he had conjured up in the name of the people that he had declared that sovereignty could be neither alienated, nor delegated, nor represented—which was to declare, in effect, that it could never be exercised. Seeking to substitute a notion of limited political authority for the tyranny of the general will, Constant was thus led to contest the language of political voluntarism itself. Reverting to the physiocratic discourse of the social, he insisted that society is not constituted by the exercise of will. On the contrary, it rests on natural relations among human beings; laws are nothing more than the declaration of these natural social relations. From this perspective, the claim to legislate by the free exercise of a sovereign will—the hallmark of the doctrine of sovereignty from Bodin to the French Revolution—involved an essential misunderstanding of the proper nature of social order. "The law is not at the disposal of the legislator. It is not his spontaneous creation. The legislator is to the social order what the physician is to nature," that is, an observer, not a creator, of the laws.

The Terror thus revealed the tyranny inherent in any notion of political voluntarism, a tyranny that could be prevented only by establishing an absolute distinction between state and civil society, a sacred boundary respecting that part of human existence that must be beyond the reach of any political power. Where the revolutionaries dreamed of a social order that would be the transparent expression of human will, Constant insisted upon the essential obscurity and impermeability of civil society in relationship to the state.

With these arguments for a necessary line of demarcation between society and the state, the doctrine of sovereignty came full circle. Early absolutist theorists had emphasized the need for a unitary sovereign authority upholding society from within, an authority that, while supreme, was also limited by the nature of the social order of which it was at once the condition and the essential expression. The growth of the active administrative state disrupted this sense of sovereignty as consubstantial with social order, prompting efforts to reclaim for society a sovereign power that now seemed to be threatening it from without rather than sustaining it from within.

Embracing the most radical of these ideas with the theory of the general will, the revolutionaries attempted to reabsorb sovereignty into society by locating its inalienable exercise in the unitary body of the nation/people. But their attempt to fulfill these conditions of unity and inalienability fed the logic of the Terror, transforming a theory of collective liberty into the practice of despotism. To this experience, the modern distinction between state and society—and the liberal insistence on their necessary separation—appears historically as the essential response.

Keith M. Baker

FURTHER READING

Bacot, Guillaume. *Carré de Malberg et l'origine de la distinction entre souveraineté du peuple et souveraineté nationale.* Paris, 1985.

Baker, Keith M. *The French Revolution and the Creation of Modern Political Culture,* vol. 1, *The Political Culture of the Old Regime.* Oxford, 1987.

Carré de Malberg, R. *Contribution à la théorie générale de l'état,* 2 vols. Paris, 1920–1922.

Franklin, Julian H. *Jean Bodin and the Rise of Absolutist Theory.* Cambridge, 1973.

Singer, Brian. *Society, Theory, and the French Revolution: Studies in the Revolutionary Imaginary.* New York, 1986.

Soboul, Albert. *Les sans-culottes parisiens en l'an II: Mouvement populaire et gouvernement révolutionnaire (2 juin 1793–9 thermidor an II).* Paris, 1958.

RELATED TOPICS

Ancien Régime	Elections	Robespierre	Suffrage
Constant	Nation	Rousseau	Terror
Constitution	Physiocrats	Sans-culottes	
Democracy	Revolutionary Assemblies	Sieyès	

VANDALISM

"Vandalism" is one of the few revolutionary neologisms for which we know both the author and the circumstances in which he invented it. The abbé Grégoire, constitutional bishop of Blois, one of the most influential deputies in the Constituent Assembly and a member of the Convention, coined the word in Year II and gave it currency in a series of reports to the Convention for the purpose, as he put it in his *Memoirs,* of "killing the thing," that is, denouncing or halting the destruction of cultural artifacts such as monuments, paintings, books, and charters, which were being destroyed as symbols of a hated past, of "feudalism," "royal tyranny," and "religious prejudice." Used for the first time in January 1794 (21 Nivôse, Year II) in Grégoire's report on inscriptions on public monuments, the term "vandalism" did not really embark on its brilliant career until after 9 Thermidor, when it was greatly aided by the three "Reports on Vandalism" submitted by Grégoire on behalf of the Committee of Public Instruction (on 14 Fructidor and 8 Brumaire, Year II, and on 24 Frimaire, Year III). Quickly assimilated, the new word was soon in widespread use. It came up frequently in Convention debates and in public and private correspondence. The "ax of vandalism" and "frenzy of vandalism" were expressions that needed no explanation. As the source of a cliché, the reports thus mark an important stage in the developing discussion of and opposition to revolutionary vandalism. In contrast to earlier denunciations of acts of defacement, which remained general and vague, Grégoire's brief included a long list of monuments, "objects of science and art," that had been destroyed: Bouchardon's works in Paris; Turenne's tomb at Franciade (formerly Saint-Denis; but note that the destruction of royal graves is not mentioned); damage to the cathedral at Chartres caused by removal of lead from its roof; entire libraries confiscated from cloisters and castles and left to rot in damp warehouses; the magnificent library of Saint-Germain-des-Prés consumed by flames; a Virgin by Houdon destroyed at Verdun; an ancient bust of Jupiter smashed at Versailles; splendid orange trees in the Indre département that someone had attempted to sell on the grounds that republicans needed apples, not oranges; and so on. It was a question not of isolated cases but of a "destructive fury" unleashed throughout the country. In the long though incomplete list cited by Grégoire (as we now know, it might have been much longer and more impressive), facts were mingled with rumor and fantasy. In Paris someone had proposed burning the Bibliothèque Nationale; in Marseilles there had been talk of burning all the libraries. In general, there had been plans to destroy *all* monuments that honored France.

From report to report the scope of Grégoire's neologism grew, and this tendency continued in the many other documents that adopted and popular-ized the word. Vandalism was not limited to monuments and objets d'art and other artifacts against which "barbarism wielded an ax." It also referred to "a veritable fanaticism determined to change the names of communes to no pur-pose," a mania carried so far that soon "the plain of Beauce will be called Mountain." And it included the mania for changing first names, for replacing Jacquot with Brutus and Pierrot with Aristide. Vandalism was above all an "organized system" against "men of talent," as evidenced by the long list of scientists, artists, and men of letters who were persecuted during the Terror. The most distressing example is Lavoisier, the shining light of French science, indeed of all science, who in Floréal, Year II, expressed his wish for two weeks' grace before mounting the scaffold in order to complete his experi-ments for the benefit of the Republic, to which plea Dumas, the president of the Revolutionary Tribunal, is supposed to have responded: "The Revolution has no need of scientists." These words, though destined to be repeated for a long time to come, were never spoken, and the circumstances reported by Grégoire were inaccurate. Nevertheless, the "antivandal" cause had found its martyr and its symbol. Condorcet became another: persecuted as a Girondin after the *journée* of May 31, he secretly wrote his *Esquisse d'un tableau du progrès de l'esprit humain,* a veritable hymn to the glory of progress and the Revolu-tion, then committed suicide on 5 Germinal, Year II, in order to avoid the scaffold.

With his reports Grégoire thus provided a matrix for the discussion of vandalism, combining a denunciation of acts of vandalism, of which he pro-vided a catalogue, with an indictment of those responsible. Grégoire, along with the antivandal movement he inspired after Thermidor, made it perfectly clear that he saw a link between terrorism and vandalism. In the aftermath of 9 Thermidor it was primarily Robespierre's personal responsibility that was attacked: Robespierre the tyrant and Robespierre the vandal were one and the same. The image of "Robespierre as vandal" became such a cliché that people often repeated it as though no proof were required, or embellished it with ornaments as rhetorical as they were demagogic: "The new Omar who wanted to burn the libraries" (Fréron); "an ignorant but ambitious man who little by little succumbed to a shameful barbary" (M.-J. Chénier); "the last tyrant, a man of crass ignorance . . . who heaped filth and bitterness on all who had engaged in important studies, all who possessed extensive knowl-edge" (Fourcroy). The Thermidorians thus exploited a key idea of the En-lightenment: that all tyranny rests naturally on ignorance and therefore fos-ters hatred of the sciences and the arts. Thus the "last tyrant" wished to make France a barbarous place, the more surely to subjugate it to his will. Quickly, however, the charges grew broader and broader. Beyond Robespierre they aimed at the so-called *vandalistes,* another neologism coined to denote those who personally committed destructive acts (particularly iconoclastic acts dur-ing the period of de-Christianization) and those who were presumed to profit from vandalism conceived as a political and cultural project. The destruction of books and art works and the persecution of artists and scientists were thus seen as so many effects of a more general phenomenon: the *encanaillement,* the degradation to rabble, of both France and the Revolution. The Terror was simply the rabble in power, and the "vandalist" was merely the other face of the "Terrorist." The increasingly vehement and protean antivandal rhetoric likened everyone involved in the Terror to a riff-raff disguised as patriots and revolutionaries not content merely to cut the throats of honest men, sow terror, rob, and steal. They debased all public life and covered it with filth; they hated culture; they destroyed books they didn't know how to read and works of art they were unable to appreciate. In a word, they vandalized France. To oppose the ravages of vandalism, which the Terror had erected into a system, the Thermidorian Convention established its own cultural institutions: the Ecole Polytechnique (September 1794), the Ecole Normale (October 1794), and the Institut (October 1795), along with subsidies for "artists." In addition, it took strong steps to put an end to iconoclasm (which nevertheless failed to halt the destruction of other types of cultural artifacts: hôtels, cloisters, châteaux, and many national properties that continued to be sold to speculators for demolition at extremely low prices). Thus the antivandal rhetoric portrayed the Thermidorian regime as it wished to be seen, in the guise of a civilizing power taking care that the country would not sink once again into vandalism and terror. This rhetoric reassured the old cultural elites, frightened and dispersed by the Terror, and encouraged the formation of new elites, which the Republic notably lacked. It brought Thermidorian and Directory leaders the added respectability, not to say legitimacy, they so badly needed in order to make people forget how badly many of them were compromised by involvement in the Terror. As the denouncer of vandalism and terrorist tyranny, the government could pose as the legitimate heir of the Enlightenment, hence of the principles of 1789. By returning to its true origins, the Revolution thus came full circle, ending a long drama; the sign under which it had begun presided over its conclusion.

If the Thermidorian period was a high point, or, more precisely, a turning point in the formulation of antivandal rhetoric, it was not the whole story. Vandalism was not a neutral term. Before Grégoire coined his new word, "vandal" stood for a whole set of images. In the language of the Enlightenment the Vandals were the "most barbaric of the barbarians." It was a commonplace of revolutionary rhetoric to describe as "barbarous" the past to be destroyed: tyranny, privileges, unjust laws, the tax system. Barbarous meant both tyrannical and ignorant. This pejorative was another commonplace of a rhetoric that was intended to be both enlightened and revolutionary: all tyranny rests on ignorance, which either brings on barbarism or is identified with it. The Ancien Régime, being barbarous and tyrannical, necessarily kept the nation in ignorance. Liberty could be based only on enlightenment. It was the natural enemy of "barbarous ignorance." Yet the accusation of "barbarity" was turned against the Revolution itself. Its adversaries used it to flay the Revolution immediately after July 14, when they directed the charge against revolutionary violence. The populace that massacred the innocent and carried their heads about on pikes had to be "barbarous." The rise of violence, especially after August 10 and the September massacres, was even more harshly denounced as barbaric and *vandale*.

VANDALISM

What is particularly perplexing about this novel figure of counterrevolutionary rhetoric, a way of expressing anger and fear as well as exorcising the Revolution, is that this time the "barbarians," the destructive forces opposed to civilization, came not from outside but from within. (They are "in our midst," said Mallet du Pan, one of the most perspicacious counterrevolutionary observers and analysts.) Of course the revolutionary ideologues angrily rejected these accusations: the Revolution was hardly a purely destructive force; on the contrary, its activities and objectives were essentially constructive. If the regeneration of the nation necessarily required a period of destruction, it was because the past was barbarous. Thus the Revolution's enemies, foreign and domestic, were identified as "barbarians" and "vandals," particularly those "hordes" unleashed against France by the coalition of tyrants, as well as the Vendean peasants, prisoners of their fanaticism.

Nevertheless, people were troubled by an unspoken fear that "barbarity" might take over the Revolution: "Let us not, as our enemies charge, make a revolution of Goths and Vandals," Mirabeau proclaimed in presenting his plan for public education in 1791. Worries that the revolutionary cause was being perverted grew more acute in subsequent years owing to the deterioration of the cultural heritage, the collapse of the educational system, and the wave of iconoclasm that swept over the country. Blame was always attributed to foreigners and malcontents and above all to ignorance, the legacy of a pernicious past; in other words, the fault lay with forces hostile to the Revolution and outside it. Still, in repeated Convention debates and in the documents of the Commission on Monuments and the Committee on Public Instruction one senses a growing malaise: how could barbarism and vandalism be denounced as forces outside of and hostile to the Revolution when quite obviously these barbarous acts were committed not by princes and priests but formed part of the patriotic and civic activity of the sans-culottes, revolutionary armies, committees of surveillance, and agents of the republic, concealed if not encouraged by certain *représentants en mission?* In the spring of Year II, following the execution of the Hébertists, the Committee of Public Safety, with Robespierre at its head, discovered that these alleged "conspirators" made an ideal scapegoat. They were accused of having plotted to undermine the government and seize power by debasing everything in sight, sinking the people in ignorance, and perverting the popular spirit. A political conspiracy was blamed for the fact that the Revolution itself had given rise to destruction of monuments, persecution of scientists, and other monstrous perversions of its noble cause. Thus it was at the height of the Terror and for the benefit of the Jacobin dictatorship that the paradigm of antivandal rhetoric was created, a paradigm that the Thermidorians would adopt and turn against the "Terrorists." By identifying vandalism with Terrorism, the Thermidorians shifted the location of the boundary between enlightened revolutionaries and "barbarous" vandals. The vandal image of course retained its primary function: to designate the *other,* the enemy of the civilization and enlightenment that were inseparable from the revolutionary cause. Yet that other, the "vandalist Terrorist" for whom Robespierre became the symbol, had somehow infiltrated the revolutionary forces, perverting the cause and turning the Revolution into its opposite, a new form of tyranny. In other words, antivandal rhetoric not only castigated vandalism but also sought to explain how a phenomenon so alien to the principles of the Revolution could have been inherent in revolutionary events as they actually developed. With its contrast between the old and the new tyranny, between monarchy and the Terror, the Thermidorian regime did battle against both the old and the new "barbarians." In this stance people saw confirmation not only of the profound identity of the Revolution and the Enlightenment, but also of the cultural and educational vocation of the government that had saved the nation from the Terror and barbarism.

Essentially ideological, the Thermidorian view expressed the ambiguities and contradictions of the moment. Hence over the long run it satisfied no one. For some it lay too heavy a burden on the Revolution, especially on the Jacobin and Montagnard period, by making it responsible for the destruction. For others, it absolved the Revolution too thoroughly, by limiting responsibility for the destructive frenzy and acts of vandalism to the Terror. Because of these ambiguities, the Thermidorian view became the point of departure for the passionate and emotional debate on revolutionary vandalism that divided French historians in the nineteenth century and whose aftermath is still evident today. It set the pattern, particularly by confounding description with denunciation, the search for origins with the assignment of blame. Before entering into this debate, I should note in passing that the meaning of the neologism has been expanding steadily ever since the Revolution to include deterioration of cultural works and public property as a result of apparently gratuitous individual or collective acts in some way expressive of hostility. (Today the destruction of telephone booths is taken as symbolic and is an object of anxious scrutiny by sociologists and psychologists.) In order to distinguish the kind of vandalism I have in mind from this more general phenomenon, I shall use the phrase "revolutionary vandalism" to describe the "thing" that Grégoire wished to "kill."

If the polemics over revolutionary vandalism took an epic turn in the late nineteenth century, it was because the stakes far exceeded the apparent object of the controversy: the destruction of cultural artifacts during the Revolution. That destruction did occur no one denied; nor did anyone in an age preoccupied with progress and civilization wish to offer an apology. The debate turned instead on the magnitude of the damage and above all the issue of responsibility. The prosecution laid stress on the specific characteristics of *revolutionary* vandalism: damages were minutely catalogued, including not only the effects of iconoclastic acts but also all damages resulting from the sale of national properties. An attempt was made to show that the destruction and devastation were not random but part of a far-reaching plan, a deliberate expression of rage inseparable from the Revolution and evident throughout its history. The defense, on the other hand, argued that "on the whole" the destruction was no more serious than during other periods of war or unrest. As much if not more damage had been done later on, during the Empire and Restoration, owing to an absence of aesthetic appreciation for ancient monuments. Above all, iconoclasm was an accident limited to certain brief periods, most notably the wave of de-Christianization that swept the country, and at odds with the overall cultural aims of the Revolution. Far from being destructive, the revolutionaries had sought to preserve the cultural heritage of the past for the nation. Like so many other historiographic polemics on the Revolution, this one merely reproduced the cleavage between the "left" and the "right." It had as much to do with the cultural policies of the Third Republic, which took pride in its revolutionary origins, as with the Revolution itself, and ideology largely outweighed substance in the debate.

Concerning the central issue, that of the revolutionary government's responsibility for the destruction, it is tempting to argue that both sides were right. There is no doubt that successive revolutionary governments did wish to preserve cultural artifacts from destruction and damage. In decree after decree the Assemblies promulgated laws concerning the protection of nationalized books, charters, paintings, and furniture, which were to be carefully inventoried and stored in special warehouses. The first measures of this kind date from November 1789; additional steps were taken in 1790 (October), 1791 (May, June), and 1792 (September). In 1790 a Commission on Monuments, composed of scholars and artists, was set up to oversee monuments and archives in Paris. At the height of the Terror, in October 1793, one month after passage of the Law on Suspects, the Convention approved "energetic" measures against abuses leading to the "destruction of monuments of the arts, sciences, and instruction" and to that end set up a special body, the Temporary Commission on the Arts. The Thermidorian Convention for its part approved a whole series of measures favorable to men of letters and scientists. (Scientists such as Monge, Guyton de Morveau, Laplace, and Fourcroy enjoyed unprecedented political and social influence; under the Directory and Consulate they became high government functionaries and ministers.) It would be easy to extend the list of orders, decrees, and institutions for the benefit of arts and letters.

Nevertheless, this list of measures, with its repetition of the same appeals and admonitions, in itself shows how ineffective or unsuitable such measures were to halt a process that, once triggered, could not be controlled. The laws to safeguard the monuments were necessary to ward off the effects of other revolutionary decisions that inevitably imperiled cultural goods. The nationalization of clerical property, the confiscation of émigré property, and the sale of both inevitably forced the wholesale removal of entire libraries and collections of charters and paintings for storage in hastily improvised and unsuitable warehouses. Damage was the inevitable result, to say nothing of theft, wild speculation on art, and sale at ridiculously low prices of châteaux and monasteries destined for demolition. The famous degree of August 14, 1792, concerning the suppression of "signs of feudalism" (and requiring the destruction of monuments "to prejudice and tyranny") spelled doom for countless monuments and works of art. To be sure, the Convention spelled out restrictions specifically in order to limit the damages, but one month after passage of the law the extent of the devastation was so obvious that it had to issue further warnings and restrictions. The end, however, was not yet in sight. During the summer and autumn of 1793 another series of laws was passed strictly prohibiting coats of arms and "emblems of royalty" in all parks, houses, churches, and enclosures. And what of the wave of de-Christianization, when bells were removed from churches, steeples destroyed, sculptures disfigured, paintings slashed, and religious artifacts melted in the name of reason and "holy equality." On the "revolutionary and republican" side it might well be objected that these abuses were denounced by the revolutionary government itself, that the de-Christianizing and iconoclastic phase of the Revolution was short-lived, that the statues and altars were for the most part victims of revolutionary army troopers whose escapades were quickly halted, and finally that certain measures were made necessary by "external circumstances," the army being in need of bronze and saltpeter. These arguments vary in merit and are easily refuted. The stalwart sans-culottes who engaged in iconoclasm in Year II were beyond any doubt encouraged by the government, and the sanctions with which they were threatened were not widely enforced. The demolitions continued for an entire year, with remarkable regularity, despite changes in the government and even after the pressure of "external circumstances" had disappeared; the example of Cluny is sufficiently eloquent in this respect.

If the participants in the debate seem to complement rather than contradict one another, the reason is that both sides reveal, each in an incomplete and partial fashion, the inherent contradictions in the Revolution's cultural policy as well as in the system of ideas that legitimated and oriented that policy. The Revolution saw itself as the child of the Enlightenment and as having a cultural, and more specifically an educational, vocation. In the case at hand, this vocation was reflected in the determination to destroy and to preserve at the same time. In effect, the revolutionary government assigned itself the role of managing nationalized cultural properties. As representative of the nation, the government was charged with putting those properties to work on the nation's behalf, with serving as protector of the arts and thus establishing the arts in a cultural space identical to the space of democratic politics. The revolutionary powers that loudly and constantly claimed this responsibility encountered practical difficulties in this management task. The volume of items to be administered was too large for the available means and resources. (Take books, for example: more than a million of them piled up and were allowed to rot in improvised warehouses across the country.) But this contradiction between goals and resources was not the only issue. More crucial was the issue of determining what the Revolution's goals in this area ought to be. As heir to the Enlightenment, the Revolution saw itself as carrying on a cultural tradition. But it defined itself as regenerating and purifying a past tainted by centuries of tyranny and prejudice. It could therefore preserve the works of the past but only on condition that it eliminate any not worthy of a regenerated people. In making this selection the revolutionary elites were certain of possessing an infallible criterion—infallible because it rested on both the achievements of the Enlightenment and the energy of the Revolution. In reality, however, that criterion was vague and constantly challenged. Hence the boundary between preservation and destruction, the two sides of "regeneration," was elusive if not impossible to grasp. These already complex issues were further complicated by the religious question that became an integral part of the revolutionary cultural experience. The significance of the de-Christianization "from above" that was launched by the revolutionary elites was not necessarily the same as that of the iconoclastic acts perpetrated by the revolutionary armies in small towns and villages. Furthermore, decrees intended to have a centralizing, unifying effect could, depending on local traditions, produce very different results in different départements and communes. To destroy a monastery in a frenzy of iconoclasm might have the same devastating effect as demolishing another in order to turn a quick profit on the capital invested in the purchase of a "national property." Yet the sociocultural significance and ideological import of the two are quite different. Although I have no wish to suggest that vandalism motivated by ideology is "nobler" than vandalism motivated only by the lure of profit, the conclusion is inescapable that there were several forms of vandalism in the Revolution just as there were several forms of de-Christianization, and that historians have been all too likely to confuse them.

Paradoxically, revolutionary vandalism helped to stimulate curiosity in the past and awaken reverence for national tradition. It revealed, if only by way of its extremist aberrations, the cultural as well as political impasse implicit in the revolutionary aim of making a radical break with the past the very principle of an effort of civilization.

The condemnation of vandalism, of the destruction of works of art, was not in itself an alternative to such a policy. That alternative began to take shape only after the decision by the Committee of Public Instruction on October 21, 1795, to accept the proposal of Alexandre Lenoir, a young painter, to set up "a historical and chronological museum in which one will be able to find the ages and sculpture in special rooms, each with the exact character and appearance of the century it represents." Thus in the former convent of the Petits-Augustins was born the Musée des Monuments français, which would remain open until the Restoration (1816). Lenoir made it into a refuge for historical monuments and a memorial to the national glory. Its various rooms housed the tombstones and busts of famous men; if no such monument was available, Lenoir had one made to order. Thus the museum contained royal tombstones of François I and Catherine de Médicis alongside the tombs of statesmen such as Michel de l'Hospital and Colbert, as well as scholars and writers from Descartes to Montesqieu. An effort was made to reproduce the characteristic "color" of each era in the décor of the rooms, while the succession of rooms expressed the idea of progress (particularly through the effect of lighting, which went from semi-obscurity in the medieval rooms to bright light in the rooms devoted to the seventeenth and eighteenth centuries).

Lenoir was criticized for having committed his own acts of vandalism in removing tombstones from their original locations and mingling old sculptures with new fabrications. The great novelty of the museum, which assured its enormous success, was nevertheless its restoration of value to the national past. Beyond the emblems, scepters, and crosses, the tombs of the great were invested with a historical value stemming from patriotic interest in a national glory that had accumulated over the centuries. The Republic set itself up as the heir and guardian of the national memory and thus confirmed itself as nation-state. Furthermore, the artificial association in one place of so many signs and traces of the past, no matter how diverse their nature and despite the lack of any relation among them other than chronological sequence, stimulated imaginations, and as Thierry and Michelet attest, gave rise to the idea of a unified national history.

Bronislaw Baczko

FURTHER READING

Despois, Eugène. *Le vandalisme révolutionnaire: Fondations littéraires, scientifiques, et artistiques de la Convention.* Paris, 1868.

Gautherot, Gustave. *Le vandalisme jacobin: Destructions adminstratives d'archives, d'objets d'art, de monuments religieux à l'époque révolutionnaire.* Paris, 1914.

Grégoire, Henri-Baptiste, abbé. *Oeuvres.* Paris, 1977. See esp. vol. 2, *Rapport à la Convention.*

Poulot, Dominique. "Alexandre Lenoir et le musée des monuments français," in Pierre Nora, ed., *Les lieux de mémoire,* vol. 2, *La nation.* Paris, 1986.

Réau, Louis. *Histoire du vandalisme: Les monuments détruits de l'art français,* 2 vols. Paris, 1959.

Robinet, Jean-François-Eugène. *Le mouvement religieux à Paris pendant la Révolution (1789–1801),* 2 vols. Paris, 1896–1898.

Rücker, Frédéric. *Les origines de la conservation des monuments historiques en France (1790–1830).* Paris, 1913.

RELATED TOPICS

Condorcet	Michelet	Robespierre
De-Christianization	Mirabeau	Terror
Enlightenment	National Properties	Thermidorians

VOLTAIRE

La faute à Voltaire, la faute à Rousseau. Like Gavroche in this famous ditty, the nineteenth century portrayed—whether to execrate or bless—the ideas of the two *philosophes* as responsible for the Revolution. "When those two men passed away," Michelet wrote, "the Revolution was achieved in the high region of the spirit." Voltaire, moreover, would have hailed as his own the idea that books govern the world. Let us not dwell, however, on this intellectualist interpretation of the Revolution's inception. Simply note the equivalence established between the two tutelary figures who stand on the threshold of the Revolution: Voltaire *and* Rousseau. For anyone aware of the war between the two *philosophes*, the coordinating conjunction was an event in itself. For Hugo, this posthumous reconciliation had required nothing less than a fantastic scene of de-Pantheonization: "The two skulls struck; no doubt a spark flew from the head that had made the *Philosophical Dictionary* to the head that had made the *Social Contract* and reconciled them."

The nineteenth century's promotion of this two-faced deity, "Voltaire-and-Rousseau," was not at all easy. As late as 1878, the centenary of both men's deaths, Louis Marc faced great difficulties in trying to organize a joint celebration, which ultimately was canceled. Usually the only way of reconciling contradictory systems and their antagonistic authors is by effecting a functional division, which may, depending on the circumstances, take the form of a division of tasks, a division of periods, or a division of minds.

A division of tasks paints a picture of the two men sharing the great labors of the Revolution between them, Voltaire presiding over the measures inspired by liberty, Rousseau presiding over those required by equality. According to Michelet, the former deserves credit for the labor of "ardent humanity," the latter for the labor of fraternity. According to Hugo, it was Voltaire who struck the universal chord, Rousseau the civic chord. According to Lanfrey, Voltaire was the wisdom of the Revolution, Rousseau the spirit. One (Voltaire) kept his eye on formal rights, the other (Rousseau) on real rights. Jaurès still echoes this felicitous division of labor.

Since the Revolution was not made in a day, this division of labor also involves a division of periods. For Louis Blanc, Voltaire expressed and summed up the eighteenth century, while Rousseau heralded the nineteenth century. Other writers assigned each thinker a period of predilection within the revolutionary process. For Quinet, the pre-Revolution was Voltaire's moment. The Constituent Assembly saw the triumph of Montesquieu. The Legislative Assembly and Convention were uncontestably the hour of Rousseau. One finds a similar division in Louis Blanc, except that for him Voltaire's reign coincides with the Constituent Assembly, after which the philosophe's influence declines only to be restored after 9 Thermidor. A brief anti-individualist interregnum is presided over by Rousseau. Auguste Comte gives a different periodization: Voltaire's authority over the Revolution coincided with the eight months of Girondin rule; then came the time of Diderot, truly a blessed period for the Comtists; finally came the moment of Rousseau.

Such periodizations obviously assume that corresponding to the division of time there is also a division of minds. In counterrevolutionary thought, it was a commonplace originated by Fiévée to see Voltaire as the predecessor of "people without morals" and Rousseau as the patron of madmen. Another cliché was to portray Voltaire as dominating masculine intelligences and Rousseau as dominating feminine hearts: Vigny attests to this polarity when he reports that his father had "a mind parallel to that of Voltaire" and his mother "to that of Jean-Jacques." The political division was more interesting. For Louis Blanc, Buchez, and Auguste Comte Voltaire's men, men "of the bourgeoisie," were the Girondins, at times supplemented by the Hébertists: a philosophic and negative sect in which hostility to Robespierre was essentially a hostility to Rousseau. Conversely, the Montagnards were supposedly consistent followers of Rousseau, although Comte excluded the Dantonists, inspired, he believed, by Diderot.

Were the men who Pantheonized "Voltaire-*and*-Rousseau"—no other men of letters passed through the portals of the Pantheon during the Revolution—aware of these divisions, and did they see them in precisely this way? What exact role, based on what images, did they assign Voltaire in the Revolution? In what ways did the memory of Voltaire help the Revolution to understand itself? If ultimately it must be admitted that the French revolutionaries gave their hearts to Rousseau—though Burke, stupefied, asked himself why—we must try to find out why they also identified so wholeheartedly with Voltaire.

The performance of *Irène* on March 30, 1778, when Voltaire's bust was crowned on stage while he looked on, has sometimes been cited as the inaugural date of the French Revolution, the dawn of an era that anointed not kings but men of letters. The Pantheonization of Voltaire on July 11, 1791, in one of the most turbulent periods of the Revolution, just a few days after the king's return from Varennes, was a second coronation. It was conceived by Charles Villette, its most energetic artisan, as a reparation for affronts that Voltaire had suffered. It was the final act in the frightful and macabre history of a sick Voltaire, obsessed with the ignominious fate reserved for the remains of Mlle. Lecouvreur and negotiating in advance with the authorities over a burial at Ferney (the authorities being no more eager than Voltaire for the scandal that would have followed denial of a burial permit), preceded if necessary by a clandestine embalming en route. An ironic turn of events had disrupted these carefully laid plans: the family had recovered the body and obtained, thanks to the zealous efforts of a nephew who was an abbé, an incongruous burial place at the abbey of Sellières. The organizers of the ceremony envisioned a plan in which, once Voltaire's remains had been wrested from the abbés, they would proceed in slow procession to Paris, where there would be a brief pause at the site of the Bastille while the coffin was perched on the summit of an artificial mountain. From there, the hearse drawn by four white horses would proceed across the city, with stops at symbolic stations: the *pavillon de Flore*, where the face-to-face confrontation between the humiliated king of the Constitution and the triumphant king of public opinion was striking to behold, according to the brochures; before the home of Charles Villette on the quai des Théâtins, renamed the quai Voltaire, where the demoiselles Calas figured prominently among the crowd in the amphitheater; and at the théâtre de la Nation for an homage to the author of *Brutus*. Last of all came apotheosis in the form of a climb to the Pantheon, a perfect image of the religion of human exemplarity dreamed of by Voltaire, the theorist who preached the supremacy of great men over kings and heroes. The anticlerical symbolism of the burial place escaped no one: Saint Genevieve seemed to forbid Voltaire to enter her church, and it had required all of Charles Villette's militant insistence and the example of Westminster Abbey to win acceptance of the choice—a Pantheon baptized a temple and carefully cleansed of all saintly patronage. Despite the syncretism of the procession— which included red-capped stormers of the Bastille, widows, and a woman in uniform designated *La femme vainqueur*—priests were kept at bay. The organizers had thought of including them, however, as is attested by an order of two hundred albs for the cortège. In the end this plan was abandoned, however, and the ceremony, which Charles Villette had hoped would be of "thoroughly religious" inspiration, was the first revolutionary festival to take place without the participation of the clergy.

Through the speeches, inscriptions, brochures, and ceremonial arrangements associated with the event we can gain a better understanding of contemporary images of the great man. For those who organized the Pantheonization, Voltaire was first of all the herald of the revolutionary upheaval. Among the men of letters credited in a general way with having foretold the future, Voltaire enjoyed the signal merit of having written to Chauvelin on April 2, 1764: "Everything I see is sowing the seeds of a revolution that will infallibly arrive and that I shall not have the pleasure of seeing." (He consoled himself by describing with delight the "lovely din" that his "grand-nephews" would enjoy.) This passage was cited and recited, boldly taken out of context (which involved "bishops' pastoral letters that are being burned every day"— Voltaire's thoughts concerned only *l'Infâme*) yet brandished everywhere as proof. Hence it was possible, on November 17, 1791, to hail Voltaire as a "precursor of the Revolution" at a tumultuous performance of *Brutus* during which his bust was carried on stage. A few months later, the artisans of the apotheosis supported their plans with this statement of belief: "Voltaire's piercing gaze read the future and saw the dawn of regeneration, of which he sowed the seeds." In the debate that began, Voltaire was honored not only for having predicted the Revolution but also for having foretold the phenomenon "as we see it." He sensed, Treilhard was certain, "that it could not be delayed." What the men of the Revolution took from Voltaire's work was thus the rumor of imminence, the certainty that a new order was on the march. "A beautiful century is in preparation," he had said. Only "two or three years perhaps" remained before that "revolution" (and it mattered little to the incense-bearers that the meaning of the word "revolution" had changed dramatically since 1764 and that Voltaire had used it very freely). The tone of triumph evident most notably in the writings on tolerance was not lost. It was possible to publish excerpts from the *Philosophical Dictionary* under the title *Cahiers de Voltaire aux Etats Généraux.*

The herald of the Revolution was also a worker, whose works, the *Courrier de Provence* wrote in July 1791, were "the very arms used in the destruction of the Bastille." It is striking to see how rapidly the view of the Enlightenment as artisan of the Revolution—an illusion of hindsight that would be developed further in the nineteenth century—became, despite grumbling, lucid, always isolated voices (such as Mounier's), a commonplace. True, in 1791 a list was drawn up of important measures already passed by the Constituent Assembly and supposedly derived from Voltaire's works: freedom of the press, unification of legal codes, reform of criminal procedure, wages for priests. One of the brochures that defended the Pantheonization of Voltaire against the Jansenist group (a shrewd choice of enemy, given that hostility to Jansenism was what unified Voltaire's life and thought) recapitulated the Voltairian principles now embodied in reality: "Religion confined within its limits, the disciples of Jesus rendering unto Caesar what is Caesar's, the power of kings limited and made subject to the law, the palaces of vengeance overthrown, petty tyrants destroyed." It was chiefly the religious policy of the Constituent Assembly that provided the occasion for this presentation of Voltairian philosophy; the debate over ecclesiastical properties was hailed at the Jacobin Club by an obscure member who rose to say that every statute approved by the Assembly could be found in Voltaire. The debate on the regular clergy was conducted by Treilhard in entirely Voltairian terms, even down to those compromises required by social utility (such as preservation of institutions in which religious cared for the sick or undertook to educate children). As for the "good curé" of the early Constituent Assembly, the one who maintained the parish birth records, kept peace in the family, and refrained from theological disputes, the model could be found in the *Philosophical Dictionary* in the person of the debonair Théotime who would not have been displeased by a "sweet, pleasant, decent wife." The brochures were therefore able to spin out the theme of a Voltaire practicing the art of being a grandfather to "his granddaughter," the Revolution.

Seldom were the Revolution's debts to Voltaire precisely spelled out in Assembly debates, however, and seldom was the man or his work so much as mentioned. Not a word about Voltaire occurs in the debate, so Voltairian in tone, on clerical property, with the exception of an obscure allusion by Garat or, again, the denial that the question had anything to do with the "new philosophy." Nor was there a word in Bergasse's report on the judiciary, though it was full of measures (publicity of prosecution, responsibility of judges) dear to the Voltairian spirit. The Revolution's image of Voltaire was not that of a man who had laid out in advance a list of reforms to be carried out. It was something much more powerful and impressive: the image of an indefatigable champion of justice. On the sarcophagus that made its way across Paris were inscribed the words: "He defended Calas, Sirven, La Barre, Montbailli." Calas' daughters, as has been mentioned, were present at the ceremony. In 1793 the Convention ordered that an expiatory column be erected in Toulouse on the place where Calas was tortured. It was "Calas' champion," the avenger of Lally, that the Revolution saw in Voltaire. It neglected Voltaire the speculator and theorist and laid stress on the Voltaire who passionately hoped to see his ideas embodied in this world. Its Voltaire was that of Michelet, "the man who suffered, the universal victim, whose throat was slit on Saint Bartholomew's day, who was burned at Seville, and whom the parlement of Toulouse broke on the wheel along with Calas." And Michelet concluded: "Old athlete, here is thy crown." And there, in the procession to the Pantheon, a crown of stars was actually brandished by the statue of Immortality over the body stretched out in the ancient manner on its sarcophagus, "in an attitude of sleep."

The old champion of justice was inseparable from the champion of liberty. Voltaire's views on the subject of liberty of course varied a great deal. He began by identifying liberty with will. Somewhat later, his reading of Locke persuaded him that the idea of free will is an absurdity (it makes no sense to say, "I want to will") and that all liberty is contained in the power to execute: for a paralytic, to be free is not to want to move but to be able to move. The *Philosophical Dictionary* made it plain that in controversies over liberty some envisioned the power to act, others the power to will, and still others the power to execute. Voltaire belonged to the last group, because his speculative uncertainties did little to modify his deep sense of liberty as the human capacity to free oneself from tradition, to define a new order and give it life. The idea of negative liberty, in which man is subject to no power other than the laws (a notion that he learned from the English and in fact revered) was always accompanied in Voltaire's mind by a positive image of man's ability to break the bonds of slavery, servitude, and perpetual vows. It was this ability that received attention from the revolutionary brochures, and not only from those devoted to freedom of the press, which were quite naturally placed under Voltaire's patronage. All honored Voltaire's tireless activism, his preaching, recruiting, and militancy, as well as the proudly independent manner in which he could write that "the past is as though it never existed" and that one must "always start from wherever one happens to be," even if they were more apt to quote this superficial Alexandrine: *Le héros conquérant n'a pas besoin d'aieux* (The conquering hero has no need of ancestors). When the Assembly first debated what honors to bestow on Voltaire, one deputy proposed that he be called the "liberator of thought." And Lamartine looked upon the coffin making its entry into Paris as "liberty, which took possession of the city and of the temple of Sainte-Geneviève," which to him proved that the Revolution had most pertinently understood itself.

Did the apotheosis of Voltaire, which coincided with the trauma of Varennes (and the final destruction of the very Voltairian idea of a beneficent king-legislator), mark the end of a reign? Did the triumph of Voltaire, which set the tone for the liberal Revolution, clear the way for the reign of Rousseau, who was more in tune with the egalitarian Revolution, and thus for a second phase of the revolutionary process according to the division of time proposed by Louis Blanc? In appearance this was the way things went. First came a series of skirmishes in which Robespierre played the leading role. The most significant of these took place at the Jacobin Club in April 1792. Robespierre intensified his attacks on the "party of intriguers," or accomplices of Narbonne, and on Guadet, Fauchet, Brissot, and Condorcet. The latter allegation nettled Brissot: how dare Robespierre attack a man who for thirty years had stood "with Voltaire and d'Alembert" in their duels with the throne and with superstition and fanaticism? Robespierre replied: "The Revolution has cut many men of the Ancien Régime down to size." Though he did not name Voltaire, he was indeed the target of Robespierre's ire in the portrait he drew of men of letters who flattered the great and fawned on kings. His major speech of 18 Floréal, Year II, concerning "the relation of religious and moral ideas to republican principles," Robespierre's true political testament, casts his suspicion of Voltaire's teachings in its definitive form. The overpraised great man belonged to the "sect" that "in politics never got as far as the people's rights" and "in morals went far beyond the destruction of religious prejudices." Furthermore, Voltaire had been among the persecutors of Jean-Jacques. This negative portrait, which gave force to Louis Blanc's interpretation, invariably resulted from a comparison with the poor vicar of Savoy, whose "Profession of Faith" was an academic exercise that Rousseau had modeled on Bernardin de Saint-Pierre. One final point is worth mentioning: the number of references to Voltaire decreased as the Revolution proceeded, an observation confirmed by the austere method of counting. In 4,500 pamphlets and brochures from the years 1791, 1792, and 1793, R. Galiani points out that in 1791 Voltaire, probably because of the battle against Catholicism, was mentioned more frequently than Rousseau; in 1792 the two writers were invoked equally often; and in 1793 Rousseau pulled ahead of Voltaire, while the overall number of references diminished steadily, as if the Revolution felt less and less need to place itself under anyone's patronage.

It is difficult, however, to accept such a sharp division between the two eras. The period supposedly dominated by Voltaire (1789–1791) was far from a time of unanimity. An incident in the very first days of the Revolution enables us to gauge Catholic hostility: the dedication to the Assembly of Voltaire's *Works*. Grégoire insisted that deliberations be postponed until it could be determined whether or not the edition would be expurgated. Preparations for the Pantheonization rekindled this opposition. A virulent group of Jansenists banded together in opposition, and a host of alternative proposals were made, some seeking to dilute the individual apotheosis in a general award of prizes (with crowns going to Montesquieu, Mably, and Rousseau as well as Voltaire), others to avoid it altogether. Lanjuinais attempted to get on with the business of the day by observing that Voltaire might have merited the gratitude of mankind but not the esteem. Some half of the pamphlets published in connection with the occasion were hostile. Concerning Voltaire, a "destructive genius" according to the authors of a petition to transport Rousseau's remains to the Pantheon in August 1791, a whole segment of revolutionary opinion was not prepared to lay down its arms. To mention only one telling example, consider the controversy that divided the editors of *La bouche de fer* in 1790—Fauchet on one side, Cloots on the other. For Fauchet, beneath Voltaire's prose one can always detect "the ordinary gentleman, the lord in his castle, the master of good form," frivolous, fickle, sarcastic, a stranger to equality, in a word an aristocrat—perhaps the least suitable of all epithets that might be applied to Voltaire. Above all it was inconceivable in honoring Rousseau to honor at the same time the man who was so hostile to him (for Sébastien Mercier in *2440* this is reason enough to burn Voltaire's works). Fauchet called for consistency, citing a wish that would often come up again for compatibility among those buried in the Pantheon. It would be illogical to engage in "discordant devotions to geniuses so absolutely opposed in sentiments and principles." Cloots replied that Fauchet understood nothing of Voltaire because he was insensitive to the "concept of French liberty." This French, wholly Voltairian idea was original in that it presented liberty as a product of the Enlightenment, whereas Fauchet—and on this point Cloots is quite perspicacious—saw it as the fruit of Christianity, an idea that to Voltaire would have seemed the height of absurdity. With the newspaper's editors and its readership divided over the issue, Bonneville attempted to mediate: Voltaire had his weaknesses, above all that of placing his hopes in an enlightened government, but these were the weaknesses of the age. One must avoid the anachronism of ascribing to Voltaire's time hopes that could not possibly have arisen then. The consequence is obviously to emancipate the Revolution from Voltaire's influence.

To put the citation counts in proper perspective, it should be said that Voltaire was not quoted in the same way as Rousseau. The men of the Revolution made extensive use of Voltairian texts (in the revolutionary decade there were six editions of his complete works and two editions of selected excerpts), but only as a repository of lapidary maxims taken out of context and well suited for inscription on banners or for calling attention to a statue's gesture or for accompanying a procession. People found a phrase for every eventuality. There were words to justify the execution of the monarch ("If man has tyrants, he ought to dethrone them"); to lambaste the Pope for condemning the execution ("In the depths of the Vatican his policy reigned"); to support revolutionary war, a use that was almost too far-fetched for an author so little given to patriotism ("How dear is the fatherland to all well-born hearts"); to celebrate liberty ("Liberty is engraved in my heart, and horror of kings"); and, more surprisingly, to celebrate equality: "*Les mortels sont égaux, ce n'est pas la naissance, c'est la seule vertu qui fait la différence"* ("Mortals are equal; it is not birth but only virtue that makes the difference"), two lines from *Mahomet* that were the most widely cited in the Revolution. We cannot say for sure whether this selective citation would have displeased a man who was no fanatical devotee of consecutive thought. It does, however, suggest a certain lack of deference, a far cry from the emotional and syncretic use made of Rousseau at the same time.

Thus it is impossible to distinguish a period in the Revolution when Voltaire reigned unchallenged over the minds of men. The Thermidorian Convention and the Directory, whose leaders invoked his name and were in any case out for vengeance against Robespierre and Rousseau, did not really belong to him; circumstances did not allow these anticlericals to pursue a steady and consistent anticlerical policy. Nor can Voltaire be used to identify a political family. Some Montagnards (Romme, for example) were fervent Voltairians, and Robespierre himself drew on Voltaire when necessary ("If God did not exist, it would be necessary to invent him"). As for the Girondins, repeatedly described as Voltaire's men because of the Guadet incident and because Condorcet had written a *Life of Voltaire,* they were actually admirers of Rousseau who saw, in the words of Brissot, an "immense gap" between the two philosophes. "O Montesquieu, O Voltaire, and you, my dear Rousseau!" exclaimed Bonneville. Buzot, Mme. Roland, and all the rest distinguished between their admiration for Voltaire and their worship of Rousseau. Even Volney, an unwavering supporter of Voltaire whose pseudonym was a compound of the first syllable of *Vol*taire and the second syllable of Fer*ney,* acknowledged this point in his *Leçons d'histoire:* "If you attack Voltaire in front of his supporters, they defend him ardently with argument and jest and see you as a person of bad taste; but if you attack Rousseau in front of his, you occasion in them a kind of religious horror, and they look upon you as a scoundrel." More sarcastically, Cloots said that Voltaire made philosophers and Rousseau, sectarians. The emotional climate in which Voltaire was cited was therefore not at all comparable with that surrounding Rousseau. Between the man who destroys and the man who rebuilds—to borrow the themes of Bernardin's comparison, the man who uses wealth and the man who uses poverty, the man who is of the city and the man who is of the fields, the man whose work impresses by breadth and the man whose work impresses by depth—the Revolution made an unambiguous choice. And when it was over, people still associated the Revolution with Rousseau. Its ties with Voltaire, on the other hand, were severed: between 1814 and 1824 alone, 1,600,000 copies of his works were printed, a fabulous figure for the time. Rémusat recounted that in the reactionary salon of his grandmother, Mme. de Vergennes, where "it would have been unsafe to advocate incautiously even the ideas of the Constituent Assembly, people continued to adore Voltaire and to declare that he had no equal."

What were the reasons for this difference, and what was it in Voltaire that prevented him from being fully assimilated by the revolutionary spirit? His lack of any inclination toward democracy springs to mind. Joseph de Maistre maintained that Voltaire would have liked only the irreligious aspect of the Revolution and "would have abhorred the rest, for no man was more hostile than he to equality of any kind." Nineteenth-century socialists would stress his tough realism, which enabled him to accept democratic egalitarianism ("a cardinal's cook can surely call himself a man, just like his master") while rejecting social equality ("the cook is a cook, at least until the Grand Turk conquers Rome"). Voltaire's obstinate insistence that a high court official would have no idea how to make shoes was singled out by hostile brochures that portrayed him as a man who poured scorn on the common people. This line of criticism was less prominent, however, than the charge that Voltaire was anti-Christian; it was as if the image of Voltaire as antidemocratic had been countered by the impact of a theater in which salvos of applause greeted the slightest allusion to equality. Similarly, *Brutus,* the most popular play in the period 1790–1793, was able to pass for a republican tragedy and make people forget about Voltaire's weakness for enlightened monarchy.

More obviously repulsive to the Revolution was the image of Voltaire as hedonist, a man who had defined pleasure as virtue's prettier name ("Mortals, in your pleasures recognize a God"). Voltaire's wariness of "meager, pale reasoners," to whom he preferred voluptuaries, played a large part in his excommunication by Robespierre, who contrasted Voltaire with Montesquieu, "the virtuous author of a famous book," and held against him his conviction that virtue "is the principle of no affair, of no political commitment." The profoundly Voltairian idea that human lives are rooted in the passions, the "wheels that make the whole machine go," was antipathetic to both reactionaries and Jacobins; for both, Voltaire was the man for "people without morals."

These remarks raise the suspicion that the Revolution's resistance to Voltaire was rooted in his anthropology. Voltaire's complaint about Mably, Rousseau, and all the "paradoxical books" was that they assumed human nature was other than what it was or believed that it could be transformed. In Voltaire's thought, despite the hymn to progress, there is a great deal of immobility: man is a creature who has his place in the chain of being, who can certainly increase his share of liberty, of intellectual vigor, and of happiness just as he can improve his physique or health, but within the limits of an essentially unalterable human condition. Voltaire's awareness of these limits fosters both pessimism (the human creature is no more than a "tiny louse," nothing at all to the vast machinery of the universe) and optimism, since this wretched creature has been given the improbable gift of reason. His pragmatism also entered into his conception of time; he fought for improvements, but the idea that the whole must be changed before changing any of its parts made no sense to him. He believed in better days to come, but the future did not control his thought any more than did the past, which cut him off so completely from the Rousseauist sensibility. The present, with which compromise was inescapable, remained his great affair. All the things his detractors attributed to conservatism—his feeling that poverty is inevitable and that inequality of conditions is insurmountable—grew out of a social imagination that moved between narrow temporal limits.

By this point we can gauge the degree of incompatibility between Voltaire and the Revolution. The very idea of revolution implied life turned on its head by an extraordinary event capable of transforming the conditions of human happiness and even the elements of human nature. In this conception the Revolution revealed its affinity with Christianity, which also depended on an extraordinary historical event capable of converting men from evil to good. At the same time we sense the reason why the men of the Revolution used Voltaire in both an emblematic and a careless way: Voltairian fixism posed a profound challenge to their enterprise, for as Louis Blanc perceptively observed, renovation of the world struck Voltaire as a "folly of moralists." Babouc, presenting a statuette to the angel Ituriel, raises a fundamental question: must it really be smashed simply because it is not made entirely of gold and diamonds? The apologist's negative answer reveals that Voltaire held firmly to two truths at once, one of which the Revolution could understand while the other was profoundly antipathetic. First, the human capacity for independence must be given its full due. Second, that independence can only be exercised within the limits of human nature. In other words, one must work for a better day but not dream of a better man. New times, perhaps; a new man, surely not.

Mona Ozouf

FURTHER READING

La bouche de fer. Paris, October 1790.

Condorcet, Marie-Jean-Antoine-Nicolas de Caritat, marquis de. *Vie de Voltaire.* Kehl, 1789.

Galiani, R. "Voltaire et les autres philosophes dans la Révolution française: Les brochures de 1791, 1792, 1793," *Studies on Voltaire* (Oxford), vol. 174, 1978.

Mailhos, G. "Le mot 'révolution' dans l'"Essai sur les moeurs' et la 'Correspondance' de Voltaire," *Cahiers de lexicologie* (Paris), no. 13, 1968.

Mounier, Jean-Joseph. *De l'influence attribuée aux philosophes, francs-maçons, et illuminés sur la Révolution de France.* Tübingen, 1801.

Pomeau, René. *La religion de Voltaire.* Paris, 1969.

Waldinger, Renée. *Voltaire and Reform in the Light of the French Revolution.* Geneva, 1956.

RELATED TOPICS

Blanc	Equality	Liberty	Quinet
Burke	Fraternity	Maistre	Robespierre
Condorcet	Girondins	Michelet	Rousseau
Enlightenment	Jaurès	Montesquieu	

Historians and Commentators

5

ACADEMIC
HISTORY OF THE
REVOLUTION

T hroughout the nineteenth century historians of the French Revolution were rarely professors or specialists in the subject. They were usually journalists, writers, activists, or politicians, and these activities were not mutually exclusive or even easy to distinguish: Louis Blanc was a journalist, Lamartine a writer, and Buchez an activist, but all shared a passion for public affairs that stimulated their curiosity about the Revolution. From one end of the century to the other, the field was wide open to all who sought the secrets of contemporary France: Thiers, Mignet, Michelet, Louis Blanc, Quinet, Tocqueville, and Taine, to mention only the most illustrious names. No one had to obtain a research permit or professional credentials from the Sorbonne: the history of the Revolution drew upon a present that it continued to shape, and for that very reason it was not taught at the Sorbonne. It was too volcanic a subject to be tamed by the university.

This was apparent at the end of the July Monarchy, when Quinet and Michelet attempted to include the Revolution in their courses at the Collège de France at the height of the battle with the Catholic Church. They were professors and historians, especially Michelet, who at this time began the vast exhumation of the archives that provided the material for his *Histoire de la Révolution française*. Nevertheless, their courses were professions of faith and ended as public meetings infused with the enthusiasm of the Latin Quarter. Quinet's was suspended in 1846, the year when Michelet chose to treat in his the subject of "French nationality," for which 1789 set the tone. The many publications devoted to the Revolution in these years, and the endless debate of which it was the focus, formed the preface to 1848, when the high drama of the late eighteenth century reappeared with all its roles.

This battle of the heirs over the legacy of the Revolution was what the university historians tried to end a hundred years later, when the history of the Revolution became an academic discipline. This ambition pursued two distinct but convergent courses.

The first was political. The founders of the Third Republic, led by Ferry and Gambetta, finally tamed the heritage of 1789. With the advent of what Ferry called the "definitive government" of France, which in any case represented a broad public consensus concerning democracy, the French Revolution was at last in power. But it was by the same token a national property, prudently administered by a government of the left, without excluding any of its periods or excommunicating any of its heroes, since it was on the Revolution as a whole that the Republic based its claim to rally the entire nation. Somewhat later Clemenceau would come up with the expression "La Révolution est un bloc" ("The Revolution is a unity"). The Republic needed a historian who would rewrite its annals for the benefit of all the children of France.

At the same time history had changed. Under the iron rule of positivism, triumphant after 1870, it reconstituted itself as scientific discourse about the past based on evidence provided by a methodical critique of contemporary documents. The historian was supposed to present, in chronological order, the duly verified facts about his subject, to analyze the relations among those facts, to weigh what uncertainties remained, and if necessary to decide what interpretation was most probable; the critical apparatus that accompanied his narrative made it possible to check his reconstruction of the facts at every point. Driven by the paradoxical ambition to become a science of the particular, and absorbed in procedures of verification, history broke with philosophy—and most of all with philosophies of history—when it subjected itself to the canonical rules of a rigorously constituted academic discipline, a knowledge both transmissible and cumulative.

The creation of a chair of the history of the French Revolution occurred at the point where these two evolutionary processes converged. In 1885 the municipal council of Paris, with its leftist majority, proposed financing a course on the subject in the capital, arguing that it was time to apply the "critical method" to this period in the national history. The first thought was to give this course at the Collège de France, the traditional place for innovations, and Renan, administrator at the time, was favorably disposed. But the minister of public instruction preferred the Faculty of Letters of Paris, where the course was instituted with Aulard assigned to teach it in February 1886. The fortunate candidate's main intellectual claim to nomination by the minister was a work entitled *L'éloquence parlementaire pendant la Révolution*, the last volume of which had just appeared. The inaugural lecture, which was delivered in a calm hall despite the pessimistic prognostications of conservatives, took place on the following March 12. A proven success, the course was transformed into a chair in March 1891 and Aulard, after election by his peers, was appointed as the first full professor of the history of the French Revolution at the Sorbonne.

From this point on, the Revolution became a distinct subject area within the history curriculum of the Faculty of Letters, for the Paris example quickly spread throughout the country, even if the new specialty was often assigned in the provinces to the chair of "modern and contemporary history." In a centralized country like France, Paris sets the tone, and there grew up around the new chair (as well as in opposition to it after Mathiez broke with Aulard in 1908) a whole network of new academic institutions encouraged by the radical Republic and, after 1900, by the Union des Gauches. In 1881 the journal *La Révolution française* was founded, edited by a society of historians and politicians who were both positivists and republicans. The creation of the Paris chair gave new impetus to the journal; Aulard quite naturally assumed its editorship in 1887. At his behest the municipal councils of Lyons and Toulouse endowed chairs similar to his own, and the government provided a small amount of money for the publication of documents. His friend Charavay, an archivist specializing in the study of Parisian electoral assemblies in the period 1789–1791, took steps that culminated in 1888 in the establishment of a Société de l'Histoire de la Révolution. Henceforth, research on 1789 was organized either around or in relation to the Paris chair. When Jaurès in December 1903 persuaded the government to establish a commission responsible for research and publication of documents concerning economic life during the Revolution, with himself as president, it was Aulard, the vice-president, who actually took charge of the commission's activities. When Mathiez broke with Aulard in 1908 he made his bastion the Société des Etudes Robespierristes, founded the previous year by Charles Vellay; and its journal, the *Annales révolutionnaires,* which first appeared in 1908, became his banner. Even after becoming once again a matter of controversy, the history of the French Revolution still inhabited the university and its fringes, and for the most part it has remained there ever since.

This evolution has not been entirely beneficial. By encouraging a rigid periodization of the national past, revolutionary historiography confined itself within a narrow interpretation of its subject. In French universities, "modern" history has ever since ended in 1789 with what the Revolution baptized the "Ancien Régime," which thus obtained, even without a birth certificate, a death warrant. The Revolution, which includes Bonaparte and the Empire, then became a separate and independent field of study, with its own chairs, professors, students, and journals. The quarter-century from 1789 to Waterloo became the watershed of French history, ending the "modern" and inaugurating the "contemporary." It divides the two, therefore defines them, and therefore "explains" them. Thus the Republic made the national past a relatively easy subject to treat as a unit in courses. In the twentieth century there have been no more of those great histories of the Revolution, so numerous in the previous century, that began with Protestantism; henceforth 1789 began in 1787 with the "crisis of the Ancien Régime."

In becoming an academic specialty the history of the Revolution became both more professionalized and more narrow. Scholarship was supposed to extend the range of knowledge and limit that of interpretation. It claimed the certainty of science and narrowed the scope of debate and disagreement. It was enough for the historian to establish the facts according to the rules of the critical method within well-marked chronological boundaries. Finally, the new course in revolutionary history gave the professor privileged rights to exploit the domain. Working with the same basic materials that had sustained the previous century's philosophical and political effervescence, it created career tracks regulated by the initiatory rite of the thesis and the power of the important "patrons" over their disciples. In every possible way it sought guarantees against excess. And in that it has been quite successful, because it has been able to maintain a certain consistency in the overall interpretation of the event over more than a century and across several generations.

It would therefore be unjust to compare the revolutionary historiography of the twentieth century with that of the nineteenth, that of the professors with that of the writers. The latter—that of the nineteenth century—is of course more brilliant and more profound, and it produced the two greatest geniuses ever to write on the subject, Michelet and Tocqueville. It threw off its last sparks during Aulard's reign with Jaurès' *Histoire socialiste,* which appeared in the first years of the twentieth century and remains the handsomest of the great monuments bequeathed to 1789 by the socialist tradition. But after Jaurès, the last writer, the last "amateur" to deal with the Revolution, it is more equitable to measure the achievements of academic history against the goals that it set for itself, given its men and its resources and the framework of its conceptions.

At the outset academic history had two ambitions: to extend our knowledge of the facts and to anchor them in a scientific vision of the event. It has been more successful in achieving the first goal than the second.

Progress in scholarship has been shaped by the curiosities of the "patrons" and by the times. The resources available have never been great: the publication of documents and collections of documents, relatively active at the beginning of the century but greatly slowed after the First World War, has not matched the importance of the subject. In an initial phase, dominated by Aulard, political history was the great beneficiary of the new academic field: the great teacher published the *Recueil des actes du Comité de Salut Public* (Anthology of the Acts of the Committee of Public Safety), followed by a similar compilation of the deliberations of the Jacobin Club. But economic and social history was already receiving aid from the Jaurès Commission, which undertook to make the *cahiers de doléances* of 1789 available to the scholarly public. Indeed, social history gradually became the central focus of original works and scholarly publications in revolutionary historiography, for reasons that are not difficult to understand. The movement of social classes, returned to prominence by Jaurès with the liberal legacy reworked by socialism, became the unchallenged *primum movens* of the Revolution and encouraged study of both the urban popular classes and the peasantry: Mathiez set an example for the first with *La vie chère et le mouvement social sous la Terreur* (1927), and Georges Lefebvre revised thinking about the second with his *Paysans du nord* (1924). Oddly, the victorious class, the bourgeoisie, aroused much less interest, and the same was true of the vanquished nobility. This was because the social interpretation of the Revolution was based not only on Marxism but on a democratic sensitivity to the common folk, the forgotten of history. By this route it made contact with, although it was not simply absorbed by, a more general trend in French historiography born in the period between the two world wars with the journal *Les annales,* which became dominant in the 1950s.

But applied to a subject like the French Revolution and combined with an ambition to become the very foundation of the subject because it touched on the causes of the event, this particular approach, commonly dominated after 1917 by the Leninist version of Marxism, was even less capable of blazing a trail toward a "scientific" interpretation. Ever since Mathiez the ghost of the Russian Revolution has haunted the history of the French Revolution, and a communist vulgate has supplanted Aulard's republican version: this interpretation was the issue implicit in the polemic between the two professors over Danton and Robespierre, in the wake of which the republican hero Danton, denounced as opportunistic and venal, was replaced by the Incorruptible, the incarnation of merciless and uncompromising battle on behalf of the people.

What strange fruit of the intellect, this French Revolution as interpreted by the academic extreme left of the twentieth century! It is simultaneously a work of necessity and an invention of men, a product of capitalism and a circumstantial improvisation, advent of the bourgeoisie and dictatorship of the people. But at least this miscellaneous synthesis has enabled historians to ignore the enigma that had so intrigued liberals—and Marx along with them—a century before, that of the contrast between the results of the Revolution and its unfolding. In any case it has allowed them to celebrate the course of events more than their consequences, to lay even greater stress on 1793 than on 1789, and to admire the Jacobins more than the Constituents. The neo-Jacobin professor was on familiar ground with the men of Year II, because the Soviet experience had demonstrated the necessity of the dictatorship and the Terror.

Thus the mechanisms that led to identification of the Revolution and its heroes with the events of the present have had as much influence on twentieth-century historians as on their nineteenth-century predecessors. Aulard had hoped to set the portrait of the Revolution within a standard frame, but Mathiez and the Russian Revolution created new space for the Jacobin imagination. Progress in academic history has come in the areas of publication of texts, unearthing of sources, and discovery of unexamined issues such as the agrarian problem, but not in the overall scheme of interpretation. The three principal witnesses to this twofold reality are Aulard, Mathiez, and Georges Lefebvre.

Born in 1849, the son of an *inspecteur d'académie,* Aulard was the scion of a Charentaise bourgeoisie loyal to the revolutionary heritage. He began his academic career at the end of the 1870s as a historian of literature after defending a thesis on "the philosophical ideas and poetic inspiration" of the great Italian Romantic, Leopardi. Nonetheless, two things made him a likely candidate for the chair created in 1886: a study of parliamentary eloquence during the French Revolution, the first volume of which appeared in 1882; and his political background, which was republican and secular, with affinities to anticlerical Freemasonry and the precursors of radicalism. A latecomer to the history of the French Revolution, he made up for it with ardent enthusiasm. The odd thing is that this positivist professor drew his reasons for undertaking this mission largely out of his convictions. The goal the great republican mandarin set for himself was to rescue the Revolution from prejudice and passion. This was the ambition of the historical method, whose purpose was to achieve not a philosophical interpretation of 1789 but a cumulative body of knowledge through the patient efforts of present and future specialists.

Energetic, active, imbued with the importance of his task, Aulard achieved an undeniable success in founding a new genre of revolutionary history based on scholarly research and "scientific" prose. In order to appreciate the difference between this genre and what went before, we may compare Aulard's *Révolution française et le christianisme* (1927) with Quinet's work of the same title published three-quarters of a century earlier. Aulard may have borrowed his title from his great republican predecessor, whom he admired (he paid homage to him in his 1886 inaugural lecture), but instead of a discussion of the relations between Christianity and the spirit of 1789 he gave a chronological account of the religious policies of the revolutionary assemblies. History had expelled philosophy, and along with it the great question that had obsessed the nineteenth century, that of the relation between Christianity and democracy; this confrontation was reduced to a narrative of "what happened" between the Catholic Church and the successive powers that embodied the Revolution.

Aulard somewhat naively brandished his fanatical scholarship against those of his predecessors, such as Taine, whom he did not like, but for reasons of a different order. This bristling erudition gives his 1907 attack on Taine's *Origines de la France contemporaine* an aggressively pedantic tone that causes it to miss its target. Nevertheless, the neophyte historian's enthusiasm for original documents and true facts encouraged him in his important and pioneering work in publishing source documents. As the chairman of two ad hoc commissions, one national, the other municipal, Aulard directed the preparation of a compilation of the acts of the Committee of Public Safety, the first volume of which was published in 1889; a short time later he was responsible for two other series of volumes on the Jacobin Club and on public opinion in Paris from 9 Thermidor to the Empire. None of these collections has been spared subsequent criticism by specialists, but all remain useful and utilized.

Aulard had a curious and open mind, as can be seen by any reader of the seven volumes that contain most of his fragmentary contributions to the history of the Revolution. He was interested in the histories of ideas, of institutions, and of revolutionary cults. He outlined a comparative history of the intellectual sources of the American Revolution and the French Revolution based on a comparison of Locke and Rousseau. In 1917 he was responsible for publication of Kant's famous 1797 text opposing the regicide, to which he joined a republican caveat. But the central core of his work, as was normal for the time, comprised a political history of the French Revolution, and the most important of his books today is still the *Histoire politique de la Révolution française,* published in 1901 with the subtitle *Origines et développement de la République, 1789–1804.* This is still the book with which one must begin in order to understand the spirit of the Revolution after it entered the Sorbonne.

The angle from which Aulard studied the political history of the Revolution was paradoxical, given the nature of the event. He was primarily interested in the new institutions and principles and relegated the actual unfolding of events to the background. For him, the Revolution represented the advent of a democratic republic, which was definitively established not by the insurrections of July 14 or August 10 but by two texts proclaiming its legal existence: the Declaration of Rights and the Montagnard Constitution. One from 1789, the other from 1793: Aulard joined the two "moments" so violently separated by so many of his predecessors. The torrent of events constituting the history of the Revolution were in his eyes so many circumstances of that Revolution, vicissitudes of its principles, external and alien to its nature; in some cases, moreover, they could contradict and temporarily delay its benefits.

Thus the Revolution did not exist where other people thought they saw it. It was not in the *journées* but in parliamentary debates, not in insurrections but in institutions. Its history could be written, like that of the Third Republic, in terms of public opinion, democratic elections, organized parties, and parliamentary majorities. Nevertheless, this historical process, within which the two fundamental texts of the new France took shape, was constantly influenced by adverse circumstances, so that the real Revolution, hampered by unfinished business, conflict, and setbacks, only partially fulfilled the promises of the ideal Revolution. The men of 1789 created the famous Declaration of Rights but established *censitaire* suffrage. The men of 1793 made suffrage universal but established the dictatorship and the Terror.

This gap between promise and achievement was where the history of the Revolution lay, yet it did not characterize or determine that history, which strictly speaking consisted solely of all actions leading to the realization of its great principles. The rest, its residue, consisted of all the baggage alien to its true nature that the Revolution inevitably carried with it. Because it was alien to the nature of the Revolution, that baggage was due to something else, to the inertia of things and above all the resistance of enemies. Thus Aulard carried the determination to exonerate the Revolution to an extreme. For him, any difference between the Revolution's proclaimed principles and what actually happened was the result of something that by definition was not the Revolution.

The problem with this kind of interpretation is one of defining externality. Circumstances were different in different periods of the history of the Revolution. While it is true that the periods and the leaders of the Revolution, those of 1789 as well as those of 1793, failed to live up to its message, they did not do so in the same way. Aulard was not an "Eighty-niner," because the Constituent Assembly established a limited suffrage regime that failed to keep the promise of equality. Nor was he a "Ninety-threer," because the dictatorship of Year II abolished the Rights of Man of 1789. But if both regimes betrayed the great principles, the first was the more culpable; its treason was written into the very text of the law, in the reestablishment of electoral privilege in favor of the bourgeoisie. By contrast, the second restored equality through universal suffrage, guaranteed by the Constitution of Year II, but declined to enforce that Constitution; it paid homage to justice but yielded to circumstances. Compared with the bourgeois monarchy of 1789–1791, the

887

democratic republic outlined by the text of June 1793 thus represented a greater fidelity to the Revolution; its lapse into terrorist dictatorship could be blamed exclusively on the circumstances of "public safety."

It is true that in other places Aulard's book gives the impression that the goal of achieving a posthumous reconciliation of the men and periods of the Revolution led him to praise them all equally and thus to join 1789 and 1793 in one uniform benediction. At times the historian's inclination is to grant them all national absolution on grounds of extenuating circumstances. Is it really necessary to say that they renounced one another? No. "Rather, there were no renegades but only good Frenchmen, who did their best in different circumstances, at different moments in our political evolution" (chap. 2, p. 46). This ecumenicism, which extends the excuse of circumstances to phenomena of various kinds, such as the *censitaire* suffrage and the terrorist dictatorship, also makes it the basis of a vague philosophy of history, according to which each period of the Revolution treated the principles of 1789 within the framework of its own specific constraints, all of which are uniformly baptized "circumstances."

What emerges, then, is the view that the Declaration of Rights, coupled with the Constitution of Year II, has ever since the Revolution constituted the fundamental charter of contemporary French history. It became "the political and social program of France after 1789." The calendar of its implementation is infinitely elastic, and so is the principle of equality itself. Hence it is not legitimate, despite the contrary opinion of so many nineteenth-century authors, to see socialism as opposed to the Declaration of Rights, for socialism, too, grew out of the Declaration by extension of the idea of equality to the social and economic sphere. In effect, the men of Year II had built a regime of circumstance, which they called the "revolutionary government." But in that temporary construction they incorporated elements that were destined to enjoy a long life, since such features as the state-controlled economy and egalitarian utopia prefigured nineteenth-century socialist ideologies. For the historian of the republican synthesis this was one more reason to assign central importance in the revolutionary saga to the year 1793. What was dictatorial in Year II could be imputed to the counterrevolution; what prefigured socialism came from its fidelity to 1789. It was thus justified both in what was contingent and in what it showed to be necessary.

The hero in whom this synthesis of the Revolution was incarnated was neither Mirabeau nor Robespierre but Danton: with this syncretistic or, if you will, national cult Aulard avoided the dilemma of choosing between the Constituent Assembly and the Committee of Public Safety, a dilemma that had bitterly divided the left in the nineteenth century. The idea came from Auguste Comte, who, hostile to the sovereignty of the people and to the Assemblies, had hailed in Danton a provisional dictatorship, a period of "naked authority" as a prelude to a government of savants, constituting a transition from the metaphysical age to the positive age (*Cours de philosophie positive*, IV, pp. 289–320). Aulard, faithful to the synthetic republican spirit, adapted this idea by democratizing it. Earlier, Jules Ferry had sought to reconcile the Comtist heritage with the ideas of 1789, the rights of man with science.

The Sorbonne professor's republican ecumenicism thus replaced the nineteenth-century historiographic debate with a conciliatory version of the Revolution. Aulard had read Louis Blanc, Michelet, and Quinet (and Tocqueville?—one wonders), but he cited them infrequently, because to his way of thinking they belonged to a dead tradition. The positivist method had relegated these "philosophical" histories to the scrap heap, and, providentially, it had dispensed its beneficiary from the need to enter into their quarrels. Instead, Aulard needed only to point to the accuracy of the "facts." He substituted a critique of sources for a critique of hypotheses, as though the former fulfilled the same function as the latter.

As a result, the historian was left with no ideas other than the political credo of the fin-de-siècle republican militant, a credo that was taken to be self-evident and yet by default straitjacketed his historical work more tightly than any explicit interpretation would have done. The Revolution was only the first act in a drama whose decisive episode was written a hundred years later with the victory of the republicans. Its history was contained less in what it was than in what it anticipated. Thus the revolutionary phenomenon was reduced to parliamentary activities and organized parties. Lacking concepts, Aulard became caught up in retrospective analogy, from which the Revolution emerged flattened out, tamed, and domesticated by the Third Republic.

In substituting what he called "historical method" for the nineteenth-century debate, Aulard therefore did not free himself, as he believed he had done, from what Quinet called the "philosophy of the Revolution." He simply settled for taking his philosophical version from the atmosphere of the time, as though the philosophy needed no justification. Its central figure was the citizen of the Third Republic, who valued liberty, equality, and secularity and thus reconciled modern individualism with the civic virtues. Citizenship formed the basis for the hope that society would become increasingly free and egalitarian as education and enlightenment progressed. The French Revolution had not been able to finish the job, but it had begun it. Because it had laid down the paths to be followed in the future, its history could be read retrospectively through that of its heir, the radical Republic. And likewise it was possible to model the First Republic on the Third, in a way that seemed almost natural to contemporaries but that very quickly grew old.

The first professor of the history of the French Revolution thought he could end, in the name of science, the intellectual debate over the object of his studies. But before he had laid down his pen, the debate resumed, in the name of science, but on the battleground marked out by so many old polemics: Mathiez took up the socialist banner against the republican Aulard. In opposition to Danton, Robespierre reappeared in the halls of the university.

Aulard's influence was considerable, not only through his works but also through his students and the theses they wrote on revolutionary history under his direction. Of these, the strongest personality was a disloyal disciple, Albert Mathiez, who soon found himself in rebellion against his master's authority and ideas. As punishment for his rebellion, he was never appointed to Aulard's chair, but he had something more: influence.

Born in 1874 into a long line of Franche-Comté peasants, Mathiez exemplified a classic type of French academic: a good student from the provinces, of modest background, who "ascended" to Paris by way of the *khâgne* (preparatory class) and the Ecole Normale Supérieure; the socialist student of the rue d'Ulm (where the Ecole Normale is located) who wore his impoverished childhood on his sleeve, even before it became a useful credential in the certified professor's political activities. Scholastic excellence was the mark of Mathiez's youth, and to it he owed an impeccable scholarly career (graduating from the Ecole Normale in 1893 and passing the *agrégation* in history in 1897) and a precocious political commitment to the left, halfway between sentimental Jacobinism and doctrinal socialism. His academic career was as classic as his pursuit of degrees except for the end, since Mathiez failed to obtain Aulard's sacrosanct chair. Awarded the doctorate in 1904 for a thesis on theophilanthropy and the *décadaire* cult (and a secondary thesis on "the origins of the revolutionary cults"), he was appointed to a teaching position in a Paris lycée in 1906 and to faculty posts at Besançon in 1911 and Dijon in 1919. Although he failed to succeed Aulard in 1923 (Philippe Sagnac was elected to the chair), he nevertheless taught in Paris from 1926 on, first as a lecturer at the Sorbonne and then with a joint appointment at the Ecole Pratique des Hautes Etudes. He died prematurely in 1932, of a stroke suffered during one of his lectures.

The great event of his professional life was his quarrel with Aulard, who had been the director of his thesis. The break came in 1908, when Mathiez joined the Société des Etudes Robespierristes, which had been founded the previous year, and contributed to the first issue of its journal, the *Annales révolutionnaires*, thus breaking the scholarly monopoly previously exercised by Aulard's journal, *La Révolution française*. As in all cases of this kind, the precise circumstances of the mutual disaffection are not well known. But the reasons for it at least seem so clear that what is surprising is that the two men had remained on good terms prior to 1908. At that time Aulard was a pontiff, a distributor of theses and credits, surrounded by disciples and clients, a man who had succeeded in identifying his subject with his chair and almost with his person. Mathiez, already the author of several books, was meanwhile pawing the ground with impatience at the lycée. He was and would remain throughout his life irascible and violent. He not only had better credentials than his master but had received better, or at any rate more standard, training in "positive" history; and he had read and loved Durkheim. All these differences, rooted in the gap between two generations, were compounded by a political difference. Aulard was a radical, Mathiez a socialist; Aulard was a republican bourgeois, Mathiez believed that it was necessary to go beyond the radicals' conception of the Republic by bringing the common people into politics. Both took their battle masks from their common field of study: Danton for Aulard, Robespierre for Mathiez. In the nineteenth century illustrious ancestors had been used as examples or foils in political battles. In the twentieth century they dropped out of the public repertory but continued to play the same part on the more limited stage of academic life. In passing from Michelet to Aulard and from Louis Blanc to Mathiez, Danton and Robespierre ceased to serve as models and became roles.

Mathiez's socialism is not easy to define, for it was more instinctual than doctrinal. Its roots, like those of Aulard's radicalism, are to be found in the revolutionary tradition that grew out of the Dreyfus Affair, in membership in the budding League of the Rights of Man, and in the Union des Gauches. Mathiez's admiration for Jaurès' *Histoire socialiste* was not all that different from Aulard's: admiration for the whole, criticism of small details. Nevertheless, the book laid greater stress on the value of the social interpretation through class conflicts and alliances. Mathiez took from Jaurès the rudiments of an elementary Marxism, which would remain the framework for his explanation of the Revolution: 1789 was the victory of the bourgeoisie, but in order to win, the bourgeoisie had had to call on the support of the people, at the cost of socialist concessions to the interests of the masses. This break with Aulard distorted Mathiez's positions all the more because it quickly led to a series of vile personal attacks by the master's one-time disciple, who thus vented his hatred of the "republican" bourgeoisie. Once again the Incorruptible brought Aulard-Danton to trial.

The summer of 1914 turned this pacifist socialist, along with his comrades, into a militant opponent of German barbarism, and he held up the centralized dictatorship of Year II as a precedent and an example: the professor from Besançon, who had become a journalist, repeatedly proposed the Convention as a model to the lackadaisical republicans who governed in Paris. In March 1917 he enthusiastically hailed the Russian Revolution, daughter of the French Revolution. Since he soon came to believe that with Kerensky it had fallen into the hands of the "Girondins," he considered the events of October as a victory for the Montagnards. But it was a victory that soon disappointed him, because the bolsheviks, instead of carrying out a policy of "public safety," made a separate peace at Brest-Litovsk.

This disaffection did not last beyond the end of the war, however. In the "blue horizon Chamber" Mathiez saw the return of the counterrevolutionaries. In opposition he joined the young communist party in 1920, once again identifying the bolsheviks with the Jacobins: "Jacobinism and bolshevism are in the same way both dictatorships, born of civil war and foreign war, two class dictatorships, employing the same means—terror, requisition, and taxes—and in the final analysis striving toward a similar goal, the transformation of society, and not just Russian society or French society but universal society" (*Le bolchevisme et le jacobinisme*, Paris, 1920). This is a key sentence, for with it Mathiez baptizes the turn in revolutionary historiography of which he was the incarnation and from which we are just emerging. After him, discourse on the French Revolution contained between the lines a second discourse on the Soviet Revolution. The historian could adduce the similarity between the two events and the apparent legacy of one to the other in substituting Russia for France in the role of avant-garde nation: the young Soviet Union inherited from the Republic of 1792 the revolutionary mission of advancing the cause of mankind. The bolsheviks had Jacobin ancestors, and the Jacobins had communist anticipations; Lenin and Robespierre fought the same battle.

From this point of view it is of relatively little importance that Mathiez did not remain a member of the communist party for very long and that, allergic to the military discipline imposed by the Comintern, he rejoined the independent extreme left in 1922. Like so many others, he left the party without giving up the intellectual model that had brought him to it. The party, moreover, continued to show a great concern for his contribution to the history of the Revolution, which gave official sanction to the notion that the rightful heirs of the Jacobin legacy were Lenin and later Stalin. In this respect, Mathiez did indeed win out over Aulard. By shifting the Jacobin investment from its natural beneficiary, the Third Republic, to a new object, the Soviet Union, Mathiez canceled out the absorption of illustrious ancestors by the radical party, a play for which he had harshly criticized his former teacher. Instead he substituted another analogy, another anachronism, another teleology through which the multifarious power of identification that the Revolution exercises on its historians manifested itself once more, but this time in an academic mode. Whereas Aulard had identified with Danton, Mathiez dedicated himself to Robespierre.

Thus the final echoes of the great nineteenth-century left-wing debates rang out in the rarefied atmosphere of the twentieth-century Sorbonne. Aulard believed that, having sculpted the Revolution's definitive mask, he had installed it amid republican furnishings. Mathiez set the debate in motion again by restoring the Revolution's status as a prefiguration of socialism. As a result, the dictatorship of Year II and its leader were now justified not by the external circumstances with which they had had to cope but by the class politics they instituted against the bourgeoisie in the service of the poor masses. For Aulard, the greatness of 1793 lay in the Montagnard Constitution, which, though never implemented, stood as an isolated monument to democracy. For Mathiez, it was the dictatorship itself that stood out as the poor classes' instrument against the wealthy classes. As a prelude to that dictatorship, the combat between the Girondins and the Montagnards set representatives of antagonistic social groups at loggerheads; and although the Montagnards, of bourgeois origin like their rivals, were not socialists, they were driven by circumstances to act as "proxies of the lower class" (*Girondins et Montagnards*, p. 11).

Both the intellectual deficiency and the political influence of Mathiez's work stem from this overall structure of interpretation. The part that has aged worst is that which concerns the Danton-Robespierre debate. Not that it added nothing to knowledge of revolutionary political history: Mathiez's implacable hatred of Aulard's false idol put him on the track of documents that enabled him to prove, or at least to make a very plausible case, that Danton was corrupt. But the latter-day prosecutor drew more from the "evidence" than it had to offer, for it is hardly enough to explain, much less to justify, the famous trial of April 1794, when Danton was prevented from speaking in order to be more easily condemned to death on Robespierre's orders. Like his favorite hero and in obedience to his example, the Jacobin historian constantly mingled private virtue with revolutionary politics, and this approach provided him with material for an indictment less hastily cobbled together than the one on which Danton was tried, but just as fraudulent as that trial, for the Terror did not rely on ironclad indictments or on investigations of morality. Mathiez loved Robespierre for the same reasons he hated Danton: because he was chaste, convinced, and virtuous. He wrote a hagiography of the Incorruptible's works, which combines moralizing naiveté with partisan fanaticism in order to turn the frightful spring of 1794 into a fleeting triumph for fraternity around the laws of Ventôse and the festival of the Supreme Being but which concludes sadly, using his hero's own vocabulary: "Alas! If Robespierre was able to unite a majority of the French in a common patriotic feeling, the moment was brief and his triumph had no future. Calumny, envy, fear, and crime would undermine his work and the Republic itself" (*Etudes sur Robespierre,* reprinted 1973, p. 183).

In Mathiez's contributions to the political history of the Revolution (among which I include his works on religious history, which actually belong to the political genre), there is always a hidden agenda that spoils the documentary aspect. The Revolution is constantly distorted by the future it was supposed to prefigure: the Constituents were not so much the inventors of the rights of man as the conservators of bourgeois liberties; the Girondins were not so much the authors of the spring 1793 Constitution as the spokesmen for the wealthy classes; and Robespierre with the laws of Ventôse prefigured the distribution of property to the people. In placing the Year II at the center of the Revolution, this anachronistic prejudice is unfaithful to its own premises, which in effect define the French Revolution as a seizure of power by the bourgeoisie. But this approach does at least have one advantage, which is to orient the history of the Revolution toward research in social history, on which Jaurès had already laid stress at the beginning of the century. In this respect, Mathiez's *La vie chère et le mouvement social sous la Terreur,* published in 1927, was a seminal work.

The book was the first systematic study of the popular classes (especially in Paris) to consider the pressure they exerted on the series of governments that ruled the Revolution from the spring of 1792 to 9 Thermidor 1794. Mathiez revealed the demands of the urban poor for economic regulation, the increasing pressure for state intervention on deputies imbued with the *laisser faire–laisser passer* ideas of the physiocrats, and the ultimate establishment of a general *maximum* on prices and wages in September 1793 in exchange for the political liquidation of the enragé leaders, whom Hébert then attempted to replace. Mathiez saw the Paris activists who clamored for controls and requisitions more as precursors of socialism than as people nostalgic for the grain policies of the monarchy. In seeking out additional ancestors for the ideas he held dear, however, he opened up a new field of study, in which many historians in subsequent generations would work.

*
***

Georges Lefebvre, born in 1874, the same year as Mathiez, was not appointed to the chair of the history of the French Revolution at the Sorbonne until 1937, after he had taught in the Faculty of Letters in Clermont-Ferrand and at Strasbourg (from 1928 on). After receiving his *docteur ès lettres* in 1924 for a thesis on the "Peasants of the North" during the French Revolution, he succeeded Mathiez in 1932 as president of the Société des Etudes Robespierristes and as editor of the *Annales historiques de la Révolution française.* Thus when he succeeded Philippe Sagnac in Aulard's chair at the age of sixty-three years, he symbolized Mathiez's posthumous revenge. The Société des Etudes Robespierristes finally occupied the throne of revolutionary history. Georges Lefebvre retired in 1945, but he remained the unchallenged master of that domain until his death in 1959.

In the best portrait we have of him, the English historian Richard Cobb portrays Lefebvre after the Second World War as a solitary and somewhat eccentric old man but still the picture of republican virtue that he had so long admired in the hero of Year II. Austere, dry, not very friendly, suspicious of life's pleasures and amenities, Georges Lefebvre was a man of two passions: equality and science. A socialist until 1940 and a fellow traveler of the communist party after the war, he may be compared in this respect to Mathiez. The two men, who though the same age did not know each other very well, were similar in the prejudice and narrowness of spirit that were so obvious, for example, in their common detestation of what preceded and what followed the Revolution: the world of the aristocracy and Thermidorian society. Similarly, both historians ignored or despised any history of the Revolution that was not done exactly as they would have done it; that they despised the version of the French academic right goes without saying, but they also detested the history that was developing with remarkable vigor in British and American universities. What were these interlopers doing in France's backyard? Mathiez understood nothing of Crane Brinton's work in comparative social history of the Revolution, and twenty years later Georges Lefebvre summarily dismissed Alfred Cobban's critiques of the social interpretation of the Revolution.

In Lefebvre, however, the scientific spirit more fully tamed political passion and narrow loyalties than in Mathiez. While Mathiez usually used archival documents the way a lawyer uses a piece of evidence, to demonstrate what he already knows in advance, his successor was a more modern and more rigorous positivist. At a very early stage in his career he immersed himself in rural history in order to discover the secrets of the Revolution in the countryside, and his 1924 thesis was a very original book compared with the Aulard-Mathiez debate, which never interested him. All his life he remained a passionate adept of social history, a tireless explorer of mountains of documents who shared with the founders of the *Annales* a taste for geography and a sociological curiosity imbibed from Durkheim and Halbwachs. He thus brought to the history of the French Revolution not simply what it already had aplenty—the Jacobin sensibility, a turn-of-the-century Marxism learned from Jaurès and Guesde, and political narrow-mindedness—but also something new: sociological history, statistical analysis of the sources, borrowings from other disciplines.

His essential contribution was in the area of rural history. Pursuing an avenue first opened up by the Russian Luchisky in the early years of the twentieth century, Lefebvre set out to determine the impact of the Revolution on the French peasantry; out of this search grew his immense monograph on the peasants of the north and the later synthetic essays in which the historian attempted to take the measure of what Michelet had called "the internal conquest of France by itself, *the conquest of the land by the man who worked it,* the greatest change that had ever taken place in property since the agrarian laws of antiquity and the barbarian invasion." Like Luchisky before him, Lefebvre set this social revolution in its proper context by showing that, to a large extent, peasants were already the owners of the land before 1789 and the sale of the national properties. But the most novel aspect of his contribution was his stress on the autonomy of the peasant movement within the Revolution and the existence of tensions and conflicts between poor peasants and *laboureurs* (that is, peasants prosperous enough to own a plow and a team of oxen). The first idea made it possible to restore autonomy to the peasantry and thus to understand that more than one revolution was at work in *the* Revolution, and that these revolutions did not always or necessarily intersect. The second illustrated the development of a rural capitalism that tended to make the poor poorer and the rich richer, particularly through the division and enclosure of communal lands. This capitalism considerably predated 1789, and its spirit had to a large extent penetrated the landed aristocracy. "The Ancien Régime," Lefebvre wrote in 1932 (*La Révolution française et les paysans*), "had started the agrarian history of France down the road of capitalism. The Revolution abruptly finished the task that the Ancien Régime had begun." Hence the poor peasantry, which rose in opposition to the seigneurs and their feudal rights in 1789 and which was encouraged by the political atmosphere of the time, was also occasionally capable of turning against the bourgeois Republic a little later on. It was the people of the countryside, also artisans of the Revolution but on their own behalf, who soon found themselves in the position of a counterweight to the development of an English-style capitalist society.

Since Lefebvre, this thesis has given rise to a vast historical literature dealing with the ambiguous relation between the anticapitalist peasantry and the "bourgeois" Revolution. It has recently been challenged by two historians from very different backgrounds, the Soviet professor Ado and the American researcher Hilton Root. Both see the poor peasantry as an anti-seigneurial class that nonetheless favored a market economy which was in every way compatible with powerful rural communities. The question, which has not been resolved and which probably has several different answers depending on regional differences, in any case demonstrates the importance of Georges Lefebvre's work in rural history. With its Marxist outlook, that work leads to a reconsideration of the problem of class alliances within the bourgeois revolution. By restoring the autonomy and historical dignity of the peasantry, it has recovered the deepest social roots of revolutionary (and in some instances counterrevolutionary) events. Just as Mathiez's *La vie chère* opened the way to the study of the urban popular classes, Lefebvre's *Paysans du nord* (published three years earlier) spawned countless historians of rural France at the end of the eighteenth century.

Lefebvre was not interested solely in reconstructing the economic and social situation of the common people. He was also interested in people's behavior and in the "mentalities" that behavior presumably reflected. This was the subject of his book on *The Great Fear of 1789*, published in 1932, which sought to trace the itineraries of the various reports and rumors that caused peasants to mobilize and arm themselves in July and August of 1789 and then, in some places, to move on to attacks against châteaux and to the burning of land registers. A diffuse hatred of seigneurial rights coalesced around widespread rumors of imaginary threats and gave rise to a powerful collective spirit.

Another topic in the history of mentalities, which Lefebvre treated in a classic 1934 article entitled "Foules révolutionnaires" ("Revolutionary Mobs"), is the punitive fanaticism of the politicized urban masses, such as the Parisian sans-culottes. Lefebvre sees this fanaticism as the source of the Terror, but he detects its obsessive presence from the very beginning of the Revolution, well before the nation found itself in any peril. He shows that this state of mind grew out of the ubiquitous idea of an "aristocratic plot" and led to collective behavior that alternated between panic and massacre. The elements of Lefebvre's psychology of revolutionary crowds were drawn from Gustave le Bon and Durkheim. In adapting them to his own subject, Lefebvre also ascribed to them a basis in the political reality of the times, since the notorious plots that were so feared by the people and denounced before the fact ultimately did come into being, so that the punitive reaction was also a defensive reaction. Thus the historian took the view that what he called the "revolutionary mentality" was a collective passion that was to some extent rational; he exonerated it of the charge of being gratuitous violence.

A word remains to be said about Lefebvre's contribution to the general history of the Revolution. Among twentieth-century historians he possessed the most extensive and trustworthy knowledge of the subject. His book *Quatre-vingt-neuf* (*Eighty-Nine*), published on the 150th anniversary of the event in 1939, usefully refocused attention on that crucial year of the Revolution. Lecture notes from his Sorbonne courses, available in reproduction, even today constitute an exceptional repository of knowledge, on which Lefebvre comments in a deliberately pedagogical and lackluster style that suited his erudite Jansenist temperament. His general work, published in 1951, and the *Napoleon* that followed it, both alert to the larger history of Europe, have not been replaced to this day. In addition, he was responsible for countless scholarly publications and for innumerable reviews in the *Annales historiques de la Révolution française*. Compared with Mathiez, Georges Lefebvre brought a more objective spirit to the event-oriented history of the French Revolution, a spirit less dominated by partisan political passions. This objectivity is typified by his judicious resolution of the Danton-Robespierre debate: Danton probably was venal, but the fact did not justify the vast range of consequences that Mathiez deduced from it. More generally, Lefebvre gives a less "socialist" analysis of the terrorist dictatorship of Year II than his predecessor and treats Robespierre as a less venerable figure. For example, he properly saw the sans-culotte demands for price controls as an archaic reaction, and he viewed the coalition of Montagnard bourgeois and egalitarian activists as a marriage of strange bedfellows, the "Popular Front" of its day, torn by contradictory forces and demands; accordingly, he was able to see Robespierre as occupying a centrist political position, the provisional leader of a fragile alliance.

The best academic historian of the Revolution also offers the best illustration of what the history of the subject has gained and lost in becoming an academic specialty. Among the gains we must count not only a more accurate knowledge of facts and events but also the enrichment of scholarship through curiosity in new areas such as the social and ideological study of the common classes. In the loss column, however, we must include the bizarre fact that, in France, academic historical science has developed since the end of the nineteenth century as the negation of philosophy. All the great questions that were raised in connection with the French Revolution in the preceding century have therefore disappeared, and it is enough to read, for example, Lefebvre's introduction to Tocqueville's *L'Ancien Régime et la Révolution* or his review of a new edition of Edgar Quinet to see that they had ceased even to be understood. In his historical work these questions were replaced either by scientistic pretensions or by his opinions. Marxism, whatever its vintage, turned out to be a providential instrument for bestowing an appearance of unity on this confused mélange. As a science of history, it is supposed to contain the secrets of interpretation and thus to eliminate any need to delve more deeply into what has already been said. Erudition remains indispensable, the hallmark of the true specialist, but its role is simply to provide a supplement to science, to fill in the blanks in an already familiar picture. As a revolutionary doctrine, a prefiguration of socialism, it also provides the left-wing professor with a body of ideas attuned to his sentiments, ideas that reinforce his devotion to the great ancestors by coupling it with loyalty to the new Jacobins of his own day. A single but telling example will suffice to show the blinding prejudice in Lefebvre's work, because it has to do with the part of revolutionary history that interested him the most. The same historian who devoted his life to the study of the peasantry as an autonomous class in its relation to the Revolution never manifested the slightest curiosity in the greatest peasant movement of the time, the Vendée. Like the Convention of 1793, he considered the Vendean peasant only in the light of the counterrevolution.

A great specialist and great scholar, Georges Lefebvre was nevertheless a narrow historian, unbeatable when it came to scouring the archives but a stranger to the great texts that defined the limits of his chosen field of research. As a result, many of the fundamental questions raised by the French Revolution eluded him. Nevertheless, of those that his training and cast of mind allowed him to embrace, such as the topic of rural France during the Revolution, he created a new historiographical discipline and brought greater objectivity to the revolutionary narrative history he inherited from his predecessors, a history to which he made many scholarly contributions. Lefebvre's work illustrates better than that of any other historian which questions academic history explored and which it avoided.

***

The results of this wedding of the history of the Revolution to the new Sorbonne of the late nineteenth century can thus be seen to be less brilliant than is alleged, a century after the fact, by the guardians of the temple, but also less impoverished than the conservative tradition has maintained. Its proponents would have us believe that the republican and socialist university has mapped out the royal road of revolutionary history, any deviation from which spells perdition. Its opponents contend that "the university, daughter of the Revolution, teaches the Revolution" (Daniel Halévy, 1939) and that the history of the Revolution it writes is nothing other than a way of continuing it.

Neither of these judgments can withstand scrutiny. It is true that the original contract between the positivist university and revolutionary history was a republican contract. But the adjective contains nothing incompatible with science; on the contrary, there was a sort of preestablished harmony between the nation, the Republic, and scientific truth; Pierre Nora in his work on Lavisse has shown how the institutional labors of academic positivism were sustained by an ambition that was inextricably political and scientific, and how "a secular monarchism coopted clerical erudition for the benefit of the republican service and its intellectual and moral reform" (Pierre Nora, *L'histoire de France* by Lavisse). Thus the republican mission in revolutionary history is inseparable from the critical method and from detailed analysis of the documents. From Aulard to Lefebvre it gave impetus to the constitution of revolutionary "monuments." Hampered by lack of funds between the two wars, this work proceeded too slowly, but the cumulative effort of several generations has produced indispensable collections of source documents, mostly at the Parisian and national level.

Nevertheless, while the academic consensus on scholarly asceticism and publication of documents may have united generations, it did not extend its benefits to the realm of interpretation. The illusion of a marriage between the Republic and science did not long outlive one of the oldest legacies of the Revolution: the quarrel between republicans and socialists, revived by the grafting of bolshevism onto French socialism. Mathiez symbolized the triumph of the most sectarian version of the Revolution, draped like Aulard's earlier version in the mantle of science. As a substitute for republican positivism, Marxism-Leninism did nothing to soften its edges. It preserved the scientistic dogmatism, compounded by an anachronistic identification with the Soviet experience. Cut off more than ever from the wealth of philosophical and historical material contained in the great debates of the nineteenth century, it imprisoned the French Revolution in a rigid and impoverished system of interpretation.

Having worked alone and outside this narrow path for many years, Georges Lefebvre in the first decades of this century produced what remains the most original part of his work: a rural history of the Revolution. But when Mathiez's death allowed him access to the supreme magistracy, he too lay down in the Procrustean bed of a methodology designed by his predecessor, and the political climate of the "liberation" did the rest, transforming this old-school positivist into a neophyte Marxist-Leninist. This transformation was the final chapter in the academic tradition of revolutionary historiography.

François Furet

FURTHER READING

Annales historiques de la Révolution française, various articles devoted to Albert Mathiez, 1932.

Annales historiques de la Révolution française, special issue on Georges Lefebvre, January–March 1960.

Cobb, Richard. "Georges Lefebvre," in *A Second Identity: Essays on France and French History.* Oxford, 1969, pp. 84–100.

Friguglietti, James. *Albert Mathiez, Revolutionary Historian (1874–1932).*

Nora, Pierre. "Lavisse, instituteur national," in *Les lieux de mémoire,* vol. 1, *La république.* Paris, 1984.

La Révolution française, special issue on Alphonse Aulard, October–December 1928.

RELATED TOPICS

Ancien Régime	Hébertists	Revolutionary Assemblies
Blanc	Jacobinism	Revolutionary Government
Buchez	Jaurès	Rousseau
Constitution	Kant	Sans-culottes
Counterrevolution	Marx	Suffrage
Danton	Michelet	Taine
Enragés	Mirabeau	Terror
Great Fear	Quinet	Tocqueville

BLANC

L
ouis Blanc began a career as a journalist in Paris in 1834, the year in
which the first volume of Buchez and Roux's monumental *Histoire parlementaire de la Révolution française* was published. The city was still aquiver
with emotion from the riots that had followed the bourgeois confiscation of
the Revolution of 1830—the "Three Glorious Days"—and it is not difficult to
imagine the newly arrived young intellectual's encounter with this enormous
tome, which set out to link the Catholic tradition with Robespierrism. In it he
found both his past and his future.

Young Louis Blanc was a child of the Ancien Régime persecuted by the
Revolution. The family hailed from Rouergue's Catholic highlands, and
Blanc's grandfather, a merchant, had been guillotined in the Terror. His father, a convinced royalist married to a daughter of the Corsican nobility,
served the imperial administration. His work took him to Madrid, where
Louis was born in 1811. Louis did well in his study of the classics in Rodez,
where he moved exclusively in Catholic, legitimist circles. The Revolution of
1830 struck not only at the family's beliefs but also at its means, for Louis
Philippe ended the pension that Louis XVIII had granted Louis Blanc's father. Young Louis and his brother Charles had just arrived in Paris and were
obliged to live on very little. Louis accepted a position as tutor in Arras, where
he read the eighteenth-century writers from whom his upbringing had protected him. Arras, moreover, was located in a province very different from
the one in which he had grown up, and there the young tutor discovered the
wretchedness of the working class and the problems of poverty. During these
years he transformed his family's nostalgia for the past into a new prophecy
for the future. In this way he was able to cling to his hatred for the bourgeois
dynasty installed by the July Revolution, a dynasty he dreamed of replacing
with a fraternal community of working men and women. The child who had
been raised by priests found employment as a young man with the left-wing
press. He joined the side of democracy and socialism yet retained the same
enemies as in the past: money and the bourgeoisie.

In 1840 he published two works that tell us something about his political leanings, at once republican and socialist. The first, a long article that was
turned into a brochure, was entitled *L'organisation du travail* (*The Organization
of Labor*) and proposed solutions to the "social problem." As the title suggests,
Blanc's idea was to replace capitalist anarchy, flourishing under the protection
of a state controlled by the bourgeoisie, with a rational economic order under
the authority of a government in the hands of representatives of the people.
The plan had affinities with other utopian socialist ideas of the period. For

example, it attached great importance to educating a "new man" free of self-interest and selfish passions. Once this change was accomplished, the new organization of production would soon meet with the approval of all. It would be protected by a similarly revamped government, composed of representatives elected by all the people and subject to recall at any time. The state would control the key industries and would regulate production through "social workshops," whose purpose was to demonstrate the superiority of cooperative labor over the competitive sector.

Blanc's second work, entitled *Histoire de dix ans* (*History of Ten Years*), can still be read with pleasure despite its length (five volumes) and preconceptions. It is a political chronicle, written with great verve and full of anecdotes and portraits; it is also a document that gives us one of the best portraits we have of the ideas and attitudes of the republican left under the July Monarchy. Beneath the hatred of the bourgeoisie, the repudiation of wealth, and the almost messianic hopes attached to universal suffrage we sense the spirit of 1848 well before it burst onto the world stage.

Having published these two best-selling works, Blanc became one of the most prominent figures of the opposition. He played an active role in the "banquet campaign" and was naturally chosen to serve as a member of the provisional government organized on February 24, 1848, after the "Paris Days." This government immediately found itself divided, with republicans of the *National* such as Dupont de l'Eure and Arago on one side and socialists associated with *Reform* such as Flocon and Blanc on the other side. Blanc for a time insisted on being named minister of progress, but in the end he received nothing more than the chairmanship of the Committee on Labor Organization, which met in the Luxembourg in early March, in the very room abandoned a few days earlier by the peers of France.

This proved to be a poisoned prize, however, a responsibility impossible to bear under the circumstances that prevailed at the time, with rampant passions unleashed by demagogues and countless utopian proposals to contend with. What is more, the public held the Committee responsible for what was in fact a decision of the Ministry of Public Works: the creation, on February 26, of the so-called National Workshops as a measure to reduce unemployment. Blanc's republican adversaries capitalized on this confusion to paint him as the instrument of the Paris workers. He was elected in May to the Constituent Assembly, but the government veered sharply to the right, and Blanc was the big loser in the Paris insurrections of May 15 and June. Soon thereafter he was indicted, stripped of his parliamentary immunity, and quickly sentenced to deportation by a special court held in Bourges. But he was tried in absentia, for he had already fled to London by way of Brussels.

In London, where he was to remain for twenty years (like Quinet refusing to accept the imperial amnesty of 1859), he wrote most of his *Histoire de la Révolution française*, whose first volume, on the causes of the Revolution, had appeared in 1847—a great year for revolutionary historiography, a year that also saw the publication of Michelet's first volume, Esquiros' *Les Montagnards*, and Lamartine's *Les Girondins*. Blanc's thirteen-volume *History* was finished in 1862 after more than ten years of work. Like Quinet's history, which was written at Veytaux on the banks of Lake Leman, it owed a great deal to circumstances, to failure and exile. But the nature of the failure and exile differed for each case.

Quinet was one of those exiled in the wake of Louis Napoleon's coup on December 2, 1851. His problem was to understand the failure of French democracy and the repetition of the history that had led from the Revolution to the Empire. By contrast, Blanc had broken his ties with the government three years earlier and had been vanquished not by the Second Empire but by the Second Republic. In his own way he was as intransigent as the hopeless republican of Veytaux. But having been driven from his homeland by the Republic, there was nothing in his experience that would have enabled him to share or even to understand the question that Quinet asked about the history of France in general and of the Revolution in particular. He was no more interested in 1852 than he had been in 1847 in forms of power and sovereignty or in the rights of citizens. He remained convinced that the abstract idea of law was a fraud, and that democracy could be established only by giving real power to the people. A Jacobin socialist, he remained all the more Jacobin because he had been exiled as the leader of socialist Jacobinism, which had suffered defeat in the streets of Paris in June. He took his revenge in the silence of the British Museum by writing his own version of the French Revolution.

*
**

The structure of the work is established immediately with the enunciation of three principles, which Blanc says have governed the course of world history or at any rate European history. The oldest is the principle of authority, according to which societies and nations are based on transcendent external beliefs and on the subjection of human beings to an intangible order and system of constraints. By contrast, the principle of individualism posits individual freedom and the consent of the governed as the central tenets of government. Society attaches great importance to the rights of individuals, even at the expense of the community. Both principles can be seen at work in Christianity, the former in Catholicism, the latter (since the time of Luther) in Protestantism. But, Blanc argues, the Protestant spirit, stripped of its religious trappings, was also responsible for the Revolution of 1789, the Rights of Man, and the work of the Constituent Assembly, and subsequently it shaped the soul of the modern world and the bourgeois nineteenth century, for which Louis Blanc had no use.

A third principle was therefore needed, a principle capable of synthesizing authority and individualism, of restoring to the atomized society of individuals a sense of the collective such as can be found in authoritarian civilizations. This restoration would take more than a simple return to a past age, for social harmony can no longer be based on coercion or belief in the sacred but only on the free participation of all citizens. Government must make room for the individual will—the obsession of modern, individualistic societies—yet block the potential for anarchy. The principle of the new order must therefore be fraternity.

Now, the word "fraternity" had figured on the banner of the French Revolution. But the Revolution, obsessed with destroying the Ancien Régime, had not at first appreciated its significance. The Constituent Assembly established first individualism and later liberty. Fraternity, however, did not re-emerge until Year II, when the Mountain seized power: that stormy period was a harbinger of things to come. The Revolution had thus summed up the work of centuries and established what still remained to be done. Blanc describes the "design and plan" of his work thus: "It must be understood that in what is commonly called the French Revolution there were in fact two distinct revolutions, both nevertheless directed against the old principle of authority. One worked in favor of individualism; it took place in 1789. The other was tumultuously tested in the name of fraternity; it fell on 9 Thermidor."

Blanc thus subscribed to the notion that there were two revolutions within the Revolution, a fundamental theme of all socialist historiography, which wants to see the event as representing both past and future. The same idea had already been proposed by Buonarroti and Buchez, each in his own fashion. As in the work of these two predecessors, for Blanc the Revolution was the occasion of a class struggle between the bourgeoisie and the people, 1789 marking the triumph of the former, 1793 the brief success of the latter. Socialist historians attacked the "middle class" championed by Guizot and his friends by resurrecting Guizot's own explanation of the bourgeoisie's victory over the nobility: on its left wing they now saw not an ally but an adversary. No longer was the dictatorship of Year II seen as Mignet saw it, a popular but temporary expedient adopted in order to save what had been won in 1789. Now it was declared to be a new stage of the Revolution, defined by new principles embodied in new actors: it was the expression of the people's interests against the interests of the bourgeoisie.

Although Blanc's *History* retains a Catholic tone acquired from his childhood and upbringing, it was not defined, as Buchez's work was, by a combination of Catholicism and French nationalism. For Blanc Catholicism was part of each individual's heritage, not a vital collective faith. It was useful for understanding the idea of community, an idea that Protestant individualism had destroyed, but not for what might come next. The Revolution belonged to the post-Catholic era, and the historian of the age of fraternity must reflect not on religion but on the Jacobin experiment. For Buchez's Catholic messianism Blanc substituted a lay teleology. Catholicism was no longer at the center of French history past, present, or future; that history was dominated now by the centralized state, the agent of progress, just as it had been dominated yesterday by equality and would be dominated tomorrow by fraternity.

Like nearly all nineteenth-century historians, Blanc delved deep into the past in search of the roots of 1789. For him the source of all the trouble lay in the sixteenth century, a time when France was partly Protestant and Catholicism was first infected with the modern virus of individualism. From there to the Rights of Man and market society the road was marked by three

903

major milestones: the Reformation, the rise of the capitalist bourgeoisie, and the philosophy of the Enlightenment. The individualist spirit, which continued right through the Revolution, was represented by the Girondins and of course by what came after 9 Thermidor, which heralded the coming of the July Monarchy and "king cash." Throughout these three centuries, however, there had also been forces contrary to this evolution, and it was here that the government of Year II found its tradition. Blanc's apologia for Jacobinism as a harbinger of things to come goes hand in hand with his admiration, evident throughout the *History,* for absolute monarchy. While absolutism may have been the vehicle of the bourgeoisie's rise, it was also the embodiment of the principle that the state is superior to the individual, independent of all special interests, and the protector of the humble. Here the socialist historian relied on his bourgeois predecessors Augustin Thierry and François Guizot and on all the other historians who had written about the communes' victory, won with the help of the absolute monarchy, over the nobility. He nevertheless ascribed to the monarchy a more specific mission than that of unifying the nation in opposition to aristocracy: namely, to establish social harmony by adopting laws to protect the social and economic rights of the poor.

Just as bourgeois individualism had its countervailing forces, Enlightenment philosophy was not uniquely bourgeois. The great philosophe of the middle class, Voltaire, who set the tone of the times, was of course bourgeois, but in opposition to him was the other great ancestor, Rousseau. Blanc writes: "There were two doctrines, not merely different but antagonistic: the aim of one was an association of equals based on the principle of fraternity; the other was based entirely on individual rights. Freedom through unity and love was what the first desired, as a direct offshoot of the Gospel; the second, the child of Protestantism, sought freedom only in the emancipation of each person taken individually. Morelly, Jean-Jacques Rousseau, Mably, and in certain respects Necker were champions of the first principle; representing the second were Voltaire, d'Alembert, Condorcet, Diderot, Helvétius, Turgot, Morellet, and so on. The first led to Robespierre; the second created Mirabeau" (*Histoire,* book 1, chap. 2).

By the middle of the eighteenth century, the elements—and even the forerunners—of the drama in two acts that would be known as the Revolution were already in place. Blanc defined both doctrines in relation to their common ancestor, Christianity, which for so many nineteenth-century authors was the mother of modern democracy. For Louis Blanc, the Christian family tree had three main branches. The Catholic yielded the authoritarian societies of the Middle Ages. The Protestant gave rise to bourgeois individualism. The third branch had yet to bear fruit, but one day a return to the Gospel spirit would yield a civil religion of fraternity, to which the eighteenth century—or at any rate one line of eighteenth-century thinkers—had pointed the way. The Revolution of Voltaire, the thinker of the bourgeoisie, would be followed by that of Rousseau, the philosopher of the people. (Blanc adds the names of Morelly, Mably, and rather bizarrely the Protestant Necker, owing to his polemics against the laissez-faire and free trade policies of the physiocrats.) Rousseau's doctrine of the general will implied strong government, and his "Savoyard vicar" looked forward to a civil religion based on mutual love among citizens. Accordingly, Blanc saw Robespierre as the heir of Jean-Jacques: "Both champions of a strong government so long as the weak needed protection and the wretched assistance, the author of the *Social Contract* and his disciple were aware that the form of a society is the confirmation of its metaphysics and theology. They therefore understood that atheism, which assumes anarchy in the heavens, consecrates disorder on earth" (*Histoire*, book 3, chap. 1). Hence Jacobinism envisioned a strong government in the service of the weak and a religion of feeling as opposed to a critical rationalist philosophy: Robespierre was for Blanc the embodiment of both.

In order to describe Robespierre in such terms, however, he first had to be extricated from the legacy of the Terror. Blanc did not follow Buchez in praising revolutionary violence for its utility. He defended the Terror cautiously, in the manner of the liberal historians of the Restoration. Terror may have been a dreadful way to govern, but the Revolution was not to blame. For one thing, it had inherited its bad habits from the Ancien Régime: social violence was primarily a curse of the past. It was provoked, moreover, by counterrevolutionary conspiracies and would not otherwise have been necessary. There was nothing original about this interpretation, which had been widely repeated ever since 9 Thermidor. Blanc's contribution was to dissociate Robespierre from the guillotine; in order to depict the Incorruptible as the founder of a new society, no matter how short-lived, the liberals' image of him as an opportunistic dictator had to be dispelled.

In Blanc's *History* the guillotine is kept busy chiefly by the Hébertists, who in the winter of 1793–94 were the dominant faction, or nearly so. Robespierre protected Danton and Camille Desmoulins from their wrath. Then, in the spring, he had the leading Hébertists arrested, judged, and executed—admittedly along with Danton and his friends. Here Blanc betrays a twinge of regret at seeing his hero abandon Danton in the name of revolutionary orthodoxy. After the "factions" have been eliminated, however, Robespierre again becomes a moderate in the midst of the "Great Terror." The Robespierrists, Blanc says, were not responsible for and were even hostile to the dreadful Law of Prairial: for him, it was the future conspirators of 9 Thermidor who were the ultraterrorists in the spring of 1794. In this way he is able to condemn both the heightening of the Terror in June 1794 and the repudiation of the Terror after Thermidor—with Robespierre now cast as the scapegoat—on the grounds that the same men were responsible for both. In other words, Robespierre the Incorruptible embodied only the good side of Jacobinism: government of the people. The bad side, the Terror, was brought on not only by the Revolution's enemies, who created the "circumstances" that made it necessary, but also by its zealots, who soon turned into reactionaries (9 Thermidor) or sank into bourgeois corruption.

What is more, Thermidor did not put an end to the Terror, for the fall of Robespierre led to the White Terror. Now terrorism was invoked "as a means not of defending the Revolution but of ending it" (book 11, chap. 1). The period after Robespierre saw one part of society again at war with another, committing uncontrollable acts of violence. For Blanc such violence was inseparable from revolution itself, but now it sought to reverse the tide of history and so dispensed with all remaining scruples, even the Revolutionary

Tribunal. Thermidor gave belated proof of Robespierre's greatness and moderation; his true legacy was the Constitution of 1793, imbued throughout with the spirit of liberty and justice.

In the historiography of the Revolution Louis Blanc thus offers, in keeping with his political convictions, the purest example of an interpretation that merges Jacobinism with socialism. The man exiled by the treacherous Republic remained, in London, the doctrinaire who had written the *Organization of Labor,* the enemy of the bourgeoisie, and the militant champion of a powerful state that would represent the general interest and enable men to overcome the tyranny of things. In his exploration of the Revolution there is a strain of Robespierrist preaching that exasperated Michelet and that has not aged well—the price Blanc paid for his political involvement. Yet the book can still be read with great pleasure for its plain charm. Blanc is a good writer, with an always eloquent if sometimes too loquacious style. He writes a classical prose, something close to Latin periods. He likes to tell stories, and has the knack. His documentation is abundant, much of it drawn from Buchez and the *Moniteur,* along with pamphlets kept in the British Museum (most of the work having been written in London). And he is so sure of his evidence that he never passes up a chance to engage in scholarly debate with Michelet, as if the work of his great predecessor remained his implicit standard of comparison. From it he took, as did all writers in this period, many parts of his story, but he never cites Michelet except to criticize him. This unwillingness to acknowledge a debt, coupled with the aggressiveness of his criticism on points of detail, says a great deal about what was left unstated, particularly the vast gulf between the socialist and the republican. Michelet, responding to Blanc in his preface of 1868, spoke of "two religions."

Running between the two *Histories* was a wall that grew up quickly in the nineteenth century between the Revolution as the undivided heritage of republicans and the Revolution as the private patrimony of socialists. The two seemed to come together in February 1848, but May and June saw fraternity give way to bullets. Those who were defeated in June saw history differently from those who were defeated on December 2. Yet old age would bring them together again: Louis Blanc did not join the Commune and, having subscribed to the republican union at the dawn of the Third Republic, ended his days as a member of parliament for the radical left. Nevertheless, his great work survives as eloquent testimony to the fact that the French Revolution did not merely divide left from right in the nineteenth century but also divided left from left.

François Furet

F<small>URTHER</small> READING

WORKS BY LOUIS BLANC

Histoire de la Révolution française, 12 vols. Paris, 1847–1862.

See also the book by Furet below and the Further Reading for the article on Buchez.

RELATED WORKS

Furet, François. *La gauche et la Révolution française au milieu du XIXe siècle: Edgar Quinet et la question du jacobinisme (1865–1870),* texts with introductions by Marina Valensise. Paris, 1986. Contains texts by Alphonse Peyrat, Jules Ferry, Emile Ollivier, Louis Blanc, Edgar Quinet, Jules Michelet.

Michel, Henry. *L'idée de l'état: Essai critique sur l'histoire des théories sociales et politiques en France depuis la Révolution.* Paris, 1896. See chap. 3, "Le socialisme autoritaire."

Vidalenc, Jean. *Louis Blanc (1811–1882).* Paris, 1948.

R<small>ELATED</small> TOPICS

Condorcet	Guizot	Mirabeau	Robespierre
Constitution	Hébertists	Necker	Rousseau
Enlightenment	Jacobinism	Quinet	Terror
Fraternity	Michelet	Rights of Man	Voltaire

BUCHEZ

P hilippe-Joseph-Benjamin Buchez, once among the most eminent historians of the French Revolution, is today all but forgotten. The very qualities that made his work influential in the past now account for his oblivion.
Hence he is of great interest to anyone who wants to understand how time
has affected the Revolution as a "historical object."

His magnum opus, written with some help from his friend Roux, is the
forty-volume *Histoire parlementaire de la Révolution française*, published in installments between 1834 and 1839 and destined to be read by a large audience. The bulk of the work consists of texts and documents from the period:
parliamentary debates, newspaper articles, minutes of club meetings and motions, and the like. It was the first work to publish source materials from the
revolutionary period. In addition, volumes one through thirty-three each
contain a preface of several dozen pages offering comments on the contents.
(There are no prefaces after volume thirty-four, which deals with 9 Thermidor, as if the author, disheartened by the death of Robespierre, chose to lay
down his pen.) In these prefaces Buchez, writing just a few years after Buonarroti, developed a new socialist interpretation of the Revolution—a socialist
interpretation notable in that it made room for religion and even for fidelity
to the Catholic Church.

Buchez's hastily compiled collection of documents did not fare well at
the hands of late-nineteenth-century positivist critics, who worked with more
reliable instruments. The *Histoire parlementaire* is like an antique shop: there
still may be a few good "finds," but let the buyer beware and investigate the
background of anything he decides to take. A socialist interpretation of the
Revolution that claimed to derive from Catholic tradition inevitably seemed
peculiar during the Third Republic, when socialist and Catholic traditions
were deemed irreconcilable. The socialist leader Jaurès measured his reading
of the Revolution against that of the anticlerical republican Michelet rather
than that of the Catholic socialist Buchez.

Yet for nearly half a century, from Louis Philippe to Gambetta, the "Buchez and Roux" was the key reference invoked by all other histories of the
Revolution and the touchstone by which the rest were measured. Everyone
used it and drew freely upon its resources: Lamartine and Marx, Louis Blanc
and Leroux, Esquiros and Quinet. Even Michelet, who had read widely in the
archives, kept the materials published in the *Histoire parlementaire* constantly
in mind—and not only the source documents but also the prefaces, which he
read but did not like. The socialist part of Buchez's interpretation was familiar
to all his successors. Some, like Esquiros and Louis Blanc, drew inspiration

from it here and there. Others, like Michelet and Quinet, argued against it. Michelet began his *Histoire de la Révolution française* in 1847 with a preface attacking those who, following the example of Buchez (who is not mentioned by name), sought to interpret 1789 as an attempt to assert "selfish individual rights." And Quinet's *Révolution française*, published eighteen years later, can be read from beginning to end as a refutation of the *Histoire parlementaire*. Both writers detect a Christian spirit at work in the Revolution, though not the same Christian spirit. And both admire the Revolution, though not the same Revolution; one celebrates 1789, the other 1793.

To read Buchez is therefore to explore a work that played a central role in mid-nineteenth-century revolutionary historiography. Such exploration can be disorienting, however, for one is likely to stumble on questions that have been lost in the mists of time.

Buchez belonged to the generation born just after the Revolution, a group that remained obsessed with the Revolution's promise. His intellectual and political odyssey was so typical of the extreme left in early nineteenth-century France that, in following it, one is inevitably reminded of Balzac's *Illusions perdues* and Flaubert's *Education sentimentale*, of the world of Arthez, or Michel Chrestien, and Deslauriers, or Sénécal. Buchez was an eclectic ideologue, who absorbed and was possessed by whatever was in the air. Born in 1796, he was the son of an official in the fiscal bureaucracy, a solid member of the middle class. Political activism soon took time from his medical studies, and he did not complete his degree until 1825. As early as 1818 he was working on behalf of secret groups opposed to the Restoration. A Freemason who found the Grand Orient Lodge too moderate for his taste, he and his friend Bazard founded the Lodge of the Friends of Truth, which exhibited republican and revolutionary leanings and quickly became involved in politics. In 1821 he took the further step of founding the charbonnerie, an uncompromising French version of the Neapolitan Carboneria hailed by Buonarroti, the survivor of the Babeuf conspiracy. The charbonnerie was not only a neo-Jacobin political party that remained faithful to its model in a time of adversity but also a clandestine paramilitary unit. Louis Blanc summed up the party's program in his *Histoire de dix ans:* "The *whereases* set down by Messrs. Bazard, Flotard, and Buchez amount to this: given that might is not right and that the Bourbons were put back on the throne by foreign powers, the charbonniers have banded together in order to restore to the French nation free exercise of its right to choose a government as it sees fit."

But the charbonnerie fizzled, and Buchez, after spending several months in prison in 1822, moved from active insurrection to revolutionary philosophizing. Still a medical student, he inclined toward a materialistic interpretation of man modeled on that of the Ideologues Cabanis and Destutt de Tracy. It was not until 1825, however, when he became a Saint-Simonian, that he discovered both a science of society and a positive politics more sophisticated than his callow charbonnier dreams of a revolutionary putsch.

This was the same year in which Saint-Simon died, just after publishing his *Nouveau christianisme*. Buchez served on the editorial board of the *Producteur* along with Enfantin, Rodrigues, Bazard, and other heirs of the master. He soon replaced Auguste Comte as the author of a column on the philosophy of science and there propounded the idea that physiology is the queen of sciences and hence ought to serve as the basis of social science.

Like Comte, Buchez later broke with the Saint-Simonians and abandoned scientism for religion. But Comte had never been part of the inner circle at the *Producteur* and left quietly. By contrast, Buchez destroyed the unity of the group in the late 1820s by challenging the orthodox "pontificate" of Bazard and Enfantin on religious matters. In April 1830 Enfantin wrote a friend: "Buchez is betwixt and between past and future, Catholicism and the Saint-Simonian religion. As usual he falls between two stools. He finds us materialists!" The "pope" correctly anticipated where the dissident was headed. Within a year or two Buchez was a Catholic and faced with a difficult task of reconciliation: if for Comte the new religion crowned the positivist edifice, Buchez was obliged to reconcile science with the most old-fashioned religious beliefs and even with the Church itself.

As was inevitable in those days, the solution took the form of a theory of history. Buchez incorporated a number of Saint-Simonian ideas: the distinction between critical periods and organic periods, the idea of progress, and the acceptance of the productive masses of workers as full participants in the human adventure. He saw history as divided into three periods: one theocratic, another revolutionary, and a third devoted to the task of "civil organization," the job of the present day. Unlike Comte, however, he did not characterize the current period as "positive." For Buchez it was at once popular and religious: at last mankind would be reconciled to the divine order through the assumption of power by the people. History, as Buchez saw it, was both scientific and messianic. It was governed by laws, but those laws were themselves subordinate to a religious end: the Christian promise of reconciliation and unity. He developed this extraordinary blend of science and Catholicism in his *Introduction à la science de l'histoire* (1833) and would later examine its consequences for the history of the French Revolution.

At the time when Buchez, aided by his disciple Roux, a former seminarian turned schoolmaster, began publishing his *Histoire parlementaire*, the Saint-Simonians, much influenced by the critiques of Maistre and Bonald, were not enthusiastic about 1789. They saw the Revolution as a major but purely "critical" event: it had destroyed feudalism, but it had also left a legacy of disorder and instability. The "organic" age was still to come—it must come—but it could not be built on revolutionary principles derived from subjective individualism. Like Comte, the Saint-Simonians condemned the dogma of freedom of religion and its temporal counterpart, popular sovereignty.

On this crucial point they were at odds with neo-Montagnard histories of the Revolution, which had also emerged during the Restoration and had proved influential with the republican left. The first neo-Montagnard historian was the ex-conventionnel Bailleul, who in 1818 defended the work of the Convention against Mme. de Staël's criticism in her celebrated *Considérations*. Bailleul, moreover, was a former Girondin, intent on defending the republican legacy—the whole republican legacy, including the Consulate—against the attacks of the baroness, on the grounds that the Revolution had been forced to deal with unprecedented circumstances. Later in the Restoration another former member of the Convention, Levasseur, set out more specifically to praise the Montagnard dictatorship in his *Memoirs*. Laurent (*Réfutation de l'histoire de France de Montgaillard,* 1828) and Buonarroti (*La Conspiration des Egaux,* 1829) took the same tack. Nostalgic for 1793, these authors saw popular sovereignty as the indispensable tool of a government of equality. They offered no philosophical critique of democracy but attempted instead to reinstate the very democratic principle that the Saint-Simonians rejected.

Buchez's position thus combined elements of two contradictory traditions: the Saint-Simonian, which repudiated democratic individualism, and the neo-Montagnard, which saw itself as keeping faith with the heritage of Robespierre and the Jacobins. Buchez sought to reconcile the idea of popular sovereignty with the establishment of an "organic" regime and to wed Jacobinism to religion.

He accomplished these feats by adopting a teleological view and by reducing world history to French history. Both devices are evident in the lengthy introduction to the *Histoire parlementaire* entitled "An Abridged History of the French." According to the introduction, the goal of world history is to bring about equality as envisioned in Jesus' teachings, and France, elect among nations, was chosen to serve as Christianity's secular arm. Ever since Clovis' baptism the French monarchy and the Church had marched shoulder to shoulder in fulfillment of God's plan. That was why the Revolution was so important: it reinforced France's election by forcefully restating the teachings of the Gospel. Yet the Revolution, like the monarchy that preceded it, was divided within: it was necessary to overcome the atomizing, individualist tendencies of 1789 in order to make possible the advent of a new age of community in 1793.

Thus Buchez's work contains many familiar themes of romantic historiography: the idea of a French "nationality" embodying and revealing the history of the world; the Christian ancestry of modern democracy; and the continuity of the history of egalitarianism from the time of the kings to the time of the Revolution. These ideas are incorporated into a work that is more ideological than it is historical, however, a work that rewrites the history of France in the light of the great schism between 1789 and 1793: selfish individualism on the one hand, fraternal egalitarianism on the other. Guizot, for example, had held that the monarchy built the French nation by equalizing and unifying the various ranks of society. Buchez accepted this idea, but in contrast to Guizot, who hailed Protestantism as a source of emancipation, Buchez was fiercely anti-Protestant. He argues, for instance, that sixteenth-century Protestants supported what he calls "aristocratic federalism" and opposed the national unity desired by the monarchy. Protestant individualism therefore did as much damage as the individualists of 1789 did two centuries later. Accordingly, the one-time Saint-Simonian turned Catholic even managed to find excuses for the Saint Bartholomew massacres: "Suffice to say that, leaving aside the motives of the Court, what drove the people to commit these terrible acts was an all too justified wrath of which something other than religious fanaticism was the cause. Their target was the nobility—a nobility that had been thwarting the country's destiny for a very long time" (*Histoire parlementaire*, I, p. 136). It comes as no surprise that the hero of this modern history of France is Cardinal Richelieu, a clergyman in the king's employ, who "finished what Louis XI began. . . . He rendered power absolute" (p. 141).

Yet Buchez had little liking for Louis XIV, in whose reign, he says, the monarchy lost contact with the people and ruptured "the bonds of French nationality." The Sun King's legacy was a divided society, which soon brought forth the two protagonists of the Revolution to come: Voltaire and Rousseau, each the leader of a school. Voltaire echoed the detestable message of Protestantism and was therefore adulated by the rich and all who promoted their own selfish interests. Rousseau, however, battled individualism on behalf of the common interest. Speaking in the name of the people, he advocated equality in the production and distribution of wealth. One must read Buchez's extravagant pages on French Enlightenment philosophy to appreciate the degree to which Voltaire and Rousseau became in the nineteenth century the keys to a revision of the history of the eighteenth century in the light of the Revolution that was its crowning achievement.

The Revolution did provide a marvelous theater for the clash of two philosophies. The *cahiers* spoke with one voice in the spirit of Jean-Jacques. But the Voltairean bourgeoisie, usurping the great popular movement of 1789 for its own benefit, slowed its progress to pursue futile goals dictated by bourgeois class interests. Here Buchez accepts the Saint-Simonian view of 1789 as the Revolution's "critical" phase and is unable to see beyond that pure negation of the social, the "individual" of the Rights of Man. The Constituent Assembly failed because of its inability to grasp the "correct doctrine": that the historical mission of the nation must take precedence over the rights of individuals and that popular sovereignty must prevail over the dogma of individual reason.

The price paid for this failure was the all but inevitable reign of violence, the Terror, which began with the September massacres, a tragic but necessary corrective: "French unity, which was nearly destroyed by the lack of a common idea and shared goal, was maintained by the terror of those executions and of the frightful violence that came after" (*Histoire parlementaire*, XIX, p. 13). For Buchez, terror could be good or bad, depending upon its ostensible purpose. Bad when used by the Roman Empire against the Christians, hence in opposition to the movement of history, it was good when used to repress "antisocial instincts" set loose in 1789. The fact that such instincts are hard to stamp out, and that they resurfaced with the Girondins, only made terror all the more necessary. The Girondins were defeated on May 31 by what Buchez calls "an act of popular sovereignty, this time carried out with governmental regularity; a coup d'état of the people organized in sections and backing its wishes with nothing less than social might" (*Histoire parlementaire,* XXVII, p. 7)—a bizarre definition, given that he is talking about an illegal use of force, but consistent if the legitimacy of violence depends on the historical purpose it is supposed to fulfill.

For Buchez, the temporarily victorious Jacobins now represented the culmination of the Revolution, and it was they who revealed the events' true meaning, too long concealed by the intrigues of the bourgeoisie: that the purpose of the Revolution was to establish a true Christian community based on equality and fraternity. Of course not all who served the dictatorship of Year II shared this just ambition or possessed the talents necessary to fulfill it. Dantonists and Hébertists remained prisoners of their misconceptions and were dishonest to boot. Buchez's hero is Robespierre, the man who proclaimed the reign of virtue, the immortality of the soul, and the existence of God. Robespierre the Incorruptible had made morality central to politics; yet, not being a Catholic, he was unable to impose his view of morality as a compulsory and irreproachable faith. Nevertheless, through him the Revolution achieved—for a few months at any rate—an "organic" dimension and bequeathed to the future the promise of a new fraternal society, destined to be the messianic fulfillment of French "nationality."

In Buchez's Catholic socialism there is a strain of nostalgia for lost community that explains his hatred of bourgeois individualism. This is an old French tradition, one that surfaced, for example, during the Wars of Religion, when Catholic commoners led by priests made war on Protestants and demanded that a Spanish Bourbon be put on the throne in place of a Protestant king. Buchez was the heir of those battles and that messianic faith, whose nature he transformed by injecting such elements of modern culture as the revolutionary idea, historicism, and a plan for the educated to reorganize society on behalf of exploited workers and peasants. His prose, though neither rigorous nor elegant, has one simple virtue: better than any other writer, he shows how the socialist critique of 1789 combined the archaic with the modern.

Consider, for example, the use he makes of Rousseau, his great hero yet an author whose argument he cannot really follow. The *Social Contract* posits the individual in order to justify the general will, hence the community: by obeying the law, the individual is only obeying himself. Buchez wants to preserve the conclusion but not the premise, since the individual will is what condemns modern society to anarchy. He fails to grasp the coherence of Rousseau's argument and therefore awards the philosopher a grade of "fair"; he himself deduces the idea of the general will from the sovereignty of God, of which it is but the temporal reflection. Hence for Buchez there is a radical contradiction between the rights of man and popular sovereignty. By restoring the transcendental dimension to Rousseau's philosophy Buchez is able to introduce a providential purpose; for him the will of God is the source of popular power, and his view of popular sovereignty is accordingly quite different from older Christian views. In classical Christian doctrine the sovereignty of the people is simply the original foundation upon which the power of kings rests; both derive their legitimacy from God. For Buchez, popular sovereignty is bestowed by God upon a nation that is not free to refuse; this grant establishes "national goals" whose achievement is recorded in the nation's history. Thus the one-time disciple of Saint-Simon turned from Rousseau to Maistre, but he did not stop there. If, as for Maistre, Robespierre was the instrument of the French nation's providential mission, that mission was not yet complete. Its ultimate goal was unprecedented in world history: a socialist regime created for the benefit of the masses, led by those who understand God's plan for France.

*
**

It is difficult today to imagine the audience that existed, under the July Monarchy, for a laboriously constructed theory that has weathered the years as badly as this one. One reason for the success of Buchez's work was of course that he made a vast array of source materials available to a broad public for the first time. Cobbled together in great haste, this compilation sold extremely well, and its sale says something about Buchez's contemporaries' curiosity about the Revolution. Yet curiosity alone cannot account for the success of Buchez's efforts to appropriate the legacy of the Revolution for his own brand of socialism *cum* Catholic messianism.

To understand this success, one has to realize that from the first years of Louis Philippe's reign the Revolution had ceased to divide proponents of the Ancien Régime from partisans of 1789, had ceased even to divide right from left; by this point the great divide fell between left and left—between those who flew the banner of 1789 and those who flaunted that of 1793. The previous decade had been inclined to exalt 1789 and to look upon Year II as an inevitable but temporary consequence: Mignet (1824) and Thiers (1823–1827) had written histories of the Revolution in this vein prior to fighting the battles of 1789 all over again in July 1830. Now, however, the opponents of the new Orleanist regime suddenly began to fly the banner of 1793: they clamored for the Republic and the Montagnard Constitution, not for the bastard regime offered by the Constituent Assembly. After Babeuf and especially by way of Buonarroti (1829) memories of Year II united advanced republicans and socialists.

Buchez wraps this legacy in a much older tradition, that of the Catholicism of the Leagues modernized with a varnish of Saint-Simon. On the scholarly or semischolarly side he brandishes the ideas of science and historical necessity. On the popular side he secularizes the image of the priest leading the community of the faithful. The Revolution had branded the Church with the stamp of the Ancien Régime and bestowed power upon an unbelieving bourgeoisie. Buchez attempted to restore the Revolution's Catholic ancestry, artificially obscured by the course of events, in order to give the people back its traditional religion under the new banner of socialism. In opposition to the individualism of the Rights of Man he mobilized both past and future. That is why he detested 1789, the bourgeoisie's only claim to govern the nation. And that is why he praised 1793, where ancient tradition joined with the promise of the future in a Jacobin dictatorship that reestablished the old alliance between a strong government and the mass of the citizenry under the auspices of the Supreme Being, just as the divine-right monarchs had joined with the people to defeat the aristocracy.

Buchez's was not a fine mind, nor was he a profound thinker. His Catholic socialism, which attracted some attention between February and May 1848, did not survive the June Days. Though finished as a doctrine, it survived in French history as a sensibility, evident for example in the Catholic left-wing extremism of the late twentieth century. Nevertheless, as a historian Buchez marks an important, perhaps an essential, stage in the interpretation of the Revolution. He was one of the first to sense the full force of the contradictions in the Revolution's legacy to French political thought: not only the Ancien Régime versus 1789—the society of corporations and communities versus the society of individuals and Christianity versus bourgeois democracy—but also 1789 versus 1793—the Rights of Man versus Jacobinism, liberty versus equality. In this sense the *Histoire parlementaire* remains a historiographic monument.

François Furet

FURTHER READING

WORKS BY BUCHEZ

Buchez, Philippe-Joseph-Benjamin, and Prosper-Charles Roux. *Histoire parlementaire de la Révolution française*, 40 vols. Paris, 1834–1838.

RELATED WORKS

Blanc, Louis. *Révolution française: Histoire de dix ans, 1830–1840*, 5 vols. Paris, 1841–1844.
Duroselle, Jean-Baptiste. *Les débuts du catholicisme social en France (1814–1870)*. Paris, 1951.
Isambert, François-André. *De la charbonnerie au saint-simonisme: Etude sur la jeunesse de Buchez*. Paris, 1966.
Reibel, Roger. "Les idées politiques et sociales de P.-J.-B. Buchez," in *Travaux et recherches de la Faculté de Droit et des Sciences Economiques de Paris*, preface by Jean-Jacques Cheavallier. Sciences Politiques, 5. Paris, 1966.

RELATED TOPICS

Blanc
Democracy
Federalism
Girondins

Jacobins
Michelet
Quinet
Revolutionary Assemblies

Robespierre
Rousseau
Sovereignty

Terror
Voltaire

BURKE

Edmund Burke burst upon the French Revolution on November 29, 1790. Two thousand copies of his just-translated *Reflections on the Revolution in France* were snapped up in Paris in two days. In London, where the work had been published on the first of the month, it had already had the effect of a bombshell. With eleven editions in less than a year, it was one of the era's best-selling books.

The counterrevolution, previously limited to parliamentary maneuvering, court intrigue, rousing of public opinion by a vehement press, and the first signs of an émigré reaction, had suddenly found a persuasive theorist capable of depicting events in the light of a philosophy of history. All Europe seized upon his facts and assimilated his ideas. Nevertheless, French historians from Thiers to Lefebvre have shown little interest in Burke. Only Jaurès attempted to read him closely and refute his arguments in detail. Recently, however, he has found his way back into the good graces of French scholars and publishers and has at last been receiving the kind of attention he deserves.

Little known in France at the time of the Revolution, Burke nevertheless occupied an important place on the English political scene. Born in Ireland in 1729, educated at Trinity College, and thoroughly familiar with Enlightenment thought through the *Annual Register,* a review he founded in 1758, Burke began his career as a man of letters with the publication in 1757 of his authoritative *Philosophical Enquiry into the Origin of Our Ideas of the Sublime and the Beautiful,* and later he entered politics. A Whig member of Parliament from 1766 onward, he was a brilliant speaker well known for his important writings and speeches on the day's burning issues: Ireland, for which he desired religious freedom; America, with which he advocated reconciliation; free trade; and the status of the East India Company. Between 1785 and 1788 he emerged as the rival of men like Fox and Thomas Paine.

His position is paradoxical, for it was as a liberal—albeit a conservative one—that he attacked the Revolution, in opposition to those in England who saw it as a reprise of English history, the eighteenth century being much given to such historical parallels. The full title of his book suggests the urgency of his concern: *Reflections on the Revolution in France and on the Proceedings in Certain Societies in London Relative to the Events, in a Letter Intended to Have Been Sent to a Gentleman in Paris.* His principal domestic adversary was the Revolution Society and its learned spokesman Richard Price, an ardent champion of the Revolution. But Price merely provided Burke with a pretext. The Revolution was a radically new and "astonishing" event, which threatened to alter the course of history. A monster had been born. Like a contagious disease, it threatened to undermine world order, and in particular it posed a menace to English stability and civilization. (Burke's book was therefore an exercise in political exorcism.) Like any abnormality, however, the Revolution was also fascinating. It therefore called for a detailed examination. Such close scrutiny, it was hoped, would also yield prophylactic benefits. Burke's diagnosis proved to be extraordinarily perceptive. With a deft style and penetrating insight he issued a prophecy: that this Revolution was unlike any other the world had ever known and, because its view of things was utopian and depraved, it would inevitably prove harmful and evil.

Burke begins by denying the assertion that the new French institutions had been modeled on English ones. Conveniently omitting mention of the 1640s, Burke shows that the Glorious Revolution of 1688 had restored legitimacy to the monarchy and set English history back on the right road of constitutional government. It was a revolution because it violated the rules governing dynastic succession, but in the context of the event those rules were outweighed by a higher national interest. In no way did the revolution of 1688 establish that the English had a right to choose their own king. Even if the people had possessed such a right before, they solemnly abjured it now. The Bill of Rights of 1689, the cornerstone of the English constitution, established an indissoluble tie between the rights and liberties of British subjects and the laws of succession to the throne. Burke's interpretation of the Glorious Revolution differs sharply from that of Locke, for whom the accomplished fact was by definition reasonable: if the government infringed upon natural rights, most notably liberty and property, then the governed had the right to rebel. Thus for Locke the revolution of 1688 was a consequence of natural law. Burke, however, adopted the classical position on legitimate disobedience. The gravity and urgency of the situation justified the use of exceptional means. The whole episode was merely "a small and temporary deviation." In essence, the Whig writer interpreted 1688 as a Tory.

Where the English Revolution had been a sober restoration of the national tradition, the French was a mad attempt to start with a clean slate. Burke saw the French Revolution not as the logical culmination of steadily growing enlightenment but as a dictatorship of reason, in the name of which the precious legacy of generations past was cast aside rather than preserved as every nation must preserve its heritage. From Locke by way of Hume, Burke took the idea that nations must plumb the past in search of sure and definite values to guide their actions. Philosophy leads to skepticism (which Burke had denounced as early as 1756 in *A Vindication of Natural Society*); its conclusions are negative, and with such conclusions it is impossible to formulate positive reforms. The past is a record of man's fundamental experiences; it determines what conventions are legitimate by transmitting them to posterity. Our culture consists of what the past teaches us about our nature. Custom, far from being a "second nature," is nature itself. Hence the "prejudices" reviled by the philosophers are also natural. They are the fund of wealth amassed by the genuine, collective wisdom of the nation, and their effectiveness demonstrates their validity. Burke thus rejects the Rousseauian social contract in the name of a philosophy of nature; for him, the legitimacy of the constitution rests on prescription, not convention. History, the slow, natural evolution of society, has seen society become more complex but without making man more perfect, for man bears the mark of original sin. Man's natural state is to live in society and progress slowly toward civilization. Like Hume, and as Bonald would later argue at great length, Burke held that man is by nature a social being.

Slowly but surely, Burke continues, the English people had built themselves a constitution. That constitution became their heritage, the increase in its value by each new generation illustrating the link between conservation and progress. One improves what one already possesses, ensuring its preservation. The past, always vital and active, continuously molds present and future. To judge where we are going, we must know how we got where we are. The existence of government is legitimate because time has shown that delegation of power by the people to their representatives serves the common interest. Such delegation is a virtue by consensus.

It is often said that Burke, the champion of tradition, was an antirationalist: he identifies reason with experience and invokes the principles of the common law. For him, empiricism is the only law that ought to guide peoples and statesmen. For Burke the question is not "What is to be done?" but "What decision will best reflect the lessons of history and do most to promote the common good?" Politics is then a matter of finding the best compromise with what actually exists in a society composed of individuals guided by self-interest. Conflicts are managed and kept within reasonable limits by the state as prescribed by the constitution. The state is also the guarantor of economic freedom. (That tireless advocate of the free market, the economist Friedrich Hayek, traces his ideological ancestry to Burke.) A legacy of history, the right to property and to free enjoyment of the fruits of one's labor is confirmed by the existence of "corporate bodies," which are veritable institutions, social organs legitimated by time, as opposed to the idealized "people" of the philosophes. The French Revolution, a philosophical construct based on the abstract individual, had done away with all corporate bodies capable of serving as reasonable representative institutions, as necessary intermediaries and buffers between the individual and the state. The primary function of modern government is to ensure the equitable distribution of opportunities; at bottom its only ideology is to be useful. Forgetting this, the Revolution sacrificed the people's genuine interests. By attempting to wipe out their prejudices and misconceptions, it left them with nothing.

Thus, natural law is made concrete by history. At the same time, a divine law is gradually revealed to man through his social practice. Nevertheless, it would be wrong to portray Burke as a theocrat, if only because of the importance he ascribes to parliament and, more generally, because of the autonomy he sees in the political process. He does, however, identify English constitutional order with world order: "Our political system is placed in a just correspondence and symmetry with the order of the world." But the English constitution is England's property alone and not exportable. The common law is compounded of history and tradition, not of abstract theories about the rights of man or myths of universal reason. For Burke the universal and the particular had come together in England in a unique way: the country enjoyed freedom by virtue of its own inalienable and inimitable history and because its laws had gradually been brought into conformity with the laws of nature.

Could France have followed a similar course, one suited to its own genius, to what Herder would have called its *Volksgeist*? Though the comparison should not be carried too far, it is worth noting that Burke, like Herder, viewed a people as a living thing. Evolution was part of his thinking about families and societies, a fact that influenced later naturalistic political philosophies.

The French revolutionaries, feverish to impose their will on society, rent the social fabric by substituting a dictatorship based on abstract principles for sound administration of natural progress. They lost contact with the concrete substance of history. Instead of acknowledging the rights of *men*, rights rooted in reality and therefore worthy of being taken seriously, France's misguided rulers proclaimed the Rights of Man, a dangerously metaphysical notion. They advocated a democratic utopia based on the absurd dogma of equality, according to which individuals were like interchangeable cogs; they severed all ancestral ties and abolished the institutions that integrated men into society. Although men are morally equal, they are in many concrete ways unequal; this is a consequence of the operation of civil society. The levelers, by attacking this factual state of affairs, this necessary evil, wreaked havoc without bringing about equality, which was in fact impossible to achieve. The fatal contradiction between the abstract and the concrete is a constant refrain in Burke's text. It was a theme that would be taken up not only by subsequent counterrevolutionary thinkers but also by adversaries of democracy.

Rationalistic folly had turned reformists into apologists of change for change's sake. Change was necessary, Burke acknowledged, but it must be moderate: "A state without the means of some change is without the means of its conservation." In contrast to counterrevolutionaries who idealized the Ancien Régime, Burke stressed the abuses of absolutism, which he said had interrupted the evolution of French society toward a harmonious equilibrium of liberty and power: "The constitution was suspended before it was perfected." Burke was overly inclined to see France through a liberal's spectacles, in which respect he resembles the royalist Ferrand, who, as a follower of Boulainvilliers before becoming a royalist, alluded in his *Essai d'un citoyen* (1789) to the "unwritten constitution . . . which collects venerable customs . . . [and] imposes specific obligations on the king, limiting his absolute power." Burke states that elements of a French constitution did exist. The Estates General could and should have used them as a basis for establishing a modern French system of government. For example, the *cahiers de doléances* proposed numerous improvements that would have neither overturned nor destroyed existing institutions. The *cahiers* reflected the true principles of the French constitution, and the inability of absolutism to wipe those principles from memory was proof of its fundamental illegitimacy. In France, 1789 should have been what 1688 was in England. But things quickly got out of hand—a theme that was to be endlessly repeated.

According to Burke, the loss of control began politically with the rejection of bicameralism in September, even if it did not manifest itself publicly until the October Days. He cites two scandalous decisions, to revoke the rights of property and to promulgate atheism. He sees a growing conflict in French society between "the landed interest" and "the moneyed interest," a point that interested Jaurès. In England these two interests formed a dynamic combination that promoted economic progress and therefore liberty, but in France conflict between them led to the victory of the moneyed interest, which Burke says was more receptive to innovation. The reasons for this difference between England and France have to do with specific features of French history: ancient customs, the nobles' relation to the land, the extent of inalienable property held by the Crown and the Church. Spurred on by the intrigues of the philosophes—"literary politicians" bent on the destruction of Christianity—the moneyed interest successfully persuaded the Assembly to confiscate the property of the Church. France was transformed: the new oligarchy that was created controlled the circulation of paper money and struck at the heart of religion, the basis of all civilization. No excess, no outrage was too great for revolutionaries hostile to the one institution that bound French society together.

Burke then paints a broad-brushed portrait of revolutionary France, a country with civil and military anarchy for a constitution; an assembly of usurpers, composed of garrulous, obscure country lawyers, simple, inexperienced rural priests, and restless, dissatisfied gentlemen; an arbitrary, abstract division of the territory, a division that threatened to destroy the unity of the nation and give undue power to Paris; streets ruled by screaming, frenzied, brutal mobs; and a passion for that unnatural monstrosity, equality, and for the law of numbers, when in fact the country was ruled by profiteers and stock-jobbers. Such was the France created by the Constituent Assembly. Generalized law-breaking had produced chaos. The Revolution had degenerated into an orgy of crime and grotesque debauch upon which people looked with a mixture of fascinated horror and astonished disbelief.

Burke was able to predict the outcome of all this chaos, as if he had discerned in it the laws of disorder. No community could be founded by abstract individuals. Hence the nation would have to seek the bond of federation in the abstraction of the state, with all its potential for despotism. The new democratic regime left the citizen directly dependent on the government, with nothing to buffer its power. The only course open to the Revolution led inexorably to tyranny. The Terror and the recourse to military rule were therefore implicit in the premises of 1789. If, moreover, the monarchy should happen to be restored, it would be totally arbitrary, for it would no longer be hampered by the checks to despotism once established by age-old tradition. What prescience! Before he died in 1797, Burke saw part of his prognosis come true, and he advocated all-out war against the perverted nation that the Revolution had engendered.

Such folly, Burke says, was totally unpredictable—and this view is perhaps one weakness of his book. Philosophy, economic and social tensions, and human weakness all bear part of the blame, but even together they cannot account for a disaster of such magnitude. In the end it is impossible to ascribe a cause to the Revolution. To go from the Estates General to the eruption of the democratic ideal required a leap—an astonishing, mystifying leap. What mysterious force can account for a nation's attempting to put a philosophy into practice? A supernatural explanation beckons: it is tempting, Burke says, to think that France, by committing some great crime, drew upon itself the wrath of heaven. Maistre would later take up the theme of the Revolution as punishment. But Burke was not out to create a religious ideology. If time is the fundamental dimension in which all societies exist, the Revolution, a Promethean aberration, committed the supreme error by seeking to establish itself as a new beginning, an origin of historical time. It went astray because it believed implicitly in the nonsensical proposition that freedom can be created out of nothing. By attempting to divinize man, it led only to a dehumanized society.

Burke's book is a veritable breviary of counterrevolution. Its formal structure is loose: without chapter or section titles, it is neither pamphlet nor treatise in political philosophy. It won an audience by its virtues alone: a sure gift for description, rigorous analysis, and powerful polemic. English opinion was divided; while the Tories and some Whigs felt that Burke's book had captured their views, radical Whigs like Mary Wollstonecraft and MacIntosh violently attacked him. Godwin, Bentham, and James Mill joined the battle as well. Above all, Thomas Paine in 1791 published *The Rights of Man*. In the debate between Paine and Burke, Pierre Manent sees an "emblem of subsequent conflicts between 'right' and 'left' that divided liberal societies and societies in search of liberal institutions." Both men accepted the liberal system of representation, but Burke interpreted that system in a conservative light, Paine in a progressive one. Translated into German in 1791, Burke's work influenced Brandes, already known for his *Political Considerations of the French Revolution* (1790), who in 1792 published a staunchly Burkean book entitled *On Some Consequences of the French Revolution Relative to Germany;* Burke's influence is also evident in Rehberg's *Research on the French Revolution* (1792) and in the work of Gentz, his translator, known as the "German Burke."

In France his fortunes were less assured, at least in the decades after the Revolution. Maistre and Bonald read him and praised the power of his work, but they saw no deep affinities between it and their own doctrines: a providentialist reading of history on the one hand, an organicist and essentially reactionary theocracy on the other, both imbued with nostalgia for the Ancien Régime and idealization of absolute monarchy. From Burke they naturally drew arguments to bolster their counterrevolutionary positions, but they were not really influenced by him. As the nineteenth century progressed, Burke's seminal importance gradually became more apparent. Taine, in particular, read Burke as confirming his own political and social naturalism, which he opposed to the abstract idealism and metaphysics of the Revolution and which helped shape his *Origines de la France contemporaine*.

Burke's wholly negative portrait of France troubled even the monarchist right, and early French liberals could not abide his deep-dyed conservatism. Some even denied that Burke was a liberal, as if traditionalism and liberalism were mutually exclusive.

French liberals agreed with Burke, however, that the Revolution had inaugurated a new chapter in French history. The French liberal tradition begins in 1789, and despite their borrowings from England and defense of the English model, Benjamin Constant and Mme. de Staël were well aware of the profound differences between a liberalism that had matured over a long period of time and a liberalism suddenly sprung on a renovated France. In 1798, in a work entitled "On the Present Circumstances Which May End the Revolution and the Principles That Ought to Underlie the French Republic," Staël elaborated a program for government based on the republican party's assuming full powers with the support of the army and for the purpose of achieving not compromise but consensus. Thereafter the government's aim would be to convert the nation gradually to its own ideology, by means of education based on sound morals and self-interest. In other words, the new France should proceed along English lines.

All the various strands of liberalism claimed the legacy of 1789, from the Doctrinaires on the right to the more left-wing Rémusat, who in 1853 published a magisterial article in the *Revue des deux mondes* in which he confidently demolished Burke's counterfactual argument that if the history of France had been different, there need not have been a Revolution. Liberal historians from Guizot to Tocqueville, along with the famous "fatalist school" discussed by Chateaubriand, saw the Revolution, including the pressure to proceed beyond the objectives originally set by the Estates General, as necessary. Burke defended continuity, the French liberals insisted on a radical break with the past, misunderstanding was inevitable. Study of this penetrating foreigner's scrutiny of France remains profitable for anyone who would understand what was truly at stake in a Revolution from which the whole modern French political tradition ultimately derives.

Gérard Gengembre

F<small>URTHER READING</small>

WORKS BY BURKE

The Political Philosophy of Edmund Burke, with an introduction by Iain Hampsher-Monk. London and New York, 1987.

Reflections on the Revolution in France. Harmondsworth, 1968.

RELATED WORKS

Butler, Marilyn. *Burke, Paine, Godwin, and the Revolution Controversy.* Cambridge, 1984.

Chevallier, Jean-Jacques. *Les grandes oeuvres politiques de Machiavel à nos jours.* Paris, 1968.

Cobban, Alfred. *Edmund Burke and the Revolt against the Eighteenth Century: A Study of the Political and Social Thinking of Burke, Wordsworth, Coleridge, and Southey.* Second edition. London, 1960.

Furet, François. "Burke ou la fin d'une seule histoire en Europe," *Le débat,* March–April 1986.

Ganzin, Michel. *La pensée politique d'Edmund Burke.* Paris, 1972.

Guicciardi, Jean-Pierre. "Burke et les lumières," *Annales historiques de la Révolution française,* vol. 253, 1983.

Manent, Pierre, ed. *Les libéraux,* a selection of texts in 2 vols. Paris, 1986. See esp. vol. 2.

R<small>ELATED TOPICS</small>

Constant	Equality	Maistre
Constitution	Emigrés	Staël
Counterrevolution	Jaurès	Taine

CONSTANT

B enjamin Constant arrived in Paris on May 25, 1795, just after the *journées* of Prairial and the defeat of the faubourgs. Then twenty-eight years old, he had made the acquaintance of Mme. de Staël the previous year. At her side and in close alliance with her he made his debut in "the sublime theater of republican ambition." So intimate were their intellectual relations in this Thermidorian period that it is often difficult to tell them apart. At the far-off court of Brunswick, Constant had been a passionate observer of the radicalization of the Revolution. He faithfully traced its steps and for a brief moment even felt sympathy for the Jacobins. Although he later repented that short lapse into extremism, his republican convictions were firm. It was in praise of republicanism and in defense of the Directory that he wrote his first political pamphlets, in a climate that was distinctly reactionary—not only politically, but more so intellectually. Even after dictatorship came to France around 1802, Constant was still working to establish that a republican constitution was possible in a large country. Despite the disappointment of his deepest hopes and the apparently disastrous turn of events, he wrote: "We are not condemned to believe that men have need of a master. We can perceive no reason for abandoning hope of liberty." It was somewhat later, around 1806, that he became a "liberal," which is to say that he began to accept the idea that political liberty is compatible with more than one form of government: in his words, "with monarchy as well as with the Republic." At bottom this view was still a dogmatic one, yet in Constant it went together with a passion, typical of the revolutionary period, to play a public role. This ambition made him more than a little adaptable, so that the frequent recantations of the politician have tended to obscure the firmness of the political theorist. Yet the compromises of the *muscadin* and the deviousness of the author of "*la Benjamine*" should not be allowed to cloud the contribution of one of the most incisive and influential interpreters of the legacy of the Revolution and of the new prospects it opened to the world.

In the early summer of 1795 the burning issue of the day was the drafting of the Constitution of Year III. For the men in power, the problem was comparable to that of squaring the circle: how could they extricate themselves from the traps in the system of 1793 and dissociate themselves from the Terror without risking their necks and placing themselves at the mercy of those bent on revenge? Constant immediately discovered at the very heart of the day's most urgent concerns the two questions that would remain central to his political thought: the practical question of how to organize a viable and secure government and, underlying that problem, the more fundamental question of why the Revolution had veered toward terror and dictatorship—a deviation that Thermidor had halted but not fully mastered. How to explain the Jacobin usurpation and the bloody Reign of Terror? What was to blame? Did the difficulty lie at the heart of the Revolution itself? Was it the inevitable consequence of the illusory goals the Revolution had set for itself? Even assuming that legitimate republicanism could be distinguished from the Montagnard deviation, how could one be sure that an elected government would function in an effective and regular manner? For Constant these were all urgent questions, and he set to work on them at once. His friend Mme. de Staël wrote her *Réflexions sur la paix intérieure* in reaction to the report submitted to the Convention on June 23 by Boissy d'Anglas. The work shows how thoroughly she was influenced by the ideas of her father, Necker. Through Staël, Constant chose Necker as the theorist with whom he would engage in continuous debate, although he rarely mentioned him by name and frequently differed with him. On July 20 and August 5 Sieyès made two famous speeches, which represent the gist of his mature thought on the question of the constitution. His fellow deputies paid them little heed, but Sieyès' texts found a most attentive reader in Constant: two of his most important ideas, the critique of sovereignty and the need for a neutral government, originated with Sieyès' speeches. Constant saw a great deal of Sieyès during the Directory. In the company of this extraordinary oracle of the political art he explored those problematic aspects of the republican constitution that were not cleared up by the Constitution of Year III. It was to Sieyès, moreover, that Constant owed his nomination to the Tribunate after Brumaire. (He was removed in 1802.)

Necker and Sieyès—Constant, a privileged newcomer, arrived on the scene with the advantage of thorough familiarity with the views of two of the leading figures in the drama of 1789. Necker, though defeated in the first act, remained to the very end a critical observer of rare penetration, while Sieyès took a leading role and even helped to prepare the final dénouement—only to become its victim. (The lucid Constant had warned him of the praetorian peril inherent in any plan that relied on Bonaparte as its instrument.) This heavy load of political experience impressed itself on a mind formed by all that was newest in European social and historical thought, Constant having gone to the University of Edinburgh to imbibe the Scottish Enlightenment at its source. Thus the young man began his career with considerable advantages. Almost alone among the Parisians of his day he was both extraordinarily intimate with public affairs and equipped with the best possible education for making sense of them.

His debt to Scottish thinkers is evident in the very originality of his view, which can be summed up as a philosophy of historical rationality. He began to philosophize at a time when European thinkers were moving away from reasoning in terms of the natural foundations of things and toward arguments based on historical change. Thus, after refuting the classical argument for social inequality, he adds in his typical manner: "Finally, even if heredity did not entail these dreadful disadvantages, there would still be against this system a decisive argument, which is that it has no hope of ever rising again"

925

(*De la force*, p. 91). The preeminent job of politics is to illuminate the nature of the present. Those involved commonly fail to grasp the true nature of the moment and the true constraints on their actions. They go astray because they literally do not know where they are. The drama of historical action, as it was revealed to Constant by the Revolution and confirmed by the emergencies that he himself was forced to confront, stems from the failure of individuals to grasp what the times require because they either fail to recognize what is irreversible in the progress of history or choose improper models to guide their actions. To elucidate the needs of the present, however, does not mean to resign oneself to the inevitability of the future. On the contrary, it means that in the midst of changing circumstances, one wants to base one's actions on firm principles. Once the temper of the times has been diagnosed, one still has to effect the transition from "first principles" to "intermediate principles" capable of making equality effective and republican government a practical and viable reality. Men not only lack direction, they also lack understanding of how to apply the abstract doctrines that dominate their minds but fail to take tranquil root in their lives. Heredity, observes Constant, "depended on a set of interrelated institutions, habits, and interests that reached into every man's innermost being" (*Réactions*, p. 71). Equality had captured men's minds, but still they could not feel at home with something so new and untried: "It penetrates the individual only to disrupt his whole manner of being." Principles were needed to put an end to this confusion. The job at hand was to render habitable a society laid waste by the sudden emergence of an idea that had no mature, stable, familiar embodiment in the body politic. From 1796 to 1806, from the topical pamphlets of the post-Thermidor period to the systematic treatises doomed to remain in obscurity under Bonaparte's dictatorship, Constant's thinking developed steadily along an unwavering line. The two books written under the Consulate and the Empire detail his thoughts on the "possibility of a republic in a large state" and "the elementary principles of liberty" first adumbrated in the two major pamphlets written under the Directory, *De la force du gouvernement actuel et de la nécessité de s'y rallier* (1796) and *Des réactions politiques*, complemented in 1797 by *Des effets de la Terreur*. Over all these years Constant's interpretation of the Revolution remained inseparable from his efforts to establish constitutional rules and collective norms that could give substance to the unfulfilled promises of the "present era."

Both the strengths and the weaknesses of Constant's position derive from this point of view. He has little to say about the process of the Revolution itself, its origins and subsequent course. As a proper philosopher of history, he is less interested in the facts than in the issues revealed by the facts, issues that make the facts intelligible: "When the harmony between institutions and ideas is destroyed, revolutions are inevitable. They tend to reestablish that harmony. This is not always the goal of the revolutionaries, but it is always the tendency of revolutions" (*Réactions*, p. 1). He is in no doubt why the Revolution of 1789 was inevitable: "Regardless of the various names that were applied to the struggle of which we were all witnesses and in many cases victims, in essence it was always a battle between the elective system and the hereditary system. That is the central question of the French Revolution and in a sense of the century" ("Constitution républicaine," NAF 14363, p. 5). The Revolution of 1789 centered on equality. On the irresistible force of this new idea (which he calls the *idée-mère*, the "mother idea") he included in his first 1796 pamphlet a flight of rhetoric that can only be compared with the more celebrated passages of Tocqueville. He sets forth the core of his whole philosophy at once: "The origin of the social state is a great riddle, but its progress is simple and steady." This sentence sums up a crucial change in the nature of political thought. Now the secret of the good society is to be sought not in its primordial institution but in its subsequent transformations: "We see the human race emerging from the impenetrable cloud that concealed its birth and advancing toward equality over the debris of many different institutions. Every step that it has taken in this direction has been irreversible" (*De la force*, p. 96). He then sketches out a chronology, of forms of inequality and milestones marking progress toward greater equality, in which we can detect the influence of Ferguson and Millar. He distinguishes four phases: castes, slavery, feudalism, and aristocracy (whose origins he situates among the primitive Europeans). The "Constitution républicaine" contains an astute analysis of the "nobility without feudalism" typical of the Ancien Régime, in which the aristocracy was an "almost imaginary corporation" that received "excessive favors" even though it played no legal role and did not even serve as an "intermediary body." The conclusion is an exhortation; wisdom demands that we not oppose the inexorable tendencies of social change: "In the end we must cede to necessity. We must cease to be blind to social progress, cease by dint of futile efforts to precipitate bloody conflict . . . [and] cease to force men to pay for their rights with crimes" (*De la force*, p. 98).

The great drawback of this kind of analysis is that, in its wish to grasp the overall meaning of what happened, it misses the actual course of events with all their attendant passions and unpredictable turns. Yes, the Revolution established equality, but why did it require an episode of dictatorship and Terror? The passage cited above touches on one possible reason that Constant would later exploit to the full: the strength of resistance born of the bitterness of the struggle. In a note, moreover, Constant cites historical examples in support of his observation that "Revolutions, which aim for the good of mankind, almost always do great harm, and the more pernicious the thing to be destroyed, the crueler the evil of revolution. . . . The scourge passes, the good remains" (*De la force*, p. 97). The logic of his position leads him to introduce another factor, however, which would assume a larger and larger role in later works: anachronism. The actors in the drama mistake the age in which they are living and therefore make poor choices of both ends and means, with the result that they wage bloody war to achieve impossible ends. This idea first appears under the head of "anticipation," which Constant uses to account for political reactions that seem enigmatic to him. If revolutions are made in order to restore harmony between prevailing opinion and institutions, why do they so often provoke reactions, even among authors—to whom Constant addresses himself particularly—who only yesterday were friends of the Enlightenment? His answer is that revolutions tend to press beyond the objects that the times would reasonably allow them to pursue. Just as the English Revolution, whose true cause was religious freedom, went too far in attacking royalty, so the French Revolution, whose target was privilege, "exceeded its limit in attacking property" (*Réactions*, p. 12). The danger of attempting to go too far is that regression is always possible.

Constant's general scheme has little power, however, to explain why republican principles ended in Jacobin dictatorship. This failure is evident from a controversy in which he engaged with a man to whom he was close politically, Lezay-Marnesia. In April 1797, not long after the publication of *Réactions politiques,* the latter, a Thermidorian like Constant, published a *realpolitische* analysis of the causes and results of the Revolution in which he argued that the Terror was an episode necessary to ensure the victory of the Revolution. Enraged, Constant responded by adding a section specifically considering the "effects of the Terror" to a new edition of his *Réactions,* published in May (see Furet, 1983). In it he vigorously rejected the idea that the Terror was *functional.* The "results" it had allegedly produced were in fact achieved in spite of it. The problem, however, was that this attempt to distinguish between what was inevitable in the Revolution and what was merely a tragic aberration made the reasons for that aberration even more enigmatic than before. If the Terror meant simply the use of extreme measures in a situation when no other resources were available, it was no great mystery. But if one refused to allow *raison d'état* as an answer, a puzzle remained. Constant thus created for himself a problem to which his writings under the Directory provided no clear answer.

By elaborating upon the concept of anachronism, however, he was able to fill this gap. By anachronism he no longer meant excessive optimism. He referred, rather, to the psychological weight of the past. The pleas of enlightened Thermidorians to "end the Revolution" would prove to be of no avail. The Republic would not be stabilized. A military despotism would end a process that apparently could not be controlled from within. In the years of Napoleon's triumph, 1802 to 1806, these prophecies became the key tenets of Constant's mature if not definitive philosophy. During those years he wrote but did not publish two books that would serve as the basis for his post-1814 writings, two books whose early drafts have only recently come to light: the still unpublished "Fragments d'un ouvrage abandonné sur la possibilité de la Constitution républicaine dans un grand pays" ("Fragments of an Abandoned Work on the Possibility of a Republican Constitution in a Large Country") and the *Principes de politique applicables à tous les gouvernements (Political Principles Applicable to All Governments)* recently published by E. Hoffmann. These works and the Thermidorian pamphlets draw upon the same source of inspiration. In the face of overwhelming popular support for authoritarian rule, Constant in 1802 continued his search for the means by which an elective liberal regime could be made workable; and he delved more deeply than he had done before into the causes that had rendered representative government uncontrollable during the Revolution. In 1806, at the height of imperial power, he gave up the cause of the republican constitution. Sidestepping the question of power, his aim now was to set forth the general principles governing the relations between authority and the individual "in the present era of the human race" and regardless of the form of government. There was no change in his fundamental convictions or in the reading of history on which they were based: mankind had reached the age of liberty, progress was irreversible, and present ills and apparent reverses were merely the passing afflictions of a painful birth. The crucial problem was to make the actors aware of their true goals, dictated by history, and of the proper means to attain them. The Revolution had erred as to ends and means. But those who concluded that because the Revolution had failed, its cause was finished, and who therefore embraced a triumphant tyrant, erred even more, for it was the height of anachronism to seek military glory in an age of commerce. This was the theme of "De l'esprit de conquête et de l'usurpation," a pamphlet that, using sections of his unpublished works, Constant hastily put together in 1814.

Lacking a proper appreciation of the difference between the ancient and modern concepts of liberty, the revolutionaries, Constant argued, had been mistaken about their goals. And in extending the concept of popular sovereignty more than was legally or realistically permissible, they had also been mistaken about their means. In both cases they suffered from having employed models of the past that concealed the needs of the present. For Constant, the primary source of the illusion from which "all the woes of the French Revolution stemmed" was the "assumption that society may exercise unlimited authority over all its members." He blamed this illusion on the fact that the very political framework against which the insurgents rose in rebellion exerted a powerful influence on their philosophical thought:

> The error of Rousseau and of the writers most partial to liberty in granting unlimited power to society comes from the way in which their political ideas were formed. In history they saw a small number of men, perhaps even a single man, in possession of an immense power that did a great deal of harm. But their wrath was directed against those who wielded that power rather than against the power itself. Rather than destroy it, they thought only of replacing it. That power was a scourge, but they saw it as a prize and bestowed it upon all of society. (*Principes*, p. 201)

This mistaken notion was supported, moreover, by a prestigious example, an illustrious embodiment of liberty coupled with social authority: the ancient republics. First the monarchy mystified power, then imitation of the civic virtue of the ancients camouflaged the unprecedented conditions of modern politics. Constant wrote:

> When the tide of events brought to the fore men who had adopted philosophy as a prejudice, those men believed they could exercise public power as they had seen it exercised in the free states of antiquity. They believed that even today all must give way before the authority of the community, that private morality must fall silent before the public interest, and that all infringements of civil liberty would be repaired by the enjoyment of the widest possible political liberty. (*Principes*, p. 40)

In the definitive version of Constant's reflections upon the liberty of the ancients, published in 1819, he would moderate the severity of his initial judgment by insisting on the "sublime genius" of Rousseau, who he said was animated by "the purest love of liberty." The substance of the judgment remains, however: "By transporting into modern times a concept of the extent of social power and collective sovereignty that belonged to other centuries, [Rousseau] offered unfortunate pretexts to more than one form of tyranny." Supported by Mably, who held an even more exaggerated view of the powers of the lawmaker, Rousseau's influence was the source of the misguided faith that had led the revolutionaries astray: that it was possible to exchange "restrictions on individual rights" for "participation in social power." To make such an argument was to ignore the great novelty of modern times, that "individual independence is the primary modern need," as well as its corollary, that "one must therefore never demand its sacrifice in order to establish political liberty" (*Liberté,* pp. 505–507). The revolutionary had sought to give people something other than what they wanted, which accounts for "their obstinate resistance to what they were offered in the guise of liberty." The result was a vicious circle: the less the revolutionaries were able to force people to accept what they were being offered, the more they were forced to resort to arbitrary rule. Inevitably they failed to achieve their goal. "Social power in every way injures individual independence without eliminating the need for it"; Constant wittily remarked that "the least of saints in the most obscure of hamlets successfully withstood the whole might of national authority ranged in battle against it" (*Liberté,* p. 190). Accordingly, "force makes still greater force necessary," so that in the end "liberty's unseeing friends, who thought they could impose it through despotism, provoked all free souls to rise against them" (*Liberté,* p. 193).

Constant does not give an analysis of the Revolution as such. Since he is primarily a politician, what he says about it is always expressed in the light of his positive, practical political goals. Whether looking at the workings of the Constitution or reflecting upon the general principles of public action, his primary concern throughout his career was to specify what conditions were necessary for the proper functioning of a social form that he believed would inevitably prevail. His critique focused initially on the false consciousness that prevented the historical actors from grasping the true nature of their roles. In his very first 1796 pamphlet he observed in typical fashion: "Those who wish to overthrow the Republic are strangely deceived by words. They have seen that a revolution is a terrible and harmful thing and conclude that what they call a counterrevolution would be a fortunate occurrence. They do not sense that this counterrevolution would itself be just another revolution" (*De la force,* p. 21). The account of changes in public opinion between July 14, 1789, and March 31, 1814, given at the end of his admirable "Fragments sur la France" is an exemplary analysis of the way in which historical actors, for all their accurate perception of events, nevertheless deceived themselves through one-sided reasoning of the sort that would later come to be known as ideological. The influence exerted by the "ghosts of the past on the brains of the living" is merely a special case of the more general phenomenon of misunderstanding—but a particularly important one. For Constant, only this influence could explain the paradox of why a timely revolution had failed and why it had turned tyrannical in its attempts to combat past abuses of authority. Against a view widely shared by his contemporaries he tirelessly argued that it was not the principles of liberty that were to blame but the fundamentally archaic way in which those principles were understood. Constant actually gave two different accounts of the influence of the past. In the narrow version, he held that the ancient model of direct democracy was responsible for the Jacobin episode. In a broader version, first adumbrated in the *Principes* of 1806 but most fully developed in one of his least known works, the *Commentaire sur l'ouvrage de Filangieri* (1822–1824), he argued that eighteenth-century reformers had been guided by an illusory belief in the capacity of laws to shape ideas and societies. No one party or school was responsible for this overestimation of the power of the legislator, a misconception that was widely shared and evident in many signs, from the obsession with Sparta to the legacy of the Enlightenment. In short, the problem lay not in the Revolution itself but in an inherited image of government that prevented the Revolution from being itself.

It would be wrong to reduce Constant's interpretation to the single question of anachronism. While maintaining the view that the goals of the Revolution were necessary but the means chosen unsuitable for attaining them, he argues that the attempt to create a representative government had bogged down in uncertainties about the best course to choose. Hence the failure of the Revolution was also an internal failure, a consequence of constitutional and political dysfunction. Here it was not the weight of precedent that was decisive, but the opposite: a novel situation that no one was able to master. Not only was sovereignty abused for want of precise limits; the very administration of sovereignty proved defective owing to the absence of any means for controlling the delegation of authority. First an assembly took the proper place of the people, then a government was reduced to impotence by internal bickering, until finally sovereignty, so difficult to conceptualize, fell into the hands of one man. How could one prevent usurpation, hinder the concentration of power, and still make sure that the actions of the representatives coincided with the wishes of those represented? Constant's discerning diagnosis of the French Republic's childhood diseases surely numbers among his finest achievements. His proposed remedy, derived from Sieyès' idea of a constitutional jury, was not widely accepted, however. The "conservative or neutral power independent of the people as well as of the executive" and charged with "defending the government against the division of the governors and the governed against the oppression of the government" was an institution that he advocated at the end of his consideration of the likelihood of success of a republican constitution, but the idea was never implemented. He himself abandoned it when he threw his support to the constitutional monarchy, in which, according to his liberal interpretation, the king served as the neutral power, since he had no direct political prerogatives but was re-

931

sponsible for monitoring the working of representative government. In the last resort those represented would thus exercise some control over their representatives.

No one has ever examined the question of the stability of republican government more lucidly than Constant. How could one prevent the alienation of representatives from the body politic that invested them with their authority? If the Revolution is to be taken seriously as a political experiment, then it must be said that Constant numbers among those who achieved the most profound understanding of the reasons for its failure. He understood that the hereditary system was doomed to be replaced by the elective, yet that inevitability did not prevent him from seeing just how difficult it would be to control the latter.

Marcel Gauchet

Further Reading

WORKS BY CONSTANT

Commentaire sur l'ouvrage de Filangieri, 2 vols. Paris, 1822–1824.

Ecrits et discours politiques, ed. Olivier Pozzo di Borgo, 2 vols. Paris, 1964. Contains reprints of *Des réactions politiques.* (n.p., Year V [1797]) and *Des effets de la terreur,* (n.p., Year V [1797]).

De la force du gouvernement actuel et de la nécessité de s'y rallier. N.p., 1796.

"Fragments d'un ouvrage abandonné sur la possibilité de la Constitution républicaine dans un grand pays." Paris, Bibliothèque Nationale, manuscripts NAF 14363–14364.

"Fragments sur la France, du 14 juillet 1789 au 31 mars 1814," in *Mélanges de littérature de politique.* Paris, 1829. Reprinted in *Oeuvres,* Paris, 1964.

De la liberté des anciens comparée à celle des modernes (1819). Text included in a selection of political writings published under the title *De la liberté chez les modernes.* Paris, 1980.

Principes de politique applicables à tous les gouvernements (1806), ed. Etienne Hoffmann, 2 vols. Geneva, 1980.

ON THE POLEMIC OF 1797

Furet, François. "Une polémique thermidorienne sur la Terreur," *Passé présent,* vol. 2, 1983, 44–55.

A full bibliography of works pertaining to Constant's early life and the period of the Revolution can be found at the beginning of Hoffmann's edition of *Principes de politique.*

Related Topics

Constitution	Elections	Napoleon Bonaparte	Sieyès	Tocqueville
Democracy	Jacobinism	Necker	Staël	
Equality	Liberty	Rousseau	Terror	

FICHTE

P rior to the summer of 1792 Fichte alluded to the French Revolution only
once and apparently took little interest in it. His journal for the month
of August 1789 does refer to a discussion "of French events," yet although his
correspondence in subsequent years occasionally touched on problems of national and international politics, it was not until he wrote to his wife on May
26, 1794, that the news from France was broached again. From this letter it
emerges that Fichte had been following developments in France in the press,
but this is hardly surprising, for by mid-1794 he had become the Revolution's
principal champion in Germany after the publication more than a year earlier
of his famous *Considerations of the French Revolution*.

Fichte's sudden interest in France has been interpreted in many ways.
Gueroult attempts to minimize its significance by showing that Fichte had at
least in theory always supported the ideas of the Revolution. The republican
spirit, he says, is "apparent in every page" of Fichte's correspondence going
back as far as his Zurich period (*Etudes sur Fichte,* p. 165). But the sources
offer little support for this assertion. Druet prefers to look to the events of
the summer of 1792, and of course the riot of August 10 that led to the
downfall of the monarchy, for the cause of Fichte's sudden conversion ("De
l'anarchie à la dictature éducative: Métaphysique et politique chez Fichte").
Previously Fichte had believed that the ideal of Plato's *Republic*—"the greatest
possible freedom"—could be achieved under an enlightened monarchy.
Events in Paris presumably opened his eyes to the true nature of monarchy,
of which the French first had to rid themselves before the goal of freedom
could be attained.

While Druet's claim is interesting and well documented, it takes no account of any purely philosophical reasons that Fichte may have had for championing the Revolution, motives internal to his philosophical system. Druet
describes the *circumstances* of Fichte's conversion. But beyond those circumstances other changes had to occur at the level of theoretical reflection in
order for a new representation of revolution to become possible: an image of
men seizing their own destiny and moving toward greater liberty. What
changed Fichte's thinking between 1788 and 1792 so that a revolution he
initially ignored became the central subject of his first important publication
in 1793? The answer is brief: his discovery of Kant. Before that discovery
Fichte's philosophical commitments were, to say the least, rather vague. As
Gueroult has shown, he subscribed to a somewhat vague determinism largely
derived from Spinoza; this combined with another idea that was part of the
larger intellectual climate, which stemmed from Leibniz and was popularized

by Herder, namely, the idea of "automatic progress that would proceed by itself in the manner of a mechanical roasting spit." We know from a letter dated August 12, 1789, that it was at this time that Fichte first immersed himself in Kant's philosophy. In his first "revolutionary" piece, the *Call to Princes*, he wrote that "our unique happiness in this world" resides in "a free spontaneity," in "an activity emanating from our own strength and pursuing its own aims through work, toil, and effort." Words like these were the first sign of an evolving defense of revolutionary activism. They became possible in the summer of 1792 perhaps in part because the riot of August 10 had opened Fichte's eyes but also, and more important, because the representation of history inherited from Leibniz and Spinoza had been shattered by Kant's second *Critique*. Fichte was thus led to draw his famous parallel between the French Revolution and the Copernican revolution that Kant had accomplished in philosophy, a parallel first expressed in a letter that is worth citing in its entirety:

> My system is the first system of freedom. Just as this nation [France] will deliver mankind from its material chains, my system will deliver it from the tyranny of the thing-in-itself and external influences. Its first principles make man into an autonomous being. The *Doctrine of Science* was born during the years when the French nation, by dint of sheer energy, brought about the triumph of political liberty. It was born in the wake of a struggle within myself against all the prejudices rooted within me, and that conquest of freedom helped to make its birth possible. I owe my exaltation to the valor of the French nation. I am indebted to it for having elicited the energy I needed to understand these ideas. While I was writing about the Revolution, the first signs, the first glimmerings of my system welled up from within as a sort of reward. To a certain extent, therefore, this system already belongs to the French nation.

This important letter sheds light on the philosophical assumptions that were to guide Fichte's defense of the Revolution against its reactionary detractors, primarily Burke and Rehberg. (For further comment on this letter, see X. Léon, *Fichte et son temps,* II, 2, p. 288; Gueroult, "Fichte et la Révolution française," p. 152; and A. Philonenko, *Théorie et praxis dans la pensée morale et politique de Fichte en 1793,* p. 78.) In the *Considerations* that defense consists essentially in applying to history Kant's revolutionary idea that knowledge of objects depends on the *subject*. In plain terms, this meant that history ought to be conceived as being founded on (or subject to) human subjectivity (or will), as we see from the following passage of the *Considerations,* which parodies the preface to Kant's first *Critique:* "We never find anything in the history of the world but what we put there ourselves. . . . Hence the French Revolution strikes me as a rich canvas on this great subject: the rights of man and the dignity of man."

Fichte's support of the Revolution in the *Considerations* is based on "semantic idealism," a moralistic view of history, and an anarchist critique of the state:

Semantic idealism. As Philonenko points out, "idealism does not consist in the assertion that the world is 'in' consciousness but in holding that . . . all experience is a 'deciphering.' . . . Idealism is based on a simple proposition: that experience takes on meaning only through the mind and its operation." This was precisely the position that Fichte took in 1793 in order to justify the events in France as a revolt of the human spirit against the weight of accumulated prejudice and—what comes to the same thing—tradition: "Experience in itself," Fichte wrote in the *Considerations*, "is like a box of type into which characters have been tossed at random. Only the human mind gives meaning to this chaos, drawing from the box now an *Iliad*, now a historical drama in the manner of Schlenkert."

Moralistic view of history. Rejecting all forms of determinism, Fichte in the *Considerations* argues forcefully that history ought to be the theater of a practical transformation of what is in the name of a moral ideal rooted in human reason. For Fichte, the Revolution erased the past and started with a clean slate, hence it was the embodiment of his idea that human societies must produce themselves (or, as we would say nowadays, that they must be self-instituted).

Anarchist critique of the state. The *Considerations* end with nothing less than a deconstruction of the state. Fichte systematically attacks the view of Hobbes (shared by Kant) that the state of nature would be a state of war: "The old idea of a state of nature, whose law would be that of a war of all against all and in which the strongest would rule the earth, is false." It is false because it sustains the reactionary view that state authority is the only way to put an end to violence and to establish the rule of law. Instead Fichte argues that the state of nature is neither good (as Rousseau maintained) nor bad (as Hobbes insisted) but merely the place where subject encounters subject in pristine purity. Hence the state is by no means necessary. It is the result of one contract among others, a contract that can and should be broken as soon as it encroaches upon man's freedom. In a celebrated passage Fichte states one of the central ideas that Marxism would retain from anarchist thought, namely, that a withering away of the state must accompany social progress.

The *Considerations* therefore tend to legitimate the Revolution. Fichte denies the value of tradition as such and undermines the notion that the state enjoys any special form of legitimacy; he argues in favor of founding history and human society on subjectivity (practical reason).

After 1793 Fichte wrote nothing more about the Revolution, but his correspondence shows that he remained attached to revolutionary France for a long time. In addition to the previously cited Baggesen letter, in which he dedicates his system to France, witness this letter to Jung, dated 29 Fructidor, Year VI: "It is doing me no more than justice to regard me as an admirer of political liberty and of the nation that promises to propagate it. . . . In this respect I desire nothing more than to devote my life to the service of the great republic and to the education of its future citizens." Many commentators have noted the apparent reservation in the words "in this respect" (*in dieser Rücksicht*), upon which Fichte would elaborate in a letter written some months later again to Jung, dated 21 Floréal, Year VII: if republican principles are indeed the best, "to this point what also emerges clearly is that inconsistencies on both sides have made their *praxis* quite similar. The truth is that the republican *praxis* often seems even worse," owing to its excesses. But Fichte's doubts about the Terror vanished after the Rastatt massacre, and his commitment could not have been more categorical, as the rest of the letter to Jung shows: "It is clear that henceforth the French Republic is the only possible fatherland for an honest man. There is no other country to which he can devote his talents, for what depends upon a French victory now is not only the most cherished hopes but the very existence of mankind." In conclusion he adds: "To sum up, I solemnly pledge my talents and my will to the Republic, not in order to benefit from this action but in order, if I can, to help." Hence it is not difficult to understand how Fichte could have written to Reinhold on May 22, 1799, that he hoped for a French victory: "I am therefore more certain of this than of anything else in the world, that if the French do not win a total victory and do not bring about a change in Germany, or at any rate in a considerable portion of Germany, then within a few years' time there will be in this country no refuge for any man known to have thought a free thought at any time in his life." In that same year, 1799, at a time when a campaign by *Eudaimonia* against Fichte's "Jacobinism" was stirring up a debate about atheism, Fichte wrote: "There can be no doubt in the mind of any reasonable man that the principles that underlie the French Republic and others molded in its image are the only ones capable of assuring the dignity of man." In other words, in 1798 and 1799 Fichte was still defending the rights of man, still championing the French side in the ongoing war, and still prepared to offer his services to the Republic. In other words, he was still a supporter of the Revolution, and as Jaurès would later write in his *Histoire socialiste,* "Fichte was an enthusiastic supporter of the rights of man and human dignity, and he was clearly prepared to take part in the bitter struggle to defend them."

From the time of his arrival in Berlin on July 3, 1799, however, Fichte, deprived of an audience precisely because of his support of the Revolution, slowly began to separate himself from the French cause. For the first time he began to speak of the regeneration of Germany and of Europe through Germany, initially in the economic sphere, since it was for the Prussian government that he wrote *The Closed Commercial State* in 1800. In the same year he broached, in *The Vocation of Man,* the idea that the French Revolution had exhausted its possibilities and that there was therefore nothing more to be expected from France: "The force that has caused all this damage in violation of accepted standards must not be allowed to recommence in the same fashion. It cannot be destined to renew itself; it must have spent all its force forever in a single explosion." Fichte now increasingly rejected France and cast his lot on the side of Prussian power: in contrast to 1799, when he had stated that Germany was for him a foreign country, in 1807 he portrayed himself as a Prussian patriot in the *Second Dialogue* and proclaimed that "only Germany can through pursuit of its national goals embrace all humanity." No longer was the "saving nation, bearer of mankind's destiny," revolutionary France, which by now had become the realm of the "nameless man," as Fichte called Napoleon, who had usurped the monarchy without belonging to any dynasty of his own. (See Philonenko, *Essais sur la philosophie de la guerre,* p. 51.) That role now devolved upon Germany, alone among nations capable of "saving the culture of mankind."

The break with the French Revolution would manifest itself on the theoretical plane in Fichte's *Machiavelli,* in which he advocates the use of force in international affairs and argues that too much importance has been attached to "the rights of man and the inherent liberty and equality of all." Thus Fichte came to question the very same principles of the Revolution that he had argued in 1799 must inevitably enlist the support of "any reasonable man," and his doubt concerning those principles became increasingly radical. By the time he came to write the *Staatslehre* in 1813, he charged, in this culmination of his political career, that the *Social Contract* had posed the problem of the state "empirically and arbitrarily." In other words, Rousseau's thought was "haphazard and without speculative principles." It was upon this thought, moreover, "that the French Revolution rests. It is not surprising that, starting from such principles, it proceeded as it did." The problem for anyone who would interpret Fichte's philosophy today is to understand the precise meaning and scope of this evolution in his political thought.

Luc Ferry

FURTHER READING

FICHTE'S WORKS IN ENGLISH TRANSLATION

Addresses to the German Nation, trans. R. F. Jones and G. H. Turnbull. Westport, Conn., 1979.
Early Philosophical Writings, ed. Daniel Breazeale. Ithaca, N.Y., 1988.
Science of Knowledge, ed. Peter Heath and John Lachs. New York, 1970.
The Vocation of Man, trans. Peter Preuss. Indianapolis, 1987.

RELATED WORKS

Druet, Pierre-Philippe. "De l'anarchie à la dictature éducative: Métaphysique et politique chez Fichte." Doctoral thesis, Liège, 1973.
——— *Fichte.* Paris, 1977.
Ferry, Luc. *Philosophie politique,* 2 vols. Paris, 1984.
Gueroult, Martial. "Fichte et la Révolution française," in Gueroult, *Etudes sur Fichte.* Paris, 1974.
Philonenko, Alexis. *Théorie et praxis dans la pensée morale et politique de Kant et de Fichte en 1793.* Paris, 1968.
——— *Essais sur la philosophie de la guerre.* Paris, 1976.
Vlachos, Georges. *Fédéralisme et raison d'état dans la pensée internationale de Fichte.* Paris, 1948.

RELATED TOPICS

Burke   Kant   Liberty   Rights of Man   Rousseau

GUIZOT

W hen Guizot embarked on public life in 1814, the Revolution was a long way from becoming history. Systematically ignored by the men of the Empire, who believed they had ended it, its ghost made a powerful resurgence in the early years of the Restoration. The ultras, who saw the Revolution as nothing but a war on priests and honest men and decent values, constantly brandished the menace of its return. The slightest disturbance was enough to evoke the crimes of the Terror. Significantly, new editions of abbé Barruel's *Mémoires pour servir à l'histoire du Jacobinisme* proliferated in this period. The struggle between the Ancien Régime and the new France seemed almost to have begun anew. Thus throughout these years the interpretation of the Revolution was of fundamental political importance. The French felt an urgent need to reread their history in order to conceive their future.

The posthumous publication in 1818 of Mme. de Staël's *Considérations sur les principaux événements de la Révolution française* set the tone for liberal historiography by distinguishing between 1789 and 1793. The publication in the same year of J.-J. Mounier's *De l'influence attribuée aux philosophes, aux francs-maçons et aux illuminés dans la Révolution française* was part of the same effort to distinguish between the Revolution's doctrine and its works. Of this work Guizot noted that "Mounier carefully distinguishes between what preceded 1789 and what followed. This distinction is more important than is thought by those who mix everything up in order to denounce it all. They do not know how many people may be inclined to mix everything up in order to excuse it all; how many people would adopt the Revolution in toto rather than abandon it altogether and who would without much difficulty resolve themselves to defend those principles that have been challenged by justifying all the consequences that have been ascribed to them." Guizot thus dismissed both the ultra and the Jacobin interpretations of the Revolution, setting himself apart from all the liberals who ignored the fact that many "good citizens" were still frightened by memories of revolutionary terror. This view was perfectly matched to the objectives of a *juste milieu* politics, which sought to find a middle way of constitutional government between the Ancien Régime on the one hand and Jacobin ardor on the other. By distinguishing between a good and a bad Revolution, Guizot hoped to provide a foundation for such a middle way. In substance this approach was neither new nor original. Like all the liberals of his day, Guizot was in fact content to reproduce without ever giving a thought to pursuing the analyses developed as early as 1795 by Benjamin Constant, Daunou, and Boissy d'Anglas to explain how the Revolution had veered out of control. Nor did the works of Mignet and Thiers, the first to be written by men of the new generation, prove innovative in this respect. Whether they invoked external circumstances, fate, or the tactics of Robespierre, their perception of the Jacobin pathology owed everything to the Thermidorians. In many cases they actually took a step backwards conceptually as compared with, say, Benjamin Constant.

Guizot's great merit was to have been the first to move beyond the Thermidorian conceptualization of the issue, which he did for reasons that were inextricably political and intellectual. Although the Thermidorians had had no choice but to distinguish between 1789 and 1793, there was no need for them to bestow legitimacy on 1789 because at that time no one challenged the positive character of the Revolution; it was taken for granted. After 1815 the situation was almost the reverse. The ultras' attacks, which were designed to discredit the Revolution as a whole, forced the liberals to give new meaning to the very principle of the Revolution and thus to relegitimate 1789. Guizot thus felt no need to write a history of revolutionary events even though the Revolution as a political and philosophical issue is at the heart of all his works. Interpreting the course of the Revolution seemed less important to him than gaining a better understanding of its deeper historical *meaning*. Significantly, he chose to devote his efforts to retracing the overall development of French civilization in order to portray 1789 as its culmination. In his 1820–1821 lectures he observes: "Revolutions must be dated from the day of their outbreak. That is the only precise era that can be assigned to them. But it is not the one in which they take place. The shocks that are called revolutions are less a symptom of what is beginning than a declaration of what has passed." Guizot wanted to understand and to explain "the revolution considered not in its acts but in its principles." The true subject of his historical works was thus modern revolution. It was on the basis of this distinction between revolution as development of a civilization and revolution as event that he approached 1789. A revolution-event is thinkable and possible only if the slow work of civilization is thwarted, in which case the function of revolution is to resynchronize the time of events with that of the principles that secretly govern them. In this respect Guizot was a precursor of historical materialism, as is shown by this astonishing excerpt from an article he published in 1818 in the *Archives philosophiques, politiques et littéraires:* "I have watched children play with oval boxes that contain other boxes of progressively smaller size. The outer box, which is the largest, contains and in a sense owns all the others. Assume that the inner boxes are alive and endowed with the faculty of growth, and that the outer box is elastic but only to a certain extent, as required by the nature of things. So long as this elasticity is sufficient to accommodate the gradual increase in size of the inner boxes, the outer box will continue to contain and own them. But a moment will come when the elasticity of the envelope reaches its limit. The inner boxes will not on that account cease to grow. Then the outer box must explode in order to make room for a power whose development it can no longer either halt or permit. . . . The old aristocracy endured this fate. For centuries it resisted and it accommodated. In 1789 its elasticity and resistance had come to the end of their rope; it succumbed."

If Guizot did not write the history of the Revolution, he did propose a theory. For him, the two major developments in European civilization were the formation of nation-states (due to the movement of centralization and the principle of unity) and the emancipation of the human spirit (due to the movement of liberty and the principle of equality). Absolutism had made the French nation-state possible, but the failure of the Reformation in France had hampered emancipation of the human spirit. In Guizot's view modernity took shape in the sixteenth century through the conjunction of these two elements. But this conjunction entailed a crisis to the extent that the principles of free inquiry and centralization of power were in some ways contradictory, "the one being the defeat of absolute power in the spiritual order, the other its victory in the temporal order." The resolution of this contradiction, Guizot argued, lay in representative government, which effected a synthesis of centralization with liberty. Guizot developed on this basis a comparative history of various European countries, which he differentiated according to several criteria: the timing and conditions of emergence of a central power, the impact of the Reformation, and the manner in which the contradiction between the two motor forces of European civilization was expressed and resolved. In this analysis, developed during the Restoration, everything, or nearly everything, was new: the stress placed on the Church's role in history, the vision of the Reformation, the perception of the conditions of social simplification (development of the state and advent of the individual working hand in hand), the role ascribed to the Third Estate and the class struggle as a source of progress, and the idea of revolution as a crisis resulting from a clash between the principles of centralization and liberty. Guizot's interpretation marked a sharp departure from the usual readings of French history, and it modified the usual image of France's future by raising two central questions: the relation of the French Revolution to the English Revolution and the consequences of the failure of the Reformation in France. For Guizot, moreover, these two questions were related. To end the French Revolution, that is, to preserve only the principles of 1789, was for him tantamount to reproducing the equivalent of 1688 while at the same time importing the principles of the Reformation. Thus the true meaning of the French Revolution remained to be realized under the Restoration. By setting 1789 in the context of the *longue durée,* Guizot integrated the positive (liberty and equality) and rejected the negative (1793 and the Napoleonic episode). In other words, he restored the conceptual truth of the Revolution by envisioning it within a proper historical framework from which it derived its authentic and ultimate meaning. This historical fatalism, for which he would be criticized by certain of his contemporaries, was also part of a political argument. By presenting the Revolution as part of a historical movement extending over nearly thirteen centuries, Guizot in effect stressed the irreversible nature of its political and sociological consequences. He thus enabled the bourgeoisie to regain its confidence in the future and to recognize itself without shame or fear in the events of 1789. This portrayal explains the bluntness of his affirmation of the rights of new France in opposition to the nostalgia of the ultras: "The Revolution," he wrote in 1820, "was a war, the true war, of the kind with which the world is familiar between alien peoples. For more than thirteen centuries France contained two peoples, one victorious, the other vanquished. For more than thirteen centuries the vanquished people fought to throw off the yoke imposed by its vanquishers. Our history is the history of that struggle. In our time a decisive battle was fought. It was called the Revolution. . . . The result of the Revolution was not ambiguous. The former vanquished people became the vanquisher."

Once this indissociably historical and social legitimation of 1789 was out of the way, Guizot was also obliged to account for the dynamic of revolutionary events themselves. "How did this great generation of 1789, which so ardently and so sincerely wanted social reform and political liberty, hurl itself or find itself dragged into the darkness and storms of the Revolution?" Guizot does not separate this question from that of the failure of Thermidor. Therein lies his originality. He attempted to understand in a unified way all the vicissitudes of the revolutionary experience without limiting himself to analysis of the Jacobin pathology. Why did the men of 1789 and of Thermidor fail in their enterprise? This question suggested to Guizot what he saw as the task of his generation: to complete and stabilize the revolutionary process. It was the same task that the Thermidorians had set themselves twenty years earlier and had failed to carry through. Guizot's thinking about the Revolution was guided by this political concern. In this respect the Doctrinaires may be considered to be neo-Thermidorians. It was their relation to Thermidor that enabled them to clarify their vision of the Revolution as well as the meaning of their political struggle.

In 1815 Guizot remembered the hopes that the fall of Robespierre had raised in France. The prayer of thanksgiving that he and his mother said on the terrace of his family home at the news of 9 Thermidor still rang in his memory. "A new France emerged from that debris," he wrote in 1818 about that period. "And anyone who failed to notice the reaction of the antirevolutionary spirit against the Jacobin spirit in this period of formation and growth was a poor observer of the progress of the revolutionary principle, which continued despite many obstacles. Although Mme. de Staël did not altogether fail to perceive that progress, she was after this point perhaps not in a position to grasp all of the symptoms or to follow it with the attention it deserved." Thus Guizot quite clearly saw himself as having broken with the generation of Sieyès and Constant. He explained that generation's failure in two ways. First, it came too soon: the whole revolutionary process had destabilizing effects because it was in effect an accelerated process of catching up. "The Revolution," Guizot pointed out, "was called upon first of all to destroy. Its first laws were merely instruments of destruction. They were used to demolish not the government of the day but power itself, considered in an abstract fashion and independent of its possessor. That had to happen; it was a matter of changing not the motor but the machine, and not only the political machine but the entire society, that is, social situations and relations." In this sense the failure of Thermidor was connected with its having taken place in a critical period, at the end of which it was necessary to move ahead and think about positive construction. Like Auguste Comte, Guizot explained the superiority of his generation in these terms: it could hope to conclude as well as regenerate the Revolution only because it came at a moment when history was about to embark on a positive period. But for Guizot, Thermidor's failure also had an intellectual dimension: it reflected the inability of the men of that time to build on ideas suitable for establishing order in conditions of liberty. The Thermidorians never thought of guiding the Revolution back to its true principles.

Guizot's objective was therefore to identify those principles and embody them in stable institutions. "The true task of our time," he said in 1838, "is to determine whether the ideas of 1789 and the social state that they introduced can give rise to a stable and regular government. There are two absolutely essential conditions that must be met if we are to hope for success. First, we must purge the principles of 1789 of any anarchical alloy. Such an alloy was natural, inevitable; it was a consequence of the initial situation, the initial use of the ideas of 1789. Those ideas were used to destroy what existed at the time, government and society. In this effort they contracted a revolutionary character. The time has come to eliminate this [character] and restore them to their true and pure sense."

In contrast to the Thermidorians, Guizot did not assume that the ideas of 1789 formed a clearly defined system, exempt from all ambiguity. That is why he could not settle for simply opposing 1789 to 1793. Ending the Revolution for him meant something more profound: redefining its intellectual foundations. The failure of the Constituent Assembly, like that of the Thermidorians, was based, he believed, on a threefold ambiguity, involving their conceptions of representation, of sovereignty, and of equality. In Guizot's judgment, the Constituents and Thermidorians did not pursue their thinking about sovereignty to the end. Since the difference between national sovereignty and popular sovereignty was not really developed, it was difficult to distinguish the liberal part of their approach (the assumption that national sovereignty implies the existence of a zone that power cannot touch) from the democratic part. Nor were they able to produce an operational concept of representation, since they alternated between a traditional approach of representation of interests and a constructivist conception of the general interest (in which parliament was seen as the organ of the nation). Finally, they clumsily associated their critique of aristocracy and privileges with a positive philosophy of civil equality. Hence they had a hard time conceptualizing the relation between equality and citizenship.

Guizot proposed clearing up this threefold ambiguity by constructing a coherent political philosophy based on the three concepts of sovereignty of reason, political capacity, and cognitive representation. The concept of sovereignty of reason made it possible to retain the subjectivist notion of sovereignty, the cornerstone of the French tradition, while constituting it in a zone effectively void of power. (In addition, it had the advantage of accommodating both spiritualist and rationalist interpretations: sovereignty of God or sovereignty of truth.) Thus Guizot was able to dismiss both Rousseau and Bonald, popular sovereignty and divine-right monarchy. The theory of the sovereignty of reason, which *Le globe* during the Restoration called the "theory of the century," was extended by the sociological theme of capacities. No one could claim to possess or incarnate reason, but certain individuals demonstrated greater capacity than others to recognize and abide by it. Thus Guizot used a kind of sociology to get beyond the practical contradictions in the thought of 1789. In this perspective, the purpose of the representative system changed. It was no longer to manipulate a complex arithmetic of interests and wills but "to gather, to concentrate all the reason that exists scattered throughout society . . . to extract from society all that it possesses in the way of reason, justice, and truth in order to apply them to its government." Implicit in the theory of the sovereignty of reason was thus a new doctrine of representation as a cognitive process: representation was not a transfer of wills but a process for constituting public reason out of elementary ideas scattered through society. "In every society there exists a certain sum of correct ideas," Guizot explained. "This sum of correct ideas is scattered among the individuals who make up the society and is unequally distributed among them. . . . The problem is to gather up all the scattered and incomplete fragments of this power, to concentrate them, and to constitute them into a government. . . . What is called representation is nothing other than the means of arriving at this result. It is not an arithmetic machine intended to collect and enumerate individual wills. It is a natural process for extracting from the bosom of society the public reason that alone has the right to govern." Radicalizing this approach, Royer-Collard went so far as to say that the goal of representation could not be anything other than a metaphor.

Guizot's principal contribution to the history of the French Revolution was thus a reformulation of its fundamental principles. The exigencies of political battle under the Restoration led him to undertake the first global critical analysis of the Revolution.

Pierre Rosanvallon

Further reading

WORKS BY GUIZOT

Four brief articles published in *Archives philosophiques, politiques et littéraires* in the form of reviews of Mounier, Montlosier, and Staël: March 1818 (vol. 3, no. 9, pp. 47–55); June 1818 (vol. 3, no. 12, pp. 385–409); June and July 1818 (vol. 3, no. 12, pp. 410–435 and vol. 4, no. 13, pp. 63–85).

Des moyens de gouvernement et d'opposition dans l'état actuel de la France. Paris, 1821.

Du gouvernement de la France depuis la Restauration et du ministère actuel. Paris, 1820.

Essais sur l'histoire de France. Paris, 1823.

Histoire de la civilisation en Europe. Paris, 1828. New edition annotated by Pierre Rosanvallon, Paris, 1985.

Histoire des origines du gouvernement représentatif, 2 vols. Paris, 1851.

Trois générations, 1789–1814–1848. Paris, 1863.

RELATED WORKS

Johnson, Douglas. *Guizot: Aspects of French History (1787–1874).* London, 1963.

Pouthas, Charles. *Guizot pendant la Restauration: Préparation de l'homme d'état.* Paris, 1923.

Rosanvallon, Pierre. *Le moment Guizot.* Paris, 1985.

Related topics

Centralization	Equality	Staël	Thermidorians
Constant	Liberty	Terror	

HEGEL

A ccording to an opinion that was widely accepted for far too long, the young Hegel's enthusiasm for the French Revolution is supposed to have given way gradually to a veritable hatred of the ideas of 1789, culminating, Rudolph Haym tells us, in a "totally antirevolutionary" attitude whose aim was to justify, through a conservative philosophy of history, reality as it existed. This contention is simply wrong, and the work of Eric Weil and Joachim Ritter has definitively refuted it. Although there is no denying that Hegel's thought evolved considerably as his ultimate philosophy of history took shape, the texts of his maturity leave no doubt about his undying admiration for the Revolution, which in his eyes remained a decisive moment in world history. The *Lessons on the Philosophy of History,* for example, still describe the great Revolution as "a superb sunrise," rightly celebrated at the time by "all thinking people": "A sublime emotion reigned in those times," and "the enthusiasm of the spirit caused the world to tremble." What Hegel admired and continued to admire in the Revolution was nothing other than the advent of subjectivity and reason in the political sphere: "Never since the sun had stood in the firmament and the planets revolved around it had it been perceived that man's existence centers in his head, that is, in thought, inspired by which he builds up the world of reality." What burst forth with the Revolution was that abstract humanism by which the individual, "because he is man and not because he is a Jew, Catholic, Protestant, German, Italian, or what have you" (*Principles of the Philosophy of Right*), becomes the true subject of the political order. The formulation is important; it sets Hegel in opposition to the theories of Burke and Maistre. It also explains why Hegel was a fierce adversary of any form of Restoration to the end of his days.

That said, it remains to understand how and why Hegel, alongside and even in intimate conjunction with this favorable judgment, drew up a veritable philosophical indictment of the Revolution and its terrorist consequences in the *Phenomenology of the Spirit* (1807).

In the dialectic of the *Phenomenology,* the Revolution is directly related to the "world of utility" that in Hegel's eyes constituted the "truth" of the *Aufklärung,* its ultimate appearance. In this world, everything is judged according to its relation to the individual will. It is clear, in fact, that the concept of utility is in itself inconsistent, that it refers to something other than itself: the useful is always useful through and for someone, so that the world of utility makes sense only in terms of that "absolute freedom" for which "the world is uniquely its will, and that will is the general will." Hegel is here taking aim at Rousseau, and the chapter of the *Phenomenology* devoted to the analysis of the Terror begins with a critique of the *Social Contract* that is essentially a reformulation of section 258 of the *Philosophy of Right* and of the whole *Philosophy of History*. What the *Social Contract* attempts to achieve, according to Hegel, is simply an absolute unification of individual wills in the concept of the general will. Hegel does not criticize this aim as such; the Hegelian state is itself portrayed as a reconciliation of the universal and the particular. What Hegel attacks in Rousseau's project and in its application to the Revolution is the fact that this reconciliation is conceived in a purely abstract and formal way, exclusive of all mediation, and that with "this formalism of freedom, with this abstraction, nothing solid is left to be established in the form of organization." "It has been said that the French Revolution grew out of philosophy, and it is not without reason that philosophy has been called universal wisdom, for it is not only truth in itself and for itself, as pure essence, but also truth as it takes on life in the world. Hence one must not rise up in opposition when it is said that the Revolution received its first impetus from philosophy. But that philosophy was first of all only abstract thought . . . which is an incommensurable difference." Hegel's reasoning is essentially this: if Rousseau's requirement, later incorporated into the ethics of Kant and Fichte, is that individual wills immediately identify themselves in a kind of fusion with the general will, two consequences inevitably follow.

First, all circumscribed social organizations, or, as Hegel calls them, "spiritual masses" (orders, corps, corporations, and so on), must disappear because in them the will is inevitably dedicated to some private purpose. Consequently, "the undivided substance of absolute freedom ascends the throne of the world with no power whatsoever in a position to resist it."

Second, the general will can never under these conditions take the form of a particular action or work: "Moving to activity and creating objectivity, it makes nothing singular but only laws and actions of state." Hence it was for an essential, not a contingent, reason that the *Social Contract* and, subsequently, the Jacobins could not abide a representative system or achieve a stable constitution or resolve the question of government in any durable manner, for "government . . . wants and at the same executes a determinate order and action. It therefore, on the one hand, excludes other individuals from its operation and, on the other hand, constitutes itself as if it were a determinate will and therefore opposed to the universal will. The government therefore cannot appear other than as a faction," so that its existence is one with its culpability.

Starting from principles like these, the Revolution could not help sinking into Terror. If absolute freedom can produce neither a positive work nor a positive operation, it has no alternative left but a negative operation. It is solely the fury of destruction, or, as Hegel wrote in the *Philosophy of Right:* "It was only abstractions that were being used; the Idea was lacking, and the experiment ended in the maximum of frightfulness and terror." The relation between general will and particular will when there is "no intermediate constituent part to unite them" can only end in the destruction of the empty singular, of the singular as such: "The unique work and operation of universal freedom is therefore death, and more precisely a death that has no inner amplitude because it accomplishes nothing. . . . It is also the coldest and flat-test of deaths, with no more significance than slicing a head of cabbage or swallowing a drink of water." The Terror turns out to lead directly to anarchy: in order to dissolve and liquidate all that is opposed to it in the form of the particular (most notably the corporations), it must institute itself, create an organization; but that organization, itself necessarily particular, is immedi-ately suspect, even guilty, so that the process of dissolution of all institutions seems neverending.

More stress is placed on this crucial point in the *Philosophy of History* than in the *Phenomenology*. With much profundity Hegel sets forth the prob-lem that the Revolution bequeathed to posterity and that remains even today one of the major aporias of our modernity: how is political stability to be conceived when the foundation of the whole social organization lies "in the principle of atoms, of particular wills?"

Compared with the *Phenomenology*, the final chapter of the *Philosophy of History* seems to me to touch on two new themes, which complement and enrich the analysis of the Revolution's intellectual origins.

For reasons of internal consistency, the *Phenomenology* treated not "the moral vision of the world" but only the *Social Contract* as the intellectual source of the Revolution. The *Philosophy of History*, like the *Philosophy of Right*, placed greater stress on the conjunction of these two moments, in fact indissoluble, in the formation of the will, Robespierre being in a sense the political symbol of their conjunction: for the insistence on subordination of the particular to the general was nothing other than the insistence on virtue that caused a cloud of "suspicion" to hover over every singular life. "Robespierre set up the principle of virtue as supreme, and it may be said that with this man virtue was an earnest matter. Virtue and Terror are the order of the day."

The second theme introduced by the *Philosophy of History* has to do with a question explicitly raised by Hegel, namely, why what "would remain quiet theory among the Germans" had to be "applied practically" by the French with the well-known consequences. For Hegel, the answer lay in the contrast between Catholicism and the Reform spirit that prevailed in Protestant Ger-many. This contrast cannot be examined in detail here, although it should be said that it marks one of the first occurrences in political philosophy of the distinction between reform and revolution. Suffice to say that for Hegel Prot-estantism was fundamentally reformist because it alone had been able "to advance to consciousness of the absolute summit of self-consciousness," that is, to true rather than merely formal consciousness of the unity of the rational and the real. And if the real is rational, the very idea of "revolutionizing" it is devoid of sense. By contrast, "in the Catholic religion, this spirit [within which God is known] is rigidly opposed in reality to the self-conscious spirit" and "only in the Protestant principle of the spirit does there exist the absolute possibility and necessity that the power of the state, religion, and the principle of philosophy coincide and the reconciliation of reality as such with the Spirit is accomplished" (*Encyclopedia of Philosophical Sciences*, section 532).

This distinction brings us to the heart of the Hegelian interpretation: if Protestantism is reformist and if the Catholicism of the Latin countries inclines them toward revolution, it is because only the former represents a just philosophy of history, which sees in the real not an obstacle to be violently transformed in the name of a virtuous ideal but the very locus of the incarnation of the rational. This goal is the ultimate reason for Hegel's twofold judgment of the Revolution, at once favorable and critical: the Revolution must be admired for what it contributed to universal history as content (the emergence of man or of subjectivity in the political sphere) but criticized for the terrorist formalism characteristic of the process by which that content was established. We must, Hegel says in the *Philosophy of History,* "consider the French Revolution in its organic connection with universal history, for in its substantial import that event is world-historical, and the formalist struggle that we discussed [earlier] must be properly distinguished from its wider bearings."

Profound as it is, the Hegelian interpretation must confront two difficulties, which are more substantial than they might seem at first sight. Here I can do no more than mention them by way of conclusion. The first has to do with the fact that the critique of moral formalism, however attractive it may appear, is in Hegel's system inseparable from the philosophy of history, which alone gives it its true significance. Hence it would be pointless, not to say incoherent, to adopt Hegel's critique of the moral vision of the world while rejecting as rationalist and metaphysical the theory of the ruse of reason that underlies it at every point. The second difficulty, very perspicaciously noted by Habermas in *Theory and Practice,* is in a sense more serious, because it is internal to the Hegelian system: if the argument that forms the basis for the critique of the Revolution is in the final analysis the same one that leads to the conclusion that the real is rational, it is no longer possible to understand what standpoint a Hegelian critique might adopt; the very content of Hegel's philosophy in a very general sense precludes taking a moral-critical stance toward the events of world history.

Luc Ferry

FURTHER READING

WORKS BY HEGEL

Hegel's Philosophy of Right, trans. T. M. Knox. Oxford, 1952.
Jenenser Realphilosophie (Natur- und Geistesphilosophie), 2 vols. Leipzig, 1939.
The Phenomenology of the Spirit, trans. J. B. Baillie. London, 1931.
The Philosophy of History, trans. J. Sibree. New York, 1956.

RELATED WORKS

Bourgeois, Bernard. *La pensée politique de Hegel.* Paris, 1969.
Habermas, Jürgen. *Theory and Practice,* trans. John Viertel. Boston, 1973.
Haym, Rudolph. *Hegel und seine Zeit.* Berlin, 1857.
Hyppolite, Jean. *Genèse et structure de la "Phénoménologie de l'esprit" de Hegel,* 2 vols. Paris, 1956.
Ritter, Joachim. *Hegel and the French Revolution,* trans. Richard Winfield. Cambridge, 1982.
Rosenzweig, Franz. *Hegel und der Staat.* Munich and Berlin, 1920.
Weil, Eric. *Hegel et l'état.* Paris, 1950.

RELATED TOPICS

Burke	Kant	Maistre	Rousseau
Fichte	Liberty	Robespierre	Terror

JAURÈS

Socialist: this was the banner-epithet under which Jaurès' history of the French Revolution appeared. And it was this aspect of the work that Aulard deemed both narrow and pedantic and, what is more, superfluous: the label could have been cut out, according to Aulard, without altering the work's import.

It is true that Jaurès' history could be read and judged in terms of strictly academic criteria. Jaurès, like all historians of the French Revolution, had carefully read his predecessors: Thiers, Michelet, Buchez and Roux, Louis Blanc, Quinet, Taine. He knew and made better use than they had done of works contemporary with the Revolution: he was familiar with Burke, Forster, and Fichte. He had explored German philosophy, a corpus neglected by the French. He had gone through the *Archives parlementaires* and *Le moniteur,* all too ingenuously according to Aulard (although subsequent historiography has tended to restore legitimacy to his confidence), and had unearthed little-known documents and individuals. It was an immense effort, whose shortcomings (including his odd silences, in particular the failure to deal with efforts to reform the monarchy; lack of references and headings to channel the flow of the prose; and the bewildering mixture of long citations from the sources with the author's commentary) have sometimes been emphasized by academic critics. But the criticisms themselves show the extent to which Jaurès and the historians of his time were exploring the same field of research using identical methods.

Yet Jaurès explicitly set out to tell the story of the Revolution from a "socialist" point of view. What did this perspective mean? Was it a book intended to be useful to political activists? Or was its purpose to show what was already socialist in the Revolution? Or was the work socialist because it availed itself of a Marxist interpretation? These three possibilities are not mutually exclusive.

The usefulness of his work was of constant concern to Jaurès. The history he set out to write was intended to be part of a vast collective effort by a group of historians to write the history of France right up to the turn of the twentieth century. It was also to be a work of militants, of socialists writing for socialists. The three thousand pages for which Jaurès assumed personal responsibility and which were published in installments between 1898 and 1903 never wavered from this pedagogical purpose. They were to help proletarians "meditate usefully." Some of the lessons were brutally stark: in contemplating the heads of Bertier and Foullon carried on pikes, symbols of the Revolution's return to the barbarity of the Ancien Régime (Jaurès had read his Quinet), proletarians would understand how a political movement could slip into imitative and archaic forms of savagery. Others were more difficult to interpret: the details of the mechanism of election to the Estates General, so minute and yet so pregnant with consequences (which Jaurès, incidentally, was the first historian to notice), were supposed to teach the proletarian never to neglect "any detail of an action, however indirect or remote." For the sake of the narrative, Jaurès introduced an imaginary socialist commentator, frequently of vehement temperament, whose responsibility was to present the proletarian point of view on each episode. Clearly, this was a history upon which the politics of the present weighed heavily. The expropriation of clerical property was seen in terms of the separation of church and state; abbé Maury's anti-Semitism was seen in terms of the Dreyfus Affair; the revolutionary war was seen in the light of the perils of the moment, an approach that made Jaurès more than a little suspicious of "patriotic" histories (Michelet's as much as the neo-Robespierrists') that linked war and revolution and made France a martyr for liberty. Jaurès, though careful not to substitute his own sensibility for that of the men of 1789, insisted on his right to "import the commitments of the present into the past," among them his socialist faith.

Did he hope that by doing so he would bring out the ways in which the French Revolution anticipated the socialist movement of the following century? There is no simple answer. First of all, Jaurès did indeed determine what was great in the Revolution by measuring it against the socialist ideal, and he did sort out the men of the Revolution according to their varying abilities to anticipate the future: he placed those, such as Rabaut-Saint-Etienne, who had no inkling of the new politics in one group, and those, like Barnave, who did have some glimmering of it in another. The visionary talents of the men of the Revolution constituted his major argument against Taine: how dare Taine accuse men who had seen so accurately and so far into the future of "abstraction"? Still, anticipation was an ambiguous concept, to be used with caution. There were false anticipations, such as the "socialisms" that Lichtenberger thought he discovered in the archaic and conventual utopias of the eighteenth century. There were also confused anticipations, such as those of Marat and the Constituent Assembly, for there was no revolutionary clairvoyance in preaching extremist measures before "the state of things made them possible or even conceivable to a large number of people." What constituted a "correct" anticipation? For Jaurès, the answer was quite simply the ability to illuminate present action and to judge, in the light of a given moment, just how far revolutionary democracy might go. Take, for example, Momoro, who shortly after the Convention convened raised the prospect of an agrarian law before the newly elected deputies, and compare him with Danton, who tried to reassure those same deputies: in this situation, it was Danton who was correct, because no one at that time possessed the "formula" of the new Revolution. In order to understand history in motion one has to look beyond the present, but such peering into the future has to be carefully controlled. Hence the socialist history of the Revolution is by no means a history of the socialist revolution.

Was Jaurès' work socialist because it was written under the patronage of Marx (as well as of Michelet and Plutarch), and thus was yet another country added to the expanding territory of Marxist interpretation? So it has been seen by Franco Venturi, Ernest Labrousse (who believed that Jaurès' thinking was "almost identical" to Marx's), and Madeleine Rebérioux. The last of these, in order to justify her argument that Jaurès permanently embraced Marx's basic methodology at the very moment when he was criticizing it as "entirely outdated," attempts to portray this sour note as a momentary consequence of strictly political difficulties during the years when Jaurès found himself at odds with the French Workers' Party and German socialism. To settle the question and measure Jaurès' debt to Marx, one might consider the importance ascribed to economics in historical causality, the interpretation of the rights of man, and the conception of the relation between freedom and necessity.

The first of these three points is the least controversial. The French Revolution was a child of wealth: that is the central argument of socialist history. At the time it was a new argument: Jaurès thus differed from both Taine and Michelet. Although he sensed, in such events as the Réveillon conflict, the danger to the bourgeois Revolution from "obscure and profound galleries of misery," he held that the economic vitality of the bourgeoisie was the very substance of the revolutionary event. This certainty was also a wish: if one grants that the French Revolution resulted from the overall good economic situation of the eighteenth century and the increasing prosperity of the bourgeoisie, then the proletariat, whose historical fate is linked to that of the bourgeoisie, can hope that its revolution will grow out of something other than destitution. Jaurès was always hostile to the idea, central to Marx's work, of an absolutely destitute class that would owe its universal character to the infinity of its suffering. In his eyes even the German proletariat was not totally naked; at the very least it possessed the historical achievements of the French proletariat. Hence proletarians always had more to lose than their chains, and Jaurès accordingly rejected any form of proletarian messianism on fundamental grounds. That repudiation explains why he had little interest in short-term crises, in particular the crisis of 1788: to have dwelt on it might have suggested that revolutions could arise out of the depths of distress. By contrast, he described as no one before him had ever done the great increase of wealth over the course of the century, the transformation of the cities, the growth of new trades, and the newfound commercial prosperity of provincial towns and port cities. In this respect Jaurès' debt to Marx and, through Marx, to Barnave was real. What he borrowed from them was the idea that the social takes precedence over the political and that the bourgeoisie was already in control of society when the Revolution broke out, so that the French Revolution was simply the culmination of a long-term process—the consecration, through the seizure of political power, of a seizure of power already accomplished in another sphere: "A new distribution of wealth leads to a new distribution of power."

The French Revolution was thus the translation into political terms of the bourgeoisie's economic domination. But it was also more than that. Jaurès repeatedly insisted on the autonomy of the political with respect to the economic. So did Marx, according to Labrousse and Rebérioux. But Jaurès' attitude was different. In closing the volume devoted to the Constituent Assembly, he expresses his regret that, because of the need to portray the growth of bourgeois interests, he was unable to give the vast intellectual achievements of the eighteenth century their due. This was not simply a somewhat negligent tip of the hat, in the Marxian manner, to the superstructure's supposed capacities of reaction. For Jaurès it was an occasion to indicate the limits of the Marxist method, which was no doubt an excellent simplifying tool well suited to a rapid reading of history but was incapable of fully exploring the depths of reality. Jaurès' analysis of the causes of the Revolution therefore emphasizes the simultaneous effects of economic and intellectual factors, not a succession first of one, then of the other. Enlightenment thought is treated on a footing of equality with bourgeois enrichment: "The bourgeoisie achieved class consciousness, while thought achieved universal consciousness."

The second test of Jaurès' originality is his interpretation of the rights of man. Did Jaurès adopt Marx's famous distinction between formal rights and real rights? Did he, like Marx, choose historical right over natural right, or did he more subtly subsume the latter in the former; or, to put it another way, did he make natural right the culmination of history? Despite the brevity of his explicit remarks on the Declaration of the Rights of Man, Jaurès' entire work treats this fundamental question—although not without difficulties.

To begin with, Jaurès was well aware of the difficulty of reconciling the two kinds of rights. If, as the Constituent Assembly asserted, man has the right "to come and go, think, live, and make use of his liberty in any way so long as it does not deny the liberty of others" (note, in passing, the euphoric accents that underscore this freedom of action), and if the social state into which man enters when he renounces the isolation of the state of nature fortifies that liberty, then obviously liberty comes first. Given that priority, what weight can historic right have, even if it involves a happy expedient such as the title of royalty, "a device suggested by the experience of centuries"? A "metaphysical abyss" thus opened up beneath the Constituents, one that was noticed among them by the more subtle thinkers such as Malouet and Mirabeau, who had little use for a Declaration of Rights because they sensed how difficult it would be to link the primary ideal of natural liberty to the "chain of historical necessities."

Does it follow, as Marx maintained, that reconciliation of the two kinds of rights is impossible? Jaurès answered in the negative, but the examples he gave sometimes illustrate the difficulty rather than eliminate it. Consider, for example, the Third Estate attempting to establish bourgeois property by abolishing feudal and ecclesiastical property and invoking both rights at once. According to Jaurès, the Third Estate was correct to do so. Yet each type of legitimation carried with it a danger. To invoke natural right was to say that bourgeois property arises out of man's free activity and that it is a right of the individual prior to any law. Very well, but that invocation treated the law of a particular period as though it belonged to the eternal order of things. On the other hand, to invoke historical right was to say that bourgeois property such as it existed at the end of the eighteenth century determined the concrete shape of individual liberty. Again very well, but to do so meant setting an expiration date to the bourgeoisie's lease. For Jaurès, the two errors were clearly not symmetrical. The first (eternalizing the historical) was of a theoretical order. The second (historicizing the eternal) was simply of a pragmatic order: to make rights subject to the pure law of time was not a conceptual error but a tactical blunder. Because no one could muster much energy in defense of a historically circumscribed right, why should revolutionaries deprive themselves of the enthusiasm set free by the idea of eternity even if it was born of illusion? Here we see how the balance that Jaurès sought to maintain between historical right and legal right breaks down in the middle of his argument because of the powerful claims of historicism.

Jaurès' distaste for the powers of illusion and his reluctance to admit that the revolutionary movement could make fools of people suggested one final argument: the Third Estate had been correct to invoke natural right not only because doing so gave a boost to activism but also because it had taken much history just to arrive at the concept of natural right. Legal abstraction was at that time the culmination of historical evolution, the long-ripened fruit of the simultaneous growth of the individual and the state, working in concert to free themselves from feudalism and the Church. It was not easy "to free oneself in a moment, by force of intellect, from all secondary and changing institutions" in order to conceive abstract liberty. Hence it was history itself that had made emancipation from history possible—an emancipation that was not the negation but the consecration of history.

One last thorny problem remained: was the historical movement that had given rise to the abstract idea of liberty likely to call it into question in the future? Presumably anyone who had "essentially changing conceptions of society and the world" would be prepared to answer this question in the affirmative: the characteristics of eternity and universality ascribed to rights would eventually disappear as history progressed. Jaurès nevertheless affirmed the existence of a *patrie* of rights both prior and superior to history. Of the decision by the Constituent Assembly to sacrifice the voting rights of the colored, Jaurès commented that this would be an understandable decision if one believed that the limits of the Revolution were defined by the essential interests of the bourgeoisie, but that it was an incomprehensible decision when made in the name of humanity. Hence there was something in the Declaration of Rights other than the masked expression of bourgeois self-interest, something that transcended history and could therefore be interpreted as a promise by the working class itself, a universal over and above its historical agents and embodiments and contemporary with the humanity in man. The grandeur of the Constituent Assembly was precisely to have wedded democratic natural law with the historical law of the monarchy (an achievement for which he praised the heroes of that compromise, such as Mirabeau) and to have revealed what was universal in bourgeois justice.

This was not an easy position to get across to others or for that matter to hold oneself. Jaurès in his Latin thesis had shown that the distinction between passive citizens and active citizens was legally absurd but offered a marvelous illustration of the inanity of formal rights in a democracy in which equality had not been achieved, a distinction very close to Marx's notion of the mask/revelation. By contrast, in the *Histoire socialiste* this distinction, for which three explanations are given (the Constituents' uneasiness about the poor, their fears that the votes of the poor would be manipulated by nobles and priests, and their awareness of the ignorance of the unfortunate), is portrayed as portending a promise of its own abolition. Jaurès singled out the remarks of Duport, who envisioned a future in which property qualifications for voting would be different and who showed that the distinction between active and passive citizens had immediately alerted "the people of toil and misery" to the need for recasting the "right to promulgate rights" in the light of natural law. Jaurès' interpretation this time is a long way from that of Marx.

Unlike Marx, Jaurès did not subsume natural right under historical right. Nor did he treat natural right as a pure culmination, a historical fulfillment. The concept had of course undergone a long historical gestation; in that sense it was indeed a culmination. But it was a right that had to be contemporary with humanity itself; in that sense it was indeed a point of departure. That is why the most admirable words of the Revolution, in Jaurès' view, were those spoken by Mirabeau: "We are entitled to believe that we are beginning the history of men." If this statement was, as Jaurès believed, an "outcry of humanity" to be remembered for the coming proletarian revolution, then clearly its purpose was not to mask/reveal the historical interests of the bourgeoisie but to free mankind from history. If the bourgeois conception of rights could be used in struggles of varying social base and historical significance, those rights must be something other than the disguised expression of bourgeois interests; they must incorporate some measure of indeterminacy. The difficulty for Jaurès lay in understanding the notion that rights are both within history and outside it. His thought is riven by divided loyalties: to Marx, who "immersed all categories in Heraclitus' river," and to Fichte, for whom history was not life's mistress.

The third area in which we may judge the degree of Jaurès' difference from Marx concerns the marriage of freedom and necessity. Historical necessity is subject to a thousand accidents: Jaurès fully subscribed to this maxim of Engels, which had become a commonplace; but in doing so he placed those "accidents" in such a light that they altered necessity itself. Few other histories of the Revolution so regularly set what might have been alongside what was. Mirabeau's political wager serves as the basis for imagining an alternative to what actually happened, and Jaurès details the possible consequences: if Louis XVI had become king of the Revolution, modern France would not have had to break with its traditions, and the French could have spared themselves the need for violence. Jaurès does not hesitate to reargue the king's trial, attempting as he does to imagine the consequences of a better, more intelligent defense. He sees the defeat of the Gironde as due largely to circumstances: the Girondins were defeated not because they identified with the bourgeoisie and could no longer claim to act in concert with the people, and not because they were doctrinaire, systematic thinkers, but because they let the reins of power slip from their hands. And above all he sees the war as a terrible stain on the Revolution and not as the result of its "natural development." Brought about by artifice, by the laborious intrigue of the Gironde, the war revealed not historical necessity but foolish and wicked human will. No doubt the torrent of the Revolution was irresistible, but the course of its flow was not laid down in advance. As a politician, Jaurès was aware at every moment of the paths it might have taken, of others it avoided, and of the limitless consequences of decisions made by a roll of the dice.

To tell the story of the Revolution in this way requires that a theoretical problem be resolved first: in a historicist account, what influence can the thoughts and actions of individuals have? Jaurès returned time and time again to this awful question: the issue was whether mankind had hitherto been "like a sleeping passenger, carried by the current of the river without contributing to the movement and awaking at intervals to remark that the landscape had changed." Jaurès' answer was no: in his preface to *Capital* he singles out a sentence in which Marx speaks of shortening socialism's gestation and alleviating its birth pangs, and from this suggestion he concludes that men can "set the common rule that guides their action" (his definition of republic, incidentally) and change the course of history.

Jaurès conceded this much to necessity, however: beyond a certain point, the consequences of revolutionary decisions were inevitable. This maxim was true of the war: once war was declared, there was no alternative but to fight to the end, if need be imposing revolutionary dictatorship on other countries. As for the *journée* of May 31, the flood of detail about the preparations for action allows room for alternatives at every point until it becomes clear that there is no choice but to go along with the coup, at which point the account is simply broken off. Jaurès' treatment of these cases reveals his own attitude toward necessity. As soon as it rears its head, Jaurès cuts short his narrative and proceeds straight to the conclusion.

This acceleration of narrative time also attests to an intellectual embarrassment. Consider Robespierre's elimination of the Hébertists and Dantonists. Jaurès is well aware of how the Committee of Public Safety's arbitrary systematization transformed "what was perhaps only a vague dream of overheated imaginations" into "a fully formed plot ready to erupt at any moment." Yet a few pages later this lethal distortion of the facts strikes him as inevitable: there was no alternative to the Terror for ensuring the unity of the Revolution. To Jaurès this way of proceeding was detestable, as was the violence done to the legal majority by the minority on May 31, but it was nevertheless legitimate in both cases on grounds of the Revolution's higher interest, a principle that is never really explained, is justified in conventional terms by foreign and domestic war, and is weakly defended. Once the Dantonist faction is eliminated, Jaurès recovers his independent attitude toward necessity: with the Dantonist party out of the way, a Dantonist policy now seems desirable and possible and the Terror a pointless routine. Never mind the difficulties of calling in Floréal for the indulgence that had been guillotined in Germinal; let us concentrate instead on Jaurès' relief in returning to the distinction between the possible and the real, value and fact, a sign that what interested him in the history he was recounting was the prodigious pace of events, of episodes not at all implicit in the causes.

These features of Jaurèsian history—the importance ascribed to ideas, the autonomous existence of natural law, the existence of deliberate, voluntary individual initiative—explain why it was a history of endless complexity (under the triple patronage of Marx, Michelet, and Plutarch, which many historians, such as Venturi, see as a symptom of lack of principles rather than as a sign of originality). There is complexity, first of all, in the circumstances, which are never identical: Jaurès excelled at demonstrating the singularity, almost the peculiarity, of those "moments" in the Revolution when the pendulum seemed to swing from one side to the other, such as the brief period of Girondin ascendancy that made the Gironde so stubborn in its pursuit of war. There is also complexity in the men; sympathy and a talented pen enabled Jaurès to produce a gallery of subtle portraits, from Dumouriez, a man of "luminous and lively egoism unclouded by any prejudice," to Mirabeau, "in whom the vehemence of the passions animated a great logical mind," to the Girondins, so "indulgent toward life's amenities and joys"—an indication of hedonism, which in Jaurès, hostile to restrictive virtues, is always a positive sign. (Such comprehension was suspect to Mathiez, who accused Jaurès "of having extended the habit of parliamentary camaraderie to the misfits and *apaisés* of the revolutionary assemblies.") And last but not least, there was complexity in the relation between men and circumstances, each man being judged in relation to the exact moment of his action. Robespierrist historiography mechanically repeats the passage in which Jaurès, called upon to choose sides in the convention, instead of taking his place, as Michelet imagines himself doing, between Cambon and Carnot (a choice that Jaurès judged not very bold), declares that he would have sat down alongside Robespierre. Yes, but when? In the summer of 1793, when it seemed to him that Robespierre's policy was identical with the direction of the Revolution itself. He has already denounced Robespierre at an earlier stage as narrow-minded, encrusted with "layers of hatred that have laid themselves down in his heart one upon another," and blind enough to slander even the great Condorcet. And later he attacks the Robespierre of Prairial, Year II, as a man in a frenzy, obsessed with bloody memories. In reality it is always the moment, sketched with extreme precision, that determines Jaurès' approval or disapproval.

Thus everything in his history depends on judgment of the "right" moment and the "appropriate" measure. Fichte had justified expropriation of clerical property on the grounds that it belonged to the Church only by virtue of a fool's bargain: it had been given in return for the promise of an invisible world, so that confiscating it meant nothing more than reclaiming the right to free thought. Jaurès observed that the Constituent Assembly asked for less: it dissociated its political activities from the question of belief. Philosophically far more timid than Fichte, the deputies were nevertheless politically bolder and more effective, for "many murmurs, beliefs, and dreams of the past continued to hover about the ancient human forest." It was judicious, therefore, to use the ax "just enough to allow the Revolution to pass." But it was difficult to say how much was "just enough," particularly when it was a question of the extent to which liberty could be suspended: this gray area is the source of the indeterminacy in Jaurès' narrative. But that indeterminacy proves fruitful, for it makes all history the history of a gap.

There is a gap between the different periods of the Revolution; and another between men's intentions and their actions; and still another between consciousness and the facts, for sometimes the former anticipated the latter (as in the case of the flight to Varennes, vindication for so many prophets), while at other times the facts were in advance of thought (as in the broad-based electoral system, ahead of its time, proposed by the Constituent Assembly). The logic of the intellect and the logic of things do not march to the same drummer. What proletarians were supposed to learn from this "socialist" history was paradoxically that the mechanism of the class struggle neither explains everything nor is responsible for everything. For example, the class struggle does not explain the Le Chapelier Law, which for Marx represented a true bourgeois coup d'état that stripped the working class of the right of association. But one must be careful, Jaurès argues, not to ascribe to that law a brutality actually conferred on it by later antagonisms, for neither Le Chapelier nor the deputies of the Constituent Assembly, who passed it unanimously in a spirit of statist individualism that led them to detest all corporations and organizations, intended to disarm the proletariat. Nor was the class struggle responsible for everything that happened, for even when it played its part it was not an inexorable or automatic mechanism. Hence it was important, Jaurès maintained, not to neglect battles with limited objectives, such as the difficult fight for the expropriation of feudalism, or ventures without immediate prospects, such as the Revolution's educational projects. If proletarians interpreted the Revolution simply as the necessary product of the class struggle, they would fail to recognize the resources available to them under democracy.

In this way Jaurès came back to the principal concern of his "socialist" history: to root tomorrow's revolution in the French democratic tradition; to teach the proletariat not to be contemptuous of the politics of amelioration or of the lengthy education of the masses that precedes rather than follows the revolution; to repeat the message that one society cannot be substituted for another at a single stroke, and that even if the Revolution cannot be "compressed into a single, indivisible point in time" and thus treated as a unified whole, it does not therefore cease to be revolutionary.

Mona Ozouf

F<small>URTHER</small> READING

WORKS BY JAURÈS

Histoire socialiste de la Révolution française, ed. Albert Soboul. Paris, 1969.

RELATED WORKS

Dommanget, Maurice. "Sur Jaurès historien de la Révolution française," in *La pensée socialiste devant la Révolution française*. Paris, 1966.

Europe, special issue on Jean Jaurès, October–November 1958.

Noland, Aaron. "Individualism in Jean Jaurès' Thought," *Journal of the History of Ideas*, March 1961.

Philonenko, Alexis. *Etudes kantiennes*. Paris, 1982.

Rebérioux, Madeleine. "Jaurès, historien de la Révolution française," in *La pensée socialiste devant la Révolution française*. Paris, 1966.

Venturi, Franco. *Historiens du XXe siècle*. Geneva, 1966.

R<small>ELATED</small> TOPICS

Barnave
Danton
Enlightenment
Fichte

Girondins
Marat
Marx
Michelet

Mirabeau
Quinet
Revolutionary Assemblies
Rights of Man

Robespierre
Taine

KANT

U nlike Fichte and Hegel, Kant never devoted a chapter or a book to the French Revolution. What is more, his complete works contain only two judgments, and those carefully hedged, on the events in France: the first can be found in paragraph 6 of section 2 of the *Streit der Fakultäten* (*Conflict of the Faculties,* 1798); the second appears in the *Nachlass.* Written at about the same time as the text in the *Conflict,* the latter adds only a few items of detail. Otherwise one has to make do with scattered remarks, most frequently in a note or appendix and dealing with important but limited aspects of the Revolution. Despite this comparative absence of comment on the Revolution, Kant was considered by contemporaries both east and west of the Rhine as one of its ardent defenders. He even had the reputation of being a Jacobin, and Charles Theremin, at the time chief of the Bureau of the Committee of Public Safety and Sieyès' confidential assistant, attempted, at Sieyès' behest, to make contact with Kant. Already quite elderly and unwilling to intervene in the affairs of a foreign country, Kant was apparently obliged to reject this approach. Sieyès was nevertheless aware of the content of Kant's philosophy thanks to Wilhelm von Humboldt, and he was able to read his project for *Perpetual Peace* (1795) in a French translation published by Jansen and Perroneau in 1796. A Königsberg gazette even announced quite officially on March 7, 1796, that Sieyès, acting on behalf of the French nation, had sent Kant a copy of the Constitution of the Republic in order to obtain the philosopher's opinion. This false news impelled a former disciple of Kant's, Materne Reuss, professor of philosophy at Würzburg, to write him on April 1, 1796: "I cannot describe the enthusiastic response—even of those who do not share your principles, and even among our ladies—to the news that you have been called to France as a legislator and peacemaker and that you have obtained your king's permission to accept." Though based on inaccurate rumor, the "enthusiasm" was real enough, and quite typical of what Kant's contemporaries took his attitude toward the Revolution to be. But was that enthusiasm well-founded?

The best way to find out is obviously to follow Kant's principal texts, beginning with the famous paragraph 6 of the *Conflict,* in which Kant's purpose is to discuss with his reader "an event of our time which demonstrates [the] moral tendency of the human race." The remarkable thing is that for Kant this event is not the Revolution itself but the way in which it is perceived *publicly* by *non-participant spectators:* "This event consists neither in momentous deeds nor in crimes committed by men. . . . It is simply the mode of thinking of the spectators which reveals itself publicly in this great game of revolutions, and manifests such a universal yet disinterested sympathy for the players on one side against those on the other, even at the risk that this partiality could become very dangerous for them if discovered. Owing to its universality, this mode of thinking demonstrates a character of the human race at large and all at once; owing to its disinterestedness, a moral character of humanity" (Gregor translation, p. 153)—which in itself already constitutes a kind of "progress." This excerpt is reason enough to moderate the judgment that Kant supported the Revolution without reservation. What he (and Hegel after him) admired in the Revolution was its humanism, its revelation of man's political nature. In this sense the Revolution was part of the *Aufklärung:* it caused man to emerge from his childlike condition, a necessity affirmed, not without courage, in *Religion within the Limits of Reason Alone.* Repeating, sometimes word for word, the arguments of *What Is Enlightenment?* Kant wrote: "I confess that I cannot accustom myself to an expression in use among reasonable men: a certain people (in the process of working out its legal liberty) is not ripe for freedom. The serfs of a landowner are ripe for freedom. And similarly men in general are not yet ripe for freedom of religion. With this kind of hypothesis, freedom will never come about, for one cannot become ripe for freedom unless one has previously been placed in a situation of freedom." Tocqueville would raise a similar argument against slavery. By order of Frederick William II, Kant was forbidden as of October 1, 1794, to publish anything on religion.

Nevertheless, Kant's admiration for the Revolution's *effect* on its *spectators* was by no means incompatible with a critique of *revolutionary action* as such, so that Kant's judgment, like Hegel's, is twofold: positive as to the *content* of the Revolution (political humanism), negative as to its *form* (the revolutionary process). This twofold attitude is expressed quite well in paragraph 6 of the *Conflict:* "The revolution of a spirited people which we have seen unfolding in our day may succeed or miscarry; it may be filled with misery and atrocities to the point that a sensible man, were he boldly to hope to execute it successfully the second time, would never resolve to make the experiment at such cost—this revolution, I say, nonetheless finds in the hearts of all spectators (who are not engaged in the game themselves) a wishful participation that borders on enthusiasm, the very expression of which is fraught with danger; this sympathy, therefore, can have no other cause than a moral predisposition in the human race" (Gregor translation, p. 153). Starting with this broad judgment, we can try to indicate more precisely what Kant deemed positive about the Revolution and what he deemed negative.

The Revolution deserved credit, first of all, for republicanism. For Kant, the republican constitution, whose principles he described in the *Doctrine of Justice* and in *Theory and Practice,* was always the one constitution not only compatible with justice but also capable of preventing "offensive warfare" and thus establishing peace. "Just as men have sometimes posited an invisible Church as the model and foundation of the visible Church outside which there is no salvation, so one may say of the political situation of states and peoples that outside the republic, there is no salvation" (*Nachlass,* XIX, 603). Under the republican constitution, people are free in the sense that they have "the capacity to obey no other (juridical) laws than those to which they have given their assent" (*Perpetual Peace*). Consequently, the risk of war is infinitely less than in an absolute monarchy, since the subject who decides to wage war (the people) is also the subject who must endure its consequences. Therein, Kant believed, lay the superiority of the French constitution over the English monarchy: "The monarch who, relying on the plenitude of his own power, can say, There must be war, whereupon war ensues, is an unlimited monarch (and his people is not free). But the monarch who must first publicly ask his people if it agrees to war, and if that people says that there must be no war, and no war ensues—that monarch is a limited monarch (and such a people is free). Now, the king of England enjoys, in accordance with his constitution, the former right, while the French Republic enjoys only the latter (for the Director must consult the representative Assembly of the entire people). Therefore the sovereign in England has an absolute power, while in France it is limited, and the people in England is not free" (*Nachlass*, XIX, 606). This text obviously adapts Rousseau's well-known judgment to the situation of the French Republic, which requires the existence of the representative system that Rousseau rejected.

Although this is not the place to delve into Kant's purely philosophical grounding of the republican constitution, we may say that the enthusiasm of the disinterested spectator was elicited by the fact that such a constitution created a public *space*.

While this positive judgment of the Revolution is crucial, it did not prevent Kant from asserting that the revolutionary state as such was, as he put in the *Anthropology*, a state "of public injustice declared to be legal." Condemnation of the right to resist state authority by violent means, even if that authority was unjust, was a constant of Kant's political thought. To be sure, when power was tyrannical, "the people's rights are violated, and it is no injustice to the tyrant to dethrone him. It is nonetheless true that subjects act in the most unjust manner in pursuing their rights in this way" (*Perpetual Peace*). Without delving into the philosophical foundations of this critique of the right of revolution, which Kant considered to be internally contradictory as well as contrary to the principle that justice must be public, it is important to guard against two errors.

Contrary to a widely held interpretation of Kant's thought, his denunciation of the revolutionary act as such does not signify adherence to legal positivism in any form. The passage cited above is quite clear in this regard. It does not deny that state power can be unjust. In other words, it does not confuse legality with legitimacy, as does Kelsen's *Pure Theory of Justice*, but merely affirms the superiority of a legal order, even an unjust one, over anarchy. A reformist rather than a revolutionary, Kant deemed the work of the Revolution totally acceptable so long as it could be regarded as being carried out with the consent of the king: "In France the National Assembly could change the constitution. . . . For they [*sic*] were the representatives of the whole people, whom the king had endowed with full powers to make the law" (*Nachlass*, XIX, 595). By the same token, he deemed the execution of Louis

XVI the revolutionaries' worst crime. Some readers may be astonished to discover that of the ten volumes of Kant's *Werke* only a few lines are devoted to the question of regicide—a fact all the more remarkable in that his entire analysis of this episode, which he judged almost "diabolical," is contained essentially in a footnote to the *Doctrine of Justice*. The point is not that Kant had little to say on the subject but that he viewed the death of Louis XVI more from the standpoint of the jurist than as a theorist of history. There is no consideration of the symbolic dimension of the event or of the division it marked between the modern world and the Ancien Régime. Yet Kant was by no means indifferent to regicide. In his eyes, the execution of the king by his people represented an extreme and scarcely conceivable act of immorality. Assassination would have been infinitely preferable, for then it would have been possible to think the act had been committed in full awareness of the transgression of the law. "Execution by due process" was the supreme evil, because its respect of legal forms, or, to put it another way, its claim of legitimacy, could be understood only as a total inversion of justice. It was not merely a violation of the law but evidence of a determination to take violation of the law as the very maxim of action. Hence with it "violence marched with its head held high; it had been raised in principle above the most sacred of rights."

Nevertheless, Kant was never a legitimist. What is more, the very reasons for which he condemned the revolutionary act reinforced his arguments justifying the content of the Revolution as forming a bulwark against any attempt at restoration: "If a revolution caused by a bad constitution managed, even by violent and illegal means, to obtain a better one, it would not be permissible to compel people to revert to the old one" (*Perpetual Peace*).

In opposition to reactionary critics of the Revolution, most notably Burke and Rehberg, Kant therefore took up his pen on two occasions: in 1793 with *Theory and Practice* and in 1795 with *Perpetual Peace*. As Philonenko points out, Burke's and Rehberg's counterrevolutionary pamphlets primarily attacked "the idea of a politics based on reason and not on facts," that is, the very thing that the leading German philosophers, Kant foremost among them, had initially appreciated about the Revolution. Thus it was the whole *Aufklärung* that was in jeopardy, and it was only to be expected that Kant, as its leading light, would respond. He did so on two levels. First, on the juridical level, he showed in *Theory and Practice* how granting liberty to the people could be reconciled with state authority by way of the synthetic concept of citizenship (in electing that authority, the citizen affirmed his free and active role, even though he then became subject to it once established). Second, at the level of philosophy of history, he rejected in *Perpetual Peace* the argument that the republican constitution was suitable only for a "people of angels," and instead he grounded the idea of political progress in the wholly amoral interplay of particular interests. No doubt Kant's deepest feelings about the French Revolution were rooted in this idea of a history that tends toward the better through the action of imperfect (selfish) individuals. Even as he denounced revolutionary activism, Kant, like Hegel after him, could not help looking favorably on the advent of a new order bearing the stamp of political humanism.

Luc Ferry

Further reading

WORKS BY KANT

The Conflict of the Faculties, trans. Mary J. Gregor. New York, 1979.
Perpetual Peace, trans. Ted Humphrey. New York, 1983.
Religion within the Limits of Reason Alone, trans. T. M. Greene and Hoyt Hudson. New York, 1960.
Werke, ed. Wilhelm Weischedel, 10 vols. Darmstadt, 1975.

RELATED WORKS

Burg, Peter. *Kant und die französische Revolution.* Berlin, 1974.
Ferry, Luc. *Philosophie politique,* 2 vols. Paris, 1984.
Philonenko, Alexis. *Théorie et praxis dans la pensée morale et politique de Kant et de Fichte en 1793.* Paris, 1968.
Schrecker, Paul. "Kant et la Révolution française," *Revue philosophique de la France et de l'étranger,* 1939.
Vorländer, Karl. "Kants Stellung zur französischen Revolution," in *Philosophische Abhandlung Hermann Cohen zum 70schen Geburtstag dargebracht.* Berlin, 1912.

Related topics

MAISTRE

J oseph de Maistre was not, strictly speaking, a historian of the French Revolution. A contemporary of the events and a pro-Restoration activist, he
always judged the news from Paris with the furious passion of a man
watching a decisive battle between good and evil. The question of the Revolution dogged him throughout his life. From the beginning he saw it as far
more than a startling series of events; for him it represented the simultaneous
emergence into the light of day of all the corrosive forces that in centuries
past had undermined the hegemony of Christianity and the sovereignty of
monarchy and that now, under the aegis of the rights of man and popular
sovereignty, were inaugurating a new era in world history. Maistre's indictment of this newborn civilization and of the causes that had brought it into
being was radical and uncompromising. Modern society, he thought, was
based on nothing, since it rested only on itself. Along with the collapse of the
Ancien Régime he witnessed the collapse of the whole scaffolding of symbols
and myths that had veiled the nakedness of power and made its aspect bearable.

The Revolution plucked a no longer young Joseph de Maistre from a
tranquil provincial life at Chambéry and revealed his vocation as a writer. The
French army's invasion of Savoy in 1792 had forced him into a long exile and
thrust him into a chaotic series of great and not easily interpreted events.
From his first meditation on the disorder came his most brilliant text, the
Considérations sur la France, published anonymously in Switzerland in 1797, in
which he develops in a concise and visionary style his own idea of the Revolution.

Maistre set out to give meaning to the upheavals of 1789, which to their
victims seemed the height of unreason. He wanted to find an order in the
general disorder. For this goal, a historical and political approach would not
suffice: what was needed was a "metaphysics" of the event, capable of identifying its "primary causes" amid a host of purely human causes. From the first
this solemn tone distinguished the *Considérations* from the mass of counterrevolutionary literature. To appreciate its originality, one has only to compare
it with the book of another great adversary of the Revolution, the Genevan
Mallet du Pan's *Considérations sur la nature de la Révolution en France, et sur les
causes qui en prolongent la durée* (1793).

Mallet du Pan's primary concern was with the inability of the governments of Europe to rise to the level of the Revolution, their stubborn persistence in combatting it with traditional arms. For him, it was obvious that the
Revolution was an abnormal phenomenon, which operated in a moral realm

inaccessible to the routine politics of sovereign states. Maistre shared this mixture of stupor and admiration before the extraordinary character of the event. For him, too, the problem was to understand the singularity of its original principle, to resolve the riddle. But where Mallet du Pan sought to interpret the mystery of the Revolution in rational historical and political terms, Maistre bowed before the majesty of the enigma; he succumbed to its diabolical fascination and drew from its mystery tangible signs not so much of the complexity of human affairs as of a superhuman intervention.

For Maistre, politics had no autonomy; it was the manifestation of a larger drama, a sacred representation being played out in the wings. The Revolution was the demonstration that the force of a higher destiny always prevails over man's will. Contrary to the political optimism of the eighteenth century, it was false to believe that the will could ever find full realization in the world of history. On the contrary, a look around is all it takes to see that results are always a long way from intentions, that the will is always disappointed, and that men never know what they are doing. "One finds in them something passive and mechanical," he wrote. "It is not men who lead the revolution, it is the revolution that employs men. He speaks well who says, It goes its own way." What accounts for the disproportion between the wretchedness of individuals and the grandeur of events, if not a superior intelligence, capable even of contradicting the natural laws of cause and effect? If men briefly believed that they were masters of their own fate, they were quickly disappointed; the revolutionary fever that began, as Bonald would say, with the Declaration of the Rights of Man must end with the declaration of the rights of God.

With that explanation we come to the central theme of the *Considérations:* Providence. Bossuet had already pointed to the hand of God in universal history. Maistre employed the same idea, but for him the problem was no longer how to show the grandeur of the French realm willed by God, but how to explain why God had willed its present misery. The explanation was that Providence pursued two different goals. One was to punish the guilty French, for there are no innocent victims. Their irresponsibility had encouraged the Revolution. The entire nation was an accomplice in regicide. Second, by means of the Revolution and its excesses, Providence was cleverly working toward the preservation of France. Maistre was among those who most eloquently recognized the national role of Jacobinism. In his eyes, the Committee of Public Safety temporarily occupied the place of the king, which had been left vacant, and by defending the Revolution by extraordinary means against foreigners, it had in reality defended the integrity of the realm.

Maistre was not the first to associate the Revolution with Providence. The theme had been broached a year earlier in a short work by Louis-Claude de Saint-Martin, one of those *illuminés* whom the Savoyard appreciated and who had adapted Gnostic and neo-Platonic themes to eighteenth-century taste. But Maistre had impressed his own original and apologetic stamp on this standard theosophical fare, justifying the impenetrable work of divine justice even in its apparently most incomprehensible and absurd aspects. If he denied in the *Considérations* that there were any innocent victims of the

Revolution, in his *Soirées de Saint-Pétersbourg* he presented an unstinting eulogy of justice (at once human and divine), which linked the mystery of evil to that of fallen human nature: "No man is punished as just, but always as man, so that it is false to say that virtue suffers in this world: it is human nature that suffers, and its suffering is always deserved."

Clearly, Maistre stands at the opposite pole from Rousseau's idea of original innocence. It is no accident that the doctrine of original sin proved so attractive to reactionary thought: where the revolutionaries with their voluntarism had set out to change the world in order to restore man to his essential goodness, reactionary thought posited the irremediable corruption of human nature, which it was the vocation of historical time to redeem. The idea that man is at the mercy of God's omnipotence is a Christian one; but Maistre's theme was totally devoid of Christian accents. It can be related, in fact, to the gnostic and heterodox roots of his religious beliefs. Indeed, there is something pagan or Judaic in the total absence of the theme of love. The God that Joseph de Maistre proposed to a Christianity worn out by a century of philosophical doubt and deism had become once again a tyrant over the world, an unfathomable, sovereign judge, whose wrath demanded expiation.

Though willed by God and guided by Providence, the Revolution was nevertheless based on purely human principles elaborated by philosophy. "Abstract rationalism" informed the conception of the rights of man and was coupled with the idea of "popular sovereignty." Maistre's polemic against the former merely repeats themes made famous by Edmund Burke in his *Reflections on the Revolution in France* (1790). "The Constitution of 1795," Maistre writes, "like its elder sisters, was made for *man*. But there is no such thing as *man* in the world. In my life I have seen Frenchmen, Italians, Russians, and so on. I even know, thanks to Montesquieu, that one can be Persian. But as for *man*, I declare I've never encountered him. If he exists, I don't know about it." A nation's only authentic constitution is the set of customs transmitted by memory and sanctified by tradition. It is the work of time, not of man, and its roots existed prior to any written law. As for the principle of popular sovereignty, Maistre evokes the contradictory and paradoxical nature of democracy: "The people is sovereign, they say. And over whom? Over itself, apparently. The people is therefore subject. Surely there is something equivocal if not erroneous in this, for the people that commands is not the people that obeys." He also rejects the idea of representation through delegation, which cannot possibly produce a genuine sovereignty.

More generally, Maistre, like all counterrevolutionaries, was diametrically opposed to the modern conception of natural law. In contrast to the philosophes, who believed that society was the result of a convention, he believed that there was no presocial state. "Strictly speaking, man never knew a time prior to society, because prior to the formation of political societies man was not entirely man." God created man as a social being by nature. Sovereignty was also natural, because it was inseparable from society.

Amalgamated into a cult of providential history, these theories were the principal ingredients of Maistre's traditionalism, or, if one prefers, of the polemical theme that elicited the greatest response from his readers. The critique of the philosophes' intellectualism and emphasis on the meaning of history were in fact topics that would meet with success in the nineteenth century, from the Romantics to the more moderate currents in liberalism. Yet Maistre's traditionalism, his steadfast refusal to accept the durability and legitimacy of the institutions created by human will and without historical roots, was also the weakest element in his polemical attack on the institutions of postrevolutionary France. In this area Maistre's thinking was not without contradictions of its own. On the one hand he conceived of the Revolution as pure nothingness, as a satanic work stemming from the negative tendency in the human condition. But on the other hand he eloquently insisted that the Revolution was not a simple episode but an epoch open to both the past and the future, an era for which precedents could be discovered by tracing the genealogy of the oppositional spirit in France (compare the *Réflexions sur le protestantisme dans ses rapports avec la souveraineté,* 1798, with *De l'église gallicane,* 1821), and whose heirs were still at work after the Restoration: "We must have the courage to admit it, madame," he wrote in 1794 to the marquise de Costa. "For a long time we did not understand the revolution of which we were witnesses. For a long time we took it to be an event. We were mistaken: it was an epoch; and woe unto the generation that witnesses the epoch of the world!"

This interpretation is a delicate point in Maistre's argument. The work of an author like Ballanche, who perfectly captured the spirit of the Restoration and who was careful to respond to both the prophets of the past and to overly radical innovators, shows how the theme of the duration or tradition of the Revolution as the work of time rather than of men could easily be developed into a dialectical image, in which each moment possesses its historical necessity and the future is just as necessary as the present and the past. And it is quite curious that Mme. de Staël, in her *Considérations sur les principaux événements de la Révolution française* (1818)—the first attempt, under the Restoration, to write a history celebrating the principles of 1789—begins with a sentence whose affinity, not to say similarity, with the passage of Maistre cited above is obvious: "The Revolution in France is one of the great epochs of the social order. Those who consider it to be an accidental event have not peered into the past or the future." The conceptual structure of Maistre's traditionalism allowed it to be assimilated equally well by intellectual tendencies close to and—like the liberal approach—very far from his own. The epochal aspect of his theory also best corresponded to the concerns of his day. But the conciliatory spirit vanishes entirely when one looks at his theory of authority.

The issue of authority was central for writers who rejected the Revolution, and its formulation could not have been simpler. Individualism had eroded the basis of all obedience, and with it the very order of society. The presocial man conceived by the philosophers, the isolated individual endowed with natural rights, was in fact a man who did not obey: he said "no," like the

Protestant, and he wanted to discuss everything because he recognized no authority other than evidence. For admirers of the ancient order, it was, as Bonald would later say, a matter of replacing the authority of evidence by the evidence of authority.

To oppose this nay-saying reason, Bonald, another theocratic and legitimist author, proposed a solution different from that of Maistre. For Bonald the answer to the problem of authority was to be found in *social* man; for him, there exists a primacy of the social over the individual, and therein lies the secret of every good constitution. The authority of social conformism must take precedence over all individual reason; it must be reproduced in all institutions and even in the education of the young. Although Maistre shared Bonald's proposed aim, his answer to the problem of authority and obedience lay in a recourse to history and religion rather than in an organicist sociology. The role of historical duration in fact lay in throwing a veil of mystery and obscurity over the origins of society and power. The virtue of history was not to unveil but to hide the beginnings: "I believe that I have read somewhere that few sovereignties are in a position to justify the legitimacy of their origin." Precisely because of this absence of original right, a symbol that veils power is more compatible with its exercise than a concept that explains and justifies it: "There exist mysterious laws," Maistre insisted, "which it is not good to divulge, which must be covered in a religious silence and revered *as a mystery.*" Similarly, the political role of religion consists not only in providing a transcendent foundation for temporal power—its acknowledged role in the legal sphere, so to speak—but even more in cloaking power in the majesty of mystery. The social function of religion stems from the fact that it is not rational and manifests itself instead in the form of dogma, prejudice, and inexplicable mysteries.

What Maistre had grasped was that a society that becomes transparent to itself is constantly threatened with dissolution, since the mechanism of authority becomes problematic. For Maistre, only a society capable of preserving the sense of mystery—about its own origins, its own functioning—can avoid this fatal end. His conclusions are unequivocal and set him diametrically against the century of Enlightenment: "I dare say that what we ought not to know is more important than what we ought to know." The classic question of political philosophy is, Why do we obey? To that question Hobbes answered that we obey out of fear and Rousseau that we obey because the people is sovereign (while La Boétie seems to have believed that we obey for the pleasure of serving). Maistre's answer would have been that we obey because of the fascination and deep astonishment we feel at the sight of a mysterious power. Man obeys because he believes: for power, like God, is absurd. Such a conception of power reveals a nihilist penchant that one might not expect in a champion of militant Catholicism. It is precisely this intuition of the arbitrary nature of sovereignty (coupled with awareness of the vanity of man's efforts to base sovereignty on anything other than force) that seems to warrant the interpretation of those who, like Carl Schmitt, have seen Maistre as a "decisionist," that is, one who believes that political authority and its decisions are fundamentally irrational. In this respect, Maistre, notwithstanding his long battle against "popular sovereignty," can be seen as one of the most ardent defenders of *sovereignty* as such, an institution destined for dissolution in the postrevolutionary world.

Liberal thought had understood that something in the absolutism of sovereign logic had been responsible for the trauma of the Revolution. Sovereignty by its very nature tends to concentrate all power in one place, whether it be the monarch or the people. The very idea of a constitution in which sovereignty is in the hands of a subject seemed fraught with peril. Divided between the sovereignty of the people and the sovereignty of God, the political theorists of the Restoration era, such as the "doctrinaires," accordingly attempted to eliminate the very concept of sovereignty, deemed to be abstract and theological. "There is no sovereignty on earth, and no sovereign," Guizot wrote. "Any *de jure* sovereignty attributed to men, whether one, several, or all, is a lie and an iniquity."

Maistre became a radical opponent of this idea, which he considered illusory: "Any kind of sovereignty is absolute by its nature. Place it on one or several heads, divide it, organize its powers any way you will: there will always be, in the final analysis, an absolute power that will be able to do harm with impunity, and that will therefore be despotic in the full sense of the word, and against which there will be no other rampart than that of insurrection. Wherever powers are divided, the battles between these various powers may be regarded as deliberations of a unique sovereign, whose reason weighs the pros and the cons. But once the decision is taken, the effect is the same in either case, and the will of any sovereign is always invincible." It is of no concern who decides or how; what matters is that a decision is taken. Against proponents of a liberal regime of laws, who might hope to eliminate "critical cases" from the world so as never to be obliged to have recourse to sovereign authority, Maistre raised a dramatic image of society at the supreme moment of decision. He thus shifted from a premodern concept of authority, in which the sovereign is the representative of a fixed order whose legitimation is accomplished by tradition, to a more modern idea, according to which the sovereign is an actor who comes out of nowhere to restore order to a society threatened with dissolution. In some ways, however, such authority is "dictatorial" rather than "legitimate." This extremist effort, understood as a "proud moral decision," by counterrevolutionaries trying to preserve a kernel of political activity, was intended to reintroduce an idea of permanent crisis into a world that seemed to want to free itself from the constant need to choose between God and his enemy. It was the primacy of this metaphysical choice in the structure of the political that Joseph de Maistre would strive to defend to the very end.

Massimo Boffa

Maistre

Further Reading

WORKS BY MAISTRE

Considérations sur la France, ed. Jean-Louis Darcel. Geneva, 1980.

Oeuvres complètes, 14 vols. Lyons, 1884–1893; reprinted in 7 vols., Geneva, 1979. Despite the title, this edition is not really complete, because part of the correspondence is left out. It can be found in *Mémoires politiques et correspondance diplomatique (1803–1810)* and in *Correspondance diplomatique (1811–1817),* ed. Albert Blanc. Paris, 1858 and 1861.

RELATED WORKS

Barbey d'Aurevilly, Jules. *Les prophètes du passé.* Paris, 1851.
Cioran, Emile M. Preface to Joseph de Maistre, *Du pape.* Monaco, 1957.
Dermenghem, Emile. *Joseph de Maistre mystique.* Paris, 1923.
Descostes, François. *Joseph de Maistre avant la Révolution.* Paris, 1893.
——— *Joseph de Maistre pendant la Révolution.* Paris, 1895.
Faguet, Emile. *Politiques et moralistes du XIXe siècle.* Paris, 1891.
Laski, Harold. *Authority in the Modern State.* New Haven, 1917.
Omodeo, Adolfo. *Un reazionario: Il conte Joseph de Maistre.* Bari, 1939.
Sainte-Beuve, Charles-Augustin. *Causeries du lundi* (4 and 15), *Portraits littéraires* (2), in Maurice Allem, ed., *Les grands ecrivains français par Sainte-Beuve.* Paris, 1930.
Schmitt, Carl. *Politische Theologie: Vier Kapitel zur Lehre von der Souveränität.* Munich and Leipzig, 1922.
Triomphe, Robert. *Joseph de Maistre.* Geneva, 1968.
Viatte, Auguste. *Les sources occultes du romantisme: Illuminisme, théosophie, 1770–1820,* 2 vols. Paris, 1928.

Related Topics

Burke	Guizot	Rousseau	Staël
Counterrevolution	Jacobinism	Sovereignty	

MARX

I t was in the period 1841–1845, the formative period of his doctrine, that Marx took his greatest and also his most fruitful interest in the French Revolution, to the point where during a stay in Paris in 1844 he envisioned writing a history of the Convention. With respect to the great event that took place in France at the end of the eighteenth century, he shared the ambivalent fascination of the German intelligentsia. Heir to a Jacobin milieu, he admired what Hegel called the "superb sunrise" of democracy that had occurred in Paris, but as a loyal son of German culture he suffered from his country's backwardness compared with France. Germany had a great philosophy but only a caricature of a history.

At least that philosophy enabled him to offer a better critique than the French of what had occurred in France. Hegel had shown the way, and the young Marx's thought opposed the master yet followed in his footsteps. What he knew about the French Revolution he had learned first from the *Phenomenology* and the *Principles of the Philosophy of Right* before turning to proper historians, primarily French historians. The interpretation of the Revolution was one of the intellectual objects out of which he gradually put together his critique of Hegel, the source of what would ultimately become Marxism. Hegel had worked out his theory of the state by way of a critique of the Revolution. Marx in turn developed a critique of the Hegelian philosophy of right by inverting the theory of the state that Hegel had developed in part from the French example.

For Hegel, the state is a totality that encompasses and transcends society. It is the symbol of reason in history, or, to put it in his own terms, "human will insofar as man wills in accordance with reason," or again, "the absolute end in itself, in which consciousness finds its higher purpose." Hence it is absurd to portray the state as Burke did, as the fortuitous consequence of layer upon layer of past practice; or as the conservatives did, as a derivative of religion; or as the liberals did, as the product of the union of individuals. Hegel acknowledged his debt to Rousseau, who had attempted to ground the state in reason and to assign it a spiritual principle, namely, the will. Where he differed from Rousseau was over the idea of a state of nature prior to the state as such, even as a theoretical construct. The state was the modern *polis*, and no more than the ancient city could it be conceived in terms of individuals joined together by contract. On the contrary, the state is, in a fundamental sense, anterior to the individuals whom it unites.

For Hegel, the French Revolution was the perfect illustration of Jean-Jacques's error. In attempting to found a state based on the free wills of the contracting parties in the form of the general will, the Revolution revealed

972

an audacity and ambition never before seen in history, but its philosophical underpinnings were false. In positing the general will as an alienation of natural will, a denaturing, a new beginning, Rousseau and the Revolution had made it seem to be a purely external form, which limited individual liberties instead of revealing the substance of liberty embodied in the state. The consequence of this abstraction was the despotism of liberty and the Terror. The Revolution, which aimed to create a new state based solely on reason, wanted to incarnate the universal in the particular. That was why in the end it could no longer recognize self-consciousness in individuals: in 1793–1794, heads fell like cabbages.

By contrast, the Hegelian state, the supreme substance of history, which was to end the public-private divorce of modern times and realize human liberty, was a creation of man, a provisional product of his alienation in the other world. Similarly, the state, which for Hegel was the place where liberty and social being were reconciled, became for Marx the imaginary figure through which the oppressed member of society formed his idea of the community. This is the gist of the famous and long unpublished 1843 manuscript, which is essential for understanding what is commonly called the young Marx, the disciple of Feuerbach.

From liberal thought, Scottish as well as Thermidorian, the young Marx inherited the distinction between civil society and the state. A characteristic feature of modern times and of the spectacular economic progress so intimately associated with the modern age was the emergence of the free individual, that is, the individual defined by his labor and his relation to the market. Out of this definition came the "abstraction" of private life, the claim that man is distinct from what constitutes him as citizen, and the complementary "abstraction" of the state, also characteristic of the modern, according to which the public sphere is now cut off from the actual activity of individuals. In Hegel the civil society/state contradiction is never developed in this radical form, since it masks a unity of opposites in the Idea and since the state is the locus of reconciliation. For the young Marx the opposite is true: civil society takes priority over the state, and what constitutes modernity above all else is the private individual, the monad defined by his work, his interests, his selfish calculations, and his pleasures, separated from his fellow men and a stranger to the very idea of community.

The French Revolution was the work of this individual. It laid bare the nature of a society based on unfettered market relations. Following Guizot and the French historians of the Restoration, Marx offered a social interpretation of the Revolution but modified its terms: the Revolution was the event through which the bourgeoisie, mistress of society, crowned its power by seizing political control. Viewed in this way, what it specifically established was an apparently autonomous but nevertheless dependent public sphere in which the political and the social were radically separate: the representative democratic state, which succeeded the monarchy. In appearance, this state was totally autonomous, since its representative character expressed the separation of the state from society, and its (universal) democratic character expressed the abstraction of egalitarian citizenship as distinct from the real situations of individual members of the society. Yet this autonomy was a lie: the state was merely a communal mask for the real society, which was that of private individualism. It expressed only an illusion of egalitarian citizenship in a world of unequal wealth. The separate individuals of modern civil society alienated themselves in the imaginary community of the state. The French Revolution with its illusion of the political established nothing other than bourgeois domination, the reality of the social. It was left to the proletarian revolution to restore what Marx called man's "species-being," that is, his true humanity, by destroying the alienation born of, and with, 1789. The end of the citizen would finally mean the advent of man.

Marx thus restored a future to humiliated Germany, which he saw as the most likely place for this ultimate emancipation to occur. At the same time he rescued the preeminent dignity of the idea of revolution, of which the French had demonstrated the extraordinary force, from Hegel's critique. Even though the French Revolution had been only the revolution of the political, at least it had put all its energy into achieving this historical goal. This interpretation accounts for the young Marx's particular admiration for Jacobinism, and more precisely for Robespierrism, the most consummate form of the illusion of the priority of the political over the social, or, to put it another way, of the idea that man's will can change society. Here, Marx followed Hegel's analysis of the French revolutionaries' abstract voluntarism, which he in fact treated as the distinctive feature of their history, predominantly shaped by Robespierrism. But his interpretation of that voluntarism drew on Feuerbach's idea of the modern citizen's alienation in the state.

The two most subtle and polished versions of Marx's interpretation are found in two texts written immediately after the critique of Hegel's philosophy of right: *The Jewish Question* (1844) and *The Holy Family* (late 1844–early 1845). During this period, moreover, Marx was in Paris, before being expelled by the July Monarchy, and he took a great interest in the French Revolution.

In the first of these two works, intended to be an analysis of the relation between modern citizenship and individual religious beliefs (in this instance Judaism), Marx refutes the idea that the one is incompatible with the other—except when, as during the Terror, there is recourse to violence. The modern state does secularize the religious spirit by transplanting the Christian idea of equality to the political sphere. But in doing so it only superimposes a new political form of alienation on the existing religious alienation, without destroying the latter but merely confining it within the private sphere. The emancipation of the citizen in the form of democratic equality is merely the modern expression of the misfortune and isolation of individuals. The bourgeois is the truth of the citizen, just as the subject was the truth of the believer.

Hence in the Declaration of the Rights of Man and of the Citizen, the quintessential charter of the French Revolution, man—that is, the individual member of civil society—invariably takes precedence over the citizen, symbol of the new democratic state; the rights of man, as distinct from those of the citizen, pertain not to man in general, to his "species-being," but to the selfish and self-contained individual of bourgeois society, to "man separated from man and the community." Liberty and equality exist only as guarantees of each individual's private pleasures.

Nevertheless, the Revolution continually asserts its absolute, primordial character. It was the event that totally destroyed the feudal and corporate structure of the Ancien Régime in the name of what Marx calls "state idealism," absorbing and unifying for its own benefit the entire political dimension; therein lay the significance not only of 1789 but even more of 1793 and the Jacobin dictatorship, in which the spirit of the Revolution bared itself fully. But in this unequal contest, in which social man was the real foundation of imaginary political man, society ultimately recaptured what the Revolution had temporarily usurped. The year 1793 was the apogee of the citizen's emancipation, but Thermidor was its truth. This dialectic of the social and the political provided Marx with a theory and a chronology of the French Revolution.

The last elements of that theory can be deciphered in *The Holy Family,* a book written in the same year as *The Jewish Question* and belonging to the same Feuerbachian cycle. In it Marx adopts the idea that Robespierre hypostasized the political state in order to make it the central reality of history and society, when in fact it was only the imaginary symbol. He adds a new interpretation of this period of the Revolution, the germ of which he probably found in Benjamin Constant. Rephrasing in his own terms an analysis dear to the author of *De la liberté chez les anciens et chez les modernes,* he showed that the illusions of Robespierre and Saint-Just were nurtured on the example of antiquity; the Terror was the result of an anachronism. The Jacobins had wanted to recreate Sparta or Rome, yet they became the unwitting champions of modern civil society. With the rights of man they believed they were reestablishing ancient democracy, whereas they were actually consecrating the inequality of bourgeois society in the guise of modern citizenship. In the modern world, as Constant had seen, citizenship had ceased to be coextensive with liberty. Because it sought to reduce a gap that was a product of history, the Terror could only end in failure. On 9 Thermidor civil society reclaimed its rights and dispelled a bloody illusion; the reign of interests and money then revealed the truth of the revolutionary process.

A few years later, however, this harmony was disrupted once again by 18 Brumaire. In effect, Bonaparte put an end to a period in which bourgeois society was represented and governed by the bourgeoisie. With the Consulate and the Empire the state regained a certain autonomy vis-à-vis civil society. To be sure, Napoleon was careful to take interests into account, and he was the creator of the Civil Code, the veritable cornerstone of the postrevolutionary world. Nevertheless, through his dictatorship he imposed on the bourgeoisie a state that had ends other than bourgeois interests, ends of its own, or, rather, that was an end unto itself, civil society being merely its "treasurer." In this sense Napoleon reinvented the Terror by assigning it a new content: conquest rather than virtue. "He achieved terrorism by replacing permanent revolution with permanent war." The imperial dictatorship was an administrative version of the Terror, with a different objective; Marx is here harking back to a central theme of liberal historiography, the direct line of descent from Robespierrism to Bonapartism seen from the standpoint of state domination of society.

Thus for Marx, the history of the revolutionary state was distinct from that of civil society and in fact formed the very substance of the period. The French Revolution, he wrote somewhat later, was the "genesis of the modern state." Alongside the development of bourgeois society and as a consequence thereof, it revealed the birth of democratic citizenship and the representative state. What is not very easy to understand in this interpretation is how this new state gained its hold on people's minds, since it was based on a collective illusion. It must be admitted that this imaginary symbol of community also functions as a real process in real history. The modern political state has a fictional yet social existence. Although not an objective reality, it exists in history as though it possessed such a reality, and it does so for the same reasons as religion: because everyone believes it.

Nevertheless, the essential reality is society, the political economy, in which money is king and social relations are relations of exploitation. By the time of the *1844 Manuscripts,* Marx had identified his primary object of research, which would lead him in the direction of English history. I am inclined to think that this focus is why he never wrote the projected work on the Convention. If the essence of the matter lay elsewhere, why waste time and energy studying the imaginary projection of individuals onto the modern state? But not writing the book also dispensed Marx from the obligation to deal with the central contradiction hidden in his interpretation. If the French Revolution revealed the birth of the modern democratic state—between 1789 and 1799, 1789 and 1815, or 1789 and 1830, depending on which chronology one prefers—it remains to be shown why that birth was accompanied by such a variety of political forms. If the history of the Revolution in the strict sense consists of the succession of political regimes that embodied the new state— constitutional monarchy, Jacobin Terror, parliamentary republic, Bonapartist dictatorship—then it is essential to understand how the same civil society, the same bourgeoisie, dominant since 1789, could account for such a plurality of political forms. What remains unexplained is the chronology of the state-society relation that gives revolutionary history its texture.

It is easy enough to conceive of the passage from 1789 to 1793, from the monarchy to the republic, in terms of a radicalization of men and ideas. But how does one explain why a system that returned to its truth—that is, to the truth of bourgeois government—in Thermidor 1794 once again slid into a new form of dictatorial state in 1799? The first Bonaparte posed for the first Marx the same problem that the second Bonaparte posed for the second Marx: that of a state installed by the bourgeoisie and partly at its service yet completely independent of it. At once bourgeois and nonbourgeois, what did Robespierre and Napoleon represent?

**

In the period that began with *The German Ideology* (1845), Marx abandoned the reference to Feuerbach in favor of historical materialism. He dropped the concept of "man's essence." History, no longer defined in terms of humanity rediscovering its nature, now obeyed only its own immanent laws. In the course of history lay the meaning of man in his relation to nature and to his fellow man. The Hegelian dialectic had migrated from thought to matter. The development of the productive forces and modes of production, the division of labor, and the class struggle replaced the figures of self-consciousness; like the creation of ideas, the creation of political forms was dependent on the development of class domination. *The German Ideology* was the instrument with which Marx set Hegel "back on his feet," and the interpretation of the French Revolution offered fertile ground on which to develop his discovery. In it he found genuine classes, antagonism between the Third Estate and the nobility, a national state, a liberal and revolutionary philosophy, and finally a revolution: all the elements of a history that had been written by French historians but that, like Hegel's philosophy, also needed to be set back on its feet.

Seen in the light of materialist analysis, the Revolution became nothing other than the consequence of the slow development of the new mode of production within the old, that is, the spectacular victory of the bourgeoisie, in the name of capitalist social relations, over the nobility and the "feudal" age. In this dialectic there is virtually no room for the political, which is subsumed by the social; the Jacobin and Napoleonic states, which in the previous period were different ways in which market society imagined itself and which therefore enjoyed at least temporary autonomy with respect to that society, were now reduced to mere appendices without real substance of their own. The bourgeoisie reigned uncontested over its own history. The priority of civil society over the state now took the form of determination of superstructures by the infrastructure, a concept that left far less room for the infinite diversity of historical cultural expression.

That reduction explains why the following years, notable for the polemical enthusiasm unleashed by Marx's discovery of dialectical materialism, were also his least productive in terms of specifically historical work, particularly on the French Revolution, that matchless theater of the political imagination. Nevertheless, Marx thought about the French experience constantly, for revolution was once again knocking at the door of European history, and the problem now was not only to emulate the energy of the late-eighteenth-century French but also to outstrip them by carrying out a proletarian social revolution, a negation-transcendence of the bourgeois political revolution.

In his writings between 1845 and 1849 Marx is farther than ever from a true history of the Revolution or even from producing a lengthy, systematic essay about it. But his numerous references to 1789 show that he continued to associate the work of the French revolutionaries with the longevity of national unity and the work of the monarchy on the one hand and with the bourgeoisie's lengthy conquest of economic, social, and finally political supremacy on the other hand. Where he differed from Thierry and Guizot was in understanding the second process to be the basis of the first. Hence the reason for all the events of the Revolution was the appropriation of the state by the new dominant class. Those events were not (as he had argued in the works of his youth) a series of alienations; 1789, 1793, and Thermidor were part of a single epic, the bourgeoisie's seizure of power.

Nevertheless, the Marx of these years shared with the author of *The*

Holy Family a special astonishment at 1793 and the Jacobin dictatorship; the Terror remained the enigma of a Revolution that had become simply bourgeois. To explain it, Marx no longer invoked ideological illusions and the ancient image of the citizen, supposedly in opposition to modern bourgeois individualism. He resorted at different times to two contradictory analyses, both based on the realities of class, now the key to universal history. His first argument was that the Terror, like the rights of man, the night of August 4, and the reign of money, was consubstantial with the establishment of bourgeois liberalism; it was the provisional and plebeian instrument of that accomplishment. By contrast, the second argument was that in 1793 the bourgeoisie lost control, and the Robespierrist and sans-culotte dictatorship (Marx, like the Restoration historians he read, did not distinguish between the two) was the incarnation of popular interests, an abortive attempt to pursue the Revolution beyond its limits which by definition was doomed to failure. With this contradiction, which he never overcame, Marx came back to the old dilemma of liberal historiography: namely, that with a social interpretation of the Revolution it is easier to think in terms of results than to account for the actual course of events.

The events of 1848 in France, the coup d'état of December 2, 1851, and the Commune of 1871 added further enigmas to Marx's ambiguities. With the Second Republic and Second Empire, history confronted the mature Marx with the questions of his youth: if the "illusion" of the modern state is mere trumpery with which the bourgeoisie disguises its undivided reign, why the interminable cascade of revolutions and coups d'état in service of the same power? Marx's most interesting answer was one that made it possible— at moments—to restore the state's independence vis-à-vis society in a cycle that stretches not from 1789 to 1830 as in his youth but from 1789 to 1871. In a few astonishing pages—astonishing because in many respects they are more "Tocquevillean" than "Marxist"—of *The Eighteenth Brumaire* and *The Civil War in France,* he analyzes the French Revolution both as the culmination of the process of forming a modern state begun by the bourgeoisie and as the veritable creation of that state, a creation capped by the achievement of Napoleon. He sees the subsequent revolutions of the nineteenth century as so many reworkings of that state, whose functions and role continued to grow. The struggles for control were all the more bitter and interminable because the state had become a parasite, independent of society. Finally, the Paris Commune heralded the end of the cycle begun in 1789.

In these brilliant overviews, Marx lays stress on a fundamental feature of France's modern history, a feature that never ceased to fascinate him: that only the Revolution of 1789 had led to a true upheaval in the state's structure and foundations, whereas the various regimes of the nineteenth century had only modified the formal organization and political balance of power. Between the two Napoleons there were many political constitutions but only one administrative constitution, unchanged in its essential elements and kept out of political conflict by a national consensus. Yet Marx never explored this potentially fruitful insight, which might have suggested a history of the state autonomous from society and even from bourgeois politics, because he always gave priority to the opposite idea of the state as the pure instrument of the dominant class and linked to its rise and fall—victor when that class was victorious, doomed when it failed. Whence came his absurd conclusion in 1871 that the state was nearing its end—proof of his total inability to conceive of history other than as a mirror image of the supposed evolution of society.

In reality, from beginning to end the enigma of the French Revolution for Marx was the enigma of all French history, in which the political is constantly in advance of the economic. Instead of the grand proof of his ideas that he believed he had found in English history, with its powerful and precocious capitalism served by a parliamentary oligarchy, France offered the spectacle of a predominantly rural economy and a state that served society as an arbiter. While England was inventing industry, France was inventing democratic equality in a world that remained precapitalist. England demonstrated the priority of the economic over the political; France refuted it. No doubt that difference explains why Marx devoted his life's great work to the modern history of England and left in regard to France only brilliant and contradictory fragments devoted to the ambiguous triumph that was the Revolution of 1789, indissociably democratic and bourgeois.

François Furet

Further reading

WORKS BY MARX
Civil War in France: The Paris Commune. New York, 1968.
Class Struggles in France.
Collected Works, 19 vols. (eventually to include some 50 vols). New York, 1975–.
The Eighteenth Brumaire of Louis Bonaparte. New York, 1963.

RELATED WORKS
Avineri, Shlomo. *The Social and Political Thought of Karl Marx.* Cambridge, 1968.
Colletti, Lucio. *Il marxismo e Hegel.* Bari, 1969.
Cornu, Auguste. *Karl Marx et Friedrich Engels: Leur vie et leur oeuvre,* 3 vols. Paris, 1955–1962.
Furet, François. *Marx et la Révolution française.* Paris, 1986.
Grandjong, Jacques. *Marx et les communistes allemands à Paris, 1844: Contribution à la naissance du marxisme.* Paris, 1974.
Ritter, Joachim. *Hegel and the French Revolution.* Cambridge, Mass., 1982.

Related topics

Burke	Guizot	Napoleon Bonaparte	Rousseau
Civil Code	Hegel	Rights of Man	Terror
Constant	Jacobinism	Robespierre	Thermidorians
Democracy			

MICHELET

I n 1843 Michelet completed the sixth volume of his *History of France* with an account of the reign of Louis XI. He had begun work on the next volume and had already written the part dealing with Charles VIII when he changed his mind. He put the last three centuries of the French monarchy aside and threw himself into the history of the French Revolution. For the next ten years he devoted himself to the five years between the meeting of the Estates General and the fall of Robespierre. These years became the subject matter of seven volumes published between 1847 and 1852 under three successive regimes—the first two volumes in 1847, the next three between 1848 and 1851, and the last two in 1852.

This change, paradoxical in that the historian wrote his account of the Revolution before writing the history of its origins, stemmed from the Revolution's being in the air. When Michelet decided to add it to the posted contents of his course at the Collège de France in 1845, he was fresh from a battle waged with all the prestige of his chair and shoulder to shoulder with Edgar Quinet against the Catholic Church's attempt to take over the university; the two professors' courses on—and against—the Jesuits had inflamed public opinion. The character of Michelet's teaching changed; less scholarly, it became a part of the politics of the day, where the religious question was central. And that question was related to the Revolution; the violence of the ongoing polemic raised the whole issue of Christianity's place in modern democracy.

Quinet devoted his 1845 course to this topic, and from his lectures he made a book, *Le Christianisme et la Révolution française,* in which, like the men of 1789, he set up a contrast between authoritarian, monarchical, dogmatic Catholicism and the true spirit of Christianity. Since Saint-Simon and Buchez, socialist sects had been dreaming of a new Christianity, which through fraternity would transcend the individualist democracy of 1789. Michelet, who already rejected the idea of a supposed affinity between orthodox Christianity and the Revolution, felt the need to intervene quickly and forcefully. While beginning to teach the Revolution he wrote, in opposition to ultramontane clericalism, a sequel to *Jésuites* entitled *Le prêtre, l'Eglise et la famille,* published in 1845. Early the following year he published *Le peuple,* in which he reworked in his own inimitable way the idea of national fraternity, the Revolution's central legacy, now threatened by both the right and the left, by both the Orleanist bourgeoisie and the socialists, mutually antagonistic proponents of the same pernicious belief in the class struggle.

Immediately after *Le peuple,* Michelet devoted his course in 1846 to "French nationality," the message of which was symbolized by 1789, and in

September he began writing the first two volumes of his *Histoire de la Révolution française*, which would appear in September 1847. With impressive industriousness, formidable endurance, and creative power Michelet established a place for himself on a crowded stage; the same year saw the publication of books by the Christian socialist Esquiros (*Histoire des Montagnards*), Lamartine (*Histoire des Girondins*), and Louis Blanc (the first volume of his *Histoire de la Révolution*). Unbeknownst to the writers, they were all learning or rehearsing the roles, drawn from the repertory left by their illustrious ancestors, which they would play in 1848. Michelet set his intentions and goals down in writing in a note dated February 8, 1847, in which he summed up the contents of his courses since 1842, ending with the following remark: "Finally, Revolution and the *Histoire de la Révolution,* vol. 1, with its religious and political introduction against Christianity and royalty. Here I have taken my stand: both against royalists (legitimists and *anglomanes*) and against terrorist republicans, against Christians and against communists: Louis Blanc" (quoted in Monod, "Michelet et l'histoire," p. 420).

The book's prehistory helps to understand its structure. Just as universal history was shaped by the contributions of nationalities—collective actors that Michelet, steeped in German thought, perceived as individuals—so was France elect among nations by virtue of the French Revolution. The events of 1789, by transforming everything particular about France into universals, possessed exemplary value for French history and French history alone. That history was characterized above all by Christianity and the Revolution, the two great principles in world history. With the former came the whole long history of the divine-right monarchy, while the latter was a radical signal of man's coming emancipation and recovery of fraternity. In this vast teleological mechanism, so typical of the Romantic period, we find elements of both Buchez, whom Michelet detested, and Quinet, his friend. In order to understand this type of interpretation, one has only to compare it with that of the liberal historians of the Restoration. For Michelet as for Buchez, the history of France was unique, incomparable, for it was the individuality of France, and France alone, that revealed world history or, rather, the ideas that guide world history. For Thierry and Guizot, man's material and moral progress, the process of civilization, followed certain laws of development. It was animated by struggle between the social classes and could be comprehended only through a comparative history of the most advanced nations, in particular England and France.

Michelet's approach was diametrically opposed to both social history and comparative history, because for him the Revolution was a spiritual event, a development as unique as the great religious annunciations. But where Buchez had celebrated a strengthening of Catholic faith in France, Michelet made the opposite diagnosis. Did he take his conclusion from Quinet? No, because where his companion saw a resurgence of the true spirit of Christianity in opposition to the Catholic Church, Michelet celebrated the advent of modern democracy on the ruins of Christianity. His French Revolution was no longer the daughter or even the distant cousin of the Gospels; it was their negation.

This argument was the heart of the long introduction to the first volume. At the outset Michelet gives his definition of the Revolution: "the advent of Law, the resurrection of Right, the reaction of Justice." Law, right, and justice are coherent enough as a definition of the content of the Revolution, but the words used to describe its form are bizarrely contradictory: an "advent" is in a sense the opposite of a "resurrection," and a "reaction" is something else entirely. In using this vague terminology Michelet probably had two things in mind. First, the most profound question about the Revolution was its relation to what preceded it, which it called the "Ancien Régime." And second, this "Ancien Régime" was at once radically distinct from what followed (as the word "advent" implies) and yet a condition of it (as "resurrection" suggests) because both were defined by Christianity. In other words, Christianity and 1789 carried with them all the baggage of the ancient and the modern, and the "socialist disputes" added nothing to this heritage. Michelet in fact detested the critique of the principles of 1789 proposed by the various socialist sects since Saint-Simon, and for the same reason that he detested Burke's critique (which was no different in its principle; the critique of modern egalitarian abstraction could be made equally well in the name of tradition or in the name of equality). For Michelet the rights of man were an absolute, transcending the subjectivity of individuals; they were the credo of the new age, the modern religion.

What was the Revolution's relation to what went before? Michelet answered: "The Revolution continued Christianity, and it contradicted it. It was at once the heir and the adversary." By this he meant something different from Hegel's concept of transcendence-conservation (*Aufheben*), namely, that while the Christian idea of fraternity had indeed been incorporated into the Revolution, there nevertheless remained a radical contradiction between the two eras and principles. For Christianity, the idea of fraternity was rooted in original sin, and the community of men was founded on an original fault and a savior. Accordingly, the institutions that developed out of the Christian spirit were marked by arbitrariness and fatality. By contrast, the Revolution established the human community in and through the human order, and therefore the realization of that community, so long forbidden by the spirit of Christianity, became a possibility.

Christianity, a religion of arbitrary salvation granted by God as a pure gift to a very small number of men without regard to merit, had as its counterpart a conception of earthly justice also subject to the arbitrary will of a single individual, modeled on the arbitrariness of divine judgment. Corresponding to the religion of grace was the monarchy of favor, reigning over a humanity deprived of its claims to moral and political activity. The much-vaunted meekness of the Christian was merely the prelude to naked violence; Saint Augustine paved the way for the Inquisition.

During the Middle Ages the monarchy was merely the temporal arm of the Church, its servant. Then came absolutism, characterized by Michelet as the emancipation of royalty, which arrogated to itself all the political and social functions of religion. The God-king became an idol, a substitute object of the French people's love. What the men of the Revolution called the "Ancien

Régime" was a sacerdotal monarchy, which rested, like the Church before it and based on the Church's example, on a mystery of incarnation: the royal person was one with the people, identical with the nation and with France.

This "Ancien Régime" succumbed to crisis toward the end of the seventeenth century owing to the widening emotional gap between the people and royalty. The people, increasingly wretched (and Michelet was already struck by accounts of the second half of Louis XIV's reign, on which he would later rely heavily for the end of his *Histoire de France*), felt that it was being treated unjustly and gradually came to see royalty as distinct from the principles of justice from which it had drawn its power of fascination. The decisive break came under Louis XV, in the middle of his reign, some time between 1744 and 1754, when "the dogma of royal incarnation perished forever." Its replacement had already been born: the "royalty of the spirit," Michelet's way of saying that in the eighteenth century opinion came to reign instead of the king. Society had no further need of the artifice of incarnation, whether religious (the Middle Ages) or secularized (absolutism). Its unity stemmed from a truer and purer principle, freed of the "material" obligation of incarnation: namely, "the profound marriage of sentiments and ideas that joins all with all." This definition of public opinion anticipates the idea of revolutionary fraternity.

While Louis XV slowly interred royalty in the depressing seraglio of the Deer Park and thus revealed the naked truth of royal incarnation, the nullity of an idol destined to endure common death in his very flesh, the philosophes were already proclaiming the new age. Of the brand-new conception of right by which the nation reclaimed a sovereignty for so long accorded to God, Voltaire was the practical and Rousseau the theoretical philosopher. Through them and their books the Revolution had already been carried out in people's minds before it took place in reality, and in all respects save one: the monarchy. "The only obscure question was that of royalty. This was not a question of pure form, as has so often been repeated, but one of substance, an intimate matter more vital than any other in France; it was a question not just of politics but of love, of religion. No other people had so loved its kings."

Thus royalty had not altogether died with Louis XV, and in any case the young Louis XVI had restored a little of its vitality. But even a good king (that is, a subjectively good king) could no longer counteract the falsehood of royalty. To bare that lie and replace it with the rights of man and the sovereignty of the people would be the quintessential meaning of the French Revolution.

Michelet had a philosophical mind befogged by his heart's effusions: what distinguished his thought was that it was always mixed with emotion. The most striking thing about his overall interpretation of 1789 is the degree to which he internalized the Revolution's central conviction about itself, namely, that it represented both a radical rupture and the advent of a new world with France in the vanguard. In order to bring out the full significance of that rupture and advent, Michelet conjured up a clash between two religions, one of which—the new one, the religion of right—was in a sense an antireligious religion because it enabled men to reclaim a sovereignty they had relinquished to God and king. In itself the concept is contradictory. When used to dramatize the break that occurred in 1789, however, it precludes consideration of one of the fundamental problems of the Revolution and of modern politics in general, namely, the ambition to institute a society without a religious foundation of any kind and based solely on the consent of individuals. Consequently, moreover, Michelet found it difficult to conceptualize the Revolution's failure: what did this new religion of right and justice signify if Bonaparte's despotism lay immediately ahead?

On the other hand, Michelet's intimacy with the revolutionary event and with the history of France in general made him extraordinarily knowledgeable about the men who made the Revolution and the symbolic stakes over which they battled. Tocqueville saw the French monarchy as a mechanism of administrative centralization and political dispossession of society, which quietly set the stage for the explosion of 1789. Michelet conjured up a whole host of images with which he was able to explain the sovereign space occupied by the monarchy, the obedience it commanded, and even the love it elicited, and subsequently the revolt of disappointed love and the people's symbolic occupation of the king's place. The two interpretations do not explain the same things, but they are not incompatible. Michelet's opens an important avenue of inquiry that leads to an understanding of the revolutionaries' overinvestment in the political sphere, their belief that the restoration of national sovereignty could work wonders and inaugurate an era of collective regeneration. No one appreciated more fully than Michelet that when the Parisian rioters took the vast, empty fortress of the Bastille on July 14 they recaptured for the people a power that had been relinquished to kings.

Thus his history of the Revolution was written from within, with an extraordinary instinct for what set so many actors, known and unknown—and especially the most important actor of all, the people—in motion for many years. If the Revolution was a great era without great men, it was so, as Michelet understood, because it constantly eluded the grasp of those who pretended to control it; he saw, too, that in order to perceive its deepest sources one must grasp the most extraordinary and novel aspect of its nature, namely, the people's entry onto the stage of power. Nothing is more alien to Michelet's method than history written in an abstract mode, such as that of Mignet, for example, in which the people exists only as one of three great collective actors, alongside the nobility and the bourgeoisie, and in which its role is set down in advance in the great book of the class struggle. For Michelet, history is not fatal; the people is not only a symbol of reason but a collection of empirical individuals whose unpredictable actions, taken together, give the Revolution its meaning.

In order to understand these individuals, Michelet had no need to delve very deep in his memory. He was in direct contact with the Revolution: born in 1798, his knowledge came from his father, an obscure Jacobin printer, from his laborious and impoverished childhood, and from his whole material and moral universe. The Paris of the Revolution was a Paris he had known and continued to know. The Tuileries, the Salle du Manège, the convents of the Jacobins and Cordeliers were not for him the abstract places that they have become for twentieth-century historians. He spent much time meditating in these small theaters that had been witness to such great events, theaters in which he conjured up the shades of the illustrious generation and shared their sentiments. Scenes and souvenirs from his promenades enriched his history of the Revolution, which he continually embellished with what he gleaned from the ubiquitous early nineteenth-century oral tradition. At times it was almost too much, all this emotion barely controlled by its author, yet this fervor was what gave the work of one of the great masters of French prose its vivid intensity, its evocative capacity, its shimmering beauty—in short, its status as a literary monument.

As always, Michelet also worked very hard. It is not easy to trace his documentation in detail, since he did not bother to indicate his sources with notes. He also shared the bad habit common to many historians of citing books and authors he did not like only when he criticized them and not when he made use of them: thus he used Buchez and Roux's monumental *Histoire parlementaire de la Révolution française,* which forms the documentary basis of many chapters of his work, although he speaks of it only with disdain. Nevertheless, his originality compared with contemporary historians of the Revolution is incontrovertible. It came from familiarity with the period and events. He had read everything his colleagues had read: the memoirs published during the Restoration and the July Monarchy, the newspapers of the day, and the two major collections of paliamentary speeches (Buchez and Roux and *Le moniteur*). But he had also made rapid yet extensive explorations in the archives. Gabriel Monod, working with bundles of Michelet's manuscript notes, was able to identify a number of sources: the Archives Centrales, where Michelet was a familiar figure and where he studied, in particular, petitions sent to the Assembly by the départemental Federations prior to the great festival of July 14, 1790; the archives of the Prefecture of Police, which contained the minutes of the sections; those of the Hôtel-de-Ville, particularly invaluable, since the records stored there burned in 1871, for the registers of the Commune; and finally, in 1851–1852 when he was living in Nantes, the archives of Loire-Inférieure, which he used in writing about the war in the Vendée. All this research added up to a considerable if somewhat hasty effort, which for a half century made Michelet's *Histoire* the principal source for specialists as well as for the merely curious. Louis Blanc took malicious pleasure in exposing its errors, yet he also plundered it shamelessly. It was Michelet who gave the great revolutionary *journées*—such as August 10 and May 31–June 2, which he recounted with maniacal knowledge of the detail and the moment, of the intrigues and the passions—the canonical place they have occupied ever since in the history of the Revolution.

For Michelet the most important period in the Revolution was the beginning, the stretch of time between the Estates General and the festival of the Federation. He wrote this part of his book in 1846–1847, years of hope and optimism for republicans; the spirit of fraternity saluted its ancestors, just as the divisions of 1848 would soon recapitulate those of 1792. What Michelet celebrated in 1789 was in fact the unity of the people and the nation in the recapture of its sovereignty and the enunciation of the law. The event was nothing at all like the "petty and selfish insular revolution" in seventeenth-century England, for it was a matter not of claiming a particular national heritage (the liberties of the English) but of founding the universal credo of the new age through the voice of an elect nation. This was Michelet's interpretation of the Declaration of the Rights of Man, and he was critical of the Constituent Assembly for having limited the significance somewhat by emphasizing the rights of individuals rather than the "Right," with a capital R, that transcends subjective rights. Probably because of his sensitivity to the numerous critiques of the philosophy of natural rights, particularly critiques from the left (Saint-Simon, Comte, Buchez, Louis Blanc), he attempted to portray the revolutionary foundation as absolute, rooted in something beyond the human.

That foundation required a fraternally united France, delivered from its feudal divisions: this was achieved on the night of August 4. It required a sovereign Assembly, freed from the royal veto: this was the work of early September. It required a vanquished monarchy, reintegrated into its reality, the people, and returned to Paris from exile in Versailles: this was the meaning of the October days. Michelet's history was the opposite of that of Burke and the French admirers of England from Lally-Tollendal and Mounier to Staël and Guizot. What he loved in the French Revolution was its philosophical universalism, its abstract radicalism, its absolutely unique character, which made it exemplary. And what he celebrated in the nation that paved the way for mankind's emancipation was not modern individualism, which on the contrary would have made it like other nations, particularly aristocratic and mercantile England, which he abominated. No, it was rather fraternity, which created the sentiment of unity and made it possible to abolish the gap and the opposition between the individual and the social. In his work, a simplification of Sieyès', there is a considerable investment in the national idea, which alone possessed the power to unify free individuals and which gave historical action the high purpose without which emancipation is impossible.

This purpose was the significance of the festival of the Federation of July 14, 1790, which for Michelet was the culmination of the Revolution, almost its genius. To appreciate the abyss that separates him from another great admirer of the same day, Tocqueville, we have only to listen to him: "It was a conspiracy for the unity of France. These provincial federations all looked toward the center; they all invoked the National Assembly, bound themselves to it, gave themselves to it, that is, to unity. All expressed gratitude to Paris for its fraternal call."

Yet the Revolution delivered less than it promised. Its downfall began in 1790 with the Civil Constitution of the Clergy, that "feeble and false" work that divided the people, revived fanaticism, and rearmed the counterrevolution; instead of affirming its own credo, the Revolution tinkered with that of its enemies. "Nothing was more disastrous for the Revolution than its failure to know itself from the religious point of view, its failure to understand that it carried within itself a religion. It did not know itself, and knew Christianity still less. It did not know whether Christianity was consistent with or contrary to it, whether it should return to it or go beyond it." What did it do? It tried to reform Christianity without believing in it, because the Revolution was a daughter of the Enlightenment, and thus it offered the "strange spectacle of a Voltaire reforming the Church, pretending to lead it back to apostolic rigor." The men of 1789 refused to make the new religion—that of the federations, of patriotic fraternity diametrically opposed to civic abdication and Christian individualism—their banner.

Thanks to eighteenth-century philosophy, these same men knew how to remedy ancient insults to the human race. They did not know how to crystallize the marvelous fraternal spirit of 1789 and perpetuate it in religious faith. As a result, division returned to opinion and the counterrevolution regained strength by organizing a vast conspiracy of the past against the new spirit, which was prevented from flourishing. Against this dreadful menace, "a conspiracy was needed. Came that of the Jacobins, and it enveloped France." Consequently, however, this "great and terrible machine, which brought the Revolution incalculable strength, which alone could save it," also denatured its original inspiration and *a fortiori* precluded its religious culmination, a task left to nineteenth-century republicans.

This misdirection, in Michelet's analysis, was a crucial turning point. The Revolution embarked on a period of foreign and civil war, social division, political dissension, and soon the Terror, although one can never quite pinpoint whether responsibility for this tragedy lay with the Revolution's enemies or with its own failings. In any case, the failure was only partial. Even reduced to the Jacobin Club, the Revolution was still the Revolution. It did not become, as Quinet would argue a short while later, its own opposite. It was now only a thin, flickering flame, ever threatened with extinction, rather than the overpowering light of 1789. It was in these terms that Michelet dealt with what was a standard question in the revolutionary historiography of his day, torn as it was between "eighty-niners" and "ninety-threers." In opposition to Buchez, Louis Blanc, and the socialists, he was fundamentally on the side of 1789. But he refused to establish a radical break between the two periods or to look upon 1793 as nothing but a negation of 1789. He did not lose his republican faith during 1849 or 1851, in the sad circumstances in which he wrote the sad parts of his *Histoire,* and by the same token he did not abandon the Revolution at the point when it was reduced to a mere ghost of its former self. The Convention and the Jacobins had substituted dictatorship and Terror for popular sovereignty, but they had saved the country.

Michelet detested the degeneration of the Revolution into small, intolerant sects. He did not like the Girondins' lack of seriousness, much less the "clerical" sectarianism of Robespierre. He condemned the antiparliamentary coup of May 31–June 2, the Parliament's capitulation to the street. But the Convention remained, before and after, the repository of the revolutionary spirit and the true heir of 1789. To understand this central figure one need only reread Michelet's truly admirable pages on the king's condemnation: the key moment, the heart of the Revolution, when the two sovereignties, the old and the new, the king and the representatives of the people, faced each other, and it became necessary to pronounce once and for all the judgment the Constituent Assembly had never dared to render, that the one was incompatible with the other. The Revolution had put the people in the king's place. It therefore became necessary to condemn the idol that had so long usurped the place of the people, to strike at the royalty in Louis XVI in order to do away with the ridiculous mystery of monarchical incarnation. To be sure, Michelet would have refrained from executing the king, in order to avoid the danger of turning him through martyrdom back into a "living head." But in the trial of the Republic's first winter he saw the Revolution's great act of justice: the affirmation of right.

The Terror was something else entirely. It was the product not only of extraordinary circumstances but of Jacobin fanaticism. For Michelet, the Jacobins of 1793 supplanted the people of 1789. Indeed, after three years of revolution, with everything in a shambles, the dominant note was one of public indifference: "The people in 1793 returned home. Before the end of that year it would become necessary to pay wages to get them to return to the sections. . . . Amid this growing apathy, and as a remedy for it, the dreadful machine that had eased up a little during 1792 was repaired and reconstructed, the machine of Public Safety and its mainspring, the Society of Jacobins." Thus the club substituted its "machine" for a revolution that had lost its popular motor and substituted its political orthodoxy for liberty. This magisterium of ideas enforced by a militarily disciplined apparatus quickly led to the dictatorship of one man and to the imposition of Terror on the Revolution. With this account Michelet refuted both the insipid interpretation of the Terror as the result of circumstances alone (an explanation shared by Mignet and Louis Blanc) and Edgar Quinet's idea of a resurgence of absolutism inside the Revolution itself. He was thus the first to propose a very modern view of the risks involved in oligarchic confiscation of democratic power in the people's name.

Nevertheless, his Revolution ended on 9 Thermidor. On arriving at that day—for Michelet it was the summer of 1853—he laid down his pen and abandoned the sequel, the Thermidorian reaction he so thoroughly disliked and whose history he would not write until much later. The spectacle of the newborn Second Empire was not such as to entice him into writing about a period in which the bourgeoisie, money, and the army would denature his Revolution for a long time to come. The monarchy had had its annals and Michelet had hoped to write those of the Republic, not to make the bourgeoisie a gift of its past or to authenticate the patents of the Bonaparte family. All histories of the French Revolution have been haunted by this dialectic between past and present, and Michelet's, by ending with 9 Thermidor, simply confirmed his loyalties.

With his history Michelet, as he had intended, erected a monument to the Republic. Not to the First Republic, or the Second, or to any particular period of the Revolution that he might have chosen as an example—for his favorite period remained the one in which the old royalty, although uprooted, still lived on after the people's self-emancipation—but to the years 1789 and 1790, when the revolutionary spirit united the French people in national fraternity. The Republic, at the moment of its birth in 1792, was unequal to its promise and scarred by war, dissension between classes and individuals, and popular indifference. None of this mattered, however, if it was only a glimmering of what tomorrow ought to be: a civilization of liberty, in which all men are brothers in service of the fatherland, the vanguard of human progress.

Michelet's Republic was thus an annunciation at once democratic and national, the fulfillment of French nationhood in and through fraternity. It was supposed to transcend the contradiction between 1789 and 1793 stressed by liberal and socialist historians: whether a celebration of 1789 at the expense of 1793 or a critique of 1789 in the name of 1793. Michelet did not care for either the Orleanist bourgeoisie or the socialist sects. He sought to restore a unique message to a Revolution composed of so many diverse episodes. That message was neither bourgeois nor socialist; it embodied a new religion of justice and fraternity, in which Michelet saw the essence of democracy.

Michelet's was a syncretic view, which drew its substance from many authors and many books (Herder, Fichte, Thierry, Buchez) and powerfully united the universal with the national. Relieved of bourgeois individualism on the right and of the terrorist heritage on the left, the Republic symbolized France's historic destiny. It prefigured what the founders of the Third Republic would soon call *laïcité* (secularism). This collection of ideas, so specifically French that it has no equivalent in any other European political culture, invokes values that retain, even in their negation of religion, something of religion's venerability: an ancient-style cult of civic equality coupled with a celebration of modern liberty. Before the school became the locus and battle-flag of this movement of religious citizenship, Michelet was its prophet. That this movement has not fared well in the twentieth century in the face of increasing individualism and a socialist critique does not alter the fact that all through the nineteenth century it was the very essence of the revolutionary heritage for republicans.

To that heritage Michelet lent his genius, combining a remarkable passion for the past with his own inimitable music to produce a book as immortal as any great work of art. Today's reader is caught up like yesterday's in the torrential narrative, captivated by the timeless truth of a scholarly history written in a poetic mode. In reconstructing the decisive drama that lasted just slightly more than five years, from the spring of 1789 to the summer of 1794, Michelet reinvented and brought back to life countless actors and minute moments, accidents and inevitabilities, passions and reasons. His power to divine both men and things makes him still the greatest of all intercessors between the French Revolution and its innumerable children.

François Furet

989

Fᴜʀᴛʜᴇʀ ʀᴇᴀᴅɪɴɢ

WORKS BY MICHELET
Histoire de la Révolution française, 2 vols. Paris, 1952.

RELATED WORKS
Furet, François. *La gauche et la Révolution française au milieu du XIXe siècle: Edgar Quinet et la question du jacobinisme (1865–1870)*. Paris, 1986.
Halévy, Daniel. *Jules Michelet*. Paris, 1928.
Maurras, Charles. *Trois idées politiques: Chateaubriand, Michelet, Sainte-Beuve*. Paris, 1898.
Monod, Gabriel. "Michelet et l'histoire de la Révolution française," *Revue internationale de l'enseignement*, vol. 59, January–June 1910, 414–437.
——— *La vie et la pensée de Jules Michelet, 1798–1852*, 2 vols. Paris, 1923.
Sainte-Beuve, Charles-Augustin. *Nouveaux lundis*, vol. 3. Paris, 1863–1870.
Viallaneix, Paul. *La voie royale: Essai sur l'idée de peuple dans l'oeuvre de Michelet*. Paris, 1971.
Wilson, Edmund. *To the Finland Station: A Study in the Writing and Acting of History*, chap. 3. New York, 1940.

Rᴇʟᴀᴛᴇᴅ ᴛᴏᴘɪᴄs

Ancien Régime
Blanc
Buchez
Burke
Civil Constitution of the Clergy
Federation
Fichte

Fraternity
Guizot
Jacobinism
King's Trial
Napoleon Bonaparte
Nation
Quinet

Rights of Man
Rousseau
Sieyès
Staël
Terror
Tocqueville
Voltaire

QUINET

B orn, like the Romantic generation, at the turn of the century, Edgar
Quinet shared its fascination with the great event that had preceded
and haunted his childhood. Having arrived in Paris from his native Franche-
Comté to make a name for himself in the field of letters, the only avenue left
open to ambitious young men under the Restoration, he did much, as a good
disciple of Victor Cousin, to familiarize the French with German philosophy
(especially Herder, whom he translated). Close, as well, to the liberal Doctrinaires and hostile to the ultraroyalist right, he hailed the July Days of 1830 as
the resurgence of the French Revolution. But these youthful loyalties did not
survive either the domestic conservatism of the new monarchy or the timidity
of its foreign policy, because the young Edgar Quinet, who in the previous
decade had been an ardent supporter of Greek independence, was a man
very sensitive to yet another legacy of the Revolution, the emancipation of
European nationalities. Having grown hostile to the bourgeois materialism
of the July Monarchy, Quinet slowly produced an abundant and uneven body
of work, ranging in content from the philosophical poem to the political essay,
in which he developed the tenets of a republican religion opposed to the
Orleanist-liberal tradition and in a spirit of fraternity with his friend Michelet. Like Michelet, and sharing his admiration for German thought and for
Vico, he attempted to decipher mankind's secrets in universal history. Appointed professor of the history of literature at Lyons in 1838 and then to the
Collège de France in 1842, he became, through his battle (again in conjunction with Michelet) against the Catholic Church's pretensions to dominate the
university, one of the leaders of the intellectual opposition to the Guizot government.

His first systematic study of the Revolution came in lectures delivered
in 1845 at the Collège de France. Quinet approached the question in a manner typical of his thinking, as one who since youth had been passionately
interested in the history of religion. He examined the relation of the French
Revolution to Christianity. What interested him was not (or at least not yet)
the history of the Revolution as such, but its philosophical antecedents and
its ability to give modern man, heir to the Christian message, a new sense of
his destiny.

For Quinet, as for Guizot and Hegel, Christianity had forged the modern individual. Its power and grandeur stemmed from its invention of the
individual conscience and man's intrinsic liberty. The Catholic Church symbolized the negation of this original content of Christianity, and the Reformation its rebirth. The former, monarchical, hierarchical, and authoritarian,

embodied the opposite of what the Gospels had proclaimed; the latter marked the reemergence of Christianity's original spirit. But Quinet was not, unlike Guizot, a Protestant. Possessed of a religious instinct but disaffected, he carried a radical philosophical individualism so far that he saw the institutionalization of the Protestant churches as the beginning of their spiritual decline. The Reformation, too, fell victim to this dialectic of the letter and the spirit.

The French Revolution was none other than the resurgence of the Christian principle that had been stamped out in the seventeenth century in a country subject to the twin disciplines of Catholicism and monarchy. Its spirit was one of "identifying with the principle of Christianity." Through democracy it sought to realize the divine promise that made each man a sovereign conscience by restoring liberty to all. The ambition it set for itself was to create a city composed of equally sovereign moral consciences, repudiating the blandishments of selfish material interests and hedonistic pleasures. With Quinet there is no public/private distinction but rather an extrapolation from the moral conscience to the civic conscience, from the Protestant to the citizen.

Nevertheless, the religious ideal, on which the modern democratic city is modeled, is not identical with the political ideal. Unlike his friend Michelet, Quinet did not see the Revolution as a latter-day religious annunciation but as a pathetic effort on the part of the human city to model its organization on the free dialogue between each individual and God—pathetic because it was condemned to encounter the resistance of historical reality, to be overwhelmed by the inertia of the past before being born again. The Revolution was an attempt by Frenchmen of the late eighteenth century to overcome a history of servitude and establish liberty—an immense, magnificent ambition, but not enough to guarantee against backsliding into the old order.

The course of events from 1848 to 1851 repeated the attempt and dramatized the failure in caricatural form. After the fraternal revolution of February came the fratricidal days of June. It all ended with another Bonapartist dictatorship, under a Bonaparte so mediocre that France could no longer blame its subjugation on circumstances or an extraordinary personality. The second of December revealed a veritable national tradition of servitude.

This tradition would be explored by Quinet, one of the new regime's prominent exiles, in a book published in 1854 entitled *Philosophie de l'histoire de France*. His 1845 course had been aimed squarely at Buchez's Catholic neo-Jacobinism. His first work in exile was a critique of the Restoration historians, especially Augustin Thierry, and of their fatalistic conception of the progress of liberty, a conception promoted initially by the Third Estate with support from the monarchy and in opposition to the aristocracy, and later by the Revolution in opposition to the monarchy. In French history Quinet saw liberty more often vanquished than victorious. It was on liberty's ruins, not in its triumph, that monarchical absolutism had prospered—hand in hand with Catholic absolutism, as the eradication of Protestantism in the seventeenth century made clear. Hatred of the nobility had led the historians of the bourgeoisie astray; in the name of the class struggle they had forgotten liberty. They saw the monarchy as the first artisan of the Revolution. Quinet saw it as the poison spring that denatured the Revolution and led it back to despotism.

*
**

Quinet's *Révolution* appeared in 1865. The central idea of the book was the failure of the illustrious ancestors, compounded by the events of December 2 and by exile; the sons and grandsons had done no better than their forebears—on the contrary. Quinet wrote his book in the same spirit in which Tocqueville had written his *Ancien Régime* ten years earlier: to understand the secret link between revolution and despotism in France before as well as after the Revolution.

Quinet's French Revolution was a twofold phenomenon. On the one hand it was the winning of civil equality, the establishment of a society based on new principles, the acquisition by numerous citizens of concrete advantages connected with the abolition of feudal property and the sale of clerical properties. On the other hand, its ambition was to make political liberty an inalienable possession of each party to the new social contract. While it easily accomplished the first set of objectives, it continually tampered with the second.

On the subject of civil equality, everything was said on August 4: on that day Ancien Régime society died, amid general enthusiasm. Quinet interpreted the unanimity of that famous night not as a sign of peasant pressure on the Assembly but as proof that the civil revolution was over before it occurred. It was in effect the expression of an evolution that, because it was necessary, had already taken place. The abolition of the Ancien Régime was nothing but a manifestation of that necessity, and it might have taken a different shape without affecting the substance of the reforms. All this change came quite early in the history of the Revolution, moreover, and without opposition; more important, it was irreversible. Somewhat later the Civil Code would institutionalize this fundamental achievement of the Revolution—the intelligible manifestation of historical necessity.

But when the question of political liberty was raised in this same period, what a contrast! What debates and battles! What a torrent of governments and regimes! What discontinuity! By setting its sights on the regeneration of man and the advent of the citizen, the Revolution illustrated the return of conscience—freedom of conscience with all its attendant unpredictability—to history.

Thus it was by establishing or reestablishing a sort of primary autonomy of the political and the religious that Quinet sought to resolve the classical problem of the nineteenth-century historian, that of continuity or discontinuity between the Ancien Régime and the Revolution. The traditional interpretation (since the Restoration at least) in terms of class struggle and the triumph of the bourgeoisie over the nobility had stressed both the inevitability of the Revolution and the central importance in it of the long-term evolution of civil society. As a result, however, 1789 seemed more a victory for a society produced by the Ancien Régime than the political inauguration of modern democracy; neither Thierry nor Guizot nor Mignet ever really overcame this dilemma, which, incidentally, they bequeathed to Marx. Quinet dealt with the question by introducing a radical distinction between two orders of reality, offering two histories proceeding at two different tempos according to two different logics. This philosophical inconsistency enabled him to isolate the economic and social on one side as the objects of a new sort of natural science, and on the other side to treat the religious and the political, where what man himself invents manifests its influence. Thus the society that emerged from August 4, 1789, was merely the product of preceding centuries, and the Revolution the sequel to the Ancien Régime. Still, the power of the Constituent Assembly was the opposite of monarchical despotism, and 1789 marked a radical break with the Ancien Régime.

The importance of revolution as a concept stemmed solely from this rupture. The concept of revolution was associated with a periodic rebirth or sudden breakthrough of a new spirit, a new irruption of the religious into the political. A revolution, in Quinet's view, is a series of events through which a specific people at a given point in space and time invents a universal future. With this concept Quinet explained how it was possible for a religious message to achieve a historical existence. Existence, however, implies nothing about necessity or even fidelity, since neither the occurrence of a revolution or its spiritual nature counts among the causal factors in social evolution.

The key problem raised by the French Revolution was to understand its spiritual nature, that is, its relation to Christianity, the matrix of modern Europe. Quinet's 1865 work (especially its fifth book, entitled *La religion*) went further in this regard than his 1845 course. In it he constrasted countries such as England, the United States, and Holland, where political revolution had crystallized preexisting religious beliefs and institutions, with late eighteenth-century France, still a Catholic monarchy. In the first-named countries the religious ground was suitable for political transformation; in France, however, the new spirit had to be invented in opposition to religion. Quinet treated a problem, previously explored by Guizot, concerning the role played in English (and by extension American) history by the precedence of religious revolution over political revolution. Like Guizot, or at any rate like the later Guizot, the Guizot of 1850, who had also repudiated the hopes of his youth, he portrayed the "success" of the English Revolution through an implicit contrast with the French case. Even more than Guizot, Quinet ascribed this success to the priority of the Protestant revolution, the true origin of English political liberty and its solid mooring.

Thus the English Revolution presented an example of the transformation of religious content into political principles, which consequently proved durable. By contrast, in the French case the historian was confronted with politics pure and simple, even though the politics in question, because it held out a promise to all mankind, had affinities with the message of the Gospel. The paradox of French history is that recovery of the spirit of Christianity came only by way of pure democracy. The French Revolution revived the language of religion without ever attaining the dignity of religion. The reason for this was that the French, who had rejected the Reformation of the sixteenth century and extirpated it from French soil by persecution in the seventeenth century, had no system of beliefs with which to conceive of modern liberty. They had at their disposal only a system of ideas shaped by "philosophy." Now, this "philosophy," an exclusive possession of the learned, was by nature ill suited to serve as a common wisdom or in the place of a popular consensus. How could a nation go in one jump from the very old to the very new, from Catholicism to the sovereignty of reason? And how were the institutions of the new spirit to be conceived with nothing more than the "philosophical" idea of tolerance?

The French Revolution did not want to institute a religion of any kind. It was content to establish tolerance and freedom of worship, in other words, to favor the influence of tradition and Catholicism. Against the Church of the past it made only a few worldly forays, without daring to see that its own principle was incompatible with the spirit of Catholicism. This combination of superficial audacity and profound cowardice was the cause of the war in the Vendée. Why did people say that the Constituents or Jacobins were too radical? They were too timid. They fought royalty by making a pact with the Church, as if the two institutions were not allied in defense of ancestral servitudes.

This idea that the Revolution was too moderate is not easy to understand, since Quinet coupled it, as we shall see, with a radical critique of the Terror. For Quinet, the Revolution's moderation reflected its fundamental ambiguity in the religious sphere: it proposed ideas that made it resemble a latter-day annunciation, yet it refused in advance to allow those ideas any religious basis or form. It sought to replace Catholicism as a political principle, but only by negating religion. Hence it established itself in a void. It declared a war that it was unable to wage. It triggered a primordial conflict while denying itself the means to fight.

Contrasting this spiritual timidity with the great religious upheavals of the sixteenth century, Quinet cited mainly conjunctural reasons, especially the determination of revolutionary leaders not to attack the beliefs of the majority of French people head on—a determination that was indeed shared by Mirabeau in 1790 and Robespierre in 1793–1794. He has less to say about the essential cause: the Revolution's claim to be regenerating man in the name of reason—what he called "philosophy"—and therefore its inability to create a religion. It was not that "philosophy" was not accessible to the people, as Quinet observed, but rather that the Revolution saw the instrument of man's salvation in history alone and thus ruled out any recourse to the transcendental. The French Revolution did indeed possess the novel ambition to establish a social pact based on nothing other than the free will of its citizens: this pact was what Quinet called "living in a social body (*corps de peuple*) without any religion." Yet even though this ambition was consubstantial with the Revolution, he never analyzed its constraints, because such an analysis would have led him to relativize his parallel between the Protestant revolutions of the sixteenth century and the French Revolution. In effect, he "reproaches" the latter for its very nature, for that which, at the end of the eighteenth century, made it unique, incomparable, and the foundation of the democratic universal. No explanation of that universal or of its relation to the religious universal is possible within Quinet's conceptual framework, which is based on the opposition between religious revolution and nonreligious revolution.

Quinet, incidentally, was probably the last of the great nineteenth-century historians to reflect on the French Revolution in terms of a comparison with England and the United States. For him, the establishment of "representative government" was no longer, as it was for Staël or Guizot, the principal term of comparison. Quinet substituted the religious question, which, he held, explained why there was success in one case, failure in the other. In doing so he made his 1865 book a much more comparative exercise than his 1845 lectures, and he took a much clearer stand in favor of English and especially American liberty—both points that distinguished him from his friend Michelet. In his own way he, too, was at bottom a critic of French revolutionary "artificialism" and of a democratic civilization based on nothing other than philosophical abstraction and man's natural rights. The tragedy of the French Revolution was that it conceived the emancipation of modern man without offering him any religious foundation.

Nevertheless, the ambition alone was enough to mark a dividing line between the past and the future, a key passage in the evolution of peoples and of mankind. Quinet combined analysis of the failure of the Revolution with celebration of its audacity, because unlike the English Revolution, which separated its objectives and first destroyed the Catholic Church before attacking absolute monarchy, France, subjected for a much longer time to the slavery of the Ancien Régime, had at least taken on both afflictions at once. There was a kind of bonus in the admirably instructive tardiness of 1789: the new world trying to be born against the old, the modern spirit facing the Middle Ages, liberty against the coupling of Church and royalty.

In opposing the Church the Revolution came up with only one weapon, which proved to be a boomerang: freedom of worship. Rather than confront its adversary on the religious battlefield, it conceded sovereignty over souls. Against royalty, the prize to be won in battle was civic liberty. This aspect of Quinet's book takes us close to Tocqueville.

In fact, the old monarchy as described by Quinet resembles Tocqueville's "Ancien Régime": excessively centralized, it had wrapped the French nation and society in the tentacles of the king's power under the usurped representation of a "royal democracy." If Quinet's diagnosis was identical to Tocqueville's, he added a remark about the origins of the monarchy's difficulties that is not to be found in the latter's work and that enabled him to absolve the national tradition of blame for the monarchical cancer: the kings of France, he argued, had imitated the chief features of the Byzantine government.

Thus the Revolution was in this respect a reassertion of the people's and the nation's power over themselves after centuries of "Byzantine" monarchical alienation. That heritage explains why the Revolution was originally and fundamentally antimonarchical. If the Constituent Assembly took so many precautions against royal authority, it was not for tactical reasons but because the genius of the Revolution itself led it to restore the "national forms" of that authority, that is, to make royal authority subject to a nation whose rights had been restored. Quinet, in exploring the notion (which he took from the texts of 1789) that the Revolution was a restoration of ancient liberties, was led to magnify the work of the Constituent Assembly, which he portrayed as the quintessential incarnation of the spirit of the Revolution. In reconstituting the old kingdom on the basis of principles opposite to those of the monarchy, in decentralizing where the monarchy had created its admin-istration, in fashioning citizens where it had dominated subjects, the Constit-uent Assembly did not mean simply to express suspicion of the king of old France. It set out in systematic fashion to destroy absolute power in order to establish the new power on a basis of liberty and democracy: this goal, accord-ing to Quinet, was the Revolution's "primary" idea.

*
**

Thus the *other* central question of the French Revolution, apart from that of its moral and religious message, was the question of power. In the historiography of the subject, Quinet's work offers one of the most profound analyses of the Revolution's political aspect. If one ignores the alleged Byz-antine genealogy of the absolute monarchy—a fantastic claim whose only purpose is to set off the contention that 1789 constituted a national restora-tion—one is left with a vision of a fundamental conflict, at the most profound level of collective representations and practices, between the old monarchy and the men of 1789. Furthermore, this conflict overlaps that between the Revolution and Catholicism, since the Church provided another model of absolute monarchy. If the last Bourbon despite his weakness did not lower his flag before the new France, it was not because he was bound hand and foot to the old society; on the contrary, he had subjugated that society. It was rather because he embodied a principle of power incompatible with liberty. And if the Constituent Assembly had been unable to make any more than the semblance of a place for him in the Constitution of 1791, it was because the Revolution had done nothing less than to invade the territory of absolute monarchy in the name of a contrary principle. Quinet lacked Tocqueville's historical genius when it came to understanding the political practices of the Ancien Régime. But because he was more interested in the symbolic form of political domination than in the administration of men and things, he was more alert than Tocqueville to the system of representation of power that supported absolutism and indeed constituted absolutism's very substance and legitimacy to the bitter end. It was this aspect of Quinet's work that established his affinity with Michelet. Like Michelet, Quinet attached central importance to the Revolution's symbolic investment in a new image of power. He under-stood that if the Revolution was a kind of annunciation, it was not because it was supposed to change society but because it was supposed to put the people in the place of the king.

For Quinet, this question of sovereignty was the crux of the second tragedy of French democracy: not only did the Revolution not dare to become a liberating religion for the new age, it also reinstituted absolute power.

This power, as we saw earlier, was the issue in the conflict between Girondins and Montagnards; it was the meaning of the Montagnard victory and the reign of Robespierre. The two parties were working toward the same goals: to regenerate France and Europe and to establish a free society. But the Girondins, who failed to appreciate the immensity of the task, thought they could complete it while remaining loyal to the new principles. The Montagnards appreciated the weight of the past; "they perceived that the question was to force a people to be free." They reconstituted absolute power in the service of the Revolution.

Accordingly, the secret of the Montagnard victory was simple: power belonged to those who reinforced revolutionary passion by coupling it with the genius of the Ancien Régime, thus combining France's two histories. While the Girondins pursued innovations and new departures, the Montagnards balanced the future against the past or conjured it away. But at the same time they annulled its promise. May 31 restored "the old political temperament of France": silence and fear. At the end of the upheaval lay 18 Brumaire and the imperial dictatorship.

The Jacobin form of this return to absolutism was the Terror. Quinet's work attacked the part of the republican tradition that had made a specialty of apology for the Terror, with or without regrets. In this respect, his originality, as an author who belonged to this tradition, was to reject not only the ritual and almost spontaneous admiration for this historical legacy but also the traditional explanation of the Terror in terms of what I have elsewhere called the "theory of circumstances": the counterrevolution, the Vendée, and danger on the borders. For Quinet, the Terror was not the result of an exceptional situation and therefore admirable or at any rate justified as the means required by the ends. Rather, it was a product of the Revolution itself in its Jacobin form, an unprecedented—and unnecessary—revival of the absolutist tradition by the revolutionary spirit.

In Quinet's eyes what was condemnable, what was absurd in the Terror was not the violence. Violence had been an intrinsic part of man's history from the beginning, as well as the midwife of progress. Luther and Calvin had not put an end to the dreadful Middle Ages by reciting peaceful homilies. The sixteenth-century Protestants inaugurated the future by smashing the statues of saints on church facades. During the French Revolution itself that practice had found imitators in the de-Christianizing movement led by sectional militants in the winter of 1793–94. But the Jacobin leaders, Robespierre foremost among them, had put an end to it, and this action Quinet deplored, because the de-Christianizers were more or less spontaneously attempting to found something new, to sever France from Catholic tradition and establish a new religion more compatible with the spirit of Christianity. Quinet thus criticized the Terror not so much for its violence as for its meaninglessness: it was an extermination process that operated in a vacuum and had no purpose other than to sacrifice individuals to the state. To that extent it revived absolutist tradition in a revolutionary mode. Not only did the guillotine fail to point the way to the future; it brought back the past. Robespierre was neither Moses nor Calvin but Richelieu. He incarnated not a new idea but the old *raison d'état*. In vain he sought to alter this image *in extremis* through the cult of the Supreme Being. But this was a bookish intellectual's fantasy and had nothing to do with religious prophecy. It was a cover for the Terror, not the institution of a new belief that could have justified the Terror.

The terrorist system as Quinet saw it had no higher logic; its purpose was not to grapple at close quarters with the old spiritual and moral world and attempt to displace it. It offered no collective purpose of civilization to justify the sacrifices it required but only hatred of individuals by other individuals. It assumed, without making its criteria explicit, that its distribution of death was just, since it recognized the liberty of its adversary, the Catholic Church. "Neither art nor subtlety will overcome this dilemma: if Terror was wanted, there should have been no tolerance; if tolerance was wanted, there should have been no Terror."

In this sense, the Terror was in contradiction with the Revolution to the extent that tolerance was a consequence of liberty: autonomy of individual consciences was bought at this price. By establishing a system of political coercion and physical extermination, the revolutionaries resorted to an ancient right in the name of a modern idea, since they simultaneously denied and acknowledged their enemies' rights. Terror for Quinet was an exclusive province of monarchical and aristocratic regimes. Its roots were older than those of French absolutism, which itself sprang from the Roman tradition. For Quinet the concept of "ancient liberty" did not exist. Conversely, the Terror was incompatible with modern democracy. What made it necessary, though still contradictory, in the French Revolution was the Jacobins' ignorance of the nature of modern democracy and its indispensable religious foundation. Instead of fighting to create the civilization of the future, the French revolutionaries borrowed their methods from the past. Consequently they were left with nothing that could serve as a purpose of their action other than action itself.

In other words, the Terror was a system whose logic was purely political, devoid of transcendent meaning. Quinet devoted the seventeenth book of his work to the subject, entitled *Théorie de la Terreur*. He first distinguished between the Terror as a popular reaction and the Terror as a system of government. He excused the former, a product of the escalating violence of the Revolution and counterrevolution, an episodic frenzy of vengeance against court intrigue and foreign invasion. What interested him, however, was the transformation of this popular sentiment into a principle of government by the members of the Committee of Public Safety: "Through them the frenzy of certain days became the fixed temperament and soul of the Revolution." This mutation was facilitated by the nature of the revolutionary idea, the indifference to the fate of individuals that it could at times encourage, the division it tended to enforce between the good and the wicked, and the impatience that it fostered at the slowness of change in a world it had promised to transform. Quinet passes very quickly over this aspect of things, however. In effect, the revolutionary Terror was not to his way of thinking a novel form of government. On the contrary, it represented a resurgence of the very substance of absolutism; the return of Louis XI, Richelieu, and Louis XIV; a renewal of Saint Bartholomew's Day and the *dragonnades;* the naked violence of power, the state as an end in itself, with the nation left to suffer in fear and servitude. The Terror marked the shackling of the Revolution to the legacy of royalty.

The proof was that the Terror could never be acknowledged as such. After 9 Thermidor this obfuscation was a visible and even prevalent lie on the part of those prominent participants in the Terror who had survived it, who already needed the mystifying excuse of circumstances. Even while the Terror still raged, however, in 1793 and 1794, the Revolution was unable to formulate its doctrine: how could it have produced an apology for government by fear without renouncing itself? How could it have adopted despotism's own system without ceasing to exist? Thus it never overcame the contradiction, which finally destroyed the system itself. In the spring of 1794, when Robespierre guillotined the Hébertists, or in other words terrorized the terrorists in an attempt to "stabilize" his dictatorship, he fell into this contradiction; but by then he had only a few months left to live.

The weakness of this interpretation is that it combines and indeed confounds two very different historical realities, the political Ancien Régime and the revolutionary government. On the subject of absolutism, which he fails to distinguish from simple despotism because he sees both as domination without justice or law, Quinet is a prisoner of the Revolution's own mythology: popes and kings alike were institutions of the "Middle Ages." Conceptually, this summary definition serves first of all to characterize the historical rupture effected by the principles of the Revolution and second to explain why the Revolution became stuck in the rut of the past. Quinet thus precludes any serious examination of what distinguished the revolutionary government from other despotisms (typologically or historically). That failure is the reason for the vague and superficial character of the passages in which he contrasts the specific character of the terrorism of Year II with the monarchy's exercise of *raison d'état.* It is also the reason for the absence of any historical analysis of the revolutionary government itself, since Quinet uses the terms centralization, Jacobinism, dictatorship, and Terror as though they were amost equivalent or at any rate necessarily related.

In another respect, however, he noticed something fundamental in the history of the Revolution, something that only Tocqueville, ten years earlier and admittedly with greater analytical powers, had noted and promised to investigate: namely, the fact that the Revolution both broke with and continued the Ancien Régime. Quinet even takes this formula literally, since he sees 1793 as a pure resurgence of royal arbitrariness, which implied that a break with the past had taken place but that the new itself had then given way to a revival of the old. Quinet does not see this era as a mere survival of the past, however, a sort of historical residue that the new age would have to overcome. Instead he depicts it as the core of what he called the French temperament, a corrupting influence in the very fabric of time, a cancer on the Revolution itself, which turned it into its opposite. He transcends the banality of the Romantic canvas with which he began, with its commonplace contrast between past and future, by conceptualizing temporal agency in terms of the opposition of absolutism to liberty, which in his eyes characterized not only the Revolution but the history that followed it and indeed his own time.

This aspect of his thought brought him closest to Tocqueville, even though he did not belong to the same milieu or even the same intellectual family as the aristocratic philosopher of democracy. It also estranged him from his friend Michelet, with whom he nevertheless fought shoulder-to-shoulder in many battles. Quinet's judgment of the French Revolution was, despite the sublimity of its principles, quite pessimistic. He believed that by adopting the political practices of the monarchy the Revolution had reinforced age-old habits of servitude and infected even the republican left with the mortal virus of absolute power. This belief was of course a shameful and unavowable passion, yet so powerful that the Europe of his day seemed to him in danger of "producing immense, servile democracies that will orbit forever around the arbitrariness from which they sprang and to which they return, while true liberal democracy will blossom in the vast, trackless wastes of North America."

This anxious questioning of the future, also adapted from Tocqueville, was inseparable from Quinet's diagnosis of the Revolution's legacy. What tended to isolate Quinet in the republican left of his day was his nonconformist position on the value of the revolutionary heritage. Though persecuted and driven into exile, he was not Jacobin enough to be a member of the family. Farther "left" than the liberal historians of the 1830s who had been his political adversaries under the July Monarchy, this exemplary republican was more severe than they in his judgment of the dictatorship of Year II. True, he did borrow from them one of the key questions of his book: how to think about the connection between 1789 and 1793. And he also shared their diagnosis; a fervent admirer of 1789, he was hostile to 1793. But the grounds for his judgment were totally different and far more serious. Thiers, Mignet, Thierry, and Guizot had not needed to condemn almost all of French history in order to criticize the Terror. On the contrary, they kept company with the monarchy for quite some time, long enough for the Third Estate to grow up under its tutelage, before abandoning it, at some point between Louis XIV and Louis XV, to the excommunicators of the "Ancien Régime." As for the Terror and the Jacobins, it sufficed to view them as unfortunate but fleeting consequences of an exceptional situation in order to exonerate not only the Revolution but the rest of French history as well.

A generation later, the republican survivor and veteran of 1848 no longer shared the triumphal optimism of the "Constitutionnels" who had wanted to, and did, remake 1789 in 1830. In his arraignment of Year II he indicted all of French history, that of the Church and that of the kings. Rejecting as idle nonsense the notorious argument that "circumstances" explained the Terror and dictatorship, he blamed instead the weight of clerical and monarchical tradition within the Revolution itself. What had seemed the most revolutionary period of all became for him literally the most reactionary. If 1789 was a people's sublime revolt against its own history, 1793 represented its woeful relapse into the servitude of its traditions. Thus the bitterness of failure, exacerbated by exile, not only made Quinet a more pessimistic historian than his *juste-milieu* predecessors but also gave his thought a more radically critical cast and a quality of interrogation of the past born from this extremism: more philosophical than political, and more libertarian than liberal.

François Furet

FURTHER READING

WORKS BY QUINET

Le Christianisme et la Révolution française. Paris, 1845. Reprinted Paris, 1984.
Philosophie de l'histoire de France. Paris, 1854.
La Révolution. Paris, 1865. Reprinted Paris, 1987.

RELATED WORKS

Furet, François. *La gauche et la Révolution française au milieu du XIXe siècle: Edgar Quinet et la question du jacobinisme (1865–1870)*. Paris, 1986.
Pochon, Jacques. "Edgar Quinet et les luttes du Collège de France, 1843–1847," *Revue d'histoire littéraire de la France,* July–August 1970.
Valès, Albert. *Edgar Quinet: Sa vie et son oeuvre*. Carrières-sous-Poissy, 1936.

RELATED TOPICS

De-Christianization
Girondins
Guizot
Hegel
Liberty
Marx

Michelet
Montagnards
Napoleon Bonaparte
Night of August 4
Revolutionary Assemblies
Revolutionary Religion

Robespierre
Terror
Tocqueville
Vendée

STAËL

Germaine de Staël's reflections on the Revolution occupied two distinct
periods in her life, separated by twenty years: Thermidor and the Restoration. Having left Paris at the time of the September 1792 massacres, she
returned in the spring of 1795 accompanied by Benjamin Constant, in circumstances more favorable to the political role it was her ambition to play.
She then wrote two topical works that would remain out of the public eye:
Réflexions sur la paix intérieure, printed but not published in 1795 (though included in the *Oeuvres complètes* published in 1820), and the more significant
*Des circonstances actuelles qui peuvent terminer la Révolution et les principes qui
doivent fonder la république en France* (On the current circumstances that may
end the Revolution and the principles that ought to found the republic in
France), which was written in 1798 and destined to remain unpublished until
1906. She returned to the subject in the final years of her life, following the
demise of the Empire, but not enough time was left to her to finish the book.
She died in 1817 at the age of fifty-one. The following year, her heirs brought
out the unfinished *Considérations sur les principaux événements de la Révolution
française.* The work caused a tremendous stir. It unleashed a polemic, of
which the critique by the former Conventionnel Bailleul was typical. This
controversy may be regarded as the first skirmish and intellectual forerunner
of the debate out of which emerged the revolutionary historiography of the
Restoration. The work of the "fatalists" Thiers and Mignet after 1823–1824
can be traced directly to this source.

It may be useful to distinguish the inspiration of the two periods in
terms of Mme. de Staël's relation to her father. Under the Directory, at the
height of her affair with Constant, she was a republican, in opposition to her
father. A letter from Necker written early in 1796 offers a glimpse of the
relations between father and daughter: "Both of them [that is, Staël and Con-
stant] are wonderfully laden with republican ideas and hopes, and they are a
little too willing to forgive the means of governments in favor of the ends. I
am a long way from sharing this view" (Grange, *Les idées de Necker,* p. 462).
Written with the shock of 18 Fructidor still fresh in mind, the *Circonstances
actuelles* states the problem of the republican constitution in terms that anticipate Constant's more systematic treatment in a book written sometime
around 1802, a work that he too would be obliged to refrain from publishing
and that benefited from the additional perspective provided by yet another—
and this time irreversible—coup d'état. By the end of Staël's life, filial sentiment had fully regained the upper hand. The *Considérations,* combining first-
hand testimony with interpretation, is a monument to the glory of Necker.

Without the slightest reservation or doubt the book justifies the actions of Louis XVI's minister and praises with almost equal fervor the perspicacious analyst of the revolutionary government. The moment was right for a work of this kind. The monarchy and representative government for which absolutism's would-be reformer had yearned in vain had become, after 1814, the rallying point of all "friends of liberty," including Constant. The hour of the republic was no more; that of the English Constitution had struck, it being "the only port in which the nation can find calm" (*Considérations*, p. 138).

That said, it remains true that the basic understanding of the event did not change from one period to the other and can be summed up as follows: the Revolution equals the Enlightenment. The 1798 text reads: "The principle of the Revolution of France is the progress of philosophy" (*Des circonstances actuelles*, p. 95). The 1818 text goes into greater detail for the benefit of those who stubbornly persist in holding that the Revolution was an accident: "The principal crises of history have all been inevitable when they were associated with the development of ideas." Once again it was the "triumph of the Enlightenment" that was involved in the Revolution of France and that made it one of the "great epochs of the social order" (*Considérations*, p. 63). The history of the great modern states can be divided into three eras: "feudalism, despotism, and representative government." "The same movement of minds produced the revolution of England and that of France in 1789. Both belong to the third era in the progress of the social order, to the establishment of the representative government toward which the human spirit is advancing everywhere" (*Considérations*, p. 69). Despite the distance in time, any of these statements might have been written by Constant around 1796 in *De la force du gouvernement actuel*. The political options had changed, but the intellectual framework remained largely the same. The signs of continuity are quite striking. The events of 18 Fructidor, for example, remained a turning point for Staël. She saw that date as marking "the introduction of military government in France." Similarly, in this final work she used one of the same arguments she had proposed under the Directory as an explanation of the Terror, and one of her sharpest polemics against those who favored reaction and a return to monarchy, namely, the corruption of the nation's moral state by the "abuses of the Ancien Régime." At the height of the Restoration she asked: "Where did the penchant for disorder that developed with such violence in the first years of the Revolution come from if not from a hundred years of superstition and arbitrary rule?" (*Considérations*, p. 304). She spoke in 1798 of the "absolute want of public morality, reduced almost to maxims," and of the depravity that was produced "in an absolute government by the inequality of ranks themselves" (*Des circonstances actuelles*, pp. 33–37).

In any case, there is ample reason to think that the mature work with all the advantages of hindsight actually falls short of the analytical acuity that might have been achieved in a topical pamphlet. The Terror offers a good example of this gap. For the Thermidorians, of course, the context lent particular urgency to this problem. To justify the Republic one had to prove that "the crimes of the Revolution are not a consequence of the republican system" (*Des circonstances actuelles*, p. 5). Staël went further. She did not stop with exoneration but turned the accusation on its head: "On the contrary, it is in this system that one finds the best and only remedy." She was thus led to develop a more substantial analysis than the one enshrined in her final work. Even the examination of the corrupting effects of inequality was more subtle in 1793 than later on. One finds, for example, this shrewd observation on the "spirit of rebellious subordination" and its difference from "true love of equality": "A man who has thought of himself as a subaltern in any kind of situation can never arrive at equality; he is the tyrant, the despot, the persecutor, but never the equal of the man who in the depths of his soul he once believed to be his master." Whence a shift in the grounds of the argument: the blame no longer lay with the principle of equality but with the legacy of inequality, which would have to be overturned once and for all in order to root out the hatred it fostered. But Staël also mentioned two other factors in the earlier work that would not appear in the 1818 text: precocity ("the Republic arrived in France before the Enlightenment that was to lay the groundwork for it") and the "false application of the principle of popular sovereignty in representative government" (*Des circonstances actuelles*, p. 33). Both themes were typical of the Constantian world view, and who can say whether he taught her or she taught him. Yet the first is so intrinsic and permanent a part of Constant's approach that one is tempted to attribute it to him. Anachronism, the disparity of time that prevents actors from being intellectual contemporaries of their times, is Constant's leitmotif. To a large extent it was the guiding principle of his work: "If institutions preceded Enlightenment, it falls to writers to bring Enlightenment up to the level of institutions." Staël remarks: "Everything that is done in accord with opinion is protected by it, but the moment one precedes or combats opinion it becomes necessary to resort to despotism. France in 1789 wanted a temperate monarchy. No terror was needed to establish one. The Republic was established fifty years before minds were ready for it. Recourse to Terror was the way it was done" (*Des circonstances actuelles*, p. 160). In passing, moreover, she makes a very acute observation on the terrorist potential in a situation that combined voluntarism in advance of its time, a common enough thing in itself, with the new necessity of democratic consent. "There was no situation more violent than a government that could not content itself with being tyrannical but also needed to compel general approval of its tyranny, to sanction despotism by popular forms" (*Des circonstances actuelles*, pp. 35–36). This perception accounts for the political and intellectual strategy of the work, as well as for its lyrical illusion: "The philosophes made the Revolution, and they will end it. The generals, considered solely in their military roles, will have much less influence on the interior of France than thinkers writing in books or speaking at the rostrum" (*Des circonstances actuelles*, pp. 273–274). To that end they must "throw floods of light" on principles and axioms, such as equality, representation, and liberty, whose nature was poorly understood. Was not political science, "whose reputation grew with each passing year," close to the age of certainty with men like Condorcet, Sieyès, Roederer, Godwin, and of course Constant? Thanks to the "philosophy of analysis" and the calculus of passions, was not the "organization of a free constitution" on the verge of achieving the rational assurance of the geometric method? By completing political science, philosophical writers would end the Revolution. "Calculus will cause weapons to fall" (*Des circonstances actuelles,* p. 281). This enthusiasm, which one might almost call prepositivist, and the proposal for detailed investigation to which it gave rise were the source of what was most original in the book, including several powerful themes that would be developed later on in Constant's private as well as published works, robustly anticipated here.

Mme. de Staël began, then, with a critique of the confusions engendered by the principle of popular sovereignty, a critique that eventually became the central element in Constant's politics. The idea was not new in 1798, far from it. It had been raised by the monarchiens early in the Revolution. It was touched on by Clermont-Tonnerre and Mounier in connection with the Constitution of 1791. Sieyès used it in his discussion of the Constitution of Year III, in which he contrasted the authentic notion of "re-public" with what he called "re-total," based on the assumption of limitless popular sovereignty. Necker echoed the same idea in his "Réflexions sur l'égalité." "The absolute principle of popular sovereignty," he argued, "may be placed among those speculative ideas that have worked against the establishment of a salutary balance among the different political powers in the organization of the French government" (*De la Révolution française*). Thus there was every reason for Staël to follow this course. In fact, she does not analyze the mechanism by which the power phantasmagorically transferred to the people was very effectively turned against it, as Constant would do in 1806. She contents herself with mere mention of the fact. Her chief concern, by contrast, is to clarify the true nature of the representative system, and her reflections on this question may well constitute the most remarkable part of her book. The central problem was how to eliminate the shorthand identification through which it became possible to declare that 750 men *were* the people assembled, as the omnipresent ideal of the ancient cities encouraged people to dream. "There is no democracy in a country where 750 deputies govern thirty million men. Pure democracy, for all its drawbacks, has great pleasures, but democracy exists only on the agora of Athens" (*Des circonstances actuelles,* pp. 158–159). The switch from a large number to a small was not just a technical expedient for overcoming the physical obstacles to a vast meeting. It completely altered the essence of the phenomenon. "Representation," Staël writes, "is not, if I may put it this way, a reductive calculus that yields a shrunken image of the people. Representation is the political combination that causes the nation to be governed by men selected and combined in such a way that they possess the will and the interest of all" (*Des circonstances actuelles,* p. 19). In no sense was there equivalence between representatives and represented. The "will and interest of all" constituted a special, abstract domain, which required a collective logic distinct from simple projection of particular interests and wishes. "It is the interests of the nation, not of the individuals who make it up, that are represented" (*Des circonstances actuelles,* p. 17). In many ways this reformulation only deepened the problem, but at least it was more clearly stated. Accepting these premises left two related questions unanswered: what impelled the action of the representatives, and what impelled the consent of the represented? The deputies' courage and virtue should not have to be relied upon to ensure fidelity to the country's wishes. The calculus of the passions provided the remedy: it was a matter of combining "the powers, number, and separation" of the proxies who governed on behalf of the nation "in such a way that their personal interest is the general interest" (*Des circonstances actuelles*, p. 23). As for the mass of citizens, clearly they did not seek the political participation for which vain efforts had been made to mobilize them. "The nation only wants results and does not care about the means." This is where the difference between the liberty of the ancients and the liberty of the moderns comes into the picture. Once again, this theme had antecedents and precursors in the eighteenth century, for example in Rousseau. Saint-Just had some astonishing things to say on the subject in *Esprit de la Révolution* (1791). But the idea did not take on its full force until it reemerged in a situation complicated by revolutionary voluntarism. Staël's formulation is quite precise though not fully developed. What was radically new about the modern era was the value assumed by the "possibility of existing in isolation from public affairs" (*Des circonstances actuelles*, p. 109). "Rome's interest encompassed the interests of all Roman citizens. Enthusiasm could always be aroused by proposing the sacrifice of personal interest. . . . But in France, where the contrary is true, it is only respect for individual existence, for private fortune, that can make the Republic beloved. *"The liberty of the present time is everything that guarantees the independence of citizens against the independence of the government. The liberty of ancient times was everything that assured citizens of playing the greatest role in the exercise of power"* (*Des circonstances actuelles*, pp. 111–112, emphasis added). Therefore, if one truly wished to give the Republic deep roots, it was essential "not to require, not to coerce," or, in other words, to avoid "a system of devotion that becomes fierce when it is not voluntary" (ibid.).

As for constitutional reform, the political opportunity on which the book had been written to capitalize (and perhaps the reason why publication proved inopportune), we may omit topical matters and confine our attention to the major ideas that later became the common property of the Thermidorian liberals: the lessons drawn from the institutional experience of the Revolution. The equation to be solved was not a simple one in this period of political disintegration, during which, to begin with, "republicans knew full well that the results of the elections, if left to themselves, would be most unfavorable to preservation of the Republic" (*Des circonstances actuelles*, p. 161). One had to act in fear of a royalist reaction against the former Conventionnels still in office, a reaction that impelled the latter to stage a coup d'état and made it necessary to envision guaranteeing them public employment. The power of property owners had to be secured against the preoccupying threat of the popular movement. In addition there were powerful prejudices to contend with, in favor of a plural executive (owing to fears of a return to royal government) and division of powers, which led to conflict. Mme. de Staël, like her father, combatted division of powers: "There is constant confusion between the necessary separation of functions and a division of powers that inevitably turns them into enemies" (*Des circonstances actuelles*, p. 179). With the benefit of hindsight the proposed solutions appear hopelessly inadequate to cope with the mess that 18 Brumaire took it upon itself to resolve, and their inadequacy verifies the adage of a "wit" whom Staël quoted in the hope of refuting: "In France only events are allowed to vote." But the spirit of the measures proposed as early as 1798 helps to clarify the reasons that would later lead the moderate republicans of that time to throw their support to the principle of constitutional monarchy. That spirit can be summed up in a phrase: republicans ought "to adopt some of the ideas of aristocracy in order to establish popular institutions on a solid footing" (*Des circonstances actuelles,* p. 164). There was a social aspect to the question: representative government was to be understood as "government by the best," the abolition of hereditary rank leading to the substitution of a "natural aristocracy" for a "factitious" one. There was also a principled side: in any government both acquisition and conservation, both "movement and duration" as Constant would later put it, must be equally represented. And there was also a constitutional side, whose roots can be traced back to Sieyès' proposal for a constitutional jury in Year III. Staël proposed that the responsibilities of the Conseil des Anciens be assigned to this body, which would become an upper house for life peers. This proposal was the point of departure for Constant's reflections on the need for a neutral power, that is, for a supplementary and paradoxical dimension, independent of the representative body but without which the latter could not function. This need was the ultimate lesson to be drawn from the great difficulties encountered in the attempt to establish a Republic in France and from the impossibility of ending the Revolution.

What new was added by the book Staël published in 1818? In substance, very little. The wide response it elicited was due mainly (at least as far as the part of the book dealing with the Revolution was concerned) to its factual density, to the writer's ability to throw a bright light on personalities and actions, and to what the author herself called "private anecdotes." The book arrived at a moment when mouths and ears were beginning to open, when surviving participants were beginning to tell their stories, and when a new public, made up largely of a new generation of readers, became avid for memoirs and documents of the sort that Berville and Barrière in 1820 began systematically to gather for their great anthology. But the Revolution occupies only a third of Staël's book. Its success was due in at least equal measure to its two other aspects: the merciless examination of Bonaparte's rise and fall and above all the plea on behalf of English-style liberty that made the book topical. It was from this angle, moreover, that Staël viewed the Revolution. Comparison of the two founding events was obligatory: "The principal analogies between the revolution of England and that of France are: a king led to the scaffold by the democratic spirit, a military leader seizing power, and restoration of the former dynasty" (*Considérations,* p. 516). There was nothing very original about this example, whose virtue was to illustrate the necessity of representative government by showing that any attempt to turn back the clock was futile. As for the revolutionary process itself, the most notable thing about the book was its unconditional acceptance of Necker's views. Apart from a few striking and frequently cited observations, the analysis often seems less acute than that of 1798. Then, all of a sudden, the reader will come upon a profound passage, such as the one concerning the "mutual antipathy" between the classes of the Ancien Régime owing to lack of contact between them. "Pride erected barriers everywhere and limits nowhere. In no other country were gentlemen so alien to the rest of the nation; they never touched the second class except to give offense. . . . The same scene was repeated from rank to rank. The irritability of a very spirited nation caused each man to be jealous of his neighbor, his superior, and his master; and individuals, not content to dominate, humiliated one another" (*Considérations,* p. 303). Concerning the Terror, however, Staël succumbs to the "eloquence of indignation" and dispatches the subject as though it were without mystery and scarcely worthy of analysis. Fortunately, however, a brilliant intelligence finds it hard to forget itself entirely, so there are occasional flashes of penetrating insight in the midst of trivial lamentation: "Political dogmas—if the name can be applied to such aberrations—reigned at that time and not men. People wanted something abstract in authority, so that everybody might be supposed to have a part in it" (*Considérations,* p. 314). Seldom has the ideocratic impersonality inherent in Jacobinism been so subtly characterized.

The *Considérations* is fundamentally a composite. It was the summation of the Thermidorian case, hence in part a survival, a work seemingly still caught up in the orbit of the Revolution. But in another respect it anticipated a new way of recounting, from a distance, the revolutionary events and their relation to one another, a method that would soon be put to use by Thiers, Mignet, and others. The *Considérations* does not belong to the richest lode of Thermidorian writing, for it fell short of the requirements of historical narrative as contemporaries understood them. The book would also fall victim, ultimately, to the discredit that later befell the liberals, who believed that they too had terminated the Revolution once and for all with their "glorious revolution" of 1830, in every way comparable to its English namesake. Taken together, these remarks show what forces of oblivion must be overcome in order to resurrect the meaning of these original attempts to imagine the ways of liberty and the chance of its invention.

Marcel Gauchet

Further reading

WORKS BY STAËL

Des circonstances actuelles qui peuvent terminer la Révolution et des principes qui doivent fonder la république en France. Published in an incomplete edition in 1906 and now available in Lucia Omacini's critical edition, Geneva, 1979.

Considérations sur la Révolution française, recently published with an introduction and notes by Jacques Godechot, Paris, 1983.

Both works contain bibliographies of Staëlian studies.

RELATED WORKS

Grange, Henri. *Les idées de Necker.* Paris, 1974.

Necker, Jacques. *De la Révolution française,* in *Oeuvres complètes,* vols. 9 and 10. Paris, 1820–1821.

Related topics

Condorcet	Enlightenment	Republic	Terror
Constant	Monarchiens	Rousseau	Thermidorians
Constitution	Napoleon Bonaparte	Sieyès	
Liberty	Necker	Sovereignty	

TAINE

"My book," Taine wrote Ernest Havet in 1878, "if I have enough strength and health to complete it, will be a medical consultation." Dr. Taine in effect sat himself down at the bedside of a country exhausted by the war and the Commune to write *Les origines,* the record of his examination of contemporary France. He never tired of comparing historical research to medical research, of demonstrating his scientific credentials, or of inventing metaphors for his profession: in his 1884 preface, introducing his study of the revolutionary government, he claims to have tracked the animal "when it lay in its lair, when it chewed, when it snatched, when it digested." He said he cared less about writing the history of the Revolution than about its "pathology." Contemporaries like Amiel thought they detected in the book the "odor of the laboratory." He insisted, moreover, that the purpose of the enterprise was therapeutic: to make a diagnosis, write a prescription, find a "social form" that the French people might take on. Like Jaurès' history, which though quite different in its choices was also immense, purposeful, and militant, Taine's *Origines* was shaped by a representation of the future. The word "militant" might seem surprising: yet Taine wrote Albert Sorel in 1870 that free minds would henceforth be obliged to mobilize for "instructive and disagreeable" lecture tours, so that by engaging in a vast, public self-critique the nation might avoid repeating its errors.

Because of its heavily didactic quality, Taine's uncompleted work, though spectacularly successful at first, fell into discredit soon after. It was easy to argue that it had been conceived and written out of a combination of political passion, fear, and resentment. For while Taine prided himself on approaching the history of the French Revolution in exactly the same spirit in which he would have treated the revolutions of Florence or Athens, his book was nevertheless intimately linked to two discoveries he had made a short while before: Germany, the fatherland of his intellect, now struck him (and also Renan and Fustel de Coulanges) as a brutal, despotic, and barbaric country; and France, the fatherland of his heart, had just witnessed the reawakening of its old revolutionary malady. Taine's prognosis, shaped by these twin traumas, was one of disaster: the "gray" idea he had always had of France now turned decidedly blacker. This pessimism was precisely what made his book unacceptable; he wrote it in the years when the history of France was converging on a republican form, when Ferry gambled and won on rebuilding national unity around the principles of 1789. Squarely aimed at those principles, Taine's history thus went against the grain. Nor was it fully assimilable by the Catholic and monarchist opposition. His portrayal of the

Ancien Régime as responsible for the revolution, his arraignment of royalty on the charge of absolutism, and his anticlericalism (never far below the surface in this fervent Stendhalian) limited the extent to which his work could be taken up by the reactionaries.

Hard to classify politically (the image of Taine as an opponent of the Empire was still fresh in the minds of contemporaries), Taine's abundant output was also hard to classify philosophically—another reason for the public's incomprehension. It was apparently empiricist, because Taine revered facts and collected them with the zeal of the genre painter who fills his canvas with details. Yet he also insisted, and it was no small claim, that history obeyed fixed laws. His work was apparently idealist as well, since the causal principle of history was for him the spirit of peoples and, for France, the classical spirit, but with the proviso that "this spirit is not distinct from the facts through which it expresses its character." And it was apparently positivist, because he believed that facts were related to one another; but positivists "relegated causes outside science," whereas Taine wanted science absolute and unbounded. His work was further influenced by materialism, which earned him the occasional sympathy of Mathiez; the materialist aspect became increasingly pronounced as the years went by and Taine's pessimism increased, to the point where he asserted that "man's masters are physical temperament, bodily needs, animal instinct, [and] hereditary prejudice." It is not hard to see why contemporaries hardly knew what to make of the massive meteorite that had somehow fallen among the flowerbeds of a history just beginning to hedge itself about with documents and preach the religion of neutrality.

The embarrassment caused by Taine's history soon turned into an indictment by the professionals. Official history charged him with having anointed himself historian without any knowledge of the historian's methods or techniques. It deplored the accumulation of anecdotes (catalogued by Aulard in an incredibly uninspired book) with which Taine sought to "pressure the distracted and flighty reader, besiege him, overwhelm him with a surfeit of sensations and proofs." It rejected the tyranny of the race-milieu-time theory already widely celebrated in literary history and transported without change to history proper. Above all, it cast a critical eye on a historian who, though dependent on circumstances himself, set little store by them in the history he wrote. Taine neglected the resistance of the refractory clergy, the flight of the king, the court's entente with Austria, the Prussian invasion, and, more generally, the foreign peril. Hence it was hardly surprising, Aulard and Seignobos agreed, that he depicted the Jacobins as madmen; eliminating circumstances and doing away with partners and adversaries alike turned crucial actions into senseless gesticulations. At once prolix and superficial, anecdotal and didactic, vague and peremptory, Taine thus exhibited all the flaws of the bad historian: the great monument already lay half in ruins, to borrow Seignobos's lapidary description.

Was Taine's work really a product of circumstances? If, as Taine himself maintained, the history of the Revolution depended on the definition of the French spirit, he had defined that spirit much earlier through comparison with England. In his *Histoire de la littérature anglaise*, the monumental work that occupied him in the 1860s, by which time he was already obsessed with his discovery of a unique explanatory principle and anxious to characterize the English spirit, he believed that with the sense of liberty he had hit upon the way to do so. The great idea of the English "is the conviction that man, having conceived alone in his conscience and before God the rules of his conduct, is above all a free, moral person." Taine traced English liberty to two fundamental sources: Protestantism, a moral religion purged of all sensuality, and participation in public life. Civic activity was embodied first of all in a "democratic aristocracy" that had had the intelligence not to cut itself off from the life of the county or parish and had thus retained not only its rank but also its purpose (Taine was a careful reader of Guizot and Macaulay). But such activity also extended well beyond the circle of notables: newspapers and meetings gave "Parliament the nation for its audience," and public affairs were linked to the lives of individuals by a thousand local roots. From this web stemmed the "superabundance of political life" that Taine discovered in England.

From his knowledge of English writers Taine very early drew the conclusion that this precious political liberty was the fruit of acceptance of inequality and toleration of disorder. The English Constitution was a complex, ancient, organic accumulation of privileges and "consecrated injustices." In this confusing mass of contracts each person could identify his rights and carve out his own protected domain, certain that no one—neither king nor lord nor community—could interfere with it. The state refrained from intervening in this ancient and often-patched edifice, whose older parts were gradually reshaped and fitted to new uses. Government offered guarantees and protections but delegated to others functions that it was incapable of carrying out—commerce, agriculture, industry—and that could be filled more effectively by free individuals, notables, or associations.

For Taine, this conservative tradition, an amalgam of civic spirit, moral virtue, and practical sense, clearly explained why revolution was unthinkable for the English. Yet they had made two revolutions: the *Times*'s reviewer reminded him how much difficulty England had had in recovering from one of them, the "little Cromwellian revolution," and Taine himself criticized Guizot for failing to convey its ferocity and energy. For him, however, the point was that these revolutions had not destroyed the monarchy. They had only forced it to adapt, thus revealing the English genius for improvisation. The English had reformed everything: "Bakewell their livestock, A. Young their industry, Adam Smith their economy, Bentham their penal code, Hutcheson, Ferguson, Joseph Butler, Reid, Stewart, and Price their psychology and their ethics."

Can it be said that it was through this encounter with the English temperament, at once practical and moral, that Taine discovered—by contrast—the "French spirit" that would become his central explanation of the revolutionary phenomenon? Or did an implicit definition of the French spirit guide the selection he made among the facts of English history? The second hypothesis is more plausible, for it is striking to see how he attenuates or sharpens characteristic features of the two countries in order to heighten the desired antithesis. If he glosses over the discontinuities in English history, if he is silent about English Catholicism, if he overstates the uncouth and rustic character of the English, it is because he desires contrast and is quietly comparing two alternative courses for European history. In the 1860s, in other words, Taine was fascinated by the idea of two peoples hurtling without their knowledge toward an inevitable clash, each heightening its own characteristic features—the one feral, Christian, inegalitarian, and conservative, the other sociable, free-thinking, egalitarian, and revolutionary. The first had not destroyed its national community even with its "revolutions," while the second had demolished its national community well before the Revolution.

In other words, the war and the Commune may have been responsible for the bitterness of *Les origines de la France contemporaine* but not for its philosophy. And Taine, much less difficult to classify and much less isolated than has been said, made use, not always with explicit acknowledgment, of the work of earlier historians, especially Burke and Tocqueville, who like him had recognized the exemplary value of English history.

From Burke, to whom he had devoted a laudatory passage in the *Histoire de la littérature anglaise,* Taine borrowed a portrait, a sentiment, and an idea, which he left unchanged in substance but amplified by rhetorical skill. The portrait was of the French revolutionaries: insane with abstraction, persuaded that the bedrock of human life was the elementary (and not the complexity in which Burke saw men immersed from the beginning), obsessed with the geometric spirit (to the point of performing surgery, as Burke put it, on their own soil), cynically reductionist (reducing man to "naked nature" by stripping him, as the revolutionaries had done to the queen Marie Antoinette over whom Burke had wept, of the gracious or decent drapery of ornament), and stupid in their pretension to create a new constitution ("rushing in where angels fear to tread"). The sentiment was one of the extreme fragility of civilized society, the slow product of compromise and adjustment, which was viable only if built on custom, enveloped in the reverence due everything that has endured, supported by church and state, and shored up by a hereditary class of notables. It is noteworthy that Taine, who rarely quoted other writers, did make an exception for Burke's statement that if a reformer laid hands on the defects of the state, he must do so as if touching "the wounds of a father, with pious veneration and a trembling hand." And finally, the idea, which Taine the scientist long hesitated to accept but which he made his own in *Les origines,* was that reason had played a limited role in the evolution of humanity. Burke had written that it was far wiser to perpetuate prejudice, with the reason it contains, than to cast aside the shroud and retain only naked reason, because prejudice makes reason effective. Taine responded: "Reason is wrong to become indignant when prejudice guides human affairs, for in order to guide them it too must become a prejudice."

Taine's debt to Burke was therefore immense. But Burke also bequeathed to Taine his perplexity at the incongruous spectacle of the French: where they might have scoured the storehouse of their history for useful remnants of their constitution, instead they had inexplicably preferred the bewilderment of a new constitution. Taine was a born explainer, however, who could not leave such strangeness alone. For him, deformity had to have a form. So where an astonished Burke saw the French ignoring a rich tradition in favor of the nudity of a clean slate, Taine responded that it all made sense if in fact the clean slate was itself a French tradition.

Thus we come to the heart of Taine's history, the celebrated hypothesis of the classical spirit. In the beginning was a *racial* trait, a fixed form of intelligence given to rational and oratorical argument. This inclination found its ideal environment in the seventeenth-century salon, and its *milieu*, the literary circle, in which an art of conversation was perfected based on ease and a stylized diction that invariably favored the general over the particular. The literary critic, familiar with English works that always informed the reader about their hero's profession, marital status, physical peculiarities, and fortune, could no longer abide a French literature filled with Damises and Cléantes (signifying employments, not individuals) and, later, with Iroquois and Persians as flat as playing cards and talking like books. Already well established by the seventeenth century, this abstract and simplifying vision was wedded in the following century, Taine argued, to the scientific spirit. This marriage might, for a scientist, have been a happy one. But French rationalism, because it was the offspring of an already mature classical spirit, had shunned the beneficial fertilization of experiment. Hence out of this wedlock came a monster: the idea of man in himself, liberated from all determinations, always and everywhere the same (physically, morally, and intellectually)—the source of all revolutionary aberrations.

Once this creature of reason entered the realm of history, the way was clear for all the philosophical offensives of the eighteenth century: that of Voltaire, directed against religion; that of the Encyclopedists and materialists, against custom; and the final efflorescence, that of Rousseau, against society. Here the philosophical nihilism of the eighteenth century found its true doctrine, and the Revolution, its true master; from then on, Taine maintained, it would do no more than fulfill the requisites of the Rousseauist vision, whose two sides were anarchy (since the form of government is subject at all times to the general will) and despotism (since individual rights are alienated in the community). This theory is the capstone of Taine's conceptual edifice: a racial trait, the classical spirit, which had long since found its milieu, in 1789 encountered its *moment*. In other words—and Taine never shrank from a striking formulation—Saint-Just and Robespierre were the direct heirs of Boileau. And far from being a rent in the fabric of the nation, the Revolution was in fact the expression of the national genius. And thus Taine discovered Tocqueville.

That discovery seems to have come rather late for the needs of his enormous book. A letter to his wife shows how much Taine admired Tocqueville's predictive powers: "What a distressing thing, to see all our ills so thoroughly understood, and yet that understanding still so little disseminated!" He studied Tocqueville to the point where he hoped to treat the very subject that Tocqueville had singled out in a letter to Kergorlay—how the Empire was able to establish itself in the midst of the society created by the Revolution—and answer its central questions: "Where did this new race come from? What produced it?" He took from Tocqueville both his summary of the Revolution's effects and his arsenal of causes. Among the effects listed by Taine we find, as in Tocqueville, the establishment of equality (not simply abstract, theoretical equality but an equality almost achieved during the Empire, with all "great lives barred," a host of petty employments, and not a single position worthy of ambition except perhaps—a Stendhalian stroke—that of bishop) and the completion of state centralization, leaving a provincial wasteland eroded by ennui. Establishment, completion: the very terminology suggests a terminal process; it attests to the deep roots that link the Revolution to the Ancien Régime. In exposing those roots Taine showed little originality. He took from Tocqueville both the material causes ("abuses," seigneurial oppression without compensating services, a useless nobility, an infuriatingly wealthy clergy, centralization and destruction by absolutism of natural groups, local life, and intermediary bodies, and fiscal irresponsibility) and the intellectual causes (the royalty of the humanities and the political radicalism of the philosophes). In the dark years while he was writing *Les origines* he was even prepared to add to this portrait the substitution of philosophy for religion, a change that deprived the popular classes of the firm mooring of faith.

These unoriginal materials were treated in a very original way, however. While Tocqueville sketched a whole host of causes and was content to lay special stress only on the *tabula rasa* created by the monarchy, a void that was quickly filled by public opinion, the true queen of kings, Taine tended to rest his entire architecture on a single pedestal, the intellectual cause. He had a far greater taste than Tocqueville for what he called the "productive element." For him, the essence of intellectual activity was to subordinate the effects of all particular causes to "the effect of a unique cause capable of accounting for the infinite complications of individuality."

This conception of causality, which dominates Taine's history, is worth exploring further. For him, the ideal type of science was deductive science. He never forgave Stuart Mill for limiting himself to inductive science by viewing causality as simply constancy of succession. He was equally hostile to Maine de Biran's concept of causality as an intimate force, a mysterious bond between cause and effect, as well as to Kant's synthetic a priori. The only conceptual model of causality left was that of the relation between the whole and its parts. In this model, cause and effect are not only inseparable but homogeneous. The world is made of one fabric. What we call cause and effect are two aspects of a single reality. This explains Taine's fondness for a phrase he coined, "causal fact," which links the abstract and the concrete: the abstract is in fact an extract, taken out of the concrete. To find a causal relation is simply to bring to light a logical relation, to apply the principle of identity to history.

Whence the rigorous atmosphere, the invariable lighting, the emotional unity, and the monotonous tone of *Les origines,* despite the abundance of facts and the dynamic appearance due to the vigorous rhythms of Taine's prose. In this deterministic history of the Revolution it is absolutely impossible for a people to resist the inclination of its national character. At times Taine seems to regret the heavy shackles he himself has forged. Since his ideal is a country with local liberties (Holland or England) or a free Protestant country (Schleiermacher's Germany), he allows himself a moment's dream: France had simply taken a wrong turn, but what if it had taken another—would these destinies be "equally open" to it? But he quickly comes to his senses: "When I say 'equally open,' I am speaking *in abstracto*. Given the circumstances, the passions, and the ideas, scarcity, the peasant's misery, bourgeois and French envy, the laws of the Constituent Assembly and the final upheaval were inevitable."

In such a static history it obviously becomes difficult to single out "moments." Unlike Tocqueville, Taine saw no bright episodes in the Revolution—not the revolution of liberty that preceded the revolution of equality nor what Louis Blanc called the revolution of Voltaire that preceded the revolution of Rousseau. The Revolution was all Rousseau's from the beginning. It is scarcely possible even to say that the Revolution became more radical. Like Bonald, Taine believed that everything was decided the moment the Estates General became the National Assembly. The total destruction of the old order was already visible, as well as all the revolutionary *journées*, all of which were alike, moreover, in that they were emblematic events, mere developments of the insurgents' invariable principle: "I am the representative of right, of the general will." Thus the Revolution did not turn to the Terror. The Terror began on July 14, as Malouet, that "impartial man," had so keenly observed. October 5 and 6 were also days of Terror, as would have been evident to any reader of Burke. By the time the September massacres came, and later the governmental Terror, Taine had already exhausted his reserves of indignation. Nor does he discriminate between Assemblies: all were anarchic as well as despotic, and the worst of all, Taine confided to Francis Charmes in 1876, was the first, the Constituent Assembly. The others had done no more than apply the system they had taken from Rousseau: "To turn France into a dust of separate, equal individuals like so many grains of sand." Taine had no regard for the Constituents' attempts to compromise, for their desperate efforts after Varennes to exonerate the king and strengthen his authority. What ought to have appealed to the adversary of universal suffrage in him, the distinction between active and passive citizens that marked the Constituent Assembly's retreat from the legitimacy of numbers, found no grace in his eyes. Even their final decision on ineligibility seemed to him to hasten the disaster (though his reasoning on this point was not very consistent).

Thus no historian was more indifferent than Taine to the vagaries of politics or worked harder to ignore circumstances. Taine described July 14 without mentioning Necker's dismissal or the stationing of troops around Paris. He recounted the September massacres without breathing a word of the foreign menace. Was this silence because of political bias, as Aulard and Seignobos maintained? It was more a matter of philosophical consistency. Taine was indifferent to circumstantial causes. Only the efficient cause mattered. Hence there was nothing random in the history he wrote: "At the moment the Estates General began, the course of ideas and events was not only determined but visible."

As one might expect, this understanding also meant that it was illusory to distinguish between one set of rulers and another. The Girondins until August 10 indulged in all the practices that would be used against them after August 10. In reality they shared the same political ideal as the Montagnards, namely (it will come as no surprise), "a state in accordance with Jean-Jacques's formula." Jacobins and Montagnards were two names for the same thing, and for Taine the Montagnard dictatorship was subsumed in that of the societies. When he dealt with individuals, he again perceived differences, the "little true facts" that he had learned to appreciate in Stendhal and the "particularization" that he admired in Sainte-Beuve; Marat's monotonous febrility, Danton's jovial cynicism, and Robespierre's literary decorum furnished the material for portraits in which one recognizes the hand of the artist. Yet since each of his heroes also has to embody and epitomize the Revolution, Taine quickly squanders the benefits of his acute observation. Marat, though mad as a hatter, was nevertheless "clever enough to pick up the fashionable foolishness, the *Social Contract.*" Danton understood "the inherent characteristic and normal procedure of the Revolution, popular brutality." Robespierre is of course even easier to reduce to the spirit of the times. In short, since Taine portrays all the revolutionaries as interpreters of the one and only revolutionary principle, he can distinguish them only by degree or moment (after three years the proper Robespierre rejoined Marat and "adopted the policy, goals, means, and works of the madman"). The diagnosis being inevitable, the patients' diversity vanishes in the uniformity of the disease, and the physician inevitably repeats the same old story. Yet his motivation, to reiterate, was not political malevolence. That sentiment did exist in Taine, quite obviously, but language and intelligibility took precedence. Taine laid out the theory in his acceptance speech to the Académie Française: since society consists of groups of people who are similar in condition, needs, and interests, "if you see one, you see them all." Science studies "each class of objects on the basis of selected samples."

Taine's favorite sample, and his primary contribution to the history of the Revolution, was the quintessential Jacobin, for if the Jacobin was defined, according to Taine, by a fixed idea, Taine also had a fixed idea of the Jacobin. Cochin hailed Taine as a man who had spent twenty years circling round the mystery of Jacobinism, yet he also noted his indifference to Jacobin procedures in themselves. This assessment is not entirely accurate, however, for it is not difficult to find in the pages of *Les origines* the same mechanisms that Cochin himself inventoried: the manipulation of electoral assemblies by a militant, active, and enterprising minority, well versed in the formulation of motions, the drafting of minutes, and the fabrication of unanimity; the tyranny exerted over the Assembly by the Jacobins and over the club itself by the galleries; the series of purges; the importance of the correspondence committee; and the vigilant presence of manipulators among the manipulated, for Taine even deals with what Cochin called the "inner circle," which he baptized "the band in the midst of the mob." Taken together, these mechanisms constituted a "machine" whose purpose was to fabricate "an artificial, violent opinion that would have the appearance of a natural and spontaneous wish."

If Taine did not pull these scattered observations together, it was because he was again concerned not so much with describing the mechanisms of power as with reducing them to the "principle" of Jacobinism. For him, that principle was the suspension of reality, or voluntary blindness: the Jacobin did not want to see, and actually did not see, individual differences, personal qualities and talents unequally distributed by nature and history, or age-old bonds among men. If he did see them, he chose to renounce them for the sake of the community. As always in Taine, the diabolical pact, once made, determined everything. With the ground thus cleared and leveled, the state was free to exercise unlimited power over people and property. It imprisoned, confiscated, and punished, but above all it sought to educate, for Taine had understood that the teacher was the king of the Revolution, and the school the temple of the Jacobin people. In other words, Jacobinism revived a backward conception of the state, eighteen centuries old, according to which a despotic power might reign legitimately over all aspects of personal life if in return the individual was allowed to share in political power. Clearly Taine incorporated his reading of Constant, in a schematic and rigid form, into his description of Jacobinism. Constant had argued that modern society became less and less susceptible to despotism as private pleasures proliferated and developed, but Taine saw modern society in its Jacobin form marching straight toward despotism. For centuries public power had grown broader and more intrusive in France at the expense of private activities. "A nation changes little": Voltairian fixity remained Taine's credo.

Dr. Taine had promised remedies he could not deliver because his book remained unfinished. At a deeper level, however, one may ask whether his method would have allowed him to formulate any prescriptions. If history is truly logic in action, if it has the capacity only to realize and never to emancipate or innovate, then how can one avoid the conclusion that the future is already implicit in the present? Taine occasionally rejected this logic: he said that "reforms *might* have sufficed" in 1789, that the intendants *might* have provided the reform movement with leaders and organization, and that the Assembly *might* not have capitulated to riot. But a Hegelian sense of the ineluctable led him to correct himself at once. The means were simply inoperative: "Nature and history made the choice for us in advance." Hence there was no "English way" for the French spirit. Taine had created a gulf between the two histories that he never could bridge.

Taine had said of Marcus Aurelius that he was a "pilot without hope." The description fits himself as well. The pessimistic determinism that is the essence of his thought prevented him from believing in remedies. Contrary to what is often said, it also quelled his reactionary passion: Taine knew that a nation can never turn back. And it also destroyed his ability to make short-term predictions. At the very moment when the Revolution's fecundity was exhausted, he thought that France was about to be caught once again "in the fatal circle of revolutions and coups d'état."

Yet even if the immediate future proved him wrong, it did not discredit his insight. His stubborn intelligence uncovered two ideas that still have currency today. First, the democratic experiment is threatened by the isolation and anonymity that it imposes on individuals. The resulting feelings of uncertainty and insecurity give rise to a renewed need for the mystical unity of community, which gives despots their opening. Bonaparte fulfilled the promise of Louis XIV: "The only way out of anarchy is despotism, with the chance of encountering in one man first a savior, then a destroyer, and the certainty of being ruled thereafter by the unknown will that genius and common sense, or imagination and selfishness, will form in a soul inflamed and deranged by the temptations of absolute power." For Taine the "bitter fruits of social dissolution" were abstraction, once again, and the common credo and secret alliance of democracy and despotism.

Taine's second idea was that the fabric of culture is extremely tenuous. Not only do bestiality and madness pose a constant threat to mankind, but murderous folly lurks at civilization's gates. Though his prescience was dimmed for the 1880s, it has been astonishing for the twentieth century, in which he divined "the promise of massacre and bankruptcy," "the exacerbation of international rancor and distrust," "the perversion of productive discoveries, the perfection of destructive applications, the backward march toward the selfish and brutal instincts, the mores and morals of the ancient city and the barbarian tribe." His suspicion of progress, his anticipation of future disasters, his obsession with signs of the inhuman, all things that made him unreadable a century ago, are precisely the things that cause us to listen to him attentively once again. The "monument half in ruins" therefore remains in excellent shape.

Mona Ozouf

FURTHER READING

WORKS BY TAINE
Correspondance, 4 vols. Paris, 1902–1907.
Les origines de la France contemporaine, 6 vols. Paris, 1876–1894.

RELATED WORKS
Giraud, Victor. *Essai sur Taine, son oeuvre et son influence.* Freiburg, 1901.
Lacombe, Paul. *Taine, historien et sociologue.* Paris, 1909.
Leroy, Maxime. *Taine.* Paris, 1933.
Roe, Frederick Charles. *Taine et l'Angleterre.* Paris, 1923.
Schaepdryver, Karl de. *Hippolyte Taine: Essai sur l'unité de sa pensée.* Paris, 1938.

RELATED TOPICS

Burke	Danton	Hegel	Kant	Rousseau
Constant	Estates General	Jacobinism	Marat	Tocqueville
Constitution	Guizot	Jaurès	Robespierre	Voltaire

TOCQUEVILLE

W hen he began work on what would become *L'Ancien Régime et la Révolution* in 1852, Tocqueville had behind him a dual career as a political writer and public figure. He had enjoyed literary success while still quite young, the first volume of *Démocratie en Amérique*, published in 1835, having made him famous at the age of thirty. The second volume, which appeared five years later, was more abstract and general than the first and was less successful; nonetheless it consolidated Tocqueville's image as the Montesquieu of the nineteenth century, which soon gained him entrance to the Académie Française (1841).

But this much honored, much admired, much consulted author was also a solitary political figure, little inclined to make the simplifications required by public life, much less the compromises necessary to win power. Elected deputy for Valognes, the district in which his family's château was located, in 1839, he never found his place among the parties and coalitions of the July Regime. Perhaps this was because he disliked playing second fiddle yet lacked the temperament of a leader, or perhaps because his political philosophy was ill-suited to practical work: too aristocratic and too democratic to embrace the bourgeois oligarchy of July, he was not sufficiently enamored of the French Revolution to be comfortable in the republican opposition. February 1848 rid him of Guizot, whom he detested, but brought back the specter of revolution with its cortège of violence and illusions.

He was reelected hands down, this time by universal suffrage, to serve as a deputy in the Constituent Assembly that met in early May, and in the face of the June uprising in Paris he shared the general reaction of the party of order; his *Souvenirs* demonstrate that even great minds were not immune to the social fear characteristic of French politics in the nineteenth century. June inaugurated the period in which Tocqueville finally found a national role, first as a member of the Committee on the Constitution, which mapped out France's new institutions, and later, in the spring of 1849, after the election of Louis Napoleon Bonaparte as president of the Republic, as the prince-president's minister of foreign affairs in the cabinet of Odilon Barrot. This parliamentary republic of notables, its existence not yet threatened by Bonaparte's nephew—elected only to a four-year term—was ultimately the regime in which Tocqueville felt least uncomfortable. But it was a brief interlude, lasting only until he could sense the outcome of the inevitable conflict between the Assembly and the president that would pose yet another threat to liberty.

The coup d'état of December 2, 1851, sent him back to his studies. For the rest of his days (he died in 1859), Tocqueville lived in a kind of internal political exile. At least the unfortunate times allowed him once again to devote himself fully to intellectual work. They even provided him with a subject, since the advent of a second Bonapartism in the wake of a Second Republic offered a rerun of the French Revolution in the middle of the nineteenth century, more than fifty years after the inauguration of the model. The French had replayed, or reendured, the Gironde, the Mountain, the Jacobins, and Thermidor only to find a second Bonaparte waiting at the end of the tale. This time they could not blame circumstances, civil and foreign war. The Second Republic had not suffered the tortures of the First, yet it had ended in the same way, in despotism. The first despot had had the incomparable charm of genius. The very mediocrity of the second revealed the workings of a mechanism independent of men and exposed the secret link between the revolutionary phenomenon and the centralized administrative state in the history of modern France. When he began work on the problem, Tocqueville was considering writing a history of the First Empire: this would have been a way of focusing his curiosity on the aftermath of the Revolution, the moment when the astonishingly paradoxical nature of its outcome became apparent in the form of a tentacular state built on the equality of its citizens.

In the end, however, he wrote a book about what preceded the Revolution. He was in part impelled by the logic of all historical work, which is to proceed backward in time in search of origins. But he was also brought back to the problem of his youth, which was also the question of his life, by the failure of the Second Republic; if the failure had revealed the permanence and prevalence of a despotic tradition in French public life, then the Revolution itself was only an episode, whose sources had to be sought in the distant past.

The first development of this idea can in fact be found in the second volume of *Democracy in America*, in the last chapter of which Tocqueville contrasts the absolutist legacy of French history with the spirit of liberty that was a fundamental element in American history because it was also the spirit of English history (*L'Ancien Régime*, book 2, part 4, chap. 4). In France, the Revolution represented the explosion of the egalitarian idea in a country that had never known or had long since forgotten political liberty, with the result that its effects were superimposed on those of the preceding era, reinforcing the state's despotic propensities.

At that time, however, the idea of continuity from the Ancien Régime to the Revolution went no further than the chronological relation between the absolutist tradition and the Napoleonic state: the French in the nineteenth century were all the less inclined toward liberty because, having been made equals by the Revolution, they had lost the habit and even the memory of liberty under the Ancien Régime. What was different in *L'Ancien Régime*, written fifteen years later, was that the relation between the two eras had ceased to be one of mere chronological succession and had become a causal link: the Ancien Régime became the *sine qua non* of the Revolution. Far from being a break with the previous era, much less an absolute break, the Revolution found its causes and the explanation of its character in the Ancien Régime and bore the stamp of its forebear. The democratic radicalism that marked its actors and its course had originated in the Ancien Régime, just as the Napoleonic regime that signaled its end had borrowed its principle from absolute monarchy.

At bottom, Tocqueville asked himself the same questions throughout his life, and the ones he treated in *L'Ancien Régime* were the same ones for which he had sought the answers in the United States, although perhaps from a different angle. What interested him was not the direction of the French Revolution, since that was implicit in a law more general than the event itself: the progress of the modern world toward equality of conditions. This "obvious fact," as such exempt from demonstration, was only a starting point of his thinking, which aimed to pinpoint the specific character of French democracy as crystallized in the Revolution. From this aim came the systematically comparative perspective, which was the reason for the American journey: Tocqueville wanted to compare a democracy such as the republic in the United States, which had not encountered any adversaries, with a democracy like the French Revolution, which had had to overturn a world. By doing so he hoped to understand what each nation owed to its particular history, and already he sought to isolate what the French democratic tradition owed to its revolutionary origins.

In the context of the 1856 book the American reference no longer made sense, for now the problem was to analyze the origins of those origins, an era that by definition did not exist in the history of the New World. But Tocqueville's ambition remained the same: to explain not so much the basis as the character of the French Revolution. He was more interested in the how than in the why; history for him was knowledge of the modalities of an event, the reconstitution of the various paths by which it came into being. What the Revolution wrought was not simply the destruction of the Ancien Régime, since that would have happened anyway. It had wrought destruction with a brutal, radical character, destruction carried out by people outside the law in the name of the interests of humanity. No such destruction had taken place in any other country in Europe, even though in most of them, Germany for example, the characteristic institutions of the Ancien Régime had remained more vigorous than in France. Tocqueville returned to the comparative method to develop his original paradox: that it was in the country where the "Ancien Régime" had disintegrated most that it was most unpopular and that it was overthrown by a radical democratic revolution. He suggested that, prior to this revolution, a different force but one comparable in its effects had worked toward the same end and laid the groundwork both in reality and in people's minds; and that there had occurred in France a prior subversion of the Ancien Régime, more fundamental than the Revolution and of which the Revolution was only its ultimate convulsion.

The idea was at once so essential and so contrary to the generally accepted wisdom about 1789, that Tocqueville chose to illustrate it once more in the final lines of Book One by examining the misinterpretation of one of his greatest predecessors, Burke. In speaking of the Ancien Régime, the Whig M.P. had lectured the French that they could have avoided the illusion of the democratic *tabula rasa* by improving the constitution of their own monarchy or even by borrowing from English common law. Tocqueville replied: "Burke did not realize that what he was looking at was the revolution, whose purpose was precisely to abolish Europe's ancient common law. He did not realize that this was precisely the issue, and nothing else." This statement was yet another way of saying that the revolution took place before the Revolution, and that what it called the Ancien Régime hid the work of subversion behind a facade of tradition.

*
**

What subversion? The subversion of the old society by the monarchical state. What was "*ancien*" about the Ancien Régime, in Tocqueville's eyes, was precisely the society that existed prior to the growth of the centralized state, a society that he called indiscriminately "feudal" or "aristocratic" to indicate that the individuals and groups of which it was composed were held together by bonds of hierarchical dependency. Political power was not distinct from social superiority and was distributed throughout the pyramid of ranks. The development of the absolutist state, on the other hand, required concentration of political power in one place, in the hands of the king, a concentration that meant that private individuals were dispossessed: the aristocracy was the first but not the only victim, since it was the entire configuration of society that was overturned.

The keystone of Tocqueville's analysis, the idea that the state had stripped society of its political power, is introduced at the beginning of Book Two, where he touches on the root of the question in discussing relations between peasants and nobles. Those relations ceased to be political, since the peasant, long since emancipated from servitude and increasingly a proprietor of his land, no longer depended on the government of his lord; yet they remained socially oppressive, in the form of seigneurial dues without any reciprocal obligations. These "feudal rights" were particularly unpopular in France, not because they were particularly oppressive but on the contrary because they had partly disappeared and those that remained had a residual character: "Feudalism remained the greatest of our civil institutions by ceasing to be a political institution. Thus diminished, it aroused more hatred than ever, and it can truly be said that the destruction of some of the institutions of the Middle Ages made those that remained a hundred times more odious."

The "Ancien Régime" is thus characterized from the first as a bastard social state, no longer truly aristocratic nor yet truly democratic. What Tocqueville knew about the period he had learned from Guizot and the historians of the Restoration. He used this knowledge to draw a contrast between the age of absolutism and the age of medieval institutions that had established a vertical chain of dependency in order to ensure solidarity in the absence of a central authority while leaving "aristocratic" liberty unfettered. Neither Guizot nor Thierry cared for the Middle Ages, during which the hard-pressed peasant was left wholly subject to the private whim of the seigneur and ignorant of the principle of public authority. Tocqueville imagined the age in a somewhat idyllic light, as a mutually beneficial exchange between the man of the soil and the man of the château. Aristocratic society was the embodiment of this age-old relation of dependency, reciprocal but unequal, which at least left the masters sovereign unto themselves. This aristocratic liberty was different from the liberty of the ancients, since the polis no longer existed, but it was a true liberty nonetheless. Yet it gradually disappeared along with the institutions of the Middle Ages, as all political and administrative functions were usurped by the state—a mechanism at work throughout society that ultimately transformed its very nature.

All the great historians of the nineteenth century were aware of the absolutist revolution. Mme. de Staël, and Guizot after her, saw it as an era in European history between feudalism and representative government. Michelet explored the idea of the nation's incarnation in the person of the king of France, a mysterious usurpation that the Revolution dispelled by restoring the people to the place previously occupied by the king. But Tocqueville was the only author to treat absolutism as a sociological phenomenon and, like the Revolution but prior to it, an instrument for subverting the network of social relations. He concentrated not so much on the divine right of kings or on the national unity constructed under their authority as on the state's methodical encroachments on society.

He was not interested in the origins of the phenomenon, however. Chapters two through seven of Book Two, which are devoted to the development of administrative centralization, say nothing about possible reasons for it: not a word about the continual wars between Bourbons and Hapsburgs over dominance in Europe, nothing about the equilibrium of classes as a factor in the absolute power of kings—a standard topic since Guizot—and nearly nothing about the seventeenth century, Richelieu, or the reign of Louis XIV, about the causes or even the crucial phases of this evolution. Once again Tocqueville gave in to an inclination of his genius that led him to explore the consequences rather than the origins of great historical facts. That was what he had done with the democratic idea in *Democratie en Amérique*. Similarly, in *L'Ancien Régime et la Révolution* he treated administrative centralization as a fundamental given in French history, the only question being the measure of its impact on society. To that end, moreover, he refused to make use of second-hand research and instead worked directly in eighteenth-century intendants' archives, exploring systematically, for example, those of the *généralité* of Tours.

Accordingly, the two central chapters of *L'Ancien Régime* are probably chapters eight and nine of Book Two, in which he analyzes the nature of the new social state born with, or rather of, the administrative monarchy. Chapter eight is entitled "How France Had Become the Country in Which Men Were Most Like Each Other." And chapter nine: "How, Though in Many Respects So Similar, the French Were Split up More Than Ever into Small, Isolated, Self-Regarding Groups." What does he mean? For one thing, that the eighteenth-century French, or at any rate the upper classes, increasingly acted and thought in the same manner, a phenomenon concomitant with growth in wealth, progress in material equality, the decline of particularisms, and the homogenizing effects of legislation. For another, that state control over society had increasingly confined the French to rival and hostile groups, obsessed with their own particular interests and nothing else. In short, that Ancien Régime society was a society with democratic tendencies and aristocratic pathologies.

It is this second part of Tocqueville's analysis that is most admirably thorough, and it is all too often neglected by commentators. The Ancien Régime was a corruption of the aristocratic principle. By this claim Tocqueville means that the structure of French society in this period could be explained primarily in terms of the constant reshaping of the feudal past by the central state. From feudalism society had inherited a vertical structure of hierarchical corporations (*corps*), which continued to constitute the social framework. But the development of the centralized administrative state stripped those corporations of their political responsibilities and powers, which were appropriated by the state. Worse yet, the state did its best to point up their social uselessness by continually selling to the highest bidders membership in the most prestigious corporations, which therefore lost status even in the eyes of their own members. These members were henceforth nothing more than the purchasers of social status and privileges granted by the king. For it was the state, always short of cash, that profited from the price of admission and that fixed and otherwise modified to its own convenience the particular advantages of each corporation, beginning with the nobility. Thus growth of the administrative machinery came at the price of an increasingly caste-like society divided into isolated corps lacking any notion of the general interest. The psychological motor of the system was the selfish passion for rank and places. Mirabeau hit on a phrase that summed it all up: the old French society was a "cascade of contempt."

The quintessential symbol of this situation was the monarchy's treatment of the nobility, that *corps* among *corps* and the first "order" of the realm. The nobility lost both its principle—blood—and its function—public service. It ceased to be an aristocracy and became a caste: by this distinction Tocqueville means not that the nobility accepted no new members but rather that those who paid for their nobility with cash bought nothing more than a guarantee of privileges. This system led to an obsession with distinctions, a jealous passion for separation, which tended to "ghettoize" the order within the nation. The nobility was at once destroyed and idolized by the Ancien Régime, and Tocqueville contrasted its evolution with that of its English counterpart, which remained open to the bourgeoisie, independent of the state, and intimately involved in its social and political role. This discussion is a famous passage, the chief points of which can already be found in Mme. de Staël's *Considérations,* but to them Tocqueville lent the brilliance and melancholy of his perspective on the milieu into which he had been born, coupled with a reconsideration of some of the ideas of his youth. Whereas the author of *Démocratie en Amérique* had no faith in the future of English liberty, that survival of aristocracy, the author of *L'Ancien Régime* looked upon English history as a missed opportunity for the society of old France.

*
**

According to Tocqueville, then, the Ancien Régime was a system subject to a paradoxical dynamic. The centralized state was constantly destroying the reality while it continually reconstructed the illusion. It stripped the nobility of its political powers yet every day created new nobles. It asserted its supremacy over the municipal assemblies yet shamelessly sold the offices of magistrates and consuls. From the top to the bottom of the social ladder it drained the old aristocratic society of its content. That society ceased to be anything more than a meticulously maintained facade, continually patched up and decked out with new ornaments but whose only remaining purpose was to fill the royal coffers with cash.

The constant use and reworking of this ancient structure gave rise to permanent and uncontrollable tensions within the absolutist system. In order to fill the space of public authority, the absolute monarchy insisted on equal obedience from all its subjects; this insistence was the condition for the uniformity of its laws. Its actions therefore tended to level society, while for financial reasons it simultaneously strove to multiply the slightest differences in status. Since these distinctions had less and less real content in terms of power, they took on more and more symbolic value in terms of *amour propre*. In the context of general submission, the more illusory superiority they offered to their beneficiaries, the more they were prized, and hence the more they were despised by all the other subjects of the king.

Thus the monarchy constantly recreated equality and inequality and fortified each passion because of what it conceded to the other. Tocqueville's Ancien Régime was compounded of pathological inequality and abortive equality. It dishonored aristocracy without creating the slightest opening for democracy. This is what Burke failed to understand: that the old monarchy bequeathed nothing to the Revolution, except possibly the negation of what it had been. The *tabula rasa* of 1789 was itself a product of this sad history.

The purpose of Book Three is to start with these "old and general facts," which had laid the groundwork for the Revolution, and, using them, to describe the specific circumstances of the crisis. Tocqueville, never one for monocausal interpretation, arranges the explanatory factors in a hierarchy based on age and generality. The ones treated in Book Three derive their character and importance in part from the preceding ones. For example, the spectacular role of men of letters in the eighteenth century is intimately related to the literary or philosophical character of the Revolution. In this case Tocqueville is adopting a standard theme of earlier historians, widely used in the late eighteenth and very early nineteenth century by Mallet du Pan, Mounier, Rivarol, Portalis, and others. What is novel is the way he links this theme to the overall structure of his analysis. If intellectuals had played such an inordinate role in eighteenth-century France, it was because the absolute monarchy had created a *tabula rasa* in two senses. By flaunting so many abusive and ridiculous privileges, it had destroyed respect for the social hierarchy and inspired the miraculous notion of natural equality. And by arrogating all administrative functions to itself, the monarchy had deprived the French, and especially the upper classes, of all practical experience and thus created a kind of national propensity for abstract theories of government on the part of both authors and their readers. Since the monarchy would not permit the formation of a political class, men of letters seized this vacant space and established in it a substitute monarchy of pure ideas.

The divorce between public opinion and Catholicism came about in the same way. Like many nineteenth-century authors, Tocqueville saw this divorce as one of the Revolution's most profound features. But whereas Michelet had celebrated it as a necessary break with the past, Tocqueville saw it as a dangerous risk for the future. In his eyes, the democratic idea was the child of Christianity, and the American experience had shown that the relationship could be harmonious. By contrast, in France, political revolution had sought to eradicate not only aristocratic society but also basic religious beliefs, and that aim was the reason for its extraordinary character and frenetic escalation as well as for the violence and durability of the passions it had aroused.

Tocqueville did not hold the Catholic Church of the Ancien Régime responsible—or even partially responsible—for the antireligious character of the French democratic tradition. He did not mention the role it had played in the violent eradication of Protestantism in the seventeenth century or the close alliance it had forged with absolute monarchy under Louis XIV, an alliance that had left it vulnerable to the monarchy's misfortunes. Faithful to his system of analysis, he blamed the monarchical state, guilty in his eyes of having plunged the upper classes into intellectual and social irresponsibility and public opinion into the abstractions of philosophy. Not that philosophy in his view had no value—Tocqueville was not one of the many nineteenth-century thinkers who held the previous century in contempt. Indeed, it had formed a generation of men remarkable for patriotism and high-mindedness as well as for the "true grandeur" of 1789. But when it attempted to take the place of religion, philosophy had cut the intellect loose from its moorings and begun the drift toward revolution.

At this point (Book Three, chapter two), however, another idea comes into play: that the Revolution was not doomed to drift in this direction forever, and that in different circumstances it might have followed a different course. What Tocqueville loved in 1789—up to the October Days, which, like Burke, he detested—was that it made liberty a part of the national consensus. Things would not have gone wrong so quickly, however, had not the general attitude of the French caused them to do so. The ambiguity of the revolutionary events was already present, Tocqueville believed, in the French philosophy of the Enlightenment, in which the idea of sweeping reforms in the name of administrative rationality was often more visible than the idea of political liberty, and of which the physiocrats were perhaps more typical than Montesquieu. The idea of reform could be embodied just as well in the despotism of one man as in the sovereignty of the people, the latter being merely a matter of substituting the nation as a unitary body for the king without changing the citizen's administrative dependency in any way.

The Ancien Régime provided democratic radicalism with an instrument for subverting authority, through the centralized state, and with a way of teaching subversion, through alienation of the body social in ideas. Circumstances provided the spark that set this tinder aflame in the form of economic prosperity, which energized private interests, public expectations, and government intervention but which simultaneously accelerated the disintegration of a rigid and discredited system that came to be detested just enough to serve as a scapegoat. The blunders and mistakes of Louis XVI's ministers did the rest. The coup de grâce was administered in 1787 with the administrative reform that made the intendants subordinate to the elected provincial assemblies. The Ancien Régime was struck down by its own hand before the Revolution signed its death warrant.

Tocqueville died before beginning work on the text that was to have been the second volume, on the Revolution itself. He did, however, leave certain preliminary drafts of paragraphs and chapters, along with numerous notes on his reading and brief reflections intended for further elaboration. For the most part these concern the beginnings of the Revolution, from 1787 to the Constituent Assembly, so that it is easier to reconstruct Tocqueville's thinking about this period than about the Jacobin dictatorship or the Terror.

Given the analysis of the Ancien Régime, the first problem is to decide whether to interpret the Revolution as a rupture or as a form of continuity. Tocqueville did not see the Ancien Régime as a precursor of or preparation for the Revolution; rather, he saw the work of the Revolution already under way and indeed accomplished before 1789. This was the great difference between him and the liberal historians of the Restoration, whom he had read extensively. They, who believed far more than he in the inevitability of the event, set—and celebrated—its occurrence in 1789 with the revolt of the Third Estate: the transformation of the Estates General into the National Assembly and the decrees of August 4–11 revealed and crystallized the work of centuries, and above all of the eighteenth century. For Tocqueville, by contrast, that work was completed before 1789, and in other forms that bore other fruits; its hallmark was not the promotion of the Third Estate against the nobility under the protection of the monarchy but the effect of centralization coupled with new ideas.

The two phenomena were related, since the abstract character of those ideas was largely determined by the fact that the administrative monarchy kept the French people out of public affairs, while in return the new ideas' influence on the enlightened classes created a uniform public opinion—the condition for an increasingly centralized power. These things preceded the Revolution: the absolute monarchy was the instrument of the first, "philosophy" the instrument of the second. And the French people in the eighteenth century were already a democratic people, a society of individuals subject to egalitarian passion and dominated by a centralized administration. In speaking, for example, of the opposition of the parlements, which first mobilized a homogeneous nation, Tocqueville said: "This did not prove that a great revolution was near, but that a great revolution had already taken place." Or again: "One frequently finds in authors who wrote before the end of 1788 words to the effect that these things happened before the revolution. This astonishes us, who are not accustomed to hearing of revolution before 1789. . . . It was in fact a very great revolution, but one that would soon be lost in the immensity of the one that was to follow and thus would disappear from history's view."

How was this "first revolution," to use Tocqueville's phrase, related to the one that followed? The answer is that it gave the latter its unique character, which made it "an event different from all others of the same type that had previously occurred in the world." With these words Tocqueville returned to the central idea of Book One, namely, that the second revolution had been conditioned by the first, which had been brought about by absolutism. But since his judgment and analysis of this unique and unprecedented event were ambiguous, it is not easy to understand what he meant.

The reason for this ambiguity is that in Tocqueville's eyes the French Revolution as such, the one that began in 1789, comprised two parts of unequal duration and radically different nature. The first was limited to 1789, concluding at the latest before the October Days: this was the revolution of liberty, carried out by the nation against despotism. It culminated in the meeting of the Estates General, the birth of a national public spirit, and the Declaration of the Rights of Man. Tocqueville loved this revolution and described it as a spectacle of incomparable beauty. The second revolution was precisely the opposite of the first, for it was the revolution of class hatred and equality, which was carried out at the expense of liberty. It lasted much longer, from the autumn of 1789 (or perhaps the middle of the summer) to the autumn of 1799. The coup d'état of 18 Brumaire cast a pall over a period that also included the dictatorship of Year II.

Tocqueville thus revived a standard distinction in liberal historiography between the two parts of the Revolution, one of which established liberty while the other destroyed it. But in so doing he altered the chronology, compared with, say, the classic work of Mignet, who dated the beginning of the second revolution from August 10. In this respect Tocqueville was closer to Staël or, going back even further, to her father, Necker, and the monarchiens. What set him apart from all his predecessors (whom he never cited, in the manner of the nineteenth century) was the nature of his analysis. For the Restoration historians the Revolution was the theater of the class struggle—the triumph of the liberty-bearing bourgeoisie over the nobility, which was bound to absolutism. If dictatorship briefly gained the upper hand over representative government, moreover, it was because the bourgeoisie, pressed by circumstances, temporarily gave way to the lower classes, who were hungry for repression. Tocqueville's interpretation shared none of these points with Mignet and Guizot.

For him, democracy was irreversible because it represented the direction of modern history. But it might or might not be related to the division of society into classes and to the victory of the middle class over the aristocracy. The French case illustrated both possibilities. In 1789 democracy was the work of the entire nation, which rallied in opposition to despotism because the effects of aristocratic liberty reinforced those of democratic liberty to tame and unify the revolutionary explosion. What followed, however, marked the return of the class spirit, which spelled the end of liberty. And it was indeed a return, since the Revolution, in drawing its sustenance from equality rather than liberty, reverted to the traditions of the monarchy, which had divided in order to rule.

In his conception of the role of social classes in relation to the progress of ideas and passions, Tocqueville was always ambiguous, and it is difficult if not impossible to reconcile the different interpretations he offers. From his notes on the Revolution, however, one can at least gain some idea of the problems he set himself as he prepared to write his second volume. Chief among these was how to explain the twofold nature of the Revolution, or, rather, putting the question in terms closer to his own, how to understand why the tragic but natural progression from Ancien Régime equality to revolutionary equality was briefly interrupted by the appearance of liberty. In this sense Tocqueville's problem was the reverse of Guizot's. Guizot saw the monarchy as having diminished the aristocracy but for the benefit of national unity, equality, and ultimately liberty: 1789 was the culmination of this long effort. What is obscure in this view is therefore not 1789 but what followed: not only Robespierre and the Terror but also the failure of free government and the dictatorship of Bonaparte. If the middle class, victorious in 1789, carried liberty in its train, why was there a return to an even worse form of despotism than before? Marx would later ask the same question in a somewhat different form, and it was a central concern of all the Restoration historians, none of whom ever gave a satisfactory answer.

By contrast, Tocqueville believed that, of the three revolutions that took place in the eighteenth century, the first fit well with the third. Absolute monarchy drained the substance from aristocracy and centralized political and administrative domination. It relied on egalitarian passions to destroy aristocratic liberty and ultimately became the instrument of a democratic form of culture or public opinion with no taste for liberty. First the Jacobins, then Robespierre, and finally Bonaparte followed the same pattern. In this sense there was continuity between the Ancien Régime and the Revolution. But 1788 or 1789? Those few months, or those two years during which the realm erupted against administrative despotism? Guizot ran up against 1793; Tocqueville made a mystery of 1789.

In fact, the degeneration from liberty to equality in 1789 can be explained in Tocqueville's system of interpretation more easily than the divine surprise of 1789. The first phenomenon illustrates a general truth developed at length in the second part of *Démocratie en Amérique*, that the passion for equality is more accessible and in any case more universal than the passion for liberty. It also demonstrates the particular truth that equality, encouraged by centralization and the movement of ideas, was the dominant passion of the

French under the Ancien Régime, and that this same source, broadened and strengthened even further, fed the French Revolution and revealed in it the same indifference to liberty as under the Ancien Régime. To the extent that "the true mother passion of the Revolution, the passion of classes, gained the upper hand," the French returned as though it were natural to the path of political servitude.

Therefore it is the sharp break that occurred in 1789 that becomes difficult to understand. That liberty's roots were recent and tenuous while hatred of inequality was as old as the decline of the society of orders can explain the fragility of 1789 but not its advent. Just as there is in Tocqueville a philosophical mystery of liberty, there is also in his vision of French history an enigma surrounding liberty's brief appearance. This question is more easily asked than answered, because Tocqueville died before he had unraveled its many strands, and it is likely in any case that he would have left in the final version a certain number of the contradictions that were an integral part of his genius. In his final letters to friends we find him still confronting the revolutionary phenomenon with a half-admiring, half-horrified surprise, whose emotional force no amount of analysis had managed to diminish. Perhaps he never believed that history would one day allow him to dispel its mystery completely.

François Furet

FURTHER READING

WORKS BY TOCQUEVILLE

The Old Regime and the French Revolution, trans. Stuart Gilbert. New York, 1955.

RELATED WORKS

Aron, Raymond. *Les grandes étapes de la pensée sociologique.* Paris, 1967.
Drescher, Seymour. *Dilemmas of Democracy: Tocqueville and Modernization.* Pittsburgh, 1968.
Furet, François. *Penser la Révolution française.* Paris, 1978.
Manent, Pierre. *Tocqueville et la nature de la démocratie.* Paris, 1982.

RELATED TOPICS

Ancien Régime	Enlightenment	Michelet	Necker
Aristocracy	Equality	Mirabeau	Physiocrats
Burke	Feudal System	Monarchiens	Staël
Centralization	Guizot	Montesquieu	
Democracy	Liberty	Napoleon Bonaparte	

Contributors
Name index
Subject index
Alphabetical list of articles

CONTRIBUTORS

Bronislaw Baczko, University of Geneva
Enlightenment, Thermidorians, Vandalism

Keith M. Baker, University of Chicago
Condorcet, Constitution, Sieyès, Sovereignty

Louis Bergeron, Centre de Recherches Historiques, Ecole des Hautes
Etudes en Sciences Sociales, Paris
National Properties

David D. Bien, University of Michigan, Ann Arbor
Aristocracy

Massimo Boffa, Institut Raymond Aron, Paris
Counterrevolution, Emigrés, Maistre

Gail Bossenga, University of Kansas, Lawrence
Taxes

Michel Bruguière, Ecole Pratique des Hautes Etudes, IVe Section, Paris
Assignats

Yann Fauchois, Institut Raymond Aron, Paris
Centralization

Luc Ferry, University of Lyons II, Institut Raymond Aron, Paris
Fichte, Hegel, Kant

Alan Forrest, University of Manchester
Army, The Revolution and Europe

François Furet, Institut Raymond Aron, Foundation Saint-Simon, Ecoles des
Hautes Etudes en Sciences Sociales, Paris
*Academic History of the Revolution, Ancien Régime, Babeuf, Barnave, Blanc,
Buchez, Chouannerie, Civil Constitution of the Clergy, Feudal System, Jacobin-
ism, Louis XVI, Marx, Maximum, Michelet, Mirabeau, Napoleon Bonaparte,
Night of August 4, Quinet, Revolutionary Government, Terror, Tocqueville,
Vendée*

Marcel Gauchet, Institut Raymond Aron, Ecole des Hautes Etudes en
Sciences Sociales, Paris
Constant, Rights of Man, Necker, Staël

Gérard Gengembre, Ecole Normale Supérieure de Fontenay-Saint-Cloud
Burke

Joseph Goy, Centre de Recherches Historiques, Ecole des Hautes Etudes en
Sciences Sociales, Paris
Civil Code

Patrice Gueniffey, Institut Raymond Aron, Paris
Carnot, Clubs and Popular Societies (with Ran Halévi), *Elections, Lafayette,
Paris Commune, Robespierre, Suffrage*

CONTRIBUTORS

Ran Halévi, Centre National de la Recherche Scientifique, Centre de Recherches Historiques, Institut Raymond Aron, Paris
Clubs and Popular Societies (with Patrice Gueniffey), *Estates General, Feuillants, Monarchiens*

Patrice Higonnet, Harvard University, Cambridge, Massachusetts
Sans-culottes

Bernard Manin, Centre National de la Recherche Scientifique, Paris
Montesquieu, Rousseau

Pierra Nora, Institut Raymond Aron, Ecole des Hautes Etudes en Sciences Sociales, Paris
Nation, Republic

Mona Ozouf, Centre National de la Recherche Scientifique, Centre de Recherches Historiques, Institut Raymond Aron, Paris
Danton, De-Christianization, Département, Equality, Federalism, Federation, Fraternity, Girondins, Jaurès, King's Trial, Liberty, Marat, Montagnards, Public Spirit, Regeneration, Revolution, Revolutionary Calendar, Revolutionary Religion, Taine, Varennes, Voltaire

Philippe Raynaud, Centre National de la Recherche Scientifique, Institut Raymond Aron, Paris
American Revolution, Democracy

Jacques Revel, Centre de Recherches Historiques, Ecole des Hautes Etudes en Sciences Sociales, Paris
Great Fear, Marie Antoinette

Denis Richet, Centre de Recherches Historiques, Ecole des Hautes Etudes en Sciences Sociales, Paris
Committee of Public Safety, Coups d'Etat, Enragés, Hébertists, Italian Campaign, Natural Borders, Revolutionary Assemblies, Revolutionary Journées, Treaties of Basel and The Hague

Pierre Rosanvallon, Centre d'Etudes Transdisciplinaires, Ecole des Hautes Etudes en Sciences Sociales, Paris
Guizot, Physiocrats

NAME INDEX

References are to article titles; a complete alphabetical list of articles can be found on page 1063. Persons known by two names are listed under their better-known name, with the variant following in parentheses. Names of persons to whom an entire article is devoted are given in capital letters. In general, historians are indexed only if their works do not appear in the relevant bibliographies; living historians are not indexed.

Abrantès, Laure Permon, dame Junot, duchesse d'
   Napoleon Bonaparte
Adams, John
   American Revolution, Constitution
Adams, John Quincy
   American Revolution
Aguesseau, Henri-François d'
   Centralization, Civil Code
Aigoin, François-Victor
   Maximum
Aiguillon, Armand-Désiré du Plessis-Richelieu d'Agenois, duc d'
   Equality, Feudal System, Night of August 4, Revolutionary Assemblies
Aimery, Jean-Louis-Claude
   Feuillants
Albitte, Antoine-Louis
   Maximum
Alembert, Jean Le Rond d'
   Blanc
Alfieri, Vittorio
   Italian Campaign
Allonville, Armand-François, comte (known as marquis d')
   Aristocracy
Alopeus, David Maximovich
   Treaties of Basel and The Hague
Alvinczy, Baron Nicolas
   Italian Campaign
Amar, Jean-Baptiste-André
   Babeuf, Coups d'Etat, Girondins, King's Trial
Amiel, Henri-Frédéric
   Taine
Anselme, Jacques-Bernard-Modeste d'
   Natural Borders
Anson, Pierre-Hubert
   Assignats
Antonelle, Pierre-Antoine, marquis d'
   Babeuf, Paris Commune

Arago, François
   Blanc
Arcq, Philippe-Auguste de Sainte-Foix, chevalier d'
   Aristocracy
Arenberg, Auguste (comte de La Marck), prince d'
   Mirabeau
Argenson, Marc-René de Voyer de Paulmy, marquis d'
   Equality, Marie Antoinette, Revolutionary Journées
Aristotle
   Montesquieu
Arnauld, Antoine
   Equality
Arndt, Ernst Moritz
   Natural Borders
Arthur, Robert-Jean-Jacques
   Paris Commune
Artois, comte d'
   See Charles X
Augereau, Pierre-François-Charles
   Carnot, Coups d'Etat, Italian Campaign, Napoleon Bonaparte, Terror, Treaties of Basel and The Hague
Augustine, Saint
   Michelet
Aulard, François-Victor-Alphonse
   Academic History of the Revolution, Centralization, Danton, Jaurès, Marat, Taine

BABEUF, François-Noël (known as Gracchus) (1760–1797)
   See Part 2
Baggesen, Jens
   Fichte
Bailleul, Jacques-Charles
   Buchez, Staël
Bailly, Jean-Sylvain

Name index

NAME INDEX

NAME INDEX

SUBJECT INDEX

References are to article titles. Subjects to which an entire article is devoted are given in capital letters.

SUBJECT INDEX

Subject index

Revolutionary cults
Revolutionary Religion
REVOLUTIONARY GOVERNMENT
See Part 3
REVOLUTIONARY JOURNEES
See Part 1
REVOLUTIONARY RELIGION
See Part 3
Revolutionary Tribunal
Republic, Revolutionary Government, Terror
Rights
Babeuf, Civil Code, Feudal System, Great Fear, Night of August 4
right to work: *Babeuf, Robespierre*
natural rights: *American Revolution, Constitution, Counterrevolution, Jaurès, Liberty*
RIGHTS OF MAN
See Part 4
Romanticism
Counterrevolution, Maistre, Michelet
Royalism
Chouannerie, Coups d'Etat, Emigrés, Federalism, Girondins, King's Trial, Revolutionary Journées, Vendée

Salons
Girondins
SANS-CULOTTES
See Part 2
Second Empire
Republic
Second Republic
Republic, Tocqueville
Sectional movement
Clubs and Popular Societies, Coups d'Etat, Enragés, Fraternity, King's Trial, Paris Commune, Revolutionary Journées, Robespierre, Sans-culottes
Secularism
Civil Code, Michelet
Seigneurie
Feudal System, Great Fear, Night of August 4
Separation of powers
American Revolution, Constitution, Liberty, Monarchiens, Montesquieu, Necker, Rights of Man, Staël
September massacres
Danton, Marat, Paris Commune, Terror
Servitude
Feudal System, Liberty, Marat
Slavery
American Revolution, Clubs and Popular Societies, Condorcet, Kant
Social contract
Buchez, Counterrevolution, Equality, Liberty, Rousseau, Sovereignty, Taxes
Socialism
Academic History of the Revolution, Babeuf, Blanc, Buchez, Democracy, Fraternity, Jacobinism, Jaurès, Republic, Revolutionary Government
Social question
Babeuf, Blanc, Buchez, Maximum, Sans-culottes
Société(s)
de l'Histoire de la Révolution: *Academic History of the Revolution*
de Pensée: *Clubs and Popular Societies*
de 1789: *Clubs and Popular Societies, Condorcet, Feuillants, Lafayette*
des Amis de la Constitution: *Clubs and Popular Societies, Feuillants, Jacobinism*
des Amis de Liberté et de l'Egalité: *Jacobinism*
des Droits de l'Homme: *Maistre*
des Etudes Robespierriste: *Academic History of the Revolution*
des Républicains Révolutionnaires: *Enragés*
des Trente: *Feuillants*
Society
civil: *Marx, Sovereignty*
secret: *Babeuf*
Sorbonne
Academic History of the Revolution
Sparta
Rousseau
Speculation
Assignats
State
Aristocracy, Centralization, Civil Code, Enlightenment, Fichte, Liberty, Marx, Montesquieu, Napoleon Bonaparte, Tocqueville
Subsistence
Revolutionary Government, Maximum
Succession, Law of
Civil Code, Equality
SUFFRAGE
See Part 3
Supreme Being
Academic History of the Revolution, Coups d'Etat, Revolution, Revolutionary Religion, Robespierre
Swamp
See Marais

TAXES
See Part 3
TERROR
See Part 1
Theocracy
Counterrevolution

Alphabetical List
of Articles

ALPHABETICAL LIST OF ARTICLES